China

中国

Joe Cummings
Robert Storey

China – a travel survival kit

3rd edition

Published by

Lonely Planet Publications Pty Ltd (ACN 005 607 983)
PO Box 617, Hawthorn, Vic 3122, Australia
Lonely Planet Publications, Inc
PO Box 2001A, Berkeley, CA 94702, USA

Printed by

Singapore National Printers Ltd, Singapore
Script: typeset by Literary Photo-Typesetting & Printing Co Hong Kong

Photographs by

Alan Samagalski (AS)
Robert Strauss (RS)
Jim Hart (JH)
Front cover: photo by Rennie Ellis, courtesy: Scoopix Photo Library
Back cover: The Stone Forest (Yun), (Richard Nebesky)

First Published

October 1984

This Edition

October 1991

Although the authors and publisher have tried to make the information as accurate as possible, they accept no responsibility for any loss, injury or inconvenience sustained by any person using this book.

National Library of Australia Cataloguing in Publication Data

Cummings, Joe
China – a travel survival kit.

3rd ed.
Includes index.
ISBN 0 86442 123 0.

1. China – Description and travel – 1976 –Guide-books.
I. Storey, Robert. II. Title.

915.10459

Joe Cummings

Joe has travelled extensively and frequently in Asia over the last 14 years. Before travel writing became a full-time job, he was a Peace Corps volunteer in Thailand, a translator/interpreter in San Francisco, a graduate student in Asian Studies (MA 1981) at the University of California (Berkeley), a columnist for the *Asia Record*, an East-West Center Scholar in Hawaii (MA 1985), a university lecturer in Malaysia and an educational consultant in the US and Taiwan.

Joe is also author or co-author of Lonely Planet guides to Thailand, Laos, Burma, Malaysia, Singapore and Indonesia. His articles and photographs have been published in the *San Francisco Examiner*, *Transitions Abroad*, *Great Expeditions*, *Conde Nast Traveler* and the *Encyclopaedia Brittanica*. He is now living in northern California.

Robert Storey

Robert, an experienced budget traveller, has spent much of his life trekking all over the backwaters of the world pursuing his favourite hobby, mountain climbing. He has had a number of distinguished careers including taking care of monkeys at a zoo and repairing slot machines in Las Vegas casinos. It was in Taiwan that Robert finally got a respectable job – teaching English. He also learned Chinese, became a computer hacker, wrote *Taiwan – a travel survival kit,* and later helped rewrite Lonely Planet's guide to Hong Kong, Macau & Canton. Now a respectable citizen, Robert often wanders around deserts and mountains carrying such essential gear as a camera and portable computer.

From the Authors

We were helped by a host of people and thanks must go to those who wrote notes and letters, or simply recognised us somewhere along the line and told us about their experiences. Special thanks to Stanley Mo (Hong Kong), whose flat become a mail drop and collection point for travel information, and Wu Hsiuchueh (Taiwan).

Thanks also to many travellers along the way, including:

Ann Barrott Wicks (USA); Caroline Deane (UK); Derek & Julie Saville (UK); Erzsebet Thomasse & Henneke Duistermaat (Nl); Jitka Lom (C); Joe Linzmeier (USA); Michelle Weinman & Richard Gamer (USA); Mick Nance (UK); Miguel Portillo & Mercè (Sp); Miriam Jenkins (USA); Takashi Kobayashi & Naofumi Yoshida (J).

Joe Cummings thanks the following individuals for their assistance while in China:

Tom Huhti, David Sheppard, Deborah Koons, Tom Domke, Tim Blaskovich, Carey Moore, Rose Reindl, Teri Snyder, Mauritz v Gurp, Rod & Kim Tutt, Julie Ellis, Wang Bo, Liu Zhi Qiang, Qin Li, Wang Jian Hua, Li Qin Shu, Qu Da Ping, Liu Tian Ju, Qian Yi, Dr Ho, Xuan Ke and Mr Lee.

This book is also a product of the hard work of people at Lonely Planet in Melbourne, Australia.

From the Publisher

Frith Pike coordinated the project and saw the book through production. She and Caroline Williamson edited the manuscript. Thanks also to Charlotte Hindle for additional copy-editing, to Chris Taylor for his work with the Chinese script and pinyin, to Felicia Zhang for checking the script and to Caroline Williamson for proofing, to Sharon Wertheim for indexing, to Dan Levin and Peter Turner for computer assistance and to Tom Smallman and Susan Mitra for editorial support.

Chris Lee Ack designed the cover and coordinated the mapping assisted by Tracey O'Mara and Ann Jeffree. Tamsin Wilson designed and illustrated this edition. Thanks also to Ann Jeffree and Andrew Gritschen for additional illustrations.

This Book

The first edition of this book appeared after Michael Buckley and Alan Samagalski spent many months on the road in China in 1983 followed by many more months at their desks. Alan Samagalski and Robert Strauss researched and wrote the second edition, preparing the way for Joe Cummings and Robert Storey for this, the third edition. All those involved in producing this book greatly appreciate the contributions of those travellers who put so much effort into writing and telling us of their experiences. Thank you: a list of people who have written to us is at the back of this book.

Warning & Request

All travel guides rely on new information to stay up-to-date. At Lonely Planet we get a steady stream of mail from travellers, and it all helps, whether it's a few lines on a postcard or a stack of closely written pages. Everywhere prices go up, new hotels open, old ones close, bus routes change – in China particularly because the country is changing so fast. So if you find something isn't exactly how it's described in the book, don't blame the authors; instead, write to Lonely Planet and help make the next edition even better. Information on hotels, restaurants, transport, new places opened to tourists, sights, cafes, cultural shows, opinions about the book itself – anything that may be of interest to other travellers – is greatly appreciated! As usual the most useful letters will earn you a free copy of the next edition, or any other Lonely Planet book if you prefer.

Contents

THE EAST

THE NORTH-EAST

THE SOUTH-WEST

THE NORTH & NORTH-WEST

TIBET & QINGHAI

Map Legend

BOUNDARIES

........International Boundary
................Internal Boundary
.... National Park or Reserve
.... The Equator
.... The Tropics

SYMBOLS

NEW DELHI ....National Capital
BOMBAY ....Provincial or State Capital
Pune ....Major Town
Barsi ....Minor Town
..........................Places to Stay
............................Places to Eat
..................................Post Office
....Airport
...................Tourist Information
............Bus Station or Terminal
66 ....Highway Route Number
...... Mosque, Church, Cathedral
........................Temple or Ruin
................................Hospital
.... Lookout
.... Camping Area
.............................Picnic Area
.........................Hut or Chalet
........................Mountain or Hill
.... Railway Station
.... Road Bridge
.... Railway Bridge
............................Road Tunnel
.........................Railway Tunnel
.................Escarpment or Cliff
....Pass
............Ancient or Historic Wall

ROUTES

.......Major Road or Highway
.... Unsealed Major Road
.... Sealed Road
..... Unsealed Road or Track
.... City Street
...............................Railway
.... Subway
....................Walking Track
.... Ferry Route
.... Cable Car or Chair Lift

HYDROGRAPHIC FEATURES

...................River or Creek
.............Intermittent Stream
........Lake, Intermittent Lake
..........................Coast Line
................................Spring
.... Waterfall
.... Swamp
.... Salt Lake or Reef
................................Glacier

OTHER FEATURES

Park, Garden or National Park
.... Built Up Area
... Market or Pedestrian Mall
.... Plaza or Town Square
............................Cemetery

Note: not all symbols displayed above appear in this book

Introduction

After being closed for repairs for almost 30 years the Middle Kingdom suddenly swung open its big red doors – but not quite all the way. Comrades, we must increase the production of tourists! China desperately needs the foreign exchange that tourism so conveniently provides, and has done very well out of the deal so far. With several million tourists flocking in every year, the tallest buildings in China are, appropriately, hotels. Come back in five years time and there'll be Marco Polo pizza parlours dotting the Great Wall.

In the late 1970s the tour groups started rolling in but the prospects for individual travel looked extremely dim. It has always been possible for individuals to travel to the People's Republic of China (PRC), but by invitation only, and until the late 1970s few managed an invite. The first regulars were people from Sweden and France (nations favoured by China) who stepped off the Trans-Siberian Railway in 1979.

In 1981 the Chinese suddenly started issuing visas to solo and uninvited travellers through a couple of their embassies overseas, but mainly through various agencies in Hong Kong. Just about anyone who wanted a visa could get one, but since there was no fanfare, news spread slowly by word of mouth. By 1983 it seemed that just about everyone who landed in Hong Kong was going to China. After all, we'd been waiting over 30 years to travel in the country unfettered by tour guides.

Nowadays the vague travellers' trails of China have been worn down to gullies tramped by baffled foreigners who notice that the image of the late '60s and early '70s – hardy peasants and sturdy workers in blue uniforms building a Communist heaven – has changed. Today they see motorcycle gangs (relatively benign) in Canton; daring punk rockers challenging the authorities in Beijing; Colonel Sanders plugging his wares in Beijing at Kentucky Fried Chicken across the street from the Mao Zedong mausoleum; Shandong peasants churning up the fields with primitive ploughs; old women making offerings in Taoist temples on Taishan; a Christian church in Tianjin packed to the steeple for a Sunday-night service; and a burgeoning black market in almost every tourist town.

Nor did China turn out to be the easiest of countries to travel in – at least not on your own. Although many early guidebooks spoke of the country in glowing terms, a lot of people quickly discovered that travel in China has its own share of hassles. Travelling in China is much easier than it used to be, and most Westerners seem to be staying longer and enjoying the place much more than those who went there a few years ago. But at some stage you'll probably find yourself at the end of your tether with both the place and the people; a lot depends on where you go, how long you stay, how you travel and how patient you are.

Many of the hassles stem from the same problems that afflict other Third World countries: too few resources and too many people. Yet the outstanding feature of China is that, after what seems like several hundred years of stagnation, it is now making a determined effort to modernise and catch up with the West. The size of the task is staggering, and now is a unique opportunity to get some whiff of what the Communists have been doing for the last 40 years. The sleeping giant stood up in 1949 and, whatever you feel about the place, China is a country that cannot be ignored.

USSR
MONGOLIA
Urümqi
Kashgar
XINJIANG
GANSU
Dunhuang
Jiayuguan
Yinchuan
NINGXIA
Golmud
Xining
Lanzhou
QINGHAI
TIBET
New Delhi
NEPAL
Kathmandu
SIKKIM
Lhasa
Thimbu
BHUTAN
INDIA
SICHUAN
Chengdu
Chongqing
GUIZHOU
Guiyang
Kunming
YUNNAN
MYANMAR
(BURMA)
VIETNAM
Hanoi
LAOS
THAILAND
China
0
300
600 km

To Ulan-Ude
To Chita
Manzhouli
HEILONGJIANG
Ulan Bator
Harbin
INNER MONGOLIA
Vladivostok
Changchun
Erenhot
JILIN
Shenyang
LIAONING
Sea of Japan
Hohhot
Beijing
Pyongyang
Tokyo
Tianjin
Seoul
HEBEI
Shijiazhuang
JAPAN
Taiyuan
KOREA
Jinan
SHANXI
Yellow Sea
SHANDONG
Xian
Zhengzhou
JIANGSU
SHAANXI
HENAN
Nanjing
Hefei
Shanghai
HUBEI
SHANGHAI
ANHUI
Wuhan
Hangzhou
East China Sea
ZHEJIANG
Nanchang
Changsha
HUNAN
JIANGXI
Fuzhou
FUJIAN
Taipei
GUANGDONG
Canton (Guangzhou)
TAIWAN
GUANGXI
Nanning
Hong Kong
Macau
South China Sea
Haikou
Sanya
Hainan Island

Facts about the Country

CHINESE DYNASTIES	
Xia	2200 – 1700 BC
Shang	1700 – 1100 BC
Zhou	1100 – 221 BC
Western Zhou	1100 – 771 BC
Eastern Zhou	770 – 256 BC
Spring & Autumn Period	770 – 476 BC
Warring States Period	476 – 221 BC
Qin	221 – 207 BC
Han	206 BC – 220 AD
Western Han	206 BC – 24 AD
Eastern Han	25 – 220 AD
Three Kingdoms Period	220 – 280
Wei	220 – 265
Shu Han	221 – 263
Wu	222 – 280
Jin	265 – 420
Western Jin	265 – 316
Eastern Jin	317 – 420
Southern & Northern Dynasties	420 – 589
Southern	
Song	420 – 479
Qi	479 – 502
Liang	502 – 557
Chen	557 – 589
Northern	
Northern Wei	386 – 534
Eastern Wei	534 – 550
Western Wei	535 – 556
Northern Qi	550 – 577
Northern Zhou	557 – 581
Sui	581 – 618
Tang	618 – 907
Five Dynasties	907 – 960
Later Liang	907 – 923
Later Tang	923 – 936
Later Jin	936 – 946
Later Han	947 – 950
Later Zhou	951 – 960
Liao	916 – 1125
Song	960 – 1279
Northern Song	960 – 1127
Southern Song	1127 – 1279
Western Xia	1038 – 1227
Jin	1115 – 1234
Yuan (Mongol)	1271 – 1368
Ming	1368 – 1644
Qing (Manchu)	1644 – 1911

CHINESE REPUBLICS	
Republic of China	1912 – 1949
People's Republic of China	1949 –

HISTORY

The Chinese have traditionally claimed a history of 5000 years, yet ancient legends tell of both celestial and mortal emperors who ruled China for tens of thousands of years before this.

First came the 'Three Sovereigns' who had human heads and the bodies in the form of snakes. Next came the mortal 'Five Sovereigns' who are credited with inventing writing, establishing the institutions of marriage and family, and teaching people many useful things about agriculture and herbal medicines.

Xia & Shang Dynasties

One of these mortal sovereigns, Yu, is said to have founded the Xia Dynasty, which held power from the 21st to the 16th century BC. The story goes that the last Xia sovereign was so tyrannical that his subjects rebelled against him. The leader of this revolt founded the Shang Dynasty which lasted until the 11th century BC. Whether the Xia actually existed is uncertain, but archaeological evidence has shown that the Shang had full-fledged urban societies built on the sites of rural villages, which in turn had developed on the sites of even older settlements of prehistoric tribes. The last despotic Shang ruler was overthrown by the king of the subject Zhou people in the west, who founded the Zhou Dynasty.

Zhou Dynasty

The Zhou period is important for the establishment of some of the most enduring Chinese political concepts. Foremost is the 'mandate of heaven' in which heaven gives wise and virtuous leaders a mandate to rule and removes it from those who are evil and corrupt. The concept of the emperor as the 'Son of Heaven' probably originated during the Zhou Dynasty.

Later, the concept of the mandate of heaven was extended to incorporate the Taoist theory that heaven expresses disapproval of bad rulers through natural disasters such as earthquakes, floods and plagues of locusts. Another refinement is the 'right of rebellion' which says that the will of heaven is expressed through the support of the people for their ruler or through the withdrawal of such support. This justified rebellions against tyrannical rulers and allowed successful rebel leaders to claim the mandate of heaven in order to rule.

The concept of the 'dynastic cycle' followed from this, maintaining that, as the moral quality of the ruling family declines, heaven passes power on to another dynasty. Thus there is an endless cycle in which governments rise, pass through a period of prosperous and just rule but gradually grow weak and corrupt until heaven has no alternative but to hand its mandate over to a new, strong and just ruler.

During the Zhou period the Chinese people also developed the concept of a separate identity. Though split into separate kingdoms, they were united by a common belief in the superiority of the Shang-Zhou culture. These kingdoms came to be known as the Zhongguo or Middle Kingdom, while outsiders were considered barbarians.

The Warring States Period

The Zhou dominated the areas north and south of the Yellow River, forming a feudal society which included over 1700 semi-independent states. Their lords swore allegiance to the emperor and gave military aid when required. However, as the power of the Zhou royal family declined, that of the feudal lords increased. Big states swallowed little ones, and by 700 BC only 200 independent states existed. Continuing annexations during the Spring and Autumn Period reduced the number to a handful.

This period and the important Warring States Period (476-221 BC) which followed was a time of turmoil, with incessant wars, unbridled power and great extremes of wealth and poverty. One of China's most influential philosophers, Confucius, lived during this time. His attempts to find a solution to its troubles led him to uphold the Zhou Dynasty as the golden age of good government on which all rulers should model themselves. Confucius' ideas resulted in the Chinese custom of venerating the alleged good government, people and literature of a distant past.

The Chinese social structure was also changing. From 500 BC onwards a landlord class developed, distinct from the long-established aristocracy of the feudal states. One explanation for the development of this class is that feudal rulers rewarded their soldiers with grants of land. Another is that the defeat of feudal lords freed large numbers of serfs and allowed them to start farming on their own. As poorer farmers foundered under the burden of increased taxes, they sold out to wealthier farmers who then rented the land to tenant farmers. The trend continued in the succeeding Qin Dynasty, during which heavy taxes ruined the peasants while the landlord class grew.

Qin Dynasty

The Warring States Period ended in the 3rd century BC when the state of Qin united the Chinese, for the first time, into a single empire. However, the First Exalted Emperor Qin Shihuang ruled only from 221 to 207 BC and is remembered mainly for his tyranny and cruelty.

Centralised control increased dramatically. The power of the aristocrats was broken by apportioning their land to private farmers. Books written before the Qin period were destroyed to wipe out ideas which conflicted with the emperor's. Prisoners of war and peasants who had lost their land were drafted into gangs to build public works like the Great Wall, which snaked across northern China and was designed to keep the northern nomads at bay. A network of roads was built connecting the capital with distant parts of the empire. Weights, measures, coinage and the writing system were standardised. The foundations of a large, unified Chinese empire were laid.

When Qin Shihuang died a rebellion broke out and the Qin capital (near modern-day Xi'an) was captured by an army led by the commoner Liu Pang. Liu took the title of emperor and established the Han Dynasty.

Han Dynasty

The Han Dynasty lasted from 206 BC to 220 AD. During this period the pattern of the modern Chinese state was established and the empire reached its zenith.

The Han emperors were rarely, if ever, able to rule with the same degree of absolute power as Qin Shihuang. Their power was shared with powerful regional governors and princes, wealthy merchant families, the landed gentry, the emperor's immediate family, relatives, servants, palace eunuchs, and the remarkably well-developed and precisely ranked government bureaucracy.

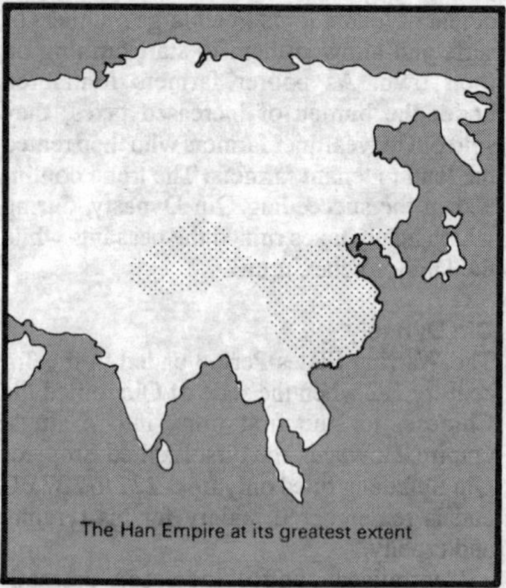
The Han Empire at its greatest extent

The fifth Han emperor, Wu, came to power in 147 BC and his far-flung military campaigns expanded the empire's boundaries furthest. Wu, an intensely autocratic monarch, decreed that knowledge of Confucian texts and teachings be a prerequisite for appointment to government positions. A university was set up in the capital to teach Confucianism, and examinations in the Confucian classics were instituted. Confucianism became the basis of education and admission to the Chinese civil service for the next 2000 years.

The Problem of Foreigners

Mountains and deserts isolated China from continental neighbours, but the expansion of the empire into central Asia brought the Han Chinese into contact with numerous foreigners. Diplomatic missions even introduced the Han to the Roman Empire, and to the Greek settlements left over from Alexander's invasion of the mountains of north-west India. However, these contacts had little or no impact on the Chinese world.

The Shang and Zhou had their own customs for dealing with those outside the Central States. The 'barbarians' were expected to 'come and be transformed' by contact with the 'higher' Chinese civilisation. They were expected to observe the rites of the Chinese court and to 'offer tribute'. In return they would be treated courteously and presented with gifts.

The Chinese continued to view themselves as a superior race through the later Han period, but the awkward fact remained that the Han armies could never quite defeat the barbarians who plagued the Chinese empire's boundaries. Often they were forced to receive the barbarian ambassadors as guests or equals, but these receptions were still officially recorded as the visits of vassals who brought tribute.

Invasions & Migrations
Strains on the empire's economy and a succession of weak rulers led to power struggles between strong regional rulers and their armies. The Han empire finally split into three separate kingdoms in 220 AD.

The rivalry between these kingdoms invited invasion by China's northern neighbours and caused great migrations of Chinese people. However, the concept of a unified empire remained and there were always rulers who aspired or claimed to be China's legitimate sovereign. During this period the north came under the control of the Turkic-speaking Tobas people, while the south split into separate Chinese kingdoms.

The conquest of northern China by the foreigners resulted in two interesting developments. The first was the growing power of Buddhism, probably introduced to China by Indian merchants accompanied by Buddhist priests. It boomed between the 3rd and 6th centuries when the northern invaders (many of whom were acquainted with the religion before they came to China) patronised the Buddhist monks, partly to build up a group of educated officials who were not Confucians.

The second development was the absorption of the northern 'barbarians' into Chinese culture. The Toba eventually disappeared as a race, either rejoining the Turkic tribes in the north or successfully assimilating the Chinese way of life. The seduction of the northern invaders by the 'civilised' style of Chinese life was repeated later with the Manchus and Mongols.

Sui & Tang Dynasties
The country was finally reunited in the 6th century under the Sui Dynasty, founded by a general of Chinese-Toba descent Yang Jian (known as Wen Di 'the Cultured Emperor') who had usurped the northern throne and conquered southern China.

The Sui Dynasty was short lived and in 618 AD the throne was again usurped, this time by the noble Li family of Chinese-Toba descent who founded the Tang Dynasty. The Chinese now look on the Tang Dynasty as a golden age of Chinese power and prosperity, and a high point in culture and creativity.

At the height of Tang power, their capital at Chang'an (on the site of modern-day Xi'an) was one of the greatest cities in the world. It held a million people within its walls and perhaps another million outside, and was a thriving imperial metropolis of commerce, administration, religion and culture. The Chinese empire covered the greatest area since the Han Dynasty. The government was highly centralised, with power concentrated increasingly in the hands of the emperor.

The Sui had instituted a nationwide examination system which enabled people from all over China to serve in the government bureaucracy in Chang'an; this system was continued and developed by the Tang. The Sui had also improved communications by building canals linking strategic parts of the empire. Canal links were further developed during the Tang Dynasty; roads and inns were built for officials, travellers, merchants and pilgrims.

These communication systems radiated out to the seaports and caravan routes which connected China to the rest of the world. The capital became a centre for international

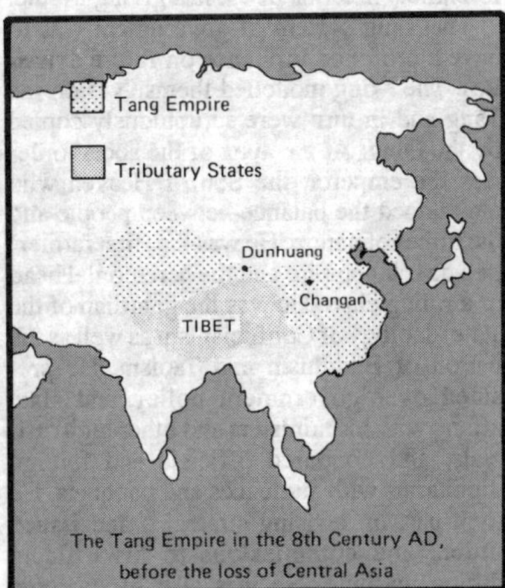

The Tang Empire in the 8th Century AD, before the loss of Central Asia

The Tang Emperor Li Shimin

trade and home to a large foreign community. Numerous religions, including Islam, the Zoroastrian sect of Persia, and the Nestorian Christian sect of Syria, established temples and mosques. During this period China was exposed to a greater variety of foreign cultures than at any time until the present. Nevertheless the foreigners had to comply with the tribute system, and the Tang government recorded official meetings with foreigners in terms of vassals giving tribute.

The Tang system of government was to have a profound influence on future dynasties. The Ming modelled themselves on the Tang and in turn were scrupulously copied by the Qing. At the apex of the social order was the emperor, the Son of Heaven who maintained the balance between people and the forces of nature. He was the 'first farmer' of a peasant empire and the ceremonial head of a ruling class. He was the guardian of the state ideology of Confucianism as well as the patron of Buddhism and Taoism. He presided over government policy and state affairs with his ministers and other high officials, and honoured officials and foreign dignitaries with audiences and banquets. He took part in devising strategies and issued orders and commissions to his officers during wartime. He was also had a large harem. The day-to-day tasks of government were handled by the emperor's personal staff, the palace eunuchs and the huge government bureaucracy.

China's Economic Revolution

Towards the end of the 8th century the Tang Dynasty started to decline. Tang armies suffered defeats at the hands of provincial warlords and Tibetan and Turkic invaders. The Tang gradually began to lose control of the transport networks and the tax collection system on which their power and prosperity depended, and the dynasty finally fell in 907 AD. China once again split into a number of independent states.

Nevertheless there was rapid economic development. When Marco Polo arrived in China in the 13th century he found huge, prosperous cities bigger than any in Europe, an orderly society and inter-regional trade on a large scale. The south had split into separate kingdoms but remained peaceful; trade and commerce developed rapidly in the absence of central government controls.

The empire was reformed in 960 AD by a southern general Zhao Kuangyin who founded the Song Dynasty using political skill rather than military means. Peace helped maintain the prosperous economic structure. In the wake of another invasion from the north in the 12th century, the Song court was forced to flee south, where Hangzhou became a highly developed commercial, political and cultural centre. Throughout the 'Southern Song' period the south remained under the control of the Han Chinese, and the north in the hands of the northern invaders. Secure behind the Great Wall, both parties were oblivious to the fury of the Mongol invasion that was about to be unleashed.

The Mongol Reign (Yuan Dynasty)

Beyond the Great Wall lay the Gobi Desert. Beyond that lay only slightly more hospitable grassland stretching all the way from Manchuria to Hungary and inhabited by nomadic Turkic and Mongol tribes who endured a harsh life as shepherds and horse-breeders. The Mongols, despised for what was considered their ignorance and poverty, occasionally went to war with the Chinese but were always defeated.

In 1206 after 20 years of internal war, Genghis Khan united the roaming Mongol tribes into a new national group, the 'Blue Mongols', under the protection of the heavenly sky. He began the invasion of China in 1211, penetrated the Great Wall two years later and took Beijing in 1215. Stubborn resistance from the Chinese rulers, conflict within the Mongolian camp, and campaigns in Russia delayed the conquest of Song China for many years. Not until 1279 did the grandson of Genghis, Kublai Khan, bring southern China under his sway. The China ruled by Kublai was the biggest country in the world – there has never been a larger country either before or since.

The Mongols made Beijing their capital, and Kublai Khan became the first emperor of the Yuan Dynasty. Kublai's government in China concentrated power in the cities and towns. The Mongols improved the road system linking China with Russia and promoted trade throughout the empire and with Europe. They instituted a famine relief scheme and expanded the canal system which brought food from the countryside to the cities.

Overall the Mongols had little effect on the Chinese and, like the Toba before them, adopted many of the ways of their conquered subjects. The Mongol rule was, however, significant because it generated European interest in the Far East. The Mongol armies had swept into eastern Europe and the whole continent was on the verge of an invasion. The invasion was called off at the last minute but it forced the Europeans to take notice of Asia. Trade and contacts across Asia were made easier by Mongol supremacy since national boundaries were cut. It was the China of the Mongols that Europeans like Marco Polo visited, their books revealing the splendours of Asia to an amazed Europe.

Ming Dynasty

Kublai Khan died in 1294, the last Khan to rule over a united Mongol empire. The Mongol reign over China was rapidly disintegrating by the 1350s, and several rebel armies vied for power. The chief contender was Zhu Yuanzhang, a man of poor peasant origins, whose powerful army secured most of southern China before attacking Beijing and driving out the Mongols.

Zhu Yuanzhang proclaimed himself the first emperor of the Ming Dynasty and took the name Hong Wu. He established Nanjing as the capital, far from the north and safe from enemy attacks. Hong Wu set about organising a new government structure. Buddhism and Taoism were made state religions, the competitive examination system to select government officials was revived, and the civil government was modelled on the Tang Dynasty system.

Hong Wu's rule is noted, however, for two developments which ultimately weakened China. The first was a dramatic increase in the power of the emperor rather than the bureaucracy; Hong Wu's rule was almost totalitarian, stifling intellectual thought and personal initiative. The second was the increased isolation of China from the rest of the world; the Ming emperors saw China as culturally superior and economically self-

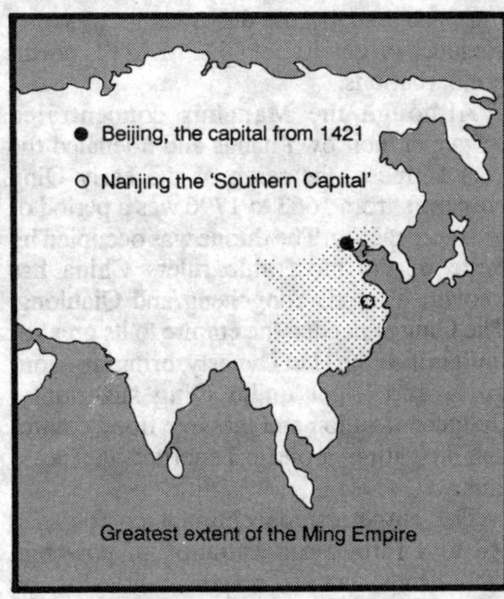

Greatest extent of the Ming Empire

sufficient, with nothing to learn from other countries. The chief exception was the third Ming emperor, Yong Le, who launched massive maritime expeditions to distant parts of the world. These came to an end when he died, and no more colonies, commercial bases or permanent contacts with other countries were established.

China was beginning to stagnate just as Europe was entering its most dynamic phase since the Roman Empire. The Ming Dynasty collapsed in the early 17th century, finishing with a line of young, weak and incompetent rulers, and a government whose power lay largely in the hands of the palace eunuchs. A severe famine in Shaanxi in 1628 precipitated the inevitable uprising, and a rebel army captured Beijing in 1644.

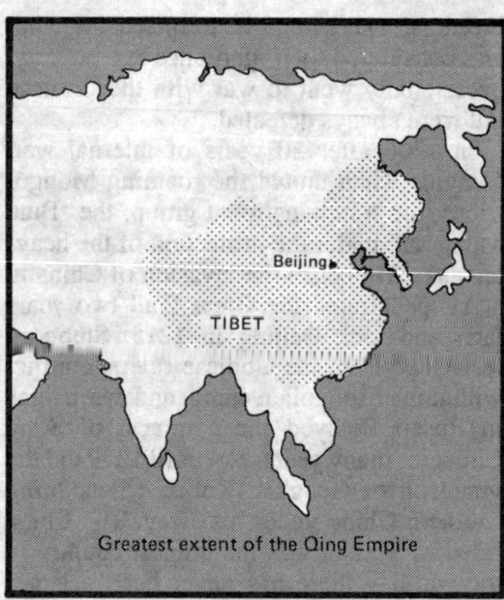

Greatest extent of the Qing Empire

Qing Dynasty

Meanwhile the Manchus to the north took advantage of the turmoil in China to launch an invasion. Initially held back by the Great Wall, they were allowed in by a Ming general and expelled the rebel army from Beijing. They set up their own dynasty, the Qing. The north succumbed to the Manchus without resistance but the south held out for 20 years. Today's Chinese 'triads' (the modern secret societies generally thought to be involved in criminal activity, especially drug trafficking), are actually the descendants of secret societies originally set up to resist the northern barbarians.

Although the Manchus concentrated power in their own hands and alienated the Han Chinese, the reign of the early Qing emperors from 1663 to 1796 was a period of great prosperity. The throne was occupied by three of the most able rulers China has known: Kangxi, Yongcheng and Qianlong. The Qing expanded the empire to its greatest limits since the Han Dynasty, bringing Mongolia and Tibet under Qing suzerainty. Reduced taxation and massive flood control and irrigation projects benefited the peasants.

The emperors' exceptional competence led to a further concentration of power in their hands, but the responsibilities of the throne became too great for the successors of Qianlong. Like the Mongols, the Manchu rulers succumbed to the ways of the Chinese and soon became culturally indistinguishable from them, modelling their government on the Ming Dynasty. Thus the isolationism and intellectual conservatism of the Ming was passed on to the Qing. China continued to be an inward-looking nation, oblivious to the technological and scientific revolutions taking place in Europe. The coming of Europeans to China hastened the fall of the Qing and helped mould the China we know today.

The Coming of the West

The Europeans couldn't be held back by the Great Wall – they came by sea. The first European ships to land in China were those of the Portuguese who arrived in 1516. Possibly as a reward for clearing nearby waters of pirates, they were permitted to set up base at Macau in 1557. Over the following century the British, Dutch and Spanish all landed in China.

The trade overtures of the foreign merchants were initially rebuffed by the Qing government, which finally opened the distant port of Canton to foreign trade in 1685. The foreigners were kept at arm's length, far from the political centre in the north. Trade flourished mainly in China's favour – although the foreigners had other ideas.

In 1773 the British started selling Indian opium to the Chinese in an effort to even up the balance of trade, since Britain was selling China some wool and spices while buying great quantities of tea, silk and porcelain. With opium addiction increasing and Chinese silver fast disappearing from the country, the emperor thundered forth with an edict in 1800 banning the trade – foreigners, Chinese merchants and corrupt officials duly ignored it.

More drastic measures were taken in 1839 when the Chinese seized 20,000 chests of opium in Canton. When subsequent negotiations broke down the British attacked Canton in the first of what became known as the 'Opium wars'. Altogether there were four Opium wars, each launched by the Westerners on some minor pretext. French troops joined the British in the Third Opium War, and the Russians and Americans lent naval support. The fourth and last Opium War was fought from 1859 to 1860.

Each war was ended by an 'Unequal Treaty'. These, along with subsequent treaties, opened more Chinese ports to foreign ships, gave foreigners the right to settle in certain areas and later let them travel freely in China. The Chinese were forced to pay large war indemnities, customs tariffs on imported Western goods were severely reduced, Western diplomats were permitted to take up residence in Beijing, freedom of movement was eventually accorded to missionaries, and foreigners were granted immunity to Chinese laws. The Russians seized the area of Siberia east of the Amur River (Heilong Jiang) in 1860, and the French seized Cochin-China from Annam, part of Vietnam today and over which the Chinese claimed suzerainty. By 1860 the opening of China was virtually complete.

Taiping Rebellion

In the second half of the 19th century there were two uprisings which could have halted this process of Chinese decay. The first was

Taiping Coin

the Taiping movement founded by Hong Xiuquan, a native of Guangdong. Convinced that he was on a mission from God and professing to be the younger brother of Jesus Christ, Hong and his followers preached Christianity while smashing Buddhist, Taoist and Confucian idols and razing their temples to the ground. Hong called his movement the 'Heavenly Kingdom of the Great Peace', and attempts by the Qing to suppress it only led him to declare open rebellion in 1851.

Marching north from Guangdong, the Taipings captured numerous towns on the Yangtse River; by 1853 they had captured Nanjing and brought southern China under their control. The army consisted of 600,000 men and 500,000 women, and was a highly organised and strictly disciplined group that adhered only to the Christian god. Gambling, opium, tobacco and alcohol were forbidden. Women were appointed as administrators and officials, and the practice of foot-binding was abolished along with slavery, prostitution, arranged marriages and polygamy. The peasants were attracted by the Taipings' policy of agrarian reform and fairer taxation. In many ways the Taipings were forerunners of the Communists of the following century.

However, the Taipings failed to gain the

support of the Western powers, who until then had remained neutral. In fact, the success of the Taipings probably worried the Westerners. It was more expedient for them to deal with a corrupt and weak Qing government than with the strong, united Taipings. After 1860 the Western powers allied with the Qing and a counter-offensive began. By 1864 the Taipings had retreated to their capital city of Nanjing. A Qing army aided by British army regulars and European and US mercenaries besieged and captured the city, slaughtering the defenders. Hong Xiuquan committed suicide and the rebellion ended.

Decline of the Qing

The years after the Taiping Rebellion were a time of further intrusion into China by the foreign powers. The Qing government grew progressively weaker and the lot of the peasants became increasingly miserable.

In 1861, when China needed a strong government more than ever, six-year-old Emperor Guangxu ascended to the throne. Real power remained in the hands of his aunt the Empress Dowager Wu Cixi, a former concubine. Wu Cixi saw reform and modernisation as a threat to the conservative power base of the Qing Dynasty. Clinging to this belief, she spent the next 48 years presiding over the disintegration of China.

China's own colonial empire began to break up. A war with France from 1883 to 1885 ended Chinese suzerainty in Indo-China and allowed the French to maintain control of Vietnam and eventually gain control of Laos and Cambodia. The British occupied Burma. In 1895 Japan forced the Chinese out of Korea and made them cede Taiwan. Britain, France, Germany and Russia rushed in to map out 'spheres of influence' in a spree of land-grabbing. By 1898 they were on the verge of carving up China; this was prevented by an US proposal for an 'open-door' policy which would leave all of China open to trade with any foreign power.

Economically the Chinese government fared disastrously. China, in debt to the Western powers and Japan, began to raise taxes, which added to the general misery of the peasants. Coastal trade by foreign ships developed at the expense of the Chinese junk trade. Foreigners built railways and telegraph lines and opened coal mines and ironworks but used them to exploit the country. Missionaries arrived in large numbers, threatening traditional Chinese society with foreign religion, science, education and morals. Chinese students returning from study abroad brought with them anti-Manchu sentiment and European-influenced political ideologies.

An attempt at 'self-strengthening' in 1881 resulted in the building of naval yards, arsenals and railways, and proved a failure when the supposedly modern Chinese army was defeated in the Sino-Japanese War of the mid-1890s. Then in 1898 the imperial court made a dramatic attempt to halt China's disintegration. Emperor Guangxu had come under the influence of the reformer Kang Youwei, who pressed for modernisation and liberalisation of China if it were to survive intact. The 'Hundred Days Reform' of 1898 was opposed by Wu Cixi. The emperor tried to have her arrested but his military officials changed sides, imprisoned him, returned Cixi to power, and executed the emperor's supporters. Kang escaped to Japan.

Boxer Rebellion

For almost 40 years the foreigners in China had been doing very much as they pleased. Bizarre retribution came with the Boxer Rebellion, the second event which might radically have changed the course of history.

The Chinese name for the Boxers clumsily translates as 'Righteous and Harmonious Fists'. They began in Shandong Province in the last years of the 19th century as an anti-Manchu organisation supported by the peasantry. At that time Shandong was in the grip of severe economic misery caused by war, floods, drought and famine. The 'boxers' developed a form of exercise aimed at harmonising mind and body in preparation for combat, and added rituals so that spirits would possess their bodies and make them invincible in battle.

The Qing failed to help the Shandong peasants, and the foreigners were blamed for disregarding the gods and angering the spirits. The slogan of the Boxers, 'Overthrow the Qing; destroy the foreigner', had immediate appeal. The Boxers suffered a heavy defeat by government troops in October 1899, but the Qing court saw the strength and popularity of the Boxers as an instrument with which to throw the foreigners out of China.

Towards the end of 1899 the Boxers and the government formed an anti-foreigner alliance. The Boxers began to massacre missionaries, other foreigners and Chinese Christians, destroying churches and ripping up railroads. They converged on Beijing in 1900 and laid siege to the foreign legations' compound. The imperial government declared war on the allied armies of Russia, Britain, Germany, France, the US, Japan, Italy and Austria.

The legations, however, held out until a relief force of foreign troops arrived to end the siege and put down the rebellion. The imperial court fled to Xi'an, and the Boxers were dispersed. Although the foreign powers punished China by executing government officials and Boxer leaders and exacting a huge indemnity, they did not break up the Chinese empire. Instead they preserved the dynasty with Cixi as ruler, thus maintaining their own supremacy. Once again the Chinese had been defeated and the foreign privileges preserved.

Fall of the Qing

With the defeat of the Boxers even the empress realised that China was too weak to survive without reform. The civil service examinations based on the irrelevant thousand-year-old Confucian doctrines were abolished, but other court-sponsored reforms proved to be a sham. By now secret societies aimed at bringing down the Qing Dynasty were being set up all over the country and by Chinese abroad. In 1905 several of these merged to form the Alliance for Chinese Revolution, headed by the Cantonese Dr Sun Yatsen.

The empress dowager died in 1908 and two-year-old Emperor Puyi ascended to the throne. The power of the central government rapidly fell apart. When the court announced the nationalisation of the railways in 1911, the move was viewed by provincial governors and wealthy merchants as an attempt to restrict their autonomy. An army coup in Wuhan seized control of the city, and the heads of many other provinces declared their loyalty to the rebels. By the year's end, most of southern China had repudiated Qing rule and given its support to the Alliance for Chinese Revolution. On 1 January 1912, Sun Yatsen was proclaimed president of the Chinese Republic.

Early Days of the Republic

Although China nominally became a republic in 1912, Sun's government in Nanjing had no substantial army with which to enforce its authority. In the north Yuan Shikai, the former chief of the imperial armies, held power; he planned to set himself up as emperor until his grandiose ambitions were cut short by his sudden death in 1916.

The combination of internal upheaval and foreign imperialism began to make China's survival as an autonomous powerful nation seem unlikely. The gravest threat came from Japan. During WW I Japan had joined the Allies and taken the German-owned port of Qingdao along with German ships, railways and industries in the Shandong Peninsula. In 1915 Japan presented China with the '21 Demands' which would have reduced China to a Japanese colony. Under the threat of a Japanese military advance out of Shandong, Yuan Shikai was forced to accept the economic concessions. However, some of the more extreme political demands, such as attaching Japanese 'political advisers' and 'police' to the provincial governments, were resisted.

Meanwhile the warlords, provincial military leaders left over from the Qing Dynasty, controlled much of China and were backed by their own armies. Supplies and requisitions for their armies were taken from the peasants, the people least able to resist. As the peasants became increasingly destitute, they were forced to join the warlord armies in order to survive by looting others. Militarism and the consequent decline in productivity led to increasing poverty – a familiar situation in China.

The Intellectual Revolution

The intelligentsia in China continued to search for solutions to China's crisis. Following Yuan's death, his opponents returned from abroad. The conservative Confucian order came under attack once again and the struggle for a new ideology which could save China resumed.

The mainstream of the intellectual revolution came from Beijing University, although in nearly all the major cities and towns there were many political organisations with their own journals. One of the leaders of the movement, Li Dazhao, worked as a librarian at Beijing University. Li became a founding member of the Chinese Communist Party and is still regarded as one of the best Chinese interpreters of Marxism; he also gave the young Mao Zedong a job in the university library and influenced Mao's political beliefs.

In 1918 Li started a society for the study of Marxism which was joined by Mao and by Zhang Guodao, a student leader at the university and later a founder of the Communist Party. Chen Duxiu, dean at the university until 1919, was another Beijing intellectual who organised Marxist study groups throughout China and also became a founder of the Chinese Communist Party.

In Tianjin a Marxist study group was started by a young scholar, Zhou Enlai. When Mao returned from Beijing to his native Changsha he started his own Marxist study group, whose members included Liu Shaoqi. In Hebei Province the 'Social Welfare Society' was formed with Lin Biao as a member.

In May 1919, the intellectual revolution was given impetus when the news reached China that the Allies at the Versailles peace conference had agreed to support Japan's claims to German concessions on Chinese territory. Student protests against the Japanese, and against the warlord regime in Beijing which had supported the treaty, were broken up by the police but did not end there. A wave of nationalist, anti-Japanese, anti-foreign, anti-warlord feeling swept through the country's intellectuals. The aims of the movement were clear: unite China, destroy the powerful warlords, establish a central government, throw off the shackles of the unequal treaties forced on China in the 19th century, and modernise sufficiently to cope with foreign powers. The question of how this was to be done, however, remained unanswered.

The Kuomintang & the Communists

After initial setbacks Sun Yatsen and the Kuomintang (the KMT or Nationalist Party), which had emerged as the dominant political force after the fall of the Qing Dynasty, managed to establish a secure base in southern China, and began training a National Revolutionary Army with which to challenge the northern warlords.

Since 1920 Russians who had taken part in the Bolshevik Revolution had been coming to China representing the Soviet government and the Communist International (Comintern), the international body dedicated to world revolution. Talks between the Comintern representatives, Li Dazhao and Chen Duxiu, eventually resulted in several Chinese Marxist groups banding together to form a Chinese Communist party (which became the CCP) at a meeting in Shanghai in 1921.

In 1922 CCP members were urged by the Moscow Comintern representatives to join the Kuomintang. There was a great deal of uneasiness within the CCP about doing this since Party members feared the Kuomintang was interested only in a national revolution to unify the country and eliminate foreign interference, rather than in a wider social revolution. The Russians insisted that a social revolution could not occur without a national revolution first. Soviet military, economic and political advisers were sent to China between 1923 and 1927 to help the Kuomintang, perhaps primarily to help form a buttress against aggressive Japanese ambitions on the Soviet Union's eastern flank. Under threat of the withdrawal of Soviet support, the CCP joined the Kuomintang.

Sun Yatsen's death from cancer in 1925 removed the unifying influence in the faction-ridden Kuomintang. A power struggle emerged between those in the political wing who were sympathetic to the social reform policies of the Communists, and those in the military wing led by Chiang Kaishek. Chiang commanded the National Revolutionary Army (NRA) and had strengthened his claim as Sun's legitimate heir by marrying Madame Sun Yatsen's sister. He opposed social reform and wished to preserve the capitalist state dominated by a privileged elite of wealthy family members and their associates, and supported by a military dictatorship.

Peasant Movement

Under the direction of Communist Party member Peng Bai, the Kuomintang set up a Peasant Training Institute in Canton where hundreds of potential peasant leaders from Guangdong, Hunan and other provinces trained for six months before returning to their home provinces to organise the peasants. The peasant organisations grew much faster than their urban industrial counterparts, and began pressing for radical changes. They demanded that land rent be reduced to only 25% of the crop, that high taxes be removed, that taking land as payment for debts be prohibited, that farm labourers be paid more, and that the landlords' private armies and gangs be abolished. Impressed by the strength of the peasant movement, Mao Zedong, who taught at the Institute during 1925-26, tried to persuade the Kuomintang leadership that the greatest potential for social revolution lay in the countryside. He was ignored as attention was focused on the impending 'Northern Expedition'.

Shanghai Coup

In 1926, in an effort to unify China, the Kuomintang embarked on the Northern Expedition to wrest power from the remaining warlords. Chiang Kaishek was appointed commander in chief by the Kuomintang and the Communists. One force of the National Revolutionary Army moved up through Hunan to take the city of Wuhan, which became the seat of the Kuomintang government. Meanwhile Chiang Kaishek's force captured Nanchang.

Following this victory Chiang tried to persuade the Soviet advisers and the political and military leaders of the Kuomintang to join him. There was now an obvious struggle for power within the Kuomintang. With the NRA about to move on Shanghai, Chiang took the opportunity to put down both the Communists and his opponents in the Kuomintang.

Shanghai was under the control of a local warlord whose strength was being undermined by a powerful industrial movement organised in the city by the Communists under Liu Shaoqi and Zhou Enlai. Kuomintang strategy called for the Shanghai workers to take over key installations in the city while the Kuomintang armies advanced on it. In March 1927 a general strike was

Chiang Kaishek

called and Shanghai industry shut down; police stations and military arsenals were seized and 5000 workers were armed. The Kuomintang army entered the city not long after.

Supported by the Shanghai industrialists who were worried about the trade union movement, and by foreigners who feared the loss of trade and privileges, Chiang let loose a reign of terror against the Communists and their sympathisers. With the help of Shanghai's underworld leaders and with financial backing from Shanghai bankers and foreigners, Chiang armed hundreds of gangsters, dressed them in Kuomintang uniforms and launched a surprise attack overnight on the workers' militia. About 5000 Shanghai Communists were killed. Massacres of Communists and various anti-Chiang factions followed in other Chinese cities. Zhou Enlai managed to escape by a hair's breadth. Li Dazhao was executed by slow strangulation.

The political leadership of the Kuomintang was thrown into turmoil once again. Since the military supported Chiang Kaishek, the Wuhan government was forced to bow to his wishes. By the middle of 1928 the Northern Expedition had reached Beijing and a national government was established with Chiang holding both military and political leadership.

The Kuomintang Government

Even at the end of the Northern Expedition only about half the country was under direct Kuomintang control; the rest was ruled by local warlords. Despite these and other problems Chiang was obsessed with his campaigns against the Communists, which he continued in the 1930s.

Any prospects of social and rural reform under the Kuomintang were lost. In the cities labourers were treated little better than beasts of burden. Children were used as slave labour in factories; they stood at machines for 12 or 13 hours a day and slept under them at night. Women and children were sold as concubines, prostitutes or domestic slaves. The destitute and starving died on the streets and strikes were ruthlessly suppressed by foreign and Chinese factory owners.

In the countryside the Kuomintang 'government' consisted of a Kuomintang-appointed county magistrate who ruled in collusion with the landlords and moneylenders and their private armed guards. Attempts at reform were blocked because it was not in the magistrates' interests to reduce rents or allow the establishment of rural banks with low interest rates for peasants. The magistrates used money made available by the government at low interest and lent it at higher interest to the poor farmers. If rural reformers persuaded farmers to use fertiliser to increase crop yields, the farmers would have to borrow money at high interest rates to buy fertiliser – then, if a better crop resulted, the local merchants would simply lower the buying price ensuring hardship for the farmers. Peasant protests were often dealt with by the private armies and gangs retained by many landlords, while the peasants' wives and children were taken into the landlords' households as domestic slaves in lieu of paying debts.

Tax collectors had police powers and could imprison peasants for failing to pay taxes and rent. Peasants who did not want to go to jail were forced to borrow money at interest rates of up to 700% a year. In some instances land taxes were collected 60 years in advance. Not only were most peasants destitute, they were terrified of taking any step which would bring them into conflict with armed authority. The Communists quickly realised that the only way to win a social revolution was with guns.

Civil War

After the massacre of 1927 the remaining Communist forces staged insurrections in several towns. Rebel units of the Kuomintang under Zhou Enlai and Zhu De (who held a high-ranking post in the Kuomintang army but was sympathetic to the Communists) seized Nanchang and held it for several days until they were driven out by loyal Kuomintang troops. The revolt was

Mao Zedong

a fiasco, but it marked the beginning of the Red Army.

In Changsha, Mao Zedong organised an uprising of the peasantry, miners and rebel Kuomintang soldiers. Mao's army moved south through Hunan, fighting Kuomintang troops, and climbed into the Jinggangshan mountains on the border between Hunan and Jiangxi. They were reinforced by Zhu De's troops, and a strategy was mapped out to first consolidate control over the Jinggang area and then slowly expand from there.

However, the Party hierarchy led by Li Lisan followed the orthodox Marxist theory that revolution must be based in the cities and towns, and ordered the Communist army to attack Nanchang and Changsha. After two costly defeats at Changsha in 1930, Mao and Zhu refused to obey Li's orders to attack Changsha again. There ensued a brief Party war in which a number of anti-Maoists were killed or imprisoned. From then on the power base of the revolution was moved squarely to the countryside and the peasants.

Communist-led uprisings in other parts of the country brought various parts of the country under their control. However, the Communist armies were still small, with limited resources and weapons. The Communists adopted a strategy of guerrilla warfare, emphasising mobility and rapid concentration and deployment of forces for short attacks on the enemy, followed by swift separation once the attack was over. Pitched battles were avoided except where their force was overwhelmingly superior. The strategy was summed up in a four-line slogan:

The enemy advances, we retreat;
The enemy camps, we harass;
The enemy tires, we attack;
The enemy retreats, we pursue.

By 1930 the ragged Communist forces had been turned into an army of perhaps 40,000, and presented such a serious challenge to the Kuomintang that Chiang had to wage a number of extermination campaigns against them. He was defeated each time, and the Red Army expanded its territory.

The Long March

Chiang's fifth extermination campaign began in October 1933, when the Communists suddenly changed their strategy. Mao and Zhu's authority was being undermined by other members of the Party who advocated meeting Chiang's troops in pitched battles, but this strategy proved disastrous. By October 1934 the Communists had suffered heavy losses and were hemmed into a small area in Jiangxi.

On the brink of defeat, the Communists decided to retreat from Jiangxi and march north to Shaanxi. In China's northern mountains the Communists controlled an area which spread across Shaanxi, Gansu and Ningxia, held by troops commanded by an ex-Kuomintang officer who had sided with the Communists after the 1927 massacres.

There was not one 'Long March' but several, as various Communist armies in the south made their way to Shaanxi. The most famous was the march from Jiangxi Province which began in October 1934, took a year to complete and covered 5000 miles over some of the world's most inhospitable terrain. On the way the Communists confiscated the property of officials, landlords and tax-collectors, redistributed the land to the peasants, armed thousands of peasants with weapons captured from the Kuomintang, and left soldiers behind to organise guerrilla groups to harass the enemy. Of the 90,000 people who started out in Jiangxi only 20,000 made it to Shaanxi. Fatigue, sickness, exposure, enemy attacks and desertion all took their toll.

The march proved, however, that the Chinese peasants could fight if they were given a method, an organisation, leadership, hope and weapons. It brought together many people who later held top positions in the China after 1949, including Mao Zedong, Zhou Enlai, Zhu De, Lin Biao, Deng Xiaoping and Liu Shaoqi. It also established Mao as the paramount leader of the Chinese Communist movement; during the march a meeting of the Communist Party hierarchy recognised Mao's overall leadership and he assumed supreme responsibility for strategy.

Japanese Invasion

In September 1931 the Japanese occupied the potentially wealthy but underdeveloped area of Manchuria, setting up a puppet state with the last Chinese emperor, Puyi, as the symbolic head.

Despite the Japanese invasion, Chiang was obsessed with putting down the Communists. 'Pacification first, resistance afterwards' was his slogan. The Communists believed that unless the Japanese were defeated there would be no China left at all, and advocated an anti-Japanese alliance with the Kuomintang. Instead, Chiang launched his extermination campaigns, the last of which forced the Communists to retreat to Shaanxi.

At the end of 1936 Chiang flew to Xi'an to oversee yet another extermination campaign against the Communists. The deadlock was broken in an unexpected manner. In what became known as the Xi'an Incident, Chiang was taken prisoner by his own generals led by Marshal Zhang Xueliang who commanded an army of Manchurian troops. (See the Shaanxi chapter for more details.) Chiang was forced to call off his extermination campaign and to form an anti-Japanese alliance with the Communists. In 1937 the Japanese launched an all-out invasion and, by 1939, had overrun eastern China. The Kuomintang government retreated west to Chongqing.

At the end of 1941 America entered the war, after the Japanese bombed Pearl Harbor. The Americans hoped to use the Chinese to tie up as many Japanese troops as possible and to use China as a base for attacking Japanese shipping and troops in South-East Asia. Chiang hoped the Americans would win the war against the Japanese and provide him with the munitions he required to finally destroy the Communists.

From 1938 until the end of the war the Japanese were never seriously harassed by the Kuomintang troops, as Chiang attempted to save his troops for renewed attacks on the Communists once the Americans had defeated the Japanese. The US general Joseph Stilwell, who was sent to China in 1942 by President Roosevelt to improve the combat effectiveness of the Chinese army, concluded that 'the Chinese government [was] a structure based on fear and favour in the hands of an ignorant, arbitrary and stubborn man...' and that its military effort since 1938 was 'practically zero'.

Defeat of the Kuomintang

Since the defeat of Japan was in America's own interest, Chiang saw no need to maintain his alliance with the Communists, reasoning that the Americans would support him regardless.

The Kuomintang-Communist alliance collapsed in 1941 when Kuomintang troops ambushed the rear detachment of one of the Communist armies. This non-combat detachment was annihilated and then its commander, Ye Ding, was imprisoned in Chongqing. Chiang then blockaded Communist forces to prevent them from receiving supplies. Although the Communists did not directly retaliate, clashes between the Kuomintang and the Communists were frequent, often developing into all-out civil war.

Nevertheless the Communist armies and guerrillas expanded into areas occupied by the Japanese. When the war against Japan ended in 1945 the Communist army numbered 900,000 and was backed by militia and several million active supporters. With the surrender of Japan in 1945, a dramatic power struggle began as the Kuomintang and Communist forces gathered in Manchuria for the final showdown.

By 1948 the Communists had captured so much US-supplied Kuomintang equipment and had recruited so many Kuomintang soldiers that they equalled the Kuomintang in both numbers and supplies. Three great battles were fought in 1948 and 1949 which saw the Kuomintang defeated and hundreds of thousands of Kuomintang troops join the Communists. The Communists moved south and crossed the Yangtse – by October all the major cities in southern China had fallen to them.

In Beijing on 1 October 1949, Mao Zedong proclaimed the foundation of the People's Republic of China (*Zhonghua Renmin Gongheguo* in Chinese). Chiang Kaishek fled to the island of Formosa (Taiwan), taking with him the entire gold reserves of the country and what was left of his air force and navy. Some two million refugees and soldiers from the mainland crowded onto the island. President Truman ordered a protective US naval blockade to prevent an attack from the mainland – the USA continued to recognise Chiang's delusion of being the legitimate ruler of all China.

Early Years of the People's Republic

The People's Republic started as a bankrupt nation. The economy was in chaos following Chiang's flight to Taiwan with the gold reserves. The country had just 19,200 km of railways and 76,800 km of usable roads, all in bad condition. Irrigation works had broken down and livestock and animal populations were greatly reduced. Industrial production fell to half that of the prewar period and agricultural output plummeted.

With the Communist takeover China seemed to become a different country. Unified by the elation of victory and the immensity of the task before them, and further bonded by the Korean War and the necessity to defend the new regime from possible US invasion, the Communists made the 1950s a dynamic period. The drive to become a great nation quickly was awesome.

By 1953 inflation had been halted, industrial production had been restored to prewar levels and the land had been confiscated from the landlords and redistributed to the peasants. In the mid-1950s industry was nationalised and farmers were encouraged to pool land and equipment in mutual-aid teams and cooperatives with a view to using resources more efficiently and increasing production.

Great Leap Forward

Despite the rapid advances China was making in both agricultural and industrial output, the Chinese government embarked on the ill-fated 'Great Leap Forward' – an ambitious plan to transform the country into a developed nation at one stroke.

The seasonally under-employed peasantry were to work on local small-scale industrial projects like steel furnaces and fertiliser plants, as well as on labour-intensive dams and irrigation networks.

While industry was being decentralised, gigantic rural communes, which would supposedly allow a more efficient use of land and resources, were being established. Having won their land, the peasants now found it being taken away again.

Inefficient management, little incentive to work in the common field, and large numbers of rural workers engaged in industrial projects, resulted in a massive slump in agricultural output. With industry in confusion and agriculture at an all-time low, China was struck by two disasters: the floods and droughts which ruined the harvests of 1959 and 1960, and the sudden withdrawal in 1960 of all Soviet aid.

Prelude to the Cultural Revolution

The withdrawal of Soviet aid, the failure of the Great Leap Forward and of the communes, unprecedented bad weather and poor harvests all contributed to the severe food shortages and famine of 1959 and 1960-61.

By 1964-65 the economy had recovered some of its equilibrium and the years of hardship were past. Industry and agriculture started to pick up and there was a general sense of optimism, clouded only by a growing fear of war with the USA spreading from Vietnam. The economic disasters, however, had opened a rift between Mao and the rest of the Communist Party. Mao found himself out of political favour and being held responsible for much of the failure of the Great Leap Forward.

A new period began in which Liu Shaoqi and Deng Xiaoping were in the ascendancy. Ownership of land was turned over to the individual villages; family ownership of land and small private plots was guaranteed; limited free markets were permitted; bonus systems and material incentives were introduced into industry. Agriculture took priority over heavy industry.

To put their policies into effect Liu and Deng built up an enormous government and Party bureaucracy, labour unions, Party schools and Communist Youth leagues over which Mao had little or no influence. However, Mao did have one power base – the army. He was still chair of the Military Affairs Commission, a post he had held since 1935. Lin Biao, his faithful disciple, was its vice-chair. Together they controlled the army – the trump card in any showdown.

The Cultural Revolution 1966-70

With the rise of Liu Shaoqi's bureaucratic elite, Mao believed that China was slipping away from the spirit of the revolution and returning to the capitalist past. In his view, the new policies reeked of 'revisionism' in which a new breed of capitalist opportunists would lead China back into the misery and oppression which the revolution had sought to destroy. China needed a 'Cultural Revolution' to put it back on track.

In August 1966 the Party Central Committee adopted a programme for the Cultural Revolution. The resolution stated that the bourgeoisie was attempting to stage a comeback using 'old ideas, culture, customs and habits of the exploiting class to corrupt the masses and capture their minds'.

The aim of the Cultural Revolution was:

> to struggle against and crush those persons in authority who [were] taking the capitalist road...and to transform education, literature, and art and all other parts of the superstructure that [did] not correspond to the socialist economic base, so as to facilitate the consolidation and development of the socialist system.

There was no doubt as to the ideological basis of the campaign; the resolution declared that:

> in the Great Proletarian Cultural Revolution, it is imperative to hold aloft the great red banner of Mao Zedong's Thought and put proletarian politics in command...Mao Zedong's Thought should be taken as the guide for action in the Cultural Revolution.

The 'Revolution' rapidly turned into political mayhem directed by Mao. Backed by his supporters in the army, he purged officials who opposed him in the Party, army and government. Thousands of government officials lost their jobs and most of them were

Stamps from the Cultural Revolution

sent to the countryside for re-education in socialism and Mao Zedong Thought, and to labour on commune farms. The Young Communist League and the Party training schools were disbanded; the army was to be the source of new cadres.

In 1967 Liu was named China's 'Khrushchev' and in 1968 he was expelled from the Communist Party, dismissed from all offices and declared a traitor; he died in prison in 1969. Deng Xiaoping was purged as the second-ranking 'Capitalist Roader'. Peng Dehuai was accused of being a counter-revolutionary and disappeared; he died in 1974. Peng Zhen, the powerful mayor of Beijing, also disappeared. Even Zhou Enlai and Zhu De were attacked in the occasional Red Guard wallposter.

Red Guards The Red Guards changed the face of the Cultural Revolution. Exactly how they started is unknown, but it seems that no-one planned or foresaw their appearance at Beijing University in May 1966. The group was initially suppressed but Mao was quick to recognise its potential. He gave his official support to the movement and unleashed a 'madness' that may have surprised even him. Millions of teenagers were given an opportunity to physically and psychologically attack and humiliate teachers, professors, cadres and others in authority.

Where conflicts about leadership arose, the Red Guard factions fought each other as well. Arms, even mortars, were seized from local militia, and the Red Guards fought each other to the brink of civil war. In 1967 Mao was forced to call in the army to end the chaos, using weapons when necessary to disarm the Guards and end the factional fighting.

Cultural Dissolution The Cultural Revolution was a time of cultural dissolution, reminiscent of the book-burning of Qin Shihuang 2000 years before. This time it was Mao's wife, Jiang Qing, a former Shanghai B-grade film star, who became the cultural supremo.

The dissolution of art and culture originated at least as far back as 1942 in Yan'an when Mao delivered his 'Talk on Arts & Letters'. He laid down the principles which were to govern the Communist Party's approach to culture. Mao said there is no such thing as art for art's sake, no art which transcends class or party, and no art independent of politics. All art and literature serve political ends and were to be made to serve the interests of the Communist Party.

Universities and secondary schools were closed for some of the Cultural Revolution; intellectuals were dismissed, killed, persecuted or sent to labour in the countryside. Publication of scientific, artistic, literary and cultural periodicals ceased. Movies, plays and operas from before the Cultural Revolution disappeared. Theatres, movies, radio, TV and loudspeakers in train carriages were dominated by Jiang Qing's 'Revolutionary Model Operas', which portrayed themes from the Chinese Revolution or the post-1949 period. Connoisseurs of music could enjoy compositions like *The Chuang Minority Loves Chairman Mao with a Burning Love* and *The Production Brigade Celebrates the Arrival in the Hills of the Manure Collectors*.

Bookstores sold the works of Mao Zedong and little else. In 1964 Lin Biao summarised Mao's teachings in the 'little red book' of Mao's quotations for the army and peasants; in 1966 copies flooded the cities. Literally hundreds of millions of 'little red books' rolled off the presses in every major language.

The Red Guards attacked writers, artists and intellectuals, destroying their works and sending them to labour in the countryside. Temples were ransacked, monasteries disbanded and monks sent to the countryside or sometimes killed. Physical reminders of China's past, including temples, monuments, and works of art considered to have been bound up with exploitation, capitalism or feudalism were consequently destroyed.

Fall of Lin Biao

Three years after Mao began his revolution, the Red Guards had risen and been suppressed, Liu Shaoqi had been locked away, and millions of people had been sent to labour in the fields. Mao's victory was so complete that at the 9th National Party Congress in 1969, Lin Biao stated that 'whoever opposes Chairman Mao Zedong's thought, at any time or under any circumstances, will be condemned and punished by the whole Party and the whole country'. Mao Zedong and Mao Zedong Thought were the unifying forces behind the Party government military, and the man was raised virtually to the level of emperor. The 1969 National Congress also adopted a new constitution, reportedly drafted by Mao himself. It designated Lin Biao, who was defence minister and vice-chairman of the Party and who was referred to as Mao's 'closest comrade in arms', as Mao's successor. It therefore came as a shock in 1972 when it was announced that Lin Biao had been killed in a plane crash in September 1971 while fleeing to the Soviet Union after a failed assassination attempt and coup against Mao.

With the army firmly in power and Lin designated as Mao's successor, it seems unlikely that he should have tried to wrest command from a man in the last few years of his life. It's possible that Lin may have been planning a coup or that Mao feared he was and had him killed. Whatever the truth, the story of the plane crash was effective in suggesting that Lin actually attempted a coup and was therefore a traitor.

Rise of Zhou Enlai

With Lin dead and Mao's health steadily deteriorating as he approached 80 years of age, Premier Zhou Enlai now exercised the most influence in the day-to-day governing of China. Remarkably, Zhou survived the Cultural Revolution, though he tended to support the same economic policies as Liu Shaoqi. His loyalty to Mao, however, appears never to have wavered since Mao assumed supreme leadership of the Party in the 1930s. As premier, Zhou's main preoccupation during the Cultural Revolution was to hold together the administrative machinery of the government.

After the 1969 Congress, Zhou set about reorganising the government structure and restoring and expanding China's diplomatic and trade contacts with the outside world – including the USA. Despite attempts at reconciliation by the Chinese in the 1950s, the US continued to follow a policy of armed 'containment' of China which aimed to isolate and eventually bring about the collapse of the Communist government.

In 1969 the Nixon administration finally cancelled most of the restrictions against trade, travel, and cultural and journalistic contacts with China; Chinese and US diplomats discussed terms of peaceful coexistence and the ceasing of US armed protection of Taiwan. The Bamboo Curtain finally parted in 1972 when Nixon stepped off the plane at Beijing airport, to be greeted by Zhou.

The Second Coming of Deng Xiaoping

In 1973 Zhou was able to return to power none other than Deng Xiaoping, vilified as China's 'No 2 Capitalist Roader' during the Cultural Revolution.

There were now two factions vying for power in the Chinese leadership. The first was the 'moderates' or 'pragmatists' led by Zhou Enlai and Deng Xiaoping. The second was the 'radicals', 'leftists' or 'Maoists'. Yet there was no open conflict between Zhou and Mao, and certainly Deng must have been brought back with Mao's approval.

The 'Maoist' faction was led by Mao's wife Jiang Qing, who rode to power during the Cultural Revolution on Mao's name and her marriage certificate. With their power threatened by the resurgence of Zhou and Deng, the radicals mounted the oddly named 'Criticise Lin Biao and Confucius' campaign – in reality an attack on Zhou and Deng.

While Zhou lived, the inevitable power struggle was kept at bay. However, his health rapidly deteriorated and, in the midst of the radical resurgence, he died in early January 1976. A memorial service was held in the Great Hall of the People in Beijing, from which Mao was inexplicably absent.

After the memorial service the period of

mourning was unexpectedly declared over. Deng Xiaoping suddenly disappeared from public view and the newspapers started to propagate the line that China was once again threatened by people in authority who were taking the 'capitalist road'. The post of acting premier went to the fifth-ranking Vice-Premier Hua Guofeng, little known in the West. Deng had been passed over for what appeared to be a compromise candidate for the job.

Tiananmen Incident 1976

In March 1976, during the Qing Ming Festival when the Chinese traditionally honour the dead, people began to lay wreaths dedicated to Zhou on the Heroes' Monument in Tiananmen Square; every night, for about a week, huge piles of paper flowers were removed from the square. More and more people came to honour Zhou with wreaths and eulogies until the square was filled with thousands of people. Wreaths were sent by ministries of the central government, departments of the central command of the People's Liberation Army and other military units as well as factories, schools, stores and communes in the Beijing area.

For the Chinese, Zhou represented both the antithesis of the madness and fanaticism of the Cultural Revolution and its instigators, and the last vestige of goodness and justice in the government – without him everything seemed lost. Though there was some scattered official support for the demonstration in Tiananmen, on the whole it was a rare, spontaneous display of how the Chinese felt about what was happening. Indirectly it was an attack on Mao and an open defiance of the leftists who had commanded that there be no more mourning for Zhou.

In the early hours of 5 April, the wreaths and poems in Tiananmen were again torn down from the square and carted away. Those who tried to prevent the removal of the tributes were arrested, and guards surrounded the monument. The same day tens of thousands of people swarmed into the square demanding the return of the wreaths and the release of those arrested, only to be attacked and dispersed by thousands of men wearing the armbands of the Workers' Militia and armed with staves. The subsequent demonstrations and riots became known as the 'Tiananmen Incident'. The demonstrations were declared counter-revolutionary and the blame was laid on Deng. On 7 April a meeting of the Politburo stripped Deng of all office and Hua Guofeng was made vice-chairman of the Party and continued as premier.

Mao was still in public view but disappeared in the middle of the year. Who had access to him, what he was being told, whether he still had the capacity to grasp and influence any of the events taking place, is unknown. The Chinese were now going through another struggle. Mao had led them against the Kuomintang, the Japan and the US in Korea, and then into the depths of the Cultural Revolution. Finally at Tiananmen his own people turned against him, just a few blocks from his home behind the walls of the Zhongnanhai government compound.

In late July the massive Tangshan earthquake struck northern China, claiming over a quarter of a million lives. For the Chinese great natural disasters foreshadow the end of dynasties, and once again it seemed as though a cycle of Chinese history had finished. With the portentous sign from heaven that he had lost the mandate to rule, Mao died in the early hours of 9 September 1976.

The Gang of Four

With Mao gone the two factions had to stand on their own feet. The meat in the sandwich was Hua Guofeng, whose authority rested largely on his status as the chosen successor to Mao Zedong.

Change came swiftly and dramatically. Less than a month after the death of Mao, Hua Guofeng had Jiang Qing and a number of other leftist leaders and their supporters arrested. She and three other principal allies of Mao – Yao Wenyuan, Zhang Chunqiao and Wang Hongwen – were selected as scapegoats for this latest ideological change and became known as the 'Gang of Four'.

Yao Wenyuan first won praise from Mao

in 1957, when as a relatively young writer he wrote an article against bourgeois influence in the arts and journalism. During the Cultural Revolution Yao became a Politburo member, responsible for Party propaganda and mass media. Zhang Chunqiao for most of his career was involved in literary propaganda work; during the Cultural Revolution he became vice-premier. Wang Hongwen was a political activist at factory-floor level in Shanghai at the beginning of the Cultural Revolution; by 1973 and before he was 40 years old he was a vice-chairman of the Communist Party.

The Third Coming of Deng Xiaoping

In the middle of 1977 Deng Xiaoping returned to power for the third time and was appointed to the positions of vice-premier, vice-chairman of the Party and chief of staff of the PLA. His return heralded yet another battle royal for the leadership – this time between Deng and Hua.

Hua did not have the unequivocal support of the Party since he was really a compromise leader for both left and right factions. Yet it was not until September 1980 that he finally relinquished the post of premier to Zhao Ziyang, a long-standing member of the Communist Party whose economic reforms in Sichuan in the mid-1970s overcame the province's bankrupt economy and food shortages and won him Deng's favour. In June 1981 Hu Yaobang, a protégé of Deng's for several decades, was named Party chairman in place of Hua.

Final power now passed to the collective leadership of the six-member Standing Committee of the Communist Party, which included Deng, Hu and Zhao. The China they took over was racked with problems – a backward country had to be modernised and the material standard of living improved. Ways had to be found to rejuvenate and replace an aged leadership (themselves) and to overcome the possibility of leftist backlash. The wasteful and destructive power struggles that had plagued the Communist Party since its inception had to be eliminated. The need for order had to be reconciled with the popular desire for more freedom; those with responsibility had to be rewarded but watched over in case of misuse of privilege; the crisis in faith in the Communist ideology had to be overcome; and a regime now dependent on the power of the police and military for its authority had to be legitimised.

Trial of the Gang of Four

The first dramatic step taken to guard against a leftist backlash was the trial of the Gang of Four and a number of its supporters at the end of 1980.

Jiang Qing was accused of framing and persecuting to death Liu Shaoqi and other high-ranking Party members and of making false charges against others. She was labelled a 'ringleader of the Lin Biao and Jiang Qing counter-revolutionary cliques' and was accused of working to overthrow the government and of 'tyrannising the people'.

The others were accused variously of working hand in glove with Jiang Qing to seize power; of making false charges against Party members; of plotting an armed rebellion in Shanghai; of agitating for a counter-revolution and being instrumental in creating violent disturbances across China in 1976; of smearing people who mourned Zhou Enlai's death as counter-revolutionaries; of falsely charging Deng Xiaoping of being the person behind the Tiananmen Incident; of engineering several incidents during the Cultural Revolution which led to the death, wounding or maiming of many innocent people; of framing Peng Dehuai; and of conspiring with Lin Biao to seize power and assassinate Mao.

The trial was reminiscent of Stalin's show-trials of the 1930s. 'Guilty' was a foregone verdict, as one political faction wreaked revenge on another, though the demise of the 'leftists' provided general relief. Jiang Qing and Zhang Chunqiao were sentenced to death but were given a two-year reprieve in which to repent their sins; their sentences were commuted to life imprisonment. The others were sentenced to long prison terms.

Resolution of a Theological Crisis

Deng was able to ward off immediate threats from the leftists by locking them up, but he still had to deal with a major crisis – what to do with Mao Zedong. One step taken was the resolution on the historical roles of Mao Zedong and Liu Shaoqi issued in 1981 by the Central Committee of the Communist Party.

Deng had every intention of pulling Mao off his pedestal and making a man out of the god. However, he couldn't denounce Mao as Khrushchev had denounced Stalin, since Mao had too many supporters in the Party and too much respect among the common people. An all-out attack would have provoked those who would otherwise have begrudgingly fallen in line with Deng and his supporters. Instead a compromise stand was taken.

The resolution cited Mao as a great Marxist and a great proletarian revolutionary, strategist and theorist saying:

> It is true that he made gross mistakes during the Cultural Revolution, but, if we judge his activities as a whole, his contributions to the Chinese Revolution far outweigh his mistakes.

The resolution went on to blame Mao for initiating and leading the Cultural Revolution which 'was responsible for the most severe setback and the heaviest losses suffered by the Party, the state and the people since the founding of the People's Republic'. The economic policies of Liu Shaoqi (who had died in prison in 1969) were given unequivocal rehabilitation.

Purge of the Party

The trial of the Gang of Four was a major step towards breaking the power of Deng's opponents. However, there were still large numbers of Maoists in the bureaucracy who could obstruct the implementation of Deng's new policies. In 1983 the Central Committee of the Communist Party launched a three-year campaign referred to as an 'overall rectification of Party style and consolidation of Party organisations' – a purge by any other name but without the violence of previous purges. Between two and four million people lost their Party membership in an effort to remove those who still supported the Gang of Four and to ensure the survival of Deng's policies beyond the grave. Deng has also elevated a number of younger supporters to the Politburo and other high-ranking government and Party positions.

Foreign Policy

Chinese relations with foreign countries are largely determined by the government's economic policies, which aim rapidly to modernise China by importing technology and teachers. A number of pressing foreign policy problems remain. These include the continued occupation of Taiwan by the Kuomintang, the status of Hong Kong after 1997, the continued occupation of Macau by the Portuguese, and China's continued role in the conflict in Cambodia.

The Taiwan problem is not ancient history and the scars of the bitter civil war run deep. Today the Beijing government no longer talks of liberating Taiwan but of a peaceful solution which would allow it to join the People's Republic, and perhaps even allow the Kuomintang to govern the island and retain its own military.

Hong Kong became a British possession as a result of the treaties forced on China in the 19th century. In 1898 the large area known as the New Territories, which joined China to the Kowloon Peninsula, was leased by Britain for 99 years. In 1984, with the lease due to expire, Britain agreed to hand the entire colony lock, stock and skyscrapers back to China in 1997.

The position of Macau is simpler. In 1974 the new left-wing government in Portugal tried to give Macau back to China as part of their drive to pack up the ragtag Portuguese empire, but the Chinese refused to take it. The Portuguese constitution now regards Macau as Chinese territory under Portuguese administration, and 1999 is the date set for its official return to China.

On China's southern borders the 'Communist monolith' theory of the 1950s and 1960s took another beating with the (disastrous) Chinese invasion of Vietnam in 1979. In their desperation to drum up support against the Vietnamese, the Chinese allied themselves with the despicable Khmer Rouge regime of Pol Pot. The Chinese have continued their support for the Khmer Rouge and appear willing to fight to the last Cambodian.

The Chinese also have a serious 'foreign policy' problem in Tibet (Xizang in Chinese). Since the 1950 invasion it has been administered as an autonomous region of China, but many Tibetans are resentful of the Chinese for their dismantling of Tibetan political and economic systems and especially, of Tibetan Buddhism. Its leader, the Dalai Lama, has been in exile in northern India since 1959, when anti-Chinese feeling led to riots.

The destruction of thousands of monasteries occurred as part of the Cultural Revolution. Violence has occurred more recently. Twenty-seven monks were arrested for demonstrating against China outside Lhasa's Jokhang Temple in October 1987. Four days later, at least eight Tibetans and six Chinese police were killed when a mob of about 2000 Tibetans stoned and set fire to a police station in the capital. Since then riots have occurred each year and foreigners have been banned from visiting Tibet except on special organised tours.

The Dalai Lama refuses to return to his homeland until the Chinese withdraw and recognise his claims, both to religious leadership and as head of the Tibetan 'government in exile'. See the Tibet chapter for more details.

Dissidence

One common characteristic of the top Communist leaders (including Mao, Zhou, Hua and Deng) is that they have been essentially authoritarian and do not accept challenges to their power. The right to set up political parties in opposition to the Communist Party, the right to publish independent opposition newspapers, and the right to voice ideas or philosophies in opposition to the Party's official line have all been suppressed, to varying degrees, by the Communist leaders.

The first major suppression resulted from the 'Hundred Flowers' campaign of 1956. In that year the Communist leadership encouraged the Chinese to speak out and voice their opinions of the new government. To the leaders' horror many intellectuals challenged the Party's right to be the sole political force in the country. The following year untold numbers of people who had expressed opposition to the Communists were arrested and imprisoned. The second great suppression was, of course, the Cultural Revolution, which raised the thoughts of Mao to a state religion and smashed those who questioned it.

Then came the 'Democracy Wall Movement' in November 1978, in which political wallposters were glued to a wall in the middle of Beijing by anyone with an opinion to air. The movement was initially supported by Deng Xiaoping, possibly to drum up mass support for his campaign against Hua Guofeng, possibly to make a good impression in the USA, which Deng was about to visit before full diplomatic relations were established in January 1979. Later that year Deng moved to close down Democracy Wall; plain-clothes police were sent in to disrupt the crowds that gathered at the wall each day, and the leading activists were arrested and imprisoned. In January 1980 Deng gave an important speech in which he insisted that the right to put up wallposters be stripped from China's constitution because it had been exploited by a 'handful of reactionaries with ulterior motives' to undermine China's 'stability and unity' and threaten its plans for economic development.

At the end of 1986 the general mood of impatience with the speed of reform was dramatically highlighted in the streets of Hefei, Wuhan, Shanghai and Beijing. In these and other cities thousands of students and workers marched and used wallposters to press for liberty, democracy and better living conditions.

The government was quick to counter these demands with honeyed words. These were followed in early 1987 by an all-out attack on 'bourgeois liberalism' (essentially the Western political concepts of democracy and freedom), and on those seeking 'all-round Westernisation'. The government deemed this incompatible with the 'four basic principles' of Party policy: adherence to the socialist road, Marxism-Leninism-Mao Zedong Thought, leadership of the Communist Party and the dictatorship of the proletariat.

Within days, the vice-president of Hefei University, Fang Lizhi (commonly known as the 'Sakharov of China'), was sacked from his post; Liu Binyan, one of China's leading intellectuals and a renowned crusader against corruption, was expelled from the Communist Party; and a liberal paper in Shanghai was placed under direct censorship. Rumours quickly circulated about the role of Hu Yaobang, general secretary of the Communist Party, whose outspoken support of reform allegedly once included the comment:

> Marx never saw a light bulb, Engels never saw an airplane, and neither of them ever visited China.

With conservative factions clamouring for sacrifice, Hu disappeared from official functions for several weeks until he made world news in January 1987 by resigning from his post.

At the time many observers took this as evidence of a conservative backlash against the reform process. But in November 1987 at the CCP's 13th Congress, Deng became the first Chinese leader to freely abdicate power when he stood down from all of his posts except central military commander, paving the way for the election of Zhao Ziyang as Party general secretary. Zhao vacated the position of premier, which then went to Soviet-educated Li Peng. Both Li and Zhao were described at the time as 'reformers with reservations'. With the appointment of several members of the new generation to the Politburo's Standing Committee, and Deng's success at persuading his fellow octogenarian Long-March veterans (the 'old comrades') to follow him into retirement, for awhile it looked as if China was headed for a new period of openness and market-oriented reform. The encouraging omens of 1987 didn't last long.

The unleashing of free (though limited) market forces, the reduction of state subsidies, and an increase in money supply all combined to bring rapid price inflation to China in 1988. Panicking consumers made a run on the banks and used their money to stock up on all manner of goods before prices could be raised. Officially, the inflation rate was reported to be 20%, but many observers thought that 30% was a more realistic figure. Remembering that inflation helped bring down the Kuomintang in 1949, conservative Communist Party leaders called for a halt to the reforms – at a time when many economists were saying that China needed even more rapid reforms.

Adding fuel to the fires of discontent were increasing reports of corruption at all levels of government. Public discontent with inflation, corruption, nepotism, the lack of individual freedom and the slow pace of reform was a recipe for protest. The catalyst turned out to be the death of Hu Yaobang.

Bloodshed in Beijing, 1989

At the age of 73, Hu Yaobang died suddenly from natural causes on 15 April 1989. Although not exactly a hero of the students when he lived, his death served as a rallying point for reformists. On 22 April during the weekend after his death, China's leaders gathered at the Great Hall of the People for an official 'mourning for Hu'. Just outside, in Tiananmen Square, approximately 150,000 students and other activists held their own ceremony which soon turned into a massive pro-democracy protest.

It didn't end there. As the weather warmed up students flocked to Beijing to camp out in the square. By the middle of May, the crowds of protesters in and around the square had swelled to nearly one million. Workers and even policemen joined in. Protests erupted in at least 20 other cities. Approximately 3000 students staged a hunger strike for democracy in the square. Railway workers assisted students wanting to come to Beijing by allowing them free rides on the trains. Students enrolled at Beijing's Art Institute constructed the 'Goddess of Democracy' in Tiananmen Square – a statue which bore a striking resemblance to America's Statue of Liberty. The students made speeches demanding a free press and an end to corruption and nepotism. Huge pro-democracy demonstrations in Hong Kong, Macau and Taiwan lent support. The arrival of the foreign press corps turned the 'Beijing Spring' into the media event of 1989.

While vehemently denouncing the demonstrations, Communist Party leaders showed surprising restraint for awhile. A major reason for this might have been the fact that Soviet leader Mikhail Gorbachev was scheduled to visit Beijing from 15 May to 18 May for the first Sino-Soviet summit since 1959 – a bloodbath just before his arrival would probably cause him to cancel the trip.

On 20 May, straight after Gorbachev's departure, martial law was declared. Zhao Ziyang was ousted from power because he had openly sympathised with the students. Li Peng assumed control of the party with the backing of Deng Xiaoping and Yang Shangkun. Troops were slow to mobilise, and when they did enter the city they found their way obstructed by huge crowds who'd set up roadblocks. A widely rumoured plan by the military to deploy forces using Beijing's subway system was halted when transit workers shut down the power supply.

Protests spread to other cities. Besides demonstrations on the Chinese mainland, 500,000 demonstrators in Hong Kong marched through the streets and held rallies. About 100,000 people demonstrated in Macau.

As troops surrounded Beijing, the enthusiasm began to shrivel. Crowds of students camped out in Tiananmen Square dwindled to around 10,000. The military assault came in the pre-dawn hours of 4 June. Tanks entered Tiananmen Square around 2 am. Just what happened next has been disputed. The government says that the students attacked troops with rocks, clubs and Molotov cocktails. The students say that tanks ploughed into the crowd and soldiers opened fire. Since the attack took place at night and thousands of troops and civilians were in the street, foreign journalists on the scene had a hard time knowing who did what. The number of deaths will never be known. While the government first claimed that there were no civilians killed in the square, some observers estimated the death toll at 3000. The truth probably lies somewhere in between, but no credible figures exist. In addition to the civilian deaths, an undetermined number of soldiers was also killed as outraged Beijing residents fought back. Many of the deaths took place in the streets near Tiananmen rather than in the square itself.

Sporadic violence continued through the next few days. Foreign journalists managed to capture a good deal of this on video tape which was subsequently broadcast around the globe, and world opinion quickly turned against China's government. Chinese students studying abroad staged large-scale protests and a number of Chinese diplomats defected.

No sooner had the blood been washed off the streets than the wave of arrests and executions began. The 'Beijing Spring' was abruptly followed by a severe winter – those caught just speaking to a foreign journalist were immediately arrested for 'rumour mongering'. Chinese television showed 'hooligans' – their faces badly swollen from beatings – confessing to 'counter-revolutionary crimes'. While ordinary people were being arrested, a political purge was also under way in the upper ranks of the Communist Party. Party general secretary Zhao Ziyang was made the scapegoat. Zhao was replaced by Jiang Zemin, well known as the 'weather vane' because of his ability to point in whatever direction the political winds are blowing.

The official government version of history is that the 'anti-government riot' was the work of counter-revolutionaries and foreign agents in the USA, Taiwan and elsewhere. The government quickly staged photo sessions with grateful little girls giving the soldiers sliced watermelons and thanking them for saving the country from the counter-revolutionaries – this was at a time when troops were ordered not to accept food from Beijing residents because the military feared it would be poisoned.

The brutal suppression of the pro-democracy movement has had a major impact on China's economy. Tourism, foreign aid and investment have fallen off sharply. Hong Kong has also been badly affected – money and talent is rapidly fleeing the colony in anticipation of the Chinese takeover, due in 1997.

For a while it looked as if Dengism would replace Maoism. Mandatory political meetings to study the thoughts of Deng Xiaoping were organised. Chinese newspapers eulogised him as China's 'great helmsman', a term not heard since the the days of Mao when people waved the little red book and sang 'Sailing the Seas Depends on the Helmsman'. Surreal propaganda reminiscent of the Cultural Revolution dominated the Chinese media. Foreign publications were banned and the government started jamming broadcasts by the BBC and Voice of America. In an attempt to break the news blockade, Chinese students in the USA, Australia and elsewhere started bombarding Chinese companies with fax messages so people inside China could know what the foreign news media was saying. In a mockery of Deng Xiaoping's exhortation to 'learn truth from facts', journalists called this new movement 'learn truth from fax'.

Many have feared that China would revert to its xenophobic past and close off to the outside world. This, at least, has not happened. A year after the protests, martial law was finally lifted and things more or less returned to normal. However, disillusionment and cynicism (both within and outside of China) remain deep. It is doubtful that the Communist Party will be able to regain the moral authority and respect it once commanded unless major reforms are instituted.

The Future

Every revolution evaporates, leaving behind only the slime of a new bureaucracy.

Franz Kafka

The 1990 Asian Games were held in Beijing and were notable for the number of sports fans who didn't show up (most foreigners stayed away and Chinese fans were barred from entering the capital for security reasons).

Able to suppress most political opposition, the Communist Party firmly controls the police and military, and there is little likelihood of another revolution in the immediate future. Yet the Communist Party suffers from an inherent instability – there has never been a means for orderly succession. The Long March veterans are mere mortals with little time left in which to shape China's destiny. China is a gerontocracy – the most powerful men in the country, including Deng Xiaoping and President Yang Shangkun, are approaching the age of 90 with no designated successors. One possible successor, Li Peng, is one of the most widely hated men in China. As when Mao died, a power struggle seems inevitable when the current wheelchair leadership departs the scene. Ever since the Communists came to power, the leadership has been engaged in constant battles between factions. The faction fights run deep throughout the Politburo, military and police. Classical Marxism vehemently denounces dynasties, yet the aging Communists in Beijing have frequently put their children into positions of power – only increasing the factional rivalries. At this point no one can predict who will come out on top and who will be purged.

No matter who gains power, the next generation of leaders will inherit enormous problems which will require a great deal of talent and imagination to solve. At the moment, China is stagnating both economically and politically. Officially, the government's policy is that there can be no compromise on the 'four cardinal principles – adherence to the socialist road, to the people's democratic dictatorship, to the lead-

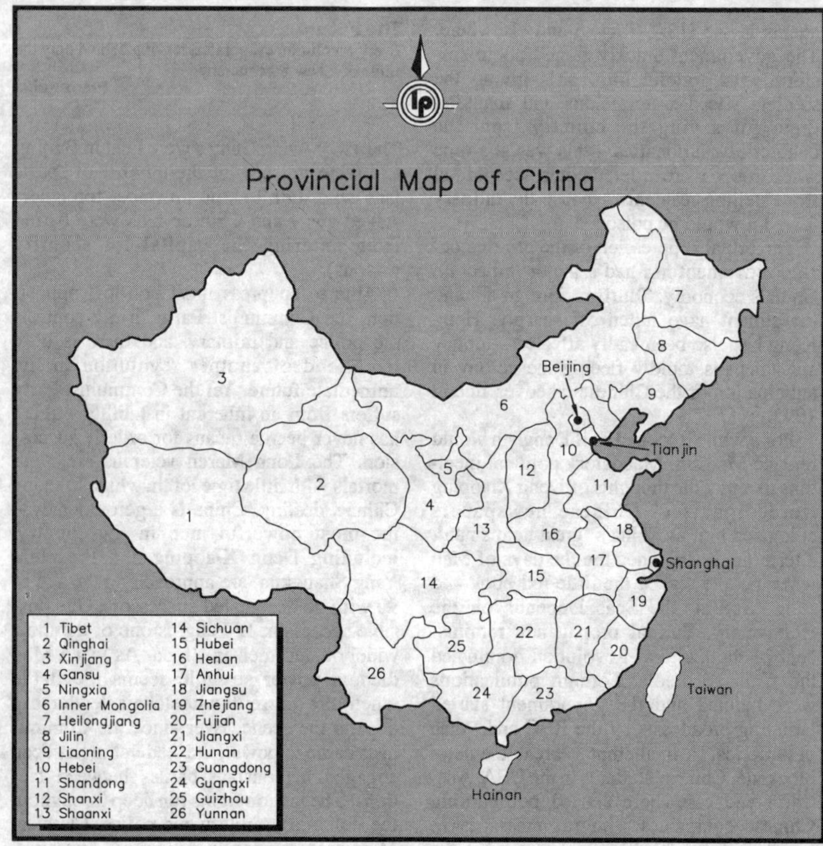

ership of the Communist Party and to Marxism-Leninism and Mao Zedong Thought'. The population, however, has become increasingly cynical and disillusioned with politics. With fast-paced reforms taking place in eastern Europe and the USSR, China is finding itself looking increasingly out-of-date in a rapidly changing world.

GEOGRAPHY

The insularity of the Chinese is very much a product of geography; the country is bounded to the north by deserts and to the west by the inhospitable Tibetan Plateau. The Han Chinese, who first built their civilisation around the Yellow River (Huang He), moved south and east towards the sea. The Han did not develop as a maritime people so expansion was halted at the coast; they found themselves in control of a vast plain cut off from the rest of the world by oceans, mountains and deserts.

China is the third largest country in the world, after the Soviet Union and Canada. Only half of China is occupied by Han Chinese; the rest is inhabited by Mongols, Tibetans, Uigurs and a host of other 'national minorities' who occupy the periphery of Han China, in the strategic border areas. The existence of numerous minority languages is why maps of China often have two spellings for the same place – one spelling being the minority language, the other being Chinese. For example, Kashgar is the same place as Kashi.

From the capital Beijing the government rules 21 provinces and the five 'autonomous regions' of Inner Mongolia, Ningxia, Xinjiang, Guangxi and Tibet. Beijing, Tianjin and Shanghai are administered directly by the central government. China also controls about 5000 islands and lumps of rock which occasionally appear above water level; the largest of these is Hainan off the southern coast. Taiwan, Hong Kong and Macau are all firmly regarded by the People's Republic as Chinese territory, and under the 1984 agreement with Britain, Hong Kong will be handed back to China in 1997. There is conflict with Vietnam concerning sovereignty over the Nansha and Xisha island groups in the South China Sea; Vietnam claims both and has occupied some of the Nansha Islands. In 1989 the Chinese took some of these islands from Vietnam by force. Other disputed islands in the Nansha group are also claimed by the Philippines, Taiwan and Malaysia.

China's topography varies from mountainous regions with towering peaks to flat, featureless plains. The land surface is a bit like a staircase descending from west to east. At the top of the staircase are the plateaus of Tibet and Qinghai in the south-west, averaging 4500 metres above sea level. Tibet is referred to as the 'Roof of the World'. At the southern rim of the plateau is the Himalayan mountain range, with peaks averaging 6000 metres high; 40 peaks rise 7000 metres or more. Mt Everest, known to the Chinese as Qomolangma Feng, lies on the China-Nepal border.

Melting snow from the mountains of western China and the Tibet-Qinghai Plateau provides the headwaters for many of the country's largest rivers: the Yangtse (Chang Jiang), Yellow (Huang He), Mekong (Lancang Jiang) and Salween (Nu Jiang) rivers. The latter runs from eastern Tibet into Yunnan Province and on into Myanmar (Burma).

Across the Kunlunshan and Qilianshan mountains on the northern rim of the Tibet-Qinghai Plateau and the Hengduanshan mountains on the eastern rim, the terrain drops abruptly to between 1000 and 2000 metres above sea level. The second step down on the staircase is formed by the Inner Mongolia, Loess and Yunnan-Guizhou plateaus, and the Tarim, Sichuan and Junggar basins.

The Inner Mongolia Plateau has open terrain and expansive grasslands. Further south, the Loess Plateau is formed of loose earth 50 to 80 metres deep – in the past the soil erosion which accompanied a torrential rainfall often choked the Yellow River. The Yunnan-Guizhou Plateau in the south-west has a lacerated terrain with numerous gorges, rapids and waterfalls, and is noted for its limestone pinnacles with large underground caverns such as those at Guilin and Yangshuo.

The Tarim Basin is the largest inland basin in the world and is the site of the Xinjiang Autonomous Region. Here you'll find the Taklamakan Desert (the largest in China) as well as China's largest shifting salt lake, Lop Nur *(lóbù bó)*, where nuclear bombs are tested. The Tarim Basin is bordered to the north by the Tianshan mountains. To the east of this range is the low-lying Turpan Depression, known as the 'Oasis of Fire' and the hottest place in China. The Junggar Basin lies in the far north of Xinjiang Province, beyond the Tianshan range.

As you cross the mountains on the eastern edge of this second step of the topographical staircase, the altitude drops to less than 1000 metres above sea level. Here, forming the third step, are the plains of the Yangtse River valley and northern and eastern China. These plains – the homeland of the Han Chinese, their 'Middle Kingdom' – are the most important agricultural areas of the country and the most heavily populated. It should be remembered that two-thirds of China is mountain, desert, or otherwise unfit for cultivation. If you exclude the largely barren regions of Inner Mongolia, Xinjiang and the Tibet-Qinghai Plateau from the remaining third, all that remains for cultivation is a meagre 15 or 20% of land area. Only this to feed a billion people!

In such a vast country, the waterways quickly took on a central role as communication and trading links. Most of China's rivers flow east. At 6300 km long, the Yangtse is the longest in China and the third longest river in the world after the Nile and the Amazon. It originates in the snow-covered Tanggulashan mountains of south-western Qinghai, and passes through Tibet and several Chinese provinces before emptying into the East China Sea.

The Yellow River, about 5460 km long and the second longest river in China, is the birthplace of Chinese civilisation. It originates in the Bayan Harshan mountains of Qinghai and winds its way through the north of China into the sea east of Beijing. The third great waterway of China, the Grand Canal, is the longest man-made canal in the world. It originally stretched 1800 km from Hangzhou in south China to Beijing in the north, though most of it is no longer navigable.

CLIMATE

China experiences great diversity in climate. Spread over such a vast area, the country is subject to the worst extremes in weather, from the bitterly cold to the unbearably hot. There isn't really an 'ideal' time to visit the country, so use the following information as a rough guide to avoid temperature extremes. The warmest regions in winter are found in the south and south-west in areas such as Xishuangbanna, the south coast and Hainan Island. In summer, high spots like Emeishan are a welcome relief from the heat.

The Yangtse River is China's dividing line for indoor heating – the government permits those living north of the river to burn coal for heat. Those living south of the river must make do with warm clothing.

North

Winters in the north fall between December and March and are incredibly cold. Beijing's temperature doesn't rise above 0°C (32°F), although it will generally be dry and sunny. North of the Great Wall, into Inner Mongolia or Heilongjiang, it's much colder with temperatures dropping down to -40°C and you'll see the curious sight of sand dunes covered in snow.

Summer in the north is around May to August. Beijing temperatures can rise to 38°C (100°F) or more. July and August are also the rainy months in this city. In both the north and south most of the rain falls during summer.

Spring and autumn are the best times for visiting the north. Daytime temperatures range from 20°C to 30°C (68°F to 86°F) and there is less rain. Although it can be quite hot during the day, nights can be bitterly cold and bring frost.

Central

In the Yangtse River valley area (including Shanghai) summers are long, hot and humid. Wuhan, Chongqing and Nanjing have been dubbed 'the three furnaces' by the Chinese.

You can expect very high temperatures any time between April and October. Winters are short and cold, with temperatures dipping well below freezing – almost as cold as Beijing. It can also be wet and miserable at any time apart from summer. While it is impossible to pinpoint an ideal time to visit, spring and autumn are probably best.

South

In the far south, around Canton, the hot, humid periods last from around April through September, and temperatures can rise to 38°C (100°F) as in the north. This is also the rainy season. Typhoons are liable to hit the south-east coast between July and September.

There is a short winter from January to March. It's nowhere near as cold as in the north, but temperature statistics don't really indicate just how cold it can get, so bring warm clothes.

Autumn and spring can be good times to visit, with day temperatures in the 20°C to 25° C (68°F to 75°F) range. However, it can be miserably wet and cold, with perpetual rain or drizzle, so be prepared.

North-West

It gets hot in summer, but at least it's dry. The desert regions can be scorching in the daytime. Turpan, which sits in a depression 150 metres below sea level, more than deserves the title of the 'hottest place in China' with maximums of around 47°C (117°F).

In winter this region is as formidably cold as the rest of northern China. In Ürümqi the average temperature in January is around -10°C (14°F), with minimums down to almost -30°C (-22°F). Temperatures in Turpan are only slightly more favourable to human existence.

Tibet

For details of this special region see the Tibet chapter in this book.

FLORA & FAUNA

Given the fact that China is a large country spanning most of the world's climatic zones, it's not surprising that there is a great diversity in plant and animal life. Unfortunately, human beings have had a considerable impact and much of China's rich natural heritage is rare, endangered or extinct. To the government's credit, more than 300 nature reserves have been established protecting over 1.8% of China's land area. Many animals are officially protected, though illegal hunting and trapping continues. A bigger problem is habitat destruction, caused by agriculture, urbanisation and industrial pollution.

Bird-watching is a possibility, especially in the spring. Some good places for this activity include the Zhalong Nature Reserve in Heilongjiang Province; Qinghai Lake in Qinghai Province; and Poyang Lake in northern Jiangxi Province – China's largest freshwater lake.

Animals are animals – in the wild they wisely avoid humans. Other than some pathetic specimens in zoos, you probably won't get to see many exotic animals in China. However, there is a good deal of wildlife on the luncheon menu – snake, monkey, pangolin, bear, giant salamander and raccoon are among the tastes that can be catered for, not to mention more mundane dog, cat and rat dishes.

Perhaps no animal better represents the both the beauty and the struggle of wildlife in China than the panda. These splendid animals are endangered by a combination of hunting, habitat encroachment and natural disasters. Sparsely populated regions of Sichuan, Tibet and Xinjiang provide a habitat for other magnificent creatures including snow leopards, argali sheep and wild yaks.

The extreme north-east part of China is inhabited by some interesting mammals – reindeer, moose, musk deer, bears, sables and tigers. There is also considerable bird life – cranes, ducks, bustards, swans and herons are among the winged creatures found in this region.

Plants have fared somewhat better under the crunch of a billion people, but deforestation, grazing and intensive cultivation have taken a toll. One of the rarest trees is the magnificent Cathay silver fir in Guangxi Province. China's last great tracts of forest are in the subarctic north-east region near the USSR border. For sheer diversity of vegetation, the area around Xishuangbanna in the tropical south is the richest part of China. This region also provides habitats for herds of wild elephants. Both the creatures and the tropical rainforest are under intense pressure from slash-and-burn agriculture.

Hainan Island also has diverse tropical plant and animal life. There are seven nature reserves on the island, though it's fair to say that more than a few endangered species still end up on the dinner plate.

Perhaps the most beautiful cultivated plant is the bamboo. Bamboo – which is actually a grass rather than a tree – comes in many varieties and is cultivated in south-east China for use as building material and food.

Other useful plants include herbs, among them ginseng, golden hairpin, angelica and fritillary.

If you're interested in delving further into China's flora and fauna, one of the best books on the subject is *Living Treasures* by Tang Xiyang (Bantam Books, 1987).

GOVERNMENT

Precious little is known about the inner workings of the Chinese government, but Westerners can make educated guesses.

The highest authority rests with the Standing Committee of the Communist Party Politburo. The Politburo comprises 25 members. Below it is the 210-member Central Committee, made up of younger Party members and provincial Party leaders. At grass-roots level the Party forms a parallel system to the administrations in the army, universities, government, and industries. Real authority is exercised by the Party representatives at each level in these organisations. They, in turn, are responsible to the Party officials in the hierarchy above them, thus ensuring strict central control.

Between 1921 and 1935 the general secretary of the Central Committee and the Politburo held overall leadership of the Party. The significance of this title changed during the Long March when Mao became the Party chairman, assuming power over both Party and government. The post of general secretary was subordinated to him and eventually abolished in 1945. Provision was then made for a chair and four vice-chairs to constitute a Standing Committee of the Politburo.

The Standing Committee of the Politburo still retains supreme power but its members are now accorded a hotchpotch of titles. Foremost on the Standing Committee is general secretary Jiang Zemin. Diminutive Deng Xiaoping no longer holds any official government posts, yet remains the most powerful man in China. Another member of the Standing Committee is the relatively youthful (in his 60s) Premier Li Peng. The post of general secretary was restored in 1956 as a top administrative job and seems to be regaining its original mantle as the foremost leadership position in the Party. However, in the Chinese political sphere titles and appearances are slippery things and often belie the holder's real power. Hu Yaobang was general secretary until he was suddenly dropped or, to put it officially, 'resigned' the post in a political upheaval in 1987. His successor, Zhao Ziyang, was even more unceremoniously dumped in 1989 and has disappeared from public view – his fate is unknown.

The day-to-day running of the country lies with the State Council, which is directly under the control of the Communist Party. The State Council is headed by the premier. Beneath the premier are four vice-premiers, 10 state councillors, a secretary-general, 45 ministers and various other agencies. The State Council implements the decisions made by the Politburo: it draws up quotas, assesses planning, establishes priorities and organises finances. The ministries include Public Security, Education, Defence, Culture, Forestry, Railways, Tourism, Minority Affairs, Radio & Television, the Bank of China and Family Planning.

Rubber-stamping the decisions of the Communist Party leadership is the National People's Congress (NPC). In theory the NPC is empowered to amend the constitution and to choose the premier and members of the State Council. The catch is that all these officeholders must first be recommended by the Central Committee, and thus the NPC is only an approving body. Its composition is surprising: there is a sizable number of women, non-Communist Party members, intellectuals, technical people and industrial managers. The army is not well represented and nor are the rural areas which supply only a small fraction of the total of NPC members.

Exactly why so much effort is made to maintain the NPC and give it publicity through TV and newspapers is unknown, but it seems important for the Chinese government to maintain the illusion of democracy. The NPC also chooses the President of the People's Republic, who at the time of this writing was octogenarian Yang Shangkun.

The president, the theoretical head of state, in fact has little political power, although Yang has gained much influence through his connections to the military – his younger half-brother, Yang Baibing, is secretary-general of the Central Military Commission which controls the army.

If the NPC is a white elephant, then the great stumbling block of the Chinese political system is the bureaucracy. There are 24 ranks on the ladder, each accorded its own particular privileges. The term 'cadre' is usually applied to all bureaucrats, but that term includes both the lowliest clerks and the political leaders with real power (from the work-unit leaders to Jiang Zemin) as well as Party and non-Party members. Despite attacks on the bureaucratic system by the Red Guards it survived intact, if many of its former members did not. Deng's three-year purge (headed by Hu Yaobang) weeded out many officials who might slow down implementation of his new economic policies. Other offenders (according to the *Selected Works of Deng Xiaoping* published in 1983) include the despotic, the lazy, the megalomaniac, the corrupt, the stubborn and the unreliable.

Problems with the Chinese bureaucracy really began with the Communist takeover in 1949. When the Communist armies entered the cities the peasant soldiers were installed in positions of authority as Party representatives in every office, factory, school and hospital. Once in power these revolutionaries, who had rebelled against the despotism of the Kuomintang, reverted to the inward-looking, conservative values of their rural homes: respectful of authority, suspicious of change, interested in their families' comfort, sceptical of the importance of technology and education, and suspicious of intellectuals. Their only real training had been in the Red Army, which had taught them how to fight, not how to run a modern state. During the 1950s Liu Shaoqi and Deng Xiaoping tried to build up a competent bureaucracy, but their training organisations were decimated by Mao's Cultural Revolution. The bureaucratic system survived but new officials had neither the technical competence nor the ideological zeal which was supposed to push China on to greater glories. The slothfulness, self-interest, incompetence and preoccupation with the pursuit of privilege continued.

At grass-roots level the basic unit of social organisation outside the family is the work unit *(dānwèi)*. Every Chinese person is a member of one, whether he or she works in a hospital, school, office, factory or village. Many Westerners may admire the cooperative spirit this system is supposed to engender, but they would cringe if their own lives were so intricately controlled. Nothing can proceed without the work unit. It issues ration coupons for grain, oil, cotton and coal, and it decides if a couple may marry or divorce and when they can have a child. It assigns housing, sets salaries, handles mail, recruits Party members, keeps files on each unit member, arranges transfers to other jobs or other parts of the country, and gives permission to travel abroad. The work unit's control extends into every part of the individual's life.

The Chinese political scene is made up of white elephants, stumbling blocks and work units. There is even a bogeyman to contend with – the army. The People's Liberation Army covers the land forces, the navy and the air force, and developed from the Chinese Workers and Peasants Red Army of the 1920s and '30s. The army is currently being trimmed down from about 4.2 million members to around three million. There are also several million workers and peasants in the local militia, which can be mobilised in time of war.

In 1949 the army took control of every institution in China. The Cultural Revolution strengthened its grasp, and there is still a considerable overlap between the Party, army and State. The death of Lin Biao was a major blow to the army's power. Deng dealt another major blow by putting on trial, and subsequently imprisoning, a number of high-ranking military leaders who had supported the Gang of Four. In a delicate transfer of power he has also tried to wean the army away from participation in the political scene and towards target practice and modernisation of equipment and fighting techniques.

Mao held that 'political power grows out of the barrel of a gun'. He also maintained that 'the Party commands the gun and the gun must never be allowed to command the Party'. The gun (or armed forces) has been a burden in Chinese politics because whoever had control of it could do away with their opponents. Mao lost almost all influence in the civilian government during the early 1960s, but his command of the army was the deciding factor in the showdown with Liu Shaoqi. Likewise, Deng Xiaoping couldn't have made a comeback after Mao's death if the military had completely supported Jiang Qing. Whichever faction can control the military is likely to control the government. As to the other manipulations involved, if you can work out how Deng could come back three times from the political grave then you have probably unlocked the secrets of political power in China today.

Political Dissidence & Repression

If you close the people's mouths and let them say only nice things, it keeps the bile inside.

from one of the last posters to appear on Democracy Wall

The events in 1989 showed that not everyone in China is content with the political system, which clearly lacks channels allowing constructive criticism to reach the higher levels of government. In the last decade a handful of extraordinarily courageous political dissidents spoke their minds and paid the price. Many such dissidents though labelled 'counter-revolutionaries' were, ironically, devoted Communists. Once a dissident is convicted as a counter-revolutionary, there is next to no legal recourse since he or she is stripped at the same time of political and civil rights.

There are several categories of dissident: members of 'democracy and human rights' movements; individuals protesting unjust treatment by officials, arbitrary arrest, or miscarriage of justice; members of religious organisations; and members of ethnic minorities protesting for political or religious reasons.

Wei Jingsheng, a leading figure in the Democracy Wall Movement, was arrested during the first 'Beijing Spring' of 1979. After a seven-hour trial Wei was sentenced to 15 years imprisonment. He spent the following years in solitary confinement in Beijing Prison No 1. Wei was reportedly transferred in 1983 to a psychiatric clinic as his mental health had suffered; it was rumoured that he was then moved to a camp in Qinghai Province. In 1986 it was reported that Wei had died in a psychiatric hospital in Jilin Province. Many other activists in the Democracy Wall Movement such as Ren Wanding, Liu Qing, Wang Xizhe and Xu Wenli were imprisoned. In 1986 there was an unconfirmed report of a government document stating that Wei Jingsheng's death should serve as a reminder of the fate of counter-revolutionaries.

Catholics in China have repeatedly been arrested and imprisoned for refusing to break with the Vatican and join the independent Roman Catholic Church in China. The Roman Catholic Bishop of Shanghai, Ignatius Gong Pinmei, consistently supported independence of the church from the government. Reportedly still detained in Shanghai's main prison, Bishop Gong was arrested in 1955. Sentenced to life imprisonment in 1960, he has spent well over 30 years in prison. Many other Roman Catholic priests and lay Catholics have been arrested and imprisoned. Father Francis Xavier Zhu Shude was first detained in a labour camp in 1953, and was repeatedly sentenced to further imprisonment for carrying out religious duties in the camp. He died there in 1983 at the age of 70, after more than 30 years in detention.

Tibetan dissidents such as Kalsang Tsering, Lobsang Chodag and Thubten Kelsang Thalutsogentsang have been arrested in Lhasa for expressing support for the Dalai Lama and Tibetan independence.

Prisoners are held in a variety of institutions, including prisons, detention centres, labour camps and corrective labour camps. Remote areas such as Tibet, Qinghai, Xinjiang and some provinces in the north-east contain large numbers of such camps, which serve as the equivalent of political exile for dissidents sent there.

The Chinese government rigorously ignores requests for information on dissidents on the grounds that this topic is beyond 'foreign interference': it is strictly an 'internal affair'. Quite possibly South Africa, which has received much criticism from China, could argue that apartheid qualifies as an internal matter. The truth is that any country which denies access to such topics invites conjecture as to the validity of its claims of justice.

More details on this topic can be found in publications such as Amnesty International's China report or *Seeds of Fire – Chinese Voices of Conscience*, edited by Geremie Barmé and John Minford.

ECONOMY

When the Communists came to power in 1949, some change in the economic conditions of the people and the country was inevitable, for the old China could not have been worse off. The cessation of war, the setting up of a stable government and redistribution of the fat of the past regimes could only improve China for the better.

China's economic policies have undergone a radical change since the death of Mao Zedong and the fall of the so-called Gang of Four. Mao had largely isolated China from the world economy, apprehensive that economic links with other countries would make China dependent on them. Believing that private enterprise would return China to the oppressive capitalism of the past, he used the Cultural Revolution to put an end to even the most basic forms of private enterprise. All aspects of the economy, from barber shops and restaurants to steel mills and paddy fields, came under state ownership and rigid state control.

Deng has reversed these policies. The official slogan is that China will develop 'socialism with Chinese characteristics'. Another Deng slogan – 'to get rich is glorious' – is much more popular with the masses. Modernisation of the country is to be achieved by turning away from the narrow path of self-reliance and centralised planning of the Mao era, and by importing foreign technology and expertise. Essentially these policies are a continuation of the work done in the early 1960s by Deng Xiaoping and Liu Shaoqi. The aim is to achieve the 'Four Modernisations' (of industry, agriculture, defence and science & technology), quadruple production of everything, boost individual income dramatically and turn China into a modern state by the year 2000.

Today the PRC's centrally planned economy has moved to a complex three-tier system. On the first rung is the state, which continues to control consumer staples (such as grains and edible oils) and industrial and raw materials. On the second rung come private purchases or sales of services and commodities within a price range set by the state. On the third rung is the rural and urban 'free market' in which prices are established between buyer and seller, except that the state can step in if there are unfair practices.

Trying to reconcile the conflict between socialist theory and the reality of the free-market reforms (which are capitalist) has been a problem for the Communist Party. The official explanation is that China is still in the 'primary stage of socialism' and that the reforms are a temporary measure to help the country out until a purer form of socialism can evolve. In no way does the Party admit that the country could be moving towards capitalism, or that capitalism could be more efficient than socialism.

Industrial Reform

Prior to 1979 a factory would be allotted a certain quantity of raw materials and told to produce a certain number of units by the appropriate ministry in Beijing. Any profit had to be remitted to the central government. It was then up to the ministry to determine how much of that profit should be returned to the factory in the form of subsidies for repairs, retooling or expansion. Factory managers were essentially cogs in a machine controlled from above.

Following decisions made at the end of 1978, centralised control was relaxed and state-controlled enterprises were thrown back on their own resources, having to find their own raw materials, set production targets, and hire and fire their own labour force instead of accepting workers assigned to them by state labour bureaus. The state gets its share of the profits through taxation, and what's left is retained by the factory to be reinvested or spent. Workers are paid overtime, and can receive bonuses if the factory does well. Early in 1983 the government began testing a system whereby workers are hired on contract, though they can be fired for causing economic losses or breaking rules.

Rural Reform

In 1978 the government introduced an agricultural 'responsibility' system which replaced the rigidly collectivised agriculture system instituted under Mao. The system is applied differently from province to province, retaining state-owned farms in the north-east where mechanised agriculture prevails, while in the south-west 'market gardening' controlled by individual villages or families is more appropriate, given the difficult terrain.

Under the system a work team or family was contracted to work a plot of state land. They decided what to grow and when, provided the government with its quota, and were then allowed to sell any surplus at rural free markets and keep the profit. In 1984 a new system was initiated whereby peasants would be granted long land leases with the right to transfer and renew their leaseholds, although it is not possible for peasants or anyone else to actually own land.

Around the end of 1984 it was decided to do away with the quota system which required peasants to sell a certain percentage of their produce to the state. The idea now is that if peasants can get more for their produce in free markets it will encourage them to increase production. The two exceptions are grain and cotton, over which the state maintains control. The state contracts for grain and cotton then purchases its requirements for more than the market price and permits the rest of the crop to be regulated by the market price. In theory, when the market price is high the state sells its reserves to bring the price down.

In early 1985, after more than 35 years of rigid price controls, the government took the crucial step of lifting those controls in Canton and Shanghai. This applied to most consumer goods in those cities including meat, eggs, fish, poultry, dairy products, fruits and vegetables. Controls continued on grain, edible oils, cotton and a few other products. The lifting of controls has created an unworkable two-tiered price system. That is, some goods can be bought on the free market at a much higher price than state-subsidised goods. The result is corruption – government officials and state-owned companies buy subsidised goods only to sell them illegally on the free market at an enormous profit. The capitalist solution would be to remove all price controls and subsidies, but this has not happened.

Foreign Investment

In sharp contrast to the extreme self-reliance of the Maoist period is China's present open-door policy on foreign investment and joint-venture enterprises with foreign companies.

In an attempt to attract foreign investment to China, the government has set up 'Special Economic Zones' such as Shenzhen County which borders Hong Kong. Low wages, reduced taxation and abundant labour have been used to encourage foreign companies to set up industries in the SEZs. Low production costs mean that Chinese goods can be competitive on the world market. Since 1984, when 14 coastal cities were opened to foreign investment along similar lines, just about every major city and town has been seeking foreign investment. There are hundreds of joint-venture enterprises, from oil and gas exploration in the South China Sea to the construction of several commercial nuclear power plants.

Not all goes smoothly – foreign business people are sometimes driven mad by the Kafkaesque paperwork for contracts, by the overcharging, or by just plain inefficiency in the use of equipment and even unwillingness on the part of the Chinese to accept advice on increasing production. Interference by government officials is a serious problem. Foreign companies are usually not free to hire and fire employees, and companies are often forced to give the best managerial jobs to those with political connections, rather than to those who are most qualified. Nor are foreign companies free to use incentives like higher pay for deserving employees. Government officials set the salaries, often at exorbitant rates, but the money is not paid to the employee – it first goes to the government, which then deducts anywhere from 50% to 90% for the state.

Another problem is that the Chinese show little respect for intellectual property. Foreign companies who set up high-technology factories in China have often found that once the Chinese learn their manufacturing techniques, the state will set up a new factory in competition with the foreign venture. Because the foreign companies are being charged exorbitant rates for land, labour and materials, they may find themselves unable to compete against the state operation – thus, they are forced to withdraw from the China market. The foreign companies may own patents and copyrights, but these hold little weight in the Chinese legal system.

Petty jealousy has long been a serious problem in Chinese society. If one individual earns too much money, he or she is persecuted by coworkers and neighbours. Thus, most workers within a company receive the same wage regardless of merit. A lack of employee incentives and worker absenteeism are two problems that continue to plague most state-run enterprises. To combat these inefficiencies, most government-owned companies now have a system where workers are paid a bonus if the company earns a profit. However, the bonuses must be paid equally to all workers in the company and the amount tends to be very small. A disproportionate share of a company's income usually goes to support the lifestyle of the cadres who enjoy such fringe benefits as free luxury cars, free travel and twice-daily free banquets.

The money to finance China's modernisation comes from a number of sources: foreign investment, loans from foreign banks and financial organisations, the tourist industry and – more recently – a fledgling stock market. To raise foreign capital, the Chinese even seem willing, for a price, to allow the Gobi Desert to be used as a dumping ground for nuclear waste from foreign reactors. China also has vast untapped oil and mineral deposits, particularly in the outlying regions of Qinghai, Tibet and Xinjiang. Another source of foreign money is the Overseas Chinese, who are courted with appeals to patriotism and encouraged to invest in the motherland. Most of the foreign money invested in the Pearl River Delta in Guangdong Province and in the Shenzhen SEZ comes from Hong Kong and Macau and from Overseas Chinese.

Foreign trade is increasing in importance, but overall China trades very little for such a large country. With over 20% of the world's population, China only accounts for 4% of world trade.

Private Enterprise

Besides the peasants who bring their produce to sell in the free markets, there's a new breed of entrepreneur in China – the private urban business person and its subspecies the pedlar. Faced with the return of rusticated youth sent away to work during the Cultural Revolution, and growing unemployment amongst young people, the government has even tended to encourage the peddling trades.

The total workforce numbers about 450 million. A quarter of these are urban employees in state-run and collective enterprises. Almost all the rest are rural workers. Statistics for 1989 estimated the number of self-employed people in the cities and towns at 21 million, yet this only represents a tiny fraction of the total workforce. The success of the new economic policies should therefore be measured in terms of their benefits to the rural population, the vast majority of Chinese.

The private businesses and street pedlars may not seem so extraordinary, but barely more than 10 years ago, during the Maoist era, they hardly existed. Free enterprise was a dirty word from the mid-60s until the death of Mao, and during that time there were no kerbside restaurants, hardly any pedlars and no throngs of shoppers browsing and haggling with merchants on the pavements.

Although small-scale private business is encouraged, large-scale enterprises are not except for joint ventures between the foreign companies and the state. Even small businesses require a licence, and it is not unusual for the authorities to pull somebody's licence when he or she starts competing against a state-run company. Thus, you will find plenty of privately run small restaurants, barber shops and clothing stores, but don't expect to see any private department stores or big hotels.

Consumerism

An ordinary urban Chinese income is around Y120 (about US$25) per month, although in some ways that figure is deceptively low. Housing rental is fixed at between 3 to 6% of a person's income (but that could mean a tiny house or flat inhabited by several people per room), and various perks (such as bus passes, free child-care services, non-staple-food allowances, haircut and public bath allowances, and bonuses) go with some jobs. Education and medical care are free, and personal income tax is nonexistent or negligible.

It's when you look at the cost of luxury or high-quality goods or household appliances that you notice the huge gap in the buying power between the Chinese and comparatively wealthy Westerners. In China a bicycle starts from around Y300, or two to three months' wages; a sewing machine is around Y300; a down jacket costs around Y250.

Over the past few years there's been a boom in the quantity and availability of luxury consumer goods in China; the Four Modernisations may not be industry, agriculture, defence and science but cassette players, washing machines, TV sets and electric fans.

The Back Door

Production of consumer goods still cannot meet demand. The country's industries have been unable to keep pace with the new demand for household appliances, colour TVs, fashionable clothes and other luxury goods by the *nouveau riche* class of farmers, urban traders and skilled workers which has arisen in the last few years. Nor are they satisfied with Chinese merchandise; they want high status foreign cigarettes, liquor, cameras, cassette players and watches.

Because of the shortages many Chinese still rely on their connections *(gūanxì)* to supply them with luxury items. Hong Kong relatives troop over the border laden down with all sorts of presents for their relatives in the People's Republic. Connections also open the 'back door'– the unauthorised means whereby goods made in state-owned factories and intended for sale in state-owned shops pass into private hands in return for favours or bribes.

The system of privilege is another means by which a few Chinese are able to accumulate a disproportionate share of available luxuries. While few individuals could afford to buy a car, high-ranking cadres will have cars placed at their disposal by the state – which amounts to much the same thing as owning one for as long as they retain their position. Likewise, better quality housing, even hot running water, is still very much the domain of the Chinese elite.

The black market in foreign currency is another product of China's new economic policies. At lower levels, currency is bought from foreigners and resold to other Chinese who use it to buy imported consumer goods. At higher levels, the buyers are usually Chinese enterprises and individuals who use foreign currency to import consumer goods or finance their children's education overseas; the sellers are usually Hong Kong and Macau residents who, having sold their foreign currency at a much higher rate than the official exchange rate, will then buy large quantities of Chinese products which they export for profit.

Results

One of China's most abundant products is statistics. Optimistic figures are constantly produced to prove that these new policies are working. The Chinese press is full of remarkable success stories of prosperous peasants and hard-working entrepreneurs who got rich because of the new economic policies.

With the increase in quantity there has been a dramatic rise in defective goods, or 'dirty radishes', to use the Chinese expression. In 1986, the *China Daily* reported that at least a third of goods produced in China were defective or did not conform to national standards. 'Red Flag' limousines continued to do nearly four km to the litre, faulty electric blankets electrocuted sleeping grannies, and hair conditioners left women bald. Members of the 1984 Chinese expedition to the Antarctic revealed that they suffered extreme discomfort when their parkas, made in Shanghai, proved neither cold-resistant nor waterproof.

The Chinese press recently also blasted counterfeiting and copyright piracy, which have become rampant. Fake Chinese and foreign cigarettes are common, as are counterfeit medicines, wines and watches.

Overall the Chinese government seems confident that living standards are rising because of the new economic policies. However, Deng's policies have not gone unchallenged within the Communist Party leadership. As late as 1985 the Chinese press was still carrying articles criticising economic policy under Mao and exhorting officials to fall in line with Deng's new policies, while reassuring them that (somehow) these policies did not conflict with Marxism nor represent a renunciation of socialism and a return to capitalism as they feared.

Even top Party leaders have been critical. In a speech in 1985, the octogenarian Chen Yun, a conservative member of the Standing Committee of the Politburo, criticised the relaxation of central planning and the view that supply and demand could blindly determine production. He said that some media reports about growing prosperity amongst the peasants were 'divorced from reality' and that 'some people, including some Party members...[were] getting rich by illegal means like speculation, swindling, graft and bribe taking'.

Against these problems has to be weighed the argument that the Chinese people are poor and the country backward, requiring some radical new policies which might work in the long run regardless of the short-term consequences. It should be remembered that Deng's policies are being applied with the intention of raising the living standard of the great mass of Chinese, both urban and rural.

POPULATION

The official figures for 1990 show mainland China (excluding Taiwan, Hong Kong and Macau) with a population of 1,115,000,000 (1.1 billion) people. Only about a fifth of the total population lives in the cities and towns; the rest live in the villages, many of which are getting so large that they may soon have to be reclassified as cities.

The huge population has to be fed with the produce of around 15-20% of the land they live on, the sum total of China's arable land. The rest is barren wasteland or can only be lightly grazed. Much of the productive land is also vulnerable to flood and drought caused by the vagaries of China's summer monsoons or unruly rivers. Since the Revolution, irrigation and flood-control schemes have improved the situation. The Communists have managed to double food production since 1952, but the population has increased by almost the same amount, leaving the quantity of food available per person pretty much what it was 30 years ago.

More than a quarter of China's billion people were rated by the census as illiterates (people 12 years of age and over who cannot read or who can only read a few words).

Those who have been to school number a respectable 600 million, but more than half of them have been to primary school only. There are 4.4 million university graduates and 1.6 million undergraduates. Given the formidable nature of the task, the Communists have certainly made considerable improvements in education. However, the statistics indicate that the staggering population still has very little technical and scientific expertise to draw upon. Even if the Chinese can be adequately fed, the prospect of substantially improving their lot and modernising the country without foreign help is a poor one – as the Chinese government has realised.

Birth Control

Birth control programmes instituted by the Communist government in the 1950s met with some success, but were abandoned during the Cultural Revolution. The responsibility lies with Mao Zedong, whose decision was probably his greatest mistake. He believed that birth control was a capitalist plot to make China weak and that the country would find strength in a large population. His ideas very much reflected his background – that of the peasant farmer for whom many hands make light work in the fields.

It was not until 1973 that population growth targets were again included in China's economic planning, and campaigns like 'Longer, Later, Fewer' were launched. Planning for the future is a nightmare. Chinese estimates of how many people the country can support range up to 1.4 billion. The current plan is to limit growth to 1.25 billion people by the year 2000, hold that figure steady somehow, and allow birth control and natural mortality to reduce the population to 700 million, which China's leaders estimate would be ideal.

Huge billboards in cities spell out the goals for the year 2000 – modernisation and population control. The posters look like ads for a Buck Rogers sci-fi movie or Fritz Lang's *Metropolis*: planes, UFOs and helicopters fill the skies, strange vehicles glide down LA-style freeways, and skyscrapers poke out of futuristic cities. Often the only people visible are a smiling couple with their one child, often a girl. The figure on the poster is 1.25 billion, the quota set for the year 2000.

China must be given some credit – it's the only major Third World country to really tackle the population problem seriously. However, it's a daunting task – although Chinese couples are legally only permitted to have one child, it has not been easy to get a billion people to procreate to meet a government-designated quota. In recent years the main thrust of the campaign in the cities is to encourage couples to sign a one-child pledge by offering them an extra month's salary per year until the child is 14, plus housing normally reserved for a family of four (a promise often not kept because of the acute housing shortage). If the couple have a second child then the privileges are rescinded, and penalties such as demotion at work or even loss of job are imposed. If a woman has an abortion it entitles her to a vacation with pay. The legal minimum age for marriage is 22 years for men and 20 for women, but if the woman delays marrying until after 25 then she is entitled to longer maternity leave. Material incentives are also applied in rural areas, sometimes meaning that farming couples get a double-sized plot if they only have one child. All methods of birth control are free; the most common ones are the IUD, female sterilisation and abortion. Forcing women to have abortions and falsifying figures are two methods taken by some local officials in their enthusiasm to meet the 'quotas' in their area.

The birth control measures appear to be working in the cities, but it's difficult to say what's happening in the villages or if the target of zero growth can ever be reached. The catch is that Chinese agriculture still relies on human muscle and farmers find it desirable to have many children. The Chinese press has often talked about 'birth guerrillas' – pregnant women who hide out in the countryside until the child is born. Such births may not even be officially recorded, but if the 'guerrilla' is discovered after she has already given birth, she can expect to face a steep fine, loss of employment and other penalties. As late as 1971 the yearly rate of population increase stood at 2.3%, which would have doubled the population again in another 30 years. By 1979 the rate was down to 1.2%, though that would still double the population in 59 years. Ominously, the rate has crept back up to 1.24% as more couples have resisted government calls to have only one child.

If the Chinese can be convinced or pressured into accepting birth control, the one thing they cannot agree to accept is the sex of their only child. The desire for male children is deeply ingrained and the ancient custom of female infanticide continues to this day – as the Chinese government and press will freely admit. In 1982 a young man in Liaoning was sentenced to 13 years imprisonment for smothering his two-month-old daughter and throwing her body down a well. According to one Chinese news source 195 female infants in a county in Anhui Province were drowned between 1978 and 1979. The *People's Daily* has even called the imbalance of the sexes a 'grave problem', and reported that in one rural area of Hebei Province the ratio of male to female children (under the age of five) was five to one. The paper also reported a case in Zhengzhou (Henan Province) in which two applications for divorce were rejected, having been made by husbands on the grounds that their wives had given birth only to female children. In one attempt to counter this age-old prejudice against female offspring the family planning billboards depict, almost without fail, a rosy-cheeked little girl in the ideal family.

PEOPLE

Han Chinese make up about 93% of the total population; the rest is composed of China's 55 or so minority nationalities, including Mongols and Tibetans. Although minorities account for a bit less than 7% of the population, they are distributed over some 50% of Chinese-controlled territory, mostly in the sensitive border regions. Some groups, like the Zhuang and the Manchu, have become so assimilated over the centuries that to the Western eye they look indistinguishable from their Han counterparts; only language and religion separate them. Other minority groups no longer wear their traditional clothing except on market or festival days. Some have little or nothing in common with the Han Chinese, like the Turkic-descended Uigurs of Xinjiang who are instantly recognisable by their swarthy Caucasian appearance, Turkish-related language, use of Arabic script and adherence to Islam.

Han migrations and invasions over the centuries have pushed many of the minorities into the more isolated, rugged areas of China. Traditionally the Han have regarded the minority groups as barbarians. Indeed, it was only with the formation of the People's Republic that the symbol for 'dog' – which was included in the characters for minority names – was replaced with the symbol for 'man'.

Minority separatism has always been a threat to the stability of China, particularly amongst the Uigurs and the Tibetans who have poor and often volatile relations with the Han and whose homelands form the border regions of China. The minority regions provide China with the greater part of its livestock and hold vast untapped deposits of minerals.

Keeping the minorities under control has been a continuous problem for the Han Chinese. Tibet and Xinjiang are heavily garrisoned by Chinese troops, partly to protect China's borders and partly to prevent rebellion among the local population. Chinese migration to minority areas has been encouraged as a means of controlling them by sheer weight of numbers. For example, 50 years ago Inner Mongolia had a population of about four million and Xinjiang had 2.5 million. Today those figures are 19 and 13 million respectively. The Chinese government has also set up special training centres, like the National Minorities Institute in Beijing, to train loyal minority cadres for these regions. Since 1976 the government has tried to diffuse discontent by relaxing some of its grasp on the day-to-day life of the minority peoples, in particular allowing temples and mosques closed during the Cultural Revolution to reopen.

Until very recently, the minorities were exempt from China's one-child family planning guidelines. In the coming decade, government officials hope to extend the one-child family policy to minorities too, but this is sure to provoke further hostility against the Han majority.

ARTS

Many people go to China expecting a profound cultural experience. This has led to a lot of disappointment. While major attractions like the Forbidden City and the Dunhuang Buddhist caves still stand intact, many of China's other ancient treasures were ransacked or razed to the ground during the Cultural Revolution. Much of China's precious art including pottery, calligraphy and embroidery was defaced or destroyed.

In the early 1970s, with the new turn in China's foreign policy towards rapprochement with the West, the Chinese government began a superficial revival of their ancient culture to present a more acceptable 'human face' towards the outside world. A few of the ransacked temples and monasteries were restored as showpieces. Exhibitions were set up to display 'archaeological objects found during the Cultural Revolution' in some attempt to cover up the vandalism of that period. These early exhibits were open only to foreigners and Overseas Chinese, as were some antique and art-reproduction shops. A few hundred copies of Chinese classics were reprinted, but these were mainly for export.

Scene from the Beijing Opera

While the Chinese government is still trying to eradicate 'feudal' ideas, it's generally accepted that beating and smashing is no way to go about it. In the past few years there's been a determined effort to restore the sites destroyed during the Cultural Revolution, but many of the temples remain derelict or are used as factories or warehouses.

China does have some sensational cultural attractions, like the Beijing Opera, the acrobats of Beijing and Shanghai, and some budding artists and musicians. But culture in China is very much like exotic food – don't expect to find it on every street corner. The Cultural Revolution almost put an end to the old culture and the country is only now starting to recover.

Calligraphy

Calligraphy has traditionally been regarded in China as the highest form of visual art. A fine piece of calligraphy was often valued more highly by a collector of art than a good painting. Children were trained at a very early age to write beautifully, and good calligraphy was a social asset. A scholar, for example, could not pass his examination to become an official if he was a poor calligrapher. A person's character was judged by their handwriting; if it was elegant it revealed great refinement.

The basic tools of calligraphy are paper, ink, ink-stone (on which the ink is mixed) and brush. These are commonly referred to as the 'four treasures of the scholar's study'. A brush stroke must be infused with the creative or vital energy which, according to the Taoists, permeates and animates all phenomena of the universe: mountains, rivers, rocks, trees, insects and animals. Expressive images are drawn from nature to describe the different types of brush strokes – for example, 'rolling waves', 'leaping dragon', 'startled snake slithering off into the grass', 'dewdrop about to fall' or 'playful butterfly'. A beautiful piece of calligraphy therefore conjures up the majestic movements of a landscape. The qualities of the brush strokes are described in organic terms of 'bone', 'flesh', 'muscle' and 'blood'. Blood, for example, refers to the quality of the ink and the varied ink tones created by the degree of moisture of the brush.

Calligraphy is regarded as a form of self-cultivation as well as self-expression. It is believed that calligraphy should be able to express and communicate the most ineffable thoughts and feelings, which cannot be conveyed by words. It is often said that looking at calligraphy 'one understands the writer fully, as if meeting them face to face'. All over China, decorative calligraphy can be found in temples, adorning the walls of caves, and on the sides of mountains and monuments.

Painting

Chinese art is like Chinese religion – it has developed over a period of more than 2000 years and absorbed many influences. Looking at Chinese paintings for the first time, the Italian Jesuit priest Matteo Ricci (who reached China in 1582) criticised Chinese painters for their lack of knowledge of the illusionistic techniques of shading, with the result that their paintings 'look dead and have no life at all'. The Chinese were in turn astonished by the oil paintings brought by the Jesuits, which to them resembled mirror images. The Chinese rejected them as paintings because they were devoid of expressive brushwork.

Chinese painting is the art of brush and ink. The basic tools are those of calligraphy, which influenced painting in both technique and theory. The brush line, which varies in thickness and tone, is the important feature of a Chinese painting. Shading is regarded as a foreign technique (introduced to China via Buddhist art from central Asia between the 3rd and 6th centuries), and colour plays only a minor symbolic and decorative role. As early as the 9th century, ink was recognised as being able to provide all the qualities of colour.

Although you will see artists in China painting or sketching in front of their subject, traditionally the painter works from memory and is not so interested in imitating the outward appearance of the subject as in capturing its lifelike qualities and imbuing the painting with the energy permeating all nature.

From the Han Dynasty until the end of the Tang Dynasty, the human figure occupied the dominant position in Chinese painting, as it did in pre-modern European art. Figure painting flourished against a Confucian background, illustrating moralistic themes. Landscape painting for its own sake started in the 4th and 5th centuries. The practice of seeking out places of natural beauty and communing with nature first became popular among Taoist poets and painters. By the 9th century the interest of artists began to shift away from figures and, from the 11th century onwards, landscape has been the most important aspect of Chinese painting.

The function of the landscape painting was to substitute for nature, allowing the viewer to wander imaginatively. The painting is meant to surround the viewer, and there is no 'viewing point' as there is in Western painting.

In the 11th century a new attitude towards painting was formulated by a group of scholar-painters led by Su Dongpo (1036-1101). They recognised that painting could go beyond mere representation; it could also serve as a means of expression and communication in much the same way as calligraphy.

Painting became accepted as one of the activities of a cultured person, along with poetry, music and calligraphy. The scholarly amateur painters were either officials or retired people who did not depend on painting for their income. They painted for pleasure and became their own patrons and critics. They were also collectors and connoisseurs of art, and the arbiters of taste. Their ideas on art were voiced in voluminous writings and in inscriptions on paintings.

Moralistic qualities appreciated in a virtuous person (in the Confucian frame of things) became the very qualities appreciated in paintings. One of the most important was the 'concealment of brilliance' under an unassuming exterior, since any deliberate display of technical skill was considered vulgar. Creativity and individuality were highly valued, but only within the framework of tradition. Artists created their own style by transforming the styles of the ancient masters, seeing themselves as part of the great continuity of the painting tradition. This art-historical approach became a conscious pursuit in the late Ming and early Qing dynasties.

When the Communists came to power, much of the country's artistic talent was turned to glorifying the revolution and bombarding the masses with political slogans. Colourful billboards of Mao waving to cheering crowds holding up the 'little red book' were once popular, as were giant Mao statues standing above smaller statues of enthusiastic workers and soldiers. Music and opera were also co-opted for political purposes.

These days artistic expression is freer, but the government still keeps painters on a tight leash. The colourful political posters glorifying socialism are still much in evidence, though Mao is not.

Funerary Objects

As early as Neolithic times (9000-6000 BC), offerings of pottery vessels and stone tools or weapons were placed in graves to accompany the departed.

During the Shang Dynasty, precious objects such as bronze ritual vessels, weapons and jade were buried with the dead. Dogs, horses and even human beings were sacrificed for burial in the tombs of great rulers. When this practice was abandoned, replicas (usually in pottery) were made of human beings, animals and precious objects. A whole repertoire of objects was produced especially for burial, making symbolic provision for the dead without wasting wealth or making human sacrifice.

Burial objects made of earthenware were very popular from the 1st to the 8th centuries AD. During the Han Dynasty, pottery figures were cast in moulds and painted in bright colours after firing. Statues of attendants, entertainers, musicians, acrobats and jugglers were made, as well as models of granaries, watchtowers, pigpens, stoves and various other things.

Close trade links with the West were illustrated among these models by the appearance of the two-humped Bactrian camel, which carried merchandise along the Silk Road, amongst funerary objects. Warriors with west Asian faces and heavy beards appeared as funerary objects during the Northern Wei Dynasty, a foreign dynasty founded by the Turkish-speaking Tobas of central Asia. The cosmopolitan life of Tang China was illustrated by its funerary wares; western and central Asians flocked to the capital at Chang'an and were portrayed in figurines of merchants, attendants, warriors, grooms, musicians and dancers. Tall western horses with long legs, introduced to China from central Asia at the beginning of the 1st century BC, were also popular subjects for tomb figurines.

Other funerary objects commonly seen in Chinese museums are fearsome military figures dressed in full armour, often trampling oxen underfoot. The figures may have served as tomb guardians and may represent the four heavenly kings. These kings guard the four quarters of the universe and protect the state; they have been assimilated into Buddhism and you see statues of them in Buddhist temples.

Guardian spirits are some of the strangest funerary objects. A common one has bird wings, elephant ears, a human face, the body of a lion, and the legs and hooves of a deer or horse, all rolled into one. One theory is that these figures represent Tubo, the earth-spirit or lord of the underworld who was endowed with the power to ward off demons and evil spirits. He was entrusted with guarding the tomb of the deceased. Those figures with human faces may have represented the legendary Emperor Yu. He is said to have been the founder of the legendary Xia Dynasty, and was transformed into Tubo after his death.

Ceramics

Earthenware production has a long history in China. As many as 8000 years ago Chinese tribes were making artefacts with clay. The primitive 'Yangshao' culture (so named because the first excavation of an ancient agricultural village was made in the region of Yangshao near the confluence of the Yellow, Fen and Wei rivers) is noted for its distinctive pottery painted with flowers, fish, animals, human faces and geometric designs. Around 3500 BC the 'Lungshanoid' culture (so named because evidence of this ancient culture was first found near the village of Lungshan in Shandong Province) was making white pottery and eggshell-thin black pottery.

Pottery-making was well advanced by the Shang period; the most important development occurred around the middle of the dynasty with the manufacture of a greenish glaze applied to stoneware artefacts. During the Han Dynasty the custom of glazing pottery became fairly common. However, the production of terracotta items – made from a mixture of sand and clay, fired to produce a reddish-brown colour, and left unglazed – continued.

During the Southern and Northern dynasties, a type of pottery halfway between Han glazed pottery and true porcelain was produced. The proto-porcelain was made by mixing clay with quartz and the mineral feldspar to make a hard, smooth-surfaced vessel. Feldspar was mixed with traces of iron to produce an olive-green glaze. The technique was perfected under the Tang but few examples survive. Tri-colour glazed vessels were also produced during the Tang Dynasty.

By the 8th century, Tang proto-porcelain and other types of pottery had found an international market, and were exported as far afield as Japan and the east coast of Africa. Chinese porcelain did not reach Europe until the Ming period, and the techniques of making it were not developed there until the 17th century.

Chinese pottery reached its artistic peak under the Song rulers. During this time true porcelain was developed. It was made of fine kaolin clay and was white, thin and transparent or translucent. Porcelain was produced under the Yuan but gradually lost the delicacy and near-perfection of the Song products. However, it was probably during the Yuan Dynasty that 'blue-and-white' porcelain made its first appearance. This porcelain had blue decorations on a white background; it was made of kaolin clay quarried near Jingdezhen, and mixed with a type of cobalt imported from Persia.

During this period three-colour and five-colour porcelain, with floral decorations on a white background, was produced. Another noted invention was mono-coloured porcelain in ferrous red, black or dark blue. A new range of mono-coloured vessels was developed under the Qing.

During the Qing period the production of coloured porcelain continued with the addition of new colours and glazes and more complex decorations. This was the age of true painted porcelain, decorated with delicate landscapes, birds and flowers. Elaborate designs and brilliant colouring became the fashion. Porcelain imitations of other materials such as gold and silver, mother of pearl, jade, bronze, wood and bamboo, also became popular.

Bronze Vessels

Bronze is an alloy whose chief elements are copper, tin and lead. Tradition ascribes the first casting of bronze to the legendary Xia Dynasty of 4000 years ago. Emperor Yu, the founder of the dynasty, is said to have divided his empire into nine provinces and then cast nine bronze tripods to symbolise the dynasty. However, the discovery in 1928 of the last Shang Dynasty capital at Anyang in Henan Province provided the first solid evidence that the ancient Chinese used bronze.

The Shang ruler and the aristocracy are believed to have used a large number of

Bronze Tripod

bronze vessels for sacrificial offerings of food and wine. hrough ritual sacrifices the spirits of ancestors were prevailed upon to look after their descendants. The vessels were often buried with the deceased, along with other earthly provisions. Most of the late Shang funeral vessels have short, pictographic inscriptions recording the names of the clan, the ancestor and the vessel's maker, along with important events. Zhou Dynasty bronze vessels tend to have longer messages in ideographic characters; they describe wars, rewards, ceremonial events and the appointment of officials.

The early bronzes were cast in sectional clay moulds, an offshoot of the advanced pottery technology's high-temperature kilns and clay-mould casting. Each section of the mould was impressed, incised or carved with the required designs. By the 5th century BC during the Eastern Zhou period (722-256 BC), bronzes with geometric designs and scenes of hunting and feasting were inlaid with precious metals and stones.

Bronze mirrors were used as early as the Shang Dynasty and had already developed into an artistic form by the Warring States Period (476-221 BC). Ceramics gradually replaced bronze utensils by Han times, but bronze mirrors were not displaced by glass mirrors until the Qing Dynasty.

In China, the mirror is a metaphor for self-inspection in philosophical discussion. The wise person has three mirrors: a mirror of bronze in which to see their physical appearance, a mirror of the people by which to examine inner character and conduct, and a mirror of the past by which to learn to emulate successes and avoid the mistakes of earlier times. The backs of bronze mirrors were inscribed with wishes for good fortune and protection from evil influence. Post-Han writings are full of fantastic stories of the supernatural powers of mirrors. One of them relates the tale of Yin Zhongwen, who held a mirror to look at himself but found that his face was not reflected – soon after, he was executed.

Jade

The jade stone has been revered in China since Neolithic times. While the pure white form is the most highly valued, the stone varies in translucency and colour, including many shades of green, brown and black. To the Chinese, jade symbolises nobility, beauty and purity. Its physical properties have become metaphors for the Confucian ideal of the *jūnzi*, the noble or superior man.

Jade is also empowered with magical and life-giving properties. Taoist alchemists, hoping to become immortal, ate an elixir of powdered jade. The stone was thought to be a guardian against disease and evil spirits. Plugs of jade were placed over the orifices of corpses to prevent the life force from escaping. Opulent jade suits, meant to prevent decomposition, have been found in Han tombs; examples can be seen in the Nanjing Museum and in the Anhui Provincial Museum in Hefei.

Music

Traditional Chinese musical instruments include the two-stringed fiddle ***(èrhú)***, three-stringed flute ***(sānxúan)***, four-stringed banjo ***(yùeqín)***, two-stringed viola ***(húqín)***, vertical flute ***(dòngxiāo)***, horizontal flute ***(dízi)***, piccolo ***(bāngdí)***, four-stringed lute ***(pípá)***, zither ***(gǔzhēng)***, ceremonial trumpet ***(sǔonà)***, and ceremonial gongs ***(dàlúo)***.

Real culture shock strikes when East meets West over the music score. China's leadership has had a hard time deciding how to react – in the beginning, Western music was vehemently denounced by the government as another form of dangerous 'spiritual pollution'. China's first concert featuring a foreign rock group was in April 1985, when the British group Wham was allowed to perform. The audience remained sedate – music fans who dared to get up and dance in the aisles were hauled off by Public Security. Since then, things have become more liberal and China has produced some notable home-grown bands.

The hip young urban Chinese like disco music. Love songs and soft rock from Taiwan and Hong Kong appeal in Canton, but in Beijing heavy metal and punk get more of a following. There are dance halls in all the major cities to cater for these crazes – sometimes with taped music, often with live bands featuring batteries of horns and electric violins.

Attempts to tailor Chinese classical music, song and dance to Western tastes have resulted in a Frankenstein's monster of Broadway-style spectacular and epic-theatre film score. Chinese rock star Cui Jian released a big hit 'Rock for the New Long March'. In an attempt to show that the geriatric leadership is also hip, government officials authorised a disco version of 'The East is Red'. There are orchestras organised on Western lines which substitute Chinese for Western instruments. A few young Chinese have even caught on to Brazil's erotic dance, the 'lambada' – a clear case of spiritual pollution if there ever was one. Exactly where all this is leading no-one knows.

Taijiquan & Gongfu

Known in the West as 'taichi', *taijiquan* (slow motion shadow boxing) has in recent years become quite trendy in many countries. It has been popular in China for centuries. It is basically a form of exercise, but it's also an art and is one form of Chinese martial arts. *Gongfu* (previously known as 'kungfu') differs from taijiquan in that the former is performed at much higher speed and with the intention of doing bodily harm. Gongfu also often employs weapons. Taijiquan is not a form of self-defence but the movements are similar to gongfu's. There are different styles of taijiquan, such as Chen and Yang.

Taijiquan is very popular among old people and also with young women who believe it will help keep their bodies beautiful. The movements are supposed to develop the breathing muscles, promote digestion and improve muscle tone.

A modern innovation is to perform taijiquan movements to the thump of disco music. Westerners find it a remarkable sight to see a large group performing their slow motion movements in the park at the crack of dawn.

Taijiquan, dancing in the park and all manner of exercises, are customarily done just as the sun rises, which means if you want to see it or participate you have to wake up the same time as the chickens, but it's well worth it.

Qigong

As much an art form as a traditional Chinese medicine, *qigong* cannot easily be described in Western terms but it's rather like faith healing. *Qi* represents life's vital energy, and *gong* is from gongfu. Qigong can be thought of as energy management and healing. Practitioners try to project their qi to perform various miracles, including driving nails through boards as well as healing others.

It's interesting to watch them do it. Typically, they place their hands above or next to the patient's body without actually making physical contact. To many foreigners this looks like a circus act, and indeed even many Chinese suspect that it's nothing but quackery. However, there are many who claim that they have been cured of serious illness without any other treatment but qigong, even after more conventional doctors have told them that their condition is hopeless.

Qigong is not particularly popular in China. Denounced as another superstitious link to the bourgeois past, rampaging Red Guards nearly obliterated qigong and its practitioners during the Cultural Revolution. It's only recently that qigong has made a comeback, but many of the highly skilled practitioners are no longer alive. In China, you are most likely to see qigong in the ever-popular gongfu movies (many imported from Hong Kong and Taiwan), where mortally wounded heroes are miraculously revived with a few waves of the hands.

Does qigong work? It's not easy to say, but there is a theory in medicine that all doctors can cure a third of their patients regardless of what method is used. So perhaps qigong gets this cure rate too.

CULTURE

Who's in Charge?

Although many Chinese workers don't seem to have much work to do, everyone fills a specialised niche. In a hotel, one person (and one person only) is in charge of changing foreign currency for FEC. When that person is off duty, foreign currency transactions cease. Similarly, one person is in charge of bicycle rentals; one person is in charge of long-distance phone calls; one person controls postcard sales at the hotel giftshop; one person has responsibilities for map sales, etc.

The Chinese are loath to do someone else's job because they may be held responsible, especially if things don't go right. You may find it difficult or impossible to conduct some essential business like getting your deposit back when trying to return a rented bicycle if the individual in charge of such important matters is on holiday. This shouldn't be much of a problem in a private business, but in a government-run organisation you never know what you'll be up against. Screaming and yelling isn't advised – unless as a last resort – and then it's unlikely to be effective.

Making Contact

Making contact with Chinese people is not usually as simple as most visitors expect. A Chinese travel guide had this to say about encountering foreign guests:

> In trains, boats, planes or tourist areas one frequently comes across foreign guests. Do not follow, encircle and stare at them when you meet. Refrain from pointing at their clothing in front of their faces or making frivolous remarks; do not vie with foreign guests, competing for a seat, and do not make requests at will. If foreign guests take the initiative to make contact, be courteous and poised. Do not be flustered into ignoring them by walking off immediately, neither should you be reserved or arrogant. Do your best to answer relying on translation. When chatting with foreign guests be practical and realistic – remember there are differences between foreign and home life. Don't provide random answers if you yourself don't know or understand the subject matter. Refrain from asking foreign guests questions about age, salary, income, clothing costs and similar private matters. Do not do things discreditable to your country. Do not accept gifts at will from foreign guests. When parting you should peel off your gloves and then proffer your hand. If you are parting from a female foreign guest and she does not proffer her hand first, it is also adequate to nod your head as a farewell greeting.

Educating a billion Chinese to be courteous to foreigners is a formidable task. For many years few foreigners set foot in the country, let alone met the common people. Whether or not most Chinese people actually like foreigners is open to debate – but they are curious about us and sometimes genuinely friendly, and on the whole it is safe to walk the streets at any time.

Making contact with Chinese people can be frustrating. Inevitably it begins with someone striking up a conversation with you on the street, in your hotel or on a train. Unfortunately many of these conversations have a habit of deteriorating into English lessons. There is also the tendency for every conversation to be a monotonous question and answer session, with the questions always being the same.

Conversations with Chinese people usually begin with 'Can I practise my English with you?' followed by 'What country are you from?' and then 'Are you married?' 'How old are you?' 'Do you have children?' Then come the questions about money – 'How much do you make?' 'Do you have a car?' 'How much does a house cost in your country?' By this time, a crowd will have gathered and everyone will be discussing (in Chinese) your income, material standard of living, and, if the numbers sound good, immigration possibilities.

If you're learning to speak Chinese, you can use these conversations to practise your Chinese. This often works out very well, but a lot depends on your linguistic ability.

You should also remember that the Chinese are highly sensitive about political issues. Almost everyone you meet will criticise the Cultural Revolution – but that's official policy nowadays. You simply can't expect people to express their real views on the present government, though many will in private. At the same time, don't expect these 'real views' to be negative just because you think they should be. Many Chinese people won't broach any political subject at all and may say that they have no interest in politics. Don't expect anyone to be too liberal with their views if they're within earshot of others, especially since a conversation with a foreigner in public places automatically attracts a crowd of onlookers.

The official policy on Chinese talking to foreigners tends to vary. Currently it's encouraged (with reservations) – modernisation of the country requires foreign technology, and if a foreign technical journal is going to be of any use you have to be able to read the thing. Fluency in English is a path to a better job, even a chance to travel overseas to work or study, and that helps explain the enthusiasm with which the Chinese are learning the language and seeking help from stray foreigners.

Not all Chinese approach foreigners out of pure curiosity, desire to practise their language skills, or a desire to make friends. Some will approach you ostensibly to practise English but what they really want is to change your Foreign Exchange Certificates for Renminbi. Others have the strange idea that foreigners can sponsor them for emigration to the USA or Australia (the two most popular destinations). American and Australian teachers in China often find themselves targeted for marriage for this reason. A foreign husband or wife is often referred to as a 'rice ticket' *(fàn piào)* by the Chinese.

Interesting people to talk to are elderly Chinese who learned English back in the 1920s and 1930s when there were large foreign communities in China. Then there are the middle-aged who were learning English just before the Cultural Revolution but were forced to stop and started to pick it up again after a gap of several years. Next comes the younger generation of Chinese who went to school or university after the Cultural Revolution and have been able to take foreign-language courses. Even the level of proficiency attained by self-taught Chinese through English-language programmes on radio or television is quite remarkable. English is now being taught in high schools, and many young kids have a rudimentary knowledge of the language. Japanese is popular at high school and university levels. You sometimes come across French, German, Russian and Spanish speakers.

If you want to meet English-speaking Chinese then go to the 'English corners' which have developed in many large Chinese cities. Usually held on a Sunday morning in a convenient park, Chinese who speak or are learning English gather to practise the language. Also seek out the 'English Salons' – evening get-togethers at which the Chinese practise English, listen to lectures or hold debates in English. Don't expect to remain a member of the audience for very long; you may soon find yourself giving the evening lecture and struggling to answer hard questions about the outside world.

If you make a Chinese friend and want to stay in contact through letters, then it's suggested that before leaving China you buy several stamps sufficient for letters from China to your home country. The first time you write to your Chinese friend enclose the stamps – say that you had them left over when you departed China, and that you're sending the stamps because you have no use for them. One of these stamps could be half a day's wage to some Chinese – so for them to write to you really does involve a sacrifice! While you're in China you can arrange meetings by having your Chinese friend phone your hotel or post a letter. Remember to get your friend to write down his/her address on several envelopes so you can post them. In the towns and cities a letter posted before 9 am should be delivered that same afternoon. It *is* possible to visit people's homes – many Chinese feel greatly honoured by your visit, though others may feel embarrassed by their humble living conditions.

Cultural Differences

The cultural gap can be a bigger obstacle to understanding than the language barrier. On the other hand, cultural differences can be fascinating – try to keep a positive attitude. Some cultural differences you may encounter in China follow.

Face Face can be loosely considered as status and many Chinese people will go to great lengths to avoid 'losing face'. For example, a foreigner may front up at a hotel desk and have a furious row with the receptionist over dorm beds which the foreigner knows exist/are vacant while the receptionist firmly denies all knowledge of the fact. Regardless of who is right or wrong, the receptionist is even less likely to back down (and 'lose face') if the foreigner throws a fit or becomes violent. Persistent waiting may lead to a 'compromise' whereby the receptionist suddenly goes off duty to be replaced by a colleague who coincidentally finds a spare dorm bed or, after the foreigner tactfully refers to a possible 'misunderstanding', discovers a cheaper alternative. There are many such social mores which can severely maul the nerves of even the most patient of foreigners. It is pointless to steer a collision course toward these barriers, but it is often possible to manipulate your way around them.

Guanxi In their daily life, Chinese often have to compete for goods or services in short supply and many have been assigned jobs for which they have zero interest and often no training. Those who have *gūanxì* (connections) usually get what they want because the 'connections' network is, of course, reciprocal. Obtaining goods or services through connections is informally referred to as 'going through the back door' *(zǒu hòu mén)*. Cadres are well placed for this activity; foreigners are not.

Speaking Frankly People often don't say what they think, but rather what they think you want to hear or what will save face for them. Thus, the staff at the CAAC office may tell you that your flight will be here 'very soon' even if they know it will delayed two days.

Smiling A smile doesn't always mean happiness. Some Chinese people smile when they are embarrassed or worried. This explains the situation where the foreign tourist is ranting and raving at the staff in the hotel lobby, while the person behind the desk stands there grinning from ear to ear.

RELIGION

Chinese religion has been influenced by three great streams of human thought: Taoism, Confucianism and Buddhism. Although each has separate origins, all three have been inextricably entwined in popular Chinese religion along with ancient animist beliefs. The founders of Taoism, Confucianism and Buddhism have been deified. The Chinese worship them and their disciples as fervently as they worship their own ancestors and a pantheon of gods and spirits.

Taoism *(dào jiào)*

It is said that Taoism is the only true 'homegrown' Chinese religion – Buddhism was imported from India and Confucianism is mainly a philosophy. According to tradition, the founder of Taoism is a man known as Laozi. He is said to have been born around the year 604 BC, but some doubt that he ever lived at all. Almost nothing is known about him, not even his name. *Laozi* translates as 'the old one' or the 'Grand Old Master'.

Legends depict Laozi as having been conceived by a shooting star, carried in his unfortunate mother's womb for 82 years, and born as a wise old man with white hair. The most popular story is that Laozi was the keeper of the government archives in a western state of China, and that Confucius consulted him.

At the end of his life, Laozi is said to have climbed on a water buffalo and ridden west towards what is now Tibet, in search of solitude for his last few years. On the way, he was asked to leave behind a record of his beliefs. The product was a slim volume of only 5000 characters, the *Dao De Jing* or *The Way and its Power*. He then rode off on his buffalo.

At the centre of Taoism is the concept of *Dao*. Dao cannot be perceived because it exceeds senses, thoughts and imagination; it can be known only through mystical insight which cannot be expressed with words. Dao is the way of the universe, the driving power in nature, the order behind all life, the spirit which cannot be exhausted. Dao is the way people should order their lives to keep in harmony with the natural order of the universe:

There is a being, wonderful, perfect;
It existed before heaven and earth.
How quiet it is!
How spiritual it is!
It stands alone and it does not change.
It moves around and around, but does not on this account suffer.
All life comes from it.
It wraps everything with its love as in a garment, and yet claims no honour, and does not demand to be Lord.
I do not know its name, and so I call it
Dao, the Way, and
I rejoice in its power.

Just as there have been different interpretations of the 'way', there have also been different interpretations of *De* – the power of the universe. This has led to the development of three distinct forms of Taoism in China.

One form held that 'the power' is philosophical. The philosophical Taoist, by reflection and intuition, orders his or her life in harmony with the way of the universe and achieves the understanding or experience of Tao. Philosophical Taoism has many followers in the West.

The second form held that the power of the universe was basically psychic in nature, and by practising yogic exercises and meditation a number of individuals could become receptacles for Tao. They could then radiate a healing, psychic influence over those around them.

The third form is the 'popular Taoism' which took hold in China. The power of the universe is the power of gods, magic and sorcery. Because popular Taoism has been associated with alchemy and the search for immortality, it often attracted the patronage of Chinese rulers before Confucianism gained the upper hand. It's argued that only philosophical Taoism actually takes its inspiration from the *Dao De Jing*, and that the other labels under which 'Taoism' has been practised used Laozi's name to give themselves respectability. As it is commonly practised in China, Hong Kong and Taiwan, popular Taoist worship is still closely bound up with ghosts, exorcisms, faith healing, fortune telling and magic.

Confucianism *(rújiā sīxiǎng)*

More a philosophy than a religion, Confucianism has nevertheless become intertwined with Chinese religious beliefs. With the exception of Mao, the one name which has become synonymous with China is Confucius *(Kǒngzi)*. He was born of a poor family around the year 551 BC – in what is now Shandong Province. His ambition was to hold a high government office and to reorder society through the administrative apparatus. At most he seems to have had several insignificant government posts, a few followers and a permanently blocked career. At the age of 50 he perceived his 'divine mission' and for the next 13 years tramped from state to state offering unsolicited advice to rulers on how to improve their governing, while looking for an opportunity to put his own ideas into practice. That opportunity never came, and he returned to his own state to spend the last five years of his life teaching and editing classical literature. He died in 479 BC, at the age of about 72.

The glorification of Confucius began after his death, and eventually his ideas permeated every level of Chinese society. To hold government office presupposed a knowledge of the Confucian classics, and spoken proverbs trickled down to the illiterate masses. During the Han Dynasty Confucianism effectively became the state religion – the teachings were made the basic discipline for training government officials and remained so until almost the end of the Qing Dynasty in 1911. In the 7th and 8th centuries temples and shrines were built to Confucius and his original disciples. During the Song Dynasty the Confucian bible *The Analects* became the basis of all education.

It is not hard to see why Confucianism took hold in China. The perpetual conflict of the Spring and Autumn Period had inspired Confucius to seek a way which would allow people to live together peacefully. His solution was tradition. Like others of his time, he believed that there had once been a period of great peace and prosperity in China. This had been brought about because people lived by certain traditions which maintained peace and social order.

Confucius

Confucius advocated a return to these traditions and also devised values which he thought were necessary for collective wellbeing. He aimed to instil a feeling of humanity towards others and respect for oneself, as well as a sense of the dignity of human life. Courtesy, selflessness, magnanimity, diligence and empathy would naturally follow. His ideal person was competent, poised, fearless, even-tempered and free of violence and vulgarity. The study of 'correct attitudes' became the primary task. Moral ideas had to be driven home to the people by every possible means – at temples, theatres, schools, at home and during festivals, in proverbs and folk stories.

All people rendered homage to the emperor, who was regarded as the embodiment of Confucian wisdom and virtue – the head of the great family-nation. For centuries administration under the emperor lay in the hands of a small Confucian scholar class. In theory anyone who passed the examinations qualified, but in practice the monopoly of power was held by the educated upper classes. There has never been a rigid code of law, because Confucianism rejected the idea that conduct could be enforced by some organisation; taking legal action implied an incapacity to work things out by negotiation. The result, however, was arbitrary justice and oppression by those who held power. Dynasties rose and fell but the Confucian pattern never changed.

There are several bulwarks of Confucianism, but the one which has probably had the most influence on the day-to-day life of the Chinese is *li*, which has two meanings. The first meaning of li is 'propriety' – a set of manners or a knowledge of how to behave in a given situation – and presumes that the various roles and relationships of life have been clearly defined. The second meaning of li is 'ritual' – when life is detailed to Confucian lengths it becomes completely ordered.

Confucian codes of conduct and clearly defined patterns of obedience became inextricably bound up in Chinese society. Women obey and defer to men, younger brothers to elder brothers, sons to fathers.

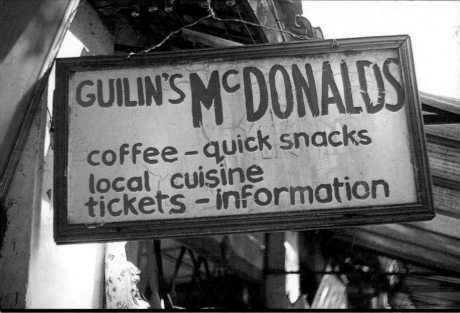

Top: Painting in Mao museum, Changsha (AS)
Bottom: Sign in Guilin (AS)

Respect flows upwards, from young to old, from subject to ruler. Age is venerated since it gives everything (including people, objects and institutions) their dignity and worth; the elderly may be at their weakest physically, but they are at the peak of their wisdom.

The family retains its central place as the basic unit of society; Confucianism reinforced this idea, but did not invent it. The key to family order is filial piety – children's respect for and duty towards their parents. Teaming up with traditional superstition, Confucianism reinforced the practice of ancestor-worship. Confucius himself is worshipped and temples are built for him. The strict codes of obedience were held together by these concepts of filial piety and ancestor worship, as well as by the concept of 'face' – to let down the family or group is a great shame for a Chinese.

Buddhism *(fó jiào)*

Buddhism was founded in India in the 6th century BC by Siddhartha Gautama of the Sakyas. Siddhartha was his given name, Gautama his surname and Sakya the name of the clan to which his family belonged.

The story goes that though he was a prince brought up in luxury, Siddhartha became discontented with the world when he was confronted with the sights of old age, sickness and death. He despaired of finding fulfilment on the physical level, since the body was inescapably subject to these weaknesses.

Around the age of 30 years Siddhartha broke from the material world and sought 'enlightenment' by following various yogic disciplines. After several failed attempts he devoted the final phase of his search to intensive contemplation. One evening as he sat beneath a bo (banyan) tree, so the story goes, he slipped into a deep meditation and emerged having achieved enlightenment. His title 'Buddha' means 'the awakened' or 'the enlightened one'.

Buddha founded an order of monks and preached his ideas for the next four decades until his death around 480 BC. To his followers he was known as Sakyamuni, the 'silent sage of the Sakya clan', because of the unfathomable mystery that surrounded him. It is said that Gautama Buddha was not the only Buddha, but the fourth, and is not expected to be the last.

The cornerstone of Buddhist philosophy is the view that all life is suffering. Everyone is subject to the traumas of birth, sickness, decrepitude and death; to what they most dread (an incurable disease or an ineradicable personal weakness), as well as separation from what they love. The cause of suffering is desire – specifically the desires of the body and the desire for personal fulfilment. Happiness can only be achieved if these desires are overcome, and this requires following the 'eightfold path'. By following this path the Buddhist aims to attain *nirvana*. Volumes have been written in attempts to define nirvana; the *suttas* (discourses of the Buddha) simply say that it's a state of complete freedom from greed, anger, ignorance and the various other 'fetters' of existence.

The first branch of the eightfold path is 'right understanding': the recognition that life is suffering, that suffering is caused by desire for personal gratification and that suffering can be overcome. The second branch

Buddha

is 'right mindedness' – cultivating a mind free from sensuous desire, ill will and cruelty. The remaining branches of the path require that one refrain from abuse and deceit; that one show kindness and avoid self-seeking in all actions; that one develop virtues and curb passions; and that one practise meditation.

The many varieties of Buddhist meditation use mental exercises to penetrate deep into the psyche, where it is believed the real problems and answers lie, and to achieve a personal experience of the verities of existence.

Buddhism developed in China from the 3rd to 6th centuries AD and was probably introduced by Indian merchants who took Buddhist priests with them on their land and sea journeys to China. Later, an active effort was made to import Buddhism into China. In the middle of the 1st century AD the religion had gained the interest of the Han Emperor Ming, who sent a mission to the West; the mission returned in 67 AD with Buddhist scriptures, two Indian monks and images of the Buddha. Centuries later, other Chinese monks like Xuan Zang journeyed to India and returned with Buddhist scriptures which were then translated from the original Sanskrit to Chinese – a massive job involving Chinese and foreign scholars from central Asia, India and Sri Lanka.

Buddhism spread rapidly in the north of China where it was patronised by various ruling invaders, who in some cases had been acquainted with the religion before they came to China. Others patronised the Buddhist monks because they wanted educated officials who were not Confucians. In the south Buddhism spread more slowly, spreading with Chinese migrations from the north. There were several periods in which Buddhists were persecuted. Their temples and monasteries were sacked and destroyed, but the religion survived. To a people constantly faced with starvation, war and poverty the appeal of this philosophy probably lay in the doctrines of reincarnation and nirvana borrowed from Indian Hinduism.

Buddhist monasteries and temples sprang up everywhere in China, and played a similar role to the churches and monasteries of medieval Europe. Monasteries were guesthouses, hospitals and orphanages for travellers and refugees. With gifts obtained from the faithful, they were able to amass considerable wealth, which enabled them to set up moneylending enterprises and pawnshops. These pawnshops were the poor man's bank right up to the mid-20th century.

The Buddha wrote nothing; the Buddhist writings that have come down to us date from about 150 years after his death. By the time these texts came out, divisions had already appeared within Buddhism. Some writers tried to emphasise the Buddha's break with Hinduism, while others tried to minimise it. At some stage Buddhism split into two major schools: *Theravada* and *Mahayana*.

The Theravada or 'doctrine of the elders' school (also called *Hinayana* or 'little vehicle' by non-Theravadins) holds that the path to nirvana is an individual pursuit. It centres on monks and nuns who make the search for nirvana a full-time profession. This school maintains that people are alone in the world and must tread the path to nirvana on their own; Buddhas can only show the way. The Theravada school is the Buddhism of Sri Lanka, Myanmar (Burma), Thailand, Laos and Cambodia.

The Mahayana or 'big vehicle' school holds that since all existence is one, the fate of the individual is linked to the fate of others. The Buddha did not just point the way and float off into his own nirvana, but continues to offer spiritual help to others seeking nirvana. The Mahayana school is the Buddhism of Vietnam, Japan, Tibet, Korea, Mongolia and China.

The outward difference between the two schools is the cosmology of the Mahayana school. Mahayana Buddhism is replete with innumerable heavens, hells and descriptions of nirvana. Prayers are addressed to the Buddha and combined with elaborate ritual. There are deities and *bodhisattvas*, a rank of supernatural beings in their last incarnation before nirvana. Temples are filled with images such as the future Buddha, Maitreya, often portrayed as fat and happy over his coming promotion, and Amitabha, a saviour who rewards the faithful with admission to a sort of Christian paradise. The ritual, tradition and superstition that Buddha rejected came tumbling back in with a vengeance.

In Tibet and in areas of Gansu, Sichuan and Yunnan a unique form of the Mahayana school is practised: Tantric or Lamaist Buddhism *(lǎmā jiào* in Mandarin). Tantric Buddhism, often called *Vajrayana* or 'thunderbolt vehicle' by its followers, has been practised since the early 7th century AD and is heavily influenced by Tibet's pre-Buddhist Bon religion, which relied on priests or shamans to placate spirits, gods and demons. Generally speaking, it is much more mystical than other forms of Buddhism, relying heavily on *mudras* (ritual postures), *mantras* (sacred speech), *yantras* (sacred art) and secret initiation rites. Priests called *lamas* are believed to be reincarnations of highly evolved beings; the Dalai Lama (see Political Dissidence & Repression) is the supreme patriarch of Tibetan Buddhism.

Chinese Religion

Taoism combines with old animistic beliefs to teach people how to maintain harmony with the universe. Confucianism takes care of the political and moral aspects of life. Buddhism takes care of the afterlife. But to say that the Chinese have three religions – Taoism, Buddhism and Confucianism – is too simple a view of their traditional religious life. At the first level Chinese religion is animistic with a belief in the innate vital energy in rocks, trees, rivers and springs. At the second level people from the distant past, both real and mythological, are worshipped as gods. Overlaid on these beliefs are popular Taoism, Mahayana Buddhism and Confucianism.

On a day-to-day level the Chinese are much less concerned with the high-minded philosophies and asceticism of Buddha, Confucius or Laozi than they are with the pursuit of worldly success, the appeasement of the dead and the spirits, and the seeking of hidden knowledge about the future. Chinese religion incorporates what the West regards as superstition; if you want your fortune told, for instance, you go to a temple. The other important thing to remember is that Chinese religion is polytheistic. Apart from Buddha, Laozi and Confucius there are many other divinities such as hearth gods and gods and goddesses for particular professions.

The most important concept in the Chinese popular religious vocabulary is luck, and the Chinese are too astute not to utilise it. Gods have to be appeased, bad spirits blown away and sleeping dragons soothed to keep luck on one's side. Geomancy *(fēngshǔi)* is the Chinese technique of manipulating or judging the environment. The location of a window, doorway or (most importantly) an ancestor's grave can have a major impact on your fortune. In Hong Kong, many of the largest skyscrapers were only constructed after careful consultation with a geomancer.

Integral parts of Chinese religion are death, the afterlife and ancestor-worship. At least as far back as the Shang Dynasty there were lavish funeral ceremonies involving the internment of horses, carriages, wives and slaves. The more important the person, the more possessions and people had to be buried with them to meet the requirements of the next world. The deceased had to be kept happy because their powers to inflict punishments or to grant favours greatly increased after death. Even today a traditional Chinese funeral can still be a lavish event.

Chinese Temples

Architecturally, the roof is the dominant feature of a Chinese temple. It is usually green or yellow and is decorated with figures of divinities and lucky symbols such as dragons and carp. Stone lions often guard the temple entrance.

Inside is a small courtyard with a large bowl where incense and paper offerings are burnt. Beyond is the main hall with an altar table, often with an intricately carved front. Here you'll find offerings of fruit and drinks. Behind is the altar with its images framed by red brocade embroidered with gold characters. Depending on the size and wealth of the temple there are gongs, drums, side altars and adjoining rooms with shrines to different gods, chapels for prayers to the dead and displays of funerary plaques. There are also living quarters for the temple keepers. There is no set time for prayer and no communal service except for funerals. Worshippers enter the temple whenever they want to make offerings, pray for help or give thanks

The dominant colours in a Chinese temple are red, gold or yellow, and green. The orange-to-red colour range represents joy and festivity. White stands for purity and is also the colour of death. Green signifies harmony, of fundamental importance to the Chinese. Yellow and gold herald heavenly glory. Grey and black are the colours of disaster and grief.

The most striking feature of the Buddhist temple is the pagoda. It was probably introduced from India along with Buddhism in the 1st century AD. Because the early pagodas were constructed of wood, they were easily destroyed by fire and subject to corrosion, so materials such as brick, stone, brass and iron were substituted. They were often built to house religious artefacts and documents, to commemorate important events, or as monuments. The Big Goose Pagoda in Xi'an is a monolithic example of pagoda construction.

During the Northern Wei period the construction of cave temples began and was continued during later dynasties. The caves at Longmen near Luoyang, at Mogao near Dunhuang, and at Yungang near Datong are some of the finest examples.

In Buddhist art the Buddha is frequently displayed in a basic triad, with a bodhisattva (a Buddhist saint who has arrived at the gateway to nirvana but has chosen to return to earth to guide lesser mortals along righteous paths) on either side. Their faces tend to express the emotions of joy, serenity or compassion. Sometimes the bodhisattvas are replaced by the figures of Buddha's first two disciples, the youthful Ananda and the older Kasyapa.

Islam *(yīsīlán jiào)*

The founder of Islam was the Arab prophet Mohammed. Strictly speaking, Muslims believe it was not Mohammed who shaped the religion but God, and Mohammed merely transmitted it from God to his people. To call the religion 'Mohammedanism' is also incorrect, since it implies that the religion centres around Mohammed and not around God. The proper name of the religion is Islam, derived from the word *salam* which primarily means 'peace', and in a secondary sense 'surrender'. The full connotation is something like 'the peace which comes by surrendering to God'. The corresponding adjective is 'Muslim'.

The prophet was born around 570 AD and came to be called Mohammed, which means 'highly praised'. His ancestry is traditionally traced back to Abraham, who had two wives, Hagar and Sarah. Hagar gave birth to Ishmael, and Sarah had a son named Isaac. Sarah demanded that Hagar and Ishmael be banished from the tribe. According to Islam's holy book the *Koran*, Ishmael went to Mecca, where his line of descendants can be traced down to Mohammed. There have been other true prophets before Mohammed, but he is regarded as the culmination of them and the last.

Mohammed said that there is only one God, Allah. The name derives from joining *al* which means 'the' with *Illah* which means 'God'. His uncompromising monotheism conflicted with the pantheism and idolatry of the Arabs. Also, his moral teachings and vision of a universal brotherhood conflicted with what he believed was a corrupt and decadent social order based on class divisions. The initial reaction to his teachings was hostile. He and his followers were forced to flee from Mecca to Medina in 622, where Mohammed built up a political base and an army which eventually defeated Mecca and brought all of Arabia under his control. He died in 632, two years after taking Mecca. By the time a century had passed the Arab Muslims had built a huge empire which stretched all the way from Persia to Spain. Though the Arabs were eventually supplanted by the Turks, the strength of Islam has continued to the present day.

Unlike in many other countries, Islam was brought to China peacefully. Arab traders who landed on the southern coast of China established their mosques in great maritime cities like Canton and Quanzhou, and Muslim merchants travelling the Silk Road through central Asia to China won converts among the Han Chinese in the north of the country. There are also large populations of Muslim Uigur people (of Turkic descent) whose ancestors first moved into China's Xinjiang region during the Tang Dynasty.

Christianity *(jīdū jiào)*

The earliest record of Christianity in China dates back to the Nestorians, a Syrian Christian sect. They first appeared in China in the 7th century when a Syrian named Raban presented Christian scriptures to the imperial court at Chang'an (Xi'an). This event and the construction of a Nestorian monastery in Chang'an are recorded on a large stone stele made in 781 AD, now displayed in the Shaanxi Provincial Museum in Xi'an.

The next major Christian group to arrive in China were the Jesuits. The priests Matteo Ricci and Michael Ruggieri were permitted to set up base at Zhaoqing in Guangdong Province in the 1580s, and eventually made it to the imperial court in Beijing. Large numbers of Catholic and Protestant missionaries established themselves in China following the invasion of China by the Western powers in the 19th century.

Judaism *(yóutài jiào)*

Kaifeng in Henan Province has been the home of the largest community of Chinese Jews. Their religious beliefs and almost all the customs associated with them have died out, yet the descendants of the original Jews still consider themselves Jewish. Just how the Jews got to China is unknown. They may have come as traders and merchants along the Silk Road when Kaifeng was the capital of China, or they may have emigrated from India. For more details, see the Kaifeng section.

Religion & Communism

Today the Chinese Communist government professes atheism. It considers religion to be base superstition, a remnant of old China used by the ruling classes to keep power. This is in line with the Marxist belief that religion is the 'opiate of the people'. Nevertheless, in an effort to improve relations with the Muslim, Buddhist and Lamaist minorities, the Chinese government is once again permitting open religious activity. However, only atheists are permitted to be members of the Communist Party. Since almost all of China's 55 minority groups adhere to one religion or another, this rule precludes most of them from becoming Party members.

Traditional Chinese religious beliefs took a battering during the Cultural Revolution when monasteries were disbanded, temples were destroyed, and the monks were sometimes killed or sent to the fields to labour. Many temples and monasteries are now derelict or have other functions. Although traditional Chinese religion is strong in places like Macau, Hong Kong and Taiwan, the temples and monasteries have a very minor religious role in mainland China.

Since the death of Mao, the Chinese government has allowed many temples (sometimes with their own contingent of monks and novices) to reopen as active places of worship. All religious activity is firmly under state control and many of the monks are caretakers within renovated shells of monasteries. Pilgrimages to burn incense, throw ***shèng bēi*** (fortune-telling wooden blocks) and make offerings to the gods by burning fake paper money appear to be common practice in temples once more. There are also stories of peasants rebuilding shrines to local gods, consulting geomancy experts before constructing buildings and graves, and burying deceased relatives with traditional religious ceremonies.

Confucius has often been used as a political symbol, his role 'redefined' to suit the needs of the time. At the end of the 19th century he was upheld as a symbol of reform because he had worked for reform in his own day. After the fall of the Qing Dynasty, Chinese intellectuals vehemently opposed him as a symbol of a conservative and backward China. In the 1930s he was used by Chiang Kaishek and the Kuomintang as a guide to proper, traditional values. During the Cultural Revolution Confucius was attacked again. Just what line to take with Confucian teachings remains a problem for the Chinese government, but they are now enjoying some kind of comeback as the government emphasises stability and respect for order and authority.

Christianity is a reminder of foreign intrusion and imperialism. The Western powers in the 19th century used the missionaries as an excuse to expand the areas on Chinese soil under their control, claiming the need to protect the missions. Besides winning religious converts, the missions posed a threat to traditional Chinese society since they introduced an alien religion, science, education and morals.

A common criticism is that many early Chinese Christians were 'rice Christians' – attracted to the power and wealth of the church rather than to the faith itself. True or not, the Chinese Christian churches survived the Communist takeover in 1949. Like the Buddhist temples, they were closed down during the Cultural Revolution; many have since been restored and are once again active places of worship.

In China today, there are believed to be 14 million Muslims, making them the largest identifiable religious group still active in the People's Republic. The government has not published official figures of the number of Buddhists, but they must be substantial since most Tibetans, Mongolians and Dai people follow Buddhism. There are around three million Catholics and four million Protestants. It's impossible to determine the number of Taoists, but the number of Taoist priests is very small.

Freedom of religion is guaranteed under the Chinese constitution, but it carries a crucial rider that 'religious bodies and religious affairs are not subject to any foreign domination'. In the late 1950s the Chinese government moved to cut off the churches from foreign influence and to place them under the control of the government. The 'Three-Self Patriotic Movement' was set up as an umbrella organisation for the Protestant churches, and the 'Catholic Patriotic Association' was set up to replace Rome as the leader of the Catholic churches.

There is much friction between the government and the Chinese Catholic church because the church refuses to disown the Pope as its leader, and because the Vatican maintains diplomatic relations with Taiwan. In March 1983, four elderly priests who had already spent long terms in prison were again given long prison sentences on charges which included subversion and collusion with foreign countries. It's thought their main offence was maintaining illicit contacts with the Vatican.

The Cultural Revolution resulted in the closure of Muslim mosques though many of these have since reopened. Of all people in China, the Tibetan Buddhists most felt the brunt of Mao's mayhem. The Dalai Lama and his entourage fled to India in 1959 when the Tibetan rebellion was put down by Chinese troops. During the Cultural Revolution the monasteries were disbanded (some were levelled to the ground) and the theocracy which had governed Tibet for centuries was wiped out overnight. Some Tibetan temples and monasteries have been reopened and the Tibetan religion is still a very powerful force among the people.

LANGUAGE

The official language of the People's Republic is the Beijing dialect, usually referred to in the West as 'Mandarin'. It's spoken mainly in the north-east and south-west. In China it's referred to as *pǔtōnghùa* or 'common speech' and the Chinese government set about popularising it in the 1950s.

Spoken

China has eight major dialects, though about

70% of the population speaks Mandarin. These days, all educated Chinese can speak Mandarin, though many people speak one of the dialects as their first language. In the countryside, people are more likely to speak only a local dialect, though most younger people will at least understand Mandarin. The other major dialect is Cantonese which is spoken in the south and is basically the same as that spoken in Hong Kong. However, Cantonese is almost unintelligible to the northerners and vice versa.

Chinese grammar is not especially difficult – indeed, it's far simpler than English. However, there are some confusing differences. One problem has to do with the use of classifiers. We have a few words in English which serve as classifiers, such as 'piece' (piece of cake) or 'ear' (ear of corn). There are over 100 classifiers in Chinese and they are used in places we would never think of in English. There is a special classifier for bicycles; a classifier for something flat and thin; a classifier for objects which are long and narrow; a classifier for rooms. Thus, a Chinese person speaking broken English may be heard saying 'one piece bicycle'; 'one piece ticket'; 'one piece stick'; or 'one piece room', etc.

To further confuse the issue, Chinese is a 'tonal' language. The difference in intonation is the deciding factor in the meaning of the word. For example, the verbs *wèn* (to ask) and *wěn* (to kiss) are only differentiated by the tone. One can only guess how many foreign students have said to their Chinese teacher 'I want to kiss you' when they meant to say 'I want to ask you'.

For all its thousands of characters, Chinese has only a bit more than 400 syllables for pronouncing them, so the tones are used to increase the number of word sounds available.

The intonation of Chinese dialects and European languages is very different which makes it difficult for people on both sides to learn each other's language. Thus the Chinese have come up with the saying 'nothing is more terrible above or below than a foreigner speaking Chinese'.

Written

Written Chinese has something like 50,000 'pictographs' – characters which symbolise objects or actions. About 5000 are in common use and you need about 1500 to read a newspaper easily.

The story goes that Chinese characters were invented by the official historian of China's mythical 'Yellow Emperor', who is supposed to have ruled over the country 4000 years ago. The earliest known characters are the *jiǎgǔwén*, simple inscriptions carved on bones and tortoise shells by primitive Chinese tribes – about 4500 such characters have been discovered. Some of these are still in use.

A system of pictographs known as *dàzhùan* continued under the Emperor Qin Shihuang, but under the succeeding Han dynasties these gave way to a system known as *lìshū*, which used constructions of dashes and dots, and horizontal and vertical strokes.

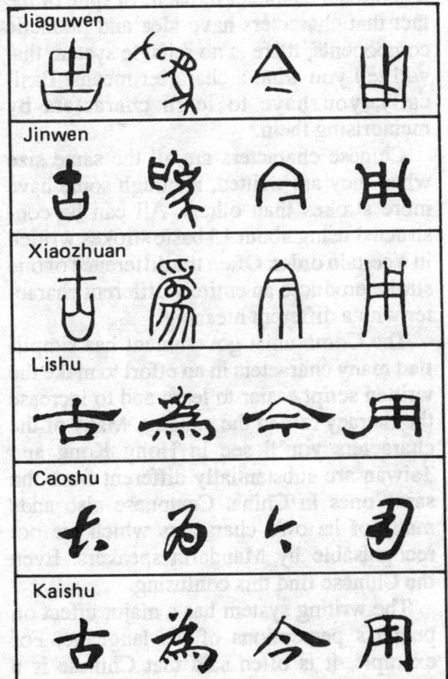

The succeeding *cǎoshū* script was written with swift brush strokes, many of them joined together to make handwriting easier. The *kǎishū* script shaped during the Wei and Jin dynasties was further simplified for ease of handwriting.

In the early stages of developing the script, each character stood for a single word. Later, two or more characters were combined to form new characters. Today, 90% of the characters in common use are made up of two or more original characters; that is, each character has two or more components.

The idea component, called a radical, often gives a clue to the meaning. Characters with related meanings usually contain the same radical. For example, the characters for mud, lake, river and oil all contain the radical which represents the character for water. There are over 200 radicals, according to which Chinese dictionaries are often arranged.

The phonetic component gives some clue to pronunciation. Like the idea component, it is often a character in itself. In spite of the fact that characters have idea and phonetic components, there is no reliable system that will tell you what a character means. Basically, you have to learn characters by memorising them.

Chinese characters are all the same size when they are written, although some have more strokes than others. All can be constructed using about 13 basic strokes written in a certain order. Often the difference of one stroke produces an entirely different character with a different meaning.

The Communist government has simplified many characters in an effort to make the written script easier to learn and to increase the literacy rate in the country. Many of the characters you'll see in Hong Kong and Taiwan are substantially different from the same ones in China. Cantonese also adds many of its own characters which are not recognisable by Mandarin speakers. Even the Chinese find this confusing.

The writing system has a major effect on people's perceptions of the language. For example, it is often said that Chinese is a monosyllabic language – that is, that each word is only one syllable long. In fact, this is not really true. Each character represents a syllable, not necessarily a whole word, though each character does have meaning (or several meanings). Most spoken words require two written characters and often three or more. For example, the Chinese character for flower *(hūa)* must be combined with two more characters to form the word for granite – flower hill rock *(hūa gāng yán)*.

Pinyin

In 1958 the Chinese officially adopted a system known as *pīnyīn* as a method of writing their language using the Roman alphabet. Since the official language of China is the Beijing dialect, this pronunciation is used. The original idea was to eventually do away with characters completely and just use pinyin. However, tradition dies hard and the idea has gradually been abandoned.

Pinyin is often used on shop fronts, street signs and advertising billboards. The popularisation of this spelling is still at an early stage, so don't expect Chinese people to be able to use pinyin. In the countryside and the smaller towns you may not see a single pinyin sign anywhere, so unless you speak Chinese you'll need a phrasebook with Chinese characters if you're travelling in these areas. Though pinyin is helpful, it's not an instant key to communication, since Westerners often don't get the pronunciation and intonation of the romanised word correct.

Since 1979 all translated texts of Chinese diplomatic documents and Chinese magazines published in foreign languages have used the pinyin system of spelling names and places. The system replaces the old Wade-Giles and Lessing systems of romanising Chinese script. Thus under pinyin, 'Mao Tse-tung' becomes *Mao Zedong*; 'Chou En-lai' becomes *Zhou Enlai*; and 'Peking' becomes *Beijing*. The name of the country remains as it has been generally written: 'China' in English and German, and 'Chine' in French – in pinyin it's 'Zhongguo'.

Maps printed in the People's Republic still retain a few spellings from minority languages such as Mongolian – thus, Chinese maps still show the city of *Hohhot (Huhehaote* in pinyin) and *Ürümqi (Wulumuqi)*.

Tones

The four basic tones are used in Mandarin, while other dialects can have as many as nine. For example, in Mandarin Chinese the word *ma* can have four distinct meanings depending on which tone is used:

high tone	— *mā* is mother
rising tone	′ *má* is hemp or numb
falling-rising tone	‿ *mǎ* is horse
falling tone	‵ *mà* is to scold or swear

In some words, the tone is not important. This so-called neutral tone is usually not indicated at all. Mastering tones is tricky for the untrained Western ear, but with practice it can be done.

The letter **v** is not used in Chinese. The trickiest sounds in pinyin are **c**, **q** and **x**. Most letters are pronounced as in English, except for the following description of the sounds produced in spoken Mandarin.

Vowels

a	like the 'a' in 'father'
ai	like the 'i' in 'I'
ao	like the 'ow' in 'cow'
e	like the 'u' in 'blur'
ei	like the 'ei' in 'weigh'
i	like the 'ee' in 'meet', or the 'oo' in 'book' when it occurs after c, ch, r, s, sh, z or zh.
ian	like in 'yen'
ie	like the English word 'yeah'
o	like the 'o' in 'or'
ou	like the 'oa' in 'boat'
u	like the 'u' in 'flute'
ui	like 'way'
uo	like 'w' followed byan 'o' like in 'or'
yu	like German umlaut 'ü' or French 'u' in 'union'
ü	like German umlaut 'ü'

Consonants

c	like the 'ts' in 'bits'
ch	like in English, but with the tongue curled back
h	like in English, but articulated from the throat
q	like the 'ch' in 'chicken'
r	like the 's' in 'pleasure'
sh	like in English, but with the tongue curled back
x	like the 'sh' in 'shine'
z	like the 'ds' in 'suds'
zh	like the 'j' in 'judge' but with the tongue curled back

Consonants (except for **n**, **ng**, and **r**) never end syllables. In pinyin, apostrophes can separate syllables – writing*(ping'an)* prevents pronouncation as *(pin'gan)*.

Gestures

Hand signs are frequently used in China. The 'thumbs-up' sign has a long tradition as an indication of excellence or, in Chinese, *gūa gūa jiào*. Another way to indicate excellence is to gently pull your own earlobe between thumb and index finger.

The Chinese have a system for counting on their hands. If you can't speak the language, it would be worth your while to at least learn Chinese finger counting. The symbol for number 10 is to form a cross with the index fingers, but in many locations the Chinese just show a fist.

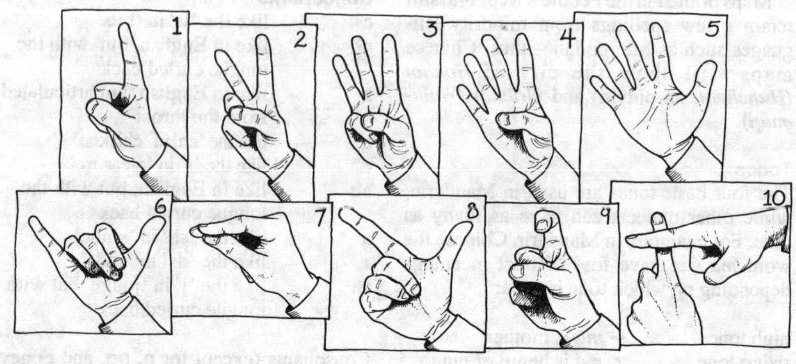

Finger Counting

Behaviour

One way to ask a question in Chinese is to place the verb together with the negative of the verb. One of the commonest examples is *yǒu méiyǒu?* (literally: have not have?). Although grammatically correct, this form of question makes it very easy for the person asked to give the reply that requires the least possible effort, namely, *méiyǒu* (not have). Nobody leaves China without having learnt this phrase! *Méiyǒu* can mean many things, such as 'not available today', 'not available for you', 'not available because I'm resting' or 'not available because I'm lazy'. To stave off this response for as long as possible, it's worth diving straight in with *wǒ yào* (I want).

I've come to the conclusion that the Chinese word for 'hello' and 'greetings' is 'meiyou'. Meiyou is what you'll hear the most and learn the first. That despised word – meiyou – was said much more often to me upon entry into an establishment than any hello I ever heard!

Deborah Koons

Máfán nǐ (literally: cause bother for you) is a useful way to butter up someone to get them to do something for you or to express gratitude for a favour they've just done you.

When you've reached an impasse by peaceful means, it often helps to ask *zěnme bàn?* (literally: what to do?). Since some Chinese people only respond to a specific question, this provides them scope to tell you about a room, bus, flight, etc you didn't know about. Sometimes the simplest things seem mighty complicated!

Phrasebooks

Phrasebooks are invaluable – but it's better to copy out the appropriate sentences in Chinese rather than show someone the book; otherwise they'll take it and read every page. Reading place names or street signs is not difficult since the Chinese name is accompanied by the pinyin form; if not you'll soon learn lots of characters just by repeated exposure. A small dictionary with English, pinyin and Chinese characters is also useful for learning a few words.

Lonely Planet publishes a *China Phrasebook* written in Mandarin as well as the *Tibet Phrasebook.*

Places

China International Travel Service (CITS)
zhōnggúo gúojì lǚxíngshè
中国国际旅行社

China Travel Service (CTS)
zhōnggúo lǚxíngshè
中国旅行社
China Youth Travel Service (CYTS)
zhōnggúo qīngnián lǚxíngshè
中国青年旅行社
embassy
dàshǐgǔan
大使馆
Foreign Language Bookstore
wàiwén shūdiàn
外文书店
Xinhua Bookstore
xīnhúa shūdiàn
新华书店

Useful Phrases

hello
nǐ hǎo
你好
good-bye
zàijiàn
再见
thank you
xièxie
谢谢
you're welcome
bùkèqì
不客气
I'm sorry
dùibùqǐ
对不起
no, don't have
méiyǒu
没有
no, not so
bù shì
不是
I am a foreign student.
wǒ shì liú xúeshēng
我是留学生.
What's to be done now?
zěnme bàn
怎么办？
It doesn't matter.
méi shì
没事.
I want...
wǒ yào...
我要…
No, I don't want it.
bùyào
不要.
I don't understand.
wǒ tīng bùdǒng
我听不懂.
I do understand.
wǒ tīngdedǒng
我听得懂.
Do you understand?
dǒng ma
懂吗？

Pronouns

I
wǒ
我
you
nǐ
你
he, she, it
tā
他，她，它
we, us
wǒmen
我们
you (plural)
nǐmen
你们
they, them
tāmen
他们

Time

What is the time?
jǐ diǎnle
几点了？
...hour...minute
...diǎn...fēn
点...分...
now
xiànzài
现在
today
jīntiān
今天
When?
shénme shíhòu
什么时候？

tomorrow
míngtiān
明天
the day after tomorrow
hòutiān
后天
three days ahead
dà hòutiān
大后天
in the morning
zǎochén
早晨
daytime
báitiān
白天
afternoon
xiàwǔ
下午
night, evening
wǎnshàng
晚上
Wait a moment.
děng yī xià
等一下.
daylight-saving time
xiàlìng shíjiān
夏令时间
Beijing (standard) time
běijīng shíjiān
北京时间

Toilets
toilet, restroom
cèsǔo
厕所
toilet paper
wèishēng zhǐ
卫生纸
bathroom (washroom)
xǐshǒu jiān
洗手间

Money
How much is it?
dūoshǎo qián
多少钱？
Is there anything cheaper?
yǒu piányì yìdiǎn de ma
有便宜一点的吗？
That's too expensive.
tài gùi le
太贵了.
Bank of China
zhōnggúo yínháng
中国银行
FEC (foreigners' money)
wài hùi jùan
外汇券
RMB (people's money)
rénmínbì
人民币
change money
hùan qián
换钱
travellers' cheque
lǚxíng zhīpiào
旅行支票

Hotel
hotel
lǚgǔan
旅馆
small hotel
lǚshè
旅社
hostel
zhāodàisǔo
招待所
tourist hotel
bīngǔan, fàndiàn, jiǔdiàn
宾馆，饭店，酒店
dormitory
duō rén fáng
多人房

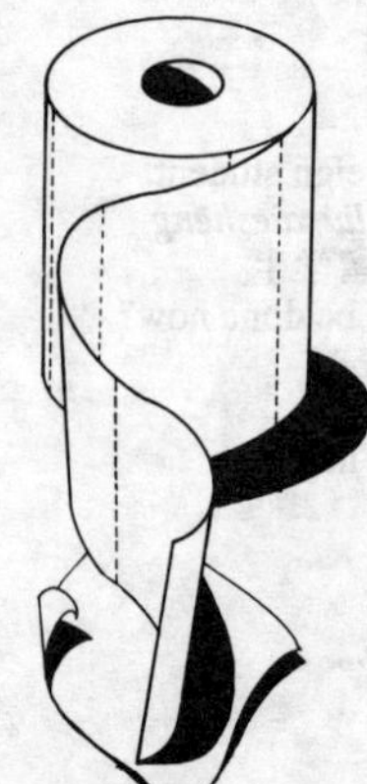

single room
dān rén fáng
单人房
double room
shūang rén fáng
双人房
bed
chúangwèi
床位
economy room
jīngjì fáng
经济房
economy room (with bath)
jīngjì tàofáng
经济套房
standard room (with bath)
biāozhǔn tàofáng
标准套房
luxury room (with bath)
háohúa tàofáng
豪华套房
hotel namecard
lǚgǔan de míngpiàn
旅馆的名片
wash clothes
xǐ yīfú
洗衣服
book a whole room
bāofáng
包房

Public Security
Public Security Bureau
gōngān jú
公安局
Foreign Affairs Branch
wài shì kē
外事科
I want to extend my visa...
wǒ yào yáncháng wǒde qiānzhèng...
我要延长我的签证
...by two weeks
...liǎngge xīngqī
两个星期
...by one month
...yíge yùe
一个月
...by two months
... liǎngge yùe
两个月

Alien Travel Permit
wàibīn tōngxíng zhèng
外宾通行证

Post & Telecommunications
post office
yóu jú
邮局
letter
xìn
信
envelope
xìn fēng
信封
package
bāo gǔo
包裹
air mail
hángkōng xìn
航空信
surface mail
píng yóu
平邮
stamps
yóu piào
邮票
postcard
míng xìn piàn
明信片
aerogramme
hángkōng yóujiǎn
航空邮件
poste restante
cún jú hòu lǐng lán
存局候领栏
telephone
diànhùa
电话
telephone office
diànxùn dàlóu
电讯大楼
fax
chúan zhēn
传真

Bicycle
bicycle
zìxíngchē
自行车

I want to hire a bicycle.
wǒ yào zū yí liàng zìxíngchē
我要租一辆自行车.
How much is it per day?
yì tiān dūo shǎo qián
一天多少钱?
How much is it per hour?
yí ge xiǎoshí dūo shǎo qián
一个小时多少钱?
deposit
yā jīn
押金

Transport
I want to go to...
wǒ yào qù...
我要去…
I want to get off
wǒ yào xià chē
我要下车
luggage
xínglǐ
行李
left-luggage room
jìcún chù
寄存处
one ticket
yì zhāng piào
一张票
I want to depart at...(time)
wǒ yào...diǎn kāi
我要 ... 点开
Could you buy a ticket for me?
kěyǐ tì wǒ mǎi yì zhāng piào mā
可以替我买一张票吗?
What time does it depart?
jǐdiǎn kāi
几点开?
What time does it arrive?
jǐdiǎn dàodá
几点到达?
How long does the trip take?
zhècì lǚxíng yào hūa dūoshǎo shíjiān
这次旅行要花多少时间?
buy a ticket
mǎi piào
买票
refund a ticket
tùi piào
退票

taxi
chūzū chē
出租车

Boat
boat
chúan
船
hovercraft
qìdiàn chúan
汽垫船
pier
mǎtóu
码头

Bus
bus
gōnggòng qìchē
公共汽车
minibus
xiǎo gōnggòng qìchē
小公共汽车
long-distance bus station
chángtú qìchē zhàn
长途汽车站
bus map
jiāotōng dìtú
交通地图
When is the first bus?
tóu bān qìchē jǐdiǎn kāi
头班汽车几点开?
When is the last bus?
mò bān qìchē jǐdiǎn kāi
末班汽车几点开?
When is the next bus?
xià yì bān qìchē jǐdiǎn kāi
下一班汽车几点开?

Train
train
hǔochē
火车
ticket office
shòu piào chù
售票处
advance rail ticket office
hǔochē piào yù shòu chù
火车票预售处

railway station
hŭochē zhàn
火车站
main railway station
zhŭyào hŭochē zhàn
主要火车站
hard-seat
yìngxí, yìngzùo
硬席，硬座
soft-seat
rŭanxí, rŭanzùo
软席、软座
hard-sleeper
yìngwò
硬卧
soft-sleeper
rŭanwò
软卧
middle berth
zhōng pù
中铺
upper berth
shàng pù
上铺
lower berth
xià pù
下铺
platform ticket
zhàntái piào
站台票
Which platform?
dì jĭ hào zhàntái
第几号站台？
upgrade ticket (after boarding)
bŭ piào
补票
first class waiting room
tóu dĕng hòuchē lóu
头等候车楼
subway (underground)
dì xià tiĕ lù
地下铁路
subway station
dì tiĕ zhàn
地铁站

Air Transport
airport
fēijīchăng
飞机场
CAAC
zhōnggúo mínháng
中国民航
charter flight
bāojī
包机
one-way ticket
dān chéng piào
单程票
round-trip ticket
lái húi piào
来回票

Emergency
police
jĭngchá
警察
Fire!
hŭo zāi
火灾
Help!
jiùmìng a
救命啊！
Thief!
xiăo tōu
小偷！

Medical
I'm sick.
wŏ shēng bìng
我生病
I'm injured.
wŏ shòushāng
我受伤
hospital
yīyùan
医院
pharmacy
yàodiàn
药店

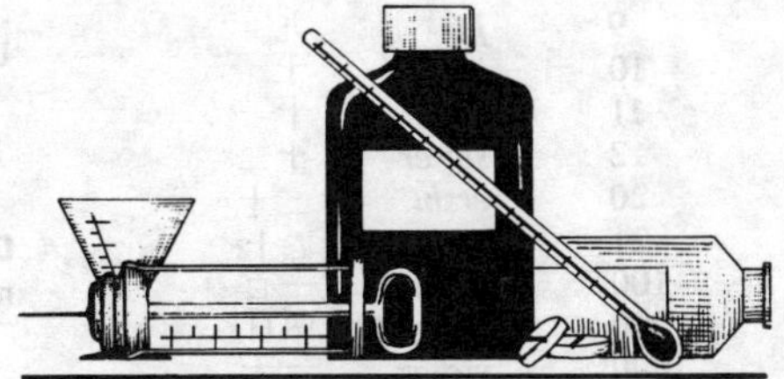

diarrhoea
lā dùzi
拉肚子

anti-diarrhoeal drug
húang liăn sù
黄连素

laxative
xiè yào
泻药

fever
fāshāo
发烧

giardia
āmībā fùxiè
阿米巴腹泻

hepatitis
gān yán
肝炎

malaria
nüèjì
疟疾

rabies
kúangqŭan bìng
狂犬病

respiratory infection (influenza)
liúxíngxìng gănmào
流行性感冒

tetanus
pò shāng fēng
破伤风

Numbers

0	*líng*	零
1	*yī, yào*	一
2	*èr, liăng*	二，两
3	*sān*	三
4	*sì*	四
5	*wŭ*	五
6	*liù*	六
7	*qī*	七
8	*bā*	八
9	*jiŭ*	九
10	*shí*	十
11	*shíyī*	十一
12	*shí'èr*	十二
20	*èrshí*	二十
21	*èrshíyī*	二十一
100	*yìbăi*	一百
200	*liăngbăi*	两百
1000	*yìqiān*	一千
2000	*liăngqiān*	两千
10,000	*yíwàn*	一万
20,000	*liăngwàn*	两万
100,000	*shíwàn*	十万
200,000	*èrshíwàn*	二十万

Countries

Australia
aòdàlìyà
澳大利亚

Britain
yīnggúo
英国

Canada
jiā'nádà
加拿大

Denmark
dānmài
丹麦

France
făgúo
法国

Germany
dégúo
德国

Netherlands
hélán
荷兰

New Zealand
xīn xīlán
新西兰

Spain
xībānyá
西班牙

Sweden
rùidiăn
瑞典

Switzerland
rùishì
瑞士

USA
mĕigúo
美国

Directions

map
dìtú
地图

Where is the...
...zài nǎlǐ
...在哪里
I'm lost.
wǒ mí lù
我迷路.
turn right
yòu zhǔan
右转
turn left
zǔo zhǔan
左转
go straight
yìzhí zǒu
一直走
turn around
xiàng húi zǒu
向回走

Streets and roads are often split up into sections *(dùan)*. Each section is given a number or (more usually) is labelled according to its relative position to the other sections using compass points. For example, Zhongshan Lu (Zhongshan Rd) might be split into an east section *(dōng dùan)* and a west section *(xī dùan)*. The east section will be designated Zhongshan Donglu and the west will be Zhongshan Xilu.

Geographical Terms

road, trail
lù
路
street
jiē, dàjiē
街，大街
boulevard
dàdào
大道
alley
xiàng, hútong
巷，胡同
north
běi
北
south
nán
南
east
dōng
东
west
xī
西
cave
dòng
洞
hot spring
wēnqúan
温泉
lake
hú
湖
mountain
shān
山
river
hé, jiāng
河，江
valley
gǔ, gōu
谷，沟
waterfall
pùbù
瀑布

Studying Chinese

Probably the two best places in the world to learn Chinese are in Beijing and Taipei. The advantage of Beijing is that the simplified writing system and pinyin are used. Living expenses are also cheaper than in Taipei, though the schools tend to rip off foreigners at every opportunity. The drawbacks to studying in Beijing are the generally uncomfortable living conditions, and a deliberate xenophobic policy of keeping foreigners separate from Chinese. Foreigners are usually assigned to a separate dormitory and not permitted to live with a Chinese family. The place where most foreigners study in Beijing is Beijing Language Institute (BLI) *(yǔyán xúeyùan)*, east of Qinghua University on the No 331 bus route. There are several other schools that accept foreign students.

In Taipei, or elsewhere in Taiwan, living expenses are high but there are opportunities to work teaching English and it's not difficult to earn enough money to meet all expenses. Of course, English teaching takes time away from your Chinese studies and it can be hard (and boring) work. Foreigners are free to live where they like in Taiwan, and it's not difficult to find some Chinese roommates. A disadvantage to studying in Taiwan is that only the old traditional characters are used, and the pinyin system is not used at all. Most foreigners also find Taipei to be a crowded, polluted and traffic clogged city.

There are many places to study in Taiwan. Probably the best is the National Taiwan Normal University (☎ (02) 3639123), Mandarin Training Centre *(táiwān shīfàn dàxúe)*, 129-1 Hoping E Rd, Section 1, Taipei.

Hong Kong is not a particularly good place for studying Mandarin, but it's fine for learning Cantonese. Although about half the population of Hong Kong can speak Mandarin, the local accent is radically different from that heard in Beijing and can be very confusing. The New Asia Yale in China Language School, at the Chinese University in the New Territories, offers courses in both Mandarin and Cantonese.

Facts for the Visitor

VISAS & EMBASSIES

Visas for individual travel in China are easy to get. China will even issue visas to individuals from countries which do not have diplomatic relations with the People's Republic. However, citizens of South Africa can only visit China on an organised tour, and must apply at least one month before their planned arrival in China.

Visas are readily available in Hong Kong and from Chinese embassies in most Western and many other countries. If you can't wait until you get to Hong Kong or if you want to fly direct to China, then enquire first at the nearest Chinese embassy.

In Hong Kong numerous travel agencies issue Chinese visas. Generally they offer a choice of a visa by itself, or a package deal including visa and transport to China. Some of the best agencies are:

Traveller Services (☎ 3674127), Room 704, Metropole Building, 57 Peking Rd, Tsimshatsui, Kowloon. They give a fast, reliable and cheap service.

Phoenix Services (☎ 7227378), Room B, 6th floor, Milton Mansion, 96 Nathan Rd, Tsimshatsui, Kowloon. Many travellers have spoken very highly of this place.

Wallem Travel (☎ 5286514), 46th floor, Hopewell Centre, 183 Queen's Rd East, Wanchai, Hong Kong Island. They specialise in travel to Communist countries.

Visa Office of the Ministry of Foreign Affairs of the PRC, 5th floor, Low Block, China Resources Building, 26 Harbour Rd, Wanchai, Hong Kong Island (☎ 8939812). They're open Monday to Friday, 9 am to 12.30 pm and 2 to 5 pm, Saturday 9 am to 12.30 pm. This place has been dispensing the cheapest visas around like a three-month visa issued in two days for HK$90.

Visa applications require two passport-size photos. Your application must be written in English, and you're advised to have one entire blank page in your passport for the visa.

The visa application form asks you a number of silly questions – your travel itinerary, means of transport, how long you will stay etc – but you can deviate from this as much as you want. You *don't* have to leave from the place you specify on your visa application form.

The cost of visas and the types of package-deal you get in Hong Kong change quite frequently, so use this information as a rough guide only. The usual price for a three-month visa issued in three days is HK$140; issued in 24 hours, HK$180; issued the same day, HK$250.

If you want more flexibility to enter and leave China several times, multiple-entry visas are available from some agencies. This is particularly useful if you intend to follow complicated routes in and out of China via Nepal, Pakistan, Thailand or Myanmar (Burma). Multiple-entry visas will cost several times as much as single-entry visas.

Some agencies in Hong Kong are now able to obtain your visa on a separate paper which you present at the Chinese border. All that is required is your passport number, nationality, date of birth and full name. Certain ports of entry such as Shenzhen are experimenting with issuing five-day visas at the border. Chinese residents of Hong Kong, Macau and Taiwan can apply for a *húi xiāng zhèng* which entitles them to multiple visa-free entry.

It should be possible to get a visa for stays longer than six months. All visas are valid from the date of issue, *not* from the date of entry, so there's no point in getting a visa far in advance of your planned entry date.

When you check into a hotel, there is usually a question on the registration form asking what type of visa you have. Most travellers aren't sure how to answer. For most, the type of visa is 'L' from the Chinese word for travel *(Lüxing)*. This letter is stamped right on the visa. There are seven types of visas, as follows:

L	Travel *(Lüxing)*
F	Business *(Fangwen)*
D	Resident *(Dingju)*
G	Transit *(Guojing)*
X	Student *(liu Xue)*
Z	Working *(ren Zhi)*
C	Stewardess *(Chengwu)*

If you ever feel encumbered by the expense and bureaucratic delays of obtaining visas, you might spare a thought for the Chinese, who are not permitted to leave their own country. While high-ranking cadres and others with the proper connections can go abroad, the overwhelming majority cannot even obtain a passport. Even those who get a passport must then secure an exit permit – even more difficult to get. However, contrary to what many foreigners believe, the Chinese can travel freely *within* their own country – the only limitation being sufficient funds to do so.

Chinese Embassies

Following are the addresses of Chinese embassies in major cities around the world.

Australia
247 Federal Highway, Watson, Canberra, 2600 ACT

Austria
Metterrichgasse 4, A-1030 Vienna

Belgium
21 Blvd Général Jacques, 1051 Brussels

Canada
411-415 Andrews St, Ottawa, Ontario KIN 5H3

Denmark
25 Oeregaardsalle, DK 2900 Hellerup, Copenhagen 2900

France
11 Ave George V, Paris 75008

Germany
5307 Wachtbergeriederbachen, Konrad-Adenauer Str, 104 Bonn

Italy
56 Via Bruxelles, Roma 00198

Japan
15-30 Minami-Azabu, 4-Chome, Minato-ku, Tokyo

Netherlands
Adriaan Goehooplaan 7, Den Haag

New Zealand
2-6 Glenmore St, Kelburr, Wellington

Spain
Trafalgar 11, Madrid

Sweden
Bragevagen 4, Stockholm

Switzerland
Kalecheggweg 10, Berne

UK
31 Portland Place, London WIN 3AG

USA
2300 Connecticut Ave NW, Washington, DC 20008. Consulates: 3417 Montrose Blvd, Houston, Texas 77006; 104 South Michigan Ave, Suite 1200, Chicago, Illinois 60603; 1450 Laguna St, San Francisco, CA 94115; 520 12th Ave, New York, NY 10036

Visa Extensions

Visa extensions are handled by the Foreign Affairs Section of the local Public Security Bureaus (the police force). The Chinese government travel organisation, China International Travel Service, has nothing to do with extensions. Extensions cost Y25. The general rule is that you can get one extension of one month's duration, though at an agreeable Public Security Bureau you may be able to wangle more, for longer, with cogent reasons (illness, transport delays, etc).

Foreign Students

Many Chinese universities take foreign students, usually for Chinese-language courses. Most students stay a year or two, but six-week summer courses and all sorts of other programmes are also available. Once you're accepted by a Chinese university you're automatically given a visa. You can then go to China to study, do your course, and be free to travel. Foreign students in China are entitled to student prices for hotel rooms and train fares. Students or foreign experts who have a resident's permit and need to leave China briefly can usually obtain a re-entry permit inside China at a Public Security Bureau for Y5. If you're a foreign student in Taiwan you'll also get student discounts, since Taiwan is considered to be part of China.

Other Useful Papers

Given the Chinese preoccupation with impressive bits of paper, it's worth carrying around a few business cards, student cards and anything else that's printed and wrapped in a plastic envelope.

These additional IDs are useful for leaving with bicycle-renters who often want a deposit or other security for their bikes – sometimes they ask you to leave your passport, but you should insist on leaving another piece of ID or a deposit. Some hotels also require you to hand in your passport as security – offer to pay in advance. An old expired passport is useful for these situations.

It's worth hanging on to cheap room or dormitory hotel receipts – the fact that you've been allowed to stay cheaply at some other hotel will weigh in your favour at the next place. Likewise, hang on to any Chinese-price tickets you happen to buy.

Officially, the only foreigners who qualify for student discounts in China are those studying in China. To receive these discounts, an official white card is needed. However, some travellers have received student discounts using Taiwanese student IDs, drivers' licences, youth hostel cards, international student cards, forgeries, made-in-Hong-Kong imitations and the like. Sometimes, it's just good enough to say (in Chinese) that you're a student. Surprisingly enough, these lies and tricks have been going on for several years but often still work. However, they don't benefit bona fide students who sometimes have their genuine cards knocked back because the person behind the hotel desk has seen so many forgeries about. One French student had a knock-down drag-out battle in Zhengzhou station with a smug booking clerk who threw her absolutely genuine card into the rubbish bin and told her it was a fake.

A supply of passport photos is useful. Although they're obtainable in China, it's more convenient if you bring them along. They're particularly useful if you're going to Europe on the Trans-Siberian, as that may require three visas (Mongolian, Soviet and Polish).

CUSTOMS

Immigration procedures are so streamlined they're almost a formality these days. The third degree at customs seems to be reserved for Seiko-smuggling Hong Kongers, who are much more of a problem than the stray backpacker.

Customs require that you declare on the Baggage Declaration for Incoming Passengers the number of cameras, wristwatches, recorders, radios, calculators, electric fans, bicycles, sewing machines, TV sets and cine cameras you're taking into China; this is to prevent you from selling them in the country or giving them away as presents.

They also ask you to declare the quantity of foreign currency you're carrying, and any gold, silver, jewellery, antiques, calligraphy and other works of art. When you leave China, you are supposed to still have all the items (minus the foreign currency). If any items you list on your form are stolen in China, you should ask Public Security to provide a Certificate of Loss (see theft section for details). Don't lose the declaration form, though if you do, *probably* nothing will happen to you.

You're allowed to import 600 cigarettes or the equivalent in tobacco products, two litres of alcoholic drink and one *pint* of perfume. You're allowed to import only 3000 *feet* of movie film, and a maximum of 72 rolls of still film. Importation of fresh fruit is prohibited.

It's illegal to import any printed material, film, tapes, etc 'detrimental to China's politics, economy, culture and ethics'. But don't be too concerned about what you take to read. As you leave China, any tapes, manuscripts, books, etc 'which contain state secrets or are otherwise prohibited for export' can be seized – as in any other country. Cultural relics, handicrafts, gold and silver ornaments, and jewellery purchased in China have to be shown to customs on leaving. You'll also have to show your receipts; otherwise the stuff may be confiscated. Don't get paranoid – they seldom search foreigners, and in the rare event that they do, they are mostly concerned that you still have your Walkman and camera with you and that you're not departing with large doses of Chinese currency.

Lastly, an item for the travelling herbalist: export of musk, toad cake, cinnabar, eucommia, gastrodia-elata, pianzihuang, caterpillar fungus, Liushen pills and Angongniuhuang pills is prohibited.

MONEY

The basic unit of Chinese currency is the *yuan* – designated in this book by a capital 'Y'. The yuan is divided into *jiao* and *fen*. Ten fen make up one jiao, and 10 jiao make up one yuan. Jiao and yuan are commonly referred to in spoken Chinese as *mao* and *kuai* respectively. There are, in fact, two types of currency in use in China: Renminbi and Foreign Exchange Certificates.

Renminbi (RMB)

Renminbi or 'People's Money' is issued by the Bank of China. Paper notes are issued in denominations of one, two, five and 10 yuan; one, two and five jiao; and one, two and five fen. Coins are in denominations of one yuan; five jiao; and one, two and five fen. The one-fen note is small and yellow, the two-fen note is blue, and the five-fen note is small and green.

Foreign Exchange Certificates (FEC)

How many countries can you name that have two currencies? The three letters most hated by foreigners and loved by Chinese are FEC. Foreign Exchange Certificates, or 'tourist money', is issued in China for use by foreigners and for compatriots from Hong Kong, Macau and Taiwan.

FEC creates numerous hassles. FEC and RMB are supposed to be worth the same, but in fact they are not. FEC is worth more, but when you pay in FEC you will often receive change in RMB. When you ask for change in FEC, the people you're dealing with will often say that they don't have it. You cannot

exchange RMB (legally) when you leave China. If you want to pay for everything in RMB (most foreigners try), you will face constant arguments. The wearisome battles over FEC and the constant solicitations from the 'change money' people can detract from your enjoyment of travelling in China. Some conspiracy theorists speculate that the government invented FEC just to prevent foreigners from becoming friendly with Chinese people.

FEC comes in seven denominations: 100 yuan, 50 yuan, 10 yuan, five yuan, one yuan, five jiao and one jiao. There are no coins. It's good to keep lots of small bills in FEC to avoid the situation where you must accept change in RMB.

You're meant to use FEC for all hotels, rail and air transport, as well as international telephone calls or fax. The government does not require that you pay for buses, taxis, postage stamps or food in FEC. In practice, the rules get bent both ways – some hotels and railway stations accept RMB from foreigners, while taxi drivers, restaurants and even some street vendors have got into the habit of demanding payment in FEC. There is no legitimate reason why you must pay in FEC for goods which are made in the People's Republic, but expect continuous vehement arguments if you stand up for your rights.

Some foreign visitors have managed to pay their whole way through China using only RMB, but this requires stamina and an official Chinese 'white' student ID card (genuine or otherwise). You'll probably need a mixture of both RMB and FEC.

Some shops and hotels operate an interesting 'price differential'. You may be asked if you want to pay a given price in FEC or pay about 50% more in RMB. Most hotels simply will *not* accept payment in RMB no matter how hard you plead, cry or rant. Some railway stations have separate booking offices for foreigners which insist on payment in FEC, and air tickets can only be bought in FEC, unless you have the magic white card.

On the other hand, in smaller towns and in the countryside where few foreigners go you'll probably find that the locals have never seen FEC, and you'll have to pay in RMB.

The FEC versus RMB battles can occupy much of your time and energy. In many youth hostels, travellers have a tendency to sit around all day and talk about FEC and changing money. Try not to let this happen to you.

Changing Money

Foreign currency and travellers' cheques can be changed at the main centres of the Bank of China, the tourist hotels, some Friendship Stores, and some of the big department stores. You'll be issued FEC and small change will be made up of RMB one, two and five-fen notes and coins. You're best off changing in the Bank of China – many tourist hotels charge a commission. The rates charged at various ports of entry (airports, wharves, Hong Kong border, etc) are usually the official rate, so don't be afraid to change as much as you need on arrival.

Always be sure to keep enough money on you to last for at least a few days. Many banks and hotels are unreliable – they run out of FEC, or the one person in charge of FEC takes a holiday and the whole operation shuts down. In some remote areas, travellers have been stuck for several days waiting for the 'FEC person' to show up for work.

Travellers' cheques from most of the world's leading banks and issuing agencies are now acceptable in China – stick to the major companies such as Thomas Cook, American Express and Bank of America, and you'll be OK.

Australian, Canadian, US, UK, Hong Kong, Japanese and most West European currencies are acceptable in China. In some of the backwaters, it may be hard to change lesser known currencies – US$ are still the easiest to change.

The Chinese government is planning to devalue its currency over the next few years, step by step. In the long term, the yuan is expected to be convertible. At the time of writing, the exchange rates were approximately:

A$1 =	Y4.00
C$1 =	Y4.50
DM1 =	Y2.00
HK$1 =	Y0.70
Y1000 =	Y40.00
UK£1 =	Y10.00
US$1 =	Y5.00
NZ$1 =	Y3.10

Credit Cards

Plastic cards are gaining more acceptance in China for use by foreign visitors in major tourist cities. Useful cards include Visa, Federal Card, MasterCard, American Express and Diners Club. It's even possible to withdraw cash against your card.

It wouldn't be worthwhile to get a credit card especially for your trip to China, but if you already have one you might find it useful. Banks in some of the outlying regions of China can take a long time to debit your account overseas.

Wiring Money

Getting money sent to you while you're in China is a real drag – try to avoid it. On the average, it takes about five weeks for your money to arrive. If you have high-placed connections in the banking system it can take considerably less time, but most travellers are not so fortunate.

Black Market

The words 'Hello, change money' have become almost as popular as spitting in China, although the number of black marketeers has decreased dramatically since the devaluation of FEC in 1991.

The exchange rate hovers more or less around the 110 RMB for 100 FEC mark, with occasional fluctuations either up or down depending on location and rumours of the FEC being done away with. There is also a bustling black market in Hong Kong and US dollars.

The reports of cheating have become so common that it cannot be recommended that you change on the street. Some people have found it fairly easy to change money in small shops, especially in areas where travellers congregate. If you need RMB, you can always get it from banks, but they'll only exchange it on a one for one basis. Some people seem to think it's illegal for foreigners to have RMB – it's not.

As for bringing things into China to sell, you'll probably find that the Chinese strike too much of a hard bargain to make it worth the trouble.

Money-Exchange Vouchers

Whenever you change foreign currency into Chinese currency (legally) you'll be given a money-exchange voucher recording the transaction. If you've got any leftover FEC when you leave the country and want to reconvert it to hard currency you *must* have those vouchers – not all of them, but at least equal to *double* the amount of FEC you want to exchange. In other words, the Chinese government is saying that you must spend at least half the money you changed while in China.

FEC can be taken in and out of the country as you please, but RMB is not supposed to be taken out. Furthermore, the banks at the border crossings will refuse to exchange RMB for foreign currency. However, there are several ways to get rid of excess RMB. Very often, the shops near the immigration station where you leave China will change RMB for Hong Kong dollars or FEC. Of course, you'll only get the black-market rate, but if you bought the RMB on the black market you should come out about even. If you do get stuck with a heap of RMB, ask around at the travellers' hang-outs in Hong Kong, as someone who's going to China will probably buy it.

Costs

How much will it cost to travel in China? That's largely up to the degree of comfort you desire – and what's cheap to one person may be expensive to another. It also depends on how much travelling you do, and what parts of China you visit. Eastern China is generally more expensive than the west, and the north-east is ridiculously expensive for hotels.

If you want to do China on a bottom-of-the-barrel shoestring budget then you have to sleep in dormitories at every hotel, get local price on all train tickets and forgo sleepers. Travelling, however, is *not* an endurance test. If you want to find out how long you can stay away and how little money you can spend doing it, go ahead, but you won't get gold stars each time you sleep on the floor of a train. Your journey can be a miserable experience if you're constantly worried about how far the money is going to stretch and if you force yourself to live in perpetual discomfort. Travelling on too low a budget only allows for a limited experience of a country – you get a one-sided view just like those people who take expensive tours and stay in posh hotels.

China just isn't going to be as cheap and as comfortable as India or South-East Asia; if you want to have a good time in the PRC then spend a bit more money. If you care about your sanity take a sleeper. Train trips in China are often long; it's no fun to sit for 30 hours in a hot, crowded hard-seat carriage where the lights are on all night and people stare at you while constantly spitting on the floor.

It is still possible to do China on US$10 a day – most of this gets spent on accommodation and transport. Develop a toleration for dormitories. Dorm beds are cheap (usually no more than Y15) and many hotels will readily dispense them. Rooms are invariably expensive – particularly if you're travelling alone, since most Chinese hotels only provide double rooms and it's unlikely they'll give you half price. Food is dirt cheap if you avoid classy restaurants. 'Eating Chinese' with a few other people not only gives you a greater variety of food to choose from, it brings the price down.

Price Gouging

Who says that China isn't a capitalist country? Foreigners will inevitably be charged more for most things in China. Avoiding this is not easy. In stores where prices are clearly marked on the labels, you probably won't get cheated. However, in restaurants, taxis, or even in hospitals, you are liable to get hit with all sorts of mysterious extra service charges because the Government-owned businesses can be just as dishonest as the private ones. Prices can be very inconsistent – it varies from place to place, person to person, or day to day. After visiting the Hanmin Canting in Yinchuan, one traveller had this to say:

> Having heard reports from several foreigners about good food and blatant overcharging, our small group of foreigners, which included a Chinese speaker, tried its luck. Sure enough, the waitress charged far in excess of the menu prices. When asked to explain the difference, she said all foreigners paid double for food. Before dropping our chopsticks and marching out in disgust, we pointed out that we were eating the same food as Chinese and that this doubling of charges had not been mentioned when we ordered.
>
> The waitress then changed tack and said that we had all received double helpings. One look at the same dishes on neighbouring tables proved that this was not true and the prices she had charged proved, on closer inspection, to have been not doubled but raised by an arbitrary sum. When we asked for the manager, we were told (as usually happens) that she was not on duty. The insolent, sneering behaviour of the waitress stung us to take the matter higher.
>
> Complaints of this kind are usually handled by a town's Shangye Ju (Office of Commerce). The relevant office in Yinchuan was near the restaurant and we finally located the bosses *(lǐngdǎo)*, who very methodically handled the problem after making a couple of phone calls to check the facts with the restaurant. Finally, a cadre took us back to the restaurant where the manager and all the staff (excluding the offending waitress) were hauled out to discuss the matter.
>
> The manager kept apologising with the lame excuse that it was a case of 'mistaken percentages'. She insisted on refunding the amount that had been overcharged. After we had refused a refund on the grounds that it was the principle, not the money which was at stake, the cadre dropped a subtle hint that our acceptance would save face for the manager. So we accepted on the understanding that in future foreigners and local Chinese would receive proper treatment.
>
> The cadre later apologised for the incident with the excuse that Yinchuan had only been opened to foreigners for a short time and the waitress didn't know there were rules. I wasn't going to waste more time arguing, but found it interesting that the waitress herself had told us it was a rule to charge foreigners double.

Situations like this are not unusual in China. To avoid problems, always ask the price first before you get the goods. If you can't speak Chinese, write it down.

Admission Fees

Gardens, parks and tourist sights usually have an admission fee of a few jiao. In some cases, fees for foreigners can be much higher, such as Y12 FEC at Beijing's Forbidden City (Chinese pay Y0.50 in RMB).

Tipping

China is one of those wonderful countries where tipping is not done and almost no one asks for it. When tips are offered in China, they are offered *before* you get the service, not after – that will ensure that you get better service. All things considered, tipping isn't a good idea because it will make it rough for foreigners who follow you.

WHAT TO BRING

The usual traveller's rule applies: bring as little as possible. It is much better to buy things as you need them than to throw things away because you've got too much to carry. If you have to get something, there are large, well-stocked department stores in almost every town.

Carrying Bags

For those carrying their own bags, the backpack is still the best form of luggage. On the other hand, packs can be cumbersome and are vulnerable to theft. Long-distance buses have very little space for stowing baggage, and city buses are so crowded that a large bag or pack will be almost impossible to lug around. A soft pack, with no frame or with a semi-rigid frame, is better all round. It's a good idea to add some theft-deterrence by sewing on a few tabs for a padlock.

A large, soft zip-bag with a wide shoulder strap is less prone to damage and a bit more thief-proof. Shoulder bags are easier to wield on crowded buses and trains, but they're hard to carry for any distance.

Whatever you bring, try and make it small. A day-pack is useful; you can dump your main luggage in a hotel or the left-luggage room at the train station and head off. It's good for hiking and for carrying extra food on long train rides.

Clothes

Clothing is one of the best bargains in China, so you needn't agonise over how many shirts and trousers to bring. However, large Western sizes can be difficult to find. If you're travelling in the north of China at the height of winter, prepare yourself for incredible cold. You can buy excellent down or quilt jackets in some of the big cities. Also very cheap and functional are the fur-lined hats with Snoopy ear covers. Sweaters are also a bargain in China. However, you might want to bring fur-lined boots and mittens, although mediocre ones can be bought in China. Shoes are generally poor quality and it's difficult to find large (Western) sizes. Western long johns are more comfortable and warmer than the Chinese variety.

Umbrellas and plastic raincoats can be bought in China – if you want a good nylon poncho then you'll have to bring it. You shouldn't need a sleeping bag since sheets and blankets are provided even in the hard-sleeper carriages of the trains. If you plan to go camping, a sleeping bag will probably be a necessity, but opportunities for camping are very limited in China.

In summer, the lightest of clothes will do for daytime wear: T-shirts, sandals and shorts. However, if you go up into the hills it can get very cold, and it can get cold on the trains at night.

The usual standards of Asian decorum apply. While shorts are less acceptable for women, plenty of Chinese women wear them and you shouldn't get any unpleasant reactions. Skirts and dresses are frequently worn in big cities – in Beijing, miniskirts are in vogue and many young women have started wearing skin-hugging tights. However, bikinis have still not made their debut in China. Make-up and jewellery are becoming increasingly popular in the cities.

The Chinese place little importance on what foreigners wear, as long as they remain within an acceptable level of modesty; casual clothes are always acceptable.

Style has made a comeback in China. Western dresses for women and suits with bell-bottom trousers for men are the standard apparel of the new breed of hip young Chinese urbanites. Forget those blue ant images from the '60s and early '70s. Many Chinese still dress like that, particularly in the poorer regions of the country, but it no longer borders on the compulsory.

Necessities

Absolutely essential is a good pair of sunglasses, particularly in the Xinjiang desert or the high altitudes of Tibet. Ditto for UV (sunblock) lotion. If you wear contact lenses, bring your own cleaning solution, eye drops and other accessories.

A water bottle can be a lifesaver, especially in the western deserts during the summer. Make sure you get one that doesn't leak.

Shaving cream is a rare item in China and good razor blades are hard to find. Mosquito repellent makes life more pleasant and guards against malaria – a good brand available in Hong Kong is Autan. Chinese nail clippers are poor quality and deodorant is unknown.

Chinese-made toothpaste is OK, but the toothbrushes are usually too hard – more suitable for removing rust than cleaning your teeth. Dental floss is hard to find in China. Tampons are unavailable in China – Chinese sanitary napkins are big and bulky.

An alarm clock is essential for getting up on time to catch your flight, bus or train. A lightweight digital model is best – make sure the battery is OK because you'll have trouble finding replacements in China. You can buy portable alarm clocks in China – the wind up style that were common in the 1950s. They're heavy, tend not to be very accurate and the relentless 'tick-tock' can keep you awake all night.

Good batteries are hard to come by in China – bring what you need for your camera and consider rechargeable batteries and a recharger (220 volts) if you can't live without your Walkman.

A gluestick is convenient for sealing envelopes and pasting on stamps. The Chinese equivalent is a leaky bottle of glue.

A medical kit is important. This is discussed in detail in this chapter in the Health section.

Luxuries

Having something to read will help preserve your sanity as well as pass the time.

Chinese tea is sold everywhere – if you need the Indian variety, you'll have to bring it. Instant coffee can be found in some of the larger shops and department stores. A mug and teaspoon are useful for those long train trips where there's a continuous supply of hot water – these can be purchased in many railway stations as well as department stores.

Many foreigners may consider Chinese cigarettes to have the gentle eastern aroma of old socks, but annual production of over 60 billion packs is a major source of tax revenue for the Chinese government. The latest additions to a vast array of Chinese cigarettes are some highly aromatic cigars. Chinese beer is of fine quality providing you stick to top brands.

Foreign-made cigarettes (and imitations) and alcohol are available from hawkers, small shops, hotel shops and Friendship Stores all over China. Top-grade foreign rocket fuel – like Morgan Rum, Napoleon Augier Cognac, even Manischewitz – can be bought at the larger tourist hotels and Friendship Stores.

Gifts

If you want to give something to a Chinese friend, then give them an English book. English is the one element of Western culture that's universally desired. Old copies of *Newsweek* and other foreign magazines will also be appreciated.

Stamps make good gifts; Chinese are avid stamp-collectors, congregating outside the philatelic sections of the post offices and dealing on the footpath. Foreign postcards are sought after, and pictures of you and your family are very popular gifts.

Don't – as some people have done – insult them by trying to give away your old jacket. Don't give away Walkmans, radios and the like unless you really have made a close friend – and make sure they're not listed on your Customs Declaration form.

TOURIST OFFICES

Among the many striking Chinese sayings, a particularly applicable one is 'With one monkey in the way, not even 10,000 men can pass'. Three of the major monkeys in China today are CITS (China International Travel Service), the PSB (Public Security Bureau) and the mass of little bits of paper collectively referred to as 'red tape'.

At one time, China was the world's most advanced nation. The Chinese invented gunpowder, rockets, the printing press and paper currency. How did such an advanced nation fall so far behind? Probably because the Chinese also invented bureaucracy.

China International Travel Service (CITS)

CITS deals with China's foreign tourist hordes, and mainly concerns itself with organising and making travel arrangements for group tours. CITS existed as far back as 1954 when there were few customers; now they're inundated with a couple of hundred thousand big-noses a year and it will take a while for them to get their act together.

CITS will buy train and plane tickets for you (and some boat tickets), reserve hotel rooms, organise city tours, and even get you tickets for the cinema, opera, acrobatics and other entertainment, as well as organise trips to communes and farms, and provide vehicles (taxis, minibuses) for sightseeing or transport.

All rail tickets bought through CITS will be tourist-priced (an extra 100% on top of the Chinese price) and there will usually be a small service charge added on to the price of rail, boat or plane tickets. CITS has nothing to do with issuing travel permits or visa extensions – for that you must go directly to the Public Security Bureaus. However, if you're on a CITS tour, they are supposed to arrange the permits for you. They can get you permits to places that are normally closed to foreigners – like Tibet – but you will have to pay heavily for the privilege.

CITS offices and desks are usually in the major tourist hotels in each town or city open to foreigners; sometimes they are elsewhere but you can get the hotel reception desk to phone them.

Service varies. Some CITS people are friendly and full of useful information about the places they're stationed in – a few may even invite you out to dinner! There are others who are downright rude and only interested in squeezing money out of foreigners. They may lie to you – claiming that a certain area is closed to foreigners (except via an expensive CITS tour) when in fact it's open. You may find CITS offices staffed by people who speak sparse or zero English and who got their jobs through the back door. Getting information out of CITS is potluck. Generally speaking, though, solo travellers will rarely have to deal with them. One thing about CITS is fairly consistent – their tours tend to be expensive. Furthermore, CITS has been known to cheat travellers outright – selling 10-day tours but just giving eight, charging for services not rendered, etc. Everything depends on who you're dealing with – some CITS offices deserve eternal praise while others deserve all the abuse you can give them.

CITS has surprisingly few overseas offices – their close cousin CTS has considerably more. Following are the addresses and telephone numbers of CITS offices in Beijing, Hong Kong and the USA:

Beijing
6 Dong Chang'an Jie, Beijing 100740 (☎ 5121122; cable CITSH, 1954 Beijing; telex 22350, 22606 CITSH CN)

Hong Kong
6th floor, Tower II, South Seas Centre, Tsimshatsui East, Kowloon (☎ 7215317, cable 2320 Hong Kong, telex 38449 CITC HX)

USA
60E 42nd St, Suite 465, New York, NY 10165 (☎ 212-867-0271)

China Travel Service (CTS)

Within China, CTS is concerned with tourists from Hong Kong, Macau and Taiwan, and with foreign nationals of Chinese descent (Overseas Chinese). Outside China they will book tours for just about anybody.

The reason why CTS doesn't normally deal with Western tourists in China is because their staff are not required to speak English or any other foreign language. Outside China, the staff will normally be able to speak English so they're happy to book tours. Staff at the Hong Kong and Macau offices also speak English, and they will issue visas and book trains, planes, hovercraft and other transport to China. The Hong Kong office is frequently crowded – avoid this by arriving there at 9 am when they open.

In China, CTS is sometimes mixed in with the CITS offices and desks in the tourist hotels, particularly in towns with only one major tourist hotel where Westerners and Overseas Chinese stay.

CTS seems to be a larger organisation than CITS and has a wider range of services. However, CTS staff are not necessarily more honest or competent than CITS. As one disillusioned traveller wrote:

Although we are seasoned independent travellers, we decided we were better off on a tour in China and contacted CTS via a Hong Kong travel agent. We were *extremely disappointed* with our trip for a number of reasons. The principle one was that the restaurants were extremely dirty and unhygienic. We were paying more than US$350 a day for two and were taken to eat in restaurants that cost Y20 (for foreigners!). The hotel restaurants (where group price was Y38 at the White Swan as an example) were 'too expensive'.

We signed up for a group tour, and when we turned up at the Hong Kong meeting point, we found there were only the two of us. At that point, it was impossible to cancel the trip without forfeiting the entire cost. Being only the two of us increased the costs considerably because we had to support the entire cost of the guide, driver and car, which meant that the value to the two of us was drastically reduced...had we known there would have been only the two of us, we would have gone on our own, stayed at good hotels, skipped some of the uninteresting spots on the itinerary, eaten at *clean* restaurants and probably saved 50% of the overall cost!

Lee S Hubert

Following are the addresses for the China Travel Service in Beijing and foreign countries:

Beijing
8 Dongjiaomin Xiang, Dongchenchu, Beijing 100005 (☎ 5129933, fax 5129008, cable 2464 Beijing, telex 22487 CTSHO CN)

Australia
Level 2, 724-728 George St, Sydney, NSW 2000 (☎ (02) 2112633, fax 2813595)

Canada
PO Box 17, Main Floor, 999 West Hastings St, Vancouver, BC V6C 2W2 (☎ (604) 6848787, fax 6843321)

France
10 Rue de Rome, 75008, Paris (☎ (1) 45-22-92-72, fax 45-22-92-79)

Hong Kong
Central Branch, 2nd floor, China Travel Building, 77 Queen's Road, Central (☎ 8533533, fax 5419777)
Kowloon Branch, 1st floor, Alpha House, 27-33 Nathan Rd, Tsimshatsui (☎ 7211331, fax 7217757)

Japan
Nihombashi-Settsu Building, 2-2-4, Nihombashi, Chuo-Ku, Tokyo (☎ (03) 2735512, fax 2732667)

Macau
Hotel Beverly Plaza, Avenida do Dr Rodrigo Rodrigues (☎ 388922)

Philippines
489 San Fernando St, Binondo, Manila (☎ 40-74-75, fax 40-78-34)

Singapore
Ground Floor, SIA Building, 77 Robinson Rd, Singapore, (☎ 2240550, fax 2245009)

Thailand
460/2-3 Surawong Rd, Bangkok 10500 (☎ (2) 2332895, fax 2365511)

UK
24 Cambridge Circus, London WC2H 8HD (☎ (071) 8369911, fax 8363121)

USA
2nd floor, 212 Sutter St, San Francisco, CA 94108 (☎ (415) 3986627, fax 3986669)
Los Angeles Branch, Suite 138, 2223E, Garvey Ave, Monterey Park, CA 91754 (☎ (818) 2888222, fax 2883464)

Complaint Hot Line

It probably doesn't do any good to complain, but it should at least make you feel better. China has recently set up English-language tourist complaint hot lines in nine locations, and it's possible that this service will be expanded. For what it's worth, the numbers are:

Beijing (☎ (01) 5130828); Shanghai (☎ (012) 4390630); Tianjin (☎ (022) 318814, 318812); Jiangsu Province (☎ (025) 301221); Zhejiang Province (☎ (0571) 556631); Guangdong Province (☎ (020) 677422); Shaanxi Province (☎ 029) 711480); Gansu Province (☎ (0931) 26860); and Guilin (☎ (0773) 226533).

Public Security Bureau (PSB)

The Public Security Bureau *(gōng'ān jú)* is the name given to China's police, both uniformed and plain-clothes. Its responsibilities include suppression of political dissidence, crime detection, mediating family quarrels and directing traffic. A related force is the Chinese People's Armed Police Force (CPAPF), which was formed several years ago to absorb cuts in the PLA. The Foreign Affairs Branch *(wài shì kē)* of the Public Security Bureau deals with foreigners. This branch is responsible for issuing visa extensions and Alien Travel Permits.

What sets the Chinese police aside from their counterparts in, say, Mexico and South America, is their amiability towards foreigners (what they're like with their own people may be a different story). They'll sometimes sit you down, give you a cup of tea and practise their English – and the number of competent English-speakers is surprisingly high. The PSB is responsible for introducing and enforcing regulations concerning foreigners. So, for example, they bear responsibility for exclusion of foreigners from certain hotels. If this means you get stuck for a place to stay, they can offer advice. Don't pester them with trivia or try to 'use' them to bully a point with a local street vendor. Do turn to them for mediation in serious disputes with hotels, restaurants, taxi drivers, etc. This often works since the PSB wields considerable power – especially in remote areas.

The only run-in you may have with the PSB is when you end up in a 'closed' place and the PSB must put you on your way. For misdemeanours such as being in a town without a permit, or being off course without a good alibi, there could be a fine which can usually be bargained down. You may even have to write a 'self-criticism' confessing your guilt. There appear to be no set rules for dealing with foreigners who have wandered into 'closed' areas. If there are, then many Public Security staff are unaware of them, so how you're treated is up to the discretion of the individual police.

One traveller covered up an expulsion order issued to him by Guiyang PSB. The Wuhan PSB caught up with him, kept him for six days, fined him US$100 and slung him out via Canton. The expulsion was not so much for visiting closed places as for overstaying his visa. (He also used an unusual device to get into Chinese hotels on the way – telling them he was from Xinjiang, where a different language is spoken and a Caucasian face is the norm. Chinese, however, carry all sorts of odd ID, like swimming licences, work-unit cards, bicycle licences and probably travel authorisation.) Some people get fined; some are told to move on; some are allowed to stay in the 'closed' area or never catch sight of Public Security. The worst you can expect is a combination of a fine and ejection from the country at your own expense.

Travel Permit
(tōngxíngzhèng)

In the early 1980s only 130 places in China were officially open to foreign tourists. Then the number swept to 244, and nowadays most of the country is open except for certain remote areas, especially those inhabited by ethnic minorities. As a rule of thumb, most of the places described in this book are open to foreigners. To find out about newly opened areas, it's best to check with the PSB in provincial capitals. Remote PSBs are often more helpful with visas, but tend to be the last to receive lists of new openings.

To travel to closed places you officially require an Alien Travel Permit (usually just called Travel Permit), obtainable from the Public Security Bureau in each place open to foreigners. They use their discretion in issuing you with a permit to a closed place. However, the choice of open places is now so extensive that the majority of travellers will have no need for this type of permit. Foreign academics and researchers usually need to front up with the right credentials or letter of introduction *(jièshào xìn)* and may then be given a free hand to pursue their lizards, steam trains, yellow-bellied sap-suckers or whatever in remote places.

One PSB turned down our request with the straight-faced logic that such permits are for places foreigners can't visit. Like the best of bureaucrats, PSB does not want to step out of line, and if they think you're asking for an unusual permit they'll just say no. There's no harm in at least asking for a permit to a strange place – you just might get it.

Travel Permits can be demanded from you at hotel registration desks, PSB offices, boat or bus ticket offices, and unusual areas during spot checks by police. If you're off the track but heading towards a destination for which you have a permit, PSB will either stop you and cancel the destination, or let you continue on your way.

The permit also lists the modes of transport you're allowed to take: plane, train, ship or car – and if a particular mode is crossed out then you can't use it. If a mode is cancelled it can be reinstated at the next PSB, but that may only be for a single trip from Point A to Point B. You could try and carry on regardless – or you could lose the permit in the next open city and start again.

If you manage to get a permit for an unusual destination, the best strategy is to get to that destination as fast as you can (by plane if possible). Other PSBs do not have to honour the permit and can cancel it and send you back. Take your time getting back – you're not likely to be hassled if you're returning to civilisation. Transit points usually don't require a permit, and you can stay the night.

BUSINESS HOURS

Banks, offices, government departments and Public Security Bureaus are open Monday to Saturday. As a rough guide only, they open around 8 to 9 am, close for two hours in the middle of the day (often one hour in winter or three during a heat wave in summer), then re-open until 5 or 6 pm. Sunday is a public holiday, but some businesses are open Sunday morning and make up for this by closing on Wednesday afternoons. CITS offices, Friendship Stores and the foreign-exchange counters in the tourist hotels and some of the local branches of the Bank of China have similar opening hours, and are generally open on Sundays as well, at least in the morning.

Many parks, zoos and monuments have similar opening hours, and are also open on Sundays and often at night. Shows at cinemas and theatres end from 9.30 to 10 pm.

Government restaurants are open for early morning breakfast (sometimes as early as 5.30) until about 7.30 am, then open for lunch and again for dinner from around 5 to 8 or 9 pm. Chinese eat early and go home early – by 9 pm you'll probably find the chairs stacked and the cooks gone home. Privately run restaurants are usually open all day, and often late into the night, especially around railway stations.

Long-distance bus stations and railway stations open their ticket offices around 5 or 5.30 am before the first trains and buses pull out. Apart from a one or two-hour break in the middle of the day, they often stay open until late at night – say 11 or 11.30 pm.

HOLIDAYS

The People's Republic has nine national holidays during the year:

New Year's Day
1 January

Spring Festival
Usually in February. This is otherwise known as Chinese New Year and starts on the first day of the old lunar calendar. Although officially lasting only three days, many people take a week off from work. Be warned: this is China's only three-day holiday and, unless you have booked a month or two in advance, this is definitely not the time to cross borders (especially the Hong Kong one) or to look for transport or accommodation. Although the demand for accommodation sky-rockets, many hotels close down at this time. Book your room in advance and sit tight until the chaos is over!

International Working Women's Day
8 March

International Labour Day
1 May

Youth Day
4 May – commemorates the student demonstrations in Beijing on 4 May 1919, when the Versailles Conference decided to give Germany's 'rights' in the city of Tianjin to Japan

Children's Day
1 June

Anniversary of the founding of the Communist Party of China
1 July

Anniversary of the founding of the Chinese People's Liberation Army
1 August

National Day
1 October – celebrates the founding of the People's Republic of China on 1 October 1949

POST & TELECOMMUNICATIONS

As well as the local post offices there are branch post offices in just about all the major tourist hotels where you can send letters, packets and parcels (the contents of packets and parcels are checked by the post office staff before mailing). In some places, you may only be able to post printed matter from these branch offices. Other parcels may require a Customs form attached at the town's main post office, where their contents will be checked.

The international postal service seems efficient, and air-mailed letters and postcards will probably take around five to 10 days to reach their destinations. An International Express Mail Service now operates in many Chinese cities. If possible, write the country of destination in Chinese, as this should speed up the delivery.

Large envelopes are a bit hard to come by; try the department stores. If you expect to be sending quite a few packets, stock up when you come across such envelopes. A roll of strong, sticky tape is a useful item to bring along and serves many purposes. String, glue and sometimes cloth bags are supplied at the post offices, but don't count on it. The Friendship Stores will sometimes package and mail purchases for you, but only goods actually bought at the store.

International Post

The ordinary postal rates for international mail (other than to Hong Kong or Macau) are listed below. There is a slightly reduced postage rate for letters and postcards to certain countries.

Letters Surface mail is Y1.50 up to 20 grams, and Y3 above 20 grams and up to 50 grams. Air-mail letters are an additional Y0.50 for every 10 grams or fraction thereof, above the surface mail rate.

Postcards Postcards are Y1.10 by surface mail and Y1.60 by air mail to anywhere in the world.

Aerogrammes These are Y1.90 to anywhere in the world.

Printed Matter Surface mail is Y1 up to 20 grams, Y1.60 from 20 grams to 50 grams, Y2.80 from 50 grams to 100 grams, Y5.40 from 100 grams to 250 grams, Y10.20 from 250 grams to 500 grams, Y16.20 from 500 grams to one kg, Y27 from one kg to two kg, and for each additional kg or fraction thereof the charge is Y11.40.

Air mail for printed matter is an additional Y0.40 for every additional 10 grams or fraction thereof.

Small Packets Surface mail charges are Y3.60 up to 100 grams, Y7.20 from 100 grams to 250 grams, Y13 from 250 grams to 500 grams, Y21.60 from 500 grams to one kg.

Top: Sign of the times, Dali (RS)
Bottom Left: Cricket cages, Lanzhou (AS)
Bottom Right: Bamboo fish traps, Erhai Lake (RS)

Air mail for small packets is an additional Y0.40 for every 10 grams or fraction thereof.

Parcels

Rates vary depending on the country of destination. Charge for a one-kg parcel sent surface mail from China to the UK is Y52, to the USA Y30.60, and to Germany Y35.60. Charge for a one-kg parcel sent air mail to the UK is Y82, to the USA Y77, and to Germany Y70.60.

Post offices are very picky about how you pack things; don't finalise your packing until the thing has got its last Customs clearance. If you have a receipt for the goods, then put it in the box when you're mailing it, since it may be opened again by customs further down the line.

Registration Fees

The registration fee for letters, printed matter and packets is Y1. Acknowledgement of receipt is Y0.80 per article.

Poste Restante

There are postes restantes in just about every city and town, and they seem to work. Unfortunately, most post offices haven't discovered alphabetical order. In large cities, the GPO will assign numbers to letters as they are received and post the number and names on a noticeboard. You have to find your name and write down the number(s) of your letters, then tell the clerk at the counter. We've seen some strange names on the noticeboards – 'Par Avion, General Delivery', and 'Hold Until Arrival'.

Some major tourist hotels will hold mail for their guests, but this doesn't always work. Many places will hold mail for several months if you write such an instruction on the outside of the letter.

It's worth noting that some foreigners living in China have had their mail opened or parcels pilfered before receipt – and some have their outgoing mail opened and read. This seems to affect tourists less, although letters with enclosures will almost certainly be opened. Your mail is less likely to be opened if it's sent to cities that handle high volumes of mail, like Beijing. Officially, the People's Republic prohibits several items from being mailed to it, including books, magazines, notes and manuscripts.

Domestic Services

Internal post is amazingly fast – say one or two days from Canton to Beijing. Within a city it may be delivered the same day that it's sent.

Domestic mail within the same city costs half the price of domestic mail being sent elsewhere. Within a city, letters (20 grams and below) cost Y0.04, postcards Y0.02. Out of town, letters are Y0.08, postcards Y0.04. The fee for registration is Y0.12.

Telephone

Many hotel rooms are equipped with phones from which local calls are free. Local calls can be made from public phones (there are some around – not many). There are also internal telex, telegram and long-distance phone services.

Direct dialling for international calls is gradually being introduced at top hotels in the major cities. You can also use the main telecommunications offices. Lines are a bit faint but usually OK and you generally don't have to wait more than half an hour before you're connected. Many large hotels now offer fax service to almost every country in the world that has direct dialling.

The usual procedure is to fill out a form with the relevant information concerning who you want to call or fax, and hand it to the attendant at the telephone desk.

Rates for station-to-station calls to most countries in the world are Y18 per minute. Hong Kong is slightly cheaper at Y12 per minute. There is a minimum charge of three minutes. Reverse-charge calls are cheaper than calls paid for in China. Time the call yourself – the operator will not break in to tell you that your minimum period of three minutes is approaching. After you hang up, the operator will ring back to tell you how much it cost. There is no call cancellation fee.

If you are expecting a call – either international or domestic – try to advise the caller beforehand of your hotel room number. The operators frequently have difficulty understanding Western names, and the hotel receptionist may not be able to locate you.

In major cities, the local directory assistance number is 114; long-distance (domestic) information is 113. However, operators only speak Chinese.

The phone system in Beijing has improved, but Li Binsheng, a well-known cartoonist, once drew a satirical cartoon which depicted an old man standing with a telephone receiver in his hand while his son and grandson waited beside him. The caption for the old man said: ' If I fail to get through, my son will follow; if he fails too, he has his son to follow'.

Fax, Telex & Telegram

Fax messages, telexes and telegrams can be sent from some of the major tourist hotels and from the central telegraph offices in some of the bigger cities.

International fax and telexes (other than those to Hong Kong or Macau) cost around Y18 per minute with a three-minute minimum charge. International telegram rates are usually around Y3.50 per word, and more for the express service. Rates to Hong Kong are less.

TIME

Time throughout China is set to Beijing time. When it's noon in Beijing it's also noon in far-off Lhasa, Ürümqi and all other parts of the country.

When it's noon in Beijing the time in cities around the world is:

Frankfurt	5 am
Hong Kong	12 noon
London	4 am
Los Angeles	8 pm
Melbourne	2 pm
Montreal	11 pm
New York	11 pm
Paris	5 am
Rome	5 am
Wellington	4 pm

The General Office of the State Council experimented with daylight saving in 1986 and was so pleased with the reduction in traffic accidents and savings in electricity that it intends to continue with the idea. The Chinese public became mighty confused figuring out what was happening. Chinese working for foreigners thought the time change only applied to Chinese, not foreigners; long-distance buses, trains and boats kept to old time; CAAC decided to postpone all flights, including those of foreign airlines, by one hour. Since Chinese consider regular hours for mealtimes a prerequisite for good health, there was considerable concern that this experiment was detrimental to health and could alter the time-balance intervals between meals.

Although the Chinese have had several years to get used to it, daylight-saving time still causes a good deal of confusion. Buses and flights usually depart one hour later during the summer, but trains do not. For several weeks after daylight-saving time begins, and again when it ends, buses depart at the wrong time, and people show up for work an hour late or leave an hour early. Some cities, especially those near Hong Kong, still refuse to follow daylight-saving time. This can cause much confusion for travellers trying to find out when buses depart, especially when local clocks say one thing and people's mouths say another.

The State Council has decreed that clocks will go forward one hour at 2 am on the first Sunday of the second 10 days of April, and will be set back one hour at 2 am on the first Sunday of the second 10 days of September.

ELECTRICITY

Electricity is 220 volts, 50 cycles AC. Plugs are usually two-pin with angled prongs like in Australia. Conversion plugs are easily purchased in Hong Kong. Battery chargers are available in some major department stores in Canton, Beijing and Shanghai, but Hong Kong would be a better place to find such things. Many of the top-class hotels cater for various makes and models of foreign electrical goods. Chinese cities are experiencing power black-outs more frequently in recent years as the demand for power has grown. This is an especially serious problem in summertime because of the increasing use of air-conditioning.

LAUNDRY

Each floor of just about every hotel in China has a service desk, usually near the elevators. The attendant's job is to clean the rooms, make the beds, and collect and deliver laundry. Almost all tourist hotels have a laundry service, and if you hand in clothes one day you should get them back a day or two later. If the hotel doesn't have a laundry, they can usually direct you to one. Hotel laundry service tends to be expensive and you might wind up doing what many travellers do – hand-washing your own clothes. If you plan on doing this, dark clothes are better since the dirt doesn't show up so much.

WEIGHTS & MEASURES

The metric system is widely used in China. However, the traditional Chinese measures are often used for domestic transactions and you may come across them. The following equations will help.

Metric		Chinese		Imperial
1 metre	=	3 chi	=	3.28 feet
1 km	=	2 li	=	0.62 miles
1 hectare	=	15 mu	=	2.47 acres
1 litre	=	1 gongsheng	=	0.22 gallons
1 kg	=	2 jin	=	2.20 pounds

BOOKS & MAPS

There is enough literature on China to keep you reading for another 5000 years of their history. A few suggestions are given here.

History & Politics

George Orwell's *1984* was ahead of its time in predicting the political trends in the communist world. *Animal Farm* is perhaps a closer approximation to post-1949 China.

Franz Kafka's *The Trial* wasn't written with China in mind, yet his book is a potent reminder of the helplessness of individuals against the all-powerful state bureaucracy.

The classic on the Chinese Revolution is *Red Star Over China* (Pelican, 1972; first published in 1937) by Edgar Snow. Snow managed to get through the Kuomintang blockade of the Communists and spent four months with them in Yan'an in 1936. His book has been criticised as naive in that it glosses over some of the worst aspects of the Communist movement, but it conveys the hope and idealism of the time.

Chinese Shadows by Simon Leys is one of the most critical books on Mao and the Cultural Revolution. It was published in 1974, based on Leys' visits to China in 1972 and 1973. It's interesting to draw comparisons between the China of the post-Mao era and the one that Leys visited.

Roger Garside's *Coming Alive – China After Mao* describes the events which led to the downfall of the 'Gang of Four' and the rise of Deng Xiaoping. Garside served at the British Embassy in Beijing from 1968 to 1970, and was first secretary from 1976 to 1979.

The issue of human rights is covered in Amnesty International's *China: Violations of Human Rights* – a grim aspect of the country that should not be ignored.

Seeds of Fire: Chinese Voices of Conscience (Far Eastern Economic Review Ltd, 1986) is an anthology of blistering eloquence from authors such as Wei Jingsheng, Liu Qing, Wang Xizhe and Xu Wenli (all currently imprisoned for their roles in the Democracy Movement) and the poet Sun Jingxuan. Wei Jingsheng's description of Q1, China's top prison for political detainees, is utterly horrific.

The Dragon Wakes by Christopher Hibbert (Penguin) is a good history from 1793 to 1911.

The Chinese People Stand Up by Elizabeth Wright (BBC) examines China's turbulent history from 1949 up to the brutal suppression of pro-democracy demonstrators in 1989.

The Soong Dynasty by Sterling Seagrave (Sidgwick and Jackson) is one of the most popular books on the corrupt Kuomintang period. Unfortunately, the author severely damaged his credibility when he later published *The Marcos Dynasty* which contains more rumour than fact.

Recent Accounts

Over the last few years, since foreign journalists were permitted to take up residence in China, there has been a spate of books delving into Chinese life, the universe and everything. Most are out of date, but if you read them in succession you can get an overview of the changes which have taken place in China since Mao died.

Fox Butterfield's *China – Alive in the Bitter Sea* (Coronet, 1983) is one of the biggest sellers. A harshly critical account, it tells you everything from the location of Chinese labour camps to how women cope with menstruation.

To Get Rich is Glorious (Pantheon Books, 1984) by American scholar and many-times China traveller Orville Schell is a concise and easy-to-read overview of the major changes in China's economic policies and political thinking over the last few years.

A dimmer view of China under Deng Xiaoping is Italian journalist Tiziano Terzani's *Behind the Forbidden Door* (Allen & Unwin, 1986). Terzani, once an avid socialist, became disillusioned after living in China from 1980 to 1984, when he was finally booted out for his critical reporting.

Chinese Lives by Zhang Xinxin and Sang Ye (Penguin) was written by two Chinese journalists who interviewed Chinese people at all levels of society.

Cultural Revolution

The best seller seems to be *Life and Death in Shanghai* by Nien Cheng (Grafton). The author was imprisoned for 6½ years, and this is her gripping story of how she survived.

Other stories from this period include *Born Red* by Gao Yuan (Stanford University Press) and *Son of the Revolution* by Liang Heng and Judith Shapiro (Fontana Paperbacks).

Post-Tiananmen

If nothing else, the 1989 killings at Tiananmen Square forced foreign journalists to take off the rose-coloured glasses and produce a few hard-hitting critical books.

Tiananmen, the Rape of Peking by Michael Fathers and Andrew Higgins (Doubleday) is probably the best book on the protests.

Beijing Spring by David and Peter Turnley is a good pictorial history of the Tiananmen events.

Tiananmen Diary by Harrison Salisbury (Unwin Paperbacks) and *Tiananmen Square* by Scott Simmie and Bob Nixon (Douglas and McIntyre) outline the same story.

Beijing Jeep by Jim Mann (Simon & Schuster) is about the short unhappy romance of American business in China.

Travellers' Tales

Then there's the sort of stuff that fits more into the 'Mad Dogs & Englishmen' genre. You won't fail to be amused by two books by Englishman Peter Fleming, written in the mid 1930s. *One's Company* describes his travels across Siberia and eastern China meeting such notables as Puyi, the puppet-emperor of Japanese-occupied Manchuria. *News from Tartary* describes his epic six-month trek on the backs of camels and donkeys across southern Xinjiang and into the north of Pakistan.

Danziger's Travels by Nick Danziger (Paladin) is a good 'Silk Road' book but the first half of it covers regions outside of China.

In Xanadu by William Dalrymple (Fontana Paperbacks) gives an account of a journey from Jerusalem to Xanadu by two British students.

Behind the Wall by Colin Thubron (Penguin) is an excellent travelogue with lots of insights into Chinese society.

The classic coffee-table book is *A Day in the Life of China* (Merehurst Press). It's very expensive but you get what you pay for.

A lively and informative book is *Cycling to Xian* (ITMB, 736A Granville St, Vancouver, BC V6Z 1G3, Canada) by Michael Buckley. The author realistically expresses both the joys and frustrations of travelling through China.

Iron and Silk by Mark Salzman (Vintage Departures) chronicles the author's studies under a Chinese martial arts teacher.

Fiction

The classic is *The Good Earth* by Pearl S Buck.

Peking by Anthony Grey (Pan Books) is your standard blockbuster by the author of *Saigon*. Not bad.

Regulations

A Guide to Aliens Visiting China, issued every June by the Exit-Entry Bureau, Ministry of Public Security, contains all the rules that concern foreigners as well as updated lists of open destinations within each province.

Living in China

If you intend to live in China, a couple of books are worth picking up.

The China Phonebook & Business Directory (published twice annually by the China Phone Book Company, Hong Kong) may be invaluable if you live in China or visit frequently. It's in English and Chinese and contains the addresses and phone numbers of industrial firms, hospitals, hotels, government departments, etc. It's available in most Hong Kong bookstores, or directly from the China Phone Book Company (☎ 8348133), 10th floor, 1001 Connaught Commercial Building, 185 Wanchai Rd, Hong Kong Island. It costs a substantial HK$375. The same company also publishes the *China Telex and Fax Directory*.

Excellent background information can be had from *China Bound: A Handbook for American Students, Researchers and Teachers* (published by the US-China Education Clearing House). It's available from the National Association for Foreign Student Affairs, 1860 19th St NW, Washington, DC 20009, USA.

Phrasebooks

If you don't speak Chinese these are essential. Lonely Planet's *China Phrasebook* includes common words, useful phrases and word lists in English, simplified Chinese characters and *putonghua*.

Some people use the *Speechless Translator*, which can be bought in Hong Kong; this has columns of Chinese characters and English translations that you string together to form sentences, with no speaking required.

Another useful book is *Instant Chinese* (Round Asia Publishing Company, 1985), which you can find in Hong Kong.

If you're visiting Tibet, you'll find Lonely Planet's *Tibet Phrasebook* useful.

Bookshops in Hong Kong

A couple of bookshops in Hong Kong carry a good selection of books from or about China. About the widest selection can be found at Swindon Books (☎ 3668033), 13-15 Lock Rd, Tsimshatsui, Kowloon.

Time Books (☎ 7217138) is on Granville Rd near the corner with Nathan Rd, Tsimshatsui, Kowloon. They have a good stock of both English and Chinese books.

The official outlet for books published in the PRC (for foreign consumption) is the Peace Book Company (☎ 8967832), 35 Kimberley Rd, Tsimshatsui, Kowloon. They have a large collection of books on language, politics, qigong, acupuncture, herbal medicine, maps, atlases, calligraphy, scroll painting, etc.

Wanderlust Books (☎ 5232042), 30 Hollywood Rd, Central, Hong Kong Island, has one of the best collections of travel books and general selection of books on China. The helpful English-speaking staff is another good reason for coming here.

Censorship

If you think it's hard deciding what to read on China, then have sympathy for the Chinese who don't have the right to choose. Books come and go in China; as the political winds change so does the availability of certain books and newspapers.

In a bookshop in Wuhan I came across a copy of a book printed in 1974 called *Criticise Lin Biao and Confucius*. It should have been removed long ago since that campaign was actually an attack on 'rightists' like Deng Xiaoping. The employees in the shop tried to take it from me when I picked it off the shelves, and despite a furious argument they refused to sell it to me. They claimed it was a damaged book (the front cover had been torn off) and they couldn't sell a damaged book. One bystander said it was an 'old' book and I couldn't learn anything from an old book. In utter frustration I left the shop. I returned the next day and all copies of the book had been taken off the shelves. So if you see something that looks interesting you'd better get it now, because in 10 years' time when the Chinese leadership is aiming in a different direction it won't be available.

Another problem with Chinese bookshops is that some books are *neibu* – restricted or forbidden except to those who have been granted access. Of course they won't tell you the book is neibu, but will make up some excuse like the book has no price on it. Books are neibu for various reasons. Sometimes it's because they're illegally printed copies of Western books and the Chinese are sensitive about infringing international copyright. A more common reason – and this one afflicts university libraries throughout China – is that only certain people have permission to use certain books. Only law students can use law books, only economics students can use economics books, and so on. To use books outside your field requires permission from the unit in charge of the library which houses those books. The rules have been relaxed recently with the exception of classics with an erotic bent, such as *Jin Ping Mei (The Golden Lotus)*. Foreign students and teachers up to professorial level are not immune to the system – even they are restricted in their access to books, and this has become one of their most serious complaints.

If you want good books to read, bring your own. US and British paperbacks are available from shops in the tourist hotels in the big Chinese cities, but the supply and range are very limited. Foreign-language bookshops cater for Chinese who are learning foreign languages, not for Western reading interests – though they often stock classic foreign fiction as well as pirated textbooks. The Beijing Friendship Store has the best foreign bookshop in China. You can now find English-language Penguin books printed in China and sold in Foreign Language Bookstores and some hotels for less than Y5 apiece. Mostly they are collections of American and British short stories, and it's not certain how many of these are printed under licence or pirated. Still, for the desperate they're a real bargain.

As a last-ditch measure, the lobbies of many hotels provide a collection of free foreign-language booklets explaining China's current version of history (subject to revision on short notice) and recent political pronouncements. Some of these can be amusing and make good collectors' items.

Foreign Newspapers & Journals

Some Western journals and newspapers are sold in a few of the major tourist hotels. The *Herald Tribune* and the Asian edition of the *Wall Street Journal* are sold in Beijing, Shanghai and Canton. *Time, Newsweek* and *Reader's Digest* have wide distribution; *Newsweek* is even sold in some foreign-language bookshops. The *Far Eastern Economic Review* and the *Economist* are also available at many tourist hotels.

When the Communist Party committee of Beijing investigated the bustling black market for foreign books, magazines and newspapers they discovered that hotel staff and garbage collectors are well-placed intermediaries for this business. Foreign hotel guests regularly leave behind several tonnes of foreign publications every month, but resident foreign experts, journalists and diplomats throw out nearly 20 tonnes. The Beijing committee analysed printed matter left behind at the Xinqiao Hotel and was pleased to discover that nearly half of the publications had good or relatively good contents. The remaining items contained 'partly erroneous' or 'problematic' material such as 'half-naked advertisements'. When the courageous committee delved into diplomatic dustbins, they discovered that 15% of their haul was 'anti-communist, anti-Chinese, obscene and pornographic' – definitely bottom of the barrel.

If you want to keep up with the world

news, a short-wave radio receiver would be worth bringing with you. There are some very compact ones available in Hong Kong.

Maps

The most useful map of China is published by Cartographic Publishing House in Beijing. The detailed map is available in both pinyin and Chinese script, and is called the *Map of the People's Republic of China (Zhonghua Renmin Gongheguo Ditu)*. You should be able to get it in your home country; otherwise it's readily available in Hong Kong and the large cities in China.

The *National Geographic* map of China has excellent coverage of minority areas. *Bartholomew's* maps are usually excellent, but not for China. Their China map is extremely detailed but uses the old Wade-Giles system of naming towns, which is a distinct nuisance. The map also leaves out Tibet and Xinjiang.

City maps are often sold by hawkers outside the railway and long-distance bus stations. These are in Chinese and show the bus routes, and in most cases are very good and definitely worth buying. Maps in English are sometimes sold at the larger tourist hotels.

Large maps of 20 major cities in China have been made by the Cartographic Publishing House and are usually available from most tourist hotels. There are versions both in Chinese and in English, and they usually come complete with sub-maps of the area around the city, and of parks and sights within the city. They carry a lot of background info on the reverse side, and are cheap. They're excellent maps, although sometimes the sights are carelessly marked and it's hard to tell whether a building is on a main street or down some side alley. Getting these maps when you need them can be difficult – if you see one you think you'll need later, then buy it! The Peace Book Company in Hong Kong is a good place to stock up.

If you're after fine detail you can sometimes get booklets of maps (in Chinese) of the counties in the individual provinces, and these usually include maps of the main towns. Booklets of detailed maps of the individual Chinese provinces (in Chinese) are sold at railway stations and Xinhua Bookstores.

If you arrive in a place where no map is available, take a look in the waiting room of the railway or long-distance bus station; large maps of the town are often hung up on the wall. They're always in Chinese, but you may be able to orientate yourself from them, and they sometimes show the bus routes.

Some of the most detailed maps of China available in the West are the aerial survey 'Operational Navigation Charts' (Series ONC). These are prepared and published by the Defense Mapping Agency Aerospace Center, St Louis Air Force Station, Missouri 63118, USA. Cyclists have recommended these highly because of their extraordinary detail. In Britain you can obtain these maps from Stanfords Map Centre, 12-14 Long Acre, London WC2E 9LP (☎ 071-836 1321) or from The Map Shop (☎ 06 846 3146), A T Atkinson & Partner, 15 High St, Upton-on-Severn, Worcestershire, WR8 OHJ.

MEDIA

News Agencies

China has two news agencies, the Xinhua News Agency and the China News Service. The Xinhua (New China) Agency is a national agency with its headquarters in Beijing and branches in each province as well as in the army and many foreign countries. It provides news for the national, provincial and local papers and radio stations, transmits radio broadcasts abroad in foreign languages, and is responsible for making contact with and exchanging news with foreign news agencies. In Hong Kong, Xinhua acts as the unofficial embassy.

Xinhua serves not only as mouthpiece but also as the 'eyes and ears' of the political elite whose decisions rely heavily on *Neibu Cankao*, the most exclusive of all restricted-circulation information bulletins in China. Few, if any, foreigners have seen this Xinhua publication which appears twice daily, once in the morning and once in the afternoon, for an estimated readership of 2000, drawn from 'responsible comrades in the central leadership'. The elite readership derives a considerable proportion of its power from this 'real' news on everything from lapses in Party discipline, religious ferment or student unrest to crime, murder, porn or even the capitalist temptations laid before staff in joint-ventures. Another better known restricted-circulation bulletin produced by Xinhua is *Cankao Ziliao*, which contains translations of international news from foreign sources.

The main function of the China News Service is to supply news to Overseas Chinese newspapers and journals, including those in Hong Kong and Macau. It also distributes Chinese documentary films abroad.

Chinese-Language Publications

There are nearly 2000 national and provincial newspapers in China. The main one is *Renmin Ribao* (the People's Daily), with nationwide circulation. It was founded in 1946 as the official publication of the Central Committee of the Communist Party. Most of these tend to be exceedingly boring though they do provide a brief rundown of world events.

At the other end of the scale there is China's version of the gutter press – several hundred 'unhealthy papers' hawked on street corners in major cities with suggestive or violent photos and stories about witchcraft, miracle cures and UFOs. These have been severely criticised by the government for their obscene and racy content – they are also extremely popular. There are also about 40 newspapers for the minority nationalities.

Almost 2200 periodicals were published at the last count, of which about half were technical or scientific; the rest were concerned with social sciences, literature, culture and education, or were general periodicals, pictorials or children's publications. One of the better-known periodicals is the monthly *Hongqi* (Red Flag), the main Communist philosophical and theoretical journal.

In China the papers, radio and TV are the last places to carry the news. Westerners tend to be numbed by endless accounts of heroic factory workers and stalwart peasants, and dismiss China's media as a huge propaganda machine. Flipping through journals like *China Today, Women of China* and *China Pictorial* only serves to confirm this view.

Nevertheless, the Chinese press does warrant serious attention since it provides clues to what is happening in China. When Deng Xiaoping returned to public view after being disposed of in the Cultural Revolution, the first mention was simply the inclusion of his name in a guest list at a reception for Prince Sihanouk of Kampuchea, printed in the *People's Daily* without elaboration or comment. Political struggles between factions are described in articles in the Chinese newspapers as a means of warning off any supporters of the opposing side and undermining its position rather than resorting to an all-out, dangerous conflict. The 'Letters to the Editor' section in the *People's Daily* provides something of a measure of public opinion, and complaints are sometimes followed up by reporters.

Newspapers and journals are useful for following the 'official line' of the Chinese government – though in times of political struggle they tend to follow the line of whoever has control over the media. For example, in the weeks after Mao's death when the 'rightists' were making a comeback, the 'leftists' controlled the media.

Foreign-Language Publications

China publishes various newspapers, books and magazines in a number of European and Asian languages. The papers you're most likely to come across are: the *China Daily*, the only English-language daily newspaper, which was first published in June 1981 and now has overseas editions printed in Hong Kong, the USA and Europe; *Beijing Review*, a weekly magazine on political and current affairs; and *China Today*, a monthly magazine. *China Today*, founded in 1952 by the wife of Sun Yatsen, used to be called *China Reconstructs*. The name was changed in 1989 because – as one official said – '37 years is a hell of a long time to be reconstructing your country'.

The government publishes impressive glossy magazines in minority languages such as Tibetan. These appear to be strictly for foreign consumption – they are not available in China.

All of China's government publications suffer from an over-supply of political rhetoric, but there are usually some interesting articles on archaeological discoveries or travel. The *China Daily* is notable for reporting crime, criminal executions and even stories about corrupt officials (a very popular theme in the papers).

Radio & TV

Domestic radio broadcasting is controlled by the Central People's Broadcasting Station (CPBS). Broadcasts are made in putonghua, the standard Chinese speech, as well as in local Chinese dialects and minority languages. There are also broadcasts to Taiwan in putonghua and Fujianese. Radio Beijing is China's overseas radio service and broadcasts in about 40 foreign languages, as well as in putonghua and several local dialects. It also exchanges programmes with radio stations in a number of countries and has correspondents in some.

The other station, Chinese Central Television (CCTV), began broadcasting in 1958, and colour transmission began in 1973.

The Chinese seem to be addicted to TV, at least in the urban areas where sets are more common. Programming has bred a desire for more TV sets and God knows how many get carried across the border every day by Hong Kong relatives! Private ownership of TVs is limited, but just about everyone has access to one: communes, factories and hotels usually buy a TV and put it in their recreation rooms or dining halls for collective viewing, or one set may serve a whole apartment block.

Although they've improved in the past few years, Chinese TV shows are designed to guide the public's moral education. Movies and soap operas urge the people to be good citizens, work and study hard, not to lie, cheat, slash foreigners' backpacks, etc. Most Chinese find their public TV boring, and those who have access to video machines consume foreign movies with a passion. Smuggled videos from Hong Kong and Taiwan are popular, but most popular of all are American police shows and war movies.

Noticeboards

Apart from the mass media, the public noticeboard retains its place as a means of educating the people or influencing public opinion. Other people who want to get a message across glue up big wallposters in public places. This is a traditional form of communicating ideas in China and if the content catches the attention of even a few people then word-of-mouth can spread it very quickly. Deng Xiaoping stripped from China's constitution the right to put up wallposters.

Public noticeboards abound in China. Two of the most common subjects are crime and road accidents. In China it's no holds barred. Before-and-after photos of executed criminals are plugged up on these boards along with a description of their heinous offences. Photos of people squashed by trucks are even more frequent. Industrial safety is another common theme.

HEALTH

Travel health depends on your pre-departure preparations, your day-to-day health care while travelling and how you handle any medical problem or emergency that does develop. While the list of potential dangers can seem quite frightening, with a little luck, some basic precautions and adequate information, few travellers experience more than upset stomachs.

Travel Health Guides

There are a number of books on travel health:

Staying Healthy in Asia, Africa & Latin America (Volunteers in Asia). This is probably the best all-round guide to carry, as it's compact but very detailed and well organised.

Travellers' Health, Dr Richard Dawood (Oxford University Press). This is comprehensive, easy to read, authoritative and also highly recommended, although it's rather large to lug around.

Where There is No Doctor, David Werner (Hesperian Foundation). This is a very detailed guide intended for someone, like a Peace Corps worker, going to work in an undeveloped country, rather than for the average traveller.

Travel with Children, Maureen Wheeler (Lonely Planet Publications). This includes basic advice on travel health for younger children.

Vaccinations

Vaccinations against cholera are required if you arrive within five days of leaving an infected area. Yellow fever vaccinations are required if you arrive within six days of leaving an infected area. If you're coming from a 'clean' area then inoculations against cholera, yellow fever and typhoid are not compulsory. However, if you're heading to South Asia after China, you probably should get all of the above.

Though not required, some vaccinations which might prove useful in China include influenza, tetanus, hepatitis B, tuberculosis, and (for Tibet) rabies. If you're bringing children, be sure they've had all the usual childhood vaccines such as polio, diphtheria, whooping cough, measles, mumps, rubella, etc.

Health Insurance

Although not absolutely necessary, it is a good idea to take out travellers' health insurance. The policies are usually available from travel agents. If you purchase an International Student Identity Card (ISIC) or Teacher Card (ISTC), you may be automatically covered depending on which country you purchased the card in. Check with the student travel office to be sure. If you're neither a student or a teacher, but you're between the ages of 15 and 25, you can purchase an International Youth Identity Card (YIEE) which entitles you to the same benefits. Some student travel offices also sell insurance to others who don't hold these cards.

Some policies specifically exclude 'dangerous activities' which may include motorcycling, scuba diving and even hiking. Obviously, you'll want a policy that covers you in all circumstances you're likely to find yourself in.

Hopefully you won't need medical care, but do keep in mind that any health insurance policy you have at home is probably not valid outside your country. The usual procedure with travellers' health insurance is that you pay in cash first for services rendered and then later present the receipts to the insurance company for reimbursement after you return home. Other policies stipulate that you call collect to a centre in your home country where an immediate assessment of your problem is made.

Medical Kit

A basic medical kit could prove useful. It should include a thermometer, Panadol for pain and fever, a pin and tweezers for removing splinters, plaster for blisters, band-aids and an antiseptic.

Medications for specific illnesses are discussed further on in this section. Briefly, useful medications include Lomotil (or Imodium) for diarrhoea, laxatives, antifungal skin ointments, antimalarial drugs, and – if you need them – contraceptives. Good all-purpose antibiotics such as tetracycline are useful *only* if you understand when and how to use them.

Basic Rules

Care in what you eat and drink is the most important health rule; stomach upsets are the most likely travel health problem but the majority of these upsets will be relatively minor.

Water The water in large Chinese cities will usually be reasonably safe. The Chinese themselves, however, will rarely drink straight from the tap. Drinking water is usually boiled, stored in a thermos flask and drunk hot, plain or with tea. Only in the hottest weather will they drink cooler water, and it will almost always be boiled first. It would be sensible to follow their example.

In the countryside and in small towns, the water supply is more likely to have been contaminated. Try to avoid drinking unboiled water unless you are quite sure it is clean.

The simplest way of purifying water is to boil it thoroughly. Technically this means boiling for 10 minutes, something which happens very rarely! Remember that at high altitude water boils at a lower temperature, so germs are less likely to be killed.

Simple filtering will not remove all dangerous organisms, so if you cannot boil water it should be treated chemically. Chlorine tablets (Puritabs, Steritabs or other brand names) will kill many but not all pathogens. Iodine is very effective in purifying water and is available in tablet form (such as Potable Aqua), but follow the directions carefully and remember that too much iodine can be harmful.

If you can't find tablets, tincture of iodine (2%) or iodine crystals can be used. Two drops of tincture of iodine per litre or quart of clear water is the recommended dosage; the treated water should be left to stand for 30 minutes before drinking. Iodine crystals can also be used to purify water but this is a more complicated process, as you have to first prepare a saturated iodine solution. Iodine loses its effectiveness if exposed to air or damp so keep it in a tightly sealed container. Flavoured powder will disguise the taste of treated water and is a good idea if you are travelling with children.

Food Most Chinese food is well cooked, and uncooked vegetables are usually pickled before being eaten. Raw vegetables and fruit should be washed with purified water or peeled where possible. Thoroughly cooked food is not safe if it has been left to cool or if it has been reheated. Take great care with shellfish or fish and avoid undercooked meat. If a place looks clean and well run and if the vendor also looks clean and healthy, then the food is probably safe. Ice-cream is more of a risk: beware of street vendors and of ice-cream that has melted and been refrozen.

Nutrition If your food is poor or limited in availability, if you're travelling hard and fast and therefore missing meals, or if you simply lose your appetite, you can soon start to lose weight and place your health at risk.

Make sure your diet is well balanced. Eggs, bean curd (tofu), beans and meat are all safe ways to get protein. Fruit you can peel (bananas, oranges or mandarins for example) is always safe and a good source of vitamins. Try to eat plenty of rice and steamed bread. Remember that although food is generally safer if it is cooked well, overcooked food loses much of its nutritional value. If your diet isn't well balanced or if your food intake is insufficient, it's a good idea to take vitamin and iron pills.

In hot weather make sure you drink enough – don't rely on feeling thirsty to indicate when you should drink. Not needing to urinate or very dark yellow urine is a danger sign. Always carry a water bottle with you on long trips. Excessive sweating can lead to loss of salt and therefore muscle cramping. Salt tablets are not a good idea as a preventative, but in places where salt is not used much adding salt to food can help.

Everyday Health A normal body temperature is 98.6°F or 37°C; more than 2°C higher is a 'high' fever. A normal adult pulse rate is from 60 to 80 per minute (children from 80 to 100, babies from 100 to 140). You should know how to take a temperature and a pulse rate. As a general rule the pulse increases about 20 beats per minute for each 1°C rise in fever.

Respiration (breathing) rate is also an indicator of illness. Count the number of breaths per minute: between 12 and 20 is normal for adults and older children (up to 30 for younger children, 40 for babies). People with a high fever or serious respiratory illness (like pneumonia) breathe more quickly than normal. More than 40 shallow breaths a minute in an adult usually means pneumonia.

Many health problems can be avoided by taking care of yourself. Wash your hands frequently – it's quite easy to contaminate your own food. Clean your teeth with purified water rather than straight from the tap. Avoid climatic extremes: keep out of the sun when it's hot, dress warmly when it's cold. Avoid potential diseases by dressing sensibly. You can get worm infections through walking barefoot. You can avoid insect bites by covering bare skin when insects are around, by screening windows or beds or by using insect repellents. Seek local advice: if you're told the water is unsafe due to jellyfish, crocodiles or bilharzia, don't go in. In situations where there is no information, discretion is the better part of valour.

Climatic & Geographical Considerations

Heat Exhaustion *(zhòng shǔ)* Dehydration or salt deficiency can cause heat exhaustion. Take time to acclimatise to high temperatures and make sure you get sufficient liquids. Salt deficiency is characterised by fatigue, lethargy, headaches, giddiness and muscle cramps, and salt tablets may help. Vomiting or diarrhoea can deplete your liquid and salt levels. Anhydrotic heat exhaustion, caused by an inability to sweat, is quite rare. Unlike the other forms of heat exhaustion it is likely to strike people who have been in a hot climate for some time, rather than newcomers.

Heat Stroke This serious, sometimes fatal, condition can occur if the body's heat-regulating mechanism breaks down and the body temperature rises to dangerous levels. Long, continuous periods of exposure to high temperatures can leave you vulnerable to heat stroke. You should avoid excessive alcohol or strenuous activity when you first arrive in a hot climate.

The symptoms are feeling unwell, not sweating very much or at all and a high body temperature (39°C to 41°C). Where sweating has ceased the skin becomes flushed and red. Severe, throbbing headaches and lack of coordination will also occur, and the sufferer may be confused or aggressive. Eventually the victim will become delirious or convulse. Hospitalisation is essential, but meanwhile get patients out of the sun, remove their clothing, cover them with a wet sheet or towel and then fan continually.

Cold Too much cold is just as dangerous as too much heat, particularly if it leads to hypothermia. If you are trekking at high altitudes or simply taking a long bus trip over mountains, particularly at night, be prepared. In regions such as Tibet you should always be prepared for cold, wet or windy conditions even if you're just out walking.

Hypothermia occurs when the body loses heat faster than it can produce it and the core temperature of the body falls. It is surprisingly easy to progress from very cold to dangerously cold due to a combination of wind, wet clothing, fatigue and hunger, even if the air temperature is above freezing. It is best to dress in layers; silk, wool and some of the new artificial fibres are all good insulating materials. A hat is important, as a lot of heat is lost through the head. A strong, waterproof outer layer is essential, as keeping dry is vital. Carry basic supplies, including food containing simple sugars to generate heat quickly and lots of fluid to drink.

Symptoms of hypothermia are exhaustion, numb skin (particularly toes and fingers), shivering, slurred speech, irrational or violent behaviour, lethargy, stumbling, dizzy spells, muscle cramps and violent bursts of energy. Irrationality may take the form of sufferers claiming they are warm and trying to take off their clothes.

To treat hypothermia, first get the patient out of the wind and/or rain, remove their clothing if it's wet and replace it with dry, warm clothing. Give them hot liquids – not alcohol – and some high-energy, easily digestible food. This should be enough for the early stages of hypothermia, but if it has gone further it may be necessary to place the victim in a warm sleeping bag and get in with them. Do not rub patients, place them near a fire or remove their wet clothes in the wind. If possible, place a sufferer in a warm (not hot) bath.

Motion Sickness *(yūn chē)* Eating lightly

before and during a trip will reduce the chances of motion sickness. If you are prone to motion sickness try to find a place that minimises disturbance – near the wing on aircraft, close to midships on boats, near the centre on buses. Fresh air usually helps, reading or cigarette smoke doesn't. Commercial anti-motion-sickness preparations, which can cause drowsiness, have to be taken before the trip commences; when you're feeling sick it's too late. Ginger is a natural preventative and is available in capsule form.

High-Altitude Sickness *(gāo shān fǎnyìng)* Tibet has a few problems all of its own caused by high altitude and thin air. Acute Mountain Sickness (AMS) is the most common problem. Rapid ascent from low altitudes, overexertion, lack of physical fitness, dehydration and fatigue will make it worse. A climber who is elderly, sick or obese is at greater risk. Symptoms include headache, dizziness, lack of appetite, nausea and vomiting. Breathlessness, sleeplessness and a pounding heart are normal at these altitudes and are not part of AMS. If you spend enough time at high elevations, your body will eventually start making more blood cells to carry extra oxygen. If you get altitude sickness, the best cure is to go to a lower altitude. A pain-killer for headache and an anti-emetic for vomiting will also help. The best prevention is to ascend slowly and avoid overexertion in the beginning. Aerobic exercises are good preparation for a trip to high elevations.

AMS is unpleasant, but a far more serious complication is high-altitude pulmonary oedema. This is usually only seen at elevations above 3000 metres about 24 to 72 hours after ascent. Symptoms include coughing up frothy sputum, which usually progresses from white to pink to bloody. A rattling sound in the chest can be heard, often without a stethoscope. The symptoms might be mistaken for pneumonia, but the suddenness of their appearance in a rapidly ascending climber should make you suspect pulmonary oedema. *This is a medical emergency!* Coma and death can follow rapidly – the only effective treatment is to get the victim to a lower elevation as soon as possible. Oxygen helps a little, but only if it's given in the early stages.

Sunburn *(shài shàng)* In Tibet and other places at high elevations, the ultraviolet rays of the sun are much more penetrating because of the thin dry air – it's easy to get sunburnt and it doesn't do your eyes any good either. UV lotion (sunblock), sunglasses and a wide-brimmed hat are good protection. You should also use zinc cream or some other barrier cream for your nose and lips. Calamine lotion is good for mild sunburn.

The same applies in the tropics, in the desert, or even in northern China on a hot summer day.

Skin Diseases *(pífū bìng)* The most common summertime affliction that visitors to China suffer from is skin disease. This is especially true in the south-east due to the hot, humid climate. The humidity is a bigger problem than the heat. The most common varieties of skin problems are 'jock itch' (a fungal infection around the groin), athlete's foot (known to the Chinese as 'Hong Kong feet'), contact dermatitis (caused by a necklace or watchband rubbing the skin) and prickly heat (caused by excessive sweating). Prevention and treatment of these skin ailments is often a matter of good hygiene.

For fungal infections, bathe twice daily and thoroughly dry yourself before getting dressed. Standing in front of the electric fan is a good way to get thoroughly dry. Apply an anti-fungal ointment or powder (ointments are better) to affected area – popular brand names are Desenex, Tinactin or Mycota, all available in Hong Kong.

The Chinese have equivalent medications but you may have a hard time getting this across to a pharmacist who doesn't speak English. Wear light cotton underwear or very thin nylon that is 'breathable' – maybe even no underwear at all if the condition gets really serious.

Wear the lightest outer clothing possible when the weather is really hot and humid. For athlete's foot, wearing open-toed sandals will often solve the problem without further treatment. Cleaning between the toes with warm soapy water and an old toothbrush also helps. Treat contact dermatitis by removing the offending necklace, bracelet or wrist-watch. Avoid anything that chafes the skin, such as tight clothing, especially elastic.

If your skin develops little painful red 'pinpricks', you probably have prickly heat. This is the result of excessive sweating which blocks the sweat ducts, causing inflammation. The treatment is the same, drying and cooling the skin. Bathe often, soak in hot soapy water to get the skin pores open and dust yourself with talcum powder after drying off. Sleeping in an air-conditioned room will help, but such rooms can be difficult to find if you're on a budget. If all else fails, a trip to the high, cool mountains – or, ironically, to the hot, dry deserts – will do wonders for your itching skin.

If you're sweating profusely you're going to lose a lot of salt, which leads to fatigue and muscle cramps. Make it up by putting extra salt in your food (a teaspoon a day is enough), but don't increase your salt intake unless you also increase your water intake.

Some Ailments

Respiratory Infection *(liúxíngxìng gǎnmào)* Travellers often refer to it as the 'China Syndrome' – it's basically an unusually severe case of influenza or the common cold. Practically the entire population is stricken during the winter and it can be much more serious than a simple case of the sniffles. Technically, the condition is called an upper respiratory infection (URI) which usually starts with a fever, chills, weakness, sore throat and a feeling of malaise normally lasting a few days. After that, a prolonged case of bronchitis sets in. Bronchitis is characterised by almost constant coughing which brings up large quantities of thick phlegm. If the phlegm is a sickening green colour with little red streaks (blood), you've got a particularly nasty case.

Why is URI so common in China? The condition is aggravated by cold weather, poor nutrition, air pollution and heavy smoking – routine hazards in China. But the biggest factor is the spitting, which spreads the disease. It's an endless cycle – people spit because they're sick and they're sick because they spit. The overcrowded conditions also increase the opportunity for infection. You'll probably be healthier if you keep away from the crowded urban centres on the east coast where *everyone* seems to be sick.

Colds are serious in China and shouldn't be neglected – bad cases can turn into pneumonia but it depends on your general state of health. Keeping warm helps, as does bed rest and drinking warm liquids. Smoking is disastrous for people with influenza and bronchitis. The coughing is usually worse at night and can make sleep nearly impossible – elevating the head with pillows helps.

The Chinese treat bronchitis with a powder made from the gall bladder of snakes. It doesn't taste nice but there is no harm trying it. Most colds cure themselves eventually without any special medications, but many travellers catch the same illness over and over. Chronic bronchitis exists in plague proportions in China and is hard to get rid of as long as you stay in the country. If you continue to cough up green phlegm and can't get well, you might eventually have to consider fleeing China. A warm beach in Thailand is a good place to nurse your battered lungs.

Serious cases that seem to be turning into pneumonia you might have to assault with antibiotics. This is not a decision to be taken lightly since antibiotics can produce unpleasant side effects. You're best off seeing a doctor unless you're knowledgeable about antibiotics. The Chinese have herbal medicines which sometimes work surprisingly well.

No vaccine offers complete protection, but there are vaccines against influenza and pneumococcal pneumonia which might help. The influenza vaccine is good for no more than a year.

Diarrhoea *(lā dùzi)* Travellers' diarrhoea has been around a long time – even Marco Polo had it. It's often caused simply by a change of diet, such as spicy and oily foods. It can also be caused by different strains of bacteria which your body isn't used to.

If you get diarrhoea, the first thing to do is nothing – it rarely lasts more than a few days. Diarrhoea can usually be managed by switching to a simple, roughage-free diet for a few days. Yoghurt, white rice, bread, bananas, pudding and boiled eggs will usually see through you through. Dehydration (a common result of diarrhoea) makes you feel worse and can be serious, so it would be wise to increase your intake of salt and liquids. Further relief can be obtained by chewing tablets of activated charcoal – unfortunately not widely available in China and somewhat inconvenient to carry.

If it persists and becomes severe, it's time to roll out the heavy artillery. Lomotil or Imodium can work wonders; in the West these are prescription drugs but you can buy them across the counter in Hong Kong and several other Asian countries. It's a useful thing to have, so stock up. However, both these drugs carry some risk – they work by paralysing the gut and are somewhat addictive; therefore such drugs should not be taken in large doses or for a long time. Chinese pharmacies also stock good anti-diarrhoeal drugs.

If the condition persists and is accompanied by fever, severe cramping and a feeling of malaise, it's probably not simple traveller's diarrhoea and you should see a doctor. It could well be dysentery, giardia or amoebiasis.

Ironically, some travellers suffer from the opposite problem – constipation. This is especially true if you wind up living on a rice and noodle diet with few vegetables or fruits. The best cure is to get some fibre in your diet, but treatment with a simple laxative should produce quick results.

Getting sick from drinking the water is less of a problem in China than it is in most other Asian countries. Even the cheap hotels have thermoses of boiled water in their rooms and dormitories. It's worth carrying a water bottle with you and refilling it in the hotels. Many trains, railway stations and ferry terminals have boilers for passengers. If you don't have any boiled water with you then you can use water purification tablets, though many types are not meant for prolonged use. If you don't have either, you have to weigh the risks of drinking unboiled water against the risks of dehydrating – the first is possible, the second is definite.

Giardia *(āmībā fùxiè)* A nasty little amoeba called giardia can be found in Tibet and some other parts of China. The problem is common in mountainous and cold regions – epidemics have been reported in Zermatt, Switzerland; Aspen, Colorado (USA); and Leningrad in the USSR. Mountaineers often suffer from this problem. Just brushing your teeth in contaminated water is sufficient to make you get it. Many kinds of mammals harbour this parasite, so you can get it easily from drinking 'pure mountain water' unless the area is devoid of animals.

Although giardia rarely causes any permanent damage, it can be most unpleasant. Symptoms include severe diarrhoea, cramping, nausea, vomiting and generally feeling lousy. If untreated, it tends to eventually go away – then come back, then go away again, then return, ad infinitum, ad nauseam. Some people manage to live with it for years – others find it unbearable.

You can usually deduce that you have giardia just from the symptoms. However, there are tests – a stool examination will often find it, but not always because the amoeba inhabit the upper portion of the intestine. Sometimes repeated examinations are needed to be sure of the diagnosis.

Most people will not bother with the stool exams and just seek treatment based on the symptoms. There is a very effective drug called Flagyl (metronidazole) which will wipe out the amoeba in just a few days, but Flagyl is a suspected carcinogen so it's not something you can eat like candy. If you take Flagyl, do not under any circumstances consume alcohol – not a drop! Flagyl is similar to the anti-alcoholism drug Antabuse. When mixed with alcohol, Flagyl produces a severe reaction that has been described as 'a feeling of imminent death'.

Flagyl is not easily obtained in China, though the Chinese have some equivalent drugs in places like Lhasa where giardia is common. If you're going to be travelling in high mountain areas, it might be prudent to keep your own stock with you.

Bilharzia *(zhùxùe xìóngbìng)*
Bilharzia is carried in water by minute worms. The larvae infect certain varieties of freshwater snails, found in rivers, streams, lakes and particularly behind dams. The worms multiply and are eventually discharged into the water surrounding the snails.

They attach themselves to your intestines or bladder, where they produce large numbers of eggs. The worm enters through the skin, and the first symptom may be a tingling and sometimes a light rash around the area where the it entered. Weeks later, when the worm is busy producing eggs, a high fever may develop. A general feeling of being unwell may be the first symptom; once the disease is established abdominal pain and blood in the urine are other signs.

Avoiding swimming or bathing in fresh water where bilharzia is present is the main method of preventing the disease. Even deep water can be infected. If you do get wet dry off quickly and dry your clothes as well. Seek medical attention if you have been exposed to the disease and tell the doctor your suspicions, as bilharzia in the early stages can be confused with malaria or typhoid. If you cannot get medical help immediately, Niridazole is the recommended treatment. The recommended adult dosage is 750 mg (1½ tablets) taken twice daily for a week. Children aged between eight and 12 years should be given 500 mg (one tablet) twice daily for a week.

Tetanus *(pò shāng fēng)* There do seem to be quite a few motor accidents in rural China. Although there is no vaccination that can protect your bus from getting hit by a logging truck, it would be prudent to get a tetanus shot before your arrival in China if you haven't had one for a few years.

Malaria *(nüèjì)* The parasite that causes malaria is spread by mosquitoes. The disease has a nasty habit of recurring in later years, even if you were 'cured' – and it can be fatal.

Malaria is not a big problem in China and you shouldn't worry about it excessively, but in summer there is a risk in the southern and south-eastern provinces of China, almost as far north as Beijing. Beijing itself and the provinces of Heilongjiang, Jilin, Inner Mongolia, Gansu, Xinjiang, Shanxi, Ningxia and Qinghai are considered to be free of malaria. Tibet is also considered free of malaria, except along the Zangbo River Valley in the extreme south-east. North of the 33°N latitude malarial transmission occurs from July to November. Between 33°N and 25°N it occurs between May and December, and south of 25°N transmission occurs all year round.

You can't be inoculated against malaria but protection is simple: either a daily or weekly tablet depending on which your doctor recommends. The tablets kill the parasites if they get into your bloodstream. You usually have to start taking the tablets about two weeks before entering the malarial zone and continue taking them for several weeks after you've left it. Resistance to two types of antimalarial tablets, chloroquine and Fansidar, has been reported in China. There is little information on the extent of the resistance, but Guangdong (including Hainan Island), Guangxi and Yunnan provinces have been reported as chloroquine-resistant areas. Fansidar should not in any case be used as a preventative; it is a powerful drug with possible side effects, and should only be used as a cure, preferably under medical supervision.

The best precaution is to avoid being bitten in the first place. A lot of Chinese hotels have mosquito nets *(wénzhàang)*. Mosquito repellent is available but you may have trouble finding it, so bring your own. Mosquito coils are readily available *(wénxiāng)*.

Weighing the benefit of taking malaria tablets against the possible side effects of long-term use is something you should do yourself.

Hepatitis *(gān yán)* Infectious hepatitis also continues to pose a minor health hazard to those visiting China. Hepatitis is a viral disease which affects the liver. There are two kinds of hepatitis – infectious (A) and serum (B).

Hepatitis A is spread amongst people if the food, water or cooking and eating utensils have been contaminated. Hepatitis is often spread in China due to the Chinese custom of everybody eating from a single dish rather than using separate plates and a serving spoon. It is a wise decision to use the disposable chopsticks now freely available in most restaurants in China, or else buy your own chopsticks and spoon.

No true vaccine exists for hepatitis A. However, there is gamma globulin, an antibody made from human blood, which is effective for just a few months. Most people don't consider it worthwhile because its effectiveness is so transitory. The best preventive measures are to eat food that is clean and well-cooked, and to use disposable chopsticks.

Hepatitis B is usually transmitted the same three ways the AIDS virus spreads: by sexual intercourse; contaminated needles; or acquired by an infant from an infected mother. For reasons unknown, infection rates are very high in China, but it is probably passed down from mother to child and then spread sexually. In recent years, it has also been spreading rapidly in developed countries due to casual sex and drug use. Innocent use of needles – ear piercing, tattooing and acupuncture – can also spread the disease.

Fortunately, a vaccine exists against hepatitis B, but the vaccine must be given before you've been exposed. Once you've got the virus, you're a carrier for life and the vaccine is useless. Therefore, you need a blood test before the vaccine can be given to determine if you're a carrier. The vaccine requires three injections each given a month apart. Unfortunately, the vaccine is expensive. It's not readily available in China, and since it needs to be administered over a three-month period, you should get it before setting out on your journey. In Asia, it's available at large hospitals in Hong Kong, Taiwan, Thailand and several other countries.

For both kinds of hepatitis, the usual symptoms are fever, loss of appetite, nausea, depression, total lack of energy and pain near the bottom of the rib cage where the liver is. The skin and whites of the eyes become yellow and urine turns a deep orange colour. There is no curative drug, but rest and good food are vital. Also stay clear of alcohol and tobacco for a full six months – the liver needs a long time to recover. Hepatitis A makes one very sick but complete recovery is the norm. You can also recover from hepatitis B but the disease can lead to liver cancer many years later – the vaccination is indeed worthwhile.

Tuberculosis *(jiéhé bìng)* The tuberculosis (TB) bacteria is transmitted by inhalation. Coughing spreads infectious droplets into the air. In closed, crowded spaces with poor ventilation (like a train compartment), the air can remain contaminated for some time. In overcrowded China, where the custom is to cough and spit in every direction, it's not hard to see why infection rates remain high.

TB in the developed world is usually a relatively mild infection; most people have it at some time in their lives without noticing it, and retain a natural immunity afterwards. In countries like China it can be more serious.

The disease is opportunistic – the patient feels fine, but the disease suddenly becomes active when the body is weakened by other factors such as injury, poor nutrition, surgery or old age. People who are in good health are less likely to catch the disease. Tuberculosis strikes at the lungs and the fatality rate once it is well established in the body is about 10%.

There are good drugs to treat tuberculosis,

but prevention is the best cure. If you're only going to be in China for a short time there is no need to be overly worried. Tuberculosis is usually developed after repeated exposures by people who are not well nourished. Budget travellers – those who often spend a long time staying in cramped dormitories and travelling on crowded buses and trains – are at greater risk than tourists who remain relatively isolated in big hotels and tour buses.

The effective vaccine for tuberculosis is called BCG and is most often given to schoolchildren because it must be taken before infection occurs. If you want to be vaccinated, you first must be tested to see if you are already immune from a previous infection – if you are, the vaccination will not be necessary. It is thought to be less effective in adults over 35. The only disadvantage of the vaccine is that, once given, the recipient will always test positive with the TB skin test. Even if you never travel, the tuberculosis vaccine could be useful – the disease is increasing worldwide.

Rabies *(kúangqǔan bìng)* China still has a serious problem with this, but the Communists deserve much credit for greatly reducing the threat. Since the Communists came to power in 1949, one of their accomplishments has been to wipe out systematically most of the stray dogs which used to roam the streets of China. This was done to control rabies, improve sanitation and preserve food. While dog lovers may not be impressed by these arguments, it's instructive to visit other poor Third World countries where disease-ridden wild dogs roam the streets, often to end their lives by starving to death.

Although the Chinese have reduced the canine population considerably, packs of wild dogs are still common in Tibetan villages and they are indeed dangerous. Other mammals, such as rats, can also transmit the rabies virus to humans. If you are bitten by an animal that may be rabid, try to get the wound flushed out immediately with soapy water. It would be prudent to seek professional treatment since rabies carries a nearly 100% fatality rate if it reaches the brain. How long you have from the time of being bitten until it's too late varies – anywhere from 10 days to a year depending on where you were bitten. Those bitten around the face and upper part of the body are in the most immediate danger. Don't wait for symptoms to occur – if you think there's good chance that you've been bitten by a rabid animal, get medical attention promptly even if it means leaving China.

By all accounts, rabies is a horrible way to go. As the disease works its way through the nervous system towards the brain, the patient experiences terribly painful muscle spasms, especially around the throat. It becomes impossible to drink water – thus, rabies is sometimes called 'hydrophobia'. Death usually occurs from paralysis of the breathing muscles.

A pre-exposure vaccine for rabies exists, though few people bother to get it because the risk of infection is so low. The vaccine will not give you 100% immunity, but will greatly extend the time you have for seeking treatment, and the treatment will not need to be nearly so extensive. If you're planning to travel in the Chinese countryside, and especially in Tibet, this might be worth considering.

Sexually Transmitted Diseases Sexual contact with an infected sexual partner spreads these diseases. While abstinence is the only 100% preventative, using condoms is also effective. Gonorrhoea and syphilis are the most common of these diseases; sores, blisters or rashes around the genitals and discharges or pain when urinating are common symptoms. Symptoms may be less marked or not observed at all in women. Syphilis symptoms eventually disappear completely but the disease continues and can cause severe problems in later years. The treatment of gonorrhoea and syphilis is by antibiotics.

There are numerous other sexually transmitted diseases, for most of which effective treatment is available. However, there is no cure for herpes and there is also currently no cure for AIDS. Using condoms is the most effective preventative.

AIDS can be spread through infected blood transfusions; most developing countries cannot afford to screen blood for transfusions. It can also be spread by dirty needles – vaccinations, acupuncture and tattooing can potentially be as dangerous as intravenous drug use if the equipment is not clean. The Chinese government has acknowledged that there are 500 HIV-positive drug users in Yunnan. If you do need an injection it may be a good idea to buy a new syringe from a pharmacy and ask the doctor to use it.

Cuts, Bites & Stings

Cuts & Scratches Skin punctures can easily become infected in hot climates and may be difficult to heal. Treat any cut with an antiseptic solution and mercurochrome. Where possible avoid bandages and Band-aids, which can keep wounds wet. Coral cuts are notoriously slow to heal, as the coral injects a weak venom into the wound. Avoid coral cuts by wearing shoes when walking on reefs, and clean any cut thoroughly.

Bites & Stings Bee and wasp stings are usually painful rather than dangerous. Calamine lotion will give relief or ice packs will reduce the pain and swelling. There are some spiders with dangerous bites but antivenenes are usually available. Scorpion stings are notoriously painful; these creatures often shelter in shoes or clothing.

Certain cone shells found in the Pacific can sting dangerously or even fatally. There are various fish and other sea creatures which can sting or bite dangerously or which are dangerous to eat. Again, local advice is the best suggestion.

Snakes To minimise your chances of being bitten always wear boots, socks and long trousers when walking through undergrowth where snakes may be present. Don't put your hands into holes and crevices.

Snake bites do not cause instantaneous death and antivenenes are usually available. Keep the victim calm and still, wrap the bitten limb tightly, as you would for a sprained ankle, and then attach a splint to immobilise it. Don't wash the wound; any venom remaining on the skin can be used to identify the snake. Then seek medical help, if possible with the dead snake for identification. Don't attempt to catch the snake if there is even a remote possibility of being bitten again. Tourniquets and sucking out the poison are now comprehensively discredited.

Jellyfish Local advice is the best way of avoiding contact with these sea creatures with their stinging tentacles. Stings from most jellyfish are simply rather painful. Dousing in vinegar will de-activate any stingers which have not 'fired'. Calamine lotion, antihistamines and analgesics may reduce the reaction and relieve the pain.

Bedbugs & Lice Bedbugs live in various places, but particularly in dirty mattresses and bedding. Spots of blood on bedclothes or on the wall around the bed can be read as a suggestion to find another hotel. Bedbugs leave itchy bites in neat rows. Calamine lotion may help.

All lice cause itching and discomfort. They make themselves at home in your hair (head lice), your clothing (body lice) or in your pubic hair (crabs). You catch lice through direct contact with infected people or by sharing combs, clothing and the like. Powder or shampoo treatment will kill the lice and infected clothing should then be washed in very hot water.

Leeches & Ticks Leeches may be present in damp rainforest conditions; they attach themselves to your skin to suck your blood. Trekkers often get them on their legs or in their boots. Salt or a lighted cigarette end will make them fall off. Do not pull them off, as the bite is then more likely to become infected. An insect repellent may keep them away. Vaseline, alcohol or oil will persuade a tick to let go. You should always check your body if you have been walking through a tick-infested area, as they can spread typhus.

Women's Health

Gynaecological Problems Poor diet, lowered resistance due to the use of antibiotics for stomach upsets and even contraceptive pills can lead to vaginal infections when travelling in hot climates. Keeping the genital area clean, and wearing skirts or loose-fitting trousers and cotton underwear will help to prevent infections.

Yeast infections, characterised by a rash, itch and discharge, can be treated with a vinegar or even lemon-juice douche or with yoghurt. Nystatin suppositories are the usual medical prescription. Trichomonas is a more serious infection; symptoms are a discharge and a burning sensation when urinating. Male sexual partners must also be treated, and if a vinegar-water douche is not effective medical attention should be sought. Flagyl is the prescribed drug.

Pregnancy The first four months of pregnancy can be a risky time to travel in remote areas as far as your own health is concerned, as most miscarriages happen during this time and they can occasionally be dangerous. The last three months should be spent within reasonable distance of good medical care. A premature baby will stand a chance of survival as early as 24 weeks if it is born in a well-equipped hospital. Pregnant women should avoid all unnecessary medication, but vaccinations and malarial prophylactics should still be taken where possible. Additional care should be taken to prevent illness and particular attention should be paid to diet and nutrition. Alcohol, nicotine and other drugs are to be avoided, particularly during the first four months of pregnancy.

Medical Clinics & Hospitals

Health care can be surprisingly good in China, at least in big urban centres. Improving public health has been one area in which the Communists have expended considerable effort. As usual, the problem is one of resources – too many people, outdated equipment and too little money. For these reasons, you probably won't want to have major surgery in China. However, Chinese doctors can do a pretty good job of diagnosing and treating most common illnesses.

In Beijing, Canton and Shanghai there are medical clinics set aside to treat foreigners, and in some of the provincial towns there are clinics in the tourist hotels. In the three main cities, these clinics are at: Friendship Hospital (☎ 338671 ext 441) *(yǒuyí yīyùan)* at 95 Yongan Lu, west side of Temple of Heaven in the Tianqiao area, Beijing; Shanghai People's No 1 Hospital (☎ 3240100), 190 Bei Suzhou Lu, Shanghai; Guangzhou No 1 People's Hospital (☎ 333090) *(dìyī rénmín yīyùan)*, 602 Renmin Beilu, Guangzhou.

Medical services are generally very cheap in China although hospitals that deal especially with foreigners charge more and ask for payment in FEC. However, they will usually give foreigners better service – Chinese patients usually have to wait for hours in long queues.

In case of accident or illness, it's best just to get a taxi and go to the hospital directly – try to avoid dealing with the authorities (police and military) if possible. One traveller who broke his leg near Dali made the mistake of calling on the police for help. They came with a Land Rover and took him to the military hospital where a cast was put on his leg – he was then charged Y10,000 for this service! A civilian hospital would have charged him less than Y100.

Medical Supplies

There are lots of well-stocked pharmacies in China supplying both Western and Chinese medicines, but you may have problems explaining what you want and then understanding what you've got and how to use it. Checking out pharmacies in China is an enjoyable pastime, but if you lack the time or really need something then bring it with you.

Blood Supplies

If you're Rh-negative, try not to bleed in China. The Chinese do not have Rh-negative blood and their blood banks don't store it. If you're a type O Rh-negative, then you're in worse luck since you can only accept a transfusion of the same and nothing else – and there aren't very many of us around!

Herbal Medicine

(zhōng yào)

Many foreigners visiting China never try Chinese herbal medicine because they either know nothing about it or simply don't believe in it. Prominent medical authorities in the West often dismiss herbalists as no better than witch doctors. The ingredients, which may include such marvellous things as snake gall bladder or powdered deer antlers, will further discourage potential non-Chinese customers. Also, even for true believers, there is a baffling assortment of herbs available on the shelves of any Chinese pharmacy and it's hard to know where to begin.

Having experimented with Chinese herbs ourselves, we've found several of them to be remarkably effective, but some warnings are in order. Chinese herbalists have all sorts of treatments for stomachaches, headaches, colds, flu and sore throat. They also have herbs to treat long-term problems like asthma. While many of these herbs seem to work, it's much more uncertain that Chinese medicine can cure serious illnesses like cancer and heart disease. All sorts of overblown claims have been made for herbal medicines, especially by those who make and sell them. Some gullible Westerners have persuaded themselves that Chinese doctors can cure any disease. A visit to any of China's hospitals will quickly shatter this myth.

Chinese medicine seems to work best for the relief of unpleasant symptoms (pain, sore throat, etc) and for some long-term conditions which resist Western medicines, such as migraine headaches, asthma and chronic backache. But for acute life-threatening conditions, such as a heart attack, it would be foolish to trust your life to herbs.

When reading about the theory behind Chinese medicine, the word 'holistic' appears often. Basically, this means that Chinese medicine seeks to treat the whole body rather than focusing on a particular organ or disease.

Using appendicitis as an example, a Chinese doctor may try to fight the infections using the body's whole defences, whereas a Western doctor would simply cut out the appendix. While the holistic method sounds great in theory, in practice the Western technique of attacking the problem directly often works better. In the case of appendicitis, removing the appendix surgically is 100% effective, though there is always some risk from the surgical procedure itself. On the other hand, in the case of migraine headaches, Chinese herbs may actually prove more effective than Western medical treatments.

Another point to be wary of when taking herbal medicine is the tendency of some manufacturers to falsely claim that their product contains numerous potent and expensive ingredients. For example, some herbal formulas may list rhinoceros horn as an ingredient. Rhinoceros horn, widely acclaimed by herbalists as a cure for fever, is so rare and so expensive that it is practically impossible to buy. Any formula listing rhinoceros horn may, at best, contain water buffalo horn. In any case, the rhino is a rare and endangered species, and you will not wish to hasten its extinction by demanding rhino-horn products.

Another benefit of Chinese medicine is that there are relatively few side effects. Compared to a drug like penicillin which can produce allergic reactions and other serious side effects, herbal medicines are fairly safe. Nevertheless, herbs are still medicines, and not candy. There is no need to gobble herbs if you're feeling fine to being with. Many Westerners believe that herbs are harmless. In fact, some herbs are mildly toxic, and if taken over a long period of time can actually damage the liver and other organs.

Before shopping for herbs, keep in mind that in Western medicine, doctors talk about broad-spectrum antibiotics, such as penicillin, which are good for treating a wide range of infections. But for many illnesses, a specific antibiotic might be better for a specific type of infection. The same is true in Chinese medicine. A broad-spectrum remedy such as snake gall bladder may be good for treating colds, but there are many different types of colds. The best way to treat a cold with herbal medicine is to see a Chinese doctor and get a specific prescription. Otherwise, the herbs you take may not be the most appropriate for your condition. However, if you can't get to a doctor, you can just try your luck at the pharmacy.

If you visit a Chinese doctor, you might be surprised by what he or she discovers about your body. For example, the doctor will almost certainly take your pulse and then may tell you that you have a slippery pulse or perhaps a thready pulse. Chinese doctors have identified more than 30 different kinds of pulses. A pulse could be empty, prison, leisurely, bowstring, irregular or even regularly irregular. The doctor may then examine your tongue to see if it is slippery, dry, pale, greasy, has a thick coating or maybe no coating at all. The doctor, having discovered that you have wet heat, as evidenced by a slippery pulse and a red greasy tongue, will prescribe the herbs for your condition.

Finally, one problem with buying herbs that there are many fake pharmaceuticals on the market. Counterfeiting is common in China, and the problem extends even to medications. If the herbs you take seem to be totally ineffective, it may be because you've bought sugar pills rather than medicine.

The following is not meant as a replacement for sound medical advice, but should give you a start when shopping for herbs. Most of these herbs are available in Hong Kong as well as China, and there are many more than those listed here.

High Fever Shinshyue Dan Granules *(xīn xǔe dān)*. This is a very bitter mixture, so if you can't stand the taste, try loading the granules into empty gelatin capsules.

Sore Throat A good brand is Superior Sore Throat Powder *(hóu fēng sǎn)*.

Headache Nothing works better than *piān tóu tòng wán*.

Phlegm Coughing and spitting up phlegm is a national pastime in China. The Chinese manufacture expectorants and decongestants from the gall bladder of snakes. Among the choices are Three Snake Gall & Fritillary Powder *(sān shé dǎn chūan bèi mò)*.

Diarrhoea Berberine hydrochloride *(húang liǎn sù)* is highly effective.

Women's tonic To help with anaemia and menstrual problems, try *sì wù tāng*.

Liniments Highly fragrant, these oils feel hot when applied to the skin. Use liniment to treat headaches, stomachaches, backaches, nausea and almost anything else. Just rub the oil on wherever it hurts, but be careful about getting it into the eyes or mouth. The Chinese sometimes put some in their nose to clear the nostrils – not very wise since these oils are mildly toxic and prolonged use will not do your liver and kidneys any good. There are many brands on the market. Look for *qīng liáng yóu* and *fēng yóu.*. White Flower Oil *(bái hūa yóu)* is a popular brand from Hong Kong.

Salves These are similar to liniments but not as strong. The most famous brand sold all over Asia is Tiger Balm.

Plaster For sprains and sore muscles, try a sticky dog skin plaster *(gǒu pí gāo yào)*, which is not made from dog skin nowadays. A popular brand is 701 Gao.

Books There are plenty of books available if you want to learn more about Chinese medicine. One of the easiest to understand is *The Web That Has No Weaver: Understanding Chinese Medicine* by Ted J Kaptchuk (Congdon & Weed, New York).

If you want a more advanced text, *The Theoretical Foundations of Chinese Medicine*, by Manfred Porkert (MIT Press, Cambridge, Mass) is good. However, the author has been criticised for introducing many Latin terms which make the book more difficult reading.

There are some old classics dealing with Chinese medicine. One of the best known is *The Treasures of Chinese Medicine (běn cǎo gāng mù)*, written in the 16th century. Another ancient reference is *The Yellow*

Emperor's Classic of Internal Medicine (húangdì nèijīng sūwén) which was first published around 2600 BC.

Acupuncture

(zhēnjiū)

Chinese acupuncture has received enthusiastic reviews from many satisfied patients who have tried it. Of course, one should be wary of overblown claims. Acupuncture is not likely to cure terminal illness, in spite of any testimonials you might read in Western countries about curing cancer holistically. Nevertheless, acupuncture is of genuine therapeutic value in the treatment of chronic back pain, migraine headaches and arthritis.

For those not already familiar with the term, acupuncture is a technique employing needles which are inserted into various points of the body. In former times, needles were probably made from bamboo, gold, silver, copper or tin. These days, only stainless steel needles of hairlike thinness are used, causing very little pain when inserted. Dirty acupuncture needles can spread disease rather than cure, so good acupuncturists sterilise their needles or use disposable ones. As many as 2000 points for needle insertion have been identified, but only about 150 are commonly used.

One of the most amazing demonstrations of acupuncture's power is that major surgery can be performed using acupuncture alone as the only anaesthetic. The acupuncture needle is inserted into the patient and a small electric current is passed through the needle. The current is supplied by an ordinary torch battery.

The exact mechanism by which acupuncture works is not fully understood by modern medical science. The Chinese have their own theories, but it is by no means certain they really know either. Needles are inserted into various points of the body, each point believed by the acupuncturist to correspond to a particular organ, joint, gland or other part of the body. These points are believed to be connected to the particular area being treated by an 'energy channel', also translated as a 'meridian', but more likely it has something to do with the nerves. By means not fully understood, it would appear the needle can block pain transmission along the meridian. However it works, many report satisfactory results.

Should you wish to try this technique, there are many hospitals of traditional Chinese medicine in major cities like Guangzhou, Beijing and Shanghai. Many of these hospitals also train Westerners who are eager to learn these methods. In Canton, one popular place with Western students is the Guangzhou Traditional Chinese Medicine Hospital (☎ 886504) *(zhōngyī yīyùan)* on Zhuji Lu near Shamian Island – they also teach herbal medicine. Some hotels also provide acupuncture services at their clinics, but these are likely to be more expensive.

If you're (justifiably) concerned about catching disease from contaminated acupuncture needles, you might consider buying your own before undergoing treatment. Good quality needles are available in major cities in China and in Hong Kong. Needles come in a bewildering variety of gauges – try to determine from your acupuncturist which type to buy.

Massage

(ànmó)

Massage has a long history in China. It's an effective technique for treating a variety of painful ailments such as chronic back pain and sore muscles. A good massage should be administered by someone who has really studied the techniques to be most effective. An acupuncturist who also practises massage would be ideal.

Traditional Chinese massage is somewhat different from the increasingly popular do-it-yourself techniques practised by people in the West. One traditional Chinese technique employs suction cups made of bamboo placed on the patient's skin. A burning piece of alcohol-soaked cotton is briefly put inside the cup to drive out the air before it is applied. As the cup cools, a partial vacuum is produced, leaving a nasty-looking but harmless red circular mark on the skin. The mark goes away in a few days. Other methods include bloodletting and scraping the skin with coins or porcelain soup spoons.

A related technique is called moxibustion. Various types of herbs, rolled into what looks like a ball of fluffy cotton, are held just near the skin and ignited. A slight variation of this method is to place the herbs on a slice of ginger and then ignite them. The idea is to apply the maximum amount of heat possible without burning the patient. This heat treatment is supposed to be good for such diseases as arthritis.

However, there is no real need to subject yourself to such extensive treatment if you would just like a straight massage to relieve normal aches and pains. Many big tourist hotels in China offer massage facilities, but the rates charged are excessive – around Y60 per hour. You can do much better than that by enquiring locally – the hotel staff might even be able to direct you to such a place if the hotel itself doesn't offer this service.

Toilets

Chinese toilets are the usual Asian-style holes in the ground over which you crouch and aim. Public toilets can often be found in the side streets of the cities and towns. Some have very low partitions (without doors) between the individual holes and some have none. The Chinese seem to crouch over these for ages reading books and newspapers. Toilet paper is not provided – always keep a stash with you.

Some toilets don't look like they've been cleaned since the Han Dynasty. Often the problem is not the filth but the smell. Nothing is wasted; your shit is eventually shovelled up and sent to the countryside where it contributes to the Chinese economy as fertiliser.

Toilet paper is readily available in China from the big department stores, although it's a good idea to hang on to whatever's left in your hotel room. Dormitory rooms are not provided with toilet paper, probably because people steal it. The tourist hotels have Western-style 'sit-down' toilets.

Remember:

men 男

women 女

WOMEN TRAVELLERS

In general, foreign women are unlikely to suffer serious sexual harassment in China. There have been reports, however, of problems in Xinjiang (a Muslim area) and Hainan. Wherever you are, it's worth noticing what local women are wearing and how they are behaving, and making a bit of an effort to fit in, as you would in any other foreign country.

While city people in China are mostly used to the sight of foreigners and their peculiar clothes and customs, the countryside is much more conservative. If you want to play safe, wear trousers or a below-the-knee skirt, with a shirt that covers your shoulders. Slip-on sandals and thongs may also be thought of as essentially indoor wear in the countryside, and more substantial shoes may improve your standing with the locals.

DANGERS & ANNOYANCES

Theft & Other Crimes

There is crime in China, as anywhere else in the world, but it probably won't affect you if you take simple precautions. It's safer to travel through China than through many other poor countries, and you're less likely to have stuff stolen. Nevertheless, a level of prudence regarding both the safety of yourself and your property is worth maintaining.

Stories from the official Chinese press paint a picture of exemplary honesty – including the Beijing shop assistant who inadvertently shortchanged a foreign tourist and finally managed to track him down in Lhasa through an advertisement she inserted in the *China Daily*. Another legend involves a foreign businessman who decided to discard a pair of trousers in his hotel room before catching a taxi to the airport. Just as his flight was called, a breathless room-attendant came racing into the airport carrying the trousers. A second attempt to jettison the trousers in another hotel met with the same defeat.

Violent crime with knives and guns is extremely rare – the most common type of theft among travellers is pickpocketing. Chinese are well aware of this, and places such as Xi'an, Beijing, Harbin, Lanzhou and Ürümqi are reportedly notorious for pickpocket schools whose 'graduates' ply specific bus routes or crowded places usually during peak hours. Razoring of bags and pockets is also prevalent on buses. A few travellers have even received serious wounds when poorly skilled pickpockets cut a little too deep in order to get at a money belt.

Since buses in China are usually so packed that passengers are virtually jammed into each other's pockets, there's plenty of scope for theft. If you want to avoid opening wallets or bags on the bus, keep a few coins or small notes ready in an accessible pocket before launching yourself onto the bus. Be careful when sleeping on trains, especially in the hard-seat section – make sure that the pocket with the money is wedged up against the wall, floor or your backpack.

Other favourite venues for petty theft include bus stations, railway stations and public toilets. Quite a few foreigners have laid aside their valuables, squatted down to business, and then straightened up again to discover that someone had absconded with the lot!

Hotels are usually safe places to leave your stuff; each floor has an attendant watching who goes in and out. If anything is missing from your room then they're going to be obvious suspects since they've got keys to the rooms. Don't expect them to watch over your room like a hawk – they don't.

Dormitories could be a problem and there have been a few reports of thefts by staff. Also, watch out for your fellow travellers! There are at least a few people who subsidise their journey by ripping off their fellow countrypeople. Most hotels have storage rooms where you check your bags in; some insist that you do. In a few hotels you may have to leave your stuff in the dormitory. This is sometimes locked so that all and sundry don't go wandering in and out. Don't leave your valuables (passport, travellers' cheques, money, health certificates, air tickets) lying around in dormitories.

A money belt is the safest way to carry valuables, particularly when travelling on buses and trains. Against its possible loss, you could leave a small stash of money (say US$50) in your hotel room, with a record of the travellers' cheque serial numbers and your passport number. Other things of little or no apparent value to the thief – like film – should be safeguarded, since to lose them would be a real heartbreak to you. Make a copy of your address book before you leave home. And note down ticket numbers – a Swedish couple whose train tickets were stolen in Chengdu were told by the railway booking office that they would have received a refund had they done so.

Small padlocks are useful for backpacks and some dodgy hotel rooms. Bicycle chain locks come in handy not only for hired bikes but for attaching backpacks to railings or luggage racks. The trendy waist-pouches often used by Hong Kong visitors are definitely *not* advisable for valuables. Street tailors are skilled at sewing inside pockets to trousers, jackets and shirts usually for a few jiao. Small padlocks are useful on camera bags. Don't rely on swivel clips to attach a camera to your waist.

The Chinese don't trust each other and there's no reason you should trust them. They run around with rings full of keys as if they were jailers, everything is scrupulously locked, the walls of buildings have jagged glass concreted to the top and iron bars are fitted on 1st-floor windows. Announcements on trains (in Chinese) advise passengers neither to entrust baggage to the care of strangers nor to leave valuables unattended during stops or when going to the dining car. You'll often see the Chinese secure their bags to the luggage racks with chain locks and you can do the same. If you wander away from your bag in a crowded railway station don't expect it to be there when you come back.

Perhaps the best way to avoid getting ripped off is to not bring a lot of junk you don't need. You'll have to make your own decisions about what gear you need for a trip to China, but Walkmans, video cameras, expensive lenses and jewellery invite theft.

Loss Reports If something of yours is stolen, you should report it immediately to the nearest Foreign Affairs Branch of the PSB. They will ask you to fill in a loss report before investigating the case and sometimes even recovering the stolen goods.

There are at least two other good reasons for obtaining a loss report. When you enter China you declare on a form all your foreign currency and valuables such as watches, cameras and calculators. When you leave China you are expected to hand in your declaration and show your valuables again – as proof that they haven't been sold. The procedure is seldom strict but there could be complications if you can't produce the items. If you lose any of the items listed on your declaration form through theft or negligence, obtaining a loss report can save possible exit hassles at the border.

If you have travel insurance (recommended), it is essential to obtain a loss report so you can claim compensation. Normally this is no problem for valuables (cameras, watches, calculators) and travellers' cheques, but some PSB offices in major cities absolutely refuse to provide a loss report for cash.

We've heard of Western women being harassed by Chinese men in Beijing's parks or while cycling alone at night, but major crimes against foreigners are very rare and the perpetrators receive the severest punishment. In March 1986, two business people from Britain and Hong Kong were robbed at knife-point in Canton by a criminal trio from north-east China. All three were later sentenced to death and their appeal was rejected. The sentence for one gang member under 18 was suspended for two years.

Kill the Rooster to Frighten the Monkey
It's hard to say how China's crime rate compares with those in other countries, though the country has its share of rapists and murderers. 'White collar' crime is also a big problem and the Chinese newspapers regularly report arrests and even the occasional execution of frauds and embezzlers.

The crackdown on corruption has been given extensive coverage in the official press. In 1986, the sons of three senior cadres were executed in Shanghai for attacks on women. Another Shanghai Party official was jailed for life for accepting over Y30,000 in bribes. Although such sentences were intended to show that all are equal before the law, the centuries-old practice of privilege for high officials and their relatives is unlikely to receive more than a dent.

A disciplinary inspection begun in 1986 within the Party has resulted in numerous warnings, dismissals and even imprisonment of Party members. The cases of accused Party members are not immediately handled by state law. The relevant Party organ must first determine the guilt of the accused before handing him or her over for conviction under state law. It's not hard to see the vested interests that could be involved when Party colleagues investigate one of their own members. When the minister and vice minister of astronautics embezzled US$46 million in foreign exchange they were rebuked with 'serious disciplinary warnings within the Party'. Meanwhile, local pickpockets get the death penalty.

Intensive investigation of illegal detention has revealed some extraordinary stories about cadres or police with a 'special privilege' mentality who abused their power and violated legal procedures. In 1984, a village Party secretary in Shaanxi Province put 72 villagers into custody under suspicion of stealing part of his bicycle bell. He then ordered torture for 17 of the villagers and forced 28 more to pay fines to cover the cost of the guards' wages during imprisonment, which in some cases lasted as long as eight days. In Baoshan, Yunnan Province, a group of police detained 201 people in 1986 for 'law-study class' which lasted as long as 80 days. Many of the detainees were forced to do manual labour, fined or tortured to confess to crimes they hadn't committed or to petty offences. As a result, two people committed suicide, one person died and many were wounded.

Juvenile crime is a growing problem in China's cities. The types of crime committed include murder, rape and theft of large sums of money. Criminal groups of youngsters are common. The official view is that they are victims of 'spiritual pollution' – influenced by images of foreign criminal cliques portrayed in mass media and by the persistent feudal idea of 'secret societies'. Other factors such as unemployment and disillusionment are rarely blamed by the leadership.

Justice in China seems to be dispensed entirely by the police, who also decide the penalty. The ultimate penalty is execution, which serves the purpose of 'killing the rooster to frighten the monkey' or, to phrase this in official terms, 'It is good to have some people executed so as to educate others'. The standard manner of execution is a bullet in the back of the head, often at a mass gathering in some sports stadium. This punishment is usually reserved for rapists and murderers. Afterwards a mugshot and maybe even a photo of the extinguished body gets plugged up on a public noticeboard. Criminals being paraded on the backs of trucks through the streets of Chinese towns are still a common sight.

A couple of years ago a tour group arriving in Xi'an witnessed one such event as they stepped out of the railway station. A protracted and embarrassed silence ensued. A public execution had just taken place and the dead bodies, with bullet holes in the backs of their necks, were lying on the pavement outside the station, surrounded by a large crowd. The police quickly dragged the corpses out of sight. China's last big purge of criminals started in 1983 with the rounding up of 100,000 suspects; estimates for the number of executions since then vary between 10,000 and 20,000. This campaign continues in tandem with a newer one to promote knowledge of the legal code amongst the masses.

Coping With China

In the first few years of individual travel to China many people came away with the impression that China was well worth the trip – but ask them if they liked it and the responses were too often negative. It was highly educational, it was different from other parts of the world, it had its moments, it was interesting, but it could also be immensely frustrating.

It still can be, but generally the problems have decreased greatly over the past few years. The Chinese are more used to foreign faces; restaurant and hotel staff are more cooperative; red tape has been reduced; and Western culture is slowly being embraced by the masses (much to the government's horror). A few years ago most travellers were leaving the place probably never to return. These days most people actually seem to enjoy China, stay for considerably longer, and might well make a return trip (especially if FEC is done away with).

The degree to which you cope with China depends on how long you stay there, where you want to go, what you want to do, how tolerant and even-tempered you are and how much money you're prepared to spend. The problems of travelling in China are usually the same as those in other Asian countries – generally they're all petty irritations, but they tend to get worse the longer you hang around.

One way to cope with China is to limit your time there. Leave with happy memories before the people and the country get irritating. Spend more time in the places you visit and less time tiring yourself out on buses and trains. The irritations of travel can make you oblivious to the good in the country. If you're in China for any length of time, then at some point you're going to explode. Sometimes this works, sometimes not. Chinese who are familiar with the eccentricities of foreigners often turn off if we get angry – the wall comes down and nothing is achieved.

Staring Squads

The programme is *Aliens*, you are the star, and cinema-sized audiences will gather to watch. You can get stared at in any Asian country, particularly when you go off the beaten track where the locals have seen few or no foreigners. But China is phenomenal for the size and enthusiasm of its staring squads. This is less of a problem in the major tourist centres where the Chinese are used to seeing foreigners, but take one step off the beaten track and you'll very quickly gather a small horde of curious onlookers.

Sometimes you don't even have to do anything to get a crowd. Stop for a minute or two on the street to look at something and several local people will also stop. Before long the number of onlookers swells until you're encircled by a solid wall of people. Travellers react differently to these crowds. Initially it can be amusing, but gradually the novelty wears off. Then it becomes tedious, and after a while it's outright aggravating to be unable to do the slightest thing without an audience.

Some people get used to being stared at and some don't. There are a few things you can do to reduce the size of audiences. You will be less conspicuous if your clothes are similar to those of local people. Don't wear fancy watches (particularly digitals), and keep the camera-case on when you're not taking a photo – Western cargo tends to attract a lot of attention. If someone comes up to talk to you on the street, then talk to them as you walk, since a conversation with a foreigner automatically attracts a crowd. If you stand on the street scribbling in a notebook someone is sure to poke their head right over the book to see what you're writing, and sometimes they'll lift it straight out of your hands for a closer inspection.

Travelling with someone else helps; if you've got somebody to talk to it's easier to ignore the crowd. Staring back or an abusive response of any kind is worse than useless. Getting out your camera and taking a photo sometimes parts the waves but doesn't send people scurrying for cover. Hiring a bicycle is a good idea – you're zooming along so fast the crowds can't accumulate. One way to deal with the staring squads is to ignore them and keep moving. Another, if you can manage a few sentences in Chinese, is to start a conversation with the nearest onlookers and establish in their minds that you too are a human being.

One of the reasons the Chinese crowd around and look at you is because foreigners often have things they don't have, like big eyes, beards, light-coloured hair, large noses, hairy arms and legs and big breasts, not to mention bizarre and brightly coloured clothes. All these have an enduring fascination for less sophisticated Chinese people. The only 'blondes' in the country are albinos and the occasional light-haired Uigur. So don't be surprised if you begin to feel like a circus freak. Curious people may even rub their fingers up and down your arm or pull at the hairs.

Noise

After you've been in China awhile, you begin to wonder if the entire nation doesn't have a hearing problem – there seems to be a competition for who can speak the loudest. In the last few years many cheap hotels have been installing television sets in every room. These are turned to full volume, so the cacophony is like a battery of jackhammers. Noise also comes from blasting radios. If you can't stand noise, God help you if you visit during the Chinese New Year when everyone detonates firecrackers.

There are a couple of ways to avoid all this: pack a good set of earplugs, go to China with the tolerance of a saint, or spend more money and stay at the tourist hotels. A noisy hotel is not what you want after a long, tiring train or bus ride.

Even in supposedly relaxing places, it's hard to escape the noise. Silence in nature is not generally appreciated by the Chinese – many parks are 'livened up' with blasting music from speakers hidden amongst the trees. More affluent Chinese carry their own boom boxes. With some effort, you might be able to find a truly quiet place to take a walk – try the deserts of north-west China.

Spitting

If you thought the Indians were champion spitters, then go to China! Everyone does it, on the streets, on the floors of train carriages and on buses. Never walk too closely beside a stationary bus full of passengers, and try not to get caught in the crossfire elsewhere!

There is a reason for all this – most Chinese suffer from chronic bronchitis which clogs the lung passages with mucus. There is much speculation as to why a billion people can't recover from the common cold, but it seems that the spitting itself spreads the very disease which makes people want to spit. If everyone could just agree to stop spitting for a few months, the whole country might be able to get well. Most foreigners who stay in China a few months fall victim to the same condition – don't be surprised if you too become a champion spitter!

Racism

Officially, the People's Republic condemns racism. The government has been a vehement critic of South Africa's apartheid policies. China's own minorities – at least in theory – hold equal legal status as the Han majority.

Despite this outward display of racial harmony, there are some sour notes. In 1997, Hong Kong is to become part of China and Hong Kong citizens will become PRC citizens. But not all – the citizenship offer only applies to those of 'Chinese descent'. There are thousands of people born in Hong Kong who are not Chinese or only partly Chinese. This is especially true of the Indians who were brought in by the British more than a century ago. When 1997 rolls around, they will become stateless because they are the wrong race. Ditto for those of mixed racial heritage.

Official policy aside, racism exists on the street level as it does in many countries. In China it is not particularly serious – most foreigners are not likely to be refused service in a restaurant or hotel because of racial considerations alone (the language barrier or the laziness of the staff is another matter).

Much depends on just which racial group you belong to. Whites normally only experience minor complications, but Blacks have reported some serious problems. A particularly ugly series of incidents occurred in 1988. The problems started at Hehai University in Jiangsu Province when some African students were found to be dating Chinese women. Riots broke out with students shouting 'kill the black devils'. The riots spread to other campuses and the African students had to be evacuated. The Chinese government mishandled the incidents and several African nations sent official notes of protest to Beijing.

Black travellers have reported that they are stared at so vigorously that they feel like a display in a zoo. White travellers get this too, but apparently Blacks get it worse. However, violence against travelling foreigners due to racial considerations appears to be extremely rare.

Queues

Basically, there are none. People tend to 'huddle' rather than queue – it resembles American-style football but without the protective gear. At larger railway stations the huddles can be a formidable obstacle to getting a ticket. Sometimes it may be worth that extra money to have CITS get your tickets or pay a Chinese person to buy them. Otherwise, be patient and accept the fact that this is China and there ain't nothing you can do about one billion people. Some large railway stations now have separate booking offices for foreigners; this means you'll always pay tourist price but at least you avoid getting trampled and have some hope of getting a sleeper on the crowded trains.

Beggars

Yes, beggars do exist in China – but at least in the cities, towns and other tourist centres there are not as many as there are in countries like India. You may see as many beggars in a week in China as you would in an hour in India. Some of them look no less wretched than their counterparts in other Asian countries. More common than beggars are the people who hang around in the public restaurants waiting to move in on the food scraps. The beggars tend not to pounce on foreigners – the chief exceptions are the kids who practically have to be removed with a crowbar once they've seized your trouser leg. Some beggars squat on the pavement beside large posters which detail their sad story. Professional beggars are common – sometimes women clutching babies who regurgitate stories about having lost their train tickets and all their money.

Drugs

China takes a particularly dim view of opium and all of its derivatives. The Chinese suffered severely from an opium epidemic which was started by British traders in 1773 and lasted until the Communists came to power – they haven't forgotten! Several heroin smugglers from Hong Kong were caught in Kunming a few years ago. Within a week they were scheduled for public execution. The local PSB issued a special invitation for the foreign press to attend.

Marijuana is often seen growing by the roadside in China, but travellers who have sampled it report that it's very poor quality. Hashish is smoked by some of China's minority groups, especially the Uigurs in Xinjiang Province.

It's difficult to say what attitude the Chinese police will take towards foreigners caught using marijuana, but there haven't been any horror stories along the lines of *Midnight Express*. Foreigners so far have been left to their own devices as long as Chinese are not included. On the other hand, turning the hotel yard into a drying factory is not likely to please Public Security. If the authorities do take an unfavourable view, you can expect a huge fine if not prison time as well. Discretion is strongly advised!

FILM & PHOTOGRAPHY

Both Chinese and foreign film can be bought at the major tourist hotels, Friendship Stores and numerous photography shops which have sprouted all over the country. The range for foreign film is rarely complete and you may not be able to get the film type or speed you need even in a major city like Beijing or Shanghai.

Film

Prices for foreign film in China are high – about 40% to 50% more than what you'll pay in Hong Kong or in the West, so take as much of the stuff as you think you'll need. Black & white film is hard to buy in Hong Kong and China, as colour photos are now the big thing. Kodak, Fujicolor and Agfacolor are commonly sold. Some Ektachrome and Fujichrome is sold but can be hard to come by when you want it. It's extremely difficult – even in Beijing and Shanghai – to find Kodachrome film. When you do find it, it's very expensive. Various brands of colour 110 print film are also sold. In general, colour slide film is hard to find, usually out-of-date when you find it, and expensive. Some brands of Polaroid film are sold in the country but it's best to bring your own supply.

You're allowed to bring in 8 mm movie cameras; 16 mm or professional equipment is not permitted without Kafkaesque red tape and paperwork. Some brands of 8 mm movie film are sold in China.

Video cameras were once subject to shaky regulations but there seems to be no problem now. One of the more amusing sights is the Japanese and Americans wearing portapaks over their shoulders with Rambo-style battery-belts, who tape everything in sight. The biggest problem is the power source and recharging your batteries off the strange mutations of plugs and voltages in China. You should be OK if you're staying in the five-star hotels where they cater for the idiosyncratic whims of foreigners, but forget it if you're backpacking. How are you going to carry the stuff without a tour bus?

Processing

You can get your film processed in 24 hours in some of the major tourist cities like Beijing, Shanghai, Canton, Guilin – usually through the major tourist hotels and Friendship Stores and at the local photography stores.

Ektachrome and Fujichrome can be processed in Beijing and Shanghai but this can be expensive, about twice what you'd pay in the West – though it may be worth it to make sure your camera's working OK.

Kodachrome film cannot be processed in China or in Hong Kong. However, in Hong Kong the photo shops can send it out by express airmail and get it back in four days. The closest countries which process them are Japan and Australia. Undeveloped film can be sent out of China and, going by personal experience only, the dreaded X-ray machines do not appear to be a problem.

Technical Problems

These include dim interiors lit by 40-watt bulbs or low-voltage fluorescent lights. The X-ray machines at airports are said to be 'film-safe' but you're still better off keeping your film in your pocket. Dust is a hazard in some places like the western deserts; keep the camera in a plastic bag and take your own cleaning devices along. Polarising and UV filters are useful. Photography from moving trains doesn't work unless you have high-speed film; if you have low-speed film then train-window shots tend to get blurred.

Prohibited Subjects

Photography from planes and photographs of airports, military installations, harbour facilities and railroad terminals are prohibited; bridges may also be a touchy subject.

These rules do get enforced if the enforcers happen to be around. One traveller, bored at the airport, started photographing the X-ray procedure in clearance. PLA men promptly pounced on her and ripped the film out. In an age where satellites can zoom down on a number plate it all seems a bit absurd, but most countries have similarly ridiculous restrictions on photography.

Taking photos is not permitted in museums, at archaeological sites and in many temples, mainly to protect the postcard and slide industry. It prevents Westerners from publishing their own books about these sites and taking business away from the Chinese-published books. It also prevents valuable works of art from being damaged by countless flash photos – but in most cases you're not allowed to take even harmless natural light photos or time exposures.

Be aware that these rules are generally enforced. If you want to snap a few photos in prohibited spots then start with a new roll of film – if that's ripped out of your camera at least you don't lose 20 other photos as well. Monks can be vigorous enforcers of this rule in temples. They can rip film out of cameras faster than you can cock the shutter – must be some special martial arts training.

People Photos

In China you'll get a fantastic run for your money; for starters there are one billion portraits to work your way through. Religious reasons for avoiding photographs are absent among the Han Chinese – some guy isn't going to stick a spear through you for taking a picture of his wife and stealing part of her soul – though the taboo may apply to some of the minority groups, and you probably won't be allowed to take photos of statues in Buddhist temples.

Some Chinese shy away from having their photo taken, and even duck for cover. Others are proud to pose and will ham it up for the camera – and they're especially proud if you're taking a shot of their kid. Nobody expects any payment for photos – so don't give any or you'll set a precedent. What the Chinese would go for, though, is a copy of a colour photo, which you could mail to them. Black & white photography is a big thing in China but colour photos are definitely preferred. People tend also to think that the negative belongs to the subject as well, and they'll ask for both the negative and the print – but through the post there's no argument.

There are three basic approaches to photographing people. One is the polite 'ask for permission and pose it' shot, which is sometimes rejected. Another is the 'no-holds-barred and upset everyone' approach. The third is surreptitious, standing half a km away with a metre-long telephoto lens. Many Chinese will disagree with you on what constitutes good subject matter; they don't really see why anyone would want to take a street scene, a picture of a beggar or a shot of an old man driving a donkeycart.

Another objection often brought up is that the subject is not 'dignified' – be it a labourer straining down the street with a massive load on his hand-cart, or a barrel of excrement on wheels. This seems a bit absurd in an age where poor peasants and workers are glorified on huge billboards, but you'll have a tough time informing your subject of this.

Chinese Photography

Shutterbugs abound in the PRC these days, although a good-quality camera is still the mark of a cadre or the nouveau-riche.

The common Chinese camera harks back to the age of the Box Brownie, or bellows-type twin-lens Rolleiflex with a top speed of 1/300th of a second using 120-size film. Top of the line is the Seagull Goeland DF, an SLR – it's a chunky-looking camera that does what most Japanese cameras can do. There is Seagull brand film to go with it. Japanese cameras are sold in some photographic stores in China; these are expensive but a few Chinese come up with the money to buy them.

A lot of Chinese cannot afford a camera in the first place, and resort to photographers at tourist places. The photographers supply dress-up clothing for that extra touch. The subjects change from street clothing into spiffy gear and sometimes even bizarre costumes and make-up for the shot. Others use cardboard props such as opera stars or boats. In Beijing one prop is a real car – after all, the average Chinese has about as much hope of owning a car as you've got of hitching on the space shuttle.

The standard shot is one or more Chinese standing in front of something significant. A temple, waterfall, heroic statue or important vintages of calligraphy are considered suitable backgrounds. In the Zhuhai Special Economic Zone (near Macau), the most popular venue for photographs is in front of a big statue of Mickey Mouse. If you hang around these places you can clip off some portrait shots for yourself – people expect photos to be taken and are more at ease with the cameras. They'll sometimes even drag you into the photo as an exotic backdrop.

ACCOMMODATION

One of the reasons tourism expanded so much in the past decade in China is that the Chinese need the foreign exchange. Hotel prices are steadily rising towards what you'd pay for a similar standard of accommodation in the West. There aren't too many bargains around, but at present the room prices in many of the middle-range hotels still compare very favourably.

The hotel situation is very much a mixed bag. On the plus side, hotel staff are friendlier and more used to dealing with foreigners than a few years ago. In the past, getting into a dormitory involved interminable arguments with staff, but these days you'll usually have no trouble getting into the dorm if the hotel has one. The construction boom in top-class hotels means that high-budget travellers and tour groups will be much better catered for than they were just a few years ago.

On the down side, prices have risen. Older hotels are being renovated, and although most travellers appreciate the new paint and carpets, someone has to pay for the improvements. Ominously, many of the renovated hotels have eliminated their dormitories – there were noticeably fewer dormitories in south China during our last trip than in previous visits.

On the whole, service has improved, but in some places the staff will tell you that the hotel is 'all full' when in fact it's empty. Since state-run hotels can't fire employees and provide few or no incentives to work, the staff prefer to keep the rooms empty so they won't have to clean them.

In many hotels, the staff manage to find a few spare rooms where they can spend the day sleeping. Many staff even in big international tourist hotels cannot speak English – in many cases, this is because they got their jobs through the back door, without qualifications.

Hotels

The hotels are tourist attractions in themselves. The enormous, rambling structures in the major cities are like mini-states, with post offices, banks, restaurants, arts & crafts shops, beauty parlours, taxi services, travel agents and specially trained staff. The White Swan Hotel in Canton is so big it has its own waterfall in the lobby. This has become a popular attraction for the locals who put on their Sunday best and spend half a day posing in front of the waterfall, potted plants and foreigners. The Jinling Hotel in Nanjing is a spectacular, gleaming white tower of 36 storeys capped with a revolving restaurant and a helipad! Room prices in these extravaganzas start at about the 5th floor and skyrocket up the elevator shaft.

One step down the ladder are the gigantic Soviet-built mammoths, constructed to house the Soviet technicians and experts who came to China in the 1950s. Then there are the older European and British-built hotels – mainly in the coastal cities and a few of the inland river cities which were once foreign concessions – often with a faded touch of the colonial era about them. These usually provide simple but comfortable rooms of sufficient standard to accommodate foreign tour groups. They often have dormitories for budget travellers, at least in the older wings.

At the bottom of the barrel are ordinary Chinese hotels – essentially large concrete boxes with echo chamber hallways. Each room might accommodate anything from four to a dozen or more people; single and double rooms are rare. Often there are only communal showers and toilets with partitions but no doors. The trend in China over the last few years has been to equip even these cheap hotels with a TV in every room – which, reverberating through the vast concrete corridors, can produce the most incredible noise. Standards of repair and cleanliness vary greatly, but are usually OK.

The Chinese method of designating floors is the same as used in the USA, but different from, say, Australia's. What would be the 'ground floor' in Australia is the '1st floor' in China, the 1st is the 2nd, and so on. However, there is some inconsistency – Hong Kong, which uses the British system, has influenced some parts of southern China.

Who Stays Where

Hotels in China fall into three main categories. In the first category are the expensive tourist hotels for high-budget tourists. In the next category are less expensive mid-range hotels which accept both foreign tourists and Chinese citizens who usually pay half the price required of foreigners. The third category includes the innumerable hotels and guesthouses *(zhāodàisǔo)* which cater solely to citizens of the People's Republic. Many of the smaller guesthouses are privately run and would gladly rent foreigners a cheap room *if* they were allowed to do so.

That's a big *if*. If you front up at a Chinese-only hotel it's really a matter of luck if you get a room or a bed. Usually they're not supposed to take you and may be worried about breaking the rules which, incidentally, are under the supervision of the Public Security Bureau. If you are really stuck for a place to stay, it sometimes helps to phone or visit the local PSB and explain your problem. Some towns apply these rules more strictly than others. In Tianjin, for example, it's almost impossible to get a room or even a dormitory bed in a Chinese hotel even though the tourist hotels are nearly always full. In other towns, the PSB doesn't give a hoot where you stay. In remote areas, there may not be any special hotels for foreigners. In this case, you have to stay in a Chinese hotel because nothing else is available. But no matter what the rules say, they could change tomorrow depending on who is in charge. As with so many things in China, it just depends on where you are and who you're dealing with.

Prices

The cost of hotel rooms depends on what you are. People's Republic Chinese stay in the cheapest hotels; those who stay in the top hotels can do so because their rank entitles them to that privilege. The 'masses' are not permitted to tread the grounds of these hotels, let alone stay there.

Foreigners pay the most. The Chinese will often try to plug you into the most expensive hotels and rooms. They do this for two reasons: they want the money, and they think you're spectacularly wealthy and that you'll want to do things in spectacular style. Fortunately for the low-budget traveller this is not as big a problem as it was in the first few years of independent China travel. Most hotels will let you stay in the dormitory if they have one.

Accommodation charges vary considerably. Generally you can get a dormitory bed for around Y10 to Y15 even in a large city, sometimes for as little as Y5 in very small towns. If possible, take a look at the rooms before handing over the cash. The standard of accommodation often bears no relation to the price – you could pay Y25 for a filthy dorm with no showers and pit toilets, then the next day find a spotlessly clean hotel with good plumbing for Y10. Some dorms are segregated by sex, but mixed dorms (foreigners only) are becoming increasingly common. Many have an attached bathroom; if not, there'll be a shower-room down the hallway often with communal showers only.

If there are no dormitories in the hotel there will often be three-bed rooms and you may be able to pay for just one bed; anyone else who comes along will get thrown in with you. In less touristed areas, spartan hostels often charge just a couple of yuan for a bed in a four-bed room. The staff may ask if you want to 'occupy the whole room' *(bāofáng)*, which means you pay for the other beds. This can make a pleasant change after a long bus trip or if you want a little more privacy.

Getting Cheaper Prices Unless you're content to stay in dormitories, it's almost impossible to say what you'll pay for hotel rooms because there is so much price variation and because so much relies on the hotel staff's willingness to give you cheap accommodation. Most Chinese hotels don't have single rooms, and if you're travelling on your own you usually have to pay the price of the double room. Sometimes they'll give you a reduction but usually not (this custom is not unique to China).

There are a few places where getting a dorm bed still involves a battle. In such a case you'll be told that there is no dormitory, or that the dormitory is full. If you keep your receipts for cheap rooms and dormitories you can show these – the fact that other hotels have given you cheap accommodation can weigh in your favour. Always ask for all the room prices if the first quote is too high for you. You'll often find that some of the staff don't know all the prices. You can bargain, but do so politely!

Watch for privately run hotels. There's been a boom in these in the last few years and you'll see people standing outside railway stations trying to rake in customers off the trains. Some Chinese-speaking Westerners have managed to find their way into these places. Unfortunately, many will not take you simply because Public Security doesn't permit it. This policy varies from city to city. If someday Public Security finally decides to leave the private hotel owners alone, travelling in China could become just as cheap and easy as in Indonesia or the Philippines.

Most of the hotels in the north-east of China still haven't got the message that foreigners aren't all millionaires travelling on expense accounts. During the peak summer season it helps to arrive early in the morning. It's important to point out that you are travelling at your own expense *(zì fèi)* and do not require prices to be doubled for the sake of inflated receipts. Since most of the hotel receptionists assume foreigners require top-quality rooms, you will often be told that only the most expensive room is available and that the other rooms have 'inadequate conditions' *(tiáojiàn bùxíng)*. Enquire about the existence of dormitories *(dūo rén fáng)* and if these don't exist then progress to an economy room *(jīngjì fáng)*. The next step up is a standard room with private bath *(biāozhǔn tàofáng)* and then luxury room *(háohúa tàofáng)*. You can also specify if you want a single room *(dān rén fáng)* or double *(shūang rén fáng)*.

Sometimes you may pick the wrong time or person and it can help to come back later or try someone else. If there is zilch response or headway, you should ask them to phone a hotel with cheaper rooms. Since the staff often spot this as a great opportunity to be rid of you, they may well do this. Be appreciative and politely ask the person phoning to ascertain room price, name of hotel and exact address. Make careful note of these details before trudging off again. The final resort is a call to the PSB or preparations for a 'relaxing' night in the hotel lobby.

Student Discount If you're a foreign student in the People's Republic you can get a discount on room prices. Students usually have to show their government-issued 'white card'. Some hotels will accept a student card from Taiwan (the official line is that Taiwan is a province of the PRC). As for other travellers, the receptionist will sometimes accept your word that you're a student and will give you a discount. Other people have used forged made-in-Hong-Kong student cards. Surprisingly enough a lot of these lies and tricks still work!

Foreign experts working in China usually qualify for the same discounts as students.

Room Service

Not good, but gradually getting better. Of course, you can't expect much in the cheap Chinese hotels, but in the tourist hotels the prices warrant some attention. The larger, foreign-built and sometimes foreign-managed hotels train their staff to handle the idiosyncrasies of foreign guests and usually provide service indistinguishable from that in a similar hotel in Hong Kong or the West. Sometimes it's rather rough around the edges but improvements made in the last few years are quite extraordinary. Lower down the price ladder, though, you can't really expect much. In mid-range hotels you'll just have to *tell* the attendants that you want the sheets and bath towels changed, the water mopped off the bathroom floor or the bathtub cleaned. A lot of foreigners don't complain because they're afraid of offending people, but unless you do, hotels won't learn that they need to improve service to attract guests.

Most hotels have an attendant on every floor. The attendant keeps an eye on the hotel guests. This is partly to prevent theft and partly to stop you from bringing locals back for the night (this is no joke). Some hotels will turn away a local person at the gate; others require that the Chinese person register name, address, work unit and purpose of visit at the reception desk. Since many people are reluctant to draw attention to themselves like this, they may be reluctant to visit you at the hotel.

Something else to be prepared for is lack of privacy. Some visitors to China adamantly maintain that the Chinese lack the concept of privacy; others say that privacy is one of their highest values. Anyway, what happens is that you're sitting starkers in your hotel room, the key suddenly turns in the door and the room attendant casually wanders in...This is becoming less of a problem as hotel workers learn how to handle foreign visitors, but it's still a frequent occurrence. Don't expect anyone to knock before entering. You could try teaching them if you like, but you have to remember that in China most people live in crowded rooms; the custom of knocking before entering is unnecessary and therefore hasn't developed. One suggestion is to tape a sign over the keyhole – it doesn't matter if it's in English because they get the idea.

It's also worth noting that privacy is another privilege of rank; the high-ranking cadres live in large houses surrounded by high walls and are driven around in cars with drawn curtains. They stay in hotel rooms (not dormitories), and if they're sufficiently high in the ranks then they stay in government guesthouses far away from the milling proletariat.

FOOD

Many people who go to China expect a marvellous banquet to be available on every street corner. There is indeed some excellent food and some fascinating culinary exotica, but China is a poor country and most people cannot afford to eat like cadres. The really outstanding food is restricted to classy restaurants in places like Canton, Shanghai, Beijing and Guilin.

Out in the backwaters, you're mostly going to find yourself living on rice (steamed or fried), a few varieties of fried meat and vegetables, dumplings, bean curd *(dóufu*, generally known in the West as tofu), noodles and soup. Food in the south is generally better than in the north, and during the winter northern Chinese food can be perfectly dreadful.

On the whole though, you'll eat far better now in China than you would have a few years ago. Restaurants have proliferated in the last few years under the free enterprise system, and since they have to compete in order to survive, the quality of the food has taken a turn for the better and prices are usually low. Beware, however, of overcharging.

Traditional Fare

Chinese cooking is famine cooking. The Chinese will eat almost anything and everything that moves, and almost no part of an animal or plant is wasted. What we now regard as Chinese culinary exotica are really an effort to make the most of everything available; they salvage the least appetising ingredients which wealthy nations reject as waste, and make them into appetising food. This has led to some interesting dishes: fish heads, ducks' feet, dog and cat meat, bird saliva, and fish lips and eyeballs, to name a few.

Even the cooking method reflects the shortage of fuel; cutting the food into small pieces and stir-frying it in a wok is more fuel-efficient than baking or spit-roasting. Pigs and chickens have always been a feature of the cuisine because they have unchoosy eating habits and can be raised on very small areas of land.

Traditional Chinese food can be divided into four major categories: Beijing (sometimes called Mandarin) and Shandong; Cantonese; Shanghainese and Jiangzhenese; and Sichuan.

Beijing & Shandong Beijing and Shandong cuisine comes from one of the coldest parts of China and uses heaps of spices and chilli to warm the body up. Bread and noodles are often eaten instead of rice.

The chief speciality is Peking duck, eaten with pancakes and plum sauce. Another speciality is beggar's chicken, supposedly created by a beggar who stole the emperor's chicken and had to bury it in the ground to cook it – the dish is wrapped in lotus leaves and baked all day in hot ashes.

Some good Beijing dishes: chicken or pork with soy sauce; bean curd (tofu) with pepper sauce; fried dried shredded beef with chilli sauce; stewed mixed vegetables; barbecued chicken; fried shrimp eggs and pork pancakes. Another speciality is Mongolian barbecue – assorted barbecued meats and vegetables cooked in a hotpot. Bird's nest soup is a speciality of Shandong cooking, as is sweet-and-sour Yellow River carp. The latter is served singed on the outside but tender inside.

Shanghainese & Jiangzhenese This cuisine is noted for its use of seafoods. It's heavier and oilier than either Beijing or Cantonese food, and uses lots of chilli and spices. Eels are popular, as is drunken chicken, cooked in *shaoshing*, a potent Chinese wine a bit like warm sherry. Other things to try are some of the cold-meat-and-sauce dishes, ham-and-melon soup, bean curd (tofu) and brown sauce, braised meat balls, deep-fried chicken, and pork ribs with salt and pepper.

Jiangzhe cooking specialises in poultry and seafood, and the dishes are cooked in their own juices to preserve their original flavour.

Sichuan This is the hottest of the four categories, and is characterised by heavy use of spices and peppers. Specialities include frogs' legs and smoked duck; the duck is cooked in peppercorns, marinated in wine for 24 hours, covered in tea leaves and cooked again over a charcoal fire. Other dishes to try are shrimps with salt and garlic; dried chilli beef; vegetables and bean curd; bear paws braised in brown sauce; fish in spicy bean sauce and aubergines in garlic.

Cantonese This is southern Chinese cooking – lots of steaming, boiling and stir-frying. It's the best of the bunch if you're worried about cholesterol and coronaries, as it uses the least amount of oil. It's lightly cooked and not as highly spiced as the other three, with lots of seafood, vegetables, roast pork, chicken, steamed fish and fried rice. Specialities are abalone, 1000-year eggs (which are made by soaking in horse's urine), shark's fin soup, roast pig and a snake dish known as 'dragon's duel tiger', which combines wild cat and snake meat.

Culinary Exotica Anteaters, pangolins *(língli* – a sort of Chinese armadillo), cats, owls, monkeys and snakes are some of the more exotic creatures on the menu. Guilin and Canton are good places to find them. The Chinese have a joke that the Cantonese are capable of doing any job except zookeeper.

Headless skinned and roasted dogs are a common sight in many of China's markets. Turtles, tortoises, toads and frogs can be found in abundance. If you like seafood then the coastal towns of Shantou, Xiamen and Quanzhou will stuff you full of prawns, squid, shellfish, octopus and other sea creatures.

One of the stranger Chinese delicacies is pig face. The meat is removed from the head and hot tar is poured over the pig's face. The dried tar is peeled off, removing the hair and leaving the skin intact, which is then used as an ingredient in soup.

Live rat embryos are supposedly a delicacy from Guizhou Province. The dish is nicknamed the 'three squeals' since the embryo squeals when you pick it up with your chopsticks, once again when you dip it in soy sauce, and finally when you put it in your mouth...or so the story goes.

Western Food

Western food is available in top-end hotels catering to large numbers of Western visitors – anything from a croissant to a slab of cow can be found somewhere in this country. Western breakfasts are common: usually only eggs with toast and jam, the toast sometimes resembling chipboard. When in Rome...In some places there's been a recent proliferation of restaurants catering to the idiosyncratic tastes of the backpacking clientele. Muesli and banana pancakes have found their way to China, and restaurants have adopted Western names like those along the travellers' trails of South-East Asia.

Vegetarianism

It's not too difficult to find vegetarian food as long as you don't eat in places that just have set meals. Long train rides could present a problem – most dishes served in the dining-cars contain meat.

Learn how to say 'I'm a vegetarian' *(wǒ chī sù)* and specify vegetable dishes when you order. This usually works though sometimes they don't seem to get the message even when you have it written down.

Fruit

Canned and bottled fruit is readily available everywhere, in department and food stores as well as in dining cars on trains. Good quality fruit – including oranges, mandarins and bananas – is commonly sold in the street markets, though you'll find that the supply and quality drop off severely in winter. Out in the deserts of the north-west, melons are abundant; pineapples and lychees are common along the south-east coast. The lychee is an evergreen tree grown mainly in Guangdong, Fujian and Guangxi. The lychee nut has a reddish skin enclosing a jelly-like pulp with sweet, milky juice. It's in season around April to August.

Ration Coupons

(yōu hùi jùan)

The Chinese can obtain rice and other grains with ration coupons, which are not issued to foreigners. Sometimes you get asked for them, but if you don't have any it usually doesn't matter. You may be charged a bit extra instead but the difference is small. These days, few things are actually rationed and the coupons are used mainly for getting a discount.

Chopsticks

For over 3000 years the Chinese have been using chopsticks and are unlikely to change the habit despite encouragement to use knives and forks from reformers in the Party. Although most meals in China seem like a chopstick battlefield, there is, according to the *China Daily*, such a thing as chopstick etiquette, in which it is bad form to insert them vertically into one's rice bowl, stir the food with them to choose a tasty morsel, pick up food with them while looking at other dishes or use them as toothpicks. Well, the masses haven't heard the rules and are surviving well without them!

Most public restaurants and privately run restaurants use wooden chopsticks. Some people think wooden chopsticks are unhealthy because they harbour dirt in the cracks and may be a source of hepatitis, so they buy their own pair. Disposable wooden chopsticks are now widely available. The best way to master chopsticks is to be hungry in a place where there are no knives and forks – see the diagrams following. They mayhelp!

Don't worry about making a mess on the table – everyone does. If you want to, raise the bowl right up to your lips and shovel in the rice. This is how the Chinese eat so don't be embarrassed, though it does take practice to master the shovelling process.

Restaurants

In the towns the government-run restaurants are the size of canteens seating several hundred people at any one time. Nor do the Chinese go in for the Western fashion of eating in dimly lit, intimate surroundings. In fact, Chinese restaurants often resemble aircraft hangers – huge, noisy and brightly lit. A few restaurants have small rooms where the elite can eat away from the crowd – cadres and their friends usually hang out in these reclusive surroundings.

There is now a multitude of privately run restaurants in China. As they do everywhere else, foreigners often end up paying more. Sometimes polite insistence will bring the price down, but at other times the locals can be frustratingly stubborn. Check prices before placing your order. Don't let the price arrive as a neat figure – ask firmly and politely for individual prices, preferably written on a receipt. You can also check the menu again, providing it has prices. In case of dispute, you can refer absolutely scandalous overcharging to the PSB or take your case to the local prices commission or office of commerce *(shāngyè jú)*. On the positive side, you'll often find these privately run restaurants much more pleasant to eat in than the large, crowded canteens. The speed of the service and sometimes the quality of the food can also be substantially better.

Many restaurants have a habit of serving enormous helpings – a real problem if you're on your own because they'll often charge you appropriately. Try asking for small help-

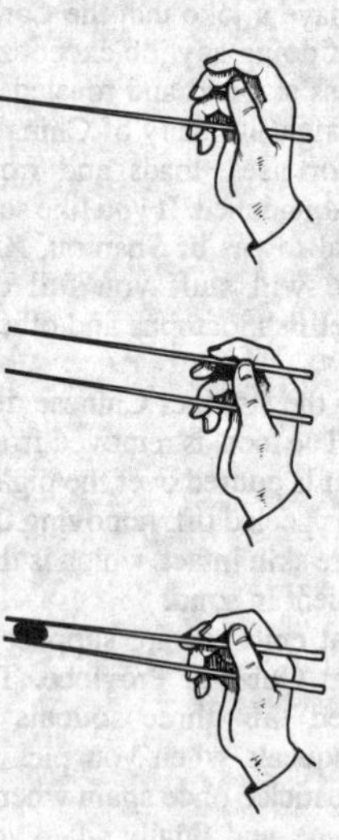

Using Chopsticks

ings – you can always order more if you're still hungry. Small street stalls are good for snacks. If you can't stand the staring any longer then flee to the restaurants in the tourist hotels; most are OK and some are much cheaper than they look.

Large government-owned restaurants have counters where you buy tickets for the food. Then you go to a window facing into the kitchen, hand in your tickets and get your food. Menus and prices are usually chalked up on a blackboard and scrubbed out as the restaurant runs out.

Unless you can speak Chinese, the best way to order a meal in a Chinese restaurant is to point at something that somebody else already has. Some restaurants are cafeteria style and you can just point to what you want. Sometimes somebody takes you in hand, leads you into the kitchen where you can point out what you want, and then buys the tickets for you. Some restaurants with a regular Western clientele have menus in English; most don't. A phrasebook is a big help if you don't speak Chinese.

Tourist hotels almost always have menus in Chinese and English. If not, there's usually someone around who speaks some English. Sometimes they dispense with menus and you pay a flat rate for a set meal.

In remote places or on long bus trips it helps to have a small bag of emergency rations such as instant noodles, dried fruit, soup extract, nuts, chocolate, etc.

Banquets

The Chinese love them and cadres try to make a habit of attending banquets about once or twice a month at state expense. Budget travellers usually don't get invited to any, though you may get to witness some incredible eating orgies in the dining rooms of the big hotels. If you come to China on business or even to teach English, there is a very good chance that you'll be invited to a banquet.

Visiting delegations, cultural groups, etc, are usually given a welcoming banquet by their host organisation. At the very highest levels there'll be formal invitations and a detailed seating plan based on rank and higher algebra. At lower levels it's a simpler affair, though the ritual and etiquette are much the same.

A formal dinner usually lasts about 1½ hours, and is preceded by 10 or 15 minutes of tea and polite conversation. The party is then seated with the host presiding at the head of the table and the high-ranking guests (that is, the leaders of the delegation) seated to his left or right.

Dishes are served in sequence, beginning with cold appetisers and continuing through 10 or more courses. Soup is usually served after the main course and is used to wash the food down.

The usual rule is to serve everyone too much. Empty bowls imply that the host hasn't served a sufficient quantity of food, so if you see a bit left in a bowl then leave it there. Similarly, though rice may be the staple, at banquets it is used only as a filler; to consume great quantities of it at a banquet implies you are still hungry and is an insult to your host.

In a formal setting it is impolite to drink alcohol alone; toasts are usually offered to neighbours or to the whole table. It is appropriate for the leader of the guests to offer a toast to everyone at the table, and the Chinese host usually begins the toasts after the first course. Avoid excessive toasting since inebriation is frowned upon.

Toasts are often made with the expression *gān bēi* (dry glass) which literally implies 'empty the cup'. In the course of a banquet there may be several gan bei toasts, but custom dictates that you need only drain your glass on the first one. Subsequent toasts require only a small sip. The Han Chinese don't clink their classes when toasting.

Don't be late for a formal banquet; it's considered extremely rude. The banquet ends when the food and toasts end – the Chinese don't linger after the meal. You may find yourself being applauded when you enter a large banquet. The Chinese custom is used as a greeting or to indicate approval and it is often OK to applaud back!

Restaurant Vocabulary
restaurant
cāntīng 餐厅
I'm vegetarian.
wǒ chī sù 我吃素
menu
cài dān 菜单
bill (cheque)
zhàng dān 帐单
set meal (no menu)
tàocān 套餐
to eat/let's eat
chī fàn 吃饭
chopsticks
kùaizi 筷子
knife and fork
dāochā 刀叉
spoon
tiáogēng 调羹

Staples
plain white rice
mǐ fàn, bái fàn 米饭，白饭
fried rice
chǎo fàn 炒饭
watery rice porridge
xīfàn 稀饭
noodles
miàn 面
fried noodles
chǎo miàn 炒面
soupy noodles
tāng miàn 汤面
dumplings
jiǎozi 饺子
bread, pastry, rolls
miànbāo 面包
steamed buns
mántóu 馒头
steamed meat buns
bāozi 包子
fried bread stick
yóutiáo 油条

Soup
soup
tāng 汤
clear soup
qīng tāng 清汤
sweet & sour soup
sūan là tāng 酸辣汤
bean curd (tofu) soup
dòufú tāng 豆腐汤
wanton soup
húndùn tāng 馄饨汤
egg soup
dàn hūa tāng 蛋花汤

Meat
beef
niú ròu 牛肉
chicken
jī ròu 鸡肉
dogmeat
gǒu ròu 狗肉
duck
yā ròu 鸭肉
goat, mutton
yáng ròu 羊肉
pork
zhū ròu 猪肉
snake
shé ròu 蛇肉

Fish & Seafood
fish
yú 鱼
crab
pángxiè 螃蟹
eel
shàn yú 鳝鱼
frogs
qīngwā 青蛙
octopus
zhāng yú 章鱼
prawns
xiā 虾
squid
yóu yú 鱿鱼

Vegetables
vegetables
shū cài 蔬菜
bamboo shoots
zhúsǔn 竹笋
bitter squash
kǔgūa 苦瓜
carrot
hóng lóbō 红萝卜

cauliflower
hūa cài 花菜
celery
qíng cài 芹菜
corn
yùmǐ 玉米
eggplant
qiézi 茄子
green pepper
qīng jiāo 青椒
mushrooms
mógu 磨菇
pickled vegetables
zhà cài 榨菜
bean curd (tofu)
dòufǔ 豆腐
tomato
xīhóngshì 西红柿

Fruit
apple
pínggǔo 萍果
banana
xiāngjiāo 香蕉
grape
pútáo 葡萄
lychee
lìzhī 荔枝
orange
chéngzi 橙子
pear
lí 梨
pineapple
bōlúo 菠萝
tangerine
júzi 橘子
watermelon
xīgūa 西瓜

Condiments
garlic
dàsùan 大蒜
ginger
jiāng 姜
black pepper
hújiāo 胡椒
hot pepper
làjiāo 辣椒
hot sauce
làjiāo jiàng 辣椒酱
ketchup
fānqié jiàng 蕃茄酱
MSG
wèijīng 味精
salt
yán 盐
sugar
táng 糖
sesame seed oil
zhīmá yóu 芝麻油
soy sauce
jiàng yóu 酱油
vinegar
cù 醋

DRINKS

Tea is the most commonly served brew in the PRC; it didn't originate in China but in South-East Asia. Indian tea is not generally available but the Friendship Stores in Beijing and Shanghai should have it. Coffee is fairly common in the large cities. Cafes – remarkably similar in both style and atmosphere to Western cafes – can be found in the larger cities and are popular with young Chinese.

Beer is probably the next most popular

drink, and by any standards the top brands are great stuff. The best known is Qingdao (Tsingtao), made with a mineral water which gives it its sparkling quality. It's really a German beer since the town of Qingdao where it's made was once a German concession and the Chinese inherited the brewery. Local brews are found in all the major cities of China and are often bland. Western liquor is sold in Friendship Stores and top-end hotels, but for a real taste of China try some of the innumerable local wines and spirits – the sort of stuff they run tanks on.

Many so-called Chinese wines are actually spirits, though China has probably cultivated vines and produced wine for over 4000 years. Chinese wine-producing techniques differ from those of Westerners. Quality-conscious wine producers in Western countries work on the idea that the lower the yield the higher the quality of the wine produced. But Chinese workers cultivate every possible sq cm of earth; they encourage their vines to yield heavily and also plant peanuts between the rows of vines as a cover crop for half the year. The peanuts sap much of the nutrient from the soil, and in cooler years the large grape crop fails to ripen sufficiently to produce a wine comparable to Western ones.

There are also basic misunderstandings between the Chinese and the Western growers brought in to advise on wine production. For example, an acre in Chinese terms is actually only a fifth of what Europeans regard as an acre. Western producers try to prevent oxidation in the wines, but oxidation produces a flavour which the Chinese find desirable and go to great ends to achieve. The Chinese are also keen on wines with different herbs and other materials soaked in them, which they drink for their health and for restorative or even aphrodisiac qualities.

Dynasty white wine is produced near Tianjin in conjunction with the French company Remy Martin, but it's essentially an export wine – not designed for the local market. Tsingtao Chardonnay is another export brand produced in Shandong Province. Hejie Jiu (lizard wine) is produced in the southern province of Guangxi; each bottle contains one dead lizard suspended perpendicularly in the clear liquid. Wine with dead bees is also desirable for its alleged tonic properties.

Coca-Cola, first introduced into China by American soldiers in 1927, is now produced in Beijing. Chinese attempts at making similar brews include TianFu Cola, which has a recipe based on the root of herbaceous peony. Fanta and Sprite are widely available, both genuine and copycat versions. Sickeningly sweet Chinese soft drinks are cheap and sold everywhere. Fresh milk is rare but you can buy it in the Friendship Store in Beijing. Bottles of sweet yoghurt are commonly sold in the larger cities.

Tibetans have an interesting brew called *qingke*, a beer or spirit made from barley. Mongolians serve sour-tasting *koumiss*, made of fermented mare's milk. *Mao tai* is a favourite of the Chinese. It's a spirit made from sorghum (a type of millet) and is used for toasts at banquets – it tastes rather like methylated spirits and you can get drunk very quickly on the stuff.

With the exception of some of the older people, Chinese women don't drink (except beer) or smoke in public, but this behaviour is considered permissible for Western women. As a rule Chinese men are not great drinkers, but toasts are obligatory at banquets – if you really can't drink, fill your wine glass with tea and say you have a bad stomach. In spite of all the toasting and beer drinking, drunkenness is strongly frowned upon though alcoholism exists in China as it does in most other countries.

Drinks Vocubulary

beer
píjiǔ 啤酒
fizzy drink (soda)
qìshǔi 汽水
Coca-Cola
kěkǒu kělè 可口可乐
tea
chá 茶

coffee
kāfēi 咖啡
water
kāi shŭi 开水
mineral water
kùang qúan shŭi 矿泉水
grape wine
pútáo jiŭ 葡萄酒
rice wine
mĭ jiŭ 米酒
ice cold
bīngde 冰的

THINGS TO BUY

Some people buy nothing in China and others come back loaded with souvenirs. Shopping and visits to arts & crafts 'factories' figure prominently on the itineraries of tour groups, and over the last few years there has been a boom in mass-produced Chinese arts & crafts. However, there are still many unique curios and beautiful pieces of art to be found.

Chinese Department Stores in Hong Kong

The Chinese government runs large department stores in Hong Kong which sell almost everything that China exports. Everything from antiques to chopsticks is available and you'll get a greater variety and often cheaper prices than you can in China itself!

There are two types of stores. The China-products-type stores such as Yue Hwa which sell the domestic, everyday items like clothing, hardware, spectacles and furniture, but also stock luxuries such as silk kimonos and negligees. The China Arts & Crafts stores stock the artsy/craftsy, curio/antiquity stuff.

Yue Hwa has several branches, but the best store is at 301-309 Nathan Rd (the northwest corner of Nathan and Jordan roads), Kowloon, right near the Jordan MTR station.

China Arts & Crafts, owned by the People's Republic, has several branches. Some popular stores in Kowloon are at the New World Centre, Salisbury Rd; the Silvercord Shopping Centre, 30 Canton Rd near Haiphong Rd; Star House, corner of Salisbury and Canton roads; and 233-239 Nathan Rd.

Friendship Stores

These stores originally stocked goods either imported from the West or in short supply in the ordinary stores. They were primarily meant for foreigners, but since many stores now sell imported goods the whole concept of the Friendship Store is a rather archaic one. Only the large Friendship Stores – in Beijing, Shanghai and Canton – are really in a class by themselves for their extraordinary range of goods.

Some Friendship Stores will pack and ship your purchases for you. Some of the goods you buy here must be paid for in FEC, while other items can be bought with RMB. Ration coupons or approval from the work unit are not needed to buy stuff in the Friendship Stores; all that's needed is the right type of money, and that's why the Chinese are so anxious to get FEC.

Department Stores

If you need something, the big department stores are the places to go. With the rebirth of consumerism these stores are stocked with all types of goods, from daily needs to luxuries, locally made and imported. Most of the goods are very expensive in relation to Chinese wages, but cheap for Westerners. Before you buy something in the Friendship Store, it's worth checking to see if it's available in the local department store where it may be cheaper.

Hotel Shops

These supply foreigners with Western and Japanese film, Western cigarettes and alcohol, Coca-Cola, biscuits, souvenirs, toothpaste, postcards, maps, foreign magazines and books.

Free Markets

Free markets, which started around 1979-80, are street markets where people sell produce and goods for their own profit. The quantity and quality of the goods has improved considerably in the past few years.

Books & Posters

Chinese political books and magazines are interesting souvenirs, as are wallposters. These are readily available in the bookshops and are very cheap. One delightful poster we've seen showed Mao Zedong, Zhou Enlai, Zhu De and Liu Shaoqi amiably chatting in what looks like a Communist heaven, surrounded by trees and flowers with a beautiful waterfall behind them! Another shows Zhu, Mao and Liu welcoming Zhou at the airport on his return from a visit to the Soviet Union in the 1950s. Older versions of this poster have Liu scrubbed out, while newer ones include Deng Xiaoping and Peng Zhen.

All over China you'll see people on the footpath presiding over shelves of little books. These are the Chinese equivalent of comic books and are popular with both children and adults, who rent them from the stall-keeper and sit down on benches to read.

The fashion magazines printed in Beijing and Shanghai are interesting mementoes, with their Western and Chinese beauties whose looks, hairstyles and dress are aeons away from the blue-garbed socialist women of the Maoist era. Racy front covers, often of semi-garbed Western models, belie more austere interiors.

Newspapers and periodicals are distributed through the post office. The major distributor of books is the Xinhua Bookstore, which has around 5000 stores throughout China. There are also Foreign Language Bookstores in the major cities. China International Book Trading Corporation *(gúojì shūdiàn)* is the chief distributor of books and periodicals abroad.

Arts & Crafts

Chinese musical instruments are sold in department stores and private shops. Some shops are devoted entirely to traditional Chinese opera costumes, so if you want something unique for the next masquerade party that's the place to go. Cassettes and records of traditional opera are also sold in these shops. You sometimes find interesting items in the Xinhua Bookstores, which are in every Chinese city.

Brushes, paints and other art materials may be worth checking out – a lot of this stuff is imported by Western countries and you should be able to pick them up cheaper at the

Paper-cuts

source. Scroll paintings are sold everywhere and are invariably expensive, partly because the material on which the painting is done is expensive. The many street artists in China sit out on the pavement drawing and painting and selling their products to passers-by.

Beautiful kites are sold in China and are worth getting, just to hang on your wall. Paper rubbings of stone inscriptions are cheap and make nice wall hangings when framed. Exquisite paper-cuts are sold everywhere.

Clothes & Jewellery

China is a hat-collector's paradise. The woven straw peasant hats vary from province to province.

In Xinjiang and in Hohhot in Inner Mongolia you can buy, or have made for you, decorative leather riding boots. Kashgar is the hat and knife-making centre of Xinjiang, and both are available in an extraordinary variety of designs. If you don't get to Kashgar, Turpan also has similar items.

Check out the cashmere jumpers, cardigans and skirts in the Beijing Friendship Store and its branch in the Beijing Hotel.

Jade and ivory jewellery are commonly sold in China – but remember that some countries like Australia and the USA prohibit the import of ivory.

Antiques

Many of the Friendship Stores have antique sections, and some cities have antique shops, but prices are high so don't expect to find a bargain. Only antiques which have been cleared for sale to foreigners may be taken out of the country. When you buy an item over 100 years old it will come with an official red wax seal attached. This seal does *not* necessarily indicate that the item is an antique though! A Canadian who bought 'real' jade for Y1500 at a Friendship Store in Guilin later discovered in Hong Kong that it was a plastic fake. After six months of copious correspondence and investigation, the Guilin Tourism Bureau refunded the money and closed down the offending store. You'll also get a receipt of sale which you must show to Customs when you leave the country; otherwise the antique will be confiscated. Imitation antiques are sold everywhere. Some museum shops sell replicas, usually at extravagant prices.

Stamps & Coins

China issues quite an array of beautiful stamps – generally sold at post offices in the hotels. Outside many of the post offices you'll find amateur philatelists with books full of stamps for sale; it can be extraordinarily hard bargaining with these guys! Stamps issued during the Cultural Revolution make interesting souvenirs. Old coins are often sold at major tourist sites; many are forgeries.

Oddities

If plaster statues are to your liking, the opportunities to stock up in China are abundant. Fat buddhas appear everywhere, and 60-cm-high Venus de Milos and multi-armed gods with flashing lights are not uncommon.

Fireworks are sold all over China. You're not allowed to bring them into Hong Kong, so customs may ask you for them or inspect your bags. Fireworks are also prohibited on aircraft, and some countries, like Australia, do not permit their import.

Lots of shops sell medicinal herbs and spices. Export tea is sold in extravagantly decorated tins; check the China Products stores in Hong Kong. In Kashgar you can buy wooden horse saddles. Hotan is the carpet-making centre of Xinjiang.

Advertising

Advertising for the foreign market is one area the Chinese are still stumbling around in. A French traveller reported seeing a TV advertisement in Paris for Chinese furs. Viewers were treated to the bloody business of skinning and cadavers in the refrigerator rooms before the usual parade of fur-clad models down the catwalk. It would be fun to handle the advertising campaigns for their more charming brand names. There's Double-Bull Underwear and Pansy Underwear (for men), and Fang-Fang Lipstick and a palindromic brand called Maxam which sounds like a vaguely familiar factor. Pamper your stud with Horse Head facial tissues. While in Canton drop into the Checkmates Disco in the China Hotel. Wake up in the morning with a Golden Cock Alarm Clock (now called the Golden Rooster). For your trusty Walkman it may be best to stay away from White Elephant Batteries, but you might try the space-age Moon Rabbit variety. Flying Eagle Safety Razors don't sound too safe either. Out of the psychedelic '60s comes White Rabbit Candy. The rarer brand to look for is the Flying Baby series, which appears to have been discontinued, and there used to be some Flying Baby toilet paper around. The ideographs for Coca-Cola are pronounced ***kěkǒu kělè*** and translate as 'tastes good, tastes happy'. But the Chinese must have thought they were really on to something good when the 'Coke Adds Life' slogan got mistranslated and claimed to be able to resurrect the dead.

Getting There & Away

There are all sorts of ways of entering and leaving China. There are international airports at Beijing, Shanghai, Canton, Kunming and other cities; rail links to the USSR, Mongolia and North Korea; boats to Hong Kong, Japan and South Korea; and, for the determined traveller, roads to the USSR, Pakistan and possibly India. The land borders with Nepal, Myanmar (Burma), Vietnam, Laos, Bhutan, and Afghanistan were all closed to foreigners at the time of writing; of these, it's worth watching Nepal, Vietnam and Laos for future developments.

The most popular entry and exit point is Hong Kong. There are direct flights from China to many Asian and Western countries, and shipping connections to Japan. Hong Kong has the cheapest air connections to Europe, Britain, the USA, Australia and many Asian countries.

From Hong Kong most people first make their way to Canton. You can get to Canton from Hong Kong by train, ferry, hydrofoil or plane. The one rule to remember is to avoid going at weekends, and even more so at holiday times like Easter and Chinese New Year! At those times everything is booked out and the crowds pour across the border from Hong Kong.

AIR

The air ticket alone can gouge a great slice out of anyone's budget, but you can reduce the cost by finding a discounted fare which may (or may not) involve restrictions on route, advance purchase requirements, cancellation charges, etc.

A common cheap ticket is the Advance Purchase one, which usually has to be purchased two or three weeks ahead of departure, has a cancellation fee, does not permit stopovers and may have minimum and maximum stays as well as fixed departure and return dates.

Also useful is combined ticketing, in which a couple of tickets are issued at the same time to cover several projected trips, therefore guarding against fare increases.

Worth considering is a ticket which will take you from point A to point B with multiple stopovers. For example, such a ticket could fly you from Sydney to London with stopovers in Denpasar, Jakarta, Hong Kong, Bangkok, Calcutta, Delhi and Istanbul.

If China is just one stop on a round-the-world trip then consider getting a 'Round the World' (RTW) ticket. With these you get a limited period in which to circumnavigate the globe, and you can make a stopover anywhere the carrying airline goes as long as you don't backtrack. Some airlines have tickets which last for a year. Sometimes two or more airlines team up to provide the service. A Round the World ticket starting and finishing in London and dropping in at Los Angeles, Honolulu, Cairns, Sydney, Perth, Hong Kong and Bangkok will cost from £1300. Similar tickets may offer you the chance to stop off in Hong Kong and travel under your own steam to Beijing, to pick up a flight there.

Travel agents offer a host of other deals. Whatever you do, buy your air ticket from one of them because the airlines don't deal directly in discount tickets. And always check what conditions and restrictions apply to the tickets you intend to buy!

If you're travelling with kids you may be surprised to hear that the agents with the cheapest adult tickets may not necessarily have the cheapest children's tickets – even if you're all taking the same flight. Unless you've got the time to get adult tickets from one agent and children's from another, probably the simplest thing to do is go to the agent who offers the lowest total price for all tickets.

CAAC

The overseas offices of the China Aviation Administration of China (also known as Air China), the domestic and international carrier of the People's Republic, are in the countries (and cities) that follow.

Australia (Melbourne, Sydney), Canada (Toronto, Vancouver), Ethiopia (Addis Ababa), France (Paris), Germany (Frankfurt, Berlin), Iraq (Baghdad), Italy (Rome), Japan (Tokyo, Fukuoka, Osaka, Nagasaki), North Korea (Pyongyang), Malaysia (Kuala Lumpur), Myanmar (Rangoon), Pakistan (Karachi), Philippines (Manila), Romania (Bucharest), Singapore, Sweden (Stockholm), Switzerland (Zurich), Thailand (Bangkok), Turkey (Istanbul), United Arab Emirates (Sharjah), UK (London), USA (Los Angeles, San Francisco, New York), USSR (Moscow) and Yugoslavia (Belgrade).

Cathay Pacific

Cathay, though partly owned by British Airways, is a Hong-Kong-based company well known for good service. It flies between Hong Kong and most major cities of the world. Most importantly, it is one of the three carriers that offer direct flights between Hong Kong and cities in China (the other two are CAAC and Dragonair).

Given a choice, most travellers prefer Cathay. However, CAAC doesn't welcome competition and the Chinese government has kept Cathay off most of CAAC's routes. At present, Cathay flies from Hong Kong to Beijing and Shanghai. You can buy a ticket from virtually any Hong Kong travel agent or directly from Cathay. There is no discounting on flights into China and prices are identical to what CAAC charges except in business class.

Dragonair

Hong Kong's fledgling airline is partly owned by the People's Republic and partly by Cathay Pacific. There has been a lot of speculation that Dragonair would go under, and it probably would have if Cathay hadn't bought into it. Rumour has it that Cathay did this to please the Chinese government.

Dragonair flies from Hong Kong to several destinations in China: Beijing, Dalian, Guilin, Haikou, Kunming, Nanjing, Shanghai and Xiamen. Within China, Dragonair tickets can be bought from CITS. In Hong Kong, their office (☎ 8108055) is on the 19th floor, Wheelock House, 20 Pedder St, Central, Hong Kong Island.

To/From Hong Kong

Most travellers heading to China from Hong Kong go by train or ferry, but flying is indeed possible. The Civil Aviation Administration of China (CAAC) and Cathay Pacific both operate direct flights between Hong Kong and a number of Chinese cities, including Beijing, Canton, Dalian, Hangzhou, Kunming, Shanghai, Tianjin and Xiamen.

There are a couple of flights a day to Canton. The fare is HK$320 and the flight takes about 35 minutes.

There are daily flights to Beijing (around HK$1600); flights six days a week to Shanghai (HK$1200); and flights twice a week to Kunming (HK$1100).

In Hong Kong flights can be booked at the CAAC office at: Ground Floor, 17 Queen's Rd, Central (☎ 8401199). There is another CAAC office at: Ground Floor, Hankow Centre, 4 Ashley Rd, Tsimshatsui, Kowloon (☎ 7390022). Both offices tend to be very crowded with long queues, so go early (9 am) when they open. After 10 am, the crowds increase substantially.

It is possible to buy all of your CAAC tickets from CITS in Hong Kong, and even from some non-Chinese airlines that have reciprocal arrangements with CAAC. However, this is generally *not* a good idea. First of all, it saves you no money whatsoever. Secondly, the tickets issued outside China need to be exchanged for a proper stamped ticket at the appropriate CAAC offices in China – a few of these offices get their wires crossed and refuse to honor 'foreign' tickets. Furthermore, CAAC flights are often cancelled, but you'll have to return the ticket to the seller in order to get a refund.

Hong Kong is a good place to pick up a cheap air ticket to almost anywhere in the world, and you have to go to the travel agents. Remember that prices of cheap tickets change and bargains come and go rapidly, and that some travel agents are more reliable than others. Travel agents advertise in the classified sections of the *South China*

Morning Post and the *Hong Kong Standard* newspapers.

Oddly enough, some of them seem to have zero interest in actually selling you a ticket. You can do your shopping around by phone; a number of agents are listed below but check the newspapers for others. There's quite a cost variance among the Hong Kong bucket shops (as ticket-discounters are known).

A popular place to buy air tickets is the Hong Kong Student Travel Bureau or HKSTB (☎ 7213269 or 3693804), Room 1021, 10th floor, Star House, Salisbury Rd, Tsimshatsui, Kowloon. Their service is reliable, though they are no longer the cheapest place.

One of the least expensive and most reliable agents is Traveller Services (☎ 3674127), Room 704, Metropole Building, 57 Peking Rd, Tsimshatsui, Kowloon. Another agent which specialises in discount tickets is Y & J Travel (☎ 3686187), Front Block, 4th floor, Wah Ying Cheong Building, 234 Nathan Rd, Kowloon.

Well worth trying is Phoenix Services (☎ 7227378) in Room B, 6th floor, Milton Mansion, 96 Nathan Rd, Tsimshatsui, Kowloon. They are friendly, helpful and reliable.

Chungking Mansions houses many travel agents. The Mansions used to be a great place to look for cheap air tickets, but in recent years more and more travellers have complained about high prices and rude service. Still, it pays to ask around the youth hostels and see what experience others have had.

Rip-Offs Be careful when you buy tickets. Rip-offs do happen. The territory has always been plagued by bogus travel agents and fly-by-night operations that appear shortly before peak holiday seasons and dupe customers into buying non-existent airline seats and holiday packages. Or you might pay a non-refundable deposit on an air ticket, and when you come to pay the balance they'll tell you the price of the ticket has risen.

A popular trick is for an agent to accept a deposit for a booking, then say when you come in to pick up the tickets that the flight is no longer available, but there is this other flight which costs X dollars more. The only way to be sure that this doesn't happen is to have the travel agent make the reservation (by telephone); you then pay for the ticket in full and get a receipt clearly showing that you have paid the total bill. You should then be able to pick up your ticket later the same day.

If you think you have been ripped off, and the agent is a member of the HKTA (Hong Kong Tourist Association), the organisation can apply some pressure (and apparently has a fund to handle cases of outright fraud). Even if an agent is a member of the HKTA it still does not have to comply with any set of guidelines.

A law was passed in mid-1985 requiring all travel agencies offering outward-bound services to be licensed. The law also set up a fund to compensate cheated customers – could be worth enquiring about if you do get ripped off.

To/From Australia

Australia is not a cheap place to fly out of, and air fares between Australia and South-East Asia are ridiculously expensive considering the distances flown. However, there are a few effective ways of cutting the cost.

Among the cheapest regular tickets available in Australia are the Advance Purchase fares. The cost of these tickets depends on your departure date from Australia. The year is divided into 'peak' and 'low' seasons; tickets bought in peak season (from December to January) are more expensive.

It's possible to get reductions on the cost of Advance Purchase and other fares by going to the student travel offices and/or some of the travel agents in Australia that specialise in cheap air tickets.

A one-way fare from Australia to Hong Kong is likely to cost from about A$650 (A$1100 return).

Travel agents advertise in the travel sections of the Saturday papers, such as the Melbourne *Age* and the *Sydney Morning Herald*. Also look in *Student Traveller*, a free newspaper published by Student Travel Australia and distributed on campuses.

Well worth trying is the Flight Shop (☎ 670 0477) at 386 Little Bourke St, Melbourne. They also have branches under the name of the Flight Centre in Sydney (☎ (02) 233 2296) and Brisbane (☎ (07) 229 9958). In Brisbane also check out the Brisbane Flight Centre (☎ (07) 229 9211).

Some good deals are available from Student Travel Australia and you don't have to be a student to use their services. They have offices in all the major Australian cities.

For tours and package deals contact Access Travel (☎ (02) 241 1128), 5th floor, 58 Pitt St, Sydney. Apart from China tours they also organise tours on the Trans-Siberian railway from Beijing to Europe, including stopovers in Ulan Bator (Mongolia), Irkutsk, Lake Baikal, Leningrad and Moscow.

To/From New Zealand

Air New Zealand and Cathay Pacific fly Auckland to Hong Kong from around NZ$1750 return, with restrictions. A flight to Beijing will cost from around NZ$1800 ($2550 return).

To/From the UK

British Airways, British Caledonian, Cathay Pacific and other airlines fly London-Hong Kong. Air-ticket discounting is a long-running business in the UK and it's wide open. The various agents advertise their fares and there's nothing under-the-counter about it at all. To find out what's going, there are a number of magazines in Britain which have good information about flights and agents. These include: *Trailfinder*, free from the Trailfinders Travel Centre in Earls Court; and *Time Out* and *City Limits*, the London weekly entertainment guides widely available in the UK.

Discount tickets are almost exclusively available in London. You won't find your friendly travel agent out in the country offering cheap deals. The danger with discounted tickets in Britain is that some of the 'bucket shops' are unsound. Sometimes the backstairs over-the-shop travel agents fold up and disappear after you've handed over the money and before you've got the tickets. Get the tickets before you hand over the cash.

Two reliable London bucket shops are Trailfinders in Earls Court; and the Student Travel Association with several offices.

You can expect a one-way London-Hong Kong ticket to cost from around £330, and a return ticket around £600. London ticket discounters can also offer interesting one-way fares to Australia with a Hong Kong stopover from around £680.

A standard-price one-way ticket with CAAC from London to Beijing will cost £300 (£550 return).

To/From Europe

Fares similar to those from London are available from other European cities.

The Netherlands, Belgium and Switzerland are good places for buying discount air tickets. In Antwerp, WATS has been recommended. In Zurich try SOF Travel and Sindbad. In Geneva try Stohl Travel. In the Netherlands, NBBS is a reputable agency.

CAAC (also known as Air China) has flights between Beijing and Belgrade, Bucharest, Frankfurt, London, Moscow, Paris, Athens and Zurich. Other international airlines operate flights out of Beijing but there are very few, if any, cut-rate fares from the Chinese end. Try the Soviet airline Aeroflot and the Rumanian airline Tarom.

To/From the USA

You can pick up some interesting tickets from North America to South-East Asia, particularly from the US west coast or Vancouver, Canada. In fact the intense competition between Asian airlines is resulting in ticket discounting operations very similar to those of the London bucket shops.

The cheapest fares are available from 'ticket consolidators'. Some tickets have restrictions, such as they can only confirm your seat a week before departure, or you must fly standby, etc.

Make sure that you understand all restrictions before you actually hand over the cash.

It definitely pays to shop around – scan the travel sections of the Sunday newspapers for likely looking agents; the *New York Times, San Francisco Chronicle-Examiner* and *Los Angeles Times* are particularly good. It's not advisable to send money (even cheques) through the post – some travellers have reported being ripped off by fly-by-night mail-order ticket agents.

One of the cheapest and most reliable travel agents on the west coast is Overseas Tours.

The Council on International Educational Exchange (CIEE), also known as Council Travel, issues International Student Identity Cards (ISIC) and International Youth Hostel (IYH) cards. They also know a lot about cheap tickets. You don't have to be a student to use their services, though they do have special fares for students and teachers. Council Travel has offices in most major US cities.

For direct flights from the USA to China the general route is from San Francisco (with connections from New York, Los Angeles and Vancouver in Canada) to Tokyo, then Beijing, Shanghai or several other cities in China. It's entirely possible to go through to Beijing and then pick up the return flight in Shanghai.

A round-trip excursion fare from San Francisco to Hong Kong is likely to cost from US$1000, and to Beijing from $1250. A single fare from San Francisco to Hong Kong will cost from US$700, with restrictions.

To/From Canada

Travel CUTS is Canada's national student travel agency and has offices in Vancouver, Victoria, Edmonton, Saskatoon, Toronto, Ottawa, Montreal and Halifax. You don't have to be a student to use their services.

Getting discount tickets in Canada is much the same as in the USA. Go to the travel agents and shop around until you find a good deal. In Vancouver try Kowloon Travel, Westcan Treks and Travel CUTS.

Canadian Pacific Airlines are worth trying for cheap deals to Hong Kong although Korean Airlines, which is booked by some of the agents mentioned above, may still be able to undercut them.

To/From Other Asian Countries

To/From Bangladesh Dragonair now has flight from Dhaka to Kunming.

To/From Singapore There are direct flights between Singapore and Hong Kong. A good place for buying cheap air tickets in Singapore is Airmaster Travel Centre. Also try Student Travel Australia. Other agents advertise in the *Straits Times* classifieds.

To/From Indonesia Garuda Airlines has direct flights from Jakarta to Hong Kong, and from Denpasar to Hong Kong via Jakarta. Cheap discount air tickets out of Indonesia can be bought from travel agents at Kuta Beach in Bali and in Jakarta. There are numerous airline ticket discounters around Kuta – several on the main strip, Jalan Legian where you can also buy discount tickets for departure from Jakarta. In Jakarta try Student Travel Australia.

To/From Thailand In Bangkok, Student Travel in the Thai Hotel is both helpful and efficient.

There is a twice-weekly flight from Beijing to Bangkok via Canton (you can pick up the flight in Canton too). There is also a very popular once-weekly flight from Kunming to Bangkok.

To/From Pakistan CAAC has direct flights from Beijing to Karachi three times weekly.

To/From Nepal There are direct flights between Lhasa and Kathmandu twice a week, but you have to book through an expensive CITS tour.

To/From Myanmar (Burma) There is a once-weekly flight from Beijing to Rangoon (Yangon) with a stopover in Kunming. You can pick up the flight in Kunming too, but must have a visa for Myanmar – available in Beijing, not Kunming. You can stay in

Myanmar for only two weeks and usually have to have an air ticket out of the country before they'll give you a visa. If the present political chaos continues, visits will remain an uncertain proposition.

To/From Japan CAAC has several flights a week from Beijing to Tokyo and Osaka, via Shanghai. Japan Airlines flies from Beijing and Shanghai to Tokyo, Osaka and Nagasaki.

To/From North & South Korea At the time of writing there were no flights between the PRC and South Korea, since the two have no diplomatic relations with each other (but see the Boat section for recent developments by sea). As for North Korea, *if* you can get a visa there are once-weekly flights between Beijing and Pyongyang.

To/From Philippines CAAC has a twice-weekly flight from Beijing to Manila and a once-weekly flight from Canton to Manila. There are also direct flights from Xiamen to Manila four times a week.

LAND

For most travellers, 'overland' to China means from Hong Kong or Macau by rail or bus. Another very popular route is the Trans-Siberian Railway from Europe. Exotic routes include Tibet to Nepal and Xinjiang to Pakistan or the Soviet Union.

The borders with Vietnam and Laos have been closed since 1979. One enterprising tour company is however planning backpackers' trips from Hong Kong through China, Vietnam, Laos and Thailand. They say they have permission from all the governments concerned, and by the time you read this the trips may be happening.

It is not possible to travel overland to Myanmar (Burma). The borders with Afghanistan and Bhutan are also out of bounds.

At the time of writing, India is about to open its border with China for trade at Garbyang, Uttar Pradesh, just north of the Nepalese border; it remains to be seen if travellers will be able to use this route.

Foreigners are not usually allowed to drive cars or motorbikes around China and are therefore not usually allowed to take them in.

To/From Hong Kong

There are several ways to make the crossing between Hong Kong and Canton, but local train is by far most popular.

Local Train The least expensive way of getting from Hong Kong to China is by local train. The trains in Hong Kong start running around 6 am, and the border stays open until 10 pm. The Kowloon-Canton Railway (KCR) local trains run from Hunghom station in Kowloon to Lo Wu at the Hong Kong/China border. From there, you walk across the border bridge to Shenzhen. You can spend some time in Shenzhen or jump on the first local train to Canton.

For most travellers, the easiest way to get on the KCR line is to first take the Mass Transit Railway (MTR) to the Kowloon Tong station, then change trains. Alternatively, you can walk to Hunghom station – easiest way is to walk along the waterfront. The fare from Hunghom to Lo Wu is HK$19 ordinary class, or HK$39 in 1st class – slightly less from Kowloon Tong station.

There are about a dozen local trains a day between Shenzhen and Canton. Tourist-price hard-seat is Y20, soft-seat Y46. Once you've been through Customs at Shenzhen station you usually have to wait a while for the Canton-bound train. The waiting hall in Shenzhen station is always packed, but there are two large restaurants upstairs if you want to eat. The trip from the border to Canton takes about 2½ to three hours. The local trains stop at the east station from where you get a bus to the centre of Canton – the express goes to the main station. Extra trains may be put on during the holiday periods like Easter and Chinese New Year, when the Hong Kongers scramble across the border.

Hong Kong-Canton Express The express

train between Hong Kong and Canton is a comfortable and convenient way of entering China. The adult fare is around HK$190 one way. For express trains, you must board at the Hunghom railway station in Kowloon.

Timetables change, so departure and arrival times are hardly worth mentioning here; check times when you're in Hong Kong. There are usually three or four express trains a day, and probably more will be put on during the holiday periods. For arrivals and departures there's usually one train early in the morning and two or more in the early afternoon. The whole trip takes a bit less than three hours.

In Hong Kong, tickets can be booked up to seven days before departure at the CTS office at 24-34 Hennessy Rd, Wanchai, and at 62 Sai Yi St, Tak Po Building, Mongkok, Kowloon. Tickets for the day of departure can be bought from Hunghom station. Return tickets are also sold, but only seven to 30 days before departure.

In theory you're allowed to take bicycles on the express train, stowed in the freight car, but this has often been difficult in practice. Some people have had their machines impounded. Cyclists note: from Macau there seems to be no problem.

In Canton you must now buy tickets for all trains, including the Hong-Kong-bound trains, at CITS – which means you will have to pay in FEC.

Bus The Chinese have built a super-highway (China's first) from Hong Kong to Canton and Zhuhai. There are still no express bus services from Hong Kong directly to Canton. However, it is possible to do a combined rail/bus trip from Hong Kong to Canton. Simply take the local train from Kowloon to Lo Wu, cross the border by foot, and hop on one of the numerous minibuses just across the street from the Customs building. Negotiate the fare in advance – they usually expect payment in Hong Kong dollars and will be surprised if you offer FEC.

Some of the luxury resort hotels in Shenzhen run weekend bus excursions across the border, but few travellers are likely to make use of such services.

To/From Macau

On the other side of the border from Macau is the Special Economic Zone (SEZ) of Zhuhai. The part of Zhuhai right on the border is called Gongbei. From Gongbei bus station, which is opposite the Customs building, you can catch buses and minibuses to Canton and other parts of Guangdong Province. You can catch minibuses to Canton on Youyi Lu just west of the Customs building. The Macau-Gongbei border is open from 7 am to 9 pm. Cyclists can ride across. Not many foreigners use this route, but it's perfectly straightforward.

There are several buses per day from Canton's long-distance bus station on Huanshi Xilu (a short walk west of the railway station) to Gongbei. The fare is Y10 on the local bus. The ride to the border takes five hours. Faster and more comfortable are the air-con minibuses which depart from just next to the Liu Hua Hotel – fare is Y20. Air-con buses also depart from the Overseas Chinese Hotel at Haizhu Square.

There is also an express bus service from Macau to Canton. You can buy tickets from Kee Kwan Motors, across the street from the Floating Casino. One bus takes you to the border at Gongbei while a second bus takes you from there to Canton, arriving four hours later.

To/From Pakistan

The Karakoram Highway leading from Kashgar in China's Xinjiang Province into northern Pakistan was closed during and after the civil disturbances in Kashgar in 1990, but is open to tour groups at the time of writing – and to individuals coming from Pakistan. Check with CITS if you want to use this route. If coming the other way, check with the Chinese Embassy in Pakistan to find out. Leaving China for Pakistan takes you through the dramatic snow-covered Karakoram mountain ranges. The road closes every winter, between about November and May, depending on the snow.

Some cyclists have succeeded in riding across the Pakistani border, some have had to put their bikes on a bus, and some have been refused permission altogether.

For details see the Xinjiang chapter.

To/From Nepal

There is a road from Lhasa to Kathmandu, but at the time of writing it was closed to foreigners. Tibet as a whole is closed to independent travellers; if you want to get there you will have to book with a tour group, and you will be charged Y3000 to Y5000 FEC for a package of five to six days in Lhasa. All this may change; check with CITS for the latest details.

One traveller reports that he entered Tibet with a tour group and then did a bunk, travelling alone for a few days. He also encountered someone who had walked from Kathmandu to Lhasa. However, the two of them met up in the Lhasa Public Security Bureau, en route to being deported, and until the political climate in Tibet relaxes a bit, similarly enterprising souls are likely to suffer the same fate.

To/From North Korea

There are twice-weekly trains between Beijing and Pyongyang. Visas can be obtained from the North Korean embassy in Beijing, but your time in North Korea will be both tightly controlled and expensive.

To/From the USSR

There are bus connections between the city of Yining in Xinjiang Province and Alma-Ata in Kazakhstan, but there are some incredible bureaucratic hassles to overcome if you choose this route. See the Xinjiang chapter of this book for details.

A great way to start or finish your China trip is to travel on the Trans-Siberian Railway. Booking tickets or obtaining visas really isn't as mind-bending as people make out, providing you think ahead. Compared with the cost of a boring old flight, the train ride is competitively priced and provides much more scope for meetings and adventures of weird and wonderful dimensions. The Soviet Union is slowly relaxing its tight and expensive grip on tourism so it is possible to visit Moscow and even a few other cities without spending a fortune. Unfortunately, Mongolia is still outrageously expensive if you break your journey there.

For the latest information, contact specialist agencies or national tourist agencies such as Intourist (USSR). For more depth, there's the *Trans-Siberian Rail Guide* by Robert Strauss (Bradt Publications, England, 1987), and the *Trans-Siberian Handbook* by Bryn Thomas (Lascelles, London 1988). Both books are now in the process of being updated.

It can be hard to book this trip during the summer peak season. In the summer of 1990 there was a two-month wait for seats in Beijing. Travel agents in Europe say that it's even difficult to get a September booking in April! Off-season shouldn't be a problem, but plan as fár ahead as possible.

There are three Trans-Siberian Railway routings, with a fourth route through Alma-Ata coming up shortly, but travellers to and from China will normally use the Trans-Mongolian and Trans-Manchurian routes:

Trans-Siberian (Moscow-Khabarovsk-Nakhodka) This is the route for those heading for Japan; from the Soviet port of

Trans-Siberian Rail Guide

Nakhodka near Vladivostok there is a boat to Yokohama and there is also one to Hong Kong. The boat only runs from May to October. You should probably allow about seven days for the Nakhodka-Hong Kong boat journey. Your Intourist rail ticket will be timed to connect with the specific sailing. The 'Rossia' express departs Moscow's Yaroslavsky station daily in the morning and the trip to Nakhodka takes about 8½ days. It is also possible to travel part of the route by air, stopping at Novosibirsk, Irkutsk or Khabarovsk, where you usually stay overnight before picking up the train connection to Nakhodka and Japan. Prices for the complete rail/ship journey from Moscow to Yokohama start from 400 roubles (about US$640) for a 2nd-class sleeper on the train and a four-berth cabin on the ship. Intourist recommends a minimum of four weeks' notice to take care of visas, hotel bookings and train reservations. Further details are available in a special Intourist folder, 'Independent Travel to the USSR – The Trans-Siberian Railway'.

Trans-Manchurian (Moscow-Manzhouli-Beijing) This is the Soviet service, twice weekly in summer, which skirts Mongolia and crosses the border at Manzhouli. The train departs Moscow on Fridays late at night, and arrives in Beijing the following Friday, early in the morning. Prices on this route from Moscow to Beijing start at US$530 for a 2nd-class sleeper in a four-berth compartment. Bought in Beijing or Hong Kong the ticket will cost around US$250. These are official prices, so some slight discounting is possible.

Trans-Mongolian (Moscow-Ulan Bator-Beijing) This one is the Chinese service (generally considered the more comfortable) which passes through Mongolia, crossing the border at Erlian. Trains depart Moscow once a week every Tuesday in the afternoon and arrive in Beijing the following Monday in the afternoon. Prices on this route from Moscow to Beijing start at about US$500 for a 2nd-class sleeper in a four-berth compartment or half that price from Beijing to Moscow.

Alma-Ata Route At the time of writing, a railway line between Ürümqi and Alma-Ata via Korgas is nearing completion, and may be open by the time you read this. This line may allow travellers to bypass Siberia and Moscow and travel through Soviet Central Asia to Warsaw via Kazakhstan.

Visas

The average time required to complete the visa and ticket hurdles is about one month. It is probably less for a simple route on a trip during winter and more for a complex routing on a trip taken in the summer peak period. Visas should be obtained in reverse order; so if you are planning on taking the Trans-Mongolian route into China you should get Chinese, Mongolian, Soviet and Polish visas in that order. A Mongolian visa is unnecessary if you take the Trans-Manchurian.

In Beijing, between seven and 10 days should be allowed for completing all visa and ticket arrangements, providing you're travelling during the quiet end of the season which lasts from December to May.

Make sure you are well supplied with FEC, cash US dollars in small denominations and visa photos. If you didn't bring visa photos with you, they can be obtained quickly at the CITIC building next to the Friendship Store in Beijing.

If you intend going to Finland from Moscow then you do not need a Polish visa – but the Soviet Embassy may not issue you a visa unless you have first obtained a Polish visa. If you are taking the Trans-Mongolian train then your Soviet visa can, if you wish, be issued for the day *after* departure from Beijing, thus giving you an extra day in the USSR since the train takes a day to go through Mongolia.

Chinese Visa There are several ways to obtain a visa for individual travel to China. The first thing to do is try the CITS office or Chinese embassy in whatever country you happen to be in; the embassy in Sweden, for example, was readily handing out visas to Swedish citizens. It is much easier now to obtain one-month or three-month visas which can be extended in the usual way in China. Failing a full tourist visa, between 1 December and 31 March the Chinese embassies will give transit visas of seven days' duration (sometimes three-day extensions are possible) – this will allow you to cross China to Hong Kong, where you can pick up a tourist visa and re-enter the country. The Chinese Embassy in Moscow is at ulitsa Druzhby 6, near Hotel Universitetskaya (nearest Metro stop is Universitet). It has been issuing visas to travellers on their way through to China, but it takes two weeks.

Soviet Visa There is a very big difference between a tourist visa and a transit visa. The Trans-Siberian only requires a transit visa. It is normally possible to arrange a stopover in Moscow for up to three days on a transit visa, and extend it after you arrive there. It's easy to extend your visa if you're staying at a legitimate hotel (as opposed to an illegal hostel). The hotel 'service bureau' will do it for you through Intourist – with hotel bookings, of course.

With a tourist visa, you can stay much longer, but you will pay heavily for the privilege. All hotels must be booked in advance through the official Soviet travel agency, Intourist. Their attitude is to milk travellers for every cent they can get (who said they aren't capitalists?). For a two-star hotel, expect to pay around US$65 outside of Moscow, and US$135 a day in Moscow. The hotel bookings must be confirmed by telex (which you will also have to pay for) and the whole bureaucratic procedure takes about three weeks. On a transit visa, you can sleep in the station or in one of the rapidly proliferating cheap private hostels.

Aside from expense, Soviet tourist visas can be a headache for another reason. Because hotel bookings must be made and paid for in advance, it's more difficult to go *to* the USSR *from* China because of unpredictable long-distance transport – you don't stand much chance of arriving when you're supposed to. But travel from the USSR to China doesn't have this problem.

With the rapid changes taking place in the USSR, it's possible that all this bureaucratic nonsense will suddenly end, maybe even by the time you read this. Let us hope so.

The USSR Embassy in Beijing (☎ 5322051) is just off Dongzhimen, Beizhongjie 4, west of the Sanlitun Embassy Compound. Hours are Monday, Wednesday and Friday from 9 am to 1 pm (the embassy is closed on 7 and 8 November; New Year's Day; 8 March; 1, 2 and 9 May; and also on 7 October). Transit visas are valid for a maximum of 10 days and tourist visas are required if the journey is broken. In practice, you can stay in Moscow for three days on a transit visa and apply for an extension when you arrive. A transit visa can be issued the same day or take three to seven days depending on how much you pay and how busy they are. Visa fees range from Y66 (seven days) to Y106 (one day). Visa charges depend on nationality. Three photos are required. The embassy does not keep your passport, so you are free to travel while your application is being processed.

If you are in Beijing and want a tourist visa rather than a transit visa, it will cost a small fortune. In Beijing, you must make bookings through China Merchant Travel Company – they charge outrageously high rates for hotel rooms, plus vast amounts for telexes (Y40 FEC per telex), a mysterious service charge (Y60 per person), a percentage of any train fares booked, etc. Even taxis to the hotel have to be booked in advance (Y190 for a taxi that should only cost Y5). The whole bureaucratic procedure takes at least three weeks. You'd do better to apply in Kong Kong. None of this applies if you just want a transit visa.

If you arrive in Moscow on a transit visa, you can sleep for free in the waiting hall of Belorussky station (not Yaroslavsky station when you arrive), but lock up your bags in the luggage lockers near the hall. Furthermore, many illegal youth hostels have sprung up in Moscow. Basically, people are turning their apartments into youth hostels and soliciting travellers who arrive off the Trans-Siberian. Costs are low – around US$5 or less per night.

Other Visas Mongolian and Polish transit visas are readily obtainable from the appropriate embassies. Mongolian visas can be issued from their embassy in London in 48 hours – they want to know the exact date you plan to enter. Mongolian visas can also be obtained in 24 hours in Irkutsk at the Mongolian Consulate, ulitsa Lapina 11. Bring passport, photos and onward ticket, with a full itinerary and a formal request for a visa.

The Mongolian Embassy in Beijing (☎ 5321203) is at 2 Xiushui Beijie, Jianguomenwai Compound. Hours are Monday, Tuesday and Friday from 8.30 to 10.30 am. You can get a visa in one day or pick it up the next day even if the visa section is closed. You don't have to show a Soviet visa to get a Mongolian visa. Prices for visas depend on nationality – most foreigners pay US$10, but UK citizens are charged US$16. For visas issued in one day, the fee rises to US$15, or US$24 for the British. It is possible to break your journey in Ulan Bator for one or two days if you book a room in advance by telex and pay a hefty ransom – enquire at the embassy. If you're taking the Trans-Manchurian train then you do not require a Mongolian visa.

The Polish Embassy in Beijing (☎ 5321235) is at 1 Ritan Lu, Jianguomenwai Compound. Hours are Monday, Wednesday and Friday, from 8.30 to 10.30 am in winter; 8 am to noon, and 2 to 5 pm in summer. Transit visas are available in two hours and are valid for two days, require two photos and cost Y26 FEC or Y20 FEC for students.

You can also get Polish visas in Canton at the Polish Consulate on Shamian Island, near the White Swan Hotel. This office issues visas in just 10 minutes. Apparently the visa can also be obtained, more expensively, on the train at the Polish-Soviet border, but this is not certain and may be risky.

The Finnish Embassy in Beijing (☎ 5321817) is at Tayuan Diplomatic Office Building, 1-10-1, 14 Liangmahe Nanlu. Many Western nationals do not need Finnish visas – if in doubt, check.

The Hungarian Embassy in Beijing (☎ 5321431) is at 10 Dongzhimenwai Dajie, open from 9 am to noon. Two photos are needed. Tourist visas are Y70 for next day service, or Y100 for visas issued in about 10 minutes.

Tickets Intourist provides an excellent timetable of the international passenger routes with rail prices. The most expensive section is usually the connection between Europe and Moscow, so you may want to save money by starting your trip in eastern Europe. You could also book an itinerary starting from Berlin or Helsinki, or you could fly to Moscow and continue from there by rail.

Other routes also exist. Prices from Budapest are astoundingly low – between US$70 and US$100 for a ticket from Budapest to Beijing (though it seems that this option is due to be spiked). These tickets are sold without reservations, and getting a reservation, especially for the return portion of the trip, can be difficult. Travelling during low season will improve your chances but don't count on it. You have to reserve a Moscow-Beijing ticket at least two months in advance at the Central Office of the Hungarian State Travel Company (IBUSZ), Tanacs Korut 3/c, Budapest V (office closes at 5 pm on weekdays and at noon on Saturdays) or at MAV-IRODA, Nepkoztarsasag utca, Budapest. Obtain your Chinese and Soviet visas as usual. The Soviet Consulate is at Nepkoztarsasag utca 104 (open Monday, Wednesday and Friday from 10 am to 1 pm). The Mongolian Embassy is on the outskirts of Budapest and issues visas within the hour for US$17 cash – price hikes are frequent, so take more cash.

Daily train services from Budapest to Moscow leave Budapest at night – it's about a 33 to 35-hour trip to Moscow. Two trains depart each night, and the earlier one is usually certain to catch the connection to

Beijing – reservations for this train should also be made well in advance. IBUSZ has offices in most countries, through which some travellers have been able to obtain Trans-Siberian tickets without trekking off to Hungary. IBUSZ sometimes sells tickets, without reservations, for the journey from Beijing to Budapest. However, buying a ticket without a reservation is always a big risk.

Travelling from China to Europe on the Trans-Siberian is easy to organise. All arrangements can be made in Beijing, but it's also possible to book (as far in advance as possible) through agencies in Hong Kong, which will add their fees to the cost of the ticket. Improve your chances by giving alternative dates, and make sure you specify which class you want to travel (deluxe, 1st or 2nd).

If you are travelling from Beijing, tickets can be obtained from the China International Travel Service (CITS) Office in Beijing, which is in the Chongwenmen Hotel, open from 9 am to 12 noon and 2 to 5 pm. Book your seat on the train before you start getting your visas. Once you have the visas, return to CITS and pay for your ticket. If you intend to travel in the peak period from June to September (summer) then you should reserve as soon as possible, preferably two months in advance. Provided your visas are in order, a ticket can be made out to any of the capital cities in eastern Europe. When you arrive in Moscow, reconfirm your onward ticket.

Prices in FEC from Beijing are as follows:

Destination	Hard	Soft	Deluxe
Berlin	1087	1577	1741
Bucharest	1091	1588	1752
Budapest	1053	1526	1690
Moscow	826	1157	1322
Prague	1134	1652	1816
Sofia	1210	1778	1942
Ulan-Bator	255	357	409
Warsaw	992	1427	1591

In Hong Kong, the specialists in the Trans-Siberian route are the staff at Monkey Business (☎ 7231376, fax 7236653), 4th floor, E-Block, Flat 6, Chungking Mansions, Tsimshatsui, Kowloon. They make all arrangements, charge reasonable prices, and seem to be able to get tickets even during the high season. A lot of travellers have had good things to say about this company. Monkey Business also maintains an office in Beijing at the Qiaoyuan Hotel (new building), room 716 (☎ 3012244, ext 716), but it's best to book through their Hong Kong office (as far in advance as possible). Hong Kong is a good place to stock up on cash US dollars in small denominations, visa photos and any foods you crave for the Siberian crossing.

Wallem Travel (☎ 5286514), 46th floor, Hopewell Centre, 183 Queen's Rd East, Wanchai, specialises in travel to the USSR and other eastern European countries. They were the first Hong Kong travel agency accredited by Intourist.

Hong Kong Student Travel Bureau or HKSTB (☎ 7213269), Room 1021, 10th floor, Star House, Salisbury Rd, Tsimshatsui, Kowloon, also arranges Trans-Siberian travel and are agents for SSTS tours. Their prices tend to be on the high side, but they are reliable.

Some Hong Kong travel agents have been selling black-market tickets. These are usually the return portion of a round-trip ticket purchased in Europe. Travellers who don't wish to use the return tickets may sell them either directly to other travellers, or to some unscrupulous travel agents in Hong Kong. The problem is that most of these tickets are open – they don't have a reservation for a definite departure date. Only the Beijing CITS can confirm the reservations for these tickets. The policy of CITS is to confirm tickets bought elsewhere two weeks in advance of departure. During the summer crunch season, it will be nearly impossible to get reservations on such short notice. In other words, these tickets are useless except during the low season (winter).

Travellers have bought these tickets in Hong Kong months in advance because they believed that they had a definite travel date, only to arrive in Beijing and find out that in fact they have no reservation at all! Unless you are absolutely sure that you've got a confirmed reservation, don't buy a black-market ticket.

Several readers have recommended Scandinavian Student Travel Service (SSTS), 117 Hauchsvej, 1825 Copenhagen V, Denmark. This organisation has branch offices in Europe, Hong Kong and North America, and provides a range of basic tours for student or budget travellers (mostly in the summer). Prices start at US$1095 for a 20-day trip from Helsinki to Yokohama via Leningrad, Moscow, Novosibirsk, Irkutsk, Khabarovsk and Nakhodka.

Pre-Departure Tips US dollars in small denominations are essential. Alcohol is not sold on the Trans-Siberian, so bring your own if you want to initiate Siberian train parties.

Food en Route Provisioning on the train is better in summer than in winter. Both food and service are poor on Soviet trains, so stock up with whatever fuels your system. Better still, if you are travelling from China, the Friendship Store in Beijing is an excellent source of all sorts of goodies like coffee, tea, bread, sausage, cakes, sweets and fruit. Apparently the Russians are uneasy about the California fruit fly and have been known to dissect incoming fruit at the border. Rolling through the Soviet Union, you'll find that the Soviet dining car has an impressive menu but 90% of it is bluff. Station kiosks en route sell buns, stuffed rolls and other food. Some travellers have reported difficulty obtaining food during the Mongolian portion of the journey. In the dining cars, you're expected to pay for food in the local currency.

Customs At the Chinese border the train's bogies are changed between narrow gauge (Chinese) and broad gauge (Soviet) while passengers wander around the terminus building. A film theatre offers some distraction. If you are leaving China, you can change FEC back into foreign currency here, but you'll have to be content with whatever foreign currency happens to be in the sack.

At the Soviet border your baggage will be searched, but Customs has lightened up a lot in the last few years. You can buy roubles at the border and in any open stopover city on the Trans-Siberian, but only with hard currency, preferably US$. On exit from the Soviet Union you can exchange roubles to the extent of your total exchange receipts, so hang onto them.

Arrival in Moscow The train usually gets into Moscow's Yaroslavsky station late – very late if you have encountered blizzards. For those who booked a hotel room the Intourist man will be waiting with a transfer taxi usually included in the hotel price. If you haven't booked, you could try sharing with someone who has. If you want to hire a taxi they are notoriously scarce (although foreign currency helps) and drivers are renowned for stinging the unwary with extravagant prices. Get the price straight first; US dollars work wonders.

The metro (underground) is another choice, providing you obtain some five-kopeck coins. Metro is baffling without help, but with a few words in Cyrillic written down by Intourist staff, you can go from Komsomolskaya metro station (beside the Yaroslavsky station) three stops to Belorusskaya station, which is beside Belorussky station (for all trains to the West) – take Koltsevaya Linia (Circle Line). There is an Intourist office at Belorussky station (open from 9 am to 8 pm) where you can buy tickets to the West. You can sleep on the seats in the huge waiting hall but do not forget to use the luggage lockers, as cameras and gear often disappear.

Stock up on food for the rest of the journey – the restaurant car sometimes disappears at the Polish border where the bogies are changed again. At the Polish border you will have your visas, currency forms and papers scrutinised and your baggage searched. For those staying a few days in Moscow you'll find foreign students very friendly and a mine of information regarding accommodation, food and currency if you're on a low budget. However, finding such students isn't particularly easy – be grateful if you run into any by chance.

Arrival in Berlin Berlin's main station is in the western part of the city (Bahnhof Zoo). You can also get off in what used to be East Berlin (Ostbahnhof). If you get off at Ostbahnhof, you can take the underground to Friedrichstrasse to reach the west part of the city.

For a cheap place to stay, try the Jugendgästehaus (Youth Hostel (☎ 2611097), Kluckstrasse 3, Tiergarten. The Mitfahrerzentrale (☎ 6939101) at Willibald-Alexis Strasse 11 offers a cheap service for lifts all over Europe. From the Busbahnhof at Masurenallee (almost opposite the Kongresszentrum ICC) excellent buses run to most major German cities and offer reductions for student-card holders. Onward train connections are available from Bahnhof Zoo. For those under 26 years of age the Transalpino tickets are recommended.

Unless you travel in a group, the selection of travelling companions for the journey is delightfully or excruciatingly random – a judgment upon which you have five or six days to ponder.

On the trip you can get stuck in the cross-fire of political debates, retreat to a chess game, an epic novel or epic paralytic drinking bouts, or teach English to the train attendant. The scenery is mostly melancholic birch trees, but there are some occasionally fascinating views – snow on the Mongolian desert and the scenery around Lake Baikal, the deepest lake in the world.

At sub-zero temperatures you can exercise along the platform, start snowball fights or wonder about the destination of teenage recruits milling around a troop train. In these stations, make sure your luggage is secure – during the few minutes that you're out on the platform, a sneak thief could pinch your camera and other valuables. A few travellers have reported such thefts.

A chess set soon makes friends. The Russians produce not only talented players but also courteous ones – perhaps as a gesture of friendship they'll quickly cede the first game but the rest are won with monotonous regularity. Prodigious amounts of alcohol disappear down Soviet throats, so expect a delighted interest in consuming your hoard of Chinese alcohol – for which there is plenty of time. On the other hand, if you want to repulse freeloaders you might try injecting them with a bottle of one of those ghastly Chinese liqueurs – the recipient is either going to stagger out in absolute revulsion or remain vaccinated and your stock is doomed.

For those interested in barter or fund-raising: tea, watches, jeans and Walkman cassette recorders are all sources of inspiration to passengers...Import of roubles is forbidden, as is changing money on the black market.

BOAT

Overnight to Canton

The Pearl River Shipping Company runs two overnight ferries between Hong Kong and Canton. They are the *Tianhu* and the *Xinghu*. One ship departs Hong Kong daily from the China Ferry Terminal in Kowloon at 9 pm and arrives in Canton the following morning at 7 am. In Canton the other ship departs at 9 pm and arrives in Hong Kong at 7 am. The ferry is one of the best and most popular ways of getting to Canton. The vessels are large, clean and very comfortable – but bring a light jacket because the air-conditioning is fierce!

For ferries to Canton you can book tickets at the China Ferry Terminal, Canton Rd, Tsimshatsui, Kowloon. Some of the agencies that issue China visas will also make bookings on this boat for you, but typically charge a HK$25 booking fee. There are no ferries on the 31st of each month. The fares per person follow.

	The *Xinghu*	The *Tianhu*
2-person cabin	HK$180	HK$180
4-person cabin	HK$160	HK$140
dormitory bunk	HK$120	HK$120
seat only	HK$90	not available

If you can't get a cabin or a bunk then buy a seat ticket, and as soon as you get on board go to the purser's office. The purser distributes leftover bunks and cabins, but act quickly if you want one.

Ferries (and some of the hovercraft) to Hong Kong depart from Canton's Zhoutouzui Wharf. For details see the Canton chapter. Fares from Canton to Hong Kong are:

	The *Xinghu*	The *Tianhu*
2-person cabin	Y90	Y90
4-person cabin	Y80	Y70
dormitory bunk	Y60	Y60
seat only	Y54	not available

Hovercraft

The hovercraft depart from the China Ferry Terminal, Canton Rd, Tsimshatsui, Kowloon and dock at Canton's Zhoutouzui Wharf in the south-west of the city. There are several departures daily. The trip takes three hours and the fare is about HK$180.

Tickets can be bought right at the China Ferry Terminal or the offices of the Hong Kong & Yaumati Ferry Company (☎ 5423081), 1st floor, Central Harbour Services Pier, Pier Rd, Hong Kong Island. Tickets can also be purchased at China Travel Service but you'll have to pay a HK$25 service charge.

Hovercraft to Hong Kong depart from Canton's Zhoutouzui Wharf. The fare is about Y90. Tickets can be bought from the CTS office at Haizhu Square and at the White Swan Hotel service desk. It's also easy to buy them at the wharf.

Macau Ferry

There is a ferry from Macau to Canton's Zhoutouzui Wharf. You can buy tickets from the China Travel Service (Ground Floor, Metropole Hotel, 63 Rua da Praia Grande) or at the ferry pier.

The ferry from Canton to Macau departs Canton's Zhoutouzui Wharf. Buy tickets at the wharf or from the White Swan Hotel.

Hong Kong to Shanghai

Two boats, the *Shanghai* and the *Haixing*, ply the south-east coast between Hong Kong and Shanghai. There are departures every five days. Many people take the boat when they leave China to return to Hong Kong – the trip gets rave reviews. Details of tickets and fares for the trip from Shanghai to Hong Kong are given in the Shanghai section. The fares for the trip from Hong Kong to Shanghai *per person* are:

Class	The *Shanghai*	The *Haixing*
Special A	2 people, HK$1060	2 people, HK$983
1st A	1-person cabin, HK$905	1-person cabin, HK$905
1st B	3-person cabin HK$826	3-person cabin, HK$826
2nd A	2 or 3 people, HK$783	3 people, HK$783
2nd B	3 people, HK$722	2 people, HK$722
3rd A	2 people, HK$665	2, 3 or 4 people, HK$665
3rd B	4 people, HK$609	2 people, HK$609
Economy	Dormitory HK$522	Dormitory HK$522

In Hong Kong, tickets for the boat can be bought from the offices of China Travel Service and from the China Merchants Steam Navigation Company (☎ 5440558, 5430945), 18th floor, 152-155 Connaught Rd, Central District, Hong Kong Island. See the Shanghai chapter for details of tickets and fares from Shanghai to Hong Kong.

Other Ships from Hong Kong

A couple of boats travel to Chinese ports on the south-east coast. These are worth investigating since the coast is one of the most attractive parts of China, and some of the most interesting towns are located here.

To/From Shantou & Xiamen The *Dinghu* plies the water between Hong Kong and Shantou, and the *Jimei* and *Gulangyu* run between Hong Kong and Xiamen. Fares from Hong Kong to Xiamen start at HK$407 for a dorm bed.

To/From Hainan Island There are direct boats from Hong Kong to Haikou and Sanya on Hainan Island. From Hong Kong to Haikou takes about 18 hours; fares start at HK$193. Hong Kong to Sanya takes about 28 hours; fares start at HK$217 (Y70 in the other direction). There are about four departures a month to both these places.

To/From Wuzhou There is a direct hovercraft from Hong Kong to Wuzhou. It departs

Hong Kong on even-numbered dates from the China Ferry Terminal at 7.20 am. The trip takes around 10 hours and the fare is HK$297. Tickets in Hong Kong can be bought at the China Travel Service and from some of the other agencies that issue China visas. Round-trip tickets can also be booked, but you must return within a month.

From Wuzhou you can get a bus to Guilin or Yangshuo, but you have to overnight in Wuzhou. Returning to Hong Kong, the hovercraft departs Wuzhou on odd-numbered dates at 7.30 am. The fare is Y80. Check the departure time before leaving.

To/From Japan

There is a regular boat service between Shanghai and Osaka/Kobe. The ship departs once weekly, one week to Osaka and the next week to Kobe, and takes two days. The cost is US$120.

To/From Korea

There is now a twice-weekly boat between Inchon in South Korea and Weihai in Shandong, leaving Inchon every Wednesday and Saturday at 4pm and arriving at Weihai the next day at 9am. The cost is US$90 (economy class), US$110 (2nd class), and US$130 (1st class). Tickets are available in China from CITS in Weihai from the boat harbour. In Seoul, tickets can be bought from the Universal Travel Service (UTS) behind City Hall, just near the Seoul city tourist information centre, or from the Unification Church's Seil Tour System, 3th, Dowon Building, 292-20 Tohwa-Dong, Mapo-Gu, Seoul (☎ 7016611). CTS in Seoul will get you a Chinese visa but will charge you US$100. It's cheaper to get a Chinese visa before coming to Korea, but don't forget that Chinese visas are only valid for three months from the date of issue. At the time of writing, there is no Chinese embassy in South Korea.

TOURS

Tour groups are still considered the darlings of Chinese who have to deal with foreigners. It is much easier for the Chinese if you arrive in a tour group, if all your accommodation is pre-booked, and if everyone sits down at the same time to eat. If there's a CITS interpreter on hand someone doesn't have to struggle with a phrasebook or pidgin English. Groups don't make a nuisance of themselves by trying to go to closed places, and they usually channel complaints through the tour leader rather than hassle the desk clerk. Most importantly, tour groups spend more money.

Are tours worth it to you? Unless you simply cannot make your own way around, then probably not. Apart from the expense, they tend to screen you even more from some of the basic realities of China travel. Most people who come back with glowing reports of the People's Republic never had to travel bottom class on the trains or battle their way on board a local bus in the whole three weeks of their stay. On the other hand, if your time is limited and you just want to see the Forbidden City and the hills of Guilin, then the brief tours from Hong Kong, though expensive, might be worth considering.

One thing you will never be able to complain about on a tour is not being shown enough. Itineraries are jam-packed and the Chinese expect stamina from their guests. The tour may include an early breakfast, a visit to a market, a morning's sightseeing, an afternoon visit to a school and a shopping session, and it may not finish until 10 pm after a visit to the local opera.

Stays in cities are short and in your few weeks in China you're whisked from place to place at a furious rate.

Nor could you complain about the quantity of food – you may complain about the quality or degree of imagination involved in the cooking, but there is no way the Chinese will let you starve.

One advantage of being on a tour is that you may get into places that individuals often can't – such as factories.

From Hong Kong & Macau

There are innumerable tours you can make from Hong Kong or Macau. The best people to go to if you want to find out what's available are the Hong Kong travel agents, the

Hong Kong Student Travel Bureau or China Travel Service.

Also worth trying is the August Moon Tour & Travel Agency (☎ 3693151), Ground Floor, Milton Mansion, 96 Nathan Rd, Tsimshatsui, Kowloon; they keep a pretty good stock of leaflets and information on a whole range of tours to China. You usually have to book tours one or two days in advance.

We could go on endlessly regurgitating all the tours to China. A lot of people seem to enjoy the one-day tours to the Special Economic Zones (SEZs) – Shenzhen near Hong Kong and Zhuhai near Macau. The tour to Zhuhai seems to be more rewarding, but there's even a tour that includes both SEZs in one day. The day tours include lunch, transport and all admission fees. Prices hover around HK$380.

There are one-day tours to Canton and tours of several days' length which include Canton, Zhongshan, Shiqi, Zhaoqing and Foshan. Many other combinations are possible.

Essentially the same tours can be booked in Macau. This can be done at the China Travel Service office (Ground Floor, Metropole Hotel, 63 Rua de Praia Grande) or the travel agents in the large tourist hotels which have English-speaking staff.

Tours further afield are also available in Hong Kong. Prices aren't cheap, but it depends on where you're going – a five-day Canton-Guilin tour costs HK$2280 and a nine-day Canton-Guilin-Beijing tour is HK$5980.

Warning We have had many negative comments from people who have booked extended tours through CTS and CITS. Although the one-day tours seem to be OK, tours further afield frequently go awry. The most significant complaints have been about ridiculous overcharging for substandard accommodation and tours being cut short to make up for transport delays. Some people have booked a tour only to find that they were the sole person on the tour. No refunds are given if you cancel – you forfeit the full amount. Other travellers report additional charges being tacked on which were not mentioned in the original agreement.

CITS drivers have been known to show up with all their relatives who want to tag along for free. One traveller reported booking a week-long tour – the female driver showed up with her boyfriend and asked if he could come along. The traveller foolishly agreed. At the first lunch stop, the driver and her boyfriend took off and left the foreigner behind – the couple then apparently spent the rest of the week enjoying a honeymoon at the traveller's prepaid hotel rooms!

From Western Countries

These tours are handled by innumerable travel agents and any of them worth their commission will still tell you that you can't go to China except on a tour. They usually offer the standard tours that whip you round Beijing, Shanghai, Guilin, Xi'an, etc.

In an attempt to spice up the offerings the Chinese have come up with some new formulas. These include honeymoon tours (how many in the group?); acupuncture courses; special-interest tours for botanists, railway enthusiasts, lawyers and potters; trekking tours to Tibet and Qinghai; women's tours; bicycle tours, and Chinese-language courses. Check with your local travel agent.

Volunteer Expeditions

Some organisations need paying helpers to assist on projects. This is a contribution to the cost of the project and you have to pay your own air fares and living expenses to and on site. On many of these projects they expect you to work hard – it may be emotionally rewarding but don't necessarily expect it to feel like a holiday.

In the USA you can order the book *Volunteer! The Comprehensive Guide to Voluntary Service in the US and Abroad* published by the Council on International Educational Exchange (CIEE). You can contact their publications office (☎ (212) 6611450), CIEE, Publications Department, 205 East 42nd St, New York, NY 10017, USA.

Mountaineering & Trekking Tours

Mountaineering and trekking tours to China are organised by various agents in the west, but the prices are too high for low-budget travellers. Trekking is administered and arranged by the Chinese Mountaineering Association under the same rules that apply to mountaineering in China. The CMA makes all arrangements for a trek with the assistance of provincial mountaineering associations and local authorities.

The first few trekkers were allowed into China only in 1980 and the first groups were organised in 1981. Because trekking comes under the mountaineering rules, all treks must be near one of the peaks open for mountaineering – these regions span the country and vary from the plains of Tibet to the lush bamboo forests of Sichuan Province and the open plains of Xinjiang.

Various travel agents will book you through to these operators. Scan their literature carefully – sometimes the tours can be done just as easily on your own. What you want are places that individuals have trouble getting into.

If you can afford it, a few mountaineering, trekking and cycling tour operators are:

USA Mountain Travel (☎ (415) 5278100), 6420 Fairmount Avenue, El Cerrito, California; Wilderness Travel (☎ (415) 5480420), 801 Allston Way, Berkeley, California; Ocean Voyages (☎ (415) 3324681), 1709 Bridgeway, Sausalito, California 94965. Also check the special outings issues of *Sierra* magazine, published by the Sierra Club (☎ (415) 7762211), 730 Polk St, San Francisco, California 94109.

Australia World Expeditions, formerly Australian Himalayan Expeditions (☎ (02) 49 6634), 159 Cathedral St, Woolloomooloo, Sydney, 2011. Tail Winds Bicycle Touring, PO Box 32, O'Connor, ACT, 2601. The Trekking Company, GPO Box 1900, Canberra, ACT 2601.

England Voyages Jules Verne (☎ 01-486 8080), 10 Glentworth St, London NW1. Society for Anglo-Chinese Understanding (☎ 01-267 9841), 152 Camden High St, London NW1. Both of these will provide individual travel arrangements (including visa) as well as tours. Voyages Jules Verne also has an office in Hong Kong at Room 214, 2nd floor, Lee Gardens Hotel, Hysan Avenue, Hong Kong Island.

Hong Kong In Hong Kong several operators organise interesting trips, such as cycling and commune living. Try the Hong Kong Student Travel Bureau or HKSTB (☎ 7213269 or 3693804), Room 1021, 10th floor, Star House, Salisbury Rd, Tsimshatsui, Kowloon; and the China Youth Travel Service, Room 904, Nanyang Commercial Bank Building, 151 des Voeux Rd, Hong Kong Island. CYTS is the younger arm of CITS and they liaise with many foreign student organisations and groups. Mera Travel Services Ltd, Room 1308, Argyle Centre, Phase 1, 688 Nathan Rd, Kowloon does trekking tours to Tibet, Nepal and India.

Getting Around

AIR

CAAC – Civil Aviation Administration of China – is China's domestic and international carrier. Its flights cover about 80 cities and towns throughout the country. For details of international flights, see the Getting There & Away chapter.

Timetables

CAAC publishes a combined international and domestic timetable in both English and Chinese in April and November each year. These can be bought at most CAAC offices in China or from the CAAC office in Hong Kong (Ground Floor, Gloucester Tower, des Voeux Rd, Central District, Hong Kong Island, (☎ 5216416)). The timetable could also serve as a useful phrasebook of Chinese place names, but it's filled with misspellings.

Fares

Foreigners pay a surcharge of 100% to 160% of the fare charged local Chinese people. Unlike the situation with trains, there is no way past this CAAC regulation, except perhaps for foreign experts. If you do somehow happen to get Chinese price and it's discovered, your ticket will be confiscated and no refund given. However, with a white card you can at least pay in RMB. Children over 12 are charged adult fare.

Cancellation fees depend on how long before departure you cancel. On domestic flights if you cancel 24 hours before depar-

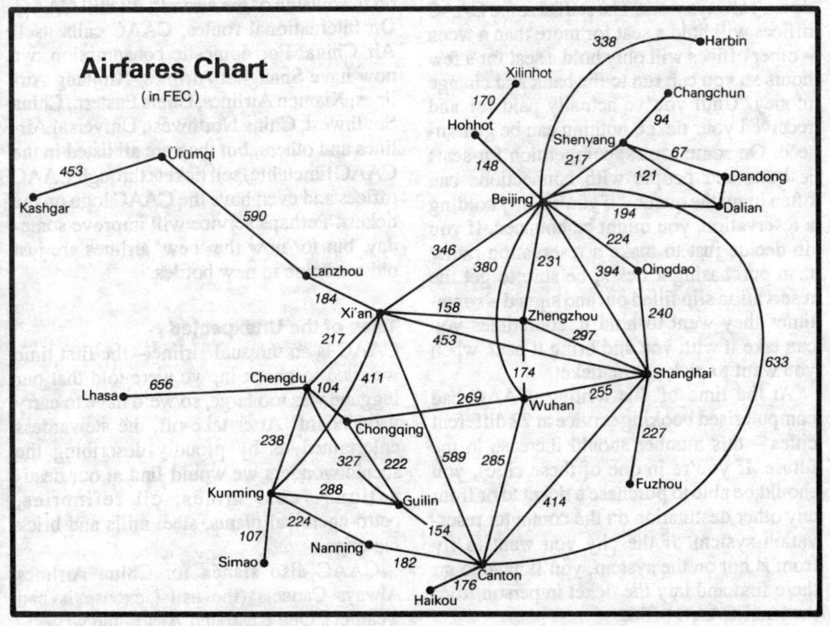

ture you lose 10% of the fare; if you cancel between two and 24 hours before the flight you lose 20%; and if you cancel less than two hours before the flight you lose 50%. If you don't show up for a domestic flight, your ticket is cancelled and there is no refund.

Baggage
On domestic and international flights the free-baggage allowance for an adult passenger is 20 kg in economy class and 30 kg in 1st class. You are also allowed five kg of hand luggage, though this is rarely weighed.

Stand-by
This does exist on CAAC flights. Some seats are always reserved in case a high-ranking cadre turns up at the last moment. If no one shows up it should be possible to get on board.

Reservations
In theory, you can reserve seats on CAAC without paying for them. In practice, this doesn't always work. The staff at some CAAC offices will hold a seat for more than a week – other offices will only hold a seat for a few hours so you can run to the bank and change money. Until you've actually paid for and received your ticket, nothing can be guaranteed. On some routes, competition for seats is keen and people with connections can often jump the queue – if you're only holding a reservation, you might be bounced. If you do decide just to make a reservation rather than purchasing a ticket, be sure to get the reservation slip filled out and signed – sometimes they want to hold it, sometimes you can take it with you and bring it back when you want to pick up the ticket.

At the time of this writing, CAAC had computerised booking service at 22 different cities – this number should increase in the future. If you're in one of these cities, you should be able to purchase a ticket to or from any other destination on the computer reservation system. If the city you want to fly from is not on the system, you'll have to go there first and buy the ticket in person from the local CAAC office.

Airport Tax
There is no airport tax on domestic flights. On international flights there is an airport departure tax of Y20.

Service
Basically there is none on domestic flights. On international flights there is however a concerted attempt to keep up appearances, and the hostesses have spiffy uniforms and make-up and get their training in Japan. On domestic flights you'll probably be given a little bag or two of sweets, or a key ring as a souvenir – almost justifies the 100% tourist surcharge.

Other Airlines
In order to spur competition and thus improve service, the Chinese government has made it a policy to break up CAAC and develop other competing airlines. While this sounds good in theory, in practice it has meant little. While they've painted new names on the outside of the aircraft, it's still CAAC. On international routes, CAAC calls itself Air China. For domestic consumption, we now have Shanghai Airlines, Xinjiang Airlines, Xiamen Airlines, China Eastern, China Southwest, China Northwest, Universal Airlines and others, but they are all listed in the CAAC timetable, sell tickets through CAAC offices and even have the CAAC logo on the tickets. Perhaps service will improve someday, but for now the 'new' airlines are just old medicine in new bottles.

Tales of the Unexpected
CAAC is an unusual airline – the first time we tried to check in, we were told that our luggage was too large, so we'd have to carry it on board! After take-off, the stewardess entertained us by proudly describing the scenic wonders we would find at our destination – coal mines, oil refineries, petro-chemical plants, steel mills and brick factories.

CAAC also stands for China Airlines Always Cancels (the usual excuse is bad weather). One frustrated Australian writes:

I don't believe Xi'an actually has an airport. It's certainly not worth trying to save time getting there by flying. Our flight was cancelled several times between Wednesday night and Friday night. It finally went on Saturday night, but we got in on the train some hours earlier. One other guidebook says that Xi'an airport has no radar. I reckon it's got no runway. Over three days of cancellations they got a bit bored with bad weather, and they came up with some beauties, like the plane having left Xi'an to fly to Beijing for us to fly back on it, but by mistake it had flown to Lengdu (or Nanso, depending on who you asked). Try to find those towns; I couldn't. Later we found it had left Lengdu (or Nanso) but they couldn't even estimate when it might arrive in Beijing. I thought I'd ask how long it usually takes to fly from Lengdu (or Nanso) to Beijing, to put an outside limit on the estimate of when we might actually do some flying ourselves, but it seems no one knows how long this flight lasts. The flight was cancelled about a half-hour after all luggage had been checked in. We'd already got a refund.

CAAC is responsible for your meals and hotels whenever a flight is delayed beyond a reasonable amount of time. Just what constitutes 'reasonable' may be subject to interpretation, but in general CAAC will take care of you. Delays are so common that almost every airport has a CAAC-run hotel where you can stay for free. Many foreign travellers don't realise this and wind up paying for a hotel when it isn't necessary.

Delays are inconvenient, but more worrisome is that CAAC also stands for China Airlines Almost Crashes. The airline's safety record appears to be a poor one – but no information on crashes or incidents is released unless there are foreigners on board.

While CAAC operates at a profit, it seems that little of that goes into maintenance, equipment, upgrading the antique planes or purchasing new aircraft. Things are improving on some runs. There are Boeing 737s out of Canton, and 707s and 747s out of Beijing and Shanghai. Yun-5, Yun-7 and Yun-10 jets (made-in-Xi'an copies of Western aircraft) have come into service.

The basic problem with CAAC is old technology. For the international runs they use nice, relatively new Boeings. But on the domestic runs it's sometimes old Russian turbo-props (like the Antonovs) designed and built back in the 1950s. The worst models are relegated to the lesser-known runs and may have no seat belts, oxygen masks, life jackets or fire extinguishers, and sometimes the freight blocks the emergency exits. Finding parts and skilled mechanics to maintain such a wide variety of vintage aircraft remains a serious problem. We don't want to scare you off flying CAAC, but these stories persist. Those who are injured or killed in CAAC domestic crashes aren't likely to receive much in the way of financial com-pensation. The CAAC timetable states that the maximum amount paid for accidental injury or death will be Y20,000 (less than US$4300) – though you may qualify for a ticket refund too.

A classic:

amused passengers watched the pilot (returning from the toilet) locked out of the cockpit by a jammed door. The co-pilot opened the door from within, then both men fiddled with the catch and succeeded in locking themselves out of the cockpit. As passengers stared in disbelief the pilot and co-pilot attacked the door with a fire-axe, pausing for a moment to draw a curtain between themselves and the audience.

Hijackings have added a new dimension to the fire-axe routine. In January 1983 a hijacker fatally shot a pilot after ordering a diversion to Taiwan; the hijacker was then axed by the navigator. Heroics in the air is the Chinese way of dealing with the menace of pirates aloft – the motherland does not like to lose planes, especially to Taiwan. In July 1982 a Shanghai-bound plane was hijacked by five Chinese youths armed with sticks of dynamite, who ordered the plane to go to Taiwan. The pilot's response was to fly around in circles until the fuel was almost exhausted, whereupon the crew led passengers in an attack on the pirates with umbrellas and mop handles. The CAAC version of this near-calamity reads, 'The heroic deeds of the crew...showed the firm standpoint of their love for the Party and our socialist motherland...they feared no sacrifice...' The captain of the flight was awarded a special title created by the State Council – 'anti-hijacking hero'. Similar honours were bestowed on the crew of a plane hijacked to South Korea on 5 May 1983.

CAAC's worst reported crash occurred in October 1990 at Canton's Baiyun Airport – 127 passengers were killed. The cause was an abortive hijacking. As a result, Taiwan's government announced that hijackers would no longer receive political asylum and would immediately be returned to the mainland – where they would most likely receive the customary bullet in the back of the head. However, Taiwan still offers large rewards (paid in gold) to defecting Chinese air force pilots because the Communists still make verbal military threats against Taiwan.

Try to score a copy of CAAC's glossy in-flight magazines (produced in Japan) – these could be a collector's item someday. They're full of heroic folk tales about air crews and their flawless safety records, doctored folk tales, how the attendant at a CAAC hostel in Beijing found a million yen and rushed after the passenger to whom it belonged. There are even some safety tips.

BUS

Long-distance buses are one of the best means of getting around the country. Services are extensive and main roads are usually good though you'll get your fair share of rough rides. Nevertheless, since the buses stop every so often in small towns and villages you get to see bits of the countryside you wouldn't if you only travelled on the trains. Bus travel is not especially cheap when compared to hard-seats on trains, but you have to take into account that there is no double-pricing system on buses. So if it's a choice between a tourist-price hard-seat ticket on the train and a bus ticket then the bus might come out slightly cheaper.

It's a good idea to book a seat in advance. All seats are numbered. Buses depart from separate bus stations which are often large affairs with numerous ticket windows and waiting halls. The symbol for a bus station is:

Safety is another consideration. Accidents are frequent, especially on winding mountain roads. Foreigners have been injured and killed in bus crashes – there is very little you can do to protect yourself. The government-run buses seem to be somewhat safer than the private ones – if a driver of a government bus causes an accident, he can be imprisoned.

If possible, try to avoid sitting at the rear of the bus since it's painful for the shock-absorbers in your back. Many long-distance buses have stereo speakers – the drivers blast out your eardrums with screeching music. Try to select a seat as far away from the speakers as possible. Chinese law requires a driver to announce his presence to cyclists, and for this he uses a tweeter for preliminaries, a bugle or bullhorn if he gets annoyed and an ear-wrenching air-horn if he really gets stirred up. Bus drivers have the peculiar habit of shutting off the engine every time they stop, even if only for a second – this is supposed to save petrol.

Astronaut-type backpacks are a near-disaster to stow on buses – there's little space under the seats, no overhead racks, and sparse space in the aisles. If you intend doing a lot of bus travelling then travel light! In China, unlike other Asian countries, people do not ride on the roof – though luggage is sometimes stowed there.

Buses do not travel at night; about eight to 14 hours a day appears to be the maximum driving time. This includes a short lunch break and assumes that there are no breakdowns; some of the geriatric models are prone to collapses on longer trips, but you'll be amazed how the old crates keep going. If the trip is a long one you'll stay overnight at a hotel en route and the bus will carry on the next morning.

TRAIN

Trains are the best way to get around in reasonable speed and comfort. The network covers every province except Tibet, and that's next. There are an estimated 52,000 km of railway lines in China, most of them built since 1949 when the system had either been blown to bits or was nonexistent in certain regions.

The safety record of the railway system is good – other than getting your luggage pinched or your pocket picked, there isn't much danger on trains. However, the Chinese have a habit of throwing rubbish out the windows even as the train moves through a station. Avoid standing too close to a passing train, lest you get hit by flying beer bottles or chicken bones.

Classes

In socialist China there are no classes; instead you have hard-seat, hard-sleeper, soft-seat and soft-sleeper.

Hard-Seat Except on the trains which serve some of the branch or more obscure lines, hard-seat is not in fact hard but is padded. But it's hard on your sanity and you'll get little sleep on the upright seats. Since hard-seat is the only thing the locals can afford it's packed out to the gills, the lights stay on all night, passengers spit on the floor, and the carriage speakers endlessly drone news, weather, information and music. Hard-seat is OK for a day trip; some foreigners don't take more than five hours of it, while others have a threshold of 12 hours or even longer. A few brave, penniless souls have even been known to travel *long-distance* this way – some roll out a mat on the floor under the seats and go to sleep on top of the gob.

Hard-Sleeper These are very comfortable and only a fixed number of people are allowed in the sleeper carriage. The carriage is made up of doorless compartments with half a dozen bunks in three tiers, and sheets, pillows and blankets are provided. It does very nicely as an overnight hotel. The best bunk to get is a middle one since the lower one is invaded by all and sundry who use it as a seat during the day, while the top one has little headroom. The worst possible bunks are the top ones at either end of the carriage or right in the middle; they've right up against the speakers and you'll get a rude shock in the morning about 6 am. Lights and speakers in hard-sleeper go out at around 9.30 to 10 pm. Few ordinary Chinese can afford hard-sleeper; those who use it are either the new class of nouveau-riche or privileged cadres on their way to conferences whose travel is being paid for by the state.

Soft-Seat On shorter journeys (such as Shenzhen to Canton) some trains have soft-seat carriages. The seats are comfortable and overcrowding is not permitted. They cost about the same as hard-sleeper and are well worth it, but soft-seat cars are a rarity.

Soft-Sleeper Luxury. Softies get the works with four comfortable bunks in a closed compartment – complete with straps to stop the top fatso from falling off in the middle of the night, wood panelling, potted plant, lace curtains, teacup set, clean washrooms, carpets (so no spitting), and often air-conditioning. As for those speakers, not only do you have a volume control, you can turn the bloody things off! Soft-sleeper costs twice as much as hard-sleeper, and almost the same price as flying (on some routes even *more* than flying!). It's relatively easy to get soft-sleeper because few Chinese (except high-ranking cadres who charge it to their state expense accounts) can afford it. Travelling in soft-sleeper should be experienced once – it gives you a good chance to meet the ruling class.

Train Types Train composition varies from line to line and also from day to night, and largely depends on the demand for sleepers on that line. A typical high-frequency train line has about 13 carriages: six hard-seat, perhaps one soft-seat, three hard-sleeper, one soft-sleeper, one dining car and one guard/baggage van.

Half or even a whole carriage may be devoted to crew quarters on the longer trips. If the journey time is more than 12 hours then the train qualifies as a dining car. The dining car often separates the hard-seat carriages from the hard-sleeper and soft-sleeper carriages.

The conductor is in a little booth in a

hard-seat carriage at the middle of the train – usually carriage No 7, 8 or 9 (all carriages are numbered on the outside). Coal-fired samovars are found in the ends of the hard-class sections, and from these you can draw a supply of hot water. The disc-jockey has a little booth at the end of one of the cars with a door marked *Boyinshi*, which apart from the reel-to-reel tape, radio and record player also contains the attendant's bed.

On some of the small branch lines there are various kinds of passenger carriages – some have long bench seats along the walls, others are just cattle cars without seats or windows.

Different types of train are usually recognisable by the train number:

Nos 1-90 These are special express and usually diesel-hauled. They have all classes and there is a surcharge for the speed and superior facilities. The international trains are included in this group.

Nos 100-350 Trains in this approximate number range make more stops than the special expresses. They have soft and hard-sleepers, but fewer of them. The speed surcharge is half that of the special expresses but the difference in overall price is minimal.

Nos 400 & 500 These are slow, and stop at everything they can find. They may have hard wooden seats and no sleepers. They should have soft-seats, but these will be equivalent to the hard-seats on the fast trains. The trains have antique fittings, lamps and wood panelling, and are usually steam-pulled. There is no speed surcharge as there is no speed.

No 700 These trains take suburban routes.

Apart from the speed breakdown, the numbers don't really tell you much else about the train. As a general rule, the outbound and inbound trains have matching numbers; thus train Nos 79/80 divide into No 79 leaving Shanghai and going to Kunming, and No 80 leaving Kunming and going to Shanghai.

However, there are for example at least six different trains listed in the Chinese train timetable under Nos 301/302, and the sequence-number match is not always reliable. Trains also appear to shift numbers from one timetable to the following year's timetable, so train No 175 becomes train No 275. Simple.

Reservations & Tickets

Buying hard-seat tickets at short notice is usually no hassle, though you will not always be successful in getting a reserved seat. Buying a ticket for a sleeper can be more problematic.

Tickets for sleepers are only sold in major cities, not in quiet backwaters. Furthermore, demand usually exceeds supply so they often sell out, especially of the hard-sleepers. Your chances of getting a sleeper increase significantly if you buy the ticket several days in advance.

Tickets can be bought in advance from CITS and CTS offices, from some major tourist hotels, from advance-booking offices or the railway stations themselves.

You can buy tickets the night before departure or on the day of departure from the railway station. This often involves long queues, and in large cities the 'queues' can become near-riots. Some stations are better than others. Tickets bought on the same day will usually be unreserved – you get on board and try and find a place for your bum.

As soon as the train pulls into the station, all hell breaks loose. In the hopes of getting a seat, hard-seat passengers charge at the train, often pushing exiting passengers back inside. Some would-be travellers climb through the windows.

Having experienced this situation many times, we've come to the conclusion that your best bet is to head for either the very front or very rear of the train if you don't have a reserved seat. Most passengers attack the middle of the train – the part closest to the platform entrance gate. If you have a reserved seat, you are spared all this – just wait for the riot to end, then quietly get on and claim your seat.

If you get on the train with an unreserved seating ticket, you can seek out the conductor and upgrade yourself to a hard-sleeper if there are any available. On some trains it's easy to get a sleeper but others are notoriously crowded. A lot of intermediary stations along the railway lines can't issue sleepers, so you just have to buy a hard-seat ticket, hop on the train and hope like everybody else.

If the sleeper carriages are full then you may have to wait until someone gets off. That sleeper may only be available to you until the next major station which is allowed to issue sleepers, but you may be able to get several hours of sleep. The sleeper price will be calculated for the distance that you used it for.

Another possibility is not to bother with a ticket at all and simply walk on to the train. To do this, you need to buy a platform ticket (*zhàntái piào*).

These are available from the station's information booth for a few jiao. You then buy your ticket on the train. This method is usually more hassle than it's worth, but may be necessary if you arrive at the station without enough time to get your ticket.

If you're buying a ticket from the railway station, then you should write down clearly on a piece of paper what you want: train number, time, date, class of travel. The appropriate characters and phrases can be copied from a phrasebook. Learn a few key phrases like 'tomorrow' and 'hard-sleeper'. English-speaking Chinese people are always willing to translate and there are usually one or two around in the larger places.

If you have a sleeper ticket the carriage attendant will take it from you and give you a metal or plastic chit – when your destination is close he or she will swap it back and give you the original ticket. Keep your ticket until you get through the barriers at the other end, as you'll need to show it there.

Black-Market Tickets These certainly exist and many travellers have made use of them. The way it works is that some local Chinese buy up hard-sleepers on the most popular lines (which frequently sell out), then sell these tickets to travellers (both Chinese and foreigners) at marked-up prices. The black marketeers usually stand outside the station hawking their tickets. This is supposedly illegal, but they may be paying off the local police too.

Since foreigners have to pay double anyway, black-market tickets can be a bargain even if they cost more than the usual Chinese price. However, be sure you know just what you're looking for as far as a legitimate ticket goes! Otherwise, you could be buying a worthless piece of cardboard, or a hard-seat when you expected a hard-sleeper.

Ticket Validity Tickets are valid from one to seven days depending on the distance travelled. On a cardboard ticket the number of days is printed at the bottom left-hand corner. If you go 250 km it's valid for two days; 500 km, three days; 1000 km, three days; 2000 km, six days; about 2500 km, seven days.

Thus if you're travelling along a major line you could (theoretically) buy one ticket and break the journey where you feel like it. This will only work for unreserved hard seats. The advantage of this method is that you can keep away from railway ticket windows for a while; you can get off, find a refreshing hotel, and get back on board the next day on the same ticket.

So much for theory – nothing is consistent in China. In some stations, the railway workers won't let you board unless you hold a ticket for the exact date and time of departure. If you buy a ticket for a morning train (unreserved hard-seat) and try to take a later train the same day, they may refuse to let you board even though the ticket is still valid!

Given the fact that the rules are subject to the unpredictable whims of various railway workers, you'll probably wind up just buying tickets for the exact time and date you intend to depart.

Timetables There are paperback railway timetables in both Chinese and English. The English timetables are hard to find in China. In Beijing, they can bought at the special ticket window for foreigners. They can also be found in Hong Kong – Swindon's Bookstore sells them. The English name is simply *China Railway Timetable*.

No matter where you get them, the timetables are so excruciatingly detailed that it's a drag working your way through them. Even the Chinese complain about this.

Thinner versions listing the major trains can sometimes be bought from hawkers outside the railway stations. Hotel reception desks and CITS offices have copies of the timetable for trains out of their city or town.

Thomas Cook publishes an overseas railway timetable, which includes China – single copies are expensive but you might get a xerox of the relevant pages from your friendly neighbourhood travel agent.

Railway Stations Some stations require that luggage be x-rayed before entering the waiting area. The reason is that China has had a big problem with people transporting huge quantities of firecrackers or gunpowder for making firecrackers – there have been several disastrous explosions. Occasional gory photographs are tacked up in stations showing the results.

If the horde of starers in the waiting room is annoying, you can usually head to the soft-class waiting rooms, which you'll often be able to use even if you've got a hard-class ticket. These soft-class waiting rooms can also serve as overnight hotels if you arrive at some disgusting hour of the morning; the staff may let you sleep there until 5 or 6 am, when you can get a bus to the hotel. You might also be able to put up here if you arrive in or are in transit through a place closed to foreigners. Some soft-class waiting rooms require a Y1 ticket which includes free tea.

Just about all railway stations have left-luggage rooms (*jìcún chù*) where you can safely dump your bags for a few jiao.

Smile – It Helps As far as foreigners are concerned many railway staff in China are exceedingly polite and can be very helpful – particularly if you look lost. Sometimes they'll invite you to sit with them or even give you their own train seats. Even when all the sleepers are supposedly full, they sometimes manage to find one for foreigners – it helps to be nice.

Costs

Calculation of train prices is a complex affair based on the length of the journey, speed of the train and relative position of the sun and moon. There are a few variables such as air-con charges, whether a child occupies a berth or not – but nothing worth worrying about. The express surcharge is the same regardless of what class you use on the train.

The most important thing to remember is the double-pricing system on Chinese trains. Most foreigners are required to pay 75% more than People's Republic Chinese for their railway tickets. Other fares apply to Overseas Chinese, Chinese students, foreign students and foreign experts in China. (All train fares mentioned in this book are standard tourist price.)

Trains are definitely cheaper than either long-distance buses or planes, but if you get a tourist-price soft-sleeper then the gap between train and air travel narrows considerably. Often the difference is so small that, given the savings in time and trouble, it's definitely worth considering flying.

Tourist price is the real crunch – it will clean your wallet out. Higher prices for foreign tourists in the hotels can be justified since the facilities and the quality of the accommodation are far better than in Chinese hotels. But on the trains and planes this doesn't apply, so the tourist pricing is purely a profit-making venture. In hard-seat you pay double to ride in the same agony!

Calculating Ticket Prices Some typical Chinese prices are given in the table. Use it as a rough guide only because fares vary slightly depending on the class of train.

Rail distance km	Prices in Y Hard-seat	Hard-sleeper	Soft-sleeper
100	10		
500	40	69	137
1000	74	120	228
1500	100	162	311
2000	125	205	390
2500	150	250	480
3000	175	283	537
3500	205	330	627

Distances by rail (km) – Major Cities

Beijing	Bei										
Shanghai	1462	Shan									
Canton	2313	1811	Can								
Changsha	1587	1187	726	Chan							
Wuhan	1229	1534	1084	358	Wuha						
Nanjing	1157	305	2116	1492	1229	Nanj					
Qingdao	887	1361	2677	1951	1593	1056	Qin				
Xi'an	1165	1511	2129	1403	1045	1206	1570	Xi'an			
Kunming	3179	2677	2216	1592	1950	2982	3512	1942	Kunm		
Chengdu	2048	2353	2544	1920	1887	2048	2412	842	1100	Chen	
Chongqing	2552	2501	2040	1416	1774	2552	2916	1346	1102	504	Chon
Zhengzhou	695	1000	1618	892	534	695	1059	511	2453	1353	1857

Distances by rail (km) – Eastern Provinces

Hangzhou	Han									
Shanghai	189	Shan								
Suzhou	275	86	Suz							
Wuxi	317	128	42	Wux						
Nanjing	494	305	219	177	Nanj					
Shaoxing	60	249	335	377	554	Shao				
Nanchang	636	825	911	953	1130	59	Nanc			
Fuzhou	972	1161	1247	1289	1466	990	622	Fuz		
Xiamen	1187	1376	1462	1504	1681	1247	838	603	Xia	
Canton	1633	1811	1897	1936	2116	1640	1042	1608	1834	Cant
Beijing	1651	1462	1376	1334	1157	1711	2005	2623	2838	2313

Distances by rail (km) – South-West Provinces

Beijing	Bei										
Shanghai	1462	Sha									
Nanchang	2005	825	Nan								
Wuhan	1229	1545	776	Wuh							
Zhuzhou	1638	1136	367	409	Zhu						
Canton	2313	1811	1042	1084	675	Can					
Liuzhou	2310	1808	1039	1081	672	1079	Liu				
Nanning	2565	2063	1294	1336	927	1334	255	Nann			
Chengdu	2048	2353	2236	1887	1869	2544	1574	1829	Che		
Chongqing	2552	2501	1732	1774	1365	2040	1070	1325	504	Cho	
Guiyang	2540	2038	1269	1311	902	1577	607	862	967	463	Guiy
Kunming	3179	2677	1908	1950	1541	2216	1246	1501	1100	1102	639
Guilin	2134	–	–	–	–	903	176	–	–	–	–

Distances by rail (km) – North-Eastern Provinces

	Bei	Tia	Jinz	Shen	Chan	Har	Qiq	Jil	Dan	Dal	Jin
Beijing											
Tianjin	137										
Jinzhou	599	462									
Shenyang	841	704	242								
Changchun	1146	1009	547	305							
Harbin	1388	1251	789	547	242						
Qiqihar	1448	1311	849	760	530	288					
Jilin	1287	1150	688	446	128	275	563				
Dandong	1118	981	519	277	582	824	1037	723			
Dalian	1238	1101	639	397	702	944	1157	84	674		
Ji'nan	494	357	819	1061	1366	1608	1668	1507	1338	1458	
Jiamusi	1894	–	–	–	–	506	–	–	–	–	–
Mudanjiang	–	–	–	–	–	357	–	–	–	–	–

Distances by rail (km) – North-West Regions

	Bei	Zhen	Xi'an	Lan	Xini	Ürüm	Hoh
Beijing							
Zhengzhou	695						
Xi'an	1165	511					
Lanzhou	1813	1187	676				
Xining	2098	1403	892	216			
Ürümqi	3774	3079	2568	1892	2108		
Hohhot	668	1363	1292	1145	1361	3037	
Yinchuan	1346	1654	1143	467	683	2359	678

Train fares are related to distance travelled, so it's possible to estimate the fare you would expect to pay for any particular journey if you know the distance. See the distance tables in this chapter.

Getting Cheaper Tickets Tourist-price tickets are slips of paper with various details scribbled all over them. Chinese-price tickets are little stubs of cardboard. Getting a Chinese-priced ticket is possible but becoming more difficult. Officially the only foreigners entitled to local Chinese-priced tickets are foreign students studying in the People's Republic, and certain foreigners authorised to live and work in China.

In the past travellers have been using all sorts of impressive-looking 'student cards' or made-in-Hong-Kong imitations of the 'white card' (which authorises foreigners to pay local price) to pass themselves off as students. Although more railway stations are catching on to these tricks, it's surprising how often they still work. It used to be possible to use a Taiwan student card (Taiwan is officially considered part of China), but this trick usually no longer works.

Officially, Overseas Chinese, Hong Kongers and Taiwanese are also required to pay tourist prices and pay in FEC. In actual practice, anyone who looks Chinese (even Japanese) can usually wind up getting local Chinese price. It appears that race is the major consideration. Most Overseas Chinese will gladly buy your ticket for you if you ask them to.

You can also get a local Chinese person to do it and give them a tip, but exercise caution – they could get into trouble, or they could pocket your money and run away. It's best to have them pay first with their own cash and then reimburse them, though many will not have the cash to do this.

Students are your best bet if you want

someone to buy tickets for you – they appreciate any tip you give them and they are usually (but not always) honest.

Most railway workers don't care if you get a Chinese-priced ticket. However, if you do get such a ticket the conductor on the train can still charge you the full fare, or you could be stopped at the railway station exit gate at your destination, have your tickets checked and be charged the full fare. In practice, this seldom happens.

Some train stations have separate booking offices for foreigners. As a rule they'll charge you tourist price, though you can sometimes wangle local price though they might make you pay in FEC. On the credit side, you don't have to wait in formidable queues and you can often get a sleeper – so if you do have to pay tourist price stop bitching and consider your money well spent!

Food Cheapest meals are the 'rice boxes' brought down the carriages on trolleys and distributed to those who previously bought meal tickets. Tickets are sold by one of the train staff who walks through the train shortly before the trolley comes through. The boxes of rice, meat and vegetables cost around Y2 – filling, though some travellers have got the runs from them.

Trains on longer journeys have dining cars. Meals cost a couple of yuan. For breakfast you've got a choice of soup and maybe two plates of meat and/or vegetables, with cheap noodles for breakfast. There is a separate sitting for passengers in the soft-class carriages – as a foreigner you can join in even if you're in hard-class, and sometimes you can get a Western breakfast. Some foreigners have been charged excessive prices for food ordered after the main sitting – check the price first.

After about 8 pm when meals are over you can probably wander back into the dining car. The staff may want to get rid of you, but if you just sit down and have a beer it may be OK. One Chinese-speaking traveller recalls getting drunk in the dining car with the train crew, one of whom stood up and loudly cursed the powers that be, saying they were all rotten to the core. He was threatened with ejection from the train at the next stop if he didn't sit down and shut up!

It's worth stocking up with your own supplies for long train trips – particularly if you're an obsessive nibbler. Jam, biscuits and fruit juice can be bought at department stores beforehand. If you like coffee or tea then bring your own – the trains have boilers at the end of the hard-class carriages. Sometimes the dining car will have canned fruit for sale, even whole chickens in plastic bags. At station stops you can buy food from the vendors.

TAXI

Long-distance taxis are usually booked through CITS or from hotels. They will usually ask excessive fees and payment in FEC – the name of the game is negotiate. Private entrepreneurs are becoming more common and they charge considerably less than CITS.

In places frequented by tourists it's possible to book private minibuses – with a group this can be worthwhile for getting to certain isolated sites. For example, it's almost essential to book a minibus to see the sights around the desert oasis of Turpan in Xinjiang Province. Drivers can usually be found hanging around bus stations and hotels. Chances are good that you won't have to look for them – they will be looking for you.

CAR & MOTORBIKE

Unless you've got money to burn, forget it. You cannot simply fly into Beijing and hire an automobile at the airport with your American Express card. Foreigners who want to operate a motor vehicle in China need special permission. It's not impossible to get, but it takes time.

Permission to operate a car is often granted to certain people who work in China – diplomats, corporate executives, etc. For travellers, there are special motor tours for car and motorcycle groups. The cost of this is high and it would take a fairly large group to make it economically feasible. In 1990, a huge car rally from London to Beijing attracted participants from all over the world.

BICYCLE

There are over 220 million bikes in China. Some are made for export, but most are for domestic use. Production can never keep up with demand because the Chinese will do anything to lay their hands on one rather than be at the mercy of the bus system. The bicycle is a workhorse, carrying anything up to a 100-kg slaughtered pig or a whole couch...you name it. Bikes are heavy and expensive – they're expected to last 15 years.

A bike licence is obligatory for Chinese but is not necessary for a foreigner. Some cities have bicycle licence plates, and in Beijing bikes owned by foreigners have special licence plates so they can't be sold to a Chinese. If a person has an accident or is drunk while riding a bike, a fine can be imposed and the bike impounded (there are posters to this effect in Chinese cities). Police also occasionally stop cyclists to do spot checks on the brakes and other equipment. Bike-repair shops are everywhere and repairs are dirt cheap (say Y2 a shot).

The cities are built for bikes – long, wide avenues flat as pancakes (one exception is hilly Chongqing where there's hardly a bike in sight) so even those heavy gearless monsters ride OK. There are now established bicycle hire shops dealing with foreigners in many tourist centres. Some bicycle hire shops are attached to Chinese hotels or operate out of an independent hire shop, of which there are many.

Day hire, 24-hour hire or hire by the hour are the norm. It's possible to hire for a stretch of several days, so touring is possible if the bike is in good condition. Rates for Westerners are typically Y1 per hour or Y5 per day – some places are more expensive depending on the competition. Some big hotels charge ridiculous rates – the Hyatt in Tianjin was asking Y10 per hour last time we checked!

If you hire over a long period you should be able to reduce the rate. Most hire places will ask you to leave some sort of ID. Sometimes they ask for your passport, which is asking a lot. Give them some other ID instead, like a student card or a driver's licence. Old expired passports are really useful for this purpose. Some hire shops may require a deposit, but that should certainly not be more than the actual value of the bike.

Before taking a bike, check the brakes (are

there any?), get the tyres pumped up hard – and make sure that none of the moving parts are about to fall off. Get the saddle raised to maximum leg-power. It's also worth tying something on – a handkerchief, for example – to identify your bicycle amidst the zillions at the bicycle parks.

In the cities bicycles are parked at designated places. Bicycle-park attendants will give you a token when you park; the charge is usually two or three jiao.

In China bicycles can be 'towed' just as illegally parked cars can be in the West; if you don't use the bike parks you may find your bike at the police station. There will be a fine – probably a few yuan.

As for accidents, there are plenty of picture displays around Chinese cities showing what happened to cyclists who didn't look where they were going and got creamed – really creamed! These displays also give tips on how to avoid accidents and show 're-education classes' for offenders who have had several accidents.

Night riding is particularly hazardous – the only time buses and cars use their headlights is to flash them on and off to warn cyclists up ahead to get out of the way – so, if you do ride at night, watch out for the motorised monsters. On country roads look out for those Mad-Max-style walking tractors; often they have no headlights. Another traffic hazard is the cyclist who spots you, glides by staring gape-mouthed, crashes into something in front and causes the traffic behind to topple like tenpins.

Remember that dogs and cyclists are enemies. Fortunately, canines are very rare in China, but Tibet is an exception – beware if cycling around Lhasa.

Bicycle theft does exist. The bicycle parks with their attendants help prevent this, but keep your bike off the streets at night, at least within the hotel gates. If the hotel has no grounds then take the bike up the lift to your room. Most hired bicycles have a lock around the rear wheel which nimble fingers can pick in seconds. You can increase security by buying and using a cable lock, widely available from shops in China.

Probably the first time the Chinese saw a pneumatic-tyred bicycle was when a pair of globe-trotting Americans called Allen and Sachtleben bumbled into Beijing around 1891 after a three-year journey from Istanbul. They wrote a book about it called *Across Asia on a Bicycle*. The novelty was well received by the Qing court, and the boy-emperor Puyi was given to tearing around the Forbidden City on a cycle.

Modern Chinese are great bicycle tourists. An 85-year-old martial arts expert has spent three years pedalling over 16,000 km across China and plans to continue for another three years. A retired Chinese couple did 10,000 km from Gansu to Guangdong in two years. A 69-year-old retired worker set off on a self-made tricycle the back of which could be converted into a bed and kitchen!

Organised bicycle tours for groups have operated in China since the beginning of 1981. The range of tours has been extended to include the Silk Road, Inner Mongolia and Tibet.

For bike tours around Guangdong, Guangxi and Hainan try Bike China Tours (☎ 9847208), GPO Box 9484, Hong Kong: very small groups, flexible and recommended by some travellers. Another company specialising in biking tours in different regions of China is Tail Winds Bicycle Touring (☎ (06) 249 6634), PO Box 32, O'Connor, ACT 2601, Australia. In the USA, trips of this nature are advertised in cycling magazines.

Prior to 1987, border guards and police officials in remote areas were often puzzled by the sudden appearance of muddy foreign bikers whizzing through from Canton to Kunming, Shanghai to Xi'an, Kathmandu to Lhasa, etc. Unfortunately, now that the novelty has worn off, officials have decided that they need to 'do something' about the influx of foreign bikers. Horror stories abound. Two Americans were intercepted at Kunming airport after flying in from Hong Kong with mountain bikes. The ensuing wrangle with Customs took several weeks before the officials, who had been coveting the bikes, graciously agreed to let the foreign couple sell them for a song to a local department store. Foreigners have crossed the border from Hong Kong and Macau without incident, only to be intercepted by local officials in remote areas and fined and even had their bikes confiscated.

The legalities of cycling from town to town are open to conjecture. In China, there is hardly any rule of law; local officials can pretty much do what they want with you. Most of the time, the police won't bother you, but some officials can't stand seeing foreigners bicycling through China – they expect you to be travelling by taxi and tour bus. After all, foreigners are universally regarded as rich and bicycles are meant for poor peasants. No respectable cadre would be caught dead riding a bicycle – they prefer limousines. Most Chinese can't figure out why foreigners would even want to cycle around China.

Furthermore, you may well pass through a closed area without knowing it's closed. One traveller, who eventually gave up and sold his bicycle, summed up his frustrations:

> It was 10 pm, it was raining, I was in the outskirts and nobody was noticing me, so I quickly hopped into a hotel. I wasn't sleeping yet and they came and took me and my stuff and my bike to the city centre, to a big hotel, of course more expensive, kept my passport and told me to come to the police station next morning.
>
> And there I was and told them about false information and all the mismanagement. I passed through so many road blocks and nobody stopped me, and if I asked a policeman on the street whether the place was open or not, he wouldn't know, so how should I, a tourist who can't speak Chinese, know that this is a closed city?
>
> 'No, this is an open city.' Ah?...so what am I doing in the police station? 'You were probably in a closed area.'
>
> I couldn't even lie, I didn't know what was open and what not.
>
> **Ze Do Rock**

If you get hauled over, it is unlikely to be on the road. PSB keeps firm tabs on transients via hotels. If you're staying overnight in closed places, try to arrive late and leave between 4 and 5 am. They will often demand a fine. Apart from bargaining down the amount of the fine, it's interesting to see the reaction when you demand a formal receipt.

Camping is possible if you can find a spare blade of grass. The trick is to select a couple of likely places about half an hour before sunset, keep pedalling and then backtrack so you can pull off the road at the chosen spot just after darkness falls.

One problem with Western bikes is that they attract a lot of attention. Another problem is the unavailability of spare parts. One Westerner brought a fold-up bicycle with him – but in most places it attracted so much attention that he had to give it to the locals to play with until the novelty wore off. One advantage of the fold-up bike is that you can stick it in a bag and stow it on the luggage racks of the trains, unfold it when you arrive at your destination and zip off, no hassles. They are, however, useless for long-distance travel and can be very expensive in the West.

It's essential to have a kick-stand for parking. A bell, headlight and reflector are good ideas. Make sure everything is bolted down, otherwise you'll invite theft. A cageless water bottle, even on a Chinese bike, attracts too much attention. Adhesive reflector strips get ripped off.

There are four basic types of bike available in China: small wheel, light roadster (14 kg), black hulk (22 kg) and farmers' models (25-30 kg). An average bicycle costs around Y120 to Y275. The average price is around Y150 or getting on for three months' wages for a city worker.

Prestigious brands are the Fenghuang (Phoenix), Yongjiu (Forever) and Tianjin-built Fei Ge (Flying Pigeon). An interesting variation is the motorised bicycle; the better ones cost almost as much as a moped. Like medicines and cigarettes, popular brands of bicycles have been part of a counterfeiting wave in China.

The standard Chinese bicycle is a copy of ye olde English Raleigh Roadster, complete to the last detail – even mimicking the crest. The Fenghuang is a heavy-duty bike, built to last with thick spokes, chaincase, upright bars, rear rack, heavy-duty tubing, wide wheelbase for heavy loads, rod-type brakes and no gears, headlights or reflectors. Dynamo sets are rare.

Then there are arrays of tricycles with spokes thicker than a motorcycle's, reinforced forks and double tubing – a sort of poor man's truck used to carry stupendous loads. Other bikes have little sidecars tacked on to carry children or invalids, or for use as makeshift pedicabs.

Providing you can get your wheels across the border with minimal bureaucratic hassles, you might want to look at the bikes in Hong Kong which are cheaper and better made than the ones across the border. There's a Raleigh agent, British Bicycle Company, and bike shops in the Mongkok area of Kowloon as well as over on Hong Kong Island. Hong Kong bikes are related to the Chinese versions, so Raleighs and Chinese-brand parts should be roughly compatible – or at least your Chinese bicycle repairer should know what they're looking at. You can also buy three-speed bikes in Hong Kong.

Bikes are not cheap to transport on trains; this can cost as much as a hard-seat fare (Chinese price). Boats are the cheapest means of transporting a bicycle; the cost is around a third of the 3rd-class passenger fare, which is not much. Trains have quotas for the number of bikes they may transport. As a foreigner you will get preferential treatment in the luggage compartment and the bike will go on the first available train. But your bike won't arrive at the same time as you unless you send it on a couple of days in advance. At the other end it is held in storage for three days free, and then incurs a small charge.

The procedure for putting a bike on a train and getting it at the other end is as follows:

1 Railway personnel would like to see a train ticket for yourself (not entirely essential).
2 Go to the baggage transport section of the station. Get a white slip and fill it out to get the two or three tags for registration. Then fill out a form (it's only in Chinese, so just fill it out in English) which reads: 'Number/ to station x/send goods person/receive goods person/total number of goods/from station y'.
3 Take the white slip to another counter, where you pay and are given a blue slip.
4 At the other end (after delays of up to three days for transporting a bike) you present the blue slip, and get a white slip in return. This means your bike has arrived. The procedure could take from 20 minutes to an hour depending on who's around. If you lose that blue slip you'll have real trouble reclaiming your bike.

Chinese cyclists spend ages at the stations mummifying their bicycles in cloth for transport. For the one scratch the bike will get it's hardly worth going through this elaborate procedure. Again, you can avoid all of this by taking a fold-up bicycle.

Transporting your bike by plane can be expensive, but it's often less complicated than by train. Some cyclists have not been charged by CAAC, others have had to pay 1% of their fare per kg of excess weight.

HITCHING

Many people have hitchhiked in China, and some have been amazingly successful. It's not officially sanctioned, so don't bother trying to get permission. The best way to get a lift is to find the outskirts of town. There are usually lots of trucks on the roads, and even army convoys are worth trying.

Much depends on where you are; in some parts the novelty of hitchhikers has worn off among the locals. Otherwise, hitching is a good way of getting to closed or isolated areas, or to places where there is poor public transport.

As far as we know, there is no Chinese signal for hitching, so just try waving down the trucks. Unless you speak Chinese, you'll need to have where you want to go written down in Chinese – otherwise there's no hope of being understood.

BOAT

Apart from the ships which ply the coast of China (see the introductory Getting There & Away chapter for details), several inland shipping routes are worth considering. For details of each trip see the appropriate sections in this book. Boat travel is the slowest but cheapest means of transport in China.

The best known trip is the three-day boat ride along the Yangtse River from Chongqing to Wuhan. Some people find this a dull trip but it's a good way to get from Chongqing to Wuhan, and it's a relief from the trains. You can also carry on down the Yangtse River and the Huangpu River to Shanghai. From Shanghai there is the boat to Qingdao.

From Canton to Wuzhou along the West (Xi) River is popular with low-budget travellers as it is the cheapest way to get from Canton to Guilin and Yangshuo, disembarking at Wuzhou and then taking a bus to Guilin or Yangshuo the next morning. The Li River boat trip from Guilin to Yangshuo is a popular tourist ride which takes six hours.

You can also travel the Grand Canal from Hangzhou to Suzhou, and flit off on various other boats in this district. There are no passenger boats on the Yellow River.

LOCAL TRANSPORT

Long-distance transport in China is not really a problem – the dilemma occurs when you finally make it to your destination. As in US and Australian cities where the car is the key to movement, the bicycle is the key in China, and if you don't have one, life is more difficult. Walking is not usually recommended, since Chinese cities tend to be very spread out.

To/From the Airport

Your plane ticket no longer includes the cost of transport between the CAAC office and the airport; expect to pay a couple of jiao for short distances and several kuai for longer ones. The departure time of the bus will be noted on your ticket. You can also take a taxi to the airport.

Bus

Apart from bikes, buses are the most common means of getting around in the cities. Services are fairly extensive and the buses go to most places you want to go. The problem is that they are almost always packed. If an empty bus pulls in at a stop then the battle for seats ensues, and a passive crowd of Chinese suddenly turns into a stampeding herd. Even more aggravating is the slow traffic. You just have to be patient, never expect anything to move rapidly, and allow lots of time to get to the railway station to catch your train. One consolation is that buses are cheap, rarely more than two jiao per trip.

Good maps of Chinese cities and bus routes are readily available and are often sold by hawkers outside the railway stations. When you get on a bus, point to where you want to go on the map, and the conductor (who is seated near the door) will sell you the right ticket. They usually tell you where to get off.

You may be offered a seat in a crowded bus, although this is becoming less common in the big cities. It's that peculiarly Chinese politeness which occasionally manifests itself, and if you're offered a seat it's best to accept as refusal may offend.

Taxi

These do not cruise the streets (anything to save petrol) except in major cities, but the situation is slowly improving due to rising affluence. You can always summon a taxi from the tourist hotels which sometimes have separate booking desks. You can hire them for a single trip or on a daily basis – the latter is definitely worth considering if you've got the money or if there's a group of people who can split the cost. Some of the tourist hotels also have minibuses on hand. Beijing taxi drivers have become notorious for ripping off foreigners (see the Beijing chapter for details), and Canton taxi drivers will often demand FEC.

Canton and Beijing taxis usually have meters – in most other cities, meters are unknown. In this case, always negotiate the fare in advance. Drivers are supposed to give you an official receipt and turn the cash over to the government. Needless to say, most would prefer to under-report the amount or not report it at all. You can help them – and negotiate a cheaper rate for yourself – if you tell them that you don't need a receipt (*wǒ bùbì fāpiào*).

Pedicab (*sānlúnchē*)

A pedicab is a pedal-powered tricycle with a seat to carry passengers. In most places it's like the pedicab you see in India, with the driver at the front and a seat for two behind him. In some places along the south-east coast it's improvised from an ordinary bicycle and a little wooden side car in which two people can sit. Beijing pedicabs don't have seats, but a flat tray at the rear on which the passenger squats. Motorised pedicabs are also common.

Pedicabs congregate outside railway and bus stations and sometimes outside the tourist hotels. Many drivers have become predatory and can be quite aggressive. Always bargain your fare! Asking prices can be as much as 10 times the standard rate, and often the drivers will simply refuse to take foreigners unless you pay it. Agree on a price beforehand, otherwise you'll be in for a furious argument when you reach your destination. If there is more than one of you, make sure the agreed fare covers both people.

Pedicabs versus rickshaws: A rickshaw is a two-wheeled passenger cart pulled by a man on foot. It was invented in Japan, where the word *jin-rikisha* means 'human-powered vehicle'. It was introduced into China in the late 19th century, where it was called *yángchē* (foreign vehicle). The rickshaw eventually became a symbol of human exploitation – one person pulling another in a cart – and disappeared from China in the 1950s. Its replacement, the pedicab – sometimes mistakenly called a rickshaw – is a tricycle with a seat for one or two passengers.

Auto-Rickshaw (Auto-Pedicab) (*sānlún mótūochē*)

The auto-rickshaw – for want of a better name – is an enclosed three-wheeled vehicle with a driver at the front, a small motor-bike engine below and seats for two passengers behind. They congregate outside the train and bus stations in larger towns and cities. Some of these vehicles have trays at the rear with bench seats along the sides so that several people can be carried at once. Tempos are a large, ugly version of the auto-rickshaw and seat five or six passengers; they're not very common.

TOURS

Most major cities have companies operating short-range tour buses which carry both Chinese and foreigners to the local sights. Regular tours include Beijing (Ming Tombs and Great Wall), Kunming (Stone Forest) and Xi'an (terracotta soldiers).

Prices are low but sometimes the buses will whiz through interesting spots and make long stops at dull places. You might have difficulty getting a ticket if the destination is closed to foreigners, if the bus is booked out or if they think you're too much trouble.

In some places CITS organises tour buses for foreigners – to the Great Wall for example. Sometimes these are good value, though usually more expensive than private minibuses. You can sometimes hitch up with a Western tour group for which you'll be charged a fee; that may be the only way of getting a look at certain places (such as factories).

SOUTHERN AND CENTRAL CHINA

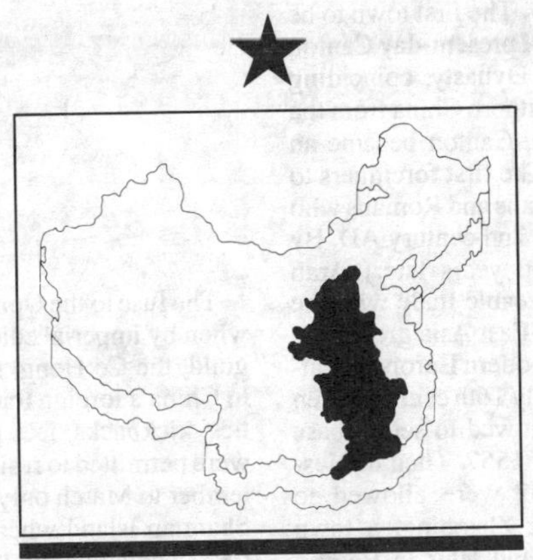

Canton 广州

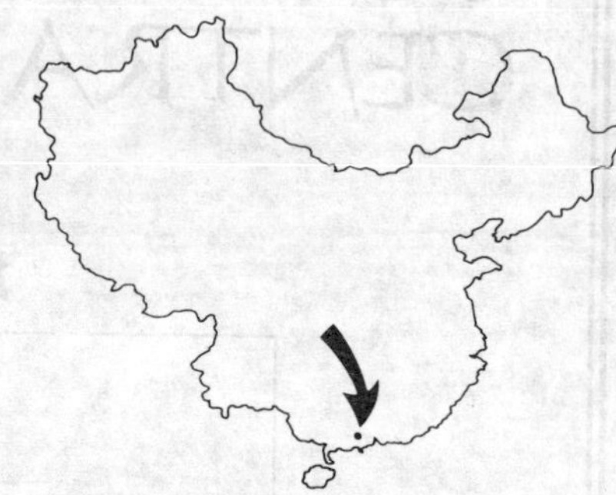

History

Known to the Chinese as Guangzhou *(gŭangzhōu)*, Canton is one of the oldest cities in China, the capital of Guangdong Province and for over a thousand years one of the main gateways to the country. The first town to be established on the site of present-day Canton dates back to the Qin Dynasty, coinciding with the conquest of southern China from the north. Close to the sea, Canton became an outward-looking city. The first foreigners to come here were the Indians and Romans who appeared as early as the 2nd century AD. By the Tang Dynasty (500 years later) Arab traders visited and a sizeable trade with the Middle East and South-East Asia grew.

Initial contact with modern European nations was made in the early 16th century when the Portuguese were allowed to set up base down river in Macau in 1557. Then the Jesuits came and in 1582 were allowed to establish themselves at Zhaoqing, a town north-west of Canton, and later in Beijing itself. The Jesuits impressed the court with their expertise in astronomy which permitted the all-important astrological charts to be produced more accurately. Some made fountains and curios or worked as painters and architects, but otherwise the Jesuit influence on China was negligible. The first trade overtures from the British were rebuffed in 1625, but the imperial government finally opened Canton to foreign trade in 1685.

British ships began to arrive regularly from the East India Company's bases on the Indian coast, and the traders were allowed to establish warehouses ('factories') near Canton as bases for shipping out tea and silk. In 1757 a new imperial edict restricted all foreign trade to Canton, indicating how little importance was placed on trade with the Western barbarians. Canton was always considered to be on the edge of a wilderness, far from Nanjing and Beijing, the centres of power under the isolationist Ming and Qing dynasties.

The fuse to the Opium wars was lit in 1757 when by imperial edict a Canton merchants' guild, the Co Hong, gained exclusive rights to China's foreign trade – paying with royalties, kickbacks, fees and bribes. Westerners were permitted to reside in Canton from September to March only, and were restricted to Shamian Island where they had their factories. They had to leave their wives and families down river in Macau and were forbidden to learn Chinese or deal with anyone except the Co Hong. The traders complained of the restrictions and of trading regulations that changed from day to day. Nevertheless trade flourished – mainly in China's favour because the tea and silk had to be paid for in hard cash, normally silver.

Trade in China's favour was not what the Western merchants had in mind. In 1773 the British unloaded 1000 chests at Canton, each containing 150 pounds of Bengal opium. The intention was to balance, and eventually more than balance, their purchases of Chinese goods. The Chinese taste for opium, or 'foreign mud' as it was called, amounted to 2000 chests a year by about 1800. Emperor Dao Guang, alarmed at the drain of silver from the country, issued an edict banning the drug trade. The foreigners had different ideas, and with the help of the Co Hong and corrupt Cantonese officials the trade expanded.

In 1839 opium was still the key to British trade in China. The emperor appointed Lin Zexu commissioner of Canton with orders to stamp out the opium trade once and for all. It took Lin just one week to surround the British in Canton, cut off their food supplies and demand that they surrender all the opium in their possession. In stiff-upper-lip tradition the British stuck it out for six weeks until they were ordered by their own superintendent of trade, Captain Elliot, to surrender 20,000 chests of opium. He tried negotiating with Kishen, Lin's representative, but when this failed he attacked Canton in the first Opium War. The attack was ended by the Convention of Chuen Pi which ceded Hong Kong Island to the British. The convention was due to be signed on 20 January 1841 but never was. Nevertheless the British ran the flag up on Hong Kong Island. A later treaty ceded the island and a piece of Kowloon 'in perpetuity'.

In the 19th century the Cantonese sense of independence, aided by Canton's distance from Beijing, allowed Guangdong to become a cradle of revolt. The leader of the anti-dynastic Taiping Rebellion, Hong Xiuquan (1814-64), was born at Huaxian north-west of Canton, and the early activities of the Taipings centred around this area. Canton was also a stronghold of the republican forces after the fall of the Qing Dynasty in 1911. Sun Yatsen, the first president of the Republic of China, was born at Cuiheng village south-west of Canton. In the early 1920s, Sun headed the Kuomintang (Nationlist Party) in Canton from where the republicans mounted their campaigns against the northern warlords. Canton was also the centre of activities of the fledgling Communist Party.

These events were nothing new. Centuries before, the southerners had gained a reputation for thinking for themselves, and rebellions and uprisings were a feature of Canton from the time of its foundation. The assimilation of southern China was a slow process, reflected in the fact that the southerners refer to themselves as men of Tang (of the Tang Dynasty 618-907 AD), while the northerners refer to themselves as men of Han (of the Han Dynasty 206 BC-220 AD). The northerners regarded their southern compatriots with disdain, or as one 19th-century northern account put it:

> The Cantonese...are a coarse set of people...Before the times of Han and Tang, this country was quite wild and waste, and these people have sprung forth from unconnected, unsettled vagabonds that wandered here from the north.

The traditional stereotype of the Cantonese – over five million of whom live in the city of Canton and its surrounding suburbs – is that of a proud people, frank in criticism, lacking restraint, oriented to defending their own interests, and hot tempered. They are regarded as shrewd in business, and quick, lively and clever in catching on to new skills.

Economy

Of all the Chinese the Cantonese have probably been influenced most by the outside world. Part of this stems from their geographical position – a mere 110 km from Hong Kong but 2300 km from the national capital.

Almost everyone in southern Guangdong has relatives in Hong Kong who for years have been storming across the border sporting the latest hairstyles and loaded down with gifts of refrigerators, TV sets or (more recently) Sony Walkmans. Despite attempts by the authorities to tear down their tall TV antennas, many Cantonese can receive the latest shows from Hong Kong.

A few years ago these shows would have been considered a ruinous influence on the moral and ideological uprightness of the Chinese people. However, ideology is not what China is all about now, especially in Canton. The Cantonese are interested in economic development and have little use for the political slogans emanating from Beijing.

'The Four Modernisations' manifest themselves in great and small ways. Their most obvious marks in Canton are the giant hotels built in the last few years, including

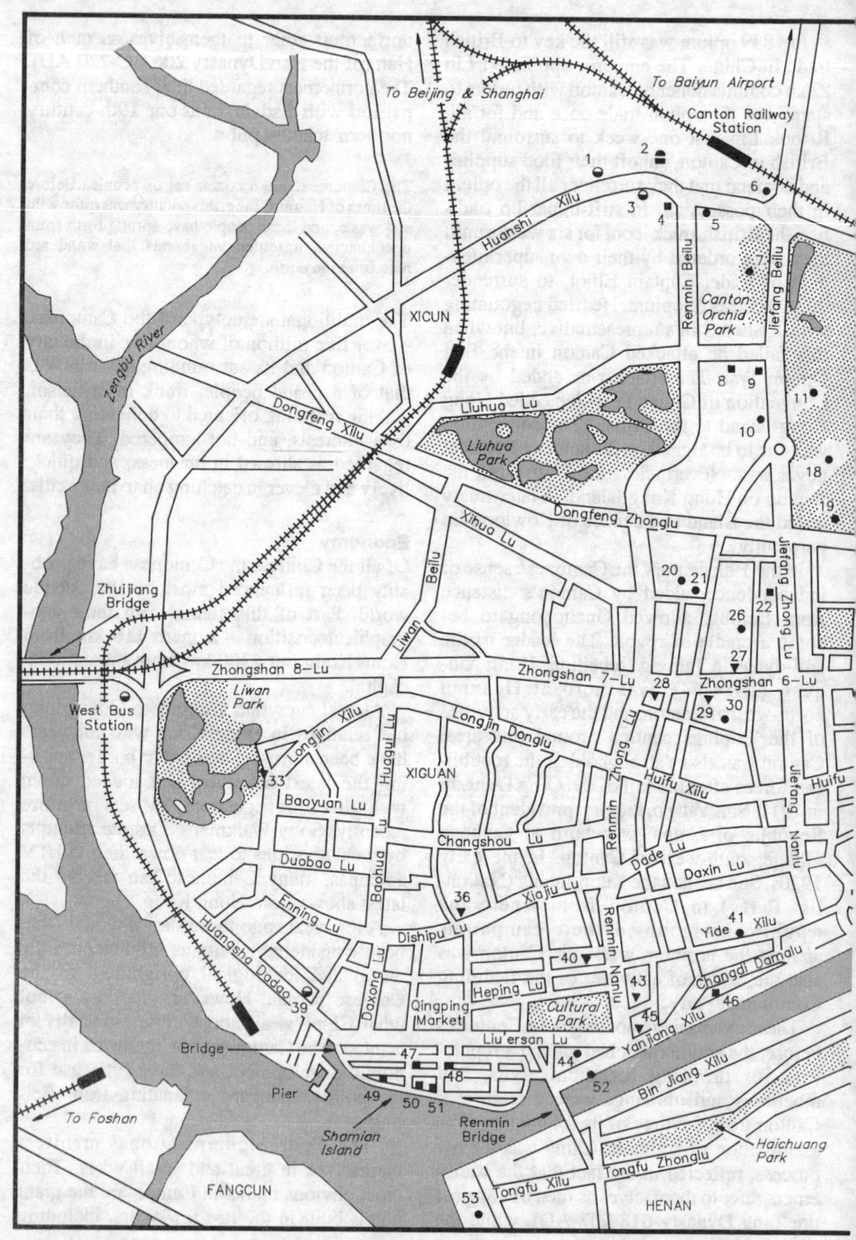
To Beijing & Shanghai
To Baiyun Airport
Canton Railway Station
Huanshi Xilu
Renmin Beilu
Jiefang Beilu
Canton Orchid Park
Zengbu River
XICUN
Dongfeng Xilu
Liuhua Lu
Liuhua Park
Dongfeng Zhonglu
Xihua Lu
Beilu
Liwan
Zhuijiang Bridge
Zhongshan 8–Lu
Zhongshan 7–Lu
Zhongshan 6–Lu
Jiefang Zhong Lu
Liwan Park
West Bus Station
Longjin Xilu
Longjin Donglu
Huagui Lu
XIGUAN
Zhong Lu
Huifu Xilu
Huifu
Jiefang Nanlu
Baoyuan Lu
Changshou Lu
Renmin
Duobao Lu
Dade Lu
Daxin Lu
Xiajiu Lu
Renmin Nanlu
Enning Lu
Baohua Lu
Dishipu Lu
Yide Xilu
Huangsha Dadao
Daxong Lu
Changdi Damalu
Heping Lu
Cultural Park
Qingping Market
Liu'ersan Lu
Yanjiang Xilu
Bridge
Pier
Bin Jiang Xilu
To Foshan
Shamian Island
Renmin Bridge
Haichuang Park
Tongfu Zhonglu
Tongfu Xilu
FANGCUN
HENAN
1
2
3
4
5
6
7
8
9
10
11
18
19
20
21
22
26
27
28
29
30
33
36
39
40
41
43
44
45
46
47
48
49
50
51
52
53

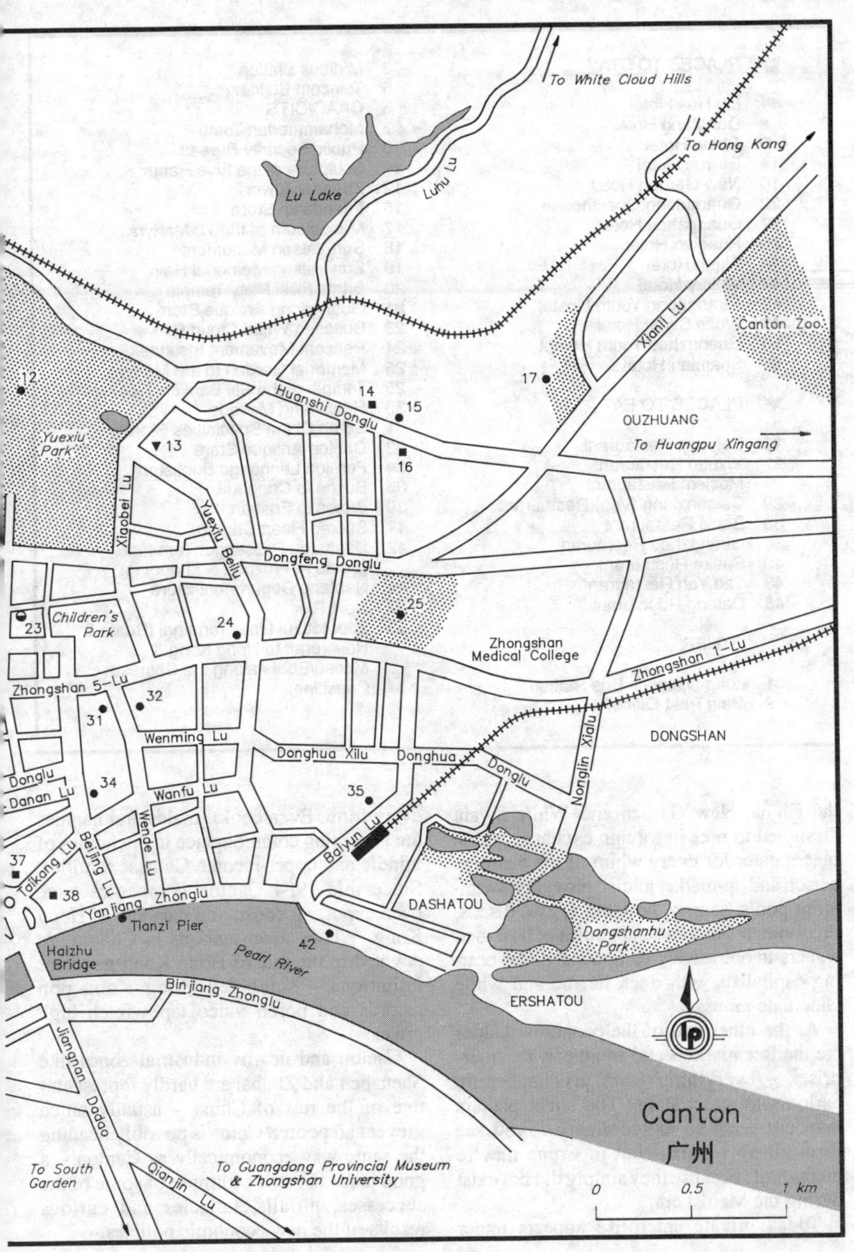
To White Cloud Hills
To Hong Kong
Lu Lake
Luhu Lu
Xianli Lu
Canton Zoo
17
12
14
15
Huanshi Donglu
13
16
Yuexiu Park
OUZHUANG
To Huangpu Xingang
Xiaobei Lu
Yuexiu Beilu
Dongfeng Donglu
25
Children's Park
23
24
Zhongshan Medical College
Zhongshan 1-Lu
Zhongshan 5-Lu
32
31
Wenming Lu
Nonglin Xialu
DONGSHAN
Donghua Xilu
Donghua
Donglu
Donglu
Danan Lu
34
Wanfu Lu
35
Wende Lu
Beijing Lu
Taikang Lu
Baiyun Lu
37
38
Yanjiang Zhonglu
Tianzi Pier
DASHATOU
42
Dongshanhu Park
Haizhu Bridge
Pearl River
Binjiang Zhonglu
ERSHATOU
Jiangnan Dadao
Canton
广州
To South Garden
Qianjin Lu
To Guangdong Provincial Museum & Zhongshan University
0
0.5
1 km

■ PLACES TO STAY

4 Liu Hua Hotel
8 Dongfang Hotel
9 China Hotel
14 Baiyun Hotel
16 New Garden Hotel
22 Guangdong Guesthouse
37 Guangzhou Hotel
38 Huaqiao Hotel
46 Aiqun Hotel
47 Victory Hotel
48 Guangdong Youth Hostel
49 White Swan Hotel
50 Guangzhou Youth Hostel
51 Shamian Hotel

▼ PLACES TO EAT

13 Beiyuan Restaurant
27 Xiyuan Restaurant
28 Moslem Restaurant
29 Caigenxiang (Veg) Restaurant
33 Banxi Restaurant
36 Guangzhou Restaurant
40 Snake Restaurant
43 Yan Yan Restaurant
45 Datong Restaurant

OTHER

1 Long-Distance Bus Station
2 Main Post Office
3 Minibus Station
5 Telecom Building
6 CAAC/CITS
7 Mohammedan Tomb
10 Public Security Bureau
11 Sculpture of the Five Rams
12 Zhenhai Tower
15 Friendship Store
17 Mausoleum of the 72 Martyrs
18 Sun Yatsen Monument
19 Sun Yatsen Memorial Hall
20 Bright Filial Piety Temple
21 Guangdong Antique Store
23 Buses to White Cloud Hills
24 Peasant Movement Institute
25 Memorial Garden to the Martyrs
26 Temple of the Six Banyan Trees
30 Huaisheng Mosque
31 South China Specialties Store
32 Canton Antique Store
34 Foreign Language Bookstore
35 Buses to Conghua
39 Buses to Foshan
41 Sacred Heart Church
42 Dashatou Passenger Terminal (Boats to Wuzhou & Zhaoqing)
44 Nanfang Department Store
52 No 1 Pier
53 Zhoutouzui Liner Terminal (Boats & Hovercraft to Hong Kong & Macau/Boats along the Chinese Coastline)

the China, New Garden and White Swan. Designed to rake in foreign exchange, these places cater for every whim of the business person and up-market tourist, providing swimming pools, saunas, bowling alleys, discos, revolving restaurants and armies of bow-tied waiters unobtrusively pampering dollar-bearing capitalists with duck terrine and white chocolate mousse.

At the other end of the economic ladder are the free markets and small private enterprises – everything from private beauty parlours to street stalls. The street pedlars may not seem so extraordinary – you see them all over Asia – but in China they're memorable because they simply did not exist during the Maoist era.

Today private enterprise appears under every form. Even cooks, maids and nannies are becoming commonplace in the homes of middle and upper-income Chinese families. Since mid-1984 Canton companies have been exporting cooks and cleaners to Hong Kong. Whole street-markets in Canton are devoted to the sale of Hong Kong goods or imitations – smuggled Hong Kong pop records and porno video tapes fetch high prices.

Canton and nearby industrial zones like Shenzhen and Zhuhai are hardly representative of the rest of China – usually much greyer and poorer. China is possibly heading the same way economically as Canton – a good place to catch a glimpse of some of the successes, pitfalls, fallacies and curious results of the new economic policies.

■ PLACES TO STAY

4 流花宾馆
8 东方宾馆
9 中国大酒店
14 白云宾馆
16 花园宾馆
22 广东迎宾馆
37 广州宾馆
38 华侨大厦
46 爱群大厦
47 胜利宾馆
48 广东青年招待所
49 白天鹅宾馆
50 广州青年招待所
51 沙面宾馆

▼ PLACES TO EAT

13 北园酒家
27 西园饭店
28 回民饭店
29 菜根香素菜馆
33 泮溪酒家
36 广州酒家
40 蛇餐馆
43 人人菜馆
45 大同饭馆

OTHER

1 广东省汽车客运站
2 邮政总局
3 小汽车出租点
5 电信局
6 中国民航/国际旅行社
7 穆罕默德墓
10 公安局
11 五羊塑象
12 镇海楼
15 友谊商店
17 黄花岗七十二烈士墓
18 孙中山纪念碑
19 孙中山纪念堂
20 光孝寺
21 广东古玩店
23 开往白云山的汽车
24 农民运动讲习所旧址
25 广州起义烈士陵园
26 六榕寺花塔
30 怀圣寺光塔
31 华东特产商店
32 广州古玩店
34 外文书店
35 开往从化的汽车
39 开往佛山的汽车
41 石室
42 大沙头码头
44 南方大厦
52 一号码头
53 洲头嘴码头

Orientation

Canton is situated at the confluence of the Pearl and Zengbu rivers – much of it lies on the north bank of the Pearl and is bounded to the west by the Zengbu. As you look out from the upper storeys of the Zhenhai Tower, the city appears a nondescript jumble of drab buildings stretching into the haze.

Canton was originally three cities. The inner city, enclosed behind sturdy walls, was divided into the new and old cities. The outer city was everything outside these walls. The building of the walls was begun during the 11th century and completed in the 16th. They were 15 km in circumference, eight metres high and five to eight metres thick.

The main thoroughfares, now called Jiefang Lu (Liberation Rd) and Zhongshan Lu and running north-south and east-west respectively, divided up the old walled city. They met the walls at the main gates. The city began to take its present form in the early 1920s: the demolition of the walls was completed, the canals were filled in and several km of motorways were built.

Outside the city walls to the west lies the Xiguan (Western Quarter). Wealthy Chinese merchants built their residences the same distance from the centre of the city as the foreign enclave of Shamian Island. The thoroughfare still known as Shibapu became the street of millionaires in the 19th century, and remained the exclusive residential district of the well-to-do class. These people patronised the famous old restaurants of the area.

In the north-east of the city is the Xiaobei (Little North) area. During the late dynastic times it was inhabited mainly by out-of-town officials as it was close to the offices of the bureaucracy. It was later developed into a residential area for civil servants.

At the west end of Zhongshan Lu is a residential district built in the 1930s using modern town-planning methods. It's known as Dongshan (East Mountain). Part of the Dongshan residential area, Meihuacun (Plum Blossom Village), is a 'model village' laid out in the 1930s with beautiful residences for high-ranking officials.

Before the Communists came to power, the waterfront on the south side of the Pearl River was notorious for its gambling houses and opium dens. The area was increasingly integrated into the city with the completion of the first suspension bridge in 1932, and was then developed as a site for warehouses and factories.

Every year an Export Commodities Fair is held from 15 April to 15 May, and 15 October to 15 November. Most hotels are fully booked at this time and prices rise. It may also be difficult to get a room, except of course at cheap youth hostels which don't attract many foreign export/import agents.

Information

CITS There's now a large, well-staffed CITS office (☎ 662447) at 179 Huanshi Lu next to the main railway station. They have English-speaking staff. Foreigners must book all train tickets out of Canton at CITS, where you can also buy tickets for the plane, hovercraft and ship to Hong Kong. The office is open from 8.30 to 11.30 am and 2 to 5 pm.

Public Security Bureau This office (☎ 331060) is at 863 Jiefang Beilu, opposite the road which leads up to the Zhenhai Tower – a 15-minute walk from the Dongfang Hotel.

Money You can change money at branches of the Bank of China in most of the large tourist hotels, including the White Swan and Liu Hua.

Post & Telecommunications Just about all the major tourist hotels have post offices where you can send letters and packets containing printed matter. The post office in the White Swan Hotel is convenient if you're staying on Shamian Island.

If you're posting parcels overseas you have to go to the post office at 43 Yanjiang Xilu near the river front and Shamian Island. You have to get the parcel contents checked and fill out a Customs form.

The telecommunications office is near the railway station on the south-east corner of Jiefang Beilu and Huanshi Zhonglu. The tourist hotels have fax, telex and long-distance telephone facilities. Most large hotels have a cheap direct-dial service to Hong Kong.

Consulates The US Consulate (☎ 669900, ext 1000) is in the Dongfang Hotel, on the 11th floor of the old wing. It's open Monday to Friday from 8.30 am to 12.30 pm and 1.30 to 5.30 pm. The Japanese Consulate (☎ 338999) is in the Garden Hotel. The Thai Consulate (☎ 886968, ext 3310) is in room 310 of the White Swan Hotel.

There is a newly opened Polish consulate on Shamian Island near the White Swan Hotel. Visas are issued in 10 minutes! There are rumours that the USSR will also open a consulate in Canton, which could prove helpful if you're planning on doing the Trans-Siberian rail journey.

Books & Bookshops An account of early Western contact with China comes from Jesuit missionary Matteo Ricci, permitted to reside at Zhaoqing in the late 16th century, and at Beijing in 1601. An English translation of his diaries has been published as *China in the 16th Century – the Journals of Matteo Ricci 1583-1610*. Other accounts are Jonathan Spence's *To Change China – Western Advisers in China 1620-1960* (Penguin, 1980) and *Kwang Tung* or *Five Years in South China* (Oxford University Press, London, 1982) by the English Wesleyan minister John Arthur Turner, a missionary in China from 1886 to 1891. The book was originally published in 1894.

A personal account of Canton in the early days of China's Republican period is *Canton in Revolution – The Collected Papers of Earl Swisher, 1925-1928* (Westview Press, USA, 1977). Swisher was a US academic and Sinologist.

Ezra F Vogel's *Canton Under Communism* (Harvard University Press, 1969) covers the years 1949 to 1968.

In Canton, the Foreign Language Bookstore (☎ 334584) at 326 Beijing Lu has trans-lations of Chinese books and magaines, as well as foreign magazines like *Time, Newsweek, Far Eastern Economic Review* and even *Reader's Digest*.

The Classical Bookstore (☎ 331551) at 338 Beijing Lu specialises in pre-1949 Chinese string-bound editions.

The Xinhua Bookstore (☎ 332002) at 336 Beijing Lu is the main Chinese bookshop in the city. If you want to investigate the state of the pictorial arts in the country today, then this is a good place to come. There are lots of wallposters as well as sets of reproductions of Chinese paintings. They also sell children's comic books (for all ages!).

Maps Hawkers outside the railway station sell excellent bus maps in Chinese. Large hotels have good English tourist maps.

Medical Services If you get sick you can go to one of the hospitals or to the medical clinic for foreigners – Guangzhou No 1 People's Hospital (☎ 333090) *(dìyī rénmín yīyùan)*, 602 Renmin Beilu.

If you're staying on Shamian Island or the river front, a nearby good hospital is the Sun Yatsen Memorial Hospital (☎ 882012) *(sūn yìxiān jìniàn yīyùan)*, 107 Yanjiang Xilu next to the Aiqun Hotel. Not much English is spoken here but medical facilities are pretty good and prices low.

Just next to Shamian Island and the Qingping Market is the Traditional Chinese Medicine Hospital *(zhōngyī yīyùan)* on Zhuji Lu. If you want to try acupuncture and herbs, this is the place to go. Many foreigners come here to study Chinese medicine rather than to be patients.

Theft Canton is easily the most dangerous city in China. Because it is widely perceived as the richest place in China, a large number of immigrants from the countryside have poured into the city searching for instant wealth. Needless to say, most become disillusioned when they find that money doesn't grow on trees, and many turn to begging and theft. Only in Canton will you see knifeproof plastic shields in the taxis separating the driver from the passengers. Before these became mandatory, many drivers were attacked and some were killed.

For foreigners, there is little danger walking the streets, but pickpocketing on buses and around the railway station is a problem. The other common danger is moneychanging. On Shamian Island, the moneychanging industry is controlled by a large gang. Almost without exception, every foreigner who changes money on the streets of Shamian Island gets ripped off. The only way to avoid this is to change money in some of the small shops on or near Shamian Island.

Peasant Movement Institute

(nóngmín yùndòng jiǎngxísǔo)
农民运动讲习所

Canton's Peasant Movement Institute was built on the site of a Ming Dynasty Confucian temple in 1924. In the early days of the Communist Party, its members (from all over China) were trained at the Institute. It was set up by Peng Pai, a high-ranking Communist leader who believed that if a Communist revolution were to succeed in China then the peasants must be its main force. Mao Zedong – of the same opinion – took over as director of the institute in 1925 or 1926. Zhou Enlai lectured here and one of his students was Mao's brother, Mao Zemin. Peng was executed by the Kuomintang in 1929, and Mao Zemin was executed by a warlord in Xinjiang Province in 1942.

The buildings were restored in 1953 and they're now used as a revolutionary museum. There's not a great deal to see: a replica of Mao's room, the soldiers' barracks and rifles, and old photographs. The institute is at 42 Zhongshan 4-Lu.

Memorial Garden to the Martyrs

(lièshì língyúan) 烈士陵园

This memorial is within walking distance of

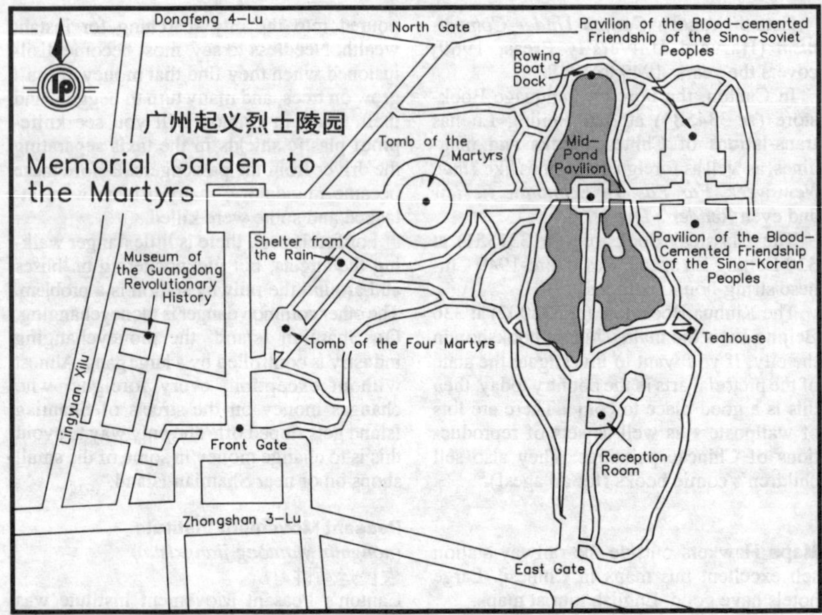

the Peasant Movement Institute, east along Zhongshan 4-Lu to Zhongshan 3-Lu. It was officially opened in 1957 on the 30th anniversary of the December 1927 Canton uprising.

In April 1927, Chiang Kaishek ordered his troops to massacre Communists in Shanghai and Nanjing. On 21 May the Communists led an uprising of peasants on the Hunan-Jiangxi border, and on 1 August they staged another in Nanchang. Both uprisings were defeated by Kuomintang troops.

On 11 December 1927 the Communists staged another uprising in Canton, but this was also bloodily suppressed by the Kuomintang. The Communists claim that over 5700 people were killed during or after the uprising. The memorial garden is laid out on Red Flower Hill *(hónghuāgāng)*, which was one of the execution grounds.

There's nothing of particular interest here, though the gardens themselves are attractive. You'll also see the Pavilion of Blood-Cemented Friendship of the Sino-Soviet Peoples and the Pavilion of Blood-Cemented Friendship of the Sino-Korean Peoples.

Mausoleum of the 72 Martyrs & Memorial of Yellow Flowers

(húanghūa gāng qīshí'èr lièshì mù)
黄花岗七十二烈士墓

This memorial was built in 1918 in memory of the victims of the unsuccessful Canton insurrection of 27 April 1911. (It was not until October 1911 that the Qing Dynasty collapsed and a Republic of China was declared in the south of the country.) The uprising had been planned by a group of Chinese organisations which opposed the Qing and which had formally united at a meeting of representatives in Tokyo in August 1905, with Sun Yatsen as leader.

Funds provided by Chinese from all over the world helped build the memorial, the most famous revolutionary monument of pre-Communist China. It's a conglomeration of architectural symbols of freedom and democracy used worldwide, since the outstanding periods of history in the rest of the world were going to be used as guidelines for the new Republic of China.

What that really means is that it's an exercise in architectural bad taste. In front, a small Egyptian obelisk carved with the words 'Tomb of the 72 Martyrs' stands under a stone pavilion. On top of the pavilion is a replica of the Liberty Bell in stone. Behind stands a miniature imitation of the Trianon at Versailles, with the cross-section of a huge pyramid of stone on its roof. Topping things off is a miniature replica of the Statue of Liberty. The Chinese influence can be seen in the bronze urns and lions on each side.

The monument stands on Yellow Flower Hill *(huánghuāgāng)* on Xianli Zhonglu, east of the Baiyun and New Garden hotels.

Sun Yatsen Memorial Hall

(sūn zhōngshān jìniàn táng)
孙中山纪念堂

This hall on Dongfeng Lu was built in honour of Sun Yatsen, with donations from Overseas Chinese and from Canton citizens. Construction began in January 1929 and was finished in November 1931. The building stands on the site of the residence of the governor of Guangdong and Guangxi during the Qing Dynasty, later used by Sun Yatsen when he became president of the Republic of China. The Memorial Hall is an octagonal Chinese monolith some 47 metres high and 71 metres wide; it seats about 4000 people.

Temple of the Six Banyan Trees

(liù róng sì hūa tǎ) 六榕寺花塔

The temple's history is vague, but it seems that the first structure on this site, called the Precious Solemnity Temple, was built during the 6th century AD, and was ruined by fire in the 10th century. The temple was rebuilt at the end of the 10th century and renamed the Purificatory Wisdom Temple; the monks worshipped Hui Neng, the sixth patriarch of the Zen Buddhist sect. Today it serves as the headquarters of the Guangzhou Buddhist Association.

The temple was given its name by Su Dongpo, a celebrated poet and calligrapher of the Northern Song Dynasty who visited the temple in the 11th or 12th century. He was so enchanted by the six banyan trees growing in the courtyard (no longer there) that he contributed two large characters for 'Six Banyans'.

Within the temple compound is the octagonal Flower Pagoda, the oldest and (reaching 55 metres) the tallest pagoda in the city. Although from the outside it appears to have only nine storeys, inside it has 17. It is said that Bodhidharma, the Indian monk considered to be the founder of the Zen sect, once spent a night here and, owing to the virtue of his presence, the pagoda was rid of mosquitoes forever.

The temple stands in central Canton, on Liurong Lu just to the west of Jiefang Beilu. Until a few years ago the three large buddha statues stood in the open courtyard. The main hall was rebuilt in 1984. The buddhas have been painted and several other shrines opened. One shrine houses a statue of Hui Neng. The temple complex is now a major tourist attraction. One reader wrote:

> I would like to suggest that you make a point of reminding readers that many of the temples listed are 'working', they're not there for tourists. At Liu Rong Si...some Americans and French were happily snapping shots of the kneeling worshippers; some even snuck up in front of the altar to do so. My Chinese friend said her blood was close to boiling...she did indeed seem awfully close to losing her temper.

Bright Filial Piety Temple

(gūangxiào sì) 光孝寺

This temple is one of the oldest in Canton. The earliest Buddhist temple on this site possibly dates as far back as the 4th century AD. The place has particular significance for Buddhists because Hui Neng was a novice monk here in the 7th century. The temple buildings are of much more recent construction, the original buildings having been destroyed by fire in the mid-17th century. The temple is on Hongshu Lu, just west of the Temple of Six Banyan Trees. A section of the complex now houses the Guangdong Antique Store.

Five Genies Temple

(wǔ xiān gūan) 五仙观

This Taoist temple is held to be the site of the appearance of the five rams and celestial beings in the myth of Canton's foundation – see the following section on Yuexiu Park for the story.

The stone tablets flanking the forecourt commemorate the various restorations that the temple has undergone. The present buildings are comparatively recent, as the earlier Ming Dynasty ones were destroyed by fire in 1864.

The large hollow in the rock in the temple courtyard is said to be the impression of a celestial being's foot; the Chinese refer to it by the name of 'Rice-Ear Rock of Unique Beauty'. The great bell which weighs five tonnes was cast during the Ming Dynasty – it's three metres high, two metres in diameter and about 10 cm thick, probably the largest in Guangdong Province. It's known as the 'Calamity Bell', since the sound of the bell, which has no clapper, is a portent of calamity for the city.

Behind the main tower stand life-size statues with 'archaic Greek' smiles; these appear to represent four of the five genies. In the temple forecourt are four statues of rams, and embedded in the temple walls are inscribed steles.

The temple is at the end of an alleyway whose entrance is on Huifu Xilu which runs westwards off Jiefang Zhonglu. Opening hours are daily from 8.30 to 11.30 am and 2.30 to 5.30 pm. Next door is 'Tom's Gym' – the equipment dates back to the Stone Age.

Sacred Heart Church

(shí shì jiàotáng) 石室教堂

This impressive edifice is known to the Chinese as the 'House of Stone', as it is built entirely of granite. Designed by the French architect Guillemin, the church is an imitation of a European Gothic cathedral. Four bronze bells suspended in the building to the east of the church were cast in France; the original coloured glass was also made in France, but almost all of it is gone.

The site was originally the location of the office of the governor of Guangdong and Guangxi provinces during the Qing Dynasty, but the building was destroyed by British and French troops at the end of the 2nd Opium War in the 19th century. The area was leased to the French following the signing of the Sino-French 'Tianjin Treaty'. Construction of the church began in 1863 and was completed in 1888. It's on Yide Lu, not far from the river front, and is normally closed except on Sundays when masses are said. All are welcome.

Another church you may find interesting is the Zion Christian Church at 392 Renmin Zhonglu. The building is a hybrid with a traditional European Gothic outline and Chinese eaves. It's an active place of worship.

Huaisheng Mosque

(húaishèng sì gūang tǎ) 怀圣寺光塔

The original mosque on this site is said to have been established in 627 AD by the first Muslim missionary to China, possibly an uncle of Mohammed. The present buildings are of recent construction. The name of the mosque means 'Remember the Sage', in memory of the prophet. Inside the grounds of the mosque is a minaret, which because of its flat, even appearance is known as the 'Guangta' or 'Smooth Tower'. The mosque stands on Guangta Lu, which runs eastwards off Renmin Zhonglu.

Mohammedan Tomb & Burial Ground

(mùhǎn mò dé mù) 穆罕默德墓

Situated in the Orchid Garden on Jiefang Beilu, this is thought to be the tomb of the Muslim missionary who built the original Huaisheng Mosque. (There are two other Muslim tombs outside the town of Quanzhou on the south-east coast of China, those of missionaries sent by Mohammed to accompany the one now buried in Canton.)

The Canton tomb is in a secluded bamboo grove behind the Orchid Garden – continue past the entrance to the garden, walk through the narrow gateway ahead and take the narrow stone path on the right. Behind the tomb compound are Muslim graves and a monumental stone arch. The tomb came to be known as the 'Tomb of the Echo' or the

'Resounding Tomb' because of the noises that reverberate in the inner chamber.

Pearl River

(zhū jiāng) 珠江

The north bank of the Pearl River is one of the most interesting areas of Canton; it's filled with people, markets and dilapidated buildings. A tourist boat-ride down the Pearl River runs daily from 3.30 to 5 pm and costs Y10. Boats leave from the pier just east of Renmin Bridge. They take you down the river as far as Ershatou and then turn around and head back to Renmin Bridge.

Liu'ersan Lu

(liùèrsān lù) 六二三路

Just before you reach the south end of Renmin Lu, Liu'ersan Lu heads west. 'Liu er san' means '6 2 3', referring to 23 June 1925, when British and French troops fired on striking Chinese workers during the Hong Kong-Canton strike.

Qingping Market

(qīngpíng shìchǎng) 清平市场

A short walk down Liu'ersan Lu takes you to the second bridge which connects the city to the north side of Shamian Island. Directly opposite the bridge, on the city side, is Qingping Market on Qingping Lu – one of the best city markets in the whole country yet one of Canton's lesser known attractions.

If you want to buy, kill or cook it yourself, this is the place to come since the market is more like a takeaway zoo. Near the entrance you'll find the usual selection of medicinal herbs and spices, dried starfish, snakes, lizards, deer antlers, dried scorpions, leopard and tiger skins, bear paws, tree bark and unrecognisable herbs and other plants.

Further up you'll find the living creatures waiting to be butchered: sad-eyed monkeys rattle at the bars of their wooden cages, tortoises crawl over each other in shallow tin trays, owls sit perched on boxes full of pigeons, fish paddle around in tubs aerated with jets of water. You can also get bundles of frogs, giant salamanders, pangolins, dogs and raccoons, alive or contorted by recent violent death – which may just make you swear off meat for the next few weeks.

The market spills out into Tiyun Lu, which cuts east-west across Qingping Lu. Further north is another area supplying vegetables, flowers, potted plants and goldfish. There are small, very cheap food stalls in the streets on the perimeter of the market.

Shamian Island

(shāmiàn) 沙面

Liu'ersan Lu runs parallel to the north bank of Shamian Island. The island is separated from the rest of Canton by a narrow canal to the north and east, and by the Pearl River to the south and west. Two bridges connect the island to the city.

Shamian means 'sand flat', which is all the island was until foreign traders were permitted to set up their warehouses (factories) here in the middle of the 18th century. Land reclamation has increased the area to its present size: 900 metres from east to west, and 300 metres from north to south. The island became a British and French concession (after they defeated the Chinese in the Opium wars) and is covered with decaying colonial buildings formerly trading offices and residences.

The French Catholic church has been restored and stands on the main boulevard. The old British church at the west end of the island has been turned into a workshop, but its past is betrayed by bricked-up Gothic-style windows. Today most of the buildings are used as offices or apartment blocks and the area retains a quiet residential atmosphere detached from the bustle across the canals.

Another 30,000 sq metres of land was added to the south bank of the island for the site of the 35-storey White Swan Hotel, which was built in the early 1980s. It's worth a walk along the north bank of Shamian Island to get a view of the houses on Liu'ersan across the canal. These are seedy three and four-storey terrace houses probably dating from the 1920s and '30s, but are a pretty sight in the morning or evening sun. A few buildings of much the same design survive in the back streets of Hong Kong Island.

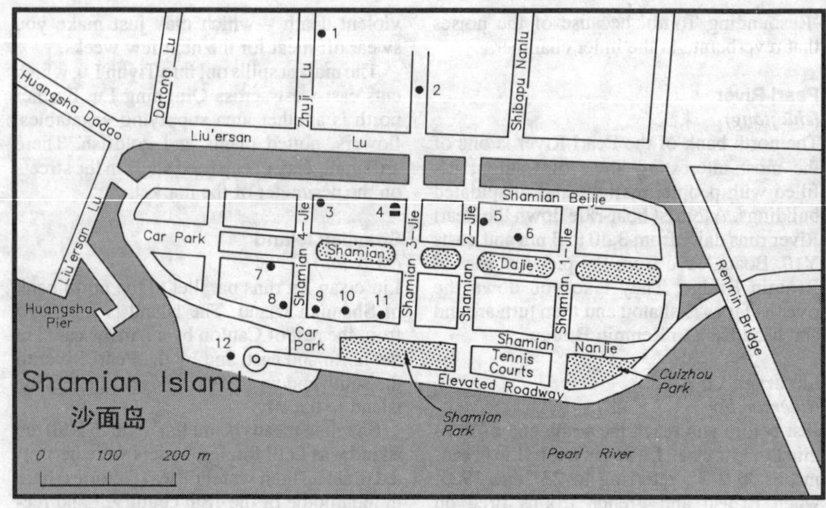

1 Traditional Chinese Medicine Hospital
2 Qingping Market
3 Victory Hotel
4 Post Office
5 Economical Restaurant
6 Guangdong Youth Hostel
7 Polish Consulate
8 Bike Hire
9 Guangzhou Youth Hostel
10 Shamian Hotel
11 Pearl Inn
12 White Swan Hotel

1 中医医院
2 清平市场
3 胜利宾馆
4 邮局
5 经济餐厅
6 广东青年旅舍
7 波兰领事馆
8 租自行车
9 广州青年招待所
10 沙面宾馆
11 夜明珠酒店
12 白天鹅宾馆

Just near the island, by the river bank on Yanjiang Lu near the Renmin Bridge overpass, stands the Monument to the Martyrs of the Shaji Massacre (as the 1925 massacre was known).

Cultural Park
(wénhùa gōngyúan) 文化公园
The Cultural Park was opened in 1956; the main entrance is on Liu'ersan Lu. Inside are merry-go-rounds, a roller-skating rink and an aquarium with exhibits from Guangdong Province. There are nightly dance classes, acrobatic shows, films and live performances of Cantonese opera (sometimes with full costume).

One of the most breathtaking motorcycle-stunt shows you'll ever see is held here in the

Top: Piling on the poultry for market (RS)
Bottom Left: Bird market, Chengdu (RS)
Bottom Right: Pressed pork in bike pannier (RS)

Top: The Bund, Shanghai (AS)
Bottom: Rice paddies at Shaoshan (AS)

evenings. Just as interesting is to watch the deadpan audience – no applause, no reaction. A foreigner walks down the street attracting lots of attention, but a motorcycle stuntman performs a 360° mid-air flip and people act like it's nothing.

The Cultural Park is usually open until 10 pm – it's worth dropping in.

Haichuang Park

(hǎichúang gōngyúan) 海幢公园

Renmin Bridge stands just east of Shamian Island and connects the north bank of the Pearl River to the area of Canton known as Henan, the site of Haichuang Park. This would be a nondescript park but for the remains of what was once Canton's largest monastery, the Ocean Banner Monastery. It was founded by a Buddhist monk in 1662, and in its heyday the monastery grounds covered 2½ hectares. After 1911 the monastery was used as a school and barracks. It was opened to the public as a park in the 1930s. Though the three colossal images of the Buddha have gone, the main hall remains and is now used at night as a dance hall (where live bands play). During the day the grounds are full of old men chatting, playing cards and chequers, and airing their pet birds.

The large stone which decorates the fish pond at the entrance on Tongfu Zhonglu is considered by the Chinese to be a tiger struggling to turn around. The stone came from Lake Tai in Jiangsu Province. During the Qing Dynasty the wealthy used these rare, strangely shaped stones to decorate their gardens. Many are found in the gardens of the Forbidden City in Beijing. This particular stone was brought back by a wealthy Cantonese merchant in the last century. The Japanese took over Canton in 1938 and plans were made to ship the stone back to Japan, though this did not happen. After the war the stone was sold to a private collector and disappeared from public view. It was finally returned to the park in 1951.

Yuexiu Park

(yùexiù gōngyúan) 越秀公园

This, the biggest park in Canton, covers 93 hectares, and includes the Zhenhai Tower, the Sun Yatsen Monument and the large Sculpture of the Five Rams.

The Sculpture of the Five Rams, erected in 1959, is the symbol of the city. It is said that long ago five celestial beings wearing robes of five colours came to Canton riding through the air on rams. Each carried a stem of rice which they presented to the people as an auspicious sign from heaven that the area would be free from famine forever. Guangzhou means 'Broad Region', but from this myth it takes its other name, City of Rams or just Goat City.

The Zhenhai Tower, also known as the Five Storey Pagoda, is the only part of the old city wall that remains. From the upper storeys it commands a view of the city to the south and the White Cloud Hills to the north. The present tower was built during the Ming Dynasty, on the site of a former structure. Because of its strategic location it was occupied by the British and French troops at the time of the Opium wars. The 12 cannon in front of the tower date from this time (five of them are foreign, the rest were made in nearby Foshan). The tower now houses the City Museum with exhibits describing the history of Canton from Neolithic times until the early part of this century.

The Sun Yatsen Monument is south of the Zhenhai Tower. This tall obelisk was constructed in 1929, four years after Sun's death, on the site of a temple to the goddess Guanyin. The obelisk is built of granite and marble blocks and there's nothing to see inside, though a staircase leads to the top where there's a good view of the city. On the south side of the obelisk the text of Dr Sun's last testament is engraved in stone tablets on the ground:

> For 40 years I have devoted myself to the cause of national revolution, the object of which is to raise China to a position of independence and equality among nations. The experience of these 40 years has convinced me that to attain this goal, the people must be aroused, and that we must associate ourselves in a common struggle with all the people of the world who treat us as equals. The revolution has not yet been successfully completed. Let all our comrades follow the principles set forth in my writings 'Plans for

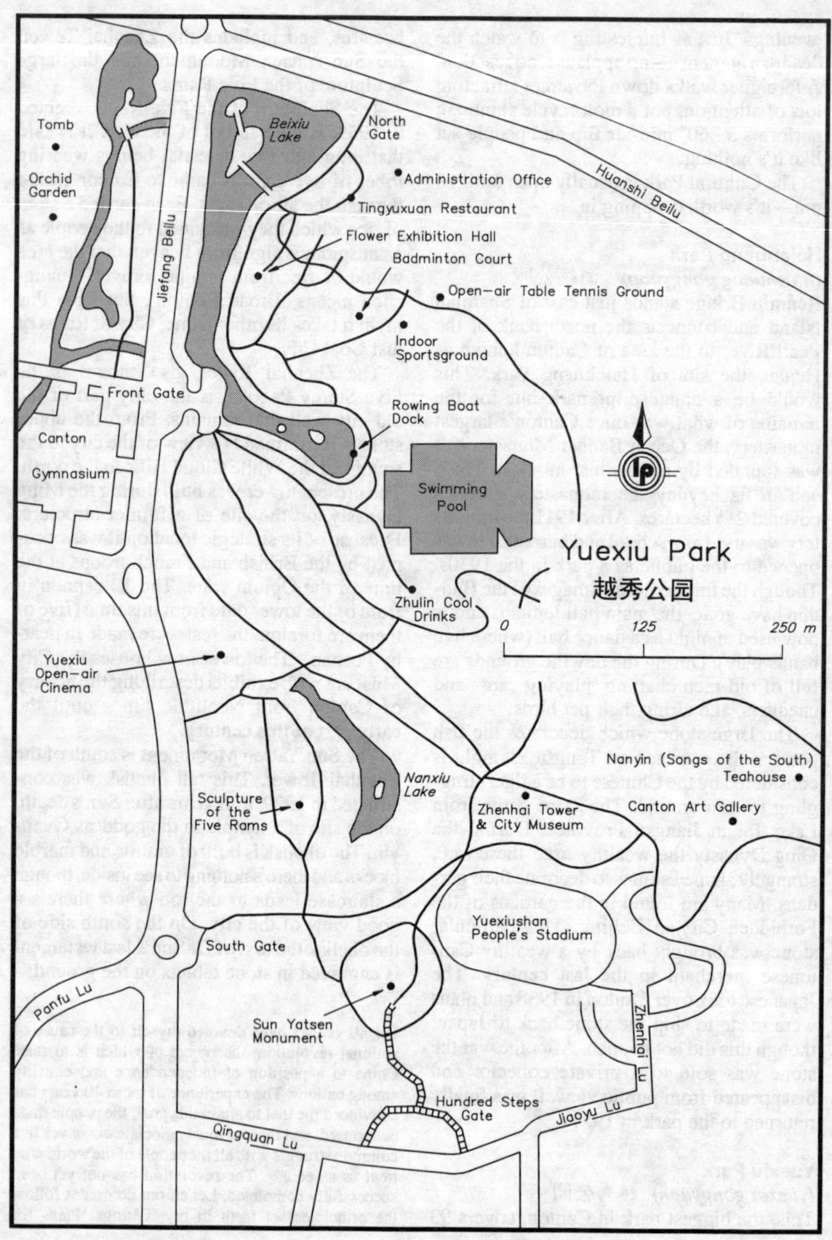
Yuexiu Park
越秀公园
Tomb
Orchid Garden
Jiefang Beilu
Beixiu Lake
North Gate
Administration Office
Tingyuxuan Restaurant
Flower Exhibition Hall
Badminton Court
Open-air Table Tennis Ground
Indoor Sportsground
Huanshi Beilu
Front Gate
Canton Gymnasium
Rowing Boat Dock
Swimming Pool
Zhulin Cool Drinks
0
125
250 m
Yuexiu Open-air Cinema
Nanxiu Lake
Sculpture of the Five Rams
Nanyin (Songs of the South) Teahouse
Zhenhai Tower & City Museum
Canton Art Gallery
Yuexiushan People's Stadium
South Gate
Panfu Lu
Sun Yatsen Monument
Zhenhai Lu
Hundred Steps Gate
Jiaoyu Lu
Qingquan Lu

National Renovation', 'Fundamentals of National Reconstruction', 'The Three Principles of the People' and the 'Manifesto of the First National Convention of the Kuomintang' and continue to make every effort to carry them into effect. Above all, my recent declaration in favour of holding a National Convention of the People of China and abolishing unequal treaties should be carried into effect as soon as possible.

This is my last will and testament.

(Signed) Sun Wen
11 March, 1925

West of the Zhenhai Tower is the Sculpture of the Five Rams. South of the tower is the large sports stadium with a seating capacity of 40,000. The park also has its own roller coaster. There are three artificial lakes: Dongxiu, Nanxiu and Beixiu – the last has rowing boats which you can hire.

Orchid Park

(lánpǔ) 兰圃

Originally laid out in 1957, this pleasant little park is devoted to over a hundred varieties of orchids. It's a great place in summer, but a dead loss in winter when all you will see are rows of flowerpots.

The Y2 admission fee includes tea by the small pond. The park, at the north end of Jiefang Beilu not far from the main railway station, is open daily from 7.30 to 11.30 am and 1.30 to 5 pm. It's closed on Wednesdays.

Nanyue Museum

(nányùe wáng hànmù) 南越王汉墓

Also known as the Museum of the Western Han Dynasty of the Nanyue King, this museum is built on the site of the palace of the second ruler of the Nanyue Kingdom dating back to 100 BC. (The Nanyue Kingdom is what the area around Canton was called back in the Han Dynasty.) It's an excellent museum with more than 500 rare artefacts on display. There are English descriptions and admission is Y3 for foreigners, Y1 for Chinese.

Liuhua Park

(liúhūa gōngyúan) 流花公园

This enormous park on Renmin Beilu contains the largest artificial lake in the city. It was built in 1958, a product of the ill-fated Great Leap Forward. The entrance to the park is on Renmin Beilu.

Canton Zoo

(gǔangzhōu dòngwùyúan) 广州动物园

The zoo was built in 1958 and is one of the better zoos you'll see in China, which is perhaps not saying much. It's on Xianlie Lu, north-east of the Mausoleum of the 72 Martyrs.

Guangdong Provincial Museum

(gǔangdōng shěng bówùgǔan)

广东省博物馆

The museum is on Yan'an 2-Lu on the south side of the Pearl River, and exhibits archaeological finds from Guangdong Province.

Zhongshan University

(zhōngshān dàxúe) 中山大学

Also on Yan'an 2-Lu, the university houses the Lu Xun Museum *(lǔ xùn bówùgǔan)*. Lu Xun (1881-1936) was one of China's great modern writers; he was not a Communist though most of his books were banned by the Kuomintang. He taught at the university in 1927.

Night Cruise

From April to October there are night cruises for tourists on the Pearl River. Departures are from Pier 39, the third pier east of the Renmin Bridge. The cruise covers a distance of 10 km and departs at 7.30 pm, returning at 8.45 pm. Check in advance to make sure that they are sailing.

Places to Stay – bottom end

Canton has quite a number of hotels to choose from, but only a few provide relatively cheap rooms and there's not much in the way of cheap dormitory accommodation.

Shamian Island is almost a happy hunting ground for cheapish hotels. To get to these, take bus No 5 from Huanshi Xilu; the stop is on the opposite side of the road and just to the west of the railway station. The bus runs along Liu'ersan Lu on the northern boundary of the canal which separates Shamian Island from the rest of Canton. Four footbridges connect Shamian Island to the city.

Near the massive White Swan Hotel is the *Guangzhou Youth Hostel* (☎ 884298) *(gǔangzhōu qīngnián zhāodàisǔo)* at 2 Shamian 4-Jie. It's the most popular hotel in Canton with low-budget travellers, and is reasonably clean and quiet. Dormitory beds cost from Y10 to Y14 and double rooms are Y40. There are no single rooms. The only negative thing is that the plumbing occasionally blows up, sending travellers scurrying across the street to the nearby White Swan to use the toilets.

Also on Shamian Island is the *Guangdong Youth Hostel* (☎ 887617) *(gǔangdōng qīngnián lǔshè)* 26 Shamian Dajie. Dorms cost from Y10 to Y14 and doubles are Y40. It's very clean and nice.

The only other place that might qualify as budget accommodation is the *CITS Hostel* (☎ 664263) *(gúolǔ zhāodàisǔo)*, right behind CITS and just east of the railway station. A dormitory bed costs Y14 in a four-bed room, but the catch is that you must supply your own roommates. So unless you can round up three friends, it will cost you Y56 to book the whole room *(bāofáng)* – hardly worth it.

Places to Stay – middle

The *Shamian Hotel* (☎ 888124) *(shāmiàn bīngǔan)* is only about five moneychangers east of the Guangzhou Youth Hostel on Shamian Island. Doubles start at Y87. They seem to have a permanent 'all full' sign on the front desk, but ask anyway because they sometimes have vacancies. Just because you manage to check in, don't think you can necessarily stay long. Big tour groups book this hotel in advance, so you might have a room today but be asked to move out the next day.

Also on Shamian Island is the *Victory Hotel* (☎ 862622) *(shènglì bīngǔan)*. There's a lack of English signs, but the hotel is easily identified – it looks like a seafood restaurant with big fish tanks outside. It's at the corner of Shamian 4-Jie and Shamian Beijie. Doubles cost Y104.

The *Aiqun Hotel* (☎ 661445) *(aìqún dàjiǔdiàn)* at 113 Yanjiang Xilu (at the corner of Changdi Damalu) is right on the river front. Singles cost Y70 and doubles Y110, a bargain for the high standard of accommodation. Some travellers have even managed to pay RMB. Take bus No 31 from the railway station; get off when you come to the river, turn left and walk up Yanjiang Lu for about 10 minutes.

The *White Palace Hotel* (☎ 882313) *(báigōng jiǔdiàn)* is a good place to stay though the staff speak little English. It's near the river at 17 Renmin Nanlu and doubles cost Y80.

Across the street from the White Palace is the *Xinya Hotel* (☎ 884722) *(xīnyà jiǔdiàn)* where doubles are Y91. The hotel is a huge, elegant-looking place popular with Hong Kongers but rather fewer foreigners.

The *GD Hotel* (☎ 883601) *(gǔangdōng dàjiǔdiàn)* is at 294 Changdi Damalu, one block north of the Aiqun Hotel. They charge Y126 for a double. No one here speaks English so they prefer foreigners who speak Chinese – otherwise they may claim to be all full.

The *Guangzhou Hotel* (☎ 338168) *(gǔangzhōu bīngǔan)* is at Haizhu (Sea Pearl) Square, east of the Aiqun Hotel. Singles cost Y135 while doubles are Y150. Bus No 29 from Huanshi Xilu near the railway station goes past the hotel. Haizhu Square is a big roundabout with a giant statue in the middle – you can't miss it.

Also on Haizhu Square is the *Huaqiao Hotel* (☎ 336888) *(húaqiáo dàxià)*, a beautiful place to stay but more inclined to take Chinese than Westerners. Doubles are from Y80 to Y140. This hotel is just next to CTS (not to be confused with CITS).

Places to Stay – top end

The *Liu Hua Hotel* (☎ 668800) *(liú hūa bīngǔan)* is a large tourist hotel at 194 Huanshi Xilu, directly opposite the railway station. It's easily recognisable by the big 'Seagull Watch' sign on the roof. Double rooms range from Y156 to Y190 and are very comfortable, though the cheaper ground-floor rooms can be very noisy.

The *Baiyun Hotel* (☎ 333998) *(báiyún*

bīngŭan), 367 Huanshi Donglu, is a huge place east of the railway station. Doubles start at Y120. Bus No 30 from the railway station goes past the hotel.

Opposite the Baiyun Hotel is the *Garden Hotel* (☎ 338989) *(hūayúan jiŭdiàn)* at 368 Huanshi Donglu, one of the most spectacular hotels in China. On top of the hotel is a revolving restaurant, and there's a snooker hall and a McDonald's-style fast-food joint on the ground floor. Doubles start at Y300.

Also in the same neighbourhood is the *Ocean Hotel* (☎ 765988) *(yŭanyáng bīngŭan)* at 412 Huanshi Donglu. It's an impressive luxury hotel with doubles from Y150 to Y200.

The *Guangdong Guesthouse* (☎ 332950) *(gŭangdōng yíng bīngŭan)*, 603 Jiefang Zhonglu, has doubles from Y180 to Y265. It's an exclusive-looking place with its own grounds and a wall around it. A sign by the lobby says that 'proper attire' is required at all times. It's a rather out-of-the-way place.

The *Dongfang Hotel* (☎ 669900) *(dōngfāng bīngŭan)* is at 120 Liuhua Lu near Jiefang Beilu and next to the China Hotel. It's a beautiful, well situated hotel. Singles cost from Y300 to Y350 and doubles from Y370 to Y420. It's about a 15-minute walk from the railway station and bus No 31 runs right by it.

Towering over the Dongfang Hotel is the gleaming *China Hotel* (☎ 666888) *(zhōnggúo dàjiŭdiàn)* which boasts wall-to-wall marble, a disco and a bowling alley. Rooms start at Y377 for singles and Y400 for doubles. It's one of the top-rated hotels and has a good Friendship Store.

The *White Swan Hotel* (☎ 886968) *(báitiāné bīngŭan)* certainly rates as one of the finest hotels in China. Aside from being magnificent (there's a waterfall in the lobby), it has a great location on Shamian Island. Of course, at Y400 for the cheapest double, it ought to be good. The White Swan is also popular with budget travellers for its post office, bank, ticket-booking office (boats and planes) and for its toilets which come in handy when the plumbing blows up at the adjacent youth hostel.

Places to Eat

There is an old Chinese saying that to enjoy the best that life has to offer, one has to be 'born in Suzhou, live in Hangzhou, eat in Canton and die in Liuzhou'. Suzhou is renowned for its beautiful women, Hangzhou for its scenery and Liuzhou for the finest wood for making coffins. Suzhou and Hangzhou are a bit overrated and who wants to die in China, but as Chinese food goes Canton ain't a bad place to stuff your face.

In this city there are dozens of famous old establishments along with heaps of smaller places, so eating out is not to be passed up. All the restaurants of any size have private rooms or partitioned-off areas if you want to get away from the crowds, but you'll pay more for the privilege.

Bakeries One of the great delights of Canton is that you can get decent bread and pastries for breakfast or snacks. The bakeries at the White Swan, China and Huaqiao hotels are cheap and very good.

Chinese Food On Shamian Island, the *Pearl Inn (yèmíngzhū jiŭdiàn)* is just to your right as you face the Shamian Hotel on Shamian Nanjie. They have good and cheap dim sum on the ground-floor restaurant. There is also a coffee shop serving Western breakfasts.

Also on Shamian Island is the *Victory Restaurant*, attached to the Victory Hotel. Prices are amazingly reasonable for such a high standard of service; there's good Chinese food, but seafood can be expensive. An English menu is available.

There are a couple of good places close to the river front. Foremost is the *Datong Restaurant* (☎ 888988) *(dàtóng jiŭjiā)* at 63 Yanjiang Xilu, just around the corner from Renmin Lu. The restaurant occupies all of an eight-storey building overlooking the river. Specialities of the house are crisp-fried chicken and roast suckling pig. The crisp-roasted pigskin is a favourite here. This is a great place for morning dim sum.

Close to the Datong Restaurant is the *Yan Yan Restaurant (rénrén càigŭan)* on Xihao

2-Lu, a side street which runs east from Renmin Lu. (Look for the pedestrian overpass which goes over Renmin Lu up from the intersection with Yanjiang Lu. The steps of the overpass lead down into a side street and the restaurant is opposite them.) The Yan Yan is easily recognisable by the fish tanks in the entrance. Get your turtles, catfish and roast suckling pig here. It's also fantastically well air-conditioned.

The *Aiqun Hotel* has a great restaurant on the 14th floor. Besides the food, it's worth coming up here just for the views overlooking the Pearl River.

One of the city's best known restaurants is the *Guangzhou* (☎ 862439) *(gǔangzhōu jiǔjiā)*, 2 Wenchang Nanlu near the intersection with Dishipu Lu. It boasts a 70-year history and in the 1930s came to be known as the 'first house in Canton'. Its kitchens were staffed by the city's best chefs and the restaurant was frequented by the most important people of the day. The four storeys of dining halls and private rooms are built around a central garden courtyard, where potted shrubs, flowers and landscape paintings are intended to give the feeling (at least to the people in the dingy ground-floor rooms) of 'eating in a landscape'. Specialities of the house include shark-fin soup with shredded chicken, chopped crabmeat balls and braised dove. It does tend to be expensive and reservations are sometimes nec-essary.

The *Moslem Restaurant* (☎ 888991) *(húimín fàndiàn)* is at 325 Zhongshan 6-Lu, on the corner with Renmin Lu. Look for the Arabic letters above the front entrance. It's an OK place, but go upstairs – the ground floor is dingy.

North of Zhongshan Lu is Dongfeng Lu, which runs east-west across the city. At 202 Xiaobei Lu is the *North Garden Restaurant* (☎ 333365) *(běiyúan jiǔjiā)*. This is another of Canton's 'famous houses' – a measure of its success being the number of cars and tourist buses parked outside. Specialities of the house include barbecued chicken liver, steamed chicken in huadiao wine, stewed fish head with vegetables, fried boneless

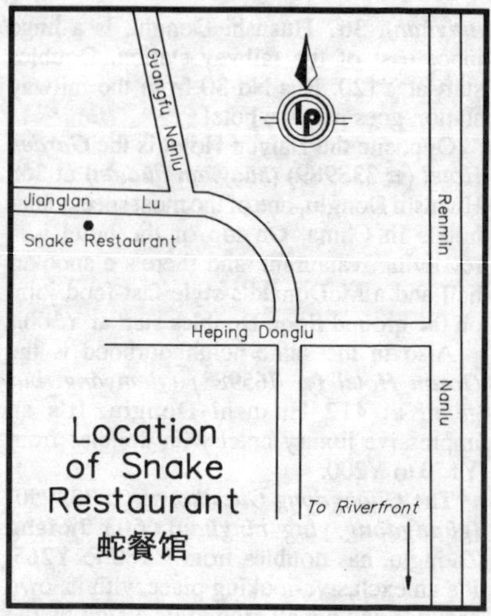

chicken,and stewed duck legs in oyster sauce. Good value.

In the west of Canton, the *Banxi* (☎ 815718) *(bànxī jiǔjiā)*, 151 Longjin Xilu, is the biggest restaurant in the city. It's noted for its dumplings, stewed turtle, roast pork, chicken in tea leaves and a crabmeat and shark-fin consommé. Its famed dim sum is served from about 5 to 9.30 am, at noon and again at night. Dim sum includes fried dumplings with shrimp, chicken gizzards, pork and mushrooms – even shark-fin dumplings! You can try crispy fried egg rolls stuffed with chicken, shrimp, pork, bamboo shoots and mushrooms. Monkey brains are steamed with ginger, spring onions and rice wine, and then steamed again with crab roe, eggs and lotus blossoms.

In the same general direction is the *Taotaoju* (☎ 887501) *(táotáojū)*, 288 Xiuli 2-Lu. Originally built as a private academy in the 17th century, it was turned into a restaurant in the late 19th century. Tao Tao was the name of the proprietor's wife. Dim sum is the speciality here; you choose sweet and savoury snacks from the selection on trolleys that are wheeled around the restaurant. Tea is the preferred beverage and is said to be made with Canton's best water – brought in from the Nine Dragon Well in the White Cloud Hills.

Beijing Lu has two of Canton's 'famous' restaurants. The *Wild Animals Restaurant (yěwèixiāng fàndiàn)* at No 247 is where you can feast on dogs, cats, deer, bear paws and snake. Once upon a time they even served tiger.

Highly recommended is the *Taipingguan* (☎ 332938) *(tàipínggǔan cāntīng)* at 344 Beijing Lu, which serves both Western and Chinese food. Zhou Enlai fancied their roast pigeon.

The *South Garden Restaurant* (☎ 448380) *(nányúan jiǔjiā)* is at 142 Qianjin Lu and the menu features chicken in honey and oyster sauce or pigeon in plum sauce. Qianjin Lu is on the south side of the Pearl River, to get to it you have to cross Haizhu Bridge and go down Jiangnan Dadao. Qianjin Lu branches off to the east.

Just to the west of Renmin Lu at 43 Jianglan Lu is the *Snake Restaurant* (☎ 883811) *(shécānguan)*, with the snakes on display in the window. The restaurant was originally known as the 'Snake King Moon' and has a history of 80 years. To get there you have to walk down Heping Lu which runs west from Renmin Lu. After a few minutes, turn right into Jianglan Lu and follow it around to the restaurant on the left-hand side. Creative snake recipes include fricasseed assorted snake and cat meats, snake breast stuffed with shelled shrimp, stir-fried colourful shredded snakes, and braised snake slices with chicken liver.

The Chinese believe that snake meat is effective in curing diseases. It is supposed to be good for dispelling wind and promoting blood circulation. It's believed to be useful in treating anaemia, rheumatism, arthritis and asthenia (abnormal loss of strength). Snake gall bladder is supposed to be effective in dispelling wind, promoting blood circulation, dissolving phlegm and soothing one's breathing. Way back in the 1320s the Franciscan friar Odoric visited China and commented on the snake-eating habits of the southern Chinese: 'There be monstrous great serpents likewise which are taken by the inhabitants and eaten. A solemn feast among them with serpents is thought nothing of'.

Cheap Eats Small government-owned dumpling *(jiǎozi)* restaurants are cheap and the food is usually good, but the service leaves a lot to be desired. Before you get your food you must pay the cashier and obtain tickets which you take to the cook. Especially when they are busy, customers tend to be ignored, so if you want something to eat you have to be aggressive. Just watch how the Chinese do it. Join the push-and-shove match, or else come back later in the off-peak hours.

Innumerable street stalls are open at night in the vicinity of the Aiqun Hotel. If you walk around the streets, and particularly along Changdi Damalu on the north side of the hotel, you'll find street stalls dishing up frogs, toads and tortoises. At your merest whim these will be summarily executed, thrown in the wok and fried. It's a bit like eating in an abattoir, but at least there's no doubt about the freshness.

Adequate but mundane food is served in the little restaurants in Zhanqian Lu, a lane which runs alongside the Liu Hua Hotel. A

Dim Sum Seller

few of these places are marginally better than the others; look around until you see something you like. Some of the restaurateurs have an aggravating habit of trying to snatch you off the street and charge ridiculous prices.

A couple of restaurants on Shamian Island are OK for a meal; they are popular with foreigners because of their proximity to the Guangzhou Youth Hostel. One restaurant worth trying is the *Economical Restaurant* (☎ 888784) *(jīngjì cāngǔan)*, 8 Shamian 2-Jie.

Vegetarian The *Caigenxiang Vegetarian Restaurant* (☎ 344363) *(càigēnxiāng sùshígǔan)*, 167 Zhongshan 6-Lu, is one of the few places in Canton where you don't have to worry about accidentally ordering dogs, cats or monkey brains.

Fast Food Kentucky Fried Chicken has not spread its wings yet in Canton, nor have the golden arches arrived on the scene, but there's the China Hotel's *Hasty Tasty Fast Food* shop (which opens on to Jiefang Beilu). It looks like and its product tastes exactly like any Hong Kong or US fast-food venue with banks of neon lights in the ceiling, laminex tables, and unremarkable food.

Another place that serves a somewhat improved version of fast food is the *Friendship Cafe*, which is next to the Friendship Store and the Baiyun Hotel on Huanshi Donglu. The 'Friendship Sandwiches' are especially recommended.

It was a hot and steamy summer afternoon. I was sitting in Hasty Tasty, Canton's premier fast-food restaurant, enjoying the air-conditioning and sipping a large Coke with ice. As I sat there contemplating where I would go next in this sizzling weather, a foreign tourist stepped up to the counter. His name was George.

George's wife was sitting at a table by the door. She wore a purple jump-suit, gaudy fake jewellery, horn-rimmed sunglasses and enough perfume to be a fire hazard. Her hair – flaming orange and held rigid by hair spray – looked like two jiao worth of cotton candy. She was carefully explaining to her two children how she would break both their arms if they didn't shut up and stop fighting with each other.

As George approached the counter, the waitress grinned at him. Perhaps she did that to all the customers, or perhaps it had something to do with the way George was dressed – in pink shorts, a flowered shirt and a white sunhat embroidered with a picture of a fish and the words 'Sea World'.

'May I take your order', the waitress said. George looked relieved, obviously pleased that the waitress could speak English. 'Excuse me, I don't want to order anything right now, but could you tell me where's the nearest McDonald's?'

'Sorry sir', the waitress replied, 'we don't have Mcdonald's in China. I have never eaten there. But they have in Hong Kong – I saw on television.'

You might as well have hit him with a freight train. Shock, horror, disbelief – you could see it in his face. George turned his back on the waitress without saying another word and trudged fearfully towards the table where his wife and two charming children were sitting.

'Well George', she bellowed, 'where's the Mcdonald's?'

'They haven't got one here', he answered coarsely. Immediately the two kids started yelling, 'We want a Big Mac!'

'Shut up!' George explained. 'We have to go back to Hong Kong!' I could see he was starting to panic. He slung his big camera over his shoulder, grabbed a shopping bag full of tourist junk purchased at the Friendship Store, and headed out the door with his wife and two children behind him. I watched from the window as they flagged down a taxi, and wondered if they were indeed heading for Hong Kong.

Robert Storey

Things to Buy

Canton's main shopping areas are Beijing Lu, Zhongshan Lu and the central section of Jiefang Lu. Beijing Lu is a most prestigious thoroughfare by Chinese standards. Names are sometimes misnomers; the Guangdong Products Exhibition Sales Centre, for example, seems to have more to do with the sale of Japanese stereos and video units than with Chinese products. Some street-markets specialise in Hong-Kong-produced goods, including posters and brand-name jeans.

Department Stores Canton's main department store is the Nanfang on Liu'ersan Lu, just to the east and opposite the main entrance to the Cultural Park.

The only other large store in the city is the Zhongshan Wulu Department Store, 250 Zhongshan 4-Lu.

Friendship Stores The Canton Friendship Store is next to the Baiyun Hotel on Huanshi Donglu, and has two or three levels selling everything from Moskovskaya Osobaya Vodka to Foshan paper-cuts and life-size replicas of the terracotta soldiers at Xi'an. They'll take a number of credit cards. Their packaging and shipping service will send stuff home for you, but they only handle goods bought from the store. The store is open from 9 am to 9.30 pm in summer, and probably for shorter hours in winter. There are arts & crafts stores in the China and New Garden hotels.

Antiques For antiques try that major tourist trap, the Guangdong Antique Store, in the Guangxiao Temple at 575 Hongshu Beilu. At 146 Wende Lu (which runs off Zhongshan Lu) is the Canton Antique Store – not as large as the Guangdong Antique Store, but worth a look.

Arts & Crafts The Jiangnan Native Product Store at 399 Zhongshan Lu has a good selection of bamboo and baskets. The Sanduoxuan on Beijing Lu, next door to the Foreign Language Bookstore at No 326, is Canton's main art-supply shop.

Getting There & Away

Canton is a transport bottleneck: from here you can travel by bus, train, plane or boat to numerous places in China. Even a few international flights pass through here (see the introductory Getting There & Away chapter for details).

Air To give pilots a challenge, the airport is right next to the White Cloud Hills, Canton's only mountains. There are daily flights to Hong Kong on CAAC and Cathay Pacific for Y190. Check the CAAC timetable for current listings. The CAAC office (☎ 662969) is at 181 Huanshi Lu, to your left as you come out of the railway station. You can also book tickets in the White Swan and China hotels.

The Airport Hotel (☎ 661700) *(báiyún jīchǎng bīngǔan)* is right next to the main terminal and is an excellent place to stay. In a nine-bed dorm, beds are Y20; Y35 in a three bed dorm; Y65 for a single and Y85 for a double. All rooms have air-con and are reasonably clean.

There are three restaurants on the 2nd floor of the terminal building – one is excellent and the other two are best avoided. The one on the balcony overlooking the passenger waiting area is cheap but has generally awful food. The plush, nearly deserted restaurant is for cadres and doesn't welcome individual travellers. The big, crowded restaurant is fantastic – excellent dim sum or set meals for around Y3, it's one of the best bargains in Canton.

Domestic flights with airfares from Canton are as follows:

Beihai Y208; Beijing Y633; Changchun Y973; Changsha Y192; Changzhou Y406; Chengdu Y475; Chongqing Y398; Dalian Y754; Dandong Y944; Guilin Y154; Guiyang Y276; Haikou Y176; Hangzhou Y369; Harbin Y1047; Hefei Y364; Hengyang Y142; Hohhot Y933; Huangshan 307; Ji'nan Y548; Kunming Y391; Lanzhou Y697; Lianyungang Y524; Liuzhou Y176; Luoyang Y463; Meixian Y110; Nanchang Y217; Nanjing 412; Nanning Y182; Ningbo Y393; Qingdao Y626; Qinhuangdao Y766; Sanya Y259; Shanghai Y414; Shantou Y127; Shashi Y302; Shenyang Y876; Shijiazhuang Y612; Taiyuan Y573; Tianjin Y663; Ürümqi Y1220; Wuhan Y285; Xiamen Y196; Xi'an Y589; Yantai Y700; Yichang Y310; Zhanjiang Y130; and Zhengzhou Y452

Bus The long-distance bus station is on Huanshi Xilu, a 10-minute walk west of the railway station. From there you can get buses to many places in and beyond Guangdong Province.

One possibility is to head up the south-east coast of China. The first major town on the route is Shantou. There are also buses to Quanzhou, Xiamen and Fuzhou.

Alternatively, head west to Zhanjiang. There are two buses daily: one air-con and one sweatbox. From Zhanjiang you can get a bus/boat combination to Haikou on Hainan Island.

There is a direct bus to Guilin which takes two days, overnighting in Wuzhou. There are one or two departures a day.

There are about eight or nine departures a

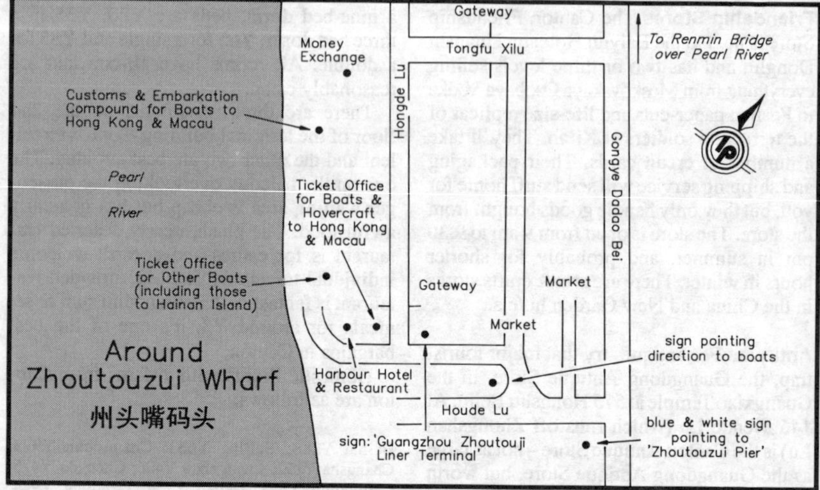

day to Zhuhai, the border town with Macau. The fare is about Y25 in an air-con minibus and Y10 in a local bus. Other air-con buses to Zhuhai leave from the Overseas Chinese Hotel in Haizhu Square, though these cost more; book with CTS at the hotel.

Train Foreigners must now buy all train tickets out of Canton from the CITS office near the main railway station. This means you'll have to pay tourist prices, but at least you avoid the formidable queues!

There are two ways of getting to Hong Kong by train. Quickest is the express train to Kowloon. Slower but cheaper is the local train from Canton to the border town of Shenzhen, where you cross the border and pick up the electric train to Kowloon. For full details see the introductory Getting There & Away chapter.

The fastest express to Beijing takes about 33 hours. The main line passes through Changsha, Wuhan, Zhengzhou and Shijiazhuang. Tourist-price fares from Canton to Beijing are Y140 hard-seat, Y233 hard-sleeper and Y444 soft-sleeper.

The express trip to Shanghai takes about 24 hours, and the line passes through Zhuzhou, Nanchang and Hangzhou. There is no direct train from Canton to Nanjing; you must first go to Shanghai and switch trains. An alternative would be to take the train as far as Hangzhou and then bus to Nanjing.

There is a direct train from Canton to Guilin. Alternatively, take a train to Hengyang and then change. The entire trip takes around 24 hours either way.

Boat Canton has two main wharves, Zhoutouzui and Dashatou. There is another harbour, Huangpu (also known as Whampoa), 25 km east of Canton.

Boats and hovercraft to Hong Kong, boats to Haikou (on Hainan Island) and boats to Macau leave from Zhoutouzui in the Henan area, on the south side of the Pearl River. For details of fares and departure times to Hong Kong and Macau see the Getting There & Away chapter.

To get to Zhoutouzui you have to cross Renmin Bridge, continue down Hongde Lu and turn into Houde Lu. Look for the sign in English pointing the way to Zhoutouzui Pier. Bus No 31 (not trolley bus No 31) from the main railway station will drop you off just near Houde Lu.

The ticket office for ferries and hovercraft to Hong Kong and Macau is at the gateway of the Guangzhou Zhoutouzui Liner Terminal. This ticket office may only sell tickets for same-day departure. Advance bookings can be made at the CTS office next to the Overseas Chinese Hotel in Haizhu Square.

Boats to Wuzhou leave from Dashatou on Yanjiang Donglu, in eastern Canton. From Wuzhou you can continue by bus to Yangshuo or Guilin. This is a very popular route.

There are four boats a day from Canton to Wuzhou. The first boat departs Canton at around 12.30 pm. The lower-class sections have accommodation reminiscent of concentration-camp bunks. Passengers are laid out like sardines in two long rows; you get a thin mat to put on the hard wooden deck, and a small partition a few inches high between you and the next person. Food is dished up on the boat, and the aisle between the rows of people is filled by a rain of chicken bones. If it really does rain then the windows are closed and the cabin can be stifling. You can also buy a combined boat/bus ticket from Canton to Yangshuo and Guilin. However, some travellers have found that when they arrived in Yangshuo, there was no bus waiting for them and the bus tickets they had bought were invalid.

Getting Around

Canton proper extends for some 60 sq km, with most of the interesting sights scattered throughout. Hence, seeing the place on foot is impractical. Just the walk from the railway station to the Pearl River is about six km.

To/From the Airport Canton's Baiyun airport is in the northern suburbs, 12 km from the city centre. There are frequent buses from the CAAC ticket office (next to railway station) to the airport – cost is 5 jiao. A taxi to the airport costs about Y15 from the White Swan Hotel.

Bus Canton has an extensive network of motor and electric trolley buses which will get you just about anywhere you want to go. The problem is that they're almost always packed, and if an empty bus pulls in at a stop then a battle for seats ensues.

Even more aggravating is the slowness with which Canton moves. Most of the streets are relatively narrow in comparison to those in other Chinese cities. They're also some of the most congested, a situation worsened in recent years by the importation of hundreds of Toyota taxis and Japanese motorcycles (many of them driven by Chinese people who seem to have picked up the kamikaze mentality as well). The end result is that even on a direct bus it can, for example, take up to 1½ hours to get from the zoo to Shamian Island in heavy traffic.

You just have to be patient, never expect anything to move rapidly and allow lots of time to get to the railway station to catch your train. Sometimes you may give up and walk. One consolation is that buses are cheap; you'll rarely pay more than two jiao per trip.

Good bus maps in Chinese are sold by hawkers outside the railway station and at some of the tourist-hotel bookshops. Get one! There are too many bus routes to list here but a couple of important ones are:

No 31 runs along Hongde Lu (east of Zhoutouzui Wharf), across Renmin Bridge, and straight up Renmin Lu to the main railway station at the north of the city.

No 30 runs from the main railway station eastwards along Huanshi Lu before turning down Nonglin Xialu to terminate in the east of the city. This is a convenient bus to take from the railway station to the Baiyun Hotel and New Garden Hotel.

No 5 takes a route similar to bus No 31, but instead of crossing Renmin Bridge it goes along Liu'ersan Lu on the north side of the canal which separates the city from Shamian Island. Get off here and walk across the small bridge to the island.

Bicycle The Guangzhou Youth Hostel on Shamian Island hires bicycles to its guests. Right across the street is another bike hire place. Rates are about Y1 per hour, or Y5 per day. A passport or deposit is necessary.

Check out Canton's unusual method of pedestrian and bicycle control. Old men and women, equipped with armbands and small flags, stand on the streets apprehending jaywalkers and hauling them before a police officer who gives an on-the-spot fine; this is not taken lightly by many offenders, whose vehement arguments are matched only by the remarkable enthusiasm of the traffic wardens for their job! Other traffic wardens put parking tickets on illegally parked bicycles.

Taxi Taxis are available from the major hotels 24 hours a day and from outside the railway station. They can be hailed in the streets; the demand for taxis is great, particularly during peak hours (from 8 to 9 am, and at lunch and dinner times).

Flagfall is around Y3 depending on the type of taxi. A ride from the White Swan Hotel to the railway station will cost about Y8. Drivers are supposed to accept RMB, but with foreigners they'll usually try to get FEC.

You can hire taxis for a single trip or on a daily basis – the latter is definitely worth considering if you've got the money or if there's a group of people who can split the cost. Beware, some drivers refuse to use their meters.

Minibus Minibuses which seat about a dozen people ply the streets on set routes. If you can find out where they're going they're a good way of avoiding the crowded buses.

AROUND CANTON

A couple of places around Canton make good full-day or half-day trips. Buses to some of these depart either from the long-distance bus station on Huanshi Xilu, or from the provincial bus station opposite the long-distance bus station. For some destinations you have to get buses from smaller bus stations around the city.

White Cloud Hills

(báiyún shān) 白云山

These hills in the north-east suburbs of Canton are an offshoot of Dayuling, the chief mountain range of Guangdong Province. The White Cloud Hills were once dotted with temples and monasteries, though no buildings of historical significance remain today. The hills are popular with the local people who come here to admire the views and slurp cups of tea – the Cloudy Rock Teahouse, on the hillside by a small waterfall, is a pleasant place to do this.

The White Cloud Hills are about 15 km from Guangzhou – a good half-day excursion. Express buses leave from Yuehua Lu near the corner with Jixiang Lu. The trip takes about 30 minutes. The bus may stop just short of the lake. About midway to the hills you go past one of China's biggest amusement parks (opened in 1985) complete with roller coasters, ferris wheels and loops.

At the southern foot of the hills is Luhu Lake – also called Golden Liquid Lake (something of a misnomer). Built for water storage in 1958, it's now used as a park. The lake is bounded by eucalyptus trees, bamboo groves and the occasional hibiscus. You can swim in it, and by the bank is a small drinks shop which rents tyre tubes.

The highest peak in the White Cloud Hills is Moxingling (Star Touching Peak) which only rises 382 metres (anything higher than a kiddie's sandcastle is a mountain in eastern China). From here there's a panorama of the city below, the Xiqiao Hills to one side, the North River and Fayuan Hills on the other side, and the sweep of the Pearl River.

The Chinese rate the evening view from Cheng Precipice as one of the eight sights of Canton. The precipice takes its name from a Qin Dynasty story. It is said that the first Qin emperor, Qin Shihuang, heard of a herb which would confer immortality on whoever ate it. Cheng On Kee, a minister, was dispatched to find it. Five years of wandering brought Cheng to the White Cloud Hills where the herb grew in profusion. When he ate the herb, the rest of it disappeared. In dismay and fearful of returning empty-handed, Cheng threw himself off the precipice. But assured immortality since he had eaten the herb, he was caught by a stork and taken to heaven. The precipice, named in his memory, was formerly the site of the oldest monastery in the area.

North of the Cheng Precipice, on the way up to Moxingling, you'll pass the Nine Dragons Well – the origins of which are also legendary. One story goes that Canton officials came to worship twice yearly and also at times of drought at the Dragon Emperor Temple that used to exist on this spot. During the 18th century, the governor of Canton visited the temple during a drought. As he prayed he saw nine small boys dancing in front of the temple. They vanished when he rose, and a spring bubbled forth from where he had knelt. A monk at the temple informed the amazed governor that these boys were, in fact, nine dragons sent to advise the governor that his prayers had been heard in heaven – hence the spring became known as the 'Nine Dragons Well'.

Lotus Mountain

(liánhūa shān) 莲花山

This interesting and exotic place is only 46 km to the south-east of Canton and makes an excellent full-day trip. The name Lotus Mountain might conjure up images of some holy mountain like Emeishan or Huangshan. In fact, it's nothing like that.

Lotus Mountain is a old quarry site. Most people wouldn't think of a quarry as being attractive, but this place happens to be an exception. The stone cutting ceased several hundred years ago and the cliffs have sufficiently eroded to a state where it looks almost natural.

Attempts to dress up the area by building pagodas, pavilions and stone steps have made it into a sort of gigantic rock garden. Dense vegetation and good views of the Pearl River add to the effect. Overall, most of the buildings fit in well with the scenery. If only someone could persuade the Chinese people to stop filling up the lotus ponds and gorges with bottles, cans and plastic bags, the area might become more popular.

However, Lotus Mountain is now a popular weekend stop-off for tour groups from Hong Kong, which means that it would be best to visit on weekdays.

There is one good restaurant on the mountain in the Lotus Mansion *(liánhūa lóu)*. It's doubtful that you'd want to spend the night here but there is one hotel, the Lotus Mountain Villa *(liánhūa shānzhūang)*.

You can get to Lotus Mountain by either bus or boat, but the boat trip is more interesting. The once-daily boat leaves Canton at 8.45 am and takes about 2½ hours to reach Lotus Mountain, departing for Canton at 4.15 pm. That gives you about five hours on the mountain, which should be about right for a relaxing hike and picnic.

The boat leaves from Tianzi Pier *(tiānzì mǎtóu)* on Yanjiang Zi Lu, one block east of Haizhu Square and the Haizhu Bridge. It's not a bad idea to buy a ticket one day in advance to avoid long lines on the day of departure. There are mahjong tables on the boat and you won't have any trouble finding partners if you want to participate.

Buses depart from the railway station area in Canton. In theory the bus should be faster than the boat but, with Canton's notorious traffic jams, it works out to be about the same. Soft drinks are available on the boat, but no food.

The major hotels in Canton also run tours to Lotus Mountain, though this will cost considerably more than doing it yourself. It also looks like they take all the fun out of the trip. You can see these tour groups, usually led by a young woman in uniform holding up a megaphone and shouting explanations as the tourist troops march by leaving a trail of rubbish.

Xiqiao Hills

(xīqiáo shān) 西樵山

Another scenic spot, these hills are 68 km south-west of Canton. There are 72 peaks in the area (the highest rises 400 metres) together with 36 caves, 32 springs, 28 waterfalls and 21 crags. At the foot of the hills is the small market town of Guanshan, and scattered around the upper levels are several stone villages which are centuries old. Most of the area is accessible by stone paths; it's popular with Chinese tourists but European visitors are rare.

Conghua Hot Springs

(cōnghùa wēnqúan) 从花温泉

The Conghua Hot Springs are about 80 km north-east of Canton. The springs are supposed to have a curative effect on neuralgia, arthritis, dermatitis and hypertension; one tourist leaflet even claims they relieve 'fatigue of the cerebral cortex' (headache?) and gynaecological problems. This major Chinese health resort is peaceful and tastefully laid out.

Buses to Conghua depart from the provincial bus station – about six times a day, maybe more frequently on weekends. The cost is Y10 for a journey of about 2½ hours. As soon as you get to the springs, buy a ticket for the return journey to Canton because buses are often full. The place is thick with bodies at the weekend, so try to avoid going then.

Guangdong 广东

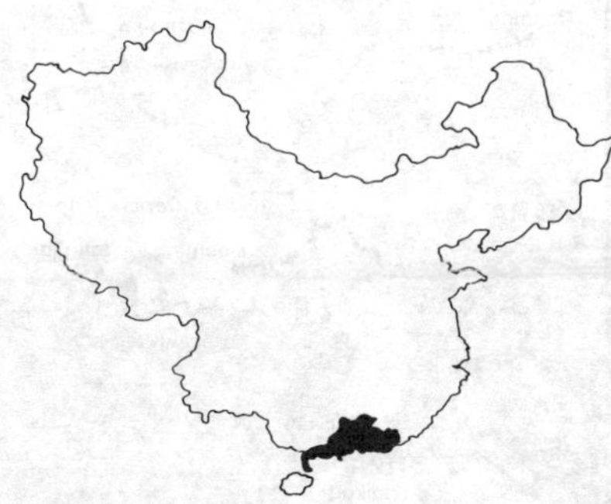

Over 2000 years ago when the Chinese were carving out a civilisation centred on the Yellow River, southern China remained a semi-independent tributary state peopled by native tribes, the last survivors of which today form minority groups. It was not until the Qin Dynasty (221-207 BC), when the northern states were united for the first time under a single ruler, that the Chinese finally conquered the southern regions. Revolts and uprisings were frequent and the Chinese settlements remained small, dispersed amongst a predominantly aboriginal population.

Chinese emigration to the south began in earnest around the 12th century AD. The original tribes were killed by Chinese armies, isolated in small pockets, or pushed further south (like the Li and Miao peoples now inhabiting the mountainous areas of Hainan Island). By the 17th century the Chinese had outgrown Guangdong *(guǎngdōng)*, and population pressure forced them to move into adjoining Guangxi Province, and Sichuan which had been depopulated after rebellions in the mid-17th century.

Because of these migrations the people of Guangdong are not a homogeneous group. The term 'Cantonese' is sometimes applied to all people living in Guangdong Province but more commonly it refers to those who shared the language and culture of a grouping of counties during the last imperial dynasties. Other inhabitants of Guangdong like the Hakka people who started moving south from the northern plains around the 13th or 14th centuries AD are distinguished from the 'Cantonese' by their language and customs.

What the migrants from the north found beyond the mountainous areas of northern and western Guangdong was the Pearl River Delta, a region richer than any in China except for the Yangtse and Yellow river areas. The Pearl River Delta lies at the south-east end of a broad plain which stretches over both Guangdong and Guangxi provinces. Because of their fertility the delta and river valleys could support very large populations. The abundant waterways, heavy rainfall and warm climate allowed wet-rice cultivation. Two crops a year could be grown (although in the past century the population increase was more than Guangdong could sustain, so grain had to be imported).

The people of Guangdong Province were the first Chinese to make (often unhappy) contact with the merchants and armies of the modern European states. They spearheaded the Chinese emigration to the USA, Canada, Australia and South Africa in the mid-19th century, spurred on by the gold rushes in those countries and by the wars and growing poverty in their own country. The image which most Westerners have today of a 'Chinatown' is based on Guangdong's chief city, Canton. It is mostly Cantonese food which is eaten and the Cantonese dialect which is most spoken among the Chinese populations from Melbourne to Toronto to London.

SHENZHEN SPECIAL ECONOMIC ZONE

(shēnzhèn jīngjì tèqū) 深圳经济特区

The Shenzhen municipality stretches across the northern border of Hong Kong from Daya Bay in the east to the mouth of the Pearl River in the west. Though hardly a place to

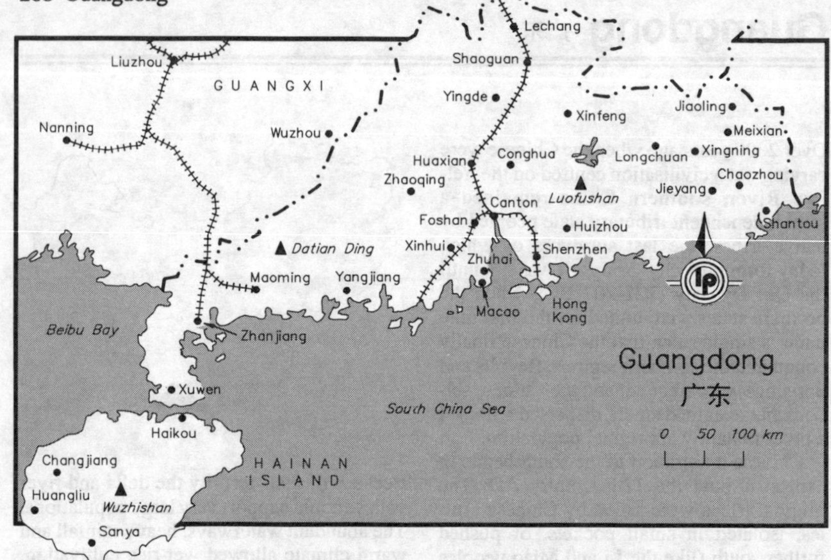

linger, Shenzhen town is worth looking around for a few hours since it is the centre of a major Special Economic Zone.

This SEZ was set up in a small part of the Shenzhen municipality in 1979. The area was chosen for several reasons: it is adjacent to Hong Kong, thus allowing easier access to the world market; most Hong Kong business people speak the same dialects and maintain kinship relations with people in Shenzhen and other parts of southern China; there is easy access to the port facilities of Hong Kong; the level land is suitable for settlement and industrial plants; there's a ready supply of raw materials for the construction industry.

Special Economic Zones in general were set up to promote foreign and Overseas Chinese investment in China using reduced taxation, low wages, abundant labour supply and low operating costs as incentives. The theory behind this is that China can be modernised quicker and more easily if it imports foreign technology and expertise. The SEZs form a sort of geographical laboratory where Western capitalist economic principles can be tested using cheap socialist labour. These zones are not a new idea and bear some resemblance to the Export Processing Zones found in 30 other countries.

In the SEZs foreigners can invest in anything which the state deems useful for the country, be it production of goods for export or construction of private-housing estates. These can be joint ventures, cooperative enterprises or wholly foreign-owned operations. A uniform income-tax rate of 15% is applied. Whether the SEZs actually benefit China is debatable. The zones were conceived of as a means of obtaining foreign technology and capital, and of producing exports with a minimum of disruption to the rest of the country's economy. One main problem has been that these zones import equipment and raw materials but most of their output is ultimately sold in China, not exported. The amount of money they produce for China may be far less than the money the government puts into them to keep them running. Most of the foreign industries set up in Shenzhen in the first years after it opened were relatively simple ones – like electronics assembly – which fell well short of the capital and technology-intensive investment that China sought.

Other problems resulted when this laissez-faire capitalism was unleashed on Chinese territory, not least of which was the booming black market in just about everything. One of the main problems in Shenzhen has been that the Hong Kong Chinese 'compatriots' as well as PRC Chinese sell Hong Kong currency at a higher black-market rate than the official rate, then buy Chinese produce at the free markets, thus undercutting the official export prices, and ship the goods off to their markets in Hong Kong and Macau. It's said that one of the things that has upset many bigwigs in the Chinese government is that black-market dealing has put their own business enterprises in Shenzhen at a disadvantage.

Various plans have been conjured up to solve these problems. One was the idea of introducing a whole new currency for use only in Shenzhen, thus halting the black-market dealing in foreign currency. The new currency would replace all other currencies in the SEZ – Renminbi, Foreign Exchange Certificates and Hong Kong dollars.

SHENZHEN TOWN

(shēnzhèn shì) 深圳市

The showpiece of the SEZ is Shenzhen town, once a fishing village but transformed in just a few years into a small town with high-rise buildings. The centrepiece is the 600-bed, 33-storey Asia Hotel complex topped by, you guessed it, a revolving restaurant. There are Friendship stores and air-con restaurants (the locals pause in the doorways for a breath of cool air), and at the nearby Xili Reservoir there are holiday resorts and golf courses for Hong Kongers searching for more breathing space.

Information & Orientation

A 'tourist service' booth near the railway station exit distributes hotel brochures and can make hotel bookings. The staff are friendly but speak little English. Many of the highrise hotels in Shenzhen can be seen from the station.

Also next to the railway station are the taxi stand and bus terminal.

Places to Stay

The *Overseas Chinese Hotel* (☎ 222811) *(huáqiáo dàshà)*, across the tracks from the railway station at 68 Heping Lu, has rooms for around Y100. Cheaper is the *Shenzhen Hotel* (☎ 238000) *(shēnzhèn lǚdiàn)*, four blocks up Jianshe Lu from the railway station. Rooms here start at Y25 per person.

Most other hotels in town cost around Y250 per room, including the *City Hotel* (☎ 257000), 2 Wenjin Lu, and the *Feng Yuan Hotel* (☎ 253268), 548 Nanfang Dongmen Hubei Lu , both in the north-west part of the city.

Getting There & Away

For full details of transport between Hong Kong, Shenzhen and Canton see the introductory Getting There & Away chapter.

Air The Huangtian International Airport is expected to open in 1992 at Shenzhen and will rival Hong Kong's proposed new airport. It will also handle domestic traffic.

Bus Outside Shenzhen railway station you can get minibuses to Canton; the fare is about Y15.

From Shenzhen there are CITS buses to Canton (Y22), and to towns on the south-east coast including Shantou (Y60) and Fuzhou, Xiamen, Zhangzhou and Quanzhou (from Y100 to Y120). The buses leave from the CITS office in the Overseas Chinese Hotel.

Train There are about a dozen local trains a day between Canton and Shenzhen. Tourist-price tickets are HK$35 hard-seat, HK$65 soft-seat (Y23 hard-seat, Y42 soft-seat). The trip takes 3½ hours.

At Shenzhen you pass through Customs and catch the electric train to Kowloon. The border closes at 10 pm (check this, it may vary throughout the year). The 2nd-class fare from the Hong Kong border station of Lo Wu to Kowloon station is HK$26. The first train to Kowloon station is at 6 am and the last is at 11.30 pm.

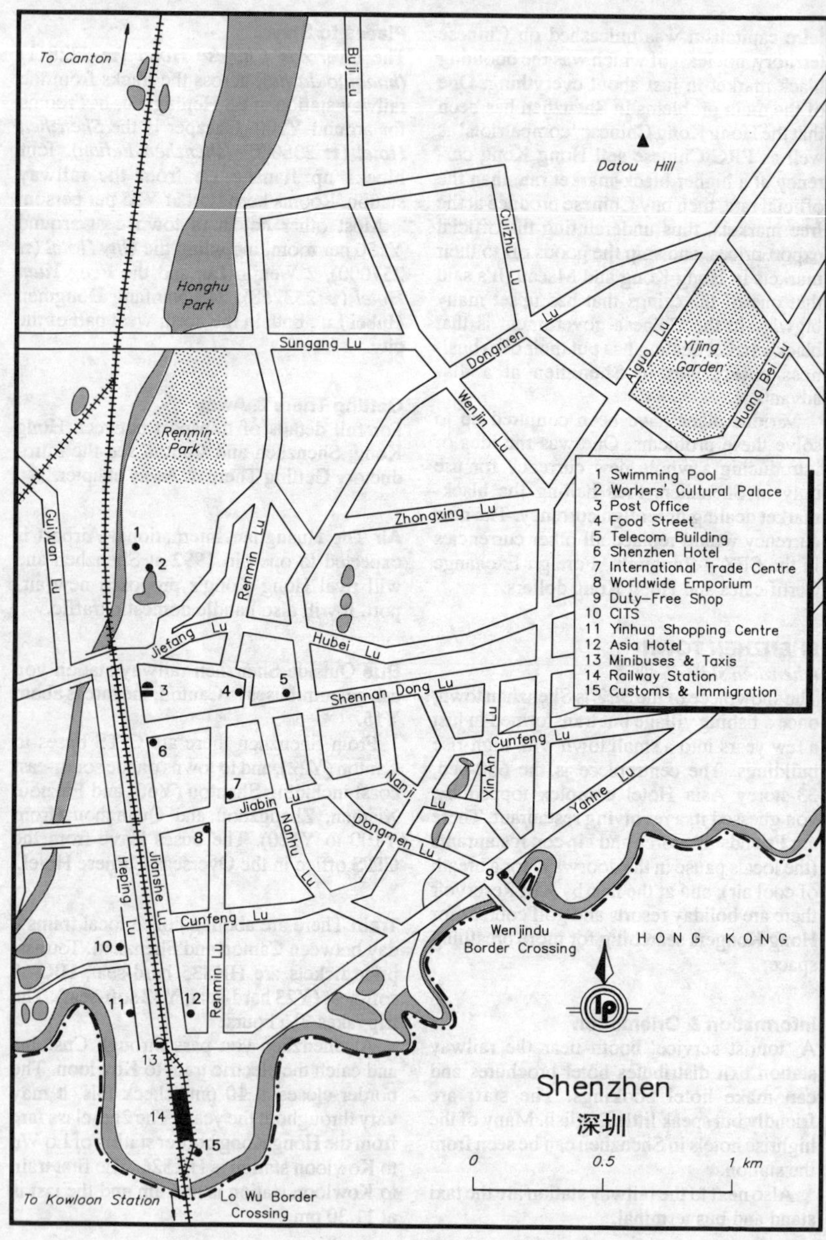
To Canton
Buji Lu
Datou Hill
Cuizhu Lu
Honghu Park
Sungang Lu
Dongmen Lu
Aiguo Lu
Yijing Garden
Huang Bei Lu
Wenjin Lu
Renmin Park
1 Swimming Pool
2 Workers' Cultural Palace
3 Post Office
4 Food Street
5 Telecom Building
6 Shenzhen Hotel
7 International Trade Centre
8 Worldwide Emporium
9 Duty-Free Shop
10 CITS
11 Yinhua Shopping Centre
12 Asia Hotel
13 Minibuses & Taxis
14 Railway Station
15 Customs & Immigration
Zhongxing Lu
Guiyuan Lu
Renmin Lu
Jiefang Lu
Hubei Lu
Shennan Dong Lu
Xin An Lu
Cunfeng Lu
Nanji Lu
Yanhe Lu
Jiabin Lu
Nanhu Lu
Dongmen Lu
Heping Lu
Jianshe Lu
Cunfeng Lu
Wenjindu Border Crossing
HONG KONG
Renmin Lu
Shenzhen
深圳
0
0.5
1 km
To Kowloon Station
Lo Wu Border Crossing

1	游泳池
2	工人文化宫
3	邮局
4	汇食街
5	电信大楼
6	深圳旅店
7	国际贸易中心
8	环球商业中心
9	免税商店
10	中国国际旅行社
11	银华购物中心
12	亚洲大酒店
13	小汽车和出租汽车出租点
14	火车站
15	海关

FOSHAN

(fóshān) 佛山

Just 28 km south-west of Canton is the town of Foshan; the name means 'Buddha Hill'. The story goes that a visiting monk from India built a hilltop temple for three buddha statues. In the following centuries the shrines and the statues were forgotten but hundreds of years later, during the Tang Dynasty (618-907 AD), the buddha figurines were suddenly rediscovered, a new temple was built on the hill, and the town was renamed.

Whether the story is true or not, from around the 10th century, Foshan has been an important religious centre. Because of its location in the north of the Pearl River Delta with the Fen River flowing through it, and its proximity to Canton, Foshan was ideally placed to take off as a market town and a trade centre as well.

From around the 10th or 11th centuries, Foshan has also been noted as one of the four main handicraft centres of old China. The other three were Zhuxian in Henan Province, Jingdezhen in Jiangxi and Hankou in Hebei. Nearby towns, since swallowed up by the expansion of Foshan, also developed distinctive crafts. Shiwan became famous for its pottery and Nanpu for metal casting. Silk weaving and paper-cutting are other popular local crafts and, today, Foshan paper-cuts are one of the most commonly sold tourist souvenirs in China.

Foshan has one other claim to fame: as Guangdong Province's top soy-sauce producer it provides half of China's soy-sauce exports to over 40 countries.

Orientation

The bus from Canton heads into Foshan from the north and pulls in outside Foshan railway station. The train line starts in Canton, passes through Foshan and continues west for about 60 km to the town of Hekou. From the railway station, walk down the Canton-Zhanjiang highway (Fenjiang Zhonglu). Turn left down any side street. Walk for about 10 minutes and you'll come to one of Foshan's main streets, Song Feng Lu. A right turn onto Song Feng Lu will point you in the direction of the town centre and the market on Lianhua Lu. Exploring the twisty streets of Foshan's older north-east section provides an interesting afternoon's diversion.

Lianhua Market

(liánhuā shìchǎng) 莲花市场

The market can't compare to Qingping Market in Canton, but it's worth a wander if you're in Foshan. Stock up on half-dead fish, turtles, snakes, crabs or skinned and roasted dogs. Other stalls offer flowers, birds and goldfish.

Ancestors' Temple

(zǔ miào) 祖庙

The Ancestors' Temple is at the south end of Zumiao Lu. The original temple was built during the Song Dynasty in the late 11th century, and was used for ancestor worship by workers in the metal-smelting trade. It was destroyed by fire at the end of the Yuan Dynasty in the mid-1300s and was rebuilt during the reign of the first Ming emperor Hong Wu. The Ancestors' Temple was con-

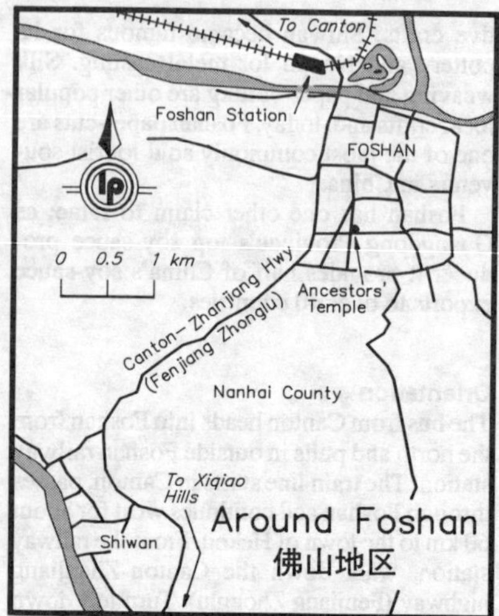

verted into a Taoist temple because the emperor worshipped a Taoist god.

The temple was developed through renovations and additions in the Ming and Qing dynasties. The structure is built entirely of interlocking wooden beams, with no nails or other metal, and is roofed with coloured tiles made in Shiwan. The latest additions are a children's amusement park in the forecourt, rows of souvenir hawkers outside, and plaster of Paris imitations to replace the original statues. In spite of all this, however, the temple-fairground is once again an active place of worship.

The main hall has an interesting collection of ornate weapons used on ceremonial occasions during the imperial days as well as a huge statue of Beidi or the Northern Emperor. Beidi is also known as the Black Emperor or Heidi, who rules over water creatures including fish, turtles and snakes.

To keep Beidi happy and to convince him not to cause floods, a frequent problem in southern China, temples are frequently built in his honour. Carved figures of snakes and turtles are also offered to this god of the waters. In the courtyard is a pool containing a large statue of a turtle with a serpent slithering over it. The Chinese throw one, two and five-fen notes (plus the odd soft-drink can) onto the turtle.

The Foshan Antiques Store is in the temple grounds. More interesting is the Chinese lantern-making workshop in the pagoda compound on Zumiao Lu, just north of the temple.

Places to Stay

The central and fairly inexpensive *Jiu Jiang (Pearl River) Hotel* (☎ 87512) *(zhūjiāng fàndiàn)* has triples without air-con that cost Y45, while doubles with air-con start at Y60.

Across the road the *Rotating Palace Hotel (xuángōng jiǔdiàn)* is Foshan's newest, which got its name because, yes, there's a revolving restaurant (or, as the English sign says, 'revolting restaurant') on top. Doubles in this glittering 16-storey tower are Y130. Even if you don't stay here, take the elevator to the observation deck on the 16th floor and look across the sea of old tiled roofs in the centre of town and the industrial smokestacks beyond; if Foshan began as a religious centre you'd hardly know it now.

The *Overseas Chinese Mansion (huáqiáo dàshà)* (☎ 86511) is on Zumiao Lu opposite the pagoda. Singles are Y75, doubles Y100. Over on Fenjiang Nanlu, near CITS, are several larger hotels that are patronised mostly by well-to-do Overseas Chinese. The flash *Foshan Hotel* (☎ 87923) *(fóshān bīnguǎn)* features doubles starting from HK$288 and up (FEC not accepted). Opposite the CITS office is the similarly priced *Golden City Hotel*. Probably one of the best bargains in town is the relatively new *Chang Cheng Hotel* (☎ 26733) at the corner of Fenjiang Nanlu and Renmin Lu; clean, air-con doubles here cost Y90.

Places to Eat

Cheap eats are to be found at the bus station on the Canton-Zhanjiang highway; squid, omelettes and chicken come in decent portions for a few yuan per person. Try the places along Songfeng Lu and Lianhua Lu; there are also several restaurants along here similar to the one at the bus station.

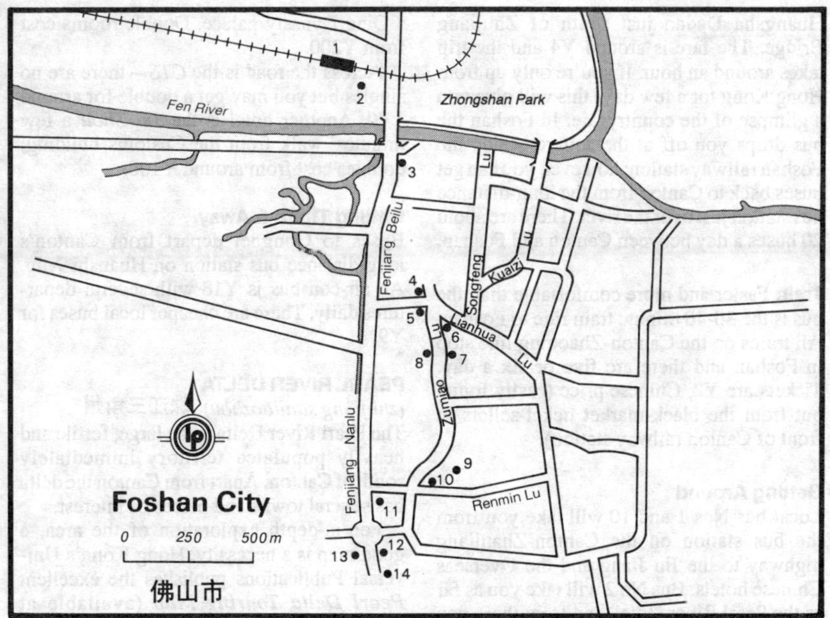

1 Railway Station
2 Buses to Canton
3 Long-Distance Bus Station
4 Post Office
5 Jiu Jiang Hotel
6 Rotating Palace Hotel
7 Pagoda
8 Overseas Chinese Mansion
9 Foshan Museum/Antiques Store
10 Ancestors' Temple
11 Chang Cheng Hotel
12 CITS
13 Golden City Hotel
14 Foshan Hotel

On Zumiao Lu near the Ancestors' Temple are two good dim sum places, the plebeian *Rose* and its classier cousin, *Fok Lam*. There are also several decent pastry shops around here.

1 火车站
2 开往广州汽车
3 长途汽车站
4 邮局
5 珠江宾馆
6 旋转餐店宾馆
7 宝塔
8 华侨大厦
9 佛山博物馆/古玩店
10 祖宗庙
11 长城宾馆
12 国际旅行社
13 金城宾馆
14 佛山宾馆

Getting There & Away

Bus Buses to Foshan from Canton leave from the bus station in west Canton, on

Huangsha Dadao just south of Zhujiang Bridge. The fare is around Y4 and the trip takes around an hour. If you're only up from Hong Kong for a few days this will give you a glimpse of the countryside. In Foshan the bus drops you off at the square beside the Foshan railway station; however, you can get buses back to Canton from the long-distance bus station just over the river. There are about 20 buses a day between Canton and Foshan.

Train Faster and more comfortable than the bus is the 30-40 minute train ride to Foshan. All trains on the Canton-Zhaoqing line stop in Foshan and there are five or six a day. Tickets are Y2, Chinese price (easily found out from the black-market ticket-sellers in front of Canton railway station).

Getting Around

Local bus Nos 1 and 10 will take you from the bus station on the Canton-Zhanjiang highway to the Jiu Jiang and the Overseas Chinese hotels. Bus No 2 will take you as far as the Pearl River Hotel, and from there you can walk to the Overseas Chinese Hotel.

GONGBEI

(gǒngběi) 拱北

Gongbei is the Chinese town bordering Macau. Like its big brother Shenzhen, it's been built from the soles up in the past few years with numerous office blocks and apartment buildings sprouting for a km or so back from the border. Yet for all this a bus ride from Gongbei to Canton reminds you that China is very much a rural society, where peasants water their fields with cans slung on poles over their shoulders, people make their way up rivers by boat standing as they push their oars, motorcyclists transport basket-loads of geese and slaughtered pigs are slung over the backs of bicycles.

Places to Stay

The *Gongbei Palace Hotel* (☎ 23831) *(gǒngběi bīnguǎn)* comes complete with disco, billiard room, swimming pool, sauna and video games. They say it's modelled on a Qing Dynasty palace. Double rooms cost from Y200.

Across the road is the *CTS* – there are no singles but you may get a double for around Y70. Another hotel is the *Jiu Zhou* a few minutes' walk from the Customs building; doubles cost from around Y100.

Getting There & Away

Buses to Gongbei depart from Canton's long-distance bus station on Huanshi Xilu. An air-con bus is Y18 with several departures daily. There are cheaper local buses for Y9.

PEARL RIVER DELTA

(zhūjiāng sānjiǎozhōu) 珠江三角州

The Pearl River Delta is the large, fertile and heavily populated territory immediately south of Canton. Apart from Canton the delta has several towns and places of interest.

For in-depth exploration of the area, a good map is a necessity. Hong Kong's Universal Publications publishes the excellent *Pearl Delta Touring Map* (available at Swindon's on Peking Rd in Kowloon), which is keyed in pinyin as well as Chinese characters. This map shows most roads and is colour-coded for elevation.

Zhuhai Special Economic Zone

(zhūhǎi) 珠海

This area immediately to the north of Macau was set up as a Special Economic Zone in 1979. The principal town is Xiangzhou, nine km north of Macau. From Gongbei you can get buses to various places in Zhuhai.

Zhongshan County

(zhōngshānxiàn) 中山县

Zhongshan County is immediately north of Zhuhai. The administrative centre is Shiqi. Zhongshan is the birthplace of Dr Sun Yatsen, who was born in the village of Cuiheng 29 km from Macau. His former house, which still stands in the village, was built in 1892 with money sent from Honolulu by his elder brother. There is also a Sun Yatsen Museum set up in 1966. South-west of Cuiheng are the Zhongshan Hot Springs,

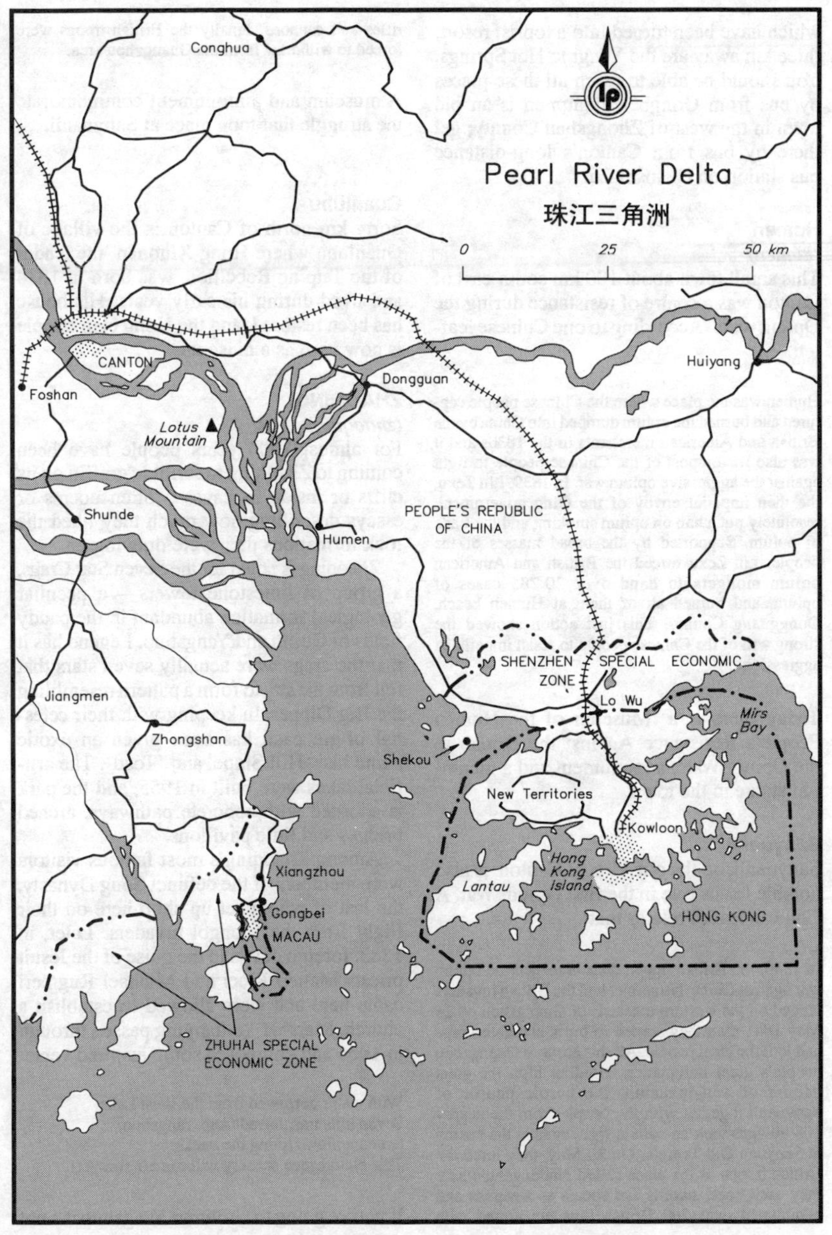
Pearl River Delta
珠江三角洲
0
25
50 km
Conghua
Huiyang
Dongguan
CANTON
Foshan
Lotus Mountain
Shunde
Humen
PEOPLE'S REPUBLIC OF CHINA
SHENZHEN SPECIAL ECONOMIC ZONE
Lo Wu
Mirs Bay
Jiangmen
Zhongshan
Shekou
New Territories
Kowloon
Hong Kong Island
Lantau
HONG KONG
Xiangzhou
Gongbei
MACAU
ZHUHAI SPECIAL ECONOMIC ZONE

which have been turned into a tourist resort; three km away are the Yungmo Hot Springs. You should be able to reach all these places by bus from Gongbei. Jiangmen is an old town in the west of Zhongshan County; get there by bus from Canton's long-distance bus station on Huanshi Lu.

Humen

(hǔmén) 虎门

This small town about 100 km south-east of Canton was a centre of resistance during the Opium wars. According to one Chinese leaflet:

> Humen was the place where the Chinese people captured and burned the opium dumped into China by the British and American merchants in the 1830s and it was also the outpost of the Chinese people to fight against the aggressive opium war. In 1839, Lin Zexu, the then imperial envoy of the Qing government, resolutely put a ban on opium smoking and the trade of opium. Supported by the broad masses of the people, Lin Zexu forced the British and American opium mongers to hand over 20,285 cases of opium...and burned all of them at Humen beach, Dongguang County. This just action showed the strong will of the Chinese people to resist imperialist aggression...

Today there is a 'Museum of the Humen People's Resistance Against the British in the Opium War', a monument and a memorial statue in the town.

Sanyuanli

Sanyuanli, on the outskirts of Canton, is also notable for its role in the first Opium War. A Chinese leaflet relates that:

> In 1840, the British imperialists launched the opium war against China. No sooner had the British invaders landed on the western outskirts of Guangzhou on 24 May 1841 than they started to burn, slaughter, rape and loot the local people. All this aroused Guangzhou people's great indignation. Holding high the great banner of anti-invasion, the heroic people of Sanyuanli together with the people from the nearby 103 villages took an oath to fight against the enemy at Sanyuan Old Temple. On 30 May, they lured the British troops to the place called Niulangang where they used hoes, swords and spears as weapons and annihilated over 200 British invaders armed with rifles and cannons. Finally the British troops were forced to withdraw from the Guangzhou area.

A museum and a monument commemorate the struggle that took place at Sanyuanli.

Guanlubu

Forty km north of Canton is the village of Guanlubu where Hong Xiuquan, the leader of the Taiping Rebellion, was born in 1814 and lived during his early years. His house has been restored, and the Hong clan temple is now used as a museum.

ZHAOQING

(zhàoqìng) 肇庆

For almost 1000 years people have been coming to Zhaoqing to scribble graffiti on its cliffs or inside its caves – often poems or essays describing how much they liked the rock formations they were drawing on.

Zhaoqing is noted for the Seven Star Crags, a group of limestone towers – a peculiar geological formation abundant in the paddy fields of Guilin and Yangshuo. Legend has it that the crags were actually seven stars that fell from the sky to form a pattern resembling the Big Dipper. In keeping with their celestial origin each has been given an exotic name like 'Hill Slope' and 'Toad'. The artificial lakes were built in 1955, and the park is adorned with concrete pathways, arched bridges and little pavilions.

Among Zhaoqing's most famous visitors were members of the defunct Song Dynasty, the last of whom set up shop here on their flight from the Mongol invaders. Later, in 1583, foreign devils in the guise of the Jesuit priests Matteo Ricci and Michael Ruggieri came here and were allowed to establish a church. Marshal Ye Jianying passed through in 1966 and composed some inspired verse:

> With water borrowed from the West Lake,
> Seven hills transferred from Yangshuo,
> Green willows lining the banks
> This picturesque scenery will remain forever!

If you're going to Guilin or Yangshuo it's not

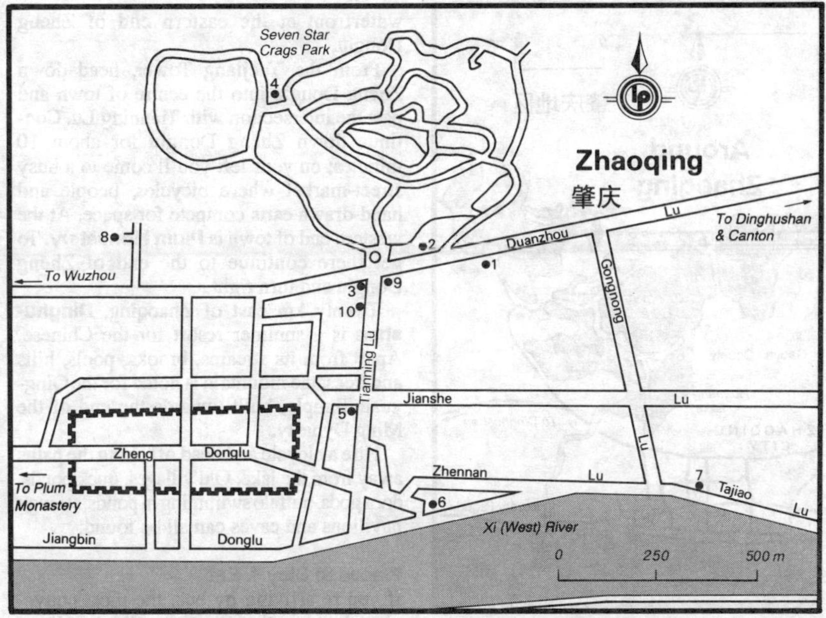

1 Long-Distance Bus Station
2 Local Bus Station
3 Overseas Chinese Hotel
4 Bohailou Hotel
5 Post Office
6 Yuejiang Tower
7 Chongxi Pagoda
8 Furong Hotel
9 Bicycle Hire
10 Duanzhou Hotel

1 长途汽车站
2 汽车站
3 华侨饭店
4 波海楼
5 邮局
6 阅江楼
7 崇禧楼
8 芙蓉宾馆
9 自行车出租店
10 端州饭店

worth coming here just to see the hills, but the ride to Zhaoqing from Canton, and the town itself are interesting.

Orientation

Zhaoqing, 110 km west of Canton on the Xi (West) River, is bounded to the south by the river and to the north by Duanzhou Lu. Zhaoqing is a small place and much of it can be seen on foot.

The long-distance bus station is on Duanzhou Lu. Turn left out of the station and walk for a few minutes to the traffic circle where you'll find the multistorey Zhaoqing Mansion and the entrance to Seven Star Crags Park. Tianning Lu is the main street with

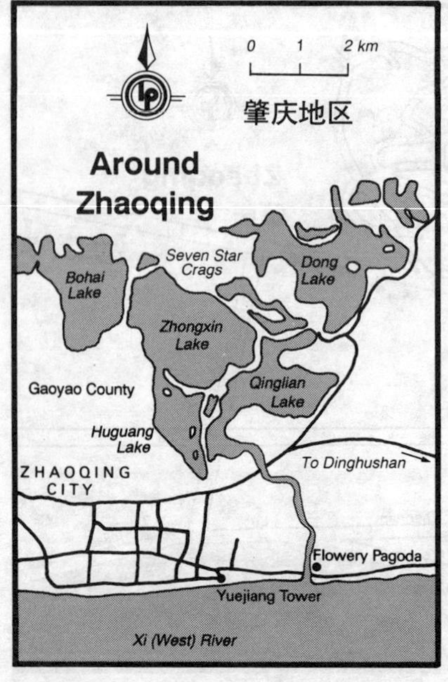

many shops, cheap restaurants and noisy canteens.

Streets to the west of it lead off into the older part of Zhaoqing. It's a 20-minute walk to Jiangbin Donglu, which hugs the north bank of the Xi River.

Things to See

Zhaoqing is a town for walking around. It's a place where the peak-hour bicycle crush goes hand-in-hand with quiet side streets, and where dilapidated houses are equipped with colour TVs and outdoor communal toilets.

The nine-storey **Chongxi Pagoda** *(chōngxīlóu)*, in a sad state until a few years ago, has been restored and stands on Tajiao Lu in the south-east. On the opposite bank of the river are two similar pagodas. Tajiao Lu, a quiet riverside street, has interesting old houses. **Yuejiang Tower** *(yuèjiānglóu)* is a restored temple about a 30-minute walk from the Chongxi Pagoda, just back from the waterfront at the eastern end of Zheng Donglu.

From the Yuejiang Tower, head down Zheng Donglu into the centre of town and past the intersection with Tianning Lu. Continue down Zheng Donglu for about 10 minutes; on your left you'll come to a busy street-market where bicycles, people and hand-drawn carts compete for space. At the western end of town is **Plum Monastery**. To get there continue to the end of Zheng Donglu and turn right.

Twenty km east of Zhaoqing, **Dinghushan** is a summer resort for the Chinese. Apart from its streams, brooks, pools, hills and trees, the mountain is noted for the Qingyuan Temple, built towards the end of the Ming Dynasty.

Hire a bicycle and head off along the paths away from the lake. Old villages, duck ponds, door gods, buffalo swimming in ponds, strange pavilions and caves can all be found.

Places to Stay & Eat

If you're arriving by bus, the most convenient hotel is the *Overseas Chinese Hotel (huáqiáo fàndiàn)* on the corner of Duanzhou Lu and Tianning Beilu. Big double rooms cost from Y75 on the ground floor (probably noisy) and Y100 upstairs – very adequate. The *Duanzhou Hotel (duānzhōu fàndiàn)* next door is similar.

In the west part of town is the *Furong Hotel (fúróng bīnguǎn)* with reasonably priced rooms beginning at Y50.

The *Bohailou Hotel (bōhǎilóu)* is on the north side of Zhong (Central) Lake in the Seven Star Crag Park. It's more attractive than many other Chinese hotels but no less cold and dreary inside. If you're here in the off-season it's extremely quiet, with farms behind it and the lake in front. Doubles cost from Y65. Between the railway station and Seven Star Crags is the similarly priced but nicer *Songtao Hotel*. Although these hotels are a bit remote from town, they have the advantage of having better scenery and being close to the railway station.

One can only hope that the Songs and the Jesuits ate somewhat better. There's nothing remarkable to be had here. The bus station has a cheap, tolerable restaurant; there are cheap restaurants along Duanzhou Lu and Tianning Lu.

Getting There & Away

Bus There are buses to Zhaoqing from Canton's long-distance bus station on Huanshi Xilu. The fare is Y10. There are half a dozen buses a day and the trip takes about 2½ hours. Try to avoid returning to Canton on a weekend afternoon; traffic jams are common on this road.

Privately run minibuses operate between Zhaoqing and Canton. In Zhaoqing the minibus ticket office is inside the main gate of the Seven Star Crags Park. The fare to Canton is Y15 and there are several buses each day.

Train Trains from Canton cost Y14 hard-seat and take about two hours. The journey to Foshan (1½ hours) costs Y11.

Boat The dock and ticket office for boats to Wuzhou and Canton is at 3 Jiangbin Donglu, just west of the intersection with Renmin Nanlu. It appears that only lower-class boat tickets can be bought here since Zhaoqing is an intermediate stop. Boats to Wuzhou and Canton depart in the early evening. Fares to both cities are Y10 in 3rd class and Y8.70 in 4th class. From Zhaoqing to Wuzhou takes around 12 hours. From Zhaoqing to Canton is a 10-hour trip.

Getting Around

The local bus station is on Duanzhou Lu, a few minutes' walk east of the intersection with Tianning Lu. Bus No 1 runs to the ferry dock on the Xi River. Bus Nos 4 and 5 go to the Plum Monastery.

Auto-rickshaws may be hired from the rank opposite the long-distance bus station. If you catch one in the street beware of overcharging. Taxis are dispatched from an office at the rear of the bus station.

The railway station is well out of town near the north-west corner of the lake. A taxi into town costs Y10 or you can grab a minibus for Y2.

The best way to get around Zhaoqing is by bicycle. There is a hire place diagonally opposite the main entrance to the Seven Star Crags. They ask exorbitant fees but will accept Y5 per day.

ZHANJIANG

(zhànjiāng) 湛江

Zhanjiang is a major port on the southern coast of China, and the largest Chinese port west of Canton. It was leased to France in 1898 and remained under French control until WW II.

Today the French are back, but this time Zhanjiang is a base for their oil-exploration projects in the South China Sea. Perhaps more importantly, Zhanjiang is a naval base and part of China's southern defences against what is construed as a threat from the Vietnamese.

You're most likely to come to Zhanjiang if you're on your way from Canton or Nanning to Hainan Island. The bus ride from Canton is an interesting trip, although Zhanjiang itself is one of the greyest towns in China.

Zhanjiang is divided into two parts separated by a stretch of countryside several km long. It's a good place to wander around at night when the crowds are out in the streets, but is rather dusty and boring during the day – too many concrete blocks, drab streets and slums.

Perhaps to liven things up the Chinese have opened some coral reefs to snorkelling and scuba diving. One of the sites is off Naozhou on an island near the Zhanjiang Peninsula. The second is off Fangji Isle east of Zhanjiang. The third site is near Dongmao and Ximao islands in Hainan Island's Sanya Bay.

Places to Stay

There is a *Chinese Hotel* you can stay at in the north part of town. Turn right out of the north bus station, and the hotel is 10 minutes up the road. It's very noisy – you won't want to hang around for too long – but otherwise it's OK. You should be able to get a bed or

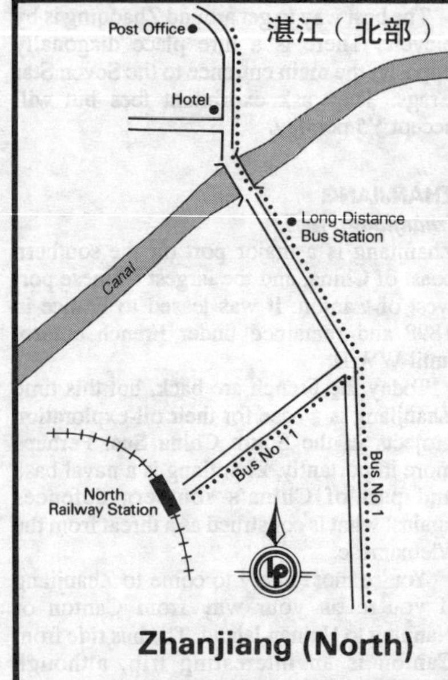

even a single room for less than Y25 – if they'll have you.

The *Canton Bay Overseas Chinese Hotel* (☎ 224996) is in the southern part of town at 22 Renmin Dadao. Double rooms start at Y70.

The *Haibin Hotel* (☎ 223555) *(hǎibīn bīnguǎn)* on Haibin 2-Lu is a Hong Kong-China joint venture on the southern outskirts of Zhanjiang. Double rooms are Y120 in the new wing and Y82 in the old wing. The hotel boasts a Hong-Kong-trained staff, Chinese restaurant, cocktail lounge, coffee shop, outdoor pool and sauna.

Getting There & Away

Air There are daily flights from Zhanjiang to Canton.

Bus You should be able to get buses to Canton from both the north and south bus stations. The trip takes about 13½ hours. The fare is Y25 in a non air-con bus, Y48 air-con.

Train Trains to Guilin and Nanning leave from the South railway station. From Zhanjiang to Guilin takes about 13 hours. From Zhanjiang to Nanning takes about 9½ hours. Tourist-price tickets from Zhanjiang to Nanning are Y36 hard-seat and Y79 hard-sleeper.

Boat You can take a bus-boat combination to Haikou on Hainan Island. A bus takes you from Zhanjiang to Hai'an on the Leizhou Peninsula (five hours), where you take a boat to Haikou (two hours). The bus station at Hai'an is about 100 metres uphill from the harbour. The harbour ticket office is a dingy place, but you can deposit baggage here or buy maps of Haikou.

Some travellers have reported persistent urchins here who dangle a slip of paper which says: 'I help you, you want to Haikou, you give me Y20, the boat leaves at...all aboard'. They'll try to hang on to the change and your baggage and generally create a nuisance until you're thankful to escape onto the boat.

Combined bus/boat tickets cost Y17.70. You should be able to buy tickets at the Chinese hotel in the northern part of Zhanjiang. If not, there's a booking office opposite the nearby post office. Or buy a separate bus ticket at the bus station and a boat ticket when you get to Leizhou Peninsula.

There's also a fast vessel (resembling a Hong Kong jetfoil) from Leizhou Peninsula to Hainan Island which takes 45 minutes; the fare is Y12.

Getting Around

There are two railway stations and two long-distance bus stations, one each in the northern and southern parts of town.

Bus No 1 runs between the two parts. This bus may be designated by a double-headed arrow (surrounded by calligraphy) rather than by a numeral.

If you arrive at the north bus station take bus No 1 to the southern part of town. This will drop you off near of the Overseas Chinese Hotel. If you arrive at the south railway station take bus No 10 to the hotel.

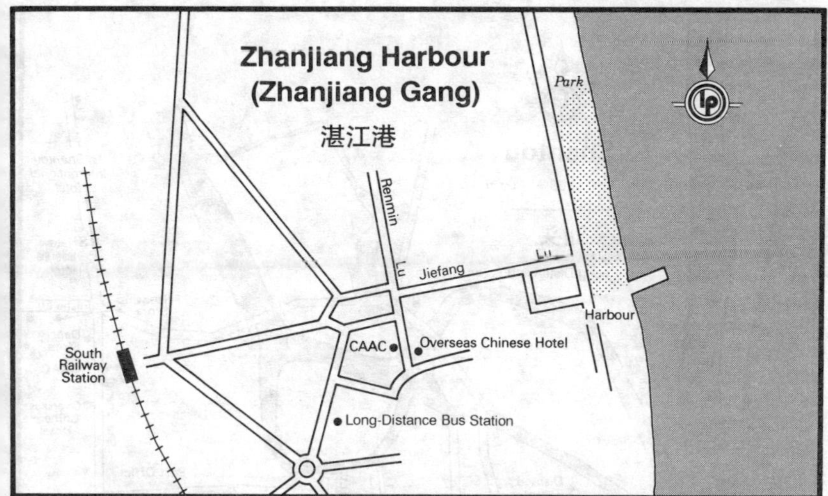

There are many motorcycles-and-sidecars cruising the streets; agree on a price beforehand or they'll charge you the earth.

SHANTOU

(shāntóu) 汕头

Considering the length of the south and south-east coasts of China, they are remarkably deficient in seaports. The main problem is the constant accumulation of silt and mud rendering the natural harbours cramped and shallow. Only a few places, like Xiamen and Hong Kong, are fortunate enough to have unlimited deep-water accommodation. On top of that, the mainland ports are handicapped by the mountainous country which surrounds many of them, making communication and transport of goods difficult. Canton's predominance is partly due to the delta waterway system which gives it a better communication and transport system than any of its rivals.

Shantou is the chief port of eastern Guangdong. As early as the 18th century the East India Company had a station on an island outside the harbour, when the town was little more than a fishing village on a mudflat. The port was officially opened up to foreign trade in 1860 with the Treaty of Tianjin, which ended another Opium War. The British were the first to establish themselves here, though their projected settlement had to relocate to a nearby island due to local hostility. Before 1870 foreigners were living and trading in Shantou town itself.

Today Shantou is the first major stop on the long haul along the coast road from Canton to Fujian. This colourful, lively place is the centre of a unique local culture that extends as far as Chaozhou. Shantou and the surrounding area has its own language (called *Chao Shan* in Mandarin – a combination of Chaozhou and Shantou – or *tae jiu* by the people themselves) and its own cuisine. Because many of the Overseas Chinese living in Thailand come from the Shantou-Chaozhou area, it's not unusual to see the occasional business sign written in the Thai language as well as Chinese.

Information & Orientation

Most of Shantou lies on a sort of peninsula, bounded in the south by the ocean and separated from the mainland in the west and the north by a river and canals. The bulk of the

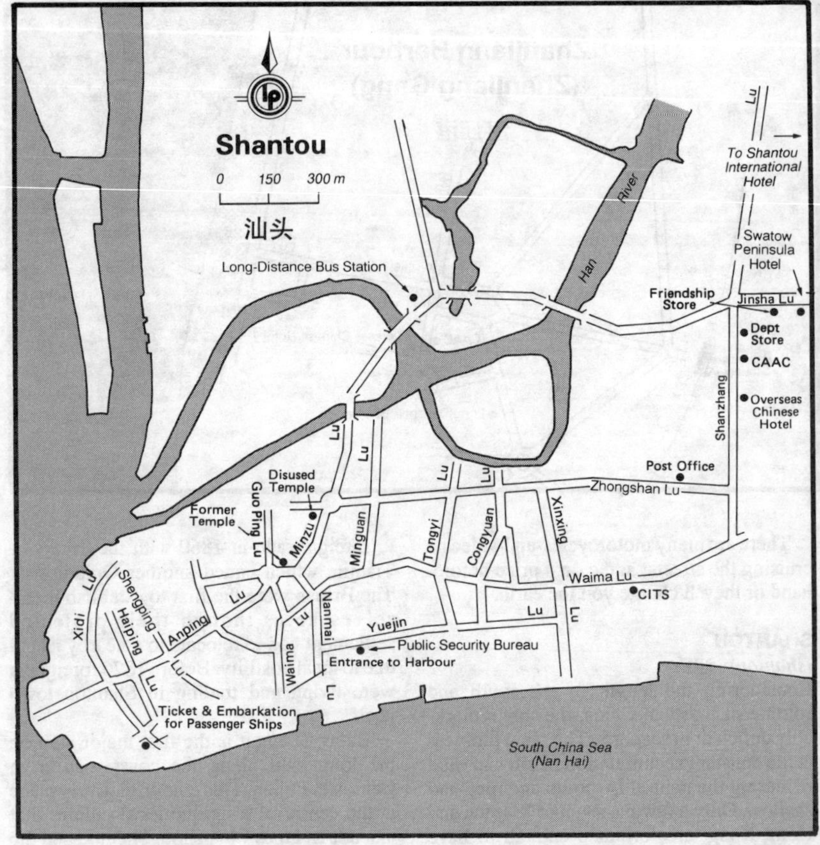

tourist facilities (CAAC, Friendship Store, Overseas Chinese Hotel) are in the western part of the peninsula along Jinsha Lu and Shanzhang Lu. From Shanzhang Lu, two main arteries Zhongshan Lu and Waima Lu lead westwards to the town centre which is the area around Minzu Lu and Shengping Lu.

In the local dialect, Shantou is often pronounced either 'Swatow' or 'Shantow'.

Public Security Bureau You'll find this office on Yuejin Lu, near the corner of Nanmai Lu.

CTS This is in the new wing of the Overseas Chinese Hotel. They sell bus tickets to Canton and Shenzhen, and boat tickets to Canton.

Money Black-market 'change-money' people are present in plague proportions around the Overseas Chinese Hotel. The Bank of China has a branch on the ground floor of the new wing of the Overseas Chinese Hotel.

Post There's a post office at 415 Zhongshan Lu, near the intersection with Shanzhang Lu.

Maps Excellent bus maps of Shantou are available from the long-distance bus station and from hawkers outside.

Things to See

There's not much in Shantou 'to see' as such, but its intrinsic interest makes it worth a visit. The town is quite small and you could do a circuit in a day.

The best area to explore is the south-western section around Anping Lu, Xidi Lu and Shengping Lu. This is a dilapidated harbourside suburb – a slum by any other name. Many of the old buildings are making way for new apartment blocks, but much of the old area is still intact. Streets like Yuejin Lu are lined with ugly little mud-and-wood shacks.

Poking around the neighbourhood, you'll find the ruins of a temple at the corner of Minzu Lu and Zhongshan Lu. Further down Minzu Lu is a shop where you can stock up on cobras and lizards. Carry on to the eastern waterfront where there's a breakwater boat shelter, fishing hovels and lean-tos with little statues of their gods.

A good day trip is to **Ma She (Ma Yi) Island** *(māyǔ)*. A boat leaves from the waterfront at 9 am every day and returns at 2.30 pm. The hour-long ride takes you through the fishing area with close-ups of the fisherfolk and their equipment. On an ordinary weekday the boat is filled with people toting bags of food and sacrificial offerings. Follow the crowd from the landing to the **Temple of the Mother of the Heavenly Emperor**, built in 1985 with funds supplied by Overseas Chinese. The site has apparently always been holy to this deity. In the village there is another temple where the fisherfolk burn incense before they leave in the morning. It's called the **Temple of the Dragon of the Sea**, is not as pretty but is rather more authentic with discarded fishing gear strewn around the crumbling building.

Evidently the island has been developed to keep pace with the worshippers' enthusiasm; there is a new hotel and restaurant building as well as marked trails for getting around the island. There are no cars, and the beaches and views are refreshing after spending several months in large Chinese cities. According to the villagers the island was settled mainly during the Japanese occupation, although there were a few people living here before then.

Places to Stay

Shantou is a popular tourist destination for Chinese Thais, who generally have less money than their Hong Kong or Taiwanese counterparts, so this keeps hotel prices lower than might be expected for such a large, modern Chinese city. The *Overseas Chinese Hotel (huáqiáo dàshà)* on Shanzhang Lu has spacious doubles in the old wing costing from Y40 with own bathroom; dorm beds are Y12. There are more expensive rooms in the new wing for Y80 and up. Take bus No 3 from the traffic circle outside the long-distance bus station, and get off at the stop outside the CAAC office.

The Swatow Peninsula Hotel (☎ 230046) on Jinsha Lu is around the corner from Shanzhang Lu. It's no relation to the Hong Kong Peninsula but is clean and quite reasonable; cheap doubles cost from Y30 to Y40, 'standard' rooms are from Y50 to 84, and 'superior' rooms from Y116 to 180. The clientele is mostly Chinese, but some English is spoken at the reception desk.

Further east on Jinsha Lu is the up-market, Hong-Kong-owned *Shantou International Hotel* (☎ 251212) *(shāntóu guójì fàndiàn)*, where modern, air-con rooms start at US$68. The Palace Revolve Restaurant on the top floor has views of the harbour and old sections of town.

Places to Eat

The best places to eat in Shantou are the street markets, where you'll find the cuisine Shantou is famous for. 'Food St' is a small street near the Overseas Chinese Hotel, running west off Shanzhang Lu. There are many evening seafood stalls here – rather like Hong Kong's Temple St night market. Rice noodles (called *kwetiaw* locally) are also a speciality. All along Minzu Lu are a number of stalls specialising in delicious won-ton *(húntun)*.

The Shantou International Hotel has a rather expensive coffee shop on the ground floor as well as restaurants specialising in Cantonese and Chaozhou cuisine on upper floors.

Things to Buy

There are several porcelain factories in the Shantou area, producing some interesting glazes and finishes not made elsewhere in southern China. They also produce the *gong fu cha* (tea) sets which are almost obligatory pieces of household ware in the Shantou area. After an introduction to this particular tea ritual you'll really know about Chinese hospitality. Embroidered cloth goods are produced in Shantou. The best place to look for these and other local products is the Arts & Crafts Services Store near the ferry docks.

Getting There & Away

The CAAC office (☎ 72355) is at 26 Shanzhang Lu, a few minutes' walk south of the intersection with Jinsha Lu.

From the long-distance bus station there are daily buses to Canton (Y30), Shenzhen (Y25), Chaozhou (Y4) and Xiamen (Y20).

Tickets for air-con coaches can be bought from the vendors outside the Overseas Chinese and Swatow Peninsula hotels, or next to CAAC. There are daily coaches to Canton (from Y35 to 43), Zhangzhou (Y25) and Shenzhen (Y34). Prices tend to vary so look around if you're on a tight budget.

There are also boats from Shantou to Canton and to Hong Kong as well as regular flights to Bangkok, Beijing, Canton, Kunming, Shanghai, Xiamen and Xi'an.

Getting Around

The incredibly dilapidated pedicabs and auto-rickshaws outside the long-distance bus station and Overseas Chinese Hotel charge about Y2 for most trips in the town centre. Other than that there are the local buses, although Shantou is small and a good deal of the town can be seen on foot.

CHAOZHOU

(cháozhōu) 潮州

Chaozhou is an ancient commercial and trading city dating back 1700 years. It is situated on the Han River surrounded by the Golden and Calabash hills.

One of the chief sights is the **Kaiyuan Temple**, which was built during the Tang Dynasty to house a collection of Buddhist scriptures sent here by Emperor Qian Long. On the cliffs at the foot of the Calabash Hills by the shores of the West Lake are the **Moya carvings** depicting local landscapes and the customs of the people, as well as poems and calligraphy; they date back 1000 years. South-east of Chaozhou is the seven-storey **Phoenix Pagoda** built in 1585.

There are frequent buses from Shantou to Chaozhou (Y4). There's also an Overseas Chinese Hotel in Chaozhou.

Top: Yak hide coracle, Samye (RS)
Bottom Left: Chickens on wheels (RS)
Bottom Right: Steer-drawn basket (RS)

Top: The Terracotta soldiers, Xian (AS)
Bottom Left: Statue of Mao Zedong (AS)
Bottom Right: Yungang caves (AS)

Hainan Island 海南岛

Hainan *(hǎinán dǎo)* is a large tropical island off the south coast of China which was administered by the government of Guangdong Province until 1988 when it became Hainan Province. The island lies close to Vietnam, and its military importance has increased over the past few years since China and Vietnam locked themselves into permanent conflict.

Consequently, the west coast of Hainan Island is dotted with naval bases, aircraft and missile bases, radio towers, radar stations and army bases. The bases are meant to defend Chinese shipping in the South China Sea and future Chinese-foreign joint ventures exploiting the oil and gas deposits in both the South China Sea and the Gulf of Tonkin (the body of water between Hainan and Vietnam). A naval force of 300,000 men is maintained on Hainan and in the mainland town of Zhanjiang, but Hainan's harbours are silted up and new ones need to be constructed to take larger warships and ocean-going cargo ships. The province has plans to expand two of the existing 11 ports and to build one deep-water port. Both the Haikou and Sanya airports are also being expanded.

The conflict with Vietnam started back in 1978, possibly initiated by the flight of as many as 250,000 ethnic Chinese from that country. In February of the following year the People's Republic invaded northern Vietnam – ostensibly to punish Vietnam for its treatment of the Chinese and for incursions on Chinese soil. When Foreign Minister Huang Hua announced on 16 March that the Chinese troops were being pulled back, the invasion was proclaimed a great success by the Chinese leadership, though clearly the PLA troops had been whipped by the Vietnamese, with probably 20,000 Chinese troops killed or wounded in just two weeks of fighting. The Chinese were afraid that the Vietnamese alliance with the Soviet Union, their domination of Laos and occupation of Cambodia were part of a Soviet plan to set up a hostile front on China's southern borders – a sort of Asian Cuba against which Hainan is being built up as a front-line defence.

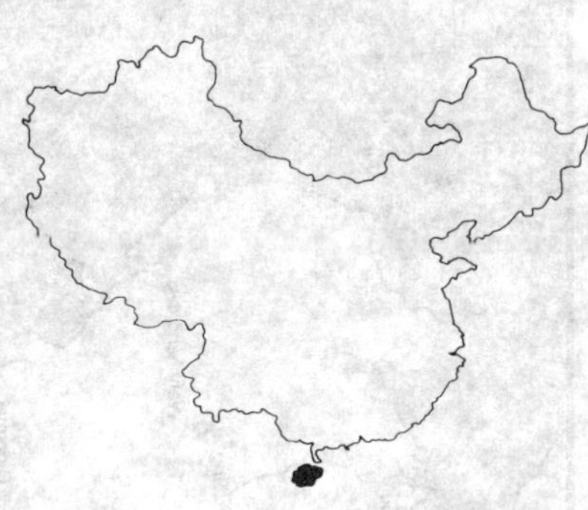

Historically, Hainan has always been a backwater of the Chinese empire, a miserable place of exile and one of the poorest regions in the country. When Li Deyu, a prime minister of the Tang Dynasty, was exiled to Hainan he dubbed it 'the gate of hell'. It is, however, rich in mineral resources: the Japanese developed an open-cut iron-ore mine at Shi Lu in the west, and there are rich deposits of other important ores like copper and titanium. The island also exports large quantities of salt from the pans on the west coast to the mainland, and it's China's main rubber producer. Plans have been made to start up a new open-cut coal mine and to restore several oil wells to provide fuel for the island's industries.

Ecology

Unfortunately, recent research shows that the island's ecosystem has been devastated. Between 1956 and 1978, deforestation reduced the island's forest cover from 27.7% to 7.05%. This has caused climatic changes, acute water shortages and severe soil erosion. Animal and bird species have been decimated.

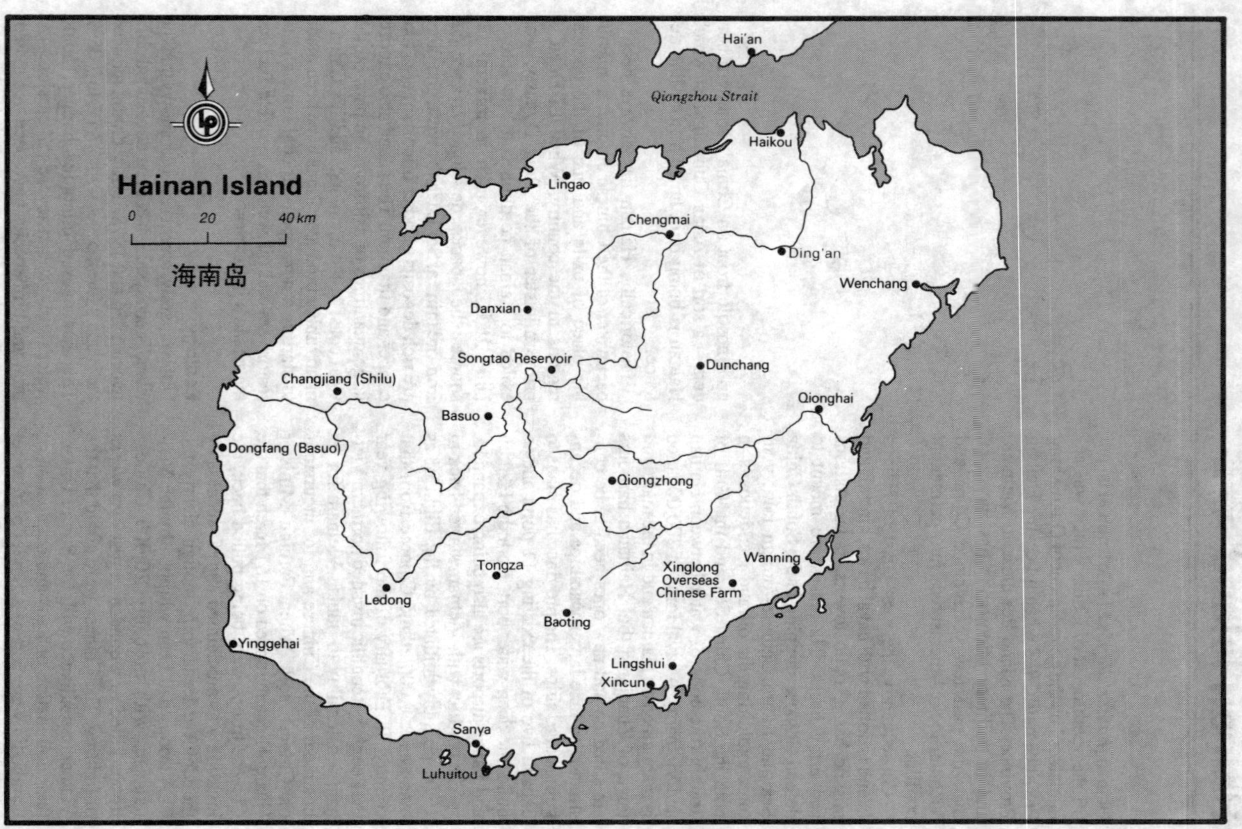

Hainan Island
0
20
40 km
海南岛
Hai'an
Qiongzhou Strait
Haikou
Lingao
Chengmai
Ding'an
Wenchang
Danxian
Songtao Reservoir
Dunchang
Changjiang (Shilu)
Basuo
Qionghai
Dongfang (Basuo)
Qiongzhong
Wanning
Xinglong Overseas Chinese Farm
Tongza
Ledong
Baoting
Yinggehai
Lingshui
Xincun
Sanya
Luhuitou

For example, the black-headed gibbon population on Hainan once numbered 20,000 – now there are perhaps 100. One of the rarest varieties of deer in the world, the Hainan deer, was once very common in the mountains, but there are now only 140 left in two nature reserves. In Wanning, we were disgusted to see rare birds brought down from the hills in packed cages for sale in the street; en route to Tongza, we were delighted when security officials at a roadblock arrested two passengers who had smuggled sacks of plants/animals out of the forest onto the bus.

Economy

Hainan has been established as a Special Economic Zone and hopes to lure foreign investment which will speed the island's development. More recently, the State Planning Commission gave Hainan authority at province level over economic management but not over financial affairs – and with good reason.

In 1985, mismanagement of the island's financial affairs caused some extremely red faces among Communist Party officials. Two years previously, Beijing had allocated Hainan massive sums of scarce foreign exchange to modernise the transport infrastructure. Officials on the island indulged, at just about every conceivable level, in a 14-month corruption bonanza. Over US$1.5 billion was used to buy 90,000 cars and trucks from Hong Kong which were then illegally 'funnelled' to the mainland where the rare goods sold like hot cakes to produce a massive profit. For good measure, the officials' shopping list included 2.9 million TV sets, 252,000 video recorders and 122,000 motorcycles.

Elsewhere in China lesser crimes are punished with a bullet in the back of the neck; on Hainan, the top three Communist Party officials in this pyramid of rake-offs were merely sacked and required to criticise their conduct.

The legacy of this absurd shopping spree is the island's unbelievable density of Japanese vehicles. Having imported more vehicles in one year than are imported annually in the whole of the rest of China, Hainan officials have been informed by Beijing that they have squandered Hainan's foreign exchange allocation for the next 10 years.

Li & Miao Tribes

The original inhabitants of the island, the Li and Miao minority peoples, live in the dense tropical forests covering the Limulingshan mountains that stretch down the centre of the island. The Li probably settled on Hainan 3000 years ago after migrating from Guangdong and Guangxi provinces. Although there has been a long history of rebellion by the Li against the Chinese, they aided the Communist guerrillas on the island during the war with the Japanese. Perhaps for this reason the island's centre was made an 'autonomous' region after the Communists came to power.

Until recently the Li women had a custom of tattooing their bodies at the age of 12 or 13. The designs were first pricked out before a blend of oil and charcoal was applied. When the scabs fell off, blue tattoos appeared. The custom seems to have died out or been suppressed; it may have been done for beautification or to mar the girls and prevent their abduction by the Chinese rulers. The *China Daily* recently produced an explanation which just happened to leave out the Chinese. According to the article, a pretty Li girl was once raped by the local headman who thus ruined the reputation of the girl and her family. From then on, all Li girls adopted tattooing to save themselves from a similar fate.

Today, almost all Li people wear standard Han dress except the elderly women. However, when a member of the Li dies, traditional Li costume is considered essential; otherwise the ancestors will not be able to recognise or accept the new arrival.

The Miao (Hmong) people spread from southern China across northern Vietnam, Laos and Thailand. In China they moved south into Hainan as a result of the Chinese emigrations from the north, and now occupy some of the most rugged terrain on the island. Theirs has also been an unhappy affair with the Chinese; land shortages led to a revolt in the 1780s which was savagely suppressed by the imperial armies. Another revolt broke out for the same reason, concurrently with the Taiping Rebellion, but once the Taipings were put down so were the Miao.

The coastal areas of the island are populated by Han Chinese. Since 1949, Chinese from Indonesia and Malaysia and most recently Chinese-Vietnamese refugees have been settled here. All told, Hainan has a population close to five million, of which about 700,000 are Li and 40,000 are Miao.

Tourism

Like Xishuangbanna in Yunnan Province, Hainan is popular as a winter refuge, but it certainly isn't the 'Asian Hawaii' dished up in some tourist brochures. Development of tourist facilities on the island is clearly geared to those Hong Kong and Overseas Chinese who favour quickie or 'auto-pilot' tours. In actual fact, the island still has a long way to go to develop a tourism infrastructure to handle group tourism. Following the 1989-90 tourist slump, most projects were put on hold.

Haikou, the capital of Hainan, and Sanya, a port with popular beaches, are the two major towns at opposite ends of the island. For road connections between these two places there's a choice of three highways: the eastern route via Wenchang and Wanning; the central route via Dunchang and Tongza (also known as Hongqizhen); and the less popular western route via Danxian (also known as Nada), Basuo and Yinggehai.

The eastern route is the most popular one. If you want to take it slowly, it's easily divided into stages on a daily basis.

The central route is worth taking if you want to explore ethnic minority areas. The best mountain scenery is between Sanya and Qiongzhong – after that it's flat and plain.

On the western route, it might be worth looking at the Institute of Tropical Plants *(rèdài zhìwù yánjiūsuǒ)* near Danxian *(dànxiàn)* and the Nature Reserve for the Protection of the Hainan Deer at Datian. To the east of Datian is the town of Xiaodongfang *(dōngfāng)*, the site of the Li minority's 'Loving Festival' on the third day of the third lunar month (around April). China's largest open-cut iron mine is at Shi Lu (also called Changjiang) *(chāngjiāng)*, which is linked by railway with Basuo, a shabby port. There is reportedly a beautiful stretch of road between Basuo and Sanya which passes the saltworks at Yinggehai.

Haikou is a fairly busy city with little to recommend it beyond a bit of old architecture. With a bit of effort you can escape for a hike around minority areas in the mountains, or without any effort at all you can sit on a beach. Winter sees all sorts down on the Sanya beaches: Beijing cadres attending meetings that might perhaps produce more suntans than dialectics; foreign students giving their nerves and stomachs badly needed R & R; droves of Scandinavians abandoning their climate to polar bears.

A few thoughtless foreigners have insisted on bathing nude, so the local men have drawn a link between porno videos, nude bathing and foreign women, who are occasionally harassed. If you want to bathe nude,

Salt Worker, Yinggehai

find a culture where it's acceptable; China is *not* the place.

Thanks to the vehicle scandal explained earlier, transport is excellent on the island. Squadrons of Japanese buses and minibuses with maniac drivers are more expensive than the slower local buses, which may be rust-traps but are marginally less lethal.

Providing you stay clear of anti-aircraft batteries and other defence installations, just about the whole island is yours to explore. Foreign tour companies offer bike itineraries round the island, and individual foreign bikers have reported happy pedalling. Gears are essential for the mountainous, central highway. The fairly flat eastern highway follows the coastline.

Typhoons *(tàifēng)* are a regular event on Hainan usually between May and October – during the past 50 years there's been at least one every year. Although they bring the island vital rain, typhoons also have an awesome capacity for destruction. If Hainan is part of your tight travel schedule, remember that typhoons can cripple all transport and communication with the mainland for several days.

HAIKOU

(hǎikǒu) 海口

Haikou, the capital of the island, lies on the northern coastline at the mouth of the Nandu River. It's a port town and handles most of the island's commerce with the mainland.

For most travellers, it's merely a transit point on the way to the beaches at the southern tip of the island. However, those interested in old southern Chinese architecture may find it worth a day or two. In the town centre, along and off Xinhua Nanlu, are rows of original buildings with the unmistakable Sino-Portuguese influence seen in Chinese colonies throughout South-East Asia: spots like Macau, Malacca and Penang. The food, also, is reminiscent of these spots – a mixture of European and Chinese.

Orientation

Haikou is split up into three fairly separate sections. The western section is the port area. A long road connects it to the northern section, which is the centre of Haikou and has the tourist facilities. Another road connects this section to a smaller urban area in the south.

Information

CITS All enquiries and tickets are handled at the offices on the ground floor of the Overseas Chinese Hotel.

Public Security Bureau This is a short walk from the Overseas Chinese Hotel. Turn right out of the hotel and walk down the road until you come to a traffic circle with a small obelisk. Turn right again and the office is a short walk further up the road on the right-hand side. They're a friendly lot here and they have an interpreter on call.

Money The Bank of China is opposite the Overseas Chinese Hotel on Datong Lu. The Overseas Chinese Hotel and the Hainan Friendship Hotel have foreign-exchange counters.

Post There is a post office in the foyer of the Overseas Chinese Hotel. There's another on the same street as the Public Security Bureau, but on the opposite side of the road and further west. A third is on the corner of the main intersection immediately east of the Public Security Bureau.

Maps Maps of Haikou and Hainan Island, in Chinese, are available from the shop in front of the Overseas Chinese Hotel.

Walking Tour

The Overseas Chinese Hotel is a good starting point for a walk around the town. Turn right from the hotel and walk for about 15 minutes to the traffic circle marked by an obelisk. Turn hard right here and then right again at the second major intersection, onto Xinhua Nanlu. Along this street you'll find the town's older buildings – reminiscent of Sino-Portuguese architecture once found from Macau to Singapore.

A few minutes' walk further down is a

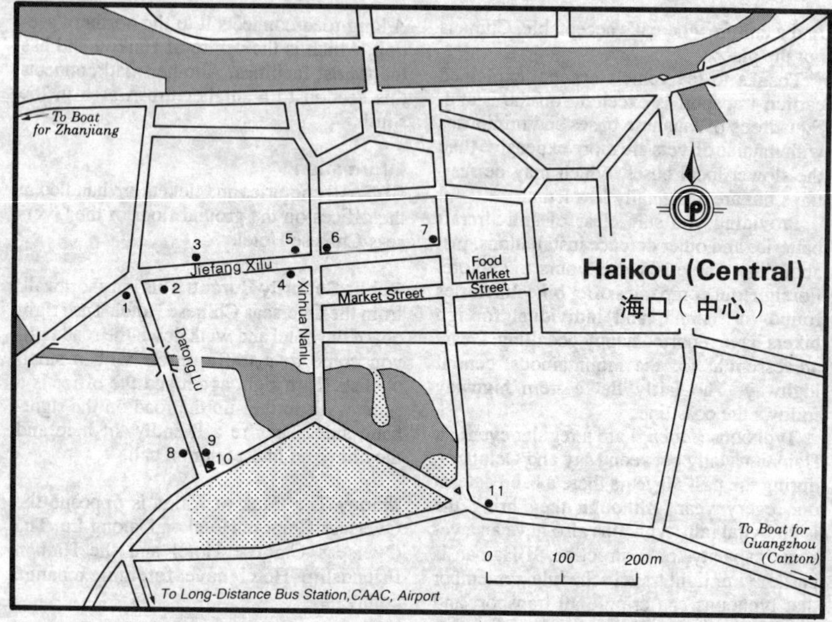

1 Friendship Hotel
2 Cafe de Rosa
3 Post Office
4 Public Security Bureau
5 Department Store
6 Post Office
7 Cinema
8 Bank of China
9 Overseas Chinese Hotel
10 Pau Tau Restaurant
11 Booking Office for Boats to Haikou & Canton (Guangzhou)

1 友谊饭店
2 Cafe de Rosa
3 邮局
4 公安局外事科
5 百货商店
6 邮局
7 电影院
8 中国银行
9 华侨饭店
10 宝岛餐厅
11 轮船售票处

jam-packed street market, with the usual array of culinary delicacies that would normally end up in a zoo in other countries. One of the best markets you'll see in China (almost on a par with the Qingping Market in Canton), it's notable for the snug-fitting, tube-shaped bamboo cages for live pigs. The area is fairly grotty, with old buildings which look like they haven't been cleaned for 30 years, but it's quite a change from the drab concrete blocks in other Chinese cities.

If you continue south along the street off which the market runs, you come to a T-junction. Immediately to the left is the large booking hall for boats to Canton and Haikou. If you turn right at the T-junction, you go past a small park and lake. Follow this road and after about 15 minutes you'll come to the road with the Overseas Chinese Hotel.

The river front in the northern part of town is lined with decaying buildings and wall-to-wall junks, oddly picturesque.

Places to Stay

There are no cheap places to stay in Haikou, unfortunately. The *Overseas Chinese Hotel* (☎ 73288) *(huáqiáo dàshà)* in the middle of town on Datong Lu is a large, well-kept structure catering to the crowds of Hong Kong and Overseas Chinese. Singles are Y79, doubles Y100. The complex contains restaurants on the ground and 6th floors; the ground floor also houses shops, a currency-exchange counter and post office.

Further north along Datong Lu is the *Ri Li Hotel* (the English sign reads 'Hainan No 3 Hotel') where clean doubles are Y100. Next door is the *Hainan Friendship Hotel (hǎinán yǒuyì fàndiàn)*; rooms are overpriced at Y130 to Y140 double, Y150 triple.

To get to Datong Lu from the harbour where the boats from Zhanjiang pull in, take a motorcycle-and-sidecar for Y2 to Y4. A pedicab should only cost about Y3. Sometimes there's a minibus for Y2 per person. If you're coming in from Canton on the ship, take bus No 3 as far as the obelisk in the centre of town and then walk the last 15 minutes to the hotel. A taxi between the hotel and the harbour should cost about Y8.

The new *CAAC office* (☎ 72615) at 9 Haixiu Lu has hotel rooms for Y100 to Y130. This is where the CAAC airport shuttle begins and terminates.

Places to Eat

The restaurants at the *Overseas Chinese Hotel* serve acceptable food, but are quite expensive.

The *Pau Tau Restaurant (bǎodǎo cāntīng)* at 17 Datong Lu is a clean, efficient place with air-con selling Chinese, Malaysian and Western food at reasonable prices. To get there, turn left outside the gates of the Overseas Chinese Hotel and walk 50 metres towards the park – it's near the corner. The Malay set dinner is excellent value for Y10. The friendly staff also serves real coffee and famous Hainan-style chicken rice; the menu is in Chinese and English.

The *Café de Rosa* is a slick fast-food restaurant which appears to be a Hong Kong joint venture. Turn right out of the Overseas Chinese Hotel and walk down the road until you come to the traffic circle with a small obelisk. Turn right again and it's the second building on the right-hand side. If you've been gasping for steak and chips, iced coffee, etc served on authentic plastic trays under fluorescent lighting, this is your chance. The restaurant also serves inexpensive Chinese food.

There is a number of cheap places in the vicinity of the main market along Xinhua Nanlu and on Jiefang Xilu. They serve the usual rice, meat and vegetable fare for Y2 or Y3. Along the north end of Datong Lu is a night market with outdoor tables and lots of seafood. You buy your fish, prawns or whatever by the *jīn* (500 grams) or *bàn jīn* (250 grams); fish prices start at around Y4 per jin and prawns should be about Y9 per jin.

Getting There & Away

Air The CAAC office (☎ 72615) is at 9 Haixiu Lu. CAAC flies daily between Haikou and Canton (Y179) and Beihai (Y66), and there are regular flights to other Chinese cities further afield as well. There are now daily flights between Haikou and Hong Kong (HK$750).

The Haikou airport is only about one km from central Haikou. You could easily walk the distance or hire a taxi for Y6.

Bus The new bus station has departures to all major destinations on the island. Ticket prices are cheapest for the dinosaur buses; for a luxury bus or minibus the tickets cost more but you also get more speed and complimentary nervous stimulation. For example, a minibus direct to Sanya takes about six hours and costs Y28. The standard buses take a couple of hours longer and cost Y17. The best Sanya buses run from the Overseas Chinese Hotel and cost Y30. They leave the hotel daily at 8.30 am.

Tickets are also sold for deluxe buses running direct to Canton (Y87), Shenzhen (Y106) and Hong Kong (Y140). However, the combined boat/bus journey can be very tedious when it includes night travel at high speed with nonstop pornographic kungfu videos.

Boat Boats leave Haikou at 11.30 am, 12.30 and 1.30 pm for the 1½-hour trip to Hai'an on the Leizhou Peninsula, where you get connecting transport to Zhanjiang. The combined bus/boat ticket is available at the harbour after 11 am for Y17.70, but in this case your bus leaves at 3 pm. It's quicker to take a minibus from Hai'an to Zhanjiang for Y9. Tickets for a new hydrofoil service between Hainan and the Leizhou Peninsula cost Y12 per person.

There are daily boats from Haikou direct to Canton; ticket prices vary between Y29.20 for 5th class to Y174.80 for deluxe class. It's worth paying a little extra to avoid the large dorm below deck, particularly if the boat is pitching and your bunk is next to the toilets. Third class will get you into an eight-bed dorm on deck. Watch out for petty thievery and take your own food – the food on board is poor. Buy tickets from the booking office in Overseas Chinese Hotel.

Two boats, the *Donghu* and *Malan*, run approximately once a week between Haikou and Hong Kong. Another boat, the *Shan Cha*, runs twice a month between Sanya and Hong Kong via Haikou. Prices vary from Y98 for 3rd class to Y178 for deluxe class. Buy tickets from the booking office for these rates; the CITS office at the Overseas Chinese Hotel charges Y113 and Y227 respectively.

Getting Around

The central area of Haikou is small and easy to walk around, but the motorcycle-and-sidecars are cheap and the buses useful. The separate sections of Haikou are connected by bus.

WENCHANG

(wénchāng) 文昌

Buses leave for Wenchang from Haikou's main bus station; or take a minibus from outside the Overseas Chinese Hotel. The 73 km could be done as a day trip. The coconut plantations called Dong Jiao Ye Lin and Jian Hua Shan Ye Lin are a short ride out of town at Qing Lan Gang. Minibuses by the riverside in Wenchang will take you to Qing Lan Gang, where you can take a ferry to the stands of coconut palms and mile after mile of beach. Another way to get to the same plantation is to take the direct bus to Dong Jiao from Haikou's main bus station.

XINGLONG

(xīnglóng) 兴隆

Since 1952, over 20,000 refugee Chinese-Vietnamese and Overseas Chinese (mostly from Indonesia or Malaysia) have settled at the **Xinglong Overseas Chinese Farm** *(xìnglóng huáqiáo cūn)* The farm concentrates on tropical agriculture and related research. Many of the members speak excellent English and are a helpful source of information. They may be able to organise transport (for about Y30) to Miao villages.

About three km from Xinglong bus station is the *Xinglong Wenchuan Hotel.* From the bus station to the hotel costs Y1 in a motorcycle-and-sidecar. The hotel is a peaceful spot for convalescence and well worth a stay. Prices start at Y40 per double with a huge bed and a bath large enough for four people. The spring water is scalding hot – if there's no cold water available, you'll just have to let it cool in the bath.

XINCUN

(xīncūn) 新村

Xincun is populated almost solely by Danjia (Tanha) minority people who are employed in fishing and pearl cultivation. In recent years, typhoons have repeatedly blown away the pearl and oyster cultivation farms, but the harbour area, fish market and nearby Monkey Island are worth an afternoon ramble.

Buses travelling the eastern route will drop you off at a fork in the road about three km from Xincun. It should then be easy to get a lift on a passing minibus and hitch or walk into Xincun. From Lingshui and Sanya frequent minibuses run directly to Xincun.

Monkey Island

(hóuzi dǎo) 猴子岛

About a thousand Guangxi monkeys (*Macaca mulatta*) live on this narrow peninsula. The area is under state protection and a special wildlife research centre has been set up to investigate all the monkey business.

A shack on the beach at Xincun functions as a booking office selling return tickets on the ferry for Y1.5. They also sell a booklet put together in Chinese by the research centre. It includes exhaustive monkey data and an appendix which lists the monkeys' favourite plants like a menu.

The ferry put-puts from Xincun to Monkey Island in 10 minutes. At the island pier, motorcycle-and-sidecars will take you to the monkey enclosure (Houzi Yuan) for Y2. You can also get there on foot. Walk along the beach road to the left for about one km, then follow the road leading uphill to the right for another 1½ km.

Guangxi Monkey

At the entrance a stall sells tickets and peanuts for the monkeys. Apart from feeding times at 9 am and 4 pm, it's a case of the monkeys seeing you and not vice versa. You can often hear them crashing around and chattering in the shrubs on the hillside; occasionally a wild, woolly head pops out of the top branches to see what's happening or to scream at you. This is one of the few places where the monkeys can run wild without being shot, trapped, tethered to table-legs, tortured in zoo cages or brutally mishandled in roadshows.

SANYA

(sānyǎ) 三亚

Sanya is a busy port and tourist resort on the southern tip of Hainan Island. The town lies on a peninsula parallel to the coast and is connected to the mainland on one side by two bridges.

The harbour area, which is mostly occupied by shabby wooden shanties, is protected to the south-east by the hilly Luhuitou Peninsula. On the western outskirts of Sanya there's a small community of Hui, the only Muslim inhabitants of Hainan.

The main part of town lacks any special features except perhaps for the local minority women who pester you to change money. A map of the area in Chinese is sold in the Luhuitou Hotel's shop.

Things to See

Most travellers head for Sanya for a few leisurely days at the beach. The popular beaches are at Dadonghai, Luhuitou Peninsula and Tianya Haijiao.

You'll find a fine beach at **Dadonghai** *(dàdōnghǎi)*, which has a hotel and plenty of sand, surf and shade. It's about three km east of Sanya and easily reached by bus for Y1. Dadonghai also has the greatest variety of places to stay.

There's only one hotel at the **Luhuitou Peninsula** *(lùhuítóu)*. The beaches are too rocky for swimming but pleasant for walks. The usual route to the hotel is not over the hills, but via a road which follows the seashore. It's possible to do this pleasant walk

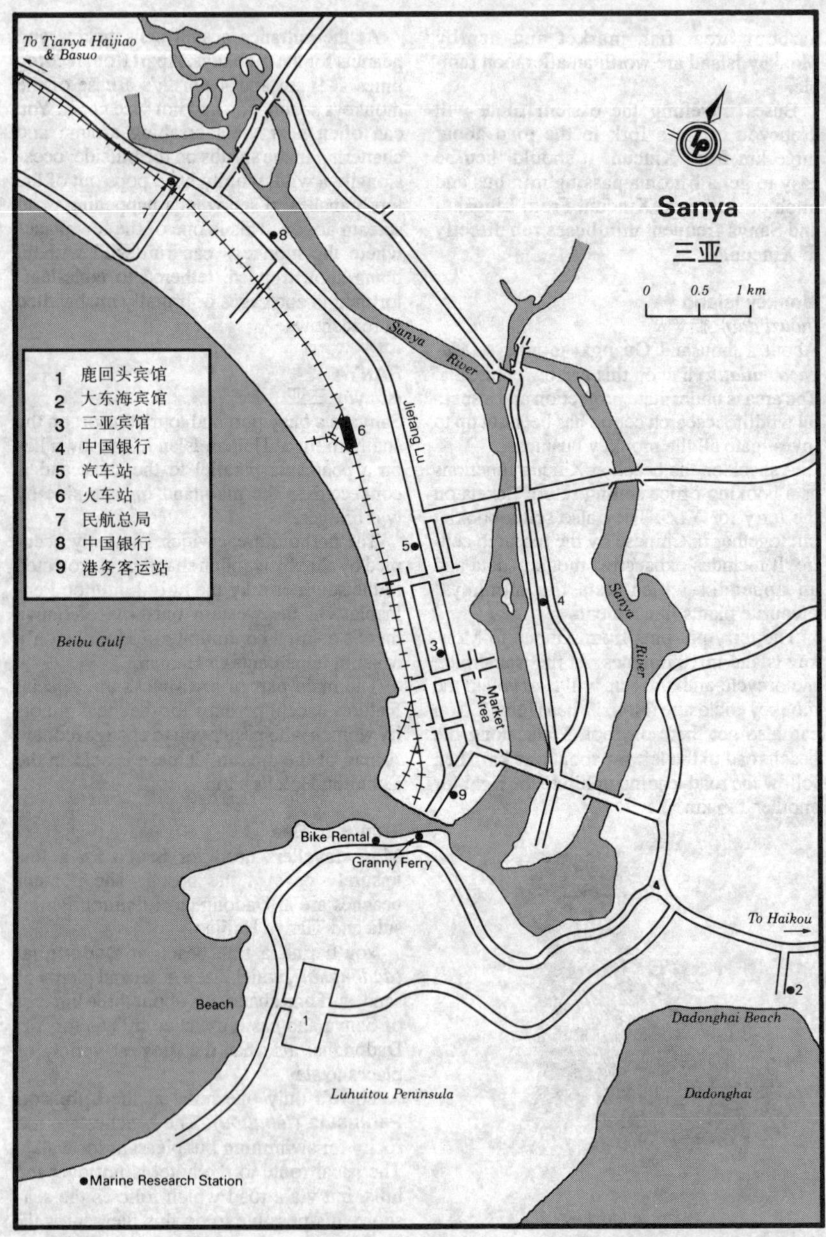
To Tianya Haijiao & Basuo
Sanya
三亚
0
0.5
1 km
1 鹿回头宾馆
2 大东海宾馆
3 三亚宾馆
4 中国银行
5 汽车站
6 火车站
7 民航总局
8 中国银行
9 港务客运站
Sanya River
Jiefang Lu
Sanya River
Market Area
Beibu Gulf
Bike Rental
Granny Ferry
To Haikou
Beach
Dadonghai Beach
Luhuitou Peninsula
Dadonghai
Marine Research Station

1 Luhuitou Hotel
2 Dadonghai Tourism Centre
3 Sanya Hotel
4 Bank of China
5 Bus Station
6 Railway Station
7 CAAC
8 Bank of China
9 Boat Ticket Office

from the town to the hotel in about an hour. You must first cross a narrow channel by ferry and then continue on by motorcycle-and-sidecar.

The name Luhuitou means 'deer turns its head' and is associated with an old legend. A young Li hunter who lived near Mt Five Fingers *(wǔzhǐshān)* pursued a young doe to the southernmost tip of the island. When the creature realised it was trapped it turned its head to gaze at the hunter. Just as he raised his bow to shoot, the doe changed into a beautiful girl and the astonished hunter dropped his bow. The two fell in love (oh dear) and lived happily ever after.

On the tip of Luhuitou Peninsula is the **Hainan Experimental Marine Research Station**, which specialises in pearl cultivation. The use of pearls in China can be traced back 4000 years; cultured pearls were created over 900 years ago during the Song Dynasty.

There's an overrated beach at **Tianya Haijiao** *(tiānyà hǎijiǎo)* (literally 'edge of the sky, rim of the sea') about 24 km west of Sanya with a few large rocks, no shade and not much else. It's popular with droves of Chinese tourists who queue to have their pictures taken in front of rocks with carved characters. Catch any bus travelling west from Sanya bus station. The trip takes about 45 minutes.

Close to Sanya are **Xidao Dongdao** *(xīdǎo dōngdǎo)* (Eastern & Western Hawksbill Islands), two coral islands clearly visible from Luhuitou Peninsula. It may be possible to find a boat from the harbour out to the islands, where the inhabitants use coral for housing and tacky souvenirs. A site close to these islands has been opened to foreigners for scuba-diving and snorkelling.

Places to Stay

Most travellers head for Dadonghai first, as this is where the best beach is. The *Dadonghai Tourism Centre Hotel (dàdōnghǎi lǚyóu zhōngxīn)* is about 2½ km out of town, a couple of hundred metres from the beach. Air-con rooms cost Y100 double, Y150 triple. In 1990, the electricity and hot water were frequently turned off while the Sanya-Haikou highway was under construction.

Right on the beach is *Dadonghai Beach Village*, a collection of thatched huts and tents that cost Y20 per night for two persons. When there are plenty of vacancies, you can easily talk the price down to Y15 a night. There are no mattresses on the wooden beds, but the staff are friendly and speak good English. Water recreation equipment can also be hired here.

Further south along the beach, hidden by tall grass that grows all around it, is a grotty motel-style place where beds are Y10 per person per night. Several other international-style hotels on Dadonghai Beach are half-finished – as tourism picks up, they'll probably open one at a time.

If you're arriving from Haikou, you could save time by asking the driver to drop you off at Dadonghai. An easy point of reference is a huge tree growing plumb in the middle of the road – traffic seems to decide at the last minute which way to go round it!

Over on Luhuitou peninsula, the *Luhuitou Hotel* (☎ 74659) *(lùhuítóu lǚguǎn)* sits in secluded semi-splendour. The mini-villas in lush gardens are a great place to rest, well worth the occasional hassle with frosty receptionists until prices, FEC, student cards etc have been sorted out. Reception is just inside the front gate. Room prices range from Y15 to Y40 per person. The cheapest rooms have no bath and no air-con; the others often have bath, air-con and separate sitting room. Complete suites are also available at higher prices. Ask at reception about deluxe buses to Haikou. Opposite reception is a shop which sells maps (in Chinese) of Sanya, canned drinks, shell necklaces and coconut shell carvings.

There are two routes to town from the Luhuitou Hotel. Cars usually drive from the gate in front of reception up over the hill and then down into town. Walkers and motorcycles-and-sidecars generally avoid the climb by taking the beach road from the back gate. Turn right outside the gate and follow the road round the peninsula for about two km. About 30 metres after passing a house with a bike-hire sign in English, turn left into the grubby alleys until you find the *mǎtóu* (ferry) on the waterfront. For Y0.20 an old woman poles you across to the other side.

The *Sanya Hotel* (☎ 74703) *(sānyà bīnguǎn)* is in the centre of town on Jiefang Lu, the main north-south road running through Sanya. If you're staying here and you want beach life, you'll have to commute. Single rooms cost Y35 to Y55, doubles Y46 to Y66. There are a few cheaper hotels near the harbour, but they appear not to accept foreigners (the *Ali Baba Hotel* near the boat ticket office might be worth a try).

Places to Eat

The little thatched-roof restaurant next to Dadonghai Beach Village has cheap, cold beer and passable food. Better food is served at the little restaurants along the road leading from the beach to the Sanya-Haikou highway. They vary in quality and popularity from season to season – most recently the *Mayflower* and the *Guangzhou (guǎngzhōu)* were quite popular with travellers. A couple of places are open early in the morning for noodles and rice.

The restaurant at the Luhuitou Hotel can be good when there are enough guests to inspire the kitchen staff. Various set meals are available at prices ranging from Y6 to Y10. Higher-priced set meals include more fancy seafood. The two restaurants just outside the back entrance of the hotel are good but overpriced.

In Sanya itself, there are plenty of restaurants and street stalls to try – nothing to be specially recommended yet.

Getting There & Away

Air There are four flights a week to Canton (Y239) via Haikou (though in 1990, no Haikou stopover was permitted, for no apparent reason). Reception at the Dadonghai Tourism Centre may be able to book plane tickets; otherwise try the CAAC office, which is miles away at the western end of town.

Bus From Sanya bus station there are frequent buses and minibuses to most parts of Hainan. Deluxe buses for Haikou (Y28 to Y30) also depart from the Luhuitou and Dadonghai hotels.

Train The sporadic passenger service between Sanya and Huangliu may soon be extended to Basuo.

Boat Boats leave Sanya twice a month (usually on the 11th and 28th) for Hong Kong. Ticket prices range from Y125 in 5th class to Y253 in deluxe class.

There is a weekly boat connection between Sanya and Canton on Friday. Ticket prices range from Y74 for 5th class to Y254.40 for 1st class.

The boat ticket office is close to the harbour, on a side street off the main north-south drag (just past the Ali Baba Hotel).

Getting Around

Apart from walking, the quickest way to get around is the motorcycles-and-sidecars which cruise the streets all day. Quite a blast, motoring around like WW II generals in a bathtub – especially if it's raining. Make sure you bargain with the drivers. The fare is per motorcycle, not per person, and is paid in RMB.

A motorcycle-and-sidecar from the centre of Sanya to Dadonghai costs about Y3. To the Luhuitou Hotel from the harbour should cost about the same.

Bikes can be hired for Y6 per day at the back gate of the Luhuitou Hotel. Another bike-rental guy operates on the back road between Sanya and the Luhuitou Hotel – look for the sign. He charges Y4 per day but wants it in FEC.

TONGSHI

(tōngshí) 通什

Tongshi is the capital of the Li and Miao Autonomous Prefecture. The town obviously had the financial backing to transform all the major buildings into modern high-rises; there's even a supermarket.

There are several hotels in Tongshi. The flashiest is the *Tongza Holiday Resort (lǚyóu shānzhuāng)* with double rooms for Y100. Minorities make the tourist cash register tinkle here – so the roof of the lobby is pyramid-shaped to give the feel of a straw hut, and minority women serve drinks or invite guests to dance and sing. A great chance for visitors to play the primitive in luxury.

The *Wuzhishan Guesthouse (wǔzhǐshān bīnguǎn)* charges Y50 for a double. A small hotel next to the bridge charges Y6 for a bed in a triple.

Minority Villages

There are several Miao villages dotted around the edge of town. From Tongshi you could take local buses, for example, to Mao'an, Maodao or Maogan.

Mt Five Fingers *(wǔzhǐshān)*, at 1867 metres Hainan's highest mountain, is close to Tongshi.

QIONGZHONG

(qióngzhōng) 琼中

The route between Tongshi and Qiongzhong passes through thick forest. Qiongzhong is a small hill-town with a lively market; the nearby waterfall at Baihuashan drops over 300 metres.

Hunan 湖南

Hunan *(húnán)* lies on some of the richest land in China. Its main period of growth occurred between the 8th and the 11th centuries when the population increased fivefold, spurred on by a prosperous agricultural industry and by migrations from the north. Under the Ming and the Qing it was one of the empire's granaries, and vast quantities of Hunan's rice surplus were shipped to the depleted regions to the north.

By the 19th century Hunan was beginning to suffer from the pressure of population. Land shortage and landlordism led to widespread unrest among the Chinese farmers and the hill-dwelling minority peoples. The increasingly desperate economic situation led to the massive Taiping Rebellion of the mid-19th century and the Communist movement of the 1920s.

The Communists found strong support amongst the poor peasants of Hunan, and a refuge on the mountainous Hunan-Jiangxi border in 1927. Some of the most prominent Communist leaders were born in Hunan, including Mao Zedong, Liu Shaoqi (both of whose villages can be visited), Peng Dehuai and Hu Yaobang. Hua Guofeng, a native of Shanxi, became an important provincial leader in Hunan.

Some 54 million people live in Hunan, most of them Han Chinese. Hill-dwelling minorities can be found in the border regions of the province. They include the Miao, Tujia, Dong (a Thai people) and Yao. In the far north of the province there is, oddly enough, a pocket of Uigurs.

Mao Zedong

Mao was Hunan's main export. Mao was born in the Hunanese village of Shaoshan, not far from Changsha, in 1893. His father was a poor peasant who had been forced to join the army because of heavy debts. After several years of service he returned to Shaoshan, and by careful saving through small trading and other enterprises managed to buy back his land.

As 'middle' peasants Mao's family owned enough

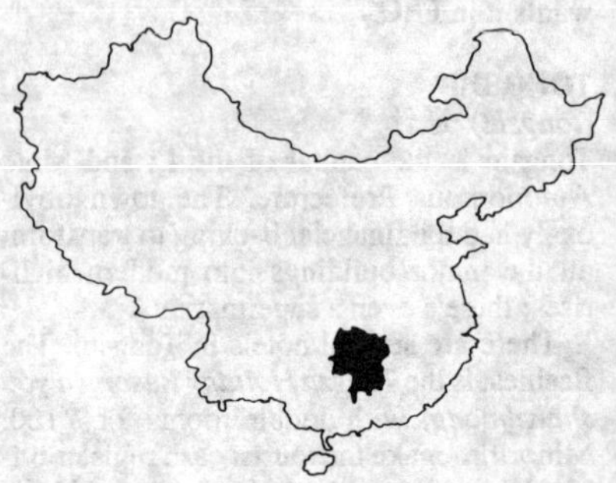

land to produce a surplus of rice with which they were able to buy more land. This raised them to the status of 'rich' peasants. Mao's father began to deal in grain transport and sales, buying grain from the poor farmers and taking it to the city merchants where he could get a higher price for it. As Mao told US journalist Edgar Snow, 'My family ate frugally, but had enough always'.

Mao began studying in the local primary school when he was eight years old and remained at school until the age of 13, meanwhile working on the farm and keeping accounts for his father's business. His father continued to accumulate wealth (or what was considered a fortune in the little village) by buying mortgages on other people's land. Creditors of other peasants would be paid off in lump sums, and these peasants would then have to pay back their loans to Mao's father, who would profit from the interest rates.

Several incidents influenced Mao around this time. A famine in Hunan and a subsequent uprising of starving people in Changsha ended in the execution of the leaders by the Manchu governor. This left a lasting impression on Mao, who '...felt that there with the rebels were ordinary people like my own family and I deeply resented the injustice in the treatment given to them'. He was also influenced by a band of rebels who had taken to the hills around Shaoshan to defy the landlords and the government, and by a radical teacher at the local primary school who opposed Buddhism and wanted people to convert their temples into schools.

At the age of 16, Mao left Shaoshan to enter middle school in Changsha, his first stop on the footpath to power. At this time he was not yet an anti-monarchist: '...indeed, I considered the emperor as well as most officials to be honest, good and clever men'. He felt

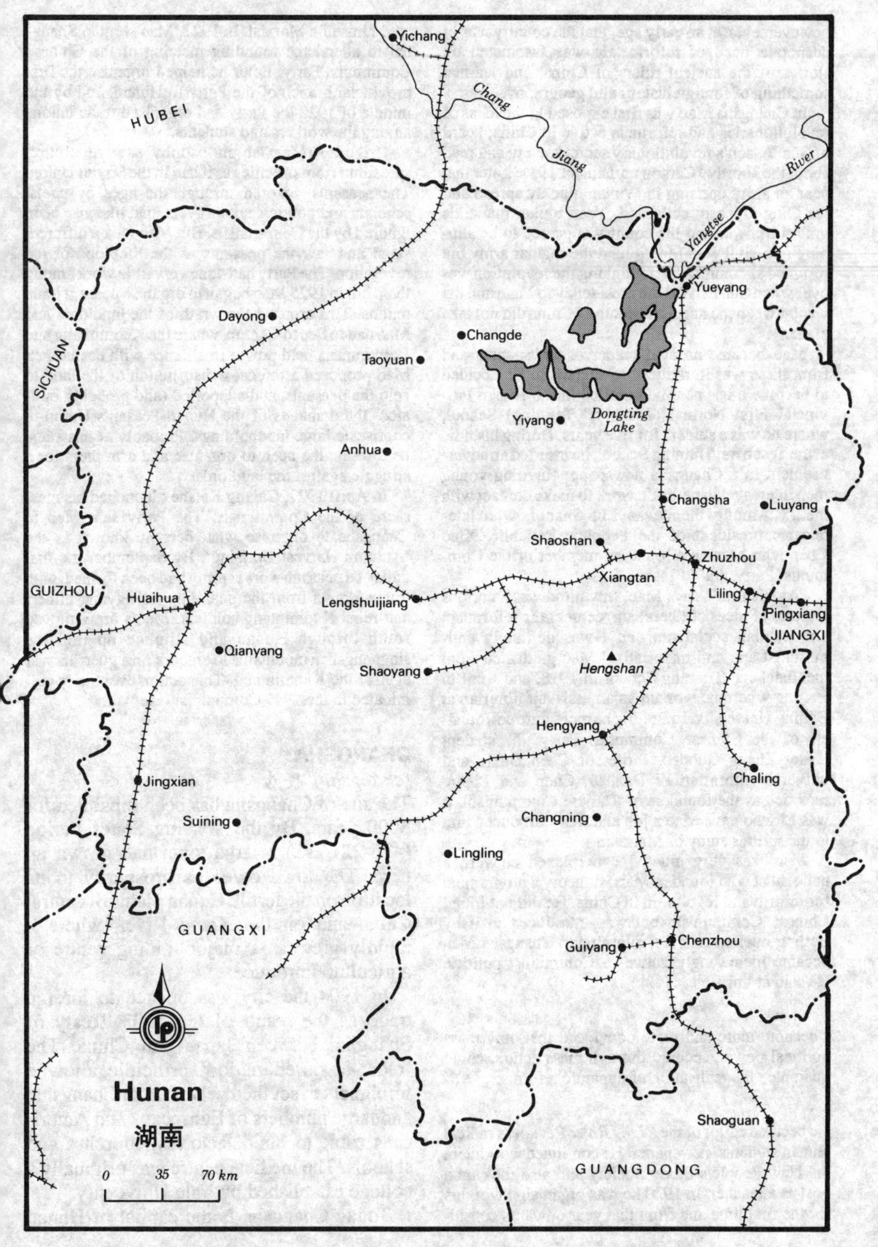
Yichang
Chang
Jiang
Yangtse
River
HUBEI
Yueyang
Dayong
Changde
Taoyuan
SICHUAN
Dongting
Lake
Yiyang
Anhua
Changsha
Liuyang
Shaoshan
Zhuzhou
Xiangtan
GUIZHOU
Huaihua
Lengshuijiang
Liling
Pingxiang
JIANGXI
Qianyang
Hengshan
Shaoyang
Hengyang
Jingxian
Chaling
Suining
Changning
Lingling
GUANGXI
Chenzhou
Guiyang
Hunan
湖南
Shaoguan
0
35
70 km
GUANGDONG

however, even at an early age, that the country was in desperate need of reform. He was fascinated by stories of the ancient rulers of China, and learned something of foreign history and geography.

In Changsha Mao was first exposed to the ideas of revolutionaries and reformers active in China, heard of Sun Yatsen's revolutionary secret society and read about the abortive Canton uprising of 1911. Later that year an army uprising in Wuhan quickly spread and the Qing Dynasty collapsed. Yuan Shikai made his grab for power and the country appeared to be slipping into civil war. Mao joined the regular army but resigned six months later, thinking the revolution was over when Sun handed the presidency to Yuan and the war between the north and south of China did not take place.

Mao became an avid reader of newspapers and from these was introduced to socialism. He decided to become a teacher and enrolled in the Hunan Provincial First Normal (Teachers' Training) School, where he was a student for five years. During his time at the Teachers' Training School, he inserted an advertisement in a Changsha newspaper 'inviting young men interested in patriotic work to make contact with me...'. Among them was Liu Shaoqi, who later became president of the People's Republic, Xiao Chen who became a founding member of the Communist Party, and Li Lisan.

'At this time', says Mao, 'my mind was a curious mixture of ideas of liberalism, democratic reformism and utopian socialism...and I was definitely anti-militarist and anti-imperialist.' Mao graduated from the Teachers' Training School in 1918, and went to Beijing where he worked as an assistant librarian at Beijing University. In Beijing he met future co-founders of the Chinese Communist Party: the student leader Zhang Guodao, Professor Chen Duxiu and university librarian Li Dazhao. Chen and Li are regarded as the founders of Chinese Communism. It was Li who gave Mao a job and first introduced him to the serious study of Marxism.

Mao was very much the perplexed convert, a nationalist who found in Marxist theory a programme for reform and revolution in China. He did not found Chinese Communism but was introduced to it by Beijing intellectuals. On returning to Changsha Mao became increasingly active in Communist politics. He said at this time:

> I became more and more convinced that only mass political power, secured through mass action, could guarantee the realisation of dynamic reforms.

He became editor of the *Xiang River Review*, a radical Hunan students' newspaper. He continued working in the New People's Study Society and also took up a post as a teacher. In 1920 he was organising workers for the first time and from that year onwards considered himself a Marxist. In 1921, Mao went to Shanghai to attend the founding meeting of the Chinese Communist Party. Later he helped organise the first provincial branch of the Party in Hunan, and by the middle of 1922 the Party had organised trade unions among the workers and students.

Orthodox Marxist philosophy saw revolution spreading from the cities as it had in the Soviet Union. The peasants, ignored through the ages by poets, scholars and political soothsayers, had likewise been ignored by the Communists. But Mao took a different stand and saw the peasants as the lifeblood of the revolution. The Party had done very little work among them but in 1925 Mao began to organise peasant trade unions. This aroused the wrath of the landlords and Mao had to flee to Canton, where the Kuomintang and Communists held power in alliance with each other. Mao proposed a radical redistribution of the land to help the peasants, and supported (and probably initiated) the demands of the Hunan Peasants Union to confiscate large landholdings. Probably at this stage he foresaw the need to organise and arm them for a struggle against the landlords.

In April 1927, Chiang Kaishek launched his massacre of the Communists. The Party sent Mao to Changsha to organise what became known as the 'Autumn Harvest Uprising'. By September the first units of a peasant-worker army had been formed, with troops drawn from the peasantry, Hengyang miners and rebel Kuomintang soldiers. Mao's army moved south through Hunan and climbed up into the Jinggangshan mountains to embark on a guerrilla war against the Kuomintang. This action eventually culminated in the 1949 Communist takeover.

CHANGSHA

(chángshā) 长沙

The site of Changsha has been inhabited for 3000 years. By the Warring States Period (476-221 BC) a large town had grown up here. The town owes its prosperity to its location on the fertile Hunan plains of central China and on the Xiang River, where it rapidly grew as a major trading centre of agricultural produce.

In 1904 the city was opened to foreign trade as the result of the 1903 Treaty of Shanghai between Japan and China. The 'most-favoured nation' principle allowed foreigners to set themselves up in Changsha, and large numbers of Europeans and Americans came to build factories, churches and schools. The medical centre was originally a college established by Yale University.

Today Changsha is the capital of Hunan

Province and has a population of around three million people.

Orientation

Most of Changsha lies on the eastern bank of the Xiang River. The new railway station is at the far east of the city. From the station Wuyi Lu leads to the river, neatly separating the city's northern and southern sections. From Wuyi Lu you cross the Xiang Bridge to the western bank, passing over Long Island in the middle of the river. Most of the sights and tourist facilities are on the east side of the river.

CITS You'll find their headquarters at the Lotus Hotel on Wuyi Lu. The Xiangjiang Hotel can assist with transport bookings as well.

Money The Bank of China is next to the CAAC office on Wuyi Lu. You can also change money at the Xiangjiang Hotel, the Lotus Hotel, or the Civil Aviation Hotel.

Post & Telecommunications The main post and telecommunications office is at the corner of Wuyi Lu and Cai'e Lu in the centre of town. There is also a post office in the Xiangjiang Hotel.

Maps There's usually a hawker or two outside the railway station selling good bus maps that cost 50 fen.

Hunan Provincial Museum

(húnán bówùguǎn) 湖南博物馆

Most of Changsha's sights are related to Mao Zedong and the Communist Revolution, but don't miss the mummified remains of the Han Dynasty woman in the Hunan Provincial Museum. The preserved body was taken from a 2100-year-old Han tomb excavated a few km east of the museum at Mawangdui.

The only sign of the tombs above ground were two earthen mounds of similar size and height standing close together. The body was found in the eastern tomb, in a chamber 16 metres underground and approached from the north by a sloping passageway. The walls of the tomb were covered in a thick layer of charcoal surrounded by a layer of compact clay, which appears to have kept out moisture and prevented the decay of the body and other objects in the tomb.

At the bottom of the tomb was a chamber made of wooden planks, containing an outer, middle and inner coffin. In the coffin was the corpse of a woman of about 50 years of age wrapped in more than 20 layers of silk and linen, with the outer layer bound in nine bands of silk ribbon.

Large quantities of silk garments and fabrics were found in the tomb as well as stockings, shoes, gloves and other pieces of clothing. One of the most interesting objects, now on display in the museum, is a painting on silk depicting the underworld, earth and heaven. The tomb also held lacquerware, pottery containing food, musical instruments (including a 25-stringed wooden instrument called a *se zither*, a set of reed pipes and a set of bamboo pitch-pipes) and a collection of wooden tomb figurines. Other finds included bamboo boxes containing vegetables and grain seeds, straw mats, medicinal herbs, seals and several hundred pieces of money made of unbaked clay with clear inscriptions. Numerous bamboo slips with writing on them listed the names, sizes and number of the objects.

The body is housed in the basement of the museum and is viewed from the floor above through perspex. Her organs have been removed and are laid out on display. Another building houses the enormous outer timber casks.

The museum is on Dongfeng Lu and is within walking distance of the Xiangjiang Hotel. Bus No 3 also runs past it.

Maoist Pilgrimage Spots

Scattered about the city are a number of Maoist pilgrimage spots. The **Hunan No 1 Teachers' Training School** *(dìyī shīfàn xuéxiào)* is where Mao attended classes between 1913 and 1918, and where he returned as a teacher in 1920-21. The school was destroyed during the civil war, but has since been restored. Although of historical interest,

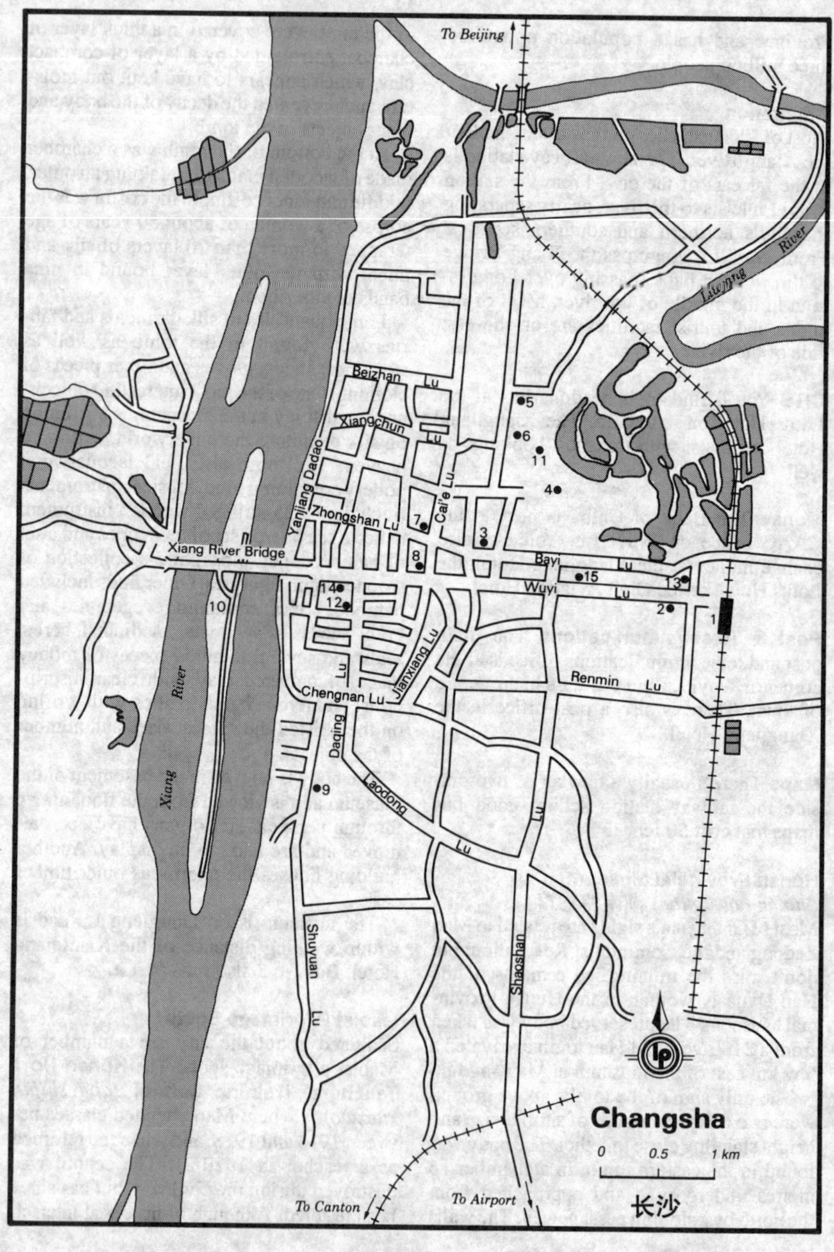
To Beijing
Liuyang River
Beizhan Lu
Xiangchun Lu
Yanjiang Dadao
Cai'e Lu
Zhongshan Lu
Xiang River Bridge
Bayi Lu
Wuyi Lu
Renmin Lu
Jianxiang Lu
Chengnan Lu
Daqing Lu
Laodong Lu
Shaoshan Lu
Shuyuan Lu
Xiang River
1
2
3
4
5
6
7
8
9
10
11
12
13
14
15
Changsha
0 0.5 1 km
长沙
To Canton
To Airport

1 New Railway Station
2 CAAC/Civil Aviation Hotel
3 Former Office of Hunan Communist Party
4 Hunan Guesthouse
5 Hunan Provincial Museum
6 Monument to the Martyrs
7 Xiangjiang Hotel
8 Post Office
9 Hunan No 1 Teachers' Training School
10 Long Island
11 Martyrs' Park
12 Public Security Bureau
13 Long-Distance Bus Station
14 CITS
15 Lotus Hotel

1 新火车站
2 中国民用航空总局
3 中国共产党早期活动的地方
4 湖南宾馆
5 湖南省博物馆
6 烈士纪念碑
7 湘江宾馆
8 邮局
9 第一师范学校
10 桔子洲
11 烈士公园
12 公安局
13 长途汽车站
14 中国国际旅行社
15 芙蓉宾馆

there's not much to see; the main attraction is a sort of Mao 'shrine' with banners, photo, candles and attendants with black armbands. Bus No 1 from outside the Xiangjiang Hotel goes straight past the school, which is still open though the shrine may have been closed.

The **Former Office of the Hunan (Xiang District) Communist Party Committee** *(zhōngguó gòngchǎndǎng zǎoqī huódòngde dìfang)* is now a museum that includes Mao's living quarters and an exhibition of photos and historical items from the 1920s. On the same grounds is a large museum containing a Mao exhibition and some archaeological relics – mainly pottery, tools, weapons and coins.

About 60 km from Changsha is the **Home & Tomb of Yang Kaihui**. Yang was Mao's first wife (discounting an unconsummated arranged childhood marriage) and is being pushed by the present government as his favourite, to counter the vilified Jiang Qing. Yang was the daughter of one of Mao's teachers at the First Teachers' Training School in Changsha, a member of a wealthy Hunanese landowning family. Mao seems to have influenced Yang Kaihui towards radicalism, and also to marriage in 1920 when she was 25 years old. She was arrested by the Kuomintang in 1930 and executed after she refused to denounce the Communist Party and Mao. Yang had two children by Mao: Mao Anqing who was taken to the Soviet Union after his mother's arrest, and the elder son Mao Anying who was arrested with his mother but later released. Mao Anying was killed in the Korean War in 1950.

Other Attractions

The **Loving Dusk Pavilion** *(aìwǎntíng)* is on Yuelu Hill on the west bank of the Xiang River, from where you can get a good view of the town. **Long Island** *(júzizhōu)* or Long Sandbank, from which Changsha takes its name, lies in the middle of the Xiang River. The only remaining part of the old city walls is **Tianxin Tower** in the south of the city.

Places to Stay

The *Xiangjiang Hotel* (☎ 26261) *(xiāngjiāng bīnguǎn)* is at 267 Zhongshan Lu. It's one of China's first-built tourist hotels, but unlike many has been well maintained. Best of all, they haven't yet got rid of their dormitories, like most hotels (probably because Changsha doesn't get hordes of well-heeled tourists). The comfortable, air-con, four-bed dorms in the old wing cost Y15 per person; hot showers are across the hall. Air-con singles with private bath in the new wing are Y70, doubles Y100 up. A four-bed room in the new wing goes for Y27 per person. To get there, take bus No 1 from the new railway station; it drops you off right outside the hotel.

Within walking distance of the railway station is the *Civil Aviation Hotel (mínháng bīngǔan)* which is attached to the CAAC office. This clean, well-run hotel has triples for Y20 per person, doubles for Y70. Opposite CAAC and west a bit on the same avenue is the *Lotus Hotel* (☎ 26246) *(fúróng bīnguǎn)*. It's a high-rise tourist place with singles for Y70 and doubles for Y100.

The *Hunan Guesthouse (húnán bīnguǎn)* near the museum is where visiting government officials usually put up. They accept foreigners, but the front desk seems very disorganised. Room rates are Y45 single, Y70 double.

Places to Eat

Hunanese food, like that of neighbouring Sichuan Province, makes use of plenty of chilli and hot spices. The Chinese restaurant at the Xiangjiang Hotel serves very tasty Hunan-style dim sum breakfasts (including shredded bean curd (tofu) skin in chilli and sesame, bamboo shoots, xi fan (rice porridge), and an assortment of buns and pastries). There are also many small, privately run restaurants in the vicinity of the Xiangjiang Hotel, including the friendly *Jing Yuan* at 152 Cai'e Beilu (the sign is in Chinese only – look for the number and a red-on-green sign).

The much-touted *Yu Yi Tsun Restaurant* (☎ 22797) *(yǒuyìcūn)*, at 116 Zhongshan Lu, is reportedly worth eating at if you know what to order.

Getting There & Away

Air CAAC (☎ 23820) is at 5 Wuyi Donglu near the railway station. Useful flights from Changsha include those to Beijing (five times a week), Canton (daily except Monday), and Chengdu, Kunming, Zhengzhou, Xi'an and Shanghai.

Bus There are three buses to Shaoshan, the birthplace of Mao Zedong, which depart from the long-distance bus station just north of the new railway station. There is also a train to Shaoshan (see following).

Train Changsha is on the main Canton-Beijing line. There are also direct trains to Guilin via the rail junction of Hengyang. Shanghai-Kunming trains pass through the railway junction of Zhuzhou just south of Changsha.

SHAOSHAN

(shāoshān) 韶山

The village of Shaoshan, about 130 km south-west of Changsha, has a significance to Chinese Communism which far overshadows its minute size, for this is where Mao Zedong was born. During the height of the Cultural Revolution it was said to have been visited by three million pilgrims a year, and a railway line and a paved road were built from Changsha to transport them. Today it's foreign tourists who are the pilgrims!

Shaoshan is hardly typical of Chinese villages, considering the number of tourists who have passed through since it was established as a national shrine. It is, however, one opportunity to get a look at the Chinese countryside. The valley is beautiful and you could wander off for days exploring the little villages nearby. Apart from its historical significance, Shaoshan is a great place to get away from those grim, grey cities.

The Great Helmsman revisited Shaoshan in June 1959, after an absence of 32 years. The visit inspired this poem:

Like a dream recalled, I curse the long-fled past,
My native soil and two and thirty years gone by.
The red flag roused the serf, halberd in hand,
While the despot's black talons held his whip aloft.
Bitter sacrifice strengthens bold resolve
Which dares to make sun and moon shine in new skies.
Happy, I see wave upon wave of paddy and beans,
And all around heroes homebound in the evening mist.

Orientation
There are two parts to Shaoshan, the railhead and the village several km away. Outside the station is a square where the bus to Shaoshan village meets the daily train from Changsha. Follow the road up the right-hand side of the park to the main street, where you'll find the long-distance bus station. At the junction of the main street and the road leading from the railway station you can catch the irregular local buses to Shaoshan village.

Mao Zedong's House
(máozédōng jiùjū) 毛泽东旧居

This is the principal shrine of Shaoshan. It's a fairly large building with mud walls and a thatched roof. There's not a great deal to see: a few utensils in the kitchen, the beds and some sparse furnishings, a photo of Mao's mother and father, but like the Chinese you can at least say you've been there. In front of the house is a pond, and on the other side a pavilion where the Chinese pose for photos with the house in the background.

Mao Zedong Exhibition Hall
(máozédōng zhǎnlǎnguǎn) 毛泽东展览馆

Devoted to the life of Mao, this museum opened in 1967 during the Cultural Revolution. It originally had two wings, exact duplicates of each other, so that more visitors could be accommodated at the same time. Today there is only one set of exhibits. Lots of Maobilia for sale – plastic Mao heads and badges of the house – so buy up, as Shaoshan is the only place left in China where you can get it.

Places to Stay
The *Shaoshan Guesthouse (shāoshān bīnguǎn)* in Shaoshan village is a pleasant, comfortable place surrounded by trees. The staff here are exceptionally friendly. The guesthouse is nearly five km from the long-distance bus station, however (local buses ply between the two). Doubles are Y60. There is a large Chinese hotel in the village, but it's unlikely you'll be able to stay there. The post office will let rooms to foreigners for Y8 per person. The guesthouse has pretty good meals.

Getting There & Away
Bus There are three daily buses from Changsha's long-distance bus station (near the new railway station) to Shaoshan – they also return. The fare is Y5 and the trip takes about four hours. In Shaoshan the long-distance bus station is on the main street at the Shaoshan railhead.

Train There is a train from Changsha to Shaoshan each morning at about 8 am. On a sunny day it's a pleasant trip past picturesque villages and attractive countryside. The train returns to Changsha in the afternoon so you can make Shaoshan a day trip if you like. One-way hard-seat fare is Y7.40 and the ride takes two to three hours (quicker than the bus).

If you don't want to return to Changsha but want to get back on the railway lines, then you can take a bus first to Xiangtan and another bus to the railway junction town of Zhuzhou. There is apparently no direct bus from Shaoshan to Zhuzhou.

YUEYANG
(yuèyáng) 岳阳

Yueyang is a stop for the Yangtse ferries from Chongqing to Wuhan. The Wuhan-Canton railway passes through this small town; if you're heading to Canton you can get off the ferry here rather than go all the way to Wuhan. Yueyang is a neat little town, untrampled by tourists. The opposite bank of the river is a vast green plain punctuated by villages. A ferry regularly takes trucks and buses across the river, and you might try some hitching and random exploration.

Information & Orientation
Yueyang lies on the southern bank of the Yangtse River. There are two sections: the southern section where you'll find the railway station, the hotel, etc, and the northern section several km away where the Yangtse ferries dock. CITS has its office at the Yunmeng Hotel. The hotel has a Chinese map of

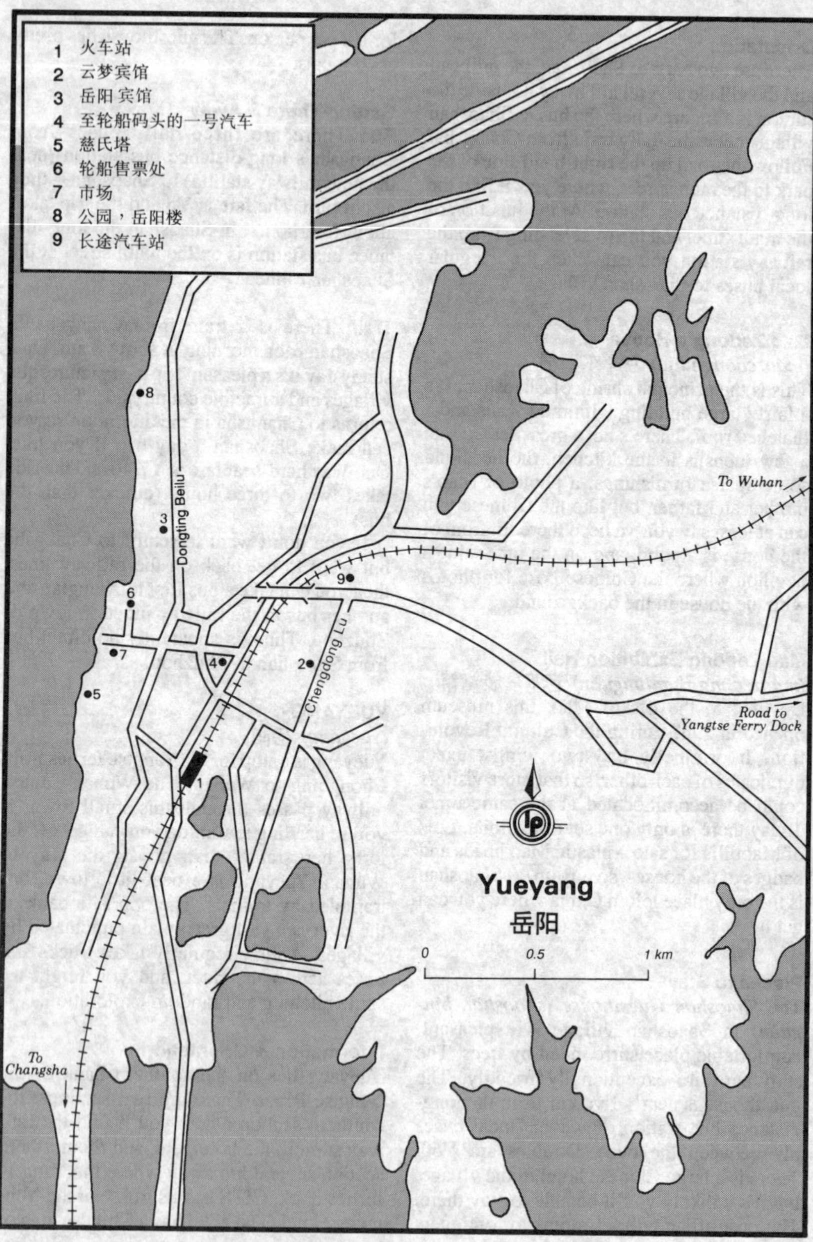
1 火车站
2 云梦宾馆
3 岳阳宾馆
4 至轮船码头的一号汽车
5 慈氏塔
6 轮船售票处
7 市场
8 公园，岳阳楼
9 长途汽车站
Dongting Beilu
Chengdong Lu
To Wuhan
Road to Yangtse Ferry Dock
To Changsha
Yueyang
岳阳
0
0.5
1 km

1 Railway Station
2 Yunmeng Hotel
3 Yueyang Hotel
4 Bus No 1 to Yangtse Ferry Dock
5 Yueyang Tower
6 Ticket Office for Boats to Junshan
7 Street Market
8 Park & Temple
9 Long-Distance Bus Station

the town and Junshan Island that is worth getting.

Things to See

Yueyang is a town for wandering and poking your nose around the alleys and street markets. The chief landmark is the leafy **Yueyang Tower (Cishi Pagoda)** *(císhì tǎ)*, an old pagoda near the riverfront. To get there, walk down the street directly in front of the railway station and turn right at the end; the tower lies up a laneway. Further north is the **Yueyang Pavilion** *(yùeyáng lóu)*, an old temple complex now used as a park. The park is something of a Mecca for Japanese tourists, apparently because of a famous poem written in its praise which Japanese kids learn at school.

To the south-west of the town is enormous **Dongting Lake** *(dòngtǐng hú)*, at 3900 sq km the second largest body of fresh water in the country. There are several islands in the lake; the most famous is **Junshan Island** *(jūnshān)*, where the Chinese grow 'silver needle tea'. When the tea is added to hot water it's supposed to remain on the surface, sticking up like tiny needles and emitting a fragrant odour.

Junshan Island can be reached by boat. To get to the boat dock walk north along the road past the Yueyang Tower. You'll come to a street market on your left. Walk to the end of the market, down the flight of steps and turn right for the ticket office and boat dock. Bus No 2 from the railway station gets you in the general vicinity. There are three or four boats a day to Junshan – worth a visit not only for the tea plantations but for the other farming activity on the island.

Places to Stay & Eat

The *Yunmeng Hotel* (☎ 24498) *(yúnméng bīnguǎn)* at 25 Chengdong Lu is a modest tourist hotel, readily identifiable by what looks like a concrete airliner tail at the front – imagination in architecture knows no bounds here. Doubles cost from Y60 for air-con, comfy double beds, private bathroom. You might manage a bed in a triple for Y15 or so but don't count on it. The hotel is about 20 minutes' walk from the railway station. Or take bus No 4 from the railway station and get off at the second stop. The hotel is five minutes' walk up the road on the left-hand side.

The fairly new *Yueyang Hotel* (☎ 23011) *(yuèyáng bīnguǎn)* on Dongting Beilu is convenient to the Yueyang Tower, Junshan boat pier, and the main market. Rooms are Y80 single, Y100 double – bargaining might be possible. To get there from the railway station, take a No 2 bus and get off at the second stop.

The Yunmeng Hotel has a fairly good restaurant. There are many other small restaurants around town, particularly near the railway station and markets.

Getting There & Away

Yueyang is on the main Canton-Beijing railway line. There are trains to Wuhan (four hours), Changsha (two hours) and Canton (13 hours). There are daily buses to Changsha (Y15) from the long-distance bus station.

The Yangtse ferries dock at the pier in the northern section of the town. Bus No 1 takes you to the pier, a 20-minute ride. The ticket office (a largish building with an anchor and star over the entrance, five minutes' walk around the corner from the bus terminal) should open about half an hour before the ferry docks. There are a number of small restaurants in the vicinity of the dock.

Up river to Chongqing takes about four days and four nights. Fares are: 2nd class Y190; 3rd class Y80; 4th class Y58 (in egalitarian China there is no 1st class). The ferry is scheduled to depart Yueyang at about 9 pm.

Down river to Wuhan takes about eight hours. Fares from Yueyang are: 2nd class Y30; 3rd class Y13; 4th class Y9. The ferry is scheduled to depart Yueyang about 7.30 am but expect delays.

ZHUZHOU

(zhūzhōu) 株州

Unlike nearby Changsha, Zhuzhou is an entirely modern town and owes its sudden development to the completion of the Canton-Wuhan railway line in 1937. Formerly a small market town, it became a river port for the shipment of coal. It later became an important railway junction town and a centre for the manufacture of railway equipment, locomotives and rolling stock. Today it harbours a diverse industry.

Places to Stay & Eat

There is at least one hotel in Zhuzhou where you can stay. Leaving the railway station, turn right along the small road in front of the station and right again at the first intersection. Cross the bridge – the hotel is a big grey concrete building a few minutes' walk ahead on the right-hand side. You should be able to get a dorm bed here for a few yuan. Best places to eat are the small food stalls near the railway station.

Getting There & Away

Zhuzhou is still a major rail junction; the Beijing-Canton and the Shanghai-Kunming railway lines intersect here. There's nothing of particular interest but you may come here to change trains.

If you're coming into Zhuzhou by bus from Xiangtan, the bus line terminates on Zhuzhou's main street. Continue straight ahead to the railway station (a half-hour walk), or take the local bus.

HENGYANG

(héngyáng) 衡阳

Hengyang is the major town of southern Hunan, and like Zhuzhou grew rapidly after the construction of the Canton-Wuhan railway line in 1937. The town became a major lead and zinc-mining centre but its industry was badly damaged during the later stages of WW II. Though it was restored after 1949, the town was overshadowed by the growth of Zhuzhou and Changsha. Today it's a rather dull industrial town on the Beijing-Canton railway line. Travellers who take the train from Canton to Guilin have to wait a couple of hours here for a connection. It's not a bad stopover.

Places to Stay & Eat

The *Hengyang Hotel (héngyáng fàndiàn)* at 54 Xianfeng Lu is a 10-minute walk down the street in front of the railway station. The CITS office is also here. Room prices may depend on who's at the desk, but spartan doubles for Y30 are possible, or triples for Y10 per person. Comfy, air-con double rooms with private bathroom are Y60. The hotel has no English signpost so look for an ornate gateway. There is a Chinese hotel next door and one across the road, but it's unlikely you'll get in. There are many small restaurants in the vicinity of the railway station.

Getting There & Away

Hengyang is a major railway junction with direct trains to Wuhan, Canton and Guilin among other places. Trains to Changsha take three hours, and tourist-price hard-seat is Y15.

XIANGTAN

(xiāngtán) 湘潭

Once a river port and market centre, Xiangtan stagnated early this century when the railway took away much of its trade. The Kuomintang gave its industry a kick in the late 1930s and the Communists expanded it. Today Xiangtan is a rather flat, hot, drab town of 300,000 people on the Shanghai-Kunming railway line.

Getting There & Away

There are regular buses from Xiangtan to Zhuzhou (1¼ hours) and buses to Changsha. There are also buses to Shaoshan which take

1½ hours to make the trip and pass several small villages on the way.

QINGYANSHAN

(qīngyán shān) 青岩山

Parts of the Qingyanshan (Blue Crag Mountains) in north-west Hunan Province have been set aside as Wuling Yuan National Park; locally the whole area is referred to as 'Zhangjiajie' *(zhāngjiājiè)*. Visitors travel by train from Changsha or Yichang (Hubei) to Dayong County, and then bus another 30 km to the Zhangjiajie Forest Park within the mountainous area. Two other parks in the area are at Souxiyu and Tianzishan. The three offer a multitude of hikes through huge, natural stone pillars, craggy peaks and clear mountain streams.

The area is largely untouristed. A couple of readers have recommended a one-week triangle trek through Sangzhi, Tianzishan, Souxiyu and Zhangjiajie; basic government accommodation is available along the way for a few yuan.

If you're coming by train from Yichang on the Yangtse River, you must change trains in Yaqueling (from Yichang to Yaqueling (one hour), from Yaqueling to Dayong (four to six hours)). Buses wait for incoming passengers at the Dayong railway station for the one-hour, Y3 trip to Zhangjiajie.

Jiangxi 江西

Jiangxi *(jiāngxī)* was incorporated into the Chinese empire at an early date, but it remained sparsely populated until the 8th century. Before this, the main expansion of the Han Chinese had been from the north into Hunan and then into Guangdong. When the building of the Grand Canal from the 7th century onwards opened up the south-eastern regions, Jiangxi became an important transit point on the trade and shipment route overland from Guangdong.

Before long the human traffic was diverted into Jiangxi, and between the 8th and 13th centuries the region was rapidly settled by Chinese peasants. The development of silver-mining and tea-growing allowed the formation of a wealthy Jiangxi merchant class. By the 19th century, however, its role as a major transport route from Canton was much reduced by the opening of coastal ports to foreign shipping – which forced the Chinese junk trade into a steady decline.

Jiangxi also bears the distinction of having been one of the most famous Communist guerrilla bases. It was only after several years of war that the Kuomintang were able to drive the Communists out onto their 'Long March' to Shaanxi.

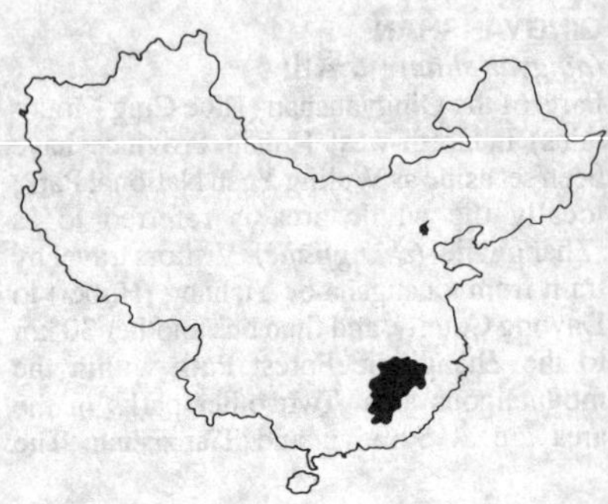

NANCHANG

(nánchāng) 南昌

The capital of Jiangxi Province, Nanchang is largely remembered in modern Chinese history for the Communist-led uprising of 1 August 1927.

After Chiang Kaishek staged his massacre of Communists and other opponents in March 1927, what was left of the Communist Party fled underground and a state of confusion reigned. At this time the Party was dominated by a policy of urban revolution, and the belief was that victory could only be won by organising insurrections in the cities. Units of the Kuomintang Army led by Communist officers happened to be concentrated around Nanchang at the time, and there appeared to be an opportunity for a successful insurrection.

On 1 August, a combined army of 30,000 under the leadership of Zhou Enlai and Zhu De seized the city and held it for several days until they were driven out by troops loyal to the Nanjing regime. The revolt was largely a fiasco, but it is remembered in Chinese history as the beginning of the Red Army. The Army retreated from Nanchang south to Guangdong, but part of it, led by Zhu De, circled back to Jiangxi to join forces with the ragtag army that Mao Zedong had organised in Hunan and led into the Jinggangshan mountains.

Not all of Nanchang's history has been so tumultuous – in fact, the name means 'southern prosperity'. It was founded back in the Eastern Han Dynasty and became a busy trading city, a major staging post on the trade route from Guangdong to Beijing, and a major distribution point for the kaolin pottery of nearby Jingdezhen. Since 1949 it has grown into another of China's multipurpose, industrial-urban sprawls with something like 2½ million inhabitants.

Orientation

Nanchang is bounded in the north by the Gan River and in the west by the Fu River, which

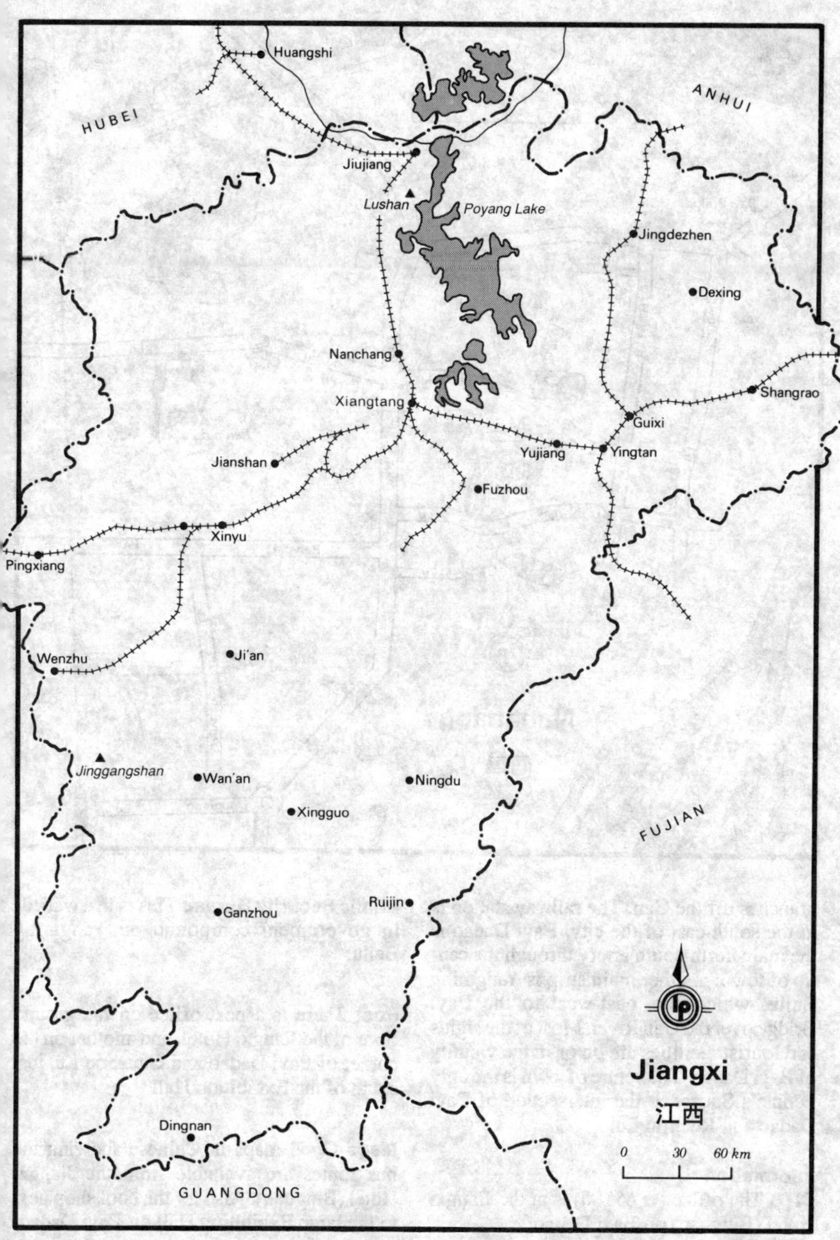
Huangshi
HUBEI
ANHUI
Jiujiang
Lushan
Poyang Lake
Jingdezhen
Dexing
Nanchang
Xiangtang
Shangrao
Guixi
Yujiang
Yingtan
Jianshan
Fuzhou
Xinyu
Pingxiang
Wenzhu
Ji'an
Jinggangshan
Wan'an
Ningdu
Xingguo
FUJIAN
Ruijin
Ganzhou
Jiangxi
江西
0 30 60 km
Dingnan
GUANGDONG

branches off the Gan. The railway station is in the south-east of the city. Bayi Dadao is the main north-south artery through the centre of town; another main strip is Yangming Beilu, which cuts east-west to the Bayi Bridge over the Gan River. Most of the sights and tourist facilities are on or in the vicinity of Bayi Dadao. The centre of town is the ugly People's Square at the intersection of Bayi Dadao and Renmin Lu.

Information

CITS The office (☎ 65180) is at the Jiangxi Hotel (Binguan) on Bayi Dadao.

Public Security Bureau This is in a walled-in government compound on Yangming Beilu.

Post There is a post office on the ground floor of the Jiangxi Hotel, and another on the corner of Bayi Dadao and Ganzhou Lu, just south of the Exhibition Hall.

Maps Good maps in Chinese showing the bus routes are available from the Jiangxi Hotel (Binguan). Also try the bookshop next to the large Exhibition Hall on Bayi Dadao.

1 Monument to the Martyrs
2 Red Flag Pavilion
3 Exhibition Hall
4 Memorial Hall to the Martyrs of the Revolution
5 Railway Station
6 Long-Distance Bus Station
7 Post Office
8 Jiangxi Hotel
9 Public Security Bureau
10 Xiang Shan Hotel

1 八一起义纪念塔
2 红旗堡
3 展览馆
4 烈士纪念馆
5 火车站
6 长途汽车站
7 邮局
8 江西宾馆
9 公安局外事科
10 香山宾馆

Things to See

A fairly nondescript city, Nanchang has been called 'the poor man's Beijing'. Bayi Dadao is colour deprivation at its worst, a length of drab, grey concrete blocks. More interesting are the side streets in the centre of town, where the occasional outdoor market livens things up.

The People's Square is the heart of it all, a dismal piazza built in the Mussolini Modern style but too small to be monolithic and too big to be comfortable. The Monument to the Martyrs stands here – a stone pillar capped by a gun. Opposite stands the immense off-yellow Exhibition Hall. On the other side of the square stands a pavilion of petrified red flags – perhaps an early comment on the state of the Chinese Revolution?

Once you've fled the piazza you might do some walking around the old residential districts near the river, where the houses are built on a more human scale.

Most of the sights are reminders of the Communist Revolution and include the **Memorial Hall to the Martyrs of the Revolution** on Bayi Dadao north of People's Square; the **Residence of Zhou Enlai & Zhu De** on Changzheng Lu; and the **Former Headquarters of the Nanchang Uprising** near the corner of Shengli and Zhongshan Lu, now a museum.

Places to Stay & Eat

The most economical place to stay (for foreigners) is the well-worn but pleasant *Xiang Shan Hotel (xiāngshān fàndiàn)* on Xiang Shan Beilu. To get there take a bus No 5 or walk south off Yangming Beilu for about eight minutes. Beds are Y10 per person in a four-bed room or Y15 in a three-bed; doubles with bath are Y40. Take bus No 2 eight stops from the railway station – the hotel is a few minutes walk further on. There's a restaurant in the hotel, quite cheap. There are also several small restaurants and street markets in the vicinity.

The *Jiangxi Hotel* (☎ 67891) *(jiāngxī bīnguǎn)* on Bayi Dadao is the big tourist joint. It's recently been renovated and is an impressive example of early post-colonial Chinese architecture. Doubles are Y120 to Y140. Take bus No 2 from the railway station.

A smaller *Jiangxi Hotel (jiāngxī fàndiàn)* (look for the Chinese characters for *fandian* rather than *binguan)* is a few doors down from its classier namesake – this gloomy rip-off costs Y100 a room.

On Yangming Beilu, about halfway between the Gan River and Bayi Dadao, is the *Hongdu Hotel (hóngdū fàndiàn)*, which was closed for renovations at the time of research. If/when it reopens, rooms will probably cost around Y100 a night.

Getting There & Away

Air The CAAC office (☎ 62368) is at 26 Zhanqian Lu. Useful connections include regular flights to Beijing, Fuzhou, Wuhan

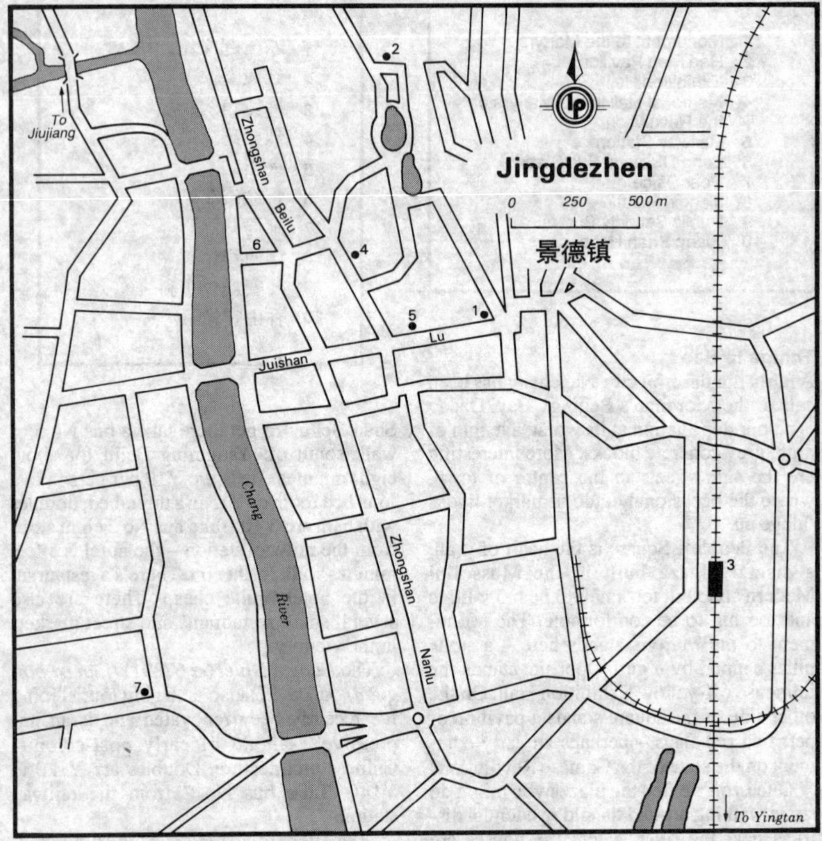

1 Jingdezhen Hotel (Fandian)
2 Jingdezhen Hotel (Binguan)
3 Railway Station
4 Public Security Bureau
5 Post Office
6 Street Market
7 Long-Distance Bus Station

1 景德镇饭店
2 景德镇宾馆
3 火车站
4 公安局外事科
5 邮局
6 市场
7 长途汽车站

and Shanghai. There are six flights a week to Canton.

Bus The long-distance bus station is on Bayi Dadao, midway between the People's Square and the railway station. From here you can take the early morning bus to Guling (Y13), the main hill-station on top of beautiful Lushan. There are also buses from Nanchang to Jiujiang on the Yangtse River, and to the porcelain-making centre of Jingdezhen.

Train Nanchang lies just off the main Canton-Shanghai railway line but many trains make the short detour north and pass through the city. There is also a railway line from Nanchang heading north to the Yangtse River port of Jiujiang.

JINGDEZHEN

(jǐngdézhèn) 景德镇

Jingdezhen is an ancient town once famous for the manufacture of much-coveted porcelain. Today Jingdezhen still makes porcelain and other ceramics – smoke stacks sprout like giant weeds all over the town – but the quality is perhaps not what it once was.

In the 12th century the Song Dynasty fled south in the wake of an invasion from the north. The Song court moved to Hangzhou and the imperial potters moved to Jingdezhen, near Gaolin village and the rich supply of kaolin clay. Today 30,000 of Jingdezhen's 250,000 people are employed in the ceramics industry. For a rundown on the history of pottery in China see the Facts about the Country chapter.

Orientation

Most of Jingdezhen lies on the eastern bank of the Chang River. The main arteries are Zhongshan Lu and Jiushan Lu; the area between the river and Zhongshan Lu is the older part of town and the more interesting. Various restaurants and hotels may be found in the city centre. Good bus maps are available from the Jingdezhen Hotel (Binguan).

Things to See

The town is filled with pottery factories, many of them cottage industries carried on in enclosed courtyards. The government showpiece is the Jingdezhen People's Porcelain Factory (☎ 4498) *(jǐngdézhèn táocíchǎng)* at 54 Fengling Lu. The Jingdezhen Porcelain Friendship Store (☎ 2231) *(jǐngdézhèn yǒuyì shāngdiàn)* is at 13 Zhushan Lu.

The best parts of the town to wander around are the side streets which lead off Zhongshan Lu, particularly those between Zhongshan Lu and the river. In the tiny streets, barely 1½ metres wide, washing is strung out between the old houses. The large wooden doors are removed in summer for ventilation.

Places to Stay

The *Jingdezhen Hotel (jǐngdézhèn fàndiàn)* is central – it almost looks imposing on its little mound of dirt above the main street, but the rooms are as basic as those in any other Chinese hotel. Doubles cost from Y45 to Y60, while triples are Y15 to Y20 per person. Take bus No 2 from either the long-distance bus station or the railway station, as it goes straight past the hotel.

The *Hua Guang Hotel (shǔguǎng fàndiàn)*, directly opposite the railway station, charges only Y5 to Y8 in multi-bed rooms, Y10 to Y16 for doubles. It's not much, but adequate, especially if you've just got in on the 3 am train from Nanchang.

Another *Jingdezhen Hotel* (☎ 4927) *(jǐngdézhèn bīnguǎn)* is about a 15-minute walk from the town centre. This is the main tourist joint and is also where most of the overseas buyers of local porcelain stay. Service is decent, and the pleasant complex is situated on a wooded lake of sorts. Doubles cost Y140.

Getting There & Away

Bus Daily buses run to Yingtan, Jiujiang and Nanchang. There is a daily bus to Tunxi; from there you can bus to Huangshan.

Train Jingdezhen is connected by a branch

line to the railway junction of Yingtan; there are two trains a day. It's a beautiful 4½-hour ride past lush paddy fields. Trains to Nanchang cost Y13 hard-seat, Y24 soft-seat (local price). If you're heading north there are trains to Tunxi and Wuhu.

Getting Around

The centre of town is small enough to walk around. Bus No 2 runs from the long-distance bus station, through the centre of town past the Jingdezhen Hotel (Fandian), and out to the railway station.

JIUJIANG

(jiǔjiāng) 九江

Jiujiang has been a river port on the Yangtse for over 1000 years. Situated near the Poyang Lake which drains into the Yangtse, Jiujiang has been a natural outlet for Jiangxi's trade. After it was opened to foreign trade in 1862 it became a port not only for Jiangxi but also for eastern Hubei and Anhui.

Today Jiujiang is a transit station for Chinese tourists on their way to nearby Lushan. The thing to do here is buy a notched walking stick and unisex sunbonnet, strut around and have your photo taken in front of something.

Information & Orientation

Jiujiang is stretched out along the south bank of the Yangtse River. The long-distance bus station is in the eastern part of town and the railway station is at the western end; the harbour is midway between the two in a narrow urban neck squashed between the river and the lake. In between the harbour and the lake are the hotels, restaurants, shops and other facilities.

Things to See

The seven-storey **pagoda** *(tǎ)* in the southeast of the town is worth a look. The local **museum** *(bówùguǎn)* is in a quaint old building set in the lake near the centre of town, connected to shore by a zigzag bridge. It's got an interesting collection of prehistoric tools and weapons but no English captions.

Places to Stay & Eat

The *Dong Feng Hotel (dōngfēng fàndiàn)* is on Xunyang Lu. They may try to send you to the Nanhu Guesthouse, but hold your ground since they are allowed to take foreigners. They're not bad for a warehouse. A dorm bed costs Y10, and a double is Y40. Rooms facing the street are very noisy. The hotel is within walking distance of the boat dock. From the long-distance bus station or the railway station, take bus No 1 and get off at the stop in front of the museum, then walk back.

The *Nanhu Guesthouse* (☎ 2272) *(jiǔjiāng nánhú bīnguǎn)* at 77 Nanhu Lu is the tourist hotel. It's a big place very inconveniently located on the eastern side of the lake. Doubles cost Y80. There don't appear to be any buses to the hotel. It's a long walk from the train, so hop on an auto-rickshaw.

There are a couple of restaurants around the dock and on the streets close to the Dong Feng Hotel – OK but not memorable.

Getting There & Away

Bus Daily buses run to Jingdezhen (about 5½ hours with many small villages on the way) and Lushan. Minibuses to Lushan leave the river dock area about every half hour for Y14. Ordinary public buses to Lushan leave less frequently and cost Y4.

Buses to Nanchang (Y12) also leave from the dock area.

Train Jiujiang is connected by rail to Nanchang, with several trains per day. A railway bridge over the Yangtse River links Jiujiang (and Nanchang) with Hefei, the capital of Anhui Province.

Boat Jiujiang lies on the Yangtse. From here you can get boats to Wuhan (Y37.60, 3rd class) or Shanghai, stopping at various ports en route. Boat tickets may be bought for the same day or following morning, but not further in advance.

Getting Around

Bus No 1 runs through Jiujiang from the long-distance bus station in the east, past the

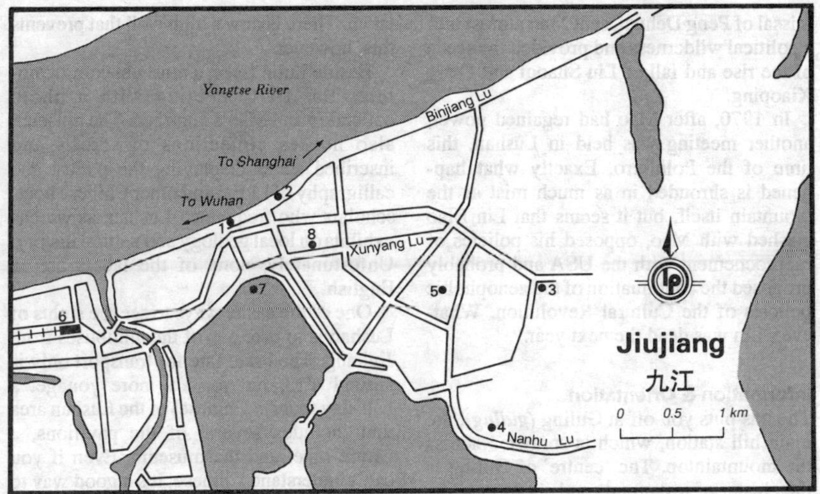

1 Local Ferry Across River
2 Yangtse River Ferry Dock
3 Long-Distance Bus Station
4 Nanhu Guesthouse
5 Pagoda
6 Railway Station
7 Museum
8 Dong Fang Hotel

1 轮渡码头
2 上海客轮码头
3 长途汽车站
4 南湖宾馆
5 塔
6 火车站
7 博物馆
8 东风饭店

South Lake *(nánhú)* to the railway station in the west. There are auto-rickshaws around the train and bus stations and the dock.

LUSHAN
(lúshān) 庐山

Every so often China throws up something that takes you completely by surprise. A village lifted lock, stock and barrel out of Switzerland and grafted onto a Chinese mountaintop is the last thing you'd expect – but here's Lushan and its chunks of European architecture decorating the foliage.

The mountain at the very north of Jiangxi Province is one of the most beautiful in China. Established as a hill resort by early foreign settlers in China, the top of the mountain is dotted with European-style stone cottages, churches and hotels which were built by Britons, Americans and Germans beginning in the late 19th century. The bus ride from the plains of Jiangxi to the top of Lushan is dramatic, as the road winds its way around the mountainside, looking down on sheer cliffs. Over the long drop below you can see immense stretches of terraced fields.

The peace of the mountain belies its significance in the destiny of a billion Chinese. It was here in 1959 that the Central Committee of the Communist Party held its fateful meeting which eventually ended in the dismissal of Peng Dehuai, sent Mao almost into a political wilderness and provided the seeds of the rise and fall of Liu Shaoqi and Deng Xiaoping.

In 1970, after Mao had regained power, another meeting was held in Lushan, this time of the Politburo. Exactly what happened is shrouded in as much mist as the mountain itself, but it seems that Lin Biao clashed with Mao, opposed his policies of rapprochement with the USA and probably proposed the continuation of the xenophobic policies of the Cultural Revolution. Whatever, Lin was dead the next year.

Information & Orientation

The bus puts you off at Guling *(gǔlǐng)*, the main hill station, which is sprawled across the mountaintop. The 'centre' of Guling is the cluster of restaurants and shops near the long-distance bus station. There are food stalls in the large building overlooking the vegetable market in Guling. The Lushan Hotel and various tourist facilities are within easy walking distance. CITS is at the Lushan Hotel. Excellent maps of Lushan are available from the shops in Guling; they show all the tracks and roads and are very detailed and accurate. The long-distance bus station is a 15-minute walk out, on the road to Jiujiang.

Things to See

The best thing to do here is take off along the innumerable paths and tracks and just explore. The old houses are tasteful affairs and it's not hard to get away from the crowds (their numbers in this favourite hill resort are phenomenal).

The mass tourist circuit takes you from the hotel to **Three Ancient Trees, Dragon Head Cliff, Fairy Cave** and back to the hotel via the lake. This takes about five to six hours in all if you don't stop or detour. The best views of the plains of Jiangxi are from the track which leads from the Fairy Cave to the sheer drop of a cliff face.

Until recently you could watch old Chinese men climbing high into the branches of the Three Ancient Trees to have their photos taken. There is now a high wall that prevents this, however.

Beside Lulin Lake, a museum commemorates the 1970 meeting with a photo collection and Mao's huge bed. The museum also houses collections of scrolls and inscribed steles displaying the poetry and calligraphy of Li Bai and other Chinese poet-scholars who frequented Lushan, as well as exhibits on local geology and natural history. Unfortunately, none of the labels are in English.

One of the easier ways to see the sights of Lushan is to take one of the minibuses from Jiujiang. The basic fare for transport only is around Y13, but for Y5 more you get a half-day tour (in Chinese) of the Lushan area that includes several of the pavilions, a nature hike, and the museum. Even if you can't understand Chinese, it's a good way to take in most of the sights without having to arrange step-by-step transport.

Places to Stay & Eat

The *Lu Shan Hotel (lúshān bīnguǎn)*, the main tourist hotel, is an old colonial building, possibly British or German-built. It offers double rooms only, no singles, that start at around Y100 – and it's often full. The hotel is a 30-minute walk from the bus terminal; go through the tunnel and down the hill.

Better value is the *Lulin Hotel* (☎ 282424) *(lúlín fàndiàn)*, which sits beside beautiful Lulin Lake. Huge rooms in the imposing stone buildings are Y90 for a single/double, Y150 for a triple, and Y140 for a quad; service is fairly efficient. The setting is very peaceful – a good location for hill walks – but several km from Guling. If you're riding in on the bus from Jiujiang, you can ask to be let off here, thus saving a walk down from Guling.

The *Yunzhong Guesthouse (yúnzhōng bīnguǎn)* has recently been enlarged and upgraded. It's a tiring walk uphill from the Lu Shan Hotel and costs Y80 to Y140 for a double. Like the Lu Shan Hotel, it's often full.

If you want to be in the heart of charming

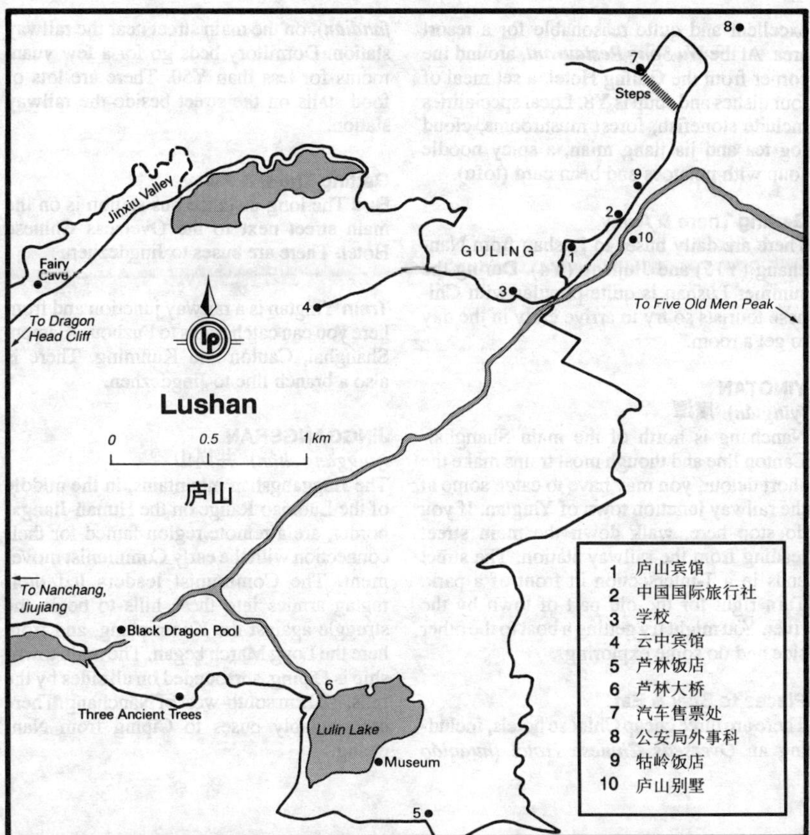

Guling, your only choice is the *Guling Hotel (gǔlǐng fàndiàn)*, where clean, spartan rooms with bath are Y18 per person. It tends to be a bit noisy but is convenient to the bank, shops, restaurants and the bus terminal.

Also in Guling, but off to one side next to the river, is the funky *Lushan Villa Hotel*, which once served as Chiang Kaishek's famous 'Mei Lu Villa'. Rooms are in separate houses, some with private bath and some without; rates are Y15 per person. The staff are friendly and the dining room serves tasty local foods.

The many small restaurants in Guling are

1 Lu Shan Hotel
2 CITS
3 School
4 Yunzhong Guesthouse
5 Lulin Hotel
6 Lulin Bridge
7 Booking Office for Bus Tours
8 Public Security Bureau
9 Guling Hotel
10 Lushan Villa Hotel

excellent and quite reasonable for a resort area. At the *Wu Song Restaurant*, around the corner from the Guling Hotel, a set meal of four dishes and soup is Y8. Local specialities include stonefish, forest mushrooms, cloud fog tea and jia jiang mian, a spicy noodle soup with potatoes and bean curd (tofu).

Getting There & Away
There are daily buses to Lushan from Nanchang (Y15) and Jiujiang (Y4). During the summer Lushan is quite popular with Chinese tourists so try to arrive early in the day to get a room.

YINGTAN
(yīngtán) 鹰潭

Nanchang is north of the main Shanghai-Canton line and though most trains make the short detour, you may have to catch some at the railway junction town of Yingtan. If you do stop here, walk down the main street leading from the railway station. The street ends in a T-intersection in front of a park. Turn right for the old part of town by the river. You might try getting a boat to the other side and do some exploring.

Places to Stay & Eat
There are three cheap Chinese hotels, including an *Overseas Chinese Hotel (huáqiáo fàndiàn)*, on the main street near the railway station. Dormitory beds go for a few yuan, rooms for less than Y50. There are lots of food stalls on the street beside the railway station.

Getting There & Away
Bus The long-distance bus station is on the main street next to the Overseas Chinese Hotel. There are buses to Jingdezhen.

Train Yingtan is a railway junction and from here you can catch trains to Fuzhou, Xiamen, Shanghai, Canton and Kunming. There is also a branch line to Jingdezhen.

JINGGANGSHAN
(jǐnggāng shān) 井岗山

The Jinggangshan mountains, in the middle of the Luoxiao Range on the Hunan-Jiangxi border, are a remote region famed for their connection with the early Communist movement. The Communist leaders led their ragtag armies into these hills to begin the struggle against the Kuomintang, and from here the Long March began. The main township is Ciping, surrounded on all sides by the hills, 320 km south-west of Nanchang. There are probably buses to Ciping from Nanchang.

Hubei 湖北

Hubei *(húběi)* comprises two quite different areas. The eastern two-thirds is a low-lying plain drained by the Yangtse and its main northern tributary the Han River. The western third is an area of rugged highlands with small cultivated valleys and basins dividing Hubei from Sichuan. The plain has been settled by the Han Chinese since 1000 BC. Around the 7th century it was intensively settled and by the 11th it was producing a rice surplus. In the late 19th century it was the first area in the Chinese interior to undergo considerable industrialisation. Site of the great industrial city and river port of Wuhan, slashed through by the Yangtse River and its many tributaries, and supporting a population of almost 50 million, Hubei is still one of China's most important provinces.

WUHAN

(wŭhàn) 武汉

With a population of three million, Wuhan is one of the largest cities in China. It's actually a conglomeration of what were once three independent cities: Hankou, Hanyang and Wuchang.

Wuchang was established during the Han Dynasty, became a regional capital under the Yuan and is now the seat of the provincial government. It used to be a walled city but the walls have long since gone.

Hankou, on the other hand, was barely more than a village until the Treaty of Nanjing opened it to foreign trade. Within a few years it was divided into British, French, German, Russian and Japanese concessions, all grouped around present-day Zhongshan Lu. With the building of the Beijing-Wuhan railway in the 1920s Hankou really began to expand and became the first major industrial centre in the interior of China.

Hanyang has been outstripped by neighbouring Hankou and today is the smallest municipality. It dates back to 600 AD, when a town first developed on the site. During the second half of the 19th century it was developed for heavy industry. The plant for the manufacture of iron and steel which was built at Hanyang in 1891 was the first modern one in China and it was followed during the early 1900s by a string of riverside factories. The 1930s depression and then the Japanese invasion totally ruined Hanyang's heavy industries and since the revolution light industry has been the main activity.

Not many people go out of their way to get to Wuhan, but a lot of people pass through the place since this is the terminal of the Yangtse ferries from Chongqing. Livelier, less grimy, more modern than Chongqing, it's a stepping-stone on the way to the comparatively sparkling, cosmopolitan citadels of Nanjing and Shanghai.

Like those cities, Wuhan has been a fortunate metropolis in unfortunate times. In Wuhan in 1911 an army revolt led to the downfall of the Qing Dynasty; in the fighting Hankou was almost totally burnt to the ground, except for the foreign concessions along the river front. The city was the centre of the bloodily suppressed 7 February 1923 strike of the workers building the Wuhan-Beijing railway line. The Kuomintang government first retreated from Nanjing to Wuhan in the wake of the Japanese invasion,

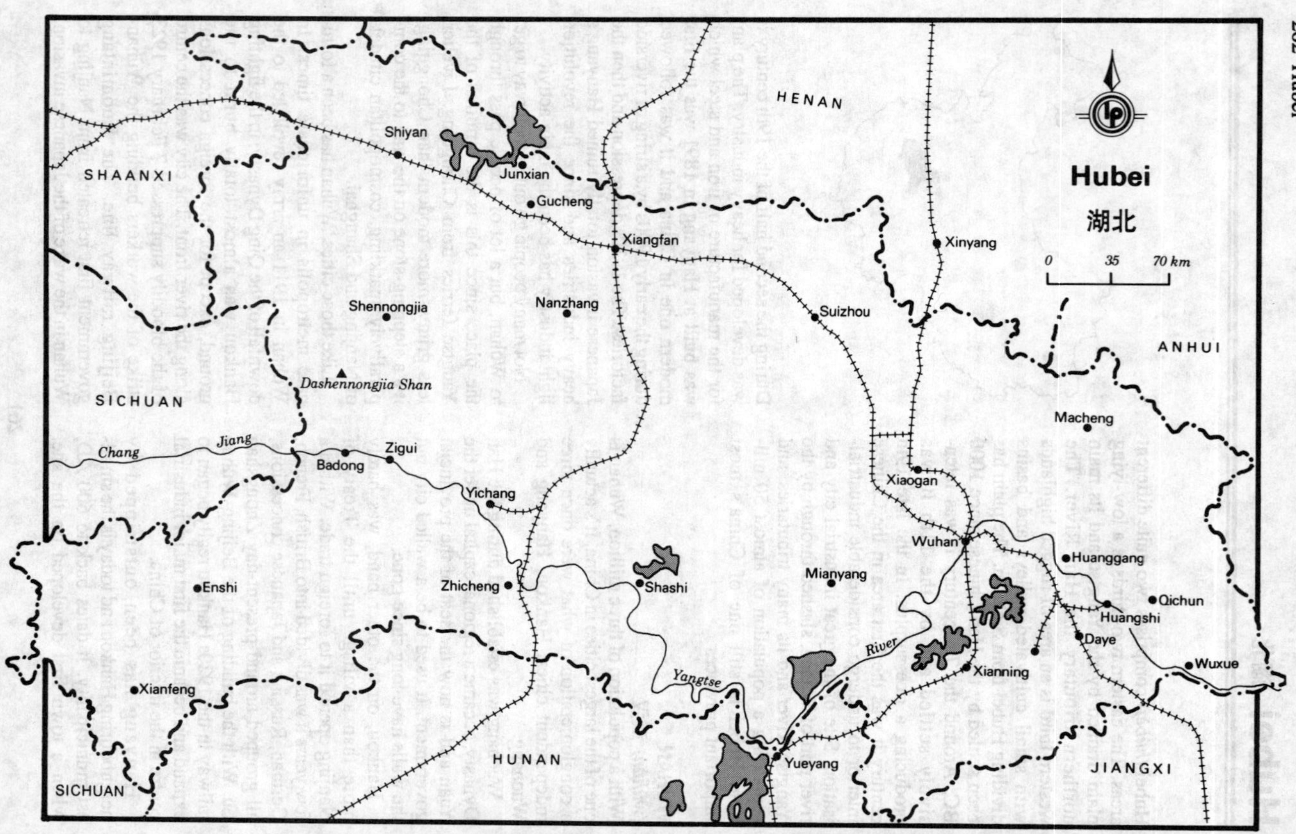
Hubei
湖北
0
35
70 km
HENAN
ANHUI
SHAANXI
SICHUAN
HUNAN
JIANGXI
SICHUAN
Shiyan
Junxian
Gucheng
Xiangfan
Xinyang
Shennongjia
Nanzhang
Suizhou
Dashennongjia Shan
Macheng
Chang
Jiang
Badong
Zigui
Yichang
Xiaogan
Wuhan
Huanggang
Enshi
Zhicheng
Shashi
Mianyang
Qichun
Huangshi
Daye
River
Xianning
Wuxue
Yangtse
Xianfeng
Yueyang

until bombing and the advance of the Japanese army forced them further west to Chongqing.

Hankou *(hànkǒu)* is the centre of Wuhan. Zhongshan Dadao is the main thoroughfare with the shops, department stores, restaurants and several market streets branching off it.

Jiefang Dadao is a market street, but there's a better one selling food and live animals south of Jiefang Dadao – it's a cobbled street lined with old houses.

The north of Hankou, around the Shengli Hotel, is a quiet residential area. Since Hankou was the foreign concession area, there are many European-style buildings, particularly along Yanjiang Dadao in the north-east part of town. Government offices now occupy what were once the foreign banks, department stores and private residences. There were five foreign concession areas in Hankou; the British arrived in 1861, the Germans in 1895, the Russians in 1896, the French in 1896 and finally the Japanese in 1898.

Wuchang is a modern district with long, wide avenues lined with drab concrete blocks. The Hubei Provincial Museum is located here. The fine Guiyuan Temple is across the river in Hanyang.

Information & Orientation

Wuhan lies on both sides of the Yangtse River. Wuchang lies on the east bank. On the west bank lie Hankou and Hanyang, separated from each other by the Han River. Hankou is the centre of things where you'll find the dock for the Yangtse ferries, the hotels and other tourist life-support systems. The main artery is Zhongshan Dadao, which cuts through Hankou roughly parallel to the Yangtse River. Most of the trains into Wuhan stop at both Hankou and Wuchang but it's more convenient to get off at Hankou.

CITS This is on Yangjiang Dadao, near the Yangtse ferry dock. It's virtually useless for individuals. It only concerns itself with tour groups, there's no-one in the office to speak with individuals, and it won't take individual bookings.

Public Security Bureau Their office (☎ 25129) is at 206 Shengli Lu, a 10-minute walk north-east of the Jianghan Hotel. They're quite friendly and helpful.

Money Change cash and travellers' cheques at the Bank of China, corner Zhongshan Dadao and Jianghan Lu, or at any of the tourist hotels.

Maps You should find hawkers selling bus maps of Wuhan near the Yangtse ferry dock and around Hankou railway station. Otherwise, try the hotel shops.

Guiyuan Temple

(guīyuǎn sì) 归元禅寺

Doubling as a curiosity shop and active place of worship is this Buddhist temple with buildings dating from the late Ming and early Qing dynasties.

The main attractions are the statues of Buddha's disciples in an array of comical poses – like the guy sprouting a second head. Two heads are better than one? Behind the dusty glass showcases, it's difficult to tell. A few years ago the statues were out in the open, and the smoking incense and sunshine filtering through the skylights gave the temple a rare magic. Alas, no longer.

Other statues in the temple include the Maitreya Buddha and Sakyamuni. Lots of beggars gather outside the temple, and lots of professional photographers inside snap souvenir shots of people posing in front of rocks and puddles. Monks occasionally bang a gong or tap a bell for the amusement of the masses, but who cares?

It's hard to say what happened to this place during the Cultural Revolution. Different people tell different stories. One local said, 'The people of Wuhan love this place so much. During the Cultural Revolution they protected it and would not let anyone in to harm it'. But 'Don't be silly', said another.' 'It looks old – but in China we are very good

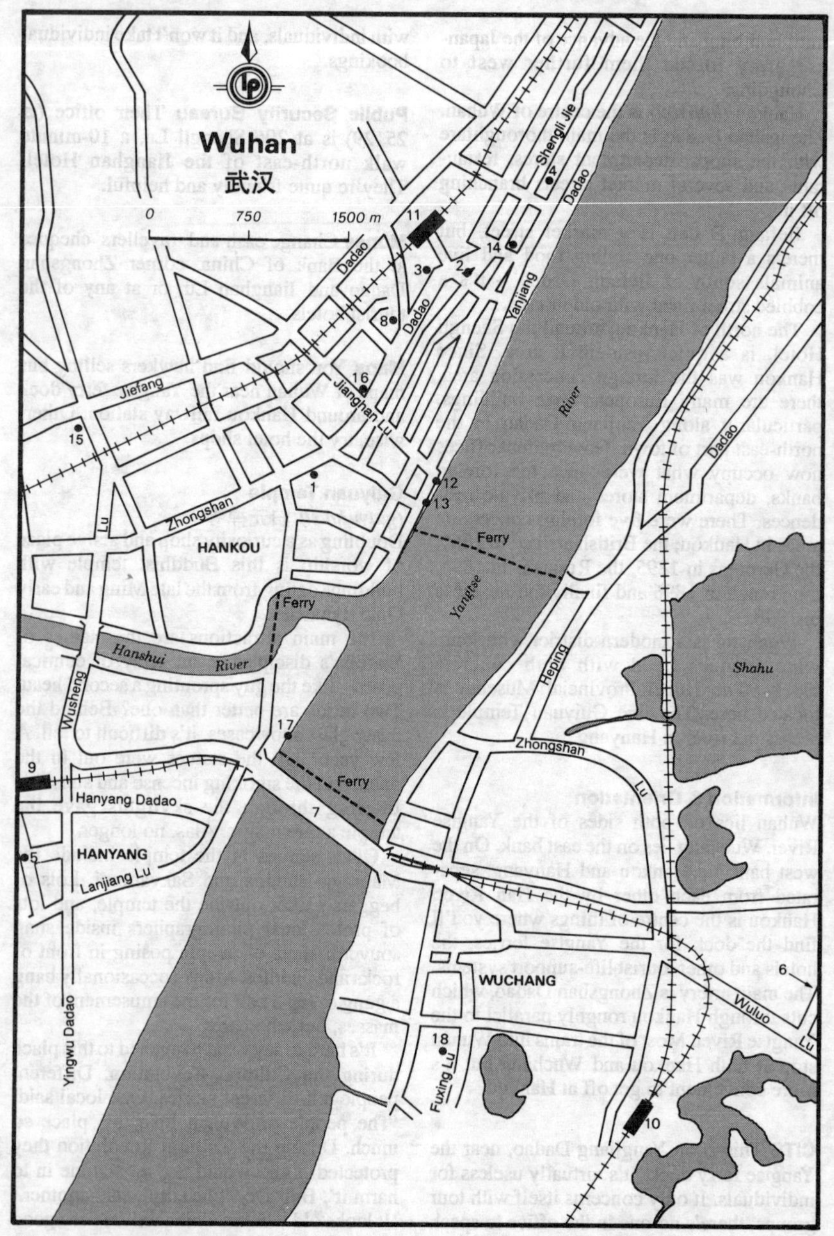
Wuhan
武汉
0
750
1500 m
HANKOU
HANYANG
WUCHANG
Yangtse
River
Hanshui
River
Shahu
Ferry
Ferry
Ferry
Shengli Jie
Dadao
Yanjiang
Dadao
Jianghan Lu
Jiefang
Zhongshan
Lu
Wusheng
Yingwu Dadao
Hanyang Dadao
Lanjiang Lu
Fuxing Lu
Heping
Dadao
Zhongshan
Lu
Wuluo
Lu
Dadao
1
2
3
4
5
6
7
8
9
10
11
12
13
14
15
16
17
18

1 Fun Palace
2 Jianghan Hotel
3 Aiguo Hotel
4 Shengli Hotel
5 Guiyuan Temple
6 Hongshan
7 Wuchang Bridge
8 Laotongcheng Restaurant
9 Hanyang Railway Station
10 Wuchang Railway Station
11 Hankou Railway Station
12 Dock for Yangtse Ferries
13 Booking Office for Yangtse Ferries
14 Public Security Bureau
15 CAAC
16 Bank of China
17 Qing Chuan Hotel
18 Hubei Province Military Region Hotel

1 民众乐园
2 江汉饭店
3 爱国旅行社
4 胜利饭店
5 归元禅寺
6 洪山
7 武汉长江大桥
8 老通城酒楼
9 汉阳火车站
10 武昌火车站
11 汉口站
12 长航客运站
13 港务局售票处
14 公安局外事科
15 中国民航
16 中国银行
17 晴川宾馆
18 湖北省军区招待所

at making things look old.' Your guess is as good as mine.

To get there take bus No 45 from the hotel district, down Zhongshan Dadao and over the bridge; there's a stop within walking distance of the temple. The temple is on Cuiweiheng Lu at the junction with Cuiwei Lu; a trinket market lines Cuiwei Lu.

Yangtse River Bridge

(wǔhàn chángjiāng dàqiáo) 武汉长江大桥

Before the Yangtse Bridge was completed in 1957, all traffic on the north-south route crossed the river by ferry. This road and rail bridge is over 1100 metres long and 80 metres high and is hailed as an example of the country's modern engineering achievements. It connects Wuchang to Hanyang. A shorter bridge spans the Han River to link Hanyang with Hankou.

Hubei Provincial Museum

(húběishěng bówùguǎn) 湖北省博物馆

The museum is a must if you're interested in archaeology. Its large collection of artefacts came from the Zhenghouyi Tomb, which was unearthed in 1978 on the outskirts of Suizhou City. The tomb dates from the Warring States Period, around 433 BC. The male internee was buried with about 7000 of his favourite artefacts, including bronze ritual vessels, weapons, horse and chariot equipment, bamboo instruments and utensils, and gold and jade objects. Most impressive is the massive set of bronze bell chimes – enough to make Mike Oldfield's eyes water. Other musical instruments found in the tomb included a wooden drum, stringed instruments and a kind of flute similar to panpipes. The museum is beside Donghu (East Lake) in Wuchang. Take bus No 14 to the terminal.

Alternatively, see the museum as part of a day's activities. From Hankou, take a ferry across the river to Wuchang, then bus No 36 to Moshan Hill. From here you take a ferry across the lake to East Lake Park, then walk to the museum, then take bus No 14 to Yellow Crane Tower, and finally a ferry back to Hankou.

Wuhan University
(wǔhàn dàxué) 武汉大学
The university was founded in 1913. Many of the rather charming traditional-style buildings date from that period. The campus, in the northern part of Wuchang, was the site of the 1967 'Wuhan Incident' – a protracted battle during the Cultural Revolution with machine gun nests on top of the library and supply tunnels dug through the hill. For a bit of Cultural Revolution nostalgia take bus No 12 to the terminal.

Places to Stay
Apart from the Qing Chuan Hotel, the tourist hotels are in the Hankou region, within walking distance of Hankou railway station. From the Yangtse ferry dock take bus No 30.

Places to Stay – bottom end Touts wait at the exit of the Wuchang railway station to steer new arrivals toward cheap hotels in the area. Most of these places cost around Y6.50 per person, but not all will take foreigners. One that will is the *Hubei Province Military Region Hotel* on Fuxing Lu. Rooms are Y30 for a double (they ask more, but this is the posted rate) or Y5.50 per person in a four-bed room. Out on Fuxing Lu are several noodle stands and 'wine houses' *(jiu jia)* with cheap eats.

The *Aiguo Hotel (àiguó lǚxíngshè)* is on Zhongshan Dadao, a 10-minute walk from Hankou railway station. Rooms range from Y16 per person in a four-bed room with shared bath to Y40 for a double with private bath. Dormitory beds are Y10. This used to be a nifty little hotel, until TVs were put in every thinly partitioned room. The noise is formidable! The showers and toilets are communal, though on the 2nd and 3rd floors there are a few private bathrooms with bathtub and toilet. There's hot water at night.

The *Shengli Hotel* (☎ 22531) *(shènglì fàndiàn)* at 11 Siwei Lu is a dreary place, a bit inconveniently located. Grungy four-bed rooms are Y10 per person. Doubles cost from Y40 to Y60, including air-con, TV and hot water – not bad value.

Places to Stay – middle The *Jianghan Hotel* (☎ 21253) *(jiānghàn fàndiàn)* at 245 Shengli Jie, a 15-minute walk from the Hankou railway station, is the place to stay if you can afford it. Built by the French in 1914 as the Demin Hotel, it's one of the best examples of colonial architecture in this part of the country. Only doubles are available, from Y120.

Places to Stay – top end Top of the range is the glittering, 24-storey *Qing Chuan Hotel* (☎ 441141) *(qíngchuān fàndiàn)* off Qingchuan Jie, near the Wuchang Bridge in Hanyang. The location is not as inconvenient as it might seem, since Hankou is a short ferry ride away. Rates very according to season; singles are Y55 to Y75 and doubles Y112 to Y180. You won't be hard done by the hotel restaurant – it's very good. Next door to the hotel is the restored Qing Chuan Pavilion.

Places to Eat
The *Laotongcheng Restaurant* (☎ 24559) *(lǎotōngchéng dòupí guǎn)*, at 1 Dazhi Lu on the corner with Zhongshan Dadao, serves a delicious snack called *dòupí* for which the all-important characters are:

While it may look like a stuffed omelette, it's actually bean curd (tofu), stuffed and fried and popular for breakfast. It's served with a jug of very greasy chicken soup. This restaurant was apparently a favourite of Mao's, though presumably he didn't have to push and shove with the proletariat to get his doupi.

There are a couple of restaurants in the vicinity of Hankou railway station. Try the *Jinghan Canguan* on Chezhan Lu (the road leading south from the railway station) for Wuchang fish from Wuhan's East Lake and for catfish. It has an English menu and gives enormous servings – best take a group of people. There are lots of noodle and dump-

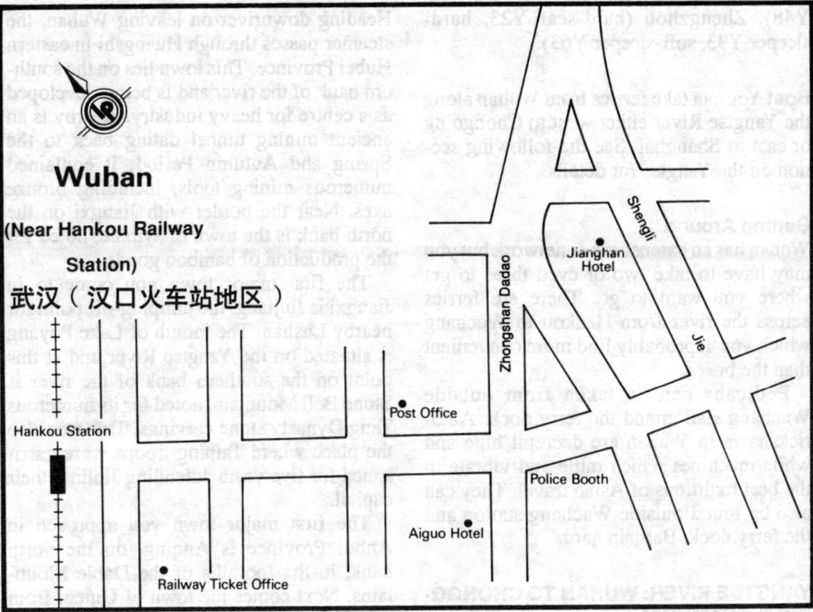

ling shops, snack bars and ice-cream places along Chezhan Lu.

Entertainment
One visitor reports finding a great evening entertainment establishment on Zhongshan Dadao in Hankou. The 'Fun Palace' or Min Zhong Le Yuan is in a vast three-storey building and re-opened in the winter of 1983-84. According to the letter:

> There are acrobats (excellent) in the central building, on top of which is a teahouse where young trendies slurp tea, spit melon seeds, and listen to Auld Lang Syne on Hawaiian guitars. There are three or four different regional operas performed simultaneously, there are stand-up comic routines, slushy Engelbert Humperdinck-type love songs, a 'speak your weight' machine – and best of all, dancing on the very top floor (but Westerners may find it hard to get in). All this, plus a wall-of-death woman motorcyclist in the courtyard, and the sight of thousands of ordinary Wuhan people enjoying themselves. To me that place alone makes Wuhan worth a visit.

Wuhan seems to have an extraordinary number of dance and live music venues. These places aren't hard to find – just look for the disco lights and listen for the batteries of out-of-tune horns.

Getting There & Away
Air CAAC (☎ 51248, 52371) is at 209 Liji Beilu, Hankou. Wuhan is connected by air to 22 Chinese cities. There are daily flights to Canton, Beijing and Shanghai and four a week to Chongqing.

Train Wuhan is on the main Beijing-Canton railway line. Express trains to Kunming and to Xi'an pass through here. The best way of heading east to Nanjing and Shanghai is by river, not by the circuitous rail route.

Some Chinese-price fares from Wuhan are: Beijing (hard-seat Y45, hard-sleeper Y70, soft-sleeper Y126), Changsha (hard-seat Y17, hard-sleeper Y25.50, soft-sleeper

Y48), Zhengzhou (hard-seat Y23, hard-sleeper Y33, soft-sleeper Y63).

Boat You can take ferries from Wuhan along the Yangtse River either west to Chongqing or east to Shanghai. See the following section on the Yangtse for details.

Getting Around

Wuhan has an extensive bus network but you may have to take two or even three to get where you want to go. There are ferries across the river from Hankou to Wuchang which you'll probably find more convenient than the buses.

Pedicabs can be taken from outside Wuchang station and the ferry dock. Auto-rickshaws in Wuhan are decrepit blue and white machines which rattle and vibrate in the best traditions of Asian travel. They can also be found outside Wuchang station and the ferry dock. Bargain hard.

YANGTSE RIVER: WUHAN TO CHONGQING & SHANGHAI

Ferries continue from Wuhan to ports further east on the Yangtse River and ultimately as far as Shanghai on the Huangpu, which branches off the Yangtse. You can also take the ferry west from Wuhan to Chongqing, which is a five-day trip.

In Wuhan, you can buy tickets for the river ferries from CITS, from the booking office at the river port (near the Yangtse ferry dock), or through the tourist-hotel service desks. There are 2nd, 3rd and 4th-class tickets. Second class is a two-person cabin, 3rd class is a 10-person dormitory and 4th class is a 20-person dormitory. Food and beer are sold on board; you can also hop off at any of the many stops along the way for provisions.

Ticket prices in yuan are:

destination	2nd class	3rd class	4th class	duration
Jiujiang	49	19	12	1 night
Wuhu	88	41.20	31.50	30 hours
Nanjing	101	46.80	35.90	36 hours
Shanghai	149	69.30	53	48 hours
Chongqing	227.30	105	80.70	5 days

Heading downriver on leaving Wuhan, the steamer passes through Huangshi in eastern Hubei Province. This town lies on the southern bank of the river and is being developed as a centre for heavy industry. Nearby is an ancient mining tunnel dating back to the Spring and Autumn Period; it contained numerous mining tools, including bronze axes. Near the border with Jiangxi on the north bank is the town of Wuxue, noted for the production of bamboo goods.

The first major town you come to in Jiangxi is Jiujiang, the jumping-off point for nearby Lushan. The mouth of Lake Poyang is situated on the Yangtse River and at this point on the southern bank of the river is Stone Bell Mountain, noted for its numerous Tang Dynasty stone carvings. This was also the place where Taiping troops were garrisoned for five years defending Jinling, their capital.

The first major town you approach in Anhui Province is Anqing, on the north bank, in the foothills of the Dabie Mountains. Next comes the town of Guichi from which you can get a bus to spectacular Huangshan (Yellow Mountain). The town of Tongling lies in a mountainous area in central Anhui on the southern bank, west of Tongguanshan. Tongling has been a copper-mining centre for 2000 years, and is a source of copper for the minting of coins. Still in Anhui Province, and at the confluence of the Yangtse and Qingyi rivers, is Wuhu, also a jumping-off point for Huangshan. Just before Anhui Province ends is the city of Manshan, the site of a large iron and steel complex.

The first large city you pass in Jiangsu Province is Nanjing, followed by Zhenjiang, then the port of Nantong at the confluence of the Tongyang and Tonglu canals. The ferry then proceeds along the Yangtse and turns down the Huangpu River to Shanghai. The Yangtse empties into the East China Sea.

WUDANGSHAN

(wǔdāng shān) 武当山

The Wudangshan mountains (otherwise known as the Canshan or the Taiheshan) stretch for 400 km across north-western Hubei Province. The highest peak rises 1600 metres, and was known as 'Pillar Propping up the Sky' or 'Heavenly Pillar Peak'.

The Wudangshan are a sacred range to the Taoists, and a number of Taoist temples were built here during the construction sprees of the Ming emperors Cheng Zu and Zhen Wu. Noted temples include the Golden Hall on Heavenly Pillar Peak, which was built entirely of gilded copper in 1416; the hall contains a bronze statue of Ming Emperor Zhen Wu, who became a Taoist deity. The Purple Cloud Temple stands on Zhanqifeng Peak, and the Nanyan Temple perches on the South Cliff.

SHENNONGJIA

(shénnóngjià) 神农架

This is an inaccessible mountain area in north-western Hubei, 160 km north of the Yangtse River gorges. The area is famous for the sightings of wild, ape-like creatures, a Chinese equivalent of the Himalayan Yeti or the North American Bigfoot. The stories are interesting, but the creatures seem to be able to distinguish between peasants and scientists – molesting the former and evading the latter. Graham Earnshaw's guidebook *On Your Own in China* gives a lengthy account of the creatures and some of the reported sightings. Apparently in Shanghai there is a club (with 3000 members) devoted to finding this thing.

YICHANG

(yíchāng) 宜昌

Yichang, regarded as the gateway to the Upper Yangtse, was once a walled city dating at least as far back as the Sui Dynasty. The town was opened to foreign trade in 1877 by a treaty between Britain and China, and a foreign concession area was set up along the river front south-east of the walled city.

Yichang is a port town and a stop for the Chongqing-Wuhan boats. There is a railway line from Yichang north to the town of Xiangfan, where you change trains and carry on to Luoyang. There are also direct trains from Yichang to Luoyang. To get from the ferry dock to the railway station in Yichang take bus No 3.

Henan 河南

The Yellow River snakes its way across the north of Henan *(hénán)*, where it all began. About 3500 years ago the Chinese were turning their primitive settlements into an urban-centred civilisation governed by the Shang Dynasty.

Excavations of Shang Dynasty towns have shown that these were built on the sites of even more ancient settlements. The Shang civilisation was not founded by people migrating from western Asia, as was once thought, but was part of a continuous line which had been developing here since prehistoric times.

The Shang Dynasty ruled from the 16th to the 11th century BC. They controlled an area which included parts of what is today Shandong, Henan and Hebei provinces. To the west of their territory the powerful Zhou people arose and conquered the Shang; the last Shang emperor supposedly hurled himself into the flames of his burning palace.

The first Shang capital, perhaps dating back 3800 years, is believed to be the site of Yanshi, west of modern-day Zhengzhou. Around the middle of the 16th century BC the capital was moved to Zhengzhou, where the walls of the ancient city are still visible. Later the capital moved to Yin, near the modern town of Anyang, in the north of Henan.

The only clues as to what Shang society was like are found in the remnants of their cities, in divining bones inscribed with a primitive form of Chinese writing, and in ancient Chinese literary texts. Apart from the walls at Zhengzhou, all that has survived of their cities are the pounded-earth foundations of the buildings, stone-lined trenches where wooden poles once supported thatched roofs, and pits used for storage or as underground houses.

Today Henan, one of the smaller Chinese provinces, is also one of the most densely populated – with over 80 million people squashed in; only Sichuan Province has

more human mouths to feed. It was the centre of Chinese civilisation during the Song Dynasty, but lost political power when the government fled south from its capital at Kaifeng, in the wake of an invasion from the north in the 12th century. Nevertheless, with such a large population on the fertile (though periodically flood-ravaged) plains of the unruly Yellow River, Henan remained an important agricultural area.

Henan's urban centres rapidly diminished in size and population with the demise of the Song. It was not until the Communist takeover in 1949 that they once again expanded. Zhengzhou was transformed into a great industrial city – Luoyang, Kaifeng and Anyang have also been industrialised but not to such a great extent.

For modern travellers, the biggest drawcard in Henan is the Longmen Caves near Luoyang.

ZHENGZHOU

(zhèngzhōu) 郑州

Zhengzhou is a 12-hour train ride from Shanghai and Beijing and a couple of decades behind them in progress. Because of its importance as a railway junction, Zhengzhou was made the capital of Henan Province after 1949. Since 1950 the popula-

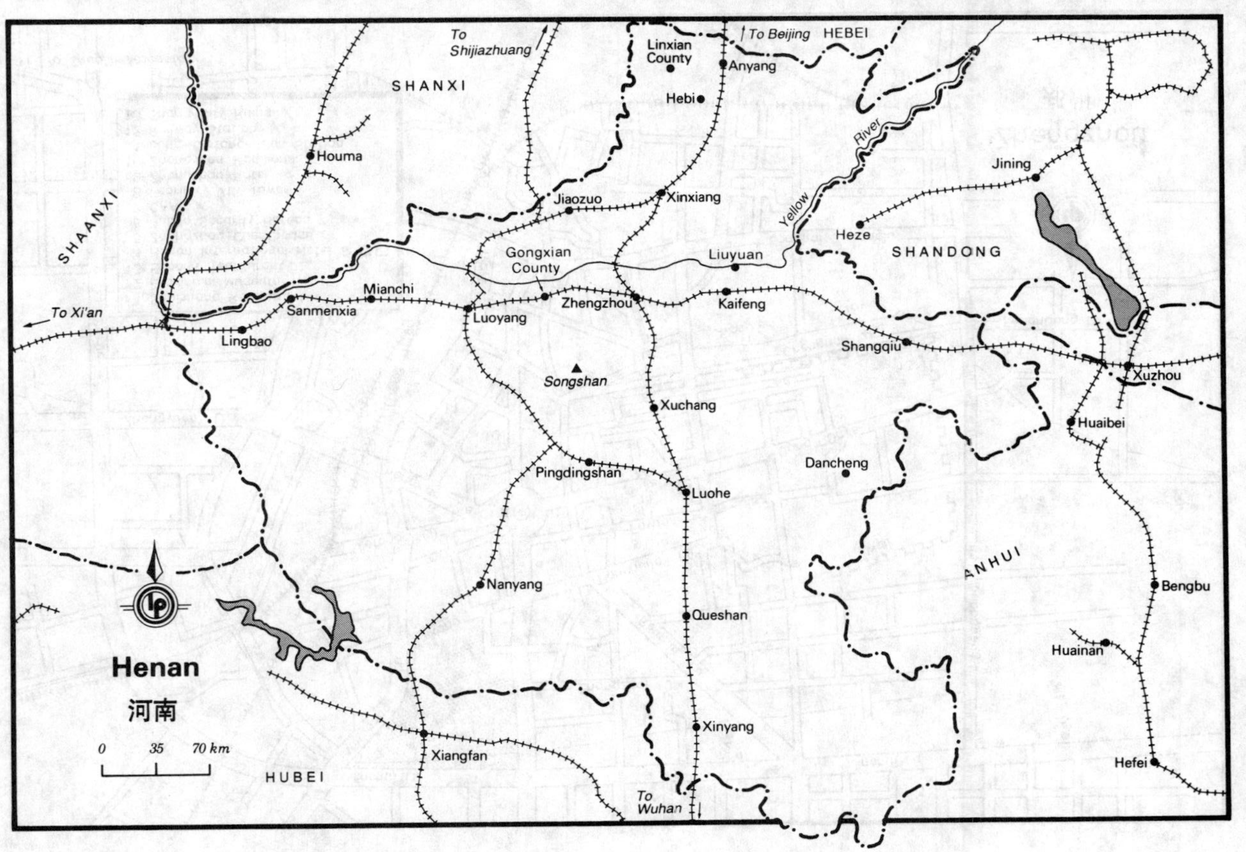
To Shijiazhuang
SHANXI
Linxian County
Hebi
Anyang
To Beijing
HEBEI
Houma
SHAANXI
Jiaozuo
Xinxiang
Yellow
River
Jining
Heze
SHANDONG
Gongxian County
Liuyuan
Mianchi
Sanmenxia
Luoyang
Zhengzhou
Kaifeng
To Xi'an
Lingbao
Shangqiu
Xuzhou
Songshan
Xuchang
Huaibei
Pingdingshan
Dancheng
Luohe
ANHUI
Nanyang
Bengbu
Queshan
Huainan
Henan
河南
Xinyang
0
35
70 km
Xiangfan
Hefei
HUBEI
To Wuhan

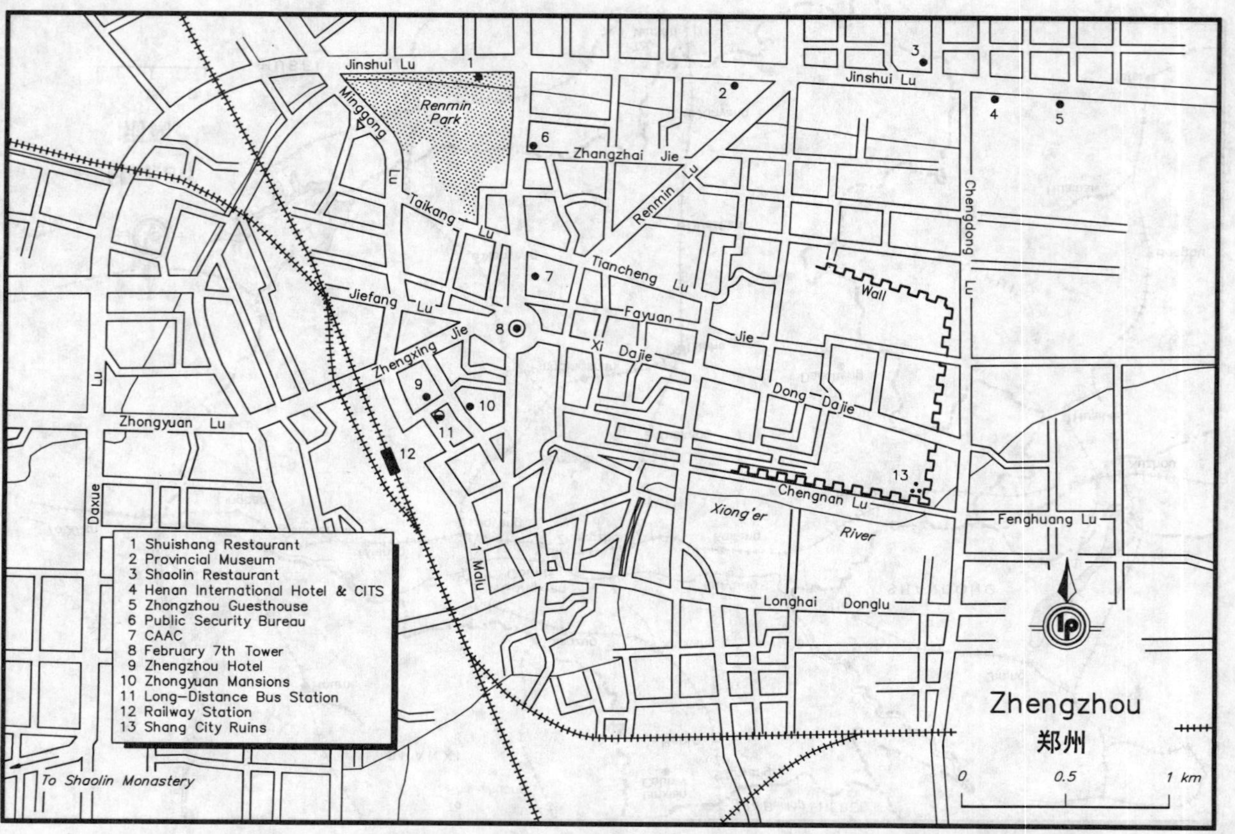
Jinshui Lu
Jinshui Lu
Renmin Park
Minggong Lu
Zhangzhai Jie
Renmin Lu
Chengdong Lu
Taikang Lu
Tiancheng Lu
Wall
Jiefang Lu
Fayuan Jie
Zhengxing Jie
Xi Dajie
Dong Dajie
Zhongyuan Lu
Daxue Lu
Chengnan Lu
Xiong'er River
Fenghuang Lu
1 Malu
Longhai Donglu
1 Shuishang Restaurant
2 Provincial Museum
3 Shaolin Restaurant
4 Henan International Hotel & CITS
5 Zhongzhou Guesthouse
6 Public Security Bureau
7 CAAC
8 February 7th Tower
9 Zhengzhou Hotel
10 Zhongyuan Mansions
11 Long-Distance Bus Station
12 Railway Station
13 Shang City Ruins
To Shaolin Monastery
Zhengzhou
郑州
0
0.5
1 km

1	水上餐厅
2	省博物馆
3	少林菜馆
4	河南国际饭店
5	中州宾馆
6	公安局外事科
7	中国航空公司
8	二七塔
9	郑州饭店
10	中原大厦
11	长途汽车站
12	火车站
13	商代遗址

tion has increased tenfold from around 100,000 people to over one million.

In Zhengzhou the Communists had a chance to build an entire city from the ground up, in whatever style they saw as the ideal or whatever resources would allow – this is what they came up with. The resulting prototype is educational – one of the most monotonous, ugly cities in China.

Seen from the top floors of the Henan International Hotel, Zhengzhou's main tourist joint, the city stretches into the distance: a sea of near identical red-brick low-rise residential blocks interspersed with factories and smokestacks. These are plonked down like lego blocks and interspersed with narrow twisting alleys. There are several main boulevards wide enough for hundreds of thousands of bicycles.

A typical group of apartment buildings consists of eight or 10 four-storey brick rectangles arranged in rows. The dirt courtyard in front of the complex is an area for playing and gossiping; the back is divided amongst tenants and used for vegetable plots and makeshift chicken coops. Each complex, which might include a hospital and the factory or office block where the tenants work, is surrounded by a four-metre wall, often topped with barbed wire or broken glass. There is only one entry gate per complex, two at most – sometimes with a gatekeeper.

Orientation

Most of the tourist facilities and sights are in the south-eastern and eastern sections of the city.

The city centre is a traffic circle on the intersection of Erqi Lu and Jiefang Lu, readily identifiable by the large February 7th Memorial Tower. South-west of the monument is the railway station, directly opposite it are Zhongyuan Mansions (one of Zhengzhou's major hotels) and the long-distance bus station. The area between the railway station and the February 7th Tower has many shops and restaurants.

Erqi Lu runs north from the monument; along it are the CAAC office, the Public Security Bureau, the post office and the February 7th Hotel. Jinshui Lu runs from east to west and intersects Erqi Lu; on it are the Provincial Museum and the Henan International Hotel.

Information

Public Security Bureau This is in a government compound at 70 Bei Erqi Lu.

CITS This is in the Henan International Hotel. Forgive the staff if they seem surprised to see you – tourists are such a rarity that they may throw a party in your honour.

Money The Bank of China (☎ 51551) is at 16 Huayuankou Lu.

Post & Telecommunications There is a post office on the ground floor of the Henan International Hotel. The main post and telephone office is beside the square in front of the railway station.

Shang City Ruins

(shāngdài yízhǐ) 商代遗址

On the eastern outskirts of Zhengzhou lie the remains of an ancient city from the Shang period. Long, high mounds of earth indicate where the city walls used to be, now cut through by modern roads. This is one of the earliest relics of Chinese urban life. The first archaeological evidence of the Shang period was discovered near the town of Anyang in northern Henan. The city at Zhengzhou is believed to have been the second Shang capital, and many Shang settlements have been found outside the walled area.

Excavations here and at other Shang sites suggest that a 'typical' Shang city consisted of a central walled area containing large buildings (presumably government buildings or the residences of important people, used for ceremonial occasions) surrounded by a ring of villages. Each village specialised in such products as pottery, metalwork, wine or textiles. The village dwellings were mostly semi-underground pit houses, while the buildings in the centre were rectangular and above ground.

Excavations have also uncovered Shang tombs. These are rectangular pits with ramps or steps leading down to a burial chamber in which the coffin was placed and surrounded with funeral objects such as bronze weapons, helmets, musical instruments, oracle bones and shells with inscriptions, silk fabrics, and ornaments of jade, bone and ivory. Among these, depending on the wealth and status of the deceased, have been found the skeletons of animals and other humans – sacrifices meant to accompany their masters to the next world. Study of these skeletons suggests they were of a different ethnic origin from the Shang – possibly prisoners of war. This, and other evidence, has suggested that Shang society was not based on the slavery of its own people. Rather, it was a dictatorship of the aristocracy with the emperor/father-figure at the apex.

There are two sites where you can see part of the ruins. The portion that still has some of the wall standing is in the south-east section of the city. Buses No 2 and 8 stop nearby – get off at the stop called East Gate *(dōng mén kǒu)*. Bus No 3 runs through the old Shang City. The other set of ruins is in Zijingshan Park *(zǐjīngshān gōngyúan)*, near the Henan International Hotel.

Henan Provincial Museum

(hénán shěng bówùgǔan) 河南省博物馆

The museum is at 11 Renmin Lu, at the intersection with Jinshui Lu, readily identifiable by the large Mao statue. It has an interesting collection of artefacts discovered in Henan Province, including some from the Shang period. There's also an exhibition on the February 7th revolt but, unfortunately, there are no English captions. The February 7th Memorial Tower, in the centre of Zhengzhou, commemorates the 1923 strike organised by workers building the railway from Wuhan to Beijing. The strike was bloodily suppressed.

Yellow River

(húanghé) 黄河

The Yellow River is just 24 km north of Zhengzhou and the road passes near the village of Huaxuankou, where Kuomintang troops blew up the river dikes in April 1938. This ingenious tactic was ordered by Chiang Kaishek. The Japanese advance was halted for a few weeks at the cost of drowning maybe a million Chinese people and making another 11 million homeless and starving. The dike was repaired with American help in 1947 and today the point where it was breached has an irrigation sluice gate and Mao's instruction, 'Control the Yellow River', etched into the embankment.

The river has always been regarded as 'China's sorrow' because of its propensity to flood. It carries masses of silt from the loess plains and deposits them on the riverbed, causing the water to overflow the banks. Consequently, the peasants along the river bank have had to build the dikes higher and higher each century. As a result, parts of the river flow along an elevated channel which is often as much as 1½ km wide and sometimes more than 15 metres high!

The river has been brought partially under control through the building of upstream dams and irrigation canals which divert the flow. The largest of these is the Longyang Dam in Qinghai Province, which is also a major source of hydroelectric power.

Mangshan is the site of Yellow River Park, on the south bank of the river. There should be buses to Mangshan from the square in front of Zhengzhou railway station or from the bus station.

Renmin Park

(rénmín gōngyúan) 人民公园

This park is interesting not for scenic beauty but for the entranceway, which looks like someone's attempt to re-create either the Lunan Stone Forest or the Tiger Balm Gardens – enough said. The park itself has little to offer but family circuses sometimes set up shop here, performing such feats as embalming their bodies in wire, or lying down with a concrete block on their stomach while dad takes to it with a sledgehammer. You can play that venerated Chinese sport of ping pong on the concrete tables in the park if you've got some bats and a ball. The entrance to the park is on Erqi Lu.

Places to Stay

Accommodation prospects in Zhengzhou are pretty dreary. There are no firmly established low-budget travellers' places to stay.

Opposite Zhengzhou railway station and next to the long-distance bus station is *Zhongyuan Mansions (zhōngyúan dàxià)*, a cavernous white tower with additions, wings, annexes and untold numbers of rooms all equipped with booming televisions. It's about the most convenient place to stay for budget travellers. Doubles are Y18 without private bath, Y40 with bath, assuming the plumbing is working – it often isn't. Some travellers have reported that they got rooms here for Y10 after much bargaining, but what they got were really grotty, cheerless dungeons.

Opposite the bus station is the *Zhengzhou Hotel (zhèngzhōu fàndiàn)*, which may be worth a try. Doubles go for around Y17, but the place tends to be filled with cadres from the countryside having meetings.

Top of the group is the *Henan International Hotel* (☎ 23413) *(hénán gúojì fàndiàn)* at 114 Jinshui Dadao Dongduan. You'll find CITS at this big tourist joint – inconveniently situated in the distant eastern outskirts of the city. Despite the hotel's great size, the rooms are pleasantly small and have comfy beds, air-con, refrigerator and attached bathroom. These were once remarkably cheap, but prices have now risen to Y100 a double. The restaurant is good.

Next door, the *Zhongzhou Guesthouse* (☎ 24255) *(zhōngzhōu bīngǔan)*, 115 Jinshui Dadao, has doubles from Y80. Bus No 2 from the railway station (the stop is in front of Zhongyuan Mansions) takes you to these hotels.

Places to Eat

Here we have more dreary prospects. The only dish which seems distinctly 'Zhengzhou' is available from food stalls around the town centre – it looks like a slimy, wok-fried, gelatinised potato. It goes for about Y1 per plate and is called *liáng fěn*.

The *Shaolin Restaurant (shǎolín càigǔan)* is on the corner of Jinshui Lu and Jing 4-Lu, a 10-minute walk west of the Henan International Hotel. It's identifiable by a large painting of the Shaolin Monastery above the very ornate entrance. The staff are friendly and the upstairs is pleasant. There have been some mixed reports about this place but give it a try.

There is a *Shuishang Restaurant (shǔishàng cāntīng)*, which means 'Restaurant over the Water', but don't expect tranquil pavilions on a pleasant lake. The restaurant is near the intersection of Erqi Lu and Jinshui Lu. Upstairs it's OK with moderate prices,

but downstairs is just like any other Chinese canteen.

The extravagant three-storey *Regent Palace* on the grounds of the Henan International Hotel is a cross between a hotel, restaurant, disco and hairdressing salon. On the 1st floor is a souvenir shop; upstairs are the Mandarin Chinese Restaurant, the Napoleon French Restaurant (serving everything from filet de boeuf Diane to screwdrivers) and the Crystal Ballroom disco.

Getting There & Away

Air Some useful air connections include Beijing (one flight weekly) Y231, Canton (daily) Y452, Xi'an (six flights weekly) Y158, Shanghai (three flights weekly) Y297, Tianjin (daily) Y230, and Wuhan (daily) Y174. The CAAC office (☎ 24339) is at 38 Bei Erqi Lu.

Bus The long-distance bus station is opposite the railway station. Buses also leave from the square in front of the railway station.

There are frequent buses to Kaifeng (two hours) and Luoyang (Y4.50, 4½ to five hours). The road to Luoyang takes you past long stretches of terraced grain fields, through dusty little towns, and past mud-brick houses and cave dwellings.

Train Zhengzhou is on the main Beijing to Canton line. It's a major rail junction and you may have to stop here overnight to change trains. There are direct trains to Beijing (12 hours), Shanghai (14 hours), Xi'an (12 hours), Canton (23 hours), Luoyang (four hours). There are also trains to Taiyuan and Datong.

Zhengzhou station has a separate ticket window for foreigners but you can sometimes get the local price on hard seats. There is an advance booking office on Erqi Lu, just north of the intersection with Hongwei Lu.

Getting Around

Zhengzhou is very spread out and walking is only recommended within the relatively narrow confines of the central city area. Bus No 2 will take you from the railway station to the Henan International Hotel. There are many taxis and auto-rickshaws in front of the railway station, together with taxi touts – beware of ridiculous overcharging.

SHAOLIN MONASTERY

(shǎolín sì) 少林寺

David Carradine never actually trained here, but at Shaolin Monastery 80 km west of Zhengzhou a form of unarmed combat was indeed developed by Buddhist monks.

Separating myth from history is hard in China and Shaolin is no exception. It's said to have been founded by an Indian monk in the 5th century, and stories are told of how the monks fought invaders and led rebellions against foreign rulers. Perhaps as a result, their monastery was burned down several times – most recently in 1928 when a local warlord had a go. That was topped off with some more vandalism by the Red Guards.

Despite the fires and vandalism, many of the monastery buildings still stand. The most impressive and photogenic form the 'forest of stupas' outside the walls, each built in remembrance of a monk. The rest of the monastery is in a very sorry state, although this does give it a certain ancient-looking charm.

Chinese people come here in droves – spurred on by a People's Republic movie which used the monastery as a set, and features high-flying unarmed gladiators inflicting punches and kicks that would wind an elephant. As a result, Shaolin is a booming Chinese tourist Mecca with convoys of buses making the trip during the high season. The unfortunate result is that the landscape is carpeted with broken beer bottles, plastic wrappers, cans, papers, etc.

The road leading to the monastery is wall-to-wall billboards, restaurants and souvenir stalls. Get your Shaolin Monastery handkerchief and imitation scimitar here. Some of the old monks are said to have returned to Shaolin in the last few years; if so, they don't come out during visiting hours.

The monastery sits on Songshan, a mountain sacred to the Taoists. On the same mountain is the Taoist Zhongyue Temple, which may have been founded during the Qin Dynasty.

Overall impression – it's not worth it. The litter, commercialisation and noisy tourists are bad enough, but the present buildings, resplendent as they may appear in the tourist brochures, are in sorry need of repair. Perhaps the best reason to visit Shaolin is to see what the Chinese people consider a major tourist attraction.

Getting There & Away

A convenient way of getting to Shaolin is on one of the local Chinese tour buses from either Zhengzhou or Luoyang. In Zhengzhou tickets can be bought from a booth in front of Zhongyuan Mansions, opposite the railway station. Their relative costs are a first for China: foreigners Y8, Chinese people Y10.

In Luoyang, the main bus station (opposite the railway station) also runs buses every morning, departing every 30 minutes between 6 and 9 am. The price is Y10 per person. There are also minibuses for Y12 available through many of the hotels. They stop off at the Zhongyue Temple and a set of underground Han tombs.

KAIFENG

(kāifēng) 开封

Kaifeng is a medium-sized city east of Zhengzhou. Its size belies the fact that this was once the prosperous imperial capital of China during Northern Song times. With the invasion from the north in 1127 the Song fled south, where their poets wrote heart-wrenching verse as their beautiful capital was pillaged.

Kaifeng never recovered from the assault and was never restored. All that remains today of the imperial splendour is a scroll painting in Beijing's Forbidden City which depicts the bustling town centre as it once was. Kaifeng's population has grown little in the past 60 years, from just 280,000 in 1923 to just over 300,000 today, which makes it something of an odd-town-out in China's urban population boom.

The most intriguing members of Kaifeng's population are the Chinese Jews. Just how the Jews came to China is unknown. The story of the scattering of the '10 tribes' is one possibility, but more likely they came as traders and merchants along the Silk Road

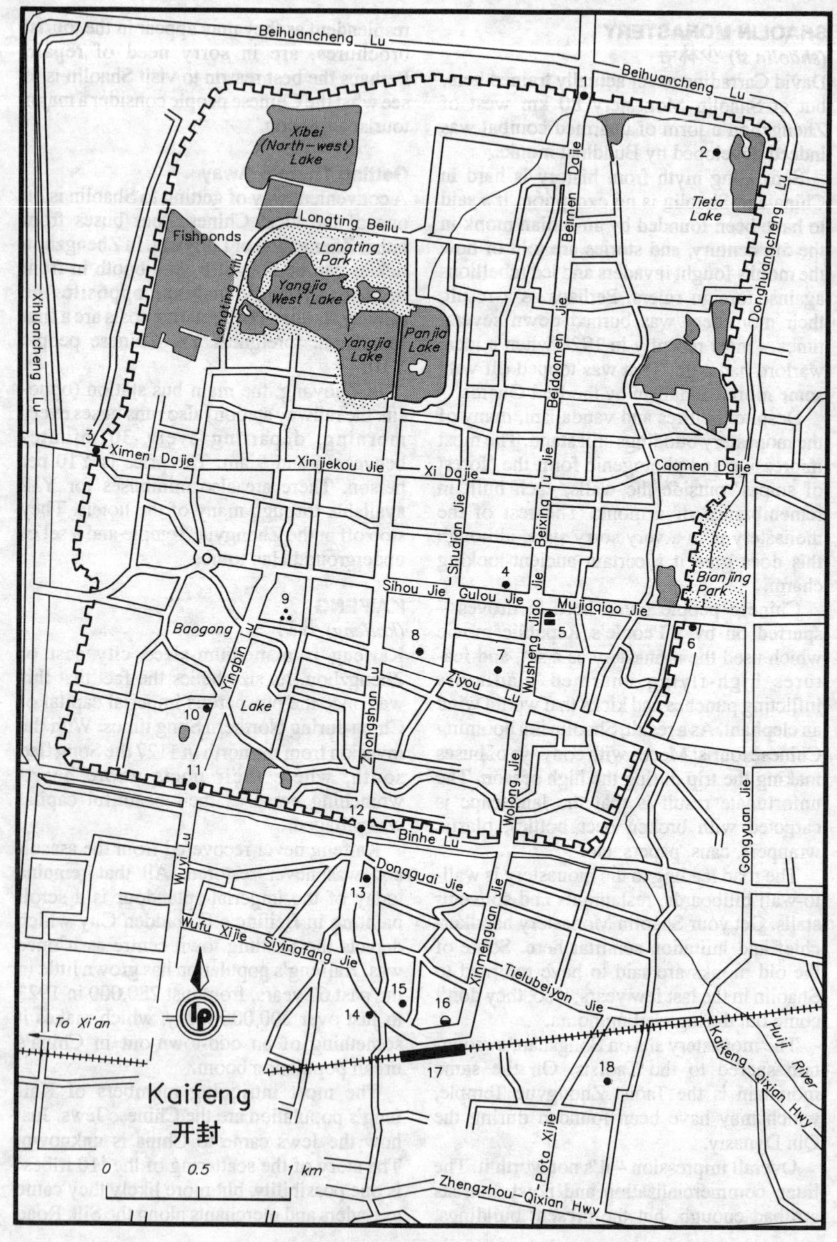
Beihuancheng Lu
Beihuancheng Lu
Xibei (North-west) Lake
Tieta Lake
Beimen Dajie
Donghuancheng Lu
Longting Beilu
Fishponds
Longting Park
Longting Xilu
Yangjia West Lake
Xihuancheng Lu
Yangjia Lake
Panjia Lake
Beidaomen Jie
Ximen Dajie
Xinjiekou Jie
Xi Dajie
Caomen Dajie
Shudian Jie
Beixing Tu Jie
Sihou Jie
Gulou Jie
Mujiaqiao Jie
Bianjing Park
Baogong Lake
Yingbin Lu
Ziyou Lu
Wusheng Jiao Jie
Zhongshan Lu
Wolong Jie
Gongyuan Jie
Binhe Lu
Wuyi Lu
Dongguai Jie
Wufu Xijie
Siyingfang Jie
Xinmenguan Jie
Tielubeiyan Jie
Huiji River
Kaifeng–Qixian Hwy
To Xi'an
Pota Xijie
Zhengzhou–Qixian Hwy
1
2
3
4
5
6
7
8
9
10
11
12
13
14
15
16
17
18
0
0.5
1 km
Kaifeng
开封

1	Beimen (North Gate)
2	Iron Pagoda
3	Ximen (West Gate)
4	Bank of China
5	Post & Telecom Office
6	Songdu Guesthouse
7	Kaifeng Guesthouse & CITS
8	Xiangguo Monastery
9	Yanqing Taoist Temple
10	Museum
11	Xi'nanmen (South-west Gate)
12	Da'nanmen (Great South Gate)
13	Xinhua Bookstore
14	Dongfeng Hotel
15	Bianliang Hotel
16	Long-Distance Bus Station
17	Railway Station
18	Fan Pagoda

when Kaifeng was the capital. Others think they emigrated from the Jewish populations of the south-west coast of India.

Father Nicola Trigault translated and published the diaries of the Jesuit priest Matteo Ricci in 1615, and based on these diaries he gives an account of a meeting between Ricci and a Jew from Kaifeng. The Jew was on his way to Beijing to take part in the imperial examinations, and Trigault writes:

When he (Ricci) brought the visitor back to the house and began to question him as to his identity, it gradually dawned upon him that he was talking with a believer in the ancient Jewish law. The man admitted that he was an Israelite, but he knew no such word as 'Jew'.

Ricci found out from the visitor that there were 10 or 12 families of Israelites in Kaifeng. A 'magnificent' synagogue had been built there and the five books of Moses had been preserved in the synagogue in scroll form for over 500 or 600 years. The visitor was familiar with the stories of the Old Testament, and some of the followers, he said, were expert in the Hebrew language. He also told Ricci that in a province which Trigault refers to as 'Cequian' at the capital of 'Hamcheu' there was a far greater number of Israelite families than at Kaifeng, and that there were others scattered about. Ricci sent one of his Chinese converts to Kaifeng, where he confirmed the visitor's story.

Today several hundred descendants of the original Jews live in Kaifeng and, though they still consider themselves Jewish, the religious beliefs and the customs associated with Judaism have almost completely died out. The original synagogue was destroyed in a Yellow River flood in 1642. It was rebuilt but destroyed by floods again in the 1850s. This time there was no money to rebuild it. Christian missionaries 'rescued' the temple's scrolls and prayer books in the late 19th century, and these are now in libraries in Israel, Canada and the USA. The Chinese government has recognised Jews as an official ethnic group and the local Jews have plans to establish a synagogue and a Jewish museum in the town.

1	北门
2	铁塔
3	西门
4	中国银行
5	邮电局
6	宋都宾馆
7	开封宾馆
8	相国寺
9	延庆观
10	博物馆
11	西南门
12	大南门
13	新华书店
14	东风旅社
15	汴梁旅社
16	长途汽车站
17	火车站
18	繁塔

A couple of other things make Kaifeng worth a visit. The old Maoist maxim, 'make one thing serve two purposes', has been given a pragmatic bent and Kaifeng's imperial relics double as temples, museums, exhibition centres, comedy venues, parks and monuments. Speaking of Maoism, Kaifeng has the notoriety of being the place where Liu Shaoqi is supposed to have ended his days in 1969.

Information

CITS This is in the Kaifeng Guesthouse.

Money The Bank of China is on Gulou Jie about half a km north of the Kaifeng Guesthouse.

Post & Telecommunications The post and telecommunications office is on Mujiaqiao Jie, near the Kaifeng Guesthouse.

Xiangguo Monastery

(xiànggúo sì) 相国寺

This is Kaifeng's chief sight, originally founded in 555 AD but frequently rebuilt over the next 1000 years. It was completely destroyed in 1644 when the Yellow River floodgates were opened in a disastrous attempt to halt a Manchu invasion. The current buildings date from 1766 and have had a thorough going-over since then. Try your hand at sharpshooting; or check out the revolutionary history museums, mummies, tacky religious statues, funfair mirrors and, oh yes, bottled human embryos. At night there's stand-up comedy, dance lessons in the shadows, chess championships and lots of hip young locals.

Iron Pagoda

(tiě tǎ) 铁塔

Built in the 11th century, the Iron Pagoda is actually made of normal bricks but covered in specially coloured tiles that look like iron. You can climb to the top of this impressive structure. The tiles on the lower levels have damaged Buddha images – possibly the result of Red Guard sledgehammers.

Other Sights

Longting Park *(lóngtíng gōngyúan)* features the Longting (Dragon Pavilion) itself and some peculiar displays. Also worth visiting is the Yanqing Taoist Temple *(yánqìng gūan)* with its interesting architecture and strange 13-metre-high pagoda. The oldest existing building in Kaifeng is Fan Pagoda *(fán tǎ)*, south-east of the railway station.

If you want to see the Yellow River then take local bus No 6 or a motorised pedicab to Liuyuan *(liǔyúan)*, 10 km north of Kaifeng. Ferries cross the river at this point too.

Places to Stay

Good news! Public Security in Kaifeng takes an easygoing attitude and puts few restrictions on where you stay. As a result, you have your choice of a wide range of cheap hotels near the railway station and you don't have to fight the usual battles of FEC versus RMB. If all of China were this relaxed, the country would undoubtedly get a lot more foreign tourists, a fact which is lost on government officials.

There are several government-run hotels and a few even cheaper private ones. The private hotels are down obscure alleys and hard to find, but runners from these hotels greet passengers on incoming trains, so you should get plenty of offers for a cheap place to stay. The government hotels are larger and marginally more comfortable.

Among the government hotels, one of the best is *Bianliang Hotel (biànliáng lǚshè)* where doubles are Y15. The hotel has large rooms, a secure luggage storage area and extremely friendly management. It is on Zhongshan Lu, about 100 metres to your left as you leave the railway station. Opposite is the *Dongfeng Hotel (dōngfēng lǚshè)* which charges similar prices.

Further down the street is the privately run *Zhongshan Hotel (zhōngshān lǚshè)* which charges Y12. All along Zhongshan Lu you'll find alleys with little hotels tucked away – again, you don't have to find them, they'll find you.

Foreign tour groups usually stay at the *Kaifeng Guesthouse (kāifēng bīngǔan)* on Ziyou Lu. It was built by the Russians and appears to have had little maintenance since they left. The run-down concrete block has doubles for Y80. Take bus No 3 from the railway station and get off at the third stop. Another expensive alternative is the *Songdu Guesthouse (sòngdū bīngǔan)* near Bianjing Park. Doubles are Y50 but cheaper accommodation may be possible.

Places to Eat

Good restaurants are hard to find but there are lots of unhealthy looking noodle shops all around the railway station and they're open late at night. There are also plenty of stalls in the vicinity of the Xiangguo Monastery.

Getting There & Away

Air There are no flights to Kaifeng and the nearest airport is at Zhengzhou.

Bus There are regular buses to Zhengzhou (two hours) from the square in front of the Kaifeng railway station. Other buses depart from the long-distance bus station east of the railway station. The fastest and cheapest way to get to Qufu is by bus along the Kaifeng-Heze-Yanzhou-Qufu route. The trip takes eight hours and you can see the Yellow River along the way. For Luoyang change buses at Zhengzhou.

Train Kaifeng lies on the railway line between Xi'an and Shanghai and trains are frequent. The train to Zhengzhou takes about 1½ hours. The trips to Shanghai and Xi'an both take around 13 hours.

To travel from north to south by rail you'll have to return to Zhengzhou first.

ANYANG

(ānyáng) 安阳

Anyang is in the far north of Henan Province, near the border of Hebei Province. It lies on the main Zhengzhou to Beijing railway line.

Close to this small town is the site of Yin, the last capital of the ancient Shang Dynasty and one of the first centres of an urban-based Chinese civilisation.

In the last few decades of the 19th century, peasants working near Anyang unearthed pieces of polished bone inscribed with an ancient form of Chinese writing – these turned out to be divining bones with questions addressed to the spirits and ancestors. Other inscriptions were found on the undershells of tortoises as well as on bronze objects, suggesting that the last capital of the Shang Dynasty once stood here.

The discoveries attracted the attention of both Chinese and Western archaeologists, though it was not until the late 1920s that work began on excavating the site. These excavations uncovered ancient tombs, the ruins of a royal palace, workshops and houses – proof that the legendary Shang Dynasty had indeed existed.

LUOYANG

(luòyáng) 洛阳

Luoyang is one of the richest historical sites in China. Founded in 1200 BC, it was the capital of 10 dynasties before losing its rank in the 10th century AD when the Jin moved their capital to Kaifeng. In the 12th century Luoyang was stormed and sacked by Jurchen invaders from the north and never really recovered from the disaster. For centuries it remained a squalid little town vegetating on the edge of a vanished capital. By the 1920s it had only 20,000 inhabitants. It took the Communists to shake the lethargy from the area. They built a new industrial city similar to Zhengzhou at Luoyang, a vast expanse of wide avenues and endless brick and concrete apartment blocks now housing over a million people.

Looking at it today, it's hard to imagine that Luoyang was once the centre of Buddhism in China. When the religion was introduced from India this was the site of the White Horse Temple *(báimǎ sì)*, the first Buddhist temple built in China. At this temple Indian Sanskrit scriptures were first translated into Chinese. When the city was the imperial capital under the Northern Wei Dynasty there were supposed to be 1300 Buddhist temples operating in the area. At the same time, work was begun on the magnificent Buddhist Longmen Cave temples outside the city.

The only real reason to visit Luoyang is the Longmen Caves. There's nothing much to see around town.

Orientation

Luoyang is spread across the northern bank of the Luo River. The main railway station is Luoyang west station. The city centre is around Jinguyuan Lu, which runs roughly south-east from the railway station and is criss-crossed by a couple of major arteries.

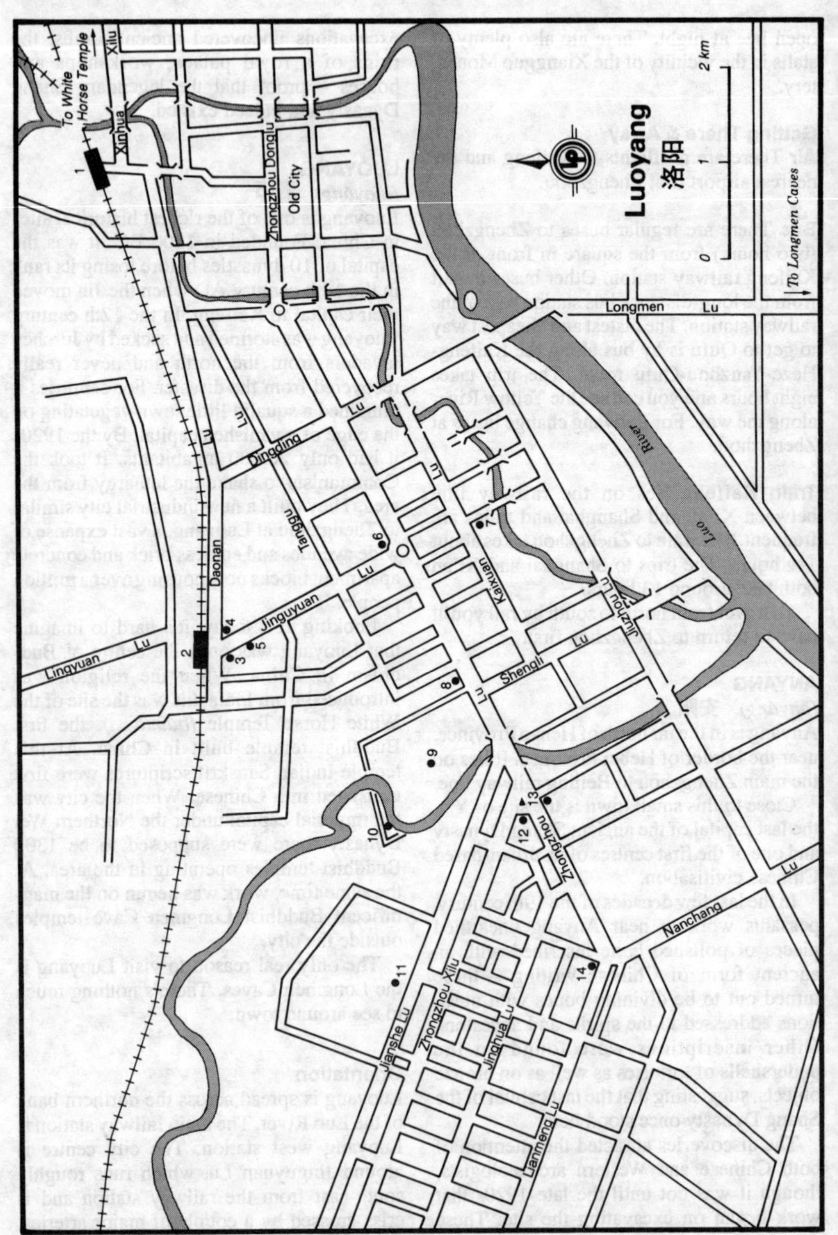
Luoyang
洛阳
0
1
2 km
To White Horse Temple
To Longmen Caves
Xilu
Xinhua
Zhongzhou Donglu
Old City
Longmen Lu
Luo River
Dingding Lu
Daonan Lu
Tanggu Lu
Jinguyuan Lu
Lingyuan Lu
Kaixuan Lu
Shengli Lu
Zhongzhou Xilu
Zhongzhou
Jianshe Lu
Jinghua Lu
Lianmeng Lu
Nanchang Lu
1
2
3
4
5
6
7
8
9
10
11
12
13
14

1	East Station
2	Main Railway Station
3	Luoyang Hotel
4	Long-Distance Bus Station
5	Tianxiang Hotel
6	Post Office
7	Public Security Bureau
8	Luoyang Museum
9	Wangcheng Park
10	Han Dynasty Tombs
11	No 1 Tractor Plant
12	Bank of China
13	Friendship Store
14	Friendship Guesthouse & CITS

1	洛阳东站
2	火车站
3	洛阳旅社
4	长途汽车站
5	天香旅社
6	邮局
7	公安局外事科
8	洛阳博物馆
9	王城公园
10	汉墓
11	第一拖拉机制造厂
12	中国银行
13	友谊商店
14	友谊宾馆

The old city is in the eastern part of Luoyang and some of the old walls can still be seen.

Information

CITS, a bank where you can change money, and a post office are in the new wing of the Friendship Guesthouse. The Public Security Bureau is on Kaixuan Lu.

White Horse Temple

(báimǎ sì) 白马寺

The Ming and Qing buildings of the White Horse Temple, perhaps the most venerable Buddhist temple in China, are built on the site of the original temple. The story of the temple's origin is interesting. In 67 AD the second emperor of the Han Dynasty sent two envoys to India to collect Buddhist scriptures. Their journey preceded that of the Tang Dynasty monk Xuan Zhuang (whose story is told in the classic novel *Journey to the West)* by 500 years. When the envoys reached Afghanistan they met two Indian monks who gave them Buddhist scriptures and statues. The four then returned to Luoyang and had the temple built. The story goes that, since the scriptures and statues were carried to Luoyang on the back of a white horse, the temple was named the White Horse Temple. In front of the temple are two Song Dynasty stone horses. To the east is a 13-storey pagoda built sometime between the 10th and 12th centuries. The two Indian monks lived in the temple, translating scriptures and lecturing on Buddhist teachings and Indian culture; they are still buried there today.

The temple stands 13 km north-east of the city. To get there take buses No 5 or 9 to the turning circle at the edge of the old city walls. Walk east to the stop for bus No 56, which will take you to the temple. On weekdays the temple tends to be a quiet and relaxing place.

Wangcheng Park

(wángchéng gōngyúan) 王城公园

The park is on Zhongzhou Lu and has two underground Han Dynasty tombs. Paintings and bas-reliefs can still be seen on the stone doors but the coffins have long gone. Other than that, the park has a tiny and decidedly dismal zoo. Freak shows (stuffed and mounted animals and pickled human foetuses) are occasionally set up in the park.

Luoyang Museum

(lùoyáng bówùgǔan) 洛阳博物馆

The museum is next to the park and houses a collection of early bronzes, Tang figurines and implements from the Stone Age. There are some eye-catching pieces but no English captions. Bus No 2 from the railway station area goes to the museum.

Luoyang No 1 Tractor Plant
(dìyī tūolājī zhìzàochǎng)
第一拖拉机制造厂

This model factory used to be known as the East is Red Tractor Plant but has been given a modern (more drab) name. Situated on Chang'an Lu, it opened in 1959 and provides social services for its workers and families, including a hospital, schools and day-care centres. If you want a tour, enquire at CITS.

Longmen Caves
(lóngmén shíkū) 龙门石窟

In 494 AD the Northern Wei Dynasty moved its capital from Datong to Luoyang. At Datong the dynasty had built the impressive Yungang Caves where works of typical Buddhist art can be seen. A common motif, for instance, is a triad in which the Buddha is flanked by bodhisattvas, though sometimes these are replaced by Ananda and Kasyapa, Buddha's first disciples. Bodhisattvas generally have expressions of benign tranquillity; they are saints who have opted to return to earth instead of entering nirvana, so that they might help others to follow the path of righteousness. You'll find many flying apsaras (celestial beings similar to angels and often depicted as musicians or bearers of flowers and incense).

At Luoyang the dynasty began work on the Longmen Caves. Over the next 200 years, more than 100,000 images and statues of Buddha and his disciples were carved into the cliff walls on the banks of the Yi River, 16 km south of the city. It was an ideal site. The hard texture of the rock, like that at Datong, made it very suitable for being carved. The caves of Luoyang, Dunhuang and Datong represent the peak of Buddhist cave art.

Apart from natural erosion, at Luoyang there has been much damage done to the sculptures during the 19th and 20th centuries by Western souvenir hunters who beheaded just about every figure they could lay their saws on. These now grace the museums and private paperweight collections of Europe and North America. Among these were two murals which were entirely removed and can now be seen at the Metropolitan Museum of Art in New York, and the Atkinson Museum in Kansas City. Oddly enough, the caves appear to have been spared the ravages of the Cultural Revolution. Even during the most anarchic year of 1967 the caves were reported to be open, no-one was watching over them and anybody could go in and have a look. Unfortunately, none of the captions at the caves are in English, even though a tourist price is charged.

The art of Buddhist cave sculpture largely came to an end around the middle of the 9th century as the Tang Dynasty declined. Persecution of foreign religions in China began, with Buddhism as the prime target. Although Buddhist art and sculpture continued in China, it never reached the heights it had enjoyed previously.

Bingyang Caves The main caves of the Longmen group are on the west bank of the Yi River. They stretch out along the cliff face on a north-south axis. The three Bingyang Caves are at the north end, closest to the entrance. All were begun under the Northern Wei and, though two were finished during the Sui and Tang dynasties, the statues all display the benevolent saccharine expressions which characterised the Northern Wei style.

Ten Thousand Buddha Cave *(wànfó dòng)* Several minutes' walk south of the Bingyang Caves is the Tang Dynasty Ten Thousand Buddha Cave, built in 680. In addition to the legions of tiny bas-relief buddhas which give the cave its name, there is a fine big Buddha and images of celestial dancers. Other images include musicians playing the flute, pipa (a plucked stringed instrument), cymbals and zheng (a 13 to 14-stringed harp).

Lotus Flower Cave *(liánhūa dòng)* This cave was carved in 527 AD during the Northern Wei Dynasty and has a large standing

Buddha, now faceless. On the ceiling are wispy apsaras drifting around a central lotus flower. A common symbol in Buddhist art, the lotus flower represents purity and serenity.

Ancestor Worshipping Temple *(fèngxiān sì)* This is the largest structure at Longmen and contains the best works of art. It was built between 672 and 675 AD, during the Tang Dynasty. The roof is gone and the figures lie exposed to the elements. The Tang figures tend to be more three-dimensional than the Northern Wei figures, standing out in high relief and rather freer from their stone backdrop. Their expressions and poses also appear to be more natural but, unlike the other-worldly figures of the Northern Wei, the Tang figures are meant to be awesome.

The seated central Buddha statue is 17 metres high and is believed to be Vairocana, the supreme, omnipresent divinity. The face is thought to be modelled on that of the all-powerful Empress Wu Zetian of the Tang Dynasty.

As you face the Buddha, to the left are statues of the disciple Ananda and a bodhisattva wearing a crown, a tassel and a string of pearls. To the right are statues (or remains) of another disciple, a bodhisattva, a heavenly guardian trampling on a spirit, and a guardian of the Buddha.

Medical Prescription Cave South of the Ancestor Worshipping Temple is the tiny Medical Prescription Cave whose entrance is filled with 6th-century stone steles inscribed with remedies for common ailments.

Guyang Cave Adjacent to the Medical Prescription Cave is the much larger Guyang Cave, cut between 495 and 575 AD. It's a narrow, high-roofed cave featuring a Buddha statue and a profusion of sculpture, particularly of flying apsaras. This was probably the first cave of the Longmen group to be built.

Shiku Cave This cave is a Northern Wei construction. It's the last major cave and has carvings depicting religious processions.

Getting to the Caves From the Luoyang railway station area, bus No 81 goes to the Longmen Caves. From the Friendship Guesthouse, take bus No 60 – it leaves from the far side of the small park opposite the hotel. Bus No 53 from the old town's west gate also runs past the caves. Many of the hotels run tour buses to them too.

Places to Stay

The cheapest place in town is the *Luoyang Hotel* (☎ 35181) *(luòyáng lǚshè)* where doubles cost Y30. It's directly opposite the train and bus stations which unfortunately means it can be incredibly noisy. Try to get a room at the back.

Just around the corner on Jinguyuan Lu is the huge *Tianxiang Hotel* (☎ 37846) *(tiānxiāng lǚshè)* where doubles range from Y68 to Y100.

The inconveniently located *Friendship Guesthouse* (☎ 22111) *(yǒuyí bīngǔan)*, at 6 Xiyuan Lu, is the high-class tourist joint. A bed in an air-con triple room in the new wing is Y150, slightly cheaper in the old wing. To get there take bus No 2 from Luoyang west railway station or from the long-distance bus station (opposite the railway station). Stay on the bus until you see the enormous Friendship Store on your left, and get off at the next stop. The hotel is about a 15-minute walk further up the road on the right-hand side. The other alternative is to get a taxi (around Y15 from the railway station, subject to bargaining).

Places to Eat

The restaurant on the second floor of the Tianxiang Hotel is excellent. It has an English menu and prices are low. Other than that, budget meals can be had from street stalls at the railway station.

Getting There & Away

Air There are flights twice weekly to Canton (Y463), Shanghai (Y319) and Ürümqi.

There are flights six days a week to Xi'an (Y117).

Bus The long-distance bus station is opposite Luoyang west railway station. Regular buses run to Zhengzhou (Y4.50, 4½ to five hours). There's one bus daily from Luoyang to Xi'an at 6 am (Y12).

Train From Luoyang there are direct trains to Beijing via Zhengzhou (16 hours), to Shanghai (18 hours), and to Xi'an (eight hours). There are some direct trains north to Taiyuan and south to Xiangfan and Yichang. Yichang is a port on the Yangtse River, where you can pick up the Chongqing to Wuhan ferry.

LINXIAN COUNTY

(línxiàn) 林县

Linxian County lies to the west of Anyang in the north-west corner of Henan Province, close to the border with Shanxi and Hebei.

It is a rural area which rates with Dazhai and Shaoshan as one of the 'holy' places of Maoism, since this is the location of the famous Red Flag Canal. To irrigate the district, a river was re-routed through a tunnel beneath a mountain and then along a new bed built on the side of steep cliffs. The Communists insist that this colossal job, carried out during the Cultural Revolution, was done entirely by the toiling masses without the help of engineers and machines.

The statistics are impressive: 1500 km of canal was dug, hills were levelled, 134 tunnels were pierced, 150 aqueducts were constructed and enough earth was displaced to build a road one metre high, six metres wide and 4000 km long. All this was supposedly done by hand and was a tribute to Mao's vision of a self-reliant China.

Critics have called it an achievement worthy of Qin Shihuang, who pressed millions into building the Great Wall. They say that this sort of self-reliance only committed the peasants and workers to endless back-breaking toil. It would have made more sense to put the energy to some productive use and, with the profit, buy a pump and lay a pipeline to bring the water straight over the hill.

GONGXIAN COUNTY

(gǒngxiàn) 巩县

Gongxian County lies on the railway line which runs west from Zhengzhou to Luoyang. During the Northern Wei Dynasty a series of Buddhist caves was cut and a temple built on the bank of the Yiluo River. However, the main attractions of the area are the great tombs built by the Northern Song emperors.

The county is bounded in the south by Songshan and in the north by the Yellow River. The Yiluo River is a branch of the Yellow River and cuts through the centre of the county.

The Buddhist cave temples are at the foot of Dalishan on the northern bank of the Yiluo River. Construction of the caves began in 517 AD and additions were made during the Eastern and Western Wei, Tang and Song dynasties. There are now 256 shrines containing over 7700 Buddhist figures.

The Song Tombs are scattered over an area of 30 sq km. Seven of the nine Northern Song emperors were buried here; the other two were captured and taken away by the Jin armies who overthrew the Northern Song in the 12th century.

After the vicissitudes of more than 800 years of history and repeated wars, all that remain of the tombs are the ruined buildings, the burial mounds and the statues which line the sacred avenues leading up to the ruins. About 700 stone statues still stand, and these have a simple and unsophisticated but imposing manner about them.

Some of the earlier statues, such as those on the Yongan and Yongchang tombs, utilise very plain lines and are characteristic of the late Tang Dynasty style. The statues of the intermediate period on the Yongding and Yongzhao tombs are carved with more exquisite, harmonious proportions. Later statues, such as thóse on the way to the

Yongyu and Yongtai tombs, tend to be more naturalistic and lifelike. The statues of people include civil officials, foreign envoys and military leaders. There are also numerous statues of animals, including a *jiaoduan*, a mythical animal which symbolises luck.

Cave Dwellings

On the road from Zhengzhou to Luoyang you'll see some of China's interesting cave dwellings. Over 100 million Chinese people live in cave houses cut into dry embankments, or in houses where the hillside makes up one or more walls. These are not peculiar to Henan Province: a third of these dwellings are found in the dry loess plateau. Some communities use both caves and houses; the former are warmer in winter and cooler in summer, but also tend to be darker and less ventilated than ordinary houses.

Sometimes a large square pit is dug first and then caves are hollowed into the four sides of the pit. A well is sunk in the middle of the yard to prevent flooding during heavy rains. Other caves, such as those at Yan'an, are dug into the side of a cliff face.

The floors, walls and ceilings of these cave dwellings are made of loess, a fine yellowish-brown soil which is soft and thick and makes good building material. The front wall may be made of loess, mudbrick, concrete, bricks or wood, depending on the availability of materials.

Ceilings are shaped according to the quality of the loess. If it is hard then the ceiling may be arched, if not, the ceiling may rise to a point. Besides the doors and windows in the front wall, additional vents may let in light and air.

Shaanxi 陕西

The northern part of Shaanxi *(shǎnxī)* is one of the oldest settled regions of China, with remains of human habitation dating back to prehistoric times. This was the homeland of the Zhou people, who eventually conquered the Shang and established their rule over much of northern China. It was also the homeland of the Qin, who ruled from their capital of Xianyang near modern-day Xi'an and were the first dynasty to rule over all of eastern China. Shaanxi remained the political heart of China until the 9th century. The great Sui and Tang capital of Xi'an was built there and the province was a crossroads on the trading routes from eastern China to central Asia.

With the migration of the imperial court to pastures further east, Shaanxi became a less attractive piece of real estate. Rebellions afflicted the territory from 1340 to 1368, again from 1620 to 1644, and finally in the mid-19th century, when the great Muslim rebellion left tens of thousands of the province's Muslims dead. Five million people died in the famine from 1876 to 1878 and another three million in the famines of 1915, 1921 and 1928. It was probably the dismal condition of the Shaanxi peasants that gave the Communists such willing support in the province in the late 1920s and during the ensuing civil war. From their base at Yan'an the Communist leaders directed the war against the Kuomintang and later against the Japanese, before being forced to evacuate in the wake of a Kuomintang attack in 1947.

Some 30 million people live in Shaanxi, mostly in the central and southern regions. The north of the province is a plateau covered with a thick layer of wind-blown loess soil which masks the original landforms. Deeply eroded, the landscape has deep ravines and almost vertical cliff faces. The Great Wall in the far north of the province is something of a cultural barrier, beyond which agriculture and human existence were always precarious ventures.

Like so much of China, this region is rich in natural resources, particularly coal and oil. The Wei River, a branch of the Yellow River, cuts across the middle of the province. This fertile belt became a centre of Chinese civilisation. The south of the province is quite different from the north; it's a comparatively lush, mountainous area with a mild climate.

XI'AN

(xī'ān) 西安

History

Once the focus of China, Xi'an vied with its contemporaries, Rome and later Constantinople, for the title of greatest city in the world. Over a period of 2000 years Xi'an has seen the rise and fall of numerous Chinese dynasties, and the monuments and archaeological sites in the city and the surrounding plain are a reminder that once upon a time Xi'an was a booming metropolis.

The earliest evidence of human habitation dates back 6000 years to Neolithic times, when the plain was lush and green and primitive Chinese tribes established their villages. The legendary Zhou established their capital on the banks of the Fen River near present-day Xi'an.

Xianyang Later, between the 5th and 3rd centuries BC, China split into five separate

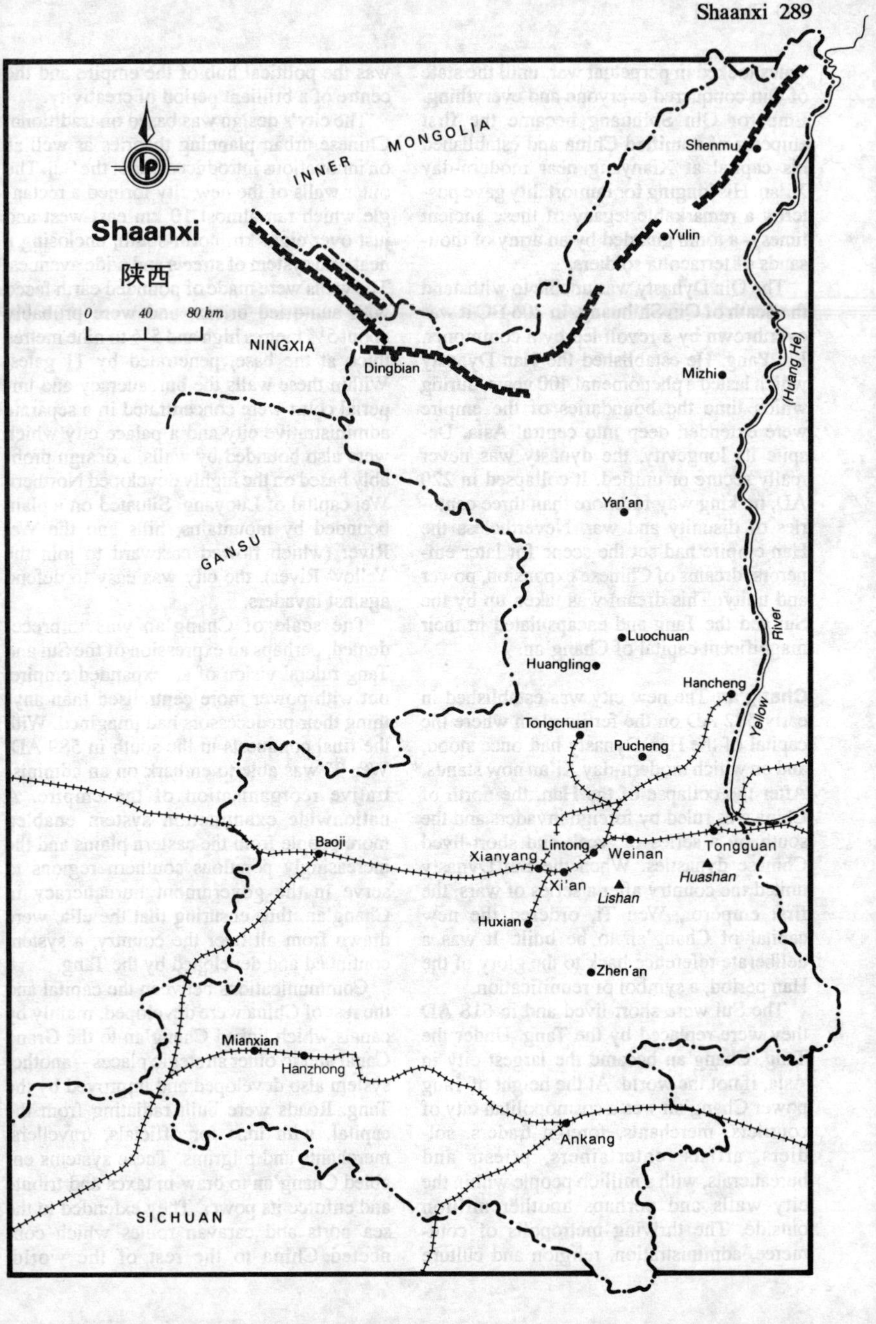

Shaanxi

陕西

0 40 80 km

INNER MONGOLIA

NINGXIA

GANSU

SICHUAN

Shenmu

Yulin

Dingbian

Mizhi

Yellow River (Huang He)

Yan'an

Luochuan

Huangling

Hancheng

Tongchuan

Pucheng

Baoji

Xianyang

Lintong

Weinan

Tongguan

Huashan

Xi'an

Lishan

Huxian

Zhen'an

Mianxian

Hanzhong

Ankang

states locked in perpetual war, until the state of Qin conquered everyone and everything. Emperor Qin Shihuang became the first emperor of a unified China and established his capital at Xianyang near modern-day Xi'an. His longing for immortality gave posterity a remarkable legacy of these ancient times – a tomb guarded by an army of thousands of terracotta soldiers.

The Qin Dynasty was unable to withstand the death of Qin Shihuang. In 206 BC it was overthrown by a revolt led by a commoner, Liu Pang. He established the Han Dynasty which lasted a phenomenal 400 years, during which time the boundaries of the empire were extended deep into central Asia. Despite its longevity, the dynasty was never really secure or unified. It collapsed in 220 AD, making way for more than three centuries of disunity and war. Nevertheless the Han empire had set the scene for later emperors' dreams of Chinese expansion, power and unity. This dream was taken up by the Sui and the Tang and encapsulated in their magnificent capital of Chang'an.

Chang'an The new city was established in early 582 AD on the fertile plain where the capital of the Han Dynasty had once stood, and on which modern-day Xi'an now stands. After the collapse of the Han, the north of China was ruled by foreign invaders and the south by a series of weak and short-lived Chinese dynasties. When the Sui Dynasty united the country after a series of wars, the first emperor, Wen Ti, ordered the new capital of Chang'an to be built. It was a deliberate reference back to the glory of the Han period, a symbol of reunification.

The Sui were short-lived and in 618 AD they were replaced by the Tang. Under the Tang, Chang'an became the largest city in Asia, if not the world. At the height of Tang power Chang'an was a cosmopolitan city of courtiers, merchants, foreign traders, soldiers, artists, entertainers, priests and bureaucrats, with a million people within the city walls and perhaps another million outside. The thriving metropolis of commerce, administration, religion and culture was the political hub of the empire and the centre of a brilliant period of creativity.

The city's design was based on traditional Chinese urban planning theories as well as on innovations introduced under the Sui. The outer walls of the new city formed a rectangle which ran almost 10 km east-west and just over eight km north-south, enclosing a neat grid system of streets and wide avenues. The walls were made of pounded earth faced with sun-dried bricks, and were probably about 5½ metres high and 5½ to nine metres thick at the base, penetrated by 11 gates. Within these walls the bureaucracy and imperial court were concentrated in a separate administrative city and a palace city which were also bounded by walls, a design probably based on the highly developed Northern Wei capital of Luoyang. Situated on a plain bounded by mountains, hills and the Wei River (which flowed eastward to join the Yellow River), the city was easy to defend against invaders.

The scale of Chang'an was unprecedented, perhaps an expression of the Sui and Tang rulers' vision of an expanded empire, but with power more centralised than anything their predecessors had imagined. With the final conquests in the south in 589 AD, Wen Ti was able to embark on an administrative reorganisation of the empire. A nationwide examination system enabled more people from the eastern plains and the increasingly populous southern regions to serve in the government bureaucracy in Chang'an, thus ensuring that the elite were drawn from all over the country, a system continued and developed by the Tang.

Communications between the capital and the rest of China were developed, mainly by canals which linked Chang'an to the Grand Canal and to other strategic places – another system also developed and improved by the Tang. Roads were built radiating from the capital, with inns for officials, travellers, merchants and pilgrims. These systems enabled Chang'an to draw in taxes and tribute and enforce its power. They extended to the sea ports and caravan routes which connected China to the rest of the world, allowing Chang'an to import the world's ideas and products. The city became a centre of international trade, and a large foreign community established itself there. Numerous foreign religions built temples and mosques, including Muslims, the Zoroastrians of Persia, and the Nestorian Christian sect of Syria. The growth of the government elite and the evolution of a more complex imperial court drew vast numbers of people to serve it: merchants, clerks, artisans, priests and labourers. By the 8th century the city had a phenomenal population of two million.

Towards the end of the 8th century the Tang Dynasty and its capital began to decline. From 775 onwards the central government suffered reverses at the hands of provincial warlords and Tibetan and Turkic invaders. The setbacks exposed weaknesses in the empire, and though the Tang still maintained overall supremacy they gradually lost control of the transport networks and the tax collection system on which their power depended. The dynasty fell in 907 AD and China once again broke up into a number of independent states. Chang'an was eventually relegated to the role of a regional centre, never to regain its former supremacy.

Xi'an The modern-day city of Xi'an stands on the site of Chang'an. In the 19th century Xi'an was a rather isolated provincial town, a condition which persisted until the completion of a railway line from Zhengzhou in 1930. After 1949 the Communists started to industrialise the city and it now supports a population of 2½ million people. The capital of Shaanxi Province, Xi'an is an example of the government's efforts to create new inland industrial centres to counterbalance the traditional dominance of the large industrial cities on the coast. At first glance the city looks little different from other modern Chinese industrial cities, but scattered about are many reminders of its imperial past. Today, Xi'an is one of the biggest open-air museums in China.

Orientation

Xi'an retains the same rectangular shape that characterised Chang'an, with streets and avenues laid out in a neat grid pattern.

The central block of the modern city is bounded by the city walls built during the Ming Dynasty within the much larger area of the Tang city, on the foundations of the walls of the Tang Forbidden City. Caves were dug into the wall as air-raid shelters when the Japanese bombed the city. During the Cultural Revolution more caves were dug to store grain. Large sections of the wall have been restored in the last few years; some sections have completely disappeared, though they're still shown on the maps.

The centre of town is the enormous Bell Tower, and from here run Xi'an's four major streets: Bei, Nan, Dong and Xi Dajie. The railway station stands at the north-east edge of the central block. Jiefang Lu runs south from the station to intersect with Dong Dajie.

Many of the city's sights, as well as most of the restaurants, tourist hotels and facilities, can be found either along or in the vicinity of Jiefang Lu or Xi and Dong Dajie. There's a scattering of sights outside the central block, like the Big Goose and Small Goose pagodas. Other sights, like the terracotta soldiers at Xianyang and at the Tomb of Qin Shihuang, and the remains of the Banpo Neolithic Village, can be found on the plain which surrounds Xi'an.

Information

CITS You'll find its office (☎ 713329) on the 2nd floor of the Jiefang Hotel, right near the railway station. There are several smaller branches of CITS in a few of the other hotels: Bell Tower Hotel (☎ 713858); Jianguo Hotel (☎ 34242); and Holiday Inn (☎ 34221). The CITS at the Jiefang is very helpful – the others are more or less useless.

Public Security Bureau This is at 138 Xi Dajie, a 10-minute walk west of the Bell Tower.

Money The Bank of China (☎ 716931) is at 223 Jiefang Lu near the corner with Dong 6-Lu. Business hours are daily from 9 am to 12 noon, and from 2.30 to 5.30 pm. It's

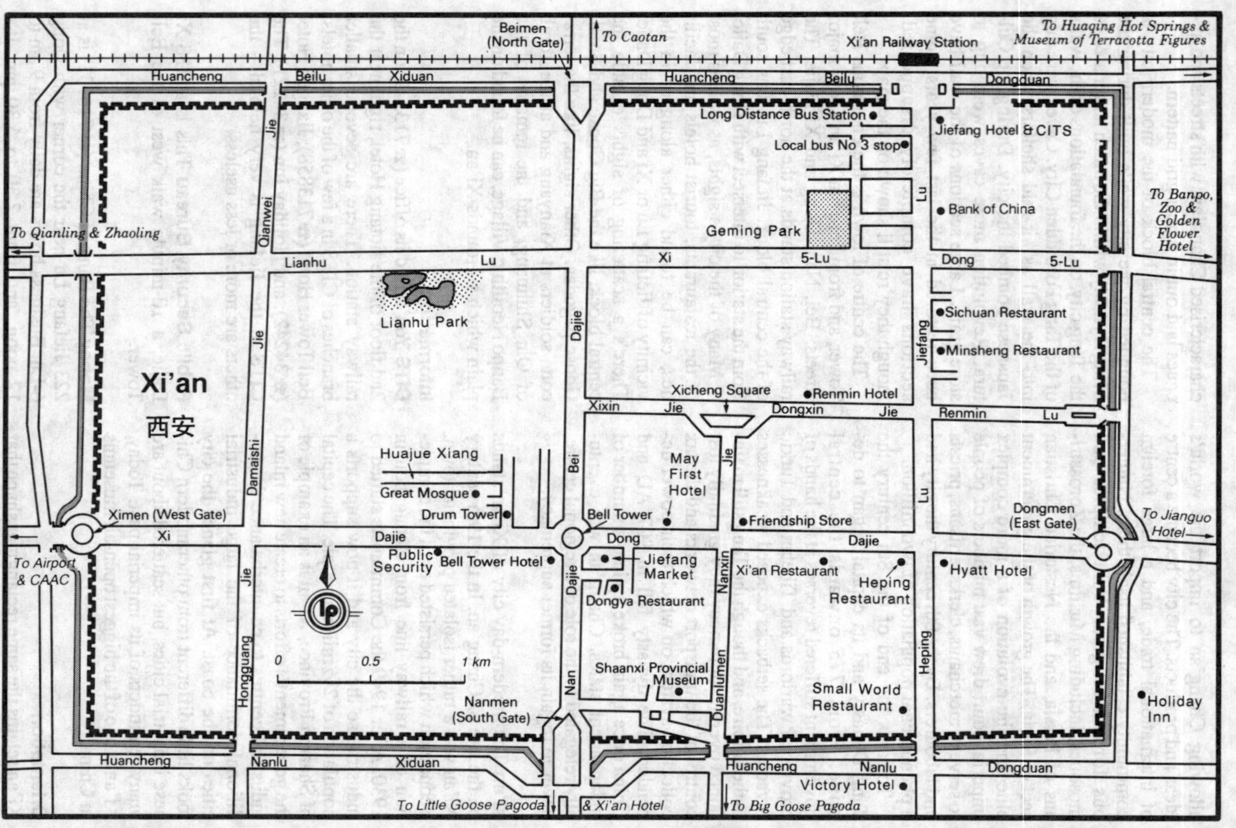

Beimen (North Gate)
To Caotan
Xi'an Railway Station
To Huaqing Hot Springs & Museum of Terracotta Figures
Huancheng
Beilu
Xiduan
Huancheng
Beilu
Dongduan
Long Distance Bus Station
Local bus No 3 stop
Jiefang Hotel & CITS
Jie
Qianwei
Lu
Bank of China
Geming Park
To Banpo, Zoo & Golden Flower Hotel
To Qianling & Zhaoling
Lianhu
Lu
Xi
5-Lu
Dong
5-Lu
Lianhu Park
Dajie
Jie
Sichuan Restaurant
Jiefang
Minsheng Restaurant
Xi'an
西安
Xicheng Square
Renmin Hotel
Xixin
Jie
Dongxin
Jie
Renmin
Lu
Damaishi
Huajue Xiang
Bei
May First Hotel
Jie
Great Mosque
Lu
Drum Tower
Bell Tower
Friendship Store
Dongmen (East Gate)
To Jianguo Hotel
Ximen (West Gate)
Xi
Dajie
Dong
Dajie
Public Security
Bell Tower Hotel
Jiefang Market
Xi'an Restaurant
Heping Restaurant
Hyatt Hotel
To Airport & CAAC
Jie
Dajie
Nanxin
Dongya Restaurant
Hongguang
0
0.5
1 km
Shaanxi Provincial Museum
Heping
Nan
Duanlumen
Small World Restaurant
Holiday Inn
Nanmen (South Gate)
Huancheng
Nanlu
Xiduan
Huancheng
Nanlu
Dongduan
Victory Hotel
To Little Goose Pagoda
& Xi'an Hotel
To Big Goose Pagoda

closed on Wednesday and Sunday afternoons.

Post The main post office is on Bei Dajie at the corner of Xixin Jie.

Bell Tower

(zhōnglóu) 钟楼

The Bell Tower is a huge building in the centre of Xi'an that you enter through an underpass on the north side of the tower. The original tower was built in the late 14th century, but was rebuilt at the present location in 1739 during the Qing Dynasty. A large iron bell in the tower used to mark the time each day, hence the name. It's usually possible to go to the top.

Drum Tower

(gǔlóu) 鼓楼

The Drum Tower is a smaller building to the west of the Bell Tower and marks the Muslim quarter of Xi'an.

City Walls

(chéng cháng) 城墙

Xi'an is one of the few old cities in China where old city walls are still visible. The walls were built on the foundations of the walls of the Tang Forbidden City during the reign of Hong Wu, first emperor of the Ming Dynasty. They form a rectangle with a circumference of 14 km. On each side of the wall is a gateway, and over each stands three towers. At each of the four corners stands a watchtower, and the top of the wall is punctuated with defensive towers. The wall is 12 metres high, with a width at the top of 12 to 14 metres and at the base of 15 to 18 metres. Some sections have completely disappeared.

Big Goose Pagoda

(dà yàn tǎ) 大雁塔

This pagoda stands in what was formerly the Temple of Great Maternal Grace in the south of Xi'an. The temple was built about 648 AD by Emperor Gao Zong (the third emperor of the Tang Dynasty) when he was still crown prince, in memory of his deceased mother. The buildings that stand today date from the Qing Dynasty and were built in a Ming style.

The original pagoda was built in 652 AD with only five storeys, but it has been renovated, restored and added to many times. It was built to house the Buddhist scriptures brought back from India by the travelling monk Xuan Zang, who then set about translating them into 1335 Chinese volumes. The impressive, fortress-like wood-and-brick building rises 64 metres. You can climb to the top for a view of the countryside and the city.

The pagoda is at the end of Yanta Lu, at the southern edge of Xi'an. Take bus No 5 down Jiefang Lu to the end of Yanta Lu and get off when it turns right into Xiaozhai Donglu. The entrance to the compound is on the southern side of the pagoda. On the western side is a former air-raid shelter now used as an amusement centre.

Little Goose Pagoda

(xiǎo yàn tǎ) 小雁塔

The Little Goose Pagoda is in the grounds of the Jianfu Temple. The top of the pagoda was shaken off by an earthquake in the middle of the 16th century but the rest of the structure, 43 metres high, is intact. The Jianfu Temple was originally built in 684 AD as a site to hold prayers to bless the afterlife of the late Emperor Gao Zong. The pagoda, a rather delicate building of 15 tiers, was built from 707 to 709 AD and housed Buddhist scriptures brought back from India by another pilgrim.

You can get to the pagoda on bus No 3, which runs from the railway station through the south gate of the old city and down Nanguan Zhengjie. The pagoda is on Youyi Xilu just west of the intersection with Nanguan Zhengjie. Climb to the top of the pagoda for a panorama of Xi'an's apartment blocks and smokestacks. Entry to the grounds is Y1.20, plus Y1 to climb the pagoda or visit the museum.

Great Mosque

(qīngzhēn dà sì) 青真大寺

This is one of the largest Islamic mosques in

China. The present buildings only date back to the middle of the 18th century, though the mosque might have been established several hundred years earlier. It stands north-west of the Drum Tower and is built in a Chinese architectural style with most of the grounds taken up by gardens. Still an active place of worship, the mosque holds several prayer services each day. The mosque is open 8 am to noon, and 2 to 6 pm. The courtyard of the mosque can be visited, but only Muslims may enter the prayer hall.

To get there, walk west along Xi Dajie and turn right at the Drum Tower. Go through the tunnel under the tower; at the second street on your left you'll see a small sign in English and Chinese pointing the direction to the mosque, which is down a small side street five minutes' walk away.

This is the large Muslim quarter of Xi'an where the narrow streets are lined with old mud-brick houses. There are some interesting shops in the vicinity of the mosque, especially on Huajue Xiang.

Shaanxi Provincial Museum

(shǎnxī bówùgǔan) 陕西博物馆

Once the Temple of Confucius, the museum houses a large collection of relics from the Zhou, Qin, Han, Sui and Tang dynasties, including a collection of rare relics unearthed in Shaanxi Province.

One of the more extraordinary exhibits is the Forest of Steles, the heaviest collection of books in the world. The earliest of these 2300 large engraved stone tablets dates from the Han Dynasty.

Most interesting is the Popular Stele of Daiqin Nestorianism. It's inscribed in Chinese and Syrian and stands just to the left of the entrance to the hall containing the collection; you'll recognise it by the small cross inscribed at the top. The Nestorians were a Syrian Christian sect whose disciples spread eastwards to China via the Silk Road. Marco Polo mentions making contact with members of the sect in Fuzhou in the 13th century.

The tablet was engraved in 781 AD to mark the opening of a Nestorian church. It describes how a Syrian named Raban came to the imperial court of Xi'an in 635 and presented Christian scriptures which were translated and then read by the emperor. The emperor, says the stone, was impressed and ordered that a monastery dedicated to the new religion be established in the city.

The Nestorians believed that Jesus had a human 'person' (that is, in the sense of having individual identity) as well as a divine person. This differs from the orthodox Christian view, which regards Jesus as one person (the 'Son' in the Father/Son/Holy Spirit trinity) but with two natures (human and divine).

Other tablets in the museum include the Ming De Shou Ji Stele which records the peasant uprising led by Li Zhicheng against the Ming, and the 114 Stone Classics of Kaichen from the Tang Dynasty inscribed with 13 ancient classics and historical records.

The rare relics exhibition is in another building. Among the artefacts is a tiger-shaped tally from the Warring States Period, inscribed with ancient Chinese characters and probably used to convey messages or orders from one military commander to another. The rare relics section has captions in English.

The museum entrance is on a side street which runs off Baishulin Lu, close to the South Gate of the old city wall. It's open daily (except Mondays) from 8.30 am to 6 pm. Admission is Y6.

Old Xi'an

In the back streets of Xi'an are little-known but exceptionally fine temples, now converted into schools and warehouses or recently restored as tourist attractions. The good thing about temple hunting is that it changes your perspective of the city. Rather than seeing Xi'an as a city of wide avenues and large grey buildings, you find mud-brick houses, cobbled alleyways, old men playing chequers, market streets, and old women lugging buckets of water from the local water pump. Temple renovation is an interesting business still carried out mainly with manual tools.

The Temple of the Eight Immortals *(bā*

xiān ān), once Xi'an's largest Taoist establishment, has been renovated and is again an active place of worship. To get there walk east along Changle Xilu until you come to a street market on the south side identifiable by the large gateway. Walk down the market street, turn right at the end, then left to the temple complex.

The East Gate *(dōngmén)* and parts of the wall have been restored. It may not be Jerusalem but for the meagre fee of Y1 you can walk or bicycle around the city walls. Entrance points are at South Gate *(nánmén)* beside the Provincial Museum, and by some obscure steps at the eastern end of the south wall.

The City God's Temple *(chéng húang miào)* is being used as a warehouse. Its sadly dilapidated buildings feature some of the most beautiful and intricate woodcraft in China. The temple is within walking distance of the Bell Tower. Go to Xi Dajie 257, then take the small lane running north through the Muslim quarter and past an active mosque on the left. Turn right at the T-junction, and right again down a cobbled alley cluttered with souvenir stalls. A right turn at the end of the alley leads you through the temple gates.

Tours CITS does a tour from 8.30 am to 4.30 pm every day for Y98. This includes Xi'an city, the Banpo Museum, Huaqing Pool and the Tomb of Qin Shihuang. An English-speaking guide is provided and you get two hours at the tomb. While the tour gives you a good chance to see everything in one day, many travellers complain that they spend too much time at the boring Huaqing Pool. Basically, it's a reasonably thorough but expensive tour, good for those whose time is limited.

Tours run by the Jiefang Hotel and Victory Hotel only cost Y10 but give you just 30 minutes each at the Tomb of Qin Shihuang, Huaqing Pool and Banpo. The guides only speak Chinese.

Places to Stay – bottom end

The *Victory Hotel* (☎ 713184) *(shènglì fàndiàn)* has become the main backpacker's haunt though it's inconveniently located just outside the city walls south of Heping Gate. It's also become increasingly dirty and the plumbing is falling apart, but it's still the cheapest place in town. Dorm beds cost Y13 and doubles are Y30. To hire a bicycle costs Y5 per day. Bus No 5 from the railway station will take you there.

The *Jiefang Hotel* (☎ 713417) *(jiěfàng fàndiàn)* is on Jiefang Lu, diagonally opposite the railway station. The 'dormitories' are simply double rooms, but they find a roommate for you if you're not travelling with someone else. They ask Y40 for this arrangement, but you can bargain them to Y35. Double rooms are exactly double, Y80. Staff are generally friendly and helpful.

The *May First Hotel* (☎ 710804) *(wǔyī fàndiàn)* is at 351 Dong Dajie, near the corner with Nanxin Jie near the Bell Tower. It's clean and friendly – doubles cost Y42.

Places to Stay – middle

The *Renmin Hotel* (☎ 715111) *(rénmín dàxià)* at 319 Dongxin Jie, one of the big tourist hotels, opened for business in 1953. Its central location has turned it into something of a meeting point for foreigners. The Soviet-style palace with Chinese architectural features has doubles for Y60, but bargaining is possible.

The *Bell Tower Hotel* (☎ 29200) *(zhōnglóu fàndiàn)* is diagonally opposite the Bell Tower in the centre of town, and resembles an aircraft hangar. Take trolley bus No 1 from the railway station and get off at the Bell Tower. Doubles cost Y258. We've had mixed reports about this place.

Places to Stay – top end

The *Golden Flower Hotel* (☎ 332981) *(jīnhūa fàndiàn)* resembles an enormous ice-block. American-built and Swedish-managed, this monument to mirrored walls stands at 8 Changle Xilu – unmistakable amidst standard grey concrete blocks. Singles/doubles cost Y500/520. There are about 200 rooms, as well as two restaurants, a bar and disco. Take bus No 11 from the railway station.

The *Holiday Inn* (☎ 333888) *(jiàrì jiǔdiàn)* is at 8 Huancheng Donglu Nanduan, at the south-eastern corner of the city wall. Doubles cost Y447.

The *Jianguo Hotel* (☎ 338888) *(jiàngúo fàndiàn)* is east of the city wall on Dongguan Zhengjie. Doubles range from Y430 to Y800.

The *Hyatt Hotel* (☎ 712020) *(kǎiyùe fàndiàn)* is at Dong Dajie and Heping Lu. Doubles start at Y480.

Places to Eat

Budget travellers staying at the Victory Hotel will no doubt want to try the line-up of restaurants catering to the backpacker trade. On Heping Lu just inside the city wall you can find the *Small World, He Sheng, Olympic Games* and *East* restaurants. All have menus in English, decent food and reasonable prices.

The restaurant on the 2nd floor of the Jiefang Hotel is good, though prices are slightly higher than you'll find outside.

For Muslim food try the stalls along Sajinqiao Lu in the Muslim quarter – peppery stodge, made from crumbled bread heated in a wok with stocks, vegetables and a touch of meat, is something to be experienced at least once.

The *May First Restaurant (wǔyī fàndiàn)* is at 351 Dong Dajie, near the corner with Nanxin Jie and next to the Foreign Language Bookstore. It's highly recommended. Although the ground floor looks none too impressive, the food is very good. The staff is helpful and friendly, and the menu is in both Chinese and English. Upstairs are the group-tour banquet rooms.

The *Dongya Restaurant (dōngyà fàndiàn)* used to be in Shanghai (founded in 1916) but moved to Xi'an in 1956. It serves possibly the best food in Xi'an. Try the ground floor's big trays of steaming dumplings. The restaurant is south-east of the Bell Tower on Luoma Shi, a small street which runs off Dong Dajie.

The *Xi'an Restaurant (xī'ān fànzhūang)* is officially rated as one of the more illustrious eating houses, but the place gets very mixed reports from travellers. One person said it's 'living on past glory and should be struck off the list as a grotty, dirty dump'. Another wrote that 'several people in our hotel who had eaten there were quite ill'. There are four levels of dining halls in the huge grey building on Dong Dajie near Juhuayuan Lu.

Others worth trying include the *Sichuan Restaurant (chūan càigǔan)* on Jiefang Lu (the cheap section at the back is very good); the *Minsheng Restaurant (mínshēng cāntīng)* one block south of the Sichuan Restaurant; and the *Heping Restaurant (hépíng fàndiàn)* at the corner of Jiefang Lu and Dong Dajie.

Things to Buy

Huajue Xiang *(hùajúe xiàng)* is a narrow alley behind the Great Mosque. It's an interesting place to browse and this is one of the best places in China to get a name chop carved. Lots of other souvenirs, clothing and other tourist paraphernalia on sale.

The Friendship Store is east of the Bell Tower, on Nanxin Jie just north of the intersection with Dong Dajie. Life-size Qin warriors go for Y20,000 apiece; if that blows your budget, try a kneeling figure for just Y5000 to Y10,000. Places like the terracotta soldier hangar are besieged by hawkers flogging everything from plastic pagodas to imitation mini-warriors. The cheapest warriors cost from Y2 to Y5, but the quality is not too good.

Getting There & Away

Train and plane are the usual means of leaving Xi'an. Centrally located and a major tourist city, it's a convenient jumping-off point for many destinations.

Air Xi'an is one of the best-connected cities in China. The airport is eight km from the city. Taxi drivers greet incoming passengers and normally ask around Y45 to take you to any of the hotels, but Y20 is the real price. The CAAC bus isn't very useful – it only takes you to the CAAC office! However, from there you can hop on a minibus (Y2) to the railway station.

The CAAC office (☎ 42861) is quite a long way out, on the south-eastern corner of Xiguan Zhengjie and Laodong Lu, 1½ km to the west of the West Gate and only one km from the airport. You may find it more convenient to buy air tickets from CITS The many places you can fly to include:

Baotou, Beijing (Y346), Canton (Y589), Changchun, Changsha (Y320), Chengdu (Y217), Chongqing (Y201), Dalian (Y117), Fuzhou (Y508), Guilin (Y369), Haikou, Hangzhou (Y408), Hanzhong (Y86), Harbin (Y686), Hohhot (Y495), Ji'nan, Kunming (Y411), Lanzhou (Y184), Luoyang (Y117), Nanchang (Y361), Nanjing (Y370), Qingdao, Qinhuangdao, Shanghai (Y453), Shantou, Shenyang (Y565), Taiyuan (Y180), Ürümqi (Y774), Wuhan (Y246), Xiamen (Y648), Xiangfan, Yan'an (Y104), Yichang, Yinchuan (Y190), Yulin (Y160) and Zhengzhou (Y158). Check the CAAC timetable for the current listings.

In addition, there are international charter flights between Xi'an and Hong Kong three times weekly for Y990 one way. However, it's significantly cheaper to fly to Canton (Y589) and take the train to Hong Kong.

Train There are direct trains from Xi'an to Ürümqi, Beijing, Shanghai, Chengdu, Taiyuan, Hefei, Qingdao and Wuhan. For Chongqing and Kunming change at Chengdu; for Guilin and Canton change at Wuhan.

Foreigners must buy their tickets in FEC from the left-most window when facing the railway station. Tourist-price tickets in yuan from Xi'an to some important destinations include:

destination	soft-seat	hard-sleeper	soft-sleeper
Beijing (22 hours)	110	170	320
Canton (43 hours)	160	250	460
Chengdu (19 hours)	83	135	240
Chongqing (29 hours)	115	200	340
Guilin (35 hours)	150	240	440
Lanzhou (15 hours)	67	85	152
Luoyang (8 hours)	55	180	140
Shanghai (26 hours)	125	200	380
Taiyuan (12 hours)	65	106	154
Ürümqi (56 hours)	180	290	570
Xining (20 hours)	86	106	184
Zhengzhou (12 hours)	65	180	320

Getting Around

As usual in China, public buses tend to be packed, but comfortable minibuses run on the same routes and charge Y2 for any destination within the city. Taxis can be readily found at the tourist hotels, railway station and airport. Bicycles may be rented from the Victory and Jiefang hotels. There are local buses to the major sights around the city such as Banpo Neolithic Village and the terracotta warriors of Qin Shihuang. To get to some of the more distant sites you may have to take a tour bus.

AROUND XI'AN

Most of the really interesting sights are outside the city. The two biggest drawcards are the Banpo Neolithic Village and the terracotta army at the Tomb of Qin Shihuang.

Banpo Neolithic Village

(bànpǒ bówùguǎn) 半坡博物馆

This rates as Xi'an's No 2 attraction, only surpassed by the terracotta soldiers. The earliest known agricultural villages in China were uncovered north of the Qinlingshan mountains, near the eastward bend of the Yellow River where it's joined by the Fen and Wei rivers. The term 'Yangshao culture' is used because the first example was found near Yangshao Village. The oldest Yangshao-type village is Banpo, which appears to have been occupied from 4500 BC until around 3750 BC. The village was discovered in 1953 and is on the eastern bank of the Chan River in a suburb of Xi'an. A large hall has been built over what was part of the

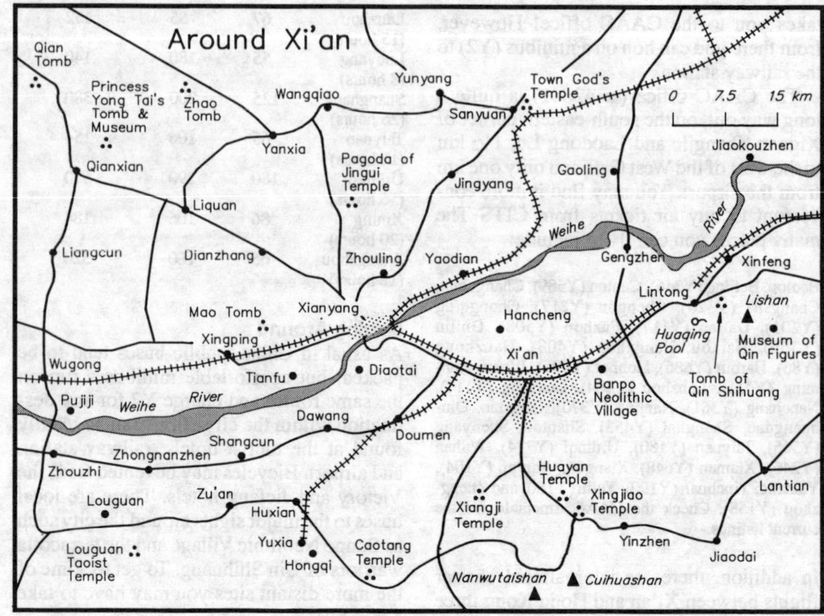

residential area of the village, and there are adjacent buildings housing pottery and other artefacts. Pottery found south of the Qinlingshan mountains has suggested that even earlier agricultural villages may have existed there, but this is speculation.

The Banpo ruins are divided into three areas: a residential area, a pottery-manufacturing area and a cemetery. These include the remains of 45 houses or other buildings, over 200 storage cellars, six pottery kilns and 250 graves (including 73 for dead children).

The earlier houses are half underground, in contrast to the later houses which stand on ground level and had a wooden framework. Some huts are round, others square, with doors facing south in both cases. There is a hearth or fire-pit in each house. The main building materials were wood for the framework and mud mixed with straw for the walls.

The residential part of the village is surrounded by an artificial moat, 300 metres long, about two metres deep and two metres wide. It protected the village from attacks by wild animals and from the effects of heavy rainfall in what was originally a hot and humid environment. Another trench, about two metres deep, runs through the middle of the village. To the east of the residential area is the pottery kiln centre. To the north of the village lies the cemetery where the adult dead were buried along with funerary objects like earthen pots. The children were buried in earthen pots close to the houses.

The villagers survived by hunting, fishing and gathering, but had begun to farm the surrounding land and keep domestic animals. Their stone tools included axes, knives, shovels, millstones, arrowheads and fishing-net sinkers. Bone objects included needles and fish hooks. Earthenware pots, bowls, basins and jars were used for storage and cooking; there was even a simple earthen vessel for steam cooking. Much of the pottery is coloured and illustrated with geometric patterns or animal figures like fish or galloping deer. The outside edges of some of the vessels are carved with what appears to be a primitive form of writing. Personal ornaments like hairpins, beads and rings were made of bone, shell, stone or animal teeth. A museum at the site sells a book called *Neolithic Site at Banpo Near Xi'an*, which describes the objects on view.

Tours to see the terracotta warriors usually take in a stop at Banpo. To get there on public transport, take bus No 8 from the stop on Dong Dajie immediately to the east of the Bell Tower. This bus stops short of the village. About five minutes walk further up the road is the stop for trolley bus No 5, which will take you the last stretch to the village. Alternatively, take trolley bus No 5 from the stop on Bei Dajie just north of the Bell Tower. This bus goes past the village. Or take bus No 11 from the train station.

Tomb of Qin Shihuang

(qín shǐhúang líng) 秦始皇陵

The emperor's tomb and the accompanying army of terracotta soldiers is *the* reason to come to Xi'an. The history of Xi'an is inextricably linked to this first emperor of a united Chinese people.

In the 3rd century BC China was split into five independent and warring states. In the year 246 BC, at the age of 13, Ying Zheng ascended the throne of the state of Qin and assumed the title 'Shi Huang' or First Emperor. One by one the Qin defeated the other states, until the last fell in 222 BC. The emperor united the country, standardising currency and written script. He also burned books and was a cruel tyrant who was secretive and suspicious in his last days, fearing assassination and searching for an elixir of immortality. His tyrannical rule lasted until his death in 210 BC. His son held out for four years until he was overthrown by the revolt which established the Han Dynasty.

When Qin Shihuang ascended the throne of Qin, construction of his final resting place began immediately. After he conquered the other states, work on the tomb was expanded on an unprecedented scale.

Qin Shihuang's tomb is covered by a huge mound of earth and has not been excavated. The *Historical Records* of Sima Qian, a famous historian of the 1st century BC, relate that the tomb contains palaces and pavilions filled with rare gems and other treasures, and is equipped with crossbows which automatically shoot intruders. The ceiling was inlaid with pearls to simulate the sun, stars and moon. Gold and silver cast in the form of wild geese and ducks were arranged on the floor, and precious stones were carved into pines. The walls of the tomb are said to be lined with plates of bronze to keep out underground water. Mercury was pumped in to create images of flowing rivers and surging oceans. At the end of the internment rites, the artisans who worked inside and the palace maids who had no children are said to have been forced to remain in the underground palace – buried alive so that none of its secrets could be revealed.

As to the size of the entire necropolis, a Ming Dynasty author in *Notes about Mount*

Terracotta Soldier from the Tomb of Qin Shihuang

Terracotta Soldiers

Lishan states that the sanctuary of the mausoleum has four gates and a circumference of 2½ km, and that the outer wall has a perimeter of six km. Modern surveys of the site show that the necropolis is indeed divided into an inner sanctuary and an outer city, and measurements of the inner and outer walls closely match the figures of the Ming author. The southern part of the complex is marked by a large mound of rammed earth below which the emperor is buried. The mound is 40 metres high and at the bottom measures about 480 by 550 metres. It's now planted with trees and surrounded by agricultural fields.

Just how far the necropolis actually extends is anyone's guess. In 1974 peasants digging a well about 1500 metres east of the tomb uncovered one of the greatest archaeological sites in the world. Excavation of the underground vault of earth and timber revealed thousands of life-sized terracotta warriors and their horses in battle formation – a whole army which would follow its emperor into immortality. In 1976, two other vaults were discovered close to the first one, but each of these was refilled with soil after excavation. The first and largest pit has been covered with a roof to become a huge exhibition hall.

The underground vault measures about 210 metres east to west and 60 metres from north to south. The bottom of the pit varies from five to seven metres below ground level. Walls were built running east to west at intervals of three metres, forming corridors. In these corridors, on floors laid with grey brick, are arranged the terracotta figures. Pillars and beams once supported a roof.

The 6000 terracotta figures of soldiers and horses face east in a rectangular battle array. The vanguard appears to be three rows of 210 crossbow and longbow bearers who stand at the easternmost end of the army. Close behind is the main force of armoured soldiers holding spears, dagger-axes and other long-shaft weapons, accompanied by 35 horse-drawn chariots. Every figure differs in facial features and expressions. The horsemen are shown wearing tight-sleeved outer robes, short coats of chain mail and windproof caps. The archers have bodies and limbs positioned in strict accordance with an ancient book on the art of war.

Many of the figures originally held real weapons of the day, and over 10,000 pieces have been sorted out to date. Bronze swords were worn by the figures representing the generals and other senior officers. Surface treatment made the swords resistant to rust and corrosion so that after being buried for more than 2000 years they were still sharp. Arrowheads were made of a lethal metal alloy containing a high percentage of lead.

The second vault, excavated in 1976 but refilled, contained about 1000 figures. The third vault contained only 68 soldiers and one war chariot and appeared to be the command post for the soldiers in the other vaults. Presumably the soldiers represent the army which is meant to protect the necropolis. These are probably just a beginning, and excavation of the entire complex and the tomb itself could take decades.

It's not permitted to take photos at the site (partly to prevent damage to the figures from flashes, though they won't even let you take a time-exposure), and if you infringe that rule you can expect to have your film confiscated. If you do sneak a few photos and get caught try to remember that the attendants are just doing their job.

Admission to the tomb is Y12, plus an additional Y10 for the museum *(qín yóng bówùgŭan)*. The museum is excellent and should not be bypassed just to save money. Student discounts are available.

Getting There & Away The tomb and terracotta soldiers are near the town of Lintong, which is 30 km east of Xi'an. To reach Lintong, take a bus from the eastern side of the Xi'an railway station. Some trains also stop in Lintong. In Lintong, get off and take another bus an additional five km to the Qin Shihuang Tomb. For information about tours, see the Getting Around section for Xi'an.

Huaqing Pool

(húaqīng chí) 华清池

At the foot of Lishan, 30 km from Xi'an, is Huaqing Pool, where water from hot springs is funnelled into public bathhouses with 60 pools accommodating 4000 people. At Lishan's summit are beacon towers built for defence during the Han Dynasty. A temple on the mountain is dedicated to the 'Old Mother' Nu Wa who created the human race and patched up cracks in the sky after a catastrophe.

Lishan is hardly worth the effort of going there as Chiang Kaishek would probably attest. His visit turned out to be most inauspicious. On 12 December 1936 he was arrested in Lishan by his own generals, supposedly clad only in his pyjamas and dressing gown, on the slopes of the snow-covered mountain up which he had fled. A pavilion marks the spot and there's a simple inscription, 'Chiang was caught here'.

In the early 1930s Kuomintang General Yang Huzheng was the undisputed monarch of those parts of Shaanxi not under Communist control. In 1935 he was forced to share power when General Zhang Xueliang arrived with his own troops from Manchuria in the wake of the Japanese occupation. Zhang assumed the office of 'Vice-Commander of the National Bandit Suppression Commission'.

In October and November 1935 the Kuomintang suffered severe defeats at the hands of the Communists and thousands of soldiers went over to the Red Army. Captured officers were given a period of 'anti-Japanese tutelage' and were then released. Returning to Xi'an, they brought Zhang reports of the Red Army's desire to stop the civil war and unite against the Japanese. Chiang Kaishek, however, stubbornly refused to turn his forces against the Japanese and continued his war against the Communists. On 7 December 1936 he flew to Xi'an to oversee another 'extermination' campaign against the Red Army.

Zhang Xueliang flew to Yan'an, met Zhou Enlai and became convinced of the sincerity of the Red Army's anti-Japanese policies. A secret truce was established. On the night of 11 December Zhang met the divisional commanders of his Manchurian army and the army of General Yang. A decision was made to arrest Chiang Kaishek. The following night the commander of Zhang's bodyguard led the attack on Chiang Kaishek's residence at the foot of Lishan and took him prisoner along with most of his general staff. In the city the 1500 'Blueshirts' (the police force controlled by Chiang's nephew and credited with numerous abductions, killings and imprisonments of Chiang's opponents) were disarmed and arrested.

A few days later, Zhang sent his plane to collect three representatives of the Red Army and bring them to Xi'an: Zhou Enlai, Ye Jianying and Bo Gu. Chiang Kaishek feared he was going to be put on trial and executed, but instead the Communists and the Manchurian leaders told him their opinions of his policies and described the changes they thought were necessary to save the country. Whatever Chiang did or did not promise to do, the practical result of the Xi'an Incident was the end of the civil war.

Zhang released Chiang Kaishek on Christmas Day and flew back with him to Nanjing to await punishment. It was a face-saving gesture to Chiang. Zhang was sentenced by a tribunal to 10 years imprisonment and 'deprivation of civil rights for five years'. He was pardoned the next day. The extermination campaign against the Red Army was called off and the Kuomintang announced that their first task now was to recover the territory lost to Japanese.

Nevertheless, Chiang began organising what he hoped would be a quiet decimation of the Communist forces. By June 1937 Chiang had moved the sympathetic Manchurian army out of Shaanxi and replaced it with loyal Kuomintang troops. He planned to disperse the Communists by moving the Red Army piecemeal to other parts of the country supposedly in preparation for the war against the Japanese. The Communists were only extricated from their precarious position by Japan's sudden and all-out invasion of China in July 1937. Chiang was forced to leave the Red Army intact and in control of the north-west.

Chiang never forgave Zhang Xueliang and never freed him. Thirty years later he was still held prisoner on Taiwan. General Yang was arrested in Chongqing and towards the end of WW II was secretly executed. Another reminder of this period is the office which the Communist Party set up in Xi'an to liaise with the Kuomintang. The office was disbanded in 1946, and after 1949 it was made into a memorial hall to the Eighth Route Army. It's on Beixin Lu, in the north of the city's central block.

Getting There & Away Like the Tomb of Qin Shihuang, the Huaqing Pool can be reached from the town of Lintong. Take a train or bus to Lintong, then another bus to the pool. The tour run by CITS stops here for two hours – too long! Most travellers find this place somewhat boring, but it's better if you go for a dip in the hot springs.

Xianyang

(xiányáng) 咸阳

This little town is a half-hour's bus ride from Xi'an. The chief attraction of Xianyang is the city museum *(xiányáng shì bówùgŭan)* which houses a remarkable collection of 3000 miniature terracotta soldiers and horses, discovered in 1965. Each figure is about half a metre high. They were excavated from a Han Dynasty tomb. Admission to the Entombed Warriors is Y12, with an extra ticket needed for entry to the special exhibition hall.

Getting There & Away To get to Xianyang from Xi'an, you take bus No 3 from the railway station to the terminal and then get bus No 59. Get off at the terminal in Xianyang. Up ahead on the left-hand side of the road you'll see a clock tower. Turn right at this intersection and then left at Xining Jie. The museum is housed in a former Ming Dynasty Confucian temple on Zhongshan Jie, which is a continuation of Xining Jie. The entrance is flanked by two stone lions. It's about a 20-minute walk from the bus terminal.

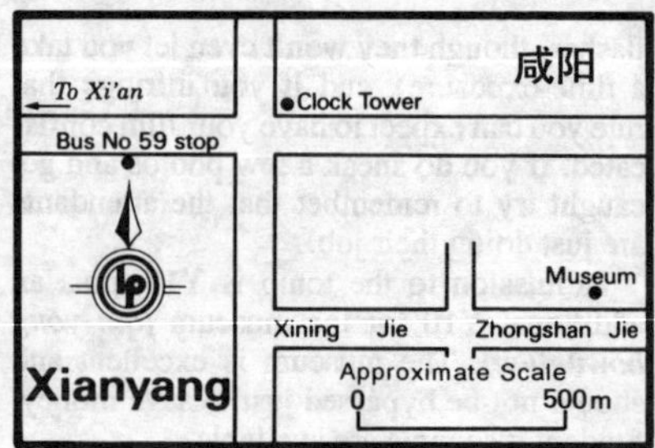

Imperial Tombs

Apart from the tomb of Qin Shihuang, a large number of other imperial tombs dot the Guanzhong plain surrounding Xi'an. The easiest way to get to these tombs is with a tour from Xi'an; see the Getting Around section for Xi'an for details.

In these tombs are buried the emperors of numerous dynasties, as well as their empresses, concubines, government officials and high-ranking military leaders. Construction of an emperor's tomb often began within a few years of his ascension to the throne and didn't finish until he died.

The Tang tombs can be visited, and there's a touch of intrigue in the stories behind them. The most famous is the Qian Tomb, the joint resting place of Tang Emperor Gao Zong and his wife Empress Wu Zetian. Gao Zong ascended the throne in 650 AD after the death of his father, Emperor Tai Zong. Empress Wu was actually a concubine of Tai Zong who also caught the fancy of his son, who made her his empress. Gao died in 683 AD, and the following year Empress Wu dethroned her husband's successor Emperor Zhong Zong. She reigned as an all-powerful monarch until her death around 705 AD. Nowadays it's fashionable to draw comparisons between Empress Wu and Jiang Qing.

Zhao Tomb *(zhāo líng)* The Zhao Tomb set the custom of building imperial tombs on mountain slopes, breaking the tradition of building tombs on the plains with an artificial hill over them. This burial ground on Jiuzongshan, 70 km north-west of Xi'an, belongs to the second Tang emperor Tai Zong, who died in 649 AD.

Of the 18 imperial mausoleums on the

Guanzhong plain, this is probably the most representative. With the mountain at the centre, the tomb fans out to the south-east and south-west. Within its confines are 167 lesser tombs of the emperor's relatives and high-ranking military and government officials.

Burying other people in the same park as the emperor was a custom dating back to the Han Dynasty. Tai Zong won support and loyalty from his ministers and officials by bestowing on them the great favour of being buried in attendance on the Son of Heaven.

Buried in the sacrificial altar of the tomb were six statues known as the 'Six Steeds of Zhaoling', representing the horses which the emperor used during his wars of conquest. Four of the statues are now in the Shaanxi Museum.

Qian Tomb *(qiánlíng)* One of the most impressive tombs is the Qian Tomb, 85 km north-west of Xi'an on Liangshan. This is the burial place of Emperor Gao Zong and Empress Wu.

The tomb consists of three peaks; the two on the south side are artificial, but the higher northern peak is natural and is the main part of the tomb. Walls used to surround the tomb but these are gone. South-west of the tomb are 17 smaller tombs of officials.

The grounds of the imperial tomb boast a number of large stone sculptures of animals and officers of the imperial guard. There are 61 (now headless) statues of the leaders of minority peoples of China and of the representatives of friendly nations who attended the Emperor's funeral.

The two steles on the ground each stand over six metres high. The 'Wordless Stele' is a blank tablet; one story goes that it symbolises Empress Wu's absolute power, which she considered inexpressible in words.

Prince Zhang Huai's Tomb *(zhāng húai mù)* Of the smaller tombs surrounding the Qian Tomb only five have been excavated. Zhang was the second son of Emperor Gao Zong and Empress Wu. For some reason the prince was exiled to Sichuan in 683 and died the following year aged 31 (a pillow across the face perhaps?). Empress Wu posthumously rehabilitated him. His remains were brought to Xi'an after Emperor Zhong Zong regained power. Tomb paintings show horsemen playing polo, but these and other paintings are in a terrible state.

Princess Yong Tai's Tomb *(yǒng tài gōng zhǔ mù)* The nearby Tomb of Princess Yong Tai is in poor shape. Unless restoration is done, it seems unlikely that the exquisite tomb paintings, some showing palace serving-girls, will survive. The line engravings on the stone outer coffin are extraordinarily graceful. Yong Tai was a granddaughter of the Tang emperor Gao Zong, and the seventh daughter of Emperor Zhong Zong. She was put to death by Empress Wu in 701 AD, but was rehabilitated posthumously by Emperor Zhong Zong after he regained power.

Mao Tomb *(mào líng)* The Mao Tomb, 40 km from Xi'an, is the resting place of Emperor Wu, the most powerful ruler of the Han Dynasty. He died in 87 BC. The cone-shaped mound of rammed earth is almost 47 metres high, and is the largest of the Han imperial tombs. A wall used to enclose the mausoleum but now only the ruins of the gates on the east, west and north sides remain. It is recorded that the emperor was entombed with a jade cicada in his mouth and was clad in jade clothes sewn with gold thread, and that buried with him were live animals and an abundance of jewels.

HUASHAN

(húashān) 华山

Huashan is one of the sacred mountains of China, 2200 metres high. It lies 120 km east of Xi'an, just south of the Xi'an-Luoyang railway line. There is only one route to the top, a north-south path about 15 km long. You can hike from the base of the mountain to the summit in a day, and stay overnight at the hotel there. The trail to the top can be dangerously crowded.

Places to Stay & Eat

There are a couple of hotels at the base of the mountain. The *Shi Er Dong Lüshe* (Twelve Caves Hotel) is good, and is run by monks from the adjacent Buddhist temple. To get there walk through the gate just behind the *Huashan Binguan* (Huashan Guesthouse). The Twelve Caves Hotel has cool and clean rooms (former monks' cells) set around a peaceful courtyard. They're ideal to rest up in during the day. Food is available from nearby stalls. Be warned that the monks running the guesthouse and monastery definitely do not like travellers who dress as if they're off to a beach party; modesty rates highly. There is another hotel halfway up the mountain, and at least three on the summit – all in old monasteries.

Getting There & Away

Xi'an is a good jumping-off point. There is a direct bus from the long-distance bus station to Huashan. Alternatively, take a train from Xi'an to Huashan station (two hours). However, few trains stop at Huashan station, so you may have to get off at Mengyuan, which is one station further down the line, and from there get a bus to Huashan.

YAN'AN

(yán'ān) 延安

This town is on a deep valley of the Yan River, 270 km from Xi'an in the far north of Shaanxi Province. Although just a small town of around 30,000 people, it vies with Mao's birthplace at Shaoshan as the No 1 Communist pilgrimage spot. Between the years 1936 and 1947 this was the headquarters of the Chinese Communists. The 'Long March' from Jiangxi ended in 1936 when the Communists reached the northern Shaanxi town of Wuqi. The following year they moved their base to Yan'an.

Numerous caves around the town were built by the Communists and the main sights are those caves in which the leaders lived and worked. Dominating the area is the Baota (Precious Pagoda), built during the Song Dynasty.

Places to Stay

The *Yan'an Hotel* charges Y40 for a good, clean double room with television and bathroom. The hotel restaurant is cheap.

Getting There & Away

There are flights twice a week from Xi'an to Yan'an; the fare is Y104. There are once-weekly flights to Yan'an from Beijing and Taiyuan.

Daily buses to Yan'an from Xi'an depart from Xi'an's long-distance bus station just off Jiefang Lu, near the train station. The fare is Y9. It's a rough ride.

An interesting alternative is the bus from Yinchuan (in the Ningxia Autonomous Region) to Yan'an. You see the Great Wall, lots of desert and cave houses on the way.

HUANGLING

(húanglíng) 皇陵

Mid-way between Xi'an and Yan'an is the town of Huangling. The tomb on nearby Qiaoshan is supposedly that of the Yellow Emperor Huang Di. Huang is said to be the father of the Chinese people, one of the 'Five Sovereigns' who reigned about 5000 years ago and by wars of conquest unified the Chinese clans. He is credited with numerous inventions and discoveries: silkworm cultivation, weaving, writing, the cart, the boat, the compass, building bricks and musical instruments. You can stay overnight in this town if you're taking the bus up from Xi'an to Yan'an.

Shanxi 山西

Shanxi *(shānxī)*, especially the southern half, was one of the earliest centres of Chinese civilisation and formed the territory of the state of Qin. After Qin Shihuang, unified the Chinese states, the northern part of Shanxi became the key defensive bulwark between the Chinese and the nomadic tribes to the north. Despite the Great Wall, the nomadic tribes still managed to break through and used Shanxi as a base for their conquest of the Middle Kingdom.

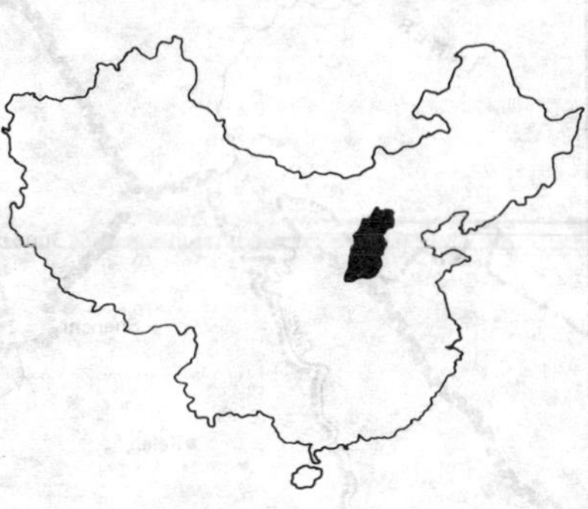

When the Tang Dynasty fell, the political centre of China moved away from the north-west. Shanxi went into a rapid economic decline, though its importance in the northern defence network remained paramount. Strategic importance coupled with isolation and economic backwardness was not an unusual situation for any of China's border regions, then or now.

It was not until the intrusion of the foreign powers into China that any industrialisation got under way. When the Japanese invaded China in the 1930s they carried out further development of industry and coal mining around the capital of Taiyuan. True to form, Shanxi was a bastion of resistance to this invasion from the north, this time through the Communist guerrillas who operated in the mountainous regions.

After 1949 the Communists began a serious exploitation of Shanxi's mineral and ore deposits, and the development of places like Datong and Taiyuan as major industrial centres. Some of the biggest coal mines can be found near these cities, and the province accounts for a third of China's known coal deposits.

Shanxi means 'west of the mountains' and is named after the Taihing range which forms its eastern border. To the west it is bordered by the Yellow River. The province has a population of about 25 million people, relatively light by Chinese standards unless you consider the fact that almost 70% of the province is mountains. The Taihing range, which also includes the Wutaishan mountains, runs from north to south and separates the province from the great North China Plain to the east. The Central Shanxi Basin crosses the central part of the province from north to south in a series of valleys. This is the main farming and economic area. Most of the farmland is used to grow crops, though the north-west is the centre of the province's animal husbandry industry.

Despite its intended future as an industrial bastion, Shanxi's wealth lies in its history. The province is literally a gold mine of temples, monasteries and cave-temples – a reminder that this was once the political and cultural centre of China. The main attraction is the Yungang Buddhist Caves at Datong.

TAIYUAN
(tàiyúan) 太原

The first settlements on the site of modern-day Taiyuan date back 2500 years. By the 13th century it had developed into what Marco Polo referred to as 'a prosperous city, a great centre of trade and industry'.

Like Datong, Taiyuan became an important frontier town, but despite its prosperity it has been the site of constant armed conflict. The trouble with Taiyuan was that it was always in somebody else's way, situated on

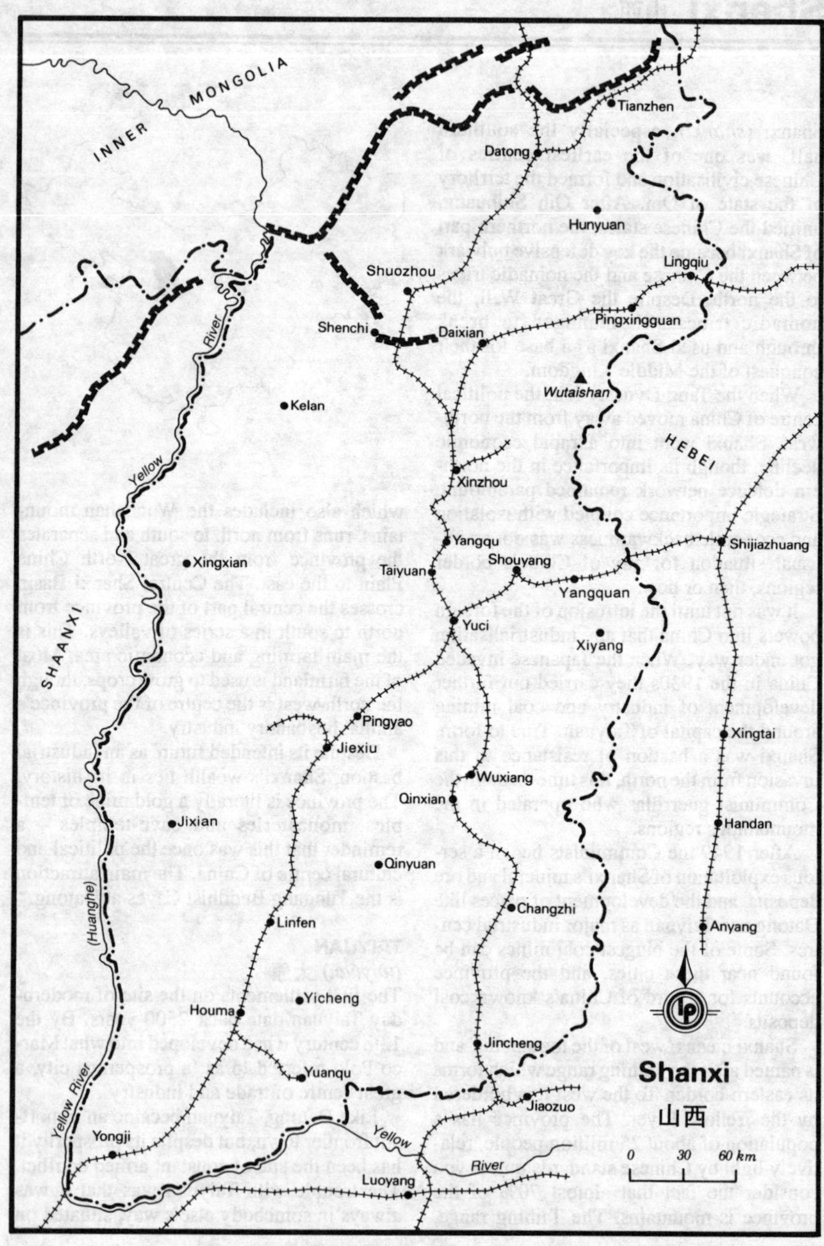
INNER MONGOLIA
Tianzhen
Datong
Hunyuan
Lingqiu
Shuozhou
Pingxingguan
Shenchi
Daixian
River
Wutaishan
Kelan
HEBEI
Yellow
Xinzhou
Yangqu
Shijiazhuang
Xingxian
Taiyuan
Shouyang
Yangquan
SHAANXI
Yuci
Xiyang
Pingyao
Jiexiu
Xingtai
Wuxiang
Qinxian
Jixian
Handan
Qinyuan
Changzhi
Linfen
Anyang
(Huanghe)
Yicheng
Houma
Jincheng
Yuanqu
Shanxi
Jiaozuo
山西
Yellow River
Yongji
Yellow
River
Luoyang
0 30 60 km

the path by which successive northern invaders entered China intent on conquest. As some indication of the importance of bloodshed in the city's life, there were once 27 temples here dedicated to the god of war.

The Huns, Tobas, Jin, Mongols and Manchus, among others, all took turns sweeping through Taiyuan. If it wasn't foreign invasion which afflicted the city, then it was the rise and fall of Chinese dynasties during periods of disunity; the town passed from one army to another as different rulers vied for power. Nevertheless, Taiyuan managed to survive.

In the latter part of the 19th century, Taiyuan moved rapidly towards industrialisation, helped by its proximity to some of the world's largest deposits of iron and coal. From 1889 it started to develop as a modern city, with the encouragement of Western powers. In the next 20 years Taiyuan gained a rail link to Hebei, electricity and a telephone system, not to mention a university and military academy. Development was pushed along by the warlord Yan Xishan, who ruled Shanxi virtually as his own private empire after the fall of the Manchu Dynasty. The coal mines were also developed by the Japanese invaders during the 1930s and '40s.

The Communists began the serious industrialisation of Taiyuan, along with other regions of Shanxi, after 1949. Today the city looks very much like its modern counterparts, Zhengzhou and Luoyang, with wide avenues and extensive residential blocks with numerous factories and smoke stacks. Amid the industrial monuments are some good Chinese Buddhist temples and artwork.

Orientation

Much of Taiyuan stretches out along the eastern side of the Fen River. The main road is Yingze Dajie. Most of the tourist facilities and many of the sights are along this road or in the immediate vicinity. The centre of town is the May 1st Square.

Information

CITS This office (☎ 441155 ext 679) is in the building adjacent to the Yingze Hotel. The helpful staff speak good English.

Public Security Bureau This is on a lane running off Wuyi Lu. Refer to the map for directions.

Money The Bank of China (☎ 666637) is on Yingze Dajie, west of Xinjian Lu. The tourist hotels also change money.

Post & Telecommunications There's a post office in the Yingze Guesthouse and a telephone office next door.

Jinci Temple

(jìncí) 晋祠

This ancient Buddhist temple is at the source of the Jin River by Xuanwang Hill, 25 km south-west of Taiyuan. It's not known for sure when the original buildings were constructed, but there have been numerous additions and restorations over the centuries right up to Qing Dynasty times. The temple probably dates back at least a thousand years.

Buses to the temple leave from the city centre. Walk one block east past the May 1st Square, turn left and walk one block to the end of that street where there's a bus terminal. Take bus No 8 to the temple.

As you enter the temple compound the first major structure is the Mirror Terrace, a Ming building used as an open-air theatre. The name is used in the figurative sense to denote the reflection of life in drama.

Zhibo's Canal cuts through the temple complex and lies west of the Mirror Terrace. Spanning this canal is the Huixian (Meet the Immortals) Bridge, which provides access to the Terrace for Iron Statues. At each corner of the terrace stands an iron figure cast in 1097 AD.

Immediately behind the statues is Duiyuefang Gate, with two iron statues out the front. The Offerings Hall behind the gate was built in 1168 to display temple offerings. To one side of the hall is a pavilion housing a large drum; the pavilion on the other side has a large bell.

Behind the Offerings Hall is a quaintly

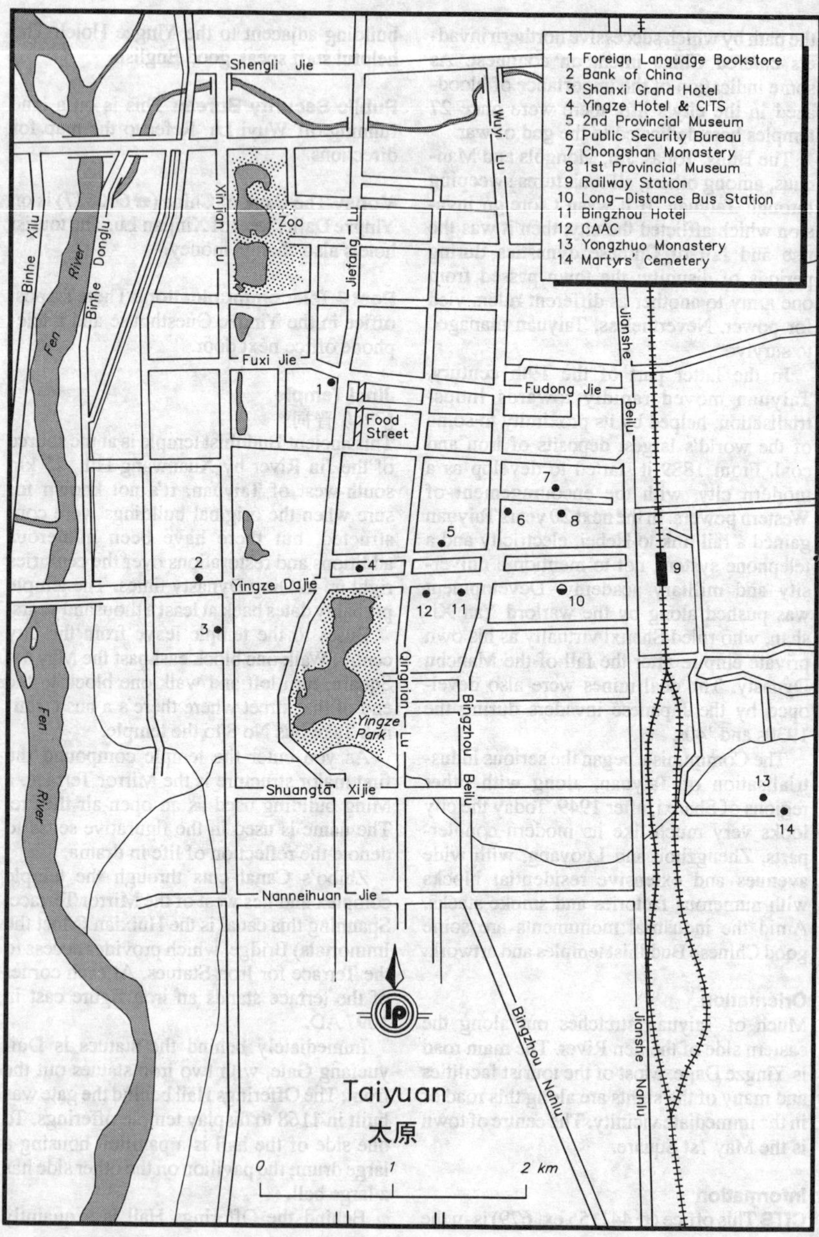
1 Foreign Language Bookstore
2 Bank of China
3 Shanxi Grand Hotel
4 Yingze Hotel & CITS
5 2nd Provincial Museum
6 Public Security Bureau
7 Chongshan Monastery
8 1st Provincial Museum
9 Railway Station
10 Long-Distance Bus Station
11 Bingzhou Hotel
12 CAAC
13 Yongzhuo Monastery
14 Martyrs' Cemetery
Shengli Jie
Wuyi Lu
Xinjian Lu
Zoo
Jiefang Lu
Binhe Xilu
Binhe Donglu
Fen River
Fuxi Jie
Food Street
Fudong Jie
Jianshe Beilu
Yingze Dajie
Yingze Park
Qingnian Lu
Bingzhou Beilu
Shuangta Xijie
Nanneihuan Jie
Bingzhou Nanlu
Jianshe Nanlu
Taiyuan
太原
0
1
2 km

1 外文书店
2 中国银行
3 山西大酒店
4 迎泽宾馆
5 第二省博物馆
6 公安局外事科
7 崇善寺
8 第一省博物馆
9 火车站
10 长途汽车站
11 并州饭店
12 中国民航
13 永祚寺
14 烈士陵园

named mediocrity, the Fish Pond with Flying Beams. The pond is one of the springs from the Jin River and is planted with 34 small octagonal stone pillars, on top of which are brackets and cross-beams supporting a bridge in the shape of a cross.

The bridge connects the Offerings Hall with the Goddess Mother Hall, otherwise known as the Sacred Lady Hall. It's the oldest wooden building in the city and one of the most interesting in the temple complex. In front of the temple are large wooden pillars with carvings of fearsome dragons. Inside are 42 Song Dynasty clay figures of maidservants standing around a large seated statue of the Sacred Lady herself. She is said to be the mother of Prince Shuyu of the ancient Zhou Dynasty, and the temple was built in her memory during the Northern Song period. It's suggested that the original building was constructed by the prince as a place to offer prayers and sacrifices to his mother. Today, people still throw money on the altar in front of the statue. Next to the Sacred Lady Hall is the Zhou Cypress, an unusual tree which has grown at an angle of about 30° for the last 900 years.

South of the Sacred Lady Hall is the Nanlao (Forever Young or Everlasting) Spring over which stands a pavilion. To the west of the spring is the two-storey Shuimou Lou (Water Goddess House, otherwise known as the Crystal Palace), originally built in 1563. On the ground floor is a statue of the goddess cast in bronze. On the upper storey is a shrine with a seated statue of the goddess surrounded by statues of her female servants.

In the north of the temple grounds is the Zhenguan Baohan Pavilion, which houses four stone steles inscribed with the handwriting of the Tang emperor Tai Zong. The Memorial Halls of Prince Shuyu include a shrine containing a seated figure of the prince surrounded by 12 Ming Dynasty female attendants, some holding bamboo flutes, pipes and stringed instruments. In the south of the temple grounds is the Sacred Relics Pagoda, a seven-storey, octagonal building constructed at the end of the 7th century.

Yingze Park

(yíngzé gōngyúan) 迎泽公园

The Ming Library *(míngdài cángjīng lóu)*, an ornate building in Yingze Park, is worth seeing. The entrance to the park is on the opposite side of the road, to the west of the Yingze Guesthouse.

Chongshan Monastery

(chóngshàn sì) 崇善寺

This Buddhist monastery was built towards the end of the 14th century on the site of an even older monastery, said to date back to the 6th or 7th centuries. The main hall contains three impressive statues; the central figure represents Guanyin, the Goddess of Mercy, with 1000 hands and eyes. Beautifully illustrated book covers show scenes from the life of Buddha. Also on display are Buddhist scriptures of the Song, Yuan, Ming and Qing dynasties.

Unfortunately the monastery only seems to be open when a tour group is visiting so you'll have to try and tag on to one. The monastery is on a side street to the west of Jianshe Beilu.

Yongzuo Monastery
(yǒngzùo sì) 永祚寺

The Yongzuo (Eternal Blessing) Monastery was built during the Ming Dynasty in the late 16th or early 17th century. It's usually referred to as the Twin Pagoda Monastery *(shūang tǎ sì)* because of its two identical pagodas, regarded as the symbol of Taiyuan. Each of these octagonal, 50-metre-high pagodas has 13 storeys and is built entirely of brick. In imitation of wooden pagodas, the bricks are carved with brackets and cornices. You'll have to walk to the pagodas – about 45 minutes from the railway station.

Provincial Museums
(shānxī shěng bówùgǔan) 山西省博物馆

The Shanxi Provincial Museum is housed in two separate complexes. The No 1 Museum is in an old Confucius Temple on Diliang-gong Lu. The No 2 Museum is in Chunyang Palace, west of the May 1st Square, and used to be a temple for offering sacrifices to the Taoist priest Lu Dongbin who lived during the Tang Dynasty. The temple was built during the Ming and Qing dynasties.

Places to Stay
There is an 'old' Chinese saying – it is easier for the tiger to fly than it is for the backpacker to check into a hotel in Taiyuan. The arrogant and lazy staff at the *Yingze Hotel* (☎ 443211) *(yíngzé bīngǔan)* are notorious for claiming that they are 'all full' even when the hotel is half empty. Fortunately, CITS is in the same compound and a call from them will magically produce rooms where, minutes before, none were available. Singles cost Y87 and doubles Y130. If you want a dormitory bed, be ready for a knock-down drag-out fight. The address is 51 Yingze Dajie, two km from the railway station. Bus No 1 takes you there.

The *Bingzhou Hotel* (☎ 442111) *(bìngzhōu fàndiàn)*, 32 Yingze Dajie, has doubles for Y90. It's a little closer to the railway station than the Yingze Hotel.

Taiyuan's only other accommodation for foreigners is the luxurious *Shanxi Grand Hotel* (☎ 443901) *(shānxī dàjiǔdiàn)*, 5 Xinjian Nanlu. It's a joint venture with Hong Kong; doubles cost Y235. You can get there on bus No 1 from the railway station.

Places to Eat
Food Street *(shípǐn jiē)* features ancient-style buildings, a traditional Chinese archway and over 30 restaurants serving good food. The street is closed to motorised traffic making it an interesting and relatively quiet place to enjoy a meal.

Don't even think about eating at the restaurant in the Yingze Hotel. It appears that only the hotel staff eat there. When a foreigner shows up, they say the restaurant is closed.

Getting There & Away
Air Useful connections from Taiyuan include direct flights to Beijing (five times weekly, Y175); Shanghai (four times weekly, Y415) and Xi'an (three times weekly, Y180).

Other destinations include Baotou, Changsha, Changzhi, Chengdu, Chongqing, Dalian, Hefei, Hohhot, Lanzhou, Nanjing, Qinhuangdao, Shenyang, Tianjin, Yan'an, Yinchuan, Wuhan and Zhengzhou.

The CAAC office (☎ 442903) is at 38 Yingze Dong Dajie.

Train From Taiyuan there are direct trains south to Xi'an, or north to Beijing via Datong.

From Taiyuan to Beijing is about 10½ hours by train and from Taiyuan to Xi'an takes 12 hours. Tourist-price hard-seats from Taiyuan to Datong are Y32; the trip takes about eight or nine hours.

Trains east to Shijiazhuang will put you on the main Canton to Beijing railway line. Alternatively, you can go to Zhengzhou, change trains and head either south to Canton or east to Shanghai.

AROUND TAIYUAN
Shuanglin Monastery
(shūanglín sì) 双林寺

This fine monastery contains exquisite painted clay figurines and statues dating from the Song, Yuan, Ming and Qing dynasties. The monastery is about 97 km south of Taiyuan and is well worth the effort getting there – you can do it as a day trip out of Taiyuan. Most of the present buildings date from the Ming and Qing dynasties, while the majority of sculptures are from the Song and Yuan dynasties. There are something like 2000 figurines in total.

To get to the temple you have to take a train from Taiyuan to Pingyao, which is on the train line heading south-west from Taiyuan. The 2½-hour journey costs a few yuan (hard-seat). When you arrive at Pingyao you can get a pedicab from the railway station to the temple – a half-hour ride.

There are several trains a day between Taiyuan and Pingyao. If you leave early in the morning you should be able to spend a couple of hours at the temple and return on one of the afternoon trains.

WUTAISHAN

(wǔtáishān) 五台山

Wutaishan is one of the sacred Buddhist mountains of China. It's actually a cluster of five peaks of which the northern peak, Yedongfeng, is just over 3000 metres high and is known as the roof of northern China.

The temples of Wutaishan are concentrated at Taihuai. The Tayuan Temple is the most prominent, with its large white bottle-shaped pagoda, built during the Ming Dynasty. The Xiantong Temple has seven rows of halls, totalling over 400 rooms. The Nanshan Temple, built during the Yuan Dynasty on the slopes of Nanshan, to the south of Taihuai, contains frescoes of the fable 'Pilgrimage to the West'. About 60 km from the Nanshan Temple is the Foguang Temple, which was originally built during the Northern Wei Dynasty.

Other sights include the marble archway of the Longquan Temple and the 26-metre-high Buddha statue and carvings of 500 arhats in the Shuxiang Temple. The Luohou Temple contains a large wooden lotus flower with eight petals, on each of which sits a carved Buddhist figure; the big flower is attached to a rotating disk so that when it turns the petals open up and the figures appear.

There are daily buses from Taiyuan to Wutaishan and the trip takes nine hours. The bus stops at Wutai, 95 km away. From Wutai you can get a bus to the Foguang Temple *(fóguang sì)*.

DATONG

(dàtóng) 大同

In 220 AD the Han Empire was separated into three kingdoms. Rivalry between them left China open to invasion from the north, and though the other kingdoms were subjugated by the Wei Kingdom (which took the dynasty name of Jin) it was a shaky unification. A series of kingdoms rose and fell in the north until the Toba, a Turkic-speaking people, came to power at the end of the 4th century and, by the middle of the 5th, had conquered all of northern China, forming the Northern Wei Dynasty.

The success of the Tobas in ruling the northern Chinese was not due to their numbers, which were relatively small, but to their adoption of a Chinese style of administration and to the intermarriage of Chinese gentry and Toba aristocracy. Northern Wei times appear to have been a very active period of development, particularly in agriculture, irrigation and trade, as well as a cultural high point, despite continuing wars and social instability. Buddhist teachings of personal salvation and nirvana began taking root among the Chinese people, and Buddhism was made a state religion.

The Northern Wei rulers established their capital at Datong, an important centre because of its strategic location just south of the Great Wall and near the border with Inner Mongolia. The town had been fortified under the Han. When the Wei set up their capital here it became the political hub of the dynasty, until the court moved to Luoyang in 494 AD. Outside the modern-day city is the greatest legacy of the period, the Yungang Buddhist Caves.

Apart from the caves, there are few reminders today that Datong was once northern China's imperial city. The city of over a million people retains one of the largest and most intact old sections left in any Chinese

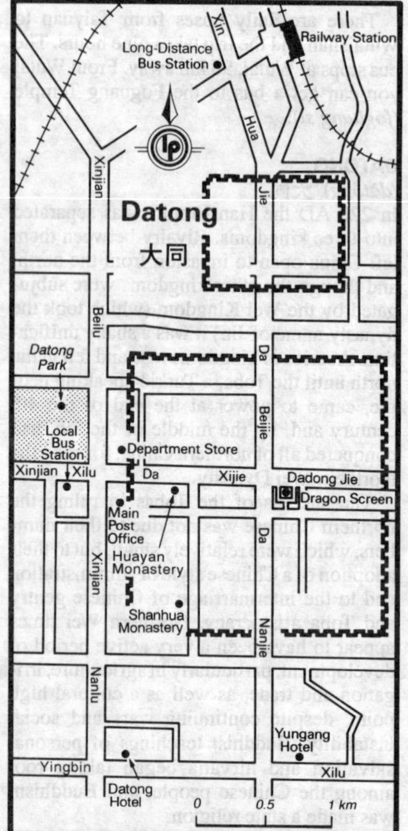

city although recent earthquakes have taken their toll. Unfortunately, it's one of the most depressing cities in China – ugly, polluted and poor. It's also Shanxi's leading coal producer.

Orientation

Datong is divided into an old city and the modern post-1949 construction. In the north of town is the long-distance bus station and the main railway station. In the centre of town are the local bus station, the Public Security Bureau, the main department store, the post office and the exhibition hall. In the south are the two tourist hotels. The old city, the Huayan Monastery and the Dragon Screen are in the east while the Yungang Caves are just outside the city.

Information

CITS This office (☎ 522265) is in the Yungang Hotel on Ying Bin Xilu.

Public Security Bureau This is next to the large department store on Xinjian Beilu.

Money Try the exchange counter in the Yungang Hotel.

Post & Telecommunications There is a post office in the Yungang Hotel. The main post and telephone office is the large central building with the clock tower (see map).

Maps Good maps of Datong are available from a booth on Xinjian Beilu near the railway station. The Datong Hotel sells the same maps, if you can find one of the lethargic staff to sell them to you. CITS also has maps but often runs out. The Xinhua Bookstore has no maps.

Datong Locomotive Factory

(dàtóng jīchē chǎng) 大同机车厂

This factory was the last one in China making steam engines for the main train lines. In 1989 they finally switched over to the production of diesel and electric engines. However, the factory still maintains a museum housing about seven old steam locomotives.

The factory is open to visitors but the only way you'll get to see it is to arrange a tour with CITS. You can only go if there's a spare seat on one of the tour buses or if you can get a group together.

The tour of the factory can best be described as educational. One US tourist said it reminded him of working in the US shipyards in the 1940s. You may be aghast at the safety conditions. After wandering through the factory you enjoy the ultimate experience of rail buffs – a ride in the cabin of one of the locomotives. Then it's off to the kindergarten where you're greeted by lines of applauding toddlers, topped off with a song-and-dance performance by some of the older children.

Dragon Screen
(jiǔlóng bì) 九龙壁
Situated in the old part of Datong on Dadong Jie, the Dragon Screen is said to have faced the mansion of the 13th son of the Ming Dynasty's first emperor, Hong Wu. The screen is eight metres high, over 45 metres long and two metres thick. On its main section, in relief, are nine stylised dragons. Unfortunately, it's in very bad condition.

Huayan Monastery
(húayán sì) 华严寺
The Huayan Monastery is on the west side of the old city. The original monastery dates back to 1140 and the reign of Emperor Tian Juan of the Jin Dynasty. Apparently about 50 monks and novices now live there.

Mahavira Hall is the main building and is one of the largest Buddhist halls still standing in China. In the centre of the hall are five gilded Ming Dynasty buddhas seated on lotus thrones. The three statues in the middle are carved out of wood while the other two are clay. Around them stand bodhisattvas, soldiers and mandarins. The ceiling is decorated with colourful paintings – originally dating to the Ming and Qing dynasties but recently restored.

Bojiajiaocang Hall (Hall for the Conservation of Buddhist Scriptures of the Bojia Order) is smaller but more interesting than the main hall. It contains 29 coloured clay figures made during the Liao Dynasty (916-1125 AD) representing the Buddha and bodhisattvas. The figures give the monastery a touch of magic lacking in other restored temples. Chinese artists come here for a bit of inspiration, and the clay replicas that are all the go.

Bus No 4 from the railway station goes past the Dragon Screen and the Huayan Monastery. The monastery can be a little difficult to find. It's set back on a small side street of its own, off Daxi Jie on the south side.

Shanhua Monastery
(shànhùa sì) 善化寺
The Shanhua Monastery at the south end of Datong is commonly called the Southern Temple. Built during the Tang Dynasty, it was destroyed by fire during a war at the end of the Liao Dynasty. In 1128 more than 80 halls and pavilions were rebuilt, and further restoration was done during the Ming Dynasty in 1445.

Mass Graves Exhibition Hall
(wàn rén kēng zhǎnlǎn gǔan) 万人坑展览馆
This is dedicated to the people executed here by the Japanese. A viewing hall has been built over the pit into which some of the bodies were thrown. Some have been exhumed and are on display in a nearby hall.

This is a difficult place to find if you don't speak Chinese, so show the Chinese characters to someone. Take bus No 6 from the local bus station to the terminal. Then change to bus No 5. Ask the conductor where to get off, and ask people on the street for more directions. If you stay on bus No 5 and take it to the terminal you'll see what Datong is really all about.

Yungang Buddhist Caves
(yúngāng shíkū) 云冈石窟
Unless you admire coal dust and grey buildings, the caves are the only outstanding sight in Datong. The Yungang Buddhist Caves are cut into the southern cliffs of Wuzhoushan mountain , 16 km west of Datong next to the pass leading to Inner Mongolia. The caves contain over 50,000 statues and stretch for about one km east to west. On top of the mountain ridge are the remains of a huge, mud-brick, 17th-century Qing Dynasty fortress. As you approach the caves you'll see the truncated pyramids which were once the watchtowers.

History Most of the caves at Datong were carved during the Northern Wei Dynasty between 460 and 494 AD. Yungang (Cloud Ridge) is the highest part of Wuzhoushan's sandstone range and is on the north bank of the river of the same name. The Wei rulers once came here to pray to the gods for rain.

The Yungang Caves appear to have been modelled on the Dunhuang Caves of Gansu Province, which were dug in the 4th century AD and are some of the oldest in China. Recent studies suggest that the Kongwang grottoes at Lianyungang, a coastal city by the Yellow Sea, were dug 200 years earlier. Buddhism may have been brought to China not only overland along the Silk Road but by sea from Burma, India and Sri Lanka.

It was in India that methods of cutting out cave temples from solid rock first developed. At the Dunhuang Caves the statues are terracotta since the rock was too soft to be carved, but here at Datong are some of the oldest examples of stone sculpture to be seen in China. Various foreign influences can be seen in the Yungang Caves: there are Persian and Byzantine weapons, lions and beards, Greek tridents and the acanthus leaves of the Mediterranean, as well as images of the Indian Hindu gods Vishnu and Shiva. The Chinese style is reflected in the form of bodhisattvas, dragons and flying apsaras (those celestial beings rather like angels).

Some think the gigantic Buddha statues at Bamiyan in Afghanistan may have inspired the Yungang statues. The first caves at Yungang had enormous Buddha images in the likenesses of five Northern Wei emperors. In fact, the first Northern Wei emperor, Daiwu, had been declared a 'living Buddha' in 416 AD because of his patronage of Buddhism.

Work on the Yungang Caves fizzled out when the Northern Wei moved their capital to Luoyang in 494. Datong then declined in importance and the caves appear to have been deliberately abandoned. In the 11th and 12th centuries the Liao Dynasty founded by northern invaders saw to some repairs and restoration. Datong itself houses some gems of Liao architecture and sculpture. More repairs to the caves were carried out during the Qing Dynasty. In comparison with the caves at Luoyang, the Datong caves are probably the more impressive and have suffered less vandalism.

From east to west the caves fall into four major groups, though their numbering has nothing to do with the order in which they were constructed. The present appearance of the caves is also misleading – the whole front of the caves was formerly covered with multistorey buildings.

Caves 1-4 These early caves with their characteristic square floor plan are at the far eastern end, separated from the others. Caves 1 and 2 each contain carved pagodas. Cave 3 is the largest in this group, though it contains only a seated Buddha flanked by two bodhisattvas. Between this group of four caves and the others is a monastery dating back to 1652, with pavilions hugging the cliff face.

Caves 5 & 6 Yungang art is seen at its best in these two caves. The walls are wonderfully carved with illustrations of Buddhist tales and ornate processions.

Cave 5 contains a colossal seated Buddha almost 17 metres high. The faded paint gives you some idea of the original colour schemes: bronze face, red lips and blue hair. Many of the smaller images in this cave have been beheaded though, on the whole, the sculptures and paintings in Caves 5 and 6 are better preserved than those in other caves since they're protected from the elements by the wooden towers built over the entrances. Cave 5 also contains a five-storey pagoda perched on the back of an elephant, carved on the upper part of the south wall.

Cave 6 contains a richly carved pagoda covered with scenes from religious stories. The entrance is flanked by fierce guardians. In the centre of the rear chamber stands a two-storey pagoda-pillar about 15 metres high. On the lower part of the pagoda are four niches with carved images, including one of the Maitreya Buddha (the future Buddha). The life story of Gautama Buddha from birth to his attainment of nirvana is carved in the east, south and west walls of the cave and on two sides of the pagoda. A relief on the east wall of the rear chamber of Cave 6 shows Prince Gautama's encounter with a sick man; the prince rides a horse while his servant protects him with an umbrella (a symbol of royalty) but cannot protect him from seeing human suffering. Pilgrims walk around the chamber clockwise.

Cave 8 Cave 8 contains carvings with Hindu influences that have found their way into Buddhist mythology. Shiva, with eight arms and four heads and seated on a bull, is on one side of the entrance. On the other side is the many-armed, multifaced Indra, perched on an eagle.

Caves 9 & 10 These caves, with pillars in front, have interesting smaller figures with humorous faces. Some carry musical instruments. Cave 12 contains apsaras with musical instruments.

Caves 16-20 These caves were carved in 460 AD and have oval floors. The roofs are dome-shaped to make room for huge Buddha statues – some standing, some sitting, all with saccharine expressions.

The cross-legged giant Buddha of Cave 17 represents the Maitreya Buddha. The cave walls are covered with thousands of tiny buddhas; carving them is considered a meritorious act.

The walls of Cave 18 are covered with sculptures of Buddha's disciples, including one near the Buddha's elbow who has a long nose and Caucasian features.

The seated Buddha of Cave 20 is almost 14 metres high. The front wall and the wooden structure which stood in front of it are believed to have crumbled away very early on, and the statue now stands exposed. It is thought to represent the son of Northern Wei Emperor Daiwu who is said to have been a great patron of Buddhism but later, through the influence of a minister, came to favour Taoism. Following a revolt which he blamed on the Buddhists, Daiwu ordered the destruction of their statues, monasteries and temples and the persecution of Buddhists. This lasted from 446 to 452 AD. Daiwu was murdered in 452 AD, though he had apparently repented of his cruel persecution. His son is said to have died of a broken heart, unable to prevent his father's atrocities, and was posthumously awarded the title of emperor. Daiwu's grandson (and successor) restored Buddhism. The statue in Cave 20 has distinctly non-Chinese features. The inlaid spot-like *urna*, a hairy wart between the brows which is a distinguishing mark of the Buddha, is missing. A carved moustache is faintly visible.

Next door is Cave 19 which is the largest cave and contains a 16-metre-high seated statue thought to represent Emperor Daiwu. It is possible he was deliberately carved with his palm facing forwards – the 'no fear' gesture – in an attempt to abate the painful memories of his persecution of Buddhism.

Cave 21 onwards These caves are small and in poor condition. Cave 51 contains a carved pagoda.

Getting to the Caves One way is to take bus No 17 to the terminal and then hop onto bus No 3. After boarding bus No 3, it's about another 30 minutes to the caves. Another route is to take bus No 6 (just outside and turn right from Datong Hotel) and let the conductor know that you want to be dropped off at the bus No 3 stop.

Admission to the caves is Y5. Slides of the caves are cheap to buy – Y8 for 20.

Places to Stay

There are only two places that accept foreigners. The cheapest accommodation is at the *Datong Hotel (dàtóng bīngǔan)* where dorms are Y10. Double rooms are available from Y75.

The more pleasant of the two hotels is the *Yungang Hotel (yúngāng bīngǔan)*. Double rooms are Y108 and, though they hate to admit it, they have a small dormitory for Y15.

Bus No 15 from the railway station drops you off at both hotels. It stops at the Datong Hotel first. Stay on for two more stops to reach the Yungang Hotel.

Places to Eat

The choices are dismal. Stalls around the

railway station rate about 85 on the vomit meter. The grocery stores might be your best bet, or eat at the Yungang Hotel.

Getting There & Away

Datong is a major junction on the north-central China railway network. There are daily express trains to Taiyuan (seven to nine hours), Beijing (seven to 8½ hours, Y14 for hard-seat, tourist-price), Hohhot (five to six hours), Lanzhou via Hohhot and Baotou, and Xi'an. If you arrive late in Datong take a motorised pedicab or auto-rickshaw from the railway station to the hotel.

An interesting alternative is to take a bus from Datong to Lingqiu (via Hunyuan near Hengshan). The bus departs Datong about 6.30 am and arrives in Lingqiu around noon. The route is very mountainous and scenic, but part of the road is very narrow, winding and somewhat dangerous. There are slow (6½ hours) afternoon trains from Lingqiu to Beijing. For the adventurous, it's a great route.

AROUND DATONG

Hanging Monastery

(xúankōng sì) 悬空寺

Dangling off Jinlong Canyon in the Heng mountains (75 km from Datong), is the peculiar Hanging Monastery. It dates back more than 1400 years but has been rebuilt several times through the centuries and now has 40 halls and pavilions. They were built along the contours of the cliff face using the natural hollows and outcrops, plus wooden beams for support. The buildings are connected by corridors, bridges and boardwalks and contain bronze, iron, clay and stone statues of gods and buddhas. There is an entry fee of Y1.80 for the lower part of the monastery, and a somewhat outrageous Y10 fee (Y5 for students) to see the upper part. It would be easier to accept these fees if the money were being used to renovate the monastery, but so far it doesn't look that way.

The easiest way to get there is with a Chinese tour bus from the long-distance bus station (at the corner of Xinjian Beilu and Xinhua Jie). Tickets are Y8. Unfortunately, you only get 30 minutes at the monastery. Many of the tours also include a stop at the Wooden Tower. The tower dates from the 11th century and is one of the oldest large wooden buildings in the world.

Alternatively, take a bus from Datong to Hunyuan. The Hanging Monastery is a pleasant 3½ km walk from there. You could stay overnight in Hunyuan and then bus back to Datong the following day. Bus No 169 leaves at 9 am, takes three hours to reach Hunyuan, and heads back at 2 pm. The fare is Y3.

There are also minibuses making this trip, either from the railway station or sometimes right from the hotel car park. Try to make arrangements the day before. The cost is Y8 (maybe less, depending on the number of passengers). It takes 1½ hours to reach the monastery. Departures are usually early, often before 7 am.

Another possibility is to take a bus from either Datong or Hunyuan to Yingxian and visit the Wooden Tower on the way to the Hanging Monastery. The bus ride to Yingxan takes 1½ hours leaving from either Datong or Hunyuan.

THE EAST

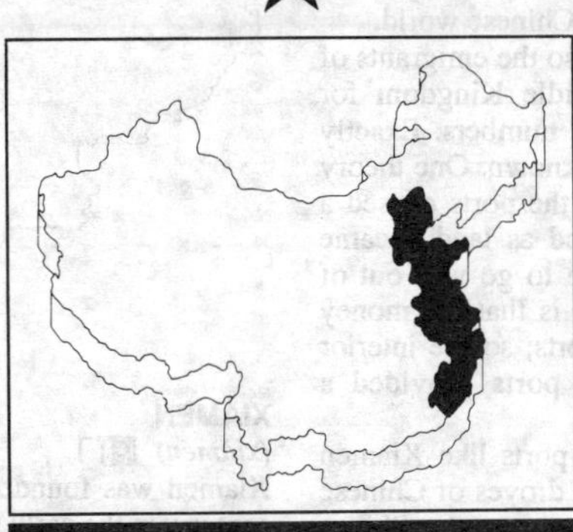

Fujian 福建

Fujian *(fújiàn)* is an odd place. The coastal region has well-established trading ports, which for centuries enjoyed substantial contact with the outside world. Early on, its great seaports developed a booming trade which transformed the region from a frontier into one of the centres of the Chinese world.

The Fujianese were also the emigrants of China, leaving the Middle Kingdom for South-East Asia in great numbers. Exactly why this happened is unknown. One theory is that the prosperity of the ports caused a population explosion, and as land became scarce the only direction to go was out of China. The other theory is that the money never got beyond the ports, so the interior remained poor but the ports provided a means of escape.

Whatever the reason, ports like Xiamen were stepping stones for droves of Chinese people heading for Singapore, the Philippines, Malaysia and Indonesia. In 1718 the Manchus attempted to halt Chinese emigration with an imperial edict recalling all subjects who were in foreign lands. Finding this ineffectual, in 1728 the court issued another proclamation declaring that anyone who did not return to China would be banished and those captured would be executed. Chinese emigration was only made legal by the Convention of Peking which ended the fourth Opium War in 1860. Even now, many descendants of the original emigrants send money to Fujian, and the Chinese government is trying to build up a sense of patriotism in the Overseas Chinese to get them to invest more money in the motherland.

Fujian is a lush, attractive province inhabited by over 26 million people. The rugged, mountainous interior of the province is closed to tourists and is said to be very poor, but the lively and prosperous port towns on the narrow coastal strip are open to foreign visitors.

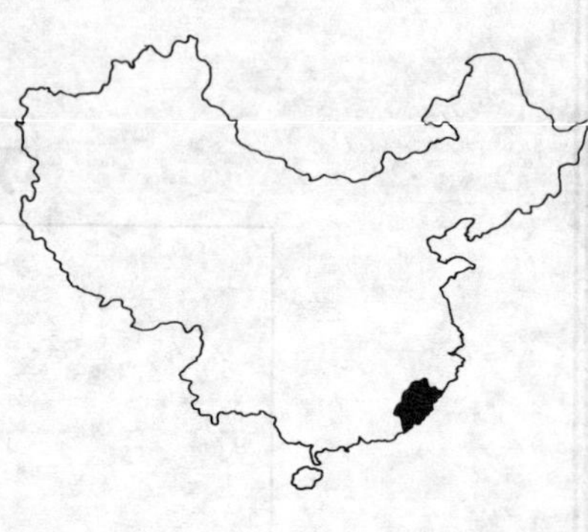

XIAMEN

(xiàmén) 厦门

Xiamen was founded around the mid-14th century, in the early years of the Ming Dynasty. There had been a town here since Song times, but the Ming built the city walls and established Xiamen as a major seaport and commercial centre. In the 17th century it became a place of refuge for the Ming rulers fleeing from the Manchu invaders. From here Ming armies fought their way north again under the command of the pirate-general Koxinga whose story follows.

When the Ming Dynasty collapsed in 1644, under the weight of the Manchu invasion, the court fled to the south of China. One after the other, a varied succession of Ming princes assumed the title of emperor, in the hope of driving out the barbarians and ascending to the Dragon Throne. One of the more successful attempts (which focused on the port of Xiamen) was by an army led by Zheng Chenggong, known in the West as Koxinga.

Koxinga's origins are a mystery. His father is said to have run away to Japan and married a Japanese woman – Koxinga's mother. His father returned to China as a pirate, raiding the Guangdong and Fujian coasts and even taking possession of Xiamen. Exactly how and why Koxinga came to be allied with the defunct Ming princes is unknown. One story claims

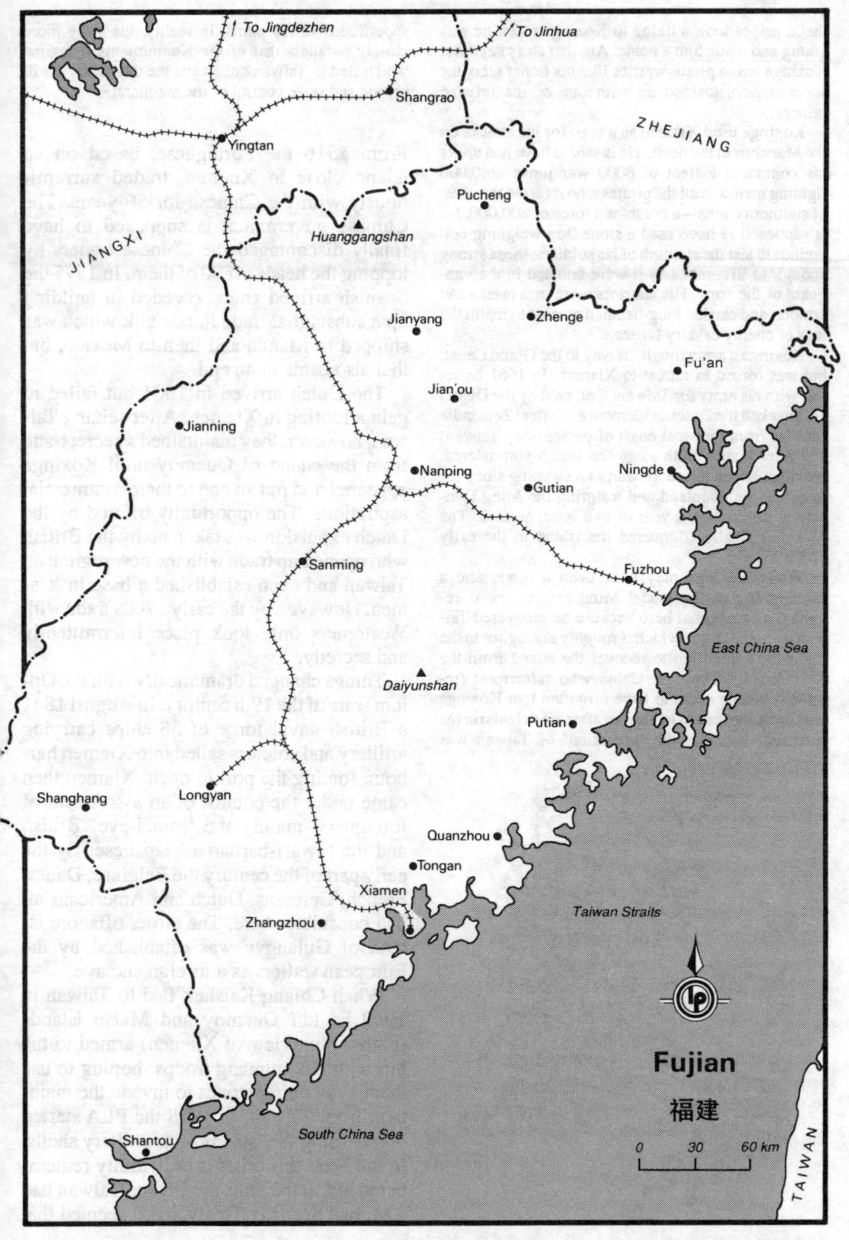

To Jingdezhen
To Jinhua
Shangrao
ZHEJIANG
Yingtan
Pucheng
Huanggangshan
JIANGXI
Jianyang
Zhenge
Fu'an
Jian'ou
Jianning
Ningde
Nanping
Gutian
Sanming
Fuzhou
East China Sea
Daiyunshan
Putian
Shanghang
Longyan
Quanzhou
Tongan
Xiamen
Taiwan Straits
Zhangzhou
Fujian
福建
Shantou
South China Sea
0
30
60 km
TAIWAN

that a prince took a liking to Koxinga when he was young and made him a noble. Another story says that Koxinga was a pirate-warrior like his father who, for some reason, teamed up with one of the refugee princes.

Koxinga used Xiamen as a base for his attacks on the Manchus in the north. He is said to have had under his command a fleet of 8000 war junks, 240,000 fighting men, and all the pirates who infested the coast of southern China – a combined force of 800,000. He is supposed to have used a stone lion weighing 600 pounds to test the strength of his soldiers; those strong enough to lift and carry it were enlisted in the vanguard of the army. His warriors wore iron masks and armour, and carried long-handled swords to maim the legs of enemy cavalry horses.

Koxinga's army fought its way to the Grand Canal, but was forced to retreat to Xiamen. In 1661 he set sail with his army for Taiwan, then held by the Dutch. He attacked the Dutch settlement at Casteel Zeelandia (not far from the west coast of present-day Taiwan) and after a six-month siege the Dutch surrendered. Koxinga hoped to use Taiwan as a stepping stone for invading the mainland and restoring the Ming Dynasty to power but, a year or two later, he died. The Manchus finally conquered the island in the early 1680s.

While Koxinga may have been a pirate and a running-dog of the feudal Ming princes, he is regarded as a national hero because he recovered Taiwan from the Dutch which is roughly analogous to the mainland's ambition to recover the island from the Kuomintang! Those in China who reinterpret (rewrite?) history seem to have forgotten that Koxinga was forced to retreat to Taiwan after his defeats on the mainland and that the 'liberation' of Taiwan was superfluous to his plans. In reality, his story more closely parallels that of the Kuomintang, a regime which fled to Taiwan but awaits the day when it will invade and seize control of the mainland.

From 1516 the Portuguese, based on an island close to Xiamen, traded surreptitiously with the Chinese for 50 years. The Chinese government is supposed to have finally discouraged the Chinese traders by lopping the heads off 90 of them. In 1575 the Spanish arrived and succeeded in building up a substantial trade in raw silk which was shipped to Manila and then to Mexico, but that also came to an end.

The Dutch arrived in 1604 but failed to gain a footing in Xiamen. After seizing Taiwan, however, they maintained a secret trade from the island of Quemoy until Koxinga appeared and put an end to their commercial aspirations. The opportunity offered by the Dutch expulsion was taken up by the British who opened up trade with the new regime on Taiwan and even established a base in Xiamen. However, by the early 1700s trade with Westerners only took place intermittently and secretly.

Things changed dramatically with the Opium wars of the 19th century. In August 1841 a British naval force of 38 ships carrying artillery and soldiers sailed into Xiamen harbour, forcing the port to open. Xiamen then came under the control of an assortment of foreigners, mainly the 'round-eye' British and the 'dwarf-barbarian' Japanese. By the early part of the century the Belgians, Danes, French, Germans, Dutch and Americans all had consulates here. The close, offshore island of Gulangyu was established by the European settlers as a foreign enclave.

When Chiang Kaishek fled to Taiwan in 1949 he left Quemoy and Matsu islands (both within view of Xiamen) armed to the hilt with Kuomintang troops, hoping to use them as stepping-stones to invade the mainland from Taiwan. In 1958 the PLA started bombarding the islands with artillery shells. In the West this crisis is only dimly remembered but, at the time, the US and Taiwan had a Mutual Security Treaty and it seemed that

Top: Pagoda in Black Dragon Park, Mt. Satseto in the background (RS)
Bottom: Interior roof of the Temple of Heaven, Beijing (AS)

Top: The Great Wall, Beijing (AS)
Bottom: Front Gate, Qianmen, Beijing (AS)

the USA was about to enter a war for the sake of Chiang's pathetic regime. Kuomintang troops still occupy the islands.

Today, Xiamen is a peaceful place. Still a thriving port, it was opened to tourists in 1980 and in the following year became a Special Economic Zone. The colonial architecture of Gulangyu is similar to that in other port towns, though better preserved. A pretty, laid-back town (if ever there was one in China), Xiamen has a very different feel from China's inland towns. The locals even have their own dialect, ***minnanhua***, which means 'south-of-the-Min-River-language'.

Orientation

The town of Xiamen is on the island of the same name, which lies just off the mainland.

The island is connected to the mainland by a long causeway which carries a railway, road and footpath. The first section of the causeway connects the town of Xinglin on the mainland to the town of Jimei at the tip of a peninsula due east of Xinglin.

The second section connects Jimei to the north of Xiamen Island. The town of Xiamen lies in the south-western corner of the island, directly opposite the small island of Gulangyu.

The railway station is at the far eastern side of Xiamen town and the long-distance bus station is in the north. The main street is Zhongshan Lu; along here you'll find the Lujiang Hotel, the Bank of China, most of the restaurants and shops and also the pier from which the ferry to Gulangyu departs. At the southern end of the town are the Nanputuo Temple and Xiamen University.

In 1912 the American missionary Reverend Pitcher described Xiamen (which was once called Amoy) in the following terms:

> A city! But not the kind of city you have in mind. There are no wide avenues, beautiful residences, magnificent public and mercantile buildings. All is directly opposite to this condition of things. The streets are narrow and crooked...ever winding and twisting, descending and ascending, and finally ending in the great nowhere. The wayfaring man, tho' wise, is bound to err therein. There is no street either straight, or one even called 'Straight' in Amoy. Then in addition to the crookedness, they must add another aggravation by making some of them very narrow. There are streets in Amoy so narrow that you cannot carry an open umbrella, but there are others ten, twelve, and fifteen feet wide. Of course they are crowded...alive with a teeming throng...Here every aspect of Chinese life passes before you, presenting grotesque pictures. Here goes the motley crowd, from the wretched beggar clothed in filthy rags to the stately mandarin adorned in gorgeous array.

Today, the streets are wider but still teem with people. The beggars whom Pitcher described as 'spending idle hours picking out the vermin from their dirty and ragged garments' are conspicuous by their absence and the mandarins have been replaced by privileged cadres, or bus-loads of Occidental toursts. Nowadays, Xiamen conveys an air of prosperity – it's a lively, colourful town of over 300,000 people, with many reminders of bygone turmoils.

Information

CTS This office (☎ 24286) is on the ground floor of the Overseas Chinese Building. The staff are friendly, but you really need to be able to speak Chinese to get much information.

Public Security Bureau Opposite the Overseas Chinese Building is a large, red-brick building; the wide footpath on the right-hand side (as you face it) leads to the Public Security Bureau.

Money The Bank of China is at 10 Zhongshan Lu, near the Lujiang Hotel. There are many black market moneychangers around the Overseas Chinese Building and along Zhongshan Lu. Both the Lujiang and Overseas Chinese hotels have exchange counters.

Books & Maps The Foreign Language Bookstore at 161 Zhongshan Lu carries several titles in English, including the informative *A Complete Guide to Xiamen*. Good bus maps are available from the following places: the counter at the railway station, the hawkers outside the railway and long-distance bus stations, and the gift shop

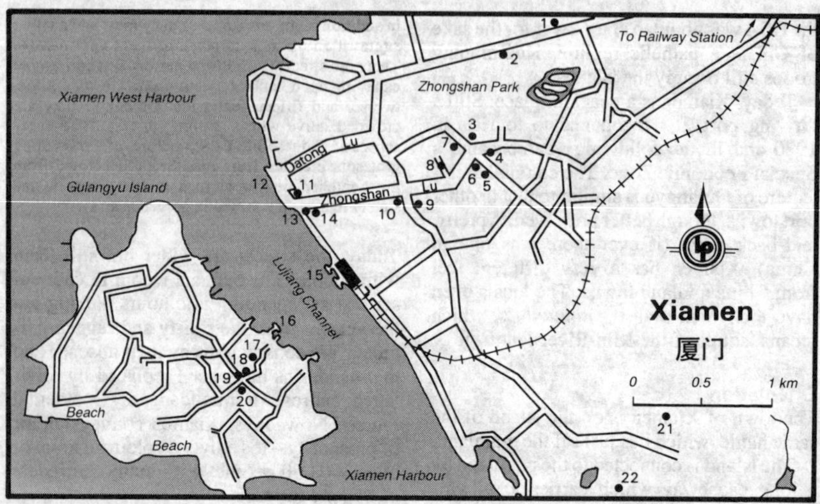

1	Long-Distance Bus Station	12	Ferry Pier (Mainland-Gulangyu)
2	Bus No 3 Stop	13	Bus No 2 Stop
3	Public Security Bureau	14	Bank
4	Bus No 1 Stop	15	Xiamen-Hong Kong Ferry Pier
5	Overseas Chinese Building	16	Ferry Pier (Gulangyu-Mainland)
6	Xin Qiao Hotel	17	Post Office
7	Post Office	18	Ke Le Restaurant
8	Xiaxi Market	19	Gulangyu Restaurant
9	Food Stalls	20	Gulangyu Tourist Hotel
10	Ludao Restaurant	21	Nanputuo Temple
11	Lujiang Hotel	22	Xiamen University

1	长途汽车站	10	绿岛饭店	16	渡船码头（鼓浪屿→大陆）
2	第三汽车站	11	鹭江大厦	17	邮局
3	公安局外事科	12	渡船码头（大陆→鼓浪屿）	18	可乐饭馆
4	第一汽车站	13	第二汽车站	19	鼓浪屿饭馆
5	华侨旅社	14	银行	20	鼓浪屿旅行社
6	新侨饭店	15	渡船码头（夏门→香港）	21	南普陀
7	邮局			22	厦大
8	市场				
9	小吃部				

on the 2nd floor of the Overseas Chinese Building.

Gulangyu Island

(gǔlàngyǔ) 鼓浪屿

Neither Gulangyu nor Xiamen were considered island paradises when Westerners landed in the 1840s. By 1860, however, they had well-established residencies on Gulangyu, and as the years rolled by, they built churches, hospitals, post and telegraph offices, libraries, hotels and consulates. In 1903 the island was officially designated an International Foreign Settlement, and a municipal council with a police force of Sikhs was established to govern it. Today, the only reminders of the settlement are the charming colonial buildings which blanket the island – and the sound of classical piano wafting from the villa-style houses! Many of China's most celebrated musicians have come from Gulangyu.

The ferry to Gulangyu leaves from the pier just north of Xiamen's Lujiang Hotel. You don't pay to go from the mainland to the island, but to get the ferry back you buy a counter at the pier on Gulangyu and drop it into a box at the barrier gate before boarding. Ferries run from about 5 am to midnight.

Transport around Gulangyu is by foot; there are no buses, cars or pedicabs. It's a small island and the sights are within easy walking distance of each other.

'In the past few years', says one of the tourist leaflets, 'many foreign visitors... plunged into the sea, indulging themselves in the waves, or lay on the golden sandy beach, being caressed by the sunshine, and made friends with the young people of Gulangyu. When the foreigners go away, they say: I am sure to come back again'. China is hardly a sun-worshipper's paradise but there are two beaches on Gulangyu, the East Beach and the West Beach. The first is overpopulated and has placid and scungy water, and the second belongs to the army and is off limits. On the beaches are a number of old, disused concrete blockhouses which appear to have ringed the entire island at one time.

Sunlight Rock *(rìguāng yán)* is the highest point on Gulangyu. It's an easy climb up the steps to the top where there's an observation platform and a great view across Gulangyu and the harbour. The large colonial building at the foot of Sunlight Rock is the Koxinga Memorial Hall *(zhèngchénggōng jìniànguǎn)*. Inside is an exhibition partly dedicated to the Dutch in Taiwan and the rest to Koxinga's throwing them out. There are no English captions but it is still worth a look and, from the verandahs of the upper storeys, there is a fine view across the island. The hall is open daily from around 8 to 11 am and 2 to 5 pm.

Nanputuo Temple

(nánpǔtuó sì) 南普陀寺

On the southern outskirts of Xiamen town, this Buddhist temple was built during the Tang Dynasty more than a thousand years ago. It was ruined in a battle during the Ming Dynasty but rebuilt during Qing times.

You enter the temple through Tian Wang (Heavenly King) Hall where the welcoming Maitreya Buddha sits cross-legged exposing his protruding belly. On either side are a pair of guardians who protect him. Standing behind the Maitreya Buddha is Wei Tuo, another Buddhist deity who safeguards the doctrine. He holds a stick which points to the ground – traditionally, this indicates that the temple is rich and can provide visiting monks with board and lodging (if the stick is held horizontally it means the temple is poor and is a polite way of saying find somewhere else to stay).

Behind Tian Wang Hall is a courtyard and on either side are the Drum and Bell towers. In front of the courtyard is Daxiongbao (Great Heroic Treasure) Hall, a two-storey building containing three buddhas which represent Sakyamuni in his past, present and future lives. The biography of Sakyamuni and the story of Xuan Zang, the monk who made the pilgrimage to India to bring back the Buddhist scriptures, are carved on the lotus-flower base of the buddha figure.

Inlaid in the buildings to the left and right of Daxiongbao Hall are eight stone tablets, inscribed in the handwriting of Emperor Qianlong of the Qing Dynasty. Four tablets are in Chinese and the others in the peculiar Manchu script. All record the Manchu government's suppression of the 'Tian Di Society' uprisings. The tablets were originally erected in front of the temple in 1789, but were inlaid in the walls when the temple was enlarged around 1920.

The Dabei (Great Compassion) Hall contains four bodhisattvas. Worshippers throw divining sticks at the feet of the statues in order to seek heavenly guidance.

At the rear of the temple complex is a pavilion built in 1936 which stores Buddhist scriptures, calligraphy, wood-carvings, ivory sculptures and other works of art – unfortunately it's closed to visitors. Behind the temple is a rocky outcrop gouged with poetic graffiti; the big red character carved on the large boulder simply means 'Buddha'.

To get to the temple, take bus No 1 from outside the Overseas Chinese Building, or bus No 2 from the intersection of Zhongshan Lu and Lujiang Lu.

Xiamen University

(xiàmén dàxué) 厦门大学

The university is next to the Nanputuo Temple, and was established with Overseas Chinese funds. The older buildings which face the shoreline are not without a certain charm, though most of the campus is a scattered collection of brick and concrete blocks. The campus entrance is next to the bus No 1 and bus No 2 terminal.

The Museum of Anthropology, on the university grounds, is worth a visit if you're down this way. After entering the campus, turn right at the first crossroads and walk until you come to a roundabout. The museum is the old stone building on the left with the cannon at the front. It has a large collection of prehistoric stone implements and pottery from China, Taiwan and Malaya, as well as human fossil remains. There are collections of porcelain, bronzes, jade and stone implements, coins, and inscribed Shang Dynasty bones and tortoise shells. You'll also see some fine calligraphy, exquisite paintings, glazed clay figurines, sculptures, clothing and ornaments from the Shang and Zhou periods through to Ming and Qing times.

Jimei School Village

(jímĕi xuéxiào cūn) 集美学校村

This much-touted tourist attraction is on the mainland north of Xiamen Island. The school is a conglomeration and expansion of a number of separate schools and colleges set up by Tan Kahkee (1874-1961). Tan was a native of the area who migrated to Singapore when he was young and became a rich industrialist. He set a fine example to other Overseas Chinese by returning some of that wealth to the mother country – the school now has around 20,000 students. The Chinese-style architecture has a certain appeal which may make a trip worthwhile.

Places to Stay – Xiamen

At the bottom end is the *Xiaxi Hotel*, next to Xiaxi Market off Zhongshan Lu, not far from the Overseas Chinese Building. Basic rooms with a communal bath cost Y20.

The well-run *Overseas Chinese Building* (☎ 25602) *(huáqiáo dàshà)* is on Xinhua Lu at the east end of Zhongshan Lu. Triple rooms cost Y22 per person (you can have the room to yourself for Y66) and doubles are Y110.

Next door, in what used to be the old wing of the Overseas Chinese Building, is the classy, refurbished *Xin Qiao Hotel* (☎ 38388) *(xīnqiáo fàndiàn)*. Singles range from Y125 to Y165 and doubles cost Y190. To get to either hotel from the railway station take bus No 1. From the bus station it's probably better to walk (about 20 minutes) or take a pedicab.

The *Lujiang Hotel* (☎ 22922) *(lùjiāng bīnguǎn)* is at 54 Lujiang Lu near the Gulangyu ferry pier. It once had the run-down charisma of an old colonial building but renovations have transformed it into a would-be luxury-class hotel. Singles range from Y145 to Y160 and doubles from Y160 to Y225, but it's often full. There's a rooftop coffee garden which is very relaxing with views across the harbour. Bus No 3 from the railway station and long-distance bus station terminates at the Gulangyu ferry pier, outside the hotel.

Between the Lujiang Hotel and the Overseas Chinese Building on Zhongshan Lu is the *East Ocean Hotel* (☎ 21111), an expensive joint-venture place without much character.

Places to Stay – Gulangyu

There are several tourist hotels on Gulangyu Island, some on the beach and some in the town. The cheapest place to stay is the *Gulangyu Tourist Hotel (gŭlàngyŭ lǚxíngshè)* where doubles cost Y70. The modern *Xiamen Gulang Island Hotel (xiàmén gŭlàngyŭ bīnguăn)* has doubles for Y140, but when vacancies are high you should be able to bargain the rates downwards.

Places to Eat – Xiamen

Xiamen is 'seafood city', with many seafood restaurants along Zhongshan Lu and its side streets. It's hardly worth recommending any one place in particular; just look around until you find something that looks good. There are plenty of fresh pineapples, frogs and peppers and a local lobster speciality called dragon shrimp *(lóngxiā)*.

Places to Eat – Gulangyu

For tasty seafood in generous helpings try upstairs at the *Gulangyu Restaurant* – don't be put off by the grotty ground floor. There are many other places on the island serving plenty of squid, crab, shrimp and sea snails.

Things to Buy

Xiaxi Market is in a long, covered alley off Zhongshan Lu, near the Overseas Chinese Building. It is open daily from dawn till dusk and offers a colourful selection of live chickens, seafood, vegetables, clothes and household items. There is also a morning market in the alley directly behind the Overseas Chinese Building.

Shops lining Zhongshan Lu between the harbour and the Overseas Chinese Building sell all manner of electronic goods. Locals claim you can buy anything here that's available in Hong Kong – a bit of an exaggeration but pretty close to the truth.

Getting There & Away

Air Xiamen Airlines has daily flights to Hong Kong and Canton as well as regular flights to practically every major city in China and Singapore. Since 1991 the airlines has also had flights to Taipei. You can book your tickets at CTS in the Overseas Chinese Building.

Bus Buses to the towns on the south-east coast depart from the long-distance bus station. Destinations include Fuzhou (twice daily, Y19); Quanzhou (about a dozen buses daily, Y6.50); and Shantou (once daily, Y20). You can also get buses straight through to Canton and Shenzhen.

There are many privately run air-con buses with ticket offices around the bus station. Destinations include Quanzhou (from Y8 to Y10), Fuzhou (Y28) and Shantou (Y29).

Train The railway line from Xiamen heads north and connects with the main Shanghai to Canton line at the Yingtan junction. Another line runs from Yingtan to Fuzhou.

From Xiamen there are direct trains to Yingtan, Shanghai, Fuzhou and possibly Canton. The train to Fuzhou takes a circuitous route, and unless you want to travel by night you're better off taking the bus.

Tourist-price fares from Xiamen to Shanghai are Y69 (hard-seat), Y117 (hard-sleeper) and Y251 (soft-sleeper).

Boat Ships to Hong Kong leave from the Passenger Station of Amoy Port Administration on Tongwen Lu, about a 10-minute walk from the Lujiang Hotel. There is a ticket office at the passenger station. There are two ships from Xiamen to Hong Kong: the *Jimei* which departs every Friday, and the *Gulangyu* which sails every Tuesday. Fares range from Y130 for a seat to Y360 in a special class berth; the trip takes 24 hours.

Getting Around

Much of the town can easily be seen on foot. The bus service is extensive but the buses are always extremely crowded. Pedicabs and auto-rickshaws congregate outside the railway station, the long-distance bus station and the Gulangyu ferry pier on the mainland side. Taxis are available from the railway station and from the tourist hotels. Bus No 1 will take you from the railway station to the Overseas Chinese Building and bus No 3 runs from the railway station and long-distance bus station to the Lujiang Hotel. There are no buses, cars or pedicabs on Gulangyu – it's feet only.

QUANZHOU

(quánzhōu) 泉州

Long before the large port of Xiamen became a centre for domestic and foreign trade, there was another city nearby, Zaiton – a major port until the end of the 14th century. There is some debate as to its site, but Zaiton is generally accepted to have been where the present-day city of Quanzhou is situated, to the north-east of Xiamen.

The port was probably one of the greatest commercial centres in the world – from it Chinese silks, satins, sugar and spices were exported to India, Arabia and western Asia. When Marco Polo visited he raved about it as:

> a great resort of ships and merchandise...for one spice ship that goes to Alexandria or elsewhere to pick up pepper for export to Christendom, Zaiton is visited by a hundred. For you must know that it is one of the two ports in the world with the biggest flow of merchandise.

Marco Polo also remembered Zaiton as a place where many people came to have figures 'pricked out on their bodies with needles'. He had seen tattooists at work elsewhere on his travels; their 13th-century methods involved the customer being tied hand and foot and held down by two assistants while the artist pricked out images and then applied ink to the incisions. Polo writes that, during this time, the victim 'suffers what might well pass for the pains of Purgatory. Many even die during the operation through loss of blood.'

Kublai Khan's invasion fleets set sail from Zaiton for Japan and Java. With tariffs imposed on all imported goods, this city was an important source of refills for the Khan's treasury.

In the middle of the 14th century, towards the end of the Yuan Dynasty, Zaiton's prosperity began to decline because of fierce fighting. When the first Ming emperor, Hong Wu, came to power his isolationist policies reduced foreign trade to a trickle and, as if that wasn't enough, the fate of the city was finally sealed by the silting up of its harbour.

Today there are few reminders of Quanzhou's former glory. Nevertheless, it's a lively little town with narrow streets, wooden houses, and numerous shops and restaurants. Of late, a number of Taiwanese citizens have built retirement homes in the area, so the ratio of old architecture to new is fast dwindling.

Orientation

Quanzhou lies on the north bank of the Jin River. The main street is Zhongshan Lu, which runs north-south and cuts the town roughly in half. Along and around this street are most of the shops and restaurants, the long-distance bus station, the Overseas Chinese Hotel and the tourist facilities. The Kaiyuan Temple, Quanzhou's main attraction, lies in the north-western part of town. There's also a scattering of sights in the hills to the north-east.

Information

CTS This office (☎ 2366) is on the ground floor of the Overseas Chinese Hotel. The staff are friendly, but don't speak much English.

Public Security Bureau This is at 334-336 Dong Jie, a few minutes' walk east of the intersection with Zhongshan Lu.

Money You can change money at the Bank of China at the corner of Jiuyi Lu and Zhong-

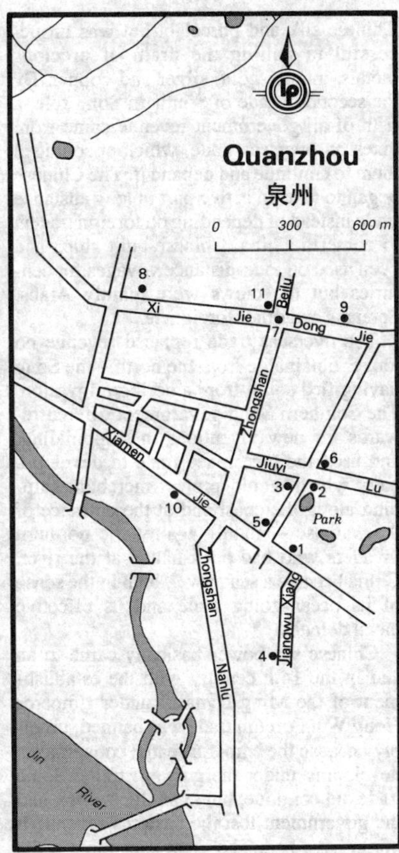

1 Qingzhen Mosque
2 Temple
3 Overseas Chinese Hotel & CTS
4 Long-Distance Bus Station
5 Seafood Restaurant
6 Bank
7 Clock Tower
8 Kaiyuan Temple & Museum of Overseas Communications History
9 Public Security Bureau
10 Post Office
11 Jin Quan Hotel

1 清真寺
2 寺
3 华侨旅行社
4 长途汽车站
5 海味类饭店
6 银行
7 钟楼
8 开元寺
9 公安局外事科
10 邮局
11 金泉宾馆

shan Lu, just north of the Overseas Chinese Hotel.

Post There is a post office at 75 Xiamen Jie and the Overseas Chinese Hotel also has one.

Kaiyuan Temple

(kāiyuăn sì)

The Kaiyuan Temple is distinguished by its pair of tall pagodas. It was founded in the 7th century during the Tang Dynasty but reached its peak during Song times when a thousand monks lived here. The present buildings, including the pagodas and the main hall, are of more recent construction. The main hall contains five large, gilded buddhas and on the ceiling above them are peculiar winged apsaras – celestial beings similar to angels. Behind the main hall stands the Guanyin Temple with its saffron-robed Buddha.

The temple is on Xi Lu, in the north-west part of town. From the Overseas Chinese Hotel the walk is lengthy but interesting.

Museum of Overseas Communications History

This museum is in the grounds of the Kaiyuan Temple behind the eastern pagoda. It contains one of *the* attractions of Quanzhou: the enormous hull of a Song Dynasty sea-going junk which was excavated near Quanzhou.

On display are also photos, coins and artefacts found in the wreck. A map shows the routes taken by Chinese junks and the foreign places they reached: from Japan to the east coast of Africa and as far south as Madagascar. The tombstones belong to Arab traders who lived in Quanzhou when it was a booming seaport.

The remains of the ship display characteristic features of Chinese ship construction: a square bow and stern, a flat bottom (no keel), and the division by bulkheads into many watertight compartments. The Quanzhou wreck has at least 11 such compartments, a construction achievement unknown in Europe at the time. A highly efficient stern rudder had been developed several centuries before, and a mariner's compass was in widespread use by the 11th century. Both the compass and the rudder had a long period of development in China from the Han period onwards. In comparison, the earliest Western records of the rudder (northern Europe) and the compass (southern Europe) date from the late 12th century.

The overseas trade of the late Tang and Song China was closely tied to the river trade. Ocean-going ships brought goods to the great ports to be carried inland along the river routes, which were slower but cheaper than the land routes and ideal for heavy loads like grain and salt. Canals were built and existing ones extended to link the major river systems, which made the nationwide trade of the Song period possible. So much trade developed that some of the cities along the water routes (such as Yangzhou on the Grand Canal) developed into big consumer and commercial centres in their own right. Zaiton became the major seaport of the Song period.

Overseas trade revolved around the import and export of luxury goods. The chief imports were aromatics, spices, dyes, cotton fabrics, gold, swords, rhinoceros horn, ivory, ebony, precious stones, peacock and kingfisher feathers (for use as insignia of rank) and slaves. The slaves were mainly Africans, usually employed as domestic servants in wealthy households. The central government encouraged the export of highly prized Chinese silk and porcelain but was unsuccessful in halting the drain of precious metals, mainly gold, silver and copper. By the second decade of Southern Song rule, a fifth of all government revenue came from taxes on overseas trade, which encouraged them to continue and expand it. The Chinese began to take an active part in long-distance trade instead of depending on foreign traders to come to China. Chinese-built ships had been used on long-distance voyages for centuries but the crews were mainly Arabs, Persians and other foreigners.

The overseas trade replaced revenue no longer obtainable from the north – the Song having fled south from a northern invasion. The Southern Song government offered rewards for new inventions in shipbuilding, and used the tax on sea trade to develop a navy which would protect merchant shipping along the coast and at the entrance of the Yangtse – mainly against the northern invaders who had been halted at the river. China became a sea power, both in the sense of its ocean-going trade and its effective naval defence.

Chinese sea power basically came to an end in the 14th century with the establishment of the Ming Dynasty under Emperor Hong Wu. Foreign trade was banned, possibly because the emperor feared conspiracies developing under the guise of trade. Some trade did continue, but in an illicit form, and the government lost the customs revenue it might have had. The great exception to the isolationist policies of the Ming period occurred during the rule of the second Ming emperor, Yong Le.

Between 1405 and 1433 Yong Le dispatched seven enormous maritime expeditions led by the palace eunuch Zheng He. The expeditions were court enterprises, not government ventures, and Zheng was the personal representative of the emperor. The motives of the expeditions were complex: possibly to impress the southern Asian countries with Chinese power, to expand the maritime trade, and to extend Chinese knowledge of the outside world with the intention of founding colonies or a commercial empire. The fleets sailed to South-East Asia, Sumatra, Java, India and the Persian Gulf, and ventured up the Red Sea and the east coast of Africa.

These expeditions came to an end with the death of Yong Le (only 64 years before Vasco da Gama finally sailed around the tip of Africa in 1497 on his way to India). One reason they stopped may have been the expense, another that the government bureaucrats were jealous of the eunuchs' power in the imperial court – so much so that in the 1470s the official records of the voyages were burnt. The restoration and improvement of the Grand Canal may also have contributed to the demise of these expeditions. With the inland trade route reopened, coastal trade dropped off and a powerful naval escort was no longer needed. One by one the shipyards closed down and China's days as a maritime power ended.

Qingzhen Mosque

(qīngzhēn sì) 清真寺

On Tonghuai Jie, just south of the Overseas Chinese Hotel, is the shell of a mosque originally built in 1009 during the Song Dynasty for Quanzhou's large Muslim population. This is the oldest mosque in eastern China. There's also a small museum which has captions in Arabic, English and Chinese.

Temples

Quanzhou has its share of temples, in various stages of repair. One is in the park opposite the Overseas Chinese Hotel; get up early to watch the taiji workouts. Another temple is on Zhenfusi Lu, a side street which runs west from the square at the north end of Zhongshan Lu, and is now used as a junior school library. More interesting, however, is the active temple next to the mosque.

Places to Stay & Eat

The *Overseas Chinese Hotel* (☎ 22192) *(huáqiáo lǚxíngshè)* is close to Zhongshan Lu and a 15-minute walk from the long-distance bus station – see the map for directions. A bed in a three-bed room with TV and own bathroom costs Y20, singles are around Y75 and doubles are Y100.

Two blocks to the west is the *Chen Chow Hotel (quánzhōu fàndiàn)*, which is mainly for Chinese people but may take foreigners. They charge about Y8 for a bed in a triple room.

The refurbished *Jin Quan* at the corner of Zhongshan Lu and Xi Jie is more up-market and doubles start at Y150.

Quanzhou is a great place for seafood – perhaps better than Xiamen – with a couple of seafood restaurants near the Overseas Chinese Hotel. Just look around until you find something you like.

Getting There & Away

Air CAAC has flights from Quanzhou to Fuzhou (Y52) and Canton (Y248). Flights can be booked at CTS in the Overseas Chinese Hotel.

Bus The long-distance bus station is in the south-east part of town. There are about a dozen buses a day to Xiamen (Y6.50, 2½ hours), an interesting ride taking you through villages with large colonnaded stone houses ostentatious enough to suggest they were built with Overseas Chinese money. There are several buses a day to Fuzhou (Y15, six hours).

Ticket offices for air-con buses are near the Overseas Chinese Hotel. There are several departures daily to Xiamen (from Y8 to Y10), Fuzhou (Y15), Canton (Y120) and Shenzhen (Y110).

Train The nearest railheads are at Xiamen and Fuzhou; see those sections for details.

Getting Around

There are no city buses in Quanzhou and transport within the city is by Quanzhou-style pedicab – a bicycle with a little wooden sidecart which seats two people (the drivers are predatory!). Buses to nearby places leave from the square at the north end of Zhongshan Lu.

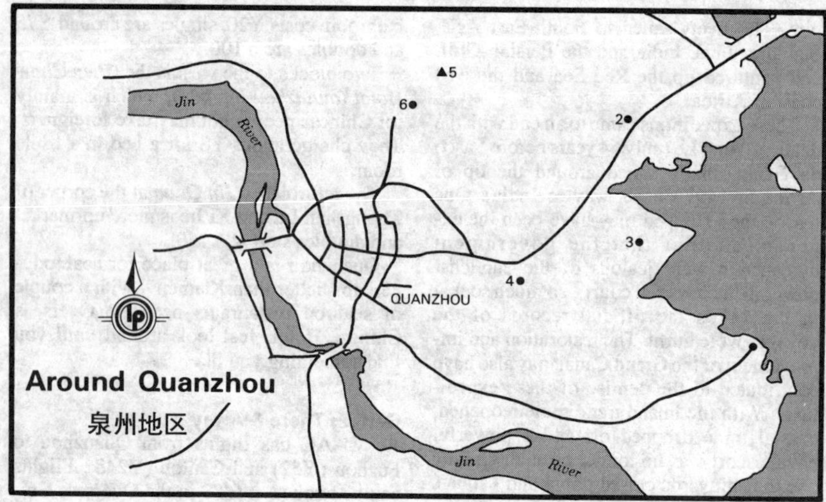

1 Ancient Bridges
2 Overseas Chinese University
3 Land Reclaimed during the Cultural Revolution
4 Lingshan Muslim Tomb
5 Lingshan
6 Laozi Statue

1 洛阳桥
2 华侨大学
3 新开垦的土地
4 圣墓
5 清源山
6 老君岩

AROUND QUANZHOU

North of Quanzhou is an unusual stubby statue of Laozi, the legendary founder of Taoism. The Chinese say that Kuomintang soldiers used the statue for target practice but there's no sign of bullet holes.

North of the statue is **Lingshan**. The Buddhist caves on the mountain were destroyed during the Cultural Revolution, though some people still pray in front of the empty spaces where the statues used to be. According to an old woman who lives on the mountain, two Red Guard factions fought each other here during the Cultural Revolution using mortars! Also found on the mountain is the 'rock that moves' (there's a large painting of it hanging in the dining room of the Overseas Chinese Hotel). It's one of these nicely shaped and balanced rocks which wobbles when you give it a nudge – we're told that to see it move you have to place a stick or a piece of straw lengthways between the rock and the ground and watch it bend as someone pushes on the rock.

The Lingshan **Muslim tomb** is thought to be the resting place of two Muslim missionaries who came to China during the Tang Dynasty. There are a number of Muslim burial sites on the north-east and south-east outskirts of Quanzhou for the thousands of Muslims who once lived at Quanzhou. The earliest dated tombstone belongs to a man who died in 1171. Many tombstone inscriptions are written in Chinese, Arabic and

Persian giving names, dates of birth and quotations from the Koran.

East of Quanzhou is a peninsula built by hand during the Cultural Revolution. The 7000 mu (about 470 hectares) of land is now used for agriculture. A village on the northern side of the peninsula was a separate island before the land was reclaimed.

Due north of the peninsula is the **Overseas Chinese University**, originally built to attract Hong Kongers and Taiwanese (only the first group came) to study in China. Like universities elsewhere in China it was closed during the Cultural Revolution. North-east of the university are two bridges built several hundred years ago which are still intact.

FUZHOU

(fúzhōu) 福州

In the 1320s the Franciscan friar Odoric spent three years in China on a missionary venture. He came via India and after landing in Canton travelled eastwards, where he:

> came unto a city named Fuzo, which contains 30 miles in circuit, wherein are exceeding great and fair cocks, and all their hens are as white as the very snow, having wool instead of feathers, like unto sheep. It is a most stately and beautiful city and stands upon the sea.

Odoric's woolly hens are in fact what poultry-breeders call Fleecy Persians, though the Chinese call them Velvet-Hair Fowls. While the Chinese still breed chickens in makeshift pens in their backyards, Fuzhou seems to have lost its fame both as a poultry farm and as a stately and beautiful city.

Although the thriving port of Fuzhou is the capital of Fujian and exports much of the region's agricultural produce, the city itself is a letdown after colourful towns like Xiamen and Quanzhou. Fuzhou looks very much like the dull industrial towns of the north, with long avenues, concrete-block buildings and expansive suburbs yet, surprisingly, the economy is still based heavily on fishing and agriculture.

Fuzhou was founded in the 6th century AD and rapidly became a commercial port specialising in the export of tea. Its name actually means 'wealthy town' and, in terms of wealth, Fuzhou was second only to Quanzhou. Marco Polo passed through Fuzhou towards the end of the 13th century, several years before Odoric's visit, and described the town as:

> an important centre of commerce in pearls and other precious stones, because it is much frequented by ships from India bringing merchants who traffic in the Indies. Moreover it is not far from the port of Zaiton (Quanzhou) on the ocean, a great resort of ships and merchandise from India; and from Zaiton ships come...as far as the city of Fu-chau (Fuzhou). By this means many precious wares are imported from India. There is no lack here of anything that the human body requires to sustain life. There are gardens of great beauty and charm, full of excellent fruit. In short it is a good city and so well provided with every amenity that it is a veritable marvel.

Despite its prosperity, Fuzhou had a reputation for revolt. Marco noted that the city had a garrison of a large number of soldiers, as there were frequent rebellions in the district. Nevertheless, Fuzhou's status as an important trading centre and port continued over the centuries and quickly drew the attention of Western traders who began to arrive in the area in the 16th century. They couldn't set up shop until 200 years later, when the Treaty of Nanking ended the second Opium War and opened Fuzhou to foreign traders in 1842.

Oddly, Fuzhou had a long history as a centre of Chinese Christianity. Marco Polo describes a Christian sect that worshipped here and writes that his father and uncle:

> enquired from what source they had received their faith and their rule, and their informants replied: 'From our forefathers'. It came out that they had in a certain temple of theirs three pictures representing three apostles of the 70 who went through the world preaching. And they declared that it was these three who had instructed their ancestors in the faith long ago, and that it had been preserved among them for 700 years.

The Christians who Polo met were probably Nestorians, descendants of a Syrian sect whose religion had been carried into China via the Silk Road. What eventually happened

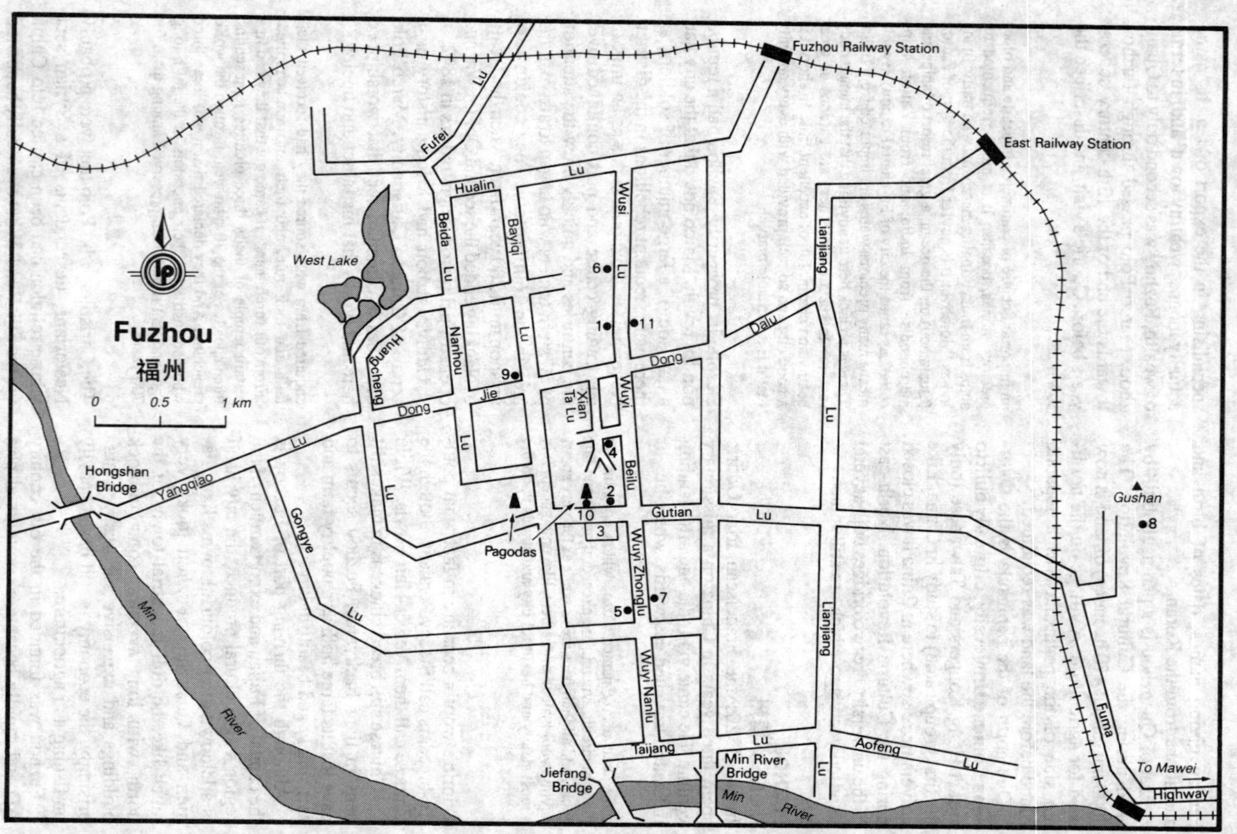
Fuzhou Railway Station
East Railway Station
Fufei
Lu
Hualin
Lu
Beida
Lu
Bayiqi
Lu
Wusi
Lu
West Lake
Fuzhou
福州
0
0.5
1 km
6
1
11
9
Huangcheng
Nanhou
Lu
Dong
Jie
Dong
Wuyi
Xian
Ta Lu
Dalu
Lianjiang
Lu
Lu
Hongshan
Bridge
Yangqiao
Lu
4
Beilu
2
10
Gutian
Lu
3
Pagodas
Gongye
Lu
Wuyi Zhonglu
7
5
Wuyi Nanlu
Lianjiang
Taijiang
Lu
Min River
Bridge
Aofeng
Lu
Lu
Jiefang
Bridge
Min
River
Min
River
Gushan
8
Fuma
To Mawei
Highway

1 Overseas Chinese Hotel, CITS & Post Office
2 Mao Statue
3 Wuyi Square
4 Public Security Bureau
5 Long-Distance Bus Station
6 Minjiang Hotel
7 CAAC
8 Yongquan Monastery
9 Banyan City & Shanghai Restaurant
10 Yu Shan Hotel
11 Foreign Trade Centre Hotel

1 华侨大厦
2 毛主席像
3 五一广场
4 公安局外事科
5 长途汽车站
6 闽江饭店
7 中国民航
8 涌泉寺
9 兵烟城与上海省饭店
10 余山宾馆
11 外国贸易宾馆

to the Nestorian Christians in Fuzhou is unknown, although Marco claims there were 700,000 such households in southern China – probably an exaggeration. A more recent addition to the Christian community was the converts made by the Western missionaries during the 19th and 20th centuries, since Fuzhou was a centre of both Catholic and Protestant missionary activity.

Information & Orientation

Most of Fuzhou lies on the northern bank of the Min River, sprawling northwards in a roughly rectangular shape. The railway station lies on the north-eastern outskirts of the city and the long-distance bus station is at the southern end. The few tourist attractions are scattered. Most of the activity is in the central part of town, roughly between the bus and railway stations, and here you'll find the hotel and tourist facilities.

There are three main roads running north-south and approximately parallel to each other, two of which cross the Min River over old stone bridges. The main road between these two is divided into sections: Wusi Lu, Wuyi Beilu, Wuyi Zhonglu and Wuyi Nanlu. Along this stretch are the long-distance bus station, the CAAC office and the Overseas Chinese Hotel.

Running east-west and cutting across all three roads is Gutian Lu – here you'll find the large town square and a pair of ancient pagodas. Further north is Dong Dalu, which is the main street for shops, restaurants and Fuzhou's nightlife.

CITS This is on the ground floor of the Overseas Chinese Hotel on Wuyi Beilu. The staff speak some English and are friendly and efficient.

Public Security Bureau This office is on Xian Ta Lu which runs off Dong Dalu – see the map.

Money There is a money-exchange counter on the ground floor of the Overseas Chinese Hotel. The main city branch of the Bank of China is on Bayiqi Lu between Dong Jie and Gutian Lu.

Post There is a post office on the ground floor of the Overseas Chinese Hotel.

Maps Good bus maps can be bought from hawkers around the railway station.

Things to See

There's not a great deal to see in Fuzhou. The northern and southern sections of the town are separated by the Min River and the two old stone bridges which link the halves have lost their former charm.

Much of the river front is a ramshackle collection of brick and wooden houses,

hanging out for demolition. On a fine day it can be interesting to watch the junks or the squadrons of sampans dredging the riverbed for sand. Across the Min River is **Nantai Island**, where the foreigners established themselves when Fuzhou became an unequal treaty port in the 19th century.

In the centre of town is a wind-swept square presided over by an enormous **statue of Mao Zedong**. The statue was erected to commemorate the 9th National Congress of the Communist Party where Maoism was enshrined as the new state religion and Lin Biao was officially declared Mao's successor.

In the north-west of Fuzhou is **West Lake Park** *(xīhú gōngyuǎn)* on Hubin Lu, where you'll find the **Fujian Provincial Museum** *(fújiànshěng bówùguǎn)*. Immediately to the east of the town, on **Drum Hill** *(gǔ shān)*, is **Yongquan Monastery** *(yǒngquán sì)*.

The hill takes its name from a large, drum-shaped rock at the summit. The monastery dates back a thousand years and is said to house a collection of 20,000 Buddhist scriptures – of which almost 700 are written in blood. There is a spa next to the monastery.

Places to Stay & Eat

The *Overseas Chinese Hotel* (☎ 557603) *(huáqiáo lǚxíngshè)* on Wusi Lu is the best place to stay. It has its act together – the shops are open, the services actually serve you, and the staff are friendly. It is one of the better hotels in China in this price range. There are no single rooms, but doubles with air-con and own bathroom cost Y75 (you may be able to knock the price down a bit). Take trolley-bus No 51 from the railway station to get there.

Just north of the Overseas Chinese Hotel is the three-star *Minjiang Hotel*, where single rooms cost Y80, and doubles are Y100.

Opposite the Overseas Chinese Hotel is the luxurious *Foreign Trade Centre Hotel* (☎ 50154) *(fújiàn wàimào zhōngxīn jiǔdiàn)* with singles for US$33, doubles for US$40 (US$ and HK$ only accepted). Its facilities include a business centre, disco, coffee shop, bar and Chinese and Western-style restaurants.

In the town centre, next to the Mao statue and an old pagoda, is the rambling *Yu Shan Hotel (yúshān fàndiàn)*, with singles for Y60 and doubles for Y80. The service is next to nil. From the railway station take trolley-bus No 51 to Gutian Lu, then walk or take bus No 8 eastwards.

Over the past few years there's been a

proliferation of small street restaurants. The central *Banyan City/Shanghai Restaurant* complex at the intersection of Dong Jie and Bayiqi Lu is quite popular. The Banyan City's speciality is seafood noodles – somewhat overrated. The Shanghai next door has good pastries and coffee. There are other restaurants at this intersection and along the north side of Dong Jie.

Getting There & Away

Air The CAAC office (☎ 51988) is on Wuyi Zhonglu, and tickets can be bought here or at CITS. Useful connections include flights from Fuzhou to Canton (five times a week), Nanchang (four times a week) and Shanghai (daily).

Bus The long-distance bus station is on Wuyi Zhonglu. Buses head south along the coast from Fuzhou to Quanzhou (from Y9.50 to Y12.40, several buses daily) and Xiamen (from Y15 to Y20, twice daily). Northbound buses go to Fuan (Y11, three buses daily) and Wenzhou (Y27, twice daily).

Just south of the Overseas Chinese Hotel are ticket offices for air-con buses. Daily buses run to Quanzhou (Y16), Xiamen (Y28), Shantou (Y60), Canton (Y110) and Hong Kong (Y145). These buses don't leave until they're very crowded (with seats down the aisles) and depraved kungfu (gongfu) movies are shown on the TV. Most buses leave from the parking lots of the Overseas Chinese and Minjiang hotels.

Train The railway line from Fuzhou heads north and connects the city with the main Shanghai-Canton line at the Yingtan junction. A branch line splits from the Fuzhou-Yingtan line and goes to Xiamen. There are direct trains from Fuzhou to Beijing, Shanghai, Nanchang and Xiamen. The rail route to Xiamen is circuitous and you'd be better off taking the bus.

Boat Passenger ships from Fuzhou depart from the nearby port town of Mawei, southeast of Fuzhou, but don't go there expecting to find a bustling harbour full of ships and junks. The port is a boring sprawl of apartment blocks with a Friendship Store and International Seamen's Club. You can get to Mawei by train from the Fuzhou railway station. There may be buses to Mawei from the large square in front of the Mao statue, but check first.

From Mawei you can take a ship to Shanghai. CITS does not handle tickets and you have to buy them either at the booking office on Dong Dajie in Fuzhou, or from the port at Mawei. Timetables vary but these boats usually go about every five days. Fares range from Y34 (5th class) to Y137 (1st class) and Y180 (special class).

Getting Around

Pedicabs will go anywhere in the central part of the city for Y5 or less. The bus network is good and bus maps are available at the railway station or at the Overseas Chinese Hotel.

Zhejiang 浙江

About 40 million residents now squash into one of China's smallest provinces. Traditionally one of the most prosperous provinces, Zhejiang *(zhèjiāng)* has always been more important than its size would indicate.

The region falls into two distinct sections. The area north of Hangzhou is part of the lush Yangtse River delta, similar to the southern region of Jiangsu Province. The south is mountainous, continuing the rugged terrain of Fujian Province. Intensely cultivated for a thousand years, northern Zhejiang has lost most of its natural vegetation cover and is a flat, featureless plain with a dense network of waterways, canals and irrigation channels. The Grand Canal also ends here – Zhejiang was part of the great southern granary from which food was shipped to the depleted areas of the north.

The growth of Zhejiang's towns was based on their proximity to the sea and their location in some of China's most productive farmland. Hangzhou, Ningbo and Shaoxing have all been important trading centres and ports since the 7th and 8th centuries AD. Their growth was accelerated when, in the 12th century, the Song Dynasty moved court to Hangzhou in the wake of an invasion from the north. Silk was one of the popular exports and today Zhejiang is known as the 'land of silk', producing a third of China's raw silk, brocade and satin.

Hangzhou is the province's capital. To the south-east of the city are several places you can visit without backtracking. A road and railway line run east from Hangzhou to Shaoxing and Ningbo. From Ningbo you could take a bus to Tiantaishan, continue south to Wenzhou and down the coast road into Fujian Province. Jiaxing, on the railway line from Hangzhou to Shanghai, is also open, as is Huzhou in the far north of Zhejiang Province on the shores of Lake Taihu.

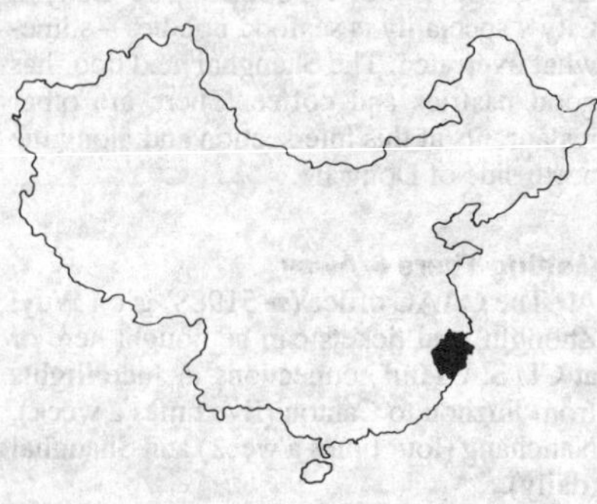

HANGZHOU

(hángzhōu) 杭州

When Marco Polo passed through Hangzhou in the 13th century he described it as one of the finest and most splendid cities in the world. Though Hangzhou had risen to prominence when the southern end of the Grand Canal reached here at the start of the 7th century, it really came into its own after the Song Dynasty was overthrown by the invading Jurchen.

The Jurchen were ancestors of the Manchus who conquered China five centuries later. The Song capital of Kaifeng, along with the emperor and the leaders of the imperial court, was captured by the Jurchen in 1126. The rest of the Song court fled south, finally settling at Hangzhou and founding the Southern Song Dynasty.

China had gone through an economic revolution in previous years, producing huge and prosperous cities, an advanced economy, and a flourishing inter-regional trade. With the Jurchen invasion, the centre of this revolution was pushed south from the Yellow River Valley to the lower Yangtse Valley and to the coast between the Yangtse River and Canton.

While the north remained in the hands of the invaders (who rapidly became

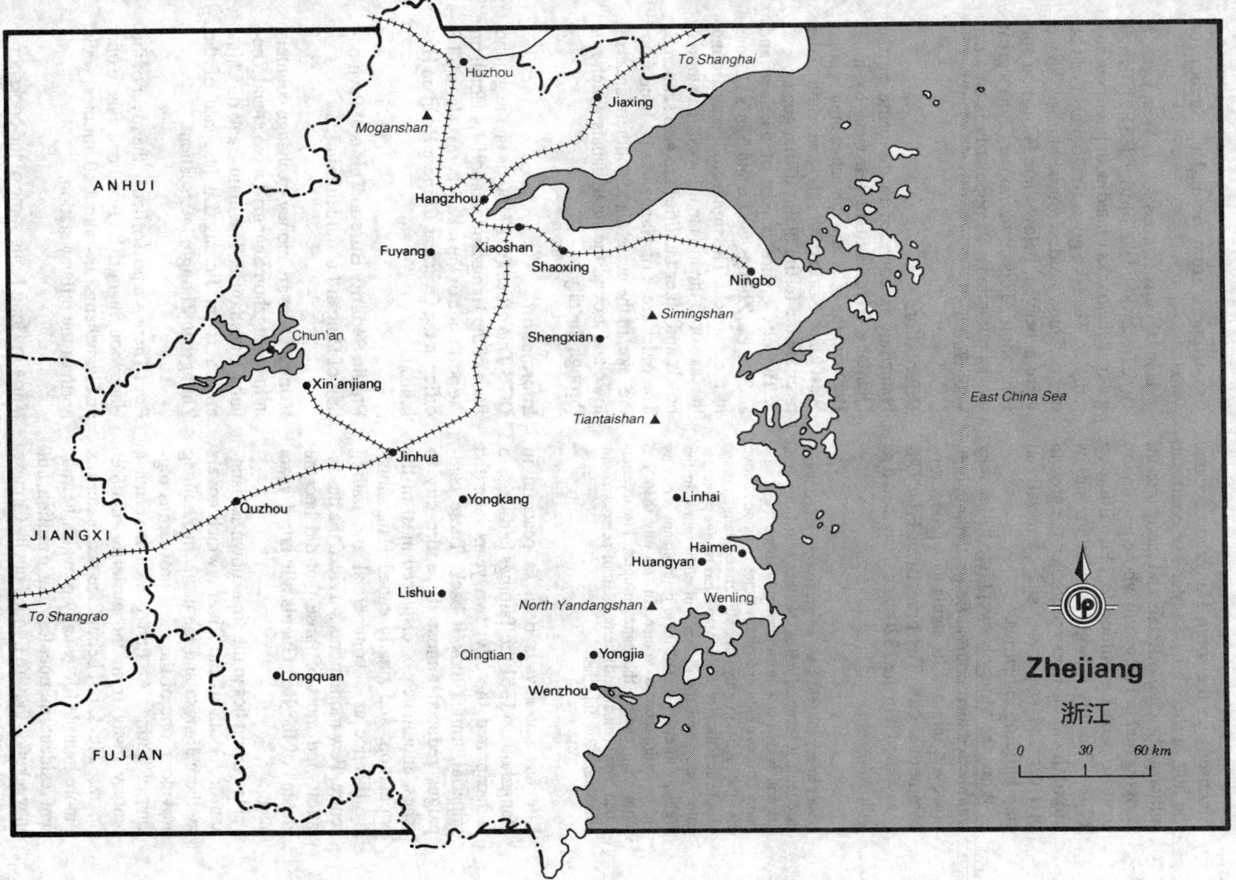
Huzhou
To Shanghai
Jiaxing
Moganshan
ANHUI
Hangzhou
Fuyang
Xiaoshan
Shaoxing
Ningbo
Simingshan
Chun'an
Shengxian
Xin'anjiang
East China Sea
Tiantaishan
Jinhua
Yongkang
Linhai
Quzhou
JIANGXI
Haimen
Huangyan
Lishui
To Shangrao
North Yandangshan
Wenling
Qingtian
Yongjia
Longquan
Wenzhou
Zhejiang
浙江
0
30
60 km
FUJIAN

Sinicised), in the south Hangzhou became the hub of the Chinese state. The court, the military, the civil officials and merchants all congregated in Hangzhou whose population rose from half a million to 1¾ million by 1275. The city's large population and its proximity to the ocean promoted the growth of river and sea trade, and of naval and ship-building industries.

When the Mongols swept into China they established their court at Beijing. Hangzhou, however, retained its status as a prosperous commercial city. The Franciscan Friar Odoric visited it in the 1320s and described it as follows:

> Never in my life did I see so great a city. It contains in circuit a hundred miles. Neither saw I any plot thereof, which was not thoroughly inhabited. I saw many houses of ten or twelve stories high, one above the other. It has mighty large suburbs containing more people than the city itself. Also it has twelve principal gates; and about the distance of eight miles, in the highway to every one of these gates stands a city as big by estimation as Venice...In this city there are more than eleven thousand bridges...I marvelled much how such an infinite number of persons could inhabit and live together.

Life has not always been so peaceful in Hangzhou. In 1861 the Taipings laid siege to and captured the city; two years later the imperial armies took it back. These campaigns reduced almost the entire city to ashes, annihilated or displaced most of the population, and finally ended Hangzhou's significance as a commercial and trading centre. Few monuments survived the devastation, and most of those that did became victims of the Red Guards a hundred years later.

Hangzhou lies in the area known as Jiangnan or 'South of the River', which covers southern Jiangsu and the northern Zhejiang provinces, one of the most prosperous regions of China. At first glance it seems a century away from the austerity of other Chinese cities, but behind the neat exteriors a more humble life usually prevails. Permanent residents number less than a million, but on weekends they're flooded out by Chinese day-trippers from Shanghai, Suzhou or Wuxi.

Hangzhou is famous for its West Lake, a large freshwater lake surrounded by hills and gardens, its banks dotted with pavilions and temples. The lake gives rise to what must be one of China's oldest tourist blurbs: 'Above there is heaven, below there is Suzhou and Hangzhou'. This city is one of China's great tourist attractions; its popularity is on a par with Guilin's.

Orientation

Hangzhou is bounded to the south by the Qiantang River and to the west by hills. Between the hills and the urban area is large West Lake. North of the city and south of the river are the fertile plains of Jiangnan.

The city centre is east of the lake and Jiefang Lu, Zhongshan Lu and Yan'an Lu are its main streets. The sights are spread around the lake or in the hills to the west. The tourist hotels and other facilities are also scattered. The older areas of Hangzhou lie back from the lake, in the eastern and southern areas of town and around the small canals which run through the city.

Information

CITS This office (☎ 27160) is on the ground floor of the Hangzhou Shangri-La Hotel, on the north side of the lake. There is also a CTS office in the Overseas Chinese Hotel on Hubin Lu.

Public Security Bureau This is at the junction of Dingan Lu and Huimin Lu.

Money There are money-exchange counters in the Hangzhou Shangri-La Hotel and Zhejiang Guesthouse. The main Bank of China branch is on Jiefang Lu just east of the Zhongshan Zhonglu intersection.

Post There is a post office in the foyer of the Hangzhou Shangri-La Hotel and a large one on Huancheng Lu – about 10 minutes' walk north of the railway station.

Maps In Hong Kong some of the bookshops

sell a map (in both Chinese and English) which covers Hangzhou, Huangshan and Moganshan and has quite a bit of background information. CTS in Hong Kong stocks a colour pamphlet which shows an isometric perspective of the West Lake with the sights and buildings labelled in English and Chinese – very useful for orientating yourself. In Hangzhou bus maps in Chinese are available from shops around the railway station and the long-distance bus station.

Temple of Inspired Seclusion

(língyǐn sì) 灵隐寺

Lingyin Si, roughly translated as 'Temple of Inspired Seclusion' or 'Temple of the Soul's Retreat', is really Hangzhou's main attraction. Originally built in 326 AD, it has been destroyed and restored no less than 16 times due to war and calamity.

The Cultural Revolution might have seen it razed for good but for the intervention of Zhou Enlai. Accounts vary as to what exactly happened, but it seems there was a confrontation between those who wanted to save the temple and those who wanted to destroy it. The matter eventually went all the way up to Zhou, who gave the order to save both the temple and the sculptures on the rock face opposite. The monks, however, were sent to work in the fields. In the early 1970s a few of the elderly and invalid monks were allowed to come back and live out their last few years in a small outbuilding on the hillside behind the temple.

The present buildings are restorations of Qing Dynasty structures. At the front of the temple is the Hall of the Four Heavenly Guardians and (in the middle of it) a statue of Maitreya, the future Buddha, sits on a platform flanked by two dragons. Behind this hall is the Great Hall, where the magnificent 20-metre-high statue of Siddhartha Gautama sits. This was sculpted from 24 blocks of camphorwood in 1956 and was based on a Tang Dynasty original. Behind the giant statue is a startling montage of 150 small figures.

Facing the temple is Feilai Feng *(fēilái fēng)*, the 'Peak that Flew from Afar'. Some praise must go to the Chinese (or the Indians) for accomplishing thc first successful solo flight of a mountain! This name, so the story goes, came from an Indian monk who visited Hangzhou in the 3rd century and said that the hill looked exactly like one in India and asked when it had flown to China. The rocky surface of the hill is chiselled with 330 sculptures and graffiti from the 10th to the 14th centuries. The earliest sculpture dates back to 951 AD and comprises a group of three Buddhist deities at the right-hand entrance to the Qing Lin Cave. Droves of Chinese people clamber over the sculptures and inscriptions to have their photo taken; the most popular backdrop is the laughing Maitreya (the fat Buddha at the foot of the ridge). There is a vegetarian restaurant beside the Temple.

To get to the temple take bus No 7 to the terminal at the foot of the hills west of Hangzhou. Behind the Lingyin Temple is Northern Peak, which can be climbed via cable car (Y2). From the summit there are sweeping views across the lake and city.

Zhejiang Provincial Museum

(zhèjiāng bówùguǎn) 浙江博物馆

This interesting museum is on Solitary Hill Island *(gūshān)*, a short walk from the Hangzhou Shangri-La Hotel. Its buildings were part of the holiday palace of Emperor Qianlong in the 18th century. Most of the museum is concerned with natural history; there's a large whale skeleton (a female *rhachianectos glaucus cope)* and a dinosaur skeleton. We had one letter from someone who said that visitors should be sure to have the Ming Dynasty eye-wash bowl demonstrated(?!).

Mausoleum of General Yue Fei

(yuèwáng miào) 岳王庙

During the 12th century when China was attacked by Jurchen invaders from the north, General Yue Fei (1103-41) was commander of the Song armies. Despite his successes against the invaders, he was recalled to the Song court where he was executed by a treacherous court official called Qin Gui.

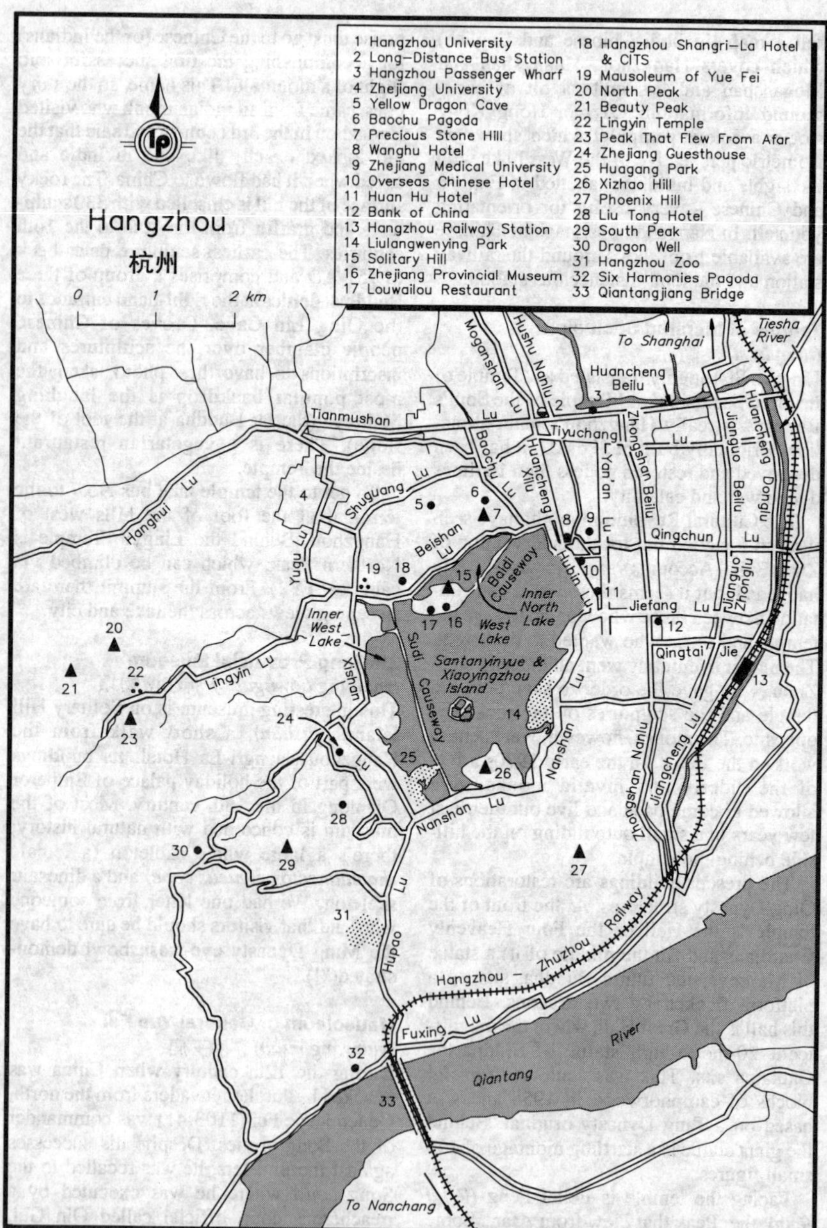
Hangzhou
杭州
0
1
2 km
1 Hangzhou University
2 Long-Distance Bus Station
3 Hangzhou Passenger Wharf
4 Zhejiang University
5 Yellow Dragon Cave
6 Baochu Pagoda
7 Precious Stone Hill
8 Wanghu Hotel
9 Zhejiang Medical University
10 Overseas Chinese Hotel
11 Huan Hu Hotel
12 Bank of China
13 Hangzhou Railway Station
14 Liulangwenying Park
15 Solitary Hill
16 Zhejiang Provincial Museum
17 Louwailou Restaurant
18 Hangzhou Shangri-La Hotel & CITS
19 Mausoleum of Yue Fei
20 North Peak
21 Beauty Peak
22 Lingyin Temple
23 Peak That Flew From Afar
24 Zhejiang Guesthouse
25 Huagang Park
26 Xizhao Hill
27 Phoenix Hill
28 Liu Tong Hotel
29 South Peak
30 Dragon Well
31 Hangzhou Zoo
32 Six Harmonies Pagoda
33 Qiantangjiang Bridge
To Shanghai
Tiesha River
Huancheng Beilu
Moganshan Lu
Hushu Nanlu
Tianmushan Lu
Tiyuchang Lu
Baochu Lu
Huancheng Xilu
Yan'an
Zhongshan Beilu
Jianguo Beilu
Huancheng Donglu
Shuguang Lu
Hanghui Lu
Yugu Lu
Beishan Lu
Baidi Causeway
Inner North Lake
Hubin Lu
Qingchun Lu
Jiefang Lu
Jianguo Zhonglu
Qingtai Jie
Inner West Lake
West Lake
Sudi Causeway
Santanyinyue & Xiaoyingzhou Island
Xishan
Lingyin Lu
Nanshan Lu
Zhongshan Nanlu
Jiangcheng Lu
Hupao Lu
Hangzhou – Zhuzhou Railway
Fuxing Lu
River
Qiantang
To Nanchang

1 杭大
2 长途汽车站
3 杭州客运码头
4 浙江大学
5 黄龙洞
6 保俶塔
7 宝石山
8 王湖宾馆
9 浙江医学院
10 华侨饭店
11 环湖饭店
12 中国银行
13 杭州火车站
14 柳浪闻莺
15 孤山
16 浙江省博物馆
17 楼外楼饭馆
18 杭州饭店
19 岳飞墓
20 北高峰
21 美高峰
22 灵隐寺
23 飞来峰
24 浙江宾馆
25 花港公园
26 夕照山
27 凤凰山
28 六通宾馆
29 南高峰
30 龙井
31 杭州动物园
32 六和塔
33 钱塘江桥

Twenty years later, in 1163, Song emperor Xiao Zong rehabilitated him and had his corpse reburied at the present site. Yue was eventually deified.

The mausoleum of this soldier-patriot is in a compound bounded by a red-brick wall on Huanhu Lu, a few minutes' walk west of the Hangzhou Shangri-La Hotel. It was ransacked during the Cultural Revolution but has since been restored.

Inside is a glazed clay statue of the general and, on the wall, paintings of scenes from his life – including one of his back being tattooed with the words 'Loyal to the Last'.

Protect Chu Tower
(bǎochù tǎ) 保俶塔

The original Baochu Ta was erected on Jewellery Hill in 938 during the Song Dynasty. It was built to ensure the safe return of Hangzhou's Prince Qian Chu from an audience with the emperor. In China there is an old saying something like, 'Keeping company with the emperor is like keeping company with a tiger' – you had to make sure you didn't get eaten. The present tower is a 1933 reconstruction, 45.3 metres high and resembling a Stone Age rocket ship. It stands just north of Huanhu Lu (follow the steps) on the northern side of the lake. In the early morning you may find elderly Chinese women practising taiji there and old men airing their birds. From the tower there are tracks south along the ridge through bamboo groves; dotted along the tracks are temples and shrines.

Six Harmonies Pagoda
(liùhé tǎ) 六和塔

To the south-west of the city stands an enormous rail-and-road bridge which spans the Qiantang River. Close by is the 60-metre-high octagonal Six Harmonies Pagoda named after the six codes of Buddhism. As a legacy of the feudal past, the pagoda was cited for demolition during the Cultural Revolution, but since this would have required an army of experts the project was called off. The pagoda was originally built as a lighthouse although it was also supposed to have some sort of magical power to halt the tidal bore which thundered up the Qiantang River in mid-September every year.

West Lake 西湖
(xī hú)

There are 30 lakes in China called Xi Hu, but this one is by far the most famous. It is a pretty sight, but if you travel 1000 km just for the water you'll probably be disappointed. The lake was originally a lagoon adjoining the Qiantang River. In the 8th century the governor of Hangzhou had it

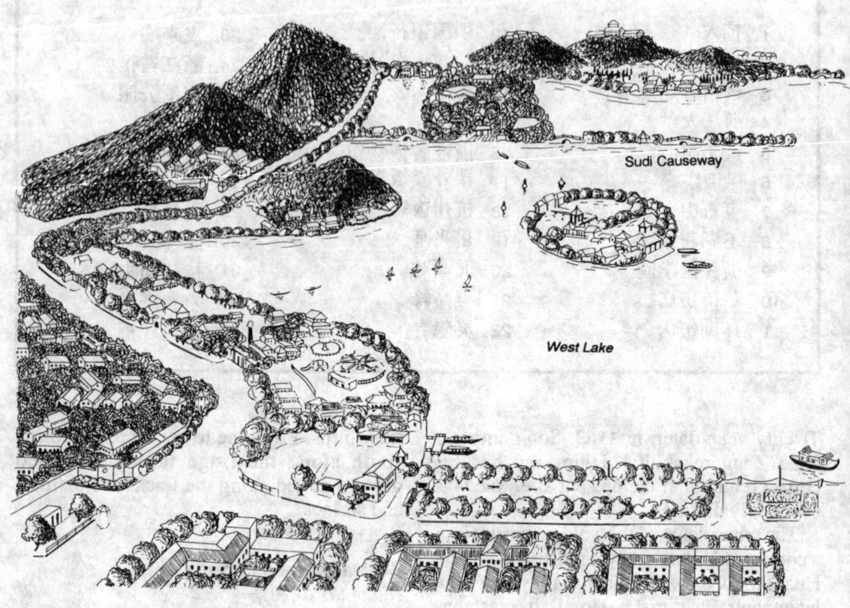

dredged; later a dike was built which cut it off from the river completely.

The lake is about three km long and a bit under three km wide. Two causeways, the Baidi and the Sudi, split the lake into sections. The causeways each have a number of arched bridges, large enough for small boats and ferries to pass under. The sights are scattered around the lake, though most of them tend to be uninspiring pavilions or bridges with fanciful names. However, the whole being greater than the sum of the parts, it's still a pretty place to wander around and has a romantic feel on a fresh night.

The largest island in the lake is Solitary Hill *(gūshān)* – the location of the Provincial Museum, the Louwailou Restaurant and Zhongshan Park *(zhōngshān gōngyuǎn)*. During the 18th century Zhongshan Park was once part of an imperial palace, but was renamed after 1911 in honour of Sun Yatsen. The Baidi causeway links the island to the mainland.

Most of the other sights are connected with famous people who once lived there – poets, perhaps an alchemist who bubbled up longevity pills, or an emperor who used to roll around his private garden there with his palace concubines. One of these sights is the Pavilion for Releasing Crane on Solitary Hill Island. It was built in memory of the Song poet Lin Hejing who, it is said, refused to serve the emperor and remained a bachelor his whole life. His only pastime was planting plum trees and fondling his crane.

Hangzhou's botanical gardens even have a sequoia presented by Richard Nixon on his 1972 visit.

Santanyinyue *(sāntán yìnyuè)* is another island in the lake. Most guidebooks and maps refer to it as 'Three Pools Mirroring the Moon' but, in fact, the island is named after three poles which stick out of the water. According to the story, in mid-August, when the moon is at its largest and roundest, it is reflected in the water between the three

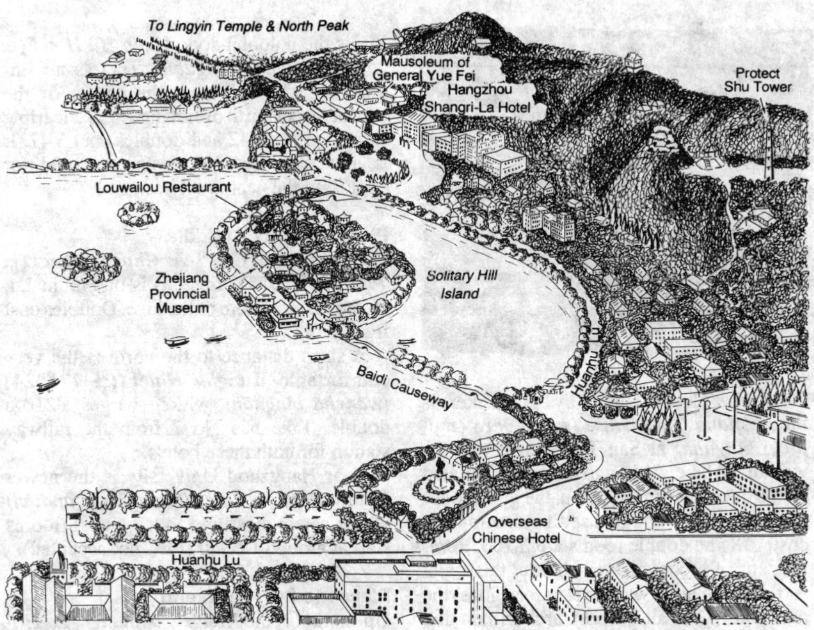

poles. At this time the locals put lighted candles in the hollow tops of the poles. Hence, the correct translation of the name should be something like 'Three Poles Fixing the Moon'. (Santanyinyue is next to Xiaoyingzhou Island in the south part of the lake).

If you want to contemplate the moon in the privacy of your own boat there are a couple of places around the lake where you can hire paddle boats and go for a slow spin. Boats can also be chartered for a lake cruise from the small docks along the east side of the lake. On Sundays and holidays, many Chinese families charter covered boats for picnic outings.

Other

Some of the more interesting areas for walking are in the eastern part of town, around the scungy canals which cut through the urban areas. There are lots of quaint brick and wooden houses, and washing hung out to dry along the narrow lanes.

The Hangzhou Zoo has Manchurian tigers, though to our untrained eyes they looked no different from other tigers.

About 60 km north of Hangzhou is Moganshan. Pleasantly cool at the height of summer, Moganshan was developed as a resort for Europeans living in Shanghai and Hangzhou during the colonial era.

Places to Stay – bottom end

The cheapest place to stay, when there's a vacancy, is the foreign students' dorm at *Hangzhou University*, north of the lake on Tianmushan Lu. Clean doubles cost Y12 per person. There are almost always vacant rooms during the summer; at other times of the year it's touch and go. To get there take a No 152 bus from the railway station and ask for *hángzhōu dàxué*. At the university gate, ask for *wàiguórénde sùshè* (foreign students' dormitory).

Another place favoured by backpackers is the *Zhejiang Guesthouse* (☎ 777988) *(zhéjiāng bīnguǎn)* at San Tai Shan 68, to the west of the lake. Although it is rather isolated on the outskirts of Hangzhou, the guesthouse is in in a quiet woodland setting. Dorm beds cost Y18 and double rooms are Y100. Reminiscent of a convalescent home, this quiet and relaxing hotel was (so the story goes) the personal HQ of all-purpose arch-villain and traitor Marshal Lin Biao. Underneath the grounds is a labyrinth of tunnels and rooms which appear to have been used as a military command post. These have been flung open to the general public, and Chinese tour groups are led through them – check out the massive indoor swimming pool. Building No 1 is supposed to have been Lin's private residence, and a dormitory for foreigners has been set up in the meeting room. To get to there take bus No 28 from near the long-distance bus station, get off anywhere north of the lake and then switch to bus No 27 to the hotel. The last No 27 bus is around 6.30 pm. From the railway station take bus No 7 to the west side of the lake and then change to bus No 27. Coming back from the hotel, bus No 27 terminates on Pin Hai Lu, which is a street running off Yan'an Lu close to the east shore of the lake.

South of the Zhejiang Guesthouse is the similar garden-style *Liu Tong Hotel* (☎ 773376) *(liùtōng bīnguǎn)* with dorms for Y15 and doubles for Y74.

Right on the east side of the lake, on Hubin Lu, is the colonial-style *Huan Hu Hotel* (☎ 25491) *(huánhú bīnguǎn)*. There's no English sign but it's near the corner of the second street north of Jiefang Lu. Basic triple rooms go for Y42 and doubles cost Y47. It is in a good area for restaurants and for exploring the nearby city centre.

Places to Stay – middle

The convenient *Overseas Chinese Hotel* (☎ 77401) *(huáqiáo bīnguǎn)* is on Hubin Lu, on the eastern shore of the lake. Doubles cost from Y147.

A short distance to the north is the very comfortable *Wanghu Hotel* (☎ 771024) *(wánghú bīnguǎn)*, which charges Y210 a double. Take bus No 7 from the railway station for both these hotels.

Near Hangzhou University is the newer *Yellow Dragon Hotel (huánglóng fàndiàn)* which caters mostly to tour groups. Rooms start at around US$40 (FEC not accepted).

Places to Stay – top end

Up-market is the *Hangzhou Shangri-La Hotel* (☎ 777951) on the north side of the lake. Single rooms, with a hillside view, cost from US$80 and doubles, with a view of the lake, cost US$135 (FEC not accepted). It is very expensive, but the facilities are great. To get there take bus No 7 from the railway station; it goes past the hotel (though if you can afford this hotel, you probably don't need to take the bus!).

Places to Eat

At the corner of Jiefang Lu and Zhongshan Lu is a friendly ground floor restaurant with oodles of noodles and more elaborate fare (shrimp, fish, eel) upstairs. There's a vegetarian restaurant on You Dian Lu, just east of the intersection with Yan'an Lu.

The *Louwailou (lóuwài lóu)* on Solitary Hill Island has good, cheap food. Its specialities are West Lake fish in vinegar sauce, and boneless fish in sauce.

Next door to the Hangzhou Shangri-La is the very trendy *Have A Bite*. Several counters offer ice-cream and you can get Chinese and Western food from around Y1 to Y6 per dish. At night the place is packed out with young Hangzhou residents partying to the sounds of a live string quartet.

There are several inexpensive restaurants along Hang Da Lu, the street that leads to the main Hangzhou University gate.

Tea Hangzhou is famous for its tea, especially longjing or Dragon Well green tea, which is grown in the Longjing district west of West Lake. Unlike most Chinese people, Hangzhou residents take great care in selecting the water and utensils with which to brew their tea, and visiting teahouses is a popular local pastime. The taste for tea carries over into Hangzhou cuisine, which features many tea-flavoured dishes. Among the local specialties are fresh-water shrimp stir-fried with Dragon Well tea leaves and carp stuffed with tea leaves.

Getting There & Away

Air The CAAC office (☎ 24259) is at 304 Tiyuchang Lu, but all foreigners are referred to CITS. Useful connections include daily flights from Hangzhou to Beijing and Canton plus regular flights to Hong Kong, Shanghai, Xiamen, Xi'an, Wuhan and other major Chinese cities.

Bus The long-distance bus station is on Hushu Nanlu just north of the intersection with Huancheng Lu. There are several buses a day to Shanghai (Y11), Tunxi (Y13), Hefei and Tiantaishan. There may be buses to Shaoxing and Ningbo; if not, take the train.

Train There are direct trains from Hangzhou to Fuzhou, Nanchang, Shanghai and Canton, and east to the small towns of Shaoxing and Ningbo. For trains to the north you must first go to Shanghai. Hangzhou railway station has a separate ticket booking office for foreigners – it's through a doorway in the main booking hall.

Tourist-price tickets from Hangzhou to Shanghai are Y14 for a hard-seat. The trip takes about three hours with numerous trains daily.

Tourist-price tickets to Canton are Y96 (hard-seat), Y146 (hard-sleeper) and Y320 (soft-sleeper). The trip takes about 28 hours, but depends on the train.

Trains to Canton go via Nanchang, the capital of Jiangxi Province, or via the rail junction of Yingtan.

From Yingtan a branch line extends to Fuzhou and Xiamen (both in Fujian Province on the south-east coast). There are direct trains from Hangzhou to Fuzhou. There is no direct train from Hangzhou to Xiamen; you must first go to Shanghai. However, you can catch a train to Fuzhou and then catch a bus to Xiamen.

Boat You can take a boat up the Grand Canal from Hangzhou to Suzhou. Boats leave twice a day at 5.30 am and 5.50 pm from the dock near the corner of Huancheng Lu and Hushu Nanlu, in the northern part of town. Tickets are available from the booking office at the dock and cost Y9, Y12, and Y20 depending on the class of service. For more details see the section on Suzhou in the Jiangsu chapter.

SHAOXING

(shàoxīng) 绍兴

Shaoxing is in the centre of the waterway system on the northern Zhejiang plain. Since early times, it's been a major administrative town and an agricultural market centre, though it never attained the same heights as neighbouring Hangzhou and Ningbo. Shaoxing is connected by train to Hangzhou (there may also be a bus connection). You can continue by bus from Shaoxing to Tiantaishan and Wenzhou.

NINGBO

(níngbō) 宁波

Like Shaoxing, Ningbo rose to prominence in the 7th and 8th centuries as a trading port from which ships carrying Zhejiang's exports would sail to Japan and the Ryukyu Islands and along the Chinese coast.

By the 16th century the Portuguese had established themselves here, working as entrepreneurs in the trade between Japan and

China since the Chinese were forbidden to deal with the Japanese.

Although Ningbo was officially opened to Western traders after the first Opium War, its once-flourishing trade gradually declined as Shanghai boomed. By that time the Ningbo traders had taken their money to Shanghai and formed the basis of its wealthy Chinese business community. Today Ningbo is a city of over 250,000 people with fishing, salt production, textiles and food processing its primary industries. Some travellers find the seaport atmosphere interesting, others a bore.

Places to Stay

Accommodation is available at the *Ningbo Hotel (níngbō fàndiàn)* for Y15 per person in multi-bed rooms, and doubles cost Y130. The nicer *Asia Gardens* costs about the same for a double but has no dorm.

Getting There & Away

Ningbo is linked by train to Hangzhou (there may also be a bus connection) and by ship to Shanghai. There are daily buses from Ningbo to Tiantaishan and Wenzhou (a small town on the Zhejiang coast). From Wenzhou buses run to Fuan in Fujian Province and on to Fuzhou and Xiamen.

QIKOU

About 60 km south of Ningbo is the small town of Qikou, the home of Chiang Kaishek. It has, surprisingly, become a Chinese tourist destination. Rumour has it that after Chiang's death, his body was secretly returned to China for burial at Qikou.

TIANTAISHAN

(tiāntái shān) 天台山

Tiantaishan is noted for its many Buddhist monasteries which date back to the 6th century. While the mountain itself may not be considered sacred, it is very important as the home of the Tiantai Buddhist sect, which is heavily influenced by Taoism.

From Tiantai it's a 3½-km hike to the **Gouqingsi Monastery** at the foot of the mountain (you can stay overnight here). From the monastery a road leads 25 km to **Huadingfeng** (over 1100 metres high) where a small village has been built. On alternate days public buses run up to Huadingfeng. From here you can continue by foot for one or two km to the **Baijingtai Temple** on the summit of the mountain.

On the other days the bus goes to different parts of the mountain, passing **Shiliang Waterfall**. From the waterfall it's a good five to six km walk along small paths to Huadingfeng.

Tiantaishan is in the east of Zhejiang. Buses link it with Hangzhou, Shaoxing, Ningbo and Wenzhou.

WENZHOU

(wēnzhōu) 温州

Wenzhou is an ancient city founded at the end of the 4th century. As a result of another treaty with Britain, its ocean port was opened to foreign trade in 1877, though no foreign settlement developed. The few foreigners who did come here were missionaries and trade officials – the latter mainly concerned with the once-profitable tea trade.

The town lies on the south-east coast of Zhejiang Province. From Wenzhou you can continue by bus to Fuan in Fujian Province, and from there buses run to the provincial capital of Fuzhou. There are also passenger ships between Wenzhou and Shanghai.

CHUN'AN COUNTY

(chún'ān xiàn) 淳安县

Chun'an County, in western Zhejiang, is known for its Lake of a Thousand Islands. Worth investigating would be a route from Hangzhou – you'd cross the lake by boat, and perhaps take a bus to Huangshan in Anhui Province.

Anhui 安徽

The provincial borders of Anhui *(ānhuī)* were defined by the Qing government and, except for a few changes to the boundary with Jiangsu, have since remained pretty much the same. Northern Anhui forms part of the North China Plain where the Han Chinese settled in large numbers during the Han Dynasty. The southern area, below the Yangtse River, was not settled until the 7th and 8th centuries. Today Anhui has a population of over 50 million.

The Yangtse cuts through the middle of this province. Most of Anhui's tourist attractions are in the south, and are more easily accessible from either Hangzhou or Shanghai than from the provincial capital of Hefei.

Most famous of the sights open to foreigners are the spectacular Huangshan (Yellow Mountains), in the far south of the province, and the nearby Jiuhuashan (Nine Flowers Mountains). On the eastern edge of the province, south of the Yangtse River, are the Ma'anshan. The Yangtse River ports of Guichi and Wuhu are convenient jumping-off points for the Jiuhuashan and Huangshan mountains.

HUANGSHAN

(huángshān) 黄山

Huangshan (Yellow Mountains) is the name of the 72-peak range lying in the south of Anhui Province, 280 km west of Hangzhou. The highest peak is Lotus Flower Peak (Lianhua Feng) at 1800 metres, followed by Bright Summit Peak (Guangming Ding) and Heavenly Capitol Peak (Tiandu Feng). In all, 30 peaks rise above 1500 metres.

The area has been a famous scenic spot for at least 1200 years, since the Tang Dynasty emperor Tian Biao gave it its present name in the 8th century. Over the centuries the range has been an inspiration for Chinese poets and painters, attracted to the jagged peaks washed by a 'sea of clouds', the ancient pines clinging to the rock face and the nearby hot springs.

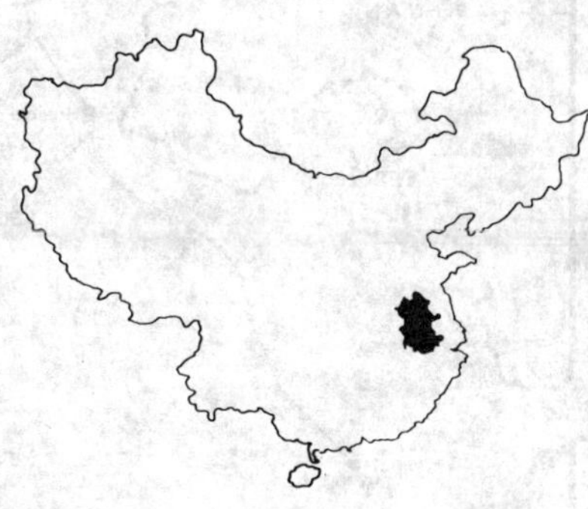

Li Bai, a Chinese poet of the Tang Dynasty, once took a trip to Huangshan and wrote:

Huangshan is hundreds of thousands of feet high,
With numerous soaring peaks lotus-like,
Rock pillars shooting up to kiss empyrean roses,
Like so many lilies grown amid a sea of gold.

Li got the altitude wrong, since most people climb Huangshan without oxygen masks. Don't expect the Himalayas, but by any standards the view from the top is worth the effort of reaching it. There's some rugged scenery, a spectacular sunrise, and the strange sight of hundreds of people scaling the endless stone staircases. This is not person-in-the-wilderness stuff; there are stone steps the whole way to the top of the mountain, concrete paths connecting the sights, and masses of Chinese tourists. With some effort, however, you can find side paths that are virtually deserted.

Information & Orientation

Buses pull into Huangshan Gate at the foot of the range, just beyond the village of Tang Kou *(tāngkǒu)*. Up a bit further is a base camp of sorts which is really an overgrown tourist resort with a few hotels, a post office,

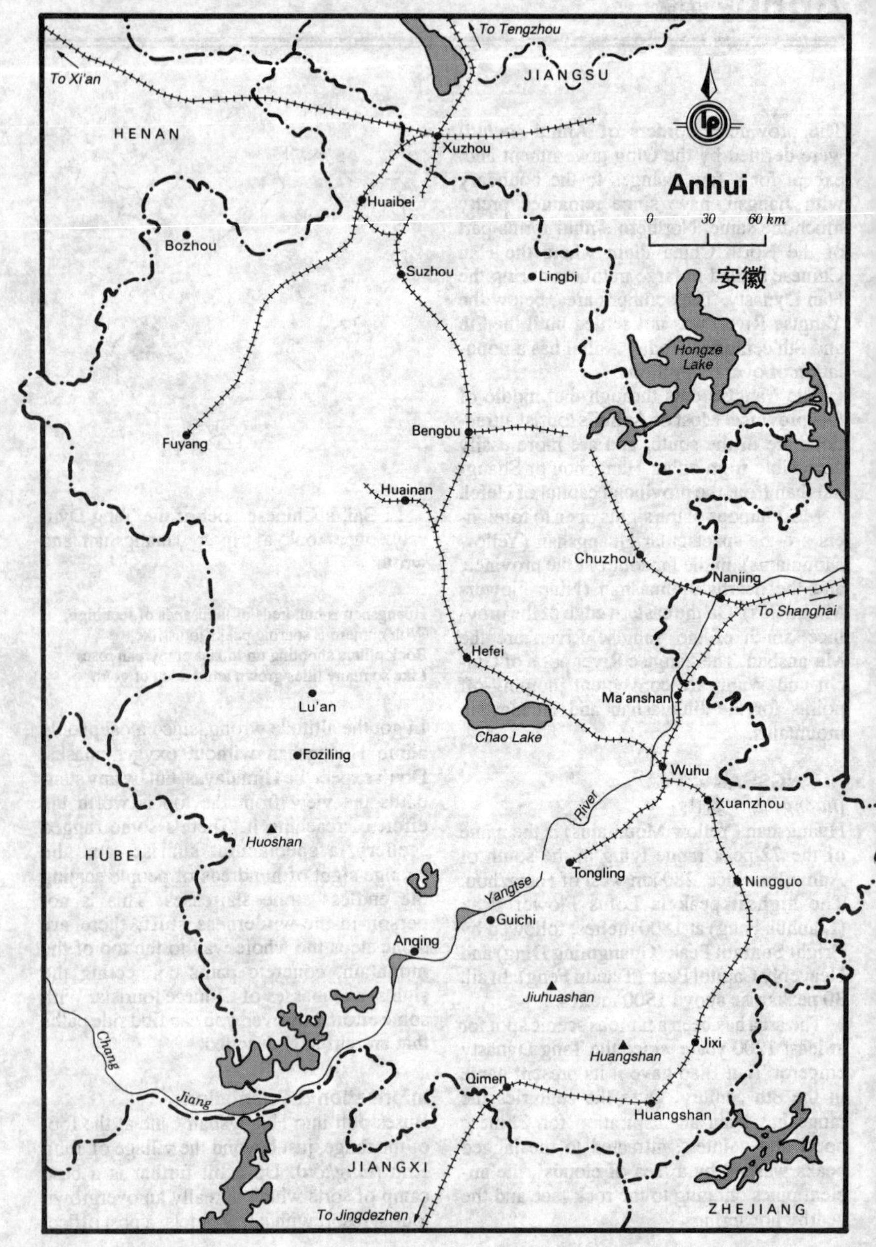
To Tengzhou
To Xi'an
JIANGSU
HENAN
Xuzhou
Anhui
0 30 60 km
Huaibei
Bozhou
Suzhou
Lingbi
安徽
Hongze Lake
Bengbu
Fuyang
Huainan
Chuzhou
Nanjing
To Shanghai
Hefei
Ma'anshan
Lu'an
Chao Lake
Foziling
Wuhu
Xuanzhou
River
Huoshan
HUBEI
Tongling
Ningguo
Yangtse
Guichi
Anqing
Jiuhuashan
Chang
Jixi
Huangshan
Qimen
Jiang
Huangshan
JIANGXI
To Jingdezhen
ZHEJIANG

a hot-springs public bath and two Friendship stores. The camp is split down the middle by a narrow stream, with the tourist facilities on either side. The next stage up is the cable-car terminal, where the main length of stair-steps also begins. At the summit is another small collection of hotels and several side trails.

Scaling the Heights

The usual Huangshan tourist experience means proceeding through four levels to reach the top of the mountain. There are at least three ways to accomplish this: the short, hard way; the long, hard way; and the very short, easy way. All ascents start from the Huangshan Gate, whether on foot or not.

Most climbers take a bus or a combination of buses between the gate and the main trail, which starts from the Yungusi cable-car terminal, about half-way up the mountain. Minibuses from the gate only go as far as the hot springs area (Y2), where you must catch a second bus to the cable-car terminal (Y2). There are also larger buses that go direct from Huangshan Gate to the terminal for Y4. If you prefer to walk, adding three more hours to the basic climb, there are steps that intersect the winding road at several points before connecting with the main trail.

From the cable-car terminal you can choose between taking the 15-minute cable-car ride to the summit or gasping up a steep 7½ km flight of steps. This climb can be done in two hours, though more comfortably in three or four. The east steps can be a killer if you push yourself too hard, but it's definitely easier than going up the west steps. Either way, there's an entrance fee of Y16 for all hikers, payable in FEC only.

If you decide to take the cable car, bring along enough cash. The round-trip charge is Y24, payable in FEC only (if you want to pay in RMB you'll be charged double). There's no way to get the Chinese price and no way to purchase a one-way ticket. You can't purchase a ticket at the summit either.

At the top of the mountain is the Beihai Hotel and, further on, the Xihai Hotel. Both have restaurants which are only open at meal times so if you happen to have arrived between meals, tough luck! From here you can make your descent via the incredibly long and steep western steps. If you came up this way don't say we didn't warn you! The western path has some spectacular scenery, which will be much more enjoyable if you're clambering down the steps rather than gasping up them. On your way down watch out for the 'Rock that Flew', a rectangular boulder perched on an outcrop as if it had flown there. Further down is a look-out point on top of a cliff from which, if the weather is good, you'll be able to see Lotus Peak. The western path leads down to the Jade Screen Tower Hotel and the Mid-Level Monastery and back to the base camp. Between the hotel and the monastery you can sidetrack up the stairway to Heavenly Capitol Peak, the third highest in the range at 1829 metres.

If you take the eastern route up and the western route down, you can do the whole circuit comfortably in about 10 hours. (If you think you're having a hard time, then spare a thought for the army of porters who carry supplies up the mountain each day – crates of drink bottles, baskets of food and armchairs strung on bamboo poles over the shoulder.) On the other hand, if you spend a night or two on the mountain, then you've got plenty of time for interesting side-trips.

Guides aren't necessary for the climb as you just follow the paths and steps, and the place is crawling with people so you can't get lost. If you do want a guide then ask CITS (a couple of private entrepreneurs will do it cheaper but you probably won't find them – and it's not worth having them if you don't speak Chinese).

If you want, you can be carried up the mountain by two porters who take you in a chair slung between bamboo poles. The rate hasn't varied in years – still Y300 for the round trip, of which Y150 goes to the government to pay insurance in case they drop you. The porters carry passengers up one day and bring them down the next.

Sunrise over Huangshan shouldn't be missed. Every morning before daybreak the Chinese throng the Fresh Breeze Terrace, in front of the Beihai Hotel, to watch the sun

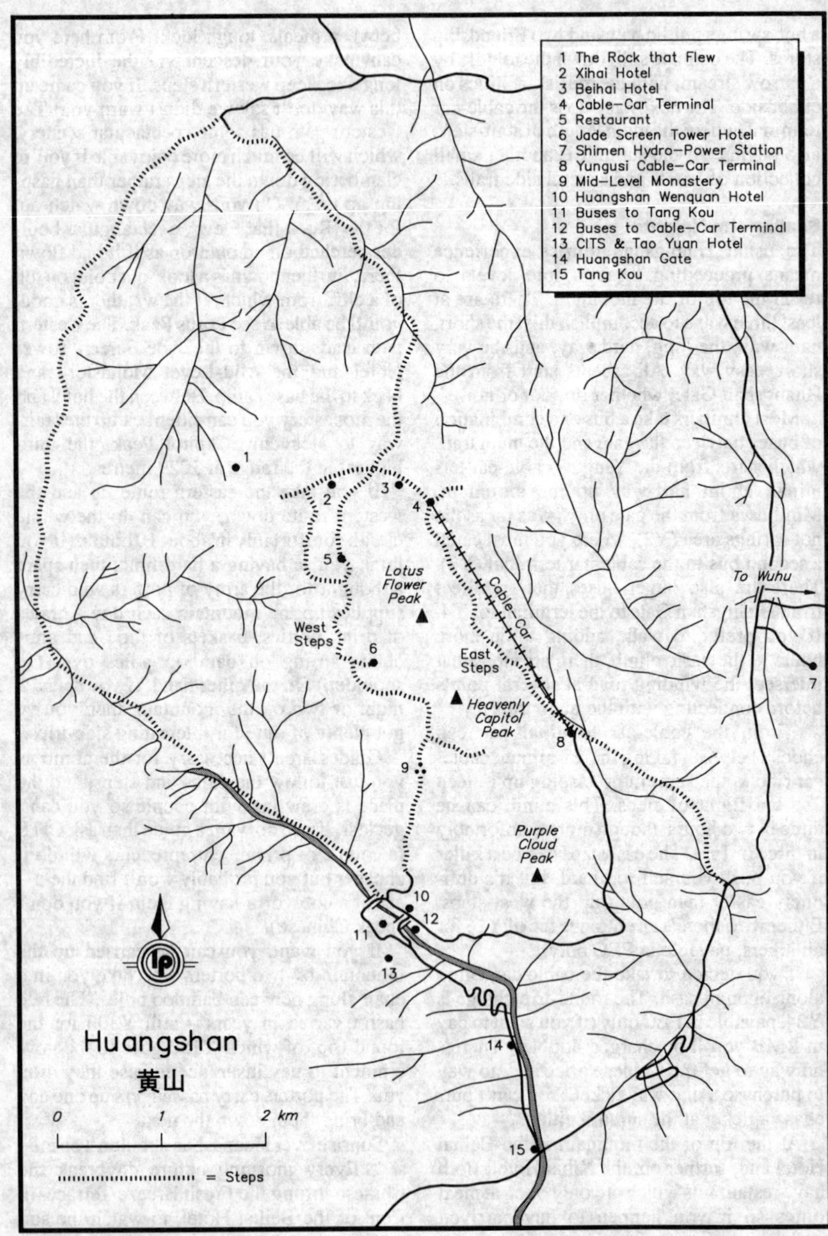
1 The Rock that Flew
2 Xihai Hotel
3 Beihai Hotel
4 Cable-Car Terminal
5 Restaurant
6 Jade Screen Tower Hotel
7 Shimen Hydro-Power Station
8 Yungusi Cable-Car Terminal
9 Mid-Level Monastery
10 Huangshan Wenquan Hotel
11 Buses to Tang Kou
12 Buses to Cable-Car Terminal
13 CITS & Tao Yuan Hotel
14 Huangshan Gate
15 Tang Kou
Lotus Flower Peak
West Steps
East Steps
Cable-Car
Heavenly Capitol Peak
Purple Cloud Peak
To Wuhu
Huangshan
黄山
0
1
2 km
= Steps

1 飞来石	6 玉屏楼	11 至汤口汽车
2 西海饭店	7 石门电话	12 至索道站汽车
3 北海饭店	8 云谷寺索道站	13 桃园宾馆
4 客运索道	9 半山寺	14 黄山大门
5 饭馆	10 黄山温泉宾馆	15 汤口

rise from the immense North Sea. The North Sea is the name given to the massive expanse of clouds covering the north of the range, through which other peaks protrude. This is communal sightseeing at its best and the noise generated by several hundred Chinese tourists is almost as incredible as the sunrise itself!

The Hot Springs, between Purple Cloud Peak and Peach Blossom Peak, is a good place to contemplate the thoughts of Wang Zhaowen, China's 'famous critic of art and literature', who makes these poignant comments about Huangshan:

> I firmly believe that the Huangshan tourist must use his own imagination. If you approach those picturesque sights with borrowed vision, the Huangshan pines, thousands upon thousands in number and so beautifully varied in shape, will not be able to catch your eye and strike your fancy.
>
> It seems to me that the tendency toward formularisation exists not only in artistic and literary creation but also in sightseeing recreation. Although the Huangshan beauties will never be diminished by stereotyped formularisation on the part of the tourist, yet the existence of such stereotypes reflects that even in tourism there exists an ideological conflict between independent thinking and slavish mentality.
>
> The pleasure of touring Huangshan cannot be obtained by painstaking effort to confirm the discoveries of other people. If one is satisfied with ready-made briefings by a tourist guide, one is sure to stand in need of originality and inventiveness in other aspects of life.

Places to Stay & Eat

In the main Huangshan climbing area there are five locations with hotels and restaurants.

Tang Kou *(tāngkǒu)* The cheapest and most accessible hotels are in the village of Tang Kou, just below Huangshan Gate on the banks of a swift-moving mountain stream. The village is also relatively free of would-be guides and hawkers selling maps (the next area up, where most tourists stay, is positively clogged with them).

Of the three hotels that take foreigners, the *Xiao Yao (Free and Unfettered) Hotel* is the best. All rooms cost Y25 per person and include a private bath with hot water (evening only) and TV.

Nearby are the *Tang Kou Hotel (tāngkǒu bīnguǎn)* and the *Tian Shan Zhuan Hotel (tiānshān zhuāng)*, which charge the same rates as the Xiao Yao but aren't as well maintained. To get to Tang Kou from Huangshan Gate, where most buses from the lowlands terminate, take either a motorcycle-taxi for Y1 (the drivers may ask more, but that's the usual rate), or walk – it's only a couple of km.

Tang Kou has several small, private restaurants on the cobblestone street next to the stream, and others scattered through the village. Local specialities include roast mountain frogs and wild mushrooms, as well as locally grown Ma Fou green tea for Y20 per katy (though vendors will ask 10 times this amount from foreigners). (The katy or catty is an ancient Chinese measurement for fruits and vegetables, equivalent to 0.6 kg.)The corner place opposite the Xiao Yao Hotel has an English menu and can prepare vegetarian dishes.

Hot Springs More expensive hotels are clustered at the next stop, where you'll find the hot-springs bathhouse and CITS office.

The big *Tao Yuan Hotel* (☎ 2295, 2381)

(táoyuán bīnguǎn) charges Y120 for a double, Y170 for a room with two double beds and Y180 for its cheaper rooms in the annexe. CITS operates the Tao Yuan and it's really poorly run.

Across the bridge from the Tao Yuan is the better *Huangshan Wenquan Hotel* (☎ 2196) *(huángshān wénquán bīnguǎn)* where rooms range from Y76 and Y140 if you have an advance booking and from Y100 and Y160 if you haven't.

Both hotels have restaurants and there are also noodle vendors on the street in the mornings and evenings.

Yungusi Cable-Car Terminal Next up, at the lower cable-car terminal, is the *Yungushan Zhuan (Huangshan Yungu Hotel)* (☎ 2444) *(yúngǔ shānzhuāng)*, a converted monastery where doubles are a steep Y200. This location has little to recommend it, unless you've climbed from Tang Kou in the afternoon and need a night's sleep before tackling the rest of the steps.

Summit (North Sea) At the summit of the mountain, near the upper cable-car terminal, are two hotels.

The *Beihai Hotel* (☎ 2555) *(běihǎi bīnguǎn)* charges Y60 per person in single or double rooms, but is almost always full so it's best to call ahead. In each room are thick padded jackets which you'll need if you go out in the early morning to watch the sunrise: depending on the time of year you may also need them during the day.

Dormitories in the large barracks nearby hold at least a hundred people each on bunk beds and cost Y10 for Chinese people – but foreigners aren't usually permitted.

A bit further along the trail is the impressive *Xihai Hotel* (☎ 2200) *(xīhǎi bīnguǎn)*, a Hong Kong-China joint venture that was designed by Swedish architects. All rooms have heaters and round-the-clock hot water; not surprisingly, everything works. For this you must part with US$65 per room (FEC not acceptable).

Both places serve food only during designated eating hours which can be a major inconvenience if you happen to arrive hungry between the posted times.

The Beihai has two restaurants on the ground floor but the set meal is expensive. Outside is a canteen where you can get basic Chinese meals for a few yuan. The Xihai has two full-service restaurants, one Chinese and one Western, plus a cafe that serves food and drinks throughout the day.

Western Path Midway down the mountain, along the western path, is the *Jade Screen Tower Hotel* (☎ 2444) *(yùpínglóu bīnguǎn)* where basic accommodation is Y30 per person. Further down is the *Mid-Level Monastery (bànshān sì)*, which is now used as a hotel and has similar rates to the Jade Screen Tower.

The Jade Screen Tower Hotel has a restaurant, and there is a small restaurant just before the hostel on your way down the mountain.

Getting There & Away

Air CAAC has flights from the nearby airport at Tunxi to Shanghai (four times weekly), Guangzhou (twice weekly), Nanjing (four times weekly), Beijing (twice weekly), and Hefei (daily).

Bus Buses from Tunxi cost Y4 and take 1½ hours to reach Huangshan Gate. Other buses come from Nanjing (Y16, eight hours), Hangzhou (Y15, seven hours) and Shanghai (Y25, 10 hours). There are also buses from Wuhu and Guichi on the Yangtse River.

Train The railway station at Yingtan is the jumping-off point for Huangshan and Jingdezhen. If you are coming from Hefei take a train to Wuhu, cross the river there and take another train to Yingtan via Tunxi.

TUNXI

(túnxī) 屯溪

South of Huangshan is the old trading town of Tunxi, which may make a worthwhile stopover. Tunxi is connected by bus to Huangshan, Hangzhou and Jingdezhen and

Top: Labrang Monastery, Xiahe (RS)
Bottom Left: Riverside houses, Fuzhou (AS)
Bottom Right: West Pagoda, Yinchuan (RS)

Top: Sunrise over Huang Shan (AS)
Bottom Left: Lake of Heaven, Changbaishan (RS)
Bottom Right: Oasis at Dunhuang (AS)

by rail to Yingtan (via Jingdezhen) and Wuhu. An airport has recently been built at Tunxi to make Huangshan more accessible to foreign tourists.

JIUHUASHAN

(jiǔhuá shān) 九华山

One way to escape the trampling hordes of Huangshan is to head north-west to Jiuhuashan, the Nine Flowers Mountains. They take their name from the poet Li Bai, who wrote:

Looking far ahead from Jiujiang,
I saw the peaks of Mount Jiuhua
Emerging from the Heavenly River
Like nine beautiful lotus flowers.

Jiuhuashan is regarded as one of China's four sacred Buddhist mountains. The others with this claim to fame are Pu Tuo in Zhejiang, Emei in Sichuan and Wutai in Shanxi. At least five other mountains (including Taishan in Shandong, which is important to the Taoists) are considered sacred or of some special significance to the Chinese people.

Getting There & Away

Jiuhuajie is the main centre of the Jiuhuashan region and there are a couple of ways to approach it. The easiest is the daily bus from Huangshan but there are also buses from Wuhu and Guichi (both ports on the Yangtse River). Another route is by train from Nanjing to Tonglingshi, and then by bus to Jiuhuajie.

WUHU & GUICHI

(wǔhú, guìchí) 芜湖和贵池

Wuhu is a Yangtse River port and a useful railway junction. Railway lines branch off south to Tunxi, east to Shanghai via Nanjing and, from the northern bank of the river, another line heads north to Hefei. There are also buses to Huangshan and Jiuhuashan from Wuhu. To the west of Wuhu is the Yangtse port of Guichi, which has buses to Huangshan and Jiuhuashan.

HEFEI

(héféi) 合肥

This nondescript industrial city is the capital of Anhui and there's not much here to recommend to tourists. It used to be a quiet market town but after 1949 was expanded to become an industrial centre and now has a population of over 500,000. The only real attraction is the local Provincial Museum with its wonderful 2000-year-old burial suit made of pieces of jade held together with silver thread.

Places to Stay

Closest to the railway station on Changjiang Lu is the *Jianghuai Hotel* where doubles cost around Y66. Cheaper are the *Meishan Hotel* and the *International Hotel*, both on Meishan Lu, where doubles cost around Y55. Further afield on Shushan Lu is the more expensive *Luyang* which charges Y150 a double.

Getting There & Away

Hefei is connected by direct trains to Ji'nan, Beijing and Zhengzhou, southwards to the port of Wuhu on the Yangtse, and westwards to Xi'an. Useful flights from Hefei include Beijing (three flights weekly), Canton (three flights weekly) and Shanghai (five times weekly). There are also direct buses between Hangzhou and Hefei ('Most pleasant, if your bladder can stand it', wrote one traveller), and buses from Hefei to Nanjing.

Shanghai 上海

Shanghai: Paris of the East, Whore of China, Queen of the Orient; city of bums, adventurers, pimps, swindlers, gamblers, sailors, socialites, dandies, drugrunners. Humiliation, indignation, starvation, back-alley corpses, coolies, rickshaw drivers, deformed beggars, child prostitutes, scab-ridden infants, student activists, strikers, intellectuals, Communists, rebels, foreign armies supporting foreign business interests. Trendsetter, snob, leader, industrial muscle, the name that keeps the Beijing bureaucrats awake at night...a hybrid of Paris and New York in the 1930s with millions trampling the streets where the millionaires once trod...one way or another Shanghai has permeated the Western consciousness.

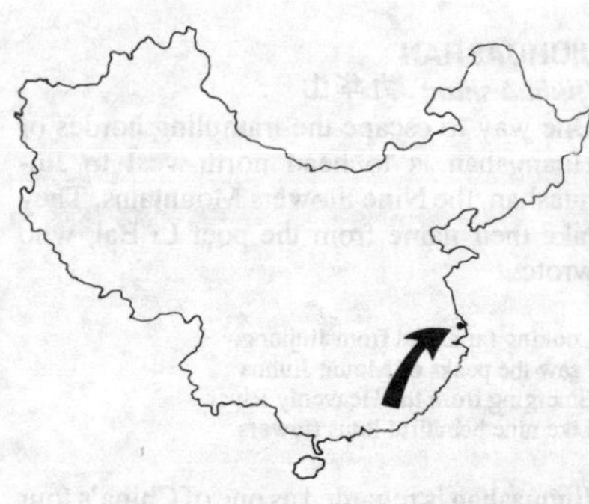

History

To seize the tail of this leviathan you have to go back to the 1840s. At that time Shanghai *(shànghǎi)* was a prosperous weaving and fishing town – but not an important one – and was walled to keep out the Japanese pirates that roamed the China coast. Shanghai, at the gateway to the Yangtse, was in an ideal position to develop as a trading port. In 1842, after the first Opium War, the British forcibly opened up a concession there, and the French followed in 1847. An International Settlement was established in 1863 and a Japanese enclave in 1895, all completely autonomous and immune from Chinese law.

Spurred on by massive foreign investment, coupled with an inexhaustible supply of cheap Chinese labour, Shanghai quickly became a booming port and industrial city. In the mid-18th century it had a population of a mere 50,000 – by 1900 it had reached its first million, partly caused by the flood of refugees who came here when the Taiping rebels took Nanjing in 1853. As for the foreign population, from a few thousand adventurers in the 1860s there were some 60,000 by the 1930s.

The International Settlement had the tallest buildings in Asia in the 1930s, the most spacious cinemas, and more motor vehicles than any eastern metropolis or in all other Chinese cities combined. Powerful foreign financial houses had set up here: the Hong Kong & Shanghai Banking Corporation; the Chartered Bank of India, Australia & China; and the National City and Chase Manhattan banks of New York. There were the blue-blood British firms of Jardine & Matheson, Sassoons and others that got their start with the opium trade, and newer but aggressive American firms that had *everything* for sale.

Guarding it all were the American, French and Italian marines, British Tommies and Japanese Bluejackets. Foreign ships and submarines patrolled the Yangtse and Huangpu rivers and the coasts of China. They maintained the biggest single foreign investment anywhere in the world – the British alone had £400 million sunk into the place. After Chiang Kaishek's coup against the Communists in 1927, the Kuomintang cooperated closely with the foreign police and with Chinese and foreign factory owners to suppress labour unrest. The Settlement police, run by the British, arrested Chinese labour leaders and handed them over to the Kuomintang for imprisonment or execution, and the Shanghai gangs were repeatedly called in to 'mediate' disputes inside the Settlement.

If you were rich you could get anything in the Shanghai of the 1920s and 1930s: dance halls, opium dens, gambling halls, flashing lights and great restaurants, plus the dimmed lights of the brothels and your choice of 30,000 prostitutes. Supporting it all were the Chinese who worked as beasts of burden and provided the muscle in Shanghai's port and factories. Shanghai was the largest manufacturing city in Asia, with more than 200,000 workers employed in the factories. American journalist Edgar Snow, who came to Shanghai in the late 1920s, wrote of the hundreds of factories where little boy and girl slave workers laboured 12 or 13 hours a day, and of little girls in silk filature factories – all of them, like most contract labour in Shanghai, literally sold into these jobs as virtual slaves for four or five years – unable to leave the heavily guarded, high-walled premises day or night without special permission.

When the Communists came to power in 1949 one of the first things they wanted to do was turn Shanghai into a showcase of how Communism really worked. Today, while housing, sanitation, water supply and pollution are still serious problems in Shanghai, it should be remembered that the housing developments, the eradication of the slums, the rehabilitation of the city's hundreds of thousands of opium addicts, and the elimination of child and slave labour are staggering achievements.

Shanghai Today

Today, Shanghai has a population bordering on 12 million people – but that figure is deceptive since it takes into account the whole municipal area of 6100 sq km. Nevertheless, the central core of some 220 sq km has over 6.3 million people, which must rate as one of the highest population densities in China, if not in the world. In 1955 a plan was announced to reduce the city's population by one million. Some estimates put the number of people moved out of Shanghai at two million since 1949; perhaps three-quarters of these were young people 'sent down' to the countryside during the Cultural Revolution. Whatever the actual figure, Chinese officials will tell you that the professionals and technicians were 'persuaded' to go to the interior to start new schools, colleges and hospitals. Meanwhile, many of the 'exiled' young people who try to creep back into the city are nabbed and shipped back out again.

Population and unemployment are severe problems in Shanghai. Some economists claim that China's switch to light industry over the last 10 years or so is due to the fact that it can absorb up to three times the number of workers that heavy industry can, and at the same time increase the general standard of living. People are so numerous in Shanghai that the weekly day off is staggered; shipyard workers don't rub shoulders with textile workers on the streets. Overcrowded as it is, Shanghai still enjoys a high living standard in comparison with the rest of China, at least in terms of wages, consumer goods and educational opportunities.

Shanghai continues to play an enormous role in the national economy. When the Communists came to power they set about downplaying this role, and priority in industrial development (under the first Five-Year Plan launched in 1953) was given to the strategically less vulnerable and poorer cities and towns of the interior. In 1956 the coastal regions were again reaffirmed as logical places for an industrial base, possibly because of the ease of import and export of goods by sea. That resulted in another boom for Shanghai, and in the late 1950s the city's limits were extended to encompass the surrounding counties, giving the city more control over its supply of food and raw materials. In 1963 Zhou Enlai put his personal seal of approval on the city, and output for certain facets of its economy was given priority. Today, the city accounts for 15% of China's total industrial output and 20% of its exports. Shanghai is now being looked upon as a source of technical expertise, which is the weak link in China's modernisation drive. Foreign business is also back in business in Shanghai with huge sums of money invested by foreign companies, like the

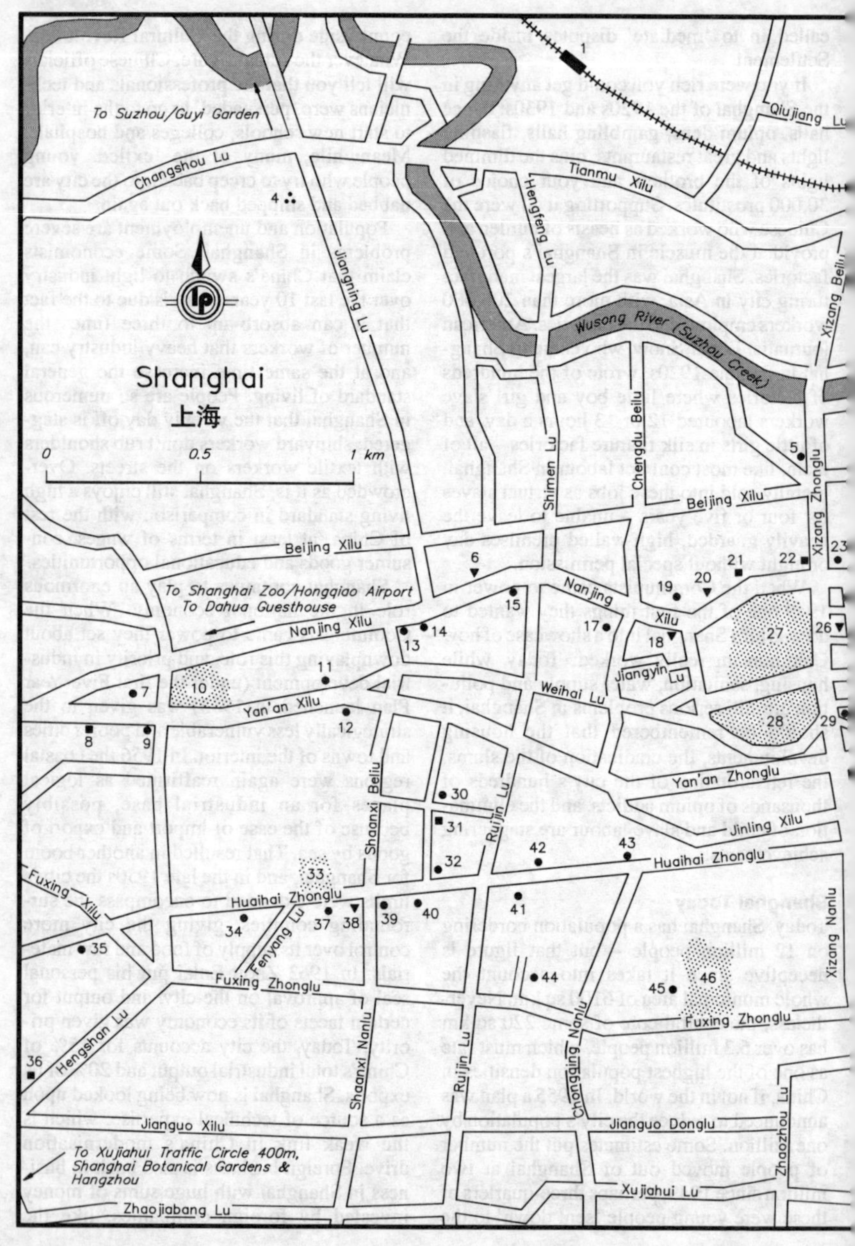
Shanghai
上海
0
0.5
1 km
To Suzhou/Guyi Garden
Qiujiang Lu
Changshou Lu
Tianmu Xilu
Hengfeng Lu
Jiangning Lu
Wusong River (Suzhou Creek)
Xizang Beilu
Chengdu Beilu
Shimen Lu
Beijing Xilu
Xizang Zhonglu
Beijing Xilu
To Shanghai Zoo/Hongqiao Airport
To Dahua Guesthouse
Nanjing Xilu
Nanjing Xilu
Jiangyin Lu
Weihai Lu
Yan'an Xilu
Yan'an Zhonglu
Shaanxi Beilu
Ruijin Lu
Jinling Xilu
Huaihai Zhonglu
Huaihai Zhonglu
Fuxing Xilu
Fenyang Lu
Fuxing Zhonglu
Fuxing Zhonglu
Hengshan Lu
Shaanxi Nanlu
Ruijin Lu
Chongqing Nanlu
Xizang Nanlu
Jianguo Xilu
Jianguo Donglu
Zhaozhou Lu
Xujiahui Lu
To Xujiahui Traffic Circle 400m, Shanghai Botanical Gardens & Hangzhou
Zhaojiabang Lu

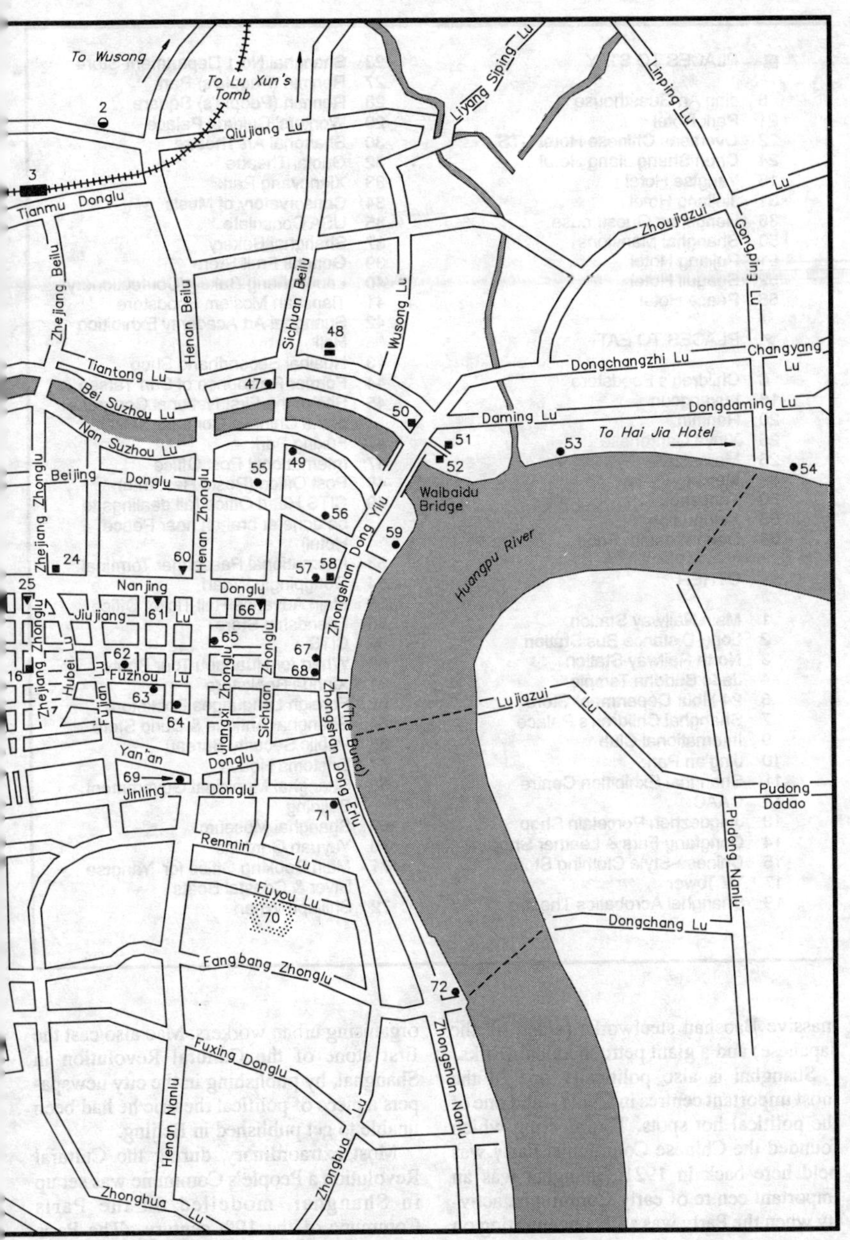
To Wusong
To Lu Xun's Tomb
2
3
Qiujiang Lu
Tianmu Donglu
Zhejiang Beilu
Henan Beilu
Sichuan Beilu
Wusong Lu
Liyang Siping Lu
Linping Lu
Zhoujiazui Lu
Gongping Lu
Changyang Lu
Dongchangzhi Lu
Dongdaming Lu
Daming Lu
To Hai Jia Hotel
48
47
50
51
52
53
54
Tiantong Lu
Bei Suzhou Lu
Nan Suzhou Lu
Beijing Donglu
Zhejiang Zhonglu
Henan Zhonglu
49
55
56
59
Waibaidu Bridge
Huangpu River
24
60
25
Nanjing Donglu
57
58
66
61
Jiujiang Lu
65
Zhongshan Dong Yilu
67
68
62
16
Hubei Lu
Fuzhou Lu
63
64
Fujian Lu
Jiangxi Zhonglu
Sichuan Zhonglu
Zhongshan Dong Erlu (The Bund)
Lujiazui Lu
Yan'an Donglu
69
Jinling Donglu
71
Pudong Dadao
Pudong Nanlu
Renmin Lu
Fuyou Lu
70
Dongchang Lu
Fangbang Zhonglu
72
Zhongshan Nanlu
Fuxing Donglu
Henan Nanlu
Zhonghua Lu

■ PLACES TO STAY

8 Jing An Guesthouse
21 Park Hotel
22 Overseas Chinese Hotel/CTS
24 Chun Sheng Jiang Hotel
16 Yangtse Hotel
31 Jinjiang Hotel
36 Hengshan Guesthouse
50 Shanghai Mansions
51 Pujiang Hotel
52 Seagull Hotel
58 Peace Hotel

▼ PLACES TO EAT

6 Children's Foodstore
18 Luyangcun
20 Renmin
25 Xinya Cantonese
26 Meiweizhai
38 Meixin
60 Yangzhou
63 Xinghualou
66 Deda Western Food

OTHER

1 Main Railway Station
2 Long-Distance Bus Station
3 North Railway Station
4 Jade Buddha Temple
5 24-Hour Department Store
7 Shanghai Children's Palace
9 International Club
10 Jing'an Park
11 Shanghai Exhibition Centre
12 CAAC
13 Jingdezhen Porcelain Shop
14 Dongfang Furs & Leather Shop
15 Chinese-Style Clothing Store
17 TV Tower
19 Shanghai Acrobatics Theatre
23 Shanghai No 1 Department Store
27 Renmin (People's) Park
28 Renmin (People's) Square
29 Workers' Cultural Palace
30 Shanghai Art Theatre
32 Guotai Theatre
33 Xiangyang Park
34 Conservatory of Music
35 USA Consulate
37 Shanghai Bakery
39 Gongtai Fruit Store
40 Laodacheng Bakery/Confectionery
41 Tianshan Moslem Foodstore
42 Shanghai Art Academy Exhibition Hall
43 Huaihai Secondhand Shop
44 Former Residence of Sun Yatsen
45 Site of the First National Congress of the Chinese Communist Party
46 Fuxing Park
47 International Post Office
48 Post Office (Poste Restante)
49 CITS Head Office (all dealings to be done at branch near Peace Hotel)
53 International Passenger Terminal
54 Gongpinglu Wharf
55 Main Advance Rail Ticket Office
56 Friendship Store
57 CITS
59 Wharf for Huangpu Tour Boats
61 Xinhua Bookstore
62 Foreign Languages Bookstore
64 Shanghai Antique & Curio Store
65 Public Security Bureau
67 Customs House
68 Shanghai Municipal Government Building
69 Shanghai Museum
70 Yuyuan Gardens
71 Main Booking Office for Yangtse River & Coastal Boats
72 Shiliupu Wharf

massive Baoshan steelworks (aided by the Japanese) and a giant petrochemical works.

Shanghai is also politically one of the most important centres in China – and one of the political hot spots. The meeting which founded the Chinese Communist Party was held here back in 1921. Shanghai was an important centre of early Communist activity when the Party was still concentrating on organising urban workers. Mao also cast the first stone of the Cultural Revolution in Shanghai, by publishing in the city newspapers a piece of political rhetoric he had been unable to get published in Beijing.

Most extraordinary, during the Cultural Revolution a People's Commune was set up in Shanghai, modelled on the Paris Commune of the 19th century. (The Paris

■ PLACES TO STAY

8 静安饭店
21 国际饭店
22 华侨饭店
24 春申江宾馆
16 长江宾馆
31 锦江饭店
36 衡山宾馆
50 上海大厦
51 浦江饭店
52 海鸥饭店
58 和平饭店

▼ PLACES TO EAT

6 儿童食品店
18 绿扬村酒家
20 人民饭店
25 斯雅粤菜饭店
26 美味宅
38 美心酒家
60 扬州饭店
63 杏花楼
66 德西餐社

OTHER

1 火车总站
2 长途汽车站
3 火车北站
4 玉佛寺
5 二十四时百货商店
7 少年宫
9 国际俱乐部
10 静安公园
11 上海展览馆
12 中国民航
13 景德镇艺术瓷器服务部
14 东方毛服装厂
15 龙风中式服装厂
17 电视楼
19 杂技场
23 第一百货商店
27 人民公园
28 人民广场
29 工人文化宫
30 艺术剧院
32 国泰剧院
33 香扬公园
34 音乐学校
35 美国领事馆
37 上海食品店
39 公泰水果店
40 老大昌食品店
41 天山回民食品店
42 画院美术馆
43 淮海旧货商店
44 孙中山故居
45 中共一大会址
46 富兴公园
47 国际邮局
48 总邮局
49 国际旅行总局
53 国际客运站
54 公平路码头
55 火车售票处
56 友谊商店
57 中国国际旅行社
59 浦江游航码头
61 新华书店
62 外文书店
64 文物商店
65 公安局外事科
67 海关楼
68 上海市人民政府
69 博物馆
70 豫园
71 轮船售票处（长江）
72 十六浦码头

Commune was set up in 1871 and controlled Paris for two months. It planned to introduce socialist reforms such as turning over management of factories to the workers' associations.) The Shanghai Commune lasted just three weeks before Mao ordered the Army to put an end to it, and thus China was finished with this form of socialism for a long time.

The so-called 'Gang of Four' had their power base in Shanghai. The campaign to criticise Confucius and Mencius was started here in 1969, before it became nationwide in 1973 and was linked to Lin Biao. Shanghai's history as the most radical city in China, the supporter of dogmatic Maoism, one of the focuses of the Cultural Revolution, and the power base of Mao's wife is rather strange when you consider that the city is now, perhaps with the exception of Canton, the most capitalist and the most consumer-oriented in China. If you can work out how a whole city can change its loyalty from orthodox Maoism to laissez-faire capitalism then you have probably gone a long way to understanding what makes the Chinese world tick.

Orientation

Landmarks are good to navigate by in Shanghai. The Peace Hotel at the intersection of the Bund and Nanjing Donglu is just about the closest thing to a centre – it's the chief tourist crossroads. On the Bund the easy direction-finder is the Customs House (with its large red star and clock tower) and the Shanghai People's Municipal Government Building – both of these are to the south of the Peace Hotel. To the north is the unmistakable looming slab known as Shanghai Mansions.

From the strip of the Bund near the Peace Hotel you can get a bus in almost any direction. Heading west along Nanjing Donglu you'll come to the Park Hotel, which roughly marks the division between Nanjing Donglu and Nanjing Xilu. From here you can easily spot the TV Tower, which is a good intermediary point to aim for when heading to the area of the old French Concession (Frenchtown). The heart of Frenchtown is marked by the colossal wings of the Jinjiang Hotel.

Other destinations are a little awkward to get to on foot. Shanghai is a big place. Some of the sights are right off the map – the zoo, for example, is near the airport.

Street names are given in pinyin, which makes navigating easy, and many of the streets are named after cities and provinces. In the central district (around Nanjing Lu) the provincial names run north-south, and the city names run east-west. Some roads are split by compass points, such as Sichuan Nanlu which means Sichuan South Rd, and Sichuan Beilu which means Sichuan North Rd. Some of the monstrously long roads are split by sectors, such as Zhongshan Dong Erlu and Zhongshan Dong Yilu, which mean Zhongshan East 2nd Rd and Zhongshan East 1st Rd, respectively – simple!

There are four main areas of interest in the city: the Bund from Suzhou Creek to the Shanghai Harbour Passenger Terminal (Shiliupu Wharf); Nanjing Donglu from the Peace to the Park Hotels, as well as the central sector to the south of this strip; Frenchtown, which is the strip of Huaihai Zhonglu from Shaanxi Nanlu to Chongqing Nanlu, plus the adjoining Jinjiang Hotel area; and the Jade Buddha Temple and the side trip along Suzhou Creek.

Information

CITS They do their dealings in an office next door to the Peace Hotel. Trains, planes and boats can be booked here. They make the standard markups on planes and trains and a surcharge on boats out of Shanghai, but they give you a good chance of getting elusive sleepers without joining the phenomenal queues at the railway stations. They will book tickets for the Trans-Siberian to Europe.

CITS has astronomically priced excursions to Suzhou, Wuxi and the other wonders as far as Nanjing. They have tours to a jade carving factory and a carpet factory, next door to each other at 25 & 33 Caobao Lu in the Xuhui District on the south-western outskirts of Shanghai. Also try the Shanghai No 1 Silk Factory in the north of the city. CITS may be able to organise visits to various other industries – a toothpaste factory, a neon signs factory, a chocolate factory, a film studio. Their city tours also take in the Children's Palace, Jade Buddha Temple and other interesting sights. They handle tickets for the Huangpu River trip, but these will be cheaper at the source, which is virtually across the road.

Shanghai CITS is hopelessly overworked – you'll just have to be patient getting information from them. Some useful info, such as train timetables to Hangzhou, is laid out on the counter under glass and behind three ranks of customers. The office remains open Saturday and for half a day on Sunday.

Public Security Bureau The office (☎ 215380) is at 210 Hankou Lu, one block north of Fuzhou Lu, near the corner with Henan Zhonglu.

Money There are money-exchange counters on the premises of the larger tourist hotels, such as the Peace, Park, Pujiang and Jinjiang hotels. Credit cards are more readily accepted in Shanghai than in other parts of China.

Most tourist hotels will accept the main ones like Visa, Amex, MasterCard, Diners, and JCB, as will banks and Friendship Stores (and related tourist outlets like the Antique & Curio Store). The Bank of China branch right next to the Peace Hotel, on the Bund, will change foreign cash and travellers' cheques.

Post & Telecommunications The larger tourist hotels have post offices from which you can mail letters and small packages.

The Express Mail Service and Poste Restante is at 276 Bei Suzhou Lu. Letters to London take just two days, or so they advertise.

The International Post & Telecommunications Office is at the corner of Sichuan Beilu and Bei Suzhou Lu. The section for international parcels is in the same building but around the corner at 395 Tiantong Lu.

Some travellers take poste restante c/o the Peace Hotel, even if they're not staying there. There is a counter on the ground floor where incoming letters are held. Check the letter drop in both the north and south buildings.

Long-distance calls can be placed from hotel rooms and do not take long to get through. The International Telegraph Office, from which you can make long-distance phone calls and send international telexes and telegrams, is on Nanjing Donglu next to the Peace Hotel.

Climate The best times to visit Shanghai are spring and autumn. Winters can drop well below freezing and are blanketed in drizzle. Summers are hot and humid with temperatures as high as 40°C. So, in short, you'll need silk longjohns and down jackets for winter, an iceblock for each armpit in summer – and an umbrella won't go astray in either season.

Foreign Consulates There are several foreign consulates in Shanghai, and it's possible to get your visas here for the Trans-Siberian journey, though Beijing is better. The consulates can also replace passports if you're unfortunate enough to have lost one.

Australia
17 Fuxing Xilu (☎ 4334604)
Belgium
Qihua Tower, 1375 Huaihai Zhonglu (☎ 4334461)
France
1431 Huaihai Zhonglu (☎ 4377414)
Germany
181 Yongfu Lu (☎ 4336951)
Hungary
Room 1810 Union Building, 100 Yan'an Donglu (☎ 3261815)
Japan
1517 Huaihai Zhonglu (☎ 4336639)
Poland
618 Jianguo Xilu (☎ 4370952)
UK
244 Yongfu Lu (☎ 4330508)
USA
1469 Huaihai Zhonglu (☎ 4336880)
USSR
20 Huangpu Lu (☎ 3242682)

Bookshops There are numerous foreign-language outlets in Shanghai, if you take the tourist hotel bookshops into account. The main Foreign Languages Bookstore is at 390 Fuzhou Lu. Next door is a stationery shop if you need writing supplies as well. Of special interest is the branch at 201 Shandong Zhonglu, which sells old books in foreign languages.

At 424 Fuzhou Lu is the Classics Bookshop. The books in the section serving foreigners are not as old as the books in the section serving Chinese customers – and the prices are higher. However, books from the foreigners' section can be exported, whereas books from the other section cannot.

There are other specialist bookshops around Shanghai, if you can read Chinese. Fuzhou Lu is the bookshop hunting ground – it always has been that way.

Back in 1949 the bookshops removed the porn from the shelves and set up displays of Marx and company overnight.

If you're hungry for Western reading material, worth checking out is the China National Publications Import & Export Corporation shop at 537 Yan'an Lu, near the Jinjiang Hotel. The retail shop on the ground floor has a good stock of Western magazines, including *Paris Match, L'Express, South* and many more.

A small range of foreign newspapers and magazines is available from the larger tourist hotels (eg Park, Jinjiang, Sheraton Hua Ting) and some shops. They include the *Wall Street Journal, International Herald Tribune, Asiaweek*, the *Economist, Time* and *Newsweek*. The latter two make good gifts for Chinese friends. The hotel shops also carry a variety of English-language paperbacks, all of which must pass government censors (this is why newer titles are conspicuously absent).

The biggest selection of Chinese periodicals is found at 16 Sichuan Beilu – and while the lingo might not make these seem worth browsing through, there are oddities like the comic book rental section to dive into. The Xinhua Bookstore at 345 Nanjing Donglu has kids' books, lots of posters, some maps, and a foreigners' section on the 2nd floor.

Get a copy of Pan Ling's *In Search of Old Shanghai* (Joint Publishing Company, Hong Kong, 1982) for a rundown on who was who and what was what back in the bad old days.

Maps There are quite a few variations around and lots of sources of them. For starters, get one from the hawkers outside the railway station. Other places to try are the bookshops in the tourist hotels, which are usually well stocked. Good English maps get snapped up fast – if you see a good map somewhere else on your travels and you're going to Shanghai, then it's wise to pick it up there and then.

The best Chinese-language map is a small fold-up one with a picture of the Peace Hotel and the Bund on the cover, costing 40 fen. It's a masterpiece of map-making though the heap of detail squashed into it may well require a magnifying glass. Another good one has the pinyin *Shanghai – shiqu jiaotongtu* on the cover and is good for working out the bus routes; it's commonly sold in Shanghai.

If you want a bilingual map, get the Hong-Kong-published *Map of Shanghai*, which is sometimes available in China (buy it at Swindon's in Hong Kong beforehand if you want to be sure of getting a copy). This map has streets and destinations written in Chinese characters as well as English – very useful.

Probably the best all-English map is *A Tourist Map of Shanghai* published by China Travel & Tourism Press. It's readily identifiable by the large advertisements for American Express, Remy Martin and Shanghai Arts & Crafts Jewellery. Another good map commonly sold in Shanghai is *A Map of Communication & Tour to Shanghai*, which also has the bus routes.

Emergency Shanghai is credited with the best medical facilities and most advanced medical knowledge in China. Western medicines are sold at the Shanghai No 8 Drugstore at 951 Huaihai Zhonglu. Foreigners are referred to Shanghai No 1 People's Hospital (☎ 240100) at 190 Bei Suzhou Lu.

Peoplewatching

Shanghai's thrills and spills are found on the streets. If the world were to run out of petrol tomorrow, it would make little difference to the noise level in Shanghai. The city has the most insane collections of hybrids on two, three and four-or-more wheels imaginable – parts cannibalised from breakdowns. Coming through the insectoid rush hour is a legless rider using his hands to crank up the rear bike drive...and then, incredibly, a semi-trailer-class tricycle with the rider pedalling backwards (using a rear sprocket and chain arrangement). The screech, squawk and jingle of the roads leading across Nanjing Donglu is offset by walls of pedestrians spilling into vacant bike lanes, while retired men with 'serve the people' armbands hurdle the railings to try and nail jaywalkers.

As early as 5 am the city is alive: mass taiji in the parks, while the younger set go for the

more energetic martial arts, and there's the inevitable jogging and frisbee-playing. Covered food markets out in the neighbourhoods are readily identified by the mounds of fresh cabbage, or the halved pig carcasses thrown on the sidewalk nearby, or simply by the queues for eggs and slabs of bean curd. It's difficult to haul yourself out of bed at these hours, but Shanghai is a place for doing things and watching people – the sort of place where unobtainable Japanese products beckon from billboards, strips of pigs' innards dangle from a dim doorway that smells of herbs and incense, pedlars maximize on street corners with shady wares and cooks pound dough behind steamy windows, or a shoe repairer sets up shop on the sidewalk.

What Was What

Time to engage in the hobby of determining what building was what, when, how, and why. It's a bit like a giant game of Monopoly: Jimmy's Kitchen, St Petersburg Restaurant, Delmonte's Casino, the Lido, Roxy's, Kabul Rd, Oxford St, Luna Park, Singapore Park. Most of the taller structures are dead wood from the 1930s, and the buildings rapidly changed function after the Japanese invasion of 1937. The Westerners got a brief respite from 1945 to 1949, but then the game was up.

The old **Chinese city** is now identified by the Zhonghua-Renmin ring road, which encloses a shoddy maze of cobbled alleyways, with some newer buildings to the south. Old walls used to be surrounded by a moat, but these walls were torn down in 1912.

The **International Settlement** *(shànghǎi zūjiè)* started off as small tracts of land on the banks of the Huangpu, north of the old Chinese city, and eventually snowballed to roughly the area shown by the map in this text. The British-dominated Settlement was a brave new world of co-operation by the British, Europeans and Americans (the Japanese were also included but were suspect). It's fairly easy to discern. If you draw a line directly north from the Jing An Guesthouse to Suzhou Creek, then the area is everything from Yan'an Lu up to Suzhou Creek in the north, and to the Huangpu River in the east. The ritziest place to live was west of today's Xizang Lu (now the Jing An district) – villas spread this way as far as the zoo. The foreign embassies were grouped on either side of the Waibaidu Bridge; the Friendship Store used to occupy the buildings of the old British Consulate, and the former Seaman's Club used to be the Soviet Consulate.

Throwing a pincer around the top of the Chinese city and lying on the southern flank of the International Settlement was the **French Concession** *(făguó zūjiè)*. The east-west dividing line between the French Concession and the International Settlement is the present-day Yan'an Lu (previously known as Avenue Foch in the west, and Avenue Edward VII in the east). The French strip of the Bund (south of Yan'an) was known as the Quai de France. Roughly, the boundaries of Frenchtown can be drawn by heading south from the Dahua Guesthouse on Yan'an Lu to the Xujiahui traffic circle, east along Zhaojiabang Lu and Xujiahui Lu to the Hunan Stadium, then up alongside the western border of the Chinese city as far as Yan'an Donglu – and then tack on the pincer between Yan'an Donglu and the northern rim of the Chinese city. Not all of Frenchtown was densely inhabited back then, and in any case the name is a bit of a misnomer as there weren't too many French there to begin with. Like the other concessions it was 90% Chinese, and in any case the most numerous foreign residents in Frenchtown were White Russians. Vietnamese troops were used by the French as a police force (just as the British used Sikhs in their concessions). For villa and mansion architecture the French concession holds the most surprises – there's a rather exclusive air to the elegant town-houses and apartment blocks. The core of things is around the present Jinjiang Hotel and Huaihai Lu.

The original **central district** *(shì zhōngxīn)* was bounded by today's Xizang Lu, Yan'an Lu, Suzhou Creek and the Huangpu River. If you bisect that with Nanjing Lu, then the key wining and dining, shopping and administrative/hotel area is the slab south of Nanjing Lu as far as Yan'an Lu, with Nanjing Donglu being the chief culprit. This is today's Huangpu District.

The area north of the central district and up as far as Suzhou Creek used to be the **American Settlement**. The area on the other side of the creek, east of Zhejiang Beilu and along the banks of the Huangpu, used to be the **Japanese Concession** *(rìběn zūjiè)*. These areas eventually became a Chinese industrial suburb, the **Hongkou District**, and are not of great interest, although the bridges above the polluted sections along Suzhou Creek are good for observing tugs and barges – there's a great deal of industry and warehouses along these banks. The major universities, Tongji and Fudan, are right up north. The main factory zones, shipyards, warehouses and new high-rise housing developments are in the sector north-east of here.

Over on the other side of the railway tracks to the west and the north of the city are rings of new industrial suburbs – **satellite towns** where the workers live in high-rises adjacent to their factories and plants – the Soviet model. The area due south of the old Chinese city and Frenchtown is similar. The housing projects sprang up, as they did in other Chinese cities, in the 1950s, and were erected outside the original city limits. The initial building programme concentrated upon the construction of about 10,000 dwelling units in north-east Shanghai, and another 10,000 in southern, northern and western Shanghai. These satellite towns are about eight km from the centre of Shanghai, and they have their own schools, day-care centres, markets and hospitals.

Beyond the industrial zones are the **market gardens** that feed the Shanghai dynamo – a long way out there from the city centre, but very close if you head due east. Directly east of the Bund, on the eastern banks of the Huangpu, is an area which was barely worked on by the Western powers. There is now a mixed residential, industrial and warehousing strip running along the eastern bank, but immediately beyond it are farming areas. There are no bridges over the Huangpu, since it would disturb the heavy shipping, but lots of ferries do the job.

The Bund
(wàitān) 外滩

The Bund is an Anglo-Indian term for the

embankment of a muddy waterfront. In Chinese it's referred to as *Waitan* and on the map it's Zhongshan Donglu (Zhongshan Rd East).

The Bund is an apt description. Between 1920 (when the problem was first noticed) and 1965 the city of Shanghai sank several metres. Correction of the problem involved pumping water back into the ground, but the Venetian threat is still there. Concrete rafts are used as foundations for high-rises in this spongy mass.

The Bund is a great meeting place for local Chinese and foreigners alike. People stroll up and down in search of vicarious excitement, often provided by street performers or free-marketeers. Pedlars sell anything from home-made underwear to naughty pictures. In the morning it's an exhibition of taiji and martial arts; at night it's a lovers' lane.

Though startling to behold in a Chinese city, the edifices that line the Bund are no special wonder. The exteriors are a solemn mix of neo-classical 1930s Chicago and New York with a bit of monumental Egyptian thrown in for good measure. To the Europeans, the Bund was Shanghai's Wall Street, and it saw a fever of trading as the city's fortunes rose and fell with each impending crisis. The buildings changed function several times as the crises got the better of traders, but originally they were banks, trading houses, hotels, residential buildings, commercial buildings and clubs.

One of the most famous traders was Jardine Matheson & Company. They registered in Canton in 1832, and dug into the China trade two years later when the British parliament abolished the East India Company's monopoly of the place. In 1848 Jardine's purchased the first land offered for sale to foreigners in Shanghai and set up shop shortly after, dealing in opium and tea. Today, Jardine Matheson owns just about half of Hong Kong and they're not finished with Shanghai either – they have an office across the way at Shanghai Mansions. James Matheson's nephew Donald, who inherited most of the Matheson side of the fortune, served in China from 1837 to 1849. By the age of 30 he'd had it, went to England, and later became the chairman of the Executive Committee for the Suppression of the Opium Trade.

At the north-west end of the Bund were, or are, the British Public Gardens (now Huangpu Park), off-limits to Chinese during the colonial era. A sign at the entrance listed regulations, which included the prohibition of Chinese and dogs from the park. A Sikh guard stood at the gateway; the British brought in an Indian force to protect themselves after the Boxer Rebellion of 1900.

While the Bund may no longer be full of noisy hawkers, tramcars, Oldsmobiles, typists, black marketeers, sailors, taipans and rickshawmen, its function is still very much the same – only this time it's the foreigners who come to kowtow to the Chinese trading establishments now set up here. The Customs House (built in 1927) is still a customs house. An exterior readily identifiable by the dome on top is the Hong Kong & Shanghai Bank, completed in 1921 – one of the most impressive hunks of granite in colonial Asia. The rowdy RAF Club used to be up in the dome. Today the bank houses the Shanghai People's Municipal Government (City Hall, CCP and PLA headquarters) so there's little chance of seeing the interior. As for the HK & Shanghai Bank, it has a more modest office further north.

The statues that lined the Bund were stripped away; the whereabouts of the pair of bronze lions that once stood outside the HK & Shanghai Bank remains a mystery. It was first thought that they were melted down for cannons by the Japanese, but later the Chinese claimed they had found them. Several Western sources mention seeing the lions in the early 1970s – it's possible that they were brought out for the making of a movie.

One interior that you can visit is the Dongfeng Hotel at the bottom of the Bund near Shiliupu Wharf; as you sweep through the double doors, cross the marble paving and bump into what looks like a railway concourse, you get an idea of how the Dongfeng started life. This was the Shanghai

Club, the snootiest little gang this side of Trafalgar Square. Membership was confined to upper-crust Brits, men only. To the left of the entrance is a Suzhou-style restaurant where you'll find the Long Bar, a 33-metre span of thick wood now hacked into three separate pieces. Opposite was the smoking room, now a Cantonese-style restaurant, where the members, replete, would doze with their copies of the *Times*, freshly ironed by the roomboys.

Nanjing Lu & the Central District

Nanjing Donglu (Nanjing Road East), from the Peace to the Park hotels, is the golden mile of China's commerce. Some display windows will stop you in your tracks! Just about everything can be found here, though back in Hong Kong it would be cheaper.

Before 1949 Nanjing Lu was a mixture of restaurants, nightclubs and coffinmakers. The most prestigious department stores were there, and still are, including Wing On's (now the No 10 Department Store), Sun Sun's (now the No 1 Food Store), and The Sun (now the No 1 Department Store).

It's entertaining to drag yourself through these places where the escalators no longer function. The stores used to be exclusive, but now they are used by crowds of eager patrons clamouring for the latest things in short supply. The one practical souvenir that travellers like to get is a black vinyl carrier bag with 'Shanghai' embossed on it – proves you've been there.

A stroll down Nanjing Lu at night offers eye-catching window displays and neon signs. Shanghai has the best reputation in China for the art of hairdressing – considered yet another facet of decadence back in the late '60s and early '70s.

By day, from 9 am to 6 pm, only buses are allowed on Nanjing Lu, which otherwise turns into a pedestrian thoroughfare. You'll see why there's such a keen one-child-only campaign in Shanghai; the human tide on Nanjing Lu has to be seen to be believed.

At the end of Nanjing Donglu you come to another shopping drag, Nanjing Xilu (once called Bubbling Well Rd, before the well was sealed over). Dividing the sections for a bit of a breather are Renmin Square and Renmin Park, once the Shanghai Racecourse. The old Racecourse Clubhouse is now the Shanghai Municipal Library, and the building is among the oldest in the city.

The nondescript parkland and the desert-like expanses of paving at Renmin Square are where all those large meetings and rallies were held back in the '60s and '70s. In April 1969, 2.7 million people poured in here to demonstrate against the Soviet Union after clashes on the border (though even that figure didn't top the peaceful 10 million who'd gathered for the May Day celebrations in Beijing in 1963). The area is also used for paramilitary training; under Renmin Square is a large air-raid shelter. Near Renmin Square is Jiangyin Lu, where you'll find Shanghai's chief goldfish market.

An interesting store at the dividing line of Nanjing Donglu and Nanjing Xilu is the *Shanghai Plants & Bird Shop*, at 364 Nanjing Xilu. It sells bonsai plants, pots, tools, birdcages, goldfish and funeral wreaths. This is possibly one of the few places in the city where you'll find fresh flowers for sale. Most Shanghainese will queue up to buy plastic flowers – they last longer and are cheaper than the real thing.

The central area bounded by Nanjing Donglu, Xizang Zhonglu, Jinling Donglu and Sichuan Zhonglu is a good place to rummage around. A lot of it is administrative, as it was under the International Settlement. Fuzhou Lu is an alleyway to explore, with bookshops and small restaurants which were once a collection of teahouses covering for brothels.

Shanghai Museum

(shànghǎi bówùguǎn) 上海博物馆

On Henan Nanlu, just off Yan'an Donglu, is the Shanghai Museum. It contains a fair collection of bronzes (graduated bells, knives, axeheads, chariot ornaments), ceramics, paintings and some terracotta figures from Xi'an. There is a shop on the 2nd floor where bronzes, scrolls and ceramics can be bought.

It's open continuously from 9 am to 3.30 pm, and admission is Y2.

Frenchtown

(făguó zūjiè) 法国租界

The core of Frenchtown – the former French concession – is the area around Huaihai Lu and the Jinjiang Hotel. The area was mainly inhabited by White Russian émigrés who numbered up to a third of the foreign population in the 1920s and '30s. They ran cafes and tailoring businesses along Huaihai, and took jobs as riding instructors, bodyguards – and prostitutes.

The cafes and tailoring outlets in today's Shanghai still centre around Huaihai Lu and the 1930s architecture is still standing. The area offers some good shopping (mainly shoes, household decorations and some secondhand goods) and excellent bakeries. The Parisian touch is about as chic as China will get. The street leading west off the northwestern tip of the Jinjiang Hotel is intriguing for its squat, double-storied architecture, where underwear flaps from the former residences of the rich, or a duck on a pole hangs out to dry.

Back in the bad old days the French Concession had a different set of laws from the International Settlement. The French licensed prostitution and opium smoking, while the Internationals just turned a blind eye. With such laws, and because of its proximity to the old Chinese city, a number of China's underworld figures were attracted to the French side of things.

On Xinle Lu, a kind of cul-de-sac which is the first diagonal street to the west of Xiangyang Park, is the Donghu Guesthouse (at No 167). This used to be the headquarters of the Great Circle Gang. Chief mobster was Du Yuesheng, boss of the gang. After a career as a sweet-potato vendor, Du got his start in the police force of the French Concession, where he used his position to squeeze money out of the local opium merchants. In 10 years he had risen to a high position in the Chinese gangs that controlled the opium trade in the Yangtse Valley – they were said to contribute the equivalent of US$20 million annually to the French authorities. In return the French allowed them to use the concession as a base for their operations. By the 1930s Du was on first-name terms with the Nanjing government leaders, and Chiang Kaishek even appointed him 'chief of the bureau of opium suppression'.

In March 1927, as the Kuomintang troops approached Shanghai on their Northern Expedition, the Communist-led workers rose in revolt and took over the Chinese part of Shanghai as planned. But Chiang had different ideas. Financed by Chiang's supporters among the Chinese bankers in Shanghai, escorted by foreign police, and provided with rifles and armoured cars by the International Settlement, Du Yuesheng's gangs launched an attack on the workers, killing between 5000 and 10,000 people, many of them Communists and left-wing Kuomintang. The attack wiped out the Shanghai Communists at a stroke, and was followed by further massacres in Canton, Changsha and Nanchang, forcing the Communists to move the focus of their movement to the countryside.

Site of the 1st National Congress of the Communist Party

(zhōnggòng dàhuìzhǐ) 中共大会址

One activity which the French, and later the Kuomintang, did not take to, was political meetings – these were illegal. The Chinese Communist Party was founded in July 1921 in a French Concession building, at a meeting of delegates from the various Communist and Socialist organisations around China.

This building is usually recorded as being at 76 Xingye Lu – but according to the street signs in the area it stands at the corner of Huangpi and Ximen Lu, further south of Xingye Lu – see the map for directions. Captions are in English and the building is closed Mondays and Thursdays.

We don't really know if the 'First Supper' was as cool, calm and collected as the present museum makes out. We don't even know if this really was where the meeting took place, exactly who was there, how many were there, the actual date or what happened. Nevertheless, the museum has been organised here in what is supposed to be the house of one of the delegates, Li Hanjun. Two foreigners are also said to have been in attendance.

Simon Leys in his book *Chinese Shadows* drops 12 names in the attendance list. According to him, what happened to them afterwards doesn't reflect too well on Communist history. Only Mao Zedong and Dong Biwu, elder statesman of the Party and a remarkable political all-rounder, survived in good standing until their natural deaths in the 1970s.

As for the others, four were executed by the Kuomintang or provincial warlords; four defected to the Kuomintang and of these four, two went over to the Japanese. Another delegate, Li Da, remained loyal to the Party and eventually became president of Wuhan University after Liberation; he is supposed to have died of injuries inflicted on him by the Red Guards in 1966. The host, Li Hanjun, appears to have left or to have been excluded from the Party early on, but his execution by the Kuomintang in 1927 rehabilitated him.

The story continues that the delegates' meeting was disrupted by the intrusion of an outsider – presumably a spy – and fearing a raid by the French police, they left the premises and later continued their meeting on a houseboat in Jiaxing, halfway to Hangzhou. The Shanghai building is supposed to have been damaged during the massacre of 1927, again at the hands of the Japanese.

Sun Yatsen's Residence
(sūn zhōngshān gùjū) 孙中山故居
At 7 Xianshan Lu, formerly the Rue Molière, is the former residence of Dr Sun Yatsen. He lived for six years in this house not far from Fuxing Park, supported by Overseas Chinese funds. After Sun's death, his wife, Song Qingling, continued to live here until 1937, constantly watched by Kuomintang plain-clothes men and French police. Her sister had married Chiang Kaishek in 1927, and her brother, T V Soong, was on-and-off finance minister to Chiang and a wheeler and dealer in banking fortunes. Song Qingling was close to the Communists, so it must have made for interesting dinner conversation. The house is set back from the street, furnished the way it used to be (it was looted by the Japanese). Gaining admission takes persistence as the staff usually tell you to come back another day to get rid of you. Fuxing Park is also worth a stroll if you're in the area – locals airing the kids off, playing chess, etc.

Arts & Crafts Research Institute
(gōngyì měishùpǐn yànjiūsuǒ)
工艺美术研究所
A French bourgeois villa is worth delving into; it's now the Arts & Crafts Research Institute at 79 Fenyang Lu. The mansion is magnifique, and the institute has something like 15 specialities including woollen embroidery, boxwood carving, lacquerware inlay, and paper-cutting. The faculty here creates the prototypes for small factories and workshops around China, examines the traditional arts, and acts as technical adviser to the specialist factories in Shanghai. The first of its kind in the PRC, the institute was created in 1956. The Conservatory of Music is on the same street – for more details see the following section on Nightlife & Entertainment.

Mandarin Gardens Bazaar
(yùyuán shāngchǎng) 豫园商场
At the north-eastern end of the old Chinese city, the bazaar area centres on what is known as Mandarin Gardens, and includes the Temple of the Town Gods. The place gets some 200,000 visitors daily, so try and stay out of it at weekends! There's nothing of historical interest left – people just come here to gawk at each other, mix, buy, sell and eat (see the Places to Eat section), but it's all entertaining enough.

The Pan family, rich Ming Dynasty officials, had **Mandarin Gardens** (*yùyuán*) built for them. The gardens took 18 years (from 1559 to 1577) to throw together and much

less time to destroy. They were bombarded during the Opium War in 1842, which is somewhat ironic since the deity lurking in the Temple of the Town Gods is supposed to guarantee the peace of the region. In the mid-19th century the gardens became the home base of the Society of Small Swords, who joined with the Taiping rebels and wreaked considerable casualties on the adjacent French Concession. The French responded promptly with thorough destruction. There's a museum devoted to the uprising and its demise within the gardens. The area was again savaged during the Boxer Rebellion. The gardens close early for lunch.

The **Temple of the Town Gods** *(chénghuángmiào)* first appeared in the Song Dynasty, and disappeared somewhere in the last paragraph. The main hall was rebuilt in 1926 with reinforced concrete and has recently undergone renovation after being used as a warehouse.

Fanning out from the temple and the gardens is the Mandarin Gardens shopping area – a Disneyland version of what the authorities think tourists might think is the real China. You enter the main action area via the **Wuxingting Teahouse** *(wǔxíng cháguǎn)*, a five-sided job set in a pond and looking as old as tea itself. It's pleasant to sit on the upper floor over a 60-fen pot of tea, but stay clear of the coffee and cocoa! The zigzag bridges leading to the teahouse were once full of misshapen beggars at every turn, something to try and visualise as you take in the present scenery. The surrounding bazaar has something like 100 small shops selling the tiny, the curious and the touristy. There are lots of places for Chinese snacks. You can get hankies emblazoned with Chinese landmarks – every time you blow your nose it will remind you of China. You can also get antiques, fans, scissors, bamboo articles, steamed ravioli, vegetarian buns, wine and meat dumplings, chicken and duck blood soup, radish-shred cakes, shell carvings, paintings, jigsaws, and so on.

The strangest thing about Mandarin Gardens Bazaar is that if you get past the 'reception centre' and the stage shows and further into the cobbled alleyways, you strike poverty. The slums have been cleared, and newer housing blocks exist to the south, but the back alleys are certainly lower-end living. There's no sanitation – everything's done with buckets and public toilets.

Jade Buddha Temple
(yùfó sì) 玉佛寺

From the Mandarin Gardens Bazaar you can hop on bus No 16 and ride all the way out to the Jade Buddha Temple. The ride takes in half of Shanghai en route, and most likely half the population will get off the bus with you.

The temple is an active one, with 70 resident monks at last count. It was built between 1911 and 1918. The exterior is readily identifiable by the bright saffron walls. Inside, the centrepiece is a 1.9-metre-high white jade buddha (some say it's alabaster), which was installed here after it had been brought by a monk from Burma to Zhejiang Province in 1882. This seated Buddha, encrusted with jewels, is said to weigh 1000 kg. A smaller, reclining Buddha from the same shipment lies on a redwood bed.

In the large hall are three gold-plated buddhas, and other halls house ferocious-looking deities. Artefacts abound, not all on display, and some 7000 Buddhist sutras line the walls. Should you arrive at the right time, a ceremony may be in progress. Also in the precincts is a branch of the Antique & Curio Store that sells miniature sandalwood drums and gongs, replicas of the larger ones used in ceremonies.

The temple was largely inactive from 1949 to 1980, as the monks were disbanded and the temple used for other functions. During the Cultural Revolution the place was only saved from destruction by a telegram (so the story goes) direct from the State Council. No doubt the recent picking up of activity is partly due to the tourist trade. The fact is that Shanghai, being so young, has few temples to show off.

The Jade Buddha Temple is popular with Overseas Chinese. No photography is permitted. The temple closes for lunch between noon and 1 pm and is open daily except on some special occasions such as the Lunar New Year in February – that's when Chinese Buddhists, some 20,000 of them, descend on the place. Admission is Y3.

An interesting route to the Jade Buddha Temple is along Suzhou Creek. It's a long walk there, and you may prefer to take the bus part of the way. The creek (water and banks heavily polluted) is home to sampans, small craft and barges, with crews delivering goods from the Yangtse reaches. There are stacks of bridges along the route and from these you'll get a decent view of the river life. Warehouses occasionally block the paths along the banks. On the way is a former church with an interesting twist – it's now a research institute for the electric-light industry.

Tomb of Lu Xun (Hongkou Park)
(hóngkǒu gōngyuǎn) 虹口公园

Lu Xun (1881-1936) was a novelist and essayist, and was regarded as the founder of modern Chinese writing. He was also revered as a scholar and a teacher. Though he was not a Communist, most of his books were banned by the Kuomintang and he had to stay in hiding in the French Concession. His message to Chinese youth read:

> Think, and study the economic problems of society...travel through the hundreds of dead villages, visit the generals and then visit the victims, see the realities of your time with opened eyes and a clear mind, and work for an enlightened society, but always think and study.

Lu Xun is best remembered for *The True Story of Ah Q*, the story of an illiterate coolie whose experiences through the first revolution of 1911 show the utter failure of that event to reach down to the ordinary people. Constantly baffled, seeing everything through a fog of ignorance and superstition, knowing words but not their meaning, he goes from one humiliation to the next, but each time rationalises his defeats into moral victories. Even when he is executed for a crime he did not commit, he goes cheerily to his death singing from a Chinese opera he does not understand: 'After 20 years I will be reborn again a hero'. His writings are published in English by the Foreign Languages Press and are widely available.

Lu Xun's tomb is some distance up Sichuan Beilu, in Hongkou Park. There's a pompous statue of the writer which would have horrified him. The statue was cast in 1961 and replaces an earlier concrete model, which would also have horrified him. His brother in Beijing wrote to another writer in Hong Kong:

> I have just seen a photograph of the statue they put up in front of Lu Xun's tomb in Shanghai; really, this is the supreme mockery! How could this personage sitting as on a throne be the effigy of someone who hated all solemn attitudes?

A museum in Hongkou Park tells the story of Lu Xun from the Communist point of view in Chinese.

Kids

Chinese kids are the most baffling section of the population. Nappyless, hardly ever

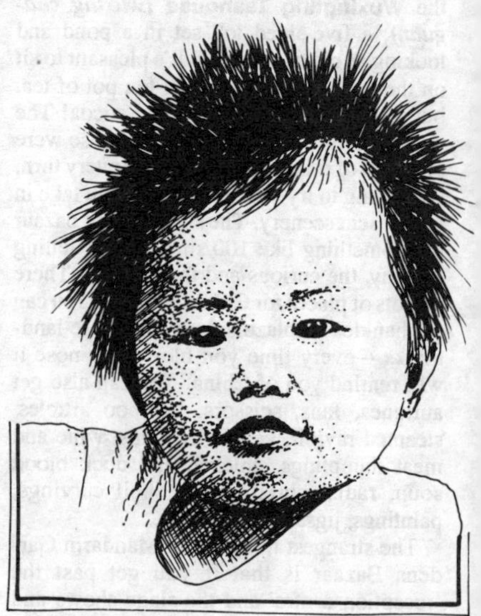

crying or looking worried – who knows what goes on inside their heads? Around the city are Children's Palaces, where extra-curricular activities take place and special interests are pursued. In theory this supplements regular schooling – but it has overtones of an elitist educational system. The one most visited by group tours (you can get in by yourself if you push) is on Yan'an Zhonglu, just west of Jing'an Park. The building really is a palace that once belonged to the Kadoorie family, and was then known as Marble House. The children here make model aeroplanes, play video games, attend classes in drawing, drama, music – and practise how to love their country and impress tourists.

A stark contrast to the kids' palace is the Peiguang Middle School. Drop down here in the early morning when the kids are doing their exercises in the courtyard just off the street (to the sound of 'Oh Canada'). The school is along Xizang Zhonglu, on the corner of Jiujiang Lu, which is one block south of Nanjing Donglu. The school used to be the notorious Laozhu Police Station in the concession days.

Children's stores are among the places where parents and their (usually one) offspring gather. Try the bookstore at 772 Nanjing Xilu, the Xiangyang at 993 Nanjing Xilu (toys, clothing and furniture), the foodstore at 980 Nanjing Xilu (cakes and cookies), the shoe and hat shop at 600 Nanjing Donglu, and the clothing store at 939 and 765 Huaihai Zhonglu.

In the entertainment line, much-publicised child prodigies pop up at the Conservatory of Music (see the Nightlife & Entertainment section). Shanghai has its own film animation studio – China's equivalent of Disneyworld products. There's also a troupe called the Children's Art Theatre.

Other Attractions

Plans for Shanghai include the erection of a 400-metre-high (!) TV tower with observation deck on the east bank of the Huangpu, to provide tourists with satellite views of the city below. If heights make you giddy then you might instead try searching out some of Shanghai's gambling dens. Chinese newspapers report that illegal gambling dens are springing up in the city, with enormous stakes laid on the tables.

A further 20 km north of Hongkou Park, towards the banks of the Yangtse and requiring a longer bus ride, is Jiading County, with a ruined Confucian temple and a classical garden.

South-west of central Shanghai and nearing a bend in the Huangpu River (within reach of Frenchtown) is the **Longhua Pagoda** *(lónghuá tǎ)*. This fell into disrepair, was used by the Red Guards as an advertising pole, and has since undergone renovation for the tourist trade. The pagoda is 40 metres high, octagonal with upturned eaves; it is said to date to the 10th century but was probably rebuilt a couple of times. The surrounding temple is largely restructured concrete, but the statuary of ferocious figures is impressive. The temple's once-famous peach blossoms have now disappeared.

The Xujiahui area bordering the western end of Frenchtown once had a Jesuit settlement, with an observatory (still in use). **St Ignatius Cathedral**, whose spires were lopped off by Red Guards, has been restored and is open once again for Catholic services. It's at 158 Puxi Lu, Xujiahui District.

Further south-west of the Longhua Pagoda are the **Shanghai Botanical Gardens** *(shànghǎi zhíwùyuǎn)*, with an exquisite collection of 9000 miniatures.

On the way to the town of Jiaxing, by rail or road, is Sunjiang County, 20 km south-west of Shanghai. The place is older than Shanghai itself. On Tianmashan, in Sunjiang County, is the **Huzhou Pagoda**, built in 1079 AD. It's the leaning tower of China, with an inclination now exceeding the tower at Pisa by 1.5 degrees. The 18.8-metre-high tower started tilting 200 years ago.

The **Shanghai Exhibition Centre** is west of the city centre. Drop in here for a mammoth view of Soviet palace architecture. There are irregular displays of local industrial wares and handicrafts.

Out near the airport is **Xijiao Park**, a zoo with a roller-skating rink, children's playground and other recreational facilities. To the west of that is the former **Sassoon Villas**. At Qingpu County, 25 km west of Shanghai, they've made up for the dearth of real antiquities and temples by creating a new scenic area for tourists to visit.

Huangpu River Trip

There are three main perspectives on Shanghai – from the gutters, from the heights (aerial views from the battlements of the tourist fortresses), and from the waters. The Huangpu River offers some remarkable views of the Bund and the river front activity. The junks that cut in and out of the harbour bring back memories so old you probably last saw them in some pirate movie. Back in the 1920s you would have arrived in Shanghai by boat, and today's touring vessels seem to ham it up, imitating the colonial style of that era. About the only negative aspect of a boat trip is the sulphurous smell of the river itself, which is severely polluted.

Huangpu tour boats depart from the dock on the Bund, slightly north of the Peace Hotel. There are several decks on the boat, but prices for foreigners are Y33 (special class A) and Y17 (special class B). Departure times are 8.30 am and 1.30 pm, with possible extra departures in the summer and on Sundays. The schedule may become erratic in winter due to bad weather.

Junk on the Yangtse River

Tickets can be purchased in advance from CITS at the Peace Hotel (there's a small surcharge), or at the boat dock – but there's no real need if you're taking upper deck since it is unlikely to be full. The boat takes you on a 3½-hour ride, 60 km round trip, northward up the Huangpu to the junction with the Yangtse River, to Wusongkou and back again along the same route. On the return run they show videos on the lower deck – usually bloodthirsty kungfu flicks.

Shanghai is one of the world's largest ports; 2000 ocean-going ships and about 15,000 river steamers load and unload here every year. Coolies used to have the back-breaking task of loading and unloading, but these days the ports are a forest of cranes, derricks, conveyor belts and forklifts. The tour boat passes an enormous variety of craft – freighters, bulk carriers, roll-on roll-off ships, sculling sampans, giant praying-mantis cranes, the occasional junk and Chinese navy vessels (which aren't supposed to be photographed).

Festivals

There are three events of significance. The Mid-Autumn Festival is held in October when they lay on the mooncakes – the festival recalls an uprising against the Mongols in the 14th century when plans for the revolt were passed around in cakes. Mooncakes are usually filled with a mixture of ground lotus, sesame seeds and dates, and sometimes duck egg. The Shanghai Music Festival is in May. The Shanghai Marathon Cup is in March and is one of the top sporting events in the country. The latter two, if not the first one, were suspended during the Cultural Revolution. Hotel space may be harder to come by at these times – also at Lunar New Year in February.

Places to Stay

Shanghai hotels are sights in their own right, a trip back to the '20s and '30s when the city was the most sophisticated of travellers' destinations. However, furnishings and art deco opulence are fading steadily, gradually replaced by the anonymous Holiday Inn-style aesthetic. Added to this is a strange armoury of electronic gadgets like closed-circuit TV, air-con, video games – all those creature comforts for today's visitor. A fair amount of renovation has been done on the buildings in the interests of tourism, though socialist plumbing is not always as successful as Western.

Apart from being navigation landmarks, the lofty upper floors of the central hotels offer stupendous views, day or night. These can be combined with a trip to restaurants serving great Chinese and Western food, the latter sometimes linked with pre-Liberation chefs and usually excellent. Shanghai's relatively decadent nightlife also happens within the walls of the hotels.

Shanghai is a headache for the low-budget traveller. As in Beijing there is simply a chronic lack of space, and a lot of what's available is permanently occupied by business people, foreign dignitaries or resident foreign experts.

Places to Stay – bottom end The *Pujiang Hotel* (☎ 3246388) *(pǔjiāng fàndiàn)* at 15 Huangpu Lu is near Shanghai Mansions, and caters to a mixed Chinese and Western clientele. The dormitories are the main attraction and the hotel is now the established backpackers' hang-out of Shanghai. If the dorms are full they may put you in a hallway with overhead walkways – rather like a cross between a military hospital and a prison. Dorm beds are Y20 a night and are usually booked by mid-afternoon (around 10 am seems to be the best time to show up). There are also four-bed rooms for Y126, triples for Y109, and doubles for Y97. The Pujiang used to be the Astor House Hotel, one of the most elegant in the early concession days, before it was dwarfed by Shanghai Mansions. Today the Pujiang is a bit run-down and can get cold and clammy in winter – otherwise it's nice enough (at least it still has character). Take bus No 65 from near the main railway station to Beijing Donglu and then walk east and left up the the Bund over Suzhou Creek to the hotel.

If the Pujiang's full, you can almost always get a bed at the *Hai Jia Hotel* (☎ 3411440) at 1001 Jiangpu Lu. Beds are only Y12 per person in five-bed rooms with communal bath. Three-bed rooms are also available for Y18 per person and doubles with air-con and private bath are Y100. To get there from the Pujiang Hotel area, take bus No 22 east along Dongdaming Lu (behind the Pujiang). The bus soon turns onto Chang Yang Lu; when you see/smell the tobacco factory, get off at the next stop, Jiangpu Lu. The Hai Jia is less than five minutes' walk north of Chang Yang Lu on the left-hand side of Jiangpu Lu. There's no English sign – look for a large, glass-fronted building with a restaurant downstairs. Coming from the main Shanghai railway station, bus Nos 310 or 70 stop almost in front of the hotel. Although it's just a bit away from the city centre, the neighbourhood around the Hai Jia is quite a bit less expensive than the Nanjing Lu or Huaihai areas.

Another place to try is the *Conservatory of Music* (☎ 4370137) *(yīnyuè xuéxiào)* at 20 Fenyang Lu off Huaihai Zhonglu in the French Concession area. The foreign student dorm will take non-students when there's room (best bet is during the summer) and costs Y20 per person in a comfortable double. To find it, take the first left after passing through the main gate, then another immediate left past the buildings on the left; the dorm will be on your right – look for the resident round-eyes wandering around.

Places to Stay – middle Just bridging the gap between budget and medium-priced accommodation is the *Chung Shen Jiang Hotel* (☎ 3205710) *(zhōngshēn jiāng)* at 626 Nanjing Donglu. Large doubles with air-con, phone, TV, and hot water are a bargain Y90. The front desk can be hopeless about bookings, however, since they don't seem to know when they're full and when they're not – if they say it's full, check with the floor maids to see if they can locate an empty room.

The *Seagull Hotel (hǎiōu bīnguǎn)* is on the waterfront and a minute's walk from the Pujiang Hotel. Clean doubles cost from Y145. A moderately priced restaurant on the 2nd floor serves Chinese and European dishes with generous helpings.

The *Yangtze Hotel* (☎ 3207880) *(chángjiāng fàndiàn)* is at 740 Hankou Lu, down an alley running east from People's Park, and is best approached from this direction. Formerly reserved for Chinese and Overseas Chinese only (when it was called the Shenjiang), the hotel has been renovated and now takes anyone who will pay from Y120 to Y148 for a double – quite reasonable value. The hotel was built back in 1934 and is an old American-style hotel. Take bus No 109 from the railway station to People's Park on Nanjing Donglu.

Places to Stay – top end This is Shanghai, and the history and the character of the Bund is one of the reasons to come here. In the not-so-distant past, travellers often splurged on a more expensive place in Shanghai just to get a wood-panelled room with a sense of history. Since the interior renovations at the Park, Shanghai Mansions, and Jinjiang, these days there's only one left that really fits the bill: the *Peace Hotel* (☎ 3211244) *(hépíng fàndiàn)* for the northern high-rise wing, 3218050 for the south building) at the junction of the Bund and Nanjing Donglu. To enjoy one of their funky old rooms, however, you'll have to put up with frosty service and a definite atmosphere of neglect. Doubles cost from Y231 and are really overpriced considering the condition of the rooms and surly service. On the ground floor of the 12-storey edifice are the sumptuous lobby, shops, bookstore, bank, video games parlour, snooker tables, cafe and barber. The scalp massage service has a good reputation. To get to the hotel take bus No 64 from the railway station. The Peace is a highly prized location for business people since it is adjacent to the Chinese trading corporations along the Bund. During the winter months, conferences are rife, large numbers of Chinese move in and it's a mite difficult to get in. Drop in and examine the decor: staggering! High ceilings, chandeliers, brass doorplates, ornate mirrors, Art-Deco lamps and fixtures, and 1930s calligraphy. Go up to the Dragon & Phoenix Restaurant on the 8th floor for great views across the Bund and the Huangpu River. The south wing used to be the Palace Hotel and was built in 1906; the brass plumbing within is original.

The Peace is a ghostly reminder of the immense wealth of Victor Sassoon. From a Baghdad Jewish family, he made millions out of the opium trade and then ploughed it back into Shanghai real estate and horses. Sassoon's quote of the day was 'There is only one race greater than the Jews, and that's the Derby'. His office-cum-hotel was completed in 1930 and was known as Sassoon House, incorporating the Cathay Hotel. From the top floors Victor commanded his real estate – he is estimated to have owned 1900 buildings in Shanghai.

The Cathay Hotel fell into the same category as the Taj in Bombay, the Stanley Raffles in Singapore and the Peninsula in Hong Kong as *the* place to stay. Sassoon himself resided in what is now the VIP section below the green pyramidal tower, complete with Tudor panelling. He also maintained a Tudor-style villa out near Hongqiao Airport just west of the zoo. Anyone who was anyone could be seen dancing in the Tower Restaurant. The likes of Noel Coward (who wrote *Private Lives* in the Cathay) entertained themselves in this penthouse ballroom.

Back in 1949 the Kuomintang strayed into the place awaiting the arrival of the Communists. A Western writer of the time records an incident in which 50 Kuomintang arrived carrying their pots and pans, vegetables and firewood, and one soldier was overheard asking where to billet the mules. After the Communists took over the city, the troops were billeted in places like the Picardie (now the Hengshan Guesthouse on the outskirts of the city), where they spent hours experimenting with the elevators, used bidets as face-showers, and washed rice in the toilets – which was all very well until someone pulled the chain. In 1953 foreigners tried to give the Cathay to the CCP in return for exit visas. The government refused but finally accepted after the payment of 'back taxes'.

The *Park Hotel* (☎ 3275225) *(guójì fàndiàn)* is at 170 Nanjing Xilu and overlooks Renmin

Park. Erected in 1934, the building is one of Shanghai's best examples of Art-Deco architecture from the city's cultural peak. The interior, however, has lost all its old world charm with recent renovations. Doubles start at Y193 plus 10% service charge. Rooms are quite comfortable and service is efficient. The best views of Shanghai are from the men's toilets on the 14th floor. Take bus No 64 from the railway station. Taxi drivers know the Park Hotel as the *Guoji Fandian* or 'International Hotel'.

Shanghai Mansions (☎ 3246260) *(shànghǎi dàshà)* is at 20 Suzhou Beilu, near the Pujiang Hotel on the same side of Huangpu River at the junction with Suzhou Creek. It's owned by the Hengshan Group, which also owns the more moderately priced Pujiang and Yangtze hotels. Double rooms (no singles) cost from Y198. For a suite toward the top of the hotel with a waterfront view and balcony and perhaps a grand piano – well, if you've got that sort of money then there's no need to ask the price. The Mansions are rather dull compared to other Shanghai hotels but try and make it to the rooftop because the views are stunning! The 20-storey brick building was constructed in 1934 as a posh British residential hotel. Since it was on the fringes of the International Settlement near the Japanese side of town, it was quickly taken over at the outset of the Sino-Japanese war in 1937. The Japanese stripped the fittings (like the radiators) for scrap metal, and the same fate befell other Shanghai hotels during the occupation. As for the billiard tables, these were sawn off at the legs to fit the smaller stature of Japanese enthusiasts. The place used to be known as Broadway Mansions; after the Japanese surrender and before 1949, the US Military Advisory Group to the Kuomintang set up shop on the lower floors, while the upper section was used by the foreign press and one floor was devoted to the Foreign Correspondents' Club.

The *Overseas Chinese Hotel* (☎ 3226226) *(huáqiáo fàndiàn)* is at 104 Nanjing Xilu – it's easily recognisable by the distinctive clock tower with the big Red Star on it, and by the fabulously ornate foyer. Doubles cost from Y187. One of Nanjing Lu's more historic hotels.

The *Jinjiang Hotel* (☎ 2582582) *(jǐnjiāng fàndiàn)* is at 59 Maoming Nanlu. It's so vast you need a map of the place to find your way around – a brochure with map is available in the north building. The colossus stretches north-south along an entire block with two gates on the western side. Doubles cost from Y275. To get to the Jinjiang take bus No 41 from the railway station; bus No 26 goes there from the Bund area.

If you don't stay at the Jinjiang you should at least drop down and have a look at it; it's located in what used to be the old French Concession, an interesting alternative to the Bund, since the surrounding area is now entirely residential. The residents of the hotel, though, need never venture out since this fortress-like building has all you need to survive. Nixon stayed here in 1972 if that's any recommendation. Apart from his fingerprints, check out the North Building, a 14-storey block once called the Cathay Mansions and built as an exclusive French apartment block with amazing wood-panelling and iron chandelier period pieces. Additional attractions of the Jinjiang include the Jin Li Restaurant on the ground floor of the new South Building (with 24-hour service); a dance hall and Western-style restaurant on the 11th floor of the North Building; and a Hong-Kong-style disco called the *Club d'Elegance* on the ground floor of the West Building (with a Y35-per-person cover charge). Check out the expensive though rather elegant *Café Reve*. You may also want to drop across the road to the Garden Hotel – formerly the Jinjiang Club (see Bars & Clubs in this chapter), which retains some of its mirrors-and-marble 1920s fittings.

Other top-end hotels in Shanghai fall into the 'modern' category. The most luxurious are huge complexes that are situated towards the south-west outskirts of city (en route to Hongqiao Airport), eg the Sheraton Hua Ting, the Yangtze New World and the Novotel Shanghai Yuan Lin. These hotel complexes attempt to create self-contained international cities (after Beijing models like the Beijing Lido), complete with multiple restaurants, lounges, discos, hair salons, swimming pools, fitness centres, business centres and shopping centres. The Sheraton Hua Ting even has a bowling alley.

Slightly less expensive are those modern hotels closer to the city centre – Shanghai Hotel, the Jing An Guesthouse and the Hengshan Guesthouse. To rates in the following list, add 10% service charge. All rooms come with a minimum of air-con, colour TV, phone, and refrigerator.

Cypress Hotel (☎ 4329388)
2419 Hongqiao Lu, US$50 to US$95
Hengshan Guesthouse (☎ 4377050)
534 Heng Shan Lu, US$45 to US$90
Hyatt Shanghai (opening 1992)
Dongtiyuhuikou, Handan Lu, US$100 up
Jing An Guesthouse (☎ 3563050)
370 Hua Shan Lu, US$40 to US$80
Hotel Nikko Longbai (☎ 2593636)
2451 Hongqiao Lu, US$85 to US$140
Novotel Shanghai Yuan Lin (☎ 4701688)
201 Bai Se Lu, US$75 to US$120
The Portman (☎ 2798888)
Shanghai Centre, 1376 Nanjing Xilu, US$90 up
Shanghai Hilton International (☎ 2550000)
250 Hua Shan Lu, US$125 to US$155
Shanghai Hotel (☎ 4312312)
505 Wulumqi Xiang, US$45 to US$95
Shanghai International Airport Hotel (☎ 2518866)
Hongqiao Airport, US$80 to US$120
Sheraton Hua Ting Hotel (☎ 4391000)
1200 Cao Xi Beilu, US$65 to US$125
Yangtze New World Hotel (☎ 2750000)
2099 Yan'an Xilu, US$95 to US$160

Places to Eat

Shanghai has a couple of its own specialities and is noted for its seafood (such as the freshwater crab that appears around October to December). Eating in the major restaurants can be an abysmal experience, as there is intense competition from the masses for tables and seats. Restaurants are forever packed in Shanghai and you really need some local help to overcome the language problems.

Lunch (around 11.30 am to 2 pm) is sometimes OK but dinner (from 5 to 7 pm) is a rat race. In these busy restaurants the waiters will try and get rid of you either by telling you that there are no tables, or by directing you to the cadre and foreigners' rooms – with their elegant decor and beefed-up prices. If it eases your digestion, back in the inflation-ridden China of 1947 a couple had dinner one evening in a Shanghai hotel and found their bill came to 250 million yuan!

If you want to spend more time eating, and at local prices, then try restaurants a bit off the track, perhaps around the old French Concession area. You could also try the smaller places on Fuzhou Lu, where the greasy-spoon prices drop to a few yuan per head. On the other hand, if it's good food (either Chinese or Western) you want, in surroundings that echo the days of the foreign concessions, then splash out on the restaurants in the old colonial hotels (details at the end of this section). It's one aspect of Shanghai not to be missed.

Also not to be missed in Shanghai is the ease and delight of snack-eating. You get waylaid for hours trying to make it along the length of Nanjing Lu, stumbling out of a pastry shop and wiping off the smudges of lemon meringue pie, chocolate and cream, only to fall immediately into the sweet store next door. The tourist hotels have a good range of cakes, chocolate eclairs and ice-cream sundaes to get you started. The offerings for breakfast from the Chinese snack shops are so good you may be converted yet!

Common Chinese breakfast fare is the *yóutiáo*, a somewhat greasy doughnut stick – but deep-fried variations in the doughnut line are smaller and much more palatable. Western snacks are a fad among the young of Shanghai; sandwiches are awful, coffee is terrible, cream cakes are fair to good, cocoa is disgusting, cold drinks are erk, but pastries are top notch. These snack hang-outs have lots of character and there are lots of characters to be observed.

One thing worth noting – if you wander into a Nanjing Lu restaurant and see a couple in matching suits, red roses in the lapels, and orange soft drinks on every table – then forget it, it's a wedding party. Around dinnertime all the Nanjing Lu restaurants seem to be occupied by them.

Nanjing Donglu Towards the Bund are two semi-Western-style coffee shops that are immensely popular with young Chinese, the *Deda Western Food Restaurant (déxī cānshè)* and *East Sea Coffee (dōnghǎi kāfēi)*. Both serve a variety of Chinese and Western dishes but almost everyone orders 'Spanish coffee', coffee with ice-cream. Further west on the right is the *Yangzhou (yángzhōu fàndiàn)* at 308 Nanjing Donglu, which has, as the name implies, Yangzhou-style food, including famous *yángzhōu chǎofàn*, a delicious fried rice dish.

The *Sichuan* (☎ 221965) *(sìchuān fàndiàn)* at No 457 has hot and spicy food, including camphor-tea duck and some rather strange-tasting chicken. Don't let them herd you into the private annexes. Stand your ground in the pleb section, where you'll get enough to fill three people for around Y12. It's a lively place at lunchtime; grab the back of someone's chair (everybody else does) and wait for them to go.

The *Xinya (Sunya) Cantonese Restaurant* (☎ 224393) *(xīnyǎ fàndiàn)* at No 719 has foreigners' cubicles on the 3rd floor with railway-carriage wood panelling and Cantonese food. Otherwise the lower floors are bare and bright like any self-respecting Chinese restaurant. Moderately priced dishes can be had for lunch and dinner, yum chas between 6.30 and 9.30 am. On the ground floor is a pastry shop that's usually empty. The *Yangunlou Restaurant* in the next block, same side of the street, is renowned for its Peking duck. Across the road is an enormous sweet and cake shop the size of a department store.

Two blocks further, turn left on Yunnan Lu and in the evenings (from 5 to 10 pm) you'll discover a marvellous 'food street' of sorts – a great place to sample local fare at local prices. Among the selections are fried wonton, noodle soups and shish kebab. Always settle on the price first before putting in an order. Nothing should cost more than Y2 or Y3.

Nanjing Xilu The *Xi Lai Lin Coffee House (xīláilín kāfēidiàn)* at No 72, near the Overseas Chinese and Park hotels, has perhaps the best pastry selection on this street. Coffee is

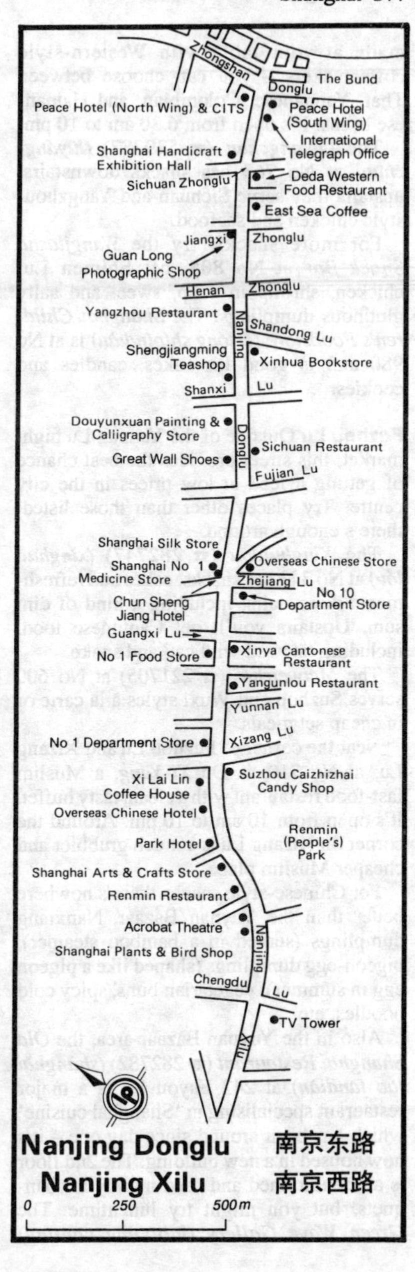

made at your table with Western-style coffeemakers – you can choose between Thai, Yunnanese, Colombian, and Hainanese beans. It's open from 6.30 am to 10 pm.

The *Luyangchun* (☎ 539787) *(lüyángchūn)* at No 763 has snacks downstairs; upstairs they serve Sichuan and Yangzhou-style chicken and seafood.

For more snacks, try the *Wangjiasha Snack Bar* at No 805, off Shimen Lu: chicken, shrimp in soup, sweet and salty glutinous dumplings. The *Shanghai Children's Foodstore (értóng shípǐndiàn)* is at No 980 and is good for cakes, candies and cookies.

Fuzhou Lu Outside of the Yunnan Lu night market, this street provides the best chance of getting a feed at low prices in the city centre. Try places other than those listed; there's enough around.

The *Xinghualou* (☎ 282747) *(xìnghuā lóu)* at No 343 has snacks, cakes and refreshments downstairs, including a kind of dim sum. Upstairs you'll get Cantonese food, including 'stewed wild cat' and snake.

The *Meiweizhai* (☎ 221705) at No 600 serves Suzhou and Wuxi styles à la carte or in cheap set meals.

Near the corner of Fuzhou Lu and Xizang Lu, at No 710, is *Da Xi Yang*, a Muslim fast-food restaurant with a clean, tasty buffet. It's open from 10 am to 10 pm. Around the corner on Xizang Lu is a much grubbier and cheaper Muslim place.

For Chinese-style snacks there's nowhere better than the Yuyuan Bazaar. Nanxiang dumplings (served in a bamboo steamer), pigeon-egg dumplings (shaped like a pigeon egg in summer), vegetarian buns, spicy cold noodles, etc.

Also in the Yuyuan Bazaar area, the *Old Shanghai Restaurant* (☎ 282782) *(shànghǎi lǎo fàndiàn)* at 242 Fuyou Lu is a major restaurant specialising in 'Shanghai cuisine' which has been around since day one – it's now housed in a new building. The 2nd floor is air-conditioned and used mainly for banquets, but you might try lunchtime. The *Green Wave Gallery (lǜbōláng cāntīng)* serves main courses and more expensive snacks; a seafood dinner may consist of black carp raised in the Lotus Pond under the winding bridge. Snacks include crabmeat buns, lotus root and bamboo shoot shortbread, three-shred eyebrow crispcakes and phoenix-tail dumplings (whatever they are).

Old French Concession Area Try the *Shanghai Western Restaurant* (☎ 374902) *(shànghǎi xīcāntīng)* at 845 Huaihai Zhonglu.

The *Meixin* (☎ 373991) *(měixīn fàndiàn)* at 314 Shaanxi Nanlu, near Huaihai Zhonglu, serves Cantonese crisp duck and chicken.

The *Red House* (☎ 565748) at 37 Shaanxi Nanlu was formerly Chez Louis and things haven't gone so well since Louis left; the food is generally terrible, but the snacks are better so long as they've got the right liqueur (baked Alaska and Grand Marnier soufflé); foreigners are expected to use the more expensive top floor but the ground floor is cheaper.

Along Huaihai Zhonglu is a string of confectionaries that will drive you bonkers! The *Canglangting* (☎ 283876) at 9 Chongqing Nanlu south of Huaihai has glutinous rice cakes and Suzhou-style dumplings and noodles. The *Tianshan Moslem Foodstore (tiānshān huímín shípǐndiàn)* at 671 Huaihai has Muslim delicacies, sweets and cakes. The *Laodacheng Bakery & Confectionery (lǎodàchēng shípǐndiàn)* at No 875 has a downstairs bakery with superb ice-cream in season; upstairs is a cafe where they spray ice-cream over everything; it also offers meringues and macaroons – open until 9.30 pm. The *Shanghai Bakery (Shanghai Foodstuff Factory) (shànghǎi shípǐndiàn)* at No 979 has French bread, wholemeal bread, cream cakes and chocolate.

Hotel Food The big tourist hotels have excellent Chinese and Western food. Dining hours are around 7 to 9 am for breakfast, 11.30 am to 2 pm for lunch and 5.30 to 8 pm for dinner. While some of the offerings in the ritzier parts of the hotels are on the expensive side, a Western breakfast can be surprisingly cheap. The coffee shop in the south wing of the *Peace Hotel* serves a breakfast of toast and three eggs for US$1 (a cup of coffee, however, will cost you another US$1). The *Dragon & Phoenix Restaurant* on the 8th floor of the north wing has Western, Shanghai, Sichuan and Cantonese food. If you examine the tableware closely you might find original Cathay crests. While the exotic seafood (like seaslug) is expensive, there are quite cheap vegetable and pork dishes – on the other hand, if you've never eaten a seaslug then this might be the time to spend some money and find out what it's like.

The *Viking Room* restaurant on the 11th floor of the north building of the *Jinjiang Hotel* serves great Western breakfasts (including yoghurt), as well as Sichuan, Cantonese and Western meals, and has some of the most opulent surroundings and incredible views to be found in Shanghai. The coffee shop on the 1st floor of the north wing serves tasty, if expensive, Italian specialities.

The *Overseas Chinese Hotel* has a few restaurants. Fujianese food is a speciality in the restaurant near the top of the nine-storey block; there's also a quaint little coffee bar to the left as you enter on the ground floor.

The *Park Hotel* has several restaurants. On the 14th floor (that's actually the 12th since two of the floors are below ground) is a restaurant that used to be called the Sky Terrace; a section of the roof could be rolled back to allow patrons to dine under the stars. Apparently the gizmo is still in place though we haven't heard of anyone getting the planetarium effect. Towards the top is the *Four Seasons Banquet Room* where extensive eight-course imperial banquets, including Beijing duck, can be ordered in advance. A less expensive Chinese restaurant on the 2nd floor specialises in Shanghai cuisine. *Le Parc Lounge* on the 1st floor is a pleasantly informal place for beer and snacks.

We hate to admit it, but the best hotel food these days is being served at the more modern joint-venture hotels, which can afford to pay for the best chefs in China. *Luigi's* at the *Sheraton Hua Ting* is reputed to have the best Italian food in Shanghai. The Sheraton's *Guan Yue Tai* serves Cantonese to the sounds of a live classical string ensemble.

The *Atrium Cafe* on the ground floor of the Singapore-run *Shanghai Hilton* has an extensive buffet of Western and Chinese dishes and occasionally serves special Indian dinners. On the 1st floor is the very expensive *Teppan Grill*, serving Japanese grills and French cuisine. Fairly moderate in price (for an international hotel) is the dim sum lunch available at the hotel's *Suiyuan*. For gourmet Sichuan there's the *Sichuan Court* and for Shanghainese, the *Shanghai Express*.

Vegetarian Food Vegetarianism became something of a snobbish fad in Shanghai at one time; it was linked to Taoist and Buddhist groups, then to the underworld, and surfaced on the tables of restaurants as creations shaped like flowers or animals. Khi Vehdu, who ran the Jing'an Temple in the 1930s, was one of the most celebrated exponents. The 1.9-metre-tall abbot had a large following – and each of his seven concubines had a house and car. The Jing'an Temple was eventually divested of its Buddhist statues and turned into a factory.

Materials for vegetarian fare include bean products, dried mushrooms, fungus, bamboo shoots, noodles, seaweed – and vegetables. It should be possible to arrange for more elaborate presentation and quality by phoning in advance and booking a vegetarian banquet.

The *Gongdelin* (☎ 580218) (*gōngdélín sùcài guǎn)* at 43 Huanghe Lu has mock crab, other mock seafood, mock duck and roasted bran-dough. Banquets can be arranged.

A couple of shops specialise in vegetarian food; these include the *Hongkouqu Grain Store* at 10 Bei Haining Lu, which is good for fresh peanut butter, tahini, grains, beans and vegetable oils. The *Sanjiaodi Vegetable Market* at 250 Tanggu Lu in the Hongkou District, north of the Bund, is a large indoor market selling fresh vegetables and beancurd products, and ready-to-cook dinners, fish and meat. The *Yuyuan Bazaar* area has snack bars serving vegetarian food.

Cafes Shanghai's cafes are open until around 10 pm and sometimes until 10.30 pm – just follow the neon. These are meeting and gossip hang-outs where coffee and cakes cost around Y2 for two people – dreadful coffee and lousy cakes, but if you've wondered what it must have been like in a Parisian cafe in the 1930s then the ambience is definitely there.

After they get booted out of all the shoe stores along Huaihai Zhonglu, young and old folk head for the upstairs section of the *Laodacheng Bakery* which is open until around 10 pm – you can choose cakes downstairs first if you want to. In case things get a bit out of hand there are little round coasters under the glass tops of the tables upstairs at the Laodacheng, reminding people of the one-child policy – with graphics of a lady feeding rabbits.

Nightlife & Entertainment

There's a bite-sized chunk of nightlife to be had here – like elsewhere in China it proceeds in fits and starts, mostly fits, and while it's pretty tame by pre-1949 standards it's rewarding enough. Back in the bad old days the acrid smell of opium hung in the streets, bevies of bar girls from the four corners draped themselves over the rich; there were casinos, greyhound and horse-racing tracks, strings of nightclubs, thousands of brothels, lavish dinners, several hundred ballrooms.

The Kuomintang dampened the nightlife by imposing a curfew. When the Communists took over they wiped out in a year what the missionaries had failed to do in a hundred years. Since the average Chinese has to get up at the crack of dawn there's a self-imposed curfew of around 10 pm – nevertheless there are Chinese couples lolling about on the walkways and park benches of the Bund late into the night. Decadent foreign devils can rage on (as much as this place will allow) until around midnight.

Before the Communist takeover one of the major sources of diversion was the Great World Amusement Centre, offering girls, earwax extractors, magicians, mah-jong, jugglers, freak shows, dancing, slot machines, story-tellers, barbers, shooting galleries, pickpockets and a bureau for writing love letters. Today the place has been turned into the Shanghai Youth Palace and stands at the corner of Yan'an Lu and Xizang Lu. Since 1983 the place has been hosting 'Youth Evenings' where 30-year-olds come in the hope of finding a husband or wife.

Bars & Clubs The Peace Hotel Jazz Bar winds up the 1930s music machine from 8 to 11 pm nightly. It's not exactly the latest material; the band pumps out polite renditions of 'Tea for Two', 'Gypsy Rag', 'When the Saints...', 'I Wonder Who's Kissing her Now?' and a sprinkling of Hong Kong pop tunes – no singing but these old-timers do a splendid job with their piano, horns and drum smashes (it seems most of them are actually trained in Western classical music). Elderly foreign guests are inspired to leap to the dance floor, but I couldn't tell if they were doing a foxtrot or a rhumba – before my time. It's time to clean out the eardrums too – what's this, they *can't* be playing Waltzing Matilda! It's a good place to meet the rest of the foreigners in the woodwork. In the background, waiters with starched napkins over their arms glide between the tables ready to dispense Hot Toddies, Manhattans, Russian Bears, Rusty Nails and Shanghai Cocktails (a mix of gin and Chinese white wine). Ice-cream sundaes and other delectables can be procured. All this takes place on the ground floor of the Peace Hotel.

Alas, the Jinjiang Club is no more. Housed in a remarkable building opposite the main gates of the Jinjiang Hotel, this place had the most extraordinary nightlife museum in the PRC. The dazzling collection of interiors was thrown up in the 1920s and was then known as the *Cercle Sportif Français* – the French Sporting Club. It closed its doors in 1949, underwent a 30-year silence (when it was rumoured to be either a military training centre or Mao's Shanghai residence) and was reopened in 1979 for foreigners and high-ranking Chinese. It has now been renovated and reopened as the luxury Garden Hotel (*huāyuǎn fàndiàn*), retaining some of the original fittings. Instead, try the Jinjiang Hotel across the road, which has a bar and (very expensive) disco.

Each of the elite Euro-American-style hotels, eg the Sheraton Hua Ting, Shanghai Hilton and Yangtze New World, has at least one international nightclub where business people and tech reps shake it as best they can.

Performing Arts There are some 70 cinemas and theatres and 35 performing troupes in Greater Shanghai – with a little help from the numerous English-speakers in this place it should be possible to delve into the local listings, which may include top-notch travelling troupes. This is probably the best place in China to get a look at the local entertainment scene: acrobatics, ballet, music, burlesque, opera, drama, puppets, sporting events...a couple of venues are listed below to give you some idea of what's in stock here.

The Shanghai Art Theatre is just down the road from the Jinjiang Hotel, and is housed in what used to be the Lyceum Theatre. The theatre was completed in 1931 and was used by the Shanghai Amateur Dramatic Society – a favourite haunt of the Brits. The theatre company of the same name started up in 1929, the first drama troupe of the Communist Party. Nowadays there are all sorts of unexpected performances here – anyone for *Equus* in Mandarin?

The Shanghai Film Studio continues to produce some of the better material in China. Film-making in Shanghai has a long tradition – as old as movie-making can be. One of the starlets of the B-grade set back in the 1930s was Jiang Qing. It's potluck whether you'll find a good movie or not, but it won't cost more than a few jiao to find out. A good gauge of a film's popularity is the bike parking outside – if it spreads for two blocks then it must be a hit!

The Conservatory of Music (☎ 4370137) *(yīnyuè xuéxiào)* at 20 Fenyang Lu off Huaihai Zhonglu in Frenchtown is a treat not to be missed by classical music lovers. The conservatory was established in 1927 and its faculty members were mainly foreign – after WW I Shanghai was a meeting place for talented European musicians. The most enthralling aspect of the conservatory is the child prodigies. Back in 1979 Yehudi Menuhin was passing through here and picked 11-year-old violinist Jin Li for further instruction in England; the kid enthralled audiences in London in 1982 with his renditions of Beethoven. Other wonders, products of the special training classes set up in the 1950s, have gone to the West on cultural-exchange visits. The conservatory was closed during the Cultural Revolution, but Beethoven et al have now been rehabilitated along with the conservatory. Performances take place on Sunday evenings at 7 pm. Tickets are usually sold out a few days before, though. Also try the opera at the People's Opera Theatre on Jiu Jiang Lu.

There are several professional orchestras in Shanghai, including the Shanghai Philharmonic and the Shanghai National Orchestra. The latter specialises in native instruments.

The largest indoor sports venue in Shanghai is the Shanghai Gymnasium at the south-west corner of the city. It's air-conditioned, has computer-controlled score boards and seats 18,000.

Acrobatics Acrobats are pure fun and they're China's true ambassadors. Donating pandas may have soothed relations but it's the acrobats who capture the international imagination. The Shenyang Acrobatic Troupe toured the USA before the two countries established diplomatic relations, and Chinese troupes have gone to 30 countries with not a dud response.

The Shanghai Acrobatics Theatre has shows most evenings. It's one of the best equipped in China for these acts. Sometimes performing tigers and pandas (not together) show up as an added bonus. Tickets for the regular shows are around Y3 but try and get them ahead of time from the office to the side of the theatre. CITS will also book seats. Or you could just try your luck and roll up when performances start, which is around 7 pm nightly – however, you may then be forced to buy the last tickets from scalpers at grossly inflated prices. Mixed reaction to the shows here; many people find the animal acts a bit sad.

The theatre is on Nanjing Xilu, a short walk west of the Park Hotel on the same side of the street.

Circus acts go back 2000 years in the Middle Kingdom; effects are obtained using simple props: sticks, plates, eggs and chairs; and apart from the acrobatics there's magic, vaudeville, drama, clowning, music, conjuring, dance and mime thrown into a complete performance. Happily it's an art which gained from the Communist takeover and which did not suffer during the Cultural Revolution. Performers used to have the status of gypsies, but now it's 'people's art'.

Most of the provinces have their own performing troupes, sponsored either by government agencies, industrial complexes, the army or rural administrations. About 80 troupes are active in China, and they're much in demand with scalpers being able to get Y5 for a Y0.40 ticket. You'll also see more bare leg, star-spangled costumes and rouge in one acrobat show then you'll see anywhere else in China – something of a revelation to see dressed-up and made-up Chinese!

Acts vary from troupe to troupe. Some traditional acts haven't changed over the centuries, while others have incorporated roller skates and motorcycles. A couple of time-proven acts that are hard to follow include the 'balancing in pairs' with one man balanced upside down on the head of another mimicking every movement of the partner below, mirror image, even drinking a glass of water! Hoop-jumping is another. Four hoops are stacked on top of each other; the human chunk of rubber going through the very top hoop may attempt a backflip with a simultaneous body-twist.

The 'Peacock Displaying its Feathers' involves an array of people balanced on one bicycle. According to the Guinness Book of Records a Shanghai troupe holds the record at 13, though apparently a Wuhan troupe has done 14. The 'Pagoda of Bowls' is a balancing act where the performer, usually a woman, does everything with her torso except tie it in knots, all the while casually balancing a stack of porcelain bowls on foot, head or both – and perhaps also balancing on a partner.

Things to Buy

Good buys in Shanghai are clothing (silks, down jackets, traditional Chinese clothing, stencilled T-shirts, embroidered clothing), antiques, tea (chrysanthemum tea from Hangzhou), stationery...the list goes on and on, so just regard this place as one big department store. All consumer urges can be catered for here.

Major shopping areas in Shanghai besides crowded Nanjing Donglu are Huaihai Zhonglu, Sichuan Beilu, Jinling Donglu and Nanjing Xilu.

Some smaller streets offer specialities. Shimen Yilu has clothing and houseware stores. Over in Frenchtown – now we're getting specialised – is the Gujin Brassiere Store at 863 Huaihai Zhonglu. In the same neighbourhood, the Straw Products Shop at 167 Rui Jin offers a fine variety of things woven of straw for bargain prices.

You can shop around the clock in Shanghai should the urge take you. For example, the Caitongde Traditional Chinese Medicine Shop at 320 Nanjing Donglu is open 24 hours a day.

The Friendship Store, once housed in the former British consulate on the Bund, has moved around the corner to a multistorey building on Beijing Donglu. It sells everything. A reader has recommended the Da Ying Woollen and Silk Shop at 897 Sichuan Beilu for good deals on wool and silk (she searched virtually all over China before deciding this was the best place to buy).

Film Shanghai is a good place to stock up on film. Limited repairs to Japanese-brand cameras are available at Seagull Photo Supplies (☎ 221004), 471 Nanjing Donglu. The shop also sells Japanese cameras. Another major photographic store is Guan Long, corner of Nanjing Donglu and Jiangxi Zhonglu.

Some brands of Western film can be processed in Shanghai and quality seems to be on par with that in the West. Enquire at the photography stores or in the large hotels (the Peace Hotel has a photo-processing service).

Getting There & Away

Shanghai has rail and air connections to places all over China, ferries up the Yangtse River and many boats along the coast, and buses to destinations in adjoining provinces.

Air Shanghai is connected by air to many

cities and towns in China. There are daily flights to Beijing, Canton, Chengdu, Chongqing, Fuzhou, Guilin, Haikou, Kunming, Nanjing, Wuhan, Xi'an and Xiamen. Other useful flights include Huangshan (two flights a week), Hangzhou (five flights a week) and Qingdao (two flights a week).

Useful international flights include those to Hong Kong (Y673, daily), Tokyo (Y1548, daily), Osaka (Y1206, six days a week) and Nagasaki (twicc a week). A few airlines (Air China, North-west, United, Canadian International) also fly to the west coasts of the US and Canada.

CAAC's offices are in the Jinjiang Hotel, Cypress Hotel, Peace Hotel, Shanghai Hotel and Sheraton Hua Ting Hotel. Their main office (☎ 523805) is at 789 Yan'an Zhonglu. Other offices are at the Lianyi Building on Yan'an Donglu and at 66 Nanjing Donglu. The enquiry office at Hongqiao airport can be reached by telephoning 2536530.

The branch of CAAC that flies out of Hongqiao airport is now called China Eastern Airways.

Several other international airlines maintain Shanghai offices:

Alitalia (☎ 2553957)
Room 824-5, Shanghai Hilton
250 Huashan Lu
Canadian Airlines International (☎ 2582582)
Room 109, Jinjiang Hotel
59 Maoming Nanlu
Cathay Pacific (☎ 4336435)
Room 123, Jinjiang Hotel
59 Maoming Nanlu
Dragon Air (☎ 4336435)
Room 123, Jinjiang Hotel
59 Maoming Nanlu
Japan Air Lines (☎ 4336337)
Ruijin Building
205 Maoming Lu
1202 Huaihai Zhonglu
Northwest Airlines (☎ 2582582)
Room 127, Jinjiang Hotel
59 Maoming Nanlu
Singapore Airlines (☎ 4330517)
Room 1341, 3/F, Jinjiang Hotel
59 Maoming Lu
United Airlines (☎ 2553333)
Shanghai Hilton Shopping Arcade
250 Huashan Lu

Bus The long-distance bus station is on Qiujiang Lu west of Henan Beilu. There are several buses a day to Hangzhou (Y11), Wuxi (Y6) and Changzhou (Y9).

There is another ticket office at Renmin Square, opposite the junction of Fuzhou Lu and Xizang Zhonglu, which has tickets for buses to Suzhou (Y4). The boarding points for the buses are marked on the ticket in Chinese (at the time of writing there were two boarding points for the Suzhou bus, one on Gongxing Lu near Renmin Square, and one on Huangpu Beilu Kou near the main station), so check where to board the bus when you buy a ticket.

Because the Shanghai-Nanjing highway corridor is so busy, rail is a better option for getting to towns along this route.

Train Shanghai is at the junction of the Beijing-Shanghai and the Beijing-Hangzhou lines. Since these branch off in various directions many parts of the country can be reached by direct train from Shanghai.

Travellers carrying elderly maps need to know that the main railway station has moved west, and that the old main station is now the north station.

Not all trains originate in Shanghai. There is one, for example, which starts in Beijing and winds up in Fuzhou on the south-east coast. Others, like the train bound for Ürümqi, do start in Shanghai.

Tourist-price train tickets and journey times on some important routes out of Shanghai are listed following.

destination	duration (hours)	hard-seat Y	hard-sleeper Y	soft-sleeper Y
Beijing	17½	125	225	420
Xi'an	27	125	200	375
Canton	33	140	225	425
Nanjing	4	31	–	–
Hangzhou	3½	14	–	–

There are over a dozen trains a day on the Shanghai-Hangzhou line, and numerous trains on the Shanghai-Nanjing line, stopping at major towns like Zhenjiang, Changzhou and Wuxi on the way. Train No

1 is a special express service to Nanjing that stops only in Wuxi.

There are direct trains from Shanghai to Guilin and Kunming but these take 29 hours and 62 hours respectively. If you can't get a sleeper, forget it! Also, keep in mind that flying is cheaper than taking soft sleeper.

There are direct trains to Qingdao in Shandong Province. The trip takes 24 hours, but this can be conveniently broken at Qufu and Tainan/Taishan.

There are direct trains from Shanghai to Fuzhou (22½ hours) and Xiamen in Fujian Province. From Fuzhou and Xiamen you can continue by bus along the coast to Canton; or take the boat from Xiamen to Hong Kong.

Getting Chinese-priced tickets is difficult in Shanghai. You could go as far as, say, Suzhou or Jiaxing, and try getting a Chinese-price ticket there. You might also try buying tickets from one of the smaller railway stations, such as Xujiahui station in the western suburbs of Shanghai, rather than from the main station.

There are five advance-ticket offices in Shanghai. The main one is at 230 Beijing Donglu and handles all destinations north of the Yangtse and south of Jinhua (Jinhua is beyond Hangzhou to the south-west). Departures for these trains are from Shanghai north (formerly main) station on Tianmu Donglu.

Foreigners are usually sent to CITS to buy their train tickets. Although you'll have to pay tourist price, the advantage is that you avoid the enormous queues and you have a good chance of getting a sleeper.

Boat Boats are definitely one of the best ways of leaving Shanghai – they're also the cheapest. For destinations on the coast or inland on the Yangtse, they may even sometimes be faster than trains, which have to take rather circuitous routes. Smaller, grottier boats handle numerous inland shipping routes.

Tickets for larger boats (like the Hong Kong-Shanghai ferries) are handled by CITS, which charges a commission. Tickets for all domestic passenger shipping out of Shanghai can be bought from the ticket office at 1 Jinling Donglu.

Considering how cheap boats are, you ought to consider taking a class or two above the crowd. It won't cost you that much more to do so.

The Hong Kong route was re-opened in 1980 after a gap of 28 years. Three passenger ships now ply the route: the *Shanghai*, the *Haixin* and the *Jinjiang*. A lot of travellers leave China this way and the trip gets rave reviews. The trip to Hong Kong takes 2½ days. There are departures every five days.

Ships depart from the International Passenger Terminal to the east of Shanghai Mansions. The address is Wai Hong Qiao Harbour, Taipin Lu No 1. Passengers are requested to be at the harbour three hours before departure.

The fares below are from CITS, aboard the *Shanghai* and the *Haixin*; fares on the *MV Jinjiang* run just a bit lower for every class except for the highest 'special class' suite, which is HK$1317. Tickets can be bought from CITS or from the ticket office at 1 Jinling Donglu.

Special Class
Two-berth cabin, HK$939 to HK$1018 per person.

1st Class
One-berth cabin, HK$782 to HK$861 per person.

2nd Class
Four, three and two-berth cabins, HK$679 to HK$739 per person

3rd Class
Two-berth and four-berth cabins, HK$565 to HK$622 per person

General Class
A large dormitory with upper and lower berths, and lights that stay on all night. Tickets cost around HK$479. It is strongly recommended that you take at least 3rd class.

When you take into account the luxurious living, the boat is cheap. Ships come complete with dance floor, library, swimming pool...just about the classiest things sailing regularly around Chinese waters.

The main destinations of ferries up the Yangtse River from Shanghai are Nantong,

Nanjing, Wuhu, Guichi, Jiujiang and Wuhan. From Wuhan you can change to another ferry which will take you to Chongqing. If you're only going as far west as Nanjing then take the train – much faster than the boat.

Tickets can be bought from the booking hall at the corner of Jinling Donglu and Zhongshan Dong Erlu. Foreigners are escorted to window No 1 on the 2nd floor to makc sure they pay the tourist price in FEC (there is a 95% surcharge on the Chinese price for foreigners). Daily departures are from Shiliupu Wharf. There is no longer a 1st class fare – the best is 2nd class. Ticket prices per person are:

destination	2nd class Y	3rd class Y	4th class Y
Nanjing	150	53	40
Wuhu	137	63	50
Jiujiang	227	105	79
Wuhan	355	150	104

Unless you can afford to fly, the most sensible way to head west from Shanghai is along the river. Wuhan, for example, is over 1500 km by rail from Shanghai. For about half the hard-sleeper train fare you can get a berth in 4th class on the boat. For a bit more than a tourist-priced hard-sleeper ticket on a train you'd probably be able to get a bed in a two-person cabin on the boat.

Other inland shipping routes have hardly been explored by Westerners. One possible route is a boat to Huzhou from Shanghai. Huzhou is on the southern shore of Lake Taihu. Worth checking out, though, are the coastal boats.

Frequency of coastal shipping varies according to destination. Some of the 5000-tonne liners have staterooms with private bath in 1st and special classes – wood panelling, red velvet curtains, the works. The ship should have a restaurant, bar, snack shops, but this depends on the boat. Second and 3rd class are split into A and B fares, with A just a bit better accommodation and service than B. The following fares are from CITS, with the 'A' fare for 2nd and 3rd classes (including the Y10 CITS surcharge – you should be able to get tickets for less at the boat office):

destination	1st class Y	2nd class Y	3rd class Y	4th class Y
Ningbo	144	110	68	35
Wenzhou	245	197	109	57
Fuzhou	350	260	115	90
Qingdao	380	280	105	70
Canton	430	370	220	170

Ships to Canton (six times a month), Qingdao (daily), Dalian and Fuzhou leave from Gongpinglu Wharf, to the east of Shanghai Mansions. Ships to Ningbo and Wenzhou leave daily from the Shiliupu dock. However, check the departure point when you buy your ticket!

The boat to Qingdao departs daily, with the exception of a few odd days of the month. It takes about 26 hours, while the train takes 24 hours. Second class on the liner is roughly equivalent to the price of a hard-seat on a train (if you get the Chinese price) and the boat would be incomparably more comfortable. Boat connections like Shanghai to Dalian, then Dalian to Tianjin, can be made, though you may find the huge number of passengers using the cheaper services a problem when getting tickets.

There may be other boats from Shanghai to points along the coast – possibly Haimen, Dinghai and Putuoshan.

Getting Around

The sights in Shanghai are spaced a fair distance apart. Not only that, but vehicles swarm everywhere, with a host of noise generators to announce their oncoming right of way: buses and traffic police have megaphones, bells, buzzers, hooters, honkers, screechers, flashing lights; taxis may just as well have a permanent siren attached; pedestrians have no early warning system and rely on fast legs. If you've got the energy, then walking through Shanghai's various neighbourhoods is fascinating.

To/From the Airport China Eastern Airlines has a bus from the CAAC office on Yan'an

Lu to the airport which costs Y1.80. The trip takes about half an hour. The Jinjiang Hotel also has an airport shuttle that costs Y8.

Bus Buses are often packed to the hilt and at times impossible to board. The closest thing to revolutionary fervour in Shanghai today is the rush-hour bus ambushes. Once on board, keep your valuables tucked away since pickpocketing is easy under such conditions, and foreigners are not exempt as targets.

Contrary to popular belief, buses are not colour coded. The bus map is. The bus map coding for trolley buses is prefixed by the following symbol, which roughly means 'electricity':

Routes 1 to 30 are for trolley buses. Those numbered 31 to 99 are city buses. Routes 201 to 220 are peak-hour city buses, and 301 to 321 are all-night buses. Buses operate from 4 am to 10 pm. Suburban and long-distance buses don't carry numbers – the destination is in characters. Some useful buses:

No 18 runs from the front of the main railway station (it originates further north-east at Hongkou or Lu Xun Park) and proceeds south down Xizang Lu, and then south to the banks of the Huangpu.

No 65 runs from behind the main railway station, passes Shanghai Mansions, crosses Waibaidu Bridge, then heads directly south along the Bund (Zhongshan Lu) as far as the Bund can go.

No 49 from the Public Security Bureau terminal heads west along Yan'an Lu. Nos 48 and 42 follow similar routes from Huangpu Park, south along the Bund, west around the Dongfeng Hotel, then link westbound along Yan'an Lu. No 26 starts in the city centre a few streets west of the Bund, drops to the Yuyuan Bazaar, then goes west along Huaihai Lu.

No 16 is a good linking bus for all those awkward destinations. It runs from the Jade Buddha Temple to Yuyuan Bazaar, then on to a ferry hop over the Huangpu River.

No 11 travels the ring road around the old Chinese city.

Other Wheels Taxis operate out of the tourist hotels. Different taxis charge different fares. The air-con minivans, commonly seen at the Shanghai railway station, charge Y10.80 for the first five km, or Y14 for 10 km. They'll take from one to five people and all the luggage that fits; this is the best deal for parties of two or more with a lot of luggage. Minimum charge for a newish VW Santana, Volvo or Nissan taxi is Y10.80, which is good for five km, and then it's Y1.20 per km after that (plus a few jiao for each bag placed in the trunk). In one of these, for example, the Peace Hotel to the Jinjiang Hotel would cost about Y12. All-day hire is possible. Cheaper are the dwindling fleet of Shanghai Saloon and Fiat taxis (usually non-air-con), which charge only Y7.20 minimum and Y0.80 per km after five km. Rates for all taxis are supposedly payable only in FEC but the Shanghai Saloons will sometimes take RMB, especially if you bargain for a flat rate. All taxis are operated by three companies, Shanghai Friendship Taxi Service (☎ 2587573), Shanghai Taxi Corp (☎ 3222999) and Shanghai Tourism Taxi Co (☎ 4382430). Theoretically they can dispatch taxis by phone, but it usually works out better if you have hotel staff call for you.

The Sheraton Hua Ting has a free hourly shuttle to the Bund and other central areas.

The gun-metal-grey Shanghai Saloons, resembling vintage Mercedes, are beautiful cars and worth a few rides but hang on to your wallet. Check the odometer; some of these things have been on the road since the 1950s! If you want to let go, then get one of those plush hearses the Red Flags, and pretend you're the would-be president of Namibia for the day.

Jiangsu 江苏

The southern part of Jiangsu *(jiāngsū)* lies in the rich Yangtse Basin, an incredibly beautiful tapestry of greens, yellows and blues offset with whitewashed farm buildings. Since the 12th century this province has been the economic heart of China. It is the most populated province, with the highest land productivity, an above-average educational level, and mellow people. Woven into this land of 'fish and rice' is a concentration of towns and cities with the third highest industrial output in the land (after Shanghai and Liaoning).

As far back as the 16th century, the towns on the Grand Canal set up industrial bases for silk production and grain storage, and they still are ahead of the rest of the nation. While heavy industry is based in Nanjing and Wuxi, the other towns concentrate more on light industry, machinery and textiles – you might term them 'hi-tech canal towns'. They're major producers of electronics and computer components, and haven't been blotted out by the scourges of coal mining or steelworks.

From Nanjing down to Hangzhou in Zhejiang Province the area is heavily touristed, full of Japanese Hino tour buses, and littered with luxury hotels. North of the Yangtse there's not really much to talk about; it's a complete contrast – decayed, backward and always lagging behind the rest of the province. In the north the major port is at Lianyungang and there's a big coal works in Xuzhou.

It's hot and humid in summer, and has overcoat temperatures in winter (visibility can drop to zero in January). Rain or drizzle can be prevalent – but it's nice rain, adding a misty soft touch to the land. The natural colourings can be spectacular in spring. Heavy rains fall in spring and summer but autumn is fairly dry.

NANJING

(nánjīng) 南京

Over Chungshan swept a storm, headlong

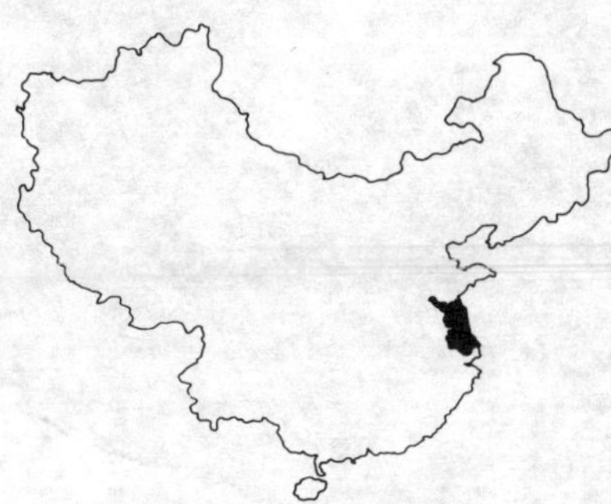

Our mighty army, a million strong, has crossed the Great River.
The city, a tiger crouching, a dragon curling, outshines its ancient glories;
In heroic triumph heaven and earth have been overturned.
Mao, from his poem *The People's Liberation Army Captures Nanjing*

The assault on Nanjing by the Communist Army in April 1949 was not the first time that the heaven and earth of the city had been overturned. In fact, the city has been conquered many times by foreigners, rebels and imperial armies. It has been destroyed, rebuilt, destroyed again, emptied of inhabitants, repopulated and rebuilt, only to be destroyed again by the occasional natural disaster.

History

The area has been inhabited for about 5000 years, and a number of prehistoric sites have been discovered either in or around Nanjing. There are also sites which date back to the Shang and Zhou dynasties.

The city's strategic position, guarded by the surrounding hills and rivers, is the source of both its prosperity and its troubles. The Yangtse narrows here and a bit further east begins to form a delta, so Nanjing became a focus of trade and communications along one of China's greatest water routes.

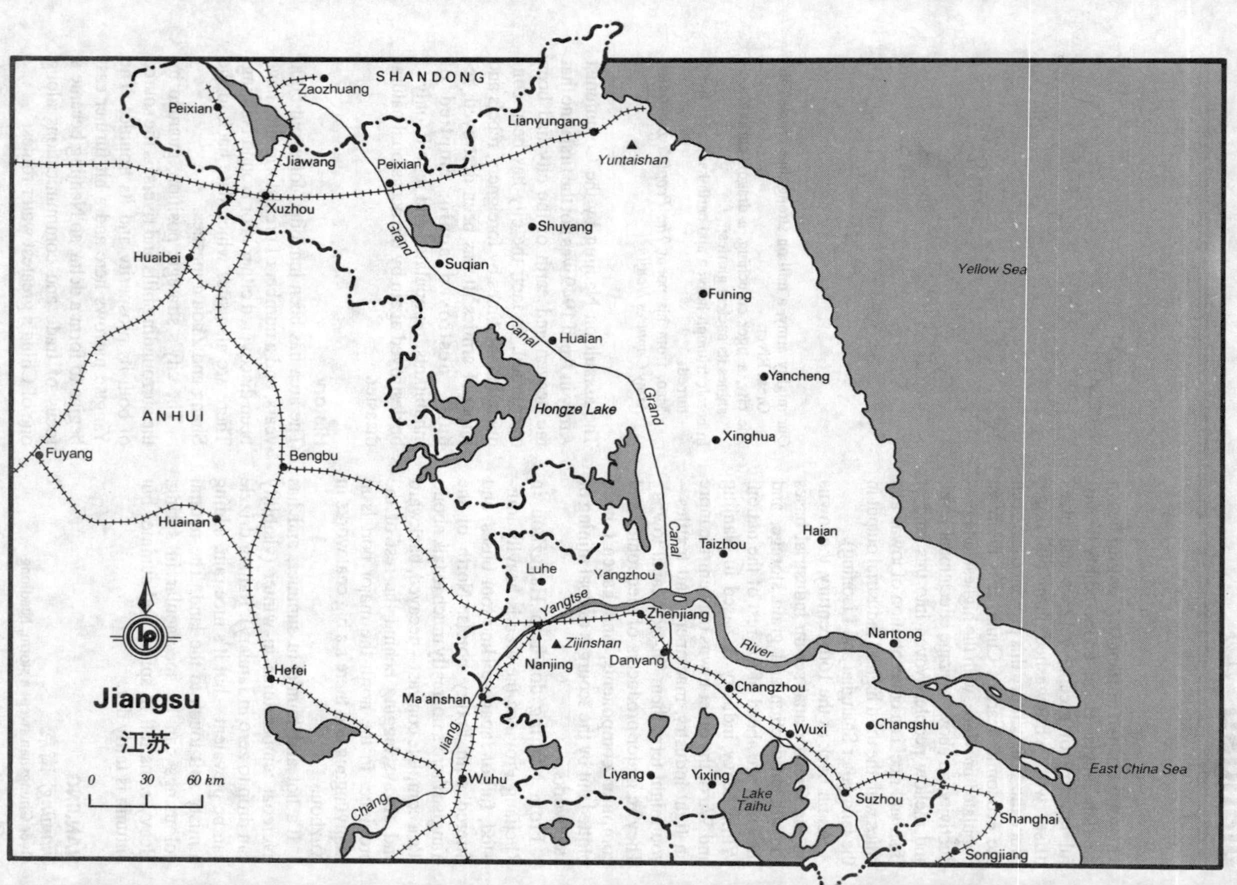
Jiangsu
江苏
0 30 60 km
Yellow Sea
East China Sea
SHANDONG
ANHUI
Grand Canal
Hongze Lake
Lake Taihu
Yangtse River
Chang Jiang
Yuntaishan
Zijinshan
Peixian
Zaozhuang
Jiawang
Xuzhou
Huaibei
Suqian
Shuyang
Lianyungang
Huaian
Funing
Yancheng
Xinghua
Haian
Taizhou
Yangzhou
Zhenjiang
Luhe
Nanjing
Danyang
Changzhou
Wuxi
Suzhou
Changshu
Nantong
Shanghai
Songjiang
Yixing
Liyang
Wuhu
Ma'anshan
Hefei
Huainan
Fuyang
Bengbu

The city's recorded history dates back to the Warring States Period (476-221 BC) when several states battled for its control, one overcoming the other and using Nanjing as a bastion to attack a third state, only to be defeated. This confusing situation was finally put to an end by the Qin Dynasty (221-207 BC); the Qin State defeated all the other states and united the country. From this period on, Nanjing grew in importance as the administrative centre of the surrounding area.

Qin rule ushered in a period of stability for the city, and during the Western and Eastern Han dynasties which succeeded the Qin, Nanjing grew as an important regional centre. In 220 AD the Eastern Han collapsed and three new states emerged. Nanjing became the capital of the state of Wu in the south when the emperor moved his court here, taking advantage of the strategic position on China's waterways and its fort which appeared impregnable.

The Wu rulers seemed to have learned as little from history as those before them. They were overthrown by the Jin who rose in the north, who in turn were overthrown by a military strongman who set himself up as the first emperor of the Song Dynasty (420-79 AD).

The early part of the 6th century was an inauspicious time to be in Nanjing. There was a terrible flood in 507, a great fire in 521 which destroyed a huge section of the imperial palace, a pestilence in 529 and another flood in 533. There were peasant rebellions in 533, 541, 542 and 544, and the upheaval was compounded by the strains imposed by large numbers of refugees and immigrants from the north.

To top it off, in 548 AD the army of General Hou Jing, who was originally allied with but now plotted to overthrow the southern emperor, attacked Nanjing and in a wave of gratuitous violence looted the city, raped the women and killed or conscripted the other inhabitants. Hou Jing took the city but after a series of palace intrigues also wound up dead.

Meanwhile in the north another general, Wen Di, who had usurped the throne of the reigning Northern Zhou dynasty, established himself as the first emperor of the Sui Dynasty and set out on a war against the south. Nanjing fell to his army in about 589. Wen Di chose to establish his capital at Xi'an and to eradicate once and for all any claims of the south to the throne of a now united China. Wen completely demolished all the important buildings of Nanjing, including its beautiful palaces, and the city ceased to be important. Although it enjoyed a period of prosperity under the long-lived Tang Dynasty, it gradually slipped back into obscurity.

Ming Dynasty

Nanjing's brightest day came in the 14th century with the overthrow of the Yuan Dynasty by a peasant rebellion led by Zhu Yuanzhang. The rebels captured Nanjing in 1356 and went on to capture the Mongol capital at Beijing in 1368. Zhu took the name of Hong Wu and set himself up as the first emperor of the Ming Dynasty (1368-1644). Under Hong Wu, Nanjing was established as the capital, partly because it was far from the north and safe from sudden barbarian attacks, and partly because it was in the most wealthy and populous part of the country. A massive palace was built, huge walls were raised around the city, and construction of other buildings proceeded at a furious pace. The city became a manufacturing and administrative metropolis and a centre of learning and culture.

However, the next Ming emperor, Yong Le, moved his capital to Beijing in 1420. Nanjing's population was halved and the city declined in importance. It was another bad century – the city suffered a succession of fires, famines, floods, typhoons, tornadoes and even a snowstorm said to have lasted 40 days. If Nanjing was down then, the Manchus to the north were up and fighting. In 1644 Beijing fell to the army under the Chinese rebel Li Zicheng, who then found himself facing a Manchu invasion. The north of China was conquered by the invaders, and though various pretenders to the Ming throne tried to hold out in Nanjing and other places in the south, in time they were all overcome. Although Nanjing continued as a major centre under the Qing, nothing much of note happened until the 19th and 20th centuries.

The Opium wars were waged right to Nanjing's doorstep in 1842 when a British naval task force of 80 ships sailed up the Yangtse River, took the city of Zhenjiang and arrived at Nanjing in August. Threats to bombard Nanjing forced the Chinese to sign the first of the 'unequal treaties' which opened several Chinese ports to foreign trade, and forced China to pay a huge war indemnity and officially cede the island of Hong Kong to Britain.

Just a few years later, one of the most dramatic events in China's history focused attention on Nanjing – the Taiping Rebellion (1851-64) succeeded in taking over most of southern China. This Chinese Christian army gained attention in the West but its success against the Qing worried the Western powers, who preferred to deal with the corrupt and weak Qing rather than the united and strong Taipings. After 1860 the Western powers allied themselves with the Qing and the counteroffensive began. By 1864 the Taipings had been encircled in their capital Nanjing. A Qing army helped by British army regulars like General Charles Gordon (of Khartoum fame) and various European and US mercenaries besieged and bombarded the city for seven months, finally capturing it and slaughtering the Taiping defenders. Hong Xiuquan, the Taiping leader, committed suicide and the rebellion ended.

The Manchus were overthrown in 1911 and Sun Yatsen established a republic with its capital first at Beijing but later at Nanjing. In 1927 Chiang Kaishek ordered the extermination of the Communists, and Yuhuatai Hill to the south of the city was one of the main execution sites. In 1937 the Japanese captured Nanjing and set about butchering the population. Just how many people died in what became known as the 'Rape of Nanjing' is unknown, though the Chinese usually put the figure at around 300,000. With the Japanese defeat in 1945 the Kuomintang government moved back to Nanjing, and between 1946 and 1947 peace talks were held there between the Kuomintang and the Communists. When these talks ran down the civil war resumed and Nanjing was captured in that 'great turning over of heaven and earth in 1949'.

True to its past, the city has not remained aloof from conflicts. On 25 March 1976, 2½ months after the death of Zhou Enlai, the 'radicals' inflamed public opinion by publishing an article in two of Shanghai's mass-circulation newspapers stating that the late premier had been a 'capitalist roader'. It was the time of the Qing Ming festival when the Chinese traditionally honour their dead. The first reaction to the article was in Nanjing, where large crowds gathered to hear speeches and lay wreaths in honour of Zhou. Slogans and posters were put up, a protest march took place through the streets and Zhang Chunqiao (later vilified as a member of the Gang of Four) was named and attacked. The story goes that the carriages of Beijing-bound trains were daubed with messages and slogans so that people in the capital would know what was happening in Nanjing, and that these contributed to the Tiananmen Incident a week later.

Today, Nanjing is an industrialised city of around three million people, rebuilt by the Communist government. Its broad boulevards are lined with thousands of trees, alleviating the heat for which this city was justifiably known as one of the 'Three Furnaces' of China. It's also an important centre for education and has one of the highest concentrations of foreign students in the country.

Orientation

Nanjing lies on the eastern bank of the Yangtse River, bounded in the west by the Zijinshan (Purple and Gold) range. The centre of town is a traffic circle presided over by the Jinling Hotel tower. The long-distance bus station and railway station are in the far north of the city. Some of the hotels and most tourist facilities are central, near the Jinling Hotel. Most of the sights are to the east of

Nanjing, in or around the Zijinshan mountains – including the Sun Yatsen Memorial, Linggu Park and the tomb of the first Ming emperor Hong Wu.

Before picking over the remnants of 3000 years of history, go and see Nanjing's prime tourist attraction, the Jinling Hotel. This 36-storey tower, one of the tallest buildings in China, was designed by a Japanese architect and built by a Singapore firm. The Chinese proletariat stands outside the fence gazing up at this thing and snapping friends' photos with the hotel as a backdrop. The Sky Palace revolving restaurant was the first of its type in China. You can dump yourself down in a comfy chair and spot the Yangtse Bridge, the observatory, the Linggu Pagoda and the Sun Yatsen Mausoleum in the distance. The Chinese receptionist wears a traditional *qipao*, the long Chinese gown split up the thigh. Drinks in the restaurant? Why not an East Meets West, Sky Lounge or Panda cocktail?

Once you've pulled yourself away from the gleaming hotel you can mull over Nanjing's extraordinary number of reminders of its splendid and not-so-splendid past. The city enjoyed long periods of prosperity – evident in the numerous buildings which successive rulers built. There is a phenomenal quantity of tombs, steles, pagodas, temples and niches scattered around. For a complete rundown get a copy of *In Search of Old Nanking* by Barry Till and Paula Swart (Joint Publishing Company, Hong Kong, 1982). Unfortunately, much of what was built has been destroyed or allowed to crumble into ruins.

Information

CITS This office (☎ 639013) is at 202 Zhongshan Beilu. They also have a ticket-booking office at the railway station which sells soft-seat and soft-sleeper tickets (open daily from 7.30 to 11.30 am and 1.30 to 5 pm).

Money The Bank of China is near the central traffic circle at 3 Zhongshan Donglu. There is also a money-exchange counter at the Jinling Hotel.

Post There are post offices in the Shuangmenlou, Jinling and Nanjing hotels. The main post office is at 19 Zhongshan Lu, around the corner from the Jinling Hotel.

Maps Good bus maps of Nanjing are available from hawkers outside the main railway station. Also check the hotel shops.

Early Remains

Nanjing has been inhabited since prehistoric times. Remains of a prehistoric culture have been found at the site of today's Drum Tower in the centre of the city and in surrounding areas. About 200 sites of small clan communities, mainly represented by pottery and bronze artefacts dating back to the late Shang and Zhou dynasties, have been found on both sides of the Yangtse.

In 212 AD, at the end of the Eastern Han period, the military commander in charge of the Nanjing region built a citadel on Qinglingshan in the west of Nanjing. At that time the mountain was referred to as Shitoushan (Stone Head Mountain) and so the citadel became known as the Stone City. The wall measured over 10 km in circumference. Today, some of the red sandstone foundations can still be seen.

Ming City Wall

Since Nanjing enjoyed its golden years under the Ming, there are numerous reminders of the period to be found. One of the most impressive is the Ming city wall measuring over 33 km – the longest city wall ever built in the world. About two-thirds of it still stands. It took from 1366 to 1386 to build and involved over 200,000 labourers. The layout is irregular, an exception to the usual square walls of these times, because much of it is built on the foundations of earlier walls which took advantage of strategic hills. Averaging 12 metres high and seven metres wide at the top, the wall was built of bricks supplied from five Chinese provinces. Each brick had stamped on it the place it came from, the overseer's name and rank, the brickmaker's name and sometimes the date. This was to ensure that the bricks were well

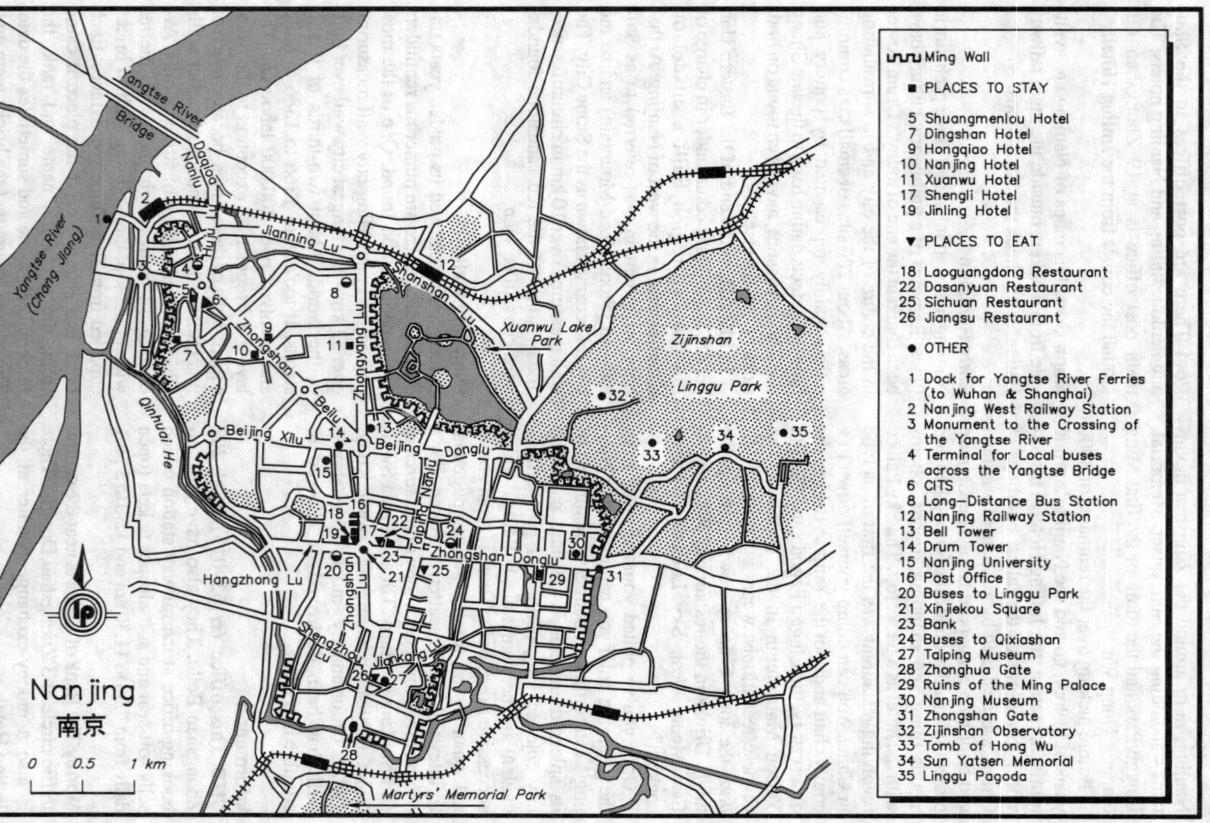
Ming Wall
■ PLACES TO STAY
5 Shuangmenlou Hotel
7 Dingshan Hotel
9 Hongqiao Hotel
10 Nanjing Hotel
11 Xuanwu Hotel
17 Shengli Hotel
19 Jinling Hotel
▼ PLACES TO EAT
18 Laoguangdong Restaurant
22 Dasanyuan Restaurant
25 Sichuan Restaurant
26 Jiangsu Restaurant
● OTHER
1 Dock for Yangtse River Ferries (to Wuhan & Shanghai)
2 Nanjing West Railway Station
3 Monument to the Crossing of the Yangtse River
4 Terminal for Local buses across the Yangtse Bridge
6 CITS
8 Long-Distance Bus Station
12 Nanjing Railway Station
13 Bell Tower
14 Drum Tower
15 Nanjing University
16 Post Office
20 Buses to Linggu Park
21 Xinjiekou Square
23 Bank
24 Buses to Qixiashan
27 Taiping Museum
28 Zhonghua Gate
29 Ruins of the Ming Palace
30 Nanjing Museum
31 Zhongshan Gate
32 Zijinshan Observatory
33 Tomb of Hong Wu
34 Sun Yatsen Memorial
35 Linggu Pagoda
Nanjing
南京
0 0.5 1 km
Yangtse River (Chang Jiang)
Yangtse River Bridge
Daqiao Nanlu
Jianning Lu
Shanshan Lu
Zhongshan Beilu
Zhongyang Lu
Xuanwu Lake Park
Zijinshan
Linggu Park
Beijing Xilu
Beijing Donglu
Taiping Nanlu
Zhongshan Donglu
Zhongshan Lu
Hangzhong Lu
Shengzhou Lu
Jiankang Lu
Qinhuai He
Martyrs' Memorial Park

■ PLACES TO STAY

5 双门楼饭店
7 丁山饭店
9 虹桥饭店
10 南京饭店
11 玄武饭店
17 胜利饭店
19 金陵饭店

▼ PLACES TO EAT

18 老广东菜馆
22 大三元酒家
25 四川饭店
26 江苏酒家

OTHER

1 中山码头
2 南京西火车站
3 渡江纪念碑
4 汽车站（大桥南路）
6 中国国际旅行社
8 长途汽车站
12 南京火车站
13 钟楼
14 鼓楼
15 南京大学
16 邮局
20 开往灵谷公园的汽车
21 新街口
23 银行
24 开往栖霞山的汽车
27 太平天国历史博物馆
28 中华门
29 牛朝门
30 南京博物院
31 中山门
32 紫金山天文台
33 明孝陵
34 中山陵
35 灵谷寺

made; if they broke they had to be replaced. Some stone bricks were used, but on the whole they were clay.

Ming City Gates

Some of the original 13 Ming city gates remain, including Heping Gate *(hépíng mén)* in the north and Zhonghua Gate *(zhōnghuá mén)* in the south. The city gates were heavily fortified and, rather than being the usual weak points of the defences, they were defensive strongholds. The Zhonghua Gate has four rows of gates, making it almost impregnable; it could house a garrison of 3000 soldiers in vaults in the front gate building. Today some of these vaults are used as souvenir shops and cafes, and are wonderfully cool in summer. Zhonghua Gate can be visited, but Heping Gate is now used as barracks.

Ming Palace

(niúcháo mén) 牛朝门

Built by Hong Wu, the Ming Palace is said to have been a magnificent structure after which the Imperial Palace in Beijing was modelled. Almost nothing remains of the Ming Palace except five marble bridges lying side by side known as the Five Dragon Bridges, the old ruined gate called Wu Men, and the enormous column bases of the palace buildings. There are also some stone blocks and a little stone screen carved with animals and scenery.

The palace suffered two major fires its first century and was allowed to fall into ruins after the Ming court moved to Beijing. The Manchus looted it, and during the Taiping Rebellion the bombardment of Nanjing by Qing and Western troops almost completely destroyed the palace.

Drum Tower

(gǔlóu) 鼓楼

Built in 1382, the Drum Tower lies roughly in Nanjing's centre, in the middle of a traffic circle on Beijing Xilu. Drums were usually beaten to give directions for the change of the night watches and, in rare instances, to warn the populace of impending danger. The Nanjing tower originally contained numerous drums and other instruments used on ceremonial occasions, though now only one large drum remains. The ground floor is used for exhibitions of paintings and calligraphy.

Bell Tower

(zhōnglóu) 钟楼

North-east of the Drum Tower, the Bell Tower houses an enormous bell dating from 1388. The bell was originally in a pavilion on the west side of the Drum Tower. The present tower dates from 1889 and is a small two-storey pavilion with a pointed roof and turned-up eaves.

Tomb of Hong Wu

(míngxiào líng) 明孝陵

This tomb lies east of the city on the southern slope of Zijinshan. Construction began in 1381 and was finished in 1383; the emperor died at the age of 71 years in 1398. The first section of the avenue leading up to the mausoleum is lined with stone statues of lions, camels, elephants and horses. There's also a mythical animal called a *xiezhi* which has a mane and a single horn on its head; and a *qilin* which has a scaly body, a cow's tail, deer's hooves and one horn. The second section of the tomb alley turns sharply northward and begins with two large hexagonal columns. Following the columns are pairs of stone military men wearing armour, and these are followed by pairs of stone civil officials. The pathway turns again, crosses some arched stone bridges and goes through a gateway in a wall which surrounds the site of the mausoleum.

As you enter the first courtyard, a paved pathway leads to a pavilion housing several steles. The next gate leads to a large courtyard where you'll find the 'Altar Tower' or 'Soul Tower' – a mammoth rectangular stone structure. To get to the top of the tower you go through stairway leading upwards in the middle of the structure. Behind the tower is a wall, 350 metres in diameter, which surrounds a huge earth mound. Beneath this mound is the tomb vault of Hong Wu, which has not been excavated.

The Ming Quarry is at Yanmenshan (also known as Yangshan) about 15 km east of Nanjing. It was from this quarry that most of the stone blocks for the Ming palace and statues of the Ming tombs were cut. The attraction here is a massive tablet partially hewn from the rock. Had the tablet been finished it would have been almost 15 metres wide, four metres thick and 45 metres high! The base stone was to be 6.5 metres high and 13 metres long. One story goes that Hong Wu wished to place the enormous tablet on the top of Zijinshan. The gods had promised their assistance to move it, but when they saw the size of the tablet even they gave up and Hong Wu had to abandon the project. It seems, however, that Yong Le, the son of Hong Wu ordered the tablet to be carved; he planned to erect it at his father's tomb. When the tablet was almost finished he realised there was no way it could be moved.

Taiping Museum

(tàipíng tiānguó lìshǐ bówùguǎn)

太平天国历史博物馆

Hong Xiuquan, the leader of the Taipings, had a palace built in Nanjing, but the building was completely destroyed when Nanjing was taken in 1864. All that remains is a stone boat in an ornamental lake in the Western Garden, inside the old Kuomintang government buildings on Changjiang Lu, east of Taiping Lu.

The Taiping Museum is housed in the former mansion of the Hongs' 'Eastern Prince' Yang Xiuqing. The garden next to the mansion is called Zhan Yuan and originally belonged to the first Ming emperor.

The museum has an interesting collection of documents, books and artefacts relating to the rebellion. Most of the literature is copied, the originals being kept in Beijing. There are maps showing the northward progress of the Taiping army from Guangdong, Hong Xiuquan's seals, Taiping coins, cannon balls, rifles and other weapons, and texts which describe the Taiping laws on agrarian reform, social law and cultural policy. Other texts describe divisions in the Taiping leadership, the attacks by the Manchus and foreigners, and the fall of Nanjing in 1864.

Sun Yatsen Memorial

(zhōngshān líng) 中山陵

Some people admire the passive symmetry of Sun Yatsen's memorial; others say it lacks imagination and falls far short of the possibilities that the expenditure would have allowed.

The man regarded as the father of modern China (by both the Communists and the Kuomintang) died in Beijing in 1925, leaving behind an unstable Chinese republic. Sun wished to be buried in Nanjing, no doubt with greater simplicity than the Ming-style tomb which his successors built for him. Less than a year after his death, construction of this immense mausoleum began.

It lies at the southern foot of Zhongmao Peak in the eastern Zijinshan mountains which ring Nanjing. The tomb itself lies on the mountain slope at the top of an enormous stone stairway, 323 metres long and 70 metres wide. At the start of the path stands a stone gateway built of Fujian marble, with a roof of blue glazed tiles. The blue and white of the mausoleum were meant to symbolise the white sun on the blue background of the Kuomintang flag.

At the top of the steps is a platform where

Lion Statue at Sun Yatsen Memorial

you'll find the memorial ceremony chamber and the coffin chamber. Across the threshold of the memorial ceremony chamber hangs a tablet inscribed with the 'Three Principles of the People' as formulated by Dr Sun: nationalism, democracy and people's livelihood. Inside is a seated statue of Dr Sun. The walls are carved with the complete text of the *Outline of Principles for the Establishment of the Nation* put forward by the Nationalist government.

Behind the hall is a crypt, in which a prostrate marble statue of Sun lies above his body. In fact, it's not known if Sun's body is still in the tomb; the story goes that it was carted off to Taiwan by the Kuomintang and has been there ever since.

Yangtse River Bridge

(nánjīng chángjiāng dàqiáo) 南京长江大桥

One of the great achievements of the Communists, and one of which they are justifiably proud, is the Yangtse River Bridge at Nanjing which was opened on 23 December 1968. One of the longest bridges in China, it's a double-decker with a 4500-metre-long roadway on top and a 6700-metre-long railway below.

The story goes that the bridge was designed and built entirely by the Chinese after the Russians marched out and took the designs with them in 1960. Given the immensity of the construction it really is an impressive engineering feat, before which there was no direct rail link between Beijing and Shanghai.

Monument to the Crossing of the Yangtse River

(dùjiāng jìniàn bēi) 渡江纪念碑

Standing in the north-west of the city on Zhongshan Beilu, this monument erected in April 1979 commemorates the crossing of the river on 23 April 1949 and the capture of Nanjing from the Kuomintang by the Communist army. The characters on the monument are in the calligraphy of Deng Xiaoping.

Nanjing Museum
(nánjīng bówùguǎn) 南京博物馆
Just east of Zhongshan Gate on Zhongshan Lu, the Nanjing Museum houses an array of artefacts from Neolithic times through to the Communist period. The main building was constructed in 1933 with yellow-glazed tiles, red-lacquered gates and columns in the style of an ancient temple.

An interesting exhibit is the burial suit made of small rectangles of jade sewn together with silver thread, dating from the Eastern Han Dynasty (25-220 AD) and excavated from a tomb discovered in the city of Xuzhou in northern Jiangsu Province. Other exhibits include bricks with the inscriptions of their makers and overseers from the Ming city wall; drawings of old Nanjing; an early Qing mural of old Suzhou; and relics from the Taiping Rebellion.

Just east of the museum is a section of the Ming city wall; there are steps leading up from the road and you can walk along the top.

Linggu Park
(línggǔ) 灵谷
To the east of the city is Linggu Park with an assortment of sights.

The **Beamless Hall** is one of the most interesting buildings in Nanjing. In 1381, when Hong Wu was building his tomb, he had a temple on the site torn down and rebuilt a few km to the east. Of this temple only the Beamless Hall (so called because it is built entirely of bricks) remains. The structure has an interesting vaulted ceiling and a large stone platform where Buddhist statues used to be seated. In the 1930s the hall was turned into a memorial to those who died in the 1926-28 revolution. One of the inscriptions on the inside wall is the old Kuomintang national anthem.

A road leads either side of the Beamless Hall and up two flights of steps to the **Pine Wind Pavilion**, originally dedicated to the Goddess of Mercy as part of the Linggu Temple. Today it houses a small shop and teahouse.

The **Linggu Temple** *(línggǔ sì)* and its memorial hall to Xuan Zang is close by; after you pass through the Beamless Hall, turn right and follow the pathway. Xuan Zang was the Buddhist monk who travelled to India and brought back the Buddhist scriptures. Inside the memorial hall is a 13-storey wooden pagoda model which contains part of his skull, a sacrificial table and a portrait of the monk.

Close by is the **Linggu Pagoda** *(línggǔ tǎ)*, which was built in the 1930s under the direction of a US architect as a memorial to Kuomintang members who died in the 1926-28 revolution. It's an octagonal building 60 metres high with nine storeys.

Places to Stay – bottom end
Most of the accommodation in Nanjing is expensive – cheaper accommodation is in short supply. One consolation is that the hotels in this city are excellent and you at least get your money's worth.

The cheapest beds in town are at *Nanjing University (nánjīng dàxué)*, off Zhongshan Lu before the Beijing Lu traffic circle. The foreign students' dorm has large doubles for Y12; if it's full, the staff can usually find you somewhere else to stay on campus. A bus No 3 from the bus station-railway station area will pass just north of the campus along Beihin Xilu, or you can take a trolley bus No 33 down Zhongshan Lu and get off just past Beijing Lu.

The clean, efficient *Shuangmenlou Hotel* (☎ 685961) *(shuāngménlóu bīnguǎn)* at 185 Huju Beilu is one of the rambling Chinese garden-style hotels that are no longer being built. The much-favoured dorm appears to have given way to doubles in the old wing (with air-con, TV and hot showers) that cost Y85; extra beds can be added for Y25 each. In the new wing, doubles start from Y110. Bus No 21 from the Nanjing West railway station stops right in front of the hotel. From the main railway station or long-distance bus station take a No 10 bus west on Jianning Lu, get off at Daqiao Nanlu and then take a No 21 south on Huju Beilu. Take bus No 16 from near the Yangtse ferry pier and get off at the second traffic circle.

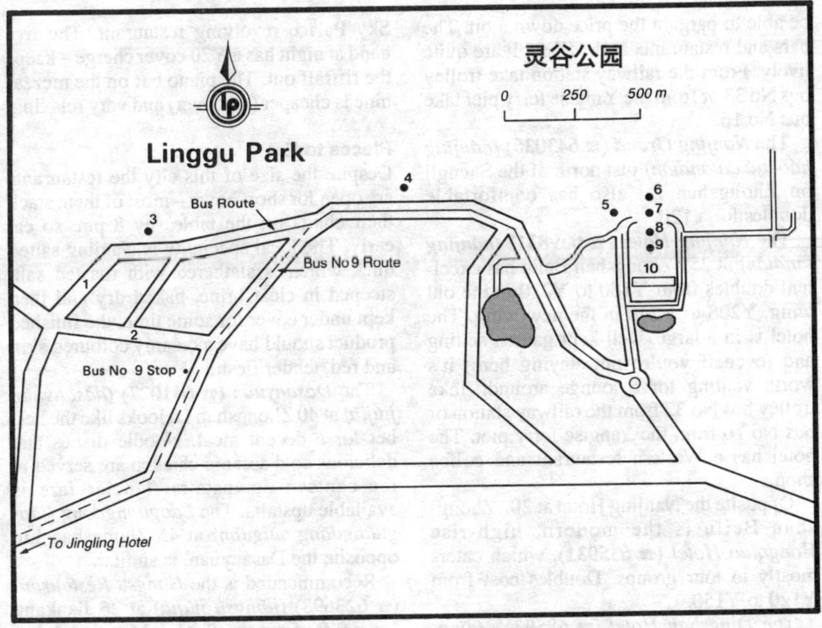

1 Avenue of Stone Figures
2 Avenue of Stone Animals
3 Tomb of Emperor Hong Wu
4 Mausoleum of Sun Yatsen
5 Linggu Pagoda
6 Pine Wind Pavilion
7 Beamless Hall
8 Gateway
9 Gateway & Surrounding Wall
10 Linggu Temple

1 石像路
2 石动物像路
3 明孝陵
4 中山陵
5 灵谷塔
6 松风阁
7 无光殿
8 门口
9 门口
10 录谷寺

The nondescript *Xuanwu Hotel* (☎ 638121) *(xuánwǔ fàndiàn)* at 192 Zhongyang Lu also has doubles from Y85. Trolley bus No 33 south from the long-distance bus or main railway station, goes right past it.

Places to Stay – middle

The going rate for almost all hotels in this range appears to be Y120. The central *Shengli Hotel* (☎ 648181) *(shènglì fàndiàn)*, at 75 Zhongshan Lu near the Jinling Hotel, is a small Hong-Kong-style hotel. The dormitory here has gone the way of most dorms in China and has been converted to double rooms. The rooms are quite nice though, for Y120; in the off-season (summer) you may be able to bargain the price down a bit. The bars and restaurants at the Shengli are quite lively. From the railway station take trolley bus No 33 or from the Yangtse ferry pier take bus No 16.

The *Nanjing Grand* (☎ 643035) *(nánjīng háohuá dàfàndiàn)* just north of the Shengli on Zhongshan Lu also has comfortable doubles for Y120.

The *Nanjing Hotel* (☎ 639831) *(nánjīng fàndiàn)* at 259 Zhongshan Beilu has excellent doubles from Y160 to Y210 in the old wing, Y208 to Y240 in the new wing. The hotel is in a large, well-kept garden setting and (even if you're not staying here) it's worth visiting for a lounge around. Take trolley bus No 32 from the railway station or bus No 16 from the Yangtse ferry pier. The hotel has a Western restaurant and coffee shop.

Opposite the Nanjing Hotel at 202 Zhongshan Beilu is the modern, high-rise *Hongqiao Hotel* (☎ 635931), which caters mostly to tour groups. Doubles cost from Y120 to Y150.

The *Dingshan Hotel* (☎ 685931) *(dīngshān fàndiàn)* is at 90 Chahaer Lu – inconveniently at the remotest part of Nanjing on top of a hill. Once a fairly plebeian place, it's been jazzed up to accommodate elderly Japanese and Overseas Chinese tourists. Doubles cost from Y130. Take trolley bus No 32 from the long-distance bus station or railway station; you have to walk the last km or two. Just look for the building with the fleet of Japanese tour buses parked outside.

Places to Stay – top end

The luxury, high-rise *Jinling Hotel* (☎ 742888) *(jīnlíng)* stands at the centre of Nanjing. This place has everything: a revolving restaurant, sauna, fitness centre, swimming pool, dual-voltage shaver sockets, and a shopping arcade – definitely one of the top hotel properties in China. Double rooms start from US$70, presidential suites US$1000. Take trolley bus No 33 from the railway station (or take a taxi if this hotel is within your budget!). If you arrive by helicopter, there's apparently a pad just metres above the Sky Palace revolving restaurant. The live band at night has a Y20 cover charge – keeps the riffraff out. The piano bar on the mezzanine is cheaper (no cover) and very relaxing.

Places to Eat

Despite the size of this city the restaurants are open for short hours – most of them stack their chairs on the tables by 8 pm, so eat early. The local speciality is Nanjing salted duck which is slathered with roasted salt, steeped in clear brine, baked dry and then kept under cover for some time; the finished product should have a creamy coloured skin and red, tender flesh.

The *Dasanyuan* (☎ 641027) *(dàsānyuǎn jiǔjiā)* at 40 Zhongshan Lu looks like the best bet for a decent meal. Noodle dishes and delicious cold sesame chicken are served in the canteen downstairs; fancier fare is available upstairs. The *Laoguangdong (lǎoguǎngdōng càiguǎn)* at 45 Zhongshan Lu, opposite the Dasanyuan, is similar.

Recommended is the *Jiangsu Restaurant* (☎ 623698) *(jiāngsū jiǔjiā)* at 26 Jiankang Lu, not far from the Taiping Museum. It has three floors of increasing excellence. Nanjing duck is the speciality – you can have it with a dish of pork and bamboo shoots – and vegetables with shrimp and rice, for a few yuan on the 3rd floor.

Other places to eat which may be worth trying are the *Sichuan Restaurant* (☎ 643651) *(sìchuān fàndiàn)* at 171 Taiping Lu and the *Luliuju Vegetarian Restaurant* (☎ 643644) *(lǜliǔjū sùcàiguǎn)* at 248 Taiping Lu.

There are several decent pastry shops along Zhongshan Beilu near Xinjiekou Square. For jiaozi (steamed dumpling), check along Zhongshan Nanlu.

Of the hotel restaurants, the Shengli and Shuangmenlou each have a couple of reasonably priced Chinese eateries that are well worth trying. The Jinling Hotel's *Plum Garden Restaurant* serves excellent Huai Yang, Sichuan and Cantonese food but is somewhat pricey; the even pricier *European Dynasty Glory Restaurant* features French cuisine accompanied by candlelight, and piano music. The more reasonable *Orchid Cafe*, on the hotel's ground floor, is open 24 hours a day and serves a variety of Chinese and Western dishes, including breakfast and lunch buffets.

Getting There & Away

Air Nanjing has regular air connections to 22 Chinese cities, including Beijing (daily), Chengdu (twice a week), Chongqing (three flights a week), Canton (daily), Huangshan (three flights a week), Shanghai (daily), Xi'an (three flights a week) and Wuhan (daily).

The CAAC office (☎ 643378) is at 52 Ruijin Lu. The Nanjing office is linked with CAAC's nationwide computer reservation service, so tickets between destinations other than Nanjing are possible. Tickets can also be purchased at the CITS office and at the Jinling Hotel.

Bus The long-distance bus station is just west of the main railway station. There are buses to Yangzhou (Y5), Yixing (Y6), Zhenjiang (Y4), Changzhou (Y6), Wuxi (Y10), Huangshan (Y16) and Hangzhou (Y15). Other buses, which may be worth checking out, depart from outside Nanjing railway station.

Train Nanjing is a major stop on the Beijing-Shanghai rail line; there are several trains a day in both directions. Heading eastwards from Nanjing, the line to Shanghai connects Zhenjiang, Changzhou, Wuxi and Suzhou.

A new, double-decker express train service has been established between Nanjing and Shanghai. This train (No 1) leaves Nanjing daily at 8.30 am, stops only in Wuxi, and arrives in Shanghai at 12.13 pm. In the opposite direction, it leaves Shanghai at 1.50 pm, arriving in Nanjing at 5.30. All cars are air-conditioned and smoking is prohibited (a first for China Railways!). The fare is Y24.

There is no direct rail link to Hangzhou; you have to go to Shanghai first and then pick up a train or bus. Alternatively, there is a direct bus from Nanjing to Hangzhou. Likewise, to get to Canton by rail you must change trains at Shanghai.

Heading west there is a direct rail link to the port of Wuhu on the Yangtse River. If you want to go further west along the river then the most sensible thing to do is take the ferry.

Boat Ferries ply the Yangtse River from Nanjing eastward to Shanghai and westward to Wuhan; they leave from the dock at the western end of Zhongshan Beilu. There are about two boats a day to Shanghai (about 19 hours) and two a day to Wuhan (two days).

Getting Around

Taxis and pedicabs hang around the railway station. They are also available from the tourist hotels. A taxi from the railway station to the Jinling Hotel will cost about Y10, a pedicab Y5.

Buses and trolley buses are the main means of local transport. The network is confusing and bus maps rarely match up with what's going on in the streets.

A good way to combine Linggu Park with the Tomb of Hong Wu and the Sun Yatsen Memorial is to take bus No 9 from Hanzhong Lu (west and opposite the Jinling Hotel) as far as the avenue of stone animals and figures, then walk to the tomb. From outside the tomb there is a shuttle bus which goes to the Sun Yatsen Memorial. Another shuttle bus leaves from opposite the gateway to the Sun Yatsen Memorial and takes you to Linggu Park.

GRAND CANAL

(dàyùnhé) 大运河

The original Grand Canal, like the Great Wall, was not one but a series of interlocking projects from different eras. The earliest parts were dug 2400 years ago in the north to facilitate troop movements. During the Sui Dynasty (581-618 AD), the ruthless Emperor Yang Di conscripted a massive workforce to link his new capital of Luoyang to the older capital of Chang'an (Xi'an). Then he extended the project down to Hangzhou in less than a decade, making it possible for junks to go along the Yangtse, up the

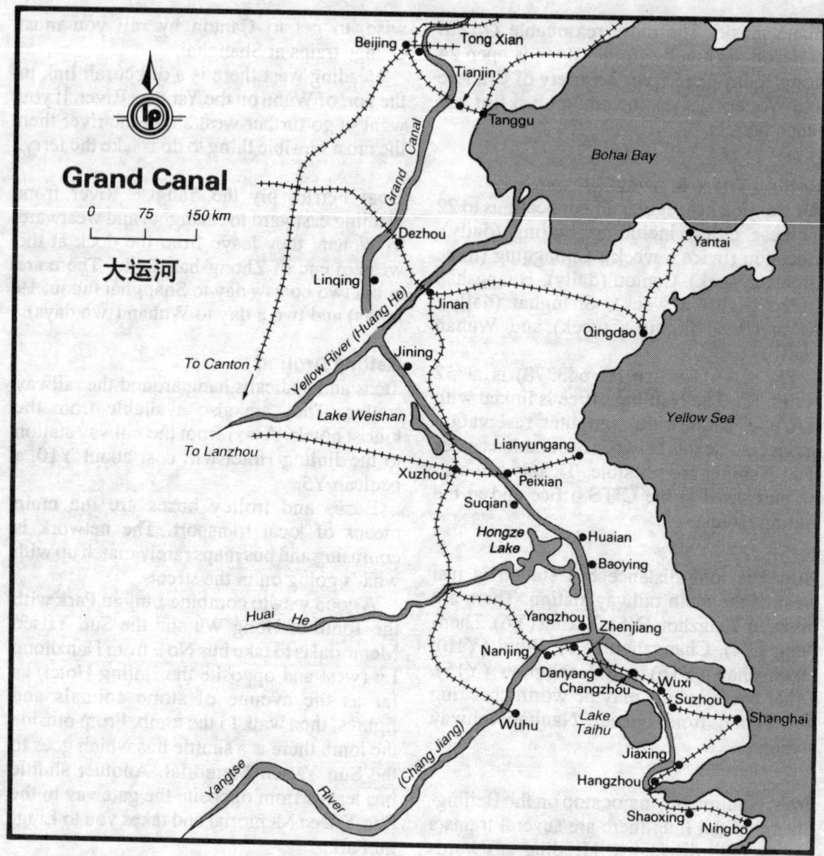

canal, and on to ports along the Yellow River – a trip that might take up to a year.

The canal at that time linked up four major east-west running rivers: the Huang (Yellow), Yangtse, Huai and Qiantang. It thus gave China a major north-south transport route, and linked the compass points. It has been said that the canal, the longest artificial waterway in the world, was built by 'a million people with teaspoons'. In fact some estimate closer to five million people, but by even the crudest mathematics the cost in lives must have been enormous.

The emperor was not so much interested in unification as subjugation. Grain from the rich fields of the south was appropriated to feed the hungry armies in the northern capitals. During the Tang Dynasty 100,000 tonnes of grain were transported annually to the north – long chains of imperial barges loaded with tax grain plied the waterways.

During the 13th century, Kublai Khan used the work of his predecessors for much the same purpose, and he did a bit of remodelling to bring the northern terminal up to Beijing, his capital. Marco Polo noted that boats were pulled along by horses with long harnesses which walked along the banks of the canal. In this way large quantities of corn and rice were shipped northward. He wrote:

> This magnificent work (the canal) is deserving of admiration; and not so much from the manner in which it is conducted through the country, or its vast extent, as from its utility and the benefit it produces to those cities which lie in its course.

Apart from bringing prosperity to the towns along its course, the canal was also a means by which the sybaritic emperors would move from point A to point B. At one stage during the Emperor Qianlong's reign, it was suggested that the grain fleets be removed from the canal so as to allow the imperial pleasure-cruisers a freer passage.

As time went by, sections of the canal fell into disuse or were engulfed by flooding from the Yellow River. In this century the growth of railways eclipsed the need for water transport. By 1980, silt, poorly planned dams, watergates and irrigation systems, or plain atrophy had reduced internal waterways mileage in China to a third of that in the 1960s.

Imperial Revival

Suddenly in 1980 the Grand Canal became a tourist attraction. A flat-bottomed cruiser with air-conditioning and all mod cons materialised out of Wuxi, and passengers coughed up several thousand dollars for a week-long run from Yangzhou to Suzhou, including overnight stopovers at the towns along the way.

Since the 'opening' hundreds of groups have made the trip. At its disposal in Wuxi CITS has a new concept – the Dragon Boat, a replica of an imperial barge with carvings, antique furniture, and a high-class restaurant on board. Tourists can dress up like emperors and strut about nibbling at the delicacies served on imperial tableware. Since then, several more boats have been added, and more are planned.

The Beijing-Hangzhou canal meandered almost 1800 km. Today perhaps half of it remains seasonally navigable. The Party claims that, since Liberation, large-scale dredging has made the navigable length 1100 km. This is an exaggeration. Canal depths are up to three metres and canal widths can narrow to less than nine metres. Put these facts together, realise that there are old stone bridges spanning the route, and you come to the conclusion that it is restricted to fairly small flat-bottomed vessels.

The section of the canal from Beijing to Tianjin has been silted up for centuries. A similar fate has befallen most sections from the Yellow River to Tianjin. The stretch from the Yellow River to Peixian (in northern Jiangsu Province) is highly dubious and is most likely silted up from the Yellow River's flooding. Jining, which lies between these two points, was once a prosperous cloth producer; the canal there now lies idle and the town is served by rail.

The canal itself is polluted with oil slicks and doubles as the local garbage bin, sewer and washing machine. There's still plenty to look at on the water: moss-stricken canal-side housing, houseboats, barges, and glimpses of life at the water's edge like women pounding their washing to a pulp and men fishing.

Touring the Canal

Heading south from the northern Chinese plains, the canal really picks up at **Peixian**. There are two Peixians – this one is in the far north-central part of Jiangsu Province near the border with Shandong. It lies east of the town of Xuzhou, to which it is linked by a railway line. Peixian is closed, but a tributary canal runs past Xuzhou, feeding into the Grand Canal.

Continuing south, you come to **Hualan** (no rail link). It's open not because of the canal but because it's Zhou Enlai's home town. Tourists (mostly Overseas Chinese) usually stop only to visit his former residence, but there are a couple of other places of interest including pavilions and pagodas. The plaster and tile housing typical of areas south of the Yangtse now give way to mud and thatched buildings. The canal runs deep here and is eminently navigable.

Further south is **Yangzhou** below which the canal passes through locks into the Yangtse. The section from Peixian to Yangzhou is part of a bold plan to divert water from the Yangtse and the rainy south to the arid, drought-racked provinces of Shandong, Hebei, Henan and Anhui. The route is also needed to ship coal to energy-hungry Shanghai from major coal producer Xuzhou. The plan, to be completed in the early 1990s, calls for dredging the section from Yangzhou to Xuzhou to a depth of four metres and a width of 70 metres at the bottom, so that 2000-tonne vessels can pass. A double ship lock is being built at Huaian. So it seems the old canal still has its major uses. The water, it appears, will be provided for irrigation as far north as Jining in Shandong Province.

South of the Yangtse the picture is much brighter, with year-round navigation. The Jiangnan section of the canal (Hangzhou, Suzhou, Wuxi, Changzhou, Danyang, Zhenjiang) is a skein of canals, rivers and branching lakes. Just as interesting as the Grand Canal are the feeder canals, many of them major thoroughfares in their own right, but sometimes it's difficult to tell which is the Grand Canal, since people may point to any canal and call it that.

Canal Ferries

Travellers have done the route from Hangzhou to Suzhou on overnight passenger boats (with sleeping berths) or on daytime 150-seater ferries. Some people regard this as the highlight of their China trip.

Others have found the boats dirty, crowded and uncomfortable, with a fair part of the trip taken up by views of high canal banks. Some words of advice: you need a good bladder since the toilets are terrible; you need some food; and try and get a window seat, both to see the scenery and escape the many smokers on the boat.

One reader wrote:

> The boat is terrible, dirty, cramped, its windows just above the waterline make it hard to see anything, but the 'toilet' won the prize as the worst in all China. It was a large bucket that was not emptied during our trip, which took 14 hours (including two hours when we were stopped by fog, which is very common in fall and winter).

Another wrote that the canal voyage was 'the highlight of our trip...a filthy but picturesque slice of life in China'.

Estimated times for the sections south of the Yangtse are:

section	duration
Hangzhou to Suzhou	14 hours, overnight berth or day boat
Suzhou to Wuxi	five to six hours, early morning day boat
Wuxi to Changzhou	four to five hours
Changzhou to Zhenjiang	eight to nine hours with a possible break in Danyang

It's possible to break the journey about halfway from Hangzhou to Suzhou at the fine canal town of **Jiaxing** which is also linked by rail to Shanghai or Hangzhou. It has textile and food-processing factories and deals in silk and rice. The pavilion to the southeast of the town, on an island lake, is reputed to be where founding members of the Chinese Communist Party sheltered when disturbed by Shanghai police in 1921. There are other connections running through Lake Taihu.

YANGZHOU

(yángzhōu) 杨州

Yangzhou, at the junction of the Grand Canal and the Yangtse, was once an economic and cultural centre of Southern China. It was home to scholars, painters, storytellers, poets and merchants in the Sui and Tang dynasties, but little remains of the greatness that Marco Polo witnessed. He served there as Kublai Khan's governor for three years and wrote that:

> Yangui has twenty-four towns under its jurisdiction, and must be considered a place of great consequence...the people are idolators, and subsist by trade and manual arts. They manufacture arms and other munitions: in consequence of which many troops are stationed in this part of the country.

Buried outside the town at Leitang, in a simple mound of earth, is Emperor Yang Di, the ruthless tyrant who completed the construction of the Grand Canal during the Sui Dynasty (518-618 AD). Yang Di is said to have levied exorbitant taxes, starved his subjects, and generally been very mean and nasty. The emperor's throne was usurped by a members of a powerful noble family who were to found the Tang Dynasty, and Yang Di was strangled by his own generals at Yangzhou in 618.

To the north-west of Yangzhou once stood the Maze Palace, a labyrinth of bronze mirrors and couches with concubines. Yang Di is supposed to have torn about here in a leopard-skin outfit, turning one night into 10 before he finally emerged to deal with affairs of state – or maybe he just couldn't find his way out again? The building was burned down, and on the ruins a structure called Jian (Warning) Building, a reminder for future generations was erected. Still there, near Guanyin Hill, it is now used as a museum of Tang relics.

During the Qing Dynasty (1644-1911), Yangzhou got a new lease of life as a salt-trading centre, and Emperor Qianlong set about remodelling the town in the 18th century. All the streets leading to the town gates were lined with platforms where story-tellers recited chapters from famous novels (the repertoire was reputed to be 30 novels). The period also saw a group of painters known as the 'Eight Eccentrics' break away from traditional methods, creating a style of natural painting that influenced the course of art in China. Merchants and scholars favoured Yangzhou as a retirement home.

The town was badly battered during the Taiping Rebellion in the 19th century. With old pavilions strangled by traffic, unkempt gardens, and amazing collections of kitsch in the central area, Yangzhou is well past its tourist prime. The air of decay hangs heavy and the population has declined drastically compared with its glorious past. Nevertheless, there's some small-town charm, a chance to escape the cities that crowd the traveller's route. It may appear presumptuous to dismiss so much history in so few words, but time has marched on!

Information

You should be able to make contact with CITS in the Yangzhou Hotel; the hotel also has a post office. Good bus maps of Yangzhou are available from the hawkers and booths around the bus station, also try the shop in the Yangzhou Hotel.

Ge Garden

(gèyuán) 个园

On Dongguan Lu this garden was landscaped by the painter Shi Tao for an officer of the Qing court. Shi Tao was an expert at making artificial rocks; the composition here suggests the four seasons.

He Garden

(héyuán) 和园

Alias Jixiao Mountain Villa, the He Garden was built in the 19th century. It contains rockeries, ponds, pavilions and walls inscribed with classical poetry.

Pavilions & Pagodas

At the north-west end of town are a couple of pavilions and a small pagoda. The three-storey octagonal pavilion at the north is **Siwang** *(sìwàng tíng)* which is more than 700 years old. The similar one to the south is **Wenchangge**, or Pavilion of Flourishing Culture – a reference to the time of its building 400 years ago.

To the west of that is the tiny **Stone Pagoda** *(shítǎ)*, which is 1100 years old and looks like someone's been at it with a sledge-hammer.

Just south-west of the bus station, **Wenfeng Pagoda** *(wénfēng tǎ)* can be scaled to the seventh level (assemble at 9 am, get out your grappling-hooks, highly recommended). It offers a bird's-eye view of the flotsam, jetsam and sampans along a canal, as well as an 'overview' of the town. Made of brick and wood, it's been rebuilt several times.

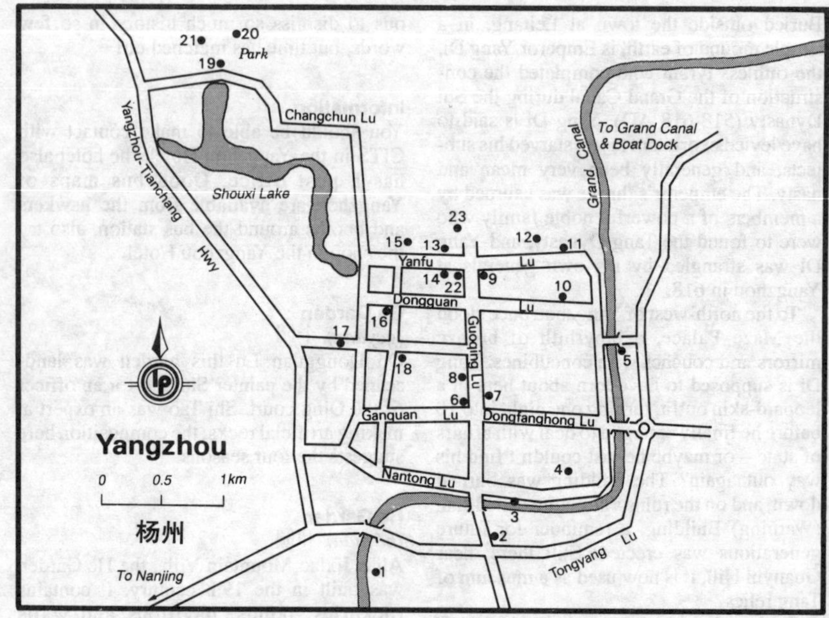

Canals

The town's busy waterlife attracted the attention of 18th-century travellers; Yangzhou used to have 24 stone bridges spanning its network of canals. It's now acquired an industrial fringe and noisy traffic.

You might like to investigate the environs – a short way out of town. The Grand Canal actually passes a little to the east of Yangzhou. The bus No 2 terminal in the north-east is a boat dock. Bus No 4 runs over a bridge on the canal. There are two ship locks to the south of Yangzhou.

North-east of the town, across the Grand Canal, is the Jiangsu Water Control Project, a large-scale plan for diverting water from the Yangtse for irrigation, drainage, power and navigation. It was completed in 1975 with foreign assistance.

Shouxi Lake

(shòu xīhú) 瘦西湖

This is the top scenic spot in Yangzhou – in the western suburbs on the bus No 5 route. 'Shouxi' means 'slender west' as opposed to the 'fat west' lake in Hangzhou. In China fat signifies happy and slender means beautiful, but this park verges toward the emaciated, desperately in need of rejuvenation.

It offers an imperial dragon-boat ferry, a restaurant and a white dagoba modelled after the one in Beihai Park in Beijing. The highlight is the triple-arched, five-pavilion Wutang Qiao, a bridge built in 1757. For bridge connoisseurs it's rated one of the top 10 ancient Chinese bridges.

Emperor Qianlong's fishing platform is in the park. It is said that the local divers used to put fish on the poor emperor's hook so he'd think it was good luck and cough up some more funding for the town.

Fajingsi Monastery

(fǎjìngsì) 法净寺

The temple complex, formerly called Daming, was founded over 1000 years ago

1	Wenfeng Pagoda
2	Long-Distance Bus Station
3	Boat Dock
4	He Garden
5	Tomb of Puhaddin
6	Renmin Department Store
7	Fuchun Teahouse (off Guoqing Lu)
8	Caigenxiang Restaurant
9	Friendship Store
10	Ge Garden
11	Lacquer Factory
12	Jade Factory
13	Museum
14	Bookstore
15	Xiyuan Hotel
16	Siwang Pavilion
17	Stone Pagoda
18	Wenchangge (Pavilion of Flourishing Culture)
19	Daming Monastery (Fajingsi)
20	Jianzhen Memorial Hall
21	Pingshan Hall
22	Yangzhou Antique Store
23	Yangzhou Hotel & CITS

1	文峰塔
2	长途汽车站
3	轮船码头
4	寄啸山庄
5	普哈丁墓
6	人民百货商店
7	富春茶社
8	菜根香饭店
9	友谊商店
10	个园
11	漆器厂
12	玉器厂
13	博物馆
14	书店
15	西园饭店
16	四望亭
17	石塔
18	文昌阁
19	大明寺（法净寺）
20	鉴真记念堂
21	平山堂
22	杨州文物店
23	杨州宾馆

and subsequently destroyed and rebuilt. Then it was finally destroyed during the Taiping Rebellion; what you see today is a 1934 reconstruction. It's nice architecture even so, and – if you time it right – you'll find the shaven-headed monks engaged in 'mysterious' ritual.

The original temple is credited to the Tang Dynasty monk Jianzhen who studied sculpture, architecture, fine arts and medicine as well as Buddhism seriously. In 742 AD two Japanese monks invited him to Japan for missionary work. It turned out to be mission impossible. Jianzhen made five attempts to get there, failing due to storms. The fifth time he ended up in Hainan. On the sixth trip, aged 66, he finally arrived. He stayed in Japan for 10 years and died there in 763 AD. Later the Japanese made a lacquer statue of Jianzhen, which in 1980 was sent to Yangzhou.

The Chinese have a wooden copy of this statue on display at the Jianzhen Memorial Hall. Modelled after the chief hall of the Toshodai Temple in Nara (Japan), the Jianzhen Memorial Hall was built in 1974 at the monastery and was financed by Japanese contributions. Special exchanges are made between Nara and Yangzhou; even Deng Xiaoping, returning from a trip to Japan, came to this monastery to cement renewed links between the two countries.

West of Fajingsi is Pingshan Hall *(píngshān táng)*, the residence of the Song Dynasty writer Ouyang Xiu who served in Yangzhou. West of that, in the Western Gardens, is No 5 Lifespring Under Heaven *(xīyuán quánshuǐ)*. These spring waters were valued by Lu Yu, a Tang Dynasty tea expert.

Tomb of Puhaddin

(pǔhādīng mù) 普哈丁墓

This tomb contains documents regarding

China's contacts with the Muslims. It's on the east bank of a canal on the bus No 2 route. Puhaddin came to China during the Yuan Dynasty (1261-1378) to spread the Muslim faith, and spent 10 years in Yangzhou, where he died. There is a mosque in Yangzhou.

History Museum

(yángzhōushì bówùguǎn) 杨州市博物馆
The museum lies to the north of Guoqing Lu, near the Xiyuan Hotel. It's in a temple originally dedicated to Shi Kefa, a Ming Dynasty official who refused to succumb to his new Qing masters and was executed. The museum contains items from Yangzhou's past. A small collection of calligraphy and paintings of the 'Eight Eccentrics' is displayed in another small museum just off Yanfu Lu near the Xiyuan Hotel.

Places to Stay

The *Yangzhou Hotel (yángzhōu bīnguǎn)* is the prime tourist joint with doubles from Y120 to Y180 but it's rather void of style. The garden-style *Xiyuan Hotel (xīyuán fàndiàn)*, which is said to have been constructed over the site of Qianlong's imperial villa, has more character. Rates at this sprawling deluxe hotel range from Y80 a double with private bath in the old wing to Y120 and up for newer rooms. Three-bed rooms are available for Y25 per person. The Xiyuan has a pretty garden setting complete with pond and geese. From the bus station take bus No 8 to the Friendship Store; the Yangzhou Hotel is the multistorey building in front of you and the Xiyuan is in a compound next door.

Places to Eat

The big wining and dining area is the crossroads of Guoqing Lu (which runs north from the bus station) and Ganquan. Yangzhou has its own cuisine but, except for a special banquet, you might have trouble finding it. Try the *Caigenxiang Restaurant (càigēnxiāng fàndiàn)*, 115 Guoqing Lu. How about buns with crab-ovary stuffing? Along Guoqing Lu and Ganquan Lu are small bakeries and cafes which sell steamed dumplings, noodles, pastries and other goodies – you can see the stuff being kneaded right behind the counter.

Both of the previously mentioned hotels have dining rooms. The *Xiyuan Hotel's* restaurant has great food, including local specialties like famous Yangzhou-style fried rice.

Another great place for local cuisine is the Fuchun Teahouse *(fùchūn cháguǎn)*, in an alley off Guoqing Lu. It's open from 6 am to 7 pm and offers a vast selection of delicious snacks and teas.

Things to Buy

The centre is full of shoe shops and housewares, but there's no sign of the lacquerware, jade, paper-cuts, woodcuts, embroidery or painting that Yangzhou is supposed to be famous for. So investigate these places if that's what you're after:

The Arts & Crafts Factory west of Xiyuan Hotel; the Friendship Store on Guoqing Lu; the Lacquer Factory *(qīqì chǎng)* which makes inlaid lacquer screens with translucent properties, due east of Xiyuan Hotel; the Jade Factory *(yùqì chǎng)* at 6 Guangchumenwai Jie; the Block Printing Co-op with handbound woodblock printed classics; the Yangzhou Antique Store *(yángzhōu wénwùdiàn)* opposite the Yangzhou Hotel; and possibly the Renmin Department Store.

Getting There & Away

The railway line gave Yangzhou a miss, one of the main reasons that this flower has wilted. Unless you're lucky enough to engineer a boat ride to Yangzhou from Nanjing or Zhenjiang, you'll have to travel by bus.

From Yangzhou there are buses to Nanjing (Y5, 2½ hours); Zhenjiang (Y3, 1½ hours with amphibious crossings of the Yangtse); Wuxi (Y9); Suzhou (Y10); Changzhou and Shanghai.

A more comprehensive route would be Nanjing, Yangzhou, Zhenjiang, Nanjing – or Changzhou, Zhenjiang, Yangzhou, Nanjing. On either of these you could also juggle with the trains. Allow an overnight stop on such routes. The railway station nearest Yangzhou is Zhenjiang.

Getting Around

The sights are at the edge of town. If you're in a hurry you might consider commandeering a 'turtle' (auto-rickshaw) – they can be found outside the bus station. The central area can easily be covered on foot.

Bus Nos 1, 2, 3, 5, 6 and 7 terminate near the bus station. Bus No 1 runs from the bus station up Guoqing Lu and then loops around the perimeter of the inside canal, returning just north of the bus station. Bus No 4 is an east-west bus and goes along Ganquan Lu.

ZHENJIANG

(zhènjiāng) 镇江

Zhenjiang takes its character not from the Grand Canal but from the Yangtse, which it faces. In other words, it's large, murky and industrial. The old silk trade still exists, overshadowed by car and shipbuilding and by textile and food-processing plants. It's a medium-sized place with 300 factories, and is home to well over 300,000 people.

Attempts have been made to 'humanise' the city by planting trees along the streets. The sights are pleasant enough since they're removed from the industrial eyesores. To the south are densely wooded areas, mountains and temples tucked away in bamboo groves but they are difficult to get to by local bus.

The city's history goes back some 2500 years. Its strategic and commercial importance, as the gateway to Nanjing, is underlined by the fact that the British and the French established concessions here. Don't be deterred by your first view of Zhenjiang from the railway station; the older part of town is a picturesque area with busy streets, small enterprises, people, bicycles and timber houses.

Information

CITS The CITS/CTS office is in the Jingkou Hotel (☎ 33567).

Maps Bus maps are available from the booth outside the railway station.

Jiaoshan

(jiāoshān) 焦山

The 'three mounts of Zhenjiang', vantage points strewn along the Yangtse, are the principal sights. The temple complexes on each are among the oldest gracing the river, and date back 1500 years.

Also known as Jade Hill because of its dark green foliage (cypresses and bamboo), Jiaoshan is to the east on a small island. There's good hiking here with a number of pavilions along the way to the top of the 150-metre-high mount, from where Xijiang Tower gives a view of activity on the Yangtse. At the base of Jiaoshan is an active monastery with some 200 pieces of tablet engravings, gardens and bonsai displays. Take bus No 4 to the terminal, then it's a short walk and a boat ride.

Beigushan

(běigùshān) 北固山

Also on the No 4 bus route, this hill has the Ganlu Temple (Ganlusi) complex featuring a Song Dynasty pagoda which offers expansive views of town. It was once six storeys high but is now four, having been vandalised by Red Guards.

Jinshan

(jīnshān) 金山

This hill has a temple arrayed tier by tier with connecting staircases on a hillside – a remarkable design. Right at the top is the seven-storey octagonal Cishou Pagoda that gives an all-embracing view of the town, the fishponds immediately below and the Yangtse beyond. There are four caves at the mount: Buddhist Sea *(fáhǎi)*, White Dragon *(báilóng)*, Morning Sun *(zhàoyáng)*, and Arhat *(luóhàn)*. Fahai and Bailong caves feature in the Chinese fairytale *The Story of the White Snake*. West of the base, within walking distance, is No 1 Lifespring Under Heaven. The spring waters of Jiangsu were catalogued by Tang Dynasty tea expert Lu Yu (No 2 is Wuxi, No 3 is Hangzhou). Take bus No 2 to Jinshan.

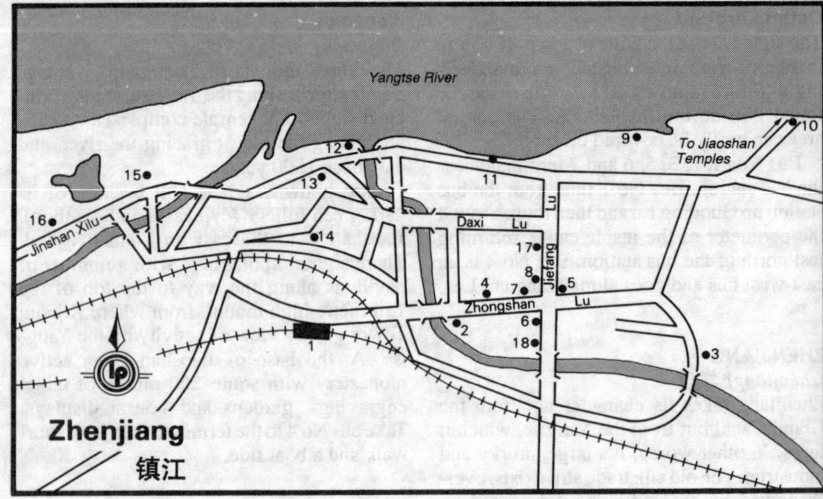

1	Railway Station & Buses to Yangzhou	火车站及开往杨州的汽车
2	Jingkou Hotel & CTS/CITS	京口饭店
3	Baotashan	宝塔山
4	Hebin Hotel	河滨饭店
5	Department Store	百货商店
6	Jingjiang Hotel/Restaurant	京江饭店
7	Pastry Shop	糕店
8	Post Office	邮局
9	Ganlu Temple	甘露寺
10	Boat to Jiaoshan Temple	焦山船码头
11	Boat Dock & Fish Factory	镇江码头
12	Ferry Dock for Yangzhou	轮渡码头
13	Museum	博物馆
14	Renmin (People's) Park	人民公园
15	Jinshan Temple	金山寺
16	Jinshan Hotel	金山宾馆
17	Arts & Crafts Store	工艺品大楼
18	Long-Distance Bus Station	长途汽车站

Museum
(bówùguǎn) 博物馆
A fourth 'mount' of interest between Jinshan and the downtown area is the old British Consulate, which is now a museum and gallery. It houses pottery, bronzes, gold, silver, Tang Dynasty paintings, and a separate

section with photographs and memorabilia of the anti-Japanese war. Its retail outlet sells calligraphy, rubbings and paintings. The museum is on the bus No 2 route, and is set high over a very old area of winding stone-laid alleys that go down to boat docks on the Yangtse. It's well worth investigating on foot.

Places to Stay

For 'foreign devils' the *Jinshan Hotel (jīnshān fàndiàn)* (☎ 32971), at 1 Jinshan Xilu, is the place to stay. It more closely resembles a motel – it started life as an Australian pre-fab – and is a 10-minute walk around the artificial lake near Jinshan Temple, at bus No 2's terminal. Doubles cost from Y100. If you're on your own you may be able to get a room for half that price.

On the main east-west drag, Zhongshan Lu is the main hotel for Overseas Chinese, the *Jingkou Hotel (jīngkǒu fàndiàn)* (☎ 33567). This is also where CTS/CITS has its offices. Doubles cost from Y75 to Y100. Nearby is the similarly priced *Hebin Hotel*.

Places to Eat

There's a pastry shop near the crossroads in the centre of town, and dumpling houses and noodle shops near the railway stations. The central *Jingjiang Hotel (jīngjiāng fàndiàn)* at 111 Jiefang Lu, reputedly has the best food in town; the ground floor has mainly jiaozi and baozi, but upstairs you can get enormous main courses very cheaply.

Things to Buy

There's a very fine Arts & Crafts Store *(gōngyìpǐn dàlóu)* at 191 Jiefang Lu which stocks embroidery, porcelain, jade and other artefacts. It may have some antiques.

Getting There & Away

Bus The long-distance bus station is in the south-east corner of the city centre. There are buses from Zhenjiang to Nanjing and Changzhou, and a bus-ferry combination to Yangzhou. You can also get buses to Yangzhou from the front of the main railway station.

Train Zhenjiang is on the main Nanjing-Shanghai line, 3½ hours by fast train to Shanghai, and an hour to either Nanjing or Changzhou. Some of the special express trains don't stop at Zhenjiang. Otherwise, there is a grand choice of schedules so check the timetable in your hotel for a destination and time to suit.

Boat A more offbeat means of departure is via the ferries on the Grand Canal or the Yangtse River.

Getting Around

The city is ideal for day-tripping. Almost all the transport (including local buses, buses to Yangzhou, taxis and auto-rickshaws) is conveniently close to the railway station.

Bus No 2 is a convenient tour bus. It goes east from the station along Zhongshan Lu to the city centre where the Friendship Store, department stores, antique shop and post office are. It then swings west into the older part of town where some speciality and second-hand stores are to be found, goes past the former British consulate, and continues on to Jin Shan, the terminal.

Bus No 4, which crosses the No 2 route in the city centre on Jiefang Lu, runs to Ganluo Temple and Jiaoshan in the east.

CHANGZHOU

(chángzhōu) 常州

Changzhou is overlooked by most guidebooks, and the CITS offices in Wuxi and Suzhou will tell you it's not worth a visit. In the former case it is an oversight and in the latter it's regional jealousy – Changzhou has zero unemployment and is doing very well economically, thank you.

Changzhou is the largest textile producer in Jiangsu Province after Shanghai. The population is around half a million and the city's history is linked with the ancient canal. Industries include textiles, food-processing, and the manufacture of machinery, chemicals, building materials, locomotives and diesel engines. Also produced are integrated circuits and electronic parts: large digital

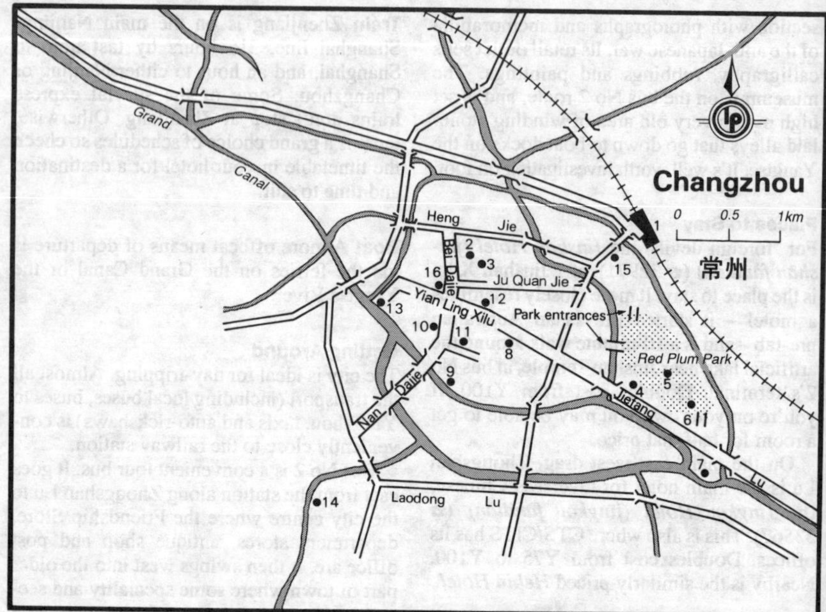

1 Railway Station
2 Changzhou Hotel
3 Municipal Government Building
4 Temple of Heavenly Tranquillity
5 Red Plum Pavilion
6 Literary Pen Tower
7 Mooring Pavilion & Boat Dock
8 CITS/CTS/Friendship Store
9 Public Security Bureau
10 Cafe
11 Xinglong Restaurant(down lane)
12 Luyang Restaurant
13 Boat Dock
14 Jiangnanchun Hotel
15 Long-Distance Bus Station
16 Post Office

1 火车站
2 常州饭店
3 市人民政府
4 天宁禅寺
5 红梅阁
6 文笔塔
7 舣舟亭
8 国际旅行社/友谊商店
9 公安局
10 咖啡馆
11 兴隆饭店
12 绿扬饭店
13 码头
14 江南春宾馆
15 长途汽车站
16 邮局

clocks around the place will tell you the time in places ranging from Moscow to Canberra.

It's a delightful mix of old and new: Changzhou has managed to retain its timeless canal housing by placing new residential areas outside the old city core. If you look at the bus map, you'll see these areas dotted around the perimeter. It is very much a back-alley town, providing some interesting sorties on foot. Tourism is a recent phenomenon. If you want to avoid the crush at Wuxi or Suzhou, Changzhou is a good place to go.

Information

Good bus maps of Changzhou are available from counters in the main railway station. CITS (☎ 24886), CTS and the Friendship Store are at 101 Yian Ling Xilu, in a compound opposite the central local bus terminal.

Canals

Changzhou has a skein of canals and is an excellent place to observe canal life. There are quite a few archaic bridges which make good vantage points – these are easily found on the bus map. Some of the bridges shelter interconnected timeworn housing. If you took the older housing away the bridges would probably fall down or vice versa! Small markets occasionally take place along canal banks near bridges.

Mooring Pavilion

(yǐzhōu tíng) 舣舟亭

This is a small park in the south-east of Changzhou right on the Grand Canal. You can sit here and watch rusty hulks drift by and churn up the oil and pollution. There's a boat dock here, and much hooting and honking on the water. The park was set up in remembrance of Su Dongpo, a great poet. Take bus Nos 3 or 7 to the Mooring Pavilion. If you take bus No 7 further, it runs straight out of town south-eastwards along the banks of the canal past dry-dock zones. In the north-west bus No 4 does a similar job. Bus Nos 4 and 7 meet at a terminal in the city centre.

Red Plum Park

(hóngméi gōngyuán) 红梅花园

North of Mooring Pavilion is Red Plum Park. The very large park has a small pagoda, a nicely sited teahouse, and boating on the nearby lake. There are one or two structures of significance – Qu Qiu Bai's house, now a museum, and Red Plum Pavilion *(hóngméi gé)*. Qu was a literary man and an early member of the Chinese Communist Party. The park itself is nondescript, in an area that looks like something from the final days of the Industrial Revolution. Around the park are shanties and other dark and gloomy housing. The Temple of Heavenly Tranquillity *(tiānníng chánsì)* – levelled, rebuilt, destroyed, renovated – is below the park at the south-west corner.

Places to Stay

The *Changzhou Hotel (Chang Chow Guesthouse)* (☎ 600713) *(chángzhōu bīnguǎn)* is central, with Chinese colonial architecture, large grounds, gardens and dining halls. It's also well off the street and quiet. The reception desk asks Y150 for a double; they have a few doubles with shared bath for only Y40, including TV and air-con. Take bus No 12 from the long-distance bus station or railway station to Ju Qian Jie and stay on the bus until just before Jua Quan Jie ends at Bei Dajie. Walk north on Hua Long Xiang and then right (east) on Chang Sheng Xiang. The hotel is at the end of Chang Sheng Xiang.

The *Jiangnanchun Hotel* (☎ 603664) *(jiāngnánchūn bīnguǎn)*, on the southern edge of town, is more difficult to get to as some hiking is involved. This is a tour-bus TV hotel. Doubles start from Y120. Take bus No 14 from the railway station, then walk.

Places to Eat

The *Xinglong Restaurant (xīnglóng fàndiàn)* is on a lane off Nan Dajie. You'll recognise it by the noise level (80 decibels) and frozen pigs at the back near the kitchen. It's got gluey, gooey Jiangsu food – if you want to post a letter, this is the place to seal it – just use the sauce. Check out the pastry shops on the same street with all sorts of pastries in 3-D animal, dragon and flower shapes.

The *Luyang Restaurant (lǜyáng fàndiàn)* gets a Four Red Star rating. A full, tasty meal can be had for a few yuan per head. They'll probably try to shuffle you away from the noisy plebs and take you upstairs where it's quieter, the furniture is plusher, the food more expensive, and you get a white tablecloth. It's not far from the Changzhou Hotel. If you take the alley that leads off the Changzhou and follow it south through a vegetable market, you'll hit the main street – the Luyang is to the right, on Yian Ling Xilu.

A small cafe on the No 2 bus route south of the Changzhou Hotel serves drinks, pastries and tasty cakes in a quaint atmosphere, remarkably like that of a Western coffee shop – a courtesy award is framed on the wall so they have to live up to it. This place is easily spotted at night – it has fairy lights strung out on the front. There are several bakeries and 'wine houses' along the same stretch.

Things to Buy

Wooden combs with imaginative designs – fish, butterflies, bottles or standing figures – are a Changzhou folk art. There's a comb factory in the western suburbs, and an Arts/Fine Arts Workshop in the centre.

Getting There & Away

Bus There are three long-distance bus stations in Changzhou. The main one is near the railway station. Another is in the north-west sector, and the third is in the south-west sector near the Jiangnanchun Guesthouse.

There are buses from Changzhou to Wuxi, Zhenjiang, Suzhou and Nanjing, but they take longer than the fast trains. However, the trains on this line are incredibly crowded and you'd be wise to take a bus if you can!

There are several buses a day to Yixing (Y3, 1½ hours). There are also direct buses from Changzhou to Dingshu, thus skipping Yixing town.

Train Changzhou is on the line from Shanghai to Nanjing. It is one hour from either Wuxi or Zhenjiang, two hours from Suzhou or Nanjing. If you're going by rail, you might consider doing some rail-hopping; buy a hard-seat ticket from, say, Suzhou to Nanjing, break the journey for a day in Changzhou, and continue with the same ticket.

Boat A more interesting route is along the Grand Canal; Wuxi, the closest major town, is five hours away by boat.

AROUND CHANGZHOU

Danyang

(dānyáng) 丹杨

Between Changzhou and Zhenjiang, Danyang is another canal town, 70 km east of Nanjing. On the banks of the Danyang main canal are some 20 stone animal statues around 1500 years old, and nearby are the tombs of the Qi emperors (the dynasty which followed the Song) and the Qixiashan Buddhist Grottoes. Danyang was the original home of the Qi royal family, so they chose to be buried here.

The Buddhist grottoes lie about 20 km east of Nanjing. The earliest caves date from the Qi Dynasty (479-502 AD), though there are others from a number of succeeding dynasties right through to the Ming.

YIXING COUNTY

(yíxīng xiàn) 宜兴县

Yixing County to the west of Lake Taihu *(tàihú)* has enormous tourist potential and provides a chance to get out of the cities. There are fertile plains, tea and bamboo plantations, undulating mountains with large caves and grottoes. The spectacular potteries of Dingshu village are, however, the real prize. Though busloads of Chinese tourists descend daily on the county from Wuxi, Nanjing and Shanghai, along with Western group tours on day trips, Yixing County has seen very few individual travellers.

The town of Yixing is *not* the place to go – you're likely to end up being the main attraction yourself. It's a small town (with about 50,000 residents) where the main business of selling noodles, zips, steamed bread, pigs' feet, pots and pans, tools and sunglasses, is all done out on the main street which terminates at the forbidding gates of the Yixing Guesthouse.

You'll probably end up in Yixing town one way or another since the only tourist hotel is there and the buses pass through. The

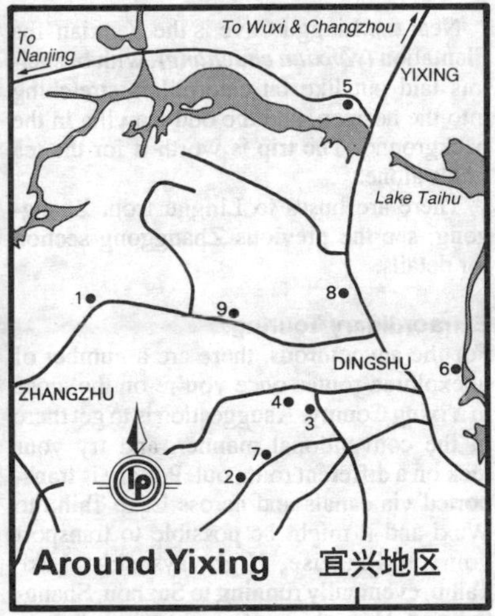

1 Shanjuan Cave
2 Linggu Cave
3 Zhanggong Cave
4 Yunutan Pool
5 Aquatic Breeding Farm
6 Purple Sandware Factory
7 Yangxian Tea Plantation
8 Chuanbei Tea Plantation
9 Furongsi Tea Plantation

1 善卷洞
2 灵谷洞
3 张公洞
4 玉女潭
5 养鱼场
6 紫砂工艺厂
7 茶场
8 川北茶场
9 芙蓉寺茶场

attractions of Yixing County are all within a 30-km range of the town. The pottery town of Dingshu can be done as a day or half-day trip.

If you have time, explore the north-east end of Yixing town with its heavy concentration of comic-book hire places (it's not just kids doing the reading) and all manner of strange transactions down side streets. This and more can be seen in Dingshu. The Confucius Temple at the north-west end of Yixing town which was in poor condition is being renovated.

Karst Caves
(shíhuī yándòng) 石灰岩洞
There are a number of these to the south-west of Yixing township, and they're a cut above average. The drab interiors are lit by the standard selection of coloured neon, but you may wish to supplement this with a torch for navigation. The caves are very wet, so take your raincoat, too. The countryside around the caves is attractive and actually worth more time than the underground. The Mandarin word for cave is *shāndòng*.

Shanjuan Cave *(shànjuǎn dòng)* This cave is embedded in Snail Shell Hill (Luoyanshan), 27 km south-west of Yixing. It covers an area of roughly 5000 sq metres, with passages of 800 metres – enough to make any speleologist delirious. It's divided into upper, middle and lower reaches, plus a water cave. An exterior waterfall provides special sound effects for this weird set.

Entry is via the Middle Cave, a stone hall with a 1000-metre floor space. From here you can mount a staircase to the snail's shell, the Upper Cave, or wander down to the lower and water caves. In the Water Cave, you can jump in a rowing boat for a 120-metre ride to the exit, called 'Suddenly-see-the-Light', where a restaurant, hotel, teahouse, Zhuling village and goodness knows what else awaits you. Good luck!

There are, of course, many legends associated with the caves – mostly about former resident hermits. One was the hermit Zhu Yingtai. At the exit is a small pavilion which she used as her 'reading room'. Zhu, as the story goes, being a Jin Dynasty lass was not permitted to attend school, so she disguised herself as a male student and took up residence in the caves.

Every piece of stalagmite and stalactite in the cave is carefully catalogued – whether it be a moist sheep, a soggy plum, a cluster of bananas or an elephant. If the commentary is in Chinese, just exercise your imagination – that's what they did.

Buses run to Shanjuan from Yixing. The trip takes one hour and costs hardly anything.

Zhanggong Cave *(zhānggōng dòng)* Nineteen km south of Yixing town are three-score chambers within caves, large and small, divided into upper and lower reaches. Their size is comparable to Shanjuan's, but the layout is different. This is upside-down caving. What you do is scale a small hill called Yufengshan from the inside, and you come out on the top with a splendid view of the surrounding countryside with hamlets stretching as far as Lake Taihu.

There are two large grottoes in this bunch of caverns. The more impressive is the Hall of the Dragon King, with a ceiling that definitely isn't sprayed-on stucco. The place would make a perfect disco! From the Hall of the Dragon King you make your way through the Dry Nostril Cave, pause to clear your sinuses, and work up to the aforementioned exit.

A little further south of Zhanggong is the Yunutan, or Jade Maiden Pond.

Buses to Zhanggong from Yixing take half an hour. From Zhanggong you can pick up a passing bus to Linggu – the end of the line. If you're stuck for transport, try to get to Dingshu village, from where bus connections are good.

Linggu Cave *(línggǔ dòng)* Eight km down a dirt road from Zhanggong, Linggu is the largest and least explored of the three caves. You could easily get lost in this one and not because of the scenery either. The cave has six large halls arrayed roughly in a semicircle, and it's a long, deep forage.

Near the Linggu Cave is the Yanxian Tea Plantation *(yánxiàn cháchǎng)*, with bushel-lots laid out like fat caterpillars stretching into the horizon, and the odd tea villa in the background. The trip is worth it for the tea fields alone.

There are buses to Linggu from Zhanggong; see the previous Zhanggong section for details.

Extraordinary Touring

For the adventurous, there are a number of unexplored routes once you're on the loose in Yixing County. Asuggestion is to get there in the conventional manner, and try your luck on a different route out. Pottery is transported via canals and across Lake Taihu to Wuxi and it might be possible to transport yourself likewise. Highways skirt Lake Taihu, eventually running to Suzhou, Shanghai and Hangzhou. If you took a bus to Changxing, a slow branch-line railway leads from there to Hangzhou. At the southern end of the lake is a cross-over point, Huzhou. A little way north of this, on Lake Taihu, is Xiaomeikou, where ferry routes are marked on the map as leading to Wuxi across the lake, and to Suzhou via Yuanshan and Xukou.

Places to Stay

The *Yixing Guesthouse (yíxīng fàndiàn)* caters chiefly to cadres holding meetings. The guesthouse is at the end of Renmin Lu on the southern edge of Yixing town. If there's not a rash of meetings, or a rare tour bus assault, the guesthouse will be empty. It's a large building, with gardens and some luxury living.

Doubles cost from around Y85 but that depends on who behind the reception desk. Figures tumble from their lips until you give up and go away, or give in and take what you get. The guesthouse reputedly has dormitory rooms. Singles might be available for Y45.

The guesthouse is a half-hour walk from Yixing bus station; turn right from the station, follow the main road south along the lakeside, cross three bridges and turn left, then right again to the guesthouse gates.

The long stretch across the bridges is the same road that runs to Dingshu, so if your bus goes to Dingshu ask the driver to let you off closer to the guesthouse. If you don't mind the stroll, and want to see the main drag of Yixing town, another way of getting to the guesthouse is to walk three blocks straight ahead from the bus station, turn right onto Renmin Lu, and keep walking until you hit the guesthouse.

Places to Eat

The guesthouse has a dining room. If you don't mind 500 people at your table (perhaps staring at you, not their food), there are small restaurants opposite the bus station. Along Renmin Lu you'll find some baked food and dumplings.

Getting There & Away

There are buses from Yixing to Wuxi (Y2, 2½ hours), Shanghai (Y9), Nanjing (Y8), Suzhou (Y6) and Changzhou (Y3, 1½ hours).

Getting Around

There are no local buses in Yixing. There are buses to the sights out of town and all of them end up in the bus stations of either Yixing town or Dingshu. There are frequent connections between the two stations. Hitchhiking is a possibility.

DINGSHU (JINSHAN)

(dīngshǔ, jīnshān) 丁蜀（金山）

In Yixing County they not only grow tea, they make plenty of pots to put it in. Small towns in China can be utterly engrossing if they specialise in some kind of product like Dingshu does.

The town has been a big pottery producer since the Qin and Han dynasties (from 221 BC to 220 AD); some of the scenes you can witness here, especially at the loading dock that leads into Lake Taihu, are timeless. Almost every local family is engaged in the manufacture of ceramics, and behind the main part of town half the houses are made of the stuff. Dingshu is *the* pottery capital of China. There are also important porcelain-making plants in Jingdezhen, Handan, Zibo and parts of Guangzhou, but few handle the wide range of ceramics that Dingshu does.

Dingshu is about 25 km from Yixing town and has two dozen ceramics factories producing more than 2000 varieties of pottery – quite an output for a population of 100,000. Among the array of products are the ceramic tables and garbage bins that you find around China, huge jars used to store oil and grain, the famed Yixing teapots, and the glazed tiling and ceramic frescoes that are desperately needed as spare parts for tourist attractions – the Forbidden City in Beijing is one of the customers.

Dingshu is also known as Jinshan. The characters for Jinshan usually appear on bus timetables, so ask for that place if Dingshu draws a blank.

Itineraries

The 'pottery-house' end of Dingshu is a good

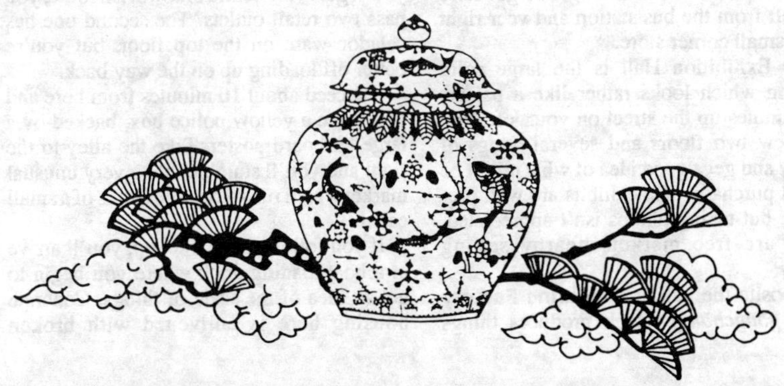

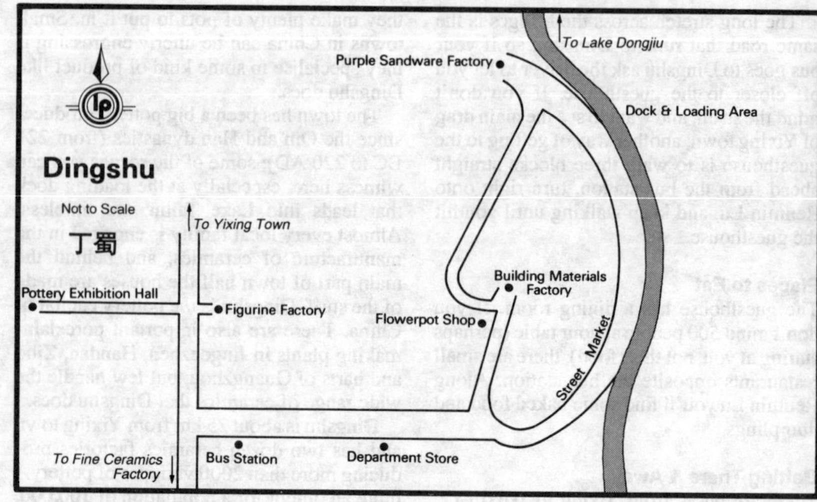

40 minutes from the bus station, but there's plenty to amuse you en route. You can get into the factories if you persist. In theory, each factory has a retail outlet; you can march in and say you're looking for the shop. If you have the bucks to sling around, CITS in Yixing town can get you into the factories of your choice at a price of their choice. Contact CITS at the Yixing Guesthouse. A suggested three-hour walking tour of Dingshu follows.

Walking Tour The logical place to get your bearings in Dingshu is the **Pottery Exhibition Hall** *(táocí zhǎnshìchǎng)*. To get there turn left from the bus station and veer right past a small corner store.

The Exhibition Hall is the large solid building which looks rather like a palace, five minutes up the street on your left. You can view two floors and several wings of pottery and get a good idea of what might be a good purchase. The exhibits are well presented, but taking photos isn't appreciated. There are free markets nearby selling pottery.

Opposite the hall is a **Figurine Factory** *(táocí gōngchǎng)* which produces things like kitsch lampstands. Yet even this factory is experimenting with glazes like tigerskin and snowflake, which is the secret of Dingshu.

Technology got off to a great start here when they introduced the new improved Dragon Kiln over a thousand years ago. Some distance north of the Exhibition Hall is the **Ceramics Research Institute** *(táocì yánjiūsuǒ)*.

Backtrack to the bus station. By now you're an expert on Dingshu pots, so ignore the little retail shop on the corner! If you go straight down the street past the bus station, you'll get to the centre of town. En route, you pass two retail outlets. The second one has celadon-ware on the top floor, but you're better off loading up on the way back.

Proceed about 10 minutes from here and you'll see a yellow police box, backed by a large billboard poster. Take the alley to the right and you'll stumble into a very unusual market which runs along the banks of a small canal.

If you follow the market up, you'll arrive at a boat-loading dock where you begin to get an idea of the scale of things. Concrete housing here is enlivened with broken ceramic tiling, and other lodgings are constructed entirely of large storage jars and pottery shards.

Further past the dock is the **Purple Sandware Factory** where they'll probably slam the door in your face. The dullish brown stoneware produced here, mostly teapots and flowerpots, is prized the world over and dates back about a thousand years. Made from local clays, the local teapots have a large and diverse export market, which might have a lot to do with their remarkable properties and aesthetic shapes. They retain the flavour and fragrance of tea for a long time; it's said that after extended use with one type of tea, no further tea leaves are necessary.

The teapots glaze themselves a darker, silkier tea-stain brown colour. It's claimed that the Purple Sands pots can be placed over a direct flame or be shoved in boiling water without cracking (though it's a different story if you drop one on the floor).

From the Purple Sands you can return to town by a different route. Go back towards the dock and take a right fork. This brings you to another road and, if you look left, you will spot the **Building Materials Factory**. This is a large operation which makes glazed tiles, garbage bins, ceramic tables and pottery pavilions. The production of pottery for civic and military use was what really got Dingshu off the ground, and is still the mainstay. Pottery is now produced for sanitation purposes, construction, daily use and the tourist industry – as well as throwing together a pavilion here, or re-tiling a temple there.

Near the gates of the Building Materials Factory is a small retail outlet selling flowerpots and the bonsai arrangements in them. Some other factories around Dingshu are the **East Wind** (garbage bins) and the **Red Star** (glazed vats, stools, tables).

Things to Buy

Pottery in Dingshu is dirt cheap, and valued by the serious as *objets d'art*. Teapots cost from Y1 to Y3 and at that price you could afford one for your hotel room to keep the tea leaves out of your mouth. The same pots can be found around Yixing County, but not with the same variety, quality, or price.

Further down the line (Wuxi, Suzhou, Shanghai), the price doubles and the selection narrows. By the time it gets to Hong Kong, the same teapot could be worth Y30 or more – quite a jump but they did get it there in one piece.

You can get matching sets of cups to go with the teapot. The teapots, because of size and other considerations, are the best buy, and you can yarn on about all the tea in the PRC while you sip from one back home.

For starters there is the tomato-shaped dragon teapot, the lid of which has a free-rolling dragon's head embedded in it. This amazing pot costs Y1. Indeed, Dingshu is the home of the world's most surprising teapots, some with ingenious musical properties involving nipples of clay in the lid.

There is a complicated ritual that should be followed for breaking in a new teapot, depending on what kind of tea – oolong, black or green – is to be brewed. Check for tight lids when purchasing and test the pouring lip by transferring water from one pot to another. Also look for the small squarish teapots; they're lighter, pack better and travel easier.

The two retail outlets along the road from the bus station are the best places to stock up, but you may spot a better deal at a factory outlet. Anyway, at Y1 you're not about to lose on the deal. Some of the locals sell on the free market; they make the pots up, then get them fired at local factories.

Also on sale, and something that can be lugged out, are flowerpots, figurines and casseroles. The casseroles are supposed to make the meat tender. In the kitsch-en-ware department are ceramic lampshades. Do they make the bulbs shine brighter?

Getting There & Away

There are direct buses from Dingshu to Yixing (Y1; 20 minutes, with departures about every 20 minutes from 6 am to 5 pm), Wuxi (Y3.80, 2½ hours), Changzhou (Y3.40), Zhenjiang (Y8) and Nanjing (Y8).

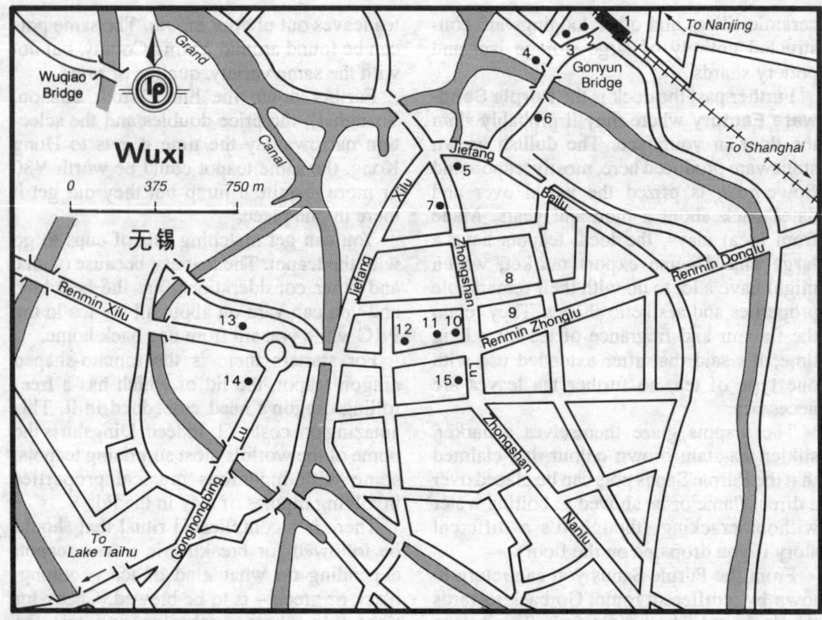

1 Wuxi Railway Station
2 CTS/CAAC
3 Long-Distance Bus Station
4 Canal Boat Dock
5 First Department Store
6 China Restaurant
7 Jiangnan Restaurant
8 Chengzhong Park
9 Free Markets (Chongansi People's Market)
10 Dongfanghong Emporium
11 Arts & Crafts Store
12 Advance Bus, Rail & Boat Ticket Office
13 Bus No 2 Stop (To Xihui Park & Taihu – starts at Station)
14 Bus No 1 Stop (Goes to Hubin & Shuixiu Hotel)
15 Dongfanghong Square

1 无锡火车站
2 中国旅行社/中国民航
3 长途汽车站
4 轮船码头
5 中百一店
6 中国饭店
7 江南菜馆
8 城中公园
9 崇安寺市场
10 东方红市场
11 工艺美术服务部
12 火车售票处
13 二路汽车站
14 一路汽车站
15 东方红广场

WUXI

(wúxī) 无锡

Just north of Suzhou is Wuxi, a name that means 'tinless' – the local tin mine that dated back to around 1066-221 BC, was exhausted during the Han Dynasty (206 BC-220 AD), not that the locals especially cared. A stone tablet dug out of Xishan hill is engraved, 'Where there is tin, there is fighting; where there is no tin, there is tranquillity'. And indeed there was tranquillity. Like Suzhou, Wuxi was an ancient silk producer, but it remained a sleepy backwater town barely altered by the intrusion of the Grand Canal (though it did once or twice come into the spotlight as a rice-marketing centre).

In this century Wuxi made up for the long sleep. In the 1930s Shanghai business people backed by foreign technicians, set up textile and flour mills, oil-extracting plants, and a soap factory. After Liberation, textile production was stepped up considerably and light and heavy industry boomed. Monstrous housing developments sprang up to accommodate a population that had surpassed Suzhou's and which today stands at 800,000. The town is ranked among the top 15 or so economic centres in China. There are hundreds of factories and an emphasis on electronics, textiles, machine manufacturing, chemicals, fishing, and agricultural crops serving the Shanghai market.

Wuxi is being promoted as a resort area, and if you have resort-type money the programme consists of cooking classes, fishing, 10-day acupuncture and massage courses, sanatorium treatments, and taijiquan lessons. At the command of CITS is a small fleet of power craft that cruise the Grand Canal and Lake Taihu. Then there are the 'dragon boats', imperial replicas.

Either of these, if they are not requisitioned by group tours, will cost you a bundle for a cruise so try your luck on the local boats first. Factory visits can no doubt be arranged through CITS, and the No 1 Silk Filature or an embroidery factory may be of interest. From May to October group tours are taken to see silkworms on a farm outside Wuxi.

Orientation

Wuxi is divided into two sections, five to 10 km apart; the hotel situation is not good in either. Because of the town's earlier stunted growth, there are few 'historical relics' and the main attraction is a natural one – Lake Taihu – which is quite a way out of town. Tourist land is out by the lakeside. If you want to observe the locals then the canal life around town is interesting.

Wuxi is shaped like a heart, with the Grand Canal its aorta and loads of capillary canals. There are concrete and factories. Apartment blocks have been built at a furious pace, in the recent decade more than doubling the living quarters built from 1949 to 1978.

Never mind, vestiges of Wuxi's former charm remain. The main thoroughfare of Wuxi is, in fact, the old Grand Canal which sees plenty of bottlenecks and frenzied activity. There are numerous waterways cutting into the canal, and more than a fair share of vantage-point bridges.

Just down from the railway station is Gongyun Bridge with a passenger and loading dock close by – well worth seeing. In the north-west of the city is an older bridge, Wuqiao, which has a great view of canal traffic and overlooks an ancient pavilion stranded on tiny Huangbudun Isle. Traffic will come at you from all directions. For for a firsthand experience, try zipping around in a small boat yourself – there are at least three boat stations within the city.

Information

CTS This office (not CITS) is conveniently in a building facing the square in front of the main railway station. Several of the staff here speak English.

Maps Good bus maps of Wuxi are available from the counters in the railway station and the long-distance bus station.

Free Markets

(zìyóu shìchǎng) 自由市场

These are not far from the corner of Renmin Lu and Zhongshan Lu. Go south on Zhongshan, turn left at Renmin, walk along a bit and you'll find the market entrance leading north again. This is about the most exciting place in Wuxi. Be prepared to bargain for foodstuffs, as the prices suddenly rocket when they see your face. There's a restaurant in the food-market area, and an antique store. If you follow the alleys in, you will eventually arrive at the delightful Chengzhong Park, a small retreat from the traffic noise and hoi polloi. It's not so attractive in itself but is a good place to observe Chinese people at leisure. Old men gather at the back of the park sipping tea at ceramic tables, smoking pipes, eyes and ears glued to their caged birds. If you wait long enough a man will appear, sweating, with a large lozenge-shaped barrel on wheels (fresh water for tea). There's taijiquan in the early morning.

Xihui Park
(xīhuì gōngyuán) 锡惠公园
By contrast, enormous and nebulous Xihui Park is hard to pin down as an attraction. It's to the west of the city on bus Nos 2, 10 or 15. The highest point in the park, Huishan hill, is 75 metres above sea level. If you climb the Dragon Light Pagoda *(lóngguāng tǎ)*, the seven-storey octagonal structure at the top, you'll be able to take in a panorama of Wuxi and Taihu. The brick and wood pagoda was built during the Ming Dynasty, burned down during the Qing Dynasty, and rebuilt in the spring many years later. For sunrises, try the Qingyun Pavilion, just to the east of the pagoda.

The park has a motley collection of pavilions, snack bars and teahouses, along with a small zoo, a large artificial lake, and a cave that burrows for half a km from the east side to the west. The western section of the park rambles off into Huishan, where you'll find the famous Ming Dynasty Jichang Garden *(jìchàng yuán)* ('Ming' refers to the garden layout – the buildings are recent), and the remaining Huishan Temple nearby was once a Buddhist monastery.

What follows for this area is the standard catalogue of inscribed stones, halls, gates and crumbled villas from the Ming, Song, Qing and Tang dynasties. Sometimes you have to wonder who is pulling whose leg. There are so many copies, permutations and fakes in China it's hard to know exactly which year you're looking at. Still, the copies are nice.

Speaking of Tang, the Second Spring under Heaven *(tiānxià dìèr quán)* is here so bring your tea mugs, or try the local teahouse brew. The Chinese patronise this watering hole to indulge in the ancient hobby of carp watching. From the Second Spring you can walk to vantage points and pavilions higher up. A major detour leads to the 329-metre peak in the north-west called Sanmao *(huīshān)*.

Lake Taihu
(tàihú) 太湖
Lake Taihu is a freshwater lake with a total area of 2200 sq km and an average depth of two metres. There are some 90 islands, large and small, within it. Junks with 'all sails set' gracefully ply the waters – a magnificent nostalgic sight.

The fishing industry is very active, catching over 30 varieties. Fish breed in the shoals, and women harvesting water-chestnuts float around in wooden tubs. On the shores are plantations of rice, tea with mulberry and citrus trees. Suitably grotesque rocks are submerged in the lake for decades, and when they're sufficiently weathered are prized for classical garden landscaping. To the north-west of the lake are hilly zones, to the south-east is a vast plain. The whole area with its fertile soil, mild climate and abundant rainfall is referred to as 'the land of fish and rice'.

Plum Garden
(méiyuán) 梅园
Once a small *peach* garden built during the Qing Dynasty, this has since been renovated or re-landscaped, and expanded. It is renowned for its thousands of red plum trees which blossom in the spring. Peach and cherry trees grow here too, and grotesque

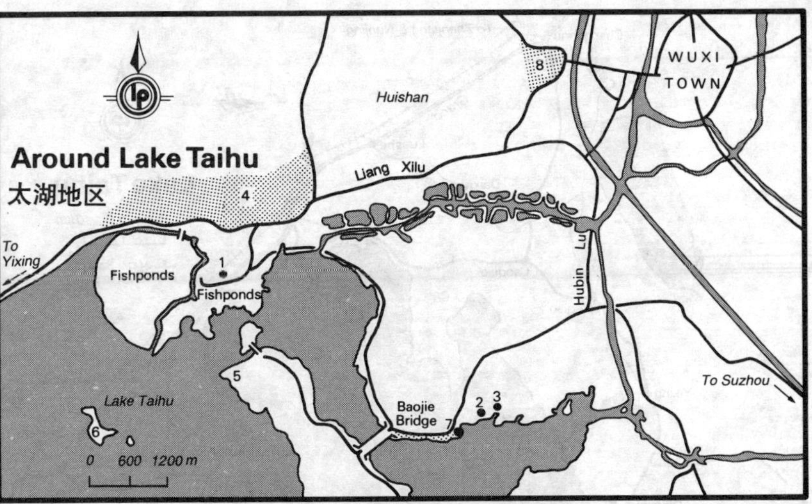

1 Taihu Hotel
2 Hubin Hotel
3 Shuixiu Hotel
4 Plum Garden
5 Turtle Head Isle
6 Three Hills Isles
7 Li Garden
8 Xihui Park

1 太湖饭店
2 湖滨饭店
3 水秀饭店
4 梅园
5 鼋头渚
6 三山
7 蠡园
8 锡惠公园

rockeries are arrayed at the centre of the garden. The highest point is Plum Pagoda, with views of Taihu. The garden is near the bus No 2 terminal.

Li Garden
(lǐyuán) 蠡园

This hideous circus is always packed out by the locals. As Chinese gardens go, this one is a goner. The whole tatty affair goes beyond bad taste – a concrete labyrinth of fishponds, walkways, mini-bridges, a mini-pagoda, and souvenir vendors hawking garish plaster and gilded figurines. Inside the garden on the shore of Taihu is a tour-boat dock for cruises to other points.

Turtle Head Isle
(guītóuzhǔ) 鼋头渚

So named because it appears to be shaped like the head of a turtle, it is not actually an island but being surrounded on three sides by water makes it appear so. This is the basic scenic strolling area where you can watch the junks on Lake Taihu.

You can walk a circuit of the area. If you continue along the shore, you come to the ferry dock for the Sanshan Isles, passing Taihujiajue Archway and Perpetual Spring Bridge *(chángchūn qiáo)*. A walkway leads

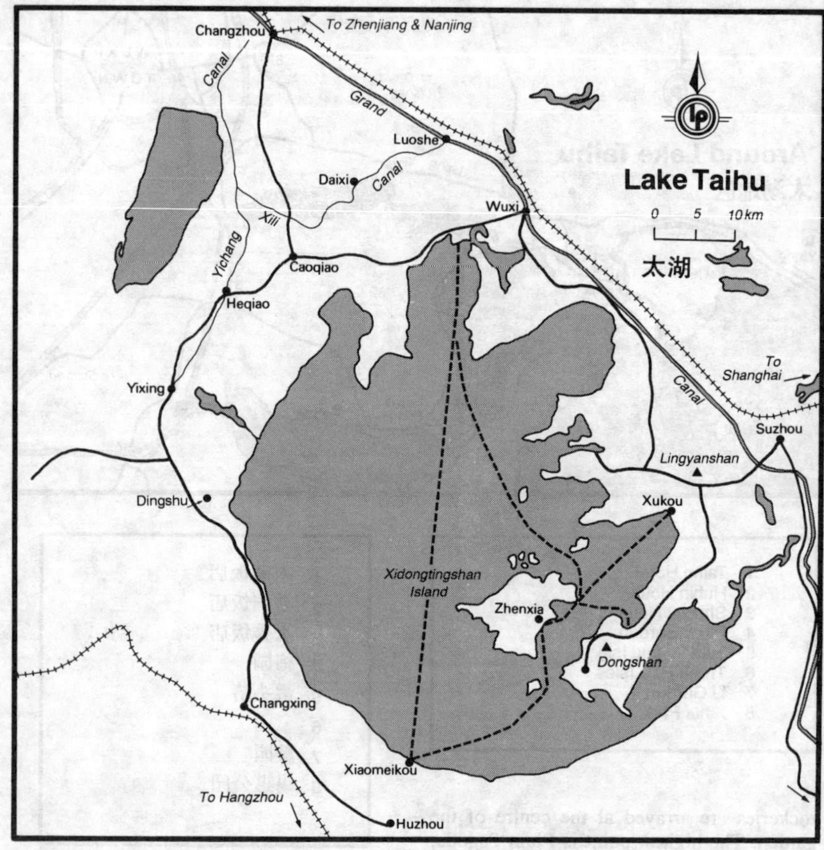

to a small lighthouse, near which is an inscribed stone referring to the island's name and several pavilions. The architecture here, like that in the Li Garden, is mostly copies of the classical examples. Inland a bit from the lighthouse is Clear Ripples (Chenglan) Hall, a very nice teahouse where you get a view of the lake.

Further along the south coast are similar vantage points: Jingsong Tower, Guangfu Temple and the 72 Peaks Villa. The highest point of Guitouzhu is the Brightness Pavilion *(guāngmíng tíng)* with all-round vistas. Back past the entrance area is a bridge leading to Zhongdu Island, which has a large workers' sanatorium – no visits without prior appointment.

To get to Guitouzhu, take bus No 1 to its terminal, or take the ferry from the dock near Plum Garden. The Chinese like to make a cycling trip out of it – the road is pleasant with no heavy traffic. A possible shortcut is around the back of Zhongdu Island leading back towards Taihu Hotel.

Three Hills Isles

(sānshān) 三山

Sanshan is an island park three km south-west of Turtle Head Isle. If you haven't seen Wuxi and the lake from every possible angle by now, try this one as well. Vantage points at the top look back toward Guitouzhu and you can work out if it really does look like a turtle head or not. As one of the picture captions in a Chinese guide puts it: 'Sight-seeing feeds chummies with more conversation-topics'. The Three-Hill Tea-house *(sānshā cháguǎn)* has outdoor tables and rattan chairs, and views. Sanshan is a 20-minute ferry ride from Guitouzhu.

Places to Stay

In the town itself is the *Liangxi Hotel* (☎ 226812) *(liángxī fàndiàn)* on Zhongshan Nanlu. Take bus No 12 from the railway station. The hotel is actually set back from Zhongshan Nanlu, on a small street which runs parallel to it; you'll have to watch out for it. They quote double rooms from Y90 but there's certainly cheaper stuff available.

The tourist hotels are around the lakeside. The *Taihu Hotel* (☎ 667901) *(tàihú fàndiàn)* has a large restaurant, telecommunications office, bank and souvenir shop, and over-looks Lake Taihu. Its air-con dining rooms serve Taihu seafood and Wuxi specialities. Three special lakeside villas are for foreign convalescents receiving treatment. The hotel is one of the key centres for group tour activity, and offers boat touring (and luxury bus) itineraries. Rooms in the old building start from Y90 a double and, in the new building from Y150 a double. Rooms in the old building are more than adequate with largish beds, TV and private bathroom. Cheaper singles with shared bath may be possible for around Y40 or even a cot in a meeting room for around Y12 a night if the staff are sympathetic. The place is a bit awkward to get to – take bus No 2 to the terminal, then walk about 20 minutes.

The *Hubin Hotel* (☎ 668812) *(húbīn fàndiàn)* on Liyuan Lu is a high-rise tour-bus hotel. It charges from Y80 a double and other prices are stiff, for a very dull atmosphere. There are 356 beds, air-con, and a full range of facilities including a bar. Take bus No 1 from the railway station.

The *Shuixiu Hotel* (☎ 668591) *(shuǐxiù fàndiàn)* is next to the Hubin Hotel. Doubles cost from around Y100. It's a squat Austra-lian prefab with koalas and kangaroos crawling over the curtains, and rooms full of fridges, phones, digital devices – you get the picture. There are rooms with views over the lake. Take bus No 1 from the railway station.

The above three hotels (the Hubin was built in 1978, the Shuixiu was assembled in 1980) are designed for the group tours – there's nothing remotely close to them in the way of shops or anything else. Anglers can drop out of the hotels toting fishing licences, tackle and bait, cruise around Lake Taihu and have their catches cooked back at the hotel. A rubbing is made first as a memento so you can have your fish and eat it too! Amateurs

are parcelled off to the fish ponds for an easy catch.

Places to Eat

The *China Restaurant (zhōngguó fàndiàn)* is recommended for its large servings and low prices. To get there, proceed directly from the railway station and across the bridge; it's on your left, second block down, on the ground floor of the China Hotel which faces Tong Yun Lu.

Other eating places can be found in the markets off Renmin Lu. The stretch along Zhongshan Lu (from the First Department Store to Renmin Lu) has lots of restaurants. Try the *Jiangnan Restaurant (jiāngnán càiguǎn)* at 435 Zhongshan Lu.

Out in the boondocks, around Taihu, choose between the hotel dining rooms, or whatever you can scrounge from stalls or teahouses at the tourist attractions. One particularly fortifying discovery was a packet of Huishan shortcake cookies (delicious), continuing a tourist tradition that dates back to the 14th century when Buddhist monasteries from Huishan hillsides doled them out to vegetarians in transit. Seasonal seafood includes crab, shrimp, eel and fresh fish. Wuxi specialities include pork ribs in soy sauce, bean curd, a kind of pancake padded out with midget fish from Lake Taihu, and honey-peach in season.

Things to Buy

The Arts & Crafts Store *(gōngyì měishù ménshìbù)* is at 192 Renmin Lu. The Dongfanghong Emporium *(dōngfānghóng shāngdiàn)* is nearby. The First Department Store *(dìyī bǎihuò shāngdiàn)* is at the top end of Zhongshan Lu. The Huishan Clay Figurine Factory *(huìshān níǒu gōngchǎng)* is near Xihui Park.

Silk products and embroidery are good buys. Apart from the places already mentioned, try the merchants in the side streets. Dongfanghong Square is the busiest shopping area.

There are some remarkably ugly clay figurines for sale around the place. A peasant folk art, they were usually models of opera stars, and after a little diversion into revolutionary heroes are back to opera and story figures again. (Wuxi has its own form of opera deriving from folk songs.) The 'Lucky Fatties' are obese babies – symbols of fortune and happiness and just the thing to fill up your mantelpiece with.

Getting There & Away

Air There are no flights to Wuxi but there is a CAAC booking office in the same building as CTS.

The advance ticket office for boat, bus and train in Wuxi is at 224 Renmin Lu. Some boats require one or two day's advance booking.

Bus The long-distance bus station is near the railway station. There are buses to Shanghai (Y7), Suzhou (Y4), Dingshu (Y3.60), Yixing (Y4), Changzhou and Yangzhou.

Train Wuxi is on the line from Beijing to Shanghai, with frequent express and special-express trains. There are trains to Suzhou (40 minutes), Shanghai (1¾ hours) and Nanjing (2¾ hours).

If you're day-tripping, get a through ticket from, say, Nanjing to Suzhou, alight at Wuxi and continue the same evening to Suzhou. Reserved seating is not necessary because of the short distances between cities and, in any case, your chances of getting a seat on these impossibly crowded trains are nil. You can dump your bags at the railway station in Wuxi and look around town.

Boat With such a large lake there is a wealth of scenery and some fascinating routes out of the town. Yixing and Suzhou lie almost on the lake, Changzhou lies north-west of Wuxi on the Grand Canal, and Hangzhou lies inland but is accessible from Wuxi.

From Wuxi there are many boat routes running along smaller canals to outlying counties as well as boats across Lake Taihu and along the Grand Canal. There are many daily boats to Yixing and Changzhou. There is another route through the Wuxi canals, across Lake Taihu and down south through a series of canals to Hangzhou. Alternatively, you can take a boat across Lake Taihu to Huzhou on the southern side and then take a bus to Hangzhou. Huzhou, where there's a tourist service, lies at the junction of routes to Shanghai, Hangzhou and Huangshan. Just north of the town is Xiaomeikou, the ferry dock. North-west of Huzhou is Changxing, and a branch-line railway running to Hangzhou.

Another interchange point for boating is at Zhenxia on the east side of Xidongtingshan Isle. From Zhenxia there are connections to Wuxi, and to Xukou near Suzhou.

Since Wuxi itself covers an area of 400 sq km which is open without a permit; day-tripping along the canals is not technically out of bounds, and there's nothing to stop you from travelling between Hangzhou, Yixing, Jiaxing, Huzhou, Wuxi and Suzhou. A variety of motorboats plies these routes, including two-deck motor barges with air-con, soft seats, a restaurant and space for over 100 passengers. You may see some Chinese-designed passenger hovercraft.

Getting Around

There are about 15 local bus lines. An alternative for faster connections is to grab an auto-rickshaw – there are ranks at the main railway station.

Bus No 2 runs from the railway station, along Jiefang Lu, across two bridges to Xihui Park, then way out to Plum Garden, stopping short of the Taihu Hotel. Bus No 2 almost crosses the bus No 1 route at Gongnongbing Square.

Bus No 1 starts on Gongnongbing Lu, and runs to Li Garden and the Hubin and Shuixiu hotels. The actual terminal of bus No 1 is further on across a bridge to the scenery on Turtle Head Isle.

A good tour bus is No 10, which does a long loop around the northern part of the city area, taking in four bridges, Xihui Park and the shopping strip of Renmin Lu.

Enquire at CITS for a special tour boat which runs from the pier near the railway station. It cuts down the Liangxi River (through the city), under Ximen Bridge, and south to Li Garden. The boat then continues to Turtle Head Isle and finally the Sanshan Isles.

A ferry runs from the south of Plum Garden to Turtle Head Isle. Li Garden is a major touring junction with a boat dock and motorboat cruises around Taihu; prices start from a few yuan for cruises lasting from one hour to half the day.

SUZHOU

(sūzhōu) 苏州

Suzhou's history goes back 2500 years, give or take a hundred – it's one of the oldest towns in the Yangtse basin. With the completion of the Grand Canal in the Sui Dynasty (589-618 AD), Suzhou found itself strategically sited on a major trading route, and the city's fortunes and size grew rapidly.

Suzhou flourished as a centre of shipping and grain storage, bustling with merchants and artisans. By the 12th century the town had attained its present dimensions, and if you consult the map the layout of the old town is distinct. The city walls, a rectangle enclosed by moats, were pierced by six gates (north, south, two in the east, two in the west). Crisscrossing the city were six north-south canals and 14 east-west canals. Although the walls have largely disappeared and a fair proportion of the canals have been plugged, central Suzhou retains its 'Renaissance' character.

A legend was spun around Suzhou through tales of beautiful women with mellifluous voices, and through the famous proverb 'In Heaven there is Paradise, on earth Suzhou and Hangzhou'. The story picks up when Marco Polo arrived in 1276. He added the adjectives 'great' and 'noble', though he reserved his finer epithets for Hangzhou. The wanderer's keen memory tells us that there were astonishing numbers of craftspeople and rich merchants, as well as great sages, physicians and magicians. He writes:

Moreover I tell you quite truly that there are six

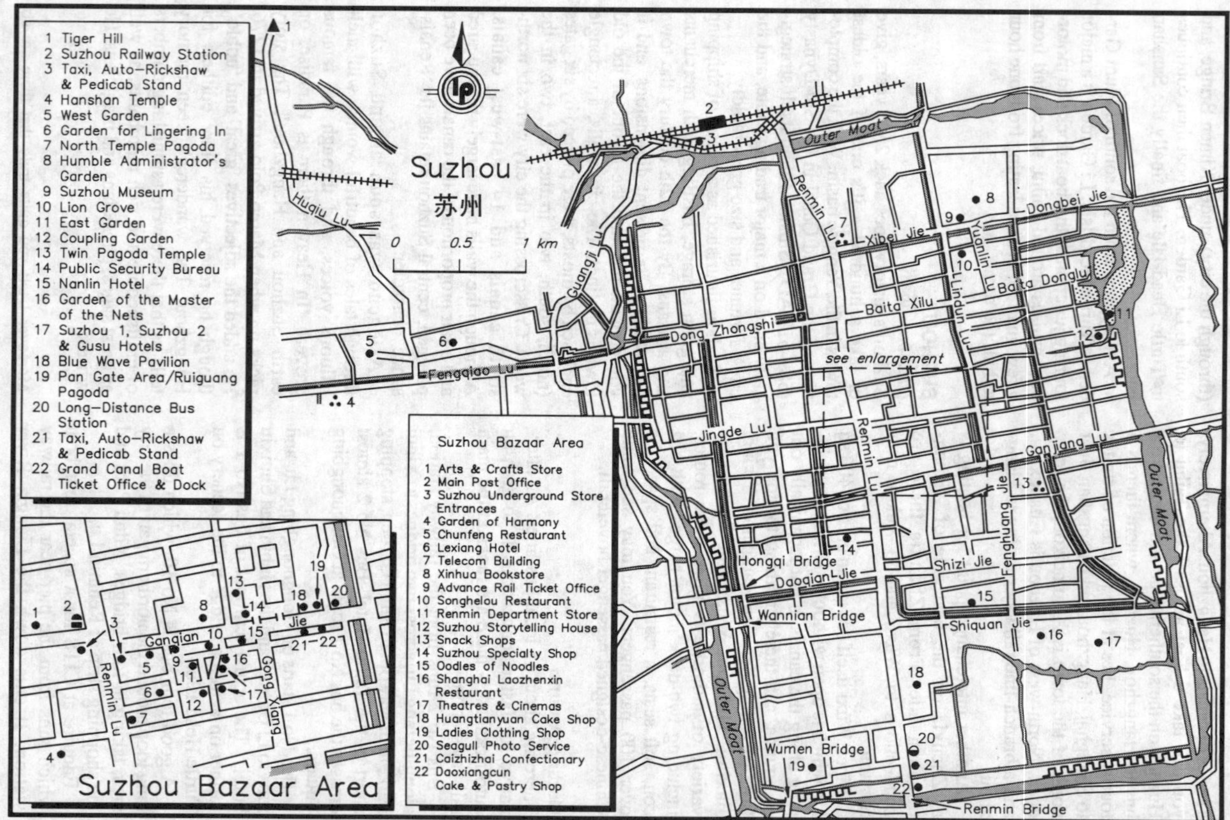

Suzhou
苏州
0
0.5
1 km
1 Tiger Hill
2 Suzhou Railway Station
3 Taxi, Auto-Rickshaw & Pedicab Stand
4 Hanshan Temple
5 West Garden
6 Garden for Lingering In
7 North Temple Pagoda
8 Humble Administrator's Garden
9 Suzhou Museum
10 Lion Grove
11 East Garden
12 Coupling Garden
13 Twin Pagoda Temple
14 Public Security Bureau
15 Nanlin Hotel
16 Garden of the Master of the Nets
17 Suzhou 1, Suzhou 2 & Gusu Hotels
18 Blue Wave Pavilion
19 Pan Gate Area/Ruiguang Pagoda
20 Long-Distance Bus Station
21 Taxi, Auto-Rickshaw & Pedicab Stand
22 Grand Canal Boat Ticket Office & Dock
Suzhou Bazaar Area
1 Arts & Crafts Store
2 Main Post Office
3 Suzhou Underground Store Entrances
4 Garden of Harmony
5 Chunfeng Restaurant
6 Lexiang Hotel
7 Telecom Building
8 Xinhua Bookstore
9 Advance Rail Ticket Office
10 Songhelou Restaurant
11 Renmin Department Store
12 Suzhou Storytelling House
13 Snack Shops
14 Suzhou Specialty Shop
15 Oodles of Noodles
16 Shanghai Laozhenxin Restaurant
17 Theatres & Cinemas
18 Huangtianyuan Cake Shop
19 Ladies Clothing Shop
20 Seagull Photo Service
21 Caizhizhai Confectionary
22 Daoxiangcun Cake & Pastry Shop
Huqiu Lu
Outer Moat
Renmin Lu
Xibei Jie
Dongbei Jie
Yuanlin Lu
Lindun Lu
Baita Donglu
Baita Xilu
Guangji Lu
Dong Zhongshi
Fengqiao Lu
see enlargement
Jingde Lu
Ganjiang Lu
Fenghuang Jie
Hongqi Bridge
Daoqian Jie
Shizi Jie
Wannian Bridge
Shiquan Jie
Wumen Bridge
Renmin Bridge
Gangian
Jie
Gong Xiang
Suzhou Bazaar Area

1 虎丘山
2 苏州火车站
3 出租汽车站
4 寒山寺
5 西园
6 留园
7 北寺塔
8 拙政园
9 苏州博物馆
10 狮子林
11 东园
12 娶园
13 双塔
14 公安局外事科
15 南林饭店
16 网师园
17 苏州和姑苏饭店
18 沧浪亭
19 盘门/瑞光塔
20 长途汽车站
21 出租汽车站
22 轮船运输公司

SUZHOU BAZAAR AREA

1 工艺美术服务部
2 邮电大楼
3 展销商店
4 怡园
5 春风饭店
6 乐乡饭店
7 南门商业大楼
8 新华书店
9 火车售票处
10 松鹤楼饭店
11 人民商场
12 书场
13 玄外观点心店
14 土特产商店
15 面店
16 上海老正兴菜馆
17 电影院
18 黄天源糕团店
19 女用品商店
20 海鸥照相馆
21 菜之斋糖果店
22 道乡村糕店

thousand bridges of stone in this city, below the greater part of which one galley or two could well pass.

He muses that if the inhabitants had turned their talents to the military arts, they would easily have overrun the whole province. But no, they were totally preoccupied with raising silkworms:

They have vast quantities of raw silk, and manufacture it, not only for their own consumption, all of them being clothed in dresses of silk, but also for other markets.

Indeed, by the 14th century Suzhou had established itself as the leading silk producer in the nation. Although Polo's estimate of 6000 bridges is a bit on the wild side, a map made 150 years before his visit shows 359 bridges, as well as 12 pagodas, more than 50 temples and numerous bathhouses. The town became a spot favoured by the Chinese aristocracy, pleasure-seekers, the leisured, famous scholars, actors and painters who set about constructing villas and garden retreats for themselves.

At the height of Suzhou's development in the 16th century, the gardens, large and small, numbered over 100. If we mark time here, we arrive at the town's tourist formula today – 'Garden City, Venice of the East' – a medieval mix of woodblock guilds and embroidery societies, whitewashed housing, cobbled streets, treelined avenues and canals.

This basically still holds true. Strangely enough Suzhou has managed to adapt itself to a modern era with old-world grace. Part of the reason is perhaps that the silk merchants in days of old succeeded, at the expense of commoners, in getting the maximum production figures.

The wretched workers of the silk sweatshops, protesting against paltry wages and the injustices of the contract hire system, were staging violent strikes even in the 15th century, and the landlords shifted. In 1860 Taiping troops took the town without a blow. In 1896 Suzhou was opened to foreign trade, with Japanese and international concessions. During WW II, it was occupied by the Japanese and then by the Kuomintang.

Somehow Suzhou has slipped through the ravages of the Cultural Revolution and 'modernisation'. Though its reliance on the Grand Canal and water transport has shifted with the coming of rail and road, the common denominator – sericulture – is still the mainstay of the economy. The worms are now partially computer-assisted!

Over 600,000 people live here, and around 500 enterprises have sprung up including electronics, machine building, optical instruments, ferro-concrete boat manufacturing and chemical industries. However, being relegated to the outskirts they've not greatly interfered with the town's central core. The artisans have regrouped and geared up for the export and tourist markets. Everything is assimilated – tourists, trains, silkworms, wheat, gardens, galleys, digital watches. They all melt into the calm rhythms of this ancient water-town.

Information

CITS This organisation has a separate building in the Suzhou Hotel compound.

Public Security Bureau This office is at 7 Dashitou Xiang.

Money The Bank of China is at 50 Guanqian Jie, but all of the major tourist hotels have foreign exchange counters as well.

North Temple

(běi sìtǎ) 北寺塔

The North Temple has the tallest pagoda south of the Yangtse – at nine storeys it dominates the north end of Renmin Lu. You can climb it for a fine aerial view of the town and the farmland beyond, which grows tea, rice and wheat. The mere fact that you can actually see this in the first place means you're in a medium sized city. The factory chimneys, the new pagodas of Suzhou, loom on the outskirts, and so does the haze and smoke they create.

The temple complex goes back 1700 years and was originally a residence. The pagoda has been burned, built and rebuilt. Made of wood, it dates from the 17th century. Off to the side of it is Nanmu Hall, which was rebuilt in the Ming Dynasty with some of its features imported from elsewhere. There is a nice teahouse with a small garden out the back.

Suzhou Museum

(sūzhōu bówùguǎn) 苏州博物馆

Situated some blocks east of the pagoda, near the Humble Administrator's Garden, the museum was once the residence of a Taiping leader, Li Xiucheng. It's a good place to visit after you've seen something of Suzhou as it helps fill in the missing bits of the jigsaw as you retrace the town's history.

The museum offers some interesting old maps (Grand Canal, Suzhou, heaven & earth), a silk and embroidery exhibition room (with Qing silk samples), Qing Dynasty steles forbidding workers' strikes, and relics unearthed or rescued from various sites around the Suzhou district (funerary objects, porcelain bowls, bronze swords).

Suzhou Bazaar

(sūzhōu shāngchǎng) 苏州商场

The area surrounding Guanqian Jie is riddled with restaurants, speciality shops, theatres, street vendors, hairdressing salons, noodle dispensaries, silk merchants and sweet shops. This maze of back alleys, the main shopping thoroughfare of Suzhou, is a strolling area with neither bicycles nor buses allowed on Guanqian Jie by day. The bazaar is also the restaurant centre of the city.

Temple of Mystery
(xuánmiàoguān) 玄妙观
The heart of Suzhou Bazaar is the Taoist Temple of Mystery. It was founded in the 3rd century (during the Jin Dynasty and laid out between 275 and 279 AD) with additions during Song times. From the Qing Dynasty on, the bazaar fanned out from the temple with small tradespeople and travelling performers using the grounds. The enormous Sanqing Hall, supported by 60 pillars and capped by a double roof with upturned eaves, dates from 1181. It was burnt and seriously damaged in the 19th century. During the Cultural Revolution the Red Guards squatted here before it was transformed into a library. Today it's been engulfed by the souvenir shops; the square in front of it hosts all manner of outdoor industries including shoe repairing, tailoring and bike parking.

Gardens
Suzhou's gardens are looked upon as works of art – a fusion of nature, architecture, poetry and painting designed to ease the mind, move it, or assist it. Unlike the massive imperial gardens, the classical landscaping of Suzhou reflects the personal taste of officials and scholars south of the Yangtse. Rich officials, once their worldly duties were performed, would find solace here in kingdoms of ponds and rockeries. The gardens were meant to be enjoyed either in solitary contemplation or in the company of a close circle of friends with a glass of wine, a concert, poetry recital or a literary discussion.

The key elements of the gardens are rocks and water. There are surprisingly few flowers and no fountains – just like the Zen gardens of Japan, they give one an illusion of a natural scene with only moss, sand and rock. These microcosms were laid out by master craftspeople and changed hands many times over the centuries. The gardens suffered a setback during the Taiping Rebellion in the 1870s, and under subsequent foreign domination of Suzhou. Efforts were made to restore them in the 1950s but during the so-called Horticultural Revolution gardeners downed tools as flowers were frowned upon. In 1979 the Suzhou Garden Society was formed, and an export company was set up to promote Suzhou-designed gardens. A few of the gardens have been renovated and opened to the public.

Each garden is meant to be savoured at a snail's pace. Remember that the flowers are best left unpicked if the garden is to be preserved. The thing to do is take along a Sunday newspaper, a pot of tea, a deckchair, a sketch pad and a bath sponge. Having said that, let us add that it is very hard to wax contemplative when there are thousands of other visitors (mostly Chinese and an amiable enough lot – mostly taking photos of each other or sketching the foliage). Old-timers come here to relax. The size of the crowds depends on the weather, the day of the week, and the garden. The gardens are usually open from early morning to dusk (from 7.30 am to 5 pm), and admission is a few mao.

A footnote on gardening in Suzhou: the common people, not having the resources for larger gardens, work at arranging miniatures (potted landscapes, courtyard cultivation). Suzhou, in fact, is the one place in China where you can count on real flowers instead of plastic. If there are any artificial ones, they will at least be silk. As you're strolling the streets it's worthwhile looking for plebeian miniatures. Potted landscapes are sold in various shops, so you can actually buy a piece of Suzhou – but what are you going to do with it?!

Humble Administrator's Garden *(zhuózhèng yuán)* Built in the early 1500s, this was a private garden belonging to Wang Xianchen, a censor with a chequered history. Some say he was demoted to Suzhou, some claim he extorted the money to have the garden constructed, others that the garden was lost to pay a gambling debt by his son.

The garden is also known as the 'Plain Man's Politics Garden' deriving from the quotation, 'To cultivate one's garden to meet one's daily needs, that is what is known as the politics of the plain man'.

There's a five-hectare water park with streams, ponds, bridges and islands of bamboo. You can sense the painter's hand in its design, meant to mimic parts of rural South China. Strong emphasis in Suzhou gardens is given to scenery not found locally. The whole garden is divided into east, middle and west sections though there's nothing of great interest in the East Garden. The Middle Garden is the best. From the Ming Dynasty Distant Fragrance Hall *(yuǎnxiāng táng)*, you can get a view of everything through lattice windows.

In the same area are the Suzhou Museum and several silk mills.

Lion Grove *(shīzilín)* Just up the street from the Humble Administrator's Garden, this grove was constructed in 1350 by the monk Tian Ru and other disciples as a memorial to their master Zhi Zheng. This guy, it appears, was some kind of cave dweller, and his last fixed address was c/o 'Lion Cliff', Tianmushan mountains, Zhejiang Province. The garden has rockeries that evoke leonine forms. The walls of the labyrinth of tunnels bear calligraphy from famous chisels. The grove encompasses one hectare; it's a bit on the dull side.

Garden of Harmony*(yíyuán)* A small Qing Dynasty garden owned by an official called Gu Wenbin, this one is quite young for a Suzhou garden. It's assimilated many of the features of other gardens and blended them into a style of its own. The garden is divided into eastern and western sections linked by a covered promenade with lattice windows. In the east are buildings and courtyards. The western section has pools with coloured pebbles, rockeries, hillocks and pavilions. The garden is off Renmin Lu, just south of Guanqian Jie.

Blue Wave Pavilion *(cānglàngtíng)* A bit on the wild side with winding creeks and luxuriant trees, this is one of the oldest gardens in Suzhou. The buildings date from the 11th century although there has been rebuilding following damage more than a few times. Originally the home of a prince, the property passed into the hands of the scholar Su Zimei who gave it its name. The one-hectare garden attempts to create optical illusions with the scenery both outside and inside – you look from the pool immediately outside to the distant hills.

Enlightened Way Hall *(míngdào táng)*, the largest building, is said to have been a site for delivery of lectures in the Ming Dynasty. On the other side of Renmin Lu, close by, is the former Confucian Temple.

Garden of the Master of the Nets *(wǎngshī yuán)* This is the smallest garden in Suzhou – half the size of Canglangting, and a tenth the size of Zhuozheng. It's so small, it's hard to find, but well worth the trouble since it's better than the others combined.

This garden was laid out in the 12th century, abandoned, then restored in the 18th century as part of the residence of a retired official. One story has it that he announced he'd had enough of bureaucracy and would rather be a fisherman. Another explanation of the name is that it was simply near Wangshi Lu.

The eastern part of the garden is the residential area – originally with side rooms for sedan-chair lackeys, guest reception and living quarters. The central part is the main garden. The western part is an inner garden where a courtyard contains the Spring-Rear Cottage *(diànchūn yī)*, the master's study. This section and the study with its Ming-style furniture and palace lanterns was duplicated and unveiled at the Metropolitan Museum of Art in New York in 1981.

A miniature model of the whole garden, using Qingtian jade, Yingde rocks, Anhui paper, Suzhou silk and incorporating the halls, kiosks, ponds, blossoms and rare plants of the original design, was produced especially for a display at the Pompidou Centre in Paris in 1982.

The most striking feature of Wangshi is its

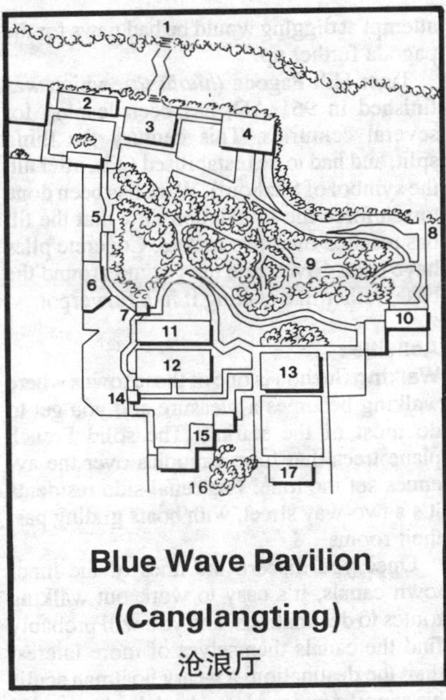

Blue Wave Pavilion (Canglangting)
沧浪厅

1 Canglangshengji Arch
2 Lotus Waterside Pavilion
3 Steles
4 Waterside House
5 Pavilion of Imperial Stele
6 Toilet
7 Buqi Pavilion
8 Pavilion for Admiring Fish
9 Canglangting Garden
10 Wenmiaoxiang House
11 Qingxiang Hall
12 Shrine of 500 Sages
13 Enlightened Way Hall
14 Yangzhi Pavilion
15 Cuilinglong Houses
16 Kanshan Tower
17 Yaohuajingjie House

1 沧浪胜迹坊
2 面水莲亭
3 碑纪
4 面水轩
5 御碑纪
6 公厕
7 步碕亭
8 观鱼处
9 沧浪亭
10 闻妙香亭
11 清香馆
12 五百名贤祠
13 明道堂
14 仰止亭
15 翠玲珑
16 看山楼
17 瑶华仙境界

use of space. Despite its size, the scale of the buildings is large, but nothing appears cramped. A section of the buildings is used by a cooperative of woodblock artists who find the peaceful atmosphere congenial to work. One should not spoil this garden's surprises any further. The entrance is a narrow alley just west of the Suzhou Hotel.

Garden for Lingering In *(liúyuán)* Extending over an area of three hectares, Liuyuan is one of the largest Suzhou gardens, noted for its adroit partitioning with building complexes. It dates from the Ming Dynasty and managed to escape destruction during the Taiping Rebellion. A 700-metre covered walkway connects the major scenic spots, and the windows have carefully selected perspectives. The walkway is inlaid with calligraphy from celebrated masters. The garden has a wealth of potted plants. Outside Mandarin Duck (Yuanyang) Hall is a 6½-metre-high Lake Tai piece – the final word on rockeries. The garden is about one km west of the old city walls. The bus there will take you over bridges looking down on the busy water traffic.

West Garden Temple

(xīyuán sì) 西园寺

About 500 metres west of Liuyuan, this temple was built on the site of a garden laid out at the same time as Liuyuan and then donated to the Buddhist community. The temple was destroyed in the 19th century and entirely rebuilt; it contains some expressive Buddhist statues.

Cold Mountain Temple

(hánshān sì) 寒山寺

One km west of Liuyuan, this temple was named after the poet-monk Hanshan, who lived in the 7th century. It was repeatedly burnt down and rebuilt, and holds little of interest except for a stele by poet Zhang Ji immortalising nearby Maple Bridge and the temple bell (since removed to Japan). However, the fine walls and the humpback bridge are worth seeing. The temple was once the site of lively local trading in silk, wood and grain. Not far from its saffron walls lies the Grand Canal. To get to the temple take bus No 4 to the terminal, cross the bridge and walk to the No 6 bus route; or take bus No 5 and then connect with bus No 6.

Tiger Hill

(hŭqiū) 虎丘

At the Tiger Hill parking lot (the bus No 5 terminal) we counted 15 Chinese tour buses, six minibuses, five Toyotas, three Shanghai taxis and two Kingswoods (modified with drawn curtains), so it seemed like a popular, interesting place. Actually, Tiger Hill is disappointingly boring. It's an artificial hill, 36 metres high, set in a park of 20 hectares. King He Lu, founding father of Suzhou, who died in the 6th century BC is buried near the top of the hill. A white tiger is said to have appeared to guard the tomb; hence the name.

Many Arthurian-type legends exist about Tiger Hill. There's a sword-testing stone with a crack in it, split by He Lu. The old boy, according to legend, is buried with his 3000 swords. A thousand builders were reputedly bumped off after making the tomb so that its secrets would not be revealed. It's apparently booby-trapped with spring water and any attempt at digging would be bad news for the pagoda further up.

Tiger Hill Pagoda *(hŭqiū tă)*, which was finished in 961 AD, has been leaning for several centuries. This century the thing split, and had to be restabilised (it is, after all, the symbol of Suzhou!). Work has been done to reinforce the foundation now that the tilt has reached over two metres. Concrete piles have been driven into the ground around the base, rather like staking it in a flowerpot.

Activities

Walking Suzhou is one of those towns where walking becomes a pleasure and you get to do most of the staring. The solid French plane trees that form canopies over the avenues set the tone. For canal-side residents it's a two-way street, with boats gliding past their rooms.

Once you discern the lines of the inner town canals, it's easy to work out walking routes to destinations, and you will probably find the canals themselves of more interest than the destination: a weary boatman sculls his sampan under a humpback bridge; an old woman nimbly bounces over the cobblestones with two laden baskets slung over a bamboo pole; a gentleman steps out of his rickety cottage to clean his teeth, his eye catching the lady opposite about to heave a nightsoil bucket into the canal; a street artist puts some final touches to a mural.

For some lively action, you really can't miss the bridges over the main moat; they offer great vantage points and often host impromptu markets. Because of their proximity to the Grand Canal, the six bridges to the west and south (Diaoqiao, Nanxin, Hongqi, Wannian, Wumen and Renmin) are especially rewarding. Two of these face docks where barges from other villages come to unload produce. Wumen Bridge is the largest single-arched stone bridge in Suzhou. Next to it is the best preserved city gate, Panmen, along with surviving fortifications. The dilapidated Ruigang Pagoda, once attached to a temple, adds a fitting dimension to the scene.

To get away from it all, the two parks

bordering the moat at the north-east end – East Garden (Dongyuan) and Coupling Garden (Ouyuan) – are not noted for their layouts, but they are uncrowded and ideal for a quiet cup of tea. In the distance, barges still patrol the waters.

Silk Factory Visits CITS tours are really your only option if you want to get into a silk-reeling, silk-weaving or silk-printing mill – you're unlikely to get in there by yourself. The silkworms are hand fed on bamboo trays by peasants. When the cocoons are spun, these are sent off to the factories where the larva cases are boiled and the filament unwound in long strands. There is also an embroidery factory, a jade-carving factory and a sandalwood-fan factory – all within the central area.

Places to Stay

The central *Lexiang Hotel* (☎ 22815) *(lèxiāng fàndiàn)* lacks ambience. It's at 18 Dajing Xiang, in the alley which runs off Renmin Lu near the Guanqian Jie markets. It's popular with travellers because of the comfortable dormitories, where beds go for Y20 per person. Double rooms cost Y160. The Lexiang is a very habitable place with quite friendly staff. To get there take bus No 1 from the railway station.

The *Gusu, Suzhou* and *Nanlin* hotels are grouped at the south-east end of town – further out but preferable and more spacious with more amenities. The Nanlin has dormitory accommodation. To get to these hotels you can take bus No 1 straight down Renmin Lu, alight at Shiquan Jie, which has wall-to-wall souvenir shops selling a mixed bag of trash and treasure, and walk east. Or take bus No 1 to Baita Lu, change to No 4 and take it eastwards directly to the hotels. The third possibility is to take bus No 2, which passes close to the north side of the Nanlin Hotel.

The *Suzhou Hotel* (☎ 24646) *(sūzhōu fàndiàn)* is at 115 Shiquan Jie. It offers air-con luxury, with a full range of services including a Friendship Store branch, theatre and extensive gardens. Doubles cost from Y169 including fridge and bath. The hotel has a rather weather-beaten appearance – on the inside!

The *Gusu Hotel* (☎ 25127) *(gūsū fàndiàn)* is in the same enclosure as the Suzhou, and is an Australian prefab. Doubles cost around Y120. It is full of electronics and outback creature comforts, angled towards Overseas Chinese. The hotel has a bar, cafe and dining rooms.

The *Nanlin Hotel* (☎ 24641) *(nánlín fàndiàn)* is at 20 Gunxiufang off Shiquan Jie. Its very pleasant gardens include a small section with outdoor ceramic tables and chairs. Doubles cost Y166 and dormitory beds cost Y25. There's a full range of facilities and a dining hall. The hotel is convenient to the long-distance bus station and boat dock. The Nanlin is not to be confused with the *Nanyuan Guesthouse* across the way, where they'll chase you around the gardens till you find out where the Nanlin is. The mysterious Nanyuan is most likely a cadre/VIP hotel.

Places to Eat

Suzhou Bazaar is the restaurant centre of the city. If there's pleasure in anticipation, then Westerners who are used to seeing items on the supermarket shelves all year round will perhaps not be too disappointed to learn that food in Suzhou is greatly dependent on the seasons. Towards autumn, the residents start salivating for a dish of a strange hairy crab, steamed with soy sauce and ginger. The crabs are caught at a freshwater lake seven km north-east of Suzhou in early autumn. The resulting feast is an annual event; Nanjingers and Shanghainese make the trip to Suzhou to sample it. There are prices to suit all wallets. You can stuff your gills for 50 fen in a noodle shop, or blow your inheritance in the Songhelou Restaurant.

Main Courses The *Songhelou Restaurant* (☎ 2066) *(sōnghè lóu)* at 141 Guanqian Jie is the most famous restaurant in Suzhou: Emperor Qianlong is supposed to have eaten there. The large variety of dishes includes squirrel fish, plain steamed prawns, braised eel, pork with pine nuts, butterfly-shaped sea cucumber, watermelon chicken and spicy duck. The waiter will insist that you be parcelled off to the special 'tour bus' cubicle at the back where an English menu awaits. The Songhelou runs from Guanqian Jie to an alley behind, where tour minibuses pull up. There have been mixed reports about this place; you may find it something of a letdown.

In the same alley at the back of the Songhelou are two large, crowded prole restaurants. The *Shanghai Laozhengxin (shànghǎi lǎozhèngxīn càiguǎn)* is one and the other is at No 19, on a corner further east. The Shanghai Laozhengxin serves pot-stewed food, cold dishes and smoked fish.

There are lots of small places to explore. Pick the most crowded, go in and see what's cooking (unfortunately, you'll have the longest waits in the most crowded places). Another indicator is the noise level: if it's over 100 decibels, it's a thumping good restaurant by Chinese standards – they like plenty of shouting, clatter and mayhem at the tables. The inner-alley sections of Guanqian Jie have a grand, almost homely feel to them with narrow doorways, ornamental windows and palace lanterns hung off some of the restaurants.

A pot of tea is the correct thing to drink with your meal. Suzhou has two native teas: Biluochun Green (Snail Spring Tea) and Jasmine.

There are a couple of other places worth trying. The *Xinjufeng Restaurant (xīnjùfēng càiguǎn)*, at 615 Renmin Lu, serves variations on duck and chicken, and regional specialities. The restaurants in the *Suzhou* and *Nanlin* hotels serve local delicacies like Suzhou almond duck and phoenix shrimp (arisen from the ashes?)

Snacks Loads of shops and vendors provide snacks. On the corner of Renmin Lu and Guanqian Jie are night food stalls with sizzling, tasty fare. In the soup line it's worth investigating a regional speciality made from Taihu aquatic plants – you might find it in a larger restaurant. In the late spring, fruit including loquats and strawberries from the shores of Lake Taihu comes to the Guanqian Jie markets.

Sweets Suzhou is famous for its sweets, candied fruits and some 170 varieties of pastries, depending on the stuffing. At the far end of Guanqian Jie is a concentration of the better known shops.

The *Huangtianyuan Cake Shop (huángtiānyuán gāobǐngdiàn)* at 88 Guanqian Jie has been in business for over a century. It serves tasty noodles, steamed leaf-wrapped dumplings and savouries, and incredible rice-based pastries with ingredients like cabbage juice, cocoa, walnuts and preserved fruits.

Almost opposite is the *Caizhizhai Confectionary (cǎizhīzhāi tángguǒdiàn)*, equally as ancient and grubby. It sells pine-nut candy and sweetened flour cakes. The candied strawberries are a real treat here, in season. Upstairs is a coffee shop.

Nearby is the *Daoxiangcun Cake & Candy Store (dàoxiāngcūn tángguǒdiàn)* at No 35 which, you must agree, could be a strain on the tooth enamel.

Entertainment

Try the barber shops and hairdressing salons on Guanqian Jie. No kidding – these places have the brightest lights and the most action in the early evening. As you're walking along, peep over the curtains of the salons to discover China's great beauty secrets. There are also a few dance halls scattered around the same district.

Suzhou has other nightlife, with over a dozen theatres and some storytelling houses. Suzhou Pingtan (ballad singing and storytelling) is where you can hear those sweet voices worked to their fullest. Most of the after hours activity takes place south of Guanqian Jie. There's a theatre at the Suzhou Hotel which occasionally has live shows.

Things to Buy

Along Guanqian Jie and in the alleys behind it, you can find Suzhou-style embroidery, calligraphy, painting, sandalwood fans, writing brushes and silk by the metre.

A curious store is Suzhou Y – no, not a dormitory, but a good place to spend WW III. This is an underground mini-department store that runs five blocks north-south on the west side of Renmin Lu, with Guanqian Jie at the northern end. It's about three metres wide (the store, not the silk) and has entrances that look like subway exits on the street.

At 274 Jingde Lu, which runs west from the intersection of Renmin Lu and Guanqian Jie, is the Arts & Crafts Store *(gōngyì mĕishù fúwùbù)* which stocks (among other handicrafts) clay figurines, traditional painting, calligraphy, musical instruments and jade carving. Never having tried embroidery ourselves, it looks nearly impossible that the Suzhou pieces were created using single filaments of silk. The double-sided hand embroidery, with its dazzling colours and striking patterns, is especially nifty.

It's worth tracking down the National Embroidery Institute display, which is in the same area as the Arts & Crafts Store. The institute specialises in hair-embroidery and the art is supposed to have been revived in Jiangsu Province since the Communists came to power. The technique uses human hair worked onto a silk backing. Suzhou embroidery is ranked among the top four needle-styles in China. Another Suzhou speciality is *kēsī*, which mixes raw and boiled-off silk in the weaving process, and is known as 'carved silk'. It was once reserved for imperial robing and can be bought in painting-scrolls or as waistbands and other items.

A little further afield at 344 Renmin Lu is an Antique & Curio Store *(wénwù shāngdiàn)*. The shop has some antique hardwood furniture, and you might delve into sandalwood fans. Actually, sandalwood is scarce and the fans are now made of other kinds of wood, like oak.

Though the Arts & Crafts Research Institute *(gōngyì mĕishù yánjiūsuǒ)* is not open to tourists, there is some fascinating activity going on there. In 1981, 32-year-old Shen Weizhong carved the world's smallest Buddha – three mm tall, with fingers as thin as hair, and a smiling face that can only be seen through a microscope. Another worker carved words onto the hair of a panda. (Now you know how they come up with those bus maps!)

Getting There & Away

Bus The long-distance bus station is at the south end of Renmin Lu. There are connections between Suzhou and just about every major place in the region including Shanghai (Y5.30), Hangzhou (Y8.90), Wuxi (Y3), Yangzhou (Y11.30) and Yixing (7.60).

Train Suzhou is on the line from Nanjing to Shanghai. To Shanghai takes about 1¼ hours, to Wuxi 40 minutes and Nanjing 3¼ hours. There are frequent expresses on this line which, if you're day-tripping, is ideal for rail hopping. Get a through ticket from, say, Nanjing to Shanghai, and break the journey in Suzhou and other towns along the way.

In Suzhou the advance booking office for the trains is at 203 Guanqian Jie.

Boat There are boats along the Grand Canal to Wuxi and to Hangzhou.

Boats from Suzhou to Hangzhou depart daily at 5.50 am and at 5.30 pm. The fare is Y9.50 to Y11.40 for a seat on the day boat and Y22.30 to 58.50 for a sleeper on the night boat, depending on the class selected. The trip takes about 14 hours. Boats from Hangzhou to Suzhou depart at 5.50 am and 5.30 pm.

Boats to Wuxi depart Suzhou at 6.10 am and at noon. The trip takes around five hours. Boats to Suzhou depart from Wuxi at 6.20 am and noon. The fare is Y2.50 for a seat.

Getting Around

The main thoroughfare is Renmin Lu with the railway station off the north end, and a large boat dock and long-distance bus station at the south end.

Bus No 1 runs the length of Renmin Lu. Bus No 2 is a kind of round-the-city bus, while bus No 5 is a good east-west bus. Bus No 4 runs from Changmen directly east along Baita Lu, turns south and runs past the east end of Guanqian Jie and then on to the Suzhou Hotel.

Taxi and auto-rickshaw ranks are outside the main railway station, down by the boat dock at the southern end of Renmin Lu, and at Jingmen (Nanxin Bridge) at the western end of Jingde Lu.

AROUND SUZHOU

While you may be right on track in Suzhou, go 20 km in any direction and you'll be off the record. The further out you go, of course, the less likely you should be there in the first place. Some of the local buses, it should be added, go for a considerable distance, such as bus No 11. You could hop on one for a ride to the terminal to see the enchanting countryside.

Grand Canal

(dàyùn hé) 大运河

The canal proper cuts to the west and south of Suzhou, within a 10-km range of the town. Suburban bus route Nos 13, 14, 15 and 16 will get you there. In the north-west, bus No 11 follows the canal for a fair distance. Once you arrive, it's simply a matter of finding yourself a nice bridge, getting out your deckchair and watching the world go by.

Precious Belt Bridge

(bǎodài qiáo) 宝带桥

Welcome to the bridge club! This is one of China's best with 53 arches, the three central humpbacks being larger to allow boats through. It straddles the Grand Canal, and is a popular spot with fishermen. The bridge is not used for traffic – a modern one has been built alongside – and is thought to be a Tang Dynasty construction named after Wang Zhongshu, a local prefect who sold his precious belt to pay for the bridge's construction for the benefit of his people. Precious Belt Bridge is about five km south-east of Suzhou. Bus No 13 will set you on the right track.

Lake Taihu Hang-outs

The following places can all be reached by long-distance buses from the station at the south end of Renmin Lu.

Lingyanshan *(língyán shān)* This is 15 km south-west of Suzhou. There are weirdly shaped rocks, a temple and pagoda (molested by Red Guards), and panoramas of mulberry trees, fertile fields and Lake Taihu in the distance – a lovely place to cycle to.

Tianpingshan *(tiānpíng shān)* This is 18 km south-west and has more of the same – plus some medicinal spring waters.

Guangfu Twenty-five km to the south-west bordering the lake, Guangfu has an ancient seven-storey pagoda and is dotted with plum trees.

Dongshan *(dōngshān)* Forty km to the south-west, this place is noted for its gardens and the Purple Gold (Zijin) Nunnery, which contains 16 coloured clay arhats and is surrounded by Lake Taihu on three sides.

Xidongtingshan Isle *(xīdòngtíng shān)* This town, also called Xishan, is a large island 60 km south-west of Suzhou. Getting there involves a 10-km ferry ride. Eroded Taihu rocks are 'harvested' here for landscaping. Take a bus from opposite Suzhou railway station to Luxian, then catch a ferry across to Zhenxia.

Changshu *(chángshú)* Fifty km north-east of Suzhou, this town is noted for its lace making. To the north-west of the town is Yushan with historical and scenic spots, including a nine-storey Song pagoda.

Luzhi In this town on the water, 25 km east of Suzhou, the canals provide the main means of commuting – in concrete flat bottomed boats. The old temple Baosheng has arhats, although that is probably not why you should come here. You could try your luck getting to places like this via canals from small docks in Suzhou.

XUZHOU

(xúzhōu) 徐州

Xuzhou does not fall into the category of a canal town, though a tributary of the Grand Canal passes by its north-eastern end. The history of the town has little to do with the canal. The colour brochure for Xuzhou shows the marshalling yard of the railway station as one of the sights and that, perhaps, is more to the point. If you're a rail buff there are plenty of lines to keep you happy since Xuzhou is at the intersection of China's two main railways: the Beijing to Shanghai line, and the Longhai line. The place has lots of cinemas, bus lines and an airport, and also the coal mines.

Orientation

The city centre is straight ahead of the main railway station, at the intersection of Huaihai Lu and Zhongshan Lu. Note that there are two railway stations, the north and main one (home to many beggars and vagrants). Take bus No 1 two stops west of the main station and you'll get to the main roundabout.

Dragon in the Clouds Hill

(yúnlóng shān) 云龙山

This hill has half the sights of Xuzhou: the Xinghua Temple, several pavilions, and a stone carving from the Northern Wei Dynasty. If you climb to the top of the hill, to the Xinghua Temple, there's a magnificent panorama of the concrete boxes that compose the Xuzhou valley and the mountains that encircle it. There are even orchards out there somewhere. Set in a grotto off the mountainside is a giant gilded Buddha head, the statue of the Sakyamuni Buddha. The park itself is circus-land with an outdoor shooting gallery and peanuts and ice-lolly sticks littering the slopes. The hill is a 10-minute walk west of the Nanjiao Hotel, or take bus Nos 2 or 11.

Monument to Huaihai Campaign Martyrs

(huáihǎi zhànyì lièshì jìniàntǎ)

淮海战役烈士纪念塔

This revolutionary war memorial and obelisk, opened in 1965, is in a huge wooded park at the southern edge of town. The Huaihai battle was a decisive one fought by the PLA from November 1948 to January 1949. The obelisk which is 38.5 metres high and has a gold inscription by Chairman Mao approached by a grand flight of stairs leading up to it. A Memorial Hall close by contains an extensive collection of weaponry, photos, maps, paintings and memorabilia – over 2000 items altogether – as well as inscriptions by important heads of state, from Zhou Enlai to Deng Xiaoping. The grounds, 100 acres of pines and cypresses, are meant to be 'symbolic of the evergreen spirit of the revolutionary martyrs'. The park lies on the bus No 11 route.

Places to Stay & Eat

The *Nanjiao Guesthouse* (☎ 38980) is the tourist joint on Heping Lu, three km from the main railway station. This is a TV hotel: most of the staff are permanently glued to the box downstairs. Double rooms start at Y85. Take bus No 2 from the main railway station. You'll find CITS here; it sells a Chinese/English map of the town.

There are no buses running in the evening, and the Nanjiao is quite a way from the railway station. Try the *Xuzhou Hotel* on the right as you come out of the railway station.

The Nanjiao has a dining room. Other places to try for a feed include the Huaihai Hotel (*Huaihai Fandian Caiguanbu*) on Huaihai Donglu between the main station and the large roundabout, south side of the street. Also the *Pencheng Hotel* close by, on a corner after an overhead bridge. There are noodle shops on the right when you come out of the main railway station.

Getting There & Away

Xuzhou lies at the junction of the main Beijing-to-Shanghai and Longhai lines. The Longhai line runs from Xi'an, Luoyang, Zhengzhou and Kaifeng in the west to the town of Lianyungang in the east.

Getting Around

The local bus station is across the square in

front of the main railway station. Auto-rickshaws are parked to the left as you leave the main railway station.

LIANYUNGANG

(liányúngǎng) 连云港

From Xuzhou, a branch line runs east to the major coastal port of Lianyungang (a six-hour ride). The town is divided into port and city sections. Yuntai Hill is the 'scenic spot' overlooking the ocean, and there are some salt mines along the shores, as well as a Taoist monastery. The mountain is reputed to be the inspiration for the Flowers and Fruit Mountain in the Ming Dynasty classic *Journey to the West* (but three other places in China make the same claim). Other sights include the 2000-year-old stone carvings at Kung Wangshan. There's an International Seamen's Club, Friendship Store, CITS office and several hotels. It may be possible to get boat connections on the east coast.

NANTONG

(nántōng) 南通

Nantong, an industrial city with over 200,000 residents, is an important textile and shipping centre for routes along the Yangtse and the canals running inland. The old walled city was on an island in the Hao River. There are no walls left, but the city administration is still on the island. There are three satellite towns outside the city core.

The most sensible way of getting to Nantong would be by boat – it's only six hours up river from Shanghai but a long way round by road. A possible land/boat route might be via Suzhou and Changshu, both of which are open to foreigners.

Shandong 山东

Shandong *(shāndōng)*, the turtle-head bobbing into the Yellow Sea, is a slow starter. The province is relatively poor and beset with economic problems, not the least of which is the rotten Yellow River which can't decide where to void itself. The river has changed direction some 26 times in its history and flooded many more times. Six times it has swung its mouth from the Bohai Gulf (north Shandong) to the Yellow Sea (south Shandong), and wreaked havoc on the residents.

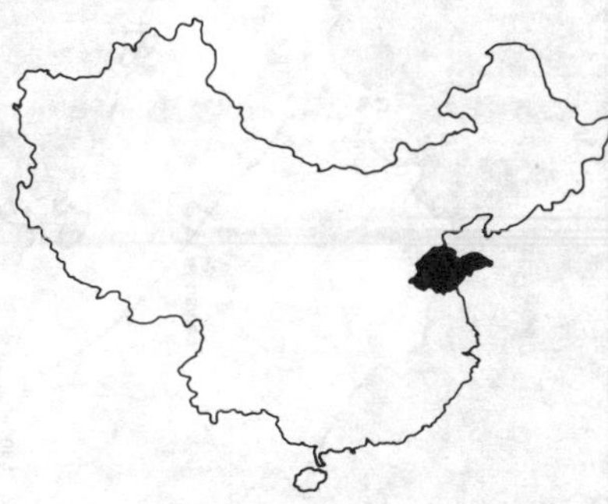

Back in 1899 the river flooded the entire Shandong Plain, a sad irony in view of the two scorching droughts which swept the area that same year and the year before. Add to that a long period of economic depression, a sudden influx of demobilised troops in 1895 after China's humiliating defeat in the war with Japan, and droves of refugees from the south moving north to escape famines, floods and drought. Then top it off with an imperial government in Beijing either incapable or unwilling to help the local people, and foreigners whose missionaries and railroads had angered the gods and spirits. All this created a perfect breeding ground for a rebellion, and in the last few years of the 19th century the Boxers arose out of Shandong and their rebellion set all of China ablaze.

Controlling the monstrous river that started it all is still going to take a fair bit of dike building. The other major problem is overpopulation. Shandong, with around 80 million people squashed into an area of just 150,000 sq km, is the third most populated province after Henan and Sichuan. And to make matters harder, about two-thirds of Shandong is hilly, with the Shandong massif (highest peak: Taishan) looming up in the south-west, and another mountain chain over the tip of the Shandong peninsula. The rest is fertile plains.

The Germans got their hands on the port of Qingdao in 1898 and set up a few factories. Shandong Province subsequently took a few quantum leaps towards industrialisation. The leading industrial town today is still Qingdao; the capital, Ji'nan, takes second place. Zibo, the major coal-mining centre, is also noted for its glassworks and porcelain. The Shengli Oilfield, opened in 1965, in northern Shandong, is the second largest crude oil source in China. As for railway lines, you can count them on the fingers of one hand, but the Shandong peninsula has some first-class harbours with good passenger links, and there is a dense road network.

Travellers tend to gloss over this province, which is unfortunate since it has quite a bit to offer. Lest it be forgotten, the Shandong tourist authorities are trying to spice it up with special-interest group tours like martial arts, fishing, calligraphy and honeymooning. Curious entry that! 'Honeymooning' – what would the special interest be in Shandong and how many in the group?

A number of places are open, including boring Ji'nan, the coastal ports of Qingdao and Yantai, Qufu and Taishan which are packed with sights, and unknowns like the Shengli Oilfield and Zibo.

Good news for peanut butter aficionados – Shandong is China's No 1 peanut producer. The thick and crunchy stuff can be tracked down in wholesome glass jars on department

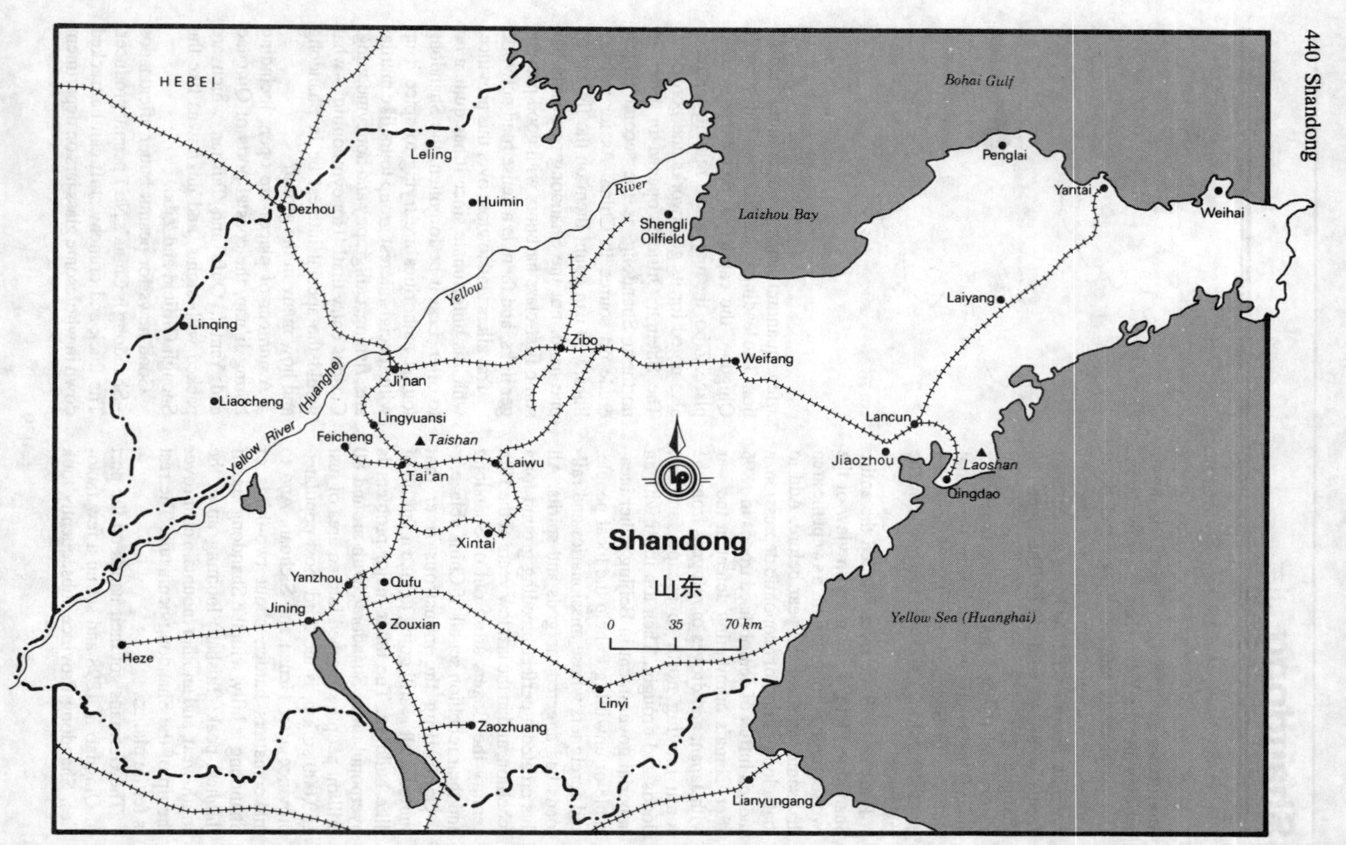
HEBEI
Bohai Gulf
Leling
Penglai
Yantai
Weihai
Dezhou
Huimin
River
Shengli
Oilfield
Laizhou Bay
Yellow
Laiyang
Linqing
Zibo
Weifang
Ji'nan
Liaocheng
Lingyuansi
Yellow River (Huanghe)
Feicheng
Taishan
Lancun
Jiaozhou
Laoshan
Qingdao
Tai'an
Laiwu
Xintai
Shandong
山东
Yanzhou
Qufu
Jining
Zouxian
0 35 70 km
Yellow Sea (Huanghai)
Heze
Linyi
Zaozhuang
Lianyungang

store shelves. Beer, wine and mineral water from Qingdao, Laoshan and Yantai are the pride of the nation.

JI'NAN

(jì nán) 济南

Ji'nan, the capital of Shandong Province, presides over a number of outlying counties and has a population of around two million in the city proper. The old city had two sets of walls – if you look at the map, you can see the squarish moats that once surrounded them and the inner wall bounded by the springs of Ji'nan. The Communists pulled down the Ming walls in 1949.

The area has been inhabited for at least 4000 years, and some of the earliest reminders of this are the eggshell-thin pieces of black pottery unearthed in the town of Longshan 30 km east of Ji'nan. Modern development in Ji'nan stems from 1899 when construction of the Ji'nan to Qingdao railway line began. The line gave the city a major communications role when completed in 1904. The Germans had a concession near the railway station after Ji'nan was opened up to foreign trade in 1906. Foreign missions were set up here and industrialisation took place under the Germans, the English and the Japanese. Steel, paper, fertiliser, cars and textiles are now produced here. The city is also an important educational centre. As for tourism, you'd be better off visiting the north pole during a snowstorm – Ji'nan is best thought of as a transit point.

Information

CITS There is an office (☎ 615858) in the Qilu Hotel.

Money The Bank of China (☎ 611855) is on Jing 2-Lu, just east of Wei 2-Lu.

Things to See

Go no further than the railway station. The further you go, the worse it gets. There is absolutely nothing better to see than that quaint piece of German railway architecture and its surreal clock gazing sternly down. Oh yes – there is something else – a safety display board just up the street showing mangled bodies amid twisted bits of truck and bicycle, with several photos in full gory colour.

Luckily I met the son of a cadre who asked me if I had any foreign video tapes. No, I didn't – how silly of me not to have stocked up in Hong Kong. He shuffled me round to a few dreary tour spots, offered me a place to stay for the night and took me to dinner with his girlfriend. He was, I guess, trying to impress her with his broken English – he certainly impressed her with the price of the meal. I stayed the night in his spacious apartment finding out how cadres' sons live – high! They have enough money or access to it to create a generation gap between themselves and parents, something that I had unwittingly been incorporated into.

The next day I set off in search of the real Ji'nan. This is the capital! There's got to be more out there. I eventually headed off to the Foreign Language Institute on the edge of the city. I asked the first foreigner I saw, 'What is there to see in Ji'nan?' 'Nothing', came the blunt answer. This from an English teacher who'd been stationed in this dump for two years, and who was nearing the end of his sentence. How he'd managed that long was beyond me.

Walking around the Institute area, the English teacher pointed out an old German church which had been converted into a sandpaper factory. Now that sounded interesting. My ears pricked up – the poetry of the situation was irresistible. I could just picture the manager at the altar, the workers bowing down to the machinery, the supervisor delivering sermons on production figures, the whole scene illuminated by shafts of sunlight filtered through stained-glass windows. 'Have you tried to get inside?' I asked with bated breath. 'Yes', said the English teacher. 'Did you succeed?' The English teacher looked at the ground. 'No', he said, 'not a peek'. Sandpaper production was obviously a state secret.

Miscellaneous Wonders You could make the trek south to Thousand Buddha Mountain *(qiānfóshān)*, which is only worth it for the views since its statues were disfigured or just disappeared during the Cultural Revolution. At the opposite end of town, past Golden Ox Park *(jīnniú gōngyúan)* (a zoo), is the dike of the Yellow River, a few km north of the No 4 bus terminal. That's on the dull side, but you pass by some dusty villages where the locals are engaged in interesting kinds of back-breaking labour.

There's also the Shandong Provincial

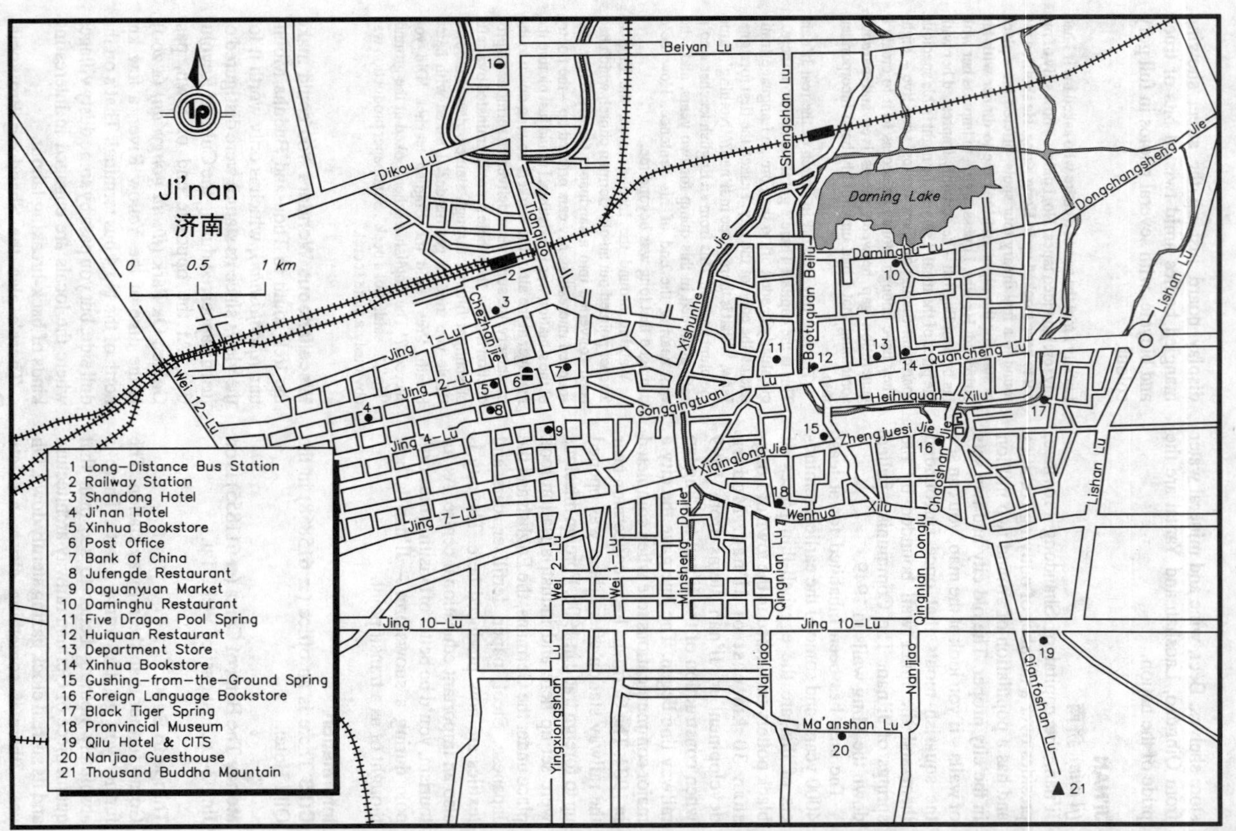

Ji'nan
济南
0
0.5
1 km
1 Long-Distance Bus Station
2 Railway Station
3 Shandong Hotel
4 Ji'nan Hotel
5 Xinhua Bookstore
6 Post Office
7 Bank of China
8 Jufengde Restaurant
9 Daguanyuan Market
10 Daminghu Restaurant
11 Five Dragon Pool Spring
12 Huiquan Restaurant
13 Department Store
14 Xinhua Bookstore
15 Gushing-from-the-Ground Spring
16 Foreign Language Bookstore
17 Black Tiger Spring
18 Pronvincial Museum
19 Qilu Hotel & CITS
20 Nanjiao Guesthouse
21 Thousand Buddha Mountain
Beiyan Lu
Shengchan Lu
Dikou Lu
Tianqiao
Daming Lake
Dongchangsheng Jie
Daminghu Lu
Lishan Lu
Baotuquan Beilu
Xishunhe Jie
Chezhan Jie
Jing 1-Lu
Jing 2-Lu
Jing 4-Lu
Jing 7-Lu
Jing 10-Lu
Wei 12-Lu
Wei 2-Lu
Wei 1-Lu
Quancheng Lu
Gongqingtuan Lu
Heihuquan Xilu
Zhengjuesi Jie
Xiqinglong Jie
Chaoshan Jie
Wenhua Xilu
Minsheng Dajie
Qingnian Lu
Qingnian Donglu
Yingxiongshan Lu
Nanjiao
Ma'anshan Lu
Qianfoshan Lu

1 长途汽车站
2 火车站
3 山东宾馆
4 济南饭店
5 新华书店
6 邮局
7 中国银行
8 聚丰德饭店
9 大观园市场
10 大明湖饭店
11 五龙潭
12 汇泉饭店
13 百货大楼
14 新华书店
15 趵突泉
16 外文书店
17 黑虎泉
18 省博物馆
19 齐鲁宾馆
20 南郊宾馆
21 千佛山

Museum *(shāndōng bówùgǔan)* sited in an old temple that turns out to be more impressive than the contents of the museum itself. The museum is divided into history and nature sections – tools, *objets d'art*, pottery, musical instruments. Otherwise, there's always Daguanyuan Market *(dàgūanyúan shìchǎng)* to browse around.

Mystery of the Springs Ji'nan's hundred-plus springs are often quoted as the main attraction, so let's set the record straight on this one. The four main parks-cum-springs are Black Tiger Spring *(hēihǔqúan)*, Pearl Spring *(zhūqúan)*, Five Dragon Pool *(wǔlóngtán)* and Gushing-from-the-Ground Spring *(bàotúqúan)*, all marvellous names but hardly accurate as adjectives. Twenty years ago they might have sprung but now they've virtually dried up. Reasons given vary – droughts, pollution from factories, increased industrial and domestic use and, more quietly, the digging of bomb shelters outside the city.

Daming Lake, covering one quarter of the city area, is also affected by this malaise which the authorities are attempting to 'correct'. Daming Lake has several minor temples, a few teahouses and a restaurant. At Baotu Spring Park there is a small memorial museum dedicated to the 11th century patriotic poetess Li Qingzhao.

Places to Stay

There isn't anything really cheap in Ji'nan. Near the railway station is the *Shandong Hotel* (☎ 20041) *(shāndōng bīngǔan)*, near the corner of Jingyi Lu and Chezhan Jie. Doubles range from Y100 to Y150, but try pushing them for a dormitory.

The sombre Soviet-style *Ji'nan Hotel* (☎ 38981) *(jì'nán fàndiàn)* at 240 Jingsan Lu also has some sobering prices – around Y100 a double. Students may manage cheaper rates. Take bus No 9 from the railway station.

The *Nanjiao Guesthouse* (☎ 23931) *(nánjiāo bīngǔan)* on Ma'anshan Lu is similar to the Ji'nan Hotel with even higher prices – Y200 for a double. To get there requires more effort – bus No 2 from the railway station and then a hike of one km. It was, so the story goes, flung up for an impending visit by Mao, who then decided to skip Ji'nan.

The *Qilu Hotel* (☎ 616688, 47981) *(qílǔ bīngǔan)* is the flashiest place in town, with doubles from Y250 to Y300. It's on Jing 10-Lu right next to Thousand Buddha Mountain Park *(qiānfóshān gōngyúan)*.

Places to Eat

Although Ji'nan isn't especially worth visiting for the fine food, with effort you can ferret out some decent fare. One of the better known eating establishments in town is the *Huiquan Restaurant* (☎ 610391) *(hùiqúan fàndiàn)*, 22 Baotuquan Beilu, which features sweet and sour carp from the Yellow River. Good Shandong food can be had at *Jufengde (jùfēngdé fàndiàn)* at the intersection of Wei 4-Lu and Jing 3-Lu. Just outside the south gate of Daming Lake Park is the *Daminghu Restaurant (dàmínghú fàndiàn)* which also serves Shandong food.

Like elsewhere in China, the railway station area always has numerous stalls, and you can always get yourself a bottle of 16% proof Tsingtao Red and hope you'll be too far gone to notice the food.

Things to Buy

Shopping territory is mostly in the area of the Ji'nan Hotel, with another strip in the older town section along Quancheng Lu. Indigenous artefacts for sale include feather paintings, inlaid mahogany boxes, gear from other parts of Shandong, and dough and wooden figurines. The Arts & Crafts Service Department is at 3 Nanmen Lu. There are a couple of antique stores, including the ones at 321 Quancheng Lu and 28 Jingsan Lu.

Getting There & Away

Air There are flights from Ji'nan to Beijing, Nanjing, Qingdao, Shanghai and Yantai. The CAAC office (☎ 33191) is at 348 Jing 2-Lu.

Train Ji'nan is a major link in the east China rail system, with over 30 trains passing through daily. From Ji'nan there are direct trains to Beijing (six hours) and Shanghai (13 hours). The trains from Qingdao to Shenyang which pass through Ji'nan sidestep Beijing and go through Tianjin instead. There are direct trains from Ji'nan to Qingdao and Yantai in Shandong Province, and to Hefei in Anhui Province. There are also direct Qingdao-Ji'nan-Xi'an-Xining trains.

Getting Around

There are about 25 urban and suburban bus lines in Ji'nan, running from 5 am to 9 pm, and two late night lines (east-west and north-south) finishing at midnight. There are also plenty of three-wheeler auto-rickshaws around the railway station.

AROUND JI'NAN

Ji'nan isn't worth much time (if any) in the way of sights; the surrounding area is slightly better.

Four Gate Pagoda
(sìméntǎ) 四门塔

Thirty-three km south-east of Ji'nan, near the village of Liubu, are some of the oldest Buddhist structures in Shandong. There are two clusters, one a few km north-east of the village and the other to the south. Shentong Monastery, founded in the 4th century AD, holds the Four Gate Pagoda, which is possibly the oldest stone pagoda in China and dates back to the 6th century. Four beautiful light-coloured buddhas face each door. The Pagoda of the Dragon and the Tiger *(lónghǔtǎ)* was built during the Tang Dynasty. It stands close to the Shentong Monastery and is surrounded by stupas. Higher up is the Thousand Buddha Cliff *(qiānfóyá)*, that has carved grottoes with some 200 small buddhas and half a dozen life-size ones. Local long-distance buses run from Ji'nan to Four Gate Pagoda, and daily tourist buses depart Ji'nan at 8 am and return at 3 pm.

Divine Rock Temple
(língyánsì) 灵岩寺

This temple is set in mountainous terrain in Changqing County, 75 km from Ji'nan. It used to be a large monastery that served many dynasties (the Tang, Song, Yuan, among others) and had 500 monks in its heyday. On view is a forest of 200 stupas commemorating the priests who directed the institution. There's also a nine-storey octagonal pagoda as well as the Thousand Buddha Temple *(qiānfódiàn)* which contains 40 fine, highly individualised clay arhats – the best Buddhist statues in Shandong. There are local long-distance buses from Ji'nan to Divine Rock Temple, but these take about three hours to get there so it's better to approach the town from Wande station (which is south of Ji'nan and 10 km from Divine Rock Temple). Tourist buses from Ji'nan depart at 7.30 am and return at 4 pm.

TAI'AN

(tài'ān) 泰安

Tai'an is the gateway town to the sacred Taishan. Apart from this, it's notable as the home town of Jiang Qing, Mao's fourth wife, ex-film actress, notorious spearhead of the all-purpose villains known as the 'Gang of Four' on whom all of China's ills are now blamed. She was later airbrushed out of Chinese history and committed suicide in May 1991.

Information

CITS This office (☎ 7020, 3259) is on the 2nd floor of 46 Hongmen Lu, which is just next to the Taishan Guesthouse. It's one of the most helpful and friendly CITS offices in China. They offer an interesting qigong tour for Y15 with an English-speaking guide.

Dai Temple

(daì miào) 岱庙

This temple is at the foot of the mountain, south of the Taishan Hotel. It was the pilgrims' first stopover and an ideal place to preview or recap the journey. It once functioned solely for that purpose, being a resting spot for the hiking emperors. The temple is a very large one of 96,000 sq metres, enclosed by high walls. The main hall is the Temple of Heavenly Blessing (Tiangong) dating back to 1009 AD. It towers some 22 metres high and is constructed of wood with double-roof yellow tiling.

The Tiangong was the first built of the 'big three' halls (the others being Taihe Hall at the Forbidden City, and Dacheng Hall at Qufu). It was restored in 1956. Inside is a 62-metre-long fresco running from the west to east walls depicting the god of Taishan on his outward and return journeys. In this case the god is Emperor Zhen Zong, who had the temple built. Zhen Zong raised the god of Taishan to the rank of emperor and there is a seven-metre-high stele to celebrate this in the western courtyard. The fresco has been painstakingly retouched by artisans of succeeding dynasties and, though recently restored, is in poor shape – but a majestic concept nonetheless.

The temple complex has been repeatedly restored; in the late 1920s, however, it was stripped of its statues and transmogrified into offices and shops. Later it suffered damage under the Kuomintang. It is gradually coming back together, not as a temple but as an open-air museum with a forest of 200-odd steles. One inscribed stone, originally at the summit of Taishan, is believed to be over 2000 years old (Qin Dynasty). It can be seen at the Eastern Imperial Hall, along with a small collection of imperial sacrificial vessels. Out-of-towners flock to Taishan Temple to copy the masterful range of calligraphy and poetry styles. Also moved from the summit is a beautiful bronze pavilion.

Around the courtyards are ancient cypresses, gingkos and acacias. At the rear of the temple is a bonsai garden and rockery. By the cypress in front of Tiangong Hall, locals and visitors can indulge in a game of luck. A person is blindfolded next to a rock, has to go around the rock three times anticlockwise, then three times clockwise, and try and grope towards the cypress, which is 20 steps away. They miss every time. Outside the main temple gates, if it's the right season, street hawkers sell watermelons with the display pieces deftly cut into rose shapes.

Places to Stay

The most popular place in town with travellers is the *Taishan Guesthouse* (☎ 4696) *(tàishān bīngǔan)*, a five-storey complex with souvenir shops, a bank and a restaurant. Dormitory beds are Y18. Double rooms cost from Y60 but can be bargained down to Y40 in the off season. The hotel is four km from the railway station and just a short walk from the start of the central route trail up Taishan. They will hold your bags for you while you climb the mountain. To get to the hotel, take bus No 3 from the railway station to the second-to-last stop. You must get this bus at the railway station – there is no city bus from the long-distance bus station. A taxi is Y10.

Somewhat less convenient is the *Overseas Chinese Hotel* (☎ 8122) *(húaqiáo dàxià)* on Dongyue Dajie. Doubles are Y160 in the low

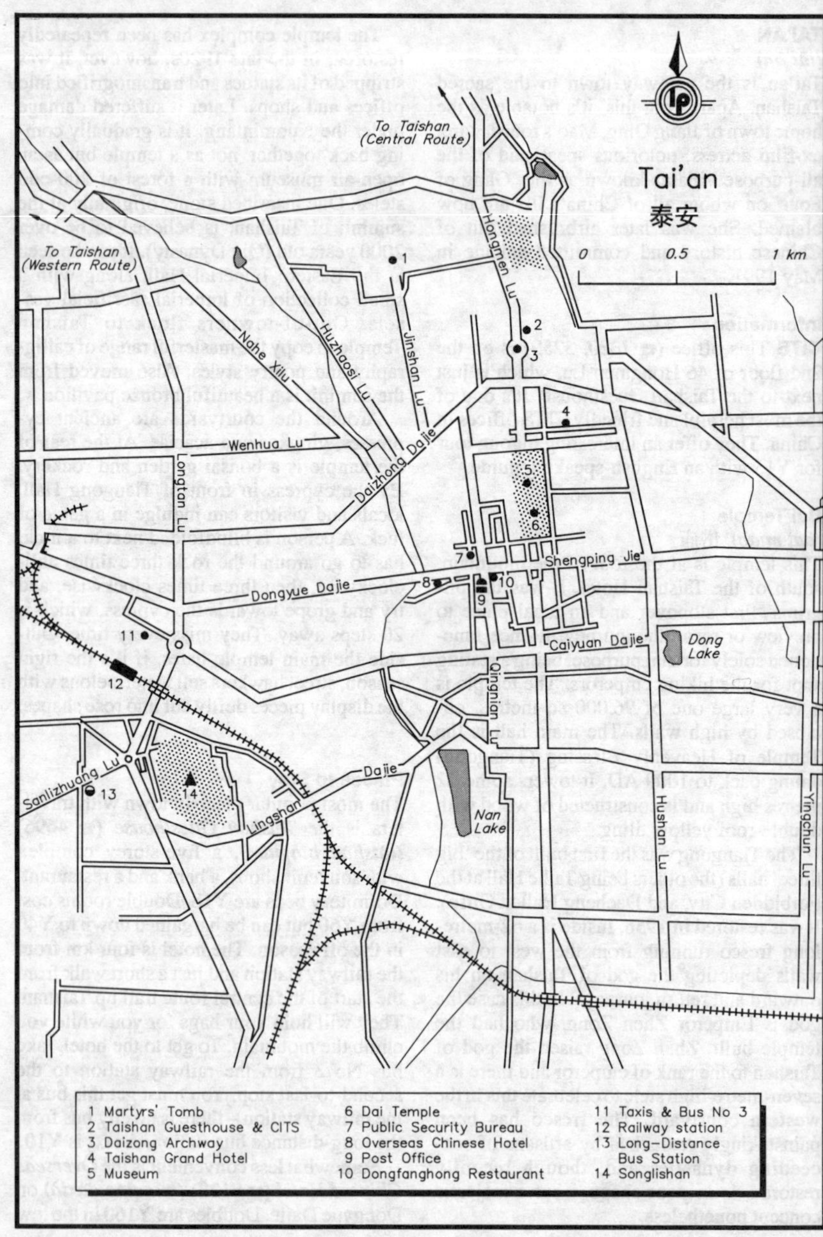
Tai'an
泰安
0
0.5
1 km
To Taishan (Central Route)
To Taishan (Western Route)
Hongmen Lu
Jinshan Lu
Huzhaosi Lu
Nahe Xilu
Daizhong Dajie
Wenhua Lu
Longtan Lu
Shengping Jie
Dongyue Dajie
Caiyuan Dajie
Dong Lake
Qingnian Lu
Hushan Lu
Yingchun Lu
Nan Lake
Sanlizhuang Lu
Lingshan Dajie
1 Martyrs' Tomb
2 Taishan Guesthouse & CITS
3 Daizong Archway
4 Taishan Grand Hotel
5 Museum
6 Dai Temple
7 Public Security Bureau
8 Overseas Chinese Hotel
9 Post Office
10 Dongfanghong Restaurant
11 Taxis & Bus No 3
12 Railway station
13 Long-Distance Bus Station
14 Songlishan

1 烈士陵园
2 泰山宾馆
3 岱宗坊
4 泰山大酒店
5 博物馆
6 岱庙
7 公安局
8 华侨大厦
9 邮局
10 东方红饭店
11 租车/3路汽车
12 火车站
13 长途汽车站
14 蒿里山

season, Y180 during peak times. Some bargaining is possible.

The only other place that takes foreigners is the *Taishan Grand Hotel* (☎ 7211) *(tàishān dàjiǔdiàn)* on Daizhong Dajie where doubles are Y120.

Places to Eat

Visitors generally keep to the set menus in the dining hall of the *Taishan Guesthouse*. The Western breakfast leaves much to be desired, but enormous Chinese set dinners are only Y10 per person. There's no dearth of restaurants around town, but after Taishan your legs may not let you go hunting (if in need, there's a roaring trade in Tai'an selling walking sticks, many neatly crafted from gnarled pieces of wood). There are many restaurants along Hongmen Lu (the street leading up to the mountain from the Dai Temple). The best known eating establishment in town is the *Dongfanghong Restaurant (dōngfānghóng fàndiàn)*, opposite the post office.

Getting There & Away

Bus Tai'an can be approached by road from either Ji'nan or Qufu and is worth combining with a trip to the latter. There are buses from the long-distance bus station to Qufu (about four times a day, two hours) Y6 and to Ji'nan (twice a day).

There are also private bus companies, some of which operate from offices just south of the Taishan Guesthouse with early morning departures to Qufu.

Train There are more than 20 express trains running daily through Tai'an with links to Beijing, Harbin, Shenyang, Nanjing, Shanghai, Xi'an, Zhengzhou, Qingdao and Ji'nan.

Tai'an station is about 1¼ hours along the line from Ji'nan. Some special expresses don't stop at Tai'an. The town is a nine-hour ride from Beijing, 11 hours from Zhengzhou and nine from Nanjing. Arrival times in Tai'an are impossible, with trains pulling in during the early hours of the morning.

Tai'an and Taishan make good stopovers on the way south from Qingdao to Qufu and Shanghai. The trip takes about 9½ hours.

Getting Around

Getting around is easy. The long-distance bus station is near the railway station, so all local transport is directed towards these two terminals. There are three main bus routes. Bus No 3 runs from the central route trailhead to the western route trailhead via the railway station, so that just about covers everything. Buses No 1 and 2 also end up near the railway station. Auto-rickshaws and pedicabs can be found outside the railway station.

AROUND TAI'AN

Taishan

(tàishān) 泰山

Also known as Dai, Taishan is the most revered of the five sacred mountains of China, adopted in turn by Taoists, Buddhists, Confucians and Maoists. From its summit imperial sacrifices to heaven and earth were offered. In China's long history, only five emperors dared to climb Taishan – Emperor Qianlong scaled it 11 times. From its heights Confucius uttered the dictum, 'The world is

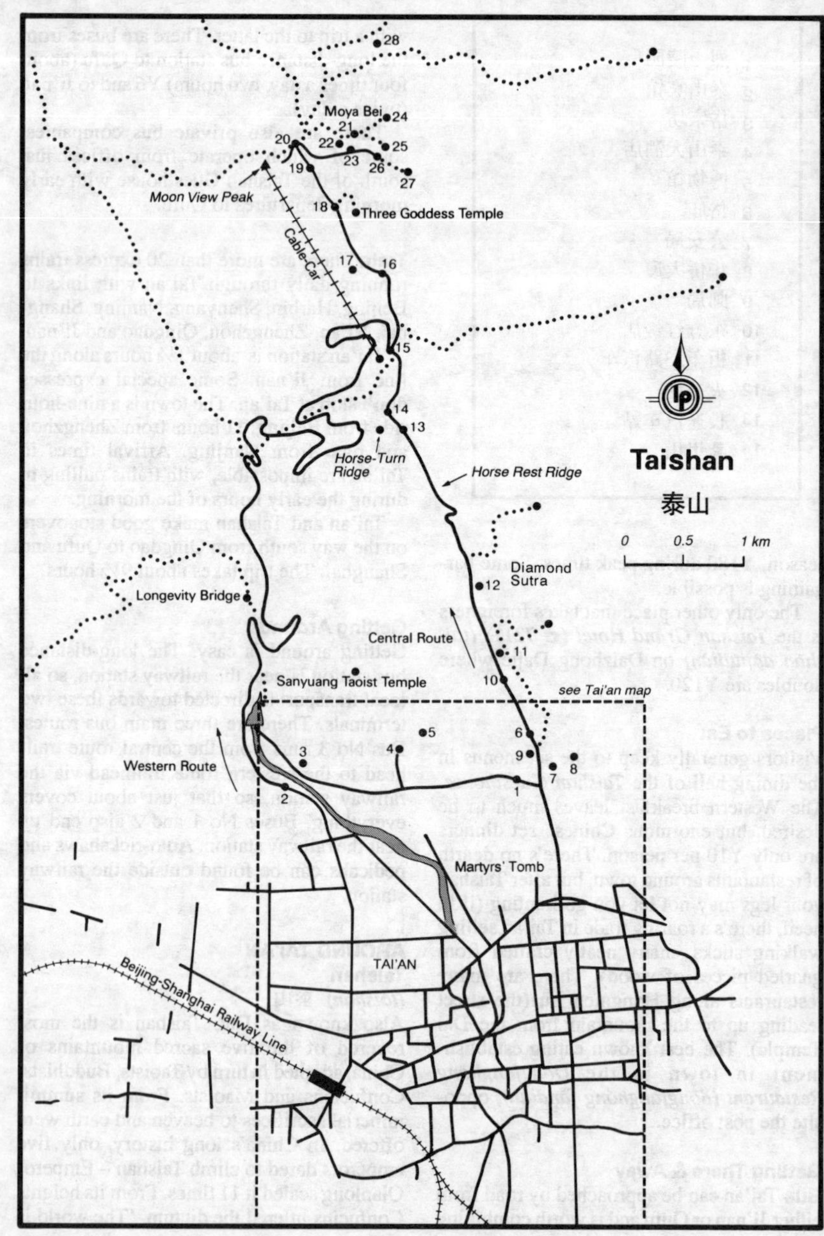

Moya Bei
Moon View Peak
Three Goddess Temple
Cable Car
Horse-Turn Ridge
Horse Rest Ridge
Taishan
泰山
0
0.5
1 km
Diamond Sutra
Longevity Bridge
Central Route
Sanyuang Taoist Temple
see Tai'an map
Western Route
Martyrs' Tomb
TAI'AN
Beijing-Shanghai Railway Line

1	Trailhead for Central Route (No 3 Bus East Terminal)	三路汽车东终站
2	Trailhead for Western Route (No 3 Bus West Terminal or No 2 Bus)	三路汽车西终站
3	Everyman's Bridge & Tomb of Feng Yuxiang	大众桥
4	Puzhao Monastery	普照寺
5	Memorial Temple	记念寺
6	Red Gate Palace	红门
7	Cloud Empress Pool	王母池
8	Tiger Mountain Reservoir	龙山水库
9	Guandi Temple	关帝庙
10	10,000 Immortals Pavilion	万仙楼
11	Monument to Revolutionary Heroes	革命烈士纪念碑
12	Doumu Hall	斗母宫
13	Hutian Pavilion	虚天阁
14	Skywalk Bridge	步天桥
15	Zhongtian Gate, Zhongtianmen Guesthouse & Cable Car	中天门
16	Cloud Bridge	云步桥
17	Five Pine Pavilion	五松亭
18	Pine Facing Pavilion	对松亭
19	Archway to Immortality	开仙坊
20	Nantian Gate (South Gate to Heaven)	南天门
21	Jade Emperor Temple	玉皇顶
22	Daiding Guesthouse	岱顶宾馆
23	Azure Clouds Temple	碧霞祠
24	Gongbei Rock	拱石
25	Sunview Peak	日观峰
26	Bridge of the Gods	仙人桥
27	Zhanlu Terrace	占鲁台
28	Rear Temple	后石坞

small'; Mao lumbered up and commented on the sunrise, 'The East is Red'.

Poets, writers and painters have found Taishan a great source of inspiration and extolled its virtues, but today one is left wondering what natural beauty is left. A long string of worshippers has left its tributes on the slopes – calligraphy cut into rock faces, temples, shrines, stairs – to which modern history has added revolutionary memorials, guesthouses, soft-drink vendors, photo booths, a weather station and the final insult – a cable car.

No matter, the pull of the supernatural (legend, religion and history rolled into one) is enough. The Princess of the Azure Clouds (Bixia), a Taoist deity whose presence permeates the temples dotted along the route, is a powerful cult figure for the peasant women of Shandong and beyond. Tribes of wiry grandmothers come each year for the ascent, a journey made difficult by bound feet. Their target is the main temples at the summit, where they can offer gifts and prayers for their progeny. It's said that if you climb Taishan you'll live to be 100, and some of the grandmothers look pretty close to that already. For the younger set, Taishan is a popular picnic destination. Tourists – foreign and Chinese – gather on the cold summit at daybreak in the hope of catching a perfect 747 sunrise. In ancient Chinese tradition, it was believed that the sun began its westward journey from Taishan.

As the old Chinese saying goes: 'The journey of a thousand miles begins with a single step'. On Taishan there are some 6000 of them that you'll remember clearly. The mountain is relatively small, but the steps are the kind that get your blood pounding. You and 5000 other climbers, that is! After a while, you realise that what you're looking at is not the mountain but the pilgrims toiling up it. The hackwork of China – the carting of concrete blocks, water, produce, goods – is a common sight on city streets, but nowhere does it appear more painful than on the sheer slopes of this mountain. Porters with weals on their shoulders and misshapen backs plod up the stairway to heaven with crates of drinks, bedding and construction for the hotels and dining halls further up. It's a time-honoured tradition, a job passed from father to son, and the cable car seems to have done little to alter it. The idea, as we understood it, was to use the cable car to transport passengers by day, and cargo by night. One wonders how many backs were broken in the building of the temples and stone stairs on Taishan over the centuries, a massive undertaking accomplished without mechanical aids.

All in all, as you may have surmised, Taishan is not the mountain climbing you might expect it to be, and it is not a particularly scenic beauty. But if you accept that, it's an engrossing experience and certainly worthwhile. If grandmother can make it up there, you should have no trouble, and it will exercise the other five walking muscles you haven't used in the streets already. The trip down, by the way, is more strenuous for the legs.

Weather The peak tourist season is from May to October. But remember that conditions vary considerably on the mountain compared to sea-level Tai'an.

The mountain is frequently enveloped in clouds and haze, which are more prevalent in summer. The best times to visit are in spring and autumn when the humidity is low, though old-timers say that the clearest weather is from early October onwards. In winter the weather is often fine but very cold.

On average, there are 16 fine days in spring, eight in summer, 28 in autumn and 35 in winter. But take care – due to weather changes, you're best advised to take a small day-pack with you to carry warm clothing, no matter what the season. You can freeze your butt off on Taishan, though you can hire padded overcoats. The average seasonal temperatures in degrees Celsius are:

	winter	spring	summer	autumn
Taishan	-3	20	24	20
Summit	-9	12	17	12

Scaling the Heights The town of Tai'an lies at the foot of Taishan and is the gateway to the mountain. (See the Tai'an section.)

Upon arrival you have several options, depending on your timing. There are three rest stops to bear in mind: Taishan Guesthouse, at the base of the trail; Zhongtianmen Guesthouse, midway up; and the Daiding Guesthouse on top of Taishan.

You should allow at least two hours for climbing between each of these points – a total of eight hours up and down, at the minimum. Allowing several more hours would make the climb less strenuous and give you more time to look around on top. If you want to see the sunrise, then dump your gear at the railway station or the Taishan Guesthouse in Tai'an and time your ascent so that you'll reach the summit before sundown; stay overnight at one of the summit guesthouses and get up early next morning for the famed sunrise (which, for technical reasons, may not be clearly forthcoming).

Chinese tourists without time or money at their disposal sometimes scale at night (with torches and walking sticks) to arrive at the peak in time for sunrise, descending shortly thereafter. Unless you have uncanny night vision or four hours of battery power, this particular option could lead to you getting lost, frozen, falling off a mountainside, or all three.

There are two main paths up the mountain: the central and the western, converging midway at Zhongtian Gate. Most people go up via the central path (which used to be the imperial route and hence has more cultural sites) and down by the western path. Other trails run through orchards and woods.

Taishan is 1545 metres above sea level, with a climbing distance of 7.5 km from base to summit on the central route. The elevation change from Zhongtian Gate to the summit is approximately 600 metres.

Cheating Your Way to the Top Minibuses run from the Tai'an railway station to Zhongtian Gate, halfway up Taishan, with several departures each morning. Occasional group tour minibuses run from the Taishan Guesthouse too.

From Zhongtian Gate there is a cable car to the top which holds 30 passengers. It takes eight minutes to travel from Zhongtian Gate to Wangfushan, near Nantian Gate, and may be useful for bird's-eye view photos. The cable cars operate in both directions. This is China's first large cableway.

Buses come down the mountain hourly between 1 and 5 pm, but don't count on the schedule or the seats.

Central Route On this route you'll see a bewildering catalogue of bridges, trees, towers, inscribed stones, caves, pavilions and temples (complex and simplex). Half the trip, for Chinese people at least, is seeing the colossal amount of calligraphy scoring the stones en route. Taishan, in fact, functions as an outdoor museum of calligraphic art, with the prize items being the Diamond Sutra (or Stone Valley Sutra) and the Moya Bei at the summit, which commemorates an imperial sacrifice.

The climb proper begins at No 1 Archway Under Heaven at the mountain base. Behind that is a stone archway overgrown with wisteria and inscribed 'the place where Confucius began to climb'. Red Gate Palace, standing out with its wine-coloured walls, is the first of a series of temples dedicated to the Princess of the Azure Clouds, who was the daughter of the god of Taishan. It was rebuilt in 1626.

Doumu Hall was first constructed in 1542 and has the more poetic name of Dragon Spring Nunnery; there's a teahouse inside.

Continuing through the tunnel of cypresses known as Cypress Cave is Horse-Turn Ridge, where Emperor Zhen Zong had to dismount and continue by sedan chair because his horse refused to go further – smart move on the part of the horse! Another emperor rode a white mule up and down the mountain and the beast died soon after the descent (it was posthumously given the title of general and its tomb is on the mountain).

Zhongtianmen (Midway Gate to Heaven) is the second celestial gate. Beyond Cloud Bridge and to the right is the place where Emperor Zhen Zong pitched his overnight tents. A little way on is Five Pine Pavilion where, one day back in 219 BC, Emperor Qin Shihuang was overtaken by a violent storm and was sheltered by the kind pines. He promoted them to the 5th rank of minister; though the three you see are, understandably, not the same ministers!

On the slopes higher up is the Welcoming Pine with a branch extended as if to shake hands. Beyond that is the Archway to Immortality. It was believed that those passing through it would become celestial beings. From here to the summit, emperors were carried in sedan chairs – eatcha heart out!

The third celestial gate is Nantianmen (South Gate to Heaven). That, and the steep pathway leading up to it, are symbolic of Taishan and of Shandong itself; the picture pops up on covers of books and on Shandong maps.

On arrival at Taishan Summit *(dàidǐng)* you will see the Wavelength Pavilion (a radio and weather station) and the Journey to the Stars Gondola (the cable car). If you continue along Paradise Rd, you'll come to Sunset Statue (where a frozen photographer sits slumped over a table with the view beyond dutifully recorded in sunrises and clipped in front of him).

Welcome to Taishan shopping centre. Here you'll see fascinating Chinese antics on the precarious rock lookouts – go and check out the Bridge of the Gods, which is a couple of giant rocks trapped between two precipices.

The grandmothers' long march ends at the Azure Clouds Temple *(bìxiácí)* where small offerings of one sort or another are made to a bronze statue, once richly decorated. The iron tiling on the buildings is intended to prevent damage by strong wind currents, and on the bronze eaves are *chiwen*, ornaments meant to protect against fire. The temple is absolutely splendid, with its location in the clouds, but its guardians are a trifle touchy about you wandering around, and parts of it are inaccessible. Little is known of the temple's history but we do know that it cost a fortune to restore or make additions, as was done in the Ming and Qing dynasties. The bronze statuette of the Princess of the Azure Clouds is in the main hall.

Perched on the highest point (1545 metres) of the Taishan plateau is Jade Emperor Temple, with a bronze statue of a Taoist deity. In the courtyard is a rock inscribed with the elevation of the mountain. In front of the temple is the one piece of calligraphy that you can really appreciate – the Wordless Monument. This one will leave you speechless. One story goes that it was set up by Emperor Wu 2100 years ago – he wasn't satisfied with what his scribes came up with, so he left it to the viewers' imagination.

The main sunrise vantage point is a springboard-shaped thing called Gongbei Rock; if you're lucky visibility could extend to over 200 km, as far as the coast. The sunset slides over the Yellow River side. On the backside of the mountain is Rear Rocky Recess, one of the better known spots for viewing pine trees; there are some ruins tangled in the foliage. It's a good place to ramble and lose the crowds for a while.

Western Route On this route there's nothing of note in the way of structures, but there's considerable variation in scenery with orchards, pools and flowering plants. The major scenic attraction is Black Dragon Pool which is just below Longevity Bridge (between the bridge and West Brook Pavilion) and is fed by a small waterfall. Swimming in the waters are some rare, red-scaled carp which are occasionally cooked for the rich. Mythical tales revolve around this pool, said to be the site of underground carp palaces and of magic herbs that turn people into beasts. Worth looking into is the Puzhao Monastery, founded 1500 years ago along the base of the mountain.

Places to Stay & Eat The *Zhongtianmen Guesthouse (zhōngtiānmén)* is a halfway house at Zhongtian Gate with little in the way of food, although there are food and drink stalls nearby. They try to charge foreigners Y80 for a double – you have to push to get into the dormitory which is only Y12. It's very quiet (provided no-one brings their stereo system).

The *Daiding Guesthouse (dàidǐng bīnguǎn)* is a recently renovated hotel on the summit and now asks Y150 for a double. There are probably cheaper dormitory beds if you do a bit of arm-twisting with the staff. If you get a room in the right place then you get excellent views. The hotel provides extra blankets and rents out heavy padded cotton overcoats, PLA-type, in lieu of heating. There's even an alarm bell which tells you when to get up for sunrise. (If you wonder where all those amazing grannies go, it seems that there are lodgings tucked down side trails, possibly former monasteries.)

As for sustenance – snacks, drinks and the like are sold on the mountain trail. Outside the Daiding Guesthouse is a green shed masquerading as a restaurant.

QUFU

(qūfù) 曲阜

Qufu is the birth and death place of the sage Confucius (551-479 BC) whose impact was not felt in his own lifetime. He lived in abject poverty and hardly put pen to paper, but his teachings were recorded by dedicated followers (in the *Analects*). His descendants, the Kong family, fared considerably better.

Confucian ethics were adopted by subsequent rulers to keep the populace in line, and Confucian temples were set up in numerous towns run by officials. Qufu acquired the status of a holy place, with the direct descendants of Confucius as its guardian angels.

The original Confucian Temple at Qufu (dating from 478 BC) was enlarged, remodelled, added to, taken away from and rebuilt. The present buildings are from the Ming Dynasty. In 1513 armed bands sacked the temple and the Kong residence, and walls were built around the town between 1522 and 1567 to fortify it. These walls were recently removed, but vestiges of Ming town planning, like the Drum and Bell towers, remain.

More a code that defined hierarchical relationships than a religion, Confucianism has had a great impact on Chinese culture. It teaches that son must respect father, wife must respect husband, commoner must respect official, officials must respect their ruler, and vice versa. The essence of its teachings are obedience, respect and selflessness, and working for the common good.

One would think that this code would have fitted nicely into the new order of Communism. However, it was swept aside because of its connections with the past. Confucius was seen as a kind of misguided feudal educator, and clan ties and ancestor-worship were viewed as a threat. In 1948 Confucius' direct heir, the first-born son of the 77th generation of the Kong family, fled to Taiwan, breaking a 2500-year tradition of Kong residence in Qufu.

During the Cultural Revolution the emphasis shifted to the youth of China (even if they were led by an old man). A popular anti-Confucian campaign was instigated and Confucius lost face. Many of the statues at Qufu also lost face (literally) amidst cries of 'Down with Confucius, down with his wife!' In the late '60s a contingent of Red Guards descended on the sleepy town of Qufu, burning, defacing and destroying. Other Confucian edifices around the country were also attacked. The leader of the Guards who ransacked Qufu was Tan Houlan. She was jailed for that in 1978 and was not tried until 1982. The Confucius family archives appear to have survived the assaults intact.

Confucian ethics have made something of a comeback, presumably to instil some civic-mindedness where the Party had failed. Confucianism is finding its way back into the Shandong school system, though not by that name. Students are encouraged once again to respect their teachers, elders, neighbours and family. If there's one thing you discover quickly travelling in China, it's that respect among the Chinese has fallen to pieces. With corruption at the top of the system, the cynical young find it difficult to reciprocate respect; the elderly remain suspicious of what has passed and afraid of the street fights and arguments.

In 1979 the Qufu temples were reopened and millions of yuan were allocated for renovations or repairs. Tourism is now the name of the game; if a temple hasn't got a fresh coat of paint, new support pillars, replaced tiling or stonework, a souvenir shop or photo merchant with a Great Sage cardboard cut-out, they'll get round to it soon. Some of the buildings even have electricity, with speakers hooked up to the eaves playing soothing flute music. Emanating from the eaves is some real music – you have to stop and listen twice to make sure – yes, real birds up there! Fully a fifth of Qufu's 50,000 residents are again claiming to be descendants of the Great Sage, though incense burning, mound-burial and ancestor-worship are not consistent with the Party line.

Whether Confucianism can take fresh root in China is a matter for conjecture, but something is needed to fill the idealist void. A few years ago a symposium held in Qufu by Chinese scholars resulted in careful statements reaffirming the significance of Confucius' historical role, and suggesting that the 'progressive' aspects of his work were a valuable legacy which had also been cited in the writings of Mao Zedong. It's simply a matter of picking Confucian hairs out of Marxist soup.

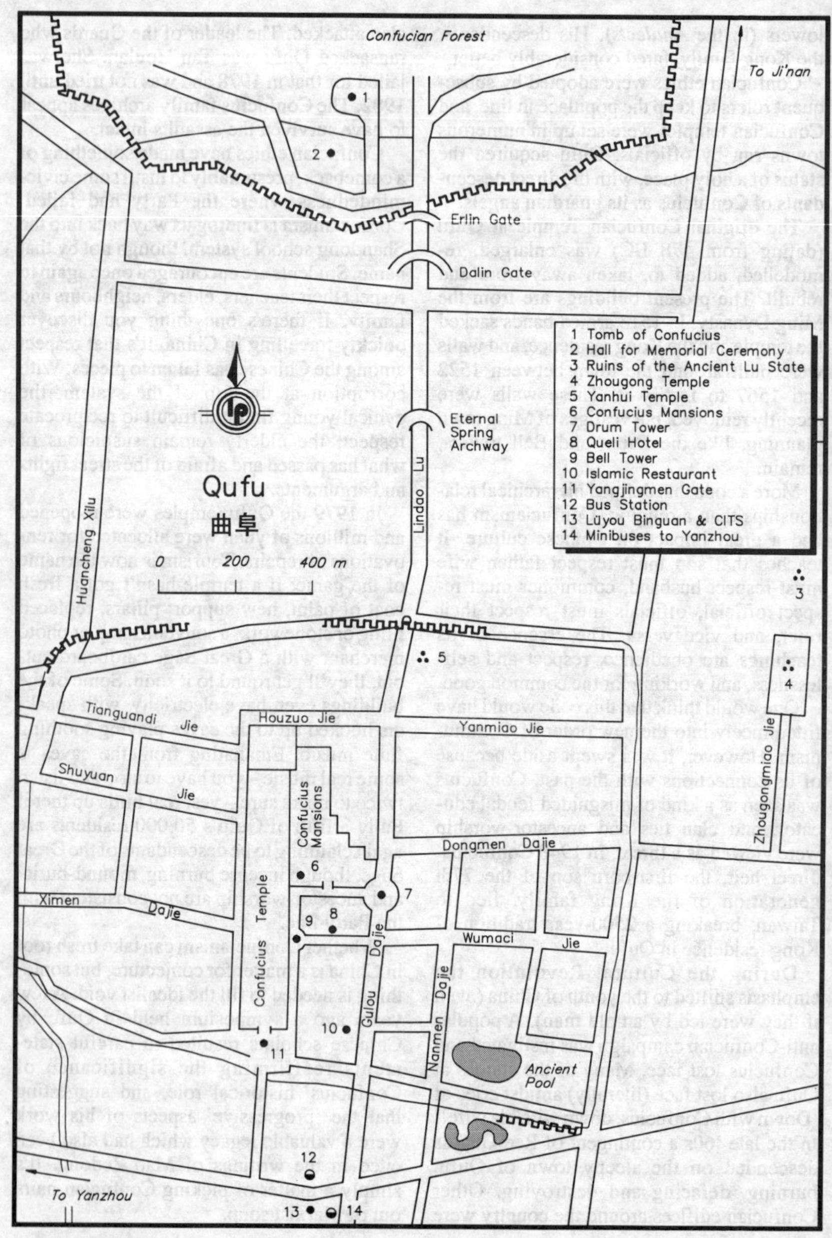

Confucian Forest
To Ji'nan
Erlin Gate
Dalin Gate
Eternal Spring Archway
Lindao Lu
Huancheng Xilu
Qufu
曲阜
0 200 400 m
1 Tomb of Confucius
2 Hall for Memorial Ceremony
3 Ruins of the Ancient Lu State
4 Zhougong Temple
5 Yanhui Temple
6 Confucius Mansions
7 Drum Tower
8 Queli Hotel
9 Bell Tower
10 Islamic Restaurant
11 Yangjingmen Gate
12 Bus Station
13 Lüyou Binguan & CITS
14 Minibuses to Yanzhou
Tianguandi Jie
Houzuo Jie
Yanmiao Jie
Shuyuan Jie
Confucius Mansions
Zhougongmiao Jie
Dongmen Dajie
Ximen Dajie
Confucius Temple
Gulou Dajie
Wumaci Jie
Nanmen Dajie
Ancient Pool
To Yanzhou

1 孔墓
2 祭奠堂
3 鲁国址
4 周公庙
5 颜庙
6 孔府
7 鼓楼
8 阙里宾舍
9 钟楼
10 回民饭店
11 仰经门
12 汽车站
13 旅游宾馆
14 往兖州小公共汽车

With the blending of stone, wood and fine imperial architecture, Qufu is an oasis of culture and elegance – the China we see on postcards and coffee-table books. It's an excellent stopover worth one or two days, and is quiet, with real birds and grass. There's plenty to see and you can see it all on foot without hassling with transport or big-city complications. It's a great place for traveller R & R (rest and recuperation).

Following a 2000-year-old tradition there are two fairs a year in Qufu, in spring and autumn – when the place comes alive with craftspeople, healers, acrobats, pedlars and poor peasants.

Information

CITS This is on the 2nd floor of the Lüyou Binguan, near the bus station. There isn't much for them to do in a small place like Qufu, but they could help you buy a bus ticket.

Confucius Temple

(kǒng miào) 孔庙

The temple started out as a simple memorial hall and mushroomed to a complex a fifth the size of Qufu. It is laid on a north-south axis, and is over one km long. The main entrance is Star Gate *(língxīngmén)* at the south, which leads through a series of portals emblazoned with calligraphy. The third entrance gateway, with four bluish characters, refers to the doctrines of Confucius as heavenly bodies which move in circles without end; it is known as the Arch of the Spirit of the Universe.

Throughout the courtyards of the Confucius Temple, the dominant features are the clusters of twisted pines and cypresses, and row upon row of steles. The tortoise tablets record in archaic Chinese such events as temple reconstructions, great ceremonies or tree plantings. There are over 1000 steles in the temple grounds, with inscriptions from Han to Qing times – the largest such collec-

tion in China. The creatures bearing the tablets of praise are actually not tortoises but *bixi*, dragon offspring legendary for their strength. The tablets at Qufu are noted for their fine calligraphy; a rubbing once formed part of the dowry for a Kong lady.

Roughly midway along the north-south axis is the Great Pavilion of the Constellation of Scholars, a triple-roofed, Jin Dynasty, wooden structure of ceremonial importance dating from 1190. Further north through Dacheng Gate and to the right is a juniper planted by Confucius – or so the tablet in front of it claims. The small Xingtan Pavilion up from that commemorates the spot where Confucius is said to have taught under the shade of an apricot tree.

The core of the Confucian complex is Dacheng Hall which in its present form dates back to 1724; it towers 31 metres on a white marble terrace. The reigning sovereign permitted the importation of glazed yellow tiling for the halls in the Confucius Temple, and special stones were brought in from Xishan. The craftspeople did such a good job on the stone dragon-coiled columns that it is said they had to be covered with silk when the emperor came to Qufu lest he felt that the Forbidden City's Taihe Hall paled in comparison.

The hall was used for unusual rites in honour of Confucius. At the beginning of the seasons and on the great sage's birthday, booming drums, bronze bells and musical stones sounded from the hall as dozens of officials in silk robes engaged in 'dignified dancing' and chanting by torchlight. The rare collection of musical instruments is displayed, but the massive stone statue of the bearded philosopher has disappeared – presumably a casualty of the Red Guards.

To the extreme north end of the Confucius Temple is Shengjidian, a memorial hall containing a series of stones engraved with scenes from the life of Confucius and tales about him. They are copies of an older set which date back to 1592.

In the eastern compound of the Confucian Temple, behind the Hall of Poetry and Rites, is Confucius' well (a Song-Ming reconstruction) and the Lu Wall where the ninth descendant of Confucius hid the sacred texts during the anti-Confucian persecutions of Emperor Qin Shihuang. The books were discovered again in the Han Dynasty (206 BC-220 AD) and led to a lengthy scholastic dispute between the scholars who escaped and remembered the books, and those who supported the teachings in the rediscovered ones.

Confucius Mansions

(kǒng fǔ) 孔府

Built and rebuilt many times, the Mansions presently date from the 16th century Ming Dynasty, with recent patchwork. The place is a maze of 450 halls, rooms and buildings, and getting around it requires a compass – there are all kinds of side passages to which servants were once restricted.

The Mansions are the most sumptuous aristocratic lodgings in China, indicative of the Kong family's former great power. From the Han to the Qing dynasties, Confucius' descendants were ennobled and granted privileges by the emperors. They lived like kings themselves, with 180-course meals, servants and consorts. Confucius even picked up some posthumous honours.

The town of Qufu, which grew around the Mansions, was an autonomous estate administered by the Kongs who had powers of taxation and execution. Emperors could drop in to visit – the Ceremonial Gate near the south entrance was only opened for this event. Because of royal protection, copious quantities of furniture, ceramics, artefacts, costumery and personal effects survived and some may be viewed. The Kong family archives, a rich legacy, also seem to have survived, and extensive renovations of the complex have been made.

The Mansions are built on an 'interrupted' north-south axis. Grouped by the south gate are the former administrative offices (taxes, edicts, rites, registration, examination halls). To the north on the axis is a special gate – Neizhaimen – that seals off the residential quarters (used for weddings, banquets, private functions). East of Neizhaimen is the

Tower of Refuge where the Kong clan could gather in case the peasants turned nasty. It has an iron-lined ceiling on the ground floor, and a staircase that is removable to the 1st floor. Grouped to the west of the main axis are former recreational facilities (studies, guest rooms, libraries, small temples). To the east is the odd kitchen, ancestral temple and the family branch apartments. Far north is a spacious garden with rockeries, ponds and bamboo groves. Kong Decheng, the last of the line, lived in the Mansions until the 1940s when he hightailed it to Taiwan.

Confucian Forest
(kǒng lín) 孔林
North of the Confucius Mansions, about 2½ km up Lindao Lu, is the Confucian Forest, the largest artificial park and best preserved cemetery in China. This timeworn route has a kind of 'spirit-way' lined with ancient cypresses.

It takes about 40 minutes to walk, or 10 minutes by auto-rickshaw. On the way, look into the Yanhui Temple *(yán miào)* which is off to the right and has a spectacular dragon head embedded in the ceiling of the main hall, and a pottery collection. The route to the forest passes through the Eternal Spring Archway, its stone lintels decorated with coiled dragons, flying phoenixes and galloping horses dating from 1594 (Ming Dynasty).

Visitors, who needed permission to enter, had to dismount at the Forest Gates. The pine and cypress forest of over 20,000 trees, planted by followers of Confucius, covers 200 hectares and is bounded by a wall 10 km long. Buried here is the Great Sage himself and all his descendants. Flanking the approach to Confucius' Tomb are a pair of stone panthers, griffins and larger-than-life guardians. The Confucian tumulus is a simple grass mound enclosed by a low wall, and faced with a Ming Dynasty stele. Nearby are buried his immediate sons. Scattered through the forest are dozens of temples and pavilions, and hundreds of sculptures, tablets and tombstones.

Mausoleum of Shao Hao
(shǎo hào líng) 少昊陵
Shao Hao was one of the five legendary emperors supposed to have ruled China 4000 years ago. His pyramidal tomb, four km north-east of Qufu, dates from the Song Dynasty and is made of large blocks of stone, 25 metres wide at the base, six metres high, with a small temple on top. Some Chinese historians believe that Qufu was built on the ruins of Shao Hao's ancient capital, but evidence to support this is weak.

Places to Stay
The place where most travellers stay is right in the Confucius Mansions themselves – the *Confucius Mansions Hotel* (☎ 412374, 412686). For genuine classical architecture, it's hard to beat. Rooms come in three standards of elegance and cleanliness, but all have private baths. Prices for doubles are Y25, Y60 and Y160. However, the food here is forgettable. When you enter the main gate at the south side of the Mansions, the hotel is just to your left – it blends in so well with the architecture that you could easily miss it.

There are a few obscure privately run hostels *(zhāodàisǔo)* along Gulou Dajie and Nanmen Dajie that will sometimes take foreigners, depending on how desperate they are for business. Prices should be no more than Y10 in the dormitories.

The new up-market place in town is the *Queli Hotel* (☎ 411300, 411303) *(quèlǐ bīnshè)*, 1 Queli St, where singles cost Y100 and doubles are Y130 – the height of luxury.

Places to Eat
Apart from the usual dirt cheap noodle stands near the bus station, there is a good *Islamic Restaurant* on Gulou Dajie with a sign in English.

Things to Buy
In the Confucius Temple there are some free-marketeers who do intricate personalised carving on chops and ballpoint pens while

you wait. The ballpoint pen engraving, done with a kind of gold leaf, can be ordered in dragon designs – with the name of a friend added it makes an excellent gift. These vendors will do a chop with an English name that the top shops in Shanghai refuse to do (because it's not 'art'). The Friendship Store is also in the Confucius Temple and sells stele-rubbings for calligraphy lovers.

Getting There & Away

Bus There are about a dozen Qufu to Yanzhou buses a day. The first bus to Yanzhou departs Qufu at 6 am, the last is at 5.40 pm – there's possibly another bus at 6.30 pm. The fare costs around Y1 and the trip takes about 30 minutes. The last bus from Yanzhou to Qufu leaves at about 5 pm.

In addition to the crowded public buses, minibuses do the trip for Y2 per person. They run late into the night as long as they can get enough passengers, or they'll serve as taxis if you pay them enough.

There are direct buses from Qufu to Tai'an for Y6 (two hours, four departures daily) and direct buses from Qufu to Ji'nan (two departures daily).

Train There's no direct railway to Qufu. When a railway station project for Qufu was first brought up, the Kong family petitioned for a change of routes, claiming that the trains would disturb the Great Sage's tomb. They won in the end – the clan still had pull in those days – and the nearest the tracks go is Yanzhou, 13 km to the west of Qufu. The railway builders haven't given up; CAAC is next in line to disturb the sage's tomb, with an airport planned at Qufu.

Yanzhou is on the line from Beijing to Shanghai. There's a fair selection of trains, but note that some special express trains don't stop at Yanzhou; others arrive at inconvenient times like midnight. Yanzhou is two hours by train from Tai'an, three from Ji'nan, about seven from Nanjing, and about nine hours from Kaifeng.

Leaving Qufu is easy enough – check at the Qufu CITS office for services connecting with the train at Yanzhou.

ZOUXIAN

(zōuxiàn) 邹县

This is the home town of Mencius *(mèngzi)* (372-289 BC) who is regarded as the first great Confucian philosopher. He developed many of the ideas of Confucianism as they were later understood. Zouxian is to the south of Qufu, a short hop on the train from Yanzhou.

ZIBO

(zībó) 淄博

Zibo is a major coal-mining centre on the railway line east of Ji'nan. Over two million people live in this city noted for its glassworks and porcelain. Not far from Zibo, at Linzhi, a pit of horses dating back some 2500 years was excavated. They are older than the horses at Xi'an and with one big difference – they are the remains of actual animals. So far, 600 horse skeletons, probably dating from Qi times (479-502 AD), have been discovered. Horses and chariots indicated the strength of the state, so it's not surprising that they were buried in the course of their master's funeral. About 90 horse skeletons are on display side by side in the pit.

QINGDAO

(qīngdǎo) 青岛

Qingdao is a remarkable replica of a Bavarian village, plonked on the Bohai Gulf – a city of red-tiled roofs and European angles, shapes and echoes, right down to the gardens. Like Shanghai, it evokes an eerie feeling of *déjà vu*. It was a simple fishing village until 1897 when German troops landed (the killing of two German missionaries having given them sufficient pretext). In 1898 China ceded Qingdao to Germany for 99 years, along with the right to build the Shandong railways and to work the mines for 15 km on either side of the tracks.

The Germans developed Qingdao as a coaling station and naval base, and when the Ji'nan to Qingdao rail line was finished in 1904, harbour facilities blossomed, electric lighting appeared, the brewery (established 1903) belched beer, and a modern town arose. It was divided into European, Chinese and business sections. The Germans founded missions and a university and, before long, Qingdao rivalled Tianjin as a trading centre, its independence from China maintained by a garrison of 2000 soldiers.

For a city with such a short history, Qingdao has seen a lot of ping pong. In 1914 the Japanese occupied it, in 1922 the Chinese wrested it back, but it fell to the Japanese again in 1938 and was then recaptured by the Kuomintang. The official history states that the people of Qingdao engaged in heroic struggles against the imperialists and the Kuomintang, and that industrial production has increased 10-fold since 1949.

The latter claim, it would seem, is not exaggerated. Behind the innocuous facade of a beach resort is a monstrous mess of factories. Not only does Qingdao brew up the nation's drinking supplies but it is also the largest industrial producer in Shandong, concentrating on diesel locomotives, automobiles, generators, machinery and light industry (watches, cameras, TVs, textiles). It has a population of 1.5 million, though its jurisdiction spreads over 5900 sq km and another 3.5 million people.

If you ignore the megalopolis behind it – and most do – Qingdao has remarkable charm and is colourful for a Chinese city (irony intended). One can indulge in the guessing game of who once occupied its well-preserved mansions, or how they operated. The present function of the larger edifices is a combination of naval base, cadre playground and sanatorium. The town is a favourite for rest and recuperation, and for top-level meetings.

Qingdao means 'green island', and the waterfront promontory, backed by undulating hills, is a true garden city. The misty beauty of the place is unmistakable with the visual stimulation of the sea, the parks and the patterns of boats and mansions. Heavy traffic is absent, and there's no sign of strenuous labour or pollution in the old German part of the city. Down this end you can't see much of the industrial zones so they don't spoil the view. Sauntering along the esplanade is the thing to do in Qingdao and, of course, sunbaking.

The German presence lingers strongly in Qingdao: in the famous beer, in the villas stretching along the beaches, in the railway station with the vintage clocks. At night you seem to travel further back in time to the pages of a Gothic novel. In the old German quarter you'll find low-powered street lamps, dimly lit apartments, smoke rising from chimneys, chinks of light in a turret or attic window, the outlines of a cathedral, the hoot of a passing train; all you need is a heavy fog. Only the shapes of cyclists, hurtling out of the darkness, break the spell – they almost run you over. But for a town that produces such copious quantities of beer, wine and spirits, Qingdao is pretty dead at night – with not a drunk in sight, and lights out at nine.

Nevertheless, there is one form of old-style 'entertainment' which appears to have made a comeback.

After more than two months of travelling in China, I was never approached by prostitutes – that is, until I got to Qingdao. No sooner had I checked into my room at the Beihai Hotel than there was a knock on my door. I opened it to find a miniskirted young lady offering her services for sale. I was amused, but turned down her offer. Congratulating myself on my moral integrity, I headed out to see the sights of the city. Less than an hour later, I was approached by another prostitute right opposite the Public Security Bureau. Why do they pick on me?

Information

CITS This office (☎ 270695) is behind the Huiquan Dynasty Hotel at 9 Nanhai Lu, but they're not particularly helpful to individual travellers. Try them for tours of the brewery, shell-carving factory and locomotive factory.

Public Security Bureau This is at 29 Hubei Lu in a beautiful old building with a clock tower, very close to the Overseas Chinese Hotel.

Money Money and travellers' cheques can be changed at the Friendship Store in the

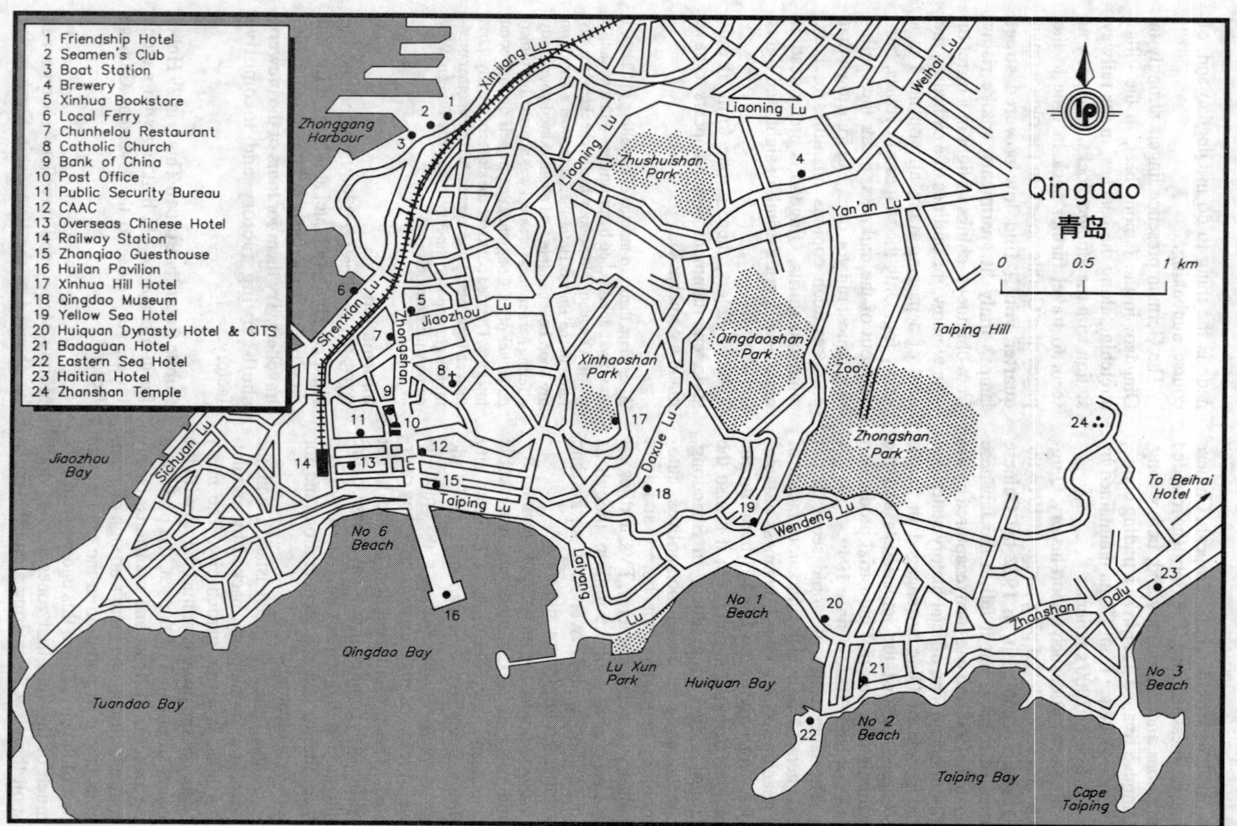
Qingdao
青岛
0
0.5
1 km
1 Friendship Hotel
2 Seamen's Club
3 Boat Station
4 Brewery
5 Xinhua Bookstore
6 Local Ferry
7 Chunhelou Restaurant
8 Catholic Church
9 Bank of China
10 Post Office
11 Public Security Bureau
12 CAAC
13 Overseas Chinese Hotel
14 Railway Station
15 Zhanqiao Guesthouse
16 Huilan Pavilion
17 Xinhua Hill Hotel
18 Qingdao Museum
19 Yellow Sea Hotel
20 Huiquan Dynasty Hotel & CITS
21 Badaguan Hotel
22 Eastern Sea Hotel
23 Haitian Hotel
24 Zhanshan Temple
Zhonggang Harbour
Xinjiang Lu
Weihai Lu
Liaoning Lu
Liaoning Lu
Zhushuishan Park
Yan'an Lu
Shenxian Lu
Zhongshan Lu
Jiaozhou Lu
Qingdaoshan Park
Taiping Hill
Xinhaoshan Park
Zoo
Zhongshan Park
Daxue Lu
Jiaozhou Bay
Sichuan Lu
Taiping Lu
To Beihai Hotel
Wendeng Lu
No 6 Beach
Laiyang Lu
No 1 Beach
Zhanshan Dalu
Qingdao Bay
Lu Xun Park
Huiquan Bay
No 3 Beach
Tuandao Bay
No 2 Beach
Taiping Bay
Cape Taiping

1	友谊饭店
2	海员俱乐部
3	海港客运站
4	青岛啤酒厂
5	新华书店
6	小港码头
7	春和楼
8	天主教堂
9	中国银行
10	邮局
11	公安局外事科
12	中国民航
13	华侨饭店
14	火车站
15	栈桥宾馆
16	回澜阁
17	迎宾馆
18	青岛博物馆
19	黄海饭店
20	汇泉王朝大酒泉
21	八大关宾馆
22	东海饭店
23	海天大酒店
24	湛山寺

Friendship Hotel. The Bank of China is at 62 Zhongshan Lu.

Post There is a small post office on the ground floor of the International Seamen's Club *(hǎiyúan jùlèbù)*, next to the Friendship Hotel. There is also one just south of the Bank of China on Zhongshan Lu (see map).

Beaches

(hǎishǔi yùchǎng) 海水浴场

Along the coast there are six beaches all with fine white sand. Taking the setting into account, they're hard to beat. The swimming season is from June to September, when the beaches are crowded, but there's also the possibility of fog and rain from June to August. Water temperature is soupy, and sea breezes are pleasant. Beaches are sheltered and have changing sheds (you can hire demure swimsuits), shower facilities, photo booths, stores and snack bars. Swimming areas are marked off with buoys and Bondi-Beach-style shark nets, lifeboat patrols, lifeguards and medical stations. Your chances of drowning at Qingdao, in other words, are absolutely nil. Don't pass up Qingdao in other seasons – spring and autumn bring out the best in local foliage and there are some spectacular flowers.

Just around the corner from the railway station is the No 6 Bathing Beach. This strip is particularly lively early in the morning when joggers, fencers, taiji exponents, old men reading newspapers and a few frisbee players turn out. Street-stall breakfast queues form, and there's a busy cottage industry that involves picking over the rocks and beach at low tide. Most of the Chinese people are on (privileged) vacation and it's quite an eye-opener to see them so relaxed.

Huilan Pavilion *(húilán gé)*, on a jetty thrusting into the sea, holds occasional art and craft exhibitions – worth the stroll, anyhow. Continuing east, around the headland past the lighthouse is Lu Xun Park *(lǔ xùn gōngyúan)* which has the combined Marine Museum & Aquarium. The Marine Museum has stuffed and pickled sea life. The Aquarium has sea life that would be better off stuffed or pickled, or in someone's soup. These tiny buildings are billed as the most famous of their kind in China; we'd hate to see the other ones.

Never mind, you're now at the start of the No 1 Bathing Beach. While it's no Cable Beach (Western Australia), it's certainly flash for China, and bodies of all shapes and sizes jam the sands in summer. This is the largest beach in Qingdao, with a 580-metre stretch of fine sand, lots of facilities, multi-coloured bathing sheds, restaurants (where you can munch prawns to 'Waltzing Matilda' on the Muzak), ridiculous dolphin statues, and high-rise blocks rather like a Chinese version of Surfer's Paradise. Plonk yourself down on the sand and all sorts of odd people will come up to you. This is the hang-out of the Chinese 'winter swimmers' whose marvellous sun-bronzed physiques don't step into the water until winter; they are said to make bad husbands because they're always at the beach. The beach also has Public Security 'moral guardians' who ensure that indecent gymnastics between consenting couples don't get out of hand.

Past the Huiquan Dynasty Hotel and the Ocean Research Institute you come to the Badaguan *(bādàgūan)* area, well known for its sanatoriums and exclusive guesthouses. The spas are scattered in lush wooded zones off the coast, and the streets, named after passes (Badaguan literally means 'Eight Passes Area'), are each lined with a different tree or flower. On Jiayuguan Lu it's maples and on Zhengyangguan it's myrtles. The locals simply call them Peach St, Snowpine St or Crab Apple St. The gardens here are extremely well groomed.

As you head out of the Eight Passes Area, bathing beaches 2 and 3 are just east, and the villas lining the headlands are exquisite. No 2 Beach is smaller, quieter and more sheltered than No 1 and is preferred when No 1 is overloaded. Facing No 2 are sanatoriums – but at the western headland is a naval installation, so don't take short cuts.

At the eastern end of the No 2 beach is the former German Governor's Residence. This castle-like villa, made of stone, is a replica of a German palace. It is said to have cost 2,450,000 taels of silver. When Kaiser Wilhelm II got the bill, he immediately recalled the extravagant governor and sacked him.

Brewery

(qīngdǎo píjiǔchǎng) 青岛啤酒场

No guide to Qingdao would be complete without a mention of the brewery, tucked into the industrial part of town, east of the main harbour. Qingdao Beer (formerly marketed as Tsingtao Beer) has gained a worldwide following.

The brewery was established early this century by the Germans who still supply the parts for 'modernisation' of the system. The flavour of the finest brew in Asia comes from the mineral waters of nearby Laoshan. First exported in 1954, the beer received the national silver medal for quality in China (as judged by the National Committee on Wines & Liquors in 1979). Pilgrimages to the brewery are reserved for tour groups, but if you want to visit the best bet would be to approach CITS at the Huiquan Dynasty Hotel to organise a guide and taxi (don't count on it though). Some people have simply fronted up at the factory and been shown around. Otherwise the drink is on tap in town, it's cheap enough in the stores and it's sold all over China.

Other

There are numerous parks in Qingdao. Zhongshan Park *(zhōngshān gōngyúan)* is north of the Huiquan Dynasty Hotel, covers 80 hectares, has a teahouse and temple and in springtime is a heavily wooded profusion of flowering shrubs and plants.

Further west of the park on Daxue Lu is the Qingdao Museum *(qīngdǎo bówùgǔan)* with a collection of Yuan, Ming and Qing paintings. Crossing the map north-west of that is an impressive piece of architecture, the Xinhao Hill Hotel *(xìnhàoshān yíng bīngǔan)*, at the edge of a park.

Off Zhongshan Lu, up a steep hill, is a structure now simply known as the Catholic Church *(tiānzhǔ jiàotáng)* – its double spires can be spotted a long way off. The church is active and services are held on Sunday mornings.

If you're into factories, Qingdao has several. Besides beer making, factories that CITS tours might observe include jade carving, shell carving, locomotives and embroidery. Enquire at CITS if interested.

Places to Stay – bottom end

The *Peace Hotel* (☎ 223231) *(hépíng bīngǔan)* and the *Friendship Hotel* (☎ 28865) *(yǒuyí bīngǔan)* are both in the complex around the Friendship Store and the boat station on Xinjiang Lu in the north-west end of town. The Friendship Hotel has become the established hang-out for budget travellers, with dormitory beds for about Y15 (bargaining is necessary), and double rooms starting at Y30. Both hotels are dumps, but you get what you pay for. The Peace Hotel is behind the Seamen's Club and Friendship Store, through a small alley to the right of the boat station.

If you arrive in Qingdao by boat, these two hotels are just a step away. If you arrive by train then it's a bit complicated. First take bus No 6 along Zhongshan Lu to the northern terminal, where it turns around. Then walk back under an overhead bridge near the terminal, turn right, and – if you can find the stop – take the No 21 bus for one stop north. If you can't find it then just walk the last stretch. (Qingdao buses are too horrendously crowded to even contemplate taking two in a row.)

Increasingly popular is the *Eastern Sea Hotel (dōnghǎi fàndiàn)* where dormitories are Y15. Bus No 26 from the railway station goes there.

Places to Stay – middle

The *Beihai Hotel* (☎ 365832) *(běihǎi bīnguǎn)* is somewhat inconvenient, eight km from the railway station in a not too attractive part of town. Doubles are Y130. You can get there on bus No 31.

The very central *Overseas Chinese Hotel* (☎ 279092) *(húaqiáo fàndiàn)* at 72 Hunan Lu, near the railway station, is often full. Doubles are Y150.

The *Yellow Sea Hotel* (☎ 270215) *(húanghǎi fàndiàn)*, 75 Yan'an 1-Lu has doubles for Y180. It's the 19-storey building to the north-west of the Huiquan Dynasty Hotel.

Places to Stay – top end

The *Badaguan Hotel* (☎ 366169) *(bādàgūan bīngǔan)*, 19 Shanhaiguan Lu, is adjacent to the No 2 Beach and has doubles for Y200. It can be reached on bus No 26.

The *Zhanqiao Guesthouse* (☎ 270502) *(zhànqiáo bīngǔan)* at 31 Taiping Lu is a marvellous old colonial villa facing the waterfront. Doubles are Y220.

The *Haitian Hotel* (☎ 366185) *(hǎitiān dàjiǔdiàn)*, 39 Zhanshan Dalu, is at the No 3 Beach. Doubles cost Y300.

The high-rise *Huiquan Dynasty Hotel* (☎ 279215) *(hùiqúan wángqiáo dàjiǔdiàn)* at 9 Nanhai Lu, presides over the No 1 Beach. Double rooms go for around Y300. To get there take bus No 6 from near the railway station.

Places to Eat

One of the best restaurants in town is supposed to be the one between the Friendship Store and the Seamen's Club, on the 2nd floor; it serves both of them. It offers a large range of seafood (swordfish, red snapper, scallops, and shellfish), all at very fishy prices (higher if you take a private booth). An attached bar serves cold dishes like jellyfish and cucumber as well as drinks. The only problem is trying to pin down the opening hours.

If you want some cheaper fare and are staying at either the Peace or the Friendship hotels, there are a couple of decent little restaurants in the general vicinity dishing up jiaozi, beer and simple Chinese dishes.

Zhongshan Lu also has several restaurants. The top one is the *Chunhelou* (☎ 227371) *(chūnhélóu)*, 146 Zhongshan Lu. The seafood is pricey but the Qingdao beer is served in real pint mugs.

For morning baozi and cakes go to the rather illustrious-looking *Tianfu Restaurant* (☎ 225205) *(tiānfū jiǔjià)*, 210 Zhongshan Lu, near the northern end of the street. It's open from 6.30 am.

There are some cafes, sidewalk stalls and up-market canteens such as the *White Spray (báilànghūa)* near the Huiquan Dynasty Hotel. They serve large plates of things like prawns, dumplings and bean curd – none of which are particularly inspiring. Take potluck – that's what the signs say.

Alcohol in this town is plentiful and cheap. There's a huge stock of Tsingtao Red in the department stores on Zhongshan Lu.

Things to Buy

The busiest shopping area is along Zhongshan Lu which has an antique store at No 40, and the Arts & Crafts Service Department at the north end. Good buys are plaited straw wares (hats, mats), shell carvings (there's a small retail shop on a side street leading from Zhongshan Lu to the station) and, for instant consumption, good cheap grog. Several market streets spill off the north end of Zhongshan Lu.

Getting There & Away

Air Qingdao is connected to Beijing (three times weekly, Y224), Canton (daily, Y626), Changchun, Chengdu, Dalian (twice weekly), Fuzhou, Harbin, Hefei, Ji'nan, Nanjing, Ningbo, Qinhuangdao, Shanghai (three times weekly, Y240), Shenyang, Wuhan, Xi'an (three times weekly), Xiamen and Zhengzhou. The CAAC office (☎ 88047) is at 29 Zhongshan Lu.

Train All trains from Qingdao go through the provincial capital of Ji'nan, except for the direct Qingdao to Yantai trains. There are two direct trains daily to Beijing (17 hours). There is only one train daily to Yantai, departing at about 9 am.

Direct trains to Shenyang (about 26 hours) pass through Ji'nan and Tianjin, sidestepping Beijing. There are direct trains to Xi'an (about 31 hours) which continue to Lanzhou and Xining.

Trains to Dalian and to Shanghai (about 24 hours) will take almost the same time as the boats. There is one train daily to Shanghai. The train is much more expensive than the boat – there's a foreigners' mark-up on the train but not on the boat.

Bus There is one bus daily to Yantai, departing at 8.50 am.

Boat There are regular boats from Qingdao to Dalian and Shanghai. There are usually five classes on these boats, including four, six and eight-berth cabins, plus a 'special class' which is about twice the price of 1st class.

The boat to Dalian (on the Liaoning Peninsula), across the Bohai Gulf, is the best way to get there from Qingdao. (It's a long way by train.) The boat takes 26 hours and leaves every four days, but sometimes there can be gaps of up to eight days. The boat is comfortable and fares range from Y10.50 in 5th class to Y59 in 1st class.

You could also take a train from Qingdao to Yantai and catch the boat from Yantai to Dalian. Fares range from Y6.20 in 5th class to Y35 in 1st class.

The boat from Qingdao to Shanghai departs Qingdao every day and the trip takes about 27 hours. Fares range from Y12.20 in 5th class to Y67.90 in 1st class. The ship is reportedly clean and comfortable, with friendly and helpful staff.

In Qingdao tickets can be bought in the large waiting hall at the boat dock near the Friendship Store.

Getting Around

Most transport needs can be catered for by the bus No 6 route which starts at the north end of Zhongshan Lu, runs along it to within a few blocks of the main railway station and then east to the area above No 3 Beach. The bus stops marked on maps of Qingdao appear to have no relation to reality. The No 6 bus stop closest to the main railway station seems to be the one on Zhongshan Lu, just north of the street leading to the Catholic Church. If you're stuck for transport then an auto-rickshaw from outside the railway station may help.

AROUND QINGDAO

Laoshan

(láoshān) 崂山

Forty km east of Qingdao is Laoshan, a mountain area covering some 400 sq km. It's an excellent place to go hiking or climbing – the mountain reaches an elevation of 1133 metres. Historical sites and scenic spots dot the area, and the local product is Laoshan mineral water. The Song Dynasty Taiqing Palace (a Taoist monastery) is the central attraction; there are paths leading to the summit of Laoshan from there. With such a large area there's plenty to explore. Due north of the Taiqing Palace is Jiushui, noted for its numerous streams and waterfalls.

An early morning bus runs from Qingdao railway station to the Taiqing Palace. Other travel agents around Qingdao have more extended itineraries, including an overnight stop in Laoshan; but it's probably hard to crash these tours unless you speak Chinese.

YANTAI

(yāntái) 烟台

Yantai, alias 'Zhifu' (at one time spelled 'Chefoo'), is a busy ice-free port on the northern coast of the Shandong Peninsula. Like Qingdao it grew from a defence outpost and fishing village but, although opened for foreign trade in 1862, it had no foreign concessions. Several nations, the Japanese and the Americans among them, had trading establishments there and Yantai was something of a resort area at one time. About 60 km east of Yantai by road, the British had a concession at Weihai around the turn of the century – it's now a major port from where a boat connects with Inchon in South Korea (see the introductory Getting There & Away chapter). Since 1949 the port and naval base at Yantai have been expanded and (apart from fishing and trading) the town is a major producer of wines, spirits and fruits.

Information

CITS There is an office (☎ 25625) in the Yuhuangding Hotel and also in the Overseas Chinese Hotel. They're set up to handle stray seamen and the tourist ships – when, for instance, a Scandinavian liner disgorges 500 passengers for five hours on their shores.

Things to See & Do

Apart from drinking and building sand castles, there's very little to see or do . Group tours are corralled off to a fish-freezing factory, a brandy distillery or the orchards behind the town. Yantai's beaches are not the greatest – they're unsheltered and prone to heavy wind-lashing.

The main one is hemmed in at the south-west side by an industrial complex and a naval establishment. Beach No 2, out by the Zhifu Hotel, is smaller and more pleasant, but difficult to get to.

A convenient tour of the town can be done on local bus No 3 which leaves from the square near the rail and boat stations. The bus cuts through Yantai, taking in the older parts of town (which are being eaten away by apartment blocks and factory chimneys), and goes past the odd colonial edifice and newer sections. It takes half an hour to get to Yantaishan Park (Yantai Hill) and then turns around at the Yantai Hill terminal. If you get off at the terminal and follow a stone wall from there up to the headland, you get a nice view of the naval dockyards, heavy shipping and even navy manoeuvres.

Yantai means 'smoke-terrace': wolf-dung fires were lit on the headland to warn fishing fleets of approaching pirates, a practice that continued during the Opium wars. If you carry on round the headland, you hit the esplanade at No 1 Beach where there is some distinctively European architecture – former foreign trading or resort housing. You can continue to the bus No 1 route, which will take you back into town.

Places to Stay

Finding a cheap and convenient place is difficult in Yantai. Right on the waterfront at the bus No 3 terminal is the *Yantai Hill Hotel* (☎ 24491) *(yāntáishān bīngǔan)*, a beautiful but expensive villa overlooking the sea. It used to be a tourist hotel but now takes Chinese people only. Doubles are Y130, if you can get in – or roll up your sleeves and fight for a dormitory. If you say you're only staying one night, leaving by train or boat the next day and the other hotels are too far out you might be lucky.

The Yuhuangding Hotel (☎ 22088) *(yùhúangdǐng bīngǔan)* on Yuhuangding Xilu is the location of CITS and is meant to be the main tourist haven in Yantai. Doubles start at Y100. From the railway station area, you can reach the hotel on bus No 7.

Another place to try is the *Overseas Chinese Hotel* (☎ 24431) *(húaqiáo bīngǔan)* at 15 Huanshan Lu. Doubles are Y100 but you can push for a cheaper room. Take bus No 7 to the terminal – the hotel is about 300 metres beyond.

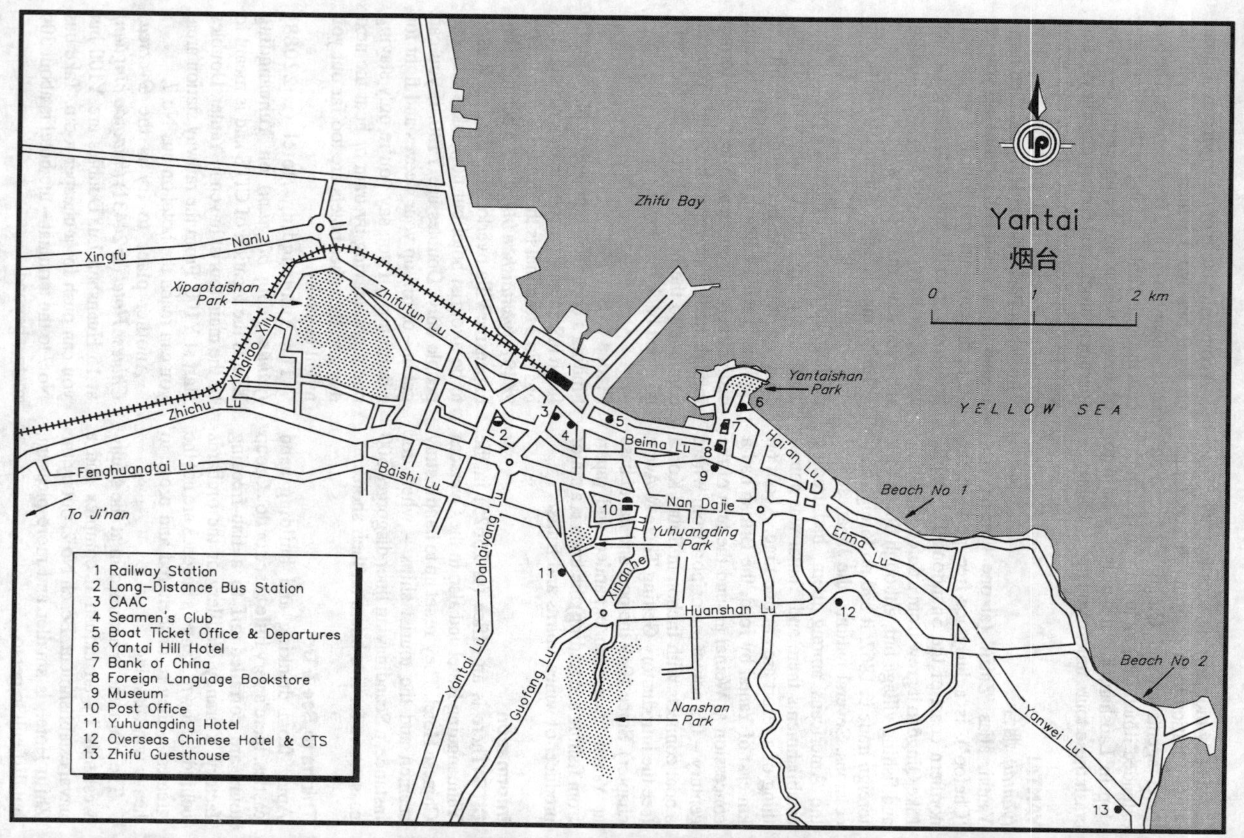
Yantai
烟台
0
1
2 km
YELLOW SEA
Zhifu Bay
Yantaishan Park
Beach No 1
Beach No 2
Xipaotaishan Park
Yuhuangding Park
Nanshan Park
Xingfu
Nanlu
Xingiao Xilu
Zhifutun Lu
Zhichu Lu
Fenghuangtai Lu
To Ji'nan
Baishi Lu
Dahaiyang Lu
Yantai Lu
Guofang Lu
Beima Lu
Hai'an Lu
Nan Dajie
Erma Lu
Xinanhe
Lu
Huanshan Lu
Yanwei Lu
1 Railway Station
2 Long-Distance Bus Station
3 CAAC
4 Seamen's Club
5 Boat Ticket Office & Departures
6 Yantai Hill Hotel
7 Bank of China
8 Foreign Language Bookstore
9 Museum
10 Post Office
11 Yuhuangding Hotel
12 Overseas Chinese Hotel & CTS
13 Zhifu Guesthouse

1	火车站
2	长途汽车站
3	中国民航
4	海员俱乐部
5	海港客运站
6	烟台山公园
7	中国银行
8	外文书店
9	博物馆
10	邮局
11	毓璜顶宾馆
12	华侨宾馆
13	芝罘宾馆

The high-rise *Zhifu Guesthouse* (☎ 24381) *(zhīfu bīngǔan)* has been built about eight km from the station. It's an expensive, nice place but a transport disaster. You need two buses to get there (Nos 3 and 5), and the last one is a rare species indeed. In other words, you could end up commuting by taxi. Otherwise it's hitching or jumping the laundry bus which runs into town from the hotel every morning. There's nothing in the vicinity of the hotel except the No 2 Beach, about 10 minutes' walk away, a set menu in the dining hall and a conference room for 200, which is for reclusive meetings (with participants ferried in by minibus).

Places to Eat

The *Yantai Restaurant* (☎ 25365) *(yāntái fàndiàn)* is a large eatery between the railway station and the boat station. There are three rooms: the central one is the cheapest and has a mass of proletarian clientele with about four chairs between them – it's stand-up noodles, dumplings, beggars and bowls of hot water. The other two sections have beer, bigger and meatier dishes – and chairs.

The *International Seamen's Club* (☎ 25127) *(hǎiyúan jùlèbù)* is just south of the railway station on Beima Lu.

As for alcohol, you can buy the stuff anywhere, including the railway station. It's very cheap, and there's some evil-looking substance that retails for less Y1. Yantai is famous for rose-petal wine *(méigūijiǔ)*, brandy *(báilándì)* and red and white wines – renowned brands are Yantai Red, Weimeisi Wine and Jinjiang Brandy.

Getting There & Away

Air There are flights to Beijing (four times weekly, Y193); Canton (three times weekly, Y700); and Shanghai (three times weekly Y293).

Train Trains approach Yantai from both Ji'nan and Qingdao. There are express trains to Beijing (about 17½ hours) and a direct but slow train to Shanghai. Both trains pass through Ji'nan (about 12 hours from Yantai).

There is only one train a day between Yantai and Qingdao (five hours).

Bus There is one bus daily between Yantai and Qingdao, departing before 9 am.

Boat The rail trip to Dalian, on the Liaoning Peninsula, takes a circuitous route. Faster are the daily boats from Yantai. From Yantai to Dalian is Y40 (1st class), Y20 (2nd class, two-bed cabin), Y12 (3rd class, four-bed cabin), Y9 (4th class, eight to 10-bed cabin) and Y8 (5th class, which you'd rather not know about). The boat leaves Yantai at 8 pm and arrives in Dalian at 6 am the next day. There are other boats between Yantai and Tianjin (berthing at Tianjin's Tanggu Harbour) which run once every five days.

AROUND YANTAI

Penglai

(pénglái) 蓬莱

About 65 km north-west of Yantai by road is the coastal castle of Penglai, a place of the gods which is often referred to in Chinese mythology. The castle *(pénglái gé)* is perched on a clifftop overlooking the sea and is about a thousand years old. The last full mirage seen from this site was in July 1981 when two islands appeared, with roads, trees, buildings, people and vehicles. This phenomenon lasted about 40 minutes (if it had lasted any longer, little red flags and factory chimneys would no doubt have appeared!). There are some pebbly beaches in the area and a seafood restaurant. Penglai is a two-hour bus ride from Yantai.

Hebei 河北

Wrapping itself around the centrally administered municipalities of Beijing and Tianjin is the province of Hebei *(hébĕi)*. It is often viewed either as an extension of Beijing, the red tape maker, or of Tianjin, the industrial giant. This is not far off the mark since, geographically speaking, they take up a fair piece of the pie. In fact, Tianjin used to be Hebei's capital, but when that came under central government administration the next largest city, Shijiazhuang, replaced it. Over 55 million people live in Hebei.

Topographically Hebei falls into two distinct parts: the mountain tableland to the north, where the Great Wall runs (and also to the western fringes of the province), and the monotonous southern plain. Agriculture, mainly wheat and cotton growing, is hampered by dust storms, droughts (five years in a row from 1972 to 1977) and flooding. These natural disasters will give you some idea of the weather. It's scorching and humid in summer and freezing in winter, with dust fallout in spring and heavy rains in July and August.

Coal is Hebei's main resource and most of it is shipped through Qinhuangdao, an ugly port town with iron and steel and machine industries.

As far as tourist sights go, there's Beidaihe, the weirdest summer resort you'll ever visit, and Chengde with its remaining palaces and temples. Shijiazhuang – the capital city – is a waste of time. There's also Tangshan, the city that disappeared in a few minutes when an earthquake registering eight on the Richter scale struck it on 28 July 1976. The big attraction here is going to be the casting section of a rolling-stock plant, with rusty equipment and rubble of walls and steel. Officials in Tangshan say there are no plans to clean it up – rather, it will be left for future generations to ponder.

Apart from all these, the best thing to see is the Great Wall, which makes everything else look insignificant.

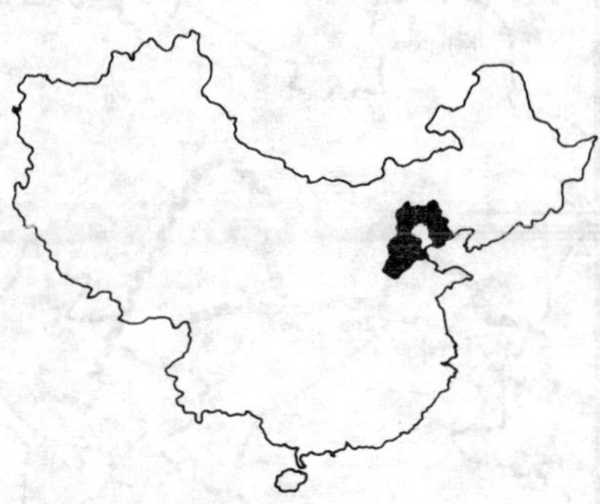

CHENGDE

(chéngdé) 承德

Chengde is an 18th-century imperial resort area, also known as Jehol. It's billed as somewhere to escape from the heat (and now the traffic) of summers in the capital and boasts the remnants of the largest regal gardens in China.

Chengde remained an obscure town until 1703 when Emperor Kangxi began building a summer palace here with a throne room and the full range of court trappings. More than a home away from home, Chengde turned into a sort of government seat, since where the emperor went his seat went too. Kangxi called his summer creation Bishu Shanzhuang (Fleeing-the-Heat Mountain Villa).

By 1790, during the reign of his grandson Qianlong, it had grown to the size of Beijing's Summer Palace and the Forbidden City combined. Qianlong extended an idea started by Kangxi, to build replicas of minority architecture in order to make envoys feel comfortable. In particular he was keen on promoting Tibetan and Mongolian Lamaism, which had proved to be a useful way of debilitating the meddlesome Mongols. The Mongolian branch of Lamaism required one male in every family to become a monk – a convenient method of channelling man-

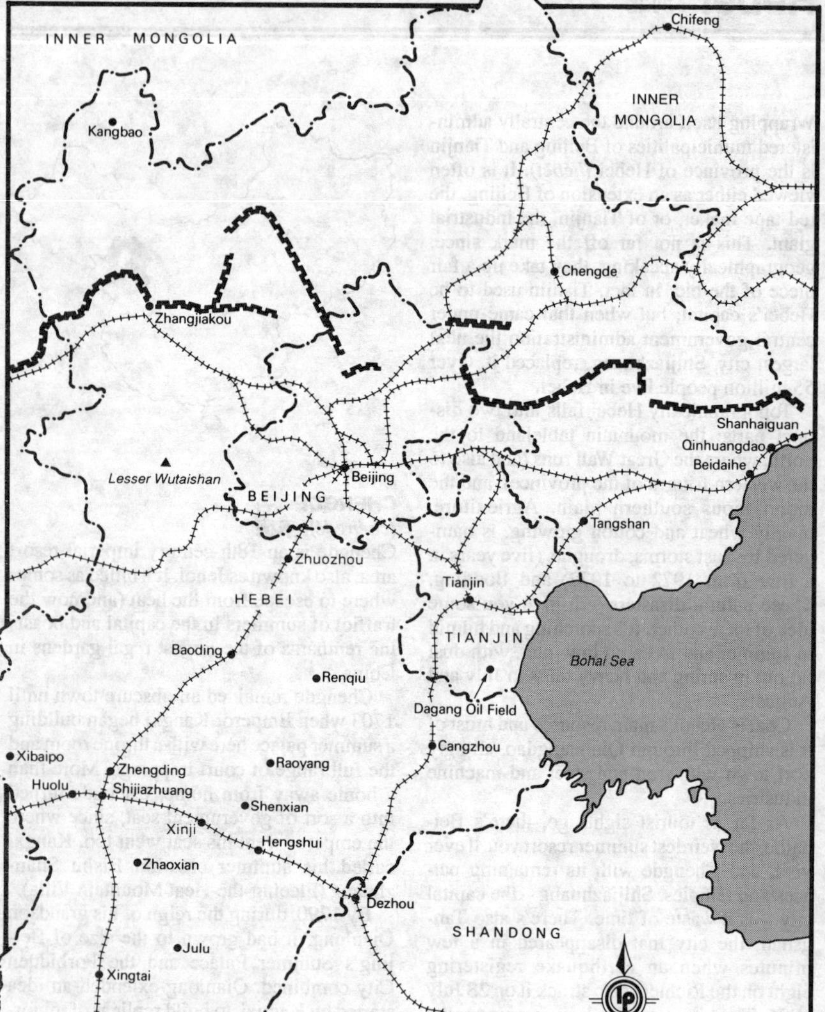

INNER MONGOLIA
Chifeng
Kangbao
INNER MONGOLIA
Chengde
Zhangjiakou
Shanhaiguan
Qinhuangdao
Beidaihe
Lesser Wutaishan
Beijing
BEIJING
Tangshan
Zhuozhou
Tianjin
HEBEI
TIANJIN
Baoding
Bohai Sea
Renqiu
Dagang Oil Field
Xibaipo
Raoyang
Cangzhou
Zhengding
Huolu
Shijiazhuang
Shenxian
Xinji
Hengshui
Zhaoxian
Dezhou
SHANDONG
Julu
Xingtai
Ji'nan
Handan
lp
Hebei
河北
0 50 100 km

power and ruining the Mongol economy. This helps explain the Tibetan and Mongolian features of the monasteries north of the summer palace, one of them a replica of the Potala Palace in Lhasa.

So much for business – the rest was the emperor's pleasure: the usual bouts of hunting, feasting and orgies. Occasionally the outer world would make a rude intrusion into this dream life. In 1793 British emissary Lord Macartney came along seeking to open trade with China. Qianlong dismissed him with the statement that China possessed all things and had no need of trade.

Chengde has very much slipped back into being the provincial town it once was, its grandeur long decayed, its monks and emperors long gone. The population of over 150,000 is engaged in mining, light industry and tourism. The Qing court has left them a little legacy, but one that needs working on. The palaces and monasteries are not what they're cracked up to be, or, alternatively, more cracked up than you'd expect them to be. The Buddhist statues are disfigured, occasionally beyond recognition, or locked up in dark corners; windows are bricked up, columns are reduced to stumps and the temples are facades – impressive from the outside but shells inside.

All this is currently being restored, in some cases from the base up, in the interests of a projected increase in tourism. It's on the cards that Chinese and Western restaurants, high-class shops, evenings of traditional music (with instruments copied from those rescued from tombs around China) and horse riding will be introduced. Meanwhile there's absolutely nothing wrong with ruins – it's just a matter of changing your expectations. Chengde has nothing remotely approaching Beijing's temples, in case you were expecting something along those lines. Chinese photography of the place is more a tribute to the skills of the photographers and lab technicians than anything else.

The dusty, small-town ambience of Chengde is nice enough and there's some quiet hiking in the rolling countryside. Chinese speakers are apparently delighted with the clarity of the local dialect (maybe because they can actually hear it in the absence of traffic).

Information

CITS You'll find them (☎ 226827) next to the Yunshan Hotel in a green sheet-metal building that looks temporary but isn't. The staff are very friendly and helpful.

Public Security Bureau This office (☎ 223091) is on Wulie Lu.

Money The Bank of China is right next to the Yunshan Hotel and CITS.

Maps Good maps of Chengde seem to be rare. A tourist map in Chinese is sold by street vendors near the Xinhua Hotel. Some of the hotel gift shops also have these.

Imperial Summer Villa

(bìshǔ shānzhūang) 避暑山庄

Otherwise known as 'Fleeing-the-Heat Mountain Villa', this park covers 590 hectares and is bounded by a 10 km wall. Emperor Kangxi decreed that there would be 36 'beauty spots' in Jehol; Qianlong delineated 36 more. That makes a total of 72, but where are they? At the north end of the gardens the pavilions were destroyed by warlords and Japanese invaders, and even the forests have suffered cutbacks. The park is on the dull side, and hasn't been very well maintained. With a good deal of imagination you can perhaps detect traces of the original scheme of things with landscaping borrowed from the southern gardens of Suzhou, Hangzhou and Jiaxing, and from the Mongolian grasslands. There is even a feature for resurrecting the moon, should it not be around – a pool shows a crescent moon created by the reflection of a hole in surrounding rocks.

Passing through Lizhengmen, the main gate, you arrive at the Front Palace, a modest version of Beijing's palace. It contains the main throne hall, the Hall of Simplicity and Sincerity, built of an aromatic hardwood called *nanmu* and now a museum displaying royal memorabilia, arms, clothing and other

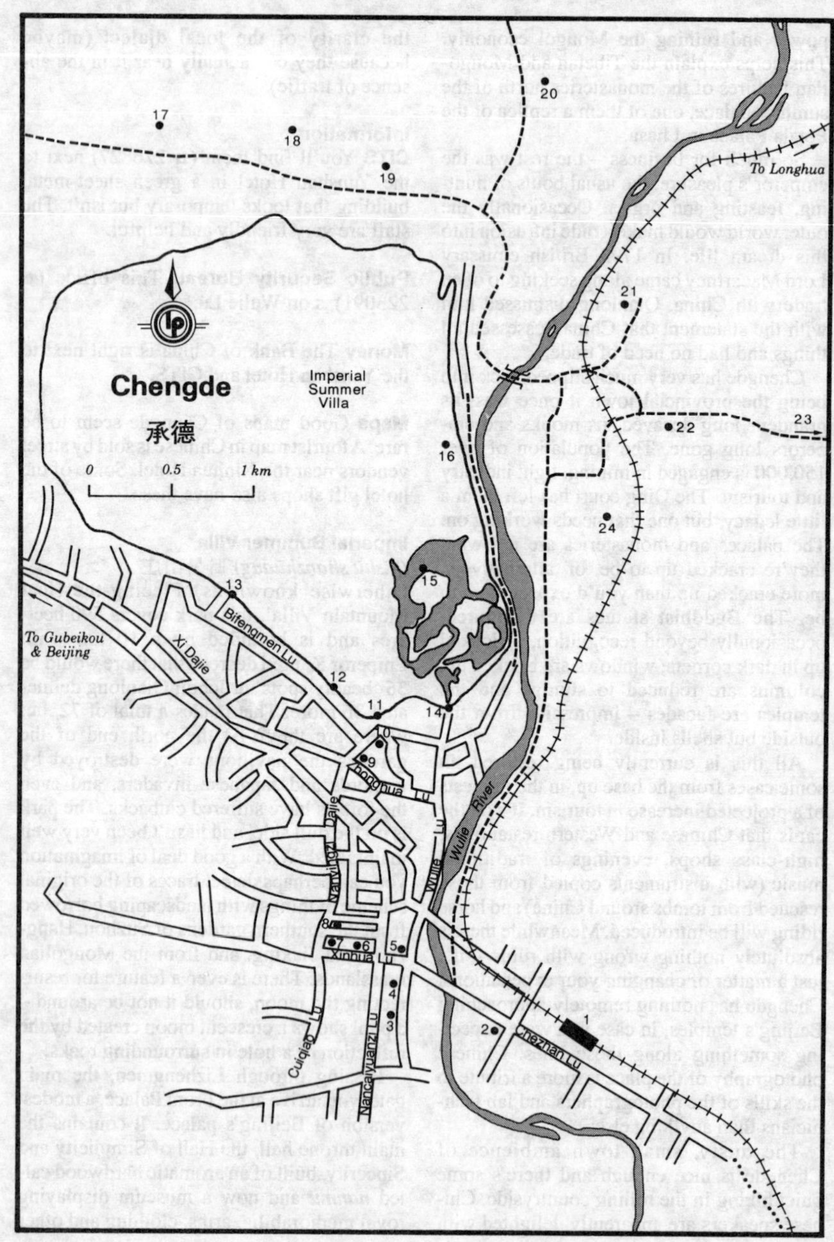
Chengde
承德
Imperial Summer Villa
To Longhua
To Gubeikou & Beijing
0
0.5
1 km
Bifengmen Lu
Xi Dajie
Zhonghua Lu
Nanyingzi Dajie
Wulie Lu
Wulie River
Xinhua Lu
Cuiqiao Lu
Nancaiyuanzi Lu
Chezhan Lu
1
2
3
4
5
6
7
8
9
10
11
12
13
14
15
16
17
18
19
20
21
22
23
24

1 Railway Station
2 Chengde Hotel (new)
3 Yunshan Hotel
4 Bank of China & CITS
5 Long-Distance Bus Station
6 Xinhua Hotel
7 Post Office
8 Chengde Hotel (old)
9 Lizhengmen Hotel
10 Mountain Villa Hotel
11 Lizhengmen (Main Gate)
12 Qiwanglou Hotel
13 Bifeng Gate
14 Dehui Gate
15 Misty Rain Tower
16 Mongolian Hotel
17 Shuxiang Temple
18 Putuozongsheng Temple
19 Xumifushou Temple
20 Puning Temple
21 Anyuan Temple
22 Pule Temple
23 Hammer Rock
24 Puren Temple

accoutrements. The emperor's bedrooms are fully furnished. Around to the side is a door without an exterior handle through which the lucky bed partner for the night was ushered and stripped and searched by eunuchs.

The double-storey Misty Rain Tower, on the north-west side of the main lake, was an imperial study. Further north is the Wenjin Chamber, built in 1773 to house a copy of the *Sikuquanshu*, a major anthology of classics, history, philosophy and literature commissioned by Qianlong. The anthology took 10 years to put together. Four copies were made but three have disappeared; the fourth is in Beijing.

Ninety per cent of the compound is taken up by lakes, hills, mini-forests and plains, with the odd vantage-point pavilion. At the northern part of the park the emperors reviewed displays of archery, equestrian skills and fireworks. Horses were also chosen and tested here before hunting sorties. Yurts were set up on the mock-Mongolian prairies (a throne, of course, installed in the emperor's yurt) and picnics were held for minority

1 火车站
2 承德大厦
3 云山饭店
4 中国银行
5 长途汽车站
6 新华饭店
7 邮局
8 承德宾馆
9 丽正门旅馆
10 山庄宾馆
11 丽正门
12 绮望楼
13 碧峰门
14 德汇门
15 烟雨楼
16 蒙古包
17 殊像寺
18 普陀宗乘之庙
19 须弥福寿之庙
20 普宁寺
21 安远寺
22 普乐寺
23 棒槌山
24 溥仁寺

princes. So, it's a good idea to pack a lunch, take your tent and head off for the day...the yurts have returned for the benefit of weary tourists.

Eight Outer Temples
(wàibā miào) 外八庙

To the north and north-east of the imperial garden are former temples and monasteries. So how many are there? The count started off at 11 many years ago, plummeted to five (Japanese bombers, Cultural Revolution), and now the number varies between five and nine. The outer temples are from three to five km from the garden's front gate; a bus No 6 taken to the north-east corner will land you in the vicinity.

The surviving temples were built between 1750 and 1780. The Chinese-style Puren Temple and the vaguely Shanxi-style Shuxiang Temple have undergone total rebuilding. Get out there in the early morning when the air is crisp and cool and the sun is shining on the front of the temples – that's the best time to take photos. Clockwise, these are the temples:

Putuozongsheng Temple *(pǔtúozōngshèng zhī miào)* Putuozongsheng (Potaraka Doctrine), the largest of the Chengde temples, is a mini-facsimile of Lhasa's Potala. It was built for the chieftains from Xinjiang, Qinghai, Mongolia and Tibet to celebrate Qianlong's 60th birthday and was also a site for religious assemblies. It's a solid-looking fortress, but is in bad shape – parts are inaccessible or boarded up and gutted by fire. Notice the stone column in the courtyard inscribed in Chinese, Tibetan, Mongolian and Manchurian scripts.

Xumifushou Temple *(xūmǐfúshòu zhī miào)* Xumifushou (the Temple of Sumeru, Happiness and Longevity) was built in honour of the sixth Panchen Lama, who visited in 1781 and stayed here. It incorporates elements of Tibetan and Han architecture and is an imitation of a temple in Shigatse, Tibet. At the highest point is a hall with eight gilded copper dragons commanding the roof ridges, and behind that sits a glazed-tile pagoda.

Puning Temple *(pǔníng sì)* Puning (the Temple of Universal Tranquillity) is also modelled on a Tibetan temple. It was built to commemorate Qianlong's victory over Mongol tribes when the subjugated leaders were invited to Chengde. A stele relating the victory is inscribed in Tibetan, Mongol, Chinese and Manchu. The main feature is an Avalokitesvara towering 22 metres; this wooden Buddha has 42 arms with an eye on each palm. The temple appears to be used as an active place of worship.

Anyuan Temple *(ānyǔan miào)* Only the main hall remains of Anyuan (the Temple of Far Spreading Peace) – a copy of a Xinjiang temple. It contains Buddhist frescoes in a very sad state.

Pule Temple *(pǔlè sì)* Pule (the Temple of Universal Happiness) is definitely the most interesting of the temples. You can scramble along the banks of the nearby rivulet to a road that leads off near a pagoda at the garden wall.

The temple was built in 1776 for visits of minority envoys (Kazakhs among them). It's in much better shape than the other temples and has been retiled and repainted. At the rear of the temple is an unusual Round Pavilion, reminiscent of Beijing's Temple of Heaven, which has a magnificent ceiling.

You can hike to Hammer Rock *(bàngchúishān)* from Pule. It has nothing to do with sharks – the rock is meant to resemble an upside down hammer. There are commanding views of the area from here. Other scenic rocks to add to your collection include Toad Rock and Monk's Hat Hill. The hiking is pleasant and the scenery is good.

Places to Stay

The old *Chengde Hotel (chéngdé bīngǔan)* on Nanyingzi Dajie has comfortable double rooms for between Y70 and Y85. A bed in a three-bed room in the Chinese wing is around Y15 – spartan but habitable. Bus No 7 from the railway station drops you right outside the hotel.

It's a half-hour walk if you arrive after the bus has stopped running. There are two hotels called the Chengde Hotel – the one close to the railway station is new, expensive and has no dorms.

Another cheap place is the *Xinhua Hotel (xīnhúa fàndiàn)* on Xinhua Lu, south of the old Chengde Hotel. Double rooms with a bath go for Y40. This hotel often claims to be full when a foreigner shows up, but you might still give it a try.

The new *Chengde Hotel* (☎ 227373) *(chéngdé dàxià)*, Chezhan Lu, is a fancy high-rise close to the railway station. Doubles cost Y120.

The classy tourist hang-out is the *Yunshan Hotel* (☎ 226171) *(yúnshān fàndiàn)*, 6 Nanyuan Jie Donglu next to CITS. Doubles range from Y120 to Y170 and are squeaky clean with plush carpeting and air-con.

Alternatively there's the *Mountain Villa Hotel (shānzhūang bīngǔan)*. Doubles start at Y90. The rooms are comfy with TVs and a private bathroom. Take bus No 7 from the railway station and then a short walk; the hotel is opposite the entrance to the Imperial Summer Villa.

There are two hotels just within the walls of the Imperial Summer Villa. On the west side is the *Qiwanglou Hotel (qǐwànglóu bīngǔan)* built in Qing Dynasty style. It's a three-star hotel with doubles ranging from Y130 to Y170. Further north and on the east side is the *Mongolian Hotel (ménggǔbāo)* where doubles cost between Y110 and Y150. It's designed in yurt style with air-con, carpet, telephone, and TV – not even Genghis Khan had it this good.

Places to Eat

There are two main market streets – one just west of the long-distance bus station, and the other just north of the post office. The local speciality is food made from haws (wine, ice-cream, sweets). Chengde Pule beer has an interesting flavour – perhaps it's the mountain water. There are lots of trolleys around town dispensing tasty baked turnip.

The Chinese restaurant on the 2nd floor of the *Yunshan Hotel* has delicious food, generous portions and is amazingly cheap given the sumptuous surroundings. There is a Western restaurant on the 1st floor of the hotel but, as the Chinese say, it's 'horse-horse tiger-tiger' (so-so).

Getting There & Away

The regular approach to Chengde is by train from Beijing. The fast train departs Beijing at 7.17 am. It's an excellent train with soft seats for Y48 – there's even a non-smoking car! The same train returns to Beijing at 2.31 pm. The one-way trip takes less than five hours. There are slower trains which take over seven hours.

An unexplored route to or from Chengde is the train from Jinzhou, which is in Liaoning Province on the way to Shenyang. There are also trains direct from Chengde to Dandong, via Jinzhou and Shenyang; sleepers are available even though the train originates in Beijing.

From Longhua, about 40 km north of Chengde, there is a fast evening train to Datong (Shanxi Province) and Hohhot (Inner Mongolia), with a brief stop at Xizhimen station in Beijing. Sleepers are available. To get to Longhua from Chengde, there are several slow trains a day.

There are also long-distance buses between Chengde and Beijing. The airport at Chengde is for military use only, though charter flights for affluent tour groups are a possibility.

Tours are available from CITS in Beijing. A complete tour to Chengde costs Y349 (two days) or Y549 (three days), but you can manage on your own more cheaply.

Getting Around

The only practical way to see all the tourist sights in one day is to take a tour. Fortunately, there are sightseeing bus tours (Chinese-speaking only) for just Y8. These depart at 8 am from the Lizhengmen Hotel *(lìzhèngmén lǚgǔan)*. This hotel is for Chinese people only, but foreigners can join the tour.

As for city buses, there are half a dozen bus lines but the only ones you'll probably need to use are the No 7 from the station to the old Chengde Hotel, and No 6 to the outer temples grouped at the north-east end of town. The best way to get around town and to the outer temples is on a bicycle; there is a rental place opposite the old Chengde Hotel. They ask you to leave some ID or a deposit. Motorised pedicabs and auto-rickshaws congregate outside the railway station.

BEIDAIHE-QINHUANGDAO-SHANHAIGUAN

The Beidaihe-Qinhuangdao-Shanhaiguan

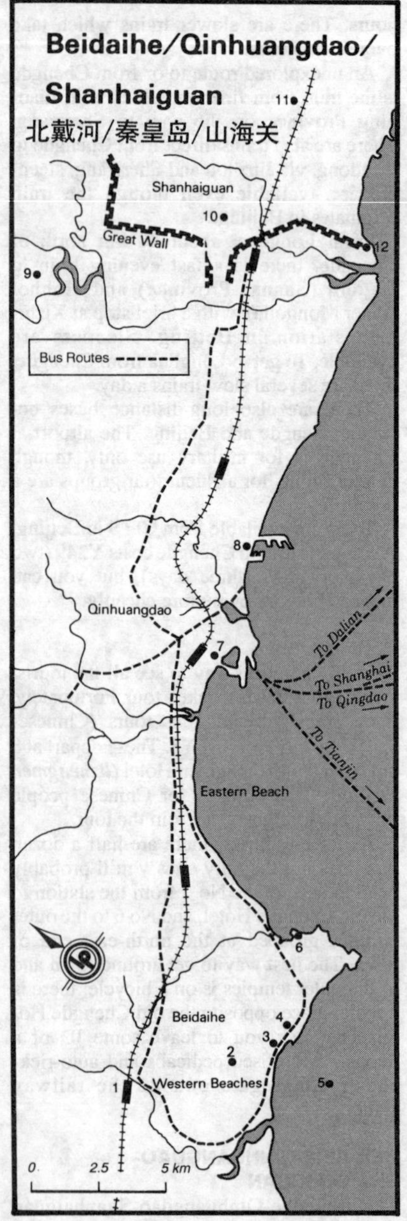

1 Beidaihe Railway Station
2 Lianfengshan Park
3 Central Beach
4 Bus Terminal/Market Area
5 Tiger Rocks
6 Pigeon's Nest
7 Seamen's Club
8 Oil Wharf
9 Yansai Lake
10 First Pass Under Heaven
11 Mengjiangnü Temple
12 Old Dragon Head

1 北戴河火车站
2 联峰山公园
3 中海滩
4 海滨汽车站
5 老虎石
6 鸽子窝
7 海员俱乐部
8 油码头
9 燕塞湖
10 天下第一关
11 孟姜女庙
12 老龙头

district, a 35-km stretch of coastline on China's east coast, borders the Bohai Sea.

Beidaihe

(běidàihé) 北戴河

This seaside resort, opened to foreigners in 1979, was originally built by Westerners but is now popular with both Chinese and non-Chinese. The simple fishing village was transformed when English railway engineers stumbled across it in the 1890s. Diplomats, missionaries and business people from the Tianjin concessions and the Beijing legations hastily built villas and cottages in order to indulge in the new bathing fad.

The original golf courses, bars and cabarets have disappeared, though there are signs that these will be revived in the interests of the nouvelle bourgeoisie. An article a few years ago in the *People's Daily* suggested: 'It does much good to both body and mind to putt and walk under fresh air'.

Something jars about this place, though the setting is right enough – hills, rocks, beaches, pine forests, a sort of Mediterranean flavour. The buildings appear too heavy to the modern eye, and lacking in glass. Then there's the occasional out-of-place Swiss alpine villa or some columnar structure better suited to Rome or Athens.

But really, who gives a damn about the architecture? Then, as now, Beidaihe is an escape from the hassles of Beijing or Tianjin. Kiesslings, the formerly Austrian restaurant, sells excellent pastries and seafood in the summer. The cream of China's leaders congregate at the summer villas, also continuing a tradition – Jiang Qing and Lin Biao had villas here, and Deng Xiaoping is said to have a heavily guarded residence.

Just to make sure nothing nasty comes by in the water, there are shark nets. It's questionable whether sharks live at this latitude – maybe they're submarine nets. Army members and working heroes are rewarded with two-week vacations at Beidaihe. There are many sanatoriums where patients can get away from the noise of the city.

That's about all you need to know about Beidaihe. The Chinese have worked the place over trying to categorise the rocks and deciding whether they're shaped like camels or tigers or steamed bread, or immortalising the rocks where Mao sat and wrote lines about fishing boats disappearing. Nobody gives a hoot – they come for the beaches.

Climate The village only comes to life in the summer (from June to September), when it's warm and fanned by sea breezes and the beaches are jammed. The average June temperature is 21°C (70°F). In January, by contrast, temperatures rest at -5°C (23°F).

Beaches There are three beaches at Beidaihe: West Beach, Middle Beach and East Beach. Rank and ethnic divisions once applied when using these beaches – the West Beach was reserved for foreigners, the Middle Beach for Chinese cadres and the like, and the East Beach for sanatorium patients – but this system appears to have been abandoned.

Other Attractions There are various hikes to vantage points with expansive views of villas or the coast. Some notable viewing places include the Sea-Facing Pavilion *(wànghǎi tíng)* at Lianfengshan Park *(liánfēngshān gōngyúan)*, about 1½ km north of the beach. Right on the shoreline is the Eagle Pavilion at Pigeon's Nest Park *(gēziwō gōngyúan)*. People like to watch the sunrise over Tiger Rocks *(lǎohǔ shí)*. The tide at the East Beach recedes dramatically and tribes of kelp collectors and shell-pickers descend upon the sands. In the high season you can even be photographed in amusing cardboard-cut-out racing boats, with the sea as a backdrop.

There may be some nightlife at the Guesthouse for Diplomatic Missions. The free market behind the bus terminal has the most amusing high-kitsch collection of sculpted and glued shellwork this side of Dalian – go and see. Handicrafts such as raffia and basketware are on sale in the stores. Some of these shops sell good maps of the area too.

Places to Stay There are only two places that accept foreigners. The *Guesthouse for Diplomatic Missions (wàijiāo rényúan bīngǔan)* has triples for Y45. It's a great place to stay, having the appearance and feel of an Indian tourist bungalow with huge verandahs, pillars and high-ceilinged rooms – all you'd need is the *dhobi* man to come knocking on the door. It's situated in a very quiet compound with a pleasant garden and its own beach. Hard-seat train tickets can be booked at the guesthouse; they need two days' notice.

Up-market there's the spick-and-span *Jinshan Guesthouse* (☎ 441678) *(jīnshān bīngǔan)* on the shorefront on Zhonghaitan Lu. Doubles cost Y165.

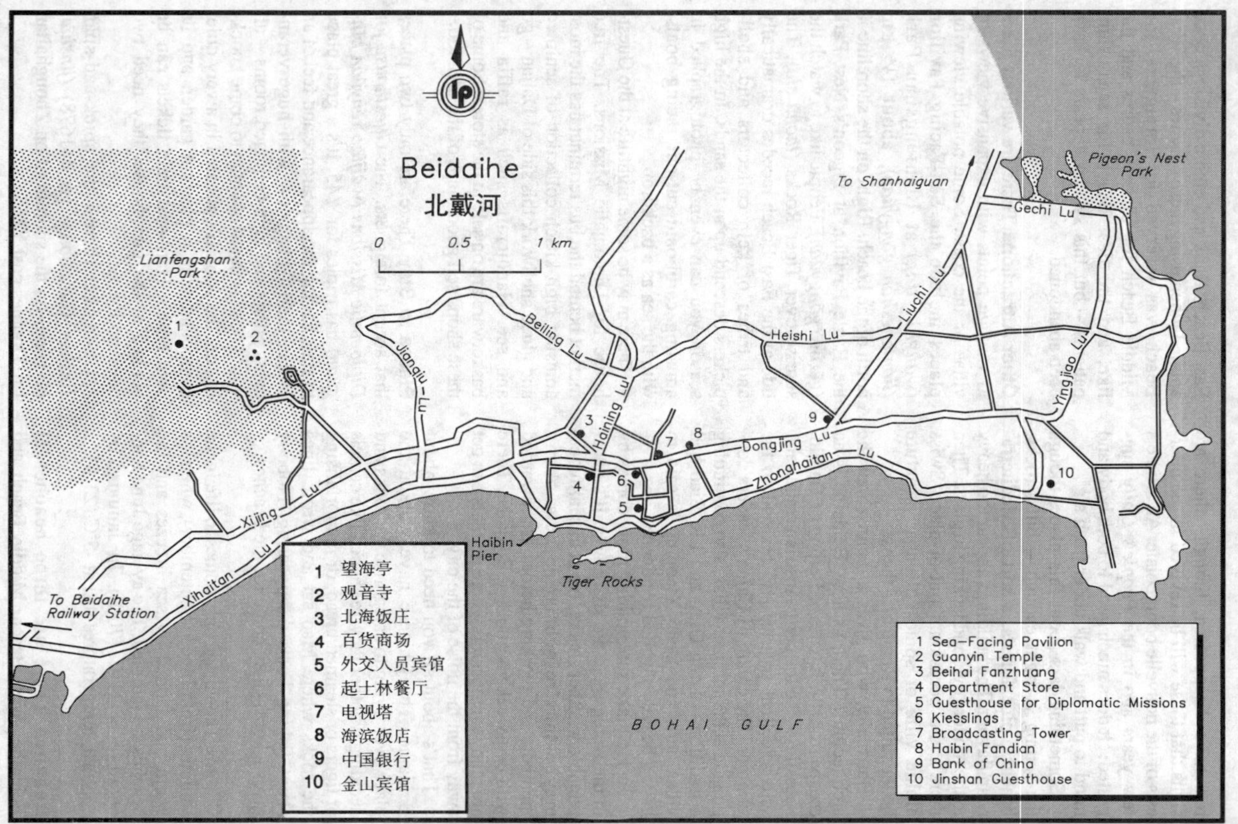

Beidaihe
北戴河
0
0.5
1 km
Lianfengshan Park
To Shanhaiguan
Pigeon's Nest Park
Gechi Lu
Liuchi Lu
Heishi Lu
Beiling Lu
Jiangiu Lu
Haining Lu
Yingjiao Lu
Dongjing Lu
Zhonghaitan Lu
Xijing Lu
Xihaitan Lu
Haibin Pier
Tiger Rocks
To Beidaihe Railway Station
BOHAI GULF
1 望海亭
2 观音寺
3 北海饭庄
4 百货商场
5 外交人员宾馆
6 起士林餐厅
7 电视塔
8 海滨饭店
9 中国银行
10 金山宾馆
1 Sea-Facing Pavilion
2 Guanyin Temple
3 Beihai Fanzhuang
4 Department Store
5 Guesthouse for Diplomatic Missions
6 Kiesslings
7 Broadcasting Tower
8 Haibin Fandian
9 Bank of China
10 Jinshan Guesthouse

Beidaihe provides a scenic backdrop to money-losing hotels that belong to individual work units. There is an Air Force Hotel, Tangshan Coal Workers Hotel, the National Traffic Bureau Hotel etc. These hotels are closed to all others and sit empty even during peak season, then suddenly fill to overflowing when the work unit has a meeting in Beidaihe. The exclusive villas are reserved for cadres.

Places to Eat In season, seafood is dished up in the restaurants. There's the *Beihai Fanzhuang* near the markets and the *Haibin Fandian* near the Broadcasting Tower. Near the Guesthouse for Diplomatic Missions is *Kiesslings (qǐshìlín cāntīng)*, which is a relative of the Tianjin branch, only operating from June to August. They have an outstanding bakery.

Getting Around There are a couple of short-run buses in Beidaihe, such as the one from the town centre to Pigeon's Nest (in summer only). Much of Beidaihe is small enough to walk around. Minibuses are easy to flag down and you can use them as taxis – negotiate the fare in advance.

There are a couple of bicycle rentals around town; look for rows of bikes. They'll charge about Y5 per day, and you'll have to leave a deposit or identification.

Qinhuangdao

(qínhúangdǎo) 秦皇岛

Qinhuangdao is an ugly port city that you'd have to squeeze pretty hard for signs of life, and even harder if you wanted to see something. It has an ice-free harbour, and petroleum is piped in from the Daqing Oilfield to the wharves.

Pollution on both land and sea is astonishing – this is *not* the place to visit. The locals will be the first to suggest that you move along to Beidaihe or Shanhaiguan.

If you do get stuck here most needs are catered for on a bus No 2 route from the railway station. This runs the short distance to the port where the Seamen's Club *(hǎiyúan jùlèbù)* has a hotel, restaurant (some seafood) and bar/store. Alternatively, you could walk in about 15 minutes.

Shanhaiguan

(shānhǎigūan) 山海关

Shanhaiguan is where the Great Wall meets the sea, or, should we say, crumbles into it. The wall, what's left of it, is in poor shape, but Shanhaiguan is well worth your time. It was a garrison town with a square fortress, four gates at the compass points, and two major avenues running between the gates. The present village is within the substantial remains of the old walled enclosure, making it a rather picturesque place to wander around. Shanhaiguan has a long and chequered history – nobody is quite sure how long or what kind of chequers – plenty of pitched battles and blood, one imagines.

First Pass Under Heaven *(tiānxià dìyī gūan)* Also known as the East Gate, this magnificent structure is topped with a two-storey, double-roofed tower (Ming Dynasty, rebuilt in 1639). The calligraphy at the top (attributed to the scholar Xiao Xian) reads the 'First Pass Under Heaven'. The words reflect the Chinese custom of dividing the world into civilised China and the 'barbarians'. The barbarians got the better of civilised China when they stormed this gate in 1644. An intriguing mini-museum in the tower displays armour, dress, weaponry and pictures. A short section of the wall attached to the east gate has been rebricked; from this vantage point you can see decayed sections trailing off into the mountains. On top of the wall at the tower are souvenir shops selling First Pass Under Heaven handkerchiefs, and a parked horse waiting for photos. How about a pair of 'First Pass Under Heaven Wooden Chopsticks' or some 'Brave Lucky Jewellery'?

Old Dragon Head *(lǎo lóng tóu)* These days the Old Dragon Head is basically just a beach – the original wall has long since crumbled away but a portion has recently been reconstructed here. The name is derived from the legendary carved dragon head that once

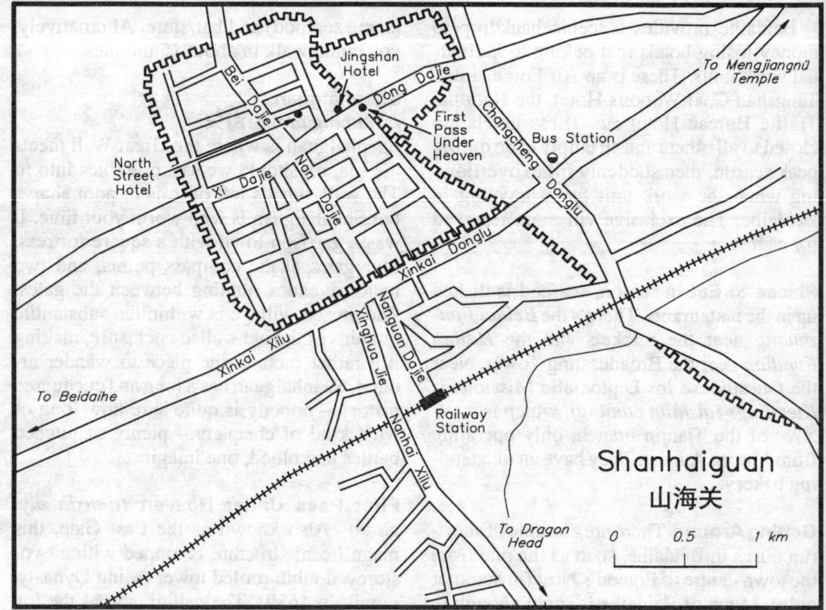

faced the sea. It's a four-km hike or taxi ride from the centre of Shanhaiguan. A more viable route is to follow (by road) the wall north to the first beacon tower. You can get part-way there by bicycle on a dirt road, and will pass a small village set in some pleasant countryside.

Yansai Lake *(yànsāi hú)* The lake is also known as Stone River Reservoir *(shíhé shǔikù)*. It's just six km to the north-west of Shanhaiguan. The reservoir is 45 km long and tourists can go boating here. Give them a few years and it could be another Guilin.

Mengjiangnü Temple *(mèngjiāngnǚ miào)* Six km east of Shanhaiguan (with a regular bus service from the south gate) is the Mengjiangnü Temple, a Song-Ming reconstruction. It has coloured sculptures of Lady Meng and her maids, and calligraphy on Looking for Husband Rock. Meng's husband, Wan, was press-ganged into wall building because his views conflicted with those of Emperor Qin Shihuang. When winter came the beautiful Meng Jiang set off to take her husband warm clothing only to discover that he had died from the back-breaking labour. Meng tearfully wandered the Great Wall thinking only of finding Wan's bones to give him a decent burial. The wall, obviously a sensitive soul, was so upset that it collapsed revealing the skeleton entombed within. Overcome with grief, Meng hurled herself into the sea from a conveniently placed boulder.

Places to Stay The cheapest place to stay is the *North Street Hotel (běijiē zhāodàisǔo)* where dorms cost Y14 and doubles are Y60, with a little bargaining. The spacious rooms come with fans and a private bathroom. The hotel is right near the First Pass (East Gate).

Also in the same neighbourhood is the up-market *Jingshan Hotel* (☎ 551130) *(jīngshān bīngǔan)* where doubles are Y80.

Top: Hawkers at Terracotta Army, Xian (AS)
Bottom Left: Scaling Tai Shan (AS)
Bottom Right: Street scene, Datong (RS)

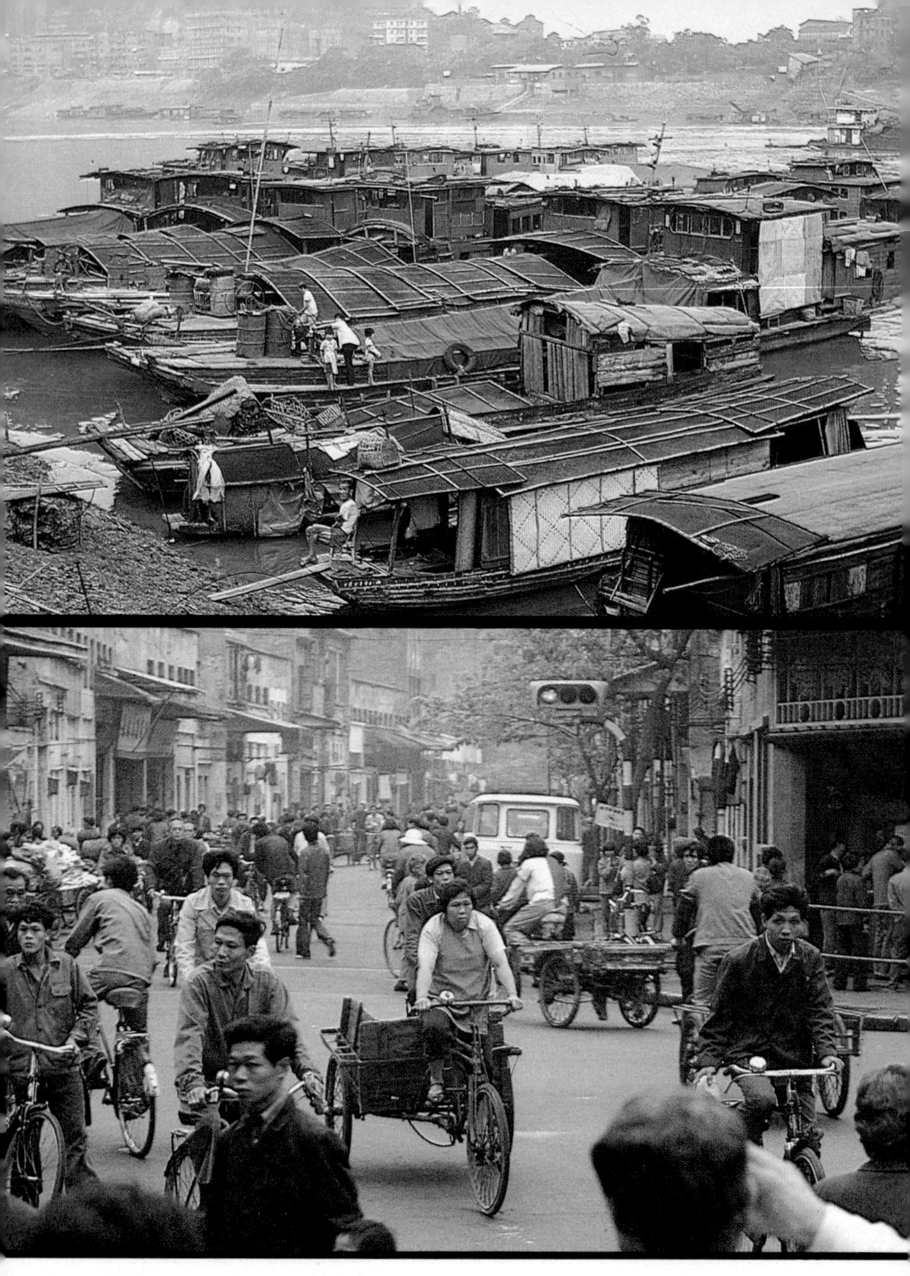

Top: River life, Wuzhou (AS)
Bottom: The blues and greys of a Canton winter (JH)

Getting There & Away

Air There is an airport at Qinhuangdao, but flights aren't frequent. The air service is used mostly by cadres on their way to meetings at the beachside in Beidaihe. Flights from Beijing, Canton and Shanghai are twice a week – all other flights are once weekly.

If you want to fly, there are flights from Beijing (Y105), Canton (Y766), Dalian, Harbin, Qingdao, Shanghai (Y452), Shenyang, Taiyuan, and Xi'an.

Train The three stations of Beidaihe, Qinhuangdao and Shanhaiguan are accessible by train from Beijing, Tianjin or Shenyang (Liaoning Province). The trains are frequent but don't always stop at all three stations or always arrive at convenient hours. The usual stop is Shanhaiguan; several trains skip Beidaihe.

The major factor to consider is that the hotel at Shanhaiguan is within walking distance of the railway station, whereas at Beidaihe the nearest hotel is at least 10 km from the station. This is no problem if you arrive during daylight or early evening – there are plenty of minibuses meeting incoming trains at Beidaihe station. However, you can't count on this at night and a taxi could be quite expensive. If you're going to arrive in the dead of night, it's better to do so at Shanhaiguan.

The fastest trains takes five hours to make it to Beidaihe from Beijing, and an extra 1½ hours to Shanhaiguan. From Shenyang to Shanhaiguan is a five-hour trip.

Alternatively, you could get a train that stops at Qinhuangdao and then take a bus from there to Beidaihe. Or you could jump a midnight train from either Beijing or Shenyang, arrive early in the morning, day-trip, and go on to the next place.

Boat There are some dubious maritime links between Qinhuangdao and Dalian, Shanghai, Qingdao and Tianjin, but it's unclear whether these carry freight or passengers. If they are passenger then the journey will be cheaper than by rail, and to Dalian the trip could also be shorter.

Getting Around

Buses connect Beidaihe, Shanhaiguan and Qinhuangdao. These generally run every 30 minutes from around 6 or 6.30 am to around 6.30 pm (not guaranteed after 6 pm). Minibuses are faster and less crowded, and can be flagged down easily. Some of the important public bus routes are:

No 5 Beidaihe railway station to Beidaihe Middle Beach, 30 minutes
No 3 & 4 Beidaihe to Qinhuangdao, 45 minutes
No 3 & 4 Beidaihe to Shanhaiguan via Qinhuangdao, one hour

SHIJIAZHUANG

(shíjiāzhūang) 石家庄

Shijiazhuang is a railway junction town about 250 km south-west of Beijing and, even though it is the capital of the province, is the odd town out in Hebei. Its population now approaches one million, but at the turn of the century it was just a small village with 500 inhabitants and a handful of buildings. With the construction of the Beijing to Wuhan Line in 1905 (financed by a Belgian company) and the Shijiazhuang to Taiyuan Line which was finished in 1907 (a Russian-French project) the town rapidly expanded to a population of 10,000 in the 1920s.

Shijiazhuang has the biggest officer training school in China; it's about two km west of the city. After the Beijing protests and subsequent killings in 1989, all the new students from Beijing University were taken to this 're-education camp' for a one-year indoctrination.

Shijiazhuang is an industrial city and the tomb of Dr Norman Bethune is just about all there is to see. Otherwise it's only useful as a transit point or a staging area for sights within the region.

Information

CYTS (☎ 615961) – a competitor of CITS – is in room 230 of the Hebei Guesthouse.

Revolutionary Martyrs' Mausoleum

(lièshì língyúan) 烈士陵园

The guerrilla doctor Norman Bethune (1890-

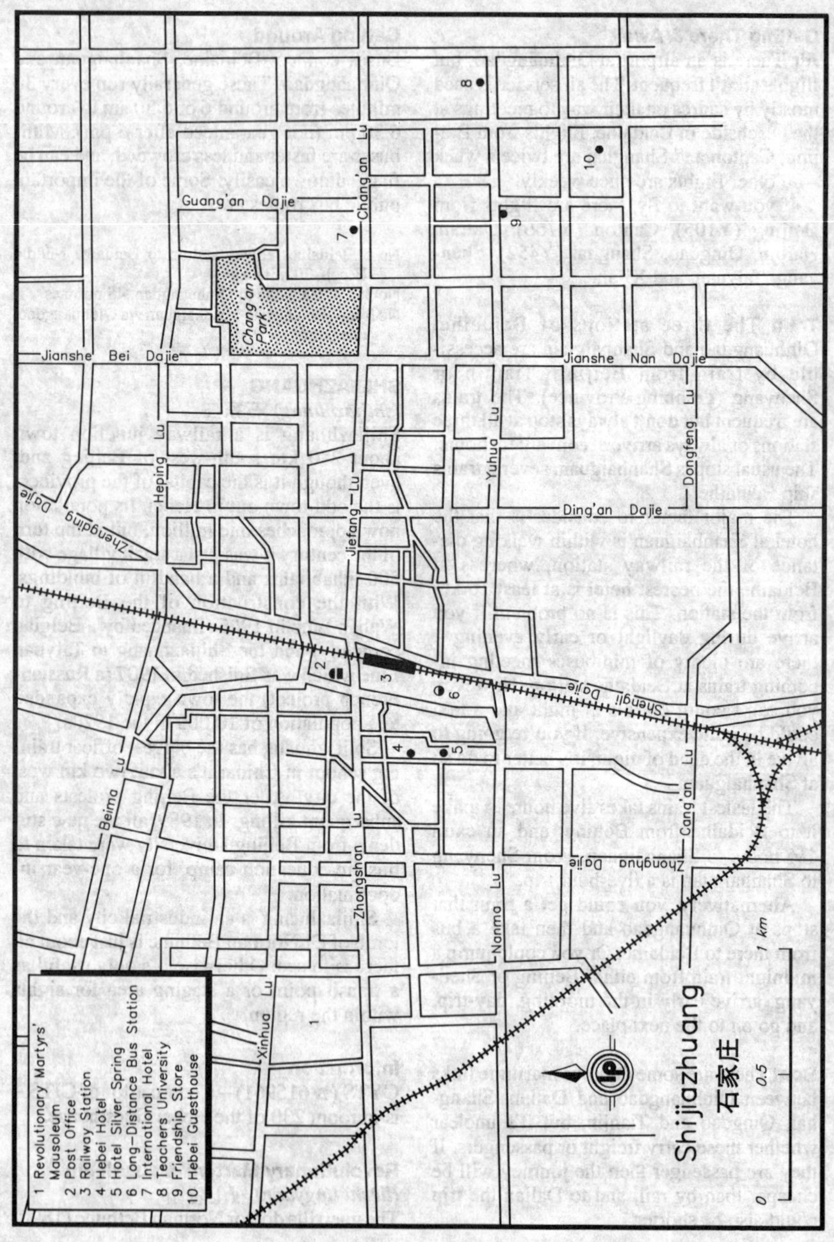
Shijiazhuang 石家庄
1 Revolutionary Martyrs' Mausoleum
2 Post Office
3 Railway Station
4 Hebei Hotel
5 Hotel Silver Spring
6 Long-Distance Bus Station
7 International Hotel
8 Teachers University
9 Friendship Store
10 Hebei Guesthouse
0
0.5
1 km
Guang'an Dajie
Chang'an Lu
Chang'an Park
Jianshe Bei Dajie
Jianshe Nan Dajie
Heping Lu
Jiefang Lu
Yuhua Lu
Dongfeng Lu
Ding'an Dajie
Zhengding Dajie
Shengli Dajie
Beima Lu
Zhongshan Lu
Nanma Lu
Cang'an Lu
Zhonghua Dajie
Xinhua Lu

1 华北烈士陵园
2 邮局
3 火车站
4 河北饭店
5 银泉酒家
6 长途汽车站
7 国际大厦
8 师范大学
9 友谊商店
10 河北宾馆

1939) is interred here: there is also a photo and drawing display depicting his life and works, and a white memorial. Bethune is the most famous 'foreign devil' in China since Marco Polo. Actually, most Chinese people don't know who Polo is, but they all know Bethune *(bái qiúēn)*. He goes down in modern history as the man who served as a surgeon with the Eighth Route Army in the war against Japan, having previously served with the Communists in Spain against Franco and his Nazi allies. Bethune is eulogised in the reading of Mao Zedong Thought: 'We must all learn the spirit of absolute selflessness from Dr Norman Bethune'.

In China, 'Bethune' is also synonymous with 'Canada' – it's about all the Chinese tend to know about the country, and bringing up the name makes for instant friendship if you're Canadian.

More than 700 army cadres and heroes buried in the cemetery died during the Resistance against Japan, the War of Liberation and the Korean War. The area is a large park; in the central alley is a pair of bronze Jin Dynasty lions dating from 1185. The Martyrs' Mausoleum is on Zhongshan Lu, west of the railway station. There is also a statue of Bethune in the courtyard of the Bethune International Peace Hospital of the PLA, a bit further west of the cemetery.

Places to Stay

The *Hotel Silver Spring* (☎ 26981) *(yínqúan jiǔjiā)* is right near the railway station. It's a bit run down, but the rooms are comfortable and the location is great. Doubles cost Y50. There is a strange rule here – you must give a Y50 deposit when you check in, which is refundable when you depart as long as you don't steal the towels or the TV.

Also near the railway station is the *Hebei Hotel (héběi fàndiàn)* where doubles range from Y87 to Y150.

The *International Hotel* (☎ 44321) *(gúojì dàxià)* is one of the up-market places in town. Doubles cost Y113. The restaurant is famous for its lousy food. You can get there on buses No 1 or 5 from the railway station.

The *Hebei Guesthouse* (☎ 615916) *(héběi bīngǔan)* is the most prestigious address in town. It's a modern eight-storey block with two restaurants and a bar. Doubles cost Y140. The hotel is at 23 Yucai Jie – take bus No 6 from the railway station, it stops close by.

Places to Eat

This may be the time to dig out that old jar of peanut butter at the bottom of your backpack. Even foreigners who have lived in Shijiazhuang for a long time (there are a few) seem to agree that if you want to eat well in this city, you'd better cook for yourself. Bethune certainly had no effect on the level of hygiene in Shijiazhuang. The restaurants and snack bars around the station come straight from Dante's *Inferno* – thick layers of dirt on the tables camouflage the greasy, disgusting food.

Getting There & Away

Air Considering that this is a major industrial city, there are amazingly few air connections. Perhaps nobody wants to come here? There are flights to Canton (twice weekly, Y612); Hohhot (four times weekly, Y135); Nanjing (once weekly, Y286); and Shanghai (twice weekly, Y380).

Train Shijiazhuang is a major rail hub with comprehensive connections: there are lines to Beijing (about four hours), Taiyuan (about five hours), Dezhou (about five hours) and Canton.

Getting Around

The long-distance bus station is north-east of the railway station and within walking distance. From there you can get buses to sights outside Shijiazhuang. Within the city there are 10 bus lines.

AROUND SHIJIAZHUANG

There's nothing spectacular in this part of Hebei, but there are a few places that you can visit.

Zhengding

(zhèngdìng) 正定

Ten km north of Shijiazhuang, this town has several temples and monasteries. The largest and oldest is the Longxing Monastery *(lóngxīng sì)*, noted for its huge, 20-metre-high bronze Buddha dating from the Song Dynasty almost 1000 years ago. The multi-armed statue is housed in the Temple of Great Mercy, an impressive structure with red and yellow galleries.

Zhaozhou Bridge

(zhàozhōu qiáo) 赵州桥

There's an old folk rhyme about the four wonders of Hebei which goes:

The Lion of Cangzhou
The Pagoda of Dingzhou
The Buddha of Zhengding
The Bridge of Zhaozhou

The bridge is in Zhaoxian County, about 40 km south-east of Shijiazhuang and two km south of Zhaoxian town. It has spanned the Jiao River for 1300 years and is possibly the oldest stone-arch bridge in China (another, believed older, has recently been unveiled in Linying County, Henan Province).

Putting the record books aside, Zhaozhou Bridge is remarkable in that it still stands. It is 50 metres long and 9.6 metres wide, with a span of 37 metres; the balustrades are carved with dragons and mythical creatures. Credit for this daring piece of engineering goes to a disputed source but, according to legend, the master mason Lu Ban constructed it overnight. Astounded immortals, refusing to believe that this was possible, arrived to test the bridge. One immortal had a wagon, another had a donkey, and they asked Lu Ban if it was possible for them both to cross at the same time. He nodded. Halfway across, the bridge started to shake and Lu Ban rushed into the water to stabilise it. This resulted in donkey-prints, wheel-prints and hand-prints being left on the bridge. Several more old stone bridges are to be found in Zhaoxian County.

Cangyanshan

(cāngyánshān) 苍岩山

About 78 km south-west of Shijiazhuang is a scenic area of woods, valleys and steep cliffs dotted with pagodas and temples. The novelty here is a bizarre, double-roofed hall sitting on a stone arch bridge spanning a precipitous gorge. It is known as the Hanging Palace, and is reached by a 300-step stairway. The palace dates back to the Sui Dynasty. On the surrounding slopes are other ancient halls.

Xibaipo

(xībǎipō) 西柏坡

In Pingshan County, 80 km north-west of Shijiazhuang, was the base from which Mao Zedong, Zhou Enlai and Zhu De directed the northern campaign against the Kuomintang from 1947 to 1948. The original site of Xibaipo village was submerged by the Gangnan Reservoir and the present village has been rebuilt close by. In 1977 a Revolutionary Memorial Museum was erected. Xibaipo has become a tourist trap, but it's still fun to visit.

Beijing 北京

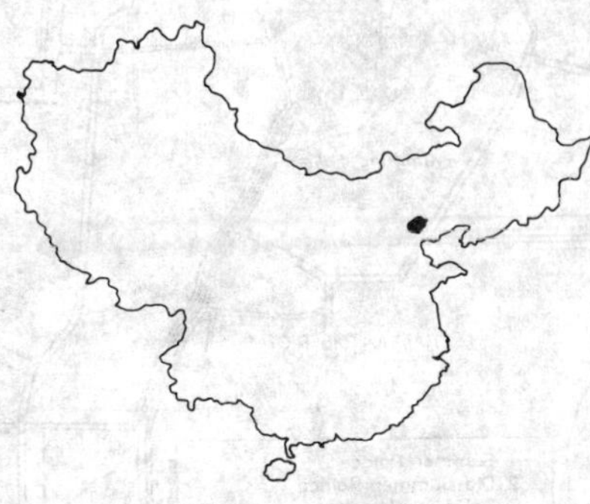

Beijing: home to stuffy museums and bureaucrats, puffy generals and backdoor elitists, host to disgruntled reporters and diplomats; a labyrinth of doors, walls, gates and entrances, marked and unmarked. As far away as Ürümqi they run on Beijing's clock; around the country they chortle in putonghua, the Beijing dialect; in the remote foothills of Tibet they struggle to interpret the latest directives from the capital. In 1983 the Chinese government announced that if the Dalai Lama were to return he'd be posted – where else? – to a desk job in Beijing. This is where they make the book and move the cogs and wheels of the Chinese universe, or try to slow them down if they're moving in the wrong direction.

All cities in China are equal, but some are more equal than others. Beijing has the best of everything in China bar the weather: the best food, the best hotels, the best transport, the best temples. But its vast squares and boulevards, its cavernous monoliths and its huge numbers of tourists are likely to leave you cold. It's a weird city – traces of its former character may be found down the back alleys where things are a bit more to human scale. Stepping off a train at the main Beijing railway station and driving up to Tiananmen Square in a bulbous Soviet Warszawa, you'd be forgiven if you were under the delusion that you'd strayed into Red Square in Moscow.

In 1981 Beijingese were gazing at imported TV sets displayed behind plate glass at the Main Department Store on Wangfujing. In 1983 the same window sported a fashion display direct from Paris. Pierre Cardin has been and gone; Arthur Miller has drifted through; Elton John dropped in to pose for photos in a Sun Yatsen jacket; Jean Michel Jarre demonstrated his laser beams and synthesisers; Muhammed Ali traded mock punches with Chinese fans; Ronald Reagan and the British Queen trod the Great Wall.

Upstairs in the department store a Western mannequin models a see-through top, nipples clearly visible. Outside the shop a worker is stopped and fined for gobbing on the footpath, part of another cleanup campaign. Further up Wangfujing, 6 pm and there's a parking problem: embassy cars and cadre limos have congregated at a restaurant for a banquet and there's nowhere to go except up on the footpath. For all its seeming liberalism, Beijing keeps an iron fist on its residents.

Perhaps nowhere else in China is the generation gap more visible. Appalled by the reforms, many older people still try to defend Chairmen Mao and the years of sacrifice for the socialist revolution. Many young people disdain socialism and are more interested in money, motorbikes, fashion and rock music.

Among the Chinese, Beijing is the promised land. Poor peasants flock to the city in search of the elusive pot of gold at the end of the rainbow – most wind up camped out on the pavement in front of the main railway station. The government tries to encourage them to go home, but the lure of the capital proves too enticing.

Tourists are often disappointed with Beijing, seeing it as a third-rate European city divested of its energy. Others, having passed

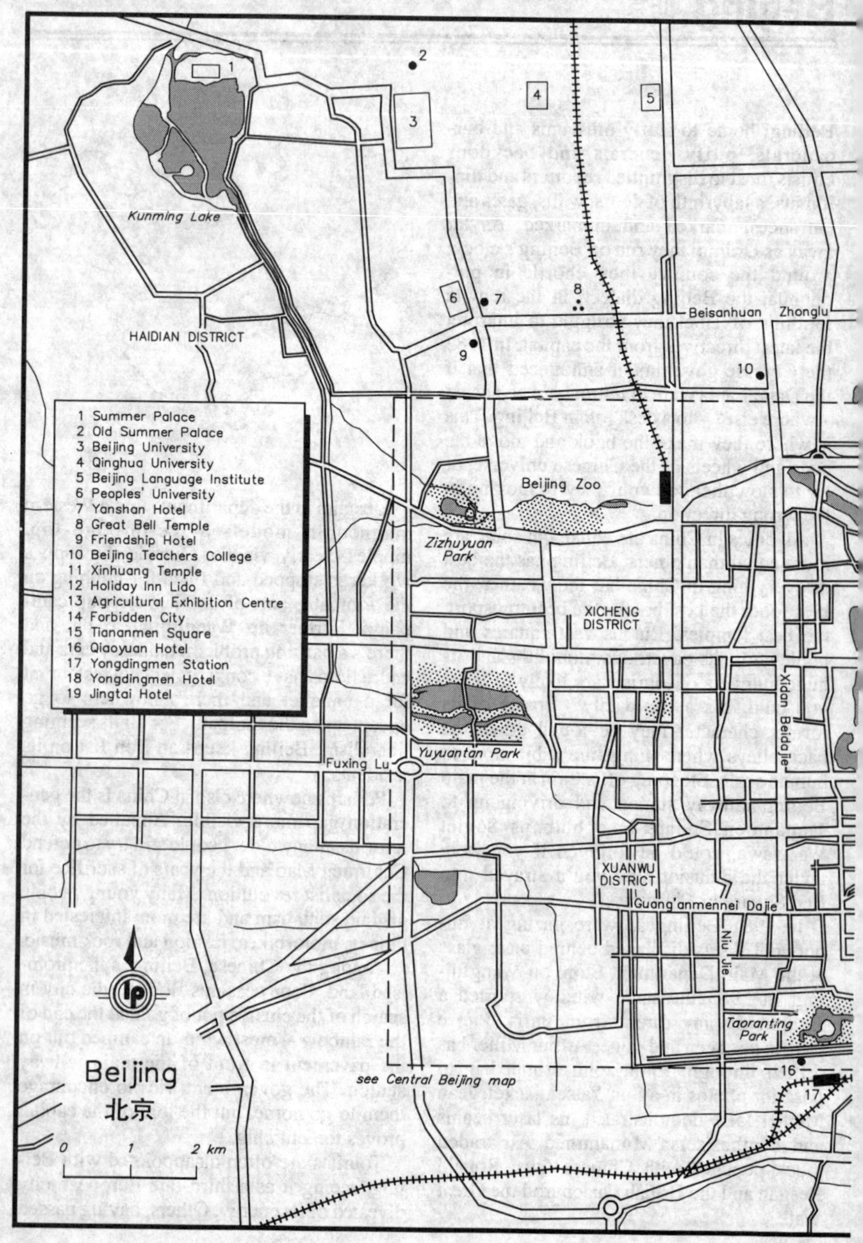
1 Summer Palace
2 Old Summer Palace
3 Beijing University
4 Qinghua University
5 Beijing Language Institute
6 Peoples' University
7 Yanshan Hotel
8 Great Bell Temple
9 Friendship Hotel
10 Beijing Teachers College
11 Xinhuang Temple
12 Holiday Inn Lido
13 Agricultural Exhibition Centre
14 Forbidden City
15 Tiananmen Square
16 Qiaoyuan Hotel
17 Yongdingmen Station
18 Yongdingmen Hotel
19 Jingtai Hotel
Kunming Lake
HAIDIAN DISTRICT
Beisanhuan
Zhonglu
Beijing Zoo
Zizhuyuan Park
XICHENG DISTRICT
Xidan Beidajie
Yuyuantan Park
Fuxing Lu
XUANWU DISTRICT
Guang'anmennei Dajie
Niu Jie
Taoranting Park
see Central Beijing map
Beijing
北京
0
1
2 km

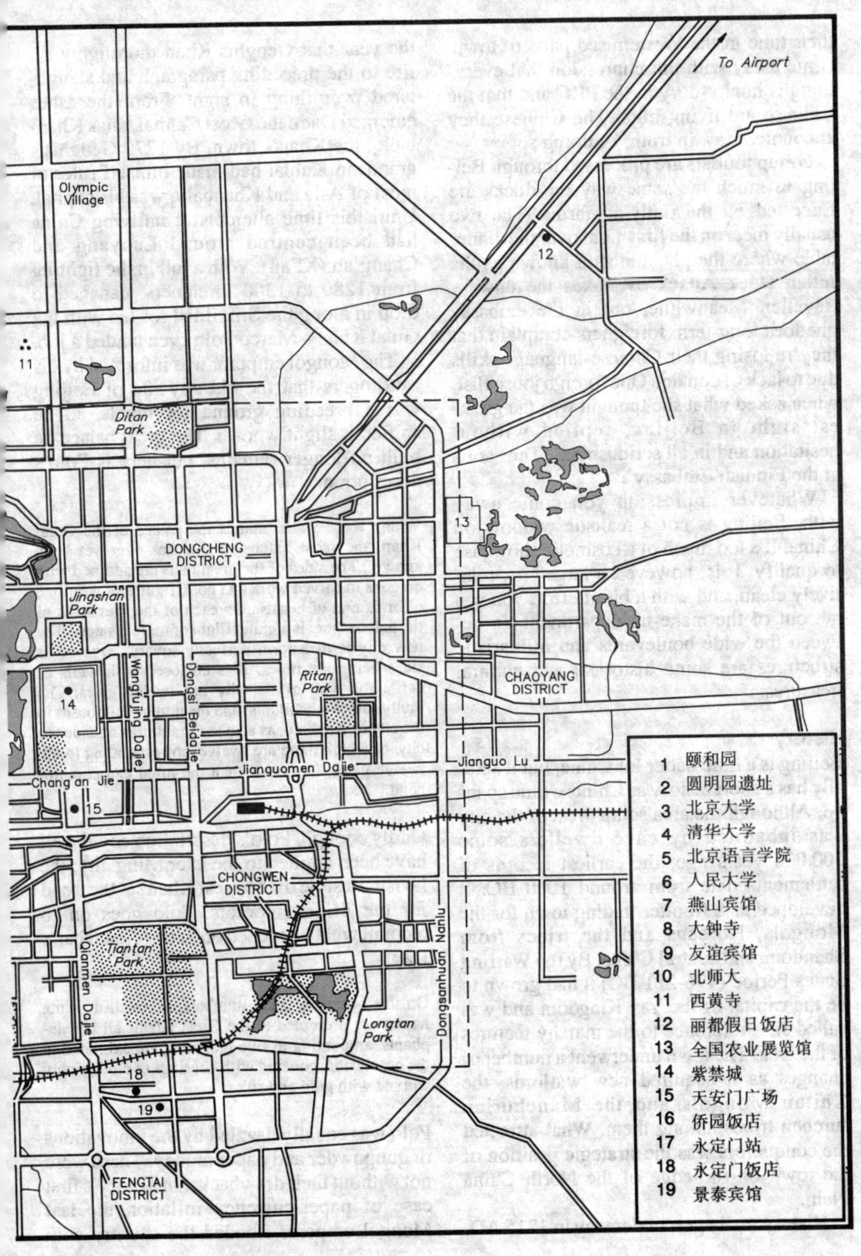
To Airport
Olympic Village
12
11
Ditan Park
13
DONGCHENG DISTRICT
Jingshan Park
Ritan Park
CHAOYANG DISTRICT
14
Wangfujing Dajie
Dongsi Beidajie
Jianguomen Dajie
Jianguo Lu
Chang'an Jie
15
CHONGWEN DISTRICT
Tiantan Park
Qianmen Dajie
Dongsanhuan Nanlu
Longtan Park
18
19
FENGTAI DISTRICT
1 颐和园
2 圆明园遗址
3 北京大学
4 清华大学
5 北京语言学院
6 人民大学
7 燕山宾馆
8 大钟寺
9 友谊宾馆
10 北师大
11 西黄寺
12 丽都假日饭店
13 全国农业展览馆
14 紫禁城
15 天安门广场
16 侨园饭店
17 永定门站
18 永定门饭店
19 景泰宾馆

their time in the Westernised parts of town, come away with the impression that everything is hunky-dory in the PRC and that the Chinese are living high. The Chinese they encounter may, in truth, be doing so.

Group tourists are processed through Beijing in much the same way the ducks are force-fed on the outlying farms. The two usually meet on the first night over the dinner table where the phenomenon known as the Jetlag Duck Attack overtakes the unwary traveller. Meanwhile, out in the embassy ghettoes long-term foreigners complain that they're losing their Chinese-language skills due to lack of contact. One foreign journalist, when asked what she thought was the greatest sight in Beijing, replied without hesitation and in all seriousness, 'The sauna at the Finnish Embassy'.

Whatever impression you come away with, Beijing is not a realistic window on China. It's too much of a cosmetic showcase to qualify. It is, however, a large city, relatively clean, and with a bit of effort you can get out of the make-up department. In between the wide boulevards and militaristic structures are some historical and cultural treasures.

History

Beijing is a time-setter for China, but it actually has a short history as Chinese time spans go. Although the area south-west of the city was inhabited by cave dwellers some 500,000 years ago, the earliest records of settlements date from around 1000 BC. It developed as a frontier trading town for the Mongols, Koreans and the tribes from Shandong and central China. By the Warring States Period (476-221 BC) it had grown to be the capital of the Yan Kingdom and was called Ji, a reference to the marshy features of the area. The town underwent a number of changes as it acquired new warlords, the Khitan Mongols and the Manchurian Jurchen tribes among them. What attracted the conquerors was the strategic position of the town on the edge of the North China Plain.

History really gets under way in 1215 AD, the year that Genghis Khan thoroughly set fire to the preceding paragraph and slaughtered everything in sight. From the ashes emerged Dadu the Great Capital, alias Khanbaliq, the Khan's town. By 1279 Genghis's grandson Kublai had made himself ruler of most of Asia and Khanbaliq was his capital. Until this time attempts at unifying China had been centred around Luoyang and Chang'an (Xi'an). With a lull in the fighting from 1280 to 1300 foreigners managed to drop in along the Silk Road for tea with the Great Khan – Marco Polo even landed a job.

The Mongol emperor was informed by his astrologers that the old city site of Beijing was a breeding ground for rebels, so he shifted it slightly north. The great palace he built no longer remains, but here is Polo's description:

> Within these walls...stands the palace of the Great Khan, the most extensive that has ever yet been known...The sides of the great halls are adorned with dragons in carved work and gold, figures of warriors, of birds and of beasts...On each of the four sides of the palace there is a grand flight of marble steps...The new city is of a form perfectly square...each of its sides being six miles. It is enclosed with walls of earth...the wall of the city has twelve gates. The multitude of inhabitants, and the number of houses in the city of Kanbalu, as also in the suburbs outside the city, of which there are twelve, corresponding to the twelve gates, is greater than the mind can comprehend.

Oddly enough, Polo's description could well have been applied to the later Ming city; the lavish lifestyle of the great Khan set the trend for the Ming emperors. Polo goes on to recount what happened on Tartar New Year's Day:

> On this occasion, great numbers of beautiful white horses are presented to the Great Khan...all his elephants, amounting to five thousand, are exhibited in the procession, covered with housings of cloth, richly worked with gold and silk.

Polo was equally dazzled by the innovations of gunpowder and paper money. These were not without their drawbacks. In history's first case of paper-currency inflation the last Mongol emperor flooded the country with worthless bills. This, coupled with a large number of natural disasters, provoked an uprising led by the mercenary Zhu Yanhang, who took Beijing in 1368 and ushered in the Ming Dynasty. The city was renamed Beiping (Northern Peace) and for the next 35 years the capital was shifted to Nanjing. To this day the Kuomintang regime on Taiwan refers to Beijing as 'Beiping' and recognises Nanjing as the capital.

In the early 1400s Zhu's son Yong Le shuffled the court back to Beiping and renamed it Beijing (Northern Capital). Millions of taels of silver were spent on refurbishing the city. Many of the structures like the Forbidden City and the Temple of Heaven were first built in Yong Le's reign. In fact, he is credited with being the true architect of the modern city. The Inner City moved to the area around the Imperial City and a suburban zone was added to the south, a bustle of merchants and street life. The basic grid of present-day Beijing had been laid and history became a question of who ruled the turf.

The first change of government came with the Manchus, who invaded China and established the Qing Dynasty. Under them, and particularly during the reigns of the emperors Kangxi and Qianlong, Beijing was expanded and renovated and summer palaces, pagodas and temples were built.

In the last 120 years of the Manchu Dynasty Beijing and subsequently China were subjected to the afflictions of power struggles, invaders and the chaos created by those who held or sought power: the Anglo-French troops who in 1860 marched in and burnt the Old Summer Palace to the ground; the corrupt regime under Empress Dowager Cixi; the Boxers; General Yuan Shikai; the warlords; the Japanese who occupied the city in 1937; followed by the Kuomintang after the Japanese defeat. A century of turmoil finally ended in January 1949 when PLA troops entered the city. On 1 October of that year Mao proclaimed a 'People's Republic' to an audience of some 500,000 citizens in Tiananmen Square.

After 1949 came a period of reconstruction. The centre of power has remained in the area around the Forbidden City, but the Communists have significantly altered the face of Beijing. Like the warlords of bygone eras they wanted to leave their mark. Under the old city-planning schemes high-rises were *verboten* – they would interfere with the emperor's view and lessen his sunlight. It was also a question of rank – the higher the building the more important the person within. The aristocrats got decorations and glazed tiling and the plebs got baked clay tiles and grey bricks. This building code to some extent prevailed over the 'house that Mao built'. Premier Zhou suggested that nothing higher than 45 metres be built within the old city wall limits, and that nothing higher than Tiananmen Gate be erected in that area.

City Planning

In the 1950s the urban planners got to work. Down came the commemorative arches, and blocks of buildings were reduced to rubble to widen Chang'an Jie and Tiananmen Square. From 1950 to 1952 the outer walls were levelled in the interests of traffic circulation. Soviet experts and technicians poured in, which may explain the Stalinesque features on the public structures that went up. Meanwhile industry, negligible in Beijing until this time, was rapidly expanded. Textiles, iron and steel, petrochemicals and machine-making plants were set up and Beijing became a major industrial city with pollution to match. The situation was exacerbated by the fact that most of the city's greenery had been ripped up. Five and six-storey housing blocks went up at a brisk pace but construction was of poor quality and it still didn't keep pace with the population boom. Agricultural communes were established on the city outskirts to feed the influx of people.

In 1982 the Central Committee of the Party adopted a new urban construction programme for Beijing, a revised version of the 1950s one. They faced tremendous challenges. On the one hand they wanted to continue the building of new roads and the widening of old streets; on the other hand they wanted to preserve the character of the old city and the historical sites. The population of the Beijing area, already well over nine million, is to be limited to 10 million by the year 2000, with four million in the metropolis, 2.5 million in satellite towns and 3.5 million in farming areas. Many new residential zones are being constructed in 12 to 16-storey blocks, but supply never meets demand and the standard of building is shoddy. In some cases the water pressure does not go above the 3rd storey, and there are usually no lifts (or sufficient electricity to run them).

The plan calls for a limitation on industrial construction, a halt to the growth of heavy industry and a shift to self-sufficient food production in the outlying counties. For the moment the self-sufficiency programme appears to be working, with extended use of greenhouses for the winter months. Another major priority shift is environmental. A massive tree-planting campaign is under way which aims to turn some 50% of the metropolitan area into recreational zones. This, however, will mean less farmland and the mushrooming of buildings in satellite locations.

Small businesses, once the mainstay of Beijing's economy, have re-emerged after having been almost wiped out in the craze to collectivise. To solve a huge unemployment problem the government has offered incentives for the self-employed such as tax exemptions and loans. Those with initiative are faring better than average; some earn incomes above Y300 a month, and privately run repair services such as those for bicycles, shoes and watches now outnumber state and collective-owned ones in Beijing.

Climate

The city is not blessed with congenial weather. Autumn (from September to October) is the best time to visit: there's little rain, it's not dry or humid, and the city wears a pleasant cloak of foliage. Winter can be interesting if you don't mind the cold; although the temperature can dip as far as -20°C and you can freeze your butt off, parts of the capital appear charming in this season. The subdued winter lighting makes the place very photogenic – the cold, dry air makes for good visibility. Winter clothing is readily available – the locals wear about 15 layers. If the wind races down the wide boulevards like Chang'an there's a particularly nasty wind-chill factor. Spring is short, dry and dusty. From April to May a phenomenon known as 'yellow wind' plagues the capital – fine dust particles blown from the Gobi Desert in the north-west sandpaper everything in sight, including your face. The locals run around with mesh bags over their heads. In the 1950s the government ordered the extermination of the city's birds, which led to an insect uprising. They then ordered the insects' habitats (grass and other greens) to be dug up, which led to even more dust being set loose. In summer (June, July and August) the average temperature is 26°C – very hot, and there's strong sunlight with heavy rains and mosquitoes in July.

Orientation

Though it may not appear so in the shambles of arrival, Beijing is a place of very orderly design. Long, straight boulevards and avenues are crisscrossed by a network of lanes. Places of interest are either very easy to find if they're on the avenues, or impossible to find if they're buried down the narrow alleys *(hútòng)*.

This section refers to the chessboard of the downtown core, once a walled enclosure. The symmetry folds on an ancient north-south axis passing through Qianmen (Front Gate). The major east-west road is Chang'an (Avenue of Eternal Tranquillity).

As for the street names: Chongwenmenwai Dajie means 'the avenue (dajie) outside (wai) Chongwen Gate (Chongwenmen)'; whereas Chongwenmennei Dajie means 'the avenue inside Chongwen Gate' (that is, inside the old wall). It's an academic exercise since the gate and the wall in question no longer exist.

Streets are also split along compass points; Dongdajie (East Avenue), Xidajie

(West Avenue), Beidajie (North Avenue) and Nandajie (South Avenue). These streets head off from an intersection, usually where a gate once stood.

A major boulevard can change names six or eight times along its length, so intersections become important. The buses are also routed through these points. It therefore pays to study your gates and intersections, and familiarise yourself with the high-rise buildings (often hotels) which serve as useful landmarks to gauge your progress along the chessboard. Other streets are named after bridges, also long gone, like the Bridge of Heaven (Tianqiao), and after features such as old temples which are still there.

The city limits of Beijing extend some 80 km, including the urban, the suburban, and the nine counties under its administration. With a total area of 16,800 sq km, Beijing municipality is roughly the size of Belgium.

For most people, Beijing starts at Beijing Zhan – that is, the main railway station. As you come out of the station there is a taxi depot straight ahead. If you keep going there are two entrances to the subway – the best and cheapest way of getting out of the area fast. Across the road from the station are various bus and minibus stops; see the Getting Around section for details.

Information

CITS One office is at the Beijing Tourist Building (☎ 5158570), 28 Jianguomenwai, near the Friendship Store. The other is in the Beijing International Hotel, just north of the railway station.

Overall, the Beijing CITS offices are among the better organised ones in the country. They come in very handy if you want tickets to the Beijing Opera, acrobatic shows or theatre. Costs are a bit higher than you'd pay at the door but at least you'll be sure of a seat. They also book the Trans-Siberian trains, but for domestic trains you have to go to the Foreigners' Booking Office in the main railway station. Bookings for the Shanghai-Hong Kong ferry cannot be made at Beijing CITS; you have to telephone Shanghai to make the booking.

Public Security Bureau This (☎ 553102) is at 85 Beichizi Dajie, the street running north-south at the east side of the Forbidden City. It's open from 8.30 to 11.30 am and 1 to 5 pm Monday to Friday; from 8.30 to 11.30 am Saturday; closed on Sundays.

Money There are money-exchange counters in many of the tourist hotels. The Beijing Hotel has an exchange counter on the ground floor and will change cash and travellers' cheques; you don't have to be staying at the hotel to use their service. The Qiaoyuan Hotel, where many low-budget travellers stay, also changes cash and travellers' cheques. The main branch of the Bank of China is on Fuchengmennei Dajie near the intersection with Fuchengmennan Dajie. This is the largest bank in the country – bus No 103 from the railway station goes there. They will cash US$ travellers' cheques and give you US$ cash if you request it. Another bank which does this is CITIC, International Building, 19 Jianguomenwai Dajie adjacent to the Friendship Store. There is another branch of the Bank of China on Dengshikou Xijie, just to the east of the Forbidden City near Wangfujing, which will advance cash against major international credit cards.

There is a booming black market in FEC and US$ in Beijing, often fronted by sleazy Uigur mobsters. Beware – rip-offs are *very* common. Always be suspicious of people who approach you on the street. One gang of rip-off merchants approaches travellers in the car park of the Qiaoyuan Hotel and offers a ridiculously generous exchange rate. Amazingly, many travellers fall for it and wind up getting cheated.

The only safe places to change money in Beijing are in the little shops catering to foreigners. In many of these shops, they'll take you into a back room and lay the money out on a table so you can count it – far safer than changing on the street. Many of the shops around the budget hotels and the stalls in the antique and silk markets will change money for you, but be careful of plain-clothes police.

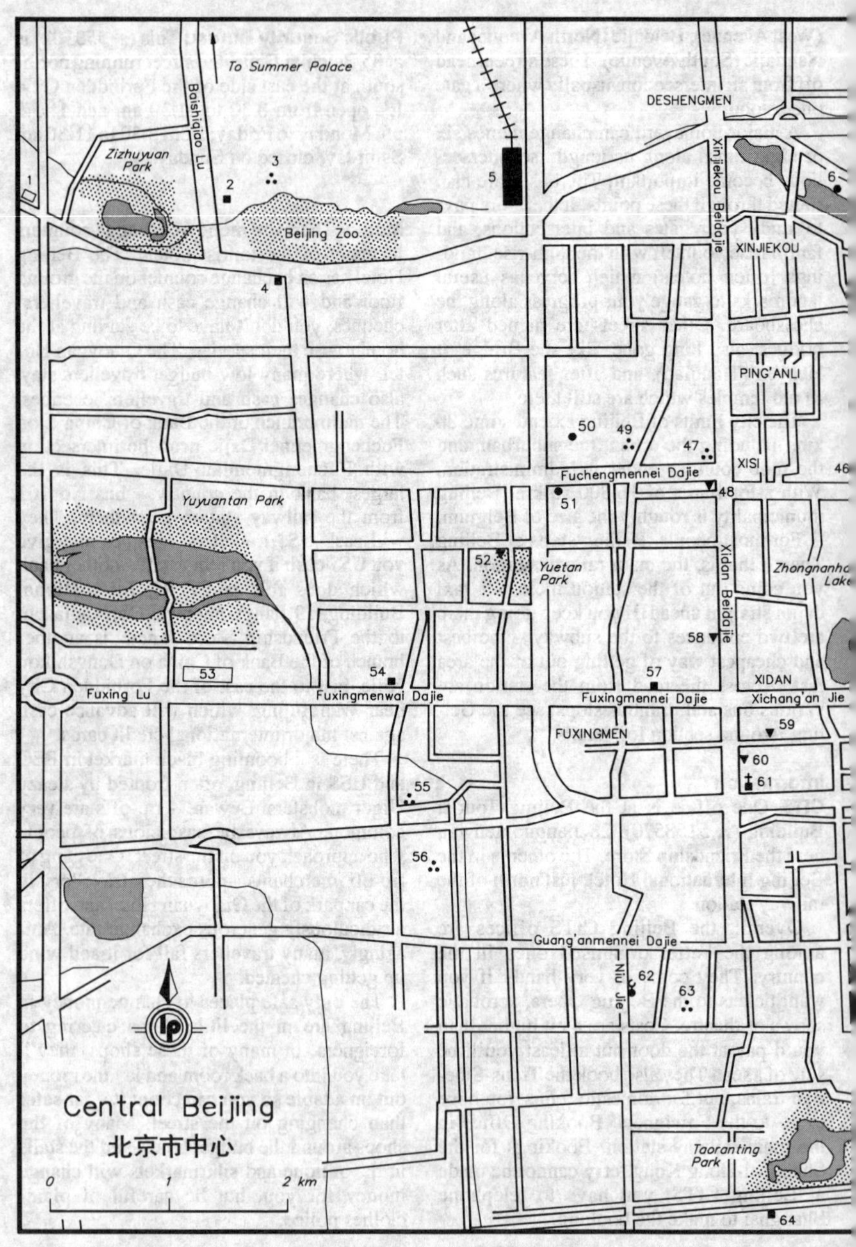

To Summer Palace
Baishiqiao Lu
Zizhuyuan Park
DESHENGMEN
Xinjiekou Beidajie
Beijing Zoo
XINJIEKOU
PING'ANLI
XISI
Fuchengmennei Dajie
Yuyuantan Park
Yuetan Park
Xidan Beidajie
XIDAN
Fuxing Lu
Fuxingmenwai Dajie
Fuxingmennei Dajie
Xichang'an Jie
FUXINGMEN
Guang'anmennei Dajie
Niu Jie
Taoranting Park
1
2
3
4
5
6
46
47
48
49
50
51
52
53
54
55
56
57
58
59
60
61
62
63
64
Central Beijing
北京市中心
0
1
2 km

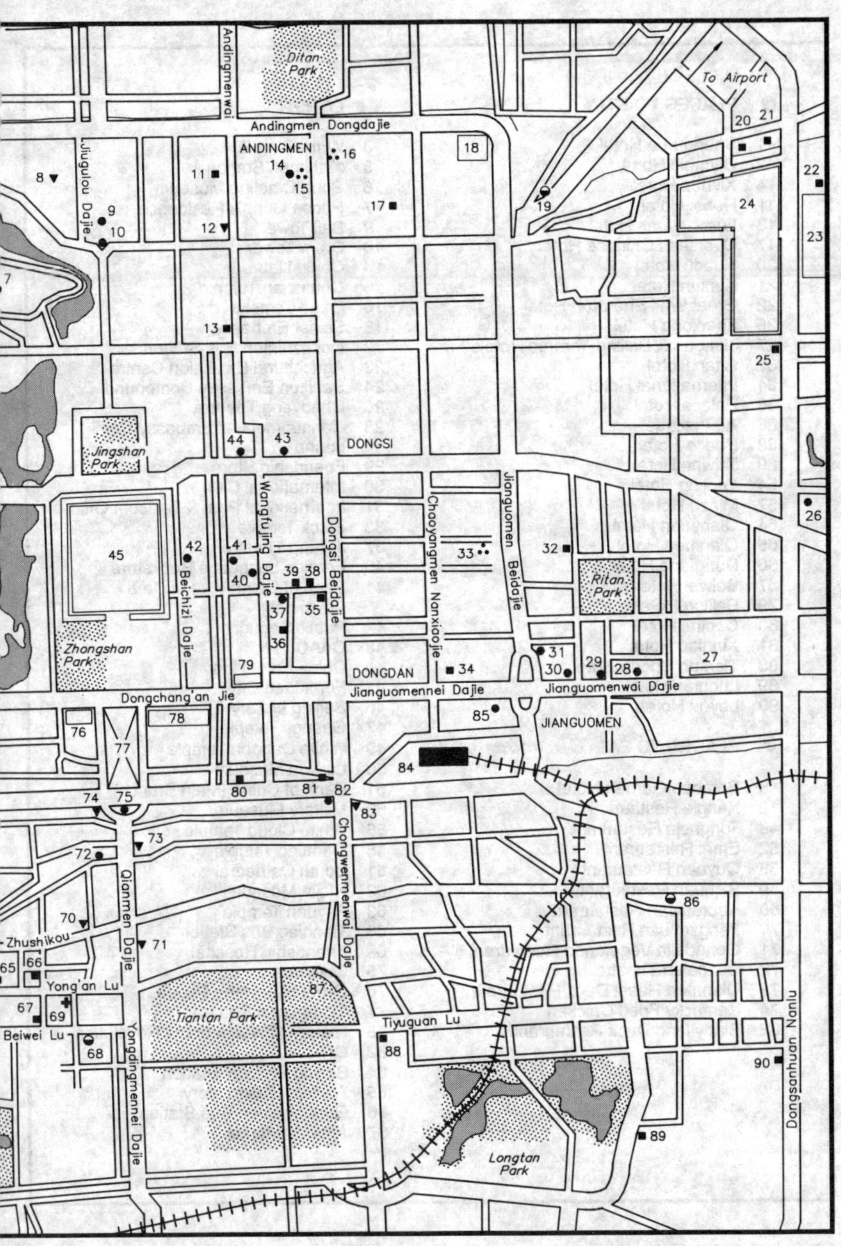
Andingmenwai
Ditan Park
To Airport
Andingmen Dongdajie
ANDINGMEN
Jiuglou Dajie
Jingshan Park
DONGSI
Wangfujing Dajie
Dongsi Beidajie
Chaoyangmen Nanxiaojie
Jianguomen Beidajie
Ritan Park
Beichizi Dajie
Zhongshan Park
DONGDAN
Jianguomennei Dajie
Jianguomenwai Dajie
JIANGUOMEN
Dongchang'an Jie
Qianmen Dajie
Chongwenmenwai Dajie
Zhushikou
Yong'an Lu
Beiwei Lu
Tiantan Park
Yongdingmennei Dajie
Tiyuguan Lu
Longtan Park
Dongsanhuan Nanlu
1
7
8
9
10
11
12
13
14
15
16
17
18
19
20
21
22
23
24
25
26
27
28
29
30
31
32
33
34
35
36
37
38
39
40
41
42
43
44
45
65
66
67
68
69
70
71
72
73
74
75
76
77
78
79
80
81
82
83
84
85
86
87
88
89
90

■ PLACES TO STAY

1 Shangri-La Hotel
2 Olympic Hotel
4 Xiyuan Hotel
11 Hebei Hotel
13 Lusongyuan Hotel
17 Overseas Chinese Hotel
20 Huadu Hotel
21 Kunlun Hotel
22 Great Wall Sheraton Hotel
25 Zhaolong Hotel
27 Jianguo & Beijing-Toronto Hotels
32 Ritan Hotel
34 International Hotel
35 Palace Hotel
36 Art Institute
38 Peace Hotel
39 Taiwan Hotel
54 Yanjing Hotel
57 Minzu Hotel
64 Qiaoyuan Hotel
65 Qianmen Hotel
66 Dongfang Hotel
67 Beiwei Hotel
79 Beijing Hotel
80 Capital Hotel
81 Xinqiao Hotel
88 Tiantan Sports Hotel
89 Longtan Hotel
90 Leyou Hotel

▼ PLACES TO EAT

8 Bamboo Garden Hotel
12 Kangle Restaurant
48 Tongheju Restaurant
52 Emei Restaurant
58 Quyuan Restaurant
59 Sichuan Restaurant
60 Kaorouwan Restaurant
70 Fengzeyuan Restaurant
71 Gongdelin Vegetarian Restaurant
72 Dazhalan Theatre
73 Qianmen Roast Duck Restaurant
74 Kentucky Fried Chicken
83 Bianyifang Duck Restaurant

OTHER

3 Wuta Temple
5 Xizhimen Station
6 Song Qingling Museum
7 Prince Gong's Residence
9 Bell Tower
10 Drum Tower
14 Capital Library
15 Confucian Temple
16 Lama Temple
18 Soviet Embassy
19 Dongzhimen Bus Station
23 Agricultural Exhibition Centre
24 Sanlitun Embassy Compound
26 Chaoyang Theatre
28 Jianguomenwai Embassy Compound
29 Friendship Store
30 International Club
31 International Post & Telecom Office
33 Black Temple
37 Jixiang Theatre
40 Foreign Language Bookstore
41 Bank of China (Credit Card Advances)
42 Public Security
43 CAAC
44 China Art Gallery
45 Forbidden City
46 Beijing Library
47 Guangji Temple
49 White Dagoba Temple
50 Lu Xun Museum
51 Bank of China (Main Branch)
53 Military Museum
55 White Cloud Temple
56 Tianning Temple
61 South Cathedral
62 Niujie Mosque
63 Fayuan Temple
68 Tianqiao Bus Station
69 Friendship Hospital
75 Qianmen
76 Great Hall of the People
77 Tiananmen Square
78 History Museum of the Revolution
82 CITS
84 Beijing Railway Station
85 Ancient Observatory
86 Guangqumen Bus Station
87 Antique Market

■ PLACES TO STAY

1 香格里拉大饭店
2 奥林匹克饭店
4 西苑饭店
11 河北饭店
13 侣松园宾馆
17 华侨饭店
20 华都饭店
21 昆仑饭店
22 长城饭店
25 兆龙饭店
27 建国和京伦饭店
32 日坛宾馆
34 国际饭店
35 王府饭店
36 美术学院
38 和平宾馆
39 台湾饭店
54 燕京饭店
57 民族饭店
64 侨园饭店
65 前门饭店
66 东方饭店
67 北纬饭店
79 北京饭店
80 首都宾馆
81 新侨饭店
88 天坛体育宾馆
89 龙潭公园
90 乐游饭店

▼ PLACES TO EAT

8 竹园宾馆
12 康乐餐厅
48 同和居饭店
52 峨嵋饭店
58 曲园酒楼
59 四川饭店
60 烤肉宛饭庄
70 丰泽园饭庄
71 功德林素菜馆
72 大栅栏戏院
73 前门全聚德烤鸭店
74 肯德基炸鸡
83 便宜坊烤鸭店

OTHER

3 五塔寺
5 西直门站
6 宋庆玲故居
7 恭王府
9 钟楼
10 鼓楼
14 首都图书馆
15 孔庙
16 雍和宫
18 苏联大使馆
19 东直门汽车站
23 全国农业展览馆
24 三里屯使馆区
26 朝阳戏院
28 建国门外使馆区
29 友谊商店
30 国际俱乐部
31 国际邮电局
33 智化寺
37 吉祥戏院
40 外文书店
41 中国银行
42 公安局外事科
43 中国民航
44 中国美术馆
45 紫禁城
46 北京图书馆
47 广济寺
49 白塔寺
50 鲁迅博物馆
51 中国银行
53 军事博物馆
55 白云观
56 天宁寺
61 南堂
62 牛街礼拜寺
63 法源寺
68 天桥汽车站
69 友谊医院
75 前门
76 人民大会堂
77 天安门广场
78 中国革命历史博物馆
82 中国国际旅行社
84 北京火车站
85 古观象台
86 广渠门汽车总站
87 古文市场

Post & Telecommunications The International Post & Telecommunications Building is on Jianguomen Beidajie, not far from the Friendship Store. Hours are from 8 am to 7 pm. It has an efficient poste restante service for both letters and parcels. Overseas parcels must be posted here; a counter sells wrapping paper, string, tape and glue. There's also an international telegraph and telephone service – this is probably the best place to make international phone calls.

Most of the tourist hotels have post offices. You can send overseas packages from these as long as they contain printed matter only.

The Telegraph Building is open 24 hours a day on Xi Chang'an Jie. Further west on Fuxingmennei Dajie is the International Telephone Office, open daily from 7 am to midnight.

Long-distance calls can be made from your hotel room if it has a phone but patience is necessary as the exchanges are overworked and the lines can sometimes be bad.

Bookshops The Friendship Store is a gold mine of US, British and European magazines, newspapers, books (lots of novels) and other saddle-bag material. Also try the Beijing Hotel, the large tourist hotels and the Foreign Language Bookstore near the Beijing Hotel. On Wangfujing there is a huge Xinhua Bookstore.

Recent copies of Western magazines make good gifts for Chinese comrades – if it's a novel, pick the raciest one you can! If you're going on the Trans-Siberian, pick the dreariest covers and contents since the Outer Mongolians and Russians may confiscate them otherwise.

Maps If you need a map in English, the best one is the *Beijing Tourist Map*, issued by the Cartographic Publishing House of Beijing (Chinese edition also available). The easiest place to find an English map is in the Friendship Store and some of the larger hotel gift shops.

If you can deal with Chinese maps, you'll find a wide variety to choose from. Good maps are available in most subway stations. One excellent map with bus routes is called *Jiaotong Lüyou Zhusutu*.

The *Beijing Shiqutu* is a large wall map in Chinese, probably the best map available of the city. It isn't convenient to carry around on the street, but if you've got a wall to hang it on, you'll find it extremely useful. There's a quarto-sized Michelin-type bundle of 32 section maps that even gets down to the nitty-gritty of the hutongs. It's called *Beijing Shiqu Dituce*. The place to look for these maps is in the Xinhua Bookstore.

Another good one is the *Map of Beijing* (China Foreign Publishing Company), which shows the sights and is bilingual throughout; you can buy it in Hong Kong, but it's hard to find in Beijing.

Emergency The clinic at the Friendship Hospital (☎ 338671 ext 441) *(yǒuyí yīyùan)* at 95 Yongan Lu, on the west side of the Temple of Heaven in the Tianqiao area, deals with foreigners. Hours are from 8 to 11.30 am and 2.30 to 5 pm.

Embassy staff have their own doctors who are sometimes willing to see patients of other nationalities. If the case merits it, you might try and get a referral or advice from your embassy.

Embassies Beijing is not a bad place to stock up on visas. There are Australian, US, Japanese, French and German consulates in Shanghai also, as well as US and Japanese consulates in Canton, and a US consulate even in Shenyang. See the chapters on those cities for details.

In Beijing there are two main embassy compounds: Jianguomenwai and Sanlitun. A visit to Embassy Land is a trip in itself – little sentry boxes with Chinese soldiers, posted not so much for the protection of staff as to scare the locals off.

The Jianguomenwai Compound is in the vicinity of the Friendship Store. The embassies here are:

Austria
5 Xiushui Nanjie (☎ 5322061)
Bulgaria
4 Xiushui Beijie (☎ 5322232)
Czechoslovakia
Ritan Lu (☎ 5321531)
Ireland
3 Ritan Donglu (☎ 5322691)
India
1 Ritan Donglu (☎ 5321908)
Japan
7 Ritan Lu (☎ 5322361)
Mongolia
2 Xiushui Beijie (☎ 5321203)
New Zealand
1 Ritan Dong 2-Jie (☎ 5322731)
Philippines
23 Xiushui Beijie (☎ 5322451)
Poland
1 Ritan Lu, Jianguomenwai (☎ 5321235)
Romania
corner of Ritan Dong 2-Jie and Ritan Donglu (☎ 5323315)
Sri Lanka
3 Jianhua Lu (☎ 5321861)
Thailand
40 Guanghua Lu (☎ 5321903)
UK
11 Guanghua Lu (☎ 5321961)
USA
Embassy: 3 Xiushui Beijie (☎ 5323831), Consulate: 2 Xiushui Dongjie
Vietnam
32 Guanghua Lu (☎ 5321125)

The Sanlitun Compound is several km north-east of Jianguomenwai, near the Agricultural Exhibition Hall. Here you'll find the following embassies:

Australia
15 Dongzhimenwai Dajie (☎ 5322331)
Belgium
6 Sanlitun Lu (☎ 5321736)
Canada
10 Sanlitun Lu (☎ 5323031)
Denmark
1 Sanlitun Dong 5-Jie (☎ 5322431)
France
3 Sanlitun Dong 3-Jie (☎ 5321331)
Germany
5 Dongzhimenwai Dajie (☎ 5322161)
Hungary
10 Dongzhimenwai Dajie (☎ 5321431)
Italy
2 Sanlitun Dong 2-Jie (☎ 5322131)
Malaysia
13 Dongzhimenwai Dajie (☎ 5322531)
Myanmar (Burma)
6 Dongzhimenwai Dajie (☎ 5321584)
Nepal
1 Sanlitun Xi 6-Jie (☎ 5321795)
Netherlands
10 Sanlitun Dong 4-Jie (☎ 5321131)
Norway
1 Sanlitun Dong 1-Jie (☎ 5322261)
Pakistan
1 Dongzhimenwai Dajie (☎ 5322504)
Spain
9 Sanlitun Lu (☎ 5323520)
Sweden
3 Dongzhimenwai Dajie (☎ 5323331)
Switzerland
3 Sanlitun Dong 5-Jie (☎ 5322736)
USSR
4 Dongzhimen Beizhongjie, west of the Sanlitun Compound in a separate compound (☎ 5322051)
Yugoslavia
56 Sanlitun Dong 6-Jie (☎ 5323516)

Tiananmen Square

(tiān'ānmén gǔangchǎng) 天安门广场

Though it was a gathering place and the location of government offices in the imperial days, the square is Mao's creation, as is Chang'an Jie leading onto it. This is the heart of Beijing, a vast desert of paving and photo-booths. The last major rallies took place here during the Cultural Revolution when Mao, wearing a Red Guard armband, reviewed parades of up to a million people. In 1976 another million people jammed the square to pay their last respects to him. In 1989, army tanks and soldiers cut down pro-democracy demonstrators here. Today the square is a place, if the weather is conducive, for people to lounge around in the evening, and a place to fly decorated kites and balloons for the kiddies. Surrounding or studding the square are a strange mish-mash of monuments past and present: Tiananmen (Gate of Heavenly Peace), the History Museum & Museum of the Revolution, the Great Hall of the People, Qianmen (Front Gate), the Mao Mausoleum and the Monument to the People's Heroes. If you get up early you can watch the flag-raising ceremony at sunrise, performed by a troop of PLA soldiers drilled to march at precisely 108 paces per minute, 75 cm per pace.

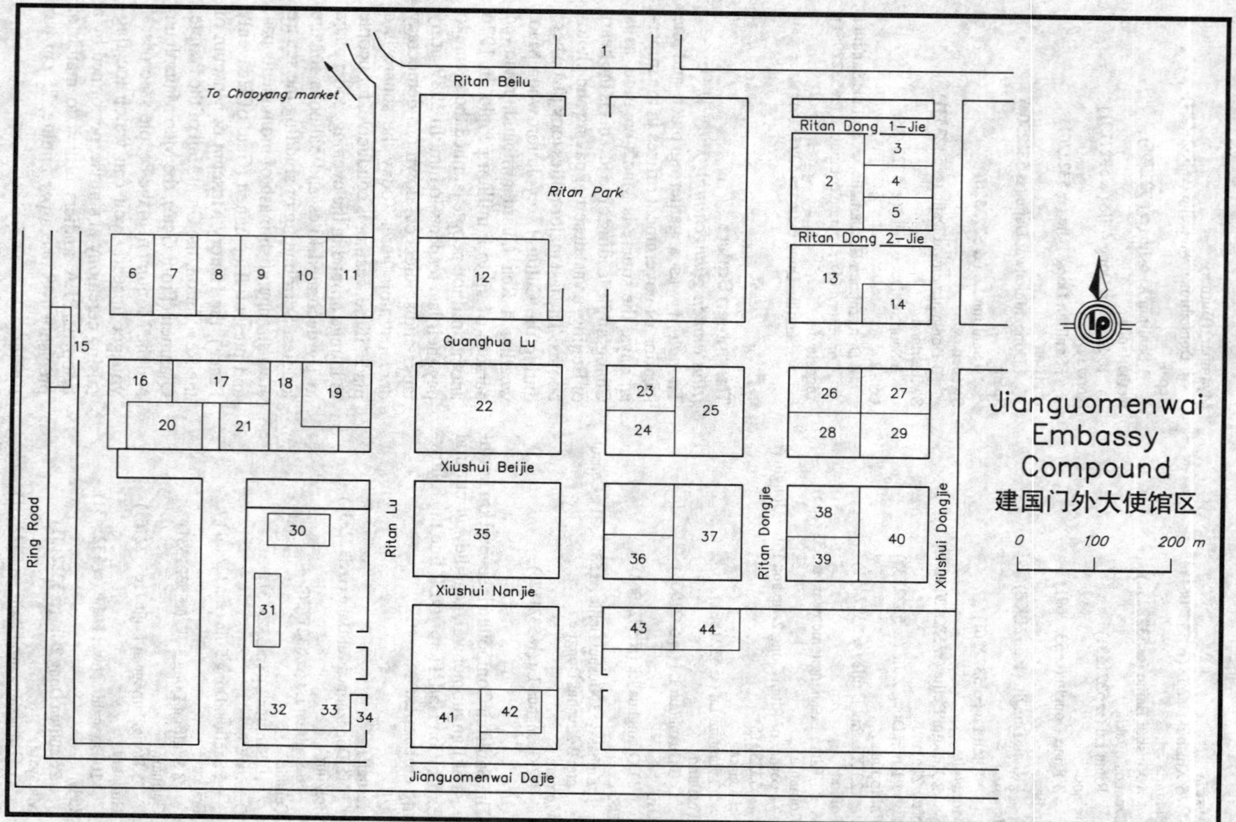
Jianguomenwai
Embassy
Compound
建国门外大使馆区
0
100
200 m
To Chaoyang market
Ritan Beilu
Ritan Park
Ritan Dong 1–Jie
Ritan Dong 2–Jie
Guanghua Lu
Xiushui Beijie
Xiushui Nanjie
Xiushui Dongjie
Ritan Dongjie
Ritan Lu
Ring Road
Jianguomenwai Dajie
1
2
3
4
5
6
7
8
9
10
11
12
13
14
15
16
17
18
19
20
21
22
23
24
25
26
27
28
29
30
31
32
33
34
35
36
37
38
39
40
41
42
43
44

1 North Korea
2 Romania
3 Senegal
4 Guyana
5 New Zealand
6 Brazil
7 Burundi
8 Kuwait
9 Chad
10 Greece
11 USA Res
12 Restaurant
13 India
14 UK
15 International Post Office
16 Bangladesh
17 Thailand
18 Rwanda
19 Gabon
20 Iraq
21 Philippines
22 Poland
23 Colombia
24 Sri Lanka
25 Vietnam
26 Finland
27 Albania
28 Egypt
29 USA
30 Tennis
31 Pool
32 Tennis
33 International Club
34 Taxi
35 Czechoslovakia
36 Cuba
37 Mongolia
38 USA
39 Ireland
40 Bulgaria
41 CITIC
42 Friendship Store
43 Austria
44 Ethiopia

1 北朝鲜
2 罗马尼亚
3 塞内加尔
4 圭亚那
5 新西兰
6 巴西
7 布隆迪
8 科威特
9 乍得
10 希腊
11 美国
12 饭馆
13 印度
14 联合王国
15 国际邮电局
16 孟加拉国
17 泰国
18 卢旺达
19 加蓬
20 伊拉克
21 菲律宾
22 波兰
23 哥伦比亚
24 斯里兰卡
25 越南
26 芬兰
27 阿尔巴尼亚
28 埃及
29 美国
30 网球场
31 游泳池
32 网球场
33 国际俱乐部
34 出租汽车
35 捷克斯洛伐克
36 古巴
37 蒙古
38 美国
39 爱尔兰
40 保加利亚
41 银行
42 友谊商店
43 奥地利
44 埃塞俄比亚

Tiananmen

(tiān'ānmén) 天安门

Tiananmen, or 'Gate of Heavenly Peace', is a national symbol which pops up on everything from airline tickets to policemen's caps. The gate was built in the 15th century and restored in the 17th. From imperial days it functioned as a rostrum for dealing with or proclaiming to the assembled masses. There are five doors to the gate, and in front of it

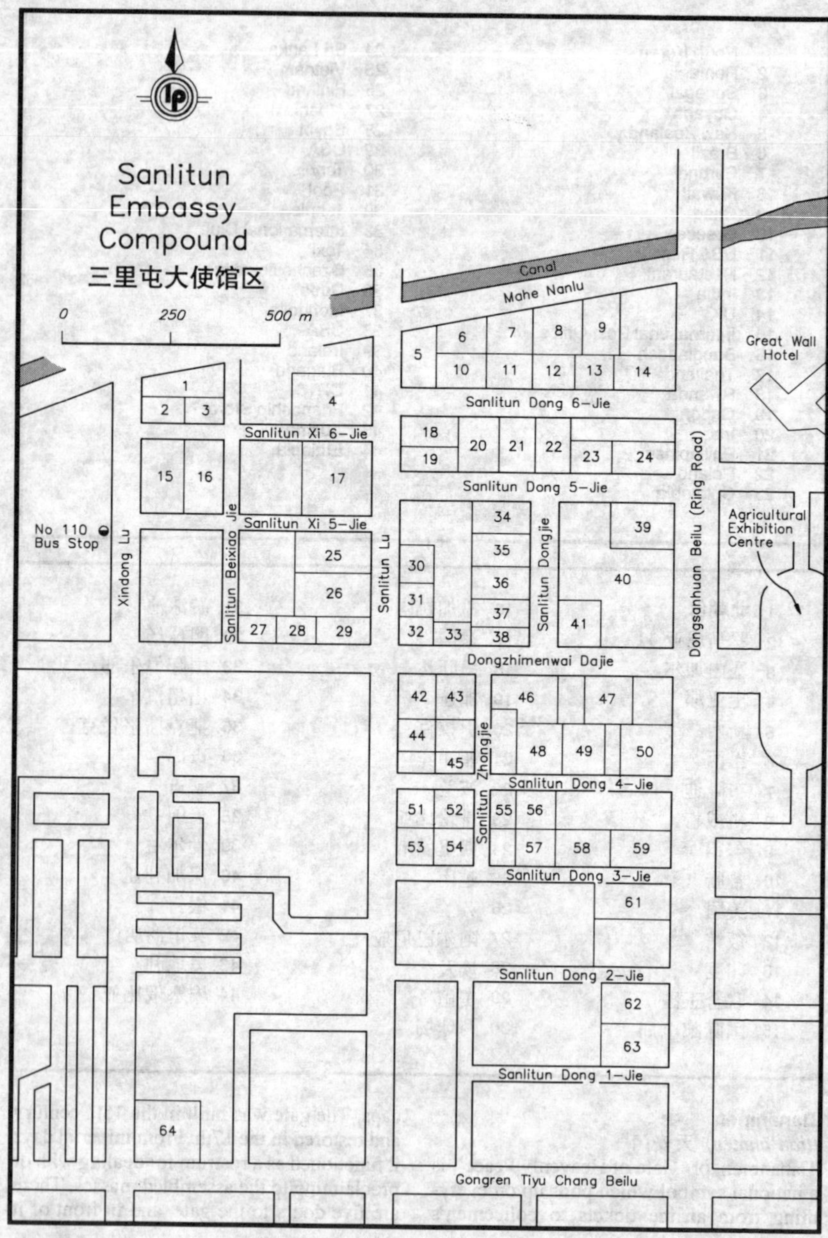
Sanlitun
Embassy
Compound
三里屯大使馆区
0
250
500 m
Canal
Mahe Nanlu
Great Wall
Hotel
Sanlitun Dong 6-Jie
Sanlitun Xi 6-Jie
Sanlitun Dong 5-Jie
Sanlitun Xi 5-Jie
No 110
Bus Stop
Xindong Lu
Sanlitun Beixiao Jie
Sanlitun Lu
Sanlitun Dongjie
Dongsanhuan Beilu (Ring Road)
Agricultural
Exhibition
Centre
Dongzhimenwai Dajie
Sanlitun Zhongjie
Sanlitun Dong 4-Jie
Sanlitun Dong 3-Jie
Sanlitun Dong 2-Jie
Sanlitun Dong 1-Jie
Gongren Tiyu Chang Beilu

1 Duty-Free Shop
2 Nepal
3 Liberia
4 Beijing International Store
5 Iran
6 Lebanon
7 Tanzania
8 Oman
9 Singapore
10 Niger
11 Burkina Faso
12 Jordan
13 Libya
14 Yugoslavia
15 Guinea
16 Kenya
17 Friendship Store
18 Somalia
19 Argentina
20 Turkey
21 Cameroon
22 Mexico
23 Switzerland
24 Denmark
25 Algeria
26 Spain
27 Australia
28 Malaysia
29 Togo
30 Belgium
31 Ghana
32 Cambodia
33 Sierra Leone
34 Zaire
35 Tunisia
36 Madagascar
37 Uganda
38 Germany
39 Nigeria
40 Pakistan
41 Sweden
42 Canada
43 Hungary
44 UNICEF
45 Laos
46 Afghanistan
47 South Yemen
48 Congo
49 Zambia
50 Chile
51 Venezuela
52 Holland
53 Morocco
54 Mauritania
55 Mali
56 Syria
57 Yemen
58 France
59 Central African Republic
60 PLO
61 Sudan
62 Italy
63 Norway
64 Sanlitun Department Store

are seven bridges spanning a stream. Each of these bridges was restricted in its use, and only the emperor could use the central door and bridge.

It was from the gate that Mao proclaimed the People's Republic on 1 October 1949, and there have been a few alterations since then. The dominating feature is the gigantic portrait of Mao, the required backdrop for any photo the Chinese take of themselves at the gate (whether they like him or not). To the left of the portrait is a slogan 'Long Live the People's Republic of China' and to the right 'Long Live the Unity of the Peoples of the World'. The grandstands are used for major reviews and can seat 20,000.

Photography is big at Tiananmen – the Chinese aspire to visit the heart of the nation almost like the Muslims aspire to visit Mecca, and Chinese schoolkids grow up singing 'I Love Tiananmen Beijing'. If you venture a short distance into the Forbidden

City through Tiananmen you'll find all kinds of bizarre cardboard cut-outs used as photo props.

History Museum & Museum of the Revolution

(zhōnggúo gémìng lìshǐ bówùgǔan)
中国革命烈士博物馆

Housed in a sombre building on the east side of Tiananmen Square, access was long thwarted by special permission requirements. From 1966 to 1978 the museum was closed so that history could be reassessed in the light of recent events.

The presentation of history poses quite a problem for the CCP. It has failed to publish

1 免税店
2 尼泊尔
3 利比里亚
4 北京国际商店
5 伊朗
6 黎巴嫩
7 坦桑尼亚
8 阿曼
9 新加坡
10 尼日尔
11 巴基那法索
12 约旦
13 利比亚
14 南斯拉夫
15 几内亚
16 肯尼亚
17 友谊商店
18 索马里
19 阿根廷
20 土耳其
21 喀麦隆
22 墨西哥
23 瑞士
24 丹麦
25 阿尔及利亚
26 西班牙
27 澳大利亚
28 马来
20 多哥
30 比利时
31 加纳
32 柬埔寨
33 塞拉利昂
34 扎伊尔
35 突尼斯
36 马达加斯加岛
37 乌干达
38 德国
39 尼日利亚
40 巴基斯坦
41 瑞典
42 加拿大
43 匈牙利
44 联合国儿童基金会
45 老挝
46 阿富汗尼
47 南也门
48 刚果
49 赞比亚
50 智利
51 委内瑞拉
52 荷兰
53 摩洛哥
54 毛里塔尼亚
55 马里
56 叙利亚
57 也门
58 法国
59 中非共和国
60 巴勒斯坦解放党
61 苏丹
62 意大利
63 挪威
64 三里屯商店

anything of note on its own history after it gained power, before, during or since the Cultural Revolution. This would have required reams of carefully worded revision according to what tack politics (here synonymous with history) might take – so it was better left unwritten.

There are actually two museums here combined into one – the Museum of History and the Museum of the Revolution. Explanations throughout most of the museums are, unfortunately, entirely in Chinese, so you won't get much out of this labyrinth unless you pick up an English-speaking student. An English text relating to the History Museum is available inside.

The History Museum contains artefacts and cultural relics (many of them copies) from Day 1 to 1919, subdivided into primitive communal groups, slavery, feudalism and capitalism/imperialism, laced with Marxist commentary. Without a guide you can discern ancient weapons, inventions and musical instruments.

The Museum of the Revolution is split into five sections: the founding of the CCP (1919-21), the first civil war (1924-27), the second civil war (1927-37), resistance against Japan (1937-45) and the third civil war (1945-49).

In 1978 a permanent photo-pictorial exhibit of the life and works of Zhou Enlai became a star attraction, and in 1983 there was an exhibit tracing the life of Liu Shaoqi. PLA soldiers are occasionally taken through the museums on tours; they snap to attention, open portable chairs and sit down in unison for explanations of each section. Whatever spiel they're given would probably be engrossing if you had someone to translate for you.

Monument to the People's Heroes

(rénmín yīngxióng jìniàn bēi)
人民英雄纪念碑

On the southern side of Tiananmen Square, this monument was completed in 1958 and stands on the site of the old Outer Palace Gate. The 36-metre obelisk, made of Qingdao granite, bears bas-relief carvings of key revolutionary events (one relief shows the Chinese destroying opium in the 19th century) as well as appropriate calligraphy from Mao Zedong and Zhou Enlai. In 1976 the obelisk was the focus of the 'Tiananmen Incident' when hundreds of thousands gathered here to protest the tyranny of the Gang of Four and to mourn the death of Zhou Enlai.

Mao Zedong Mausoleum

(máo zhǔxí jìniàn táng) 毛主席纪念堂

Behind the Monument to the People's Heroes stands this giant mausoleum built to house the body of Chairman Mao. Mao died in September 1976, and the mausoleum was constructed over a period of 10 months from 1976 to 1977. It occupies a prominent position on the powerful north-south axis of the city, but against all laws of geomancy this marble structure faces north. At the end of 1983 the mausoleum was re-opened as a museum with exhibitions on the lives of Zhou Enlai, Zhu De, Mao and the man he persecuted, Liu Shaoqi. Mao's body still remains in its place.

Whatever history will make of Mao, his impact on its course will remain unchanged: enormous. Easy as it now is to vilify his deeds and excesses, many Chinese show deep respect when confronted with the physical presence of the man. Shoving a couple of museums into the mausoleum was meant to knock Mao another rung down the divine ladder. Nevertheless the atmosphere in the inner sanctum is one of hushed reverence, with a thick red pile carpet muting any sound.

The mausoleum is open daily from 8.30 to 11.30 am (probably closed all winter). Join the enormous queue of Chinese sightseers, but don't expect more than a quick glimpse of the body as you file past the sarcophagus. The body is apparently lowered into the ground for the winter months, and not on view. The story goes that the Chinese had problems embalming Mao and had to call the Vietnamese to the rescue (Ho Chi Minh was also embalmed).

CITS guides freely quote the old 7:3 ratio on Mao that first surfaced in 1976. Mao was 70% right and 30% wrong (what, one wonders, are the figures for CITS itself?) and this is now the official Party line. His gross errors in the Cultural Revolution, it is said, are far outweighed by his contributions. What young people think of him now is quite another matter.

Don't forget, by the way, to buy some souvenirs of your visit. Mao Zedong Mausoleum keyrings, thermometers, face towels, handkerchiefs, sun visors, address books and cartons of cigarettes (a comment on the guy's chain-smoking?) are sold in souvenir bungalows outside the building.

Qianmen

(qiánmén) 前门

Silent sentinel to the changing times, Qianmen (Front Gate) has had its context removed. It's one of the few old gates left, and a great landmark to get around by. It guarded the wall division between the ancient Inner City and the outer suburban zone, and dates back to the reign of Emperor Yong Le in the 15th century.

Great Hall of the People

(rénmín dàhùi táng) 人民大会堂

This is the venue of the rubber-stamp legislature, the National People's Congress. It's open to the public when the Congress is not sitting. You tramp through the halls of power, many of them named after provinces and regions of China and decorated appropriately. You can see the 5000-seat banquet room where Nixon dined in 1972 and the 10,000-seat auditorium with the familiar red star embedded in a galaxy of lights in the ceiling. There's a sort of museum-like atmosphere in the Great Hall, with *objets d'art* donated by the provinces, and a snack bar and restaurant. The hall was completed over a 10-month period, from 1958 to 1959.

Forbidden City
(zǐjìnchéng) 紫禁城

The Forbidden City, so called because it was off limits for 500 years, is the largest and best preserved cluster of ancient buildings in China. It was home to two dynasties of emperors, the Ming and the Qing, who didn't stray from this pleasure-dome unless they absolutely had to.

The Forbidden City is open daily except Mondays, from 8.30 am to 5 pm. Two hundred years ago the admission price would have been instant death, but this has dropped considerably to Y12 for foreigners and Y0.50 for Chinese. Student discounts are available, but there are additional charges for some of the special exhibition halls. Just inside the gate, for Y20 you can rent a cassette tape player and tape for a self-guided tour – this requires a Y100 deposit. You must enter the Forbidden City from the south gate and exit from the north.

The basic layout was built between 1406 and 1420 by Emperor Yong Le, commanding battalions of labourers and craftspeople – some estimate up to a million of them. From this palace the emperors governed China, often rather erratically as they tended to become lost in this self-contained little world and allocated real power to the court eunuchs. One emperor devoted his entire career to carpentry – when an earthquake struck, an ominous sign for an emperor, he was delighted since it gave him a chance to renovate.

The buildings now seen are mostly post-18th-century, as with a lot of restored or rebuilt structures around Beijing. The palace was constantly going up in flames – a lantern festival combined with a sudden gust of Gobi wind would easily do the trick, as would a fireworks display. There were also deliberate fires lit by court eunuchs and officials who could get rich off the repair bills. The moat around the palace, now used for boating, came in handy since the local fire brigade was considered too common to quench the royal flames. Some of the emperors enjoyed the spectacle of fires, but Emperor Jiajing was so disturbed by them that he ordered a hall built in honour of the 'Fire-Pressing God'. Three fires caused by lightning broke out during his reign, including the biggest bonfire of the lot in 1557. A century later, in 1664, the Manchus stormed in and burned the palace to the ground.

It was not just the buildings that went up in smoke, but rare books, paintings, calligraphy, anything flammable. In this century

there have been two major lootings of the palace: first by the Japanese forces, and second by the Kuomintang, who on the eve of the Communist takeover in 1949 removed thousands of crates of relics to Taiwan, where they are now on display in Taipei's National Palace Museum – considered one of the top three museums in the world. The gaps have been filled by bringing treasures, old and newly discovered, from other parts of China.

The palace is so large (720,000 sq metres, 800 buildings, 9000 rooms) that a permanent restoration squad moves around repainting and repairing. It's estimated to take about 10 years to do a full renovation, by which time the beginning is due for repairs again. The complex was opened to the public in 1949.

The palace was built on a monumental scale, one that should not be taken lightly. Allow yourself a full day for exploration, or perhaps several separate trips if you're an enthusiast. The information given here can only be a skeleton guide; if you want more detail then tag along with a tour group for explanations of individual artefacts. There are plenty of Western tour groups around, and overall the Forbidden City gets 10,000 visitors a day. Tour buses drop their groups off at Tiananmen and pick them up again at the north gate; you can also enter the palace from the east or west gates. Even if you had a separate guidebook on the Forbidden City, it would be rather time-consuming to match up and identify every individual object, building and so forth – a spoken guide has more immediacy.

On the north-south axis of the Forbidden City, from Tiananmen at the south to Shenwumen at the north, lie the palace's ceremonial buildings.

Restored in the 17th century, Meridian Gate (Wumen) is a massive portal which in former times was reserved for the use of the emperor. Gongs and bells would be sounded upon royal comings and goings. Lesser mortals would use lesser gates – the military used the west gate, civilians used the east gate. The emperor also reviewed his armies from here, passed judgment on prisoners, announced the new year calendar and surveyed the flogging of cheeky ministers.

Across Golden Stream, which is shaped to resemble a Tartar bow and is spanned by five marble bridges, is Supreme Harmony Gate (Taihemen). It overlooks a massive courtyard that could hold an imperial audience of up to 100,000.

Raised on a marble terrace with balustrades are the Three Great Halls, the heart of the Forbidden City.

The Hall of Supreme Harmony (Taihedian) is the most important and the largest structure in the Forbidden City. Built in the 15th century and restored in the 17th century, it was used for ceremonial occasions such as the emperor's birthday, the nomination of military leaders, and coronations. Flanking the entrance to the hall are bronze incense burners. The large bronze turtle in the front is a symbol of longevity and stability – it has a removable lid and on special occasions incense was lit inside so that smoke billowed from the mouth. To the west side of the terrace is a small pavilion with a bronze grain-measure and to the east is a sundial; both are symbolic of imperial justice. On the corners of the roof, as with some other buildings in the city, you'll see a mounted figure with his retreat cut off by mythical and real animals, a story that relates to a cruel tyrant hung from one such eave. Inside the hall is a richly decorated Dragon Throne where the emperor would preside (decisions final, no correspondence entered into) over trembling officials. The entire court had to hit the floor nine times with their foreheads; combine that with thick veils of incense and battering of gongs and it would be enough to make anyone dizzy. At the back of the throne is a carved Xumishan, the Buddhist paradise, signifying the throne's supremacy.

Behind Taihedian is the smaller Hall of Middle Harmony (Zhonghedian) which was used as a transit lounge for the emperor. Here he would make last-minute preparations, rehearse speeches and receive close ministers. On display are two Qing Dynasty sedan chairs, the emperors' mode of transport around the Forbidden City. The last of the

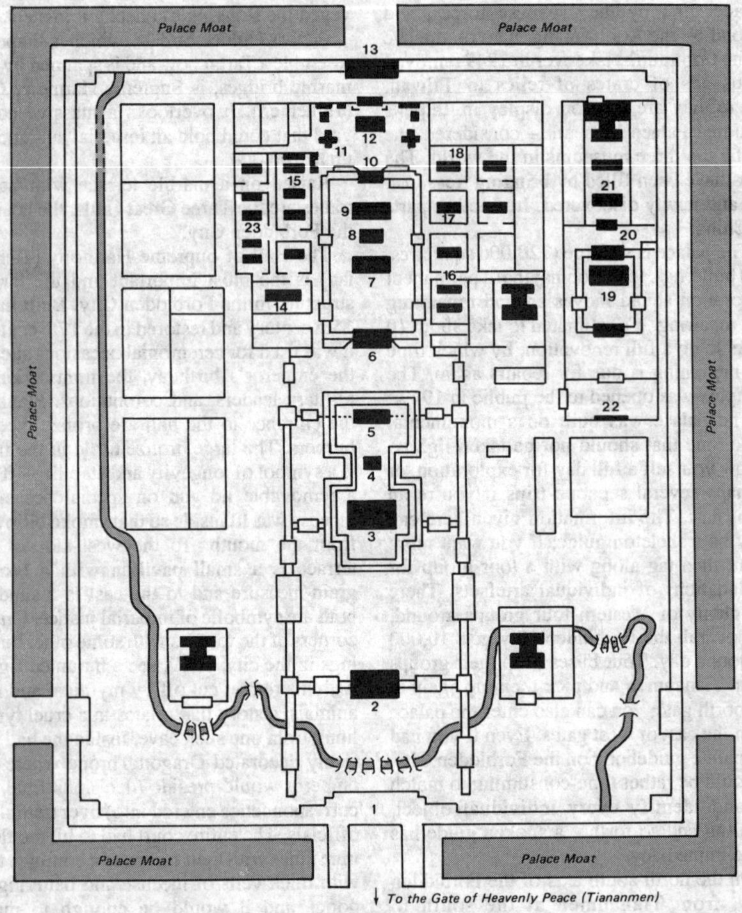

Palace Moat

Palace Moat

13

12

11

10

18

15

9

21

23

8

17

20

7

16

19

14

6

22

5

Palace Moat

Palace Moat

4

3

2

1

Palace Moat

Palace Moat

↓ *To the Gate of Heavenly Peace (Tiananmen)*

Palace Area of Forbidden City

紫禁城的宫殿地区

1 Meridian Gate (Wumen)
2 Supreme Harmony Gate (Taihemen)
3 Hall of Supreme Harmony (Taihedian)
4 Hall of Middle Harmony (Zhonghedian)
5 Hall of Preserving Harmony (Baohedian)
6 Gate of Heavenly Purity (Qianqingmen)
7 Palace of Heavenly Purity (Qianqinggong)
8 Hall of Union (Jiaotaidian)
9 Palace of Earthly Tranquillity (Kunninggong)
10 Imperial Garden
11 Thousand Autumns Pavilion
12 Hall of Imperial Peace
13 Gate of Divine Military Genius (Shenwumen)
14 Hall of Mental Cultivation (Yangxindian)
15 Western Palaces Nos 16, 17 & 18 (residential palaces now used as museums)
16 Exhibition of Bronzes
17 Exhibition of Ceramics
18 Exhibition of Ming & Qing Dynasty Arts & Crafts
19 Exhibition of Paintings (Hall of Imperial Supremacy)
20 Hall of the Cultivation of Character
21 Exhibition ofJewellery (Hall of the Cultivation of Character)
22 Nine Dragon Screen
23 Palace of Eternal Spring (Changchungong)

1 午门
2 太和门
3 太和殿
4 中和殿
5 保和殿
6 乾清门
7 乾清宫
8 交泰殿
9 坤宁宫
10 御花园
11 千秋亭
12 钦安殿
13 神武门
14 养心殿
15 宫廷史迹陈列
16 青铜器馆
17 陶瓷馆
18 明清工艺美术馆
19 绘画馆
20 养性殿
21 珍馆
22 九龙壁
23 长春宫

Qing emperors, Puyi, used a bicycle and altered a few features of the palace grounds to make it easier to get around.

The third hall is the Hall of Preserving Harmony (Baohedian) used for banquets and later for imperial examinations. It now houses archaeological finds. The Baohedian has no support pillars, and behind it is a 250-tonne marble block carved with dragons and clouds which was moved into Beijing on an ice path. The outer housing surrounding the Three Great Halls was used for storing gold, silver, silks, carpets and other treasures.

The basic configuration of the Three Great Halls is mimicked by the next group of buildings, smaller in scale but more important in terms of real power. In China, real power traditionally lies at the back door, or in this case, the back gate.

The first structure is the Palace of Heavenly Purity (Qianqinggong), a residence of Ming and early Qing emperors, and later an audience hall for receiving foreign envoys and high officials.

Immediately behind it is the Hall of Union, which contains a clepsydra – a water clock with five bronze vessels and a calibrated scale. Water clocks date back several thousand years but this one was made in 1745. There's also a mechanical clock on display, built in 1797, and a collection of imperial jade seals.

At the northern end of the Forbidden City is the Imperial Garden, a classical Chinese garden of 7000 sq metres of fine landscaping, with rockeries, walkways and pavilions. A good place to take a breather, with snack bars, WCs and souvenir shops. Two more gates lead out through the large Gate of Divine Military Genius (Shenwumen).

North of Shenwumen and outside the present confines of the Forbidden City is Coal Hill (Jingshan Park) *(jǐngshān gōngyúan)*, which contains an artificial mound made of earth excavated to create the palace moat. If you clamber to the top pavilions of this regal pleasure garden you get a magnificent panorama of the capital and a great overview of the russet roofing of the Forbidden City. On the east side of the park is a locust tree where the last of the Mings, Emperor Chongzhen, hanged himself (after slaying his family) rather than see the palace razed by the Manchus. The hill supposedly protects the palace from the evil spirits – or dust storms – from the north, but didn't quite work for Chongzhen.

The western and eastern sides of the Forbidden City are the palatial former living quarters – once containing libraries, temples, theatres, gardens, even the tennis court of the last emperor. These buildings now function as museums and often require separate but nominal admission fees. Opening hours are irregular and no photos are allowed without prior permission. Special exhibits sometimes appear in the palace museum halls – check the *China Daily* for details.

On the western side of the Forbidden City, towards the north exit, are the six Western Palaces which were living quarters for the empress and the concubines. These are kept in pristine condition, displaying furniture, silk bedcovers, personal items, and fittings such as cloisonné charcoal burners.

Of particular interest is the Palace of Eternal Spring (Changchungong), decorated with mural scenes from the Ming novel *A Dream of Red Mansions*. This is where the Empress Dowager Cixi lived when she was still a concubine.

Nearby is the Hall of Mental Cultivation (Yangxindian), a private apartment for the emperors. It was divided into reception rooms, a study where important documents were signed and a bedchamber at the rear.

On the eastern side of the City, six more palaces duplicate the rhythms and layout of those on the west. There are museums here for bronzes, ceramics, and Ming Dynasty arts and crafts. Further east is a display of gold and jade artefacts and Ming and Qing paintings, sometimes augmented with Song and Yuan paintings. Just south, protecting the gateway to two of the palaces, is the polychrome Nine Dragon Screen built in 1773.

A few more interesting aspects of the Forbidden City include the watchtowers at the four corners of the city which stand on top of the walls. Structural delights, they have three storeys, are double-roofed and measure 27.5 metres high.

Zhongshan Park *(zhōngshān gōngyúan)*, otherwise known as Sun Yatsen Park, is in the south-west of the Forbidden City and was laid out at the same time as the palace. Here you'll find the Altar of Land and Grain, which is divided into five sections, each filled with earth of a different colour (red, green, black, yellow and white) to symbolise all the earth belonging to the emperor. There is also a concert hall and a 'modernisation' playground in the park.

The Workers' Cultural Palace *(láodòng rénmín wénhùa gōng)* in the south-east sector of the Forbidden City is a park with halls dating from 1462 which were used as ancestral temples under the Ming and Qing; they come complete with marble balustrades, terraces and detailed gargoyles. The park is now used for movies, temporary exhibits, cultural performances and the odd mass wedding. There's boating at the north end and skating in winter on the frozen moat.

A Day in the Life... Four hundred years ago the Jesuit priest Matteo Ricci spent 20 years in China, much of that time at the imperial court in Beijing. He recorded in his diary:

> Just as this people is grossly subject to superstition, so, too, they have very little regard for the truth, acting always with great circumspection, and very cautious about trusting anyone. Subject to this same fear, the kings of modern times abandoned the custom of going out in public. Even formerly, when they did leave the royal enclosure, they would never dare to do so without a thousand preliminary precautions. On such occasions the whole court was placed under military guard. Secret servicemen were placed along the route over which the King was to travel and on all roads leading into it. He was not only hidden from view, but the public never knew in which of the palanquins of his cortège he was actually riding. One would think he was making a journey through enemy country rather than through multitudes of his own subjects and clients.

Behind the Wall If ceremonial and administrative duties occupied much of the emperor's time, then behind the high walls of the Forbidden City it was the pursuit of pleasure which occupied much of his attention. One of the imperial bedtime systems was to keep the names of royal wives, consorts and favourites on jade tablets near the emperor's chambers – sometimes as many as 50 of them.

By turning the tablet over the emperor made his request for the evening, and the eunuch on duty would rush off to find the lucky lady. Stripped naked and therefore 'weaponless' she was wrapped in a yellow cloth, and the little bound-footed creature was piggybacked over to the royal boudoir and dumped at the feet of the emperor; the eunuch recorded the date and time to verify legitimacy of a possible child.

Financing the pleasure-dome was an arduous affair that drew on the resources of the empire. During the Ming Dynasty there were an estimated 9000 maids of honour and 70,000 eunuchs serving the court. Apart from the servants and the concubines there were also the royal elephants to upkeep. These were gifts from Burma and were stabled south-west of the Forbidden City. Accorded rank by the emperor, when one died a period of mourning was declared. Periodically the elephant keepers embezzled the funds intended for elephant chow. When this occurred, the ravenous pachyderms went on a rampage.

While pocketing this cash was illegal, selling elephant dung for use as shampoo was not, and it was believed to give the hair that extra sheen. Back in the harem the cosmetic bills piled up to 400,000 taels of silver. Then, of course, the concubines who had grown old and gone out of active service were still supposed to be cared for. Rather than cut back on expenditure, the emperor sent out eunuchs to collect emergency taxes whenever money ran short.

As for the palace eunuchs, the royal chop was administered at the Eunuch Clinic near the Forbidden City, using a swift knife and a special chair with a hole in the seat. The candidates sought to better their lives in the service of the court but half of them died after the 'operation'. Mutilation of any kind was considered grounds for exclusion to the next life, so many eunuchs carried their appendages around in pouches, believing that at the time of death the spirits might be deceived into thinking of them as whole.

Museums & Libraries

The best museums are in the Forbidden City, and the biggest are the combined History Museum & Museum of the Revolution in Tiananmen Square. The most interesting are the temporary exhibits held in parks or places like the Nationalities Cultural Palace. Museums in Beijing are poorly maintained and presented, and little research work is done.

Military Museum *(jūnshì bówùgǔan)* Perhaps more to the point than the Museum of the Revolution, this traces the genesis of the PLA from 1927 to the present and has some interesting exhibits: pictures of Mao in the early days, mind-boggling Socialist Realist artwork, captured American tanks and other tools of destruction. After the bloody suppression of pro-democracy demonstrators in 1989, obviously staged photos of burnt carcasses dressed in immaculate unburnt army uniforms were displayed in a pathetic attempt to prove that the students massacred innocent soldiers. The museum is on Fuxing Lu on the western side of the city; to get there take the subway to Junshibowuguan.

Lu Xun Museum *(lǔ xùn bówùgǔan)* Dedicated to China's No 1 Thinking Person's Revolutionary, this museum contains manuscripts, diaries, letters and inscriptions by the famous writer. To the west of the museum is a small Chinese walled compound where Lu Xun lived from 1924 to 1926. The museum is off Fuchengmennei Dajie, west of the Xisi intersection on the north-western side of the city.

Beijing Library *(běijīng túshūgǔan)* This holds around five million books and four million periodicals and newspapers, over a third of which are in foreign languages. Access to books is limited and access to rare books is even rarer, though you might be shown a microfilm copy if you're lucky. The large collection of rare books includes surviving imperial works such as the *Yong Le Encyclopedia* and selections from the old Jesuit library. Of interest to Ming-Qing scholars is the special collection, the *Shanbenbu*. The library is near Beihai Park on the south side. Beijing University Library also has a large collection of rare books.

Capital Museum & Library *(shǒudū túshūgǔan)* Formerly a Confucian temple, the museum houses steles, stone inscriptions, bronzes, vases and documents. It's near the Lama Temple out northwards towards Ditan Park.

China Art Gallery *(zhōnggúo měishù gǔan)* Back in the post-Liberation days one of the safest hobbies for an artist was to retouch classical-type landscapes with red flags, belching factory chimneys or bright red tractors. You can get some idea of the state of the arts in China at this gallery. At times very good exhibitions of current work including photo displays are held in an adjacent gallery. Check the *China Daily* for listings. The arts & crafts shop inside has an excellent range of woodblock prints and papercuts. The gallery is west of the Dongsi intersection.

Xu Beihong Museum *(xú bēihóng bówùgǔan)* Here you'll find traditional Chinese paintings, oils, gouaches, sketches and memorabilia of the famous artist, noted for his galloping horse paintings. Painting albums are on sale, as well as reproductions and Chinese stationery. The museum is at 53 Xinjiekou Beidajie, Xicheng District.

Song Qingling Museum *(sòng qìnglíng gùjū)* Madam Song was the wife of Sun Yatsen, the founder of the Republic of China. After 1981 her large residence was transformed into a museum dedicated to her memory and to that of Sun Yatsen. The original layout of the residence is unchanged and on display are personal items and pictures of historical interest. The museum is on the north side of Shisha Houhai lake.

Zhongnanhai
(zhōngnánhǎi) 中南海

Just west of the Forbidden City is China's new forbidden city, Zhongnanhai. The name means 'the central and south seas' in this case after the two large lakes in the compound. The southern entrance is via Xinhuamen (Gate of New China) which you'll see on Chang'an Jie; it's guarded by two PLA soldiers and fronted by a flagpole with the red flag flying. The gate was built in 1758 and was then known as the Tower of the Treasured Moon.

The compound was first built between the 10th and 13th centuries as a sort of playground for the emperors and their retinue. It was expanded during Ming times but most of the present buildings only date from the Qing Dynasty. After the overthrow of the imperial government and the establishment of the Republic it served as the site of the presidential palace.

Since the founding of the People's Republic in 1949, Zhongnanhai has been the site of the residence and offices of the highest-ranking members of the Communist Party. People like Mao Zedong, Zhou Enlai, Liu Shaoqi and Zhu De have all lived and worked in the area. The offices of the Central Committee of the Communist Party and of the State Council, the Central People's Government and the Military Commission of the Party Central Committee are here.

Prior to the arrival of the new batch of tenants Zhongnanhai had been the site of the emperor's ploughing of the first symbolic furrow of the farming season, and the venue for imperial banquets and the highest examinations in martial arts. Empress Dowager Cixi once lived here; after the failure of the 1898 reform movement she imprisoned Emperor Guangxu in the Hall of Impregnating Vitality where, ironically, he later died. Yuan Shikai used Zhongnanhai for ceremonial occasions during the few years of his presidency of the Chinese Republic; his vice-president moved into Guangxu's death-house.

Beihai Park

(běihǎi gōngyúan) 北海公园

Approached by four gates, and just north-west of the Forbidden City, Beihai Park is the former playground of the emperors. It's rumoured to have been the private pleasure domain of the great dragon lady/witch Jiang Qing, widow of Mao who, until her death in May 1991, was serving a life sentence as No 1 of the Gang of Four. The park covers an area of 68.2 hectares, half of which is a lake. The island in the lower middle is composed of the heaped earth dug to create the lake – some attribute this to the handiwork of Kublai Khan.

The site is associated with the Great Khan's palace, the belly-button of Beijing before the creation of the Forbidden City. All that remains of the Khan's court is a large jar made of green jade, in the Round City near the south entrance. A present given in 1265, and said to have contained the Khan's wine, it was later discovered in the hands of Taoist priests who used it to store pickles. In the Light Receiving Hall, the main structure nearby, is a 1½-metre-high white jade Buddha inlaid with jewels – a gift from Burma to Empress Dowager Cixi.

From the 12th century on, Beihai Park was landscaped with artificial hills, pavilions, halls, temples and covered walkways. In the present era the structures have been massively restored and Beihai Park is now one of the best examples of a classical garden found in China. Dominating Jade Islet on the lake, the White Dagoba is a 36-metre-high pop-art 'Peppermint Bottle' originally dating from 1651. It was put up for a visit by the Dalai Lama and was rebuilt in 1741. It's believed that Lamaist scriptures, robes and other sacred objects are encased in this brick-and-stone landmark.

On the north-east shore of the islet is the handsome double-tiered Painted Gallery – with unusual architecture for a walkway. Near the boat-dock is the Fangshan Restaurant, dishing up recipes favoured by Empress Cixi. She liked 120-course dinners with about 30 kinds of desserts. The restaurant is expensive and high class, and reservations are necessary (but check out the decor!). Off to one side, however, is a snack bar that dispenses royal pastries much more cheaply.

From this point you can catch a barge to the north-west part of the park or, if energetic, double back and hire a rowing boat (there's another rowing-boat hire place on the north-west side). The attraction on the north side is the Nine Dragon Screen, five metres high and 27 metres long, made of coloured glazed tiles. It's one of the three most famous ones in the PRC, and is in good shape. The screen was to scare off evil spirits; it stands at the entrance to a temple which has disappeared. To the south-west of the boat dock on this side is the Five Dragon Pavilion dating from 1651, where the emperors liked to fish or camp out at night to watch the moon.

On the east side of the park are the 'gardens within gardens'. These waterside pavilions, winding corridors and rockeries were summer haunts of the imperial family, notably Emperor Qianlong and Empress

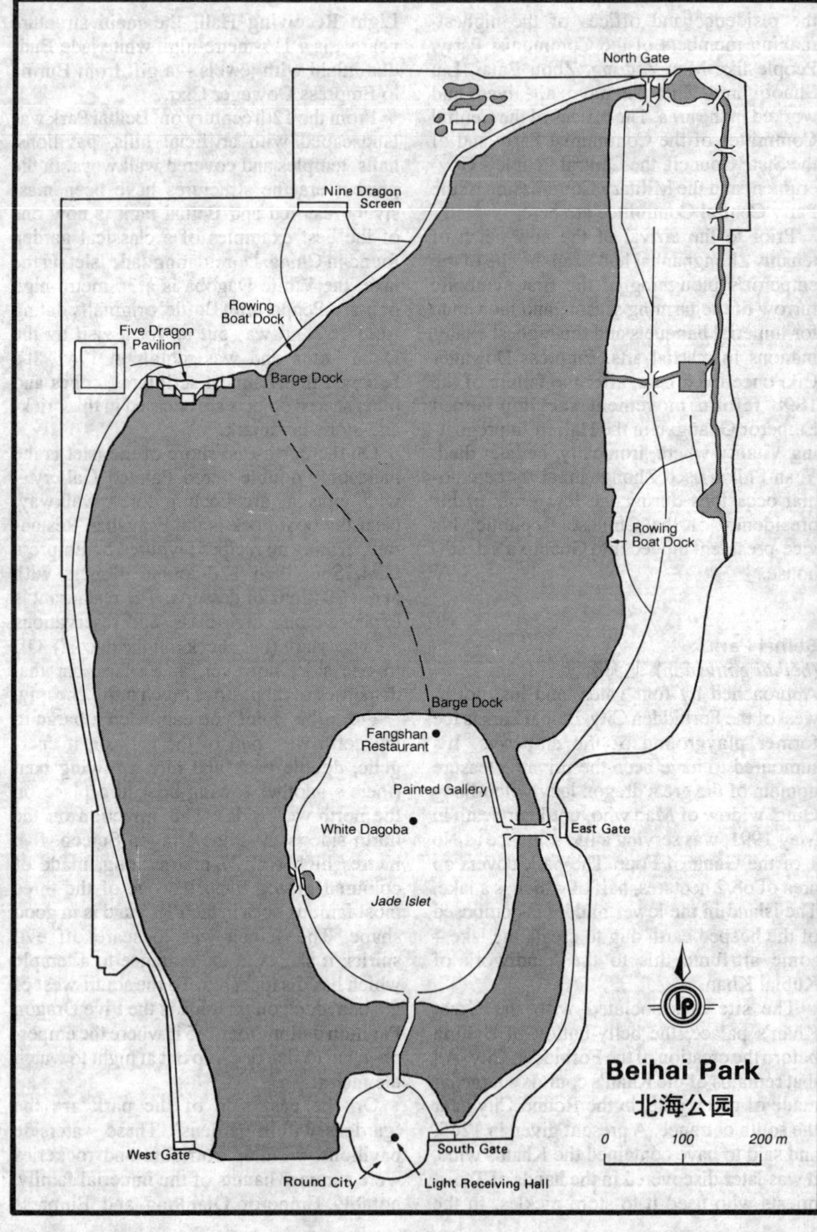

North Gate
Nine Dragon Screen
Rowing Boat Dock
Five Dragon Pavilion
Barge Dock
Rowing Boat Dock
Barge Dock
Fangshan Restaurant
Painted Gallery
White Dagoba
East Gate
Jade Islet
Beihai Park
北海公园
0
100
200 m
West Gate
South Gate
Round City
Light Receiving Hall

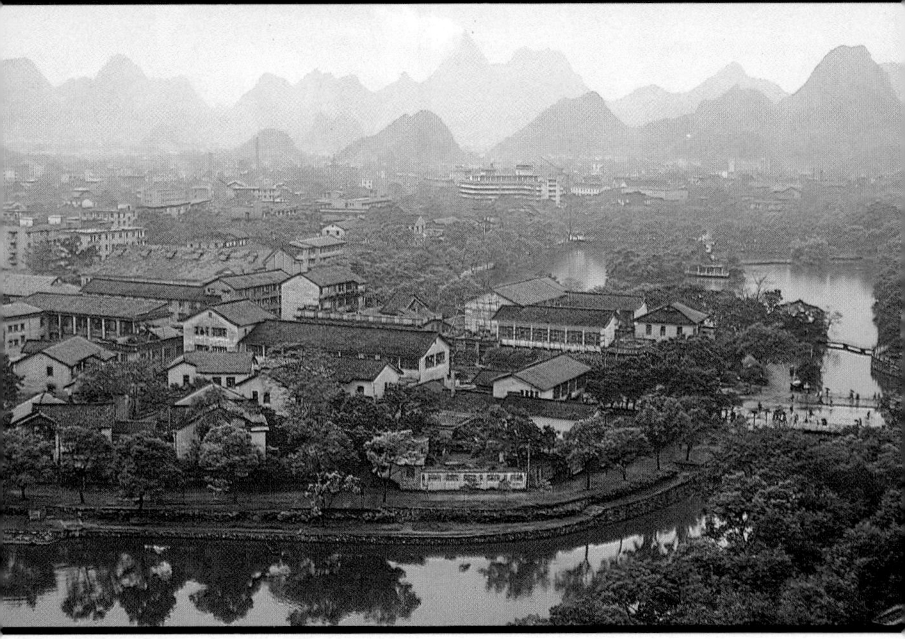

Top: The Pearl River, Canton (AS)
Bottom: View from Lijiang Hotel, Guilin (AS)

Top: Keeping an eye on the masses, Dali (RS)
Bottom Left: Upright official declining foreign enticement, Xiahe (RS)
Bottom Right: Apprehended criminals, Guilin (AS)

Cixi. They date back some 200 years, with structures like the Painted Boat Studio and the Studio of Mental Calmness. Until 1980 the villas were used as government offices.

Beihai Park is a relaxing place to stroll around, grab a snack, sip a beer, rent a rowing boat or, as the Chinese do, cuddle on a bench in the evening. It's crowded at weekends. Some people dive into the lake when no-one's around – swimming is not permitted. In winter there's skating. This is nothing new in China – skating apparently goes back to the 18th century when Emperor Qianlong reviewed the imperial skating parties here.

Other Parks

In imperial days the parks were laid out at the compass-points: to the west of the Forbidden City lies Yuetan (Temple of the Moon) Park *(yùetán gōngyúan)*; to the north lies Ditan (Temple of Earth) Park *(dìtán gōngyúan)*; to the south lies Taoranting (Happy Pavilion) Park *(táorántíng gōngyúan)* and to the east is Ritan (Temple of the Sun) Park *(rìtán gōngyúan)*. To the south-east of the Forbidden City is the showpiece of them all, Tiantan (Temple of Heaven) Park *(tiāntán gōngyúan)*.

All of these parks were venues for ritual sacrifices offered by the emperors. Not much remains of the shaman structures, bar those of Tiantan, but if you arrive early in the morning you can witness taiji, fencing exercises, or perhaps opera-singers and musicians practising. It's well worth investigating the very different rhythms of the city at this time. Other notable parks are Zi zhuyuan (Purple Bamboo) Park *(zǐzhúyùan)*, west of the zoo; Longtan (Dragon Pool) Park *(lóngtán gōngyúan)*, east of Tiantan; and Yuyuantan (Jade Hole Pool) Park *(yùyūantún gōngyúan)* on the west side of the city.

Temporary exhibitions take place in the parks, including horticultural and cultural ones, and there is even the odd bit of open-air theatre as well as some worthy eating establishments. Just to the north of Yuetan Park is the Emei Restaurant, which serves hot Sichuan food with no compromise for foreign palates – Sichuan food addicts prefer it to the Sichuan Restaurant itself. The Ritan Restaurant in Ritan Park serves jiaozi in an older-style pavilion and is very popular with Westerners for snacks. If you take up residence in Beijing, the parks become very important for preserving sanity. They are open late too, typically until 8 pm.

Tiantan

(tiāntán) 天坛

The perfection of Ming architecture, Tiantan (the Temple of Heaven) has come to symbolise Beijing. Its lines appear on countless pieces of tourist literature (including your five jiao tourist bill), and as a brand name for a wide range of products from Tiger Balm to plumbing fixtures. In the 1970s the complex got a facelift and was freshly painted after pigment research. It is set in a 267-hectare

park, with four gates at the compass points, and bounded by walls to the north and east. It originally functioned as a vast stage for solemn rites performed by the Son of Heaven who came here to pray for good harvests, seek divine clearance and atone for the sins of the people.

With this complicated mix in mind, the unique architectural features will delight numerologists, necromancers and the superstitious – not to mention acoustic engineers and carpenters. Shape, colour and sound take on symbolic significance. The temples, seen in aerial perspective, are round, and the bases are square, deriving from the ancient Chinese belief that heaven is round, and the earth is square. Thus the north end of the park is semicircular and the south end is square (the Temple of Earth is on the northern compass point and the Temple of Heaven on the southern compass point).

The Temple of Heaven was considered highly sacred ground and it was here that the emperor performed the major ceremonial rites of the year. Just before the winter solstice, the emperor and his enormous entourage passed down Qianmen Dajie to the Imperial Vault of Heaven in total silence – commoners were not permitted to view the ceremony and remained cloistered indoors. The procession included elephant chariots, horse chariots and long lines of lancers, nobles, officials and musicians, dressed in their finest, flags fluttering. The next day the emperor waited in a yellow silk tent at the south gate while officials moved the sacred tablets to the Round Altar, where the prayers and sacrificial rituals took place. The least hitch in any part of the proceedings was regarded as an ill omen, and it was thought that the nation's future was thus decided. This was the most important ceremony although other excursions to Ditan (Temple of Earth) also took place.

Temple of Heaven, Beijing

Admission to the park is 1 jiao, and an additional Y2 for the Hall of Prayer for Good Harvests.

Round Altar The five-metre-high Round Altar was constructed in 1530 and rebuilt in 1740. It is composed of white marble arrayed in three tiers, and its geometry revolves around the imperial number nine. Odd numbers were considered heavenly, and nine is the largest single-digit odd number. The top tier, thought to symbolise heaven, has nine rings of stones, each ring composed of multiples of nine stones, so that the ninth ring has 81 stones. The middle tier – earth – has the 10th to 18th rings. The bottom tier – man – has the 19th to 27th rings, ending with a total of 243 stones in the largest ring, or 27 times nine. The number of stairs and balustrades are also multiples of nine. If you stand in the centre of the upper terrace and say something, the sound waves are bounced off the marble balustrades, making your voice appear louder (nine times?).

Echo Wall Just north of the altar, surrounding the entrance to the Imperial Vault of Heaven, is the Echo Wall, 65 metres in diameter. This enables a whisper to travel clearly from one end to your friend's ear at the other – that is, if there's not a group tour in the middle.

In the courtyard are the Triple Echo Stones. If you stand on the first one and clap or shout, the sound is echoed once, on the second stone twice, and on the third, three times. Should it return four times, you will almost certainly not get a railway ticket that

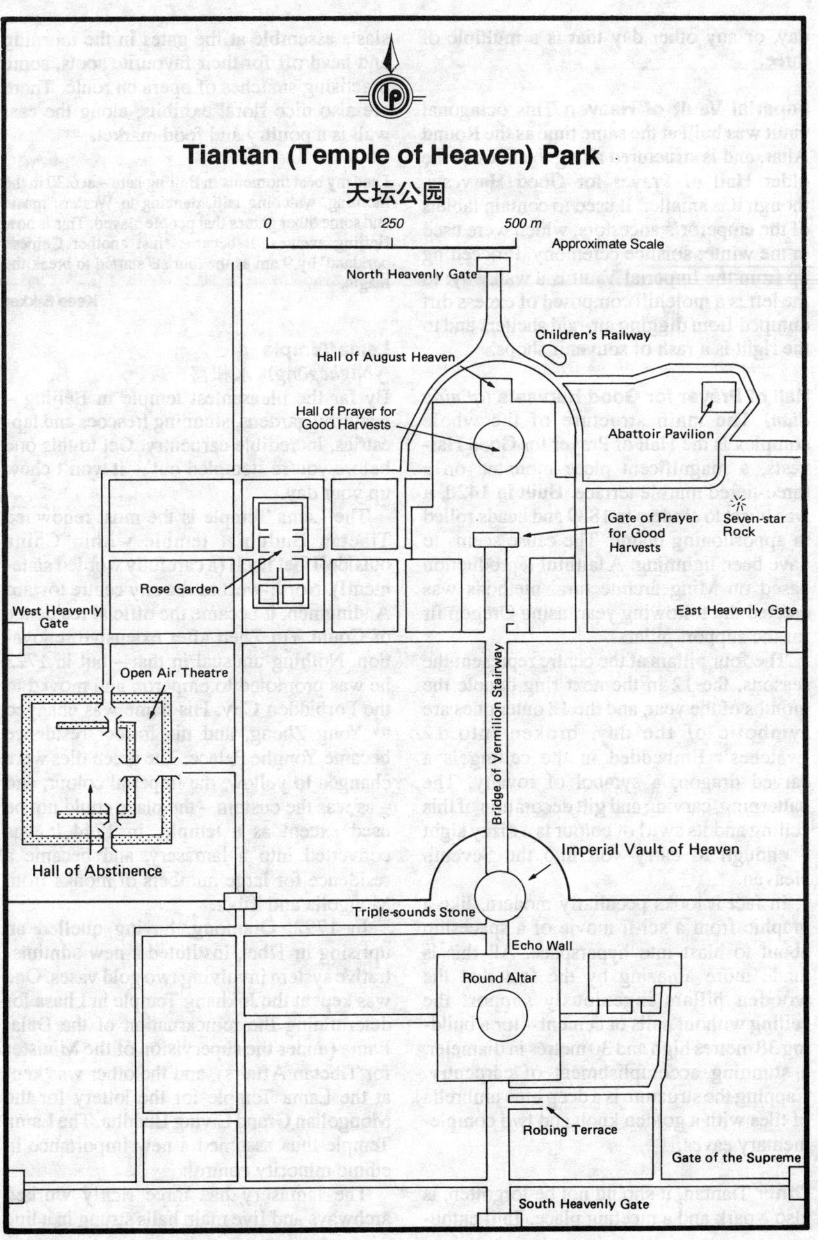
Tiantan (Temple of Heaven) Park
天坛公园
0
250
500 m
Approximate Scale
North Heavenly Gate
Children's Railway
Hall of August Heaven
Hall of Prayer for Good Harvests
Abattoir Pavilion
Gate of Prayer for Good Harvests
Seven-star Rock
Rose Garden
West Heavenly Gate
East Heavenly Gate
Open Air Theatre
Bridge of Vermilion Stairway
Imperial Vault of Heaven
Hall of Abstinence
Triple-sounds Stone
Echo Wall
Round Altar
Robing Terrace
Gate of the Supreme
South Heavenly Gate

day, or any other day that is a multiple of three.

Imperial Vault of Heaven This octagonal vault was built at the same time as the Round Altar, and is structured along the lines of the older Hall of Prayer for Good Harvests, though it is smaller. It used to contain tablets of the emperor's ancestors, which were used in the winter solstice ceremony. Proceeding up from the Imperial Vault is a walkway: to the left is a molehill composed of excess dirt dumped from digging air-raid shelters and to the right is a rash of souvenir shops.

Hall of Prayer for Good Harvests *(qí nián diàn)* The main structure of the whole complex is the Hall of Prayer for Good Harvests, a magnificent piece mounted on a three-tiered marble terrace. Built in 1420, it was burnt to cinders in 1889 and heads rolled in apportioning blame. The cause seems to have been lightning. A faithful reproduction based on Ming architectural methods was erected the following year, using Oregon fir for the support pillars.

The four pillars at the centre represent the seasons, the 12 in the next ring denote the months of the year, and the 12 outer ones are symbolic of the day, broken into 12 'watches'. Embedded in the ceiling is a carved dragon, a symbol of royalty. The patterning, carving and gilt decoration of this ceiling and its swirl of colour is a dizzy sight – enough to carry you into the Seventh Heaven.

In fact it looks peculiarly modern, like a graphic from a sci-fi movie of a spaceship about to blast into hyperspace. All this is made more amazing by the fact that the wooden pillars ingeniously support the ceiling without nails or cement – for a building 38 metres high and 30 metres in diameter, a stunning accomplishment of carpentry. Capping the structure is a deep blue umbrella of tiles with a golden knob and two complementary eaves.

Other Tiantan, it should not be forgotten, is also a park and a meeting place. Taiji enthusiasts assemble at the gates in the morning and head off for their favourite spots, some practising snatches of opera en route. There are also nice floral exhibits; along the east wall is a poultry and food market.

I had my best moments in Beijing here – at 6.30 in the morning, watching taiji, dancing to Western music and some other games that people played. This is how Beijing awakes. It became 'just another Chinese parkland' by 9 am as the tourists started to break the magic.

Kees Bikker

Lama Temple

(yōnghégōng) 永和宫

By far the pleasantest temple in Beijing – beautiful gardens, stunning frescoes and tapestries, incredible carpentry. Get to this one before you're 'templed out' – it won't chew up your day.

The Lama Temple is the most renowned Tibetan Buddhist temple within China outside Tibet itself (a carefully worded statement!). North-west of the city centre toward Andingmen, it became the official residence of Count Yin Zhen after extensive renovation. Nothing unusual in that – but in 1723 he was promoted to emperor, and moved to the Forbidden City. His name was changed to Yong Zheng, and his former residence became Yonghe Palace. The green tiles were changed to yellow, the imperial colour, and – as was the custom – the place could not be used except as a temple. In 1744 it was converted into a lamasery, and became a residence for large numbers of monks from Mongolia and Tibet.

In 1792, Qianlong, having quelled an uprising in Tibet, instituted a new administrative system involving two gold vases. One was kept at the Jokhang Temple in Lhasa for determining the reincarnation of the Dalai Lama (under the supervision of the Minister for Tibetan Affairs), and the other was kept at the Lama Temple for the lottery for the Mongolian Grand Living Buddha. The Lama Temple thus assumed a new importance in ethnic minority control.

The lamasery has three richly worked archways and five main halls strung in a line down the middle, each taller than the preceding one. Styles are mixed – Mongolian, Tibetan and Han, with courtyard enclosures and galleries.

The first hall, Lokapala, houses a statue of the Maitreya (future) Buddha, flanked by celestial guardians. The statue facing the back door is Weituo, guardian of Buddhism, made of white sandalwood. Beyond, in the courtyard, is a pond with a bronze mandala depicting Xumishan, the Buddhist paradise.

The second hall, Yonghedian, has three figures of Buddha – past, present and future.

The third hall, Yongyoudian, has statues of the Buddha of Longevity and the Buddha of Medicine (to the left). The courtyard following it has galleries with some nandikesvaras – joyful buddhas tangled up in multi-armed close encounters. These are coyly draped lest you be corrupted by the sight, and are to be found in other esoteric locations.

The Hall of the Wheel of Law, further north, contains a large bronze statue of Tsongkapa (1357-1419), founder of the Yellow Sect, and frescoes depicting his life. This Tibetan-style building is used for study and prayer.

The last hall, Wanfu Pavilion, has an 18-metre-high statue of the Maitreya Buddha in his Tibetan form, sculpted from a single piece of sandalwood and clothed in yellow satin. The smoke curling up from the yak-butter lamps transports you momentarily to Tibet, which is where the log for this statue came from.

In 1949 the Lama Temple was declared protected as a major historical relic. Miraculously it survived the Cultural Revolution without scars. In 1979 large amounts of money were spent on repairs and it was restocked with several dozen novices from Inner Mongolia, a token move on the part of the government to back up its claim that the Lama Temple is a 'symbol of religious freedom, national unity and stability in China'. The novices study Tibetan language and the secret practices of the Yellow Sect.

The temple is very much active again. Prayers take place early in the morning, not for public viewing, but if you enquire discreetly of the head lama you might be allowed to return the following morning. No photography is permitted inside the temple buildings, tempting as it is – in part due to the monkish sensitivity to the reproduction of Buddha images, and partly perhaps to the postcard industry. The temple is open daily, except Monday, from 9 am to 4 pm.

Confucian Temple & Imperial College

(kǒng miào) 孔庙

Just down the hutong opposite the gates of the Lama Temple is the former Confucian Temple and Imperial College ***(gúozijiān)***. The Confucian Temple is the largest in the land after the one at Qufu. The temple was re-opened in 1981 after some mysterious use as a high-official residence and is now used as a museum – in sharp contrast to the Lama Temple.

The forest of steles in the temple courtyard look forlorn. The steles record the names of those successful in the civil service examinations (possibly the world's first) of the imperial court. To see his name engraved here was the ambition of every scholar, but it wasn't made easy. Candidates were locked in cubicles (about 8000 of them) measuring roughly 1½ by 1½ metres for a period of three days. Many died or went insane during their incarceration.

The Imperial College was the place where the emperor expounded the Confucian classics to an audience of thousands of kneeling students, professors and court officials – an annual rite. Built by the grandson of Kublai Khan in 1306, the former college was the only institution of its kind in China; it's now the Capital Library. Part of the 'collection' are the stone tablets commissioned by Emperor Qianlong. These are engraved with 13 Confucian classics – 800,000 characters or 12 years' work for the scholar who did it. There is an ancient 'Scholar-Tree' in the courtyard.

Celestial Potpourri

There are heaps of smaller temples and other divine edifices scattered around the capital, all in varying states of preservation, decay or renovation. These have now been put to use as warehouses, residences, schools, army barracks, factories and so on. They may even be open to visitors or quick peepers. Some are listed following.

Wuta Temple *(wǔtǎ sì)* This is an Indian-style temple with five pagodas, first constructed in 1473 from a model presented to the court. North-west of the zoo, it's difficult to find but has been restored and re-opened. Take Baishiqiao Lu north from the zoo for almost one km to a bridge, and turn east to the temple, which lies in the middle of a field.

Great Bell Temple *(dàzhōngsì)* This temple is almost two km due east of the Friendship Hotel on Beisanhuan Xilu, and has an enormous 46-tonne bell inscribed with Buddhist sutras. The bell was cast during the reign of Ming Emperor Yong Le in 1406 and the tower was built in 1733. This monastery is one of the most popular in Beijing and was re-opened in 1980.

White Dagoba Temple *(báitǎ sì)* The dagoba can be spotted from the top of Jingshan, and is similar (and close to) the one in Beihai Park. It was used as a factory during the Cultural Revolution but reopened after restoration in 1980. The dagoba dates back to Kublai Khan's days and was completed with the help of a Nepalese architect, though the halls date only from the Qing Dynasty. It lies off Fuchengmennei Dajie.

Guangji Temple *(gǔangjì sì)* The Guangji (Universal Rescue) Temple is on the north-west side of Xisi intersection, and east of the White Dagoba Temple. It's in good shape and is the headquarters of the Chinese Buddhist Association. It is said to contain some of the finest Buddhist statues in China and may be open to the public.

Xihuang Temple *(xīhúang sì)* The Xihuang (West Yellow) Temple can be seen from Beihuan Donglu ring road (south side). It is a fair distance out of the city centre, north-west of the intersection of Andingmen and Andingmenwai Dajie. The temple has a distinctive gold-and-white dagoba and was used as the residence for visiting Panchen Lamas from Tibet in the 17th century.

Niujie Mosque *(niújiē lǐbài sì)* In the south-west sector of Beijing, south of Guang'anmennei Dajie, is a Muslim residential area with a handsome mosque facing Mecca. Niujie (Ox St) is an area worth checking out with a feel all its own. In a lane further east of the mosque is the Fayuan (Source of Law) Temple. The temple was originally constructed in the 7th century and is still going strong – it's now a Buddhist college, open to visitors.

White Cloud Temple *(báiyúngūan)* This is in a district directly south of Yanjing Hotel and west of the moat. It was once the Taoist centre of North China and the site of temple fairs. Check a map for directions. Walk south on Baiyun Lu and cross the moat. Continue south along Baiyun Lu and turn into a curving street on the left; follow it for 250 metres to the temple entrance.

Further south of the White Cloud Temple is the Tianningsi pagoda, looking pretty miserable in a virtual industrial junkyard. The temple once attached has disappeared.

Cathedrals The East Cathedral *(dōngtáng)* at 74 Wangfujing was built on the site of the house of the Jesuit priest Adam Schall. It was founded in 1666 and was later used by the Portuguese Lazarists. It has been rebuilt several times and is now used as a primary school during the week; Catholic services are held early on Sunday mornings.

South Cathedral *(nántáng)*, on Qianmen at the Xuanwumen intersection (north-east side) above the Metro station, is built on the site of Matteo Ricci's house (first built 1703 and destroyed three times since then).

North Cathedral *(běitáng)*, or the Cathedral of Our Saviour, was built in 1887. It was badly damaged during the Cultural Revolution and converted to a factory warehouse. It was re-opened at the end of 1985 after restoration work was completed. The cathedral is at Xishiku, in the West District.

Black Temple *(zhìhùa sì)* So nicknamed because of its deep blue tiling, this is a pretty example of Ming architecture (dating from 1443) but there's nothing else of note. If you strain over the bus map, looking north of the main railway station, you will find a hutong called Lumicang, which runs east off Chaoyangmen Nanxiaojie (about 1½ km north of the station). The temple is at the east end of Lumicang. The coffered ceiling of the third hall of the Growth of Intellect Temple is not at the east end of Lumicang – it's in the USA. Lumicang hutong had rice granaries in the Qing Dynasty.

Underground City
(dì xià chéng) 地下城
With a Soviet invasion supposedly hanging over them in the late '60s, the Chinese built huge civil defence systems, especially in northern China. This hobby started before 1949 when the PLA used the tunnelling technique to surprise the enemy. Pressed for space, and trying to maximise the peacetime possibilities of the air-raid shelters (aside from the fact that the shelters are useless in the event of nuclear attack) Beijing has put them to use as warehouses, factories, shops, restaurants, hotels, rollerskating rinks, theatres and clinics.

CITS has tours to the Underground City for Y10, often combined with a visit to the Mao Mausoleum. The section you see on the brief tour is about 270 metres long with tunnels at the four, eight and 15-metre levels. It was constructed by volunteers and shop assistants living in the Qianmen area – about 2000 people and 10 years of spare-time work with simple tools – though the shelters were planned and construction was supervised by the army. The people reap a few benefits now such as preferential treatment for relatives and friends who can stay in a 100-bed hotel, use of the warehouse space – and there's a few bucks to be made from tourists. Some features of the system you can see are the telecommunications and first-aid rooms and ventilation system.

There are roughly 90 entrances to this particular complex. The guide claims that 10,000 shoppers in the Dazhalan area can be evacuated to the suburbs in five minutes (what about the other 70,000?!) in the event of an attack. Entrances are hidden in shops – the one you descend by is an ordinary-looking garment shop. It's got the flavour of a James Bond movie with a bit of the apocalypse thrown in. A terse lecture is given by a Civil Air Defence man at the end, complete with fluorescent wall map – oh, and a cup of tea before you surface.

If you want to give the CITS tour a miss then there are two bits of the underground city that are easy to get to yourself – the subway and the Dongtian Underground Restaurant.

Dongtian Restaurant The Dongtian (Cave Heaven) Restaurant is just north of Chang'an at 192 Xidan Beidajie, east side – look for a display of pictures of subterranean scenes that mark the entrance. Descending 60 steps, you'll come to four small dining rooms, all served by the same restaurant. They have the decor of an American greasy-spoon truck-stop as interpreted by a crazed neoclassical Sino-Italian decorator.

Dongtian is one of about a dozen underground restaurants operating in Beijing. What better way to get there than by subway? Take the tube to Xuanwumen, then hop on a bus north for about two stops.

Chang'an Inn Next to the Dongtian, but not accessible to the public (you can try) is the Chang'an Inn with its 400 beds. There are some 100 underground hotels in Beijing with a total of 10,000 beds. While the views may not be great, the rooms are insulated by several metres of earth from traffic noise, dust, wind and pesky mosquitoes. Young Chinese honeymooners visiting the capital can rent one of the Chang'an Inn's special Double Happiness rooms, decorated with bright red calligraphy wishing them joys when they surface and re-enter the real world. As the Chinese saying goes, 'Make one thing serve two purposes'.

Beijing Subway *(dì xià tiě lù)* The Beijing Subway runs 15 to 20 metres underground and is a major link in the air-raid shelter system, providing fast evacuation of civilians to the suburbs. The east-west line, though opened in 1969, was for a time restricted to Chinese with special passes – and foreigners were not permitted to use it until 1980. Like most subways it loses money – several million yuan per year. One reason is that it employs a lot of people who give orders but do very little work. Unlike most other subways the crime rate is low (there is the odd pickpocket), graffiti is non-existent, it's very clean, and messy suicides are said to be rare (one every couple of years supposedly). The 'Underground Dragon' is mostly tiled, and has austere marble pillars. Some platforms are enlivened with brushwork paintings, illuminated ads – and, surprise, surprise, Hong-Kong-based English-only advertising.

A good idea to familiarise yourself with urban and suburban Beijing is to hop off the subway at random, explore, and pop back down again. It's only four jiao per ride, you can't get lost, and it gives you some very fast first impressions of different sectors of Beijing, painlessly. The subway is open from 5.30 am to 10.30 pm and trains run every few minutes. It can get very crowded but it sure beats the buses! (See the maps in the Getting Around section of this chapter.)

Ancient Observatory
(gǔgūan xiàngtái) 古观象台
One interesting perspective on Beijing is the observatory mounted on the battlements of a watchtower, once part of the city walls. Dwarfed by embassy housing blocks, it lies in a no-man's-land of traffic loops and highways just west of the Friendship Store. The views themselves are worth the visit. This is one of the sights that you can visit in safety – small in scope, interesting, some English explanation. The observatory dates back to Kublai Khan's days when it was north of the present site. The Great Khan, as well as later Ming and Qing emperors, relied heavily on astrologers before making a move.

The present Beijing Observatory was built from 1437 to 1446, not only to facilitate astrological predictions but to aid seafaring navigators. Downstairs are displays of navigational equipment used by Chinese shipping. On the 1st floor are replicas of five 5000-year-old pottery jars, unearthed from Henan Province in 1972 and showing painted patterns of the sun. There are also four replicas of Han Dynasty eave tiles representing east, west, north and south. There is a map drawn on a wooden octagonal board with 1420 stars marked in gold foil or powder; it's a reproduction of the original, which is said to be Ming Dynasty but is based on an older Tang map. Busts of six prominent astronomers are also displayed.

On the 'roof' is a variety of astronomical instruments designed by the Jesuits. The Jesuits, scholars as well as proselytisers, found their way into the capital in 1601 when Matteo Ricci and company were permitted to work with Chinese scientists. The emperor was keen to find out about European firearms and cannons from them.

The Jesuits outdid the resident Muslim calendar-setters and were given control of the observatory, becoming the Chinese court's advisors. Of the eight bronze instruments on display (including an equatorial armilla, celestial globe and altazimuth), six were designed and constructed under the supervision of the Belgian priest Ferdinand Verbiest, who came to China in 1659 to work at the Qing court. The instruments were built between 1669 and 1673, and are embellished with sculpted bronze dragons and other Chinese craftwork, a unique mix of east and west. The azimuth theodolite was supervised by Bernard Stumpf, also a missionary. The eighth instrument, the new armilla, was completed in 1754. It's not clear which of the instruments on display are the originals.

During the Boxer Rebellion, the instruments disappeared into the hands of the French and the Germans. Some were returned in 1902, while others came back under the provisions of the Treaty of Versailles (1919). Bertrand Russell commented that this was 'probably the most important benefit which the treaty secured to the world'. The observatory the Jesuits set up in Shanghai was used for meteorological predictions, and is still used for that purpose. The Jesuits even had some influence over architecture in Beijing, and designed the Italian rococo palaces at the Old Summer Palace (destroyed in 1860) using Versailles as a blueprint.

More recently, government officials were caught off guard when local and foreign rock bands got together and staged a dance party in the ancient tower. The observatory is open daily, except Mondays, from 9 to 11 am and 1 to 4 pm.

Beijing Zoo

(běijīng dòngwùyúan) 北京动物园

For humans the zoo is OK – an enormous park, lovely lakes, good birds – but after you've been there you'll probably look as pissed off as the animals do. No attempt has been made to re-create their natural environments. The animals live in tiny cages with little shade or water. The Panda House, right by the gates, has four dirty specimens that would be better off dead. Parents can buy their children miniature plastic rifles with which they can practise shooting the animals. The children also enjoy throwing rocks at the monkeys and jabbing them with sticks.

The zoo is in the north-west corner of the city; the former Ming Dynasty garden was converted to a zoo in 1908. It contains 400 species and is the largest in China. Some rare animals reside here, including golden monkeys from Sichuan, Yangtse alligators, wild Tibetan donkeys, the snow leopard and the black-necked crane.

Nearby are the Beijing Planetarium and the bizarre Soviet-style Beijing Exhibition Hall (irregular industrial displays, theatre, Russian restaurant) which looks like some crazed Communist architect's wedding-cake decoration.

Hutong Hopping

A completely different side of Beijing emerges in the hutongs or back lanes. The original plan of the city allowed for enclosed courtyards buried down alleys, and though the politics have changed many of the courtyards remain. Given the choice between a high-rise block and a traditional compound, most residents of Beijing would opt for the latter. The compounds have loads more character – and offer courtyards to grow vegetables in.

There are over 3000 hutongs in Beijing, so there's a lot out there to discover. The word derives from Mongolian and means a passageway between tents or yurts. Many of the hutongs are named after markets (fish, pig, rice, sheep) or trades (hats, bowstrings, trousers) once conducted along them. Others took their names as the seats of government offices, or specialised suppliers to the palace (granaries, red lacquer, armour). Yet others were named after dukes and officers.

Around the Forbidden City of yore there were some very odd industries. Wet-Nurse Lane was full of young mothers who breastfed the imperial offspring. They were selected from around China on scouting trips four times a year. Clothes-Washing Lane was where the women who did the imperial laundry lived. The maids, grown old in the service of the court, were packed off to faraway places for a few years so that their intimate knowledge of the royal undergarments would be out of date by the time they got round to gossiping.

Walking along the hutongs kind of destroys the advantage of a lightning visit, and may well lead to you acquiring a Chinese entourage. Charging off on a bicycle is the best way to go. If you see an interesting compound, you can stop and peer in – maybe even be invited in; the duller bits you can cruise by.

Beijing University

(běidà) 北大

Beijing University and Qinghua University *(qīnghúa dàxúe)* are the most prestigious institutes in China. Beida was founded at the turn of the century; it was then called Yanjing University and was administered by the Americans. Its students figured prominently in the 4 May 1919 demonstrations and the later resistance to the Japanese. In 1953 the university moved from Coal Hill to its present location. In the 1960s the Red Guards first appeared here and the place witnessed some scenes of utter mayhem as the battles of the Cultural Revolution took place. Today there are hundreds of foreign students at Beida, studying a range of subjects.

The shopping district for Beida is the Haidian area to the south, where students congregate in the small restaurants and where locals come from surrounding communes to stock up on provisions.

Beijing has about 50 colleges and universities. A curious one is the Minorities Institute *(mínzú xúeyùan)*, just north of the zoo. The institute trains cadres for the regions where ethnic minorities live.

Beida is on the bus No 332 route from the zoo, or about a 45-minute cycle-ride from the city centre. Further east, past Qinghua University, is the Beijing Language Institute (BLI) *(yǔyán xúeyùan)* with its own contingent of foreign students. The institute is on the No 331 bus route.

Old Summer Palace

(yúanmíngyúan) 圆明园

The original Summer Palace was laid out in the 12th century. By the reign of Emperor Qianlong, it developed into a set of interlocking gardens. Qianlong set the Jesuits to work as architects for European palaces for the gardens – elaborate fountains, baroque statuary, and kiosks.

In the second Opium War (1860), British and French troops destroyed the place and sent the booty abroad. Since the Chinese pavilions and temples were made of wood they did not survive fires, but a marble facade, some broken columns and traces of the fountains stick out of the rice-paddies.

The ruins are a favourite picnic spot for foreigners living in the capital and for Chinese twosomes seeking a bit of privacy. The ruins can be reached on foot (about half an hour) or by bike from Beida. They aren't signposted so they're easy to miss. Go north from Beida, turn right along the road to Qinghua University, detour left into the rice fields – and then ask whoever happens to be wandering by.

There are some pleasant round trips to the area. Take bus No 332 from the zoo to the Old Summer Palace and to the Summer Palace; change to bus No 333 for the Fragrant Hills; change to bus No 360 to go directly back to the zoo.

Another round-trip route is to take the subway to Pingguoyuan (the last stop in the west) and then take bus No 318 to the Fragrant Hills; change to No 333 for the Summer Palace, and then to No 332 for the zoo.

Summer Palace

(yíhéyúan) 颐和园

This is one of the best sights in Beijing – don't miss it! The Summer Palace is an immense park containing some newish Qing architecture. The site had long been a royal garden and was considerably enlarged and embellished by Emperor Qianlong in the 18th century. He deepened and expanded Kunming Lake with the help of 100,000 labourers – and reputedly surveyed imperial navy drills from a hilltop perch. It was later abandoned.

Empress Dowager Cixi began rebuilding in 1888 using money that was supposedly reserved for the construction of a modern navy – but she did restore a marble boat that sits immobile at the edge of the lake. She had this ugly thing fitted out with several large mirrors and used to dine at the lakeside.

In 1900 foreign troops, annoyed by the Boxer Rebellion, had another go at roasting the Summer Palace. Restorations took place a few years later and a major renovation occurred after 1949, by which time the palace had once more fallen into disrepair.

The original palace was used as a summer residence, an escape from the ferocious heat. The residents of the Forbidden City packed up and decamped here for their holidays, so the emphasis is on cool features – water, gardens, hills. It was divided into four sections: court reception, residences, temples and strolling or sightseeing areas. Three-quarters of the park is occupied by Kunming Lake, and most items of structural interest are towards the east or north gates.

The main building is the Hall of Benevolence & Longevity, just off the lake toward the east gate. It houses a hardwood throne and has a courtyard with bronze animals. In it the emperor-in-residence handled state affairs and received envoys.

Along the north shore of the lake is the Long Corridor, over 700 metres long, which is decorated with mythical scenes. If the paint looks new it's because a lot of pictures were whitewashed during the Cultural Revolution.

On artificial Longevity Hill is a number of temples. The Pavilion of Precious Clouds on the western slopes is one of the few structures to escape destruction by the Anglo-French forces. It contains some elaborate bronzes. At the top of the hill sits the Buddhist Temple of the Sea of Wisdom, made of glazed tiles; good views of the lake can be had from this spot.

Other sights are largely associated with Empress Cixi, like the place where she kept Emperor Guangxu under house arrest, the place where she celebrated her birthdays, and exhibitions of her furniture and memorabilia. A very Disneylandish atmosphere pervades this 'museum'; tourists can have their photos taken, imperial dress-up fashion.

The Tingliguan Restaurant serves imperial banquet food – fish from Kunming Lake, velvet chicken, dumplings – on regal tableware lookalikes. It has a splendid alfresco location and exorbitant prices, and is housed in what was once an imperial theatre, with attached souvenir shops.

Another noteworthy feature of the Summer Palace is the 17-arch bridge spanning 150 metres to South Lake Island; on the mainland side is a beautiful bronze ox. Also note the Jade Belt Bridge on the mid-west side of the lake; and the Garden of Harmonious Interest at the north-east end which is a copy of a Wuxi garden.

You can get around the lake by rowing boat. Boating and swimming are popular pastimes for the locals (windsurfing for the richer ones) and in winter you can skate on the lakes. As with the Forbidden City Moat, slabs of ice are cut out of the lake in winter and stored for summer use.

The park is about 12 km north-west of the centre of Beijing. Take bus No 332 from the zoo. You can also get there by bicycle – it takes about 1½ to two hours from downtown. If you consult a bus map, you'll see the Beijing-Miyun Irrigation Canal feeding from Yuyuan Lake to Kunming Lake. The route is good for biking although it's a dirt road. The bus map will show which side of various sections of the canal is bikable.

Fragrant Hills Park

(xiāngshān gōngyúan) 香山公园

Within striking distance of the Summer Palace, and often combined with it on a tour, are the Western Hills, another former villa-resort area. The part of the Western Hills closest to Beijing is known as the Fragrant Hills. This is the last stop for the city buses – if you want to get further into the mountains, you'll have to walk, bicycle or take a taxi. You can scramble up the slopes to the top of Incense-Burner Peak, or take the crowded cable car. From the peak you get an all-embracing view of the countryside. The

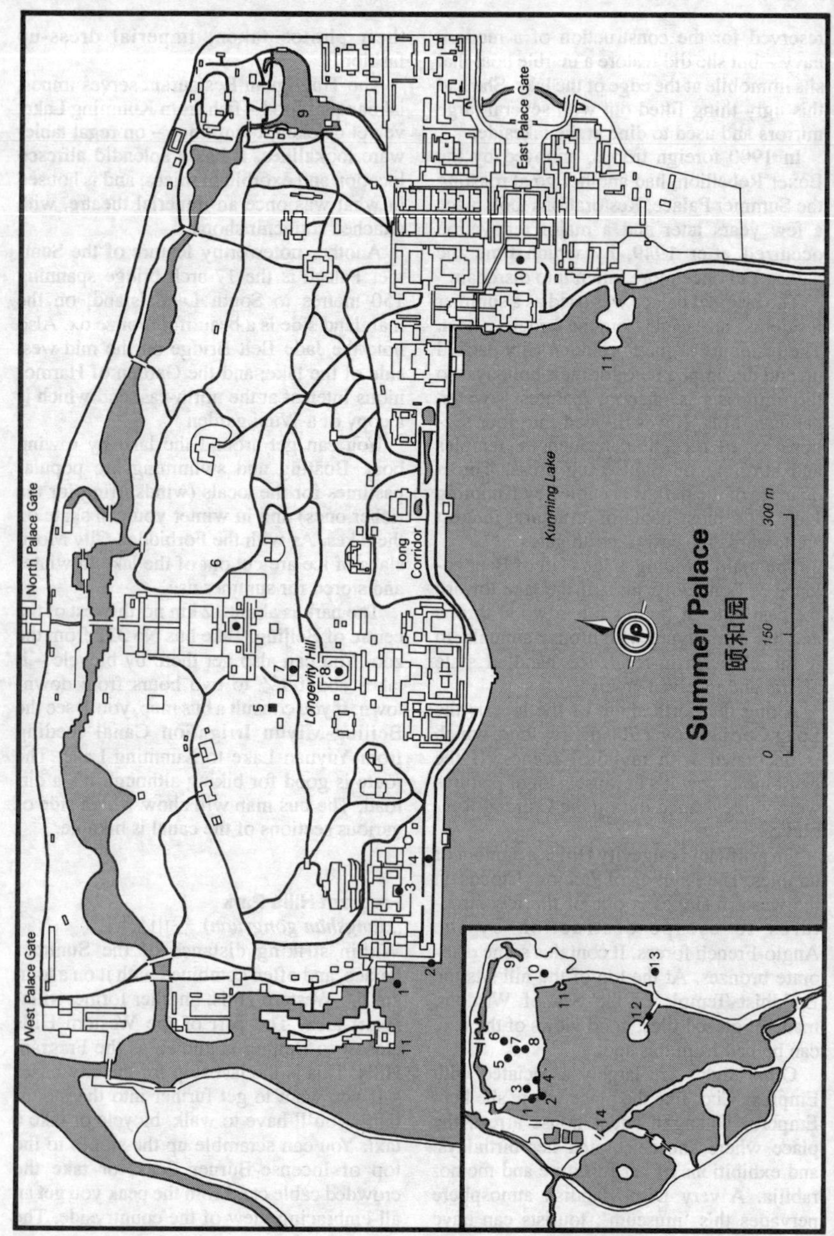
Summer Palace
颐和园
West Palace Gate
North Palace Gate
East Palace Gate
Longevity Hill
Long Corridor
Kunming Lake
0
150
300 m

1	Marble Boat
2	Ferry Dock
3	Listening to the Orioles Restaurant
4	Long Corridor
5	Pavilion of Precious Clouds
6	Hall of Buddhist Tenants
7	Temple of the Sea of Wisdom
8	Temple of Buddhist Virtue
9	Garden of Harmonious Interest
10	Hall of Benevolence & Longevity
11	Rowing Boat Dock
12	Pavilion of Knowing in the Spring
13	Bronze Ox
14	Jade Belt Bridge

1	清晏船
2	码头
3	听鹂馆
4	长廊
5	排云殿
6	香崇宗印之阁
7	智慧海
8	佛香阁
9	谐趣园
10	仁寿殿
11	划船码头
12	知春亭
13	铜牛
14	玉带桥

cable car is a good way to get up the mountain, but it tends to spray you with black grease – an umbrella might be helpful! Starting from the Fragrant Hills, you can hike further into the Western Hills and leave the crowds behind.

The Fragrant Hills area was also razed by foreign troops in 1860 and 1900 but a few bits still poke out. A glazed-tile pagoda and the remains of the Zhao Temple, a mock-Tibetan temple built in 1780, are both in the same area. The surrounding heavily wooded park was a hunting ground for the emperors, and once contained a slew of pavilions and shrines. It's a favourite strolling spot for Beijingers, many of whom go to gaze through the gates of the Xiangshan Hotel. You might also like to hunt for a restaurant, called the Xiangshan but not linked with the hotel – service is said to be slow so some people place their orders, ramble off around the 150 hectares of parkland, and come back to the table.

A bicycle trip to the Fragrant Hills is beautiful but exhausting. There are a couple of ways of getting to the Fragrant Hills by public transport: bus No 333 from the Summer Palace, bus No 360 from the zoo, and bus No 318 from Pingguoyuan (the last stop in the west on the subway).

Temple of the Sleeping Buddha

(wòfó sì) 卧佛寺

On approach to the Fragrant Hills is the Temple of the Sleeping Buddha. During the Cultural Revolution the buddhas in one of the halls were replaced by a statue of Mao (since removed). The draw card is the huge reclining Buddha, 5.2 metres long, cast in copper. The history books place it in the year 1331 but it's most likely a copy. Its weight is unknown but could be up to 50 tonnes. Pilgrims used to make offerings of shoes to the barefoot statue.

Azure Clouds Temple

(bìyún sì) 碧云寺

A short distance from the North Gate of Fragrant Hills Park is the Azure Clouds Temple, whose landmark is the Diamond Throne Pagoda. Of Indian design, it consists of a raised platform with a central pagoda and stupas around it. The temple was first built in 1366, and was expanded in the 18th century with the addition of the Hall of Arhats, containing 500 statues representing disciples of Buddha. Dr Sun Yatsen's coffin was placed in the temple in 1925 before being moved to Nanjing. In 1954 the govern-

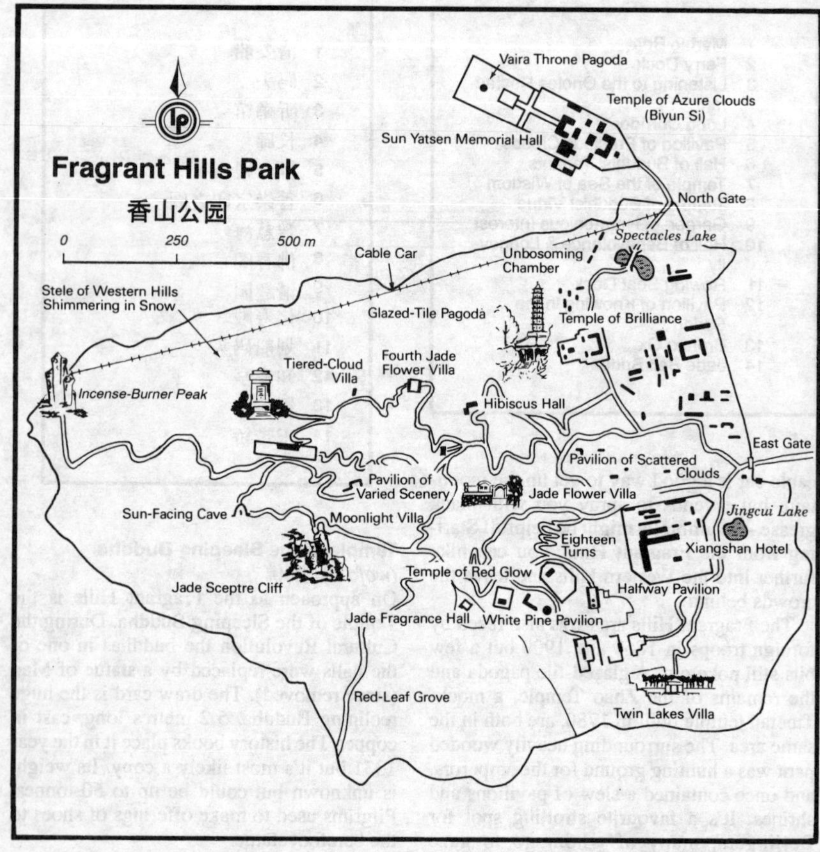

ment renovated Sun's memorial hall, which has a picture display of his revolutionary activities.

Badachu

(bādàchù) 八大处

Directly south of the Fragrant Hills is Badachu, the Eight Great Sites, also known as Eight Great Temples *(bādà sì)*. It has eight monasteries or temples scattered in wooded valleys. The Second Site has the Buddha's Tooth Pagoda, built to house the sacred fang and accidentally discovered when the Allied army demolished the place in 1900. Unfortunately, Badachu seems to be part of a military zone and foreigners are not allowed in. This may change in the future as the demand for more tourist sites increases, so check out the situation when you get there.

You might end up at Badachu on a magical mystery tour from the Qianmen ticket/tour office. Otherwise take bus No 347, which runs there from the zoo (it crosses the No 318 route).

Beijing Buster Bicycle Tour

Lama Temple – Confucian Temple – Bamboo Garden Hotel – Drum Tower – Bell

Tower – Northern Lakes – Jingshan Park – Forbidden City – Beihai Park – Zhongnanhai – Tiananmen – Qianmen – Dazhalan

Obviously this is far too much to attempt in one day, and it's not recommended that you see everything unless you have only one whirlwind day to dive-bomb the capital. The Forbidden City alone is worth a full day's exploration. Attractions like this, however, can be visited several times rather than cased in one fell swoop. This bike tour takes in some of the many moods of Beijing – not, one hopes, just the temples. If the Lama Temple is closed then the Temple of Heaven would make a good substitute at the end of the tour.

Nonstop cycling time is about 80 minutes – Chinese bike, Western legs, average pace. If you have trouble, there are two bike-repair shops on Dongdan (112 Dongdan Beidajie and 247b Dongsi Nandajie) and one at 107 Qianmen Dajie.

The starting point is outside the CITS office at the Chongwenmen Hotel. What better place to begin a self-guided tour that will cost you all of two yuan? Launch yourself into the sea of cyclists, throw your legs into cruising speed, and cycle the length of Dongdan north to the Lama Temple – about a 20-minute haul. Dongdan is a mildly busy shopping area, and this straight stretch is a good way to find your Beijing bicycle-legs and learn to watch for Chinese cyclists and buses cutting you off. The Lama Temple is the most refreshing, well-groomed temple you'll see in Beijing. Note that it's closed on Mondays.

Take the hutong running west opposite the gates of the Lama Temple. You'll pass through several decorated lintels; these graceful archways *(páilóu)*, which commemorate mandarin officials or chaste widows, were ripped out of the thoroughfares of Beijing in the 1950s. The reason given was the facilitation of traffic movement. Some have been relocated in parks. The ones you see in this hutong are rarities.

On your right, a short way down the hutong, is the former Confucian Temple & Imperial College, now a museum/library complex. Unless you can read stele-calligraphy, it's not of great interest. A stele standing in the hutong ordered officials to dismount at this point but you can ignore that.

Continue west on this hutong, and to your right, further down, you will spot a coal briquette factory. If you peer in you will see – and hear – the grimy production of these noxious bricks, which are the major heating and cooking source for Beijing residents and the cause of incredible pollution in winter. In imperial days, Fuel-Saving Lane, down by the palace, supplied the court with coal and firewood. Some 400 years later it seems this factory is performing a similar task. Marco Polo marvelled at the black lumps that produced heat; you may react differently.

The hutong eventually runs into a smaller one. Continue straight on until it ends at Jiugulou Dajie. Make a small detour here. If you go north on Jiugulou and take the first hutong to the left, you will arrive at the Bamboo Garden Hotel *(zhúyúan bīngǔan)*, which is a wonderful illustration of the surprises that hutongs hold. This was originally the personal garden of Sheng Xuanhuai, an important Qing official. There are exquisite gardens, beautiful courtyards, renovated compound architecture, and expensive restaurant (English menu, alfresco in summer). It's a quiet place to sip a drink.

Go back to Jiugulou Dajie and head south following the bus No 8 route. Follow Jiugulou to a T-junction, turn left and you will come to the Drum Tower *(gǔlóu)*. It was built in 1420 and has several drums which were beaten to mark the hours of the day – in effect the Big Ben of Beijing. Time was kept with a water clock. It's in pretty sad shape, but an impressive structure nonetheless with a solid brick base. Occasional exhibitions take place here since the tower is connected with local artisans. Admission is Y2.

Behind the Drum Tower, down an alley directly north, is the Bell Tower *(zhōnglóu)*, which was originally built at the same time as the Drum Tower, but burnt down. The present structure is 18th-century, and the

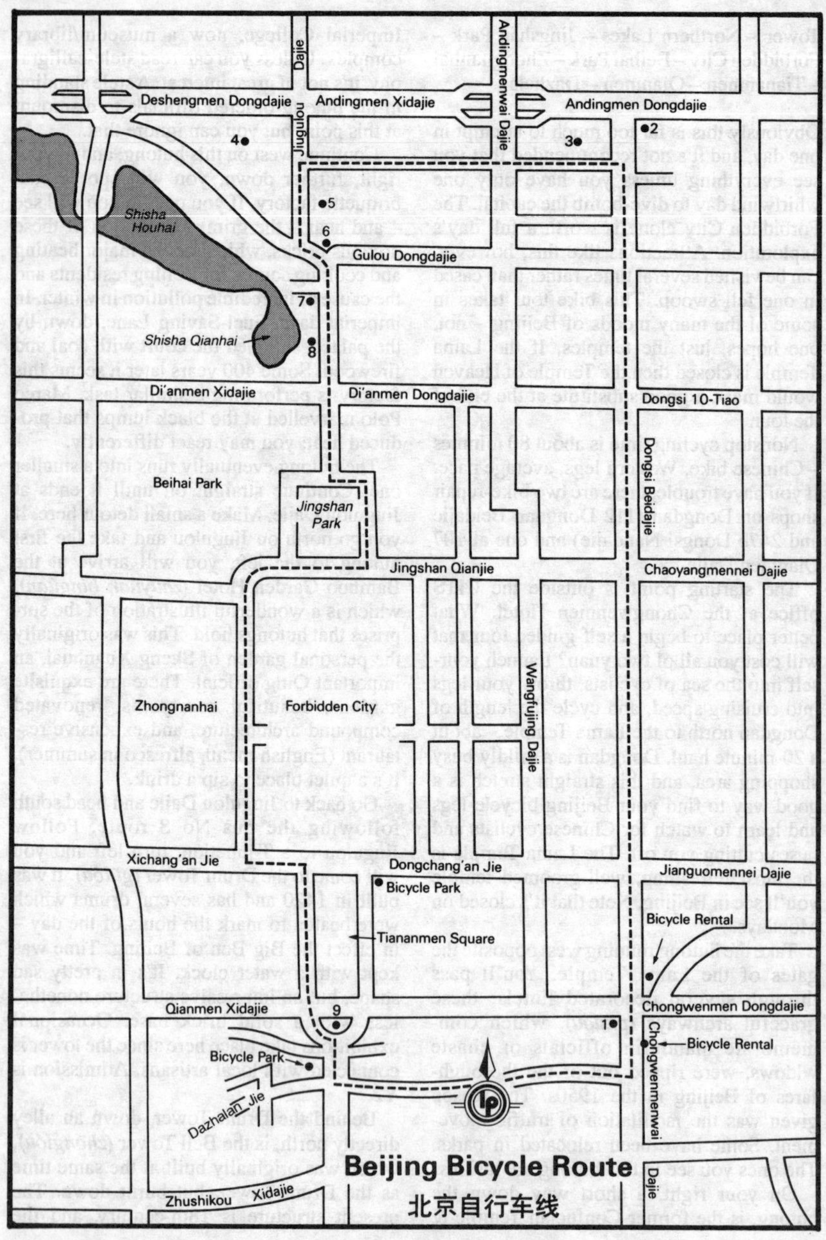
Deshengmen Dongdajie
Andingmen Xidajie
Andingmen Dongdajie
Andingmenwai Dajie
Jiugulou Dajie
Shisha Houhai
Gulou Dongdajie
Shisha Qianhai
Di'anmen Xidajie
Di'anmen Dongdajie
Dongsi 10-Tiao
Dongsi Beidajie
Beihai Park
Jingshan Park
Jingshan Qianjie
Chaoyangmennei Dajie
Wangfujing Dajie
Zhongnanhai
Forbidden City
Xichang'an Jie
Dongchang'an Jie
Bicycle Park
Jianguomennei Dajie
Bicycle Rental
Tiananmen Square
Qianmen Xidajie
Chongwenmen Dongdajie
Bicycle Rental
Bicycle Park
Dazhalan Jie
Chongwenmenwai Dajie
Zhushikou Xidajie
1
2
3
4
5
6
7
8
9
Beijing Bicycle Route
北京自行车线

1	Chongwenmen Hotel/CITS
2	Lama Temple
3	Confucian Temple
4	Bamboo Garden Hotel
5	Bell Tower
6	Drum Tower
7	Kaorouji Restaurant
8	Farmers' Market
9	Qianmen

1	崇文门饭店
2	雍和宫
3	孔庙
4	竹园宾馆
5	钟楼
6	鼓楼
7	烤肉季饭店
8	农贸市场
9	前门

gigantic bell which used to hang there has been moved to the Drum Tower. Legend has it that the bellmaker's daughter plunged into the molten iron before the bell was cast. Her father only managed to grab her shoe as she did so, and the bell's soft sound resembled that of the Chinese for 'shoe' *(xié)*. The same story is told about a couple of other bells in China.

As you head due south of the Drum Tower, the first hutong to the right provides a very interesting excursion into the Northern Lakes area. This district is steeped in history; if you consult a Beijing map you will see that the set of lakes connects from north to south. In the Yuan Dynasty, barges would come through various canals to the top lake (Jishuitan), a sort of harbour for Beijing. Later the lakes were used for pleasure-boating, and were bordered by the residences of high officials.

The larger lake to the north-west is the Shisha Houhai (Lake of the Ten Back Monasteries). Below that is the Shisha Qianhai (Lake of the Ten Front Monasteries). There's little evidence of the splendour left, but check out the Shoudu Karouji Restaurant which has balcony dining in summer; the restaurant is buried down a hutong. For those with some more time, it's possible to circumnavigate the lakes. It's a peaceful area and a good place to see what the locals are up to. You can't really get lost – just keep the lakes in sight.

Worth checking out is Prince Gong's Residence *(gōngwángfǔ)*, which lies more or less at the centre of the arc created by the lakes running from north to south. It's reputed to be the model mansion for Cao Xueqin's 18th-century classic, *A Dream of Red Mansions* (translated as the *The Story of the Stone* by David Hawkes, Penguin, 1980). It's one of the largest private residential compounds in Beijing, with a nine-courtyard layout, high walls and elaborate gardens. Prince Gong was the son of a Qing emperor.

Back on track. Return to the Drum Tower. Looking south from it you can see the outlines of pavilions on Jingshan (Coal Hill), which is where you're heading. From this point, you are tracing the historic north-south axis, travelling the ancient hourglass that filters into Qianmen Dajie. Continuing south of the Drum Tower, you come into a fairly busy shopping street. About half-way down you cross a small stone bridge (with buildings around it). If you turn right immediately after the bridge you'll arrive at a farmer's market on the shores of Shisha Qianhai lake – explore!

Continuing down Di'anmen Dajie, you'll bump into the back of Jingshan Park. Proceed to the front, where there is bicycle parking. Jingshan Park is a splendid place to survey the smog of Beijing, get your bearings with 360° views, and enjoy a good overview of the russet roofing of the Forbidden City opposite. There are snack bars both in the park and at the north end of the Forbidden City.

Hop back on your trusty hulk and follow the moat west. Just beyond the traffic lights is the entrance to Beihai Park, where you can exercise your arms as well as your legs – hire a rowing boat. There's a cafe near the south gate overlooking Beihai Lake, where you can get beer, coffee, tea or cold drinks.

Back-pedal a bit to the traffic lights, hang a right, and you're heading into the most sensitive part of the capital – the Zhongnanhai Compound. On the left, going down Beichang Jie, you pass some older housing that lines the moat. On the right is a high wall that shields from view the area where top Party members live and work (it was decided not to rip down this section of the old walls). In 1973, when the new wing of the Beijing Hotel shot up, the Public Security Bureau suddenly realised that guests with binoculars could observe activity in Zhongnanhai, so a fake building was erected along the western wall of the Forbidden City to short-circuit that possibility. Mysterious buildings, indeed, abound in this locale (also on the strip back at the traffic lights along the way to Jingshan Park), including private theatres for viewing foreign films and so on.

At the end of the street is an archway that brings you into Chang'an Jie and Tiananmen Square. Traffic is one way for north-south avenues on either side of the square. If you want to go to Tiananmen, dismount after the archway and wheel the bike to the parking areas along the sidewalk. Bicycles cannot be ridden across Tiananmen Square (apparently tanks are OK), but you can walk the bike.

From Tiananmen it's a short ride to the Qianmen gate, and if you continue down Qianmen Dajie you'll see a large bike-parking area on your right, open to 9 pm. It's right at the entrance to Beijing's most fascinating hutong, Dazhalan. Your bicycle is absolutely useless in the crowded streets so park it. From Dazhalan, you're within reach of good restaurants, and there's an acrobat theatre on Dazhalan itself.

The fast route back to the Chongwenmen Hotel is to go back to Qianmen gate and take the wide avenue to the right. More interesting, but slower, is to take the eastern extension of Dazhalan. This hutong will run you right back to your starting point. You have to walk your bike for the first 50 metres or so, then the crowds thin out. Ride slowly since this is a market-type hutong and a shopping area (called Fishmouth Lane) and things can jump out at you.

Weary legs? Why not try the public baths? There's one at the Qianmen entrance side of the hutong. The baths are a bit like the Japanese communal tubs in concept, but are split into men's and women's sections. There's a variety of services including massage, foot-treatment and haircutting. Tubs are at different temperatures including lukewarm, hot and searing. The locals are unabashed and a hairy, sweaty cyclist is bound to attract attention. The baths reach nowhere near Japanese hygiene standards so try and get there early in the day before the water thickens. Private rooms may be possible and prices are low.

Places to Stay

Beijing has chronically overbooked hotel space, a situation that is aggravated in peak seasons. New hotels are going up to alleviate the problem, but if you want a bed for the night you are likely to encounter problems for some time to come. Hotels in Beijing fall into different categories: those permanently occupied by foreign business people, diplomats and visiting dignitaries; those used by foreign experts; the group-tour hotels; the Overseas Chinese hotels; the 'cadre' hotels; and the scarcer low-budget hotels.

Hotels perform a number of functions other than lodging and this listing provides a guide to what those functions might be. The listing is by no means complete, nor are your chances of getting into these hotels. Even if you have the money and you look like the kind of person the hotel deems acceptable, you could be turned away for any number of reasons or whims. Those who have the correct ID (like foreign experts) can usually get much cheaper prices.

Places to Stay – bottom end The best established low-budget, backpacker's hotel in Beijing is the *Qiaoyuan Hotel* (☎ 338861) *(qiáoyúan fàndiàn)* on Dongbinhe Lu in the south of the city near the Yongdingmen railway station. Dorm beds are Y11, double rooms cost from Y36 to Y60 with shower, triples Y40. To get there take bus No 20 or 54 from the main Beijing railway station to the terminal (Yongdingmen) and walk for about 10 minutes along the canal (there's a sign in English) to the hotel. Or from just north of the Chongwenmen Hotel take trolley bus No 106 to the terminal. There are also minibuses for Yongdingmen which leave from the bus No 20 stop opposite the main railway station; these cost Y2 and run all night. From the airport, take the airport bus to Dongzhimen, then bus No 106 to Yongdingmen. The hotel can change money, but in general the place is poorly managed – sneering employees and an abysmal restaurant are real downers. Fortunately, there are numerous services for travellers just outside the hotel – restaurants, bike hire, laundry service, second-hand bookshop, etc. In summer, the area becomes a true travellers' hang-out almost up to the decadent standards of Bali and Kathmandu, complete with banana muesli pancakes and hashish vendors.

Increasingly popular with budget travellers is the *Jingtai Hotel* (☎ 764675) *(jǐngtài bīngǔan)*, 65 Yongwai Jingtaixi, a small alley running off of Anlelin Lu in the south of the city. This place is rapidly developing into an alternative to the Qiaoyuan. Dorm beds cost Y10, doubles Y40 and triples Y50. The hotel is clean and pleasant, has hot water all day, and a bar that serves cold beer. Bus No 45 will drop you off at the intersection of Yongdingmennei Jie and Anlelin Lu, a 10-minute walk from the hotel. Bus No 25 goes right down Anlelin Lu and will drop you off near the hotel – this bus both terminates and starts at the Anlelin Lu's east end. Another way to get there from the railway station is to take bus No 39 to the first stop after it crosses the canal – the name of the bus stop is *Puhuangyu*. From there, you've got a 15-minute walk west on Anlelin Lu.

Just a two-minute walk from the Jingtai Hotel is the *Yongdingmen Hotel (yǒngdìngmén fàndiàn)*, another budget place gaining in popularity. It's right on Anlelin Lu. Triple rooms cost Y30 to Y50. Both the Jingtai and Yongdingmen will (reluctantly) accept RMB.

A few travellers have stayed at the *Longtan Hotel (lóngtán fàndiàn)*, which has friendly staff and a good, cheap restaurant, and beds for Y30 in three-bed rooms. The hotel is opposite Long Tan Park in the south of the city, close to a hospital. Bus No 51 (to the last stop) lets you out near the hotel.

Places to Stay – University Hostels Typical prices are Y20 for dormitories, Y40 for double rooms. Most of these places have no beds – just Japanese-style tatami mats – but they're reasonably comfortable. There are some problems with staying in these places; they aren't hotels, so staff are only on duty from around 8 am to 5 pm with the usual two-hour lunch break. Few staff speak English, and if you start arguing with them about FEC and dirty toilets, you'll be asked to leave. They really don't have to take foreigners, so be on your best behaviour here or risk getting kicked out. They provide no special amenities like laundry service or bike rentals, but they often have cheap student cafeterias, although these are only open for short hours, like from 5 to 6 pm. Overall, it's usually better to stay in the budget hotels, but the university hostels offer an alternative if the hotels are packed out.

The most central place is the *Art Institute* (☎ 55473) *(měishù xúeyùan)*, in an alley off Wangfujing near the Beijing Hotel. The main problem with this place is that it's very popular – beds are hard to get, so give them a call first. This school built the now famous 'Goddess of Democracy' which came to symbolise the democracy movement during the Tiananmen protests in 1989. From the main railway station take bus 103 to Wangfujing.

The second best place to stay is *Beijing University (běidà)*. It's a beautiful campus, but a bit far out from things in the north-west part of the city. Bus Nos 331 and 332 stop near the campus. It's relatively easy to get into here.

The third best place to stay is *Beijing Teachers' College (běishīdà)*. Also in the northern part of the city, bus Nos 16, 22, 38 and 47 stop nearby.

Just to the north of Beijing University is *Qinghua University (qīnghúa dàxúe)*. Bus Nos 331, 365 and 375 stop nearby.

Also in the north-west part of the city is the Peoples' University *(rénmín dàxúe)*. You can get there on bus Nos 302 and 320.

One other university that accepts foreigners is the *Beijing Language Institute* (☎ 890351) *(yǔyán xúeyùan)*. Many foreigners come here to study Chinese. Bus No 331 stops in front of the school.

Places to Stay – middle Middle-range hotels in Beijing usually offer air-con rooms with colour TV, phone, bath and desk.

Tiantan Sports Hotel (☎ 752831) *(tiāntán tǐyù bīngǔan)*, 10 Tiyuguan Lu, derives its name from its position between the Temple of Heaven and the gymnasium. It hosts sports-minded group tours but will take whoever else turns up. The hotel has a YMCA tinge to it but is a bright, airy place in a good location with friendly staff. It even boasts the *Shanghai Jakarta Restaurant*, which dishes up decent Indonesian-style food like *gado-gado*. To get there take the subway one stop from the main railway station to Chongwenmen, then bus Nos 39, 41 or 43. Singles are Y85 and doubles Y100 – a good place to stay if you want something comfortable but not ridiculously expensive.

Beiwei (☎ 338631) *(běiwěi fàndiàn)* is on the west side of the Temple of Heaven at 13 Xijing Lu on the corner with Beiwei Lu. It caters for a similar clientele to the Sports Hotel but will also take whoever fronts up. Take the subway two stops from the main railway station, then bus No 5 south. Or you can take bus No 20 direct from the main railway station. Double rooms only (no singles) are Y180.

The *Lüsongyuan* (☎ 440436) *(lüsōngyúan bīngǔan)*, one of the best cheapish hotels, is at 22 Jiao Dou Kou Lu (South Eight Lane). It's difficult to find – directly north of China Art Gallery, second hutong north of Di'anmen, turn left. This is a very pleasant place with courtyard-style architecture, no high-rise and plenty of sunlight. There are about three dozen double rooms at Y120 each, as well as a bar and dining hall with basic food. Take bus No 104 from the main railway station.

The *Chongwenmen Hotel* (☎ 5122211) *(chóngwénmén fàndiàn)* is the home of CITS. It's not really a great place to stay but it is central. Double rooms cost Y132.

The *Xinqiao* (☎ 557731) *(xīnqiáo fàndiàn)* at the north-west side of the Chongwenmen intersection was built in the '50s, Soviet style, but is now undergoing renovation. It should be open by the time you read this and rooms will probably start at Y200 for a double.

The *Leyou* (☎ 784761) *(lèyóu fàndiàn)*, 13 Dongsanhuan Nanlu at the intersection with Jingsong Lu, costs Y72 for a single. Take bus Nos 28 or 52 to the terminal.

The *Friendship Hotel* (☎ 890621) *(yǒuyí bīngǔan)* is on Baishiqiao Lu, north of the zoo. It was originally built for Soviet advisers and is now primarily used by Western experts and their families, though it does have some tourist accommodation. Double rooms cost from Y144. Facilities are legendary, including the full-size swimming pool (open to all), theatre, tennis courts and a foreign experts' club. It's a long way out – up past the zoo in the north-west – but it runs its own bus service to the city centre. The nightlife here is worth checking out, with movies, dances and multinational congregations of partygoers. The hotel has a staggering 2600 rooms and you practically need a map of the grounds to find your way around. Bus No 332 runs past the hotel.

The *Minzu Hotel* (☎ 6014466) *(mínzú fàndiàn)* is west of Xidan intersection on Fuxingmennei. It's an 11-storey Russian monolith. Doubles are from Y195 to Y377, and triples are Y704. The ground-floor restaurant is pleasant.

The *Yanjing Hotel* (☎ 868721) *(yànjīng fàndiàn)* is near the Muxudi subway on Fuxingmenwai. The 20-storey hotel which opened in 1981 was formerly called the 'Fuxing', which came across rather strongly when pronounced with a thick Scottish accent. Inside are some impressive modern murals; the one on the 1st floor is a glazed ceramic fresco with a Silk Road theme. Singles cost Y150 and doubles Y250.

The *Qianmen Hotel* (☎ 3016688, 336556) *(qiánmén fàndiàn)* at the corner of Yongan Lu and Hufang Lu, south-west of Qianmen Gate, is an eight-storey mid-50s block with fountains in the snazzy foyer. Singles are from Y170 to Y190, but a few foreigners claim to have bargained them down to Y90.

Right next door is the *Dongfang Hotel* (☎ 3014466) *(dōngfāng fàndiàn)* with doubles from Y195 to Y350.

The *Ritan Hotel* (☎ 5125588) *(rìtán bīngǔan)* on Ritan Lu, near the corner with Ritan Beilu, has doubles from Y150.

The *Huadu Hotel* (☎ 5001166) *(húadū fàndiàn)* is at 8 Xinyuan Nanlu, in the eastern suburbs near Dongzhimen gate. The six and five-storey blocks are managed by CITS and cost from Y230 to Y370.

Places to Stay – top end Keeping up with the top-end hotels in Beijing is an exasperating task. No sooner does one extravaganza open its doors than the foundations for an even more voluptuous building are laid.

The *Beijing Hotel* (☎ 5137766) *(běijīng fàndiàn)*, Dong Chang'an Jie, is the most central hotel in the capital and is therefore prized by business people, embassy staff and dignitaries. Standard doubles cost from Y310 to Y470. Rooms are also used on a long-term basis. The roof of the west wing commands a great view of Tiananmen Square and the Forbidden City.

The *Capital Hotel* (☎ 5129988) *(shǒudū bīngǔan)* is one block south of the Beijing Hotel at 3 Qianmen Dongjie. Doubles are Y466.

Beijing's newest hotel is the *Taiwan Hotel* (☎ 5136688) *(táiwān fàndiàn)*, 5 Jinyu Hutong, Wangfujing. Needless to say, it caters to Taiwanese tourists but anyone with money is welcome. Doubles cost Y400.

Adjacent to the Taiwan Hotel on the same side of the street is the *Peace Hotel* (☎ 5128833) *(hépíng bīngǔan)* where doubles cost a cool Y460. Across the street is yet another elegant high-rise, the *Palace Hotel* (☎ 5128899) *(wángfǔ fàndiàn)* where doubles are Y753.

The *Zhaolong Hotel* (☎ 5002299) *(zhàolóng bīngǔan)* is at the corner of Dongsanhuan Beilu and Gongren Tiyuchang Beilu in the east part of the city. Doubles start at Y300.

The *Yanshan* (☎ 2563388) *(yànshān dàjiǔdiàn)* is in the Haidian district. Doubles are Y240.

The *Fragrant Hills Hotel* (☎ 2565544) *(xiāngshān fàndiàn)* is in the far north-west of Beijing – too far away from the city to be practical for anyone but tour groups. Doubles start at Y268 and deluxe triples are Y1884. If you want to see what a well-behaved, well-dressed Chinese hotel-staffer looks like, visit this place. The locals stand at the gate and have their picture taken against this wonder of the Western world.

The *Great Wall Sheraton Hotel* (☎ 5005566) *(chángchéng fàndiàn)* is on Donghuan Beilu, near the Agricultural Exhibition Centre in embassy-land, north-east Beijing. Standard double rooms cost from Y470 to Y700 plus 10% service charge. There are restaurants, lounges (Le France, Silk Road, Cosmos Club), an indoor swimming pool, tennis courts and a beauty salon.

In the same neighbourhood as the Sheraton is the *Kunlun Hotel* (☎ 5003388) *(kūnlún fàndiàn)* where doubles cost from Y270 to Y595.

Further to the north-east towards the airport is the *Holiday Inn Lido* (☎ 5006688) *(lìdū jiàrì fàndiàn)*. Doubles start at Y290.

The *Shangri-La Hotel* (☎ 8412211) *(xiānggé lǐlā fàndiàn)* is in the west part of town and room prices begin at Y480.

Close to the Shangri-La is the *Olympic Hotel* (☎ 8316688) *(àolín pīkè fàndiàn)*, one of the newest and best hotels with prices starting at Y450.

The *Jianguo Hotel* (☎ 5002233) *(jiàngúo fàndiàn)* on Jianguomenwai Dajie is just east of the Friendship Store. The hotel was opened in 1982 and has the distinction of being China's first joint-venture hotel. The

Chinese staff of about 600 have no spittoons and are not allowed newspapers, cigarettes, naps or even chairs. As a compensation prize they can rake in as much as three times an ordinary Beijinger's salary. Single and double rooms start from Y540 and go to Y1295.

Next door to the Jianguo Hotel is the equally extravagant *Hotel Beijing-Toronto* (☎ 5002266) *(jīnglún fàndiàn)* with doubles from Y376 to Y989. There are great buffet lunches – a few shoestring travellers who have footed the bill say it's worth every fen!

The *Xiyuan Hotel* (☎ 8313388) *(xīyùan fàndiàn)* is in Erligou out by the zoo, far away from the centre. It's a huge, modern place with a revolving disco on top of the 26-storey block, coffee shop, bar and fitness centre. The restaurants serve Muslim, Chinese and Western food. Doubles are from Y296 to Y706, and a deluxe suite a mere Y2688.

Temple of Heaven Crashpad

Getting a cheap bed in Beijing wasn't always as easy as stumbling into the Qiaoyuan Hotel and smiling at the bleary-eyed receptionist. Back in 1983, when we were researching the first edition of this book, dormitory accommodation was hard to come by and to get it often required some aggressive arm-wrestles with uncooperative hotel managers. Michael Buckley witnessed the creation of such a dormitory:

Scene 1 The meeting room, ground floor, Tiantan Sports Hotel. I roll in at 11 pm – good timing – the next hotel is miles off, and the manager knows even before he picks up the phone that everything else in town is chock-a-block. After a laborious wait, he allows me a couch in the meeting room. Two more travellers, I discover, are already snoozing on the couches within. Cost is Y3 per night per couchette. Three days later, travellers discover there is another meeting room on the 4th floor – the word spreads.

Scene 2 A traveller strides straight past the manager, backpack on. 'Where are you going?' he demands. 'To the meeting room,' she answers, taking the stairs three at a time, not looking back, unrolls sleeping bag on arrival. Manager scratches head – she didn't even bother to ask if there were any rooms free. Manager, driven crazy by travellers' preference for the low-priced meeting rooms, transforms the one on the 4th floor into a dorm with camp beds, Y8, men only. Female travellers quickly point out the injustice – a conference is held, where else, in the ground-floor meeting room and, amazingly enough, a third meeting room is found (2nd floor) and designated a women's dorm. Both of these former meeting rooms, now established dorms, are large and filled with camp beds entirely surrounded by facing armchairs, a somewhat surreal decor.

Scene 3 Word has spread along the travellers' grapevine as far as Hong Kong, but CITS has received neither news nor reservations. A fresh group of travellers steps into the Tiantan off the Trans-Siberian and heads straight for the dorms – later they set up a disco near the restaurant. The manager has given up denying that the dorms exist: the camp beds are given a shakedown, spruced up, and the price jumps to Y10.

Scene 4 Much later. The dorms are full, *really* full. I am sharing a room with two people, one sleeping on the floor. I pass the desk as two travellers argue with the manager, refusing to believe the dorms are really really full, otherwise known as 'aw-full'. The room I'm in is large – space for two more on the floor, so I offer the travellers the option if they get stuck and tell them the room number. When I return in the evening, there are about seven travellers in the room arguing with the manager about floor space, and I quietly slip back out again. Ah yes, time to leave Beijing before another crashpad is created.

Places to Eat – Pigging Out in Beijing

In a daring denunciation of cadre corruption, Chinese rock musician Cui Jian wrote the 'Official Banquet Song':

I'm a big official, so I eat and drink, eat and drink;
To the Mongolian restaurant we go for hotpot;
To Quanjude for Peking duck;
Anyway, it's not my money;
So eat and drink and all be merry!

In 1949 Beijing had an incredible 10,000 snack bars and restaurants; by 1976 that number had dwindled to less than 700. Restaurants, a nasty bourgeois concept, were all to have been phased out and replaced by

revolutionary dispensaries dishing out rice. We could hazard some wild guesses about what happened to some of the chefs – they were allocated jobs as bus drivers while the bus drivers were given jobs as chefs. Anyhow the number of eateries is well on the rise again. While there are still not enough to cater for the million-odd Chinese customers, they certainly present ample variety for the average gastronome and there's no way you'll get through them all. Most of the regional and minority styles are represented in the capital.

When & Where Location and timing have a lot to do with whether you get your meal. At around 5 pm, a strange eating hour for Westerners (the internal alarm clock hasn't got the message yet), dinner is under way, and the panic is on. Where's the nearest hotpot? Which bus? Listed below are some favourite restaurants and a brief rundown of some others. It's the tip of the epicurean iceberg. Go and hunt for more. Eating out in the capital is a true adventure, one that should be seized with both chopsticks. Dining hours are from 5 to 7 pm sharp but try and get there by 6 pm. Lunch is from 11 am to 1 pm and is less crowded. If you miss out, there's always, of course, predictable hotel food.

Table Manners Forget those! We speak here of the popular prole section of a restaurant – waiters are in the nasty habit of intercepting foreigners and detouring them to private cubicles where the furniture is plusher, crowds are nonexistent, prices skyrocket and the kitchen is exactly the same. Any number of tactics will be employed to steer you away from the popular section. Never mind, throw yourself in anyway. Fighting for your supper increases the appetite, and your table company will be congenial enough once you manage to land a seat.

Order by pointing to your neighbour's dishes. Make sure your finger gets within an inch of the food and that you didn't order three of that dish. Beer is usually obtained with tickets at a separate counter, but you can solve this by arriving with your own beer from a nearby store. At the established restaurants you can reserve tables by phoning ahead. This will mean cubicles, banquet-style and more expensive food, although some dishes can only be obtained by phoning ahead with a group order.

Specialities Northern cuisine specialities are Peking duck, Mongolian hotpot, Muslim barbecue and imperial food. Imperial cuisine is served up in the restaurants of Beihai Park, the Summer Palace and the Fragrant Hills – very expensive, but go for the cheaper snacks. Mongolian hotpot is a winter dish – a brass pot with charcoal inside it is placed at the centre of the table and you cook thick strips of mutton and vegetables yourself, fondue fashion, spicing as you like. Muslim barbecues use lamb, a Chinese Muslim influence; shish kebabs are called *shashlik*.

Peking duck is the capital's famous invention, now a production line of sorts. Your meal starts at one of the agricultural communes around Beijing where the duck is pumped full of grain and soybean paste to fatten it up. The ripe duck is lacquered with molasses, pumped with air, filled with boiling water, dried, and then roasted over a fruitwood fire. The result, force-fed or not, is delicious.

We forgot to mention that the poor duck is killed somewhere along the line. In fact, the story goes that the original roast duck was not killed. In Chang'an, where the dish is said to have been devised 1200 years ago, two nobles placed live geese and ducks in an iron cage over a charcoal fire. As the heat increased the thirsty birds would drink from a bowl filled with vinegar, honey, malt, ginger and salt until they passed away.

Peking Duck Otherwise known as the 'Big Duck', the *Qianmen Roast Duck Restaurant* (☎ 7011379) *(qiánmén qùanjùdé kǎoyādiàn)* is at 32 Qianmen Dajie, on the east side, near Qianmen subway. This is one of the oldest restaurants in the capital, dating back to 1864. Prices are moderate, and there's a cheaper section through the right-hand doorway. Same duck, same kitchen. The cheap section is very crowded – if you don't get there by 6 pm, forget it. Beer is brewed on the premises. The duck is served in stages. First come boneless meat and crispy skin with a side dish of shallots, plum sauce and crêpes, followed by duck soup made of bones and all the other parts except the quack. Language is not really a problem; you just have to negotiate half or whole ducks. The locals will show you the correct etiquette, like when to spit on the floor.

The *Beijing Hotel* has a number of top-class restaurants. Of interest is the genial west-wing dining room on the 7th floor, where you can get painless Peking duck. Some think the food's not up to scratch, but perhaps their taste buds are more finely tuned than most. Other gourmet novelties like bear paws are served if you've got the bucks.

The *Bianyifang Duck Restaurant* (☎ 750505) *(biànyífāng kǎoyādiàn)* at 2 Chongwenmenwai Dajie is just east of CITS but don't let that ruin your appetite – they've been in business for aeons. It uses a slightly different method of preparation – a closed oven.

Sichuan The place to go is the *Sichuan* (☎ 336356) *(sìchūan fàndiàn)* at No 51 Rongxian Hutong. To get there go south from Xidan intersection (where Xidan meets Chang'an), turn left into a hutong marked by traffic lights and a police-box, and continue along the hutong till you find the grey wall entrance. In contrast to the bland interiors and peeling paint of most of the capital's restaurants, this one is housed in the sumptuous former residence of Yuan Shikai (the general who tried to set himself up as an emperor in 1914). The compound decor is spectacular, and the several dining rooms will clean out your wallet very fast. For cheaper food continue to the back of the courtyard, veer right, and there's a dining room with good meals for a few yuan per head if you're sharing dishes. You'll need some drinks for this one! It's a good idea to bring your own in case they've run out (or better still, a flask of yoghurt to cool the flames). The food is out of this world: fiery pork, explosive prawns, bamboo shoots, bean curd (tofu), beef dishes, some seafood, and side dishes of cucumber. In the more expensive parts of the restaurant variety is greater, but the back dining room will sate the appetite.

Another favourite haunt is the *Emei Restaurant* (☎ 863068) *(éméi fàndiàn)* on Yuetan Beijie, with very cheap, hot Sichuan food and friendly staff.

Next to the *Qianmen Roast Duck Restaurant* you'll find the *Lili* (☎ 751242) *(lìlì cāntīng)* at 30 Qianmen. The Sichuan-style spicy chicken and hot noodles with peanuts and chillies are very good. They serve some of the best dumplings in Beijing too.

Also try the *Shuxiang* (☎ 545176) *(shǔxiāng cānguǎn)* at 40 Chongwenmennei near the Xinqiao Hotel.

Shandong The *Fengzeyuan Restaurant* (☎ 7211336) *(fēngzéyúan)* at 83 Zhushikou Xidajie, off Qianmen Dajie, serves Shandong-style cuisine. It's highly rated by gourmets and is famous for seafood and soups. Specialities include sea cucumber braised with scallion, snowflake prawns and chicken puffs with shark skin. They also serve duck, crisp chicken, duck-marrow soup and turtle soup with egg. For dessert there's silver-thread rolls, toffee apples and almond curd with pineapple. Despite the restaurant's grubby appearance the food is very good.

The *Tongheju Restaurant* (☎ 2017433) *(tónghéjū fànzhūang)* is near the intersection of Xidan Beidajie and Fuchengmennei Dajie. They serve Shandong-style crispy spiced duck, seafood and a renowned pudding made of cggs, lard and flour.

The crowded *Cuihualou (cùihúalóu fànzhūang)* at 60 Wangfujing, north of Dongfeng Market, has Shandong-style seafood, velvet chicken and toffee apples.

Hunanese The *Quyuan* (☎ 662196) *(qǔyúan jiǔlóu)* is at 133 Xidan Beidajie north of Chang'an, west side, in a red-fronted building by an overhead bridge. The Hunan food served here is hot and spicy like Sichuan cuisine. If the French can do it with frogs, how often do you get a chance to digest dog? Anyone for hot dog? On the menu is onion dog, dog soup (reputed to be an aphrodisiac) and dog stew. For those with canine sensibilities, perhaps a switch to Hunan-style duck spiced with hot pepper, or some seafood, and several styles of noodles. The desserts with lychees are good; they can be varied or custom-made if you phone in advance. The food is cheap and the management nice.

The *Xiangshu* (☎ 558351) *(xiāngshǔ cāntīng)* is on the Wangfujing side of Dongfeng Market. The food is a combination of Sichuan and Hunan, highly recommended. Try the Xiangshu for the 'silver-thread rolls' which are Beijing's best pastry.

Mongolian Hotpot & Muslim Barbecue *Kaorouwan* (☎ 657707) *(kǎoròuwǎn fànzhūang)* at 102 Xuanwumennei, south of Xidan intersection, on the east side of the street, serves Muslim barbecues, and you can do your own skewers if the wind is blowing in the right direction.

Hongbinlou (☎ 655691) *(hóngbīnlóu fànzhūang)* at 82 Xi Chang'an Jie, just east of Xidan intersection, serves shashlik (kebabs), Peking duck and Mongolian hotpot. Lamb banquets can be ordered in advance.

Shoudu Kaorouji (☎ 445921) at 37 Shichahai is difficult to find but worth it in summer. Go to the Drum Tower *(gǔlóu)* area, turn into a hutong to the left immediately before the Drum Tower as you go north, and follow it down to the lakeside. The dowdy interiors of most Chinese restaurants make you feel boxed in with no windows, but here you've got a view of the lake, the alleys and the activity in the area. In summer tables are moved onto the balcony. This is a place for potless hotpot and Muslim barbecue.

Shanxi *Jinyang* (☎ 331669) *(jìnyáng fàndiàn)* is at 241 Zhushikou Xidajie, in a red-fronted building west of the Fengzeyuan. You can dine on Shanxi-style salty duck, squirrel fish, noodles and onion cakes in a pleasant atmosphere.

Shanghai *Laozhengxing* (☎ 5112148) *(lǎozhèngxīng fàndiàn)* at 46 Qianmen is a Shanghai-style place with a range of sea-

food, including fish, eel, and hairy crabs when in season.

Cantonese *Guangdong Restaurant* (☎ 894881) *(gŭangdōng cāntīng)* in the Xijiao market opposite the zoo serves up Peking duck and Cantonese-style cuisine, including turtle and snake.

Vegetarian The Yangzhou-style *Gongdelin Vegetarian Restaurant (gōngdélín sùcài-gŭan)* at 158 Qianmen Dajie is probably the best in the city. It gets rave reviews and serves up wonderful veggie food with names to match. How about the 'peacock in pride' or 'the fire is singeing the snow-capped mountains'? The helpings are generous, the prices low and the staff friendly.

Other Chinese Restaurants *Huaiyang Fanzhuang* at 217 Xidan Beidajie has a Jiangsu-cuisine section serving hairy crab in season.

Shaguoju Restaurant (☎ 661126) *(shā-gūojū fànzhūang)*, in a tacky building at 60 Xisi Nandajie, is further north toward the Xisi intersection. Pork is served in many forms, some dishes in earthenware pots; the food is cheap.

Kangle Restaurant (☎ 443884) *(kānglè fàndiàn)* at 259 Andingmennei is further east of the Drum Tower near the Jiaodaokou intersection. This place serves up Fujian and Yunnan styles of food. Expensive 'across-the-bridge noodles' must be ordered in advance for a minimum of four people. Also try Yunnan-style steamed chicken, seafood and *san bu zhan* (sweet sticky pudding).

Russian Overall, not too good, but you may find it a welcome break from the noodle and rice dishes. The *Moscow Restaurant* (☎ 894454) *(mòsīkē cāntīng)* is on the west side of the Soviet-designed Exhibition Centre in the zoo district. The vast interior has chandeliers, a high ceiling, fluted columns. Foreigners are shuffled to a side room overlooking the zoo (which has, by the way, no connection with the menu). The food gets mixed reviews, but it's definitely Russian – borsch, cream prawns au gratin, pork à la Kiev, beef stroganoff, black bread, soups and black caviar, moderately priced.

Western All the large tourist hotels serve Western food of varying quality and price. Travellers pining for a croissant or strong coffee will be pleased to know that Beijing is the best place in China to find such delicacies.

The *Friendship Store (yoŭyí shāngdiàn)* is the best place to assemble breakfast, though a mite on the expensive side. The deli adjacent to the supermarket has sliced ham, bread rolls, scotch eggs and sausage. It also offers a range of pastries and croissants that can be heated up in a microwave. You can get yoghurt in ceramic flasks – though both the yoghurt and the pastries can be found in other locations around Beijing. Fresh milk and fruit juice are available in the supermarket. Occasionally the deli stocks an excellent Heilongjiang cheese, comparable to Gouda: look for a red cannonball. This is one of the very few places in China where you can get those cheese-enzymes working again.

Good bets for Western meals are the *Beijing, Xinqiao* and *Minzu* hotels. The *Jianguo Hotel* serves Holiday Inn, California home-style cooking at greater than Californian prices. Check the ads in the *China Daily* for novelty events; anyone for a Texas spare-rib barbecue at the *Great Wall Sheraton Hotel*?

For some light relief try *Maxim's* (☎ 5122110) *(bālí măkèxīmŭ cāntīng)* within the precincts of the Chongwenmen Hotel. The joint China-French venture initiated by Pierre Cardin is a copy of Maxim's in Paris and opened in October 1983. The Paris-trained, French-speaking staff have picked up some strange habits and will knock back those wearing shorts and runners. Dinner for two – *sacré bleu* – is a cool Y200 or so excluding that Bordeaux red or the Alsatian Gerwürtzraminer. The pissoir is reputed to be the best in China.

The *Huadu Restaurant* (☎ 557208) *(húa-dū cāntīng)* at 76 Dongdan Beidajie is a small place that serves pizzas! The dish was first introduced by tourists.

And finally there is *Kentucky Fried Chicken* across the street from Mao's mausoleum in Tiananmen Square – if this doesn't make the late Chairman turn over in his grave, nothing will.

Snacks Off da Trax Beijing has a fair number of snack bars, noodle bars, dumpling shops and cake shops – nowhere near the number it used to have, but sufficient to sate the curiosity. A Beijing newspaper suggested there weren't nearly enough snack bars and that the locals should resort to selling hot dogs!

Snacks can be found at roadside stalls, especially around breakfast time. Also try the market areas, and the ground floor of restaurants (the masses section). Small vendors are making a comeback, ever since the return of the ice-cream soda in 1980 after an absence of 14 years. In fact a health problem exists with the unsupervised production of popsicles by home entrepreneurs.

A few suggestions for snack-trackers are given, but you're better off thinking of it as 'chance food'. When you see something you like, jump at it. You've got nothing to lose but your taste buds. The street market behind the Beijing Hotel is a good, cheap place to start.

Near Wangfujing is the Art Institute *(měishù xúeyùan)*, which has a cheap cafeteria that does good meals for Y3.

The Qianmen area in bygone Beijing had the largest concentration of snack bars, and is a good place to go hunting. Down Qianmen Dajie is the *Zhengmingzhai Cakeshop*. The *Jinfeng* at 157 Qianmenwai sells Beijing-style baozi dumplings.

The *Duyichu* at No 36 Qianmen and close to Dazhalan is an ancient restaurant serving *shaomai* (steamed dumplings).

Off the beginning of Dazhalan on Liangshidian hutong is *Zhimielou*, which sells dragon-whisker noodles – strands as fine as silk, an old Qing recipe.

For baozi and jiaozi try the *Hongxinglou* at 1 Beiwei Lu on the west side of the Temple of Heaven. It also serves shaomai and noodles. Twenty different kinds of jiaozi (in season) can be ordered and there's even frozen take-away. The crowded ground floor has two kinds of jiaozi, beer and cold cuts. The next floor has jiaozi and Shandong-style seafood and pork dishes. The seafood is not cheap, but if you stick to jiaozi this can be a very inexpensive place to eat.

The *Ritan Park Restaurant* to the north of the Friendship Store has classy jiaozi and Western snacks. It's patronised by Westerners and housed in a classical-style building.

Near Xisi, on Xianmen Dajie, is a genuine coffee and teahouse, a private business called the *Daoshanzhuang*. Refreshments are served to music by Chopin, Mozart and Schubert, or to light foreign and Chinese music. Art on the walls is by the manager-owner, Su Daoshan.

In 1982 a group of Beijing chefs set about reviving the imperial pastry recipes. They even went so far as to dig up the last emperor's brother to try their products out on. The same year, an Overseas Chinese outfit was permitted to start up a snack bar specialising in South-East Asian snacks. Snacking is where you can experience the free market. Jobless youths have carved out small businesses for themselves, and there are licensed family-owned restaurants. The other person you'll meet is the snacker, someone who can't afford a full-course meal. It will cost you next to nothing to sample these places, all highly educational.

Fast Food For a taste of China's gastronomic future try *Minim's*, the poor person's Maxim's. No joke; it's one door down from its famous big sister in the Chongwenmen Hotel – lots of tin-foil and surly staff, mediocre coffee, OK chocolate mousse, and the tomato soup is said to be good. Otherwise, it has few redeeming features.

Across the road is *Rosenbac's* which has a fine bakery dispensing real bread, croissants and pastries. Behind it is a glossy fast-food joint indistinguishable from a university cafeteria.

Nightlife & Entertainment

Foreigners who live in this city say a night out in Beijing is no fun at all. The town goes to bed early – most cultural events start around 7 pm and are finished by 9.30 pm, when transport becomes infrequent. The Chinese mostly stick to restauranting or playing chess in the gutters at midnight; young people go to the Chinese-only discos.

Discos Back in the late '70s, Saturday Night Fever (1940s style) hit Beijing. Discos popped up in various hotels and notably in the Nationalities Cultural Palace on Chang'an Jie, where dancing was punctuated by a floor show with minority groups. The authorities reasoned that the high admission price of Y10 would keep the locals out, but they misjudged the craze for the joys of dancing. Due to problems of mixing and drinking, the music died, and even the Life Disco at the Jianguo Hotel had trouble getting started. Many of the large tourist hotels have discos; the best way to check which dance floor is still operating (and how much it will cost) is to phone ahead.

Fun with the Foreign Community Embassy staff and journalists, bored with Beijing's 'nightlife', have created their own. At one time in the '70s the sole source of decadence in Beijing was the 'Down Under Club' in the basement of the Australian Embassy, which got such a reputation that taxi drivers refused to collect passengers late at night (this problem was overcome by summoning a taxi to the Malaysian Embassy next door). They started something of a precedent, which has evolved into a Friday night get-together at varying embassies or residences – the news sometimes hits the lobby of the Beijing Hotel. The Brits have imported their nightlife – there's a British pub called The Bell inside the grounds of the UK Embassy, but the last time we heard, the place was not exactly open to the public.

Clubbing Sporting, recreational and club facilities are to be found in the Friendship Hotel, the International Club and the Minority Nationalities Cultural Palace. The International Club is pretty lifeless, patronised by dozy diplomats, and has signs around the place telling you what not to do. There are dusty tennis courts, billiard tables, a full-sized swimming pool, a bowling alley (a bummer – you have to set up your own pins) and a bar/restaurant (it's debatable whether the chef isn't in fact a can opener).

The Nationalities Cultural Palace is a toffee-nosed Chinese and foreign hang-out with a large range of amenities including ping pong, a bowling alley, bar, restaurant and ballroom and banquet rooms. Of interest here might be minority singing and dancing events by night (or shows which have nothing to do with minorities) and occasional exhibitions featuring minority wares by day. If you get to the upper floors of this massive group of buildings there are some very nice views.

What's On Back in the days of Mao, 'cultural events' often meant revolutionary operas featuring evil foreign and Kuomintang devils who eventually were defeated by brave workers and peasants inspired by the Little Red Book. Fortunately, performances have improved considerably. The *China Daily* carries a listing of cultural evenings recommended for foreigners. Offerings include concerts, theatre, minority dancing and some cinema. There are about 35 theatres and 50 cinemas in the capital. You can reserve ahead by phoning the box office via your hotel, or pick up tickets at CITS for a surcharge – or take a risk and just roll up at the theatre.

Entertainment is dirt cheap, Y3 being a typical price if you buy the tickets yourself rather than through your hotel or CITS. Beijing is on the touring circuit for foreign troupes, and these are also listed in the *China Daily*. They're somewhat screened for content, but lately they've been beefing up what's available. In 1983 Arthur Miller's *Death of a Salesman* was acted out by Chinese at the Capital Theatre, and held over for two months by popular demand.

The same theatre staged some avant-garde Chinese theatre. It put on two plays by Gao Zingjian, incorporating theatre of the absurd and traditional Chinese theatrical techniques. One of the plays, *Bus-stop*, is based on eight characters who spend 10 years at the bus stop to discover that the service was cancelled long ago. That's either a vicious comment on the Beijing bus service, or a sly reference to Gao's stint in re-education camp during the Cultural Revolution – or else it's a direct steal from Samuel Beckett or Luigi Pirandello.

In the concert department they've presented Beethoven's Ninth played on Chinese palace instruments, such as tuned bells copied from those found in an ancient tomb. Other classical instruments are being revived for dance-drama backings. Bizarre performances are often staged for foreign tour groups and some of these have to be seen to be believed. Perhaps trial runs before touring overseas with cultural shows tailored to Western tastes? Some of this stuff would go down great in Las Vegas!

Film is out of the boring stage and starting to delve into some contemporary issues, even verging on Cultural Revolution aftershock in a mild manner. The International Club near the Friendship Store shows Chinese films with English subtitles or simultaneous translation into English, every Saturday night at 7 pm. The Friendship Hotel shows old foreign and Chinese films (with simultaneous translation) every Friday night.

Television, if you're that kind of addict, brings a lot of different types of Chinese entertainment directly into your hotel room, if you have that kind of room. There are a couple of channels, and if you have the right kind of electronic hookups perhaps some naughty Hong Kong video. Programmes are listed in the *China Daily*. TV is actually a good way of studying Chinese, especially the kids' programmes with fascinating forms of Chinese animation.

As for other events, you might like to delve into items listed in the local newspapers. If you can read Chinese or get a translation you can find out about sporting events, puppet theatre, storytelling and local cinema. These may be sold out, but scalpers do a roaring trade.

You can even set yourself up as an English teacher at the Beijing 'English corner' in Purple Bamboo Park, near the Capital Stadium in the Haidian District.

Opera *(píngjù)* It used to be the Marx Brothers, the Gang of Four and the Red Ballet – but it's back to the classics again these days. Beijing Opera is one of the many forms of the art and the most famous, but it's only got a short history. The year 1790 is the key date given; in that year a provincial troupe performed before Emperor Qianlong on his 80th birthday. The form was popularised in the West by the actor Mei Lanfang (1894-1961) who played *dan* or female roles, and is said to have influenced Charlie Chaplin. There is a museum devoted to Mei Lanfang at 9 Huguosi Lu, in western Beijing.

Earlier in the century, teahouses, wine shops and opera were the main nightlife in Beijing; of these, only the opera has survived (just). The opera bears little resemblance to its European counterpart. The mixture of singing, dancing, speaking, mime, acrobatics and dancing can go on for five or six hours; an hour is usually long enough for a Westerner. Plots are fairly basic so the language barrier is not really a problem – the problems are the music, which is searing to Western ears, and the acting, which is heavy and stylised.

When you get bored after the first hour or so, and are sick of the high-pitched whining, the local audience is with you all the way – spitting, eating apples, breast-feeding an urchin on the balcony, or plugging into a transistor radio (important sports match?). It's a lively prole audience viewing entertainment fit for kings.

Another problem is trying to find a performance that really is Beijing Opera. All you can do is patiently troop around the theatre circuit until you hit the one that's still dishing up the real thing. Most performances start around 7 or 7.30 pm.

The best bets are the Dazhalan Theatre *(dàzhàlán xìyùan)* on Dazhalan Jie; the Jixiang at 14 Jinyu Hutong, off Wangfujing; and the Chaoyang *(cháoyáng xìyùan)*, at

Dongsanhuan Beilu and Chaoyang Beilu out in the east part of the city.

Some others that might be worth a try include the Chang'an theatre at 126 Xi Chang'an Jie, just east of the intersection with Xuanwumennei Dajie; the Erqi on Fuxingmenwai Dajie; the Tianqiao at 30 Beiwei Lu near the Temple of Heaven; the Renmin on Huguosi Dajie.

The oldest in Beijing is the Guanghe at 24-26 Qianmen Dajie – it's actually down an alleyway leading off Qianmen.

Beijing Opera is usually regarded as the *crème de la crème* of all the opera styles prevalent in China. Traditionally it's been the opera of the masses. In some ways it's very similar to the ancient Greek theatre, with its combination of singing, dialogue, acrobatics and pantomime, the actors wearing masks and the performance accompanied by loud and monotonous rhythms produced with percussion instruments. The themes are usually inspired by disasters, natural calamities, intrigues or rebellions. Many have their source in the fairy tales and stock characters and legends of classical literature. Titles like *The Monkey King, A Drunken Beauty* and *A Fisherman's Revenge* are typical.

The music, singing and costumes are products of the opera's origins. Formerly, Beijing Opera was performed mostly on open-air stages in markets, streets, teahouses or temple courtyards. The orchestra had to play loudly and the performers had to develop a piercing style of singing which could be heard over the throng. The costumes are a garish collection of sharply contrasting colours because the stages were originally lit by oil lamps.

The movements and techniques of the dance styles of the Tang Dynasty are similar to those of today's Beijing Opera. Provincial opera companies were characterised by their dialect and style of singing, but when these companies converged on Beijing they started a style of musical drama called *kunqu*. This developed during the Ming Dynasty, along with a more popular variety of play-acting with pieces based on legends, historical events and popular novels. These styles gradually merged by the late 18th and early 19th centuries into the Beijing Opera we see today.

The musicians usually sit on the stage in plain clothes and play without written scores. The erhu is a two-stringed fiddle which is tuned to a low register, has a soft tone and generally supports the huqin, another two-stringed fiddle tuned to a high register. The yueqin, a sort of moon-shaped four-stringed guitar, has a soft tone and is used to support the erhu. Other instruments are the *sheng* (reed pipes) and the pipa (lute), as well as drums, bells and cymbals. Last but not least is the *ban*, a time-clapper which virtually directs the band, beats time for the actors and gives them their cues.

There are four types of actors' roles: the *sheng, dan, jing* and *chou*. The sheng are the leading male actors and they play scholars, officials, warriors, etc. They are divided into the *laosheng* who wear beards and represent old men, and the *xiaosheng* who represent young men. The *wensheng* are the scholars and the civil servants. The *wusheng* play soldiers and other fighters, and because of this are specially trained in acrobatics.

The dan are the female roles. The *laodan* are the elderly, dignified ladies such as mothers, aunts and widows. The *qingyi* are aristocratic ladies in elegant costumes. The *huadan* are the ladies' maids, usually in brightly coloured costumes. The *daomadan* are the warrior women. The *caidan* are the female comedians. Traditionally, female roles were played by male actors.

The jing are the painted-face roles, and they represent warriors, heroes, statesmen, adventurers and demons. Their counterpart is the *fujing*, ridiculous figures who are anything but heroic. The chou is basically the clown. The caidan is sometimes the female counterpart of this male role.

Apart from the singing and music, the opera also uses acrobatics and mime. Few props are used, so each move, gesture or facial expression is symbolic. A whip with silk tassels indicates an actor riding a horse. Lifting a foot means going through a doorway. Language is often archaic Chinese, music is ear-splitting (bring some cotton wool), but the costume and make-up are magnificent. The only action that really catches the Western eye is a swift battle sequence – the women warriors involved are trained acrobats who leap, twirl, twist and somersault into attack.

There are numerous other forms of opera. The Cantonese variety is more 'music hall', often with 'boy meets girl' themes. Gaojia Opera is one of the five local opera forms from Fujian Province and is also popular in Taiwan, with songs in the Fujian dialect but influenced by the Beijing Opera style.

Strange as it may sound, Chinese music is actually quite closely related to Western music. The 12 notes worked out by the ancient Chinese correspond exactly to those of the ancient Greeks (on which Western music is based). Although most Chinese musical instruments were introduced from India and central Asia, Chinese music is tonally closer to Western music. Western music, however, uses groupings (scales) of eight notes whereas Chinese music uses groupings of five notes. The five-note scale is one of the main reasons Chinese music sounds different from Western music. The other important difference (shared with Indian music) is a lack of harmony, generally considered very important in Western music.

Acrobatics *(tèjì biǎoyǎn)* Two thousand years old, and one of the few art forms condoned by Mao, acrobatics is the best deal in town. You can forget CITS, forget railway stations, forget hotels, forget language problems. Magic!

Acts take place in various locations, normally advertised in the *China Daily*. For authentic atmosphere, try the Acrobat Rehearsal Hall on Dazhalan, once the major theatre area in Beijing. CITS and the Qiaoyuan Hotel also sell tickets for around Y15 but you can usually roll up, roll in and get a seat for Y3. The show starts at 7.15 pm and acts change nightly. The shows are sometimes cancelled, and the place is always closed on Saturdays. Dazhalan is a hutong off the subway end of Qianmen Dajie. For a rundown on some popular acrobatic stunts see the Shanghai chapter.

Song & Dance Shows These come in different varieties, from Western style to Chinese or occasionally in the style of China's ethnic minorities. They advertise in the *China Daily*, but note that these shows are frequently cancelled even if advertised in the newspapers.

The Unusual A golfing club in China? Try the Beijing International Golf Club, a Chinese-Japanese joint venture opened in mid-1986, 35 km north of Beijing near the Ming Tombs – a spectacular golf course with good scenery. Visitor fees are Y200 weekdays, Y250 weekends and public holidays.

If hitting balls isn't quite your style then try hitting targets. There are reports of a firing range near Beijing where redneck foreigners, presumably with a copy of *Soldier of Fortune* tucked under one arm, are able to play with weapons and live ammo.

Things to Buy

Once upon a time in China you got what you paid for. A mixed blessing: if the man said it was top-quality jade then it was top-quality jade and you'd pay through the nose for it. These days there are all sorts of forgeries and imitations about, from Tibetan jewellery to

Qing coins and even phony packets of Western cigarettes. This doesn't apply in Friendship Stores and other government-run emporiums, so there's no need for paranoia about being ripped off with fakes in these places. Be aware that out in the streets and free markets it's a different story.

Bargains can still be had on certain goods. Prices are sometimes higher than in other Asian countries but lower than in the West. How about a blouson-style leather jacket to beat around in for just US$50? For heftier goods you have to take into account the sometimes outrageous tariffs for shipping. It therefore makes sense to go for smaller or lighter items that you can carry yourself. Some Chinese emporiums are like Aladdin's Caves – tourist attractions in themselves.

Shopping Districts Fast shopping can be done at the Friendship Store, which stocks most things that you'd want, and also carries luxury items not available elsewhere.

More fun and a bit cheaper for hard-to-find items is to rummage around with the Chinese. Shopping is concentrated in three busy areas: Wangfujing, Qianmen (in the Dazhalan hutong) and Liulichang (antiques). Other mildly interesting shopping streets are Xidan and Dongdan, north of Chang'an.

Tourist attractions like the Temple of Heaven, as well as major hotels, have garish souvenir shops stocking arts and crafts. Otherwise, speciality shops are scattered around the city core. Stores are generally open from 9 am to 7 pm seven days a week; some are open from 8 am to 8 pm. Bargaining is not a way of life in the stores, but on the free market it certainly is.

Down jackets are one of the best bargains you can find in Beijing, and will certainly come in handy if you plan to visit China in the winter. Good buys are stationery (chops, brushes, inks), prints, handicrafts, clothing (fur, silk, and antiques). Small or light items to buy are silk scarves, T-shirts, embroidered purses, papercuts, wooden and bronze Buddhas, fold-up paper lanterns and kites.

Friendship Store The Friendship Store at 21 Jianguomenwai (☎ 593531) is the largest in the land, with guards posted near the entrance to keep the Chinese out.

The top floor carries furniture, carpets, arts & crafts (stones, paintings, carvings, cloisonné). On the middle floor are clothing items, fabrics, cosmetics, toys and 'daily necessities'. The ground floor has tinned and dried imported/local foods, tobacco, wines, spirits, Chinese medicines, film, foreign books and magazines. To the right are a supermarket, deli and florist.

If you can't find the food you want, try the branch at 5 Sanlitun Lu. The Friendship Store also has tailors (alterations and made-to-measure), taxi service, money exchange, and a packing and shipping service.

Wangfujing This street just east of the Beijing Hotel is lined with a number of speciality stores, and has Beijing's largest department store. Opposite the department store is the Dongfeng, a covered market with a similar selection of dry goods.

This is the classiest shopping area in the capital, with largest-of-the-kind stores and appropriately sized crowds on weekends and holidays. In pre-'49 days it was known as Morrison Street, catering largely for foreigners.

Swiss and Seiko have moved in – among the first foreign businesses to set up shop in Beijing. Many foreigners will find the Xinhua Bookstore (No 212) an interesting place to browse. The name Wangfujing derives from a 15th-century well, the site of which is now occupied by the offices of the *People's Daily*.

Wangfujing is the place to go to buy film, though if you're willing to pay more, you can find film at the Friendship Store and hotel shops. Slide film is a rare item – usually out of date and expensive. Nevertheless, last year's slide film is better than none. Try to avoid this situation by bringing a sufficient supply with you.

Wangfujing is also the place to go for processing. Print film can be processed in one day and quality isn't bad. The Beijing Hotel and International Club also do processing, but at a higher price. Slides can also be developed but quality varies from acceptable to abysmal. If your slides mean anything to you, wait until you get home to have them processed.

If you need passport-type photos, Wangfujing is also a good place to go, or try the CITIC Building out by the Friendship Store.

Qianmen Area If Wangfujing is too sterile for you, the place to go and rub shoulders is Dazhalan, a hutong running west from the top end of Qianmen. It's a heady jumble of silk shops, department stores, theatres, herbal medicine, food and clothing specialists and some unusual architecture. The hutong is really more of a sight than a place to shop, but you might find something that catches your eye.

Dazhalan has a definite medieval flavour to it, a hangover from the days when hutongs sold specialised products – one would sell lace, another lanterns, another jade. This one used to be called Silk Street. The name Dazhalan refers to a wicket-gate that was closed at night to keep undesirable prowlers out.

In imperial Beijing, shops and theatres were not permitted near the city centre, and the Qianmen-Dazhalan district was outside the gates. Many of the city's oldest shops can be found along or near this crowded hutong.

Just off the beginning of Dazhalan at 3 Liangshidian Jie is Liubiju, a 400-year-old pickle-and-sauce emporium patronised by discriminating shoppers. Nearby is the Zhimielou Restaurant, which serves imperial snacks. On your right as you go down Dazhalan is a green concave archway with columns at No 5; this is the entrance to Liufuxiang, one of the better-known material and silk stores and a century old.

Next door to that is the entrance to the Acrobat Rehearsal Hall. Dazhalan at one time had five opera theatres. The place used to be thronged with theatre-goers both day (cheap rehearsals) and night (professionals). The nightlife lingers on with two performing theatres, and pedicab men wait for the post-theatre crowds as the rickshaw drivers did many years ago. No 1 Dazhalan was once a theatre.

Another famous shop is the Tongrengtang at No 24, selling Chinese herbal medicines. It's been in business since 1669, though it doesn't appear that way from the renovations. It was a royal dispensary in the Qing Dynasty, and derives its pills and potions from secret prescriptions used by royalty. All kinds of weird ingredients – tiger bone, rhino horn, snake wine – will cure you of anything from fright to encephalitis, or so they claim. Traditional doctors are available on the spot for consultation; perhaps ask them about fear of railway stations (patience pills?).

Dazhalan runs about 300 metres deep off Qianmen. At the far end where the hubbub dies down is a bunch of Chinese hotels, and if you sense something here...yes, you're right, Dazhalan was the gateway to Beijing's red-light district. The brothels were shut down in 1949 and the women packed off to factories.

Qianmen Dajie, and Zhushikou Xidajie leading off to the west, are interesting places to meander. On Qianmen Dajie there are pottery stores at Nos 99 and 149, minority musical instruments at Nos 18 and 104, and a nice second-hand shop at No 117.

Tiantan Area The antique market at the north-east corner of Tiantan Park across from the silk factory is great! You can buy a Little Red Book for Y10 (be sure to bargain). There are plenty of antiques, though most are under 100 years old and some are replicas. A favourite buy for foreigners is a 'youth of China' alarm clock with a picture of a rosy-cheeked female Red Guard enthusiastically waving the Little Red Book.

Second-hand Shopping Shopping for second-hand goods is one of the favourite pastimes of embassy staff in Beijing. This is reputedly worked on a rota-system so that anything of real value can be snapped up the moment it hits the shelf. Most of the second-hand or commission shops sell recycled radios, TVs and household goods, but some are specialised and are unmarked and hard to find. Here are a few.

Arts & Crafts Trust Company, 12 Chongwenmennei Dajie, just north of Xinqiao Hotel and CITS, has a very pleasant atmosphere. It sells theatrical costumes, used furs and clothing, jewellery and a large selection of antiques including a wonderful array of clocks. The antiques and clocks aren't necessarily Chinese – some are European or Japanese. A separate section next door sells furniture, carpets and embroidery.

Beixinqiao, 30 Dongsi Beidajie, has old chests of all shapes and sizes, some made of camphor and mahogany. Other second-hand furniture can be found in the shops at 32 Chongwenmenwai and 56 Wangfujing. It's all expensive stuff.

Possibly the best antique furniture shop in town is at 38 Dongsi Nandajie. They will also repair furniture for you, although the last we heard, mailing goes through the Friendship Store, which will identify antiques.

Qianmen Trade Commission House, 117 Qianmen, has furs and fur-lined coats and jackets. The older style of wealth was all about having it, not displaying it, so long coats look cheap from the outside but have a 'silver lining' – an expensive skin such as fox. This is one of Beijing's largest second-hand goods stores, with all sorts of other goods for sale.

Markets With the resurgence of individual trading, going to a market is a good way of observing some lively interaction between locals. Markets are a bit difficult to locate. 'Market' on a bus map basically means department store.

The lower end of Qianmen Dajie, west Zhushikou Lu and the Tianqiao area are pretty brisk. Along the north-east wall of the Temple of Heaven is a very busy market with poultry and gardening supplies.

The Dongsi People's Market in a hutong near the CAAC building may be worth a visit for another reason – the newer store is in an old area once occupied by the Longfu Temple, the remains of which are still visible.

There's a bird-and-fish market west of Pinganli intersection, near the zoo. There's a large fruit-and-vegetable market near the Beitaipingzhuang intersection north-west of Deshengmen – follow Xinjiekouwai Dajie.

Pigeon racing is coming back into style in China; there is a pigeon market on Changping Lu, about three km north of Deshengmen on the way to the Ming Tombs.

Getting There & Away

Getting to Beijing is no problem – one of those rail or air lines will lead you to the capital sooner or later. The real problem is getting away, and your exodus is best planned well in advance. There are planes from Beijing to numerous destinations but most people will probably leave the city by train – get in early to get a sleeper.

Air You can get to just about anywhere in the world from Beijing. Many budget travellers

Street Market

make use of the direct flight to Hong Kong with CAAC or Cathay Pacific. The cost is Y1000. For more information about international flights to Beijing see the introductory Getting There & Away chapter in this book.

Beijing Capital Airport, operational since 1980, was built as part of the 'Four Modernisations' drive, and is modelled on Paris's Orly Airport. It's 29 km north-east of the city.

To get to the airport you can take the CAAC bus (Y2.50) which leaves the office in the city centre at irregular times – likewise coming from the airport to Beijing.

Alternatively take a taxi. Split between a maximum of four passengers, the fare is not too bad; plus the taxi leaves from your hotel – an important consideration if your plane leaves at 6 am. The journey takes half an hour. Local bus No 359 runs to the airport from Dongzhimen.

The partially computerised CAAC ticket office (☎ 4014441 for domestic reservations; ☎ 4012221 for international reservations; and ☎ 554415 for enquiries) is at 117 Dongsi Xidajie.

The CAAC aerial spider web spreads out in every conceivable direction, with daily flights to major cities and quite a few minor ones. For the most current information, get a CAAC timetable. The following is a list of all domestic direct flights from Beijing and ticket prices:

Baotou Y194; Canton Y663; Changchun Y313; Changsha Y484; Changzhou Y340; Chaoyang Y129; Chengdu Y570; Chifeng Y112; Chongqing Y550; Dalian Y194; Dandong Y284; Fuzhou Y564; Guilin Y621; Guiyang Y684; Haikou Y837; Hailar Y476; Hangzhou Y403; Harbin Y338; Hefei Y321; Hohhot Y148; Huangshan Y393; Ji'nan Y138; Kunming Y760; Lanzhou Y454; Lianyungang Y236; Mudanjiang Y482; Nanchang Y469; Nanjing Y328; Nanning Y742; Ningbo Y448; Qingdao Y224; Qinhuangdao Y105; Qiqihar Y424; Shanghai Y394; Shantou Y651; Shenyang Y217; Taiyuan Y175; Tianjin Y60; Tongliao Y216; Ulanhot Y334; Ürümqi Y954; Wuhan Y380; Xiamen Y595; Xi'an Y346; Yan'an Y278; Yantai Y193; Yinchuan Y370; Zhengzhou Y231

Enquiries for all airlines can be made at Beijing International Airport (☎ 552515). The individual offices of airlines are at:

Aeroflot Soviet Airlines
  Hotel Beijing-Toronto (☎ 5002412)
Air France
  2716 China World Trade Centre, 1 Jianguomenwai (☎ 5051818)
All Nippon Airways
  West Building, Beijing Hotel (☎ 5125551)
British Airways
  Room 210, 2nd floor, SCITE Tower, 22 Jianguomenwai (☎ 5124070)
CAAC
  155 Dongsi Xidajie (☎ 558861). There is also a booking office in the Beijing Hotel.
Canadian Airlines
  China World Trade Centre, 1 Jianguomenwai (☎ 5001956)
Cathay Pacific
  Room 152, Jianguo Hotel (☎ 5003339)
Finnair
  18-5 CITIC Building, 19 Jianguomenwai (☎ 5127180)
Japan Airlines
  Room 2279, Hotel Beijing-Toronto (☎ 5002221)
JAT Yugoslav Airlines
  Room 427, Kunlun Hotel (☎ 5003388 ext 426)
LOT Polish Airlines
  Room 139, Jianguo Hotel (☎ 5002233)
Lufthansa
  SCITE Tower, 22 Jianguomenwai (☎ 5123535)
Northwest Airlines
  Room 101-103, Jianguo Hotel (☎ 5004529)
Pakistan International
  Diplomatic Apartments, 12-43 Jianguomenwai (☎ 5323274)
Philippine Airlines
  12-53 Jianguomenwai (☎ 5323992)
Qantas
  5th floor, Beijing Fortune Building, 5 Dongsanhuan Beilu, Chaoyangqu (☎ 5002481)
Romanian Air Transport
  Romanian Embassy Compound, Ritan Lu, Dong 2-Jie, Jianguomenwai (☎ 5323552)
SAS-Scandinavian Airlines
  18th floor, SCITE Tower, 22 Jianguomenwai (☎ 5120575)
Singapore Airlines
  1-2 CITIC Building, 19 Jianguomenwai (☎ 5044138),
Swissair
  Room 201, SCITE Tower, 22 Jianguomenwai (☎ 5123555)
Thai International
  Room 204, SCITE Tower, 22 Jianguomenwai (☎ 5123881)
United Airlines
  Room 204, SCITE Tower, 22 Jianguomenwai (☎ 5128888)

Bus Beijing is approachable by bus from outlying locations – the roads are bumpy except for the highway from Tianjin, which is in good nick.

Long-distance bus stations within Beijing are on the perimeter: at Dongzhimen (north-east), Guangqumen (south-east) and Tianqiao (near the theatre on the west side of Temple of Heaven).

There are two bus stations near Yongdingmen station, another at the Ganjiakou intersection south of the zoo, and one off Deshengmenwai Dajie. They are usually part-way along the direction you want to travel.

These bus stations also have cheaper alternatives to tour buses, such as cheap, local buses to out-of-town locations like the Ming Tombs.

Train There is a Foreigners' Ticketing Office at the main Beijing railway station. Enter the station and it's to the rear and left side – there's a small sign in English saying 'International Passenger Booking Office'. The ticketing office is inside the foreigners' waiting room. It's open daily, from 5.30 to 7.30 am, 8 to 11.30 am, 1 to 5.30 pm and 7 pm to 12.30 am. They sell timetables in English for Y8. There are lockers inside the waiting room – Y10 per day for large lockers and Y5 per day for small ones. Tickets can be booked several days in advance. Your chances of getting a sleeper (hard or soft) are good so long as you book ahead.

You can pay in RMB at the Foreigners' Ticketing Office provided you have a genuine (or genuine-looking) white card. Getting a Chinese person to buy your ticket from the regular ticket windows involves major tactical difficulties – mainly that the ticket windows, some two dozen of them, can't be seen half the time for the crowds!

The following is a table of approximate train fares out of Beijing for hard-seat, hard-sleeper and soft-sleeper. Variations in fares and travel times may arise because of different routings of different trains. For example, the journey to Shanghai can take between 17 and 25 hours depending on the train.

Advance train ticket offices are scattered around Beijing. The offices listed below sell hard-seat and hard-sleeper for one, two or three days in advance of intended departure. These offices may refuse to sell you a ticket and direct you back to the Foreigners' Ticket Office in the main Beijing station. With such heavy demand for tickets it's likely that the Foreigners' Ticket Office is your only chance of getting a ticket anyway, particularly if you want a sleeper.

Qianmen Ticket Office At the east side of the loop at the top end of Qianmen Lu but set back from the street by the cinema, you can buy tickets to Kunming, Chongqing, Ürümqi, Canton, Baotou, Chengde, Shijiazhuang, Taiyuan, Chengdu, and Lanzhou.

Xizhimen Ticket Office On the approach to Xizhimen station, you can buy tickets to Nanchang, Qingdao, Suzhou, Shanghai, Xiamen, and Hohhot. There are also non-express services to Baotou and regular Chinese trains to the Great Wall.

Dongdan Ticket Office You'll find this office on Dongdan Beidajie, third block north of Chang'an up Dongdan, on the left-hand side. You can buy tickets to all of the north-east lines such as Shenyang, Harbin, etc.

Getting Around

Bus Sharpen your elbows, chain your money to your underwear and muster all the patience you can – you'll need it. Overstuffed buses are in vogue in Beijing, and can be particularly nauseating at the height of summer when passengers drip with perspiration. They're cosy in winter if you haven't frozen to the bus stop by the time the trolley arrives, but difficult to exit from – try the nearest window.

There are about 140 bus and trolley routes, which make navigation rather confusing, especially if you can't see out of the window in the first place. Bus maps are listed in the Information & Orientation section of this chapter.

Buses run from around 5 am to 11 pm. A minor compensation for the crowding is that the conductor rarely gets through to you. Bus

Destination	Rail Distance (km)	Approx Travel Time (hours)	Hard-Seat (Y)	Hard-Sleeper (Y)	Soft-Sleeper (Y)
Baotou	–	17	56	97	193
Beidaihe	–	6	33	55	106
Canton	313	35	140	233	444
Changchun	1043	17	83	135	257
Changsha	1587	23	107	172	331
Chengde	–	5	26		
Chengdu	2048	34	129	210	400
Chongqing	2552	40	133	216	411
Dalian	1238	19	76	131	261
Dandong	1118	16	83	132	247
Datong	382	7	35	57	108
Fuzhou	2623	43	163	265	505
Guilin	2134	31	133	216	411
Guiyang	2540	49	156	253	480
Hangzhou	1651	24	109	174	328
Harbin	1285	17	97	157	300
Hefei	1107	19	71	119	237
Hohhot	668	12	54	87	167
Ji'nan	494	9	44	72	132
Kunming	3179	59	191	310	589
Lanzhou	1882	35	121	196	373
Luoyang	–	14	63	93	195
Nanchang	2005	36	107	182	359
Nanjing	1157	20	86	139	265
Nanning	2565	39	157	252	476
Qingdao	887	17	69	112	211
Shanghai	1462	17	119	193	366
Shenyang	738	11	65	106	202
Shijiazhuang	283	3	27	49	96
Suzhou	–	25	83	143	286
Taiyuan	514	11	41	71	141
Tianjin	137	2	13	–	–
Ürümqi	3774	75	221	356	676
Wuhan	1229	21	89	144	274
Xi'an	1206	22	89	144	274
Xining	2098	44	114	197	392
Yantai	–	18	66	113	224
Yinchuan	1343	25	93	152	290
Zhengzhou	695	12	54	88	165

stops are long and far between. It's important to work out how many stops to go before boarding. Avoid these sardine cans like the plague at rush hours or on holidays.

Buses are routed through landmarks and key intersections, and if you can pick out the head and tail of the route, you can get a good idea of where the monster will travel. Major terminals occur near long-distance junctions: the main Beijing railway station, Dongzhimen, Tianqiao, Yongdingmen, Qianmen. The zoo (Dongwuyan) has the biggest pile-up with about 15 lines, since it's where inner and outer Beijing get together.

One or two-digit bus numbers are city core, 100-series buses are trolleys, and 300-series are suburban lines. If you can work out how to combine bus and subway connections, the subway will speed up part of the trip. Some useful buses are:

No 1
: travels east-west across the city along Chang'an, from Jianguo Lu to Fuxing Lu

No 5
: travels the north-south axis, from Deshengmen/Gulou and down the west side of the Forbidden City to Qianmen/Tianqiao; it ends at Youanmen

No 44
: follows the Circle Line subway in a square on the ring road

No 15
: zigzags from the Tianqiao area to the zoo and passes several subway stops

No 7
: runs from the west side of Qianmen gate to the zoo (Dongwuyuan)

No 20
: zigzags from the main Beijing railway station to Yongdingmen station via Chang'an and Qianmen Dajie. This bus gets you to the Qiaoyuan Hotel.

No 54
: runs from the main Beijing railway station, terminates at Yongdingmen station and (like bus No 20) is an ideal way to get to the Qiaoyuan Hotel

No 103
: trolley runs from the main railway station to the zoo via Chongwenmen, Wangfujing, Art Gallery, Jingshan and Beihai parks

No 106
: runs from Dongzhimenwai via Chongwenmen Dajie to Yongdingmen station

No 116
: travels from the south entrance of the Temple of Heaven up Qianmen Dajie to Tiananmen, east along Chang'an to Dongdan and directly north on Dongdan to the Lama Temple – a good sightseeing bus

No 332
: Dongwuyan (zoo), Minzuxueyuan (Institute for Nationalities), Weigongcun, Renmindaxue (People's University), Zhongguancun, Haidian, Beijingdaxue (Beijing University) and Yiheyuan (Summer Palace). There are actually two Nos 332: regular and express – both make good sightseeing buses. The express bus has fewer stops and is at the head of the queue near the zoo.

Subway *(dì xià tiě)* The Underground Dragon is definitely the best way of travelling around. Trains can move at up to 70 km/hour

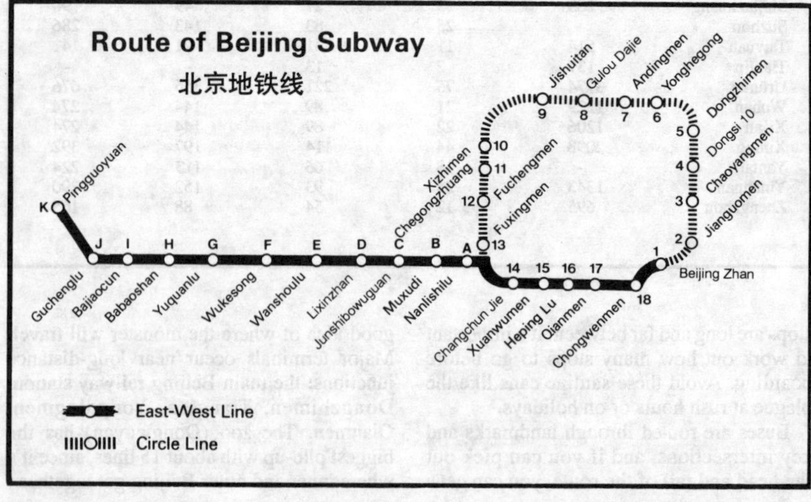

– a jaguar compared to the lumbering buses. The subway is also less crowded per sq cm than the buses, and trains run at a frequency of one every few minutes during peak times. The carriages have seats for 60 and standing room for 200. Platform signs are in Chinese and pinyin. The fare is a flat four jiao regardless of distance. The subway is open from 5 am to 11 pm.

East-West Line The 24-km line has 17 stops and runs from the main station to Pingguoyuan which is, no, not the capital of North Korea, but a western suburb of Beijing. It takes 40 minutes to traverse the length of the line. The stops are Beijing Zhan (the main railway station), Chongwenmen, Qianmen, Heping Lu, Xuanwumen, Changchun Jie, Nanlishilu, Muxudi, Junshibowuguan (Military Museum), Lixinzhan, Wanshoulu, Wukesong, Yuquanlu, Babaoshan, Bajiaocun, Guchenglu and Pingguoyuan. It takes 40 minutes to traverse the length of the line. It's a five-minute walk between station A on the East West Line and station 13 on the Circle Line and there is no direct connection between them.

Circle Line This 16-km line presently has 13 stations: Beijing Zhan (railway station), Jianguomen, Chaoyangmen, Dongsi 10, Dongzhimen (the subway here tunnels right around the USSR Embassy), Yonghegong, Andingmen, Gulou Dajie, Jishuitan, Xizhimen (the north railway station and zoo), Chegongzhuang, Fuchengmen and Fuxingmen.

Bicycle The scale of Beijing is suddenly much reduced on a bike, which can also give you a great deal of freedom. Beijing is as flat as a chapatti. An added advantage is that Beijingers will ride up alongside you to chat. You can check your bearings with them, but it's not claustrophobic like being on the pavement, and you can break off at any time. Just push those pedals!

Bicycles can be hired at the Qiaoyuan Hotel for about Y3 per day. Another good place is the bike shop near the Chongwenmen intersection, on the north side at No 94. Bikes can be rented for longer periods, say three days continuous. The renter may demand you leave your passport, but a deposit of about Y100 will usually do.

Make sure the tyres are pumped up, the saddle is adjusted to the correct height (fully extended leg from saddle to pedal) and, most important, that the brakes work. Brakes are your only defence – and the roller-lever type on Chinese bikes are none too effective to begin with. What you get in the way of a bike is potluck. It could be so new that all the screws are loose, or it could be a lethal rustbin. If you have problems later on, adjustments can be made at any bike shop, dirt cheap.

Traffic rules for bikes: there are none. Cyclists pile through red lights, buses sound warning horns and scatter a slew of bikers over a bus stop, taxis zip past the mess and the police look the other way. Traffic police have no power to fine cyclists, and if they stop one, everybody will gather to jeer the cop. In the absence of any law and order, it's best not to adopt a 10-speed mentality in Beijing. Cruise slower and keep your eyes peeled. A constant thumb on a clear bell is good fun, but nobody takes any notice. You're better off screaming in a foreign language. Insurance – what's that?

Several shopping areas are closed to cyclists from 6 am to 6 pm; Wangfujing is one. Parking is provided everywhere for peanuts – compulsory peanuts since your velo can otherwise be towed away. Beijingese peak hours can be rather astounding – a roving population of three million plus bicycles, a fact explained by the agony of bus rides. This makes turning at roundabouts a rather skilled cycling procedure. If nervous, dismount at the side of the road, wait for the clusters to unthicken, try again. Beijing in winter presents other problems, like slippery roads (black ice) and frostbite. You need to rug up and be extra careful.

Car Resident foreigners such as embassy staff and journos are allowed to drive their own cars in the capital, and to drive the Beijing-Tianjin highway. Most are not permitted to drive more than 40 km from the capital without special permission. Cars and minibuses can be hired from some of the major hotels. All vehicles are chauffeur-driven. Try Beijing Car Company (☎ 594441) and Capital Car Company (☎ 867084).

Taxi They usually have a sticker on the window indicating their per-km charge. If you don't get one with a meter, be sure to negotiate the fare in advance. You can usually get a cheaper rate if you tell them in advance that you don't need an official receipt *(wǒ bùbì fāpiào)*. Pricing also depends on size, make, age of car, backway subsidy, air-con, heating, waiting time – we could go on. In general, if you want a cheap ride, search for the oldest, smallest, most decrepit-looking bomb you can. The light-brown Soviet Warszawas (Polish-made, Soviet licence, Stalin era, known as Huashache) are not only half the price of regular cabs but you're riding an antique. Taxis can be summoned to a location of your choosing or hailed in the streets. They're scarce at certain hours such as drivers' dinner time (from 6 to 8 pm) or the sacred lunch-time siesta. Beware of the tyrannical ways of some Beijing taxi drivers. A letter to the *China Daily* relates:

It has happened several times now that we had bad experiences in trying to get a taxi...to return to Beijing

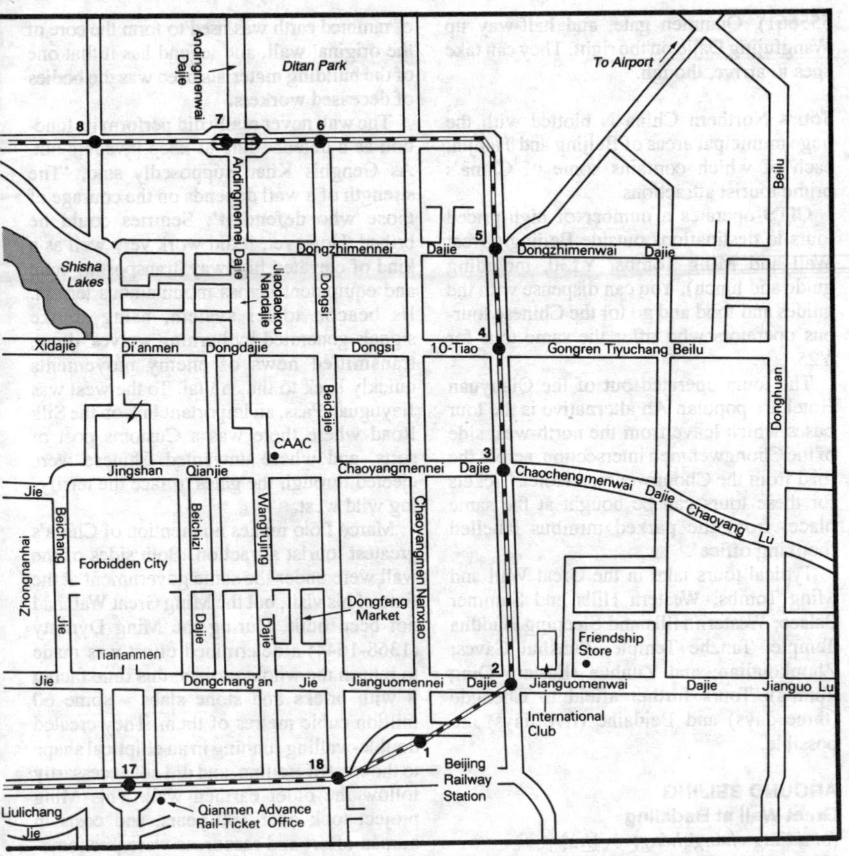

University. If one has to return in the evening, the drivers seem to find it normal to set their own tariff...Drivers wanted to take us to the university only after we agreed to pay a fixed amount of money beforehand, refusing to use their meters. This was Y30. One driver who agreed to take us for Y25 was sneered at by his colleagues who found he was 'too cheap'. One driver who charged us Y35 after arrival at the university agreed suddenly to accept Y20 when we threatened to contact his company. Arguing about rules with these drivers was quite useless since as far as they were concerned it was a matter of 'Take it or walk to Beijing University'.

Beijing taxi drivers, incidentally, pull in around Y500 a month, and there have been reports that some make as much as Y2000. In the nonprofit public sector, bus drivers average just Y150 per month and conductors Y100 per month.

Auto-Rickshaw Far cheaper than cars, auto-rickshaws are good to get your adrenalin up, but they usually ask double the real price, so bargain heavily. They can be summoned by phone. Some of their congregation points can be discerned from the bus map; a few rough locations are the main train station (☎

555661), Qianmen gate, and half-way up Wangfujing Dajie on the right. They can take ages to arrive, though.

Tours Northern China is blotted with the huge municipal areas of Beijing and Tianjin, each of which contains some of China's prime tourist attractions.

CITS operates a number of high-priced tours to destinations outside Beijing (Great Wall and Ming Tombs, Y130, including guide and lunch). You can dispense with the guides and food and go for the Chinese tour-bus operators who offer the same tour for Y25.

The tours operated out of the Qiaoyuan Hotel are popular. An alternative is the tour buses which leave from the north-west side of the Chongwenmen intersection, across the road from the Chongwenmen Hotel. Tickets for these tours can be bought at the same place, from the parked minibus labelled 'booking office'.

Typical tours take in the Great Wall and Ming Tombs; Western Hills and Summer Palace; Western Hills and Sleeping Buddha Temple; Tanzhe Temple; Yunshui Caves; Zhoukoudian; and Zunhua (Eastern Qing Tombs). Tours further afield to Chengde (three days) and Beidaihe (five days) are possible.

AROUND BEIJING

Great Wall at Badaling

(bādálǐng chángchéng) 八达岭长城

Known to the Chinese as the '10,000 Li Wall' (5000 km), the Great Wall stretches from Shanhaiguan Pass on the east coast to Jiayuguan Pass in the Gobi Desert, crossing five provinces and two autonomous regions.

The undertaking was begun 2000 years ago during the Qin Dynasty (221-207 BC), when China was unified under Emperor Qin Shihuang. Separate walls, constructed by independent kingdoms to keep out marauding nomads, were linked up. The effort required hundreds of thousands of workers, many of them political prisoners, and 10 years of hard labour under General Meng Tian. An estimated 180 million cubic metres of rammed earth was used to form the core of the original wall, and legend has it that one of the building materials used was the bodies of deceased workers.

The wall never really did perform its function as a defence line to keep invaders out. As Genghis Khan supposedly said, 'The strength of a wall depends on the courage of those who defend it'. Sentries could be bribed. However, it did work very well as a kind of elevated highway, transporting men and equipment across mountainous terrain. Its beacon tower system, using smoke signals generated by burning wolves' dung, transmitted news of enemy movements quickly back to the capital. To the west was Jiayuguan Pass, an important link on the Silk Road where there was a Customs post of sorts, and where unwanted Chinese were ejected through the gates to face the terrifying wild west.

Marco Polo makes no mention of China's greatest tourist attraction. Both sides of the wall were under the same government at the time of his visit, but the Ming Great Wall had not been built. During the Ming Dynasty (1368-1644) a determined effort was made to rehash the whole project, this time facing it with bricks and stone slabs – some 60 million cubic metres of them. They created double-walling running in an elliptical shape to the west of Beijing, and did not necessarily follow the older earthen wall. This Ming project took over 100 years, and costs in human effort and resources were phenomenal.

The wall was largely forgotten after that, but now it's reached its greatest heights as a tourist attraction. Lengthy sections of it have been swallowed up by the sands, claimed by the mountains, intersected by road or rail, or simply returned to dust. Other bits were carted off by local peasants to construct their own four walls – a hobby that no-one objected to during the Cultural Revolution. The depiction of the wall as an object of great beauty is a bizarre one. It's really a symbol of tyranny, like the Berlin Wall used to be.

Most travellers see the wall at Badaling, 70 km north-west of Beijing at an elevation

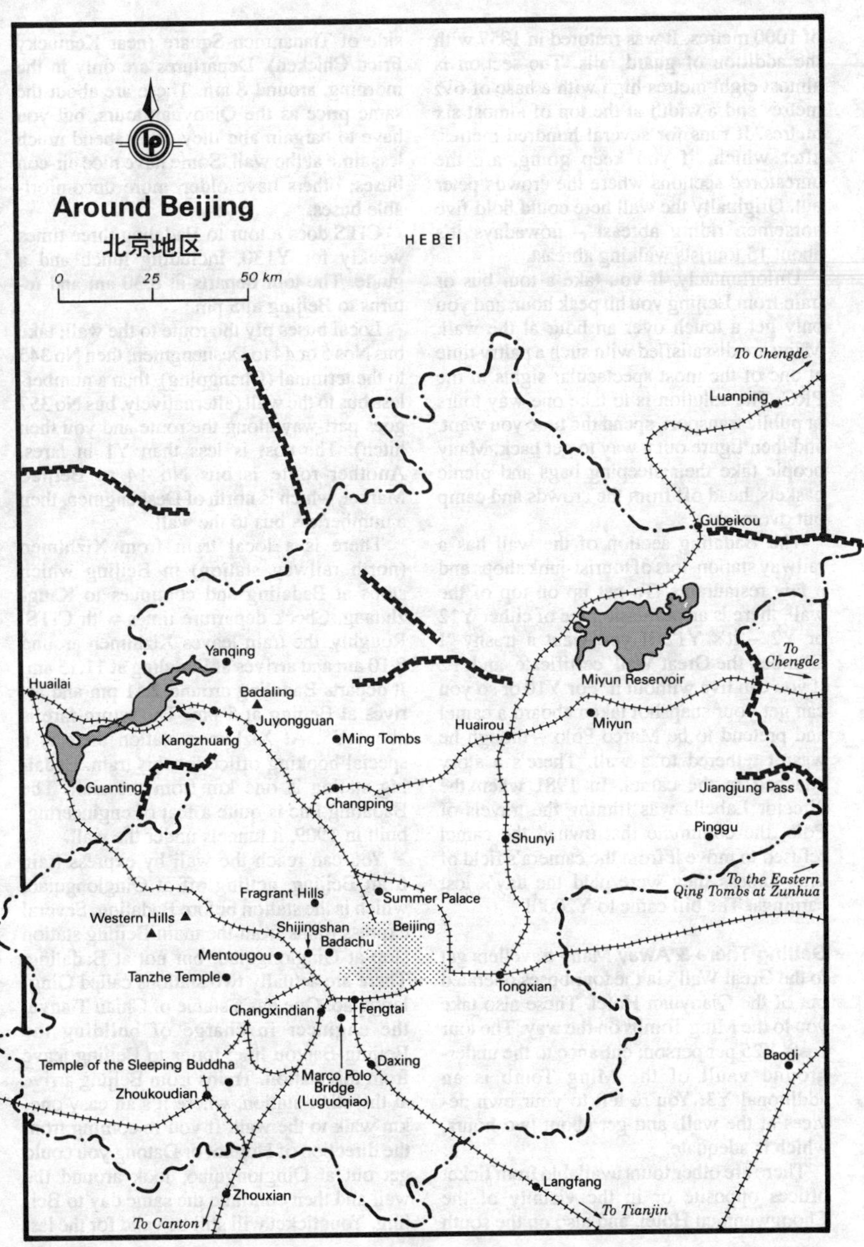
Around Beijing
北京地区
0
25
50 km
HEBEI
To Chengde
Luanping
Gubeikou
To Chengde
Miyun Reservoir
Yanqing
Huailai
Badaling
Juyongguan
Kangzhuang
Ming Tombs
Huairou
Miyun
Guanting
Changping
Jiangjung Pass
Pinggu
Shunyi
To the Eastern Qing Tombs at Zunhua
Fragrant Hills
Summer Palace
Western Hills
Shijingshan
Beijing
Badachu
Mentougou
Tanzhe Temple
Tongxian
Changxindian
Fengtai
Daxing
Temple of the Sleeping Buddha
Marco Polo Bridge (Luguoqiao)
Zhoukoudian
Baodi
Langfang
Zhouxian
To Tianjin
To Canton

of 1000 metres. It was restored in 1957 with the addition of guard rails. The section is almost eight metres high with a base of 6½ metres and a width at the top of almost six metres. It runs for several hundred metres, after which, if you keep going, are the unrestored sections where the crowds peter out. Originally the wall here could hold five horsemen riding abreast – nowadays it's about 15 tourists walking abreast.

Unfortunately, if you take a tour bus or train from Beijing you hit peak hour, and you only get a touch over an hour at the wall. Many are dissatisfied with such a paltry time at one of the most spectacular sights in the PRC. The solution is to take one-way tours or public transport, spend the time you want, and then figure out a way to get back. Many people take their sleeping bags and picnic baskets, head off from the crowds and camp out overnight.

The Badaling section of the wall has a railway station, lots of tourist-junk shops and a few restaurants. To get up on top of the wall, there is an admission fee of either Y12 or Y2 – it's Y12 if you want a trashy 'I Climbed the Great Wall' certificate, and Y2 if you can live without it. For Y10 or so you can get your snapshot taken aboard a camel and pretend to be Marco Polo – though he wasn't tethered to a wall. There's a story attached to the camel. In 1981 when the director Labella was filming the travels of Polo, the commune that owned the camel refused to move it from the camera's field of view unless they were paid the day's lost earnings. The bill came to Y2000!

Getting There & Away Many travellers get to the Great Wall via the tour buses operated out of the Qiaoyuan Hotel. These also take you to the Ming Tombs on the way. The tour costs Y25 per person; entrance to the underground vault of the Ming Tomb is an additional Y3. You're left to your own devices at the wall, and get about two hours, which is adequate.

There are other tours available from ticket offices opposite or in the vicinity of the Chongwenmen Hotel, and also on the south side of Tiananmen Square (near Kentucky Fried Chicken). Departures are only in the morning, around 8 am. These are about the same price as the Qiaoyuan tours, but you have to bargain and they often spend much less time at the wall. Some have nice air-con buses; others have older, more uncomfortable buses.

CITS does a tour to Badaling three times weekly for Y130, including lunch and a guide. The tour departs at 8.30 am and returns to Beijing at 5 pm.

Local buses ply the route to the wall; take bus Nos 5 or 44 to Deshengmen, then No 345 to the terminal (Changping), then a numberless bus to the wall (alternatively, bus No 357 goes part-way along the route and you then hitch). The cost is less than Y1 in fares. Another route is bus No 14 to Beijiao Market, which is north of Deshengmen, then a numberless bus to the wall.

There is a local train from Xizhimen (north railway station) in Beijing which stops at Badaling and continues to Kangzhuang. Check departure times with CITS. Roughly, the train leaves Xizhimen around 8.10 am and arrives at Badaling at 11.15 am. It departs Badaling around 2.11 pm and arrives at Beijing at 5 pm. The return fare is about Y5. At Xizhimen station there is a special booking office for this train. Badaling station is one km from the wall. The Badaling line is quite a feat of engineering; built in 1909, it tunnels under the wall.

You can reach the wall by express train from Beijing, getting off at Qinglongqiao, which is the station before Badaling. Several express trains from the main Beijing station stop at Qinglongqiao, but not at Badaling. There are actually two stations called Qinglongqiao. One has a statue of Chian Tianyu, the engineer in charge of building the Beijing-Baotou line; trains to Beijing leave from this station. Trains from Beijing arrive at the other station, where it's an easy one-km walk to the wall. If you're coming from the direction of Hohhot or Datong you could get out at Qinglongqiao, look around the wall and then continue the same day to Beijing. Your ticket will still be valid for the last stretch to Beijing and you can dump your bags in the left-luggage room at Qinglongqiao station while you look around.

A taxi to the wall and back will cost at least Y200 for an eight-hour hire with a maximum of four passengers.

Great Wall at Mutianyu

(mùtiányù) 慕田峪

This part of the wall is much less touristy and more attractive than Badaling. This area has begun to attract self-propelled travellers who are tired of the souvenir shops and armadas of Japanese tour buses. Just how long before Mutianyu becomes another Disneyland is anybody's guess, but so far most of the mass tourism has concentrated on Badaling.

The Qiaoyuan Hotel operates a minibus directly to the wall at Mutianyu for Y25, and it's about the easiest way to get there. A small number of Chinese tour buses also go to Mutianyu – look for them near the Chongwenmen Hotel or the Kentucky Fried Chicken near Tiananmen. Entrance to the wall at Mutianyu costs Y2.

To go by yourself is complicated and doesn't save much money. If you're starting from the Qiaoyuan Hotel area, take bus No 106 (from Yongdingmen) to Dongzhimen (last station). From there walk across the street to the long-distance bus station and take a bus to Huairou, then it's another 20 km by local minibus (these are scarce), taxi or bicycle.

Other Parts of the Wall

Most other parts of the wall are difficult to reach except by taxi. About 10 km south-east of Badaling, Juyong Pass was a garrison town dating back to the Mongol period. There remains a solid stone and marble gateway, Cloud Terrace, built in 1345 and now entirely rebuilt. The vault of the archway bears superb bas-reliefs of the Four Heavenly Guardians, and inscribed on the walls are incantations in six different languages – Sanskrit, Tibetan, Mongolian (Phagspa script), Uigur, Chinese and Tangut (a rare language from a 13th-century Gansu kingdom) – all of which drive philologists crazy!

Other parts of the wall open to foreigners are those stretches at Jiayuguan in Gansu Province and Shanhaiguan in Hebei Province. More bits and pieces are scattered around. To ease the squeeze on Badaling, another section has been renovated at Jinshanling (Shalinkou), 130 km north-east of Beijing on the bus route to Chengde. It's 10 km east of Gubcikou Pass and with a combined package to Chengde it should be a real money-raker.

This section of the wall dates from the Ming Dynasty and has some unusual features like 'obstacle-walls', which are walls-within-walls used for defending against enemies who'd already scaled the Great Wall. Small cannon have been discovered here, as well as evidence of rocket-type weapons such as flying knives and flying swords.

An early Western visitor was Lord Macartney, who crossed Gubei Pass on his way to Chengde in 1793. His party made a wild guess that the wall contained almost as much material as all the houses in England and Scotland.

In the early 1970s a Gubeikou PLA unit destroyed about three km of the wall to build barracks, setting an example for the locals, who did likewise. The story goes that in 1979 the same unit was ordered to rebuild the section torn down.

Along the route to Jinshanling, another plus is the Miyun Reservoir, a huge artificial lake slated to become a holiday resort for foreigners. It already has touring vessels but they're limited to group tours. Trains running to Chengde stop at Miyun, which is 90 km from Beijing. Gubeikou is on the Beijing-Tongliao line.

Ming Tombs

(míng líng) 明陵

The general travellers' consensus on the tombs is that you'd be better off looking at a bank vault, which is, roughly, what the tombs are. Each held the body of an emperor, his wives and girlfriends, and funerary treasures. The scenery along the way is charming though, and the approach through a valley is rewarding.

The seven-km 'spirit way' starts with a triumphal arch, then goes through the Red Gate, where officials had to dismount, and passes a giant tortoise (made in 1425) bearing the largest stele in China. This is followed by a guard of 12 sets of stone animals. Every second one is in a reclining position, legend has it, to allow for a 'changing of the guard' at midnight. If your tour bus driver whips past them, insist on stopping to look – they're far more interesting than the

tombs – because the drivers like to spend half an hour at the Ming Tombs Reservoir, which is dead boring. Beyond the stone animals are 12 stone-faced human statues of generals, ministers and officials, each distinguishable by headgear. The avenue culminates at the Dragon and Phoenix Gate.

Dingling is the only one of the tombs that has been excavated, although 13 of the 16 Ming emperors are buried in this 40-sq-km area, often referred to as the Thirteen Tombs *(shísānlíng)*. The other tombs, such as Changling, can be viewed from the exterior. Changling, which was started in 1409 and took 18 years to complete is the tomb of Emperor Yong Le and, so the story goes, of 16 concubines who were buried alive with his corpse.

Dingling, the tomb of Emperor Wan Li (1573-1620), is the second largest tomb. Over six years the emperor used half a million workers and a heap of silver to build his necropolis and then held a wild party inside the completed chambers. It was excavated between 1956 and 1958 and for Y3 you can now visit the underground passageways and caverns. The underground construction covers 1195 sq metres, is built entirely of stone, and is sealed with an unusual lock stone. The tomb yielded up 26 lacquered trunks of funerary objects, some of which are displayed on site; others have been removed to Beijing museums and replaced with copies.

Wan Li and his royal spouses were buried in double coffins surrounded by chunks of uncut jade. The jade was thought to have the power to preserve the dead (or could have bought millions of bowls of rice for starving peasants), so the Chinese tour literature relates. Meanwhile cultural relics experts as well as chefs are studying the ancient cookbooks unearthed from Dingling with a view to serving Wan Li's favourite dishes to visitors, using replicas of imperial banquet tableware. Until they figure that one out, you might have to be content with the amusing cardboard cutouts and other props used by Chinese photographers at the site.

The tombs lie 50 km north-west of Beijing

and four km from Changping. The tour buses usually combine them with a visit to the Great Wall. You can also get there on the local buses. Take bus Nos 5 or 44 to Deshengmen terminal. West of the flyover is the terminal of bus No 345 which you take to Changping, a one-hour ride. Then take bus No 314 to the tombs (or hitch the last stretch).

It's only fair to mention that many people find the Ming Tomb a wipeoff. 'What a monumental disappointment!' said one letter. 'There isn't anything down there, and you pay Y6 just to walk into a four-storey deep hole and back out again.' Another letter complained that 'other than seeing that they knew how to make deep excavations in China several centuries ago, there is nothing to justify the trip'. Perhaps true, but that's a bit like saying that all the Great Wall proves is that Chinese were capable of putting one brick on top of another for a very long distance. There may not be anything inside the tombs, but like the Wall and the Mao Zedong Mausoleum, it's interesting to see the product of an incredible amount of misspent human labour.

Tanzhe Temple

(tánzhè sì) 潭柘寺

About 45 km directly west of Beijing is Tanzhe Temple, the largest of all the Beijing temples, occupying an area 260 metres by 160 metres. The Buddhist complex has a long history dating as early as the 3rd century (Jin Dynasty); structural modifications date from the Liao, Tang, Ming and Qing dynasties. It therefore has a number of features – dragon decorations, mythical animal sculptures and grimacing gods – no longer found in temples in the capital.

The temple takes its name from its proximity to Longtan (the Dragon Pool) and some rare *zhe* trees. Locals come to the Dragon Pool to pray for rain during droughts. The zhe trees nourish silkworms and provide a yellow dye. The bark of the tree is believed to cure women of sterility, which may explain why there are so few of these trees left at the temple entrance.

To get there take bus No 336 from Zhanlanguan Lu, which runs off Fuchengmenwai Dajie north-west of Yuetan Park. Take this bus to the terminal at Mentougou and then hitch. A direct route is bus No 307 from Qianmen to the Hetan terminal and then a numberless bus to the temple. Alternatively, take the subway to Pingguoyuan, bus No 336 to Hetan and the numberless bus to the temple.

Marco Polo Bridge

(lúgōuqiáo) 芦沟桥

Publicised by the great traveller himself, the Reed Moat Bridge is made of grey marble, is 260 metres long, and has over 250 marble balustrades supporting 485 carved stone lions. First built in 1192, the original arches were washed away in the 17th century. The bridge is a composite of different eras, lately widened in 1969.

The bridge stands near the little town of Wanping and will probably be most remembered in Chinese history not for its

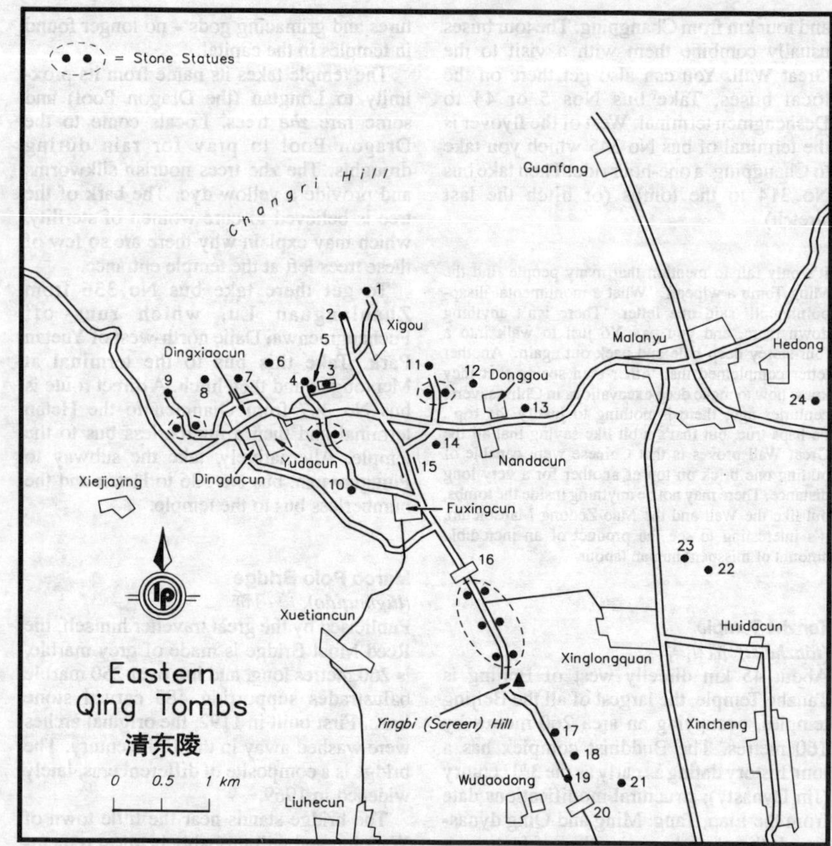

connection with Marco Polo but as the site of an incident which sparked off full-scale war with the Japanese in 1937. On the night of 7 July, Japanese troops illegally occupied a railway junction outside Wanping, Japanese and Chinese soldiers started shooting at each other, and that gave Japan enough of an excuse (as if they really needed one) to attack and occupy Beijing.

You can get to the bridge by taking bus No 109 to Guang'anmen and then catching bus No 339. By bicycle it's about a 16-km trip.

Zhoukoudian

(zhōukǒudiàn) 周口店

Site of those primeval Chinese, the Peking Men, Zhoukoudian is 48 km south-west of Beijing. There's a dig-site here and a fossil exhibition hall – you'd have to be a fossil to stay at either for more than 15 minutes. On display are models, stone tools and the skeletons of prehistoric creatures. Over the years the cave has suffered serious damage and pollution.

The museum is open from 9 am to 4 pm, Wednesday to Sunday, but check before you go. You could get a suburban train from

1	Xiaodong Tomb	13	Taifei (Two Imperial Concubines of Emperor Kangxi) Tombs
2	Xiaoling Tomb	14	Stele Tower
3	CITS	15	Seven-Arch Bridge
4	Yuling (Emperor Qianlong) Tomb	16	Longfeng (Dragon-Phoenix) Gate
5	Foreign Guest Reception Centre	17	Stele Tower
6	Yufei Tomb	18	Robing Hall
7	Dingdong (Empress Cixi) Tomb	19	Dagong Gate
8	Dingfei Tomb	20	Stone Archway
9	Dingling Tomb	21	Zhaoxi Tomb
10	Stele Tower	22	Huiling Tomb
11	Jingling Tomb	23	Huifei Tomb
12	Jingfei Tomb	24	Princess Tomb

1	孝东陵	9	定陵	17	石碑楼
2	孝陵	10	石碑楼	18	理服廊
3	中国国际旅行社	11	景陵	19	大宫门
4	乾隆裕陵	12	景妃陵	20	石孔门
5	外宾招待中心	13	太妃陵	21	昭西陵
6	裕妃陵	14	石碑楼	22	惠陵
7	定东陵	15	七孔桥	23	惠妃陵
8	定妃陵	16	龙凤门	24	公主陵

Yongdingmen station, or a bus from the Tianqiao bus station (near Tianqiao Theatre, west side of Temple of Heaven). The Tianqiao bus station serves south-west Beijing. There may be CITS tours to the site.

There is an interesting story attached to the Peking Man skull. Early this century, villagers around Zhoukoudian found fossils in a local quarry and took them to the local medicine shop for sale as 'dragon bones'. This got back to Beijing, and archaeologists – foreign and Chinese – poured in for a dig. Many years later, a molar was extracted from the earth, and the hunt for a skull was on. They found him in the late afternoon on a day in December 1929, *Sinanthropus Pekinensis* – a complete skullcap. The cap was believed to be half a million years old – if so then it rates as one of the missing links in the evolutionary chain. Research on the skull was never carried out. When the Japanese invaded in 1937 the skullcap was packed away with other dig results and the whole lot vanished. The Chinese accused the Americans, the Americans accused the Japanese, the mystery remains. Other fragments surfaced from Zhoukoudian after 1949, but no comparable treasure was found.

Yunshui Caves

(yúnshŭi dòng) 云水洞

In the direction of Zhoukoudian in Fangshan County are the more pedestrian Yunshui Caves, with coloured lights, passageways and snack bar. There are some recently discovered caves in the same area, too.

Western Qing Tombs

(qīng xīlíng) 青西陵

These tombs are in Yixian County, 110 km south-west of Beijing. If you didn't see enough of Dingling, Yuling, Yongling and Deling, well, there's always Tailing, Changling, Chongling and Muling – the latter four being part of Xiling.

The tomb area is vast and houses the corpses of the emperors, empresses and other members and hangers-on of the royal family. The tomb of Emperor Guangxu (Chongling) has been excavated – his was the last imperial tomb and was constructed between 1905 and 1915.

Eastern Qing Tombs

(qīng dōnglíng) 青东陵

The Eastern Qing Tombs area is Death Valley – five emperors, 14 empresses and 136 imperial consorts. In the mountains ringing the valley are buried princes, dukes, imperial nurses, and so on.

The approach to the tomb area is a common 'spirit way', similar to that of the Ming Tombs but with the addition of marble-arch bridges. The materials for the tombs come from all over China, including 20-tonne logs pulled over iced roads, and giant stone slabs.

Two of the tombs are open. Emperor Qianlong (1711-99) started preparations when he was 30, and by the time he was 88 the old boy had used up 90 tonnes of his silver. His resting place covers half a sq km. Some of the beamless stone chambers are decorated with Tibetan and Sanskrit sutras; the doors bear bas-relief bodhisattvas.

Empress Dowager Cixi also got a head start. Her tomb, Dingdong, was completed some three decades before her death. The phoenix, symbol of the empress, appears above that of the dragon (the emperor's symbol) in the artwork at the front of the tomb – not side by side as on other tombs. Both tombs were plundered in the 1920s.

In Zunhua County *(zūnhùa xiàn)*, 125 km east of Beijing, the Eastern Qing Tombs have a lot more to see in them than the Ming Tombs – although you may be a little jaded after the Forbidden City. Of course, the scenery helps make the visit worthwhile.

The only way to get there is by bus and it's a rough ride. Tour buses are considerably more comfortable and take three or four hours to get there; you have about three hours on site. It may be possible to make a one-way trip to Zunhua and then take off somewhere else rather than go back to Beijing. A little way north along the road to Chengde is a piece of the Great Wall.

Jixian

(jìxiàn) 蓟县

Halfway to Zunhua the tour bus makes a lunch stop at Jixian, more interesting than Zunhua. One way of getting to Jixian is to hop on a regular long-distance bus from Guangqumenwai bus station, south-east of the main Beijing railway station. Jixian is also connected by a direct rail link to Tianjin.

The Jixian area is about 90 km due east of Beijing and is little explored by individuals. In the west gate is the Temple of Solitary Joy *(dúlè sì)*. The main multistorey wooden structure, the Avalokitesvara Pavilion, qualifies as the oldest such structure in China at 1000 years vintage. It houses a 16-metre-high statue of a bodhisattva with 10 heads which rates as one of China's largest terracotta statues. The Buddha is Liao Dynasty and the murals inside are Ming Dynasty. The complex has been recently restored.

To the north-west of Jixian are the Panshan hills *(pánshān)*, ranked among the 15 famous mountains of China – wooded hills, springs, streams.

Tianjin 天津

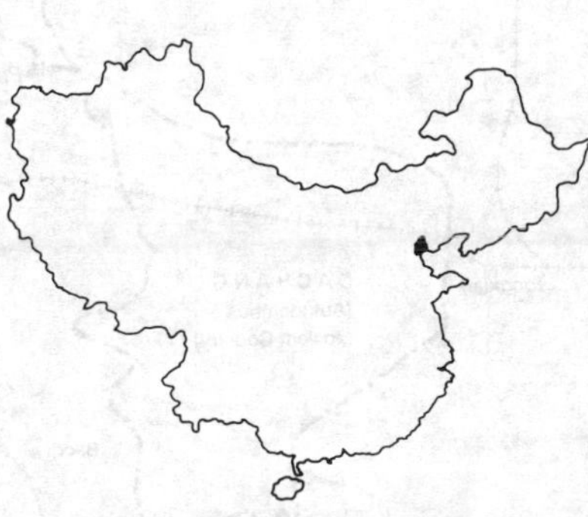

Tianjin *(tiānjīn)* is the 'Shanghai of the North' – a reference to its history as a foreign concession, its heavy industrial output, its large port, and its direct administration by the central government.

The city's fortunes are, and always have been, linked to those of Beijing. When the Mongols established Beijing as the capital in the 13th century, Tianjin first rose to prominence as a grain storage point. Pending remodelling of the Grand Canal by Kublai Khan, the tax grain was shipped along the Yangtse River, out into the open sea, up to Tianjin, and then through to Beijing. With the Grand Canal fully functional as far as Beijing, Tianjin was at the intersection of both inland and port navigation routes. By the 15th century, the town was a walled garrison. In the 17th century Dutch envoys described the city thus:

> The town has many temples; it is thickly populated and trade is very brisk – it would be hard to find another town as busy as this in China – because all the boats which go to Beijing, whatever their port of origin, call here, and traffic is astonishingly heavy.

For the sea-dog Western nations, Tianjin was a trading bottleneck too good to be passed up. In 1856 Chinese soldiers boarded the *Arrow*, a boat flying the British flag, ostensibly in search of pirates. This was as much of an excuse as the British and the French needed. Their gunboats attacked the forts outside Tianjin, forcing the Chinese to sign the Treaty of Tianjin (1858), which opened the port up to foreign trade and also legalised the sale of opium. Chinese reluctance to take part in a treaty they had been forced into led the British and French to start a new campaign to open the port to Western trade. In 1860 British troops bombarded Tianjin in an attempt to coerce the Chinese into signing another treaty.

The English and French settled in. Between 1895 and 1900 they were joined by the Japanese, Germans, Austro-Hungarians, Italians and Belgians. Each of the concessions was a self-contained world with its own prison, school, barracks and hospital. Because they were so close together, it was possible to traverse the national styles of architecture in the course of a few hours, from Via Vittorio Emanuele to Cambridge Road. One could cross from the flat roofs and white housing of the Italian concession, pass the Corinthian columns of the banks along the Rue de France, proceed down to the manicured lawns of Victorian mansions, and while away the wee hours of the morning dancing at the German Club (now a library).

This palatial life was disrupted only in 1870 when the locals attacked the French-run orphanage and killed, among others, 10 of the nuns – apparently the Chinese thought the children were being kidnapped. Thirty years later, during the Boxer Rebellion, the foreign powers levelled the walls of the old Chinese city.

Meanwhile, the European presence stimulated trade and industry including salt, textiles and glass manufacture. Heavy silting of the Hai River led to the construction of a new port at Tanggu, 50 km downstream, and Tianjin lost its character as a bustling port. The Japanese began the construction of an

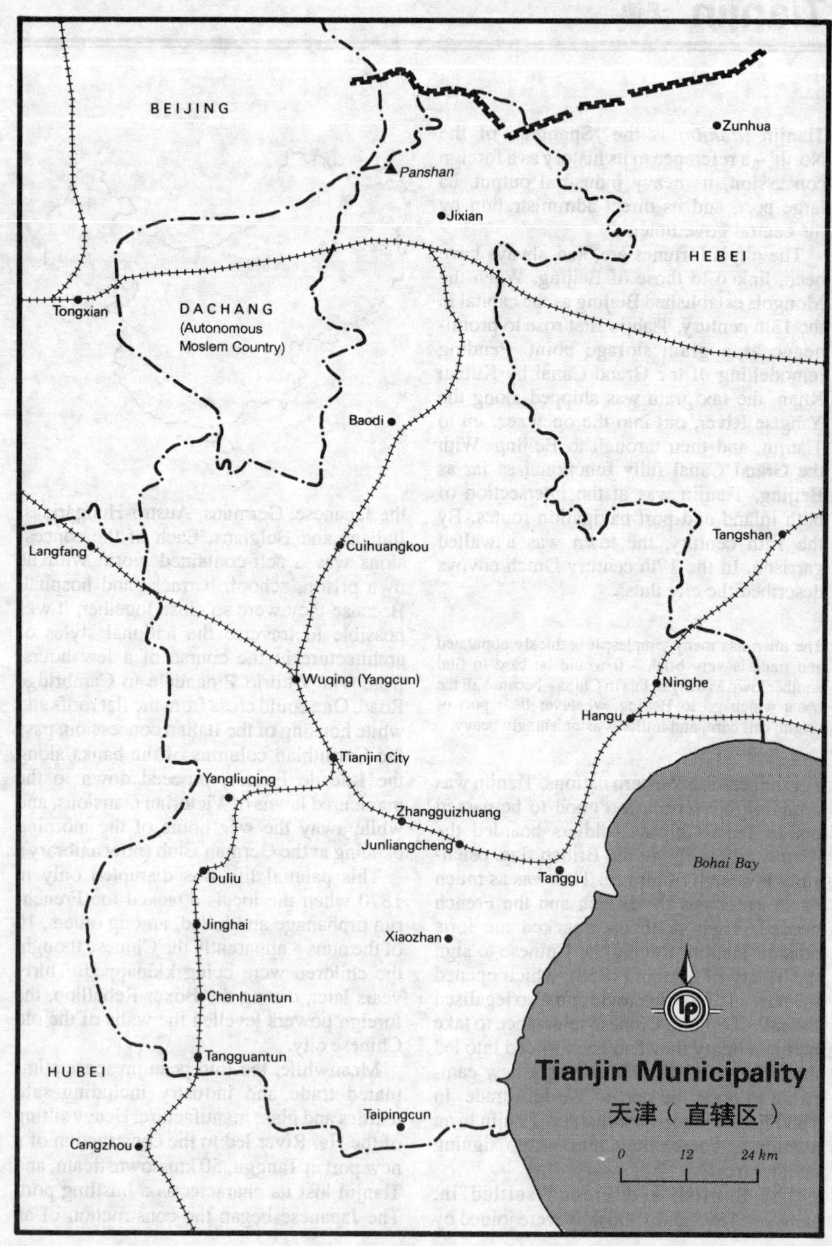
BEIJING
Zunhua
Panshan
Jixian
HEBEI
Tongxian
DACHANG
(Autonomous
Moslem Country)
Baodi
Tangshan
Langfang
Cuihuangkou
Ninghe
Wuqing (Yangcun)
Hangu
Tianjin City
Yangliuqing
Zhangguizhuang
Junliangcheng
Bohai Bay
Duliu
Tanggu
Jinghai
Xiaozhan
Chenhuantun
Tangguantun
HUBEI
Tianjin Municipality
天津（直辖区）
Taipingcun
Cangzhou
0
12
24 km

artificial harbour during their occupation (1937-45) and it was completed by the Communists in 1952, with further expansions in 1976 for container cargo. The Tanggu-Xingang port now handles one of the largest volumes of goods of any port in China.

Since 1949 Tianjin has been a focus for major industrialisation. It produces a wide range of consumer goods, heavy machinery and precision equipment, with over 3000 industrial enterprises. Industries include rubber products, elevators, carpets, autos, steel, electronics, chemical products and engineering machinery. Brand names from Tianjin are favoured within China for their quality – from Flying Pigeon bicycles to Seagull watches. The suburban districts and the five outlying counties are important sources of wheat, rice, cotton, corn and fish in northern China. Tianjin itself is a major education centre with two universities and numerous institutes and colleges.

The 1976 earthquake, with its epicentre at Tangshan (the greatest natural disaster to befall a nation in recent memory), severely affected Tianjin. The city was closed to tourists for two years. Five and six-storey housing blocks have been constructed on the outskirts as part of the rehousing programme. The population of Tianjin's city and suburbs is some 5½ million, though the municipality itself takes in a total of around eight million. The hotels are impossible, but you can travel down here from Beijing in just two hours on the train. A day or two in Tianjin is really quite enough. One of the specialities of the place is the two-day kite-flying festival held in early April or late September.

Information

CITS The office (☎ 318550) is at 20 Youyi Lu, just opposite the Friendship Store.

Public Security Bureau This (☎ 223613) is at 30 Tangshan Dao.

Money The Bank of China (☎ 312020) is at 80 Jiefang Beilu.

Post & Telecommunications The international post office is the Dongzhan Post Office, next to the main railway station; overseas parcels can be mailed and long-distance phone calls can be made here. For letters there is another post office conveniently located on Jiefang Beilu, a short walk north of the Astor Hotel.

Maps Besides the usual maps from hawkers and the Xinhua Bookstore, a better map is the *Communications Map of Urban District of Tianjin* produced by the Tianjin Commission of Foreign Economic Relations & Trade Foreign Affairs Office. It's in both Chinese and English and is available from some of the hotels.

Art Museum

(yìshù bówùguǎn) 艺术博物馆

The Art Museum is at 77 Jiefang Beilu, one stop from the main railway station. It's easy to get to, and is pleasant to stroll around. The gallery is housed in an imposing rococo mansion and has a small but choice collection of brush paintings, painting and calligraphy from bygone eras on the ground floor, and folk-art products such as New Year pictures, Zhang family clay figurines and Wei family kites from the Tianjin area on the 2nd floor. The top floor features special displays.

Other Museums

There are five or so in Tianjin and none are really worth the trouble unless you're an enthusiast. The Natural History Museum *(zìrán bówùguǎn)* is down the fossil-end of town on Machang Dao.

The History Museum *(lìshǐ bówùguǎn)* over the south-eastern side of the Hai River, at the edge of a triangular park called the No 2 Workers' Cultural Palace *(dì èr gōngrén wénhùa gōng)*, contains 'historical and revolutionary relics of the Tianjin area'.

The Zhou Enlai Memorial Hall *(zhōu ēnlái jìniàn guǎn)* is on the western side of the city in the Nankai District. It's in the eastern building of Nankai School. Zhou Enlai studied here, so his classroom is

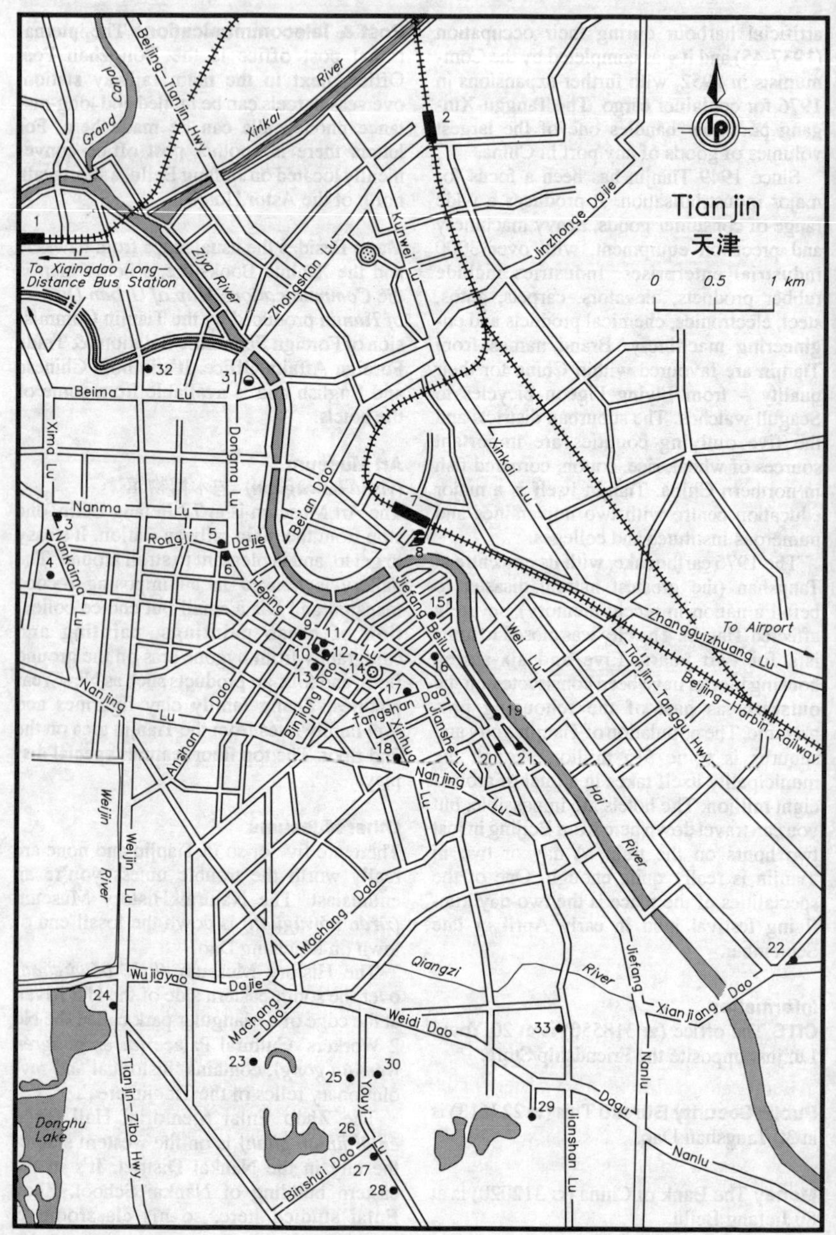
Tianjin
天津
0
0.5
1 km
Beijing–Tianjin Hwy
Grand Canal
Xinkai River
Ziya River
To Xiqingdao Long-Distance Bus Station
Zhongshan Lu
Kunwei Lu
Jinzhonge Dajie
Xinkai Lu
Beima Lu
Xima Lu
Dongma Lu
Nanma Lu
Rongji Dajie
Nankaima Lu
Bei'an Dao
Heping Lu
Binjiang Dao
Jiefang Beilu
Zhangguizhuang Lu
To Airport
Wei Lu
Tianjin Tanggu Hwy
Beijing–Harbin Railway
Nanjing Lu
Anshan Dao
Tangshan Dao
Jianshe Lu
Xinhua Lu
Hai River
Weijin River
Weijin Lu
Machang Dao
Wujiayao Dajie
Qiangzi River
Weidi Dao
Xianjiang Dao
Jiefang Nanlu
Tianjin–Zibo Hwy
Youyi Lu
Binshui Dao
Jianshan Lu
Dagu Nanlu
Donghu Lake
1
2
3
4
5
6
7
8
9
10
11
12
13
14
15
16
17
18
19
20
21
22
23
24
25
26
27
28
29
30
31
32
33

1	West Railway Station	18	Friendship Hotel
2	North Railway Station	19	Astor Hotel
3	5th Subway Exit	20	Tianjin No 1 Hotel
4	Zhou Enlai Memorial Hall	21	Tianjin Hyatt Hotel
5	Yanchunlou Restaurant	22	History Museum
6	Quanjude Restaurant	23	Natural History Museum
7	Main (East) Railway Station	24	Balitai Long-Distance Bus Station
8	Post & Telecom Office	25	CITS
9	CAAC	26	Crystal Palace Hotel
10	Roast Duck Restaurant	27	Tianjin Grand Hotel
11	Quanyechang Emporium	28	Geneva Hotel
12	Chuansu Restaurant	29	Park Hotel
13	Goubuli Restaurant	30	Friendship Store
14	Zhongxin (Central) Park	31	Dongbei Long-Distance Bus Station
15	Art Museum	32	Eardrum Fried Spongecake
16	Bank of China	33	18th Street Dough Twists
17	Public Security Bureau		

1	火车西站	12	川苏菜馆	23	自然博物馆
2	火车北站	13	狗不理饱子铺	24	长途汽车站
3	地下铁道第五站	14	中心公园	25	中国国际旅行社
4	周恩来纪念馆	15	艺术博物馆	26	水晶宫饭店
5	燕春楼饭庄	16	中国银行	27	天津宾馆
6	全聚德饭店	17	公安局外事科	28	津利华大酒店
7	天津火车站	18	友谊宾馆	29	乐园饭店
8	邮电局	19	利顺德大饭店	30	友谊商店
9	中国民航	20	天津第一饭店	31	东北长途汽车站
10	天津烤鸭店	21	凯悦饭店	32	耳鼓炸糕
11	全夜长商场	22	历史博物馆	33	十八街小吃部

enshrined and there are photos and other memorabilia from his youth (1913-17).

Streetscapes

Far more engrossing than any of the preceding is the fact that Tianjin itself is a museum of European architecture from the turn of the century. One minute you're in little Vienna, turn a corner and you could be in a London street, hop off a bus and you're looking at some vintage French wrought-iron gates or a neo-Gothic cathedral.

If you're an architecture student, go no further – Tianjin is a textbook of just about every style imaginable, a draughtsman's nightmare or a historian's delight, depending on which way you look at it. Poking out of the post-earthquake shanty rubble could be a high-rise castle of glass and steel; and anyone with a sense of humour will be well satisfied with some of the uses to which the bastions of the European well-to-do have been put.

Tianjin traffic is equally mixed: horse

carts, cyclists with heavy loads struggling to make it across an intersection before an ambush from a changing light cuts them off, a parent with a kid in a bicycle sidecar. Judiciously selected buses will take you through as many former concessions as you want – and presuming that you have a window seat, this kind of random touring will be quite rewarding, architecturally speaking.

There's enough action on the main shopping drags of Tianjin and around the former Chinese city to keep even the most hardened of alley-cats interested. Some of these features are described in the following touring section, but should one have the time, there's much more than this to see.

Touring Tianjin

The following is a combined bus, subway and foot tour which will whip you round the streets, the eating holes and the buy-and-sell stretches – allow at least three hours. The route follows an elliptical shape in a clockwise direction, starting at the main railway station and taking in the Art Gallery, Kiesslings, the old Chinese sector, Heping Lu and the city centre. Because opening and closing hours for places mentioned may not fit your own schedule, you might skip some places, or return to them later, or do the route in reverse, or just scrap the whole thing and use the information as you see fit. If you have a bit more time, then more walking is preferable at the beginning and end of the tour.

Step One – main railway station Turn right out of the main railway station; you'll find the 24-hour baggage room with its windows facing onto the street – dump your bags here. Get a bus map – they're available from booths near the station and also from the post office near the station. To catch the elusive bus No 13, continue past the baggage offices to the end of the street, turn left, walk 1½ blocks south and you'll find the terminal queue (bus No 13 actually goes back towards the station first before heading over Jiefang Bridge into town).

Step Two – bus No 13 route First stop is the former French concession and the Art Museum. If you're interested in Tianjin folk art in the buying sense, this would be a logical stopover, as the best examples are to be found within.

Second stop – you are now entering the former British concession.

Third stop is the park near the Tianjin No 1 Hotel and the Astor Hotel.

Fourth stop, get off. This lands you between the Friendship Hotel and Kiesslings. Just ahead of the bus stop is Kiesslings Restaurant on Zhejiang Lu – check out their bakery.

Step Three – the subway Walk south to Nanjing Lu and then west to the first subway station. Tianjin's subway opened in 1982; the cars shuttle back and forth on a single track. There's nothing to see down in the depths except the subterranean bathroom tiling, but it saves a lot of paperwork with buses. Ride it to the fifth stop. When you surface you're within walking distance of the old Chinese town.

Step Four – Chinatown Apologies for this misnomer – couldn't resist it. The old Chinese sector can easily be identified on the bus map as a rectangle with buses running around the perimeter. Roughly, the bounding roads are Beima (North Horse), Nanma (South Horse), Xima (West Horse) and Dongma (East Horse). Originally there was one main north-south street, crossing an east-west one within that (walled) rectangle.

Within this area you can spend time fruitfully exploring the lanes and side streets where traditional architecture remains, and perhaps even find a dilapidated temple or two. Basically, though, this is a people-watching place, where you can get glimpses of daily life through doorways. There's a good run of shops on Nanma, Dongma and Beima Lu.

Step Five – Heping Lu A massive shopping drag extends from the west station down via Beima Lu, where it meets another shopping drag coming from the north station along

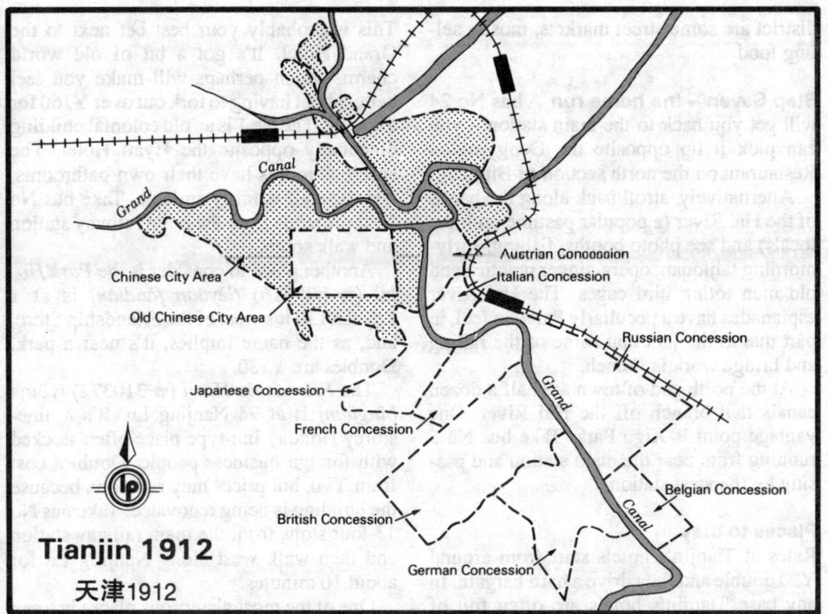

Zhongshan Lu. Both of these snake down the length of Heping Lu as far as Zhongxin Park.

If you make your way on foot along Nanma Lu, the southern fringe of 'Chinatown', you'll arrive at the top end of Heping Lu. Going south on Heping, you will find a busy alley, Rongji Dajie, leading off to the right – plenty more food, but try to save some space in the lower intestines for the Goubuli dumpling shop which is a little way off yet.

From Rongji Dajie you can walk south, or jump a bus several stops down Heping to the heart of the shopping district.

Step Six – city centre This area buzzes with activity till late in the evening. It's crammed with theatres, speciality shops, restaurants, large department stores, ice-cream parlours. The street to walk on is Binjiang Dao, with alleyways and other shopping streets gathered around it – something like eight whole blocks of concentrated shopping.

You can find just about anything – from silk flowers to a hot bath – in the many boutiques, curio stores and emporiums. The area is particularly lively between 5 and 8 pm, when the streets are thronged with excited shoppers and in-going theatre fans.

Quanyechang (Encouraging Industrial Development Emporium) is Tianjin's largest department store and is at the corner of Heping Lu and Binjiang Lu. Besides selling a large variety of consumer goods, the emporium has two theatres and some electronic amusement facilities. The original smaller Quanyechang has a fascinating balcony interior. If you follow the galleries around they will eventually lead into the main seven-storey block. The older section was founded in 1926.

Some Western trends in the central district include public phone boxes (a rare item on the streets of China) and an eyewear shop (next to the second-hand store on Binjiang). At the south-eastern fringes of the central district are some street markets, mostly selling food.

Step Seven – the home run A bus No 24 will get you back to the main station – you can pick it up opposite the Dengyinglou Restaurant on the north section of Binjiang.

Alternatively, stroll back along the banks of the Hai River (a popular pastime with the locals) and see photo booths, fishing, early-morning taijiquan, opera-singer practice and old men toting bird cages. The Hai River esplanades have a peculiarly Parisian feel, in part due to the fact that some of the railing and bridge work is French.

At the north end of town are half a dozen canals that branch off the Hai River. One vantage point is Xigu Park. Take bus No 5 running from near the main station and passing by the west station.

Places to Stay

Rates at Tianjin's hotels start from around Y90 double and they drive a hard bargain. In any case Tianjin's hotels are often full of foreign business people who stay for one or two months or longer. Tianjin can be a hard place to find a room, let alone a cheap room. You have no hope of getting into the Chinese hotels.

Unless you've got the money, or can work your way into a Chinese hotel, or ingratiate yourself into one of the university residences or the Foreign Language Institute (or a church or bathhouse?), you may end up back at the station. A smart move is to dump your luggage at the station (there's a 24-hour left luggage) so if the worst comes to the worst, you can stay up late somewhere without having to cart your gear around. Ideally, make Tianjin a day trip from Beijing.

About the cheapest place in town is the *Tianjin Grand Hotel* (☎ 319000) *(tiānjīn bīngŭan)* is on Youyi Lu, Hexi District. And grand it is: 1000 beds in two high-rise blocks built in 1960, but now showing signs of age. Doubles cost from Y90. Take bus No 13 from the main railway station.

The *Tianjin No 1 Hotel (tiānjīn dìyī fàndiàn)* (☎ 316438) is at 198 Jiefang Beilu. This is probably your best bet next to the Grand Hotel. It's got a bit of old world charm, which perhaps will make you feel better about having to fork out over Y160 for a double. The No 1 is an old colonial building diagonally opposite the Hyatt Hotel. The spacious rooms have their own bathrooms, and the staff is fairly amiable. Take bus No 13 three stops from the main railway station and walk south.

Another place to consider is the *Park Hotel* (☎ 809816) *(lèyúan fàndiàn)* is at 1 Leyuan Lu. It's west of the Friendship Store, and, as the name implies, it's near a park. Doubles are Y130.

The *Friendship Hotel* (☎ 310372) *(yǒuyí bīngŭan)* is at 94 Nanjing Lu. It's a nine-storey Holiday Inn-type place often stocked with foreign business people. Doubles cost from Y90, but prices may rise soon because the building is being renovated. Take bus No 13 four stops from the main railway station and then walk west along Nanjing Lu for about 10 minutes.

One of the most glamorous places in town is the *Crystal Palace Hotel* (☎ 310567) *(shŭijīnggōng fàndiàn)* on Youyi Lu. Doubles start at Y330.

Also in the neighbourhood is the new *Geneva Hotel* (☎ 342222) *(jīnlìhúa dàjiŭdiàn)*, 30 Youyi Lu, where doubles are Y330.

At the top of the range is the peculiar-looking *Tianjin Hyatt* (☎ 318888) *(kăiyùe fàndiàn)* at 219 Jiefang Beilu overlooking the Hai River. Singles and doubles cost from Y330 plus 10% tax.

The *Astor Hotel* (☎ 311112) *(lìshùndé fàndiàn)* at 33 Tai'erzhuang Lu, dates from early this century but has been completely refurbished. Doubles cost from Y240 to Y305. The hotel is near the Hyatt; take bus No 13 three stops from the main railway station.

Places to Eat

There are some wonderful digestibles in Tianjin. If you're staying longer, you can get a small group together, phone ahead, and negotiate gourmet delights. 'Tianjin flavour' specialities are mostly in the seasonal seafood line and include crab, prawns, cuttlefish soup and fried carp.

City Centre The *Tianjin Roast Duck Restaurant (tiānjīn kǎoyā diàn)* (☎ 23335) is at 146 Liaoning Lu. You can get Peking duck here – either the full works or a cheaper basic duck. This place has Mao Zedong's seal of approval (one doesn't really know if that's positive or positively embarrassing advertising these days) and on the restaurant walls are a couple of black & white photos of a relaxed-looking Mao talking to the chefs and autographing the visitors' book.

The *Chuansu Restaurant* (☎ 25142) is on Changchun Dao, between Xinhua Lu and Liaoning Lu, very close to the Tianjin Roast Duck. It serves hot Sichuan food and other styles.

Rongji Dajie This is an alley running west off the north end of Heping Lu, and has a fair share of restaurants. The *Quanjude* (☎ 20046) is at 53 Rongji Dajie. Upstairs are banquet rooms – moderate to expensive prices. Seafood is expensive (like sea-cucumber, a delicacy that chefs love to foist on foreigners). Peking duck and Shandong food are also served.

Directly opposite the Quanjude is the *Yanchunlou* (☎ 22761) at 46 Rongji Dajie. It serves Muslim food, lamb dishes and hotpot in winter.

Finger Food A permanent cake box clipped to a bicycle rack is one of the eccentricities of Tianjin residents – and a prerequisite for a visit to friends.

Yangcun rice-flour cake is a pastry produced in Wuqing County suburbs since the Ming Dynasty, so they say. It's made from rice and white sugar.

Eardrum Fried Spongecake, made from rice powder, sugar and bean paste, and fried in sesame oil, is so named from the proximity of the shop that makes it to Eardrum Lane (Erduoyan). Another speciality that takes its name from the shop location is 18th Street Dough-Twists. They sell bars made of sugar, sesame, nuts and vanilla.

The best area to go snack-hunting is the city centre, where you can find both the Chinese and the Western varieties – well, mock Western. The 'coolest' places to be are the ice-cream parlours or the sandwich and refreshment hangouts in this district.

King of the dumpling shops is *Goubuli* (☎ 23277) *(gǒubùlǐ)* on Shandong Lu, between Changchun Lu and Binjiang Dao. Very crowded, this place serves some of the finest dumplings in the nation – so you might as well dine in style, and it won't cost you an arm or a leg to do so. You can back up the dumplings with tea, soup or beer, and you get upper-crust lacquered chopsticks with which to spear the slippery little devils on your plate. The shop has a century-old history. The staple of the maison is a dough bun, filled with high-grade pork, spices and gravy, that disintegrates on contact with the palate. Watch for the baozi with the red dot since this indicates a special filling like chicken or shrimp. 'Goubuli' has the alarming translation of 'dogs won't touch them' or 'dog doesn't care'. The most satisfying explanation of this seems to be that Goubuli was the nickname of the shop's founder, a man with an extraordinarily ugly face – so ugly that even dogs were turned off by him. US President George Bush ate here often when he was ambassador to China.

Should you wish to fortify a main meal, an ice-cream or a coffee, Tianjin produces a variety of liquid substances. There's Kafeijiu, which approximates to Kahlua, and Sekijiu, which is halfway between vodka and aviation fuel.

Things to Buy

The four traditional arts and crafts in Tianjin are New Year posters, clay figurines, kites and carpets. You can also go hunting for antiques and second-hand goods – Tianjin is less picked-over than Beijing.

The Quanyechang Department Store, the Overseas Chinese store and the other department stores are mainly directed toward consumer goods and the craft stocks are low or nonexistent, so it's a matter of finding the speciality shops or going to the factory source, where the selection is wider.

For a taste of things to come check out the Tianjin International Market at the junction of Binjiang Dao and Nanjing Lu. It stocks anything from Japanese felt-tipped pens to Sanyo medical freezers and dental chairs.

Rugs & Carpets If you're serious about carpets (that's serious money!) the best bet is to get to a factory outlet. There are eight carpet factories in the Tianjin municipality. Making the carpets by hand is a long and tedious process – some of the larger ones can take a proficient weaver over a year to complete. Patterns range from traditional to modern. The No 3 Carpet Factory (☎ 281712) *(tiānjīn dìtǎn sānchǎng)*, 99 Qiongzhou Dao, is in the Hexi District. Small tapestries are a sideline.

Kites Kites are not easily found. Again it's better to go directly to the source, which is the Arts & Crafts Factory (☎ 272855) *(tiānjīn gōngyì měishùchǎng)* at the western end of Huanghe Dao, in the Nankai district. The Wei kites were created by master craftsman Wei Yuan Tai at the beginning of the century, although the kite has been a traditional toy in China for thousands of years. One story has it that Mr Wei's crow kite was so good that a flock of crows joined it aloft. The body of this line is made of brocade and silk, the skeleton made of bamboo sticks. Wings can be folded or disassembled, and will pack into boxes (the smaller ones into envelopes). Different kite varieties are made in Beijing, where there is a Kite Arts Company and a Kite Society. One member, Ha Kuiming, made a kite with a diameter of eight metres, which needed two men to hold it back once it got going.

Clay Figurines The terracotta figures originated in the 19th century with the work of Zhang Mingshan: his fifth-generation descendants train new craftspeople. The small figures take themes from human or deity sources and the emphasis is on realistic emotional expressions. Master Zhang was reputedly so skilful that he carried clay up his sleeves on visits to the theatre and came away with clay opera stars in his pockets. In 1900, during the Boxer Rebellion, Western troops came across satirical versions of themselves correct down to the last detail in uniforms. These voodoo dolls were ordered to be removed from the marketplace immediately! Painted figurines are now much watered down from that particular output; the workshop is at 270 Machang Dao, Hexi District (south end of Tianjin). The Art Gallery on Jiefang Lu has a collection of earlier Zhang family figurines.

New Year Posters A batch of these is also on display at the Art Gallery. They first appeared in the 17th century in the town of Yangliuqing, 15 km west of Tianjin proper. Woodblock prints are hand-coloured, and are considered to bring good luck and happiness when posted on the front door at the Lunar New Year – OK if you like pictures of fat babies done in dayglo colour schemes. Rarer are the varieties that have historical, deity or folk-tale representations. There's a salesroom and workshop on Changchun Jie, between Xinhua Lu and Liaoning Lu.

Other There are second-hand stores selling mostly chintz, though some older fur clothing can be found. A few of these stores are downtown; also try Dongma Lu. The Yilinge Antique Store at 161 Liaoning Lu has bronzes, ceramics, carvings, paintings and calligraphy, and will engrave seals or arrange artist-commission work. The Wenyuange at 191 Heping Lu is another curio store, mainly dealing in hardwood furniture, and will arrange packing, customs and delivery.

Getting There & Away

Air CAAC (☎ 701224, 704045) is at 242 Heping Lu. Tianjin has air connections to Beijing (daily, Y60); Canton (daily, Y663); Changchun (once weekly); Dalian (once weekly, Y254); Hong Kong (daily, Y870); Shanghai (three times weekly, Y380); Shenyang (daily, Y278); Taiyuan (twice weekly);

Wuhan (daily, Y362); and Zhengzhou (daily, Y211).

Bus For buses to Beijing look around Tianjin main railway station. Many buses depart from this area for the capital. The trip takes about three hours. Buses don't leave until they're full, so in this regard they're less reliable than the trains. They drop you off near the main Beijing railway station.

There are three long-distance bus stations, with buses running to places that are not in the lexicon of the average traveller's catalogue.

Bus stations are usually located partway along the direction of travel. Nanzhan (Balitai) is on the north-east edge of the Water Park south-west of the city centre. Xizhan (Xinqingdao) is at 2 Xiqing Dao near Tianjin west railway station.

The bus station of interest is Tianjin Zhan (Dongbei), which has the most destinations and the largest ticket office. It's just west of the Hai River, in the north end of Tianjin. Bus No 24 from city centre will land you in the general vicinity. From the Dongbei station you can get buses to Beijing, Jixian, Zunhua and Tangshan. A road route worth considering (also served by rail) is from Tianjin to Beijing via Jixian.

The bus station in Beijing for buses to Tianjin is Yongdingmen.

Train Tianjin is a major north-south rail junction with frequent trains to Beijing, extensive links with the north-eastern provinces, and lines southwards to Ji'nan, Nanjing, Shanghai, Fuzhou, Hefei, Yantai, Qingdao and Shijiazhuang.

There are three railway stations in Tianjin: main, north and west. Ascertain the correct station. For most trains you'll want the main station. Some trains stop at both main and west, and some go only through the west station (particularly those originating in Beijing and heading south). Through trains to north-east China seem to stop only at the north station.

If you have to alight at the west station, bus No 24 connects the west station to the main station, passing through the central shopping district.

The main station is one of the cleanest and most modern in China. You purchase tickets on the second floor.

Express trains take just under two hours for the trip between Tianjin and Beijing. Normal trains take about 2½ hours. The last train to Beijing leaves Tianjin around 4 pm, so your time in the city is rather limited if you're only day-tripping. Tourist-price hard-seat from Beijing to Tianjin is Y13.

Since Tianjin is only two hours from Beijing and three to four hours from Beidaihe/Shanhaiguan, it may be worth buying a through ticket from Beijing to Beidaihe and making Tianjin a stopover. You can then continue on to Beidaihe on the same day using the same ticket.

Other rail routes worth considering (also served by road) are Tianjin to Beijing via Jixian, and Tianjin to Qingdao in Shandong Province (direct trains).

Boat Tianjin's port is Tanggu, which was renamed Xingang (New Harbour), so just refer to Tanggu Xingang *(tánggū xīn gǎng)* and everyone will know what you're talking about. The port is 50 km from the centre of Tianjin.

Boats to Dalian depart 12 times a month. The trip takes about 20 hours. Tickets range from Y7.40 in 6th class to Y50.10 in 1st class.

Boats to Yantai depart about four times a month. The trip takes about 30 hours. Tickets range from Y7.30 in 6th class to Y48.90 in 1st class. Due to the large numbers of passengers on the boats, it's recommended that the traveller stick to 4th class (Y10.40) and higher. The liners are comfortable, can take up to 1000 passengers, and are equipped with a bar, restaurant and movies.

In Tianjin tickets can be bought at 5 Pukou Jie. This tiny street runs west off Taierzhuang Lu and is difficult to find. Pukou Jie is roughly on the same latitude as the enormous smokestack which stands on the opposite side of the river.

Tickets can also be purchased at Tanggu

port opposite the Tanggu Theatre, but you'll be best off buying in Tianjin. The embarkation/disembarkation point in Tanggu is opposite Tanggu south railway station.

To get to Tanggu from Tianjin, take a train from Tianjin south railway station. There are also buses. There are direct trains between Beijing and Tanggu, and between Tanggu and Tangshan.

Car Foreigners with their own cars, ie diplomatic corps or similar, are permitted to drive along the Beijing-Tianjin highway.

Getting Around

A pox on local transport in this city! Tianjin is one of the most confusing places you can take on in China, compounded by the fact that your visit there may turn, by necessity, into a very short one. If your time is indeed limited, refer to the touring section and save yourself the trouble – it's a real mess out there trying to find bus stops. Your chances of getting on a bus at rush-hour are about 2% – and you'll get a unique chance to find out what it feels like to be buried alive in a pile of people. If you must use a bus then try and ambush it at the point of origin.

Key local transport junctions are the areas around the three railway stations. The main (that is, the east) station has the biggest collection: bus Nos 24, 27 and 13, and further out toward the river are Nos 2, 5, 25, 28, 96. At the west station are bus Nos 24, 10 and 31 (Nos 11 and 37 run past west station); at the north station are bus Nos 1, 7 and 12.

Another major bus terminal point is around Zhongxin Park, at the edge of the central shopping district. From here you'll get bus Nos 11 and 94, and close by are bus Nos 9, 20 and 37. To the north of Zhongxin Park are bus Nos 1, 91, 92, 93.

A useful bus to know is the No 24, running between main station and west station 24 hours a day. Other bus services run from 5 am to 11 pm.

A few alternatives to the buses are the auto-rickshaws or the taxis from the railway stations. The subway can be useful – it runs all the way from Nanjing Lu to the west railway station. Unfortunately, there doesn't seem to be anywhere to hire bicycles. The central shopping area can be covered on foot – in fact, some streets are closed to motor traffic.

AROUND TIANJIN

Were it not for the abysmal hotel situation, Tianjin would make a fine staging point for trips directly north (to Jixian, Zunhua, Tangshan, Beidaihe), and a launching pad for roaring into the north-east (Manchuria). Preliminary bus tours have been set up for some northern routes, but it's expensive stuff.

Jixian

(jìxiàn) 蓟县

Jixian is rated as one of the 'northern suburbs' of Tianjin, though it's actually 125 km from Tianjin city proper. For more details see the section on Beijing. The Pan Hills *(pánshān)*, 12 km north-west of Jixian, and the Eastern Qing Tombs *(qīng dōnglíng)* are about 40 km due east of Jixian in Hebei Province. A suburban-type train runs to Jixian from Tianjin; you can also get there by bus from the Dongbei bus station.

Tangshan

(tángshān) 唐山

Tangshan was devastated in the earthquake of July 1976 and since rebuilt. Over 240,000 people (almost a fifth of Tangshan's population) were killed in the quake and over 160,000 seriously injured; with casualties from Beijing and Tianjin added, the figures could be considerably higher. A new Tangshan has arisen from the rubble. As early as 1978 it was claimed that industrial output (steel, cement, engineering) was back to 1976 levels. The present population of the city is around 1.4 million. You could drop off in Tangshan for a few hours en route by train from Beijing to Beidaihe.

Tanggu

(tánggū) 塘沽

There are three harbours on the Tianjin municipality stretch of coastline: Hangu (north), Tanggu-Xingang (centre) and Dagang (south).

Tanggu is about 50 km from Tianjin proper. The road and rail route from Tianjin to Tanggu passes by salt-works which furnish roughly a quarter of the nation's salt. There's a Friendship Store and International Seamen's Club *(hǎiyúan jùlèbù)* in Tanggu. The harbour is where 'friends from all over the world' come to drop anchor, so Tanggu is used to foreign faces. The port is kept open by ice-breakers in winter.

THE NORTH-EAST

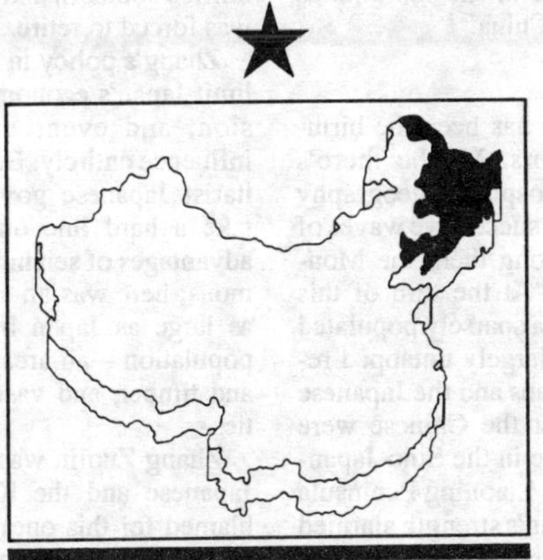

The North-East

Steam trains, ice-cream, dusty roads, mud houses, Mao statues, chimney stacks, logging towns, Soviet-clone hotels, red maples, snowcaps...Manchuria, the north-east, is relatively unvisited by travellers, but has played more than its fair share in the tumultuous events of 20th-century China.

HISTORY

Historically, Manchuria has been the birthplace of the conquerors. Maybe there's something about the inhospitable geography of this region that drives successive waves of people southwards, among them the Mongols and the Manchus. At the turn of this century Manchuria was a sparsely populated region, but it had rich, largely untapped resources. Both the Russians and the Japanese eyed it enviously. After the Chinese were defeated by the Japanese in the Sino-Japanese War of 1894-95, the Liaoning Peninsula was ceded to Japan. Japan's strength alarmed the other foreign powers, Russia among them, and Japan was forced to hand the peninsula back to China. As a 'reward' for this intervention, the Russians were allowed to build a railway across Manchuria to their treaty port of Port Arthur (Lüshun). The Russians moved troops in with the railway, and for the next 10 years effectively controlled north-east China.

The Russo-Japanese War of 1904-05 put an end to Russia's domination of Manchuria. The land battles were fought on Chinese soil, and when the Russians surrendered Japan gained control of the trans-Manchurian railway and Port Arthur. Meanwhile, the overall control of Manchuria moved into the hands of Zhang Zuolin. When the Russo-Japanese War broke out Zhang had been a bandit-leader in control of a large and well-organised private army. Lured by promises of reward, he threw his lot in with the Japanese and emerged from the war with the strongest Chinese army in Manchuria. By the time the Qing Dynasty fell he held 'the power of life and death' in southern Manchuria, and between 1926 and 1928 ran a regional government recognised by foreign powers. Zhang was ousted by the Kuomintang's Northern Expedition which unified southern and northern China, and he was forced to retire.

Zhang's policy in Manchuria had been to limit Japan's economic and political expansion, and eventually to break Japan's influence entirely. But by the 1920s the militarist Japanese government was ready to take a hard line on China. To them, the advantages of seizing Manchuria were enormous; here was an area of land three times as large as Japan but with a third of her population – an area of undeveloped mines and timber, and vast agricultural possibilities.

Zhang Zuolin was assassinated (both the Japanese and the Kuomintang have been blamed for this one); control of Manchuria passed to his son, Zhang Xueliang, with the blessing of the Kuomintang government in Nanjing. The Japanese invasion of Manchuria began in September 1931, and the weak Kuomintang government in Nanjing either couldn't or wouldn't do anything about it. Chiang Kaishek urged 'reliance' (whatever that meant) on the League of Nations and continued to organise his annihilation campaigns against the Communists. Manchuria fell to the Japanese, who renamed it the independent state of Manchukuo – a Japanese puppet state. The exploitation of the region began in earnest: heavy industry was established and extensive railway lines were laid.

The Japanese occupation of Manchuria was a fateful move for the Chinese Communist forces locked up in Shaanxi. The invasion forced Zhang Xueliang and his 'Dongbei' (North-Eastern) army out of Manchuria – these troops were eventually moved into Central China to fight the Communists. Up until the mid-1930s Zhang's loyalty to

Chiang Kaishek never wavered, but he gradually became convinced that Chiang's promises to cede no more territory to Japan and to recover the Manchurian homeland were empty ones. Zhang made a secret truce with the Communists, and when Chiang Kaishek flew to Xi'an in December 1936 to organise yet another extermination campaign against the Communists, Zhang had Chiang arrested. This forced Chiang to call off the extermination campaign and to form an alliance with the Communists to resist the Japanese.

1945 & After

When WW II ended the north-east suddenly became the focus of a renewed confrontation between the Communist and Kuomintang troops. In February 1945 the meeting of Allied leaders at Yalta discussed the invasion of Japan. Roosevelt was anxious that the Russians should take part, but in return for Soviet support Stalin demanded that Mongolia (part of the Chinese empire until 1911) should be regarded as independent (in fact, a Soviet satellite) and that Soviet rights in Manchuria, lost to Japan, should be restored – that meant the restoration of Soviet control over trans-Manchurian railways, the commercial port of Dalian and the naval base of Port Arthur (Lüshun). Chiang Kaishek wished to keep the Russians favourably disposed and began negotiations for a treaty with the USSR on the basis of the Yalta agreements. A treaty was eventually signed which pledged that each side would work together in close and friendly collaboration and 'render each other every possible economic assistance in the post-war period' – Stalin had sold out the Communists and thrown Soviet support behind the Kuomintang. At the Potsdam conference of July 1945 it was decided that all Japanese forces in Manchuria and North Korea would surrender to the Soviet army; those stationed elsewhere would surrender to the Kuomintang.

After the A-bombs obliterated Hiroshima and Nagasaki in August 1945 and forced the Japanese government to surrender, the Soviet armies moved into Manchuria, engaging the Japanese armies in a brief but bloody conflict. The Americans started transporting Kuomintang troops by air and sea to the north, where they could take the surrender of Japanese forces and regain control of north and central China. The US navy moved in to Qingdao and landed 53,000 marines to protect the railways leading to Beijing and Tianjin and the coal mines which supplied those railways.

The Communists, still in a shaky truce with the Kuomintang, also joined the rush for position. Although Chiang Kaishek told them to remain where they were, the Communist troops marched to Manchuria on foot, picking up arms from abandoned Japanese depots as they went. Other Communist forces went north by sea from Shandong. In November 1945 the Kuomintang attacked the Communists even while US-organised peace negotiations were taking place between the two. That attack put an end to the negotiations.

All these moves came within days of the Japanese surrender. The Soviet troops established themselves along the railways and the main cities of Manchuria like Harbin, Changchun, and Dalian. Since the Kuomintang troops could not move in to replace them by the agreed date of mid-November, Chiang asked the Russians to stay in the cities to prevent the Chinese Communist forces from entering the Soviet-controlled zones. The Russians complied and did not withdraw until March 1946 when the Kuomintang troops were finally installed. In the meantime the Russians stripped the Manchurian cities of all the Japanese military and industrial equipment. Whole factories including machinery, machine tools and even office furniture were dispatched by train to the USSR; even the railway tracks were taken up and shipped out; and gold in the Manchurian banks was taken away. The Russians remained in Port Arthur and Dalian, and the last of the US troops were not withdrawn until March 1947, though Qingdao (in Shandong Province) continued to be used by the US navy.

The Rise of the Communists

The Communists, meanwhile, occupied the countryside, setting in motion their land-reform policies, which quickly built up their support among the peasants. There was a tremendous growth of mass support for the Communists, and the force of 100,000 regulars who had marched into Manchuria rapidly grew to 300,000, as soldiers of the old Manchurian armies that had been forcibly incorporated into the Japanese armies flocked to join them. Within two years the Red Army had grown to 1½ million combat troops and four million support personnel.

On the other side, though the Kuomintang troops numbered three million and had Soviet and US arms and support, its soldiers had nothing to fight for and either deserted or went over to the Communists – who took them in by the thousands. The Kuomintang armies were led by generals whom Chiang had chosen for their personal loyalty to him rather than for their military competence; Chiang ignored the suggestions of the US military advisers whom he himself had asked for.

In 1948 the Communists took the initiative in Manchuria. Strengthened by the recruitment of Kuomintang soldiers and the capture of US equipment, the Communists became both the numerical and material equal of the Kuomintang. Three great battles led by Lin Biao in Manchuria decided the outcome. In the first battle of August 1948, the Kuomintang lost 500,000 people. In the second battle (from November 1948 to January 1949) whole Kuomintang divisions went over to the Communists who took 327,000 prisoners.

The Kuomintang lost seven generals who were killed, captured or deserted; seven divisional commanders crossed sides. The third decisive battle was fought in the area around Beijing and Tianjin; Tianjin fell on 23 January and another 500,000 troops came across to the Communist camp. It was these victories which sealed the fate of the Kuomintang and allowed the Communists to drive southwards.

CLIMATE

The weather tends to extremes in the north-east – mostly cold. Up in Harbin, come January, they'll all be huddled round their Soviet stoves drinking vodka – and so would you be if it was -30°C outside, with howling Siberian gales. Activity slows to a crunch in this snowflake-spitting weather, while the animals pass the season over totally and sensibly hibernate.

At the higher latitudes along the Sino-Soviet border there's a nine-month snow period (from September to May); moving south to Harbin this lessens to a cold snap from November to March; by the time you get to Dalian, it lasts from about December to February. Highest rainfalls are from June to August.

This is not to say that you should avoid winter, but merely to suggest that it would be a damn good idea if you did! If, however, you know how to deal with the cold and have a good pair of earmuffs, you may be attracted by the winter sports. You'll be able to get around more freely from May to September. Mohe, in northern Heilongjiang, has the record for the coldest temperature recorded in China, a mere -52.3° C.

ECONOMY

With almost a century of perpetual turmoil behind them, the north-eastern regions are being developed into China's industrial backbone; attempts are being made to turn them into a bread-basket with state-run farms out on the prairies – it's the same sort of economic possibility which the Japanese sought to exploit and which the Soviet Union stripped bare. To preserve the ailing forests – the last great timber reserves in the land – zones (less than 1% of China's total land area) have been placed off limits to hunters and lumberjacks. A vigorous tree-planting campaign has also been started.

Of the three north-eastern provinces – Liaoning *(liáoníng)*, Heilongjiang (*(hēilóngjiāng)* and Jilin *(jílín)* – Liaoning is China's richest in natural resources. It has large deposits of coal and iron ore, as well as magnesium and petroleum. It also has the heaviest industry and the densest rail network. While there is much hoopla about this year's production of knitted underwear exceeding that of last year by x per cent, and exceeding that of 1949 by xxx per cent, the PRC has kept very quiet on the subject of industrial pollution. A rare snippet on the topic comes from the *Beijing Review* in a 1983 article which says:

> Then in 1949, with the Liberation, progress arrived, and with it chimneys belching coal smoke into blue skies, factory sluices emptying into once-clear rivers, and an ever-growing and hungry populace indiscriminately clearing ancient forests in their search for arable land.

Those keen on delving into heavy industry and the accompanying soot, grime and fallout, can find no better place than Liaoning – the city of Benxi stands out as a prime example. Seeing this aspect of China is probably as valid as visiting its temples, but success at getting into the factories is not guaranteed. In lieu of an expensive CITS liaison it pays to befriend a high-ranking factory worker.

POPULATION & PEOPLE

The population of the north-east has increased dramatically over the last 35 years. Heilongjiang now has over 32.6 million people, Jilin has 22.5 million, and Liaoning 35.7 million. These people are mostly Han Chinese immigrants or their progeny. Of the local minority groups, the Manchus have sunk without a trace; the Koreans are over a million strong (mostly in the south-east of Jilin Province); and in the freezing far north of Heilongjiang are pockets of Oroqens (few in number), hunters who have only recently been persuaded to give up their nomadic ways.

TOURISM

Tourism in the north-east is the proverbial 'good news, bad news'. The good news: almost all of the north-east is open now (only the Soviet border regions require permits) with offerings dangled for well-heeled visitors ranging from backpacking, fishing and hunting in Heilongjiang, to skiing in Jilin. The bad news: most of the north-east is monotonous. There are only two small, reasonably accessible places whose natural

Oroqen Women Embroidering Wolf Skins

beauty stands out – the Changbaishan mountains (Changbaishan Nature Reserve) along the North Korean border, and Jingbo Lake in Heilongjiang. There are some good bird-watching areas near Qiqihar, but most of the north-east has been given over to agriculture and industry. Temples, museums and other cultural edifices are few and far between.

The industrial city landscapes are supposed to look (starkly) beautiful in winter with photogenic blacks and whites, and some extra-sooty greys. If you can survive the cold, Harbin has an interesting ice festival in winter. Deep in the woods north-east of Harbin, CITS organises hunting and winter-sports expeditions. A few whitewater enthusiasts have rafted down the Erdao Songhua River in Jilin. In Bei'an (Dedu County), way up north of Harbin, a set of volcano crater lakes and a volcano museum have recently opened. Sino-Soviet tourism has re-emerged and there's talk of running boat trips down the Heilong River (Amur River). CITS in Shenyang has started to organise trips to North Korea. All in all, the north-east remains a place for specialised interests including pharmacology, ornithology and metallurgy.

Most visitors to the north-east are with tours or on business. Backpackers are few and far between – there are few easily accessible sights, and hotel prices are high. Dormitories are almost nonexistent; you can expect to pay from Y60 to Y140 per night for a double room. The Public Security Bureau certainly hasn't helped by placing many perfectly acceptable hotels off limits to foreigners...unless you pull out every imaginable stop. The most enjoyable parts are out in the backwoods where you get the opposite treatment – very spartan places to stay but really friendly, helpful locals.

SKIING

Yes, it is possible to ski in the People's Republic. Don't expect to find another St Moritz or Aspen, but you can pursue the art of sliding downhill in China. There are a number of skifields: locals consider Jilin more suitable for beginners while Heilongjiang could cater for the more advanced. You're well advised to bring your own equipment. The Chinese make wood and fibreglass skis; you could hire some, but the quality and size of boots and so on cannot be vouched for.

Twenty km from Jilin town (in Jilin Province, east of the capital Changchun) are the Songhua Lake skifields of Daqingshan, with a 1700-metre cableway, lounge, drying rooms and restaurant. Another skifield is at Tonghua, where championships have been held. In Heilongjiang there's the Qingyun skifield, in Shangzhi County, south-east of Harbin; it has a cableway, a guesthouse with room for 350 people, and stone cottages. North of Shangzhi, and approachable by bus, is the Yanzhou County skifield. There's snow for a long time (see the Climate section in this chapter) – the main season is from late November to early April.

TIGERS

China has three subspecies of tiger: the Bengal, the South China and the North-Eastern or Manchurian. All told there are no more than 400 tigers left in China.

The South China subspecies is the most endangered and numbers only about 50 in the wild and about 30 in zoos both in China and abroad. (Even when India launched its Project Tiger in 1973 there were 1800 Royal Bengal tigers left in its territory – a number that was considered perilously low.) Unlike the Bengal and Manchurian tigers which are found in several countries, the South China tiger is peculiar to China only. Its plight began in the 1950s, with indiscriminate hunting and deforestation. At that time tigers were still fairly numerous in many southern provinces, especially in Hunan, Fujian, Guizhou and Jiangxi. Throughout the '50s and early '60s there were 'anti-pest' campaigns and many areas had their entire tiger populations wiped out. Today the subspecies only exists in the mountainous regions of south-west and south-east Hunan, and in northern Guangdong.

The Manchurian tiger seems doomed since it now numbers only 30 in the wilds of

Jilin and Heilongjiang; zoos account for about 100 more and some are still found in the Soviet Union and North Korea.

The exact number of Bengal tigers in China is not known; they live in the Xishuangbanna Autonomous Region and southern Yunnan near Burma and Laos, in a few counties in western Yunnan bordering Burma, and in the subtropical mountainous region of south-eastern Tibet and neighbouring Assam.

In Mengxian County on the Yellow River, Henan Province, an old man He Guangwei makes a living catching the big cats *barehanded* – with a bit of help from the martial arts. In over 50 years he's captured at least 230 leopards and seven tigers, as well as killing 700 wild boars and 800 wolves. If you do happen to come across one of the beasties his advice is to go for the muzzle:

> The most sensitive part of a leopard or tiger is on the muzzle between the eyes and the nose. A quick hard blow there will make its eyes water, and it stops to rub them. But the blow must be sharp and accurate. If several blows aren't effective, you're in trouble. You have to kick the animal quickly and hard in vulnerable places like the ears or the belly. But this usually kills the animal. So I don't do it unless my life is at stake.

Good luck.

THE EAST IS STEAM

For train buffs, a trip through some parts of China can be like a trip back through time. The following article was sent to us by Patrick Whitehouse for our first edition – updates from train buffs are very welcome.

The first railway in China was the line from Shanghai to Woosung, built by foreign capital. Negotiations for its construction began in 1865 and, after fierce opposition, the first eight km out of Shanghai were completed in 1876. The line was pushed on until a Chinese person was knocked down and killed, and the resulting riots caused the whole line to close. Subsequently the Chinese government bought and re-opened it but, after completing payments in 1878, they closed the line, took up the permanent way, and sank it in the sea with all the rolling stock and equipment!

A few lines were built within the next decade but it was not until after the Sino-Japanese War in 1894 that railway building really got going. With the formation of the Chinese Republic in 1912 came nationalisation, and considerable construction took place in the next two decades. The Japanese made their mark on the Manchurian railways after 1931. Their influence extended into China as the country was overrun during WW II; a high proportion of locomotives and rolling stock in operation after the war was of Japanese manufacture or design. During this period a large number of US-built locomotives were sent to China to help rehabilitate the railways, and many of these survive as Class 'KD' 2-8-0s. At the time of Liberation China's railways lay in ruins after 15 years of war. Before 1935 the country had approximately 20,000 km of railway, but by 1949 less than half of it was in working order.

The new government was faced with the gigantic task of reconstructing its war-torn network. The first five-year plan envisaged the building of 55 new railways and the reconstruction or double-tracking of 29 existing lines. In the first 15 years, to 1964, the length of operating railways was estimated to have reached 35,000 km; today the total length is close to 40,000 km and still expanding – only Tibet is without at least some railway facility. There was hardly any signalling 15 years ago; today, China Railways have some of the most modern and sophisticated signalling. Before WW II China imported practically all its rolling stock, equipment and supplies; now it manufactures its own. About 500 locomotives of all types are built each year; imported diesels to date have come from France and Romania.

The major development plan calls for main line electrification. Today a small proportion of lines have wire (Baoji to Chengdu; Yangpingquan to Xiangfan). Also being electrified are the Beijing-Baotou and the Guiyang-Kunming lines. Diesel will be kept to a minimum since that fuel is deemed too precious for railway combustion; the jump is direct from steam to electricity. The system employed is 25,000V AC single-phase 50Hz, with overhead conductor. The French electrical industry has assisted in the initial development of electrification, although the Chinese are becoming increasingly self-reliant in this work.

Three grateful Brits joined a small party of Australians in an official 'rail visit' to Manchuria. As always in China, we were treated as honoured guests – and if our dedication to railways was deemed to be slightly unusual, this was never made known. On this trip everything really begins at Shenyang, the capital of Liaoning Province, and both the largest industrial centre and the communications hub of north-east China. From the rail-fan's point of view, Shenyang is one of the most important rail centres in the country. Six lines converge on the city, and with the coal traffic from Fushun and other mines in the area, with the inbound iron ore and outbound steel to and from nearby Anshan, and with the chemical and manufacturing goods flowing from and through Shenyang itself, freight traffic is plentiful – and in China that means steam!

Space forbids a detailed description of the Fushun mine complex with its attendant steam and electrified railway system – except to say that it's immense. The highlight of the visit to Shenyang was Sugintun steam depot, which is all freight and consequently almost 100% 'QJ' class 2-10-2s, and 'JS' class 2-8-2s. Like most Chinese depots, Sugintun shed is fully equipped to carry out heavy repair work, but not boiler fitting. The 'two-star' attractions were found hidden away. These were two Japanese Pacifics sitting at the back of the shed – a class 'SL8' No 296 (in steam) and a class 'SL7' (very dead). Both were pre-war Manchurian express classes of note, the former being used on the Port Arthur (Luda, near Dalian) to Harbin overnight service on the South Manchurian Railway, and the latter between Port Arthur and Shenyang. The 'SL7s' made their trip with fully air-conditioned trains (some of the first in the world) and ran at an average speed of 110 km per hour (68.75 miles per hour).

From Shenyang we journeyed to Jilin, behind steam 'SL' class Pacifics hauling 12 bogies of about 518 tonnes, which is a good load for these engines over a steeply graded route. At least eight sizeable rivers are bridged during the trip. As foreign guests we travelled extremely comfortably in a soft-class coach with tea on hand at any time from the blue-uniformed coach attendant. Jilin provided an opportunity for that most relaxing of railway pursuits – railway sauntering, at a place called Dragon Pond Hill station. Locomotive variety here was classes 'QJ' 2-10-2, 'JF' 2-8-2 and, on the passenger runs, 'RM' Pacifics.

At Changchun, further along the line, there are two railway factories: a Locomotive Works and a Passenger Coach Works. The Locomotive Works built the first of the big 'Heping' (Peace) steam locomotives, as well as the power cars for the Peking Metro. The Passenger Coach Works was built in 1957 to help overcome the shortage of passenger stock and today builds lightweight coaches for 160 km-per-hour operation, deluxe coaches and sleeping cars. The plant has been modernised and expanded since 1978; technological aid comes from Japan's largest railway vehicle builders, Nippon Sharyo Seizo Kaisha. The Locomotive Works and the Carriage Works have been visited by foreigners, as have the social complex with its schools, housing and hospital. Other Changchun joys included line-side photography and an early-morning visit to the steam shed. The latter was so fantastic – clean engines, variety and hospitality – that I just stood there in the sunshine for a moment and said out loud, 'I just don't believe it!' In addition to the usual tender engines, the depot sported two different classes of 2-6-4T Class 'DB2' No 89, a Japanese-built locomotive dating from 1934-36, and 'DB1' No 28, an Alco of 1907. The main classes based here are the 'QJ' 2-10-2, 'RM' 4-6-2 and 'SL' 4-6-2, with a shed allocation for around 100. As with Sugintun depot, Changchun was equipped for overhauls at 100,000-km intervals. A heavy general overhaul is carried out on steam locomotives at the main works after 300,000 km.

Our last stop northwards was Harbin, some 500 km north of Vladivostok and at one time on the Trans-Siberian Railway; the Manzhouli-to-Harbin and Harbin-to-Mudanjiang lines form most of the original route. Harbin itself is the junction of two major and three secondary lines. Winter comes to Harbin early and line-side photography included snow scenes, albeit dull ones from the weather point of view. Even so, it was impossible not to be thrilled by the sight of heavy double-headed freights hauled by thundering 'QJs', headlights on in the gloom, pounding up the bank at Wang Guang on their way south. Of particular interest was one of China's three named engines – *General Zhu De*, No 2470. Passenger trains were 'RM' hauled.

At a further shed there was another gem hiding in the yard – a Tangshan-built 2-6-2T of 1949-50, No PL275. Harbin is the area freight depot containing the usual high quota of 'QJs' (still being built at Datong). The shed itself dates from 1899 and has a working staff of some 2600 for the 100% steam allocation of approximately 100 locomotives. Winter is the busy season as the roads become impassable, and 70 locomotives from the shed are in daily service, with an equal number coming in for servicing.

Suffice it to say that our visit covered only a small section of China's rail network, but along the way we saw a great deal of Manchuria. Help was always at hand, and we were fortunate enough to find interpreters and guides who showed a positive interest in our hobby – purchasing technical books and crawling over engines for special identification points. One guide had worked his service out on the installation of the Tan Zam Railway ('Uhuru' or 'Freedom' Railway). The Tan Zam Railway was completed in 1975, linking Zambia's copper mines with Tanzania's ports, thus enabling the two countries to bypass the usual South African export routes. Twenty thousand Chinese worked on the project alongside 36,000 Africans. That particular guide had some fascinating stories to tell.

Patrick Whitehouse
Millbrook House Ltd
England, 1984

Liaoning 辽宁

SHENYANG

(shěnyáng) 沈阳

A major industrialised and prosperous city on the north-east route, Shenyang has the distinction of being the only one to have historical interest. It is the cradle of the Manchus, and started as a trading centre for nomads as far back as the 11th century, becoming established as the capital in the 17th century. With the Manchu conquest of Beijing in 1644, Shenyang became a secondary capital under the Manchu name of Mukden, and a centre of the ginseng trade.

The city was occupied by the Russians around the turn of the century as part of their 'railway colonialism', and was a key battleground during the Sino-Japanese War (1904-05). Shenyang rapidly changed hands – in turn dominated by warlords, the Japanese (1931), the Russians (1945), the Kuomintang (1946) and the CCP (1948). The present population is around six million (for an area of 8500 sq km, the urban population is 4.2 million), which reflects more than a tenfold increase since 1949.

Shenyang's latest claim to fame is its role as a guinea pig for new bankruptcy laws. Another astoundingly capitalist arrival is the new stock exchange, which is booming.

Shenyang is the centre of the Liaoning Province Industrial Effort; six major rail lines converge on the city, including those freight lines from Anshan, the steel giant, and Fushun, the coal capital. Industrial output of Shenyang rivals that of Shanghai and includes machinery, aircraft, trams, textiles, pharmaceuticals, rubber products – you name it. The latest products can be viewed at the Liaoning Industrial Exhibition Hall, and factory visits are on the group-tour agenda.

Information

CITS You'll find them (☎ 466953) at 113 Huanghe Nandajie which is south of the Liaoning Mansions.

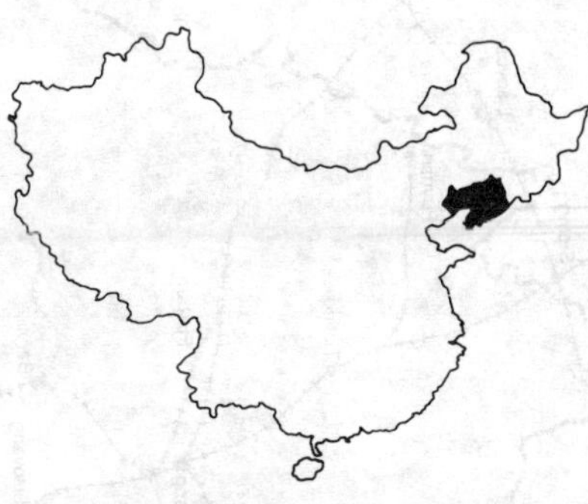

Public Security Bureau This is just off the traffic circle on Zhongshan Lu near the Mao statue (see map).

Money The Bank of China is at 75 Heping Beidajie.

Post The main post office is at 32 Zhongshan Lu, Section 1.

US Consulate Odd as it might seem, Shenyang has a US consulate (☎ 290035) at 40 Lane 4 Section 5, Sanjing Jie, Hepingqu.

Mao Statue (Zhongshan Square)

(zhōngshān gǔangchǎng) 中山广场

Of all the bizarre statues in north-east China (Soviet war heroes, mini-tanks on top of pillars...), this Mao statue takes the cake. Like some kind of strange machine, it zooms out of Red Flag Square, a giant epoxy-resin Mao at the helm, flanked by vociferous peasants, soldiers and workers. The last word on the personality cult and the follies of the Cultural Revolution, this is a rare item, erected in 1969. The statue is in Zhongshan Square at the intersection of Zhongshan Lu and Nanjing Beijie.

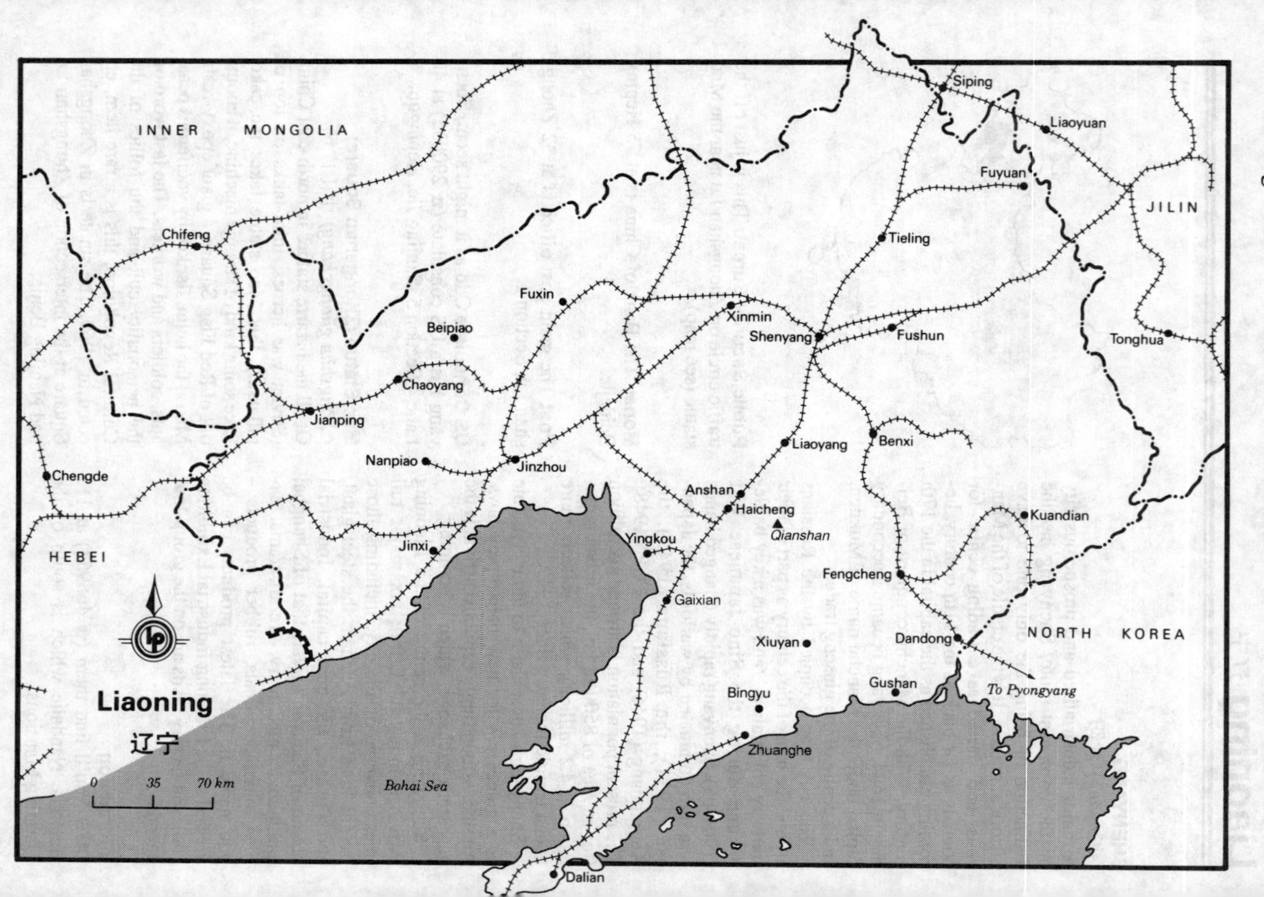
INNER MONGOLIA
JILIN
HEBEI
NORTH KOREA
Siping
Liaoyuan
Fuyuan
Chifeng
Tieling
Fuxin
Xinmin
Beipiao
Shenyang
Fushun
Tonghua
Chaoyang
Jianping
Benxi
Liaoyang
Nanpiao
Jinzhou
Chengde
Anshan
Haicheng
Kuandian
Qianshan
Yingkou
Jinxi
Fengcheng
Gaixian
Dandong
Xiuyan
Gushan
To Pyongyang
Bingyu
Zhuanghe
Liaoning
辽宁
0
35
70 km
Bohai Sea
Dalian

North Tomb

(běilíng) 北陵

Also known as Zhaoling, this is the finest sight in Shenyang. Set in a huge park, the North Tomb is the burial place of Huang Taiji (1592-1643), who founded the Qing Dynasty (although he did not live to see the conquest of China). The tomb took eight years to build, and the impressive animal statues on the approach to it are reminiscent of the Ming tombs. The larger buildings, used as barracks by various warlords, are in a state of disrepair, though some attempt has been made to restore them. The tumulus of the tomb is a grassy mound at the rear. To get to the North Tomb take bus No 220 from the railway station, bus 213 from the Imperial Palace or bus No 6.

East Tomb

(dōnglíng) 东陵

Also known as Fuling, this tomb is set in a forested area eight km from Shenyang. Entombed here is Nurhachi, grandfather of Emperor Shunzhi who launched the invasion of China in 1644. Nurhachi is entombed with his mistress. Construction of the tomb started in 1626 and took several years to complete, with subsequent additions and renovations. It's similar in layout to the North Tomb, but smaller, and is perched on a wooded hilltop looking over a river. To get to the East Tomb take bus No 18 from the imperial palace and then walk.

Imperial Palace

(gùgōng) 故宫

This is a mini-Forbidden-City model in layout, though it's far smaller and the features are Manchu. The main structures were started by Nurhachi and completed in 1636 by his son, Huang Taiji.

Straight through the main gate at the far end of the courtyard is the main structure, the octagonal Dazheng Hall with its coffered ceiling and an elaborate throne. It was here that Emperor Shunzhi was crowned before setting off to cross the Great Wall in 1644. In the courtyard in front of the hall are the Banner Pavilions, formerly administrative offices used by tribal chieftains. They now house displays of 17th and 18th-century military equipment – armour, swords,and bows. The central courtyard west of Dazheng Hall contains a conference hall, some living quarters, and some shamanist structures (one of the customs of the Manchus was to pour boiling wine into a sacrificial pig's ear, so that its cries would attract the devotees' ancestors). The courtyard to the western fringe is a residential area added on by Emperor Qianlong in the 18th century, and the Wenshu Gallery to the rear housed a copy of the Qianlong anthology.

The Shenyang imperial palace functions as a museum, with exhibitions of ivory and jade artefacts, musical instruments, furniture, and Ming and Qing paintings. Admission is Y5 and there are extra charges to visit some of the pavilions. You must leave bags at the door and photography is prohibited inside. The captions to exhibits are all in Chinese. If you've visited the Forbidden City in Beijing, Shenyang's Imperial Palace may come as a disappointment, but history buffs may find it interesting. It's in the oldest section of the city; bus No 10 will get you there.

Places to Stay

All the provinces in the north-east have attempted to 'standardise' prices for foreigners. Liaoning pitches in with single rooms starting at Y60 FEC, and Y140 FEC for a double is not unusual. You may be able to improve on this, but it can be tough.

The *Hua Sha Hotel (húaxià fàndiàn)* is near the railway station at 3 Zhongshan Lu. Singles cost Y70 and doubles are Y130, but they often claim to be 'all full' and mostly cater to Overseas Chinese – China Travel Service (CTS) is here too.

The *Dongbei Hotel* (☎ 368120) *(dōngběi fàndiàn)*, is at 100 Tianjin Beijie – one block south of Taiyuan Beijie, the main shopping street. It's also known as the Dongning Hotel. This may be your best bet if you don't require a dormitory. Of course they do have cheap dorms, but for Chinese only. Singles cost Y70 and doubles are Y85.

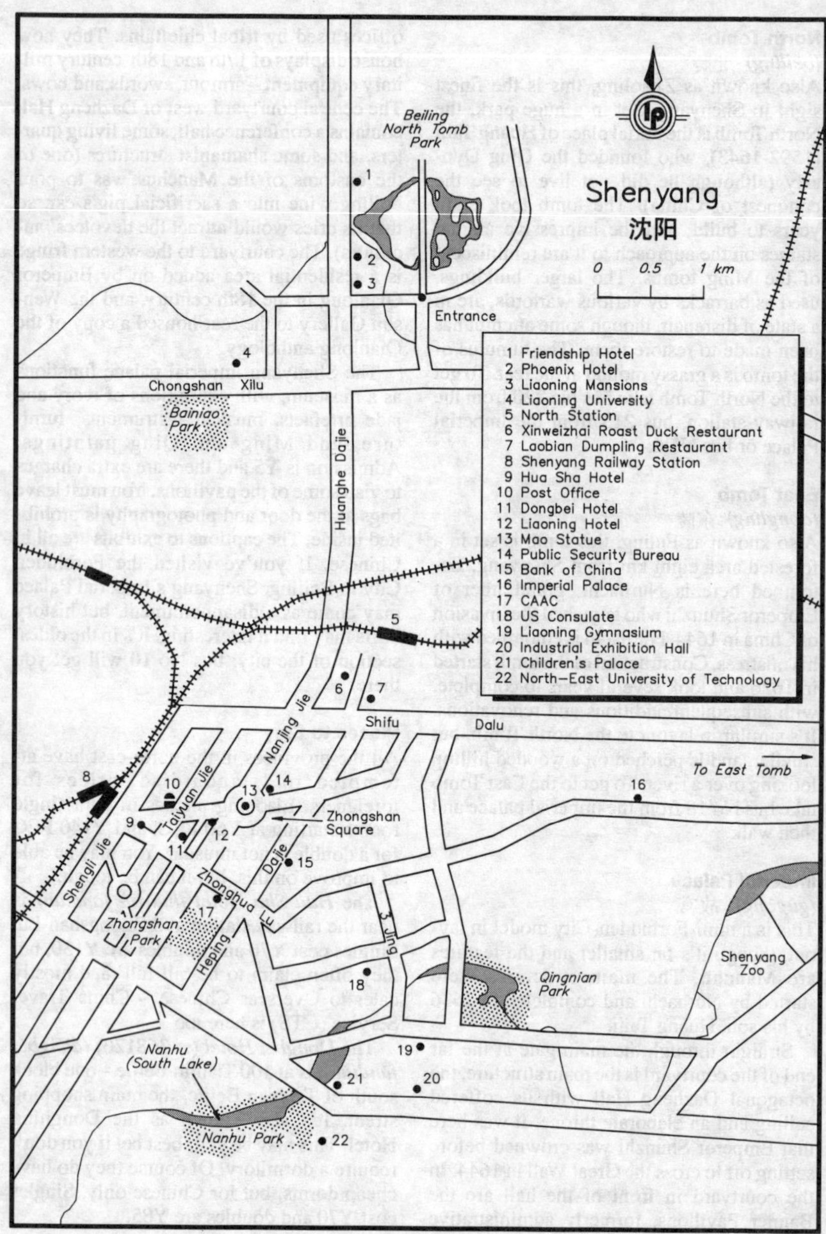
Shenyang
沈阳
0 0.5 1 km
Beiling North Tomb Park
Entrance
Chongshan Xilu
Bainiao Park
Huanghe Dajie
Shifu
Dalu
To East Tomb
Nanjing Jie
Taiyuan Jie
Zhongshan Square
Shengli Jie
Dajie
Zhonghua Lu
Heping
Zhongshan Park
3 Jing
Qingnian Park
Shenyang Zoo
Nanhu (South Lake)
Nanhu Park
1 Friendship Hotel
2 Phoenix Hotel
3 Liaoning Mansions
4 Liaoning University
5 North Station
6 Xinweizhai Roast Duck Restaurant
7 Laobian Dumpling Restaurant
8 Shenyang Railway Station
9 Hua Sha Hotel
10 Post Office
11 Dongbei Hotel
12 Liaoning Hotel
13 Mao Statue
14 Public Security Bureau
15 Bank of China
16 Imperial Palace
17 CAAC
18 US Consulate
19 Liaoning Gymnasium
20 Industrial Exhibition Hall
21 Children's Palace
22 North-East University of Technology

1	友谊宾馆	9	华厦饭店	17	中国民航
2	凤凰饭店	10	邮局	18	美国领事馆
3	辽宁大厦	11	东北饭店	19	辽宁体育馆
4	辽宁大学	12	辽宁宾馆	20	工业展览馆
5	火车北站	13	中山广场	21	少年宫
6	新味斋烤鸭店	14	公安局外事科	22	东北工学院
7	老边饺子馆	15	中国银行		
8	沈阳火车站	16	故宫		

The *North-East University of Technology* (☎ 393000) *(dōngběi gōng xúeyùan)* near Nanhu Park often allows foreigners to stay, but don't arrive too late. Their doubles cost Y40. Take trolley bus No 11. Another university that sometimes takes foreigners is *Liaoning University* (☎ 462541) *(liáoníng dàxúe)* on Chongshan Lu across from Bainiao Park. Bus No 205 stops there.

The *Liaoning Hotel (liáoníng bīngǔan)* facing Zhongshan Square was constructed in 1927 by the Japanese; it's got 77 suites, a billiard room with slate tables, and art nouveau windows. Doubles cost from Y120 to Y150.

The *Liaoning Mansions* (☎ 462536) *(liáoníng dàxià)* is at 1 Huanghe Dajie, Section 6, going towards the North Tomb. It's a long way from the railway station and therefore tends to serve tour groups. This is an enormous Soviet-style place complete with chandeliers. Doubles are Y90.

The *Phoenix Hotel* (☎ 466500) *(fènghúang fàndiàn)*, 109 Huanghe Nandajie, is the best hotel in town. Doubles are Y140. It's just to the north of the Liaoning Mansions, 10 km from the railway station.

The *Friendship Hotel* (☎ 466581) *(yǒuyí bīngǔan)* is at 1 Huanghe Beidajie, Huangguqu, north of the Phoenix Hotel. It's a villa-style place used for state guests. Doubles start at Y100.

Places to Eat

Mouth-watering banquet fare will undoubtedly surface in the classier hotels for a hefty price, but on the streets the level of sanitation will quickly cure your hunger pangs without you having to eat anything! The area around the railway station has numerous noodle and rice places, and is the best bet for budget travellers.

One of the better-known eating establishments in town is the *Laobian Dumpling Restaurant* (☎ 447941) *(lǎobiān jiǎozi gǔan)*. It's on a small street called Beishichang Jie, which runs off of Shifu Dalu. The restaurant can be reached on bus No 325, but really isn't too convenient unless you take a taxi – from almost anywhere, it's too far to walk. On the same street is *Xinweizhai Roast Duck Restaurant (xīnwèizhāi kǎoyā diàn)*, another one of Shenyang's famous houses.

More convenient is the large *Lumingchun Restaurant (lùmíngchūn fàndiàn)*, not far from the CAAC booking office. It serves up various seafood and chicken dishes.

Entertainment

The Shenyang Acrobatic Troupe is one of China's best and definitely worth chasing up.

Things to Buy

The Lianying Corporation, opened in 1983, is an enormous (clean) four floors of glassed-in counters and muzak that is superior to any department store in Beijing. It stocks arts & crafts. Shenyang seems to be one long bout of buying and selling, with a high density of department stores. Taiyuan Jie is the major shopping street. The Overseas Chinese come to raid the medicine shops of Shenyang.

Getting There & Away

Air Shenyang is connected to the following cities:

Beijing (three times daily, Y217); Canton (twice daily, Y876); Changchun (Y94); Changsha (Y735); Chaoyang (Y90); Chengdu (Y787); Chifeng (Y138); Chongqing; Dalian (Y121); Dandong (Y67); Fuzhou (Y685); Haikou (Y1056); Harbin (Y164); Hohhot (Y352); Kunming; Mudanjiang (Y211); Nanjing (Y547); Qingdao (Y241); Qinhuangdao (Y129); Shanghai (daily, Y460); Shantou; Taiyuan (Y392); Tianjin (daily, Y278); Ürümqi; Wuhan (Y624); Xi'an (four times weekly, Y565); Xiamen (Y752); Yanji (daily, Y183); and Zhengzhou (daily, Y448).

The CAAC office (☎ 363705) is at 31 Zhonghua Lu, Section 3.

Train Shenyang is the hub of the north-eastern rail network and there are frequent departures to all major destinations. From Shenyang to Beijing takes nine hours; to Changchun is five hours; to Harbin, nine hours; to Dandong, five hours; and to Dalian, six hours.

Getting Around

You can hire bicycles from some of the sheds off Taiyuan Jie.

AROUND SHENYANG

Qianshan

(qiānshān) 千山

Qianshan is an abbreviation for Qianlianshan (Thousand Lotuses Mountain). According to legend (do you really want to hear another one?), there was once a fairy who wanted to bring spring to the world by embroidering pretty clouds on lotuses. Just as she was making the 999th lotus, the gods found it, accused her of stealing the clouds and had her arrested. The fairy put up a fight and during the struggle all the lotuses dropped to earth, where they immediately turned into green hills. In memory of the fairy, people began to call the mountain 'Thousand Lotuses Mountain' or just Qianshan. Later, when a monk arrived and actually counted the peaks he discovered there were only 999, so he built an artificial one to make a round number.

About 50 km from Shenyang, Qianshan is a preferable place to stay or visit. It takes two hours to get there by bus from the Shenyang long-distance bus station. Another approach is from Anshan, which is 25 km from the mountain – take bus No 8 which leaves from a side street about 50 metres in front of Anshan station. If you just want to make a day trip, luggage can be left at the station. The last bus in either direction leaves at 6.30 pm.

The bus drops you off at the entrance to the Qianshan park. Food, drink, Qianshan T-shirts, locally made clickers and knobbly walking sticks are available from hawkers. Maps can be bought from hawkers near the gate or from the ticket office.

You can hike around the hills, which have a motley scattering of Tang, Ming and Qing temples. The mountain is steep in parts and it takes about three hours to reach the summit. At the southern foot of the mountain (approached along a different bus route) is the Tanggangzi Hot Spring.

The last Qing emperor, Puyi, used to bathe here with his empresses. Tanggangzi has hot springs which are piped into ordinary baths, and a sanatorium for those with chronic diseases – there is some hotel accommodation.

There are several other places to stay at Qianshan: to the right of the park entrance is the Qianshan Binguan. The Lucui Binguan is in a pleasant spot about 100 metres into the park on the right. Taoist temples on the hills also accept guests overnight. Prices for a double vary between Y25 and Y40 depending on the standard of the room. The mountain gets very crowded on Sundays and holidays.

DALIAN

(dàlián) 大连

Dalian is known under a jumble of names – Dalny, Dairen, Lüshun, and Luda. Lüshun is the part further south (formerly Port Arthur, now a naval base), and Lüshun and Dalian comprise Luda. In the late 19th century the Western powers were busy carving up pieces of China for themselves and, to the outrage of Tsar Nicholas II, Japan gained the Liaoning Peninsula under an 1895 treaty (after creaming Chinese battleships off Port Arthur in 1894). Nicholas II gained the support of the French and Germans and managed to get the Japanese to withdraw from Dalian; the Russians got the place as a concession in 1898 and set about constructing the port of their dreams – as opposed to the only partially ice-free port of Vladivostok.

To Russia's further dismay, however, the Japanese made a comeback, sinking the Russian East Asia naval squadron in 1902, and decimating the Russian Baltic squadron off Korea in 1905. The same year, Dalian passed back into Japanese hands, and the Japanese completed the port facilities in 1930. In 1945, the Soviet Union reoccupied Dalian and did not withdraw definitively until 10 years later.

Dalian is a major port, on a par with Tianjin; Dalian's harbour facilities have been expanded and deepened, with a new harbour completed in 1976 for oil tankers (with a pipeline coming in from Daqing). The city is also an industrial producer in its own right with shipbuilding, petroleum refining, food-processing, diesel engineering and chemical, glassware, and textile industries. These developments have polluted Dalian Bay and affected the fishing enterprises, but efforts are being made to clean it up with waste treatment and oil-reclaiming ships.

Dalian was the first of the 14 open coastal cities to offer a package of attractive terms to foreign investors who had expressed great dissatisfaction with previous discriminatory practices.

It has also become China's 'first rat-free city'. With military precision, local residents planned an intensive eradication campaign and chose April 1986 (when the rats were celebrating peak powers of performance and pregnancy) as the time of assault. A team of rodent specialists from Liaoning Province was later called in for an official inspection of the city. The *China Daily* reported that the inspection method involved the spreading of talcum powder in favourite rat haunts such as grain depots, shops, factories, schools, ports, etc. After 21 days of powdering, only 0.353% of the total powdered space showed paw prints. The inspection showed that the density rate of rats in key areas of the city met the country's 2% requirement: 0.46% at the harbour, 0.16% at the railway station and 0.83% at the airport. Sounds like the rats had packed their bags and were hastily emigrating by boat, train or plane!

The city of Dalian itself is remarkably clean, orderly and attractive with wide avenues. It's well designed, quiet and atypically uncrowded. The credit for this goes to Dalian's Municipal Construction Planning Department, which has made a real effort at replacing the previously ugly matchbox buildings with eye-pleasing structures. Dalian's urban and suburban population amounts to over 1.3 million people living in an area of 1000 sq km – the Dalian jurisdiction area (including five counties) extends to 12,000 sq km with a population of 4.4 million. It's also a prime apple-growing region.

Information

Public Security Bureau This is just to the north-east of Zhongshan Square (see the map).

CITS This office (☎ 335795) is on the 4th floor, 1 Changtong Jie, on the west side of Laodong Park near the Civil Aviation Hotel and CAAC.

Money The Bank of China (☎ 235167) is at 9 Zhongshan Square.

Post & Telecommunications The post and telephone office is at 10 Zhongshan Square, near the Bank of China.

Stalin Square

(sīdàlín gǔangchǎng) 斯大林广场

Stalin seems to be held in high esteem in this part of China. The square commemorates liberation from Japan in 1945 and the memorial was set up in 1954. During the Cultural

Revolution, Stalin Square was used for political rallies. It's on the west end of Zhongshan Lu (on the south side) near the city government building.

Beaches

Dalian is actually a health resort of a kind, so beaches with their attached parks are the attraction. The beach five km to the south-east is for Western VIPs and is bordered by the exclusive Bangchuidao Guesthouse. Laohutan Park *(lǎohǔtān gōngyúan)* has a rocky beach that's rather poor for swimming (you can get there on bus No 102 from the city centre). Small Fujiazhuang Beach *(fùjiāzhūang hǎishǔi yùchǎng)* is the best – and has fine sand and surreal rock outcrops in the deep bay, is excellent for swimming but has few facilities. Like the other beaches, this one has a sanatorium nearby; the patients sometimes venture out in their pyjamas to assist rubber-booted fisherfolk hauling in their catch.

The beach is a fair way out of town – take bus No 102 and then change to bus No 5. Xinghai Park & Beach *(xīnghǎi gōngyúan)* is five km to the south-west – it's crowded and a little on the slimy side, but it's got a

1 North Railway Station
2 Dalian Railway Station
3 Holiday Inn
4 CAAC
5 Civil Aviation Hotel
6 CITS
7 Bus to Dandong
8 Dong Fang Hotel
9 Dalian Hotel
10 Dalian Hotel
11 Post Office
12 Bank of China
13 Public Security Bureau
14 International Hotel
15 Furama Hotel
16 International Seamen's Club
17 Friendship Store/Hotel
18 Harbour Passenger Terminal
19 Nanshan Hotel

1 大连北站
2 大连火车站
3 九州假日酒店
4 中国民航
5 民航大厦
6 中国国际旅行社
7 往丹东汽车
8 东方饭店
9 大连宾馆
10 大连饭店
11 邮局
12 中国银行
13 公安局外事科
14 国际大酒店
15 富丽华酒店
16 海员俱乐部
17 友谊商店/宾馆
18 海港客运站
19 南山宾馆

good seafood restaurant (take bus No 2, or else take tramcar No 201 and then change to tramcar No 202).

Other Sights

For the individual traveller, access to the port facilities (probably one of Dalian's top sights) is limited. You'll have to be content with the large Natural History Museum *(zìrán bówùgǔan)* behind the station with its stuffed sealife. It's open Tuesday, Thursday, Saturday and Sunday from 8 am to 4 pm. Laodong Park *(láodòng gōngyúan)*, in the centre of town, offers good city views. There's also an assortment of handicraft factories, whose products include glasswork and shell mosaic.

Places to Stay

Dalian sees few individual travellers – mostly cruise-ship passengers or seamen. A few hotels sometimes have dormitories, sometimes don't – you have to *push* and results are not guaranteed. Here's a quick summary of the hotel battlefield.

The *Friendship Hotel* (☎ 234121) *(yǒuyí bīngǔan)* is on the 3rd floor, above the Friendship Store at 137 Sidalin Lu. Doubles cost from Y72 to Y100. It's one of the cheapest places to stay, but is rather a long way from the railway station.

The *Dong Fang Hotel (dōngfāng fàndiàn)* is at 28 Zhongshan Lu, not far from the railway station. It was being renovated at the time of this writing. Double rooms are projected to rise to over Y100. It used to provide dorms for Y10, but this may no longer be true after the renovation is complete.

The seven-storey *Dalian Hotel* (☎ 233171) *(dàlián fàndiàn)* is at 6 Shanghai Lu. Single rooms go for Y96.

There is another *Dalian Hotel* (☎ 233111) *(dàlián bīngǔan)* at 7 Zhongshan Square, but the Chinese name is different. Singles cost Y130 and doubles are Y240. This hotel was used in a scene in the movie *The Last Emperor*.

The *Nanshan Hotel* (☎ 238751) *(nánshān bīngǔan)*, 56 Fenglin Jie, Zhongshanqu, has a dozen villas tucked into very pleasant

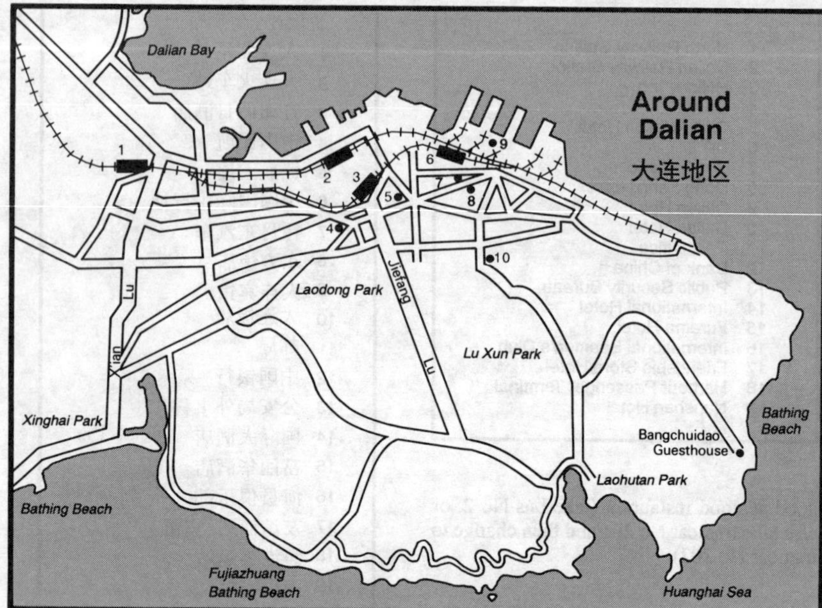

1 Shahekou Railway Station
2 North Railway Station
3 Dalian Railway Station
4 CAAC
5 Dalian Hotel
6 East Railway Station
7 International Seamen's Club
8 Friendship Store/Hotel
9 Harbour Passenger Terminal
10 Nanshan Hotel

1 沙河口站
2 大连北站
3 大连火车站
4 中国民航
5 大连饭店
6 大连东站
7 海员俱乐部
8 友谊商店/宾馆
9 海港客运站
10 南山宾馆

gardens. It once had the atmosphere of a country club, but has now been renovated and resembles a battleship. Doubles cost from Y100 to Y140. To get there take the round-the-city unnumbered bus; or take tramcar No 201 and then change to bus No 12 or walk uphill.

The *International Hotel* (☎ 238238) *(gúojì dàjiǔdiàn)*, 9 Sidalin Lu, has doubles for Y260.

The *Civil Aviation Hotel* (☎ 333111) *(mínháng dàxià)* is run by CAAC and is next to their ticket office. Doubles cost a whopping Y280. If you're booked on one of CAAC's hopelessly delayed flights, you might even get to stay here for free.

The *Furama Hotel* (☎ 230888) *(fùlìhúa jiǔdiàn)* at 74 Sidalin Lu is the glitziest hotel in town. It's an Overseas Chinese hang-out and even has its own Friendship Store. Doubles start from Y330.

The *Holiday Inn* (☎ 808888) *(jiǔzhōu jiàrì jiǔdiàn)* costs Y305 for a single. It's unique among Dalian's luxury hotels in that it is convenient – right next to the railway station.

Another possibility is the *Bangchuidao Guesthouse* (☎ 235131) *(bàngchúidǎo bīngǔan)* to the east of the town on the coast. It's next to an exclusive beach and there is no way to reach it except by taxi. A lot of tour groups stay here.

Places to Eat

People make the trip to Dalian to gorge themselves on seafood – a pleasant change of diet. The *Haiwei Seafood Restaurant (hǎiwèi fàndiàn)*, near the railway station at 85 Zhongshan Lu, will serve up prawns and sea urchins and other unusual and interesting seafood. Tianjin Jie is the wining-dining-shopping street. It's within walking range of the station, and boasts a number of restaurants and snack bars.

The *International Seamen's Club (hǎiyúan jùlèbù)*, on the east end of Sidalin Lu, has several dining sections on the 2nd floor. It's not cheap, but you can have a peaceful plate of fried dumplings *(gūotiē)*. Xinghai Park, out by the beachfront, has a kind of elevated club house with beach umbrellas – you'll be charged about Y20 a head for giant prawns, fish and beer, which is not bad for an open-air location overlooking windsurfers and sunbathers.

Entertainment

The Copacabana of Dalian is the International Seamen's Club *(hǎiyúan jùlèbù)*, open until 10.30 pm, with dining and banquet rooms, a bar where sailors doze with their stale beers to the chirp of video-game machines, and a disco. It has a full-size theatre with weekend offerings – Beijing Opera or perhaps a film or an acrobat show.

Things to Buy

Worth looking into are the two Friendship stores – the old one at 137 Sidalin Lu and the new one in the Furama Hotel.

Getting There & Away

Air Dalian has both domestic and international air connections. CAAC and Dragonair fly to Hong Kong. CAAC and All Nippon Airways go to Tokyo. All Nippon Airways has its office in the International Hotel, but you can book through CITS. Domestic flights include:

Beijing (daily, Y194); Canton (daily, Y754); Changchun (Y217); Changhai; Chengdu (Y668); Chongqing; Fuzhou; Harbin (four times weekly, Y286); Hefei; Nanjing (Y324); Qingdao (Y133); Qinhuangdao; Shanghai (daily, Y378); Shenyang (Y121); Taiyuan; Tianjin (Y254); Ürümqi; Wuhan (Y490); Xi'an (Y480); Xiamen; and Yanji.

The CAAC office (☎ 35884) is just next to the Civil Aviation Hotel opposite CITS.

Bus There are buses to Dandong, Fushun and Jinzhou. The government-run long-distance bus station is one block south of the railway station. There is a private bus station just next to CITS. These buses are slightly cheaper, but don't look as safe. Book your ticket peacefully the day before or arrive at the last minute and fight for it. Several buses leave daily for Dandong between 6 and 8 am. The trip takes nine hours

Train There are nine trains daily to Shenyang and the trip takes six hours. From Shenyang there are direct trains to Beijing and Harbin.

Boat The booking office is at the boat terminal, east of the Seamen's Club, and has a left-luggage office (modern facilities, too). Providing you have a ticket, you can sleep in the comfy building beside the booking office. Since the rail lines from Dalian have to go all the way round the peninsula before proceeding south, boats can actually save you time as well as money.

There are boats to Yantai or Shanghai daily, to Qingdao every other day, to Canton every four to six days, to Tanggu (the port of Tianjin) every four to six days. There are other departures to Weihai, Longkou, Shidao and Yingkou. To Shanghai takes about 40 hours, to Qingdao it's about 28 hours, and to Yantai takes about eight hours. Even 3rd class is comfortable, but avoid cargo class. Meals cost around Y5 and the seasickness pills are free.

Getting Around

Bus No 13 runs from the railway station area, along behind the Friendship Store, and to the boat terminal. Tramcar No 201 starts from the railway station, heads in the same direction as bus No 13, but turns south before the Friendship Store and proceeds east (it's good for getting part-way to the Nanshan Hotel). There is a round-the-city bus with no number, but the characters for circle route *(húan lù)* appear on the destination sign. This bus is useful for a tour through Dalian.

BENXI

(běnxī) 本溪

About two hours' drive south-east of Shenyang is Benxi, an iron, steel and coal-mining town, with a cement works. Liaoning Province accounts for some a tenth of national coal production, with eight large-scale mining areas.

Benxi is notable for being one of the most polluted cities in China. Big chimneys belch flames and thick black smoke – a scene straight from hell. It does make interesting photography though. The train between Shenyang and Dandong stops here briefly – long enough for most travellers.

The main reason some tourists traipse out to Benxi is to see the Benxi Water Cavern *(běnxī shǔidòng)* 27 km east of town. There are boat trips through the cave. It's chilly inside but you can hire an overcoat. The Chinese have given the stalactites and stalagmites weird names, and the associated stories may require an almighty leap of imagination.

TIELING

(tiělíng) 铁岭

Tieling, north of Shenyang on the railway line, was opened to tourism fairly recently. A British couple we met were probably among the first individual tourists to arrive there. The local tourism committee, after recovering from the shock of actually receiving a tourist, decided to solve the problem by chauffeuring the couple around in a sedan and providing two blow-out banquets in a row. Zhou Enlai spent his youth in Tieling so one of the 'highlights' is a model replica of the town as he knew it – complete with fairy lights to show the route he used to take to school.

BINGYU VALLEY

(bīngyù gōu) 冰峪谷

According to CITS, this is Liaoning's answer to Guilin and Yangshuo. The valley has a number of towering, vertical rock formations with a river meandering between them. It's pretty, but it's not likely to replace Guilin on the travellers' circuit. Still, you might want to have a look.

The valley is 250 km north-east of Dalian. Take a bus from the long-distance bus station to Zhuanghe *(zhūanghé)*, a town about halfway between Dalian and Dandong. Then take another bus to Bingyu Scenic Area *(bīngyù fēngjǐn qū)*. There is a very basic hotel or you can camp for Y10, tent included.

DANDONG

(dāndōng) 丹东

Dandong lies at the border of Liaoning Province and North Korea. Along with Dalian and Yingkou, this is one of the three key trading and communication ports for the whole north-eastern area. The city has been designated one of Liaoning Province's major export production centres and is being revamped for greater light industry production of things like wristwatches, knitwear, printing and foodstuffs. This is the home of *Ganoderma*, wrinkle-killer face cream. You can buy tussah silk at the local silk factory.

Dandong isn't a cultural Mecca, but it's clean, leafy, easy to cover and doesn't suffer from overcrowding. However, there isn't

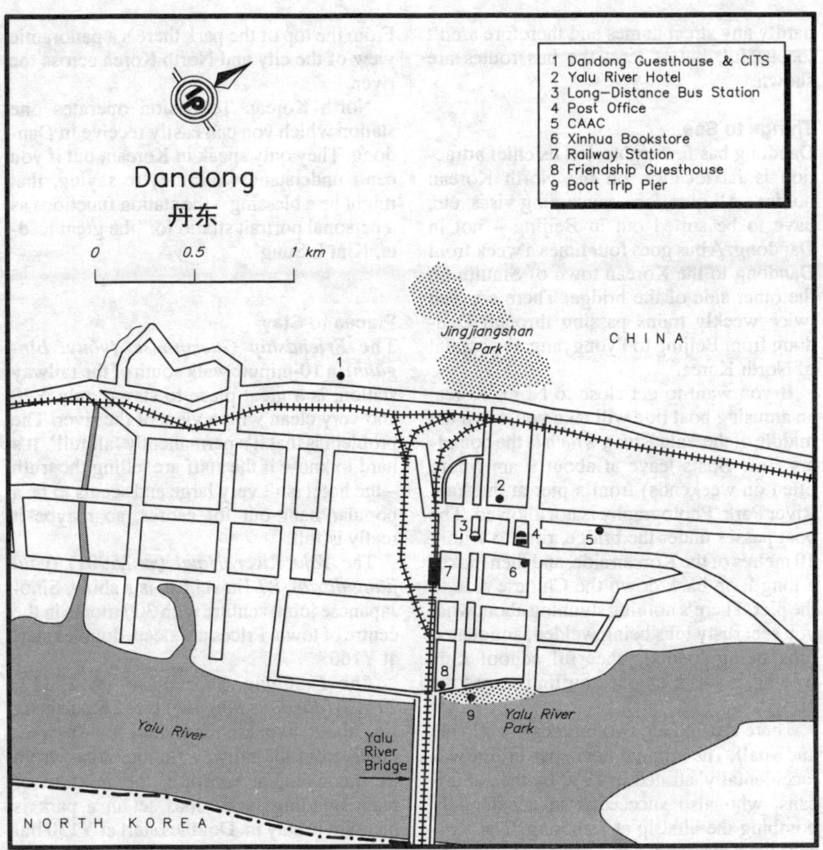

much to see here other than the view of North Korea across the Yalu River.

Information

CITS The office (☎ 27721) is inside the Dandong Guesthouse and will supply a brochure but no maps. The staff doesn't know which side of a postage stamp to lick, but at least they're friendly.

Maps Available only from Xinhua Bookstore, near the post office. The maps show hardly any street names and therefore aren't too useful, but at least the bus routes are shown.

Things to See

Dandong has few sights, but its chief attraction is its location on the North Korean border. All questions concerning visas, etc, have to be sorted out in Beijing – not in Dandong. A bus goes four times a week from Dandong to the Korean town of Sinuiju on the other side of the bridge. There are also twice weekly trains passing through Dandong from Beijing to Pyongyang, the capital of North Korea.

If you want to get close to North Korea, an amusing boat ride will take you down the middle of the Yalu River, which is the boundary line. Boats leave at about 9 am (more often on weekends) from a pier at the Yalu River Park. Photography is not allowed. The boat passes under the bridge, runs to within 10 metres of the Korean side, and then makes a long loop back down the Chinese side to the pier. There's nothing stunning about what you see: rusty tubs being welded, antiquated tubs being loaded, cheerful school kids waving, a steam engine chuffing across the bridge.

There are, in fact, two bridges – well, one and a half. The original steel-span bridge was 'accidentally' strafed in 1950 by the Americans, who also succeeded in accidentally bombing the airstrip at Dandong. The Koreans have dismantled this bridge as far as the mid-river boundary line. All that's left is a row of piers on the Korean side and half a bridge (still showing shrapnel pockmarks) on the Chinese side. The present bridge runs parallel to the old one.

Yalu River Park *(yālù jiāng gōngyúan)* is a favourite picnic site, full of photographers trying to squeeze Mum, Dad, kids, Gran and Granpa into the standard 'I visited the Sino-Korean border' shot which has to include the bridge as a backdrop. You can even get your portrait taken in the cockpit of a Chinese MIG fighter.

Jinjiangshan Park *(jǐnjiāng shān gōngyúan)* is close to the Dandong Guesthouse. From the top of the park there's a panoramic view of the city and North Korea across the river.

North Korean Television operates one station which you can easily receive in Dandong. They only speak in Korean, but if you can't understand what they're saying, that might be a blessing – the station functions as a personal portrait studio for 'the great leader, Kim Il Sung'.

Places to Stay

The *Friendship Guesthouse (yǒuyí bīngǔan)*, a 10-minute walk south of the railway station, is a great place to stay – only Y20 and very clean with a view of the river. The problem is that it's permanently 'all full'. It's hard to know if the staff are telling the truth – the hotel isn't very large and seems to be a popular hang-out for cadres, so maybe it really is full.

The *Yalu River Hotel* (☎ 25901) *(yālù jiāng dàxià)*, 87 Jiuwei Lu, is a shiny, Sino-Japanese joint-venture with 300 rooms in the centre of town. Prices are steep, doubles start at Y160.

The *Dandong Guesthouse* (☎ 27312, 27313) *(dāndōng bīngǔan)* is at 2 Shanshang Jie, about two km or a half-hour's walk uphill from the railway station. Apart from its inconvenient location, the mixture of main buildings and villas set in a park is pleasant to stay in. Doubles start at Y150 but can be bargained down to Y80 or less after much wrangling and showing student ID. The rooms all have TV – turn off the telly and it's just serenading crickets and the lonesome whistling of steam locos shunting outside.

Places to Eat

The *Dandong Guesthouse* offers pricey (FEC only) and unexciting food, including Western breakfasts. The food scene is more lively downtown, where the free-enterprise merchants have set up red lanterns and neon lights to attract passers-by. At a pinch, stalls in the railway station sell food all night long.

Getting There & Away

Air There are regular flights to Beijing (Y284), Canton (Y944) and Shenyang (Y67). There is a CAAC ticket office east of the Yalu River Hotel (see map).

Bus The bus station is a five-minute walk from the railway station. Helpful staff try hard to get foreigners on the right bus.

A bus leaves daily for Tonghua at 6.30 am. Thc trip takes 10 hours.

My bus appeared to have been overbooked, but the inventive staff placated irate travellers by producing collapsible chairs! The route follows mostly dirt roads through villages with the typical thatched houses of the Korean minority. At the lunch stop, the drivers invited the foreigners to eat with them – a delicious meal of egg and onions, aubergines and sliced cucumber with garlic. Shortly after passing a bus that had plunged off the road and almost landed in a reservoir, the bus ground to a halt again. In the middle of the road was a large, mobile office which had embedded itself in an overhanging branch and slipped off its trailer.

The bus from Dandong will drop you off in Tonghua about three km from the station. To continue to the station, cross to the opposite side of the road outside the bus station and take a city bus from the next bus stop – ask for the railway station *(hŭochē zhàn)*.

Several buses leave daily between 5.10 and 6.40 am for the nine-hour trip to Dalian.

Whichever bus you take, it's a gamble. The express bus trip from Dalian to Dandong was some ride. About 10 minutes after departure, considering the speed – perhaps I should say take-off – the lovely Korean girl sitting in front of me was already looking green and fumbling for the window catch. Her well-meaning companions were insistent that the best solution for her problem was to eat more tomatoes.

Meanwhile the driver decided to improve his banshee act by using not only his double air-horns but also the outside loudspeaker to harangue traffic in front. His tactic was to move up within three inches of the back bumper of the vehicle in front and then scream in Chinese, 'Move it, move it, let the vehicle behind overtake'. Donkey-carts, walking tractors, jeeps scattered like buckshot.

The Korean girl succumbed to motion sickness and threw up out of the window. Since the window was very small, the girl had quite a struggle before she finally managed to get her head outside. Traffic coming from the other direction came within a hair's breadth of knocking her block off. The driver kept flying along, turned the internal loudspeaker on and blasted the girl: 'Hey you behind, get your head in, get it in, observe safety, observe safety'. While his voice rose to a frenzy, he turned in his seat to look back and the bus swayed violently.

The scenery along this route is meant to be beautiful, but I can't give an honest opinion because this girl gave my window a nauseating landscape.

Train There are direct trains to Dandong from Shenyang and Changchun; the trip from Shenyang takes five hours. The combination train from Pyongyang to Moscow and Pyongyang to Beijing passes through Dandong on Saturday at about 3 pm. Buy a platform ticket and watch the international crowds of passengers (mostly Russians, North Koreans and Chinese) buying luxury items.

AROUND DANDONG

About 52 km north-west of Dandong is the town of Fengcheng. The nearby mountain, Fenghuangshan, is 840 metres high and dotted with temples, monasteries and pagodas from the Tang, Ming and Qing dynasties. The Fenghuang Mountain Temple Fair takes place in April and reportedly attracts thousands of people. Fenghuangshan is one hour from Dandong by either train or bus. The express train does not stop here, but you do get a view of the mountain.

Wulongbei Hot Springs *(wŭlóngbēi wēnqúan)* is about 20 km north of Dandong on the road to Fengcheng. There's a guesthouse here and you could try the springs.

Dagushan, where there are several groups of Taoist temples dating from the Tang Dynasty, lies close to the town of Gushan – about 90 km south-west of Dandong.

Jilin 吉林

CHANGCHUN

(chángchūn) 长春

Changchun, with its broad leafy avenues, is a well laid-out but rather dull city. The Japanese, who developed it as the capital of 'Manchukuo' between 1933 and 1945, built the uninspiring militaristic structures. In 1945 the Russians arrived in Changchun on a looting spree; when they departed in 1946, the Kuomintang moved in to occupy the cities of the north-east, only to find themselves surrounded by the Communists in the countryside (roving around blowing up railway lines). The Communists had assembled a formidable array of scrounged and captured weaponry, even former Japanese tanks and US jeeps, and Changchun saw more than a few of them in action. The Communists took over the city in 1948.

Information

CITS This office (☎ 882401) is directly behind the Changbaishan Hotel in the Bank of China Building (this Bank of China does not change money). The staff here is very friendly. They have a useful bilingual city bus map plus other literature.

Public Security Bureau This is on the south-west corner of Renmin Square near the Bank of China.

Money The Bank of China is on the north-west corner of Renmin Square *(rénmín gŭangchăng)* – on the corner of Xi'an Dajie and Sidalin Dajie.

Post The post office is on Sidalin Dajie, two blocks south of the railway station.

Puppet Emperor's Palace & Exhibition Hall

(wěihúanggōng) 伪皇宫

No, this place has nothing to do with seeing puppet shows. Henry Puyi was the last person to ascend to the dragon throne. He was two years old at the time and was forced to abdicate just six years later when the 1911 revolution swept the country. He lived in exile in Tianjin and in 1935 was spirited away to Changchun by the Japanese invaders and set up as the 'puppet emperor' of Manchukuo in 1932. He lived in Changchun for the next 14 years. Puyi was captured by the Russians in 1945 and was only returned to China sometime in the late 1950s, where he was allowed to work as a gardener at one of the colleges in Beijing. He died of cancer in 1967, thus ending a life which had largely been governed by others. His story was the basis for the award-winning film *The Last Emperor*.

South Lake Park

(nánhú gōngyúan) 南胡公园

The largest park in the city is South Lake Park. It has the usual ponds, pavilions and wooden bridges and is right near the Changbaishan Hotel. From the station, take trolley Nos 62 or 63.

Changchun Film Studio

(chăngchūndiànyǐng zhìpiànchăng)

长春电影制片厂

The studio got its start during the civil war, making documentaries. You aren't likely to

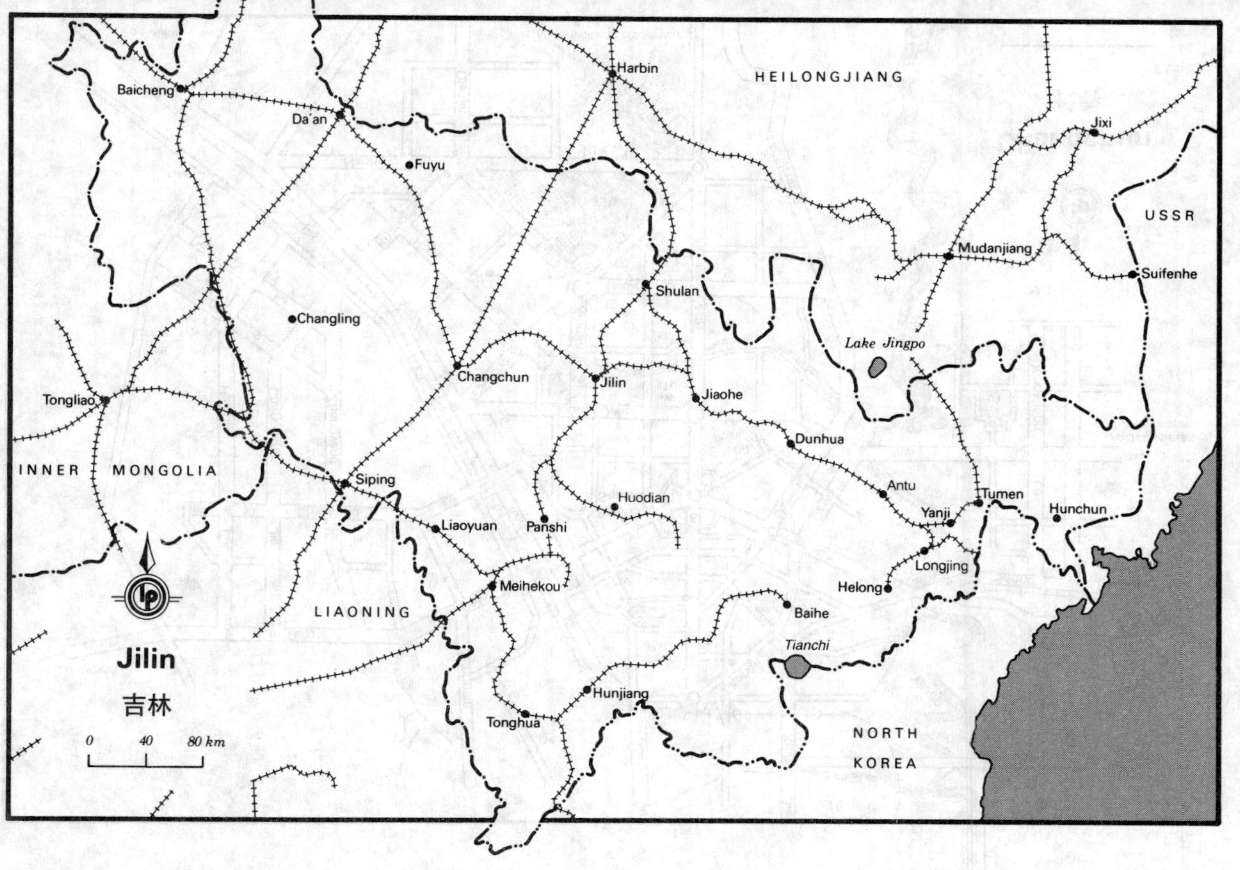
Harbin
HEILONGJIANG
Baicheng
Da'an
Jixi
Fuyu
USSR
Mudanjiang
Suifenhe
Shulan
Changling
Lake Jingpo
Changchun
Jilin
Tongliao
Jiaohe
Dunhua
INNER MONGOLIA
Siping
Antu
Tumen
Hunchun
Huodian
Yanji
Liaoyuan
Panshi
Longjing
Meihekou
Helong
LIAONING
Baihe
Tianchi
Jilin
吉林
Hunjiang
Tonghua
NORTH KOREA
0
40
80 km

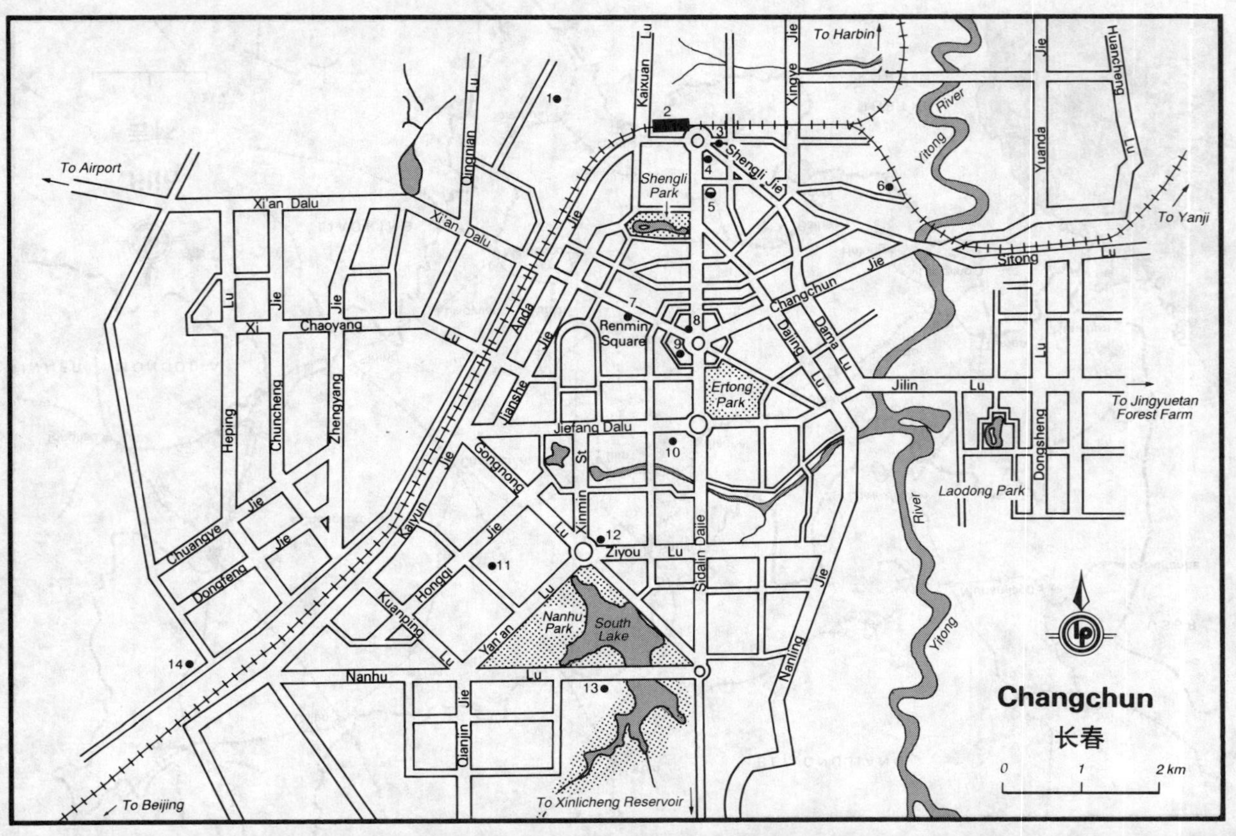

Changchun
长春
0
1
2 km
To Harbin
To Airport
To Yanji
To Jingyuetan Forest Farm
To Beijing
To Xinlicheng Reservoir
Kaixuan Lu
Xingye Jie
Huancheng Lu
Yuanda Jie
Yitong River
Shengli Jie
Shengli Park
Qingnian Lu
Xi'an Dalu
Sitong Lu
Changchun Jie
Dajing Lu
Dama Lu
Jilin Lu
Dongsheng
Laodong Park
Renmin Square
Ertong Park
Jiefang Dalu
Anda Jie
Jianshe Jie
Chaoyang Lu
Xi Lu
Jie
Jie
Heping
Chuncheng
Zhengyang
Gongnong Jie
Xinmin St
Ziyou Lu
Sidalin Dajie
Nanling Jie
Kaiyun Jie
Honggi Jie
Chuangye Jie
Dongfeng Jie
Kuanping Lu
Yan'an Lu
Nanhu Park
South Lake
Nanhu Lu
Qianjin Jie
1
2
3
4
5
6
7
8
9
10
11
12
13
14

1 Railway Carriage Factory
2 Railway Station
3 Advance Rail Ticket Office
4 Chunyi Guesthouse
5 Post Office
6 Puppet Emperor's Palace & Exhibition Hall
7 Changchun Hotel
8 Bank of China
9 Public Security Bureau
10 Jixiang Hotel
11 Film Studio
12 Changbaishan Hotel & CITS
13 Nanhu Guesthouse
14 No 1 Automobile Factory

1 客车工厂
2 火车站
3 火车售票处
4 春谊宾馆
5 邮局
6 傀儡帝宫殿和展览馆
7 长春宾馆
8 中国银行
9 公安局外事科
10 吉香宾馆
11 电影制造厂
12 长白山宾馆
13 南湖宾馆
14 第一汽车制造厂

get inside unless you join a CITS tour, but a Chinese tour may be possible.

Factories

China's first car-manufacturing plant was set up here in the 1950s with Soviet assistance, starting with 95 horsepower Jiefang (Liberation) Trucks, and moving on to make bigger and better things like the Red Flag limousines. CITS can arrange a tour. Lesser factories (tractor, locomotives, train coach, carpet, fur, wood-carving) may be accessible.

Places to Stay

Like elsewhere in the north-east, many excellent Chinese hotels are off limits to foreigners. Furthermore, most of the hotels in Changchun have been renovated and are charging renovated prices. None of the hotels as yet have dormitories, though it never hurts to ask.

On the south side of town, there are two universities which *might* let you stay in their dormitories, but this depends on the stars and the wind direction. The two campuses are the *North-east Normal University (dōngběi shīfàn dàxúe)* and *Jilin Polytechnic University (jílín gōngyè dàxúe)*, both on Sidalin Dajie. It's nine km from the railway station – take bus No 6.

The *Tianchi Fandian* is right in front of the railway station. Doubles are Y70 but it's a real battle to get in and may not be worth the trouble. They usually tell foreigners to go across the street to the Chunyi Guesthouse.

The *Chunyi Guesthouse* (☎ 35951) *(chūnyí bīngŭan)*, 2 Sidalin Dajie, is one block south of the railway station. They charge Y100 for big, beautiful double rooms with private bath. The staff is friendly.

The main tourist place is the *Changbaishan Hotel* (☎ 883551) *(chángbáishān bīngŭan)*. Doubles cost Y140 in renovated rooms, Y80 in old rooms, but all the rooms will be renovated eventually. CITS is in the Bank of China building behind the hotel. It's nine km from the railway station – take trolley Nos 62 or 63.

The *Changchun Hotel* (☎ 822661) *(chángchūn bīngŭan)*, 10 Xinhua Lu, is a short walk west of Renmin Square. Doubles cost Y120.

The *Jixiang Hotel (jíxiáng dàjiŭdiàn)* is on Jiefang Dalu and gets rather few foreign visitors. Doubles cost Y120.

The main cadre hang-out is the exclusive *Nanhu Guesthouse (nánhú bīngŭan)*, about 10 km south of the railway station. Doubles cost from Y130 to Y160, and villas cost a trifling Y900.

Getting There & Away

Air There are flights to Beijing (daily, Y313); Canton (daily, Y973); Chengdu (Y883); Dalian (Y217); Nanjing; Qingdao; Shanghai (three times weekly, Y570); Shenyang (Y94); Tianjin; Wuhan; Xiamen; Xi'an; Yanji (daily, Y121); and Zhengzhou. The CAAC office (☎ 39772) is at 2 Liaoning Lu.

Train The advance railway ticket office is one block east of the railway station on the 2nd floor. You can pay in RMB.

There are frequent trains heading north to Harbin (four hours) and south to Shenyang (five hours). Trains are also frequent to Jilin, and there is an overnight train for Yanji (departs 6.40 pm, arrives 6.30 am), which is the route you take to Changbaishan.

JILIN

(jílín) 吉林

East of Changchun is the city of Jilin. A Chinese pamphlet puts it in a nutshell:

> Under the guidance of Chairman Mao's revolutionary line, it has made rapid progress in industrial and agricultural production...From a desolate consumer city, Kirin (Jilin) has become a rising industrial city with emphasis on chemical and power industries.

Three large chemical plants were built after 1949. The Fengman Hydroelectric Station, built by the Japanese, disassembled by the Russians and put back together by the Chinese, fuels these enterprises, and provides Jilin with an unusual tourist attraction: water passing from artificial Songhua Lake through the power plant becomes a warm, steamy current that merges with the Songhua River and prevents it from freezing. Overnight, vapour rising from the river meets the minus 20 ° C weather, causing condensation on the branches of pines and willows on a 20-km stretch of the bank. During the Spring Festival (25 January), hordes of Japanese and Overseas Chinese come for the resulting icicle and spraypaint show. To reach this hydroelectric station, take bus No 9 from the roundabout north of the Xiguan Hotel.

If you want to try some elementary ski slopes, there's the Songhuahu ski-ground at Daqingshan (935 metres elevation) which is 16 km from Jilin, and just west of Fengman. CITS can provide further details about snow conditions, lift operation, transport and hire of equipment.

Jilin, like Harbin, has an ice-lantern festival, held at Beishan Park. In 1976, the Jilin area received a heavy meteorite shower, and the largest bit, weighing 1770 kg, is on view in the meteorite exhibition hall (take bus No 3 from outside the Dongguan Hotel). It's also possible to visit the Jilin Special Products Research Centre *(lóngtánshān lùchǎng)*, where there is a deer park, ginseng garden and a collection of sables. Take bus No 12 from the station and get off on the other side of the bridge over the Songhua River.

Information

CITS The office (☎ 453773) is in the Xiguan Hotel.

Places to Stay

The *Xiguan Hotel (xīgūan bīngǔan)*, at 661 Songjiang Lu, is about seven km from the station. Take bus No 1 from the station to its terminal beside a roundabout; from there it's about a two-km walk along the riverside. This place is inconvenient to reach. Doubles start at Y110.

The *Dongguan Hotel* (☎ 454272) *(dōnggūan bīngǔan)*, at 223 Songjiang Lu, is about three km from the station and has doubles for Y100. Take trolley bus No 3 from the station.

1 火车站
2 长途汽车站
3 清真寺
4 天主教堂
5 东关宾馆
6 西关宾馆

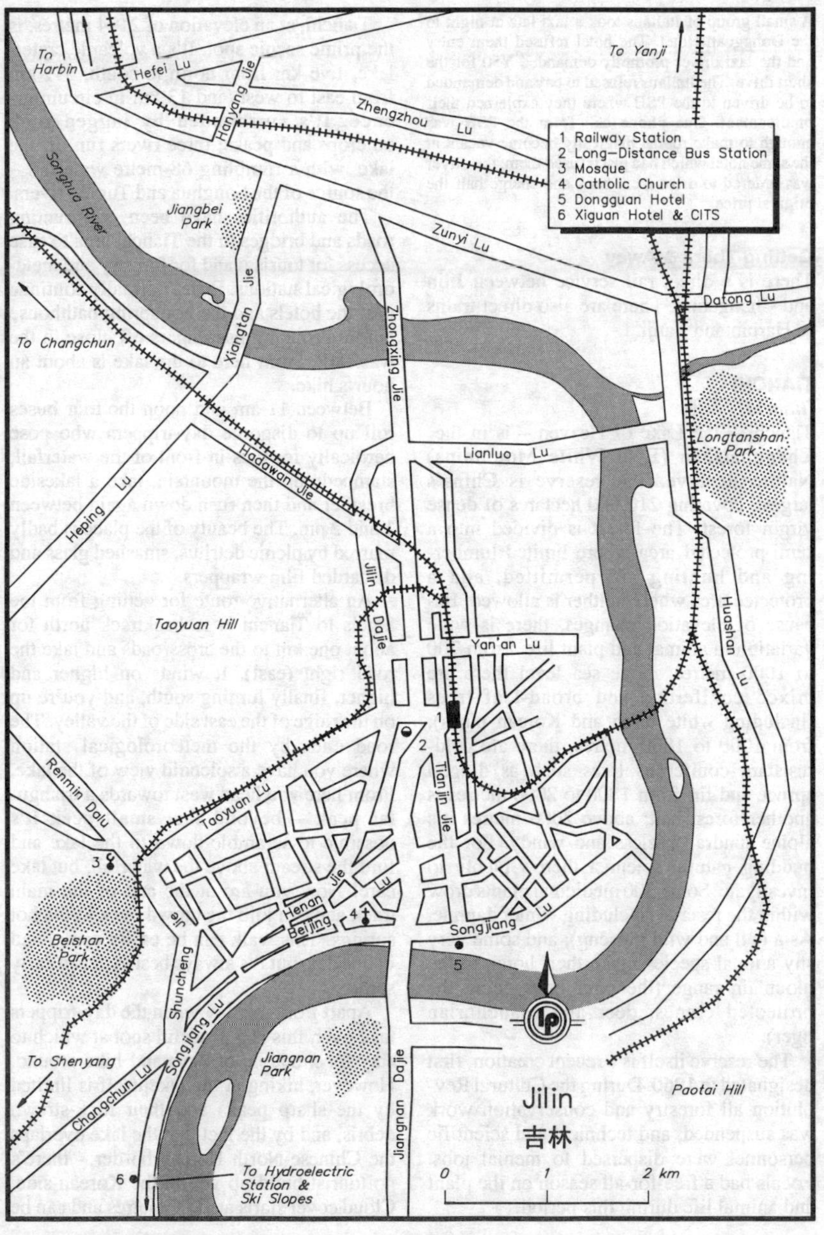
1 Railway Station
2 Long-Distance Bus Station
3 Mosque
4 Catholic Church
5 Dongguan Hotel
6 Xiguan Hotel & CITS
To Harbin
Hefei Lu
Hanyang Jie
Zhengzhou Lu
To Yanji
Songhua River
Jiangbei Park
Zunyi Lu
Datong Lu
To Changchun
Xiangtan Jie
Zhongxing Jie
Longtanshan Park
Lianluo Lu
Hadawan Jie
Heping Lu
Jilin Dajie
Taoyuan Hill
Yan'an Lu
Huashan Lu
Renmin Dalu
Taoyuan Lu
Tianjin Jie
Henan Jie
Beijing Lu
Songjiang Lu
Beishan Park
Shuncheng Jie
Songjiang Lu
To Shenyang
Jiangnan Park
Jiangnan Dajie
Paotai Hill
Changchun Lu
Jilin
吉林
To Hydroelectric Station & Ski Slopes
0
1
2 km

A small group of Italians took a taxi late at night to the Dongguan Hotel. The hotel refused them entry and the taxi driver promptly demanded Y50 for the short drive. The Italians refused to pay and demanded to be driven to the PSB where they explained their predicament. One phone call from the PSB was enough to make rooms magically become vacant at the same hotel which had just refused them; the driver was ordered to drive them back and charge half the original price.

Getting There & Away

There is a direct rail service between Jilin and Changchun. There are also direct trains to Harbin and Yanji.

TIANCHI

(tiānchí) 天池

Tianchi – the Lake of Heaven – is in the Changbaishan (Ever-White Mountains) Nature Reserve. The reserve is China's largest, covering 210,000 hectares of dense virgin forest. The forest is divided into a semi-protected area where limited lumbering and hunting are permitted, and a protected area where neither is allowed. Because of elevation changes, there is wide variation in animal and plant life. From 700 to 1000 metres above sea level there are mixed coniferous and broad-leaf trees (including white birch and Korean pines); from 1000 to 1800 metres, there are cold-resistant coniferous trees such as dragon spruce and fir; from 1800 to 2000 metres is another forest belt; above 2000 metres it's alpine tundra, treeless and windy. For the budding natural scientist there's plenty to investigate. Some 300 medicinal plants grow within the reserve (including winter daphne, Asia bell and wild ginseng); and some very shy animal species make their home in the mountain range (the rarer ones being the protected cranes, deer and Manchurian tiger).

The reserve itself is a recent creation, first designated in 1960. During the Cultural Revolution all forestry and conservation work was suspended, and technical and scientific personnel were dispersed to menial jobs. Locals had a free-for-all season on the plant and animal life during this period.

Tianchi, at an elevation of 2194 metres, is the prime scenic spot. It's a volcanic crater-lake, five km from north to south, 3½ km from east to west, and 13 km in circumference. It's surrounded by jagged rock outcrops and peaks; three rivers run off the lake, with a rumbling 68-metre waterfall – the source of the Songhua and Tumen rivers.

The authorities have been constructing roads and bridges in the Tianchi area to ease access for tourism and for forestry and meteorological stations. Buses normally continue past the hotels and the hot-spring bathhouse before dropping passengers off close to the waterfall. From here to the lake is about an hour's hike.

Between 11 am and noon the tour buses roll up to disgorge day-trippers who pose heroically for pics in front of the waterfall, stampede up the mountain, take a lakeside breather and then rush down again between 1 and 2 pm. The beauty of the place is badly marred by picnic detritus, smashed glass and discarded film wrappers.

An alternative route for getting from the hotels to Tianchi is to backtrack north for about one km to the crossroads and take the road right (east). It winds on higher and higher, finally turning south, and you're up on the ridge of the east side of the valley. The road ends by the meteorological station where you have a splendid view of the lake. From here you head west towards a triangular peak – beyond that small peak it's possible to scramble down to the lake and ford the stream above the waterfall, but take care! Now you are at the end of the main track and can join the crowd back to the hot springs. This walk can be easily completed in one day, but it's always best to get an early start.

Apart from midday when the day-trippers take over, this is a peaceful spot at which to stay for a couple of days and hike around. However, hiking at the lake itself is limited by the sharp peaks and their rock-strewn debris, and by the fact that the lake overlaps the Chinese-North Korean border – there's no tourist build-up yet on the Korean side. Cloud cover starts at 1000 metres and can be prevalent. The highest peak in the Changbaishan range is 2700 metres.

Enchanting scenery like this would not be complete in the Chinese world without a legend or mystique of some sort. Of the many myths, the most intriguing is the origin of the Manchu race. Three heavenly nymphs descended to the lake in search of earthly pleasure. They stripped off for a dip in the lake; along came a magic magpie which deposited a red berry on the dress of one of the maidens. When she picked it up to smell it, the berry flew through her lips into her stomach. The nymph became pregnant and gave birth to a handsome boy with an instant gift of the gab. He went on to foster the Manchus and their dynasty.

Dragons, and other things that go bump in the night, were believed to have sprung out of the lake. In fact, they're still believed to do so. There have been intermittent sightings of unidentified swimming objects – China's own Loch Ness beasties or aquatic yetis or what have you. Tianchi is the deepest alpine lake in China – plumbed to a depth estimated at between 200 and 350 metres. Since it is frozen over in winter and temperatures are well below zero, it would take a pretty hardy monster to survive (even plankton can't). Sightings from the Chinese and North Korean sides point to a black bear, fond of swimming, and oblivious to the paperwork necessary for crossing these tight borders. On a more profound note, Chinese couples throw coins into the lake, pledging that their love will remain as deep as Tianchi, and as long lived.

The local post office, next to the guesthouses, has scenic first-day covers. The hot-spring bathhouse, where water from lake and underground sources is mixed, is close to the hotels. It costs Y1 for a communal dip and Y5 for a private cubicle. If you cross the nearby river via either the tree trunk or the bridge lower down, there's a forest path which leads to the dark, brooding Lesser Tianchi Lake.

Places to Stay

There are several places to stay, but getting a cheap dormitory will be a battle. The *Birch Hotel (yùehúa lóu)* has doubles for Y110. Some cheaper alternatives include the *Nature Reserve Bureau Hotel (bǎohù jú bīngǔan)* for Y80 and the *Meilinsong Guesthouse (měilínsōng bīngǔan)* for Y90.

The largest hostel is the *Tianchi Hotel (tiānchí fàndiàn)* where doubles cost Y120.

You may have to fight to get into any hotel, especially if you want a cheap room or dormitory. Sometimes, the only way is to park yourself in the lobby and refuse to move. If you have a sleeping bag, you might consider camping.

In Changbaishan, none of the guesthouses would take me in and the staff were most unhelpful. I had my own tent and camped by Lesser Tianchi Lake together with a Danish guy I met on the bus from Baihe. Camping is not permitted but no officials bothered us. There were many curious Chinese tourists of course. The place was quite badly littered and the rusty pedal-boats in the lake disturbed the silence with their squeaking.

Getting There & Away

The Changbaishan area is remote, and it's quite an expedition getting there: you're advised to bring loads of ginseng, frog-oil tonic and other supplies and refreshments with you, plus good hiking gear (because of high altitudes, sudden thunderstorms are not uncommon).

The *only* season when there's transport access (when the road from Baihe to Changbaishan is open) is from late June to September, when snow and ice cover is reduced. Chinese hikers come to see the autumn colourings – so the peak season with a high local turnover is from mid-July to mid-August. Although Changbaishan was only opened to foreigners in 1982, it has been on the Chinese tour map for some time, with something like 30,000 visitors from the north-eastern provinces arriving each year between July and September.

There are two 'transit points' to Changbaishan: Antu and Baihe. Starting from Changchun, the route via Antu is faster and more common. Before you go, get a weather forecast from someone in Jilin, Changchun or Shenyang (during July and August will be no problem). Allow about five days for the round trip from, say, Shenyang. Tour buses go up the mountain in the July and August, but at other times you may have trouble finding a bus from Baihe. The only other local transport is logging trucks and official jeeps – the latter are expensive to rent, the drivers of the former are very reluctant to give rides.

Antu Route There are trains to Antu from Changchun – the trip takes 10 hours. The evening train departs from Changchun at 6.40 pm. There are sleepers available on this train, but you might have to book them all the way to Yanji. If you arrive in Antu at night you can sleep in the station waiting room. There is also a small hotel in Antu.

Buses for Baihe depart from 7.20 to 10.30 am. You can also get buses to Baihe from Yanji (further down the rail line) but then you'll have to backtrack. From Antu it takes five hours to travel the 125 km. Unless you arrive early in Baihe, you may find yourself waiting till the next morning for transport to Changbaishan, a further 40 km.

Special tourist buses run from Antu to the Changbaishan Hot Springs area in July and August – some of these have a three-day package trip, but you'll be with a mob of noisy, camera-clicking tourists. There are some trains from Shenyang to Antu.

Baihe Route Baihe is the end of the line as far as trains go – a scrapyard for locos. To get to Baihe from Jilin, Changchun or Shenyang, you must take a train or bus to Tonghua and then change to a train for Baihe. The morning train leaves Shenyang at 6.30 am for Tonghua. From Dandong, there are buses to Tonghua departing at 6.30 am.

The two daily trains between Tonghua and Baihe have two steam locos (one pushing, the other pulling); there are no sleepers, only carriages with soft seats (green velvet) and hard wooden benches (ouch!). The 500-series trains take 10 hours of chuggalugging to cover the 277 km between Tonghua and Baihe. If you're overnighting, it's worth paying extra for soft-seat in lieu of a sleeper. The soft-seat waiting room at Tonghua

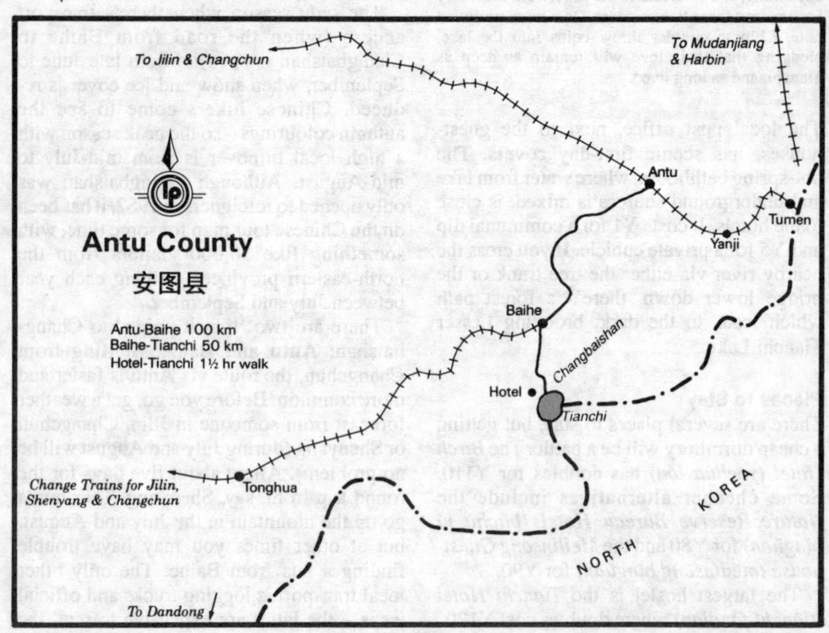

station is the lap of luxury. Look for the sign saying 'soft-seat waiting room' beside the packed hard-seat waiting room, and ring the red bell.

The early morning train arrives in Baihe at 5.20 am and is met by an excursion bus *(yóulǎn chē)*, which takes you about three km into the town with its grubby shacks for breakfast before a change of buses for the two-hour trip to the mountain. Buses usually return from the mountain at 2 pm. There are several cheap places to stay in town, all within a few minutes of the bus station.

Buses leave between 5.30 and 6.40 am for Antu and Yanji. The bus bounces past tobacco fields, villages with thatched roofs and log chimneys, stockaded gardens, pigs on mud heaps and howling dogs. Allow five hours to Antu or seven hours to Yanji. Close to Yanji, watch out for an airfield with low-flying, antique MIG fighters (Chinese copies) practising scrambles – the Soviet Union is just a few minutes' flying time away.

THE COUNTRYSIDE

The Changbaishan region presents you with some possibilities for shaking off the cities and traipsing through the wilderness, and gives you some good reasons for doing so: virgin forest, babbling brooks, and some rough travel and rough trails, as well as rough toilets – if you can find one.

The whole zone is the Yanbian (Chaoxian) Korean Autonomous Prefecture. The local people – of Korean descent – are often indistinguishable in dress from their Chinese counterparts. If you visit this area around mid-August, you can join in the 'Old People Festival'. The Koreans are a fairly lively lot, who enjoy eating spiced cold noodles and dog meat, and singing and dancing – and offering hospitality. They can also drink you under the table. Yanbian has the greatest concentration of Korean and Korean-Han groups in China, mostly inhabiting the border areas north and north-east of Baihe, extending up to Yanji.

Transport by rail is faster, as opposed to spine-jangling dirt roads. Apart from public buses the only other means of getting around is by jeeps or logging trucks. Off the main track, the trains are puffing black dragons, possibly of Japanese vintage. The fittings are old and the uncrowded trains have no sleepers.

Food in general leaves a lot to be desired – in the Korean places you can get by on cold noodles topped with a pile of hot spices or some meat and egg.

In a Tonghua restaurant I was rather relieved when two beggars fought it out and wolfed down the remaining grey dumplings on my plate – I was feeling off-colour from the ones I'd already eaten. A bus lunch-stop along the way yielded a hell's kitchen, with pig's heads bloodying the floor, fires going in corners, and mysterious concoctions bubbling away in cauldrons.

YANJI

(yánjí) 延吉

Yanji is the capital of the autonomous zone – both Korean and Chinese languages are spoken here, and some semblance of traditional costume and custom is maintained. The surrounding countryside is sprinkled with clusters of thatched cottages. However, there's nothing to see in Yanji – consider it a transit stop.

Information

CITS This office (☎ 515018 or 517906) at 19 Gongyuan Jie Yanxi Lu arranges expensive day trips to see a genuine Korean family and a Korean museum.

Places to Stay

The *Yanji Binguan* charges Y62 for doubles between June and August and Y38 at other times. Reception at the door includes a fancy female flunky who whirls you inside with a flourish; reception at the desk then ignores your existence.

A far better bet is the *Minzu Fandian*, which has helpful staff and charges a down-to-earth Y40 for a double. Both hotels are about 40 minutes from the station on foot, or ask the bus driver to drop you nearby if you're coming from Baihe. There's a train from Yanji to Tumen at 5.49 am.

Getting There & Away

There are daily direct flights from Changchun to Yanji for Y121. Since Yanji lies on the railway line between Antu and Tumen (and thence to Mudanjiang in the south-east of Heilongjiang Province) it should not be too difficult to drop in for a visit. There are buses between Yanji and Baihe (Tianchi).

TUMEN

(túmén) 图门

Tumen is a small city on the North Korean border. You could spend a few hours there strolling through the riverside park or climb the hill for an elevated view of the border area.

Places to Stay

The *Dongfang Fandian*, close to the station, charges Y15 for a dorm bed. The *Tumen Binguan* charges Y50.

Getting There & Away

The most convenient train departs from Tumen at 8.23 am heading for Mudanjiang; it takes 6½ hours and costs Y10 soft-seat.

Heilongjiang 黑龙江

HARBIN

(hā'ěrbīn) 哈尔宾

As the provincial capital, Harbin is the educational, cultural and political centre of Heilongjiang *(hēilóngjiāng)*. This city used to be a fishing village on the Songhua River – the name in Manchu means 'place for drying nets'. In 1896 the Russians negotiated a contract for shoving a railway line through Harbin to Vladivostok (and Dalian). The Russian imprint on the town remained in one way or another until the end of WW II; by 1904 the 'rail concession' was in place, and with it came other Russian demands on Manchuria. These were stalled by the Russo-Japanese war (1904-05), and with the Russian defeat the Japanese gained control of the railway. In 1917 large numbers of White Russian refugees flocked to Harbin, fleeing the Bolsheviks; in 1932 the Japanese occupied the city; in 1945 the Soviet Army wrested it back for a year and held it until 1946 when the Kuomintang troops were finally installed, as agreed by Chiang Kaishek and Stalin.

As the largest former Russian settlement outside the USSR, Harbin has been acutely aware of Soviet colonial eyes, and the outward manifestation is the large-scale air-raid tunnelling in the city. On the ethnic score, there is nothing to fear as there are hardly any Russian settlers left (the total population of Harbin is 2.6 million, including the outlying areas). Perhaps the Chinese have more to fear from each other – during the Cultural Revolution, according to one source, rival factions took to the air to drop bombs on one another.

Heilongjiang Province has recently started to develop cross-border trade and tourism with the Soviet Union; a Soviet consulate is planned in Harbin. For travellers on the Trans-Siberian Railway, Harbin is a possible starting or finishing point.

The city's industry grew with its role as a transport hub and predominantly includes

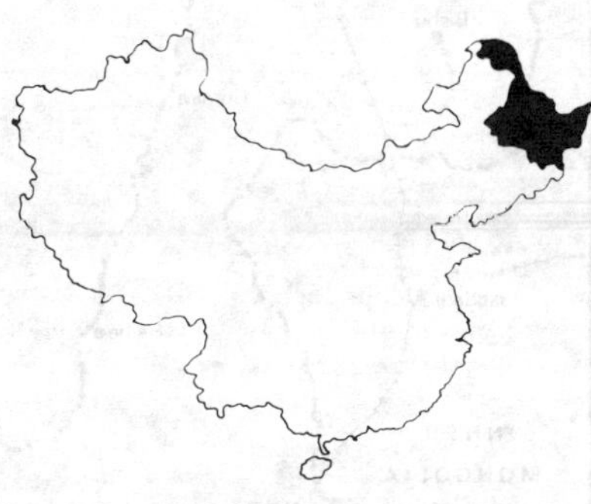

food-processing and the manufacture of machinery, tools, cement, paper, pharmaceuticals, electric motors and steam turbines. Factory wastes have taken their toll on the Songhua River, where the fish population has been decimated (there are reports of mercury poisoning) and the water level has dropped.

Information

CITS This office (☎ 221088) is in a separate building in the grounds of the Swan Hotel *(tiāné fàndiàn)*, at 73 Zhongshan Lu on the No 3 bus route. CITS can arrange specific tours for diverse needs and tastes, including elderly health build-up, bicycling, Chinese law, trade unions, steam locos, hunting, welding technology, honey production, abacus twiddling, etc.

Public Security Bureau This is on Zhongyang Dajie (see map).

Money The Bank of China is on Hongjun Jie near the International Hotel.

Post & Telecommunications The post office is at the corner of Dongda Zhijie and Fendou Lu. The telecommunications office

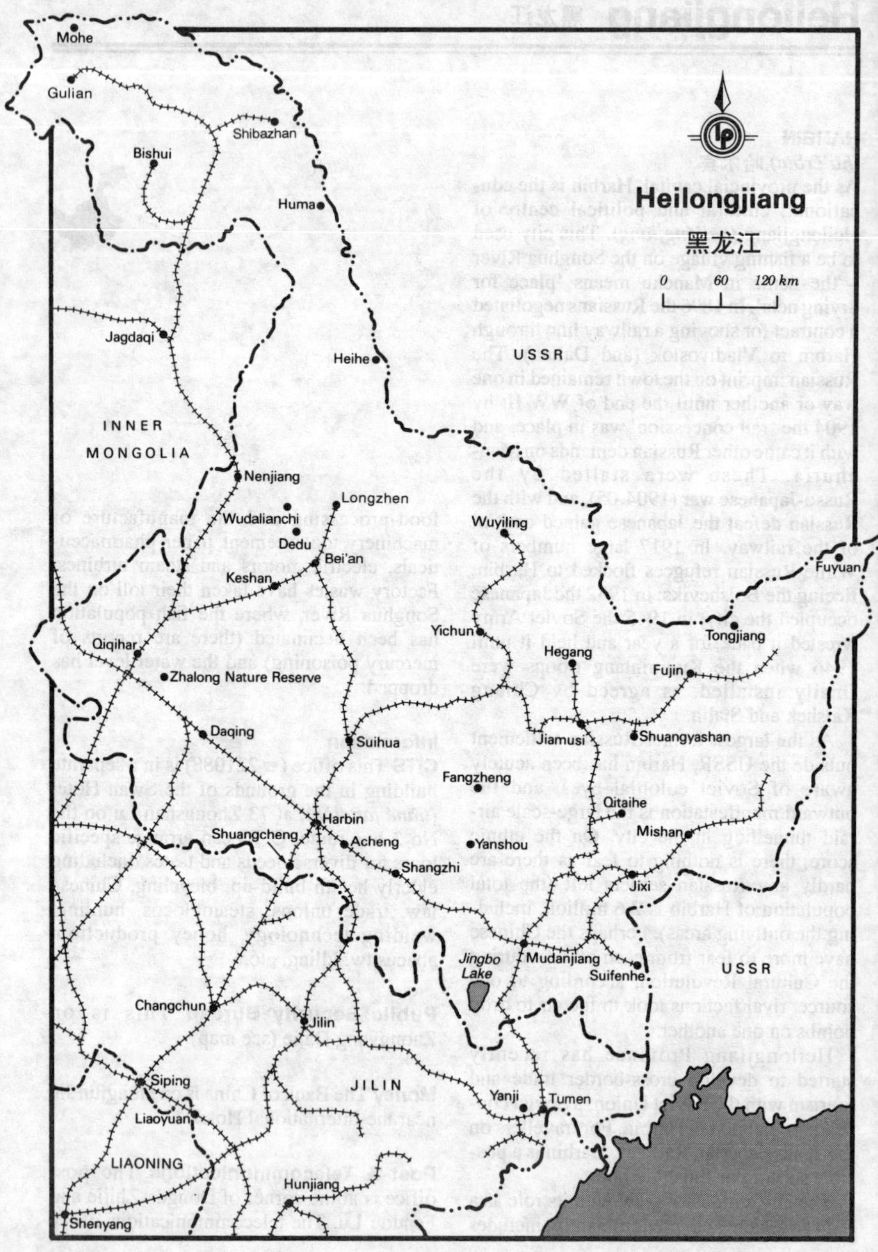
Heilongjiang
黑龙江
0 60 120 km
Mohe
Gulian
Shibazhan
Bishui
Huma
Jagdaqi
Heihe
USSR
INNER
MONGOLIA
Nenjiang
Longzhen
Wudalianchi
Dedu
Bei'an
Keshan
Wuyiling
Fuyuan
Yichun
Tongjiang
Hegang
Fujin
Qiqihar
Zhalong Nature Reserve
Daqing
Suihua
Jiamusi
Shuangyashan
Fangzheng
Qitaihe
Harbin
Shuangcheng
Acheng
Yanshou
Mishan
Shangzhi
Jixi
Mudanjiang
Suifenhe
USSR
Jingbo
Lake
Changchun
Jilin
JILIN
Siping
Yanji
Tumen
Liaoyuan
LIAONING
Hunjiang
Shenyang

is also on Fendou Lu, two blocks from the post office.

Architecture

Put wandering around the market areas and the streets high on your list. There's a very different kind of architectural presence in Harbin – Soviet spires, cupolas and scalloped turreting. The area known as Daoliqu, near Zhongyang Lu, is good to investigate.

Harbin has several dozen Orthodox churches, but most were ransacked during the Cultural Revolution and have since been boarded up or converted for other uses. A few stray onion-domes punctuate the skyline.

The Daoliqu district, in the section toward the banks of the Songhua River, also has the best speciality shops and some market activity, and is worth your time on foot. Another shopping and market area is to be found north-east of the International Hotel, a short walk away at Dazhi Dajie.

Children's Railway

(értóng gōngyúan) 儿童公园

This railway in the Children's Park was built in 1956. It has two km of track plied by a miniature diesel pulling seven cars with seating for 190; the round trip (Beijing-Moscow?) takes 20 minutes. The crew and administrators are kids under the age of 13.

Stalin Park

(sīdàlín gōngyúan) 斯大林公园

Down by the river, this is a tacky strip stacked with statues; it's the main perambulating zone, with recreation clubs for the locals. A 42-km embankment was constructed along the edge to curb the unruly Songhua River – hence the Flood Control Monument which was built in 1958. The sandy banks of the Songhua take on something of a beach atmosphere in summer, with boating, ice-cream stands,and photo booths. It's possible to travel on tour boats arranged through CITS but you might like to investigate local docks for a quick sortie down the Songhua.

During winter the river becomes a road of ice (when it's one metre thick it can support a truck) and the Stalin Park/Sun Island area is the venue for hockey, skating, ice-sailing, sledding and sleighing – equipment can be hired.

Sun Island

(tàiyángdǎo gōngyúan) 太阳岛公园

Opposite Stalin Park and reached by a ferry hop is Sun Island, a sanatorium-recreational zone still under construction. The island covers 3800 hectares and has a number of artificial features – a lake, hunting range, parks, gardens, forested areas – all being worked on to turn this into Harbin's biggest touring attraction. In summer there's swimming and picnics; in winter it's skating and other sports. There are a number of restaurants and other facilities on Sun Island.

Japanese Germ Warfare Experimental Base – 731 Division

(rìběn xìjūn shíyàn jīdì) 日本细菌实验基地

If you haven't visited concentration camps such as Belsen or Auschwitz, a similar lesson in the horrors of extermination can be learnt at this base. Take bus No 338 from the main railway station to the terminal, which is close to Pingfangqu.

In 1939 the Japanese army set up a top-secret, germ-warfare research centre here. Japanese medical experts experimented to their hearts' content on Chinese, Soviet, Korean, British and other prisoners. Over four thousand were exterminated in bestial fashion: some were frozen or infected with bubonic plague, others were injected with syphilis, and many were roasted alive in furnaces. When the Soviets took back Harbin in 1945, the Japanese hid all trace of the base. The secret would probably have remained buried forever, but a tenacious Japanese journalist dragged out the truth only recently. Japan's medical profession was rocked by the news that some of its leading members had a criminal past which had hitherto escaped detection. Another disturbing angle to the story was the claim that the Americans granted freedom to the perpetra-

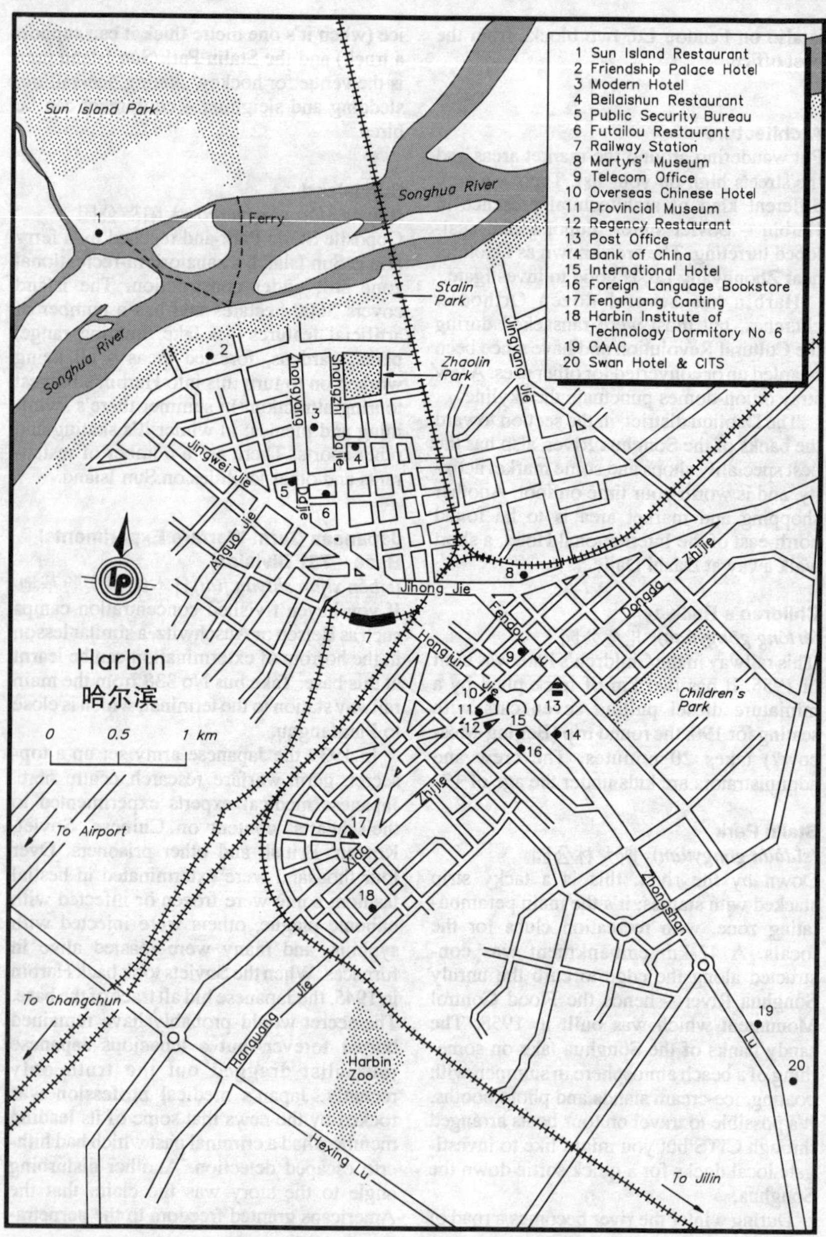
1 Sun Island Restaurant
2 Friendship Palace Hotel
3 Modern Hotel
4 Beilaishun Restaurant
5 Public Security Bureau
6 Futailou Restaurant
7 Railway Station
8 Martyrs' Museum
9 Telecom Office
10 Overseas Chinese Hotel
11 Provincial Museum
12 Regency Restaurant
13 Post Office
14 Bank of China
15 International Hotel
16 Foreign Language Bookstore
17 Fenghuang Canting
18 Harbin Institute of Technology Dormitory No 6
19 CAAC
20 Swan Hotel & CITS
Sun Island Park
Songhua River
Ferry
Stalin Park
Zhaolin Park
Jingyang Jie
Zhongyang Dajie
Shangzhi Dajie
Jingwei Jie
Anguo Jie
Dajie
Jihong Jie
Hongjun Jie
Fendou Lu
Dongdazhijie
Children's Park
Zhongshan Lu
Harbin
哈尔滨
0 0.5 1 km
To Airport
To Changchun
Hanguang Jie
Harbin Zoo
Hexing Lu
To Jilin

1 太阳岛餐厅
2 友谊宫
3. 马迭尔宾馆
4 北鹿彝饭店
5 公安局外事科
6 福泰楼饭店
7 火车站
8 东北烈士馆
9 电信局
10 华侨饭店
11 省博物馆
12 丽晶美食中心
13 邮局
14 中国银行
15 国际饭店
16 外文书店
17 凤凰餐厅
18 哈尔滨工业大学 第六宿舍
19 中国民航
20 天鹅饭店

tors of these crimes in return for their research data.

Other Attractions & Non-Attractions

Skiers can head for Shangzhi close to Harbin, but it's best to bring your own equipment and first check whether the lift is operating with CITS. In warmer times there's the Harbin Music Festival, a 12-day event that takes place in July (it was suspended during the Cultural Revolution).

The **Retirement Home for Foreigners** *(wàiqiáo yǎnglǎo yùan)* at 1 Wenjing Jie is unique in China. Koreans, Americans, Japanese, Russians or stateless persons spend their last years here. Many of them have interesting tales to tell and many were stranded here as a result of wars and were unable to return to their homeland (the White Russians for example). A few were born in China and even had citizenship during the Kuomintang era, but lost it when the Communists came to power because they had the wrong racial background.

The **Provincial Museum** *(shěng bówùgǔan)* is opposite the International Hotel and has some boring historical and natural history sections; the **Industrial Exhibition Hall** is dead boring; the **zoo** *(dòngwùyúan)* is lukewarm but does have some Manchurian tigers and red-crowned cranes. The **Martyrs' Museum** *(dōngběi lièshì gǔan)* in the centre of town has relics from the anti-Japanese campaign.

Ice Lantern Festival

(bīngdōng jié) 冰灯节

If you don't mind the cold, then try not to miss Harbin's main drawcard, the Ice Lantern Festival held from 1 January to early March (the Lunar New Year) in Zhaolin Park. Fanciful sculptures are made in the shapes of animals, plants, buildings or motifs taken from legends. Some of the larger ones have included a crystalline ice bridge and an ice elephant that children could mount from the tail in order to slide down the trunk. At night the sculptures are illuminated from the inside, turning the place into a temporary fantasyland.

Places to Stay

The only budget place to stay is the *Harbin Institute of Technology* (☎ 228383, ext 4673) *(hā'ěrbīn gōngyè dàxúe)*. It's supposedly for foreign teachers, but if you're polite you can talk your way in. Dormitory No 6 is on Hanguang Jie – rooms go for Y25.

The *International Hotel* (☎ 31441) *(gúojì fàndiàn)*, at the intersection of Xida Zhijie and Hongjun Jie, is less than one km from the railway station. Singles cost Y96 and doubles are Y120. It's run-down and overpriced – only the location is good.

The *Overseas Chinese Hotel (húaqiáo fàndiàn)* is on Honglun Jie, even closer to the railway station than the International. It was under renovation at the time of this writing. When it reopens, prices for singles are projected to cost around Y100 and doubles, Y120. It's impossible to say at this time if they will have dormitories – before renovation, they didn't.

The *Swan Hotel* (☎ 220201) *(tiānė fàndiàn)*, 73 Zhongshan Lu, is the classiest place in town. Doubles range from Y98 to Y120. It's a nice place to stay, but is a long way from the station. CITS is installed in the same compound and CAAC is nearby. Frequent minibuses that run down Zhongshan Lu can take you to the hotel for Y1.

The *Modern Hotel* (☎ 465842) *(mǎdié'ěr bīngǔan)* is not modern at all. It's an old place with character on Zhongyang Dajie in one of Harbin's more colourful neighbourhoods. Doubles range from Y80 to Y120. Beware of overcharging in the hotel's restaurant.

The *Friendship Palace Hotel (yǒuyí gōng bīngǔan)* is a classy place next to the Songhua River. Doubles start at Y120.

Places to Eat

A practice almost unique to Harbin is that red lanterns hang above the door outside every restaurant. It's a rating system – the more lanterns, the higher the standard and price. It's very convenient for budget travellers – if you see five lanterns out the front, you'd better avoid the place unless you want to splurge.

The *Har Har Le Restaurant (hāhālè fàndiàn)* is in the same building as the Overseas Chinese Hotel. It's cafeteria-style, with good food and cheap prices; there's no need to look at menus, just point to what you want.

The *Fenghuang Canting* is small but has great food and is very popular. It's off Xida Zhijie (see map).

There are a couple of places around Stalin Park. On the edge of Zhaolin Park at 113 Shangzhi Dajie is the *Beilaishun Restaurant* (☎ 49027) *(běiláishùn fàndiàn)* serving Muslim beef and mutton dishes upstairs and also hotpot in winter. The *Futailou Restaurant* (☎ 417598) *(fútàilóu fàndiàn)* at 19 Xi Shisandao Jie serves Beijing roast duck and other dishes, but you need to order two days in advance for regional specialties.

As for the hotels, the *International* sells a lot of expensive exotica. Anyone for grilled bear paws? Or some stewed moose nose with monkey-leg mushrooms? This place seems to be popular with Soviet tourists.

The top of the line in terms of food and prices is the *Regency Gourmet Centre (lìjīng měishí zhōngxīn)* across the street from the International Hotel, under the Northern Theatre. There's good food and good service, but it's expensive.

If you visit Sun Island, you can get a good meal at the *Sun Island Restaurant (tàiyángdǎo cāntīng)*.

Getting There & Away

Air From Harbin there are flights to Beijing (twice daily, Y338); Canton (daily, Y1047); Chengdu; Chongqing; Dalian (Y286); Fuzhou; Heihe (daily, Y172); Jiamusi (daily, Y124); Mudanjiang (once weekly, Y100); Qingdao; Qinhuangdao; Shanghai (six days a week, Y623); Shenyang (daily, Y164); Ürümqi (Y1293); Xi'an (twice weekly, Y686); and Xiamen (Y917).

CAAC (☎ 52334) has its office at 87 Zhongshan Lu close to the Swan Hotel.

Bus There is a long-distance bus station near Sankeshu railway station which takes care of a large proportion of bus departures. Other buses depart from the main railway station.

Train There are frequent departures to Beijing, Shanghai and points in between. Harbin to Changchun takes four hours; to Shenyang, nine hours; to Beijing, 18 hours. Rail connections to Qiqihar, Mudanjiang and Jiamusi are regular but slow.

Boat Boat services operate from mid-April to late November. A regular service between Harbin and Jiamusi takes 27 hours. Buy tickets from the boat dock on Bei Qidao Jie.

Getting Around

There are over 20 bus routes in Harbin; buses start running at 5 am and finish at 10 pm (9.30 pm in winter). Bus No 1 or trolley bus No 3 will take you from the hotel area to

Stalin Park. CITS has a boat tour along the Songhua River which lasts 2½ hours and costs Y15 per head.

JINGBO LAKE

(jìngbó hú) 镜泊湖

The name means 'mirror lake', and it's probably the most impressive sight in Heilongjiang. The lake covers an area of 90 sq km; it's 45 km long from north to south, with a minimum width of 600 metres and a maximum of six km, and is dotted with islets. The nature reserve encompasses a strip of forest, hills, streams, pools and cliffs around the lake and there is a lava cave in the area. The main pastime is fishing (the season is from June to August); tackle and boats can be hired (prices negotiable). Different varieties of carp (silver, black, red-tailed, crucian) are the trophies.

It's best to avoid peak season (July and August) – autumn is nice when the leaves are changing colour. Get out on the lake in a rowing boat – there are loads of stars at night. Be sure to visit the Diaoshuilou Waterfall. Lots of trees, hills, pavilions, rock gardens, and pleasant walks around the lake, but during the peak summer season you'll have to hike through the jostling mob of photo posers, litter collectors and knick-knack sellers. The Chinese say it's only fun when it's crowded.

The name Mirror Lake comes from a legend related to a wicked king who sent his minister out every week to find a beautiful girl – if the girl didn't suit him, he'd have her killed. A passing monk gave the king a mirror to aid in the selection, saying that this mirror would retain the reflection of a true beauty, even after she turned away. The minister duly trotted off, found a beautiful girl at the lake, and discovered that the mirror test worked. The king immediately asked for the lady's hand. 'What is the most precious thing in the world?' asked the girl. The king thought for some time. 'Power', he replied. Upon hearing this, the girl threw the mirror into the lake, a storm broke out, and she vanished.

Places to Stay

The centre of operations is *Jingbo Villa (jìngbó shānzhūang)*, at the north end of the lake. Double rooms start from Y50 – dormitories exist but it will be a battle to get into one. There are other, cheaper hotels around the lake but they aren't allowed to take foreigners. The smallish Diaoshuilou Waterfall (20 metres high, 40 metres wide) is north of Jingbo Villa and within easy hiking distance of it.

Getting There & Away

The best approach is by rail from Harbin. Take a train to Dongjing *(dōngjīng)*. From there, it's one hour by minibus to the lake.

Some trains only go as far as Mudanjiang, a city of 700,000 people. If you get off at Mudanjiang, it's three hours by bus to Jingbo Lake. Buses depart between 6 and 7 am from the square in front of Mudanjiang station, summer only (from June to September). There are two or three trains a day between Harbin and Mudanjiang. If you have to spend a night in Mudanjiang, turn right outside the station (right over the railway bridge) and walk for 20 minutes to the Beishan Hotel (☎ 25734) *(běishān bīngǔan)*, on Xinhua Lu opposite the park. Doubles go for Y64. CITS is in room 105.

From Mudanjiang and Dongjing, there are also slower connections by rail to Tumen (one train daily, about six hours), Suifenhe (one train daily, five hours from Mudanjiang) and Jiamusi (two trains a day, about 10 hours).

There are flights between Mudanjiang and Harbin once a week for Y100 – the same flight continues on to Beijing.

SUIFENHE

(sūifēnhé) 绥芬河

This town achieved commercial importance in 1903 with the opening of the South Manchurian Railway, which was a vital link in the original Trans-Siberian route running from Vladivostok to Moscow via Manchuria.

The railway was later rerouted via Khabarovsk to Vladivostok and Nakhodka. In recent years, cross-border trade has livened up here and there's even some Soviet tourism. The grandiose nickname of 'Little Moscow of the East' certainly suits the

Russian atmosphere in Suifenhe, but there's little else to do unless you like a lusty Sino-Soviet friendship evening when, according to a local tourist brochure, Soviet visitors sing 'Evening in Suburban Moscow'. Although the whole place is Chinese, most of the buildings are Russian leftovers in the elegant, gingerbread style from the turn of the century – reminders of pre-Revolutionary times. There's one train (daily at 6.45 am) from Mudanjiang to Suifenhe; the trip takes about six hours and returns from Suifenhe at 1.12 pm.

WUDALIANCHI

(wǔdàliánchí) 五大连池

Wudalianchi, which means 'the five large connected lakes', is a nature reserve and health spot which has also been turned into a 'volcano museum'. To get there, take a six-hour train ride northwards from Harbin to Bei'an, where there are regular buses covering the 60 km to the lakes.

This area has a long history of volcanic activity. The most recent eruptions were during 1719 and 1720 when lava from craters blocked the nearby Bei River and formed this series of five barrier lakes. The malodorous mineral springs are the source of legendary cures and thus the No 1 attraction for hordes of chronically sick, who slurp the waters or slap mud onto themselves. To increase blood pressure, immerse your feet in a basin of the water; to decrease blood pressure, immerse your head. Baldness, cerebral haemorrhages, skin diseases and gastric ulcers are a few of the ailments helped by drinking the water or applying mud packs. Some of the cures are only temporary.

HEILONG RIVER BORDERLANDS

(hēilóngjiāng biānjìng) 黑龙江边境

Much of the north-eastern border between China and the Soviet Union follows the course of the Heilongjiang (Black Dragon River), also known to the Soviets as the Amur River. Several places along this river are open to foreigners, so it should now be possible to see some Siberian forest and the dwindling settlements of Siberian tribes such as the Oroqen, Ewenki, Hezhen and Daur.

The Oroqen minority lived, until recently, the nomadic life of forest hunters. Recent estimates put their numbers at about 4000, scattered over a vast area. Their traditional tent, called a *xianrenzhu*, is covered with birch bark in the summer and deerskin in the winter. Hunting as well as the raising of reindeer are still their main activities. A major source of income is deer hunting since the deer's embryo, antlers, penis and tail are highly prized in Chinese medicine.

The Oroqen lifestyle is changing rapidly, although they retain their self-sufficiency. Boots, clothes and sleeping bags are made from deerskins; baskets, eating utensils and canoes are made from birch bark; horses or reindeer provide transport. Their food consists mostly of meat, fish and wild plants. Oroqens are particularly fond of raw deer liver washed down with fermented mare's milk. Meat is often preserved by drying and smoking.

Interesting facets of their religion included (and probably still do to a lesser degree) a belief in spirits and consulting shamans. It was once taboo to kill bears. If this happened, perhaps in self-defence, a complicated rite was performed to ask the bear's 'forgiveness' and its bones were spread in the open on a tall frame of willow branches. This 'wind burial' was also the standard funeral for a human. Our word 'shaman' means an 'agitated or frenzied person' in the Manchu-Tungus language. Such persons could enter

Oroqen Man

a trance, become 'possessed' by a spirit and then officiate at religious ceremonies.

It's hard to determine how much of their culture the Oroqens have kept. Official publications trumpet stories of a wondrous change from primitive nomadism to settled consumerism. The following extract from a *China Daily* article about sedentary Oroqen at Shiba Zhan in 1986 clearly demonstrates the Han assumption that they know what's best for a minority:

Meng Pinggu, a venerable senior citizen in the community, started hunting at age 12. At his home, bear skins and a hunting rifle hang on the walls, and a birch canoe is under the eaves. But a colour TV set and washing machine overshadow the old furniture.

Meng has shifted from hunting to forestry. In the evening, the family gets together and watches TV. 'Now we Oroqens can see movies at home,' he said.

The Oroqens – China's Nomadic Hunters by Qiu Pu (Foreign Languages Press, Beijing, 1983) is a surprisingly informative publication, providing you skip the political salad dressing.

In Harbin the CITS office runs boat tours between Huma, Heihe and Tongjiang. Telescopes on the boats will give you a better look at Soviet settlements or even at Blagoveshchensk, a large Soviet port opposite Heihe.

Assuming you have at least two weeks to spare and are flexible about transport, an independent trip should also be viable during the summer – take some iron rations and insect repellent. Connections between Harbin and this region include the fast option of a flight to Heihe, the much slower option of a train at least as far as Jagdaqi, possibly further, and, of course, buses – God bless the old bangers! – to the ends of the wilderness. Remember, this is a border region where it's best to tread softly, since Caucasian features can easily be mistaken for those of a visitor from the other side.

Mohe

(mòhé) 漠河

Natural wonders are the attraction at Mohe, China's northernmost town, sometimes known as the 'Arctic of China'. In mid-June, the sun is visible in the sky for as long as 22 hours. The northern lights (aurora borealis) are another colourful phenomenon seen in the sky at Mohe. China's lowest absolute temperature of -52°C was recorded here in 1965; on normal winter days temperatures of -40°C are common.

During May 1987 this area was devastated by China's worst forest fire in living memory. The towns of Mohe and Xilinji were completely gutted, more than 200 people died and over one million hectares of forest were destroyed.

Try for a permit at the Public Security Bureau in Jagdaqi *(jiāgédáqí)* in Inner Mongolia. To reach Mohe would require a rail trip north from Jagdaqi to Gulian, followed by a 34-km bus ride.

Heihe

(hēihé) 黑河

Heihe borders the Soviet Union. Due to the recent thawing in relations between the two countries, there is a steadily increasing amount of cross-border trade and even a fledgling tourist industry. Chinese tour groups now are able to cross the border to Blagoveshchensk. Soviet tourists visiting Heihe like to eat Chinese food and stock up on goods which are apparently hard to find in the USSR. Chinese tourists don't find much to buy in the Soviet Union, but are impressed to see a city where nobody spits and people actually stand in line.

There are still problems for foreigners wishing to visit Blagoveshchensk. A Soviet visa is needed, and a re-entry visa for China would also be necessary. All this must be arranged in Beijing, not in Heihe. In theory, one could cross the border at Blagoveshchensk and take a train 109 km to Belogorsk, which is on the Trans-Siberian Railway, then continue on to Europe. This would require a tourist visa (as opposed to a transit visa). This is expensive – you are required to pay for all hotels in advance and rates are exorbitant. Furthermore, the Soviet travel agency, Intourist, has no hotel in either Blagoveshchensk or Belogorsk which they are willing to book Westerners into. Consequently, they will not issue a visa for those places. Therefore, the most you might be able to manage is a day trip from Heihe to

Blagoveshchensk and back again. In other words, if you want to do the Trans-Siberian, you'll have to depart from Beijing, not Heihe. Perhaps this will change some day – especially if Intourist realises that there is money to be made by opening this route to foreigners.

There are daily flights between Harbin and Heihe for Y172. Boats also connect Heihe with Mohe and Tongjiang. The railway does not reach Heihe.

Tongjiang

(tóngjiāng) 同江

Tongjiang lies at the junction of the Songhua and Heilong rivers. They swell to a combined width of 10 km but their respective colours, black for the Heilong and yellow for the Songhua, don't mix until later.

The Hezhen minority, a mere 1300 people, lives almost entirely from fishing in this region. A local delicacy is sliced, raw fish with a spicy vinegar sauce. Apart from carp and salmon, the real whopper here is the huso sturgeon *(húang yú)* which can grow as long as three metres and weigh up to 500 kg!

Tongjiang has boat and bus connections with Jiamusi; boats also connect with Heihe.

Fuyuan

(fǔyǔan) 抚远

The earliest sunrise in China starts at 2 am in Fuyuan. Close to Fuyuan is the junction of the Heilong and Ussuri rivers. On the Soviet side is the city of Khabarovsk; on the Chinese side, there's the tiny outpost of Wusu which has 20 inhabitants who see visitors only during the salmon season in September.

JIAMUSI

(jiāmùsī) 佳木斯

North-east of Harbin is Jiamusi. Once a fishing village, it mushroomed into a city of half a million people. It now smelts aluminium, manufactures farm equipment and refines sugar, and has a paper mill, plastics factory and electrical appliances factory.

Among the sights are **Sumuhe Farm**, in the suburbs of Jiamusi. This farm grows ginseng and raises over 700 head of sika and red deer for the antlers. Martens, close kin to the weasel, are also raised. It's not really such a strange combination – in fact the 'three treasures' of the north-east are ginseng, deer antlers and sable pelts. Each of these are also well represented further south in Jilin Province, where production is largely domesticated. Wild ginseng from the Changbaishan area fetches astronomical sums on the Hong Kong market.

Another curious item in the north-eastern pharmacopoeia includes frog oil, taken from a substance in the frog's ovary. These and other ingredients will arrive in soups or with stewed chicken if a banquet is ordered at a ritzy hotel. (Non-banquet food on grease-laden dining tables is abysmal in the north-east region, so a visit to the local medicine shop is obligatory for stays of more than a week's duration.)

The **New Friendship Farm** is about 110 km east of Jiamusi on the railway line, a state-run frontier enterprise that is the pride of Heilongjiang – the pioneers who built it arrived in the 1950s and now number around 100,000, organised into numerous agricultural brigades.

The **Village of Fools** is not the pride of Heilongjiang. It's in Huachuan County to the east and north-east of Jiamusi. The cretins and bearers of bulbous goitre are being studied at Jiamusi Medical College – the cause of their problems is suspected to be a dietary deficiency.

Getting There & Away

Jiamusi is connected by rail to Harbin (15 hours), Dalian and Mudanjiang. Steamers ply the Songhua River so it may be possible to travel between Harbin and Jiamusi by water. There are also flights between Harbin and Jiamusi.

DAQING

(dàqìng) 大庆

Daqing is an oil-boom town which appeared in the swamplands in 1960. This is one of those triumph-of-the-spirit towns, and demonstrates China's awesome ability to mobilise large numbers of people for the cause. The first drilling began in the 1950s with Soviet technical assistance; when the Russians withdrew in 1959, the Chinese decided to carry on alone. Shortly after, the first well gushed, and a community of tents, wooden shanties and mud housing erupted in the sub-zero wilderness. By 1975, Daqing was supplying 80% of the PRC's crude oil, but production has since tapered off. Most of the oil is piped to the coast near Dalian.

There's no town centre in Daqing as such – some 8000 oil wells with small communities attached are scattered throughout the 5000-sq-km area. Saertu, however, serves as the administrative, economic and cultural sector, with residential and office buildings, a library, stores, 'modernisation' playground, exhibition halls and greenhouses. The population of the Daqing area has swelled to 800,000. There's a spartan hotel in Saertu, and you may be allowed to view model sections of the Daqing area such as medical facilities, the school or recreational props.

QIQIHAR

(qíqíhā'ěr) 齐齐哈尔

Qiqihar is the gateway to the Zhalong Nature Reserve, a bird-watching area 35 km to the south-east. It's also one of the oldest settlements in the north-east. The town itself is industrialised with a population of over a million and produces locomotives, mining equipment, steel, machine tools and motor vehicles. There's not much to see here – a zoo, a stretch of riverside and the ice-carving festival from January to March.

The Hubin Hotel is a bargain at Y16. The more modern Crane City Hotel behind the Hubin is not recommended. You can reach the Hubin Hotel on trolley bus No 15 – it's seven stops from the railway station.

CITS (☎ 72016) is in the Hubin Hotel and the staff are very friendly. They can give you a lot of advice about the best places for watching birds.

Qiqihar is linked directly by rail to Beijing (about 22 hours) via Harbin (about four hours).

ZHALONG NATURE RESERVE

(zhálóng zìrán bǎohù qū)

The modest Zhalong Hotel has dormitories for Y15, double rooms for Y50, and offers tours through the freshwater marshes of the reserve for Y40 per day, in flat-bottom boats. The area is mainly of interest to the patient binoculared and rubber-booted ornithologist.

The Zhalong Reserve is at the north-west tip of a giant marsh, made up of about 210,000 hectares of reeds, moss and ponds. It lies strategically on a bird-migration path which extends from the Soviet Arctic, around the Gobi Desert, and down into South-East Asia, and some 180 different species of bird are found there, including storks, swans, geese, ducks, herons, harriers, grebes and egrets. The tens of thousands of winged migrants arrive from April to May, rear their young from June to August, and depart from September to October.

Birds will be birds – they value their privacy. While some of the cranes are over 1.5 metres tall, the reed cover is taller. The best time to visit is in spring before the reeds have a chance to grow.

The nature reserve, one of China's first, was set up in 1979. In 1981 the Chinese

Ministry of Forestry invited Dr George Archibald (director of the ICF, the International Crane Foundation) and Wolf Brehm (director of Vogelpark Walsrode, West Germany) to help set up a crane centre at Zhalong. Of the 15 species of cranes in the world, eight are found in China, and six are found at Zhalong. Four of the species that migrate here are on the endangered list: the red-crowned crane, the white-naped crane, the Siberian crane and the hooded crane. Both the red-crowned and white-naped cranes breed at Zhalong (as do the common and demoiselle cranes), while hooded and Siberian cranes use Zhalong as a stopover.

The centre of attention is the red-crowned crane, a fragile creature whose numbers at Zhalong (estimated to be 100 in 1979) were threatened by drainage of the wetlands for farming. The near-extinct bird is, ironically, the ancient symbol of immortality and has long been a symbol of longevity and good luck in the Chinese, Korean and Japanese cultures. With some help from overseas experts, the ecosystem at Zhalong has been studied and improved, and the number of these rare birds has risen. A small number of hand-reared (domesticated) red-crowned and white-naped cranes are kept in a pen at the sanctuary for viewing and study. On the eve of their 'long march' southwards in October, large numbers of cranes can be seen wheeling around, as if in farewell. The birds have been banded to unlock the mystery of their winter migration grounds (in either Korea or southern China).

Since the establishment of the International Crane Foundation, George Archibald and Ron Sauey have managed to create a 'crane bank' in Wisconsin, USA, stocking 14 of the 15 known species. They've even convinced the North Koreans to set up bird reserves in the mine-studded demilitarised zone between North and South Korea, and the travel baggage of these two countries includes suitcases full of Siberian crane-eggs picked up in Moscow (on one trip a chick hatched en route was nicknamed 'Aeroflot'). Last on the egg-list for the ICF is the black-necked crane, whose home is in remote Tibet and for whom captive breeding may be the final hope.

Getting There & Away

Zhalong is linked to Qiqihar by a good road, but there's not much traffic along it. There are occasional buses – you'll have to enquire to find them. The other alternative is to get a taxi, which will cost around Y30 after some bargaining. Hitching may be possible.

THE SOUTH-WEST

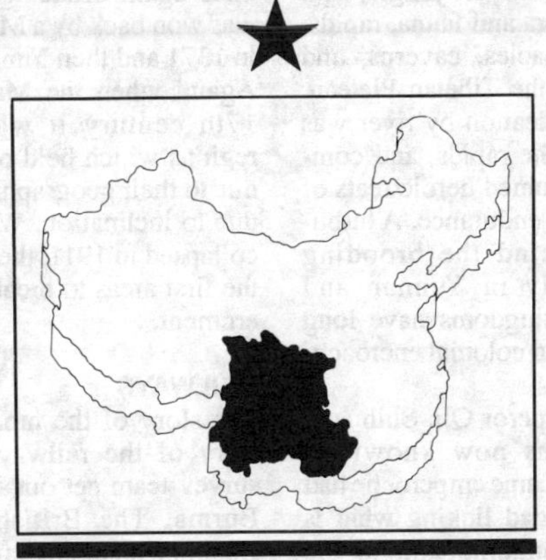

The South-West

INTRODUCTION

The south-west of China is a region of immense mountains and precipitous cliffs, covered by dense subtropical forests, and cut through by mountain rivers fed by melting snows. This is China's backyard jungle, with fertile basins, exotic flora and fauna, rapids, jagged limestone pinnacles, caverns, and peaks on the edges of the Tibetan Plateau. For centuries, communication by river was hazardous because of the rapids, and communication by road assumed heroic feats of human engineering and endurance. A turbulent history lies behind the brooding landscapes, especially in Yunnan and Sichuan where tribal kingdoms have long resisted Han Chinese and colonial encroachment.

The ancestors of Emperor Qin Shihuang conquered the regions now known as Sichuan, and after he became emperor he had his engineers build a road linking what is now Chengdu to Chongqing and to the regions further south. This road stretched 1600 km from the capital at Xianyang (near modern-day Xi'an). A third of its length is said to have been a 150-cm-wide wooden balcony cantilevered out from the sheer cliff, supported by wooden brackets driven into the rock face. Despite this new means of communication, and the creation (on paper) of new administrative divisions, the chiefs of the people south of Sichuan in the areas now known as Guizhou and Yunnan continued to rule the region themselves. In the later Han period they were given titles and ranks as tribute bearers to the imperial court, and gifts of silk in return for 'protecting' the southern borders of the Chinese empire – but their loyalty to the empire was mainly an invention of the Han and later Chinese historians.

After the fall of the Han Dynasty another thousand years was to pass before much of the south-west could be effectively integrated into the empire, and even then it continued to revert to independence at every opportunity. In the mid-13th century the region was almost pounded into final submission – this time by the Mongol armies of Mangu Khan. When the Mongol rule collapsed in 1368 the south-western regions once again broke with the north; Sichuan was won back by a Ming military expedition in 1371 and then Yunnan the following year. Again, when the Manchus invaded in the 17th century it was the south-western regions which held out the longest – partly due to their geographical location and partly due to inclination. When the Qing Dynasty collapsed in 1911, the south-west was one of the first areas to break with the central government.

RAILWAYS

The story of the modern south-west is the story of the railways. In 1875, a British survey team set out from Bhamo, in upper Burma. The British dream was to link Bhamo with Shanghai, easily 3000 km away. At about the same time, China's first railway tracks were coming out of Shanghai. They proceeded a short distance before they were torn up by superstitious mobs; an even worse fate befell the survey captain from Bhamo. By the early 1900s, various foreign railway gauges – Russian, Japanese, Anglo-American, German, Belgian-French – were running from the treaty ports as far as was necessary for trading and exploiting raw materials, but the south-west was almost forgotten. The only spur was a narrow-gauge French line, completed in 1910, linking Hanoi with Kunming. During WW II another spur was added in Guangxi, trailing off toward Guizhou. The first major link was the Baoji-Chengdu line (1956), which connected with the Chengdu-Chongqing line (1952), and thus with what for centuries was the south-west's lifeline, the Yangtse River.

The railway lines that today's travellers take for granted were completed with great difficulty and loss of life over recent decades. More than 5000 km of added track have sliced literally months off travel time in the south-west. The crowning achievement is the Kunming-Chengdu line. It took some 12 years to make and was finished in 1970, after workers bored through solid rock and bridged deep ravines and treacherous rivers.

Apart from Sichuan, the south-west region is relatively underpopulated. Since its (substantial) natural resources remain largely untapped, the mainstay is agriculture. Its industrial contribution to China as a whole is therefore negligible. The opening of the Chengdu-Kunming line has boosted various industries (including the manufacture of iron, steel, farm machinery and chemical fertilisers) in the cities along the way. It has also caused a gravitation of population to the railway havens. This railway line can be added to China's list of impossible projects that have become fact.

GETTING THERE & AROUND

Itineraries

Distances are stretched in the south-west (from Guangzhou to Kunming is 2216 km by rail) and the only way to speed it up is to fly between some points or cut out destinations. The well-worn (and proven) route is to take a boat from Canton to Wuzhou, then a bus to Guilin, and then to travel by train from Guiyang to Kunming, Emei, Chengdu, and Chongqing. From Chongqing people usually take the Yangtse ferry to Yichang or further. You can also proceed directly from Guiyang to Chongqing. Another option is to bypass the Yangtse trip and head directly to Xi'an from Chengdu.

Air

A favourite plane trip is from Canton to Guilin. It costs only Y133, and gives you an amazing view of the landscape as you fly in. The view is virtually guaranteed since CAAC will not take off if there is a rain cloud in the sky (though that can lead to lengthy delays). One of the newer services for tourists in Guilin is a flight over the karst formations – but you can get an aerial tour by flying there in the first place. You should also remember that the train ride from Canton to Guilin takes 20 hours(!) while flying takes 1½. The other useful flight is from Guilin to Kunming which costs Y225 and takes 1½ hours as compared with 33 hours on the train.

Many savvy travellers interested only in south-west China fly in directly from Bangkok to Kunming on one of the weekly CAAC flights, making Kunming a base for exploring the south-west. This saves having to get to Guilin, Guiyang or Kunming from Canton. There are also Dragonair flights from Dhaka.

An exit to consider is the flight from Kunming to Bangkok or Rangoon, but it needs to be planned well in advance. See the Getting There & Away chapter for the difficulties of getting to Myanmar.

Trains

Trains, the horrors of hard-seat travel in the south-west, are a pain in the neck. The problems arise, as they always do, with hard-class seating. No person in their right mind would want to endure hard-seat travel for more than 12 hours – although some masochistic travellers have survived 48-hour ordeals and arrived somewhat dazed, to put it mildly. Hard-sleeper is very comfortable (no crowding permitted), but the tickets may require as much as four days of waiting to get. In a place like Kunming, where you're likely to spend several days anyway, this is OK – just book a ticket out of the place immediately upon arrival.

If you wish to speed things up and carry on regardless, there's a slight chance of being able to upgrade your hard-seat to a hard-sleeper once you're on the train. This is eminently possible in northern China but not in the south-west. Soft-class sleepers will be available, but most low-budget travellers find them prohibitively expensive. You could try for a soft-seat, which is about the same price as a hard-sleeper ticket, but the trains in the south-west don't seem to include this class very often.

Apart from lack of sleepers, crowding is another big problem. Sichuan has the highest population of any province in China and Yunnan has the fewest rail lines so, at times, it seems that a whole quarter of humankind is hurtling down those tracks. Often the train is packed out before it even gets to the south-west, having loaded up in Shanghai. (The No 79 Shanghai-Kunming express is a good example – if you get on board at Guilin you have about zero hope of getting a hard-sleeper, and you may not even get a soft-sleeper.)

On some trains hard-seat carriages have people hanging from the rafters, watering their turtles in the wash basins, spitting everywhere. On one train two Westerners almost came to fisticuffs with locals over musical chairs in the unreserved section. If a foreigner got up to go to the toilet, a local would take the seat and refuse to budge; if the same displaced foreigner tried to pull the same stunt, all hell would break loose. At night, people are toe-to-toe in the aisles, or curled in foetal positions on the furniture. Hong Kongers refer to a phenomenon known as 'fishing' – which is when your head bobs up and down all night, with intermittent jerks.

One has to retain one's sense of humour in such situations – it pays to distract yourself. Compensation can be found in the sheer magnificence of the scenery along much of the route – you should try to travel by day as much as possible to downplay the discomfort of night. The Chengdu-Baoji train, for our money, is one of the most scenic rides. The Kunming-Chengdu route can be disappointing: engineering marvel that it is, it has tunnels every few metres (427 tunnels and 653 bridges to be exact, 40% of the route) – and these plunge one into a darkness that precludes any attempt to talk, read or view the landscape.

Since the actual act of travelling in the south-west eats up so much of your time there, some strategy is called for. It's better to stop in fewer places, get to know people and leave time for decent train reservations (intermediary stations are not empowered to issue hard-sleeper tickets). If you want to upgrade from hard seat to hard sleeper, check with the conductor in the car immediately behind the dining car – where his or her office is. If you're really in a bind in hard-class seating, can't upgrade and you've had all you can take, consider getting off at some intermediary station; tickets can be valid for up to seven days, and no re-purchase is necessary – you just use the same ticket to hop back on the next train heading in your direction. You'll be back in the same situation on the next train, but at least you'll get a refreshing night's sleep out of the stop (the 1st-class waiting room at the station can be wonderfully comfortable upon a midnight arrival). Another booster is to hang out in the dining-car after meal time – the staff may let you stay or they may kick you out, but it's worth a try.

Food supplies on south-west trains are not the greatest – you should stock up like a squirrel for the long journey ahead where possible (coffee, fruit, bread, chocolate?). Don't forget to carry a large mug, like every Chinese passenger does (enamel-coated metal mugs are best, since they don't break). The endless supply of hot water from the boiler at one end of every passenger car is useful not only for brewing tea or coffee but for making instant noodle soups, which can be purchased in larger railway stations.

Approximate rail prices can be calculated using the distance tables in the introductory Getting Around chapter. A hard-sleeper ticket from Guilin to Kunming will cost you around Y88 (Chinese price) – if you can get Chinese price, and if any hard-sleepers are available

Boat

An unexplored option is boating. The hovercraft from Hong Kong considerably speeds up the trip to Wuzhou, and from Wuzhou it should be possible to navigate to Nanning (this would be a very slow trip, but possibly a scenic one – larger boats anchor in mid-stream due to difficulties with rapids).

Guangxi 广西

Guangxi *(guǎngxī)* first came under Chinese sovereignty when a Qin Dynasty army was sent southwards in 214 BC to conquer what is now Guangdong Province and eastern Guangxi. Like the rest of the south-west the region was never firmly under the Chinese foot; the eastern and southern parts of Guangxi were occupied by the Chinese, while a system of indirect rule through chieftains of the aboriginal Zhuang people prevailed in the west.

The situation was complicated in the northern regions by the Yao (Mien) and Miao (Hmong) tribespeople, who had been driven there from their homelands in Hunan and Jiangxi by the advance of the Han Chinese settlers. Unlike the Zhuang, who easily assimilated Chinese customs, the Yao and Miao remained in the hill regions, often cruelly oppressed by the Han. There was continuous trouble with the tribes, with major uprisings in the 1830s and another coinciding with the Taiping Rebellion.

Today China's largest minority, the Zhuang, well over 13 million people, is concentrated in Guangxi. They're virtually indistinguishable from the Han Chinese. The last outward vestige of their original identity is their linguistic links with the Thai people. Back in 1955 Guangxi Province was reconstituted as the Guangxi Zhuang Autonomous Region; the total population numbers about 40 million people. Besides the Zhuang, Miao and Yao minorities, Guangxi is home to smaller numbers of Dong, Maonan, Mulao, Gin and Yi peoples.

The province remained a comparatively poor one until the present century. The first attempts at some modernisation of Guangxi were made during 1926-27 when the 'Guangxi Clique' (the main opposition to Chiang Kaishek within the Kuomintang) controlled much of Guangdong, Hunan, Guangxi and Hubei. After the outbreak of war with Japan the province was the scene of major battles and substantial destruction.

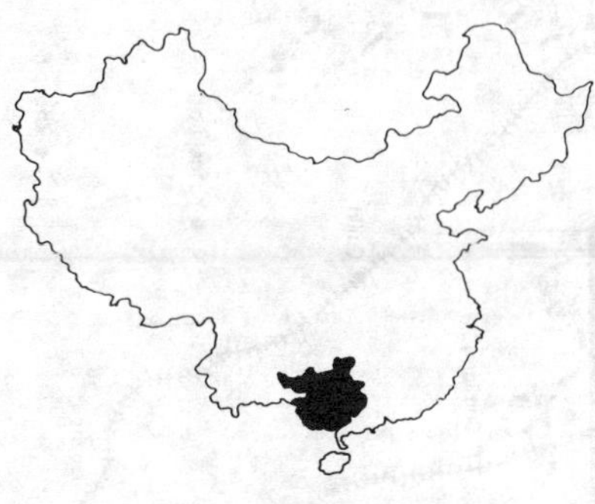

On a pleasanter note Guangxi also has Guilin, one of China's great attractions and the jumping-off point for exploring the bizarre landscape for which the region is famous. If Guilin seems too congested and touristy there's always the backpackers' Mecca of Yangshuo, a couple of hours down the Li River.

WUZHOU

(wúzhōu) 梧州

Situated at major and minor river junctions, Wuzhou was an important trading town in the 18th century. In 1897 the British dived in there, setting up steamer services to Canton, Hong Kong and later Nanning. A British consulate was established – which gives some idea of the town's importance as a trading centre at the time – and the town was also used by British and US missionaries as a launching pad for the conversion of the heathen Chinese.

The period after 1949 saw some industrial development with the establishment of a paper mill, food-processing factories, and machinery and plastics manufacturing, among other industries. During the Cultural Revolution, Guilin and the nearby towns appear to have become battlegrounds for

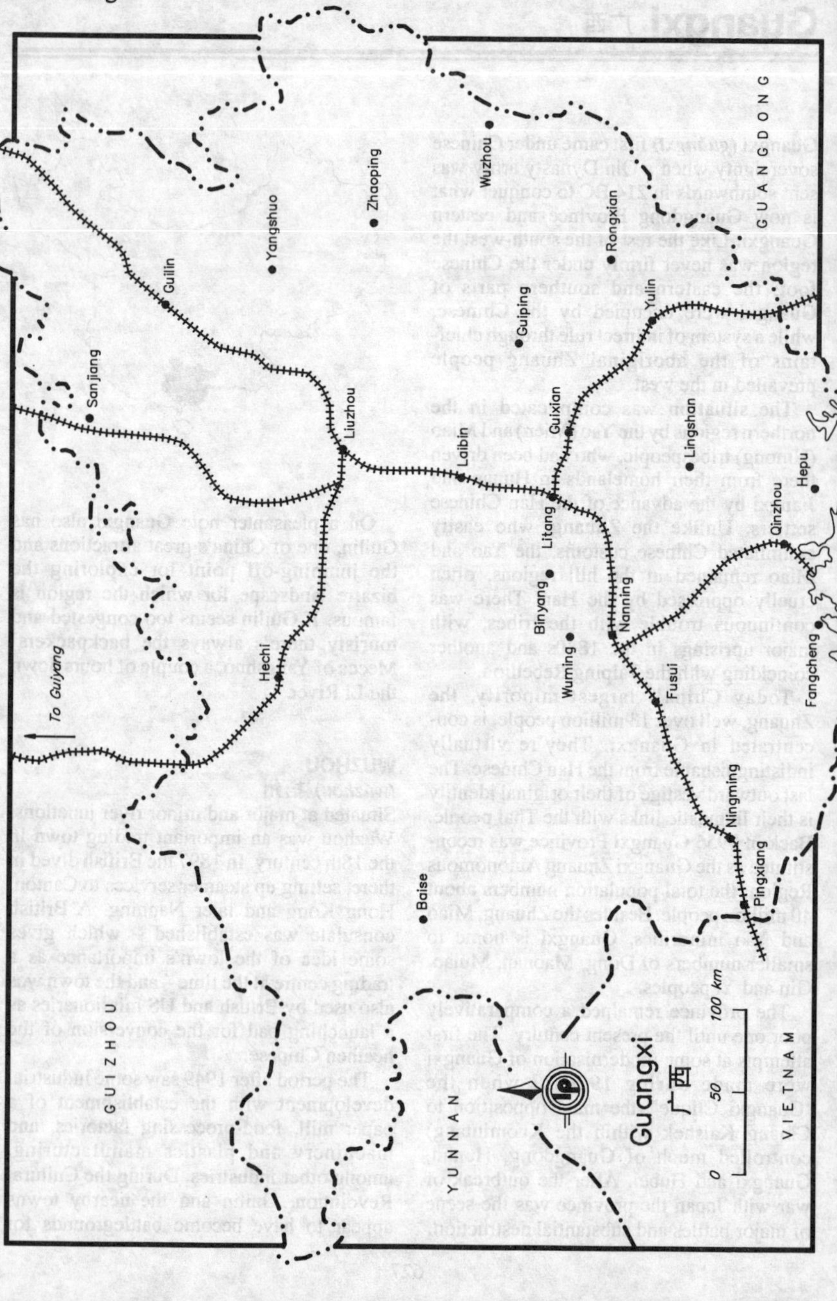

Guangxi 广西

GUANGDONG
GUIZHOU
YUNNAN
VIETNAM

To Guiyang

Zhaoping
Wuzhou
Yangshuo
Rongxian
Guilin
Yulin
Guiping
Sanjiang
Guixian
Liuzhou
Lingshan
Laibin
Hepu
Litang
Qinzhou
Binyang
Nanning
Wuming
Hechi
Fangcheng
Fusui
Ningming
Pingxiang
Baise

0 50 100 km

rivals, both claiming loyalty to Mao. In something approaching a civil war half Wuzhou was reportedly destroyed.

Today, the town has large snake depositories, probably the one thing of interest, but we don't know if you can see these. More than one million snakes are transported annually to Wuzhou (from places like Nanning, Liuzhou and Yulin) for export to the kitchens of Hong Kong, Macau and other countries. They're kept in cages at a storehouse in the north-east section of town.

Wuzhou also has some fine street markets, tailors, tobacco, herbs, roast duck and river life to explore. If you need a corn or wart removed then this is the place to come. Sidewalk beauticians armed with blades, needles and solutions will whip the nasties out in a jiffy, much to the interest of the crowd of onlookers.

For the most part travellers use Wuzhou as a stopover on the popular trip from Canton to Guilin/Yangshuo, taking a boat from Canton to Wuzhou and then a bus to Yangshuo or Guilin. A walk in Wuzhou turns up some unusual sights. Check out the industrial and residential areas on the west bank if you've got the time. The river level rises as much as 20 metres during the summer monsoon rains, which is why the town is perched high up on the banks.

Just north of town on a hill is the Western Bamboo Temple *(Xi Zhu Si)*, where around 20 Buddhist nuns live. The vegetarian restaurant there, open only for lunch, is excellent. You can walk to the temple along Zhongshan Lu from the bus station area in about half an hour.

Information

The post office is on Nanhuan Lu, just before the bridge. Good maps of the city, with bus routes, are available from shops near the boat dock and long-distance bus station. CITS has an office at the Beishan Hotel, but you shouldn't have to deal with them at all if you're just passing through – all onward tickets can easily be purchased at the boat dock or bus station.

Places to Stay

Along Xijiang Yilu, which runs parallel to the Xijiang River waterfront, are several inexpensive, adequate hotels. All hotels in Wuzhou apparently offer Overseas Chinese guests a 20-25% discount; prices quoted below are for non-Chinese.

The gloomy *Xinxi Hotel (xīnxī fàndiàn)*, two blocks west of the bus station on Xijiang Yilu, has somewhat dingy rooms for Y15 to Y25.

A bit farther west along Xijiang Yilu on the right is the better *Yuan Jiang Hotel (yuānjiāng fàndiàn)*, with basic doubles for Y10 to Y25 per person with private bath, Y8 in a triple with communal bath. The hotel directly opposite the bus station (Zhong Shan Hotel) *(zhōngshān fàndiàn)* doesn't take foreigners, in spite of the English signs reading 'Welcome'.

In the opposite direction on Xijiang Lu, east from the bus station/dock area, is the somewhat nicer *Baiyun (White Cloud) Hotel* (☎ 26683) *(báiyún fàndiàn)*, where triples are Y58, and doubles from Y70 to Y120.

If all of these above hotels are full (not likely), try the *Hebin Hotel (hébīn fàndiàn)*, across the Gui River near the bridge. Doubles cost around Y50 a night, but it's a bit of a concrete hulk.

The top spot in town is the *Beishan Hotel (běishān fàndiàn)* at 12 Beishan Lu up Dazhong Lu to the north of the city centre. They offer basic doubles starting at Y85. However, it's not very conveniently located for an overnight stay if you have an early boat or bus to catch.

Places to Eat

There's no shortage of small restaurants, especially in the vicinity of the boat docks and bus station. The illuminated mirages by the river bank are floating restaurants à la Aberdeen (Hong Kong) with extravagant names such as *Water City Paradise*.

If that doesn't appeal to you, there are other small restaurants along the east bank of the Gui River on Guijiang Erlu.

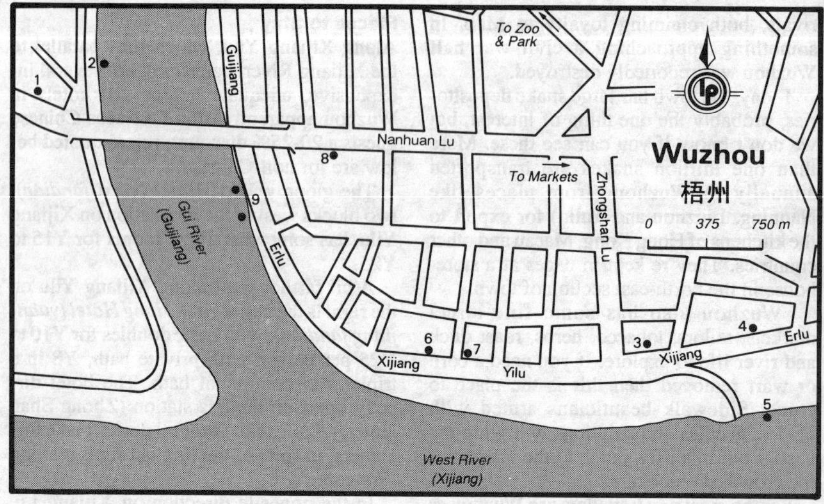

1 Hebin Hotel
2 Swimming Enclosure
3 Long-Distance Bus Station
4 Booking Office
5 Ferry Dock
6 Yuan Jiang Hotel
7 Xinxi Hotel
8 Post Office
9 Floating Restaurants

1 河滨饭店
2 游泳区
3 长途汽车站
4 售票处
5 渡船码头
6 燕江饭店
7 新西宾馆
8 邮局
9 水上饭店

Getting There & Away

Bus From Wuzhou's long-distance bus station there are two buses a day to Yangshuo (Y13) and Guilin (Y16). There are also daily departures to Nanning (Y30) and Canton (Y25).

You can also take an air-con bus to Nanning or Yangshuo. Tickets can be bought from the booth outside the Hebin Hotel, or from vendors near the long-distance bus station. Fares are about Y5 more than for the ordinary buses. It's really only worth it if the passengers keep the windows of the bus closed – unlikely unless the weather is bad).

All buses leave early in the morning. Be sure you confirm the time of departure vis-à-vis local time, since Wuzhou does not follow Beijing time during the summer. The ticket vendors may quote Beijing time even though the bus actually leaves according to local time (or vice versa). Even if your Chinese is good, this may mean pointing to the hands on your watch, since the locals have a habit of saying one time when they mean another; this can only be ascertained by the pointing method.

The trip from Wuzhou to Yangshuo takes seven hours, with another two hours to Guilin. The scenically impressive marathon from Wuzhou to Nanning takes 15 hours.

Boat There are daily boats between Wuzhou and Hong Kong; for details see the Getting There & Away chapter at the start of this book. Every other day (assuming the river level is sufficiently high) there are boats to Nanning (Y20, 36 hours) and Canton. Tickets can be bought from the booking office just east of Wuzhou's long-distance bus station. This office also sells tickets for the ferries to Canton and Zhaoqing.

GUILIN

(guìlín) 桂林

Guilin has always been famous in China for its scenery and has been eulogised in innumerable literary works, paintings and inscriptions since its founding. For many Western visitors Guilin *is* the landscape of China. For the Chinese it's the most beautiful spot in the world – the world of course meaning China.

The town sits in the midst of huge limestone peaks which jut haphazardly out of the plains. Except for these, Guilin looks like other modern Chinese towns, with its long wide streets lined with concrete blocks and factories. The place bursts with Chinese and Western tourists as well as modern high-rises, delivering a very disappointing first impression for most travellers.

The tourist scene is actually what makes Guilin so interesting. Despite 35 years of Communism and the brutal Cultural Revolution, the Chinese didn't forget the meaning of private enterprise. Very early on in the tourist boom there was a proliferation of privately run shops with souvenirs and exorbitant prices catering for the foreign horde. Travellers' coffee shops, bicycle hire shops, a substantial black market and one or two shonky discount-tour-ticket operators got off to an early start. Guilin was, and still is, a great place to learn about capitalism! However, most of the cheaper, backpacker-oriented operations have moved south to Yangshuo.

The city was founded during the Qin Dynasty and developed as a transport centre with the building of the Ling Canal which linked the important Pearl and Yangtse river systems. Under the Ming it was a provincial capital, a status it retained until 1914 when Nanning became the capital. During the 1930s and throughout WW II Guilin was a Communist stronghold and its population expanded from about 100,000 to over a million as people sought refuge here. Today it's the home of over 300,000.

All that said, it's not the place to see those magnificent peaks. A combination of heat, hazy skies, industry, congested streets, enormous crowds and over-development has sent the backpackers packing south to the smaller town and finer scenery of Yangshuo and beyond. Summer is the worst time to be in Guilin – but Yangshuo does not pale.

Information & Orientation

Most of Guilin lies on the west bank of the Li River. The main artery is Zhongshan Lu, which runs roughly parallel to the river on its western side. At the southern end of this street – that is, Zhongshan Nanlu – is Guilin south railway station where most trains pull in. The length of Zhongshan Lu is a hotchpotch of shops and tourist hotels and a gourmet's delight of restaurants.

Closer to the centre of town is Banyan Lake to the west of Zhongshan Lu, and Fir Lake on the eastern side. Further up is the main Zhongshan Lu/Jiefang Lu intersection. In this area you'll find the CITS office, the Public Security Bureau and places to hire bicycles, as well as one of Guilin's original up-market hotels and landmarks, the large Li River Hotel.

Jiefang Lu runs east-west across Zhongshan Lu. Heading east, it runs over Jiefang (Liberation) Bridge to the large Seven Star Park, one of the town's chief attractions. This is also where you'll find the upscale Ramada Renaissance Riverside Hotel. Most of the limestone pinnacles form a circle around the

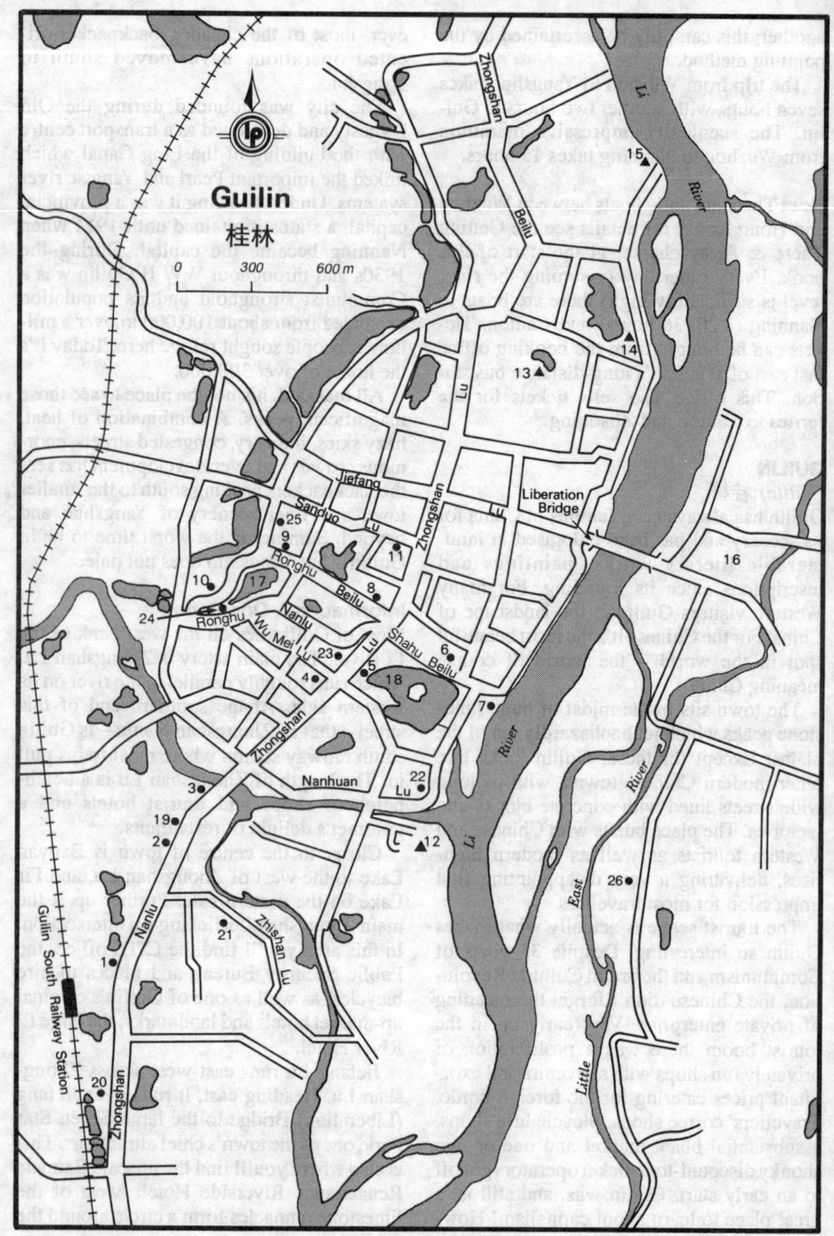
Guilin
桂林
0 300 600 m
Zhongshan Beilu
Li River
Jiefang Lu
Sanduo Lu
Liberation Bridge
Zhongshan Lu
Ronghu Beilu
Ronghu Nanlu
Wu Mei Lu
Shahu Beilu
Zhongshan
Nanhuan Lu
Nanlu
Zhishan Lu
Zhongshan
Guilin South Railway Station
Little East River
Li River
1
2
3
4
5
6
7
8
9
10
11
12
13
14
15
16
17
18
19
20
21
22
23
24
25
26

1	Hidden Hill Hotel
2	Long-Distance Bus Station
3	Osmanthus Hotel
4	South Hotel
5	CAAC
6	Li River Hotel
7	Pier for Tour-Boats down the Li River
8	Hubin Hotel
9	CITS
10	Ronghu Hotel
11	Public Security Bureau
12	Elephant Trunk Hill
13	Solitary Beauty Peak
14	Whirlpool Hill
15	Folded Brocade Hill
16	Seven Star Park
17	Banyan Lake
18	Fir Lake
19	Taihe Hotel
20	Guilin Overseas Chinese Mansion
21	Grand Hotel
22	Yu Gui Hotel
23	Post Office
24	Holiday Inn Guilin (North Side of Ronghu Nanlu)
25	Rongshuluo Hotel
26	Guishan Hotel

1	隐山饭店
2	长途汽车站
3	丹桂饭店
4	南方酒店
5	中国民用航空总局
6	漓江饭店
7	游船码头
8	湖宾饭店
9	旅行社
10	榕湖饭店
11	公安局
12	象鼻山
13	独秀峰
14	伏波山
15	叠采山
16	七星山
17	榕湖
18	杉湖
19	大喜宾馆
20	桂林华侨大厦
21	锦桂饭店
22	Yu Gui Hotel
23	邮局
24	假日桂宾馆
25	Rongshuluo Hotel
26	桂山酒店

town, though a few pop up within the city limits.

For the best views of the surrounding karst formations you either have to climb to the top of the hills or get out of the town altogether. The peaks are not very high and are often obscured by the buildings – the best views are from the top of the Li River Hotel.

CITS The office (☎ 2648) is at 14 Ronghu Beilu, facing Banyan Lake. The staff are friendly and reasonably helpful.

Public Security Bureau This (☎ 3202) is on Sanduo Lu, a side road which runs west off Zhongshan Lu, in the area between Banyan Lake and Jiefang Lu.

Money The Bank of China is on Jiefang Lu. All the tourist hotels, including the Hidden Hill, have foreign exchange services which you can usually use even if you're not staying at the hotel. The black market for FEC has cooled considerably in Guilin in recent years.

Post & Telecommunications The Post & Telecommunications building is on Zhongshan Lu. There is a second post office by the large square in front of the railway station; you can also make long-distance phone calls there. Some of the large hotels, such as the Li River Hotel, have post offices.

Solitary Beauty Peak
(dúxiùfēng) 独秀峰
The 152-metre pinnacle is at the centre of the town. The climb to the top is steep but there are good views of the town, the Li River and surrounding hills. The nephew of a Ming emperor built a palace at the foot of the peak in the 14th century, but only the gate remains. The site of the palace is now occupied by a teachers' college.
Bus No 1 goes up Zhongshan Lu past the western side of the peak. Or take bus No 2, which goes past the eastern side along the river. Both buses leave from Guilin south railway station.

Whirlpool Hill
(fúbōshān) 洑波山
Close to Solitary Beauty and standing beside the west bank of the Li River, this peak offers a fine view of the town. There is an odd story about how the hill gets its name – something to do with torrents of water plunging into the Li River and forming whirlpools. Try not to get caught in the rush.

On the southern slope of the hill is Returned Pearl Cave *(huánzhū dòng)*. The story goes that the cave was illuminated by a single pearl and inhabited by a dragon; one day a fisherman stole the pearl but he was overcome by shame and returned it.

Near this cave is Thousand Buddhas Cave *(qiānfó dòng)* – a misnomer since there seem to be a couple of dozen statues at most, dating from the Tang and Song dynasties. Admission to the hill is 10 fen, and there's a bicycle park at the entrance. Bus No 2 runs past the hill.

Seven Star Park
(qīxīng gōngyuán) 七星公园
Seven Star Park is on the eastern side of the Li River. Cross Liberation Bridge *(jiěfàng qiáo)* and the Ming Dynasty Flower Bridge to the park.

The park takes its name from its seven peaks, which are supposed to resemble the star pattern of the Ursa Major (Big Dipper) constellation. There are several caves in the peaks, where visitors have inscribed graffiti for centuries – including a recent one which says, 'The Chinese Communist Party is the core of the leadership of all the Chinese People'. It takes a lot of imagination to see the 'Monkey Picking Peaches' and 'Two Dragons Playing Ball' in the stalagmites and stalactites. Otherwise, try the pitiful zoo.

To get to the park take bus Nos 9, 10 or 11 from the railway station. From the park, bus No 13 runs back across the Li River, past Whirlpool Hill and down to Reed Flute Cave.

Reed Flute Cave
(lúdíyán) 芦笛岩
Ironically, the most extraordinary scenery Guilin has to offer is underground. If you see nothing else then try not to miss the Reed Flute Cave – rather like a set from *Journey to the Centre of the Earth*. At one time the entrance to the cave was distinguished by clumps of reeds used by the locals to make musical instruments, hence the name.

One grotto, the Crystal Palace of the Dragon King, can comfortably hold about 1000 people, though many more crammed in here during the war when the cave was used as an air-raid shelter. The dominant feature of the cave is a great slab of white rock hanging from a ledge like a cataract, while opposite stands a huge stalactite said to resemble an old scholar. The story goes that a visiting scholar wished to write a poem worthy of the cave's beauty. After a long time he had composed only two sentences and, lamenting his inability to find the right words, turned to stone.

The other story is that the slab is the Dragon King's needle, used as a weapon by his opponent the Monkey King. The Monkey King used the needle to destroy the dragon's army of snails and jellyfish, leaving their petrified remains scattered around the floor of the cave. You can no doubt invent your own stories.

The cave is on the north-western outskirts of town. Take bus No 3 from the railway station to the last stop. Bus No 13 will take you to the cave from Seven Star Park. Otherwise, it's an easy bicycle ride. For a guided tour try tagging on to one of the Western tour groups. Try to avoid the cave in the tourist (carnival) season, when the magic goes on holiday.

Ling Canal

(líng qú) 灵渠

The Ling Canal is in Xingan County, about 70 km north of Guilin. It was built during the 2nd century BC in the reign of the first Qin emperor, Qin Shihuang, to transport supplies to his army. The canal links the Xiang River (which flows into the Yangtse) and the Tan River (which flows into the Pearl River), thus connecting two of China's major waterways.

You can see the Ling Canal at Xingan, a market town of about 30,000 people, two hours by bus from Guilin. The town is also connected to Guilin by train. Two branches of the canal flow through the town, one at the north end and one at the south. The total length of the Ling Canal is 34 km.

Other Hills

Time to knock off a few more peaks. North of Solitary Beauty is **Folded Brocade Hill** *(diécăi shān)*. Climb the stone pathway which takes you through the Wind Cave, with walls decked with inscriptions and Buddhist sculptures. Some of the damage to faces on the sculptures is a legacy of the Cultural Revolution. Great views from the top of the hill. Bus No 1 runs past the hill.

There's a good view of **Old Man Hill** *(lăorén shān)*, a curiously shaped hill to the north-east, from Whirlpool Hill. The best way to get there is by bicycle as buses don't go near it. At the southern end of town, one of Guilin's best known sights is **Elephant Trunk Hill** *(xiàngbí shān)* which stands next to the Li River and is a lump of rock with a large hole in it.

At the southern end of Guilin, **South Park** *(nán gōngyuán)* is a pretty place. You can contemplate the mythological immortal who is said to have lived in one of the caves here; look for the carving of him. Admission to the park is 10 fen.

There are two lakes near the city centre, **Banyan Lake** *(róng hú)* on the west side and **Fir Lake** *(shān hú)* on the east side. Banyan Lake is named after an 800-year-old banyan tree on its shore. The tree stands by the restored South City Gate *(nán mén)* originally built during the Tang Dynasty.

A word of warning about hiking in the hills: a Chinese-US tourist was recently attacked and robbed by log-wielding bandits near Elephant Trunk Hill; the wound on her leg required stitches at the local hospital (the stitches were apparently very poorly done). In remote areas it would probably be best not to hike alone.

Places to Stay – bottom end

Guilin has almost nothing in the way of budget hotels. The Guilin Municipal Tourism Bureau has the sole authority to issue licences that permit hotels to accept foreigners. All those that admit foreigners bear a blue plaque featuring an osmanthus blossom symbol and must meet the minimum 'one-star' standard, which means they must post minimum rates of US$15 per night or the Chinese FEC equivalent. Two-star hotels post a minimum of US$24, three-stars a minimum of US$40 and on up to four-stars which must charge a minimum of US$50 per night per room.

This means that of the dozen or more inexpensive Chinese hotels along Zhongshan Lu, only two admit foreigners at the time of writing. All the dorms that were travellers' stand-bys in earlier years have been converted into doubles in order to meet the municipal standard.

A few minutes walk north from the Guilin south railway station is the *Hidden Hill Hotel (yǐnshān fàndiàn)* on Zhongshan Nanlu, with a money-exchange service and restaurant. In spite of the posted rates, which conform to municipal regulations, the Hidden Hill charges Y15 per person in a triple, from Y20 to Y25 for a single room and Y35 to Y40 for a double, all with private bath. Rooms are pretty shabby, however, and the word is that the Hidden Hill may soon lose its 'foreigner licence'.

The *Hubin Hotel (húbīn fàndiàn)*, on

Shahu Beilu facing Fir Lake, is in a similar position to the Hidden Hill – just hanging on to its licence and charging Y30 to Y50 per room. The *Rongshuluo Hotel*, just round the corner from CITS, has similarly priced rooms. Yet a fourth place in the 'one-star' category is the *South Hotel (nánfāng jiǔdiàn)* on Wu Mei Lu, just off Zhongshan Lu – same rates, same conditions.

Places to Stay – middle

Despite the requirement that 'two-star' hotels start at US$24, the hotels in this category will actually charge from Y60 to Y80 per room – in other words, about half the legal rate. The relatively new *Taihe Hotel* (☎ 33504) *(tàihé fàndiàn)* is next to the long-distance bus station on Zhongshan Nanlu. Their basic doubles cost from Y60 to Y70.

The wonderful old top-floor dorm at the *Osmanthus Hotel (dānguì fàndiàn)*, just before the first bridge on Zhongshan Lu, has gone; double rooms now go from Y65 to Y99 in the old wing, Y180 in the new 'international' wing. The *Yu Gui Hotel (yùguì fàndiàn)* on Nanhuan Lu near the Li River costs Y80 for a double and they even take credit cards (unusual for a hotel in this category).

Off Zhongshan Lu near the fire station is the newish and quite well-appointed *Grand Hotel* (☎ 335831) *(jǐnguì fàndiàn)*, 15 Zhishan Lu. Rooms here cost from Y70 to Y100 and represent three-star value (including an English-speaking staff) for two-star rates.

Another good value in this category is the *Guilin Overseas Chinese Mansion* (☎ 33573) *(guìlín huáqiáo dàshà)* at 29 Zhongshan Nanlu, a few minutes south of the railway station. Cheapest are the doubles with shared bath and fan, which are only Y37.60. A four-bed room with private bath and fan is Y57; very nice 'standard' doubles with air-con, hot water, phone and TV are Y70. There are also nicer doubles and triples for Y112 and Y141 respectively.

Places to Stay – top end

The *Banyan Lake Hotel (rónghú fàndiàn)* at 17 Ronghu Lu once catered only for Overseas Chinese. Indeed, you practically needed a map of the hotel grounds and a fluent command of the local dialect to find the reception desk! Since then a new wing has been added, the range of clientele expanded and room prices have shot up. Doubles start at US$50 in the new wing and rise astronomically. The old wing has doubles for US$20; you might even be able to talk them down further if occupancy is low. It's a bit inconveniently located unless you have a bicycle.

The *Li River Hotel* (☎ 222881) *(lǐjiāng fàndiàn)* at 1 Shahu Beilu was once the main tourist hotel in Guilin. It's right in the middle of town and the roof provides a panoramic view of the encircling hills. Double rooms are US$50, no singles. Once a fairly plebeian hotel, it's now got the full works: post office, barber, bank, restaurants, tour groups and bellboys in monkey suits. Take bus Nos 1 or 11 from Guilin south railway station. Get off when you cross Banyan Lake Bridge, the second bridge on Zhongshan Lu. Then walk for about 15 minutes up Shahu Beilu beside Fur Lake.

The US-style *Holiday Inn Guilin* (☎ 3950) *(jiàrì guìbīnguǎn)* at 14 Ronghu Nanlu has doubles posted at US$80, but when occupancy is low you can negotiate this to US$50 or less. Another brand-name place is the *Ramada Renaissance Riverside Hotel* (☎ 442411) on Yanjiang Lu near Seven Star Park. Rooms start here at US$75.

Opposite Elephant Trunk Hill is the flash four-star *Guishan Hotel (guìshān jiǔdiàn)*, where rooms start at US$100 a night. The Guishan also hires apartments in the compound that go for as low as US$300 a *month*. The foreign-managed *Sheraton Guilin Hotel* (☎ 225588) at 9 Binjiang Nanlu also starts at US$100.

Places to Eat

Guilin food is basically Cantonese. Traditionally the town is noted for its snake soup, wild cat or bamboo rat, washed down with snake-bile wine. You could be devouring some of these animals into extinction. The pangolin (a sort of Chinese armadillo) is a protected species but still crops up on restaurant menus. Other protected species include the muntjac horned pheasant, mini-turtle, short-tailed monkey and gem-faced civet. Generally the most exotic stuff you should come across is eels, catfish, pigeons and dog.

Many small, cheapish eateries have sprung up along Zhongshan Lu in the last few years. It's really not worth mentioning any one in particular; if you just walk down the street, they'll find you. Another good area for restaurants is along Zhishan Lu.

Just north of the Osmanthus Hotel on Zhongshan Lu is *Beer Street*, a half-indoor, half-outdoor place with a good variety of Chinese dishes and cold beer at fair prices.

The Guilin Overseas Chinese Mansion has a cosy little coffee shop that's quite reasonable. Next door is a small restaurant with cheap Western breakfasts.

The Chinese restaurant in the Grand Hotel has fabulous dim sum – it's very popular among Taiwanese tourists.

Getting There & Away

Guilin is connected to many places by bus, train, boat and plane. Give serious thought to flying in or out of this place, as train connections are not good.

Air Worth considering is the daily flight from Guilin to Kunming. The fare is Y275, which is less than the tourist-price soft-sleeper on the train (Y310).

Other useful connections include Canton (daily), Chengdu (four days a week), Chongqing (five days a week) and Shanghai (daily). CAAC has an office (☎ 3063) at 144 Zhongshan Lu, just to the south of the intersection of Zhongshan Lu and Shahu Beilu.

Bus The long-distance bus station is on Zhongshan Lu, a short walk from Guilin south railway station. There are daily buses from Guilin to Yangshuo (Y2 to Y4, depending on the bus, 1½ hours, a dozen buses per day) and to Wuzhou (Y16), where you can pick up a boat or bus to Canton.

There are daily buses from Guilin to Liuzhou (Y10). From Liuzhou you can carry on by rail to Nanning and Zhanjiang, or to Guiyang and Kunming.

Daily buses to Canton (Y40) take two days with an overnight stopover in Wuzhou. Alternatively, you can buy a bus/boat combination ticket which takes you by bus to Wuzhou and then by boat to Canton.

Train There are useful train connections to Guilin, but some of these (like the Kunming-Guiyang-Guilin-Shanghai route) tend to involve long hauls on unbelievably crowded carriages. Guilin railway station has a separate ticket office for foreigners; this means you'll have to pay tourist price but at least you avoid the impossible queues.

Direct trains out of Guilin include those to Kunming (about 33 hours), Guiyang (18 hours), Zhanjiang (about 13 hours), Liuzhou (three hours) and Nanning. For Chongqing change trains at Guiyang.

The train to Kunming via Guiyang comes through from Shanghai and is extremely crowded. It's virtually impossible to get a seat, let alone a sleeper, if you pick it up midway. You may manage a soft-sleeper but for much the same price you could fly, which is what many people are now doing. To book a sleeper from Guilin to Kunming, you have to line up at the FEC counter in the station no later than 7 am. Only six hard-sleepers a day are sold for this train and you must book three days in advance. Tourist-price tickets from Guilin to Kunming are Y90 hard-seat, Y185 hard-sleeper and Y310 soft-sleeper.

There is a direct train to Canton. Tourist-price fares are Y69 hard-seat, Y116 hard-sleeper and Y215 soft-sleeper. Otherwise you have to stop at Hengyang and change trains. The indirect route will take about 24 hours and fares are a few yuan cheaper.

If you're heading east on the train, consider breaking your journey at the rail junction of Hengyang. Tourist-price hard-seat from Guilin to Hengyang is only Y25, and from there you can continue your trip east to Shanghai, north to Changsha and Beijing, or south to Canton. In any case, by the time the train reaches Hengyang you might get off whether you planned to or not! A direct train to Changsha is Y38 hard-seat, Y75 hard-sleeper.

Getting Around

Taxi & Bus Taxis are available from the major tourist hotels for Y5 to Y10 per trip, depending on the distance. Pedicabs charge Y2 to Y5 per trip.

Most of the city buses leave from the terminal at Guilin south railway station and will get you to many major sights, but a bicycle is definitely better.

A taxi to the airport is Y25 (but there are also CAAC buses from the city office to airport for only Y2.50).

Bicycle Bicycles are definitely the best way to get around Guilin. There's been a proliferation of bicycle hire shops over the last few years – just look along Zhongshan Lu for the signs. Most charge about Y0.50 to Y0.60 per hour, but you may be able to negotiate a cheaper day rate.

Boat A popular tourist trip is the boat ride from Guilin down the Li River to Yangshuo. Although this is still popular with tour groups (whole fleets of boats do the run every day in the high season), low-budget travellers have been put off by the exorbitant ticket prices. Standard prices for foreigners are now Y132 return; no one-way tickets are available. If you don't mind paying this much, you can purchase your ticket at the CITS office or at any tourist hotel. The boats leave from a dock on the Li River about 100 metres north of Elephant Trunk Hill.

Much less expensive boat trips are available from Yangshuo, where the scenery is just as good if not better.

YANGSHUO

(yángshuò) 阳朔

The place to escape the congestion of Guilin is Yangshuo, 80 km and 1½ hours by bus to the south. Yangshuo is a tiny country town set amidst the limestone pinnacles, and from here you can explore the small villages in the countryside. In fact, the scenery around Yangshuo makes giving Guilin a complete miss no hardship at all. As the Chinese tourist leaflets say:

> The peaks surrounding the country town are steep and delicate, rising one higher than another like piled-up petals. Their inverted images mirrored in the river are just like green lotuses shooting up from the water, elegant and graceful. The scenery of Yangshuo will make you enjoy the beauty of the natural world whenever you come. On fine days they bathe in the sunlight; in the rainy season they are in the misty rain; in the morning the glory casts upon them; at dusk the mountain haze enwraps them – all in all, they are colourful and in different postures, and make you feel intoxicant.

Yangshuo is a laid-back town if ever there was one in China, and offers a rare opportunity to relax and explore the villages and countryside. Hire a bicycle and take off along the tracks which lead to old settlements. A lot of people have stayed overnight in the villages, and if you want to go camping on the mountains you shouldn't have any problem. It's probably not permitted to camp out, but who's going to climb a 200-metre peak to bring you down? There are caves in the peaks, unlit by fairy lights, many no doubt untrod by human feet.

In 1983, when the first edition of this book was being researched, there wasn't much in Yangshuo. The tourist market by the dock catered to the flotilla of tour boats bearing Chinese, Japanese and Westerners who swept through like a plague of locusts before being bundled on buses and whisked back to Guilin. Three hotels (one of which they wouldn't let you stay at, and another which didn't have toilets) and a couple of soupy noodle dispensaries catered to the meagre number of backpackers who found their way here. Today you can munch on banana pancakes and muesli, slurp coffee and hang out in half a dozen or more travellers' cafes with Midnight Oil and Dire Straits tapes playing in the background.

Information

CITS There's an office (☎ 2256) on the grounds of the Yangshuo Hotel. You can get

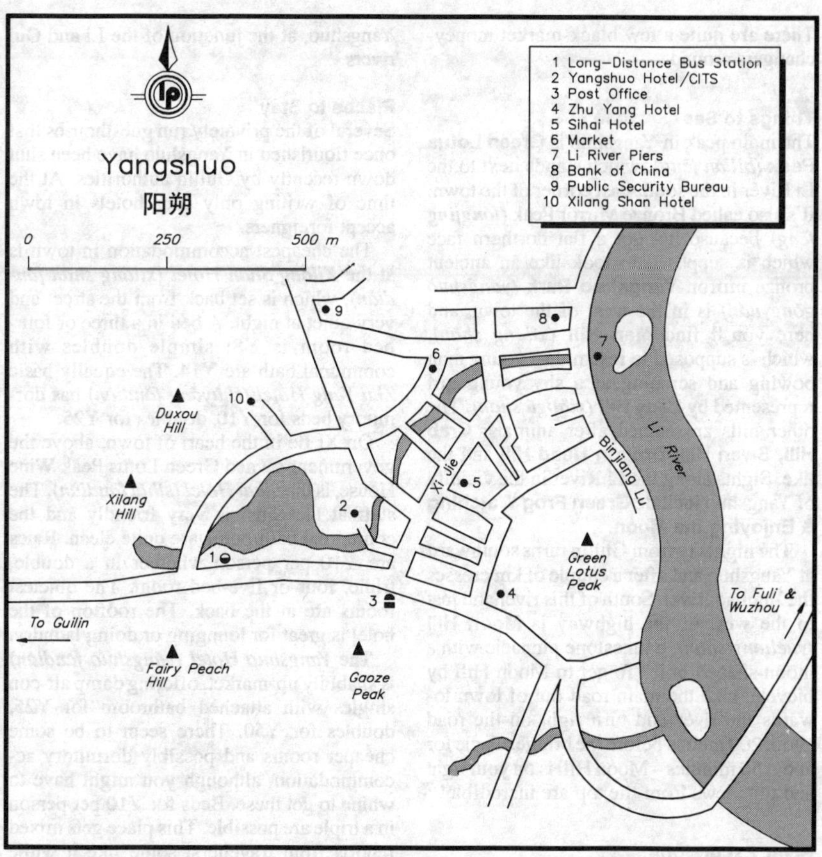

useful maps of Yangshuo and the surrounding area which show villages, paths and roads. They advertise visits to local factories, schools and villages; fishing trips; and acupuncture and massage services. They were planning to provide guides for local hiking and caving – could be worth enquiring about.

Money The Bank of China on Binjiang Lu will change cash and travellers' cheques.

There are quite a few black-market money-changers around.

Things to See

The main peak in Yangshuo is **Green Lotus Peak** *(bìlián fēng)*, which stands next to the Li River in the south-east corner of the town. It's also called Bronze Mirror Peak *(tóngjìng fēng)* because it's got a flat northern face which is supposed to look like an ancient bronze mirror. **Yangshuo Park** *(yángshuò gōngyuán)* is in the west of the town, and here you'll find **Man Hill** *(xīláng shān)*, which is supposed to resemble a young man bowing and scraping to a shy young girl represented by **Lady Hill** *(xiǎogū shān)*. The other hills are named after animals: **Crab Hill, Swan Hill, Dragon Head Hill** and the like. Sights along the Li River in the vicinity of Yangshuo include **Green Frog Watching & Enjoying the Moon**.

The highway from Guilin turns southward at Yangshuo and after a couple of km crosses the Jingbao River. South of this river and just to the west of the highway is **Moon Hill** *(yuèliang shān)*, a limestone pinnacle with a moon-shaped hole. To get to Moon Hill by bicycle, take the main road out of town towards the river and turn right on the road about 200 metres before the bridge. Cycle for about 50 minutes – Moon Hill is on your right and the views from the top are incredible!

River Excursions

There are many villages close to Yangshuo which are worth checking out. A popular riverboat trip is to the picturesque village of **Fuli** *(fùlì)* a short distance down the Li River, where you'll see stone houses and cobbled lanes. There are a couple of boats a day to Fuli from Yangshuo (foreigners are usually charged Y8, but you might try looking around for local boats); you can bring a bicycle and pedal back. Friday is market day and the main street is packed with people from the outlying villages buying and selling everything from herbal medicines to piglets in bamboo cages. **Pinglo** *(píngluò)* is a small, industrialised river town 35 km from Yangshuo, at the junction of the Li and Gui rivers.

Places to Stay

Several of the privately run guesthouses that once flourished in Yangshuo have been shut down recently by Guilin authorities. At the time of writing only four hotels in town accept foreigners.

The cheapest accommodation in town is at the *Xilang Shan Hotel (xīláng shān fàndiàn)*, which is set back from the street and very quiet at night. A bed in a three or four-bed room is Y8; simple doubles with communal bath are Y14. The equally basic *Zhu Yang Hotel (zhūyáng fàndiàn)* has dormitory beds for Y10, doubles for Y25.

On Xi Jie in the heart of town, above the government-owned Green Lotus Peak Wine House, is the *Sihai Hotel (sìhǎi fàndiàn)*. The staff at the Sihai is very friendly and the communal bathrooms are quite clean. Rates are Y10 per person whether in a double, triple, four or five-bed room. The quietest rooms are at the back. The rooftop of the hotel is great for lounging or doing laundry.

The *Yangshuo Hotel (yángshuò fàndiàn)* is shabbily up-market, offering damp air-con singles with attached bathroom for Y25, doubles for Y50. There seem to be some cheaper rooms and possibly dormitory accommodation, although you might have to whine to get these. Beds for Y10 per person in a triple are possible. This place gets mixed reports from travellers: some like it while others find it dingy and the staff unfriendly. Could depend on what level of accommodation you take. CITS has its office on the hotel grounds.

Places to Eat

There are several small private restaurants along Xi Jie, in amongst the many souvenir shops. All of them serve a mixture of Chinese food and traveller perennials like muesli and pancakes; in fact, the menus are almost identical, even so far as to look like they were all painted by the same person (they probably were). The food at the *Green Lotus Peak Wine House (bìlián fēng jiǔdiàn)*, below the

Sihai Hotel, is usually reliable and inexpensive. There is another restaurant by the same name further south at the main intersection that isn't quite as consistent or friendly.

Sarah's, also on Xi Jie, is very small but very popular and probably serves the best coffee in town. Other established places include *Lisa's*, *Hard Rock Cafe* and *Suzannah's Cafe*.

If you get tired of the 'international' spots, hop over to the narrow street east of and parallel to Xi Jie; here you'll find a number of *yóutiáo* and noodle vendors.

Fresh fruit is sold down at the wharf where the tour boats dock. The best of the local beers seems to be the Liquan brand.

Getting There & Away

There are over a dozen buses a day from Yangshuo to Guilin, the first departing Yangshuo about 8 am and the last about 6.30 pm. The fare is Y2.30 for the local bus, which leaves from the main terminal area, or Y4 for the tourist buses which leave from near the gate of the Yangshuo Hotel. Depending on the bus, the trip takes 1½ to two hours.

If you're heading to Canton you can take a bus/boat combination from Yangshuo; you go by bus to Wuzhou and then take a boat from Wuzhou to Canton. Get tickets from Yangshuo's long-distance bus station, where an unfathomable confusion reigns regarding departure times and availability of seats. The fare to Wuzhou is Y13.

There are also daily buses from Yangshuo to Liuzhou, from where you can carry on by train to Nanning, Zhanjiang, or Guiyang and Kunming.

Getting Around

The town itself is small enough to walk around easily, but if you want to get further afield then hire a bicycle. Just look for rows of bikes and signs at the south end of Xi Jie. The charge is about Y2 per day.

CITS organises half-day river trips for around Y5 per person, and full-day trips for around Y12 per person. Check the signs near the boat dock for what's available.

LI RIVER

(lǐ jiāng) 漓江

The Li River is the connecting waterway between Guilin and Yangshuo and is one of the main tourist attractions of the area. A thousand years ago a poet wrote of the scenery around Yangshuo: 'The river forms a green gauze belt, the mountains are like blue jade hairpins'. The 83-km stretch between the towns is hardly that but you do see some extraordinary peaks, sprays of bamboo lining the river banks, fishermen in small boats and picturesque villages.

As is the Chinese habit, every feature along the route has been named. **Paint Brush Hill** juts straight up from the ground with a pointed tip like a Chinese writing brush. **Cock-fighting Hills** stand face to face like two cocks about to engage in battle. **Mural Hill** just past the small town of Yangti is a sheer cliff rising abruptly out of the water; there are supposed to be the images of nine horses in the weathered patterns on the cliff face.

Tour boats depart from Guilin from a jetty about 100 metres north of Elephant Trunk Hill each morning at around 7.30 am. The trip takes about six hours round trip. Many people find that the time drags by the end. It's probably not worth it if you're going to be spending any length of time in Yangshuo, unless you decide to overnight in Xingping at the halfway point. Back in Yangshuo, buses meet the incoming boats to take passengers on to Guilin, pausing at a tourist market and photo stop near Moon Hill.

Xingping

(xīngpíng) 兴坪

This scenic little town sits on the banks of the Li River about three hours downstream from Yangshuo. The mountain scenery around Xingping is even more breathtaking than around Yangshuo and there are many unexplored caves in the area. People residing in some of the caves manufacture gunpowder for a living. The Sunday market can be colourful.

Few travellers spend the night in Xingping, but it's certainly worth considering a

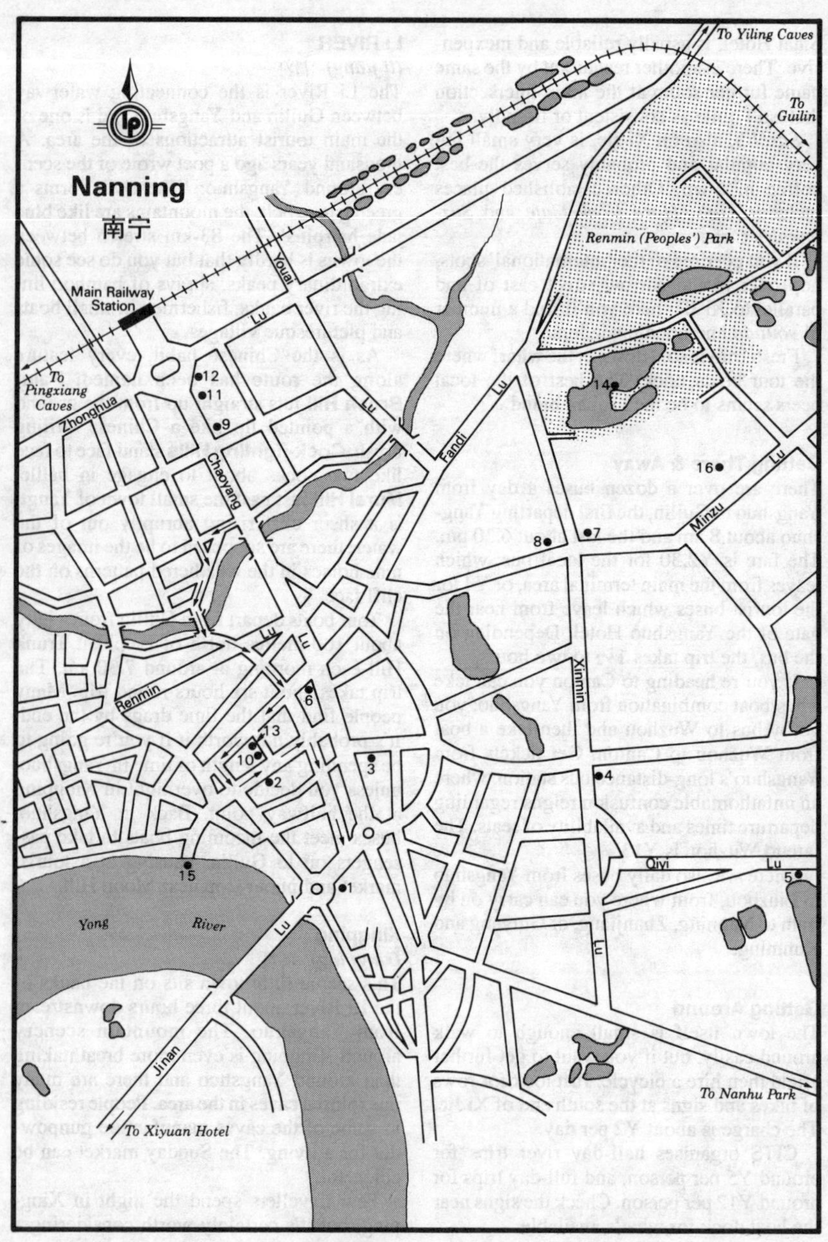
Nanning
南宁
To Yiling Caves
To Guilin
Renmin (Peoples') Park
Main Railway Station
To Pingxiang Caves
Youai
Lu
Zhonghua
Chaoyang
Lu
Fandi
Lu
Xinmin
Lu
Minzu
Lu
Renmin
Lu
Lu
Qiyi
Lu
Yong
River
Jinan
Lu
To Xiyuan Hotel
To Nanhu Park
1
2
3
4
5
6
7
8
9
10
11
12
13
14
15
16

1	Yongjiang Hotel	10	Foreign Language Bookstore
2	Nanning Restaurant	11	CAAC Office
3	Bike Rental	12	Chaoyang (Chinese) Hotel & Travel Agency
4	Friendship Store	13	Arts & Crafts Service Department
5	Guangxi Provincial Museum	14	Bailongdong Restaurant
6	Chaoyang Department Store	15	Boat Dock
7	Mingyuan Hotel (CITS)	16	Exhibition Hall
8	Yongzhou Hotel		
9	Long-distance Bus Station		

1	邕江饭店	7	明园饭店	13	工艺美术服务部
2	南宁酒家	8	邕州饭店	14	白龙饭店
3	出租自行车店	9	长途汽车站	15	港客运码头
4	友谊商店	10	外文书店	16	展览馆
5	广西省博物馆	11	中国民航		
6	朝阳百货大楼	12	朝阳旅社		

stay here. One small hotel sits on a point that juts out into the river; basic rooms are Y10 per person. A couple of doll's house restaurants with bilingual menus keep everyone fed (take care that they don't overcharge).

Getting There & Away Some travellers come to Xingping by boat from Yangshuo and then pedal back to Yangshuo on bicycles they've hired and brought on the boat. The boat costs Y20 per person (tourist price, you may be able to get a lower fare) and takes 2½ to four hours depending on the river level.

The 25-km Yangshuo-Xingping road winds through rice fields, lush vegetable gardens and twisty peaks and only takes a couple of hours by bike, going slowly. By bus (Y1.80) it's only 45 minutes to an hour away.

NANNING

(nánníng) 南宁

By way of introduction, here are a few statistics to dwell upon about Nanning. According to Chinese sources, the number of factories in the city shot from four in 1949 to 400 by 1979. From 1949 to 1981 the area of Nanning city increased twelvefold. From 1976 to 1983 it appears that the population doubled (from 1949 to 1979 it quadrupled) and now stands at over 650,000. A prestigious list of light and heavy industry could be rattled off here, but perhaps you already have a picture in mind.

At the turn of the century Nanning was a mere market town; now it's the capital of Guangxi. Apart from the urban expansion that the post-1949 railway induced in the south-west, Nanning became important as a staging post for shipping arms to Vietnam. The railway line to the border town of Pingxian was built in 1952, and was extended to Hanoi, giving Vietnam a lifeline to China. In 1979, with the Chinese invasion of Vietnam, the train services were suspended indefinitely. The border with Vietnam in Guangxi and Yunnan is a hot one these days, and (ridiculous as it is) the Vietnamese are considered a threat to Chinese oil exploration in the Gulf of Tonkin.

At street level, the town of Nanning is a

poor one, with a promise of progress in the solid-looking department stores. Elsewhere the city is a motley collection of cracked, peeling, stained, crumbled, worn, seedy, ramshackle walls, facades and fittings. The population in the Nanning region is mostly a Zhuang-Han mix, though the rest of the Zhuang are scattered over Guangxi's rural areas.

There's a plethora of free markets in Nanning. You can follow a series of different outdoor markets (spices, medicinal herbs and potions, clothing, sunglasses, housewares, eating stalls...) by taking the route marked on the map in this book. There are food stalls at the northern and southern sections of the route. Check out the unusual street commerce in progress – strips of car tyre, dead rats, desiccated cockroaches, dried snakeskins. For the rice-weary there's an abundance of subtropical fruit in season. Another market strip is Fandi Lu, the road leading diagonally to the north-east toward Renmin Park. If you happen to be a smoker there are shaggy mounds of tobacco lying around the markets, and you can order it rolled in filter packs on the spot. To the south and west of the Yongjiang Hotel, along the river banks on the same side, is the older section of town. Check out the underground bomb-shelter disco/amusement hall in Renmin Park.

Nanning is also a jumping-off place for visits to Wuming, Yiling, Binyang, Guixian, Guiping and Beihai.

Information

CITS The office (☎ 22986) is in the Mingyuan Hotel. They're quite helpful.

Guangxi Provincial Museum

(guǎngxī bówùguǎn) 广西省博物馆

The museum is in Nanhu Park, and has a collection of tribal, archaeological and Taiping relics. Take bus No 3 to the terminal. The museum's opening hours are variable, and lunchtime is definitely not one of them.

Dragon Boat Races

As in other parts of the south-west (and Guangdong and Macao), Nanning has Dragon Boat races on the fifth day of the fifth lunar month (some time in June) in which large numbers of sightseers urge the decorated rowing vessels along the Yong River. The oarsmen are coordinated by a gong-player on board.

Places to Stay

The *Yongjiang Hotel* (☎ 28123) *(yōngjiāng bīnguǎn)* on Jinan Lu has two wings: a high-rise for foreigners and for Hong Kong and Macau citizens, and a squat building for People's Republic Chinese. Rooms in the high-rise are luxurious and start from Y68 a double. Rooms in the old wing are Y38; dorm beds are available for Y10. Local buses running to the Yongjiang from the railway station are Nos 2 and 5. There are great views of the city from the restaurant on the 8th floor.

The *Yongchuan* (☎ 22450) *(yōngchuān)* on Xinmin Lu is of a similar standard to the Yongjiang. Single rooms with hard beds and own bathroom start at Y26 and doubles at Y45. Once the TV in the corridor goes off it's rather quiet. Not a bad place, if a bit tattered round the edges. It's rather awkward to get to – you take bus No 2 one stop from the railway station, alight and walk left to the next big intersection, and then take bus No 1 for two stops.

Close to the Yongchuan is the CITS *Mingyuan Hotel* (☎ 22986) *(míngyuán fàndiàn)* on Xinmin Lu. Foreigners are sent off to the new wing, which is a snazzy building with singles from around Y75 and doubles from Y100. There are comfy rooms, soft beds, own bathroom, TV and enough lights per room to illuminate a rock concert.

You may or may not be able to get into the *Xiyuan Hotel* (☎ 29923) *(xīyuán fàndiàn)* by the riverside, at 38 Jiangnan Lu, but take bus No 5 from the railway station. Rooms are Y25-60. The similar *Nanning Hotel (nánníng fàndiàn)* at 38 Minsheng Lu is even cheaper, but they don't usually take foreigners.

Places to Eat

Market-stall food is good – snakes and snails

and puppy dogs' tails, glazed chicken, roast duck and fruit are all part of the menu. Opposite the Foreign Language Bookstore is a large restaurant where the specialities include turtle, snake, ants and fruit-eating fox. Turn left out of the Yongjiang Hotel and then left again to encounter a world of street restaurants and fruit stalls. Between April and November, nothing on this street closes before midnight. The food is cheap and good.

In Nanhu Park there's a fish restaurant where the creatures are taken from tanks – not too expensive. Take bus No 2 to the terminal.

The penthouse dining room in the high-rise block of the *Yongjiang Hotel* is a bit pricey, but has nice views. The *Mingyuan Hotel* has a decent bar.

Renmin Park, with a market run leading up to it (Fandi Lu), has a teahouse and restaurant, the *Bailongdong (báilóng fàndiàn)*.

Getting There & Away

Air CAAC flies daily to Canton, thrice weekly to Beijing and four times a week to Kunming. The airline office (☎ 23333) is at 64 Chaoyang Lu.

Bus Daily buses to Wuzhou, from Nanning's long-distance bus station, cost Y20 and take up to 15 hours. Buses to Canton are Y40 and take 21 hours (although it's a gruelling trip, this is the cheapest way to get to Canton from Nanning). There are also regular buses to Liuzhou (Y14, seven hours) and Beihai (Y14, six hours). Tickets for more expensive air-con buses can be bought from the tourist hotels.

Train Plan your railway trips ahead of time, as the choice of departures is not great.

There are special direct trains (No 91) from Nanning to Guilin every other day. Chinese-price tickets are Y38 hard-seat, Y76 soft-seat. The trip takes about eight hours.

Trains to Liuzhou take about five hours and cost Y23 hard-seat, Y49 soft-seat, Chinese price.

If you're continuing from Nanning to Guiyang you have to change at Liuzhou. There are also special express trains direct from Nanning to Beijing and Chongqing.

There are direct trains from Nanning to Zhanjiang on the coast of Guangdong Province. From Zhanjiang you can get a ferry to Haikou on Hainan Island, a direct bus to Canton, or a direct overnight boat to Hong Kong. Tourist-price tickets from Nanning to Zhanjiang are Y39 hard-seat and Y60 hard-sleeper (Chinese prices). The trip takes about 9½ hours.

Boat Leaving Nanning by boat is possible though trips are slower and less frequent than the equivalent bus trips. When the river level is sufficiently high, there are boats every other day to Wuzhou via Guixian and Guiping. The trip takes 36 hours and costs Y20. There are also boats to Canton for only Y38 that take about 72 hours.

The Binyang-Guixian-Guiping route, going north-east from Nanning, is useful for getting to Wuzhou cross-country. The roads are rough, the areas backward, and it's a sugar cane/grain basin. It's 90 km by road from Nanning to Binyang; 90 km by road from Binyang to Guixian; and 70 km by boat from Guixian to Guiping. From Guiping there are boats to Wuzhou, a 10-hour trip. Guixian can also be reached by rail from Nanning, and the line continues to Zhanjiang.

There are a couple of cultural sights along the way, but nothing of note. Just 25 km north-west of Guiping is Jintiancun, the wellspring of one of the weirdest chapters in Chinese history. Hong Xiuquan, a schoolteacher possibly suffering from hallucinations generated by an illness, declared himself the brother of Jesus Christ and took upon himself the mission of liberating China from the Manchus. These were the seeds of the Taiping Rebellion (1850-64), which sought to distribute land equally among all Chinese and to establish equality between the sexes. The extremely puritanical Christian sect that Hong developed eventually established a

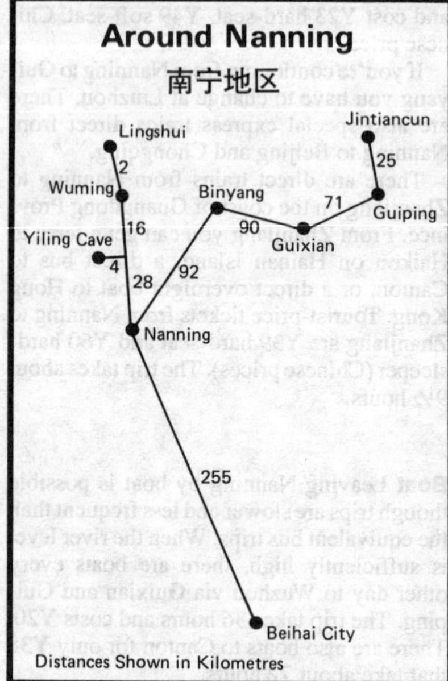

standing army of over a million which swept across 17 provinces in an effort to defeat the Qing dynasty, at the loss of 20 million lives. After Hong's army was finally surrounded by Qing forces in Nanjing in 1864, he committed suicide along with nearly 100,000 of his followers.

One approach to Hainan Island is via Beihai, which is 255 km from Nanning. **Beihai** is a port town and a very sensitive naval base but there is a pretty white-sand beach, **Baihutou**, just outside of town. The bus trip from Nanning takes eight hours. From Beihai you can continue to Zhanjiang and get a bus/boat combination to Haikou on Hainan Island.

Getting Around

There are at least two bicycle-hire places, but they're difficult to find. The one marked on the map in this book is hidden by a (crowded) bus stop. Look for a batch of numbered bikes near the bus stop. The owner will want to know at which hotel you're staying.

Pedicabs and auto-rickshaws can be found at the town centre and outside the major hotels. Taxis are available from the hotels.

AROUND NANNING

Yiling Caves & Wuming

(yǐlíng yán) 伊岭岩

Twenty-five km to the north-north-west of Nanning are these caves with their stalagmites and galactic lights; 15 minutes is enough for the caves, but the surrounding countryside is worth exploring.

Wuming is 45 km from Nanning, on the same road that leads to the Yiling Caves. There are CITS-organised visits to the local Two-Bridge Production Brigade which you probably won't get on. A few km further up the line is Lingshui Springs, which is a big swimming pool.

To get to either Wuming or the Yiling Caves, take a bus from Nanning's long-distance bus station. Also try the Nanning Tourist Company which operates out of the Chaoyang Hotel near the railway station – they cover short round trips.

LIUZHOU

(liǔzhōu) 柳州

Liuzhou, with a population of over 500,000, is the largest city on the Liu River and an important south-west China railway junction. The place dates back to the Tang Dynasty, at which time it was a dumping ground for disgraced court officials. The town was largely left to its mountain wilds until 1949, when it was transformed into a major industrial city. The city is also known for medicinal herbs, fruit and coffins. Liuzhou is the only place in China where you can buy an exquisitely wrought ashtray-sized wooden coffin.

Liuzhou is Guilin's poor cousin with similar but less impressive karst scenery on the outskirts. Try some cave-lake-park sightseeing. River transport is the best way of viewing the karst landscape.

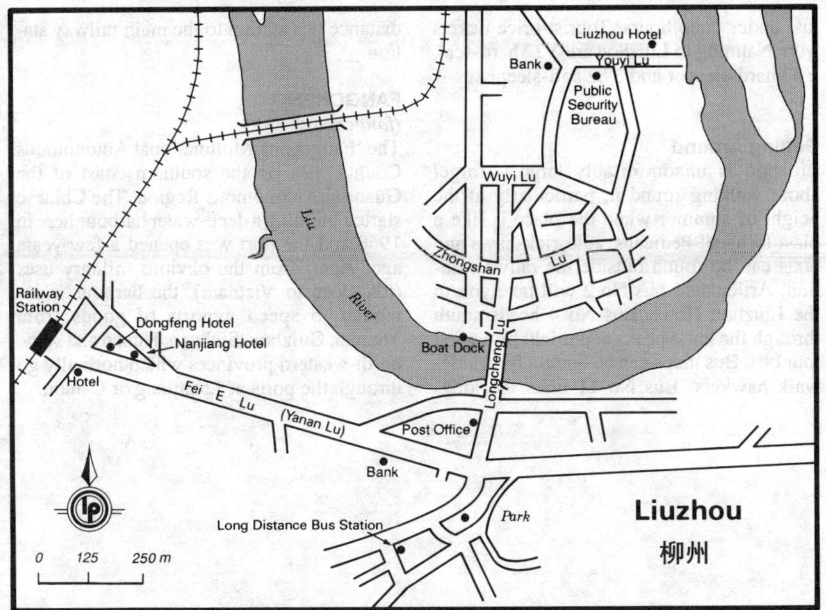

Places to Stay & Eat

A few minutes' walk from the main railway station down Fei E Lu is the large *Nanjiang Hotel* which will take foreigners (there's no English or pinyin sign – see the map for directions). Singles cost Y25, doubles Y45 with hard beds and your own TV and mouldy bathroom. You may manage a cheaper room with a bit of effort. Dormitory beds are Y10. Not a bad place all told, with friendly staff.

The *Liuzhou Hotel (liŭzhōu fàndiàn)* is the centre of tourist operations. The hotel is quite remote. From the railway station get an articulated bus No 2. This takes you most of the way, followed by a short walk – ask the conductor where to get off. Double rooms cost from Y60. Some people have managed to get fairly cheap rooms by bargaining.

Apparently women of the Dong minority are known to serve *youcha* or oil-tea (actually a kind of soup) within the confines of the Liuzhou Hotel. The women seem a bit far from home, since the heartland of the Dongs is 200 km or more north of Liuzhou in Songjiang County. Songjiang is the area where the borders of Guizhou, Guangxi and Hunan meet.

On the streets there's not much to recommend – more noodles, boiled eggs, jiaozi and baozi.

Getting There & Away

Bus There are daily buses from Liuzhou's long-distance bus station to Guilin (Y14) and Yangshuo (Y10).

Train Liuzhou is a railway junction which connects Nanning to Guilin. Trains from Guilin to Kunming pass through Liuzhou. If you're coming up from Nanning you'll probably have to change trains in Liuzhou to get to Kunming.

Tourist-price hard-seat fare from Liuzhou to Guilin is around Y14, and the trip takes just under three hours. Tourist-price tickets from Nanning to Liuzhou are Y22 hard-seat, Y42 hard-sleeper and Y82 soft-sleeper.

Getting Around

Liuzhou is uncomfortably large – forget about walking round it, particularly at the height of summer when the place is like a blast furnace! Pedicabs, auto-rickshaws and taxis can be found outside the railway station. Articulated bus No 2 will take you to the Liuzhou Hotel. Bus No 4 heads south through the karst peaks and might be a good tour bus. Bus maps can be bought from sidewalk hawkers. Bus No 11 links the long-distance bus station to the main railway station.

FANGCHENG

(fángchéng) 防城

The 'Fangcheng Multinational Autonomous County' lies on the southern coast of the Guangxi Autonomous Region. The Chinese started building a deep-water harbour here in 1968 and the port was opened a few years ago. Apart from the obvious military uses (it's close to Vietnam), the harbour is intended to speed exports of goods from Yunnan, Guizhou, Sichuan, Hunan and some north-western provinces which normally go through the ports at Zhanjiang or Canton.

Guizhou 贵州

HISTORY

Until recent times Guizhou *(guìzhōu)* was one of the most backward and sparsely populated areas in China. Although the Han Dynasty set up an administration in the area, the Chinese merely attempted to maintain some measure of control over the non-Chinese tribes who lived here, and Chinese settlement was confined to the north and east of the province. The eastern areas were not settled until the 16th century, when the native minorities were forced out of the most fertile areas. Another wave of Chinese immigration in the late 19th century brought many settlers in from overpopulated Hunan and Sichuan. But Guizhou remained impoverished and backward, with poor communications and transport.

When the Japanese invasion forced the Kuomintang to retreat to the south-west, the development of Guizhou began; roads to the neighbouring provinces were constructed, a rail link was built to Guangxi, and some industries were set up in Guiyang and Zunyi. Most of the activity ceased with the end of WW II, and it was not until the construction of the railways in the south-west under Communist rule that some industrialisation was revived.

Recent analyses in the Chinese press have provided grim warnings about backwardness and poverty. Eight million of the province's population are living below the national poverty line. Between 60% and 70% of the population are illiterate and nearly 50% of the villages are not accessible by road.

However, in typical Han fashion the blame was laid at the door of the minorities who were castigated for 'poor educational quality'; more self-righteous arguments were levelled at cave-dwellers because 'the temptations of modern life have failed to lure these Miao out of their dark, unhealthy cave'. These self-sufficient minorities living without TV, radio, electricity etc are certainly poor, but they show few signs of embracing consumer life and throwing away their cultural identity as a reward for assimilation with the Han.

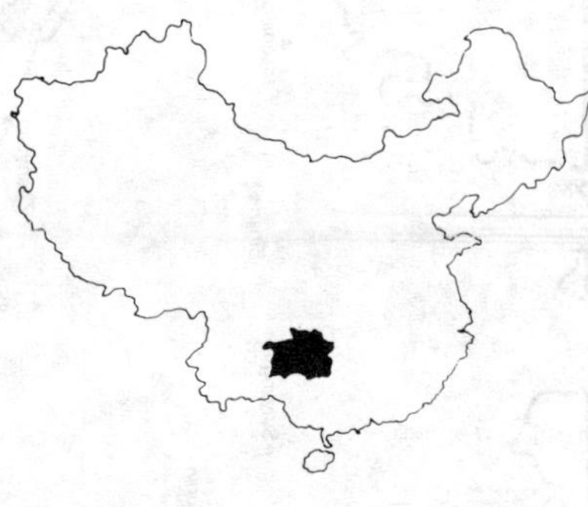

Today the population of Guizhou is 31.3 million, of which about 75% is Han and the rest a flamboyant mixture of minorities such as Miao, Bouyei, Dong, Yi, Shui, Hui, Zhuang, Bai, Tujiao and Gelao. Between them these minorities celebrate nearly 1000 festivals each year which preserve fascinating customs and elaborate skills in architecture, dress and handicrafts.

The province's most famous export is Maotai liquor, named for the village of its origin in Renhuai County. This fiery white spirit is sold in distinctive white bottles with a diagonal red label. Millions of Chinese tuned in to national television in 1972 when Zhou Enlai and Richard Nixon toasted each other with three successive cups of Maotai.

GEOGRAPHY

Mountains and plateaus make up some 87% of Guizhou's topography, which has an average altitude of 1,000 metres above sea level. A recent drive to increase income from tourism should see more remote regions of Guizhou opening for foreigners to explore caves, waterfalls and minority areas. The star

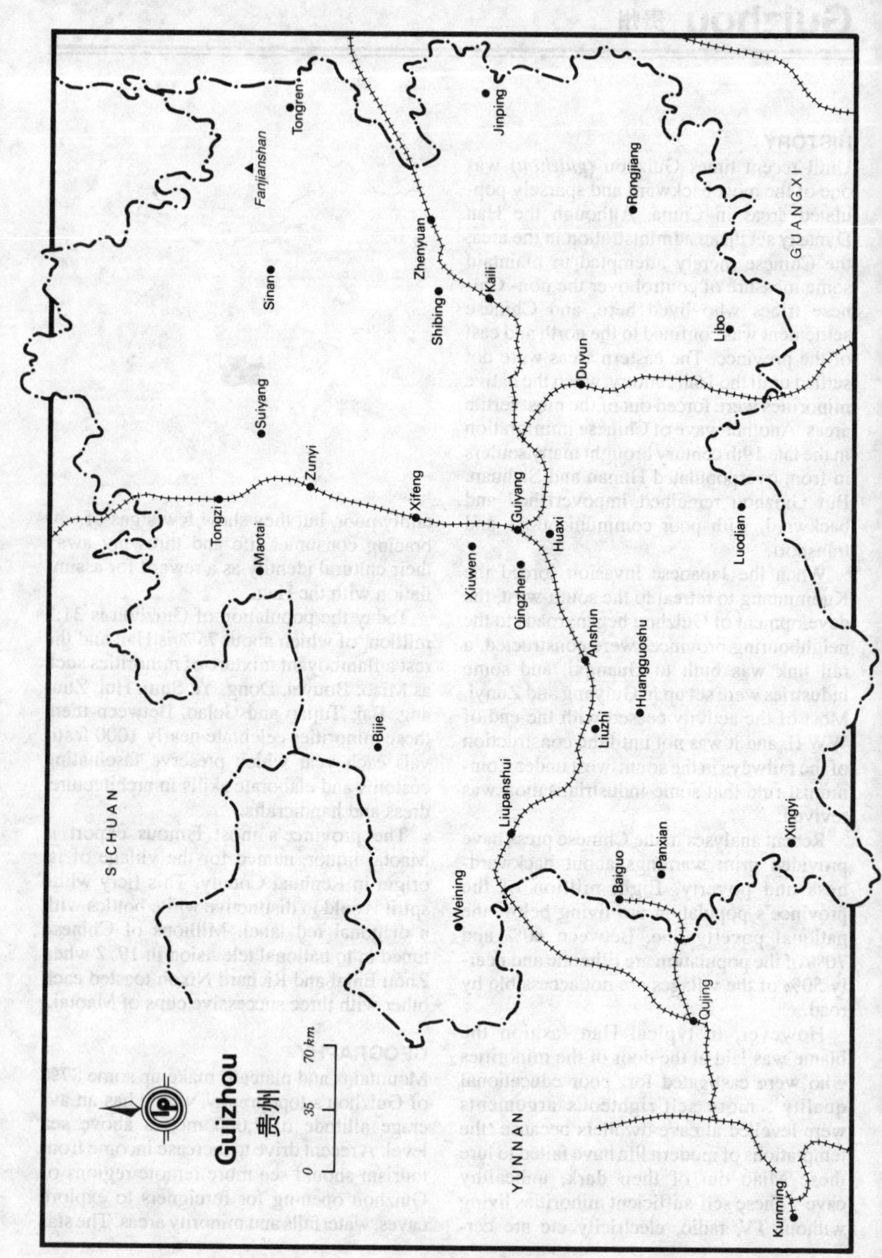
Guizhou
贵州
0 35 70 km
SICHUAN
YUNNAN
GUANGXI
Fanjianshan
Tongren
Jinping
Rongjiang
Zhenyuan
Sinan
Shibing
Kaili
Libo
Duyun
Suiyang
Zunyi
Xifeng
Tongzi
Guiyang
Huaxi
Maotai
Xiuwen
Qingzhen
Luodian
Anshun
Huangguoshu
Luzhi
Bijie
Liupanshui
Panxian
Weining
Baiguo
Xingyi
Qujing
Kunming

attraction close to Guiyang is the Huangguoshu Falls, China's biggest. The neighbourhood also presents opportunities for hiking and stumbling around some of China's all-too-little-visited villages.

FESTIVALS

Festivities amongst the minorities in Guizhou offer plenty of scope for exploration. Festivals take place throughout the lunar calendar at specific sites and are technicolour spectaculars which can feature bullfighting, horse racing, pipe playing, comic opera, singing contests and gigantic courting parties.

There are several festivals in **Guiyang** during the first lunar month (usually February or March), fourth lunar month (around May) and sixth lunar month (around July). Some of these take place in Huaxi.

Another town open to foreigners is **Kaili** *(kǎilǐ)*, on the railway line east of Guiyang. A profusion of festivals is held in nearby minority areas such as Lei Gongshan, Xijiang, Danxi, Qingman and Panghai. The town of Zhijiang, about 50 km from Kaili, is also a festival centre.

Further east on the railway line is **Zhenyuan**, recently opened to foreigners, which is renowned for its festivals between April and July. This town was once an important staging point on the ancient post road from central China to South-East Asia.

GUIYANG

(guìyáng) 贵阳

Guiyang, the capital of Guizhou Province, has a mild climate year-round; its name means 'Precious Sun' and may be a reference to the fact that the sun rarely seems to shine through the clouds and drizzle. A rush of post-Liberation factories, including manufacturers of diesel engines, machinery, textiles and the like, has added a polluting dimension, and rapid population expansion has created nightmares in concrete and brick over the top of what was formerly little more than a village.

A few old neighbourhoods and temples remain and with some effort the place can be appreciated for the funky conglomeration of town and village that it is. For most people, however, Guiyang is simply a transit point to somewhere else (if you're on your way to Chongqing from Guilin, for example, you'll have to change trains at Guiyang) or a jumping-off point for the Huangguoshu Falls or other places rapidly opening to foreigners in the province.

Information

CITS This office (☎ 25121) is staffed by two extremely friendly and helpful gentlemen; one speaks good English and the other speaks French; exactly why their talents have been placed in Guiyang, where there's really nothing to see, is one of the ironies of the China International Travel Syndrome. Bus Nos 2 or 1 from the railway station will get you to the office. It's in a government compound of colonnaded buildings, in the building to the right of the compound's main gateway.

Things to See

The distinctive architectural characteristic of Guiyang's handful of Mussolini-modern buildings is the columns – like the ones at the Provincial Exhibition Hall. The main street leading down from the railway station harbours one of the largest glistening white statues of Mao Zedong in China. For details on the scenic bus loop around the city, see the Getting Around section.

Sights on the edges of the city are of the dreary cave-lake-park type, but the **Huaxi Caves** *(huāxī dòng)* in Huaxi Park *(huāxī gōngyuán)* did yield a surprise – photocells along the underground path are activated by the guide's torch, triggering strings of coloured bulbs and neon signs as well as musical effects. There are other sights that may (or may not) be worth checking out: the late Ming Dynasty **Hongfu Monastery** *(hóngfú sì)* in Qianlingshan Park *(qiánlíng shān gōngyuán)* to the north-west of the city; and the **Kanzhu Pavilion** *(kànzhú tíng)* on top of the mountain, which is the vantage point overlooking the city. Five km to the

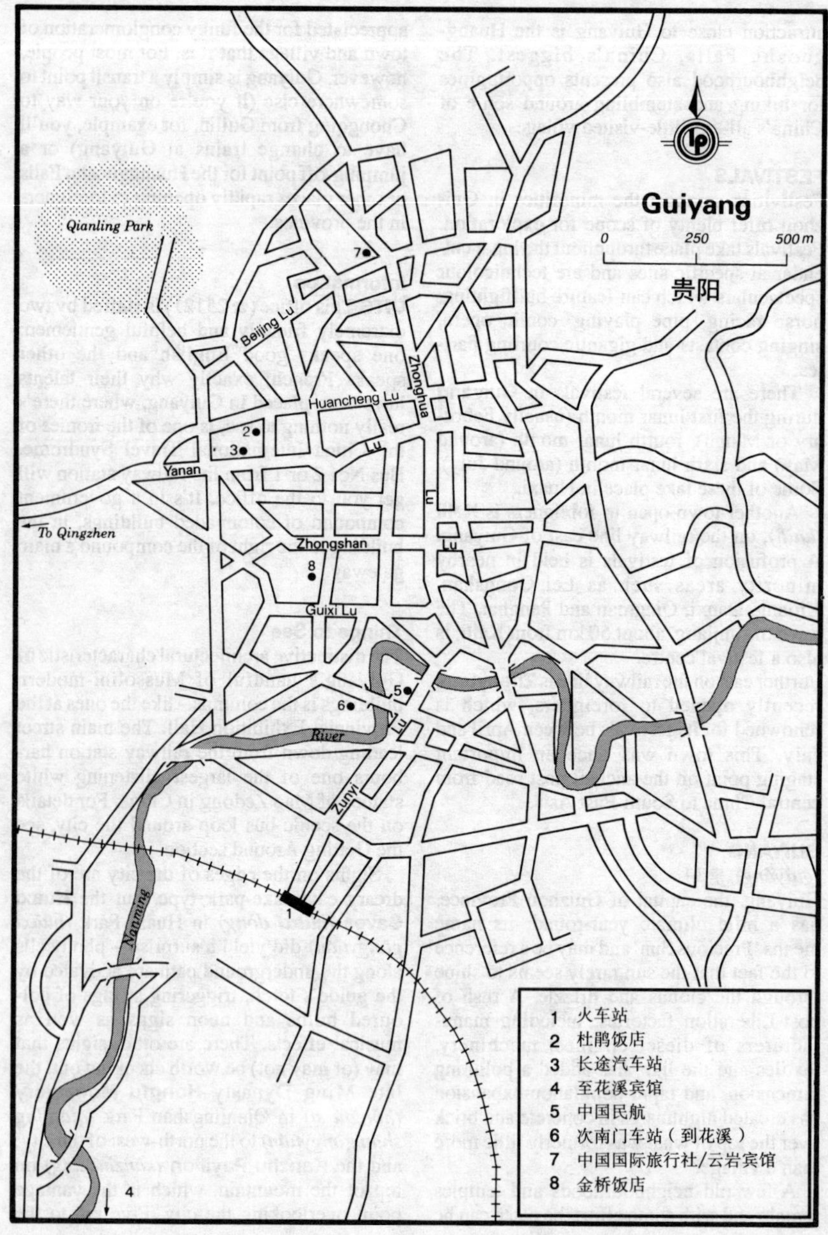
Guiyang
0
250
500 m
贵阳
Qianling Park
To Qingzhen
Beijing Lu
Zhonghua
Huancheng Lu
Lu
Yanan
Lu
Lu
Zhongshan
Guixi Lu
River
Lu
Zunyi
Nanming
1 火车站
2 杜鹃饭店
3 长途汽车站
4 至花溪宾馆
5 中国民航
6 次南门车站（到花溪）
7 中国国际旅行社/云岩宾馆
8 金桥饭店

1	Railway Station
2	Dujuan Hotel
3	Long-Distance Bus Station
4	To Hua Xi Hotel
5	CAAC
6	Cinanmen Bus Depot (Buses to Huaxi)
7	CITS/Yunyan Hotel
8	Jinqiao Hotel

south-west of Guiyang is **Nanjiao Park** *(nánjiāo gōngyuán)*, noted for its caves.

Places to Stay

If you're changing trains and stranded (going to Chongqing, for example), or attempting to get to the Huangguoshu Falls and in need of overnight lodgings, then try and use the 1st-class waiting room at the railway station. It's on the upper floor; on the ground floor there's a 24-hour baggage cage. Some students hang around the railway station waiting to catch a glimpse of the outside world, and you're a prize catch.

The official tourist hotel is the *Hua Xi Hotel* (☎ 551129) *(huāxī bīnguǎn)*, which is 20 km south-west of the city, halfway to the airport. The dun-coloured buildings are on a hill in a landscaped and mini-forest area. Rooms go for Y100, but you can usually bargain that down to Y45 for one person. Triples are from Y35 to Y45 per person. The problem is that this hotel is a logistical disaster for transport; from the railway station it requires bus No 2 to Xi'nanmen (south-west bus depot), then a no-number bus (it's sometimes identified as No 16) to Huaxi Park, then a two-km walk – by this time you're almost in the countryside so it's not a bad two-km walk. But the last bus connection to Huaxi Park is around 6 pm. A taxi from the railway station would cost at least Y15. Taxis and minibuses are available for hire at the hotel, and if you're in town CITS should be able to get you one. The other problem is that there's little chance of an early-morning bus connection from the hotel to the Guiyang long-distance bus station to catch an early-morning bus to Huangguoshu – that would also require a taxi.

Much more convenient is the *Dujuan Hotel (dùjuān fàndiàn)* on the block between Yan'an Lu and Huancheng Lu, just a short walk from the bus station. Doubles start at Y40 or you can share a three or four-bed room for Y10 per person. The *Jinqiao Hotel* (☎ 25872) *(jīnqiǎo fàndiàn)* at 34 Ruijin Zhonglu (on the bus No 1 route) has been upgraded since the last edition of this book. It's no longer a particularly cheap place to crash; doubles are now Y80.

At the north end of town is the older, Chinese-garden-style *Yunyan Hotel* (☎ 23324) *(yúnyán bīnguǎn)*, 68 Beijing Lu. Rates vary widely depending on the wing; most rooms in the older sections are in the Y50 to Y100 range. It may be possible to get into a triple for Y35 per person. In the newer wing rooms start at around Y100.

Places to Eat

For munchies try the restaurants on the perimeter of the square around the railway station. The *Huaxi Hotel* and *Yunyan Hotel* have pleasant, reasonably priced dining rooms.

Some food stalls in Guiyang sell traditional snacks such as *kǎo dòufu* (roasted bean curd), *liángfěn* (bean jelly), *huájié tángyuán* (sweet dumpling) and *kǎo bāogǔ* (roast corn).

In 1986, drinkers in Guiyang received a very raw deal when local bootleggers laced Maotai liquor with methanol to cut costs and add more kick before selling it to local merchants. Within days, 20 people had died and teams of medical workers were treating hundreds of seriously sick boozers. The mayor of Guiyang went on TV to warn the public about the evil brew, which contained 300 times the permitted level of methanol.

Getting There & Away

Air Guiyang is connected by air to Beijing, Canton, Haikou, Kunming, Guilin, Shanghai, Wuhan, Chengdu and Changsha. The CAAC office (☎ 23000) is at 170 Zunyi Lu.

Bus Buses to the Huangguoshu Falls (Anshun) depart from the long-distance bus station in the north-west of the city. The bus station is a distinctive building, an old temple-like structure. For details, see the section on Huangguoshu.

Train Direct trains run to Kunming, Guilin, Chongqing and Nanning. For Zhanjiang you may have to change trains at Liuzhou. Some sample fares: *Chinese price*, hard-sleeper, are:

to Guilin, 18 hours, Y50; to Liuzhou, 15 hours, Y41; to Kunming, 15 hours, Y40; to Chongqing, 11 hours, Y30.

Getting Around

If you want to do a city-loop tour, then across the square from the railway station are two round-the-city buses, Nos 1 and 2. They follow the same route but No 2 goes clockwise while No 1 goes anti-clockwise. These will get you to most places (bar the Huaxi Binguan) – the round trip from the station takes about 45 minutes for the grand sum of Y0.15. You can get a good window seat since you get on at the terminal; the same cannot be said if you choose to alight at random for a foot-sortie. The main shopping street is on the bus No 1 route heading north.

AROUND GUIYANG

Hong Feng Hu *(hóngfēng hú)* (Red Maple Lake) lies close to Qingzhen, which is 33 km west of Guiyang. This complex of four lake districts covers over 74 sq km. The main attractions seem to be boating to some of the hundreds of small islands and exploring caves.

Huangguoshu Falls

(huángguǒshù dàpùbù) 黄果树大瀑布

Located 155 km south-west of Guiyang, China's premier cataract reaches widths of 81 metres, with a drop of 74 metres into the Rhinoceros Pool. For a preview, there is a drawing of the falls on the 10-fen Foreign Exchange Certificate. Huangguoshu provides an excellent chance to go rambling through the superb rural minority areas on foot. Once you're there, you'll have no transport problems as everything you need is within walking range or, if you wish to go further, hiking range. Take a raincoat if you're off to waterfalls and a warm jacket or sweater if you're descending into caves, which can be chilly.

The thunder of Huangguoshu Falls can be heard for some distance, and the mist from the falls carries to the local villages during the rainy season, which lasts from May to October. The falls are at their most spectacular about four days after heavy rains. The dry season lasts from November to April, so during March and April the flow of water can become a less impressive trickle.

The main falls are the central piece of a huge waterfall, cave and karst area, covering some 450 sq km. It was only explored by the Chinese in the 1980s as a preliminary to harnessing the hydroelectric potential. They discovered about 18 falls, four subterranean rivers, and 100 caves, many of which are now being gradually opened up to visitors.

At the edge of the falls is **Water Curtain Cave** *(shuǐlián dòng)*, a niche in the cliffs which is approached by a slippery (and dangerous) sortie wading across rocks in the Rhino Pool – from the cave you'll get an interior view of the gushing waters through six 'windows'.

One km above the main falls is **Steep Slope Falls** *(dǒupō pùbù)*, which are easy to reach. Steep Slope Falls is 105 metres wide and 23 metres high, and gets its name from the crisscross patterning of sloping waters. Eight km below Huangguoshu Falls are the **Star Bridge Falls** *(tiānshēng qiáo)*.

Ten km north-west of the Huangguoshu area (there may be a bus) are the **Gaotan Falls**, which lie on another river system. The falls here have a graduated drop of 120 metres.

About 30 km from the Gaotan Falls is a spectacular series of underground caverns called **Longgong** *(lónggōng)* or Dragon Palace which form a network through some 20 mountains. Charter boats tour one of the largest water-filled caves, often called the

'Dragon Cave'. The caverns lies in Anshun County, at the Bouyei settlement of Longtan *(lóngtǎn zhài)* (Dragon Pool). Other scenic caves in the vicinity include **Daji Dong**, **Chuan Dong** and **Linlang Dong**.

Huangguoshu (Yellow Fruit Tree) is in the Zhenning Bouyei and Miao Autonomous County. The Miao are not in evidence around the falls, but for the Bouyei, who favour river valleys, this is prime water country. The Bouyei are the 'aboriginals' of Guizhou. The people are of Thai origin and related to the Zhuangs in Guangxi. They number 2.1 million, mostly spread over the south-west sector of Guizhou Province. Bouyei dress is dark and sombre, with colourful trimmings; 'best' clothes come out on festival or market days. The Bouyei marry early, usually at 16, but sometimes as young as 12. Married women are distinguished by headgear symbols.

The Bouyei are very poor, showing signs of malnutrition and wearing clothes that are grubby and tattered. The contrast with the postcard minority image of starched and ironed costumes, or the ring-of-confidence sparkling teeth is obvious. The Bouyei tribespeople are also shy and suspicious of foreigners.

Batik (cloth wax-dyeing) is one of the skills of the Bouyei. The masonry at Huangguoshu is also intriguing – stone blocks comprise the housing, but no plaster is used; the roofs are finished in stone slates. There is a Bouyei festival in Huangguoshu lasting 10 days during the first lunar month (usually February or early March).

Places to Stay & Eat At the bus park near the Huangguoshu Falls are some food stalls. Below them, down the cliff, is a teahouse and souvenir shop. The viewing area for the falls is a short downhill walk from the bus park. Further away from the bus park is *Huangguoshu Guesthouse (huángguǒshù bīnguǎn)*, which is only for foreigners. Clean rooms with bathroom start at Y20 per person. Its decent restaurant charges Y4 for set meals; buy tickets at the reception desk.

Just before the bridge on the way into town from Anshun is the *Tianxing Hotel* with cheaper accommodation for Y10 per person. Other doss houses in the village with no facilities charge Y2 per night, but the authorities may require foreigners to stay in one of the sanctioned hotels.

Getting There & Away You can get to Huangguoshu Falls from either Guiyang or Anshun – both have logistical obstacles but Anshun is preferable.

The falls are 150 km by road from Guiyang. A bus (usually No 103) leaves Guiyang's long-distance bus station at 7 am; the fare is around Y6 or Y8, and the trip takes four to five hours. Tour buses depart the falls for Guiyang at around 3 or 4 pm.

Guiyang CITS offers minibus tours to the falls, departing from the Hua Xi Hotel in Guiyang. Prices are in the region of Y0.50 to Y0.80 per km, dependent on the size of the group and vehicle. For a same-day return trip to the falls you'd be looking at, say, Y230 – no food, no guide. The same deal, but considerably cheaper, can be got in Anshun.

Anshun lies on the Guiyang-Kunming railway line, about two hours from Guiyang. Anshun is 50 km from the falls, so a local bus takes about 1½ hours to get there; the fare is Y2.50. If you arrive in Anshun by train you may have problems with a bus connection to Huangguoshu, so you may have to stay overnight in Anshun and take a bus out the next morning. The bus service between Anshun and the falls is sporadic; on weekdays buses depart from Anshun at around 7.30 am and noon, and there may be one as late as 2.30 pm. Bus frequencies at weekends are higher than on weekdays.

Alternatively, you could go from Anshun to Zhenning, which is near the falls. The trip takes an hour and costs Y0.80. There are five morning buses from Anshun to Zhenning and five afternoon buses.

There's a local bus from Huangguoshu to Guiyang at 12.30 pm; other buses depart Huangguoshu for Anshun at 10.30 am, 2 pm, 3 pm, 4 pm and 4.30 pm. These will probably connect with trains leaving Anshun for Guiyang or Kunming.

As a rule of thumb, you have a better chance of getting a hard-sleeper on the section between Kunming and Anshun if you start out from Kunming and buy your ticket in advance there. There's usually little chance of buying a hard-sleeper ticket from Anshun to Kunming.

You could take the bus between Kunming and Huangguoshu. Some travellers spurn the trains between Guizhou and Yunnan provinces and simply take buses via Panxian and Qujing. A bus from Anshun to Panxian is Y10.

The bus to Panxian passes through Huangguoshu daily at about 9 am and will stop outside the ticket office if you flag it down. The trip costs Y7.50 and takes 10 hours. Panxian has a hostel at the bus station with beds for Y10. The bus from Panxian to Qujing leaves at 7.30 am, takes six hours and costs Y6. The hotel in Qujing is about 20 minutes walk from the bus station. Follow the road which runs from the other side of the roundabout directly opposite the front of the bus station. After passing a modern house (pagoda style) on your left, take the first road on the right. The hotel is about 200 metres down this road on the left. The bus from Qujing to Kunming departs at 7.30 am, takes four hours and costs Y6.

ANSHUN

(ānshùn) 安顺

Anshun, once an opium-trading centre, remains the commercial hub of western Guizhou but is now known for its batiks. At the north-east end of town is a large Confucian temple. The town lies on the Guiyang-Kunming railway line, a two-hour ride from Guiyang.

You can make Anshun a jumping-off point for the Huangguoshu Falls. The bus from the Hongshan Hotel is sometimes sent to the station if they receive word that foreigners are looking lost there. You'll then be charged Y4 for the ride to the hotel. If you avoid being intercepted at the railway station, you may be able to get down to Huangguoshu on the same day.

Walk straight ahead from the railway station for about 1½ km, and the bus station is on your left – ask for 'Huang Guo Shu, Duan Tu Qi Che Zhan' (Huangguoshu, short-distance bus station). If you intend to come back on the same day, dump your bags at the left-luggage room at the Anshun railway station.

Spending a day or two in Anshun isn't the worst of fates, actually, since the karst valley setting is pleasant and some of the narrow streets are lined with interesting old wooden houses.

Places to Stay

Near the bus station are a couple of convenient places. The *Xixiushan Hotel (xīxiù bīnguǎn)* opposite the station has cheap dorm beds but is sometimes reluctant to give them to foreigners. Doubles cost around Y40.

The *Minzu Hotel (mínzú fàndiàn)* on Tashan Donglu, on the east side of town near the highway to Guiyang, has doubles for Y40 to Y50. There's a fair Muslim restaurant on the second floor.

The main tourist joint, inconveniently located on the northern outskirts of Anshun, is the *Hongshan Hotel* (☎ 23454) *(hóngshān bīnguǎn)*, 39 Baihong Lu. It's definitely lacking in the electricity and plumbing departments, but it's solid. The hotel gardens overlook an artificial lake. Double rooms cost from Y50 to Y60. The hotel is completely isolated but the dinner-bell of the hotel dining room is loud enough to warn of impending food shortages.

CITS (☎ 3173) has an office here which organises trips to Huangguoshu and the surrounding area. The bus station is four km away and the railway station three km. The hotel minibus charges about Y5 per person for transfer to the railway station.

Sichuan 四川

There is a Chinese saying that the real riches in life are not jade or pearls, but the five grains (rice, soya beans, wheat, barley and millet). These are well represented in the fertile Sichuan Basin, under irrigation since the 3rd century BC and the PRC's greatest rice producer.

Sichuan *(sìchuān)* is the largest province in China but also the most heavily populated, with almost 100 million people. It is the eastern region of Sichuan, the great Chengdu plain, that supports one of the densest rural populations in the world, while the regions to the west are mountainous and sparsely populated, mainly by Tibetans.

Possibly because this is the home of Deng Xiaoping (who was born here in 1904), Sichuan has become a testing ground for the dissolution of the commune system; he has called the commune a utopian dream of 'reaching heaven in one step'. The efforts now are towards decentralisation of agriculture, greater autonomy of decision making, establishment of free markets at which peasants can sell their produce, and greater individual incentives. Xindu County, outside Chengdu, was one of the first experimental stations; farms are state-owned, but if peasants meet the required quota, any surplus is theirs. They also decide what to plant and when. If the streets of Chengdu are any indication, the 'responsibility system' is a howling success.

Roughly the size of France, give or take Luxembourg, Sichuan has rich natural resources. Wild mountainous terrain and fast rivers kept it relatively isolated until the present era, and much of the western fringe is still remote. The capital is Chengdu; the largest city is Chongqing, which is also the stepping-stone for the ferry ride down the Yangtse River.

The remote mountains of Sichuan, Gansu and Shaanxi provinces are the natural habitat of the giant panda. Of China's 1174 species of birds, 420 species of mammals and 500

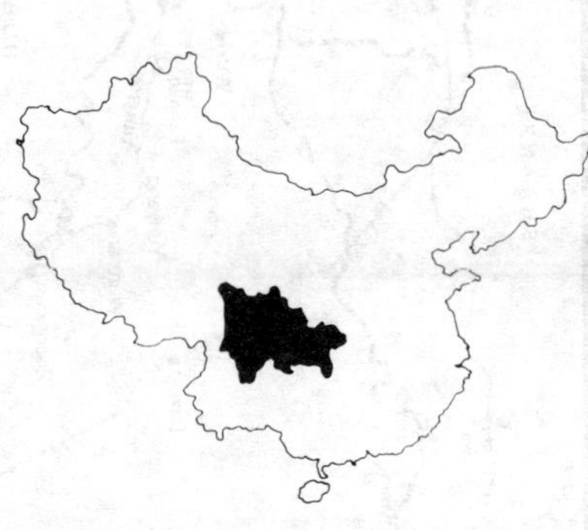

species of reptiles and amphibians, the one animal which Westerners automatically associate with China is the giant panda. This is probably due to the Chinese fondness several years ago for giving them away as presents to foreign governments.

CHENGDU

(chéngdū) 成都

Chengdu is Sichuan's capital and the administrative, educational and cultural centre, as well as a major industrial base. It boasts a 2500-year history, linked closely with the art and craft trades. During the Eastern Han Dynasty (25-220 AD) the city was named Jinjiang Cheng (Brocade City), due to its thriving silk manufacture. Like other major Chinese cities, the place has had its share of turmoil. First it was devastated by the Mongols in retaliation for fierce fighting put up by the Sichuanese. From 1644 to 1647 it was presided over by the rebel Zhang Xiangzhong, who set up an independent state in Sichuan, ruled by terror and mass extermination. Three centuries later the city was set up as one of the last strongholds of the Kuomintang. Ironically, the name 'Chengdu' means Perfect Metropolis – and today 2.5 million people inhabit the perfect

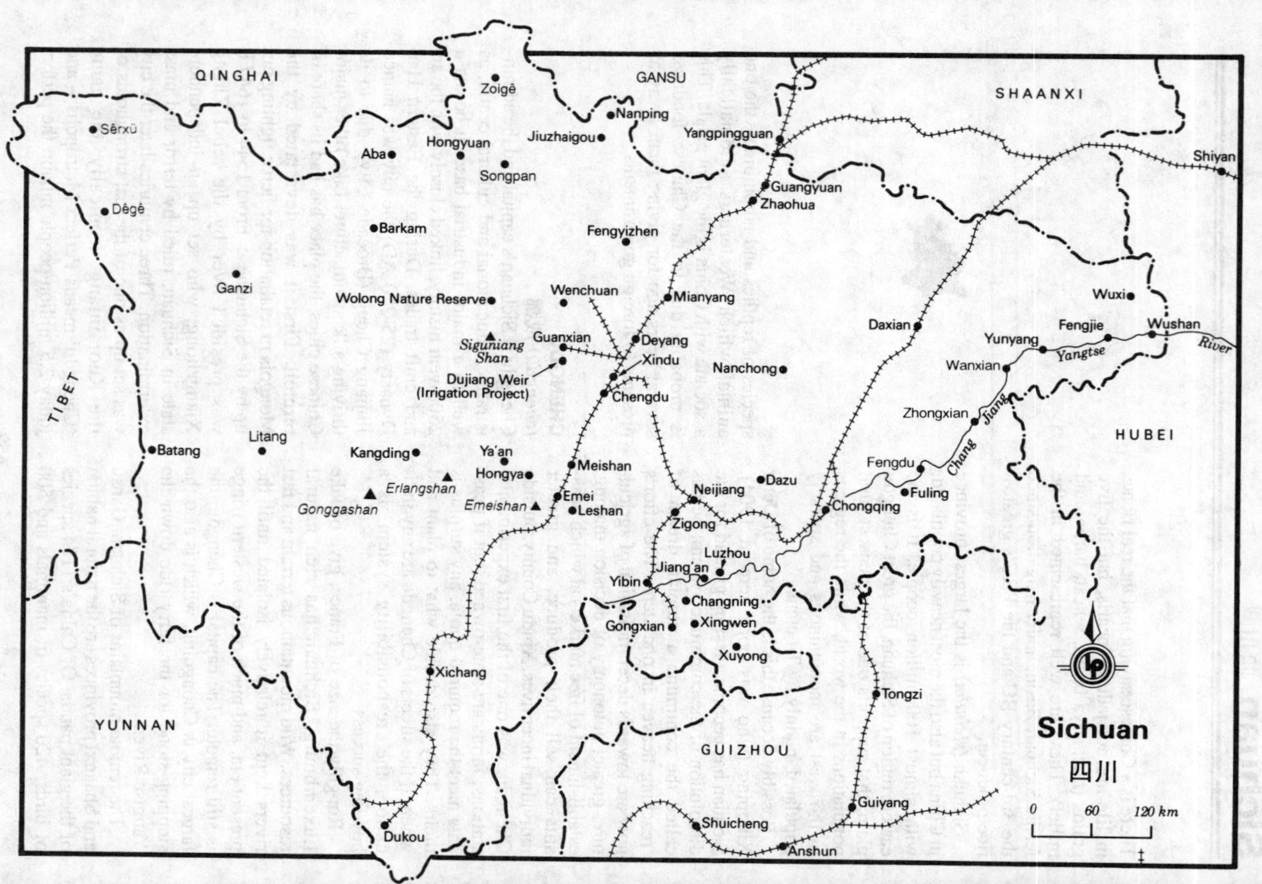
QINGHAI
GANSU
SHAANXI
TIBET
YUNNAN
GUIZHOU
HUBEI
Sêrxü
Dêgê
Zoigê
Nanping
Jiuzhaigou
Yangpingguan
Shiyan
Aba
Hongyuan
Songpan
Guangyuan
Zhaohua
Barkam
Fengyizhen
Ganzi
Wolong Nature Reserve
Wenchuan
Mianyang
Daxian
Wuxi
Fengjie
Wushan
Yunyang
Yangtse
River
Wanxian
Siguniang Shan
Guanxian
Deyang
Xindu
Nanchong
Dujiang Weir (Irrigation Project)
Chengdu
Zhongxian
Chang Jiang
Batang
Litang
Kangding
Ya'an
Hongya
Meishan
Fengdu
Fuling
Erlangshan
Gonggashan
Emeishan
Emei
Leshan
Neijiang
Dazu
Chongqing
Zigong
Luzhou
Jiang'an
Yibin
Changning
Gongxian
Xingwen
Xuyong
Xichang
Tongzi
Sichuan
四川
Guiyang
Shuicheng
Anshun
Dukou
0 60 120 km

city proper, or nearly four times that if you count the surrounding metropolitan area.

The original city was walled with a moat, gates at the compass points, and the Viceroy's Palace (14th-century) at the heart. The latter was the imperial quarter. The remains of the city walls were demolished in the early 1960s, and the Viceroy's Palace was blown to smithereens at the height of the Cultural Revolution. In its place was erected the Soviet-style Exhibition Hall. Outside, Mao waves merrily down Renmin Lu; inside, the standard portraits of Marx, Engels, Lenin, Stalin and Mao gaze down in wonder at rampant capitalism. So much for the revolution. (In Beijing's Tiananmen Square, the four portraits have been removed, to be resurrected for special occasions.)

Comparisons between Chengdu and Beijing are tempting – the same city-planning hand at work – but Chengdu is an altogether different place, with far more greenery, overhanging wooden housing in the older parts of town, and a very different kind of energy coming off the streets. One of the most intriguing aspects of the city is that its artisans are back. These small-time basket-weavers, cobblers, itinerant dentists, tailors, houseware merchants and snack hawkers could be one of the greatest strengths of the Chinese economy, as they fill basic needs. Chengdu has built up a solid industrial base since 1949, and traditional handicrafts such as lacquerware and embroidery are produced in bulk. Most of Chengdu's industries are well outside the city limits although the air suffers throughout the city, especially in the summer months. One of the biggest is China Chengdu Aircraft Industries, which makes aircraft noses for the USA's McDonnell-Douglas Aircraft Corporation.

Free markets, flea markets, black markets, pedlar markets – whatever they are, Chengdu is cooking with them. Each twist and turn down the back alleys seems to reveal a new speciality. Around the corner comes a florist shop on wheels – a bicycle laden with gladioli – or you chance upon a meat market, a vegetable market, a spice market, or a side street devoted to a species of household repair. Add to this the indoor food markets, and you're looking at a thriving small business economy.

There is a busy poultry market a short walk from the Jin Jiang Hotel. To get there cross the bridge to the south and turn left. If you go north and then take an alley to the left, off Renmin Lu, before you reach Shaanxi Jie, you'll find an outdoor factory of sorts, where the street is lined with women at their sewing machines. Further west, bordering the south-east edge of Renmin Park, is a small strip devoted entirely to the sale of eggs.

Engrossing to stroll through is the tinker-and-tailor free market (for lack of better terminology) which runs north from near the Chengdu Restaurant, and then turns east along another alley leading to Chunxi Lu – this one is a local Mecca for clothing and on-the-spot tailoring. It appears that the market is not affected by cotton-ration coupons, and it also appears that those with fast scissors can earn double what a factory worker gets.

At night during warm-weather months, Chengdu exhibits what may be the liveliest street life in all of China.

Orientation

Chengdu has echoes of boulevard-sweeping Beijing in its grand scale, except that here flowering shrubs and foliage line the expanses. As in Beijing there is a ring road right around the outer city. The main administrative-type boulevard is Renmin Beilu, Zhonglu and Nanlu, north to south. The nucleus of the shopping-dining-theatre district is a large pentagonal shape bounded by the boulevards Dongfeng Lu, Shangdong Dajie, Hongxing Lu and Shuncheng Jie.

The best landmark is the colossal Mao statue outside the Exhibition Hall. There seems to be a shifting of street numbers and street names around Chengdu, as well as boulevard reconstruction; if you follow the numbers in one direction you meet another set of numbers going the other way, which leaves the poor family in the middle with five

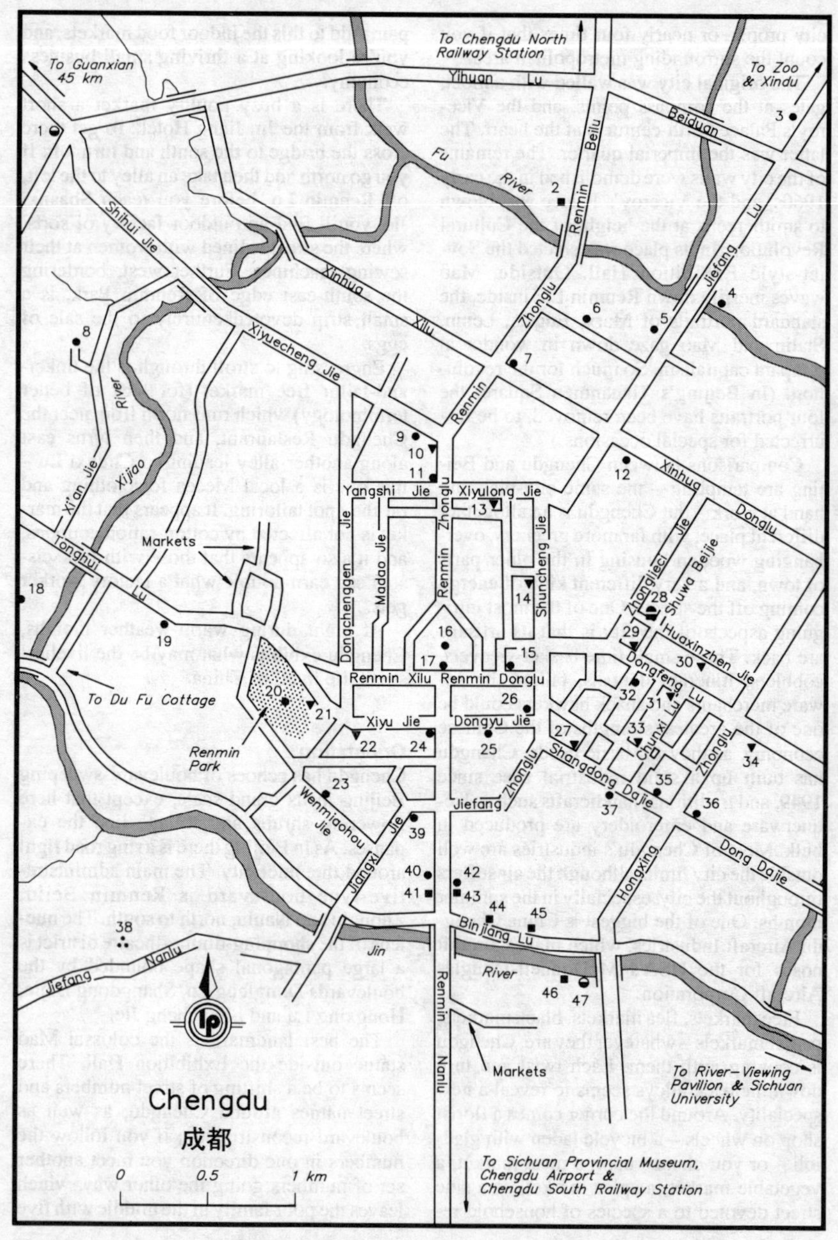
To Chengdu North Railway Station
To Guanxian 45 km
To Zoo & Xindu
Yihuan Lu
Beiduan
Fu River
Renmin Beilu
Jiefang Lu
Shihui Jie
Xinhua Xilu
Xiyuecheng Jie
Renmin Zhonglu
Xi'an Jie
Xijiao River
Yangshi Jie
Xiyulong Jie
Xinhua Donglu
Zhongjieci Jie
Shuwa Beijie
Huaxinzhen Jie
Markets
Tonghui Lu
Dongchenggen Jie
Madao Jie
Renmin Zhonglu
Shuncheng Jie
Dongfeng Lu
Chunxi Lu
Renmin Xilu
Renmin Donglu
To Du Fu Cottage
Xiyu Jie
Dongyu Jie
Renmin Park
Shangdong Dajie
Zhonglu
Zhonglu
Wenmiaohou Jie
Jiangxi Jie
Jiefang
Hongxing
Dong Dajie
Binjiang Lu
Jin River
Jiefang Nanlu
Renmin Nanlu
Markets
To River-Viewing Pavilion & Sichuan University
Chengdu
成都
0 0.5 1 km
To Sichuan Provincial Museum, Chengdu Airport & Chengdu South Railway Station

■ PLACES TO STAY

2 Tibet Hotel
41 Jin Jiang Hotel/CITS
43 Minshan Hotel
44 Binjiang Hotel
45 Black Coffee Hotel
46 Jiaotong (Traffic) Hotel

▼ PLACES TO EAT

4 Teahouse
10 Rong Le Yuan Restaurant
13 Chen Mapo (Granny's Beancurd) Snackshop
14 Xiao Yuan Teahouse & Bar
21 Renmin Teahouse
22 Wang Pang Duck Restaurant
27 Chengdu Restaurant
29 Zhong Shuijiao Ravioli Restaurant
30 Shi Mei Xuan Restaurant
31 Lai Tangyuan Rice-Ball Restaurant
33 Yaohua Restaurant
34 Snackshops (Sweets)

OTHER

1 Ximen Bus Station (Buses for Guanxian)
3 Bamboo Weaving Factory
5 Sichuan Embroidery Factory
6 Wenshu Monastery
7 Chengdu Theatre
8 Tomb of Wang Jiang
9 Drum & Cymbal Shop
11 Foreign Languages Bookstore
12 Public Security Bureau
15 Telecommunications Building
16 Sichuan Exhibition Hall
17 Mao Statue
18 Cultural Park & Qingyang Palace
19 Lacquerware Factory
20 Monument to the Martyrs of the Railway Protecting Movement 1911
23 Public Security Bureau (Exit/Entry Administration)
24 Xinhua Bookstore
25 Advance Rail Ticket Office
26 Renmin Market
28 GPO
32 Bank of China
35 Bicycle Hire Shop
36 Bicycle Hire Shop
37 Friendship Store
38 Temple of Wuhou
39 Bicycle Hire Shop
40 Bicycle Hire Shop
42 China Southwest Airlines/Blue Sky Hotel
47 Chengdu Bus Terminal (Xinnanmen Bus Station)

sets of numbers over their doorway. Street names, also, seem to change every 100 metres or so. If the numbers (or even streets) in this text are a little askew, hopefully the map locations won't be.

The area where Renmin Nanlu crosses the Jin River, near the Jin Jiang and Traffic hotels, has become the city's tourist ghetto. This is where you'll find most of the restaurants and arts & crafts shops catering for foreigners. The 'English Club' meets among the trees near the intersection of Renmin Nanlu and Binjiang Lu on Tuesdays, Fridays and Sundays at 7.30 pm. Although some travellers can't stand being surrounded by small crowds of inquisitive Chinese people, those that can will be amply rewarded by some interesting chat. Conversations can be surprisingly candid.

Information

CITS This office (☎ 28731) is next to hopeless, and mainly interested in raking up group-tour money. They're in the Jin Jiang Hotel. Try the front-desk staff as they make a lot more sense, and their English is superior. Good sources of information are the budget-tour guides who hang out at the Flower Garden Snack Bar, next to the Traffic Hotel.

Public Security Bureau The office (☎ 6577) is on Xinhua Donglu, east of the intersection with Jiefang Zhonglu. This is the place to report thefts etc.

For permits to visit 'closed' areas in Sichuan, you must apply to the Exit-Entry Administration branch of the Sichuan PSB on Wenmiaohou Jie, which is off Jiangxi Jie

■ PLACES TO STAY

2 西藏饭店
41 锦江宾馆
43 岷山饭店
44 滨江饭店
45 黑咖啡饭店
46 交通饭店

▼ PLACES TO EAT

4 解放北路茶馆
10 荣乐饭店
13 陈麻婆豆腐
14 晓园茶馆
21 人民茶馆
22 王胖鸭店
27 成都餐厅
29 钟水饺饭店
30 市美轩餐厅
31 赖汤元饭店
33 耀华饭店
34 小吃（东风路）

OTHER

1 西门汽车站
3 竹编工艺厂
5 蜀绣厂
6 文殊院
7 成都剧院
8 王建墓
9 鼓店
11 外书店
12 公安局外事科
15 电讯大楼
16 四川省展览馆
17 毛泽东像
18 文化公园
19 漆器厂
20 烈士纪念碑
23 省公安局厅出入境理处
24 新华书店
25 火车售票处
26 人民市场
28 邮总局
32 中国银行
35 出租自行车店
36 出租自行车店
37 友谊商店
38 武侯祠
39 出租自行车店
40 出租自行车店
42 中国西南航
47 新南门汽车站

to the west of the Jin Jiang Hotel. Certain members of the staff speak excellent English. This office is open Monday and Wednesday from 8.30 to 11 am and from 3 to 5 pm, and on Saturday from 8.30 to 11 am.

Money All of the hotels mentioned in Places to Stay have foreign exchange counters. The Jin Jiang Hotel has a branch of the Bank of China on the ground floor. On the streets in the vicinity of the Jin Jiang and Traffic hotels you'll be pestered by hordes of money-changers – the black-market rate in Chengdu is usually a bit above average.

Post The main post office is on the corner of Huaxinzhen Jie and Shuwa Beijie. Poste restante mail is kept behind the window marked 'International Post' – names of addressees for poste restante parcels are marked on a blackboard.

Poste restante service at the GPO is generally efficient. Nonetheless, since it's across town from the Jin River tourist area, many tourists have their mail addressed to the Jin Jiang Hotel. In our experience this hotel is not an especially good place to receive mail if you're not staying there. If you do attempt to pick up mail at the Jin Jiang, be sure to check both the reception desk and the hotel's post office.

Consulates The US Consulate General has an office in Chengdu in the Jin Jiang Hotel. Telephone direct on 51912 or 52791, or dial 24481 and ask for extension 138.

Maps City bus maps can be found at railway stations, the Jin Jiang Hotel and Xinhua bookshops. Three different maps in Chinese provide excellent detail for Sichuan Province, Chengdu city or its surrounding areas. The English 'Tourist Map of Chengdu', available at the Jin Jiang Hotel's gift shop, is very useful for city excursions.

Reading & Music The Foreign Language Bookstore has mildly captivating tourist literature and general data, as well as the usual collection of English-teaching materials, *Jane Eyre*, US and British short story collections and Grimm's fairy tales. And while you're here, there's a counter selling watery versions of Western music and traditional Chinese music in cassette form (the store shares the same corner as a Xinhua Bookstore).

Dangers & Annoyances There have been several reports of foreigners becoming targets for rip-offs and theft in Chengdu.

To avoid getting ripped off by taxis, pedicab drivers and restaurants, always get the price at the start of proceedings. Pickpockets are common around bus stations, railway stations and post offices, and watch out for gangs who razor your bags on buses (the No 16 bus is the most notorious). It's a good idea to use a money belt. If you want to play it safe with train tickets, make a note of the ticket numbers. If the tickets are stolen you'll be given replacements, providing you can supply the numbers of the old ones.

Should things get out of hand, use the phone (☎ 6577) to locate an English-speaker at the Gong An Ju, Wai Shi Ke (Public Security Bureau, Foreign Affairs Section); they might be of use.

Renmin Park

(rénmín gōngyuán) 人民公园

This is one Chinese park well worth recommending. It's to the south-west of the city centre. The teahouse here is excellent (see the Places to Eat section), and just near the entrance is the candyman, producing works of art in toffee. China's back-street merchants can be truly amazing. While most of the action, or relaxation, is around the entrance to Renmin Park, the rest of it is not too shabby – a bonsai rockery, a kids' playground, a few swimming pools (for locals), and the Monument to the Martyrs of the Railway-Protecting Movement (1911). Apparently this obelisk, decorated with shunting and tracks, marks an uprising of the people against officers who pocketed cash raised for the construction of the Chengdu-Chongqing Line. Since Renmin Park was also at the time a private officer's garden, it was a fitting place to erect the structure.

Temple Parks

Of perhaps more middling interest are the temple parks of Chengdu. These are all a fair distance from the Jin Jiang Hotel, although a cycle out to them would be a rewarding exercise in itself.

The celebrated Tang poet Du Fu (712-70 AD) lived at the thatched **Du Fu Cottage** *(dùfǔ cǎotáng)*. Something of a rover, Du Fu was born in Henan and left his home turf to see China at the tender age of 20. He was an official in Chang'an (the ancient capital on the site of modern-day Xi'an) for 10 years, was later captured by rebels after an uprising, and fled to Chengdu, where he stayed for four years. He built himself a humble cottage and penned over 200 poems on the sufferings of the people.

The present grounds – 20 hectares of leafy bamboo and luxuriant vegetation – are an expansion over time of the original cottage area. It's also the centre of the Chengdu Du Fu Study Society, and houses Chinese and Western editions of the poet's works, a Du Fu statue and miniature calligraphy (a miniaturist might be on hand to engrave rings). From the time of his death in exile (in Hunan), Du Fu acquired a cult status, with the poems themselves being great inspiration for painting (which is displayed on site).

Praise for Du Fu comes from the highest source, Chairman Mao. The Great Helmsman seems to have overdone it a bit – the right-hand section of the park is largely devoted to commemorating his visit in 1958. The park offers tranquil strolling in tea gardens and is about five km west of the city centre.

The **Temple of Wuhou** *(wǔhòu sì)* is in Nanjiao Park *(nánjiāo gōngyuán)* in the city's southern suburb. Wuhou or Zhu

Geliang was a famous military strategist of the Three Kingdoms Period (220-65 AD). He was the prime minister of the state of Shu, and shares the tomb space and shrine with his emperor, Liu Bei. Chengdu was the capital of Shu state. Structures at the site date to the Tang Dynasty, with renovations and enlargements from the 17th and 20th centuries. There's some fine stele calligraphy, and statues of military and civic officers. To the west of the temple is a large park with a lake, places for picnicking, a nice teahouse, and a small antique store at the north end.

The position of **River Viewing Pavilion** *(wàngjiāng lóu)* is as the name suggests. It is to the south-east of Chengdu, near Sichuan University. The pavilion is a four-storey Qing wooden structure with a teahouse and restaurant. Lush forests of bamboo of over 100 types surround the building. The bamboos range from skyscrapers to bonsai-sized potted plants, so this might be a good place to escape the summer heat. The pavilion was built to the memory of Xue Tao, a Tang Dynasty poet. Nearby is a well, said to be the place where she drew water to dye her writing paper.

These three temple parks are open from 7.30 am to 6 pm.

To the west of the city centre is **Cultural Park** *(wénhuà gōngyuán)*, the site of Qingyang Gong, an ancient Taoist temple. The Lantern Festival is held here at Chinese New Year.

Tomb of Wang Jian

(wángjiàn mù) 王建墓

To the north-west of Chengdu, the tomb's exhibition hall features a display of relics, including a jade belt, mourning books, imperial seals, and warrior and musician sculptures. Wang Jian (847-918 AD) was emperor of Shu in the 10th century. The hall is open daily except Monday, from 9 am to noon and from 2 to 5.30 pm.

Sichuan University Museum

(sìdà bówùguǎn) 四大博物馆

The museum is on the 1st and 3rd floors of Sichuan University's Liberal Arts building. Founded in 1914 by American scholar D S Dye, it underwent several closings and name changes before re-opening under its current name in 1984. The six exhibition rooms display, on a rotating basis, a collection of over 40,000 items. The collection is particularly strong in the fields of ethnology, folklore and traditional arts. The Tibetan Art Exhibition Room, for example, is designed like a family worship hall and contains Buddha images, thangkas (religious paintings), Tibetan musical instruments and various other cultural artefacts. The ethnology room exhibits artefacts from the Yi, Qiang, Miao, Jingpo, Naxi and Tibetan cultures. The Chinese painting and calligraphy room displays works from the Tang, Song, Yuan, Ming and Qing dynasties. Some labels are in English.

The museum is open Monday to Saturday, from 9 am to noon and from 2.30 to 5.30 pm. The university grounds are within easy walking distance of Jiuyanqiao bus station, next to the Nine-Arch Bridge. A No 35 bus east from Binjiang Lu will terminate near the bridge. From there, walk south across Yihuan Nanlu to the university.

Monastery of Divine Light

(bǎoguāng sì) 宝光寺

This monastery in the north of Xindu County is an active Buddhist temple. It comprises five halls and 16 courtyards, surrounded by bamboo. Pilgrims, monks and tourists head for Xindu, which makes for lively proceedings and attracts a fine array of hawkers. The temple was founded in the 9th century, was subsequently destroyed, and was reconstructed in the 17th century.

Among the monastery treasures are a white jade Buddha from Burma, Ming and Qing paintings and calligraphy, a stone tablet engraved with 1000 Buddhist figures (540 AD), and ceremonial musical instruments. The temple is rich in artefacts, but most of the more valuable items are locked away and require special permission to view them – you may be able to get this if you can find whoever's in charge around here.

The Arhat Hall, built in the 19th century, contains 500 two-metre-high clay figurines representing Buddhist saints and disciples. Well, not all of them: in among this spaced-out lot are two earthlings – emperors Kangxi and Qianlong. They're distinguishable by their royal costumes, beards, boots and capes. One of the impostors, Kangxi, is shown with a pockmarked face, perhaps a whim of the sculptor.

The temple has an excellent vegetarian restaurant where a huge array of dishes is prepared by monastic chefs (special requests can be catered for). Be punctual if you want to make certain of lunch, which is served between 11 am and noon. The temple is open daily, from 8 am to 6 pm. The countryside around Xindu is fertile, with bracing farm scenery. About one km from Baoguangsi is Osmanthus Lake and its bamboo groves, lotuses, and osmanthus trees. In the middle of the lake is a small memorial hall for Ming scholar Yang Shengan.

Xindu is 18 km north of Chengdu: a round trip on a bicycle would be 40 km, or at least four hours' cycling time on a Chinese bike. Otherwise, buses leave from the traffic circle south of the Chengdu north railway station; the bus trip takes about 40 minutes. Hitching is another possibility, but better done returning from Xindu.

Zoo

(dòngwù yuán) 动物园

For the humans there are lush, beautiful grounds (the animals get concrete, but at least some attempt has been made to make them feel at home). Since Sichuan is the largest panda habitat, Chengdu Zoo is the best place to see them in China. About eight pandas are on hand for observation; during the hottest summer months, however, they're not very active.

The zoo is about six km from Chengdu city centre, and is open from 8 am to 6 pm daily. The easiest way to get there is to take bus No 302 from the northern railway station – it terminates at the zoo. You can also be dropped off by the Xindu bus. It's half an hour by bicycle from Chengdu.

Wenshu Monastery

(wénshū yuàn) 文殊院

Whatever its background, Wenshu (God of Wisdom) Monastery offers a spectacle that few PRC temples do: it's so crowded with worshippers that you may have trouble getting in there on weekends. The object of veneration drawing the burners of incense appears to be a Buddhist statue made in Tibet. Wenshu dates back as far as the Tang Dynasty, with reconstruction in the 17th century. Various halls contain Buddhist artefacts, but you may not be permitted to view all of these. There is also a teahouse, and a gallery displaying paintings and calligraphy. It is open daily, 8 am to 8 pm. The alley on which Wenshu is located is a curiosity in itself, with joss-stick vendors, foot-callus removers, blind fortune-tellers with bamboo spills, and flower and firework sellers. The alley runs eastwards off Renmin Zhonglu.

Places to Stay – bottom end

The *Jiaotong (Traffic) Hotel* (☎ 52814) *(jiāotōng fàndiàn)*, next to Xinnanmen bus

station, is the backpacker's palace. It's clean, comfortable, fairly quiet and close to a number of good dining spots. A bed in a triple is Y14, with immaculate showers and toilet down the hall. A double with communal bath is Y28, but there are only four of them and they're usually booked out. A double with private bath is Y50 per person; a bed in a four-bed dorm costs Y4. The staff at reception are friendly and there's a noticeboard with travel info next to the counter. Another useful service here is a baggage room where you can leave heavy backpacks for a few days while you head off to Emeishan, Jiuzhaigou or wherever. To get here from the northern railway station, take a trolley bus No 1 till it terminates at the Xinnanmen bus station.

Even cheaper is the *Binjiang Hotel* (☎ 24451) on Binjiang Lu, across the river from the Jiaotong toward Renmin Lu. This big, noisy hotel is not as pleasant as the Jiaotong overall, but some travellers claim they prefer it (hooked on the TV blare, no doubt). Per-person rates in the six-bed dorms are Y9, in a four-bed Y11, triple (with private bath) Y14. Doubles with bath are available for Y25 or Y43 with air-con. Students and Overseas Chinese can obtain a discount from these rates, but in the winter the hotel charges an additional Y1 heating charge. This is one of those hotels where every room seems to have its TV on at full volume most of the time.

At the very bottom of the cheapies is the *Black Coffee Hotel (hēi kāfēi fàndiàn)*, a few minutes' walk east of the Binjiang Hotel. This is a unique hostelry, a bomb shelter which has been converted into an underground hotel. It's a bit dank and airless, but at least it's fairly quiet. Doubles cost Y14 per person; a bed in a four-bed room costs Y5. Scattered throughout the musty maze of rooms are a disco, a bar, a restaurant, and small sitting rooms where local Chinese couples go for some furtive fumbling.

Another budget possibility is CAAC's *Blue Sky Hotel* next door to the China Southwest Airlines office on Renmin Nanlu. Doubles are Y45, triples Y16 per person. The staff seems terribly disorganised here, however, and the rooms are nothing special.

Places to Stay – middle

The *Tibet Hotel* (☎ 33401) *(xīzàng fàndiàn)* at 10 Renmin Beilu is about five blocks south of Chengdu north railway station. Rooms are clean and service is efficient. A small outdoor café on the Renmin Beilu side of the hotel is a pleasant spot for a cup of coffee and a book. All rooms are air-con; triples cost Y54 and doubles cost from Y88 to Y110. A few dorm beds are available for Y12 but they're often full.

Places to Stay – top end

The *Jin Jiang Hotel* (☎ 24481) *(jīnjiāng bīnguǎn)* at 180 Renmin Nanlu was once the headquarters for all travellers who came to Chengdu, whether business people, tourists, or backpackers. After extensive renovations in the mid-80s, it's now strictly a posh act (or at least it tries to be) and all the dorms and cheap triples are gone. The acres of reflective surfaces require the ministrations of full-time polishers and presumably are also the justification for rocketing room prices. The Jin Jiang's rooms have been transformed into typical modern tourist hotel rooms, but at least the facade of the building has maintained its character. If you want to leap in at the top, there's a deluxe suite for Y1500 or the simple version for Y202. Standard doubles and singles are Y173, which isn't bad value in this range.

This 1000-bed mini-state deluxe block with high walls has all the usual facilities but they don't quite measure up to those of the international hotels in Beijing, Shanghai or Canton. The swimming pool behind the hotel seems to be in a state of permanent decay. At peak hour the elevators are jammed with an odd mix of touring Europeans, resident foreign experts, business people, chirpy Hong Kongers, even a stray Tibetan dignitary with flowing robes may be caught in the crush. Everyone seems to use the facilities, but it's hard to tell who's actually staying here.

In the lobby there's a taxi counter which

can also arrange minibuses or Landcruisers for trips further afield. The open plan coffee shop is useful as a meeting point or rest-stop – pick up your copy of the *China Daily* from the reception desk.

To find the CITS office, walk through the lobby and past the bank, and it's just before the rear exit on your left.

The bank is on the ground floor; go through the lobby in the direction of the rear exit. Efficient staff change most currencies and you can use credit cards to draw up to Y500 daily. Unorthodox money-changing takes place outside the hotel gates.

The telephone office, next to the bank, operates until 11 pm. Overseas connections are erratic as one operator is helpful, the other stroppy. Next to the telephone office is a business centre.

Opposite the bank and the telephone office are two shops. One sells export-quality food and drink; the other sells handicrafts and tourist paraphernalia. Between the two you should be able to stock up on Kodachrome, Johnny Walker, Nescafe and other items close to your heart.

The corridor to the right as you enter the lobby once used to house the post office and telex rooms and a photo-processing centre but was undergoing renovations at the time of writing. A temporary hotel post and telex office has been constructed outside the main building in the south of the compound.

There's a bicycle hire place conveniently located on the wall along Renmin Lu (see the Getting Around section). Of course, the Jin Jiang charges the highest rates in town.

Opposite the Jin Jiang on Renmin Nanlu is the newer, 21-storey *Minshan Hotel* (☎ 583333) *(mínshān fàndiàn)*, which does a brisk tour-group business. Modern doubles start at Y232. The Minshan has a couple of bars, a teahouse and three restaurants.

Places to Eat

Sichuan cuisine is world famous and in a class of its own. It emphasises extremities of the tastebuds, with an armoury of spicing designed, it seems, to force you to pay attention to your food. Sichuan chefs have a slogan that signifies the diversity of Sichuanese cooking styles – ***bǎicài, bǎiwèi*** – which means 'a hundred dishes, a hundred flavours'. Many local dishes use some variation of a sauce that relies on a fusion of fiery red pepper with a local peppercorn that causes a 'numb' sensation in the mouth – ostensibly so you won't be as painfully affected by the hot spices.

Another typical Sichuan seasoning is 'fish-flavour sauce', which blends red pepper pickled in fish brine with ginger, Sichuan salt, soya sauce, garlic, sugar and vinegar. A so-called 'lychee sauce' is concocted from Sichuan salt, soya, vinegar, sugar, rice wine, garlic, ginger and green onion. This is the sauce used in guo ba rou pian (crispy rice with pork), a dish that many travellers are wild about. Other famous dishes in Chengdu are tea-smoked duck (zhang cha ya), diced chicken with chilli and peanuts (gongbao jiding), beef in hot and spicy sauce (shui zhu niu rou), fish simmered in preserved bean sauce (dou chi yu), fish-flavoured meat shreds (yu xiang rou si) and bean curd simmered in numb-and-spicy sauce (mapo doufu).

Famous Restaurants The *Chengdu Restaurant* (☎ 7301) *(chéngdū cāntīng)* at 642 Shangdong Dajie is one of the largest and best in the city, a favourite with travellers. Good atmosphere, decent food, reasonable prices – downstairs is adequate. Try to assemble a party of vagabonds from the hotel before sallying forth, since tables are large, and you get to sample more with a bigger group. It's about a 20-minute walk along a side alley opposite the Jin Jiang Hotel. Arrive early.

The *Rong Le Yuan* (☎ 24201) *(rónglè yuán)* is at 48 Renmin Zhonglu. It's hard to find – look for a small, red-fronted doorway that leads to a larger courtyard. It's open for lunch and dinner, and the servings are more than honest here – order dishes one by one. Mapo doufu is Y1, large soups Y0.50, main courses Y1 to Y2. A nice setting with outdoor breezes that pass under the high roof. The two back rooms are for weddings or special occasions. Examine dishes of other diners carefully because they may not be to your liking if duplicated.

For guo ba rou pian, you can't beat the *Shi Mei Xuan (shìměixuān cāntīng)* opposite the Jinjiang Theatre on Huaxinzhen Jie. A large plate of the crispy rice in pork and lychee sauce costs around Y8, plenty for two. The restaurant has lots of other great dishes, too, and the proprietors don't seem to mind if you walk through the kitchen and point. Large, clean dining rooms with wooden tables and ceiling fans make eating here even more enjoyable.

Another main-course restaurant in the heart of the city is the *Yaohua* (☎ 6665) *(yàohuá fàndiàn)* at 22 Chunxi Lu. On the edge of Renmin Park, to the south side of Tonghunen Jie, is *Nuli Canting (nǔli cāntīng)*, which translates as 'Great Effort Restaurant'. It may not be worth making the Great Effort, but if you happen to be in the vicinity, drop by and check it out – this small place bears the numbering (or renumbering) 55 57 59 61 63 65 67.

A special treat for ailing vegetarians is to ride out to *Xindu Monastery*, 18 km north of Chengdu, in time for lunch (11 am to noon). You can also get a good, cheap, vegetarian lunch at Wenshu Monastery. For details of the bus service see the Things to See section.

Riverside Restaurants Along the south side of the Jin River between the Jin Jiang and Traffic hotels is a short string of restaurants and teahouses with outdoor tables. All serve Sichuan specialities as well as Chinese standards and a few Western dishes and are well worth trying; perhaps the best is the *Jinjiang Restaurant*, which offers tasty mapo doufu and dandan mian (noodles in a spicy peanut sauce) at reasonable prices.

Down at the very end of the row, close to the Traffic Hotel, is the popular *Flower Garden Snack Bar*, where travellers talk over Jiuzhaigou adventures or trade tips on getting permits for western Sichuan and beyond. This is also a good place to enquire about train tickets and 'unauthorised' budget tours of Chengdu and northern Sichuan. The food? Consistently good, from noodles to more elaborate dishes. There are a few Western dishes (breakfasts and sandwiches) on the bilingual menu. Don't miss the peach custard, which is marked on the menu as 'Phoenix & Dragon Soup'.

Hotel Food On the 1st floor of the *Jin Jiang Hotel* is the immense *Shuxing Restaurant*, which serves fixed price, à la carte, and buffet Chinese meals – not bad. On the 2nd floor is a restaurant that's reserved for tour groups, and there are 14 different banquet halls for special groups and visiting dignitaries. The *Garden Restaurant* on the 9th floor is divided into Western and Chinese dining sections. The hostesses always steer foreigners toward the Western section but if you indicate that you want to sample the Cantonese menu, they'll allow you to sit in the Chinese section. Although the food in the indoor dining area does not represent particularly good cuisine or value, the outside terrace is pleasant enough for a drink with a view across the city haze. Hours are from 6.30 am to midnight.

The *Tai Bai Lou* Chinese restaurant in the *Minshan Hotel* serves Sichuan-style dim sum (including many of the dishes listed under Snacks) from breakfast until mid-afternoon. The *Bai Cao Yuan* in the same hotel specialises in 'health food', dishes that are considered therapeutic in Chinese culture.

The restaurant in the *Traffic Hotel* isn't worth writing about – most people staying here eat in the restaurants along the river.

Snacks Many of Chengdu's specialities originated from xiao chi or 'little eats'. The snack bars are great fun and will cost you next to nothing. In fact, the offerings can be outdone in no other Chinese city – and if you line up several of these places you will get yourself a banquet in stages. The offerings run through the whole vocabulary – dandan mian, ma la liang mian (noodles in spicy sesame butter), meats fried in thin pancakes, steamed buns of various kinds, ju yer tian pa (sweet cakes steamed in banana leaves), flower cakes (made to resemble a white chrysanthemum) and hong you chao shou (dumplings in hot chilli oil), to name a few.

The best area for snack-hunting is along Dongfeng Lu and the side streets running north and south off Dongfeng. A few of the more renowned snack outlets follow.

Pock-marked Grandma's Bean Curd (chén mápō dòufu) serves mapo doufu with a vengeance. Small squares of bean curd are accompanied by a fiery meat sauce (laced with garlic, minced beef, salted soybean, chilli oil, numbing peppercorn – enough to make you shut up for a few days). As the story goes, the madame with the pock-marked face set up shop here (reputed to be the same shop as today's) a century ago, providing food and lodging for itinerant pedlars (the clientele look to be roughly the same today too, as does the decor). Bean curd is made on the premises and costs less than Y1 a bowl. Beer is served to cool the fires. The restaurant has grotty, greasy decor – but those spices will kill any lurking bugs, as well as take care of your sinus problems. Also served are spicy chicken and duck, and plates of tripe. Situated at 113 Xiyulong Jie, the small white shop has a green front.

Ming Xiao Chi Dian (Chengdu Snack Bar) serves noodles, baozi and a kind of jaffle. *Zhong Shuijiao (Chef Zhong's Ravioli)*, at 107 Dongfeng Lu, is renowned for its boiled dumplings. At the south end of Chunxi Lu, Nos 6 and 8 are two of the better-known noodle shops – they will also make up sugar jaffles. No 8 is *Cook Long's Soup-Dumpling Restaurant (lóng cháoshǒu fàndiàn)*.

Off the north end of Chunxi Lu, and situated on Dongfeng, is *Lai's Rice-balls*. Lai started off as a street-stall vendor, and has moved up in the world. You get four dumplings in a soup, and a side dish of sesame sauce. Each dumpling has a different sweet stuffing – preserved rose petals or mandarin oranges, for example – and they should be dipped in the sugar-sesame sauce before devouring. Further east on Dongfeng, past the intersection with Hongxing Zhonglu, is a sweet-tooth snack shop, at No 75 – elaborate decor, jaffles, sweet and sticky concoctions.

Hotpot Although it is said to have originated in Chongqing, *huǒ guō* or hotpot is quite popular in Chengdu. You'll see lots of sidewalk hotpot operations in the older section of town near the Chunxi Lu market as well as along the river. Big woks full of hot, spiced oil (not to be confused with the mild Mongolian version, which employs simmering soup broth) invite passers-by to sit down, pick out skewers of raw ingredients and make a do-it-yourself fondue. You pay by the skewer – it's best to ask the price of a skewer before you place it in the oil. During the winter months the skewered items on offer tend to be meat or 'heavy' vegetables like potatoes. In the summer months lighter, mostly vegetarian fare is the norm.

Duck Platters Chengdu has lots of cold duck places. Some are nondescript, and serve duck in a disappointing fashion. Care should be taken because these are not snacks – you are moving out of the pittance price bracket. The next trick is getting that duck heated up!

On a corner, at the foot of Dongchenggen Jie (and south-east of Renmin Park) is *Wang Pang (Fat Mr Wang's Duckshop) (wángpàng yādiàn)* – it is one of the better known places. The nicest duck shop sighted is *Weiyuelou* at No 46 Renmin Zhonglu. It's friendly and clean. Outside it has brown-tiled frontage under an apartment block; inside are marble table tops, paintings, calligraphy and real windows. American beer is served in bowls. Half a chopped stone-cold duck goes for Y5. The restaurant's name translates to 'tasty and delicious chamber', and the place does not fall short of it.

Teahouses The teahouse, or *chádiàn*, has always been the equivalent of the French cafe or the British pub in China – or at least this was true of the pre-'49 era. Activities ranged from haggling over the bride's dowry to fierce political debate. The latter was especially true of Sichuan, which historically has been one of the first areas to rebel and one of the last to come to heel.

Chengdu's teahouses are thus somewhat special – as in other Chinese cities, they were closed down during the Cultural Revolution because they were thought to be dangerous assembly places for 'counter-revolutionaries'. With faction battles raging in Sichuan as late as 1975, re-emergence of this part of daily life has been slow – but you can't keep an old tea addict down! Teahouses sprawl over Chengdu sidewalks (in back-alley sections), with bamboo armchairs that permit ventilation of one's back. In the past, Chengdu teahouses also functioned as venues for Sichuan opera – the plain-clothes variety, performed by amateurs or retired workers. There's been a revival of the teahouse opera, but such places (and the times of performances) are difficult to locate, so it's best to find a local to take you there (try asking at the Flower Garden Snack Bar). Other kinds of entertainment include storytelling and musicians, while some teahouses cater entirely for chess players.

Most Chinese teahouses cater for the menfolk, young and old (mostly old), who come to meet, stoke their pipes or thump cards on the table. Chengdu, however, offers some family-type teahouses. More in the old-man teahouse variety, with a nice balcony view, is a chadian parked by a bridge on Jiefang Lu (see map for location). In the city centre on Shuncheng Jie is a pleasant interior teahouse, the *Xiao Yuan (xiǎoyuán cháguǎn)*. It's very popular and has a certain sophistication.

A more comfortable setting is the *Renmin Teahouse (rénmín cháguǎn)* in Renmin Park, which is a leisurely tangle of bamboo armchairs, sooty kettles and ceramics, with a great outdoor location by a lake. It's mixed, a family-type chadian – crowded on weekends. In the late afternoon workers roll up to soothe shattered factory-nerves – and some just doze off in their armchairs. You can do the same. A most pleasant afternoon can be passed here in relative anonymity over a bottomless cup of stone-flower tea at a cost so ridiculous it's not worth quoting. When enough tea-freaks appear on the terrace, the stray earpicker, with Q-tips at the ready, roves through (advertising to improve the quality of conversation?), and paper-profile cutters with deft scissors also make the rounds.

Another charming indoor family-type teahouse is to be found in Wenshu Monastery, with a crowded and steamy ambience. Other major Chengdu sights have chadians attached to them – and the back lanes hold plenty more.

Nightlife & Entertainment

Nightlife can be fruitful hunting in Chengdu, and you will have to hunt. If you don't speak Chinese, ask around among the English-speaking staff at the riverside restaurants for entertainment ideas. If something strikes your fancy, get it written down in Chinese, and get a good map location – these places are often hard to find, especially at night. If you have more time, try and get advance tickets. Offerings include teahouse entertainment, acrobatics, cinema, Sichuan Opera, Beijing Opera, drama, art exhibits, traditional music, story-telling, shadow plays, sporting events and visiting troupes.

Chengdu is the home of Sichuan Opera, which has a 200-year tradition and features slapstick dress-up, eyeglass-shattering songs, men dressed as women and occasional gymnastics. There are several opera houses scattered throughout the older sections of town. Some offer only a couple of performances per week while others are open daily.

One of the easier Sichuan Opera venues to find is the *Jinjiang Theatre (jǐnjiāng jùyuàn)* on Huaxinzhen Jie, which is a combination teahouse, opera theatre and cinema. Sichuan Opera performances here are frequent and of a high standard – performance times are listed on boards near the entrance (you may have to enlist a Chinese-reading acquaintance to figure out what's what). Mr Lee at the Flower Garden Snack Bar offers an inexpensive Sichuan Opera tour in which he reserves front row seats at a local opera house, explains the storylines and takes his charges backstage to meet the actors.

Cinemas abound – there's the Sichuan Cinema a block north of the Jin Jiang Hotel (same side of street) – pot luck, but at 50 fen a seat it's not about to break the piggy-bank.

On the Jin Jiang Hotel's 8th floor, the billiards room and disco is now operating again after renovation. Expect to pay around Y10 FEC to enter the disco, which has amazingly short hours – from 8 to 11 pm. The ballroom disco held on Saturdays (possibly more frequently now) on the ground floor is for Chinese only – no dogs or foreigners.

A hired bicycle is a useful adjunct to nightlife since bus services are low frequency or unreliable after 9 pm (also packed to the hilt).

Things to Buy

Chengdu has a large range of handicrafts of excellent quality. If you want to see an even larger range of a particular output, try and get to the factory source (the brocade and filigree factories are to the west, towards Du Fu Cottage).

Chunxi Lu is the main shopping artery, lined with department stores, art dealers, secondhand bookstores, stationers, spectacle shops and photo stores. At No 10 is the Arts & Crafts Service Department Store *(chéngdū měishùpǐn fúwùbù)*, dealing in most of the Sichuan specialities (lacquerware, silverwork, bamboo products). This place also has branches in the Jin Jiang Hotel, the airport and the Exhibition Centre. At No 13 Chunxi Lu is a musical instrument shop selling hand-tempered brass gongs and cymbals. At No 14 is a cavernous teahouse for resting weary shopping legs. At No 51 is Shi Bi Jie, specialising in mounting artwork and in calligraphy and Chinese stationery. Right at the north end of Chunxi Lu is the Sichuan Antique Store (on Shangyechang Jie) *(sìchuān wénwù shāngdiàn)*, also a largest-of-the-kind, with branches in the Jin Jiang Hotel and Exhibition Centre; it deals in porcelain, jewellery, embroidery, bamboo wares, ivory and jadeite.

Along Renmin Nanlu to the north of the Jin Jiang Hotel is a string of antique and handicraft shops. A lot of the merchandise is tacky but if you spend some time looking, you may find some nice stuff among the dross. Although few Tibetans drift into Chengdu, there are a number of Tibetan items here and there from the high plateaus and grasslands of western and northern Sichuan. Some of the stuff has undoubtedly been spirited away from Tibet by entrepreneurial Chinese as well. And some of it is probably fake – buyer beware.

At No 22 Chunxi Lu is the Derentang Pharmacy *(déréntán yàodiàn)*, largest of its kind in Chengdu, a century old. It offers, among other elixirs, caterpillar fungus (a mix of the fungus and larva of a moth species – good for TB, coughs, restoring the kidneys) and the rhizome of chuanxiong (pain reliever, blood purifier).

The Exhibition Hall *(zhǎnlǎn guǎn)*, which actually does have industrial exhibitions, has Friendship wares with a capital F scattered on the ground floor, 3rd floor and 5th floor. Antiques are sold on the 5th floor. These expanses of counters are staffed by mild-mannered clerks who tot up strenuous hours of newspaper-reading in between tour-bus assaults. The largest section is the 5th floor, where you can find anything from a sword to an antique bird cage to your aunt's lost wedding ring. There's double-sided embroidery (Sichuan Shu embroidery is famous in China), stage costumes, palm-wood walking sticks, lacquerware screens, bamboo-thread-covered tea-sets – a list as long as your arm.

The Friendship Store is disappointing for foreigners on a shopping spree, but its stocks are popular with Chinese who may hang around outside to exchange their lucre for yours. Of the Chinese shopping variety are the speciality stores – but they're difficult to locate. There's a very nice place selling drums, cymbals and brass gongs at the eastern end of Hongguang Donglu (near Renmin Zhonglu). At 154 Renmin Nanlu Sanduan is a household goods store selling cane furniture, baskets, bamboo and porcelain.

Renmin Market *(rénmín shìchǎng)* is a

maze of daily necessity stuff – worth poking your nose into but not of great interest for purchases. Further north of that, along Jiefang Zhonglu, are small shops selling fur-lined and sheepskin coats and jackets (as well as heavy PLA-type overcoats) – a good selection, not found in too many other places.

Getting There & Away

Transport connections in Chengdu are more comprehensive than in other parts of the south-west.

Air The CAAC branch with its headquarters here is called China Southwest Airlines. The main office is diagonally opposite the Jin Jiang Hotel. This office is linked with the national CAAC reservation network and is a good place to purchase tickets between China destinations other than Chengdu.

The smaller Sichuan Provincial Airlines has its office on Renmin Donglu near the Shuncheng Jie intersection (just east of the Telecommunications Building).

China Southwest Airlines has plenty of air connections out of Chengdu, including Beijing (Y570), Canton (Y430), Changsha (Y340), Chongqing (Y100), Guilin (Y313), Guiyang (Y170), Kunming (Y220), Lanzhou (Y302), Lhasa (Y629), Nanjing (Y522), Shanghai (Y500), Wuhan (Y336), and Xi'an (Y208).

Sichuan Provincial Airlines has cheaper regional fares but flies hand-me-down planes from CAAC, eg the Soviet-made YUN-7. Sample fares include Chongqing (Y87), Dazu (Y82), Kunming (Y199), and Xi'an (Y181).

Bus The main bus station is Xinnanmen Chezhan (New South Gate bus station), conveniently next to the Jiaotong (Traffic) Hotel. It handles departures for Emei (Y9.70), Leshan (Y7), Dazu, Zigong, Ya'an, and Kangding.

The Ximen Chezhan (Ximen bus station), in the north-west of the city, runs buses to Guanxian (irrigation project and its vicinity) and to places on the Jiuzhaigou route such as Nanping, Songpan and Barkam. The best way to get there from the Jin Jiang or Traffic hotels is to take bus No 35 west to the terminal at Qingyang Gong bus station and then change to bus No 5 – ask to get off at Ximen Chezhan.

Train Most rail traffic proceeds from Chengdu north (main) railway station. Ticket offices in Chengdu may try to sell foreigners soft-sleepers and deny that hard-sleepers are available. The advance rail ticket office, a smaller building on Dongyu Jie, is for Chinese-priced tickets only. CITS has also been known to dish out Chinese-priced tickets (especially for soft-sleepers) to foreigners. Perhaps this is because they're mixed in with CTS. Their top speed for obtaining tickets seems to be four days. For more information on trains in the south-west, see the introductory South-West section. There are also plenty of black-market train tickets for sale on the streets – either in front of the railway station or wherever foreigners congregate. Expect to pay a mark-up of 50% or more for a black-market hard-sleeper ticket (still cheaper than the tourist price – and you can pay in RMB instead of FEC).

From Chengdu there are direct trains to Emei (three hours, Y7 hard-seat, Chinese price), Kunming (25 hours, Y150 hard-sleeper, tourist price), Chongqing (11 hours, Y80 hard-sleeper, Y40 hard-seat, tourist price) and Xi'an (about 20 hours, Y110 hard-sleeper, tourist price).

For the routing to Kunming via Lijiang and Dali, travel to Jiujiang (railhead for Dukou) on the Chengdu-Kunming line and then take buses. For some reason, the timetables don't include train No 91 which leaves Chengdu at 7.53 pm and arrives in Jiujiang at 10.40 am – Y70 hard-sleeper, tourist price.

There are also direct trains to Lanzhou, Hefei and Beijing. For more information, see the introduction in the chapter on the south-west region.

Combination Tickets Combination rail/bus/boat tickets are sold at Chengdu north railway station, window No 14. You may have trouble trying to get one of these – we couldn't even find half the places these tickets take you to on our Chinese map! There are at least 15 combinations, and some brief details are given here for the sake of interest. Rail/bus tickets are sold for the route from Chengdu via Jiujiang to Leshan, Wutong Qiao and Mabian. There is a combined rail/bus ticket from Chengdu via Longchuan to Luzhou, Fushun, Naxi, Xuyong, Gusong, Guilin, etc. Another option is a rail/boat/bus ticket from Chengdu via Jiujiang, Leshan and then along the Min River to wherever. Also on sale is a combined ticket which will take you by rail to Chongqing, and then by ferry to Shanghai. There is a similar combination ticket service in Chongqing.

Getting Around

Bus The most useful bus is No 16, which runs from Chengdu north railway station to the south railway station, passing by the Public Security Bureau, the Foreign Language Bookstore and the Jin Jiang Hotel. Bus maps carry colour coding for trolleys and ordinary buses – bus Nos 1, 2, 3, 4 and 5 can also be trolleys bearing the same number. Trolleys have wires; it's easy to work out which colour is the wiring – it can only go so far around the city. Trolley bus No 1 runs from Xinnanmen bus station to Chengdu north railway station. Ordinary bus No 4 runs from the Ximen bus station (north-west end of town) to the south-east sector, and continues service until 1 am (most others cease around 9.30 to 10.30 pm).

Bicycle There are bike hire shops throughout the city. The most expensive are those at the Jin Jiang Hotel, Traffic Hotel, and Flower Garden Snack Bar, each of which charges 60 fen per hour or about Y5 per day. You'll find cheaper rates at shops along Dong Dajie near the Hongxing Lu intersection – average Y2.50 per day.

Get there early if you want to choose something halfway roadworthy from the typical fleet of decrepit crates. You can hire bikes for more than a day and get a discount. Don't park a hired bike outside hotel gates overnight, as it may be towed away. One traveller had a hired bike towed from outside a shop and, after a complex enquiry, found it in what turned out to be the local police station. There are usually specific parking areas for bikes – look around before you park.

Buses are very crowded in Chengdu, and hired bikes come as a relief. More than this, however, they give access to back alleys where thriving markets and strange industries are in progress (comic-book libraries, teahouses, small shops, weathered housing). Some areas are for pedestrians only by day (Chunxi Lu), but you can always use back streets to get to your destination. You may get lost, so best to have the destination written in Chinese.

If you have good reflexes, good night vision and a strong sense of compass points, night-riding is a dangerous sport that yields a different side of Chengdu. Headlights are only used to warn cyclists that something large is speeding through; no Chinese bikes carry lamps (the cost is too high), very few carry reflectors. Add to this the complete disdain of red lights (manually operated, the police box nearby may be empty), and some accidents are bound to occur.

The back alleys are a little safer in terms of the number of large random objects coming towards you, but more hazardous in terms of small random objects. With reduced visibility, it is advisable to ride slower. Although Beijing is soundly snoring by 9.30 pm, Chengdu hangs in there for a bit longer – the glow of TV tubes visible from dark house doorways, the occasional cluster of night markets, theatre crowds spilling onto the streets, and the brilliant blues, greens and reds of the ice-cream parlours and snack bars.

AROUND CHENGDU

Guanxian

(guànxiàn) 灌县

The **Dujiangyan Irrigation Project**, some 60 km north-west of Chengdu, was undertaken in the 3rd century BC to divert the

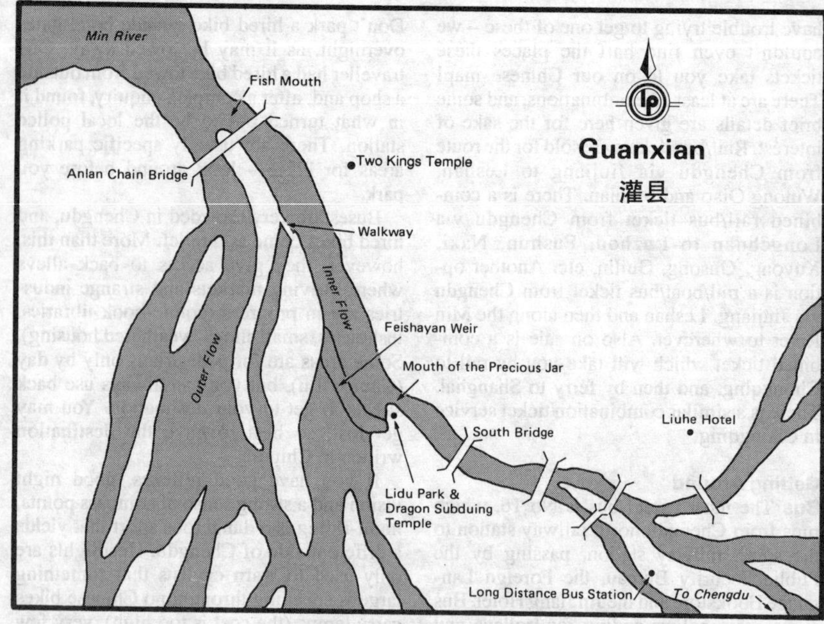

fast-flowing Min River and rechannel it into irrigation canals. The Min was subject to flooding at this point, yet when it subsided droughts could ensue. A weir system was built to split the force of the river, and a trunk canal (Mouth of Precious Jar) was cut through a mountain to irrigate the Chengdu Plain. Thus the mighty Min was tamed, and a temple (Fulong) was erected to commemorate the occasion during the Jin Dynasty (265-420 AD).

The project is ongoing – it originally irrigated some 1.2 million hectares of land, and since Liberation this has expanded to 3.2 million hectares. Most of the present dams, reservoirs, pumping stations, hydro-electric works, bridgework and features are modern; a good overall view of the outlay can be gained from **Two Kings Temple** *(èrwáng miào)*. The two kings are Li Bing, governor of the Kingdom of Shu and father of the irrigation project, and his son, Er Lang, who were given the titles posthumously – this makes for a rather unusual and dilapidated engineering temple. Inside is a statue of Li Bing, shockingly lifelike; in the rear hall is a standing figure of his son holding a dam tool. There's also a Qing Dynasty project map, and behind the temple there is a terrace saying in effect, 'Mao was here' (1958).

Although Guanxian is of immense importance to specialists interested in the progress of agriculture in China, other visitors may find that dams and irrigation offer less scope for enthusiasm. Of local flavour there is precious little. A nice teahouse is sited on **South Bridge** *(nánqiáo)*, near Lidu Park entrance. The *Liuhe Hotel*, about 15 minutes' walk from the Guanxian bus station, has beds from Y3.

Buses run to Guanxian from Ximen bus station in Chengdu every half-hour from 7 to 11.30 am, and hourly from 1 to 6 pm. They cost Y2, and the trip takes 1½ hours over bumpy roads. You'd do better to take a bus directly to Two Kings Temple (a further half hour beyond the Guanxian bus station), and work your way back to Guanxian township. If you can't get a direct bus from Chengdu to the temple, then change buses at Guanxian bus station.

Wolong Nature Reserve

(wòlóng zìrán bǎohùqū) 卧龙自然保护区

Wolong Nature Reserve lies 40 km north-west of Chengdu, about nine hours of rough roads by bus (via Guanxian). It was set up in the late 1970s and is the largest of the 13 reserves set aside by the Chinese government especially for panda conservation. Of these 13 reserves, 11 are in Sichuan. The United Nations has designated Wolong as an international biosphere preserve. Estimates place the total number of giant pandas at a round figure of 1000, most of which are distributed in approximately 28 counties of north and north-western Sichuan (with further ranges in Gansu and Shaanxi). Other animals protected here are the golden monkey, golden langur, musk deer and snow leopard. The reserve is estimated to have some 3000 kinds of plants and covers an area of 200,000 hectares. To the north-west is Siguniangshan (6240 metres) and to the east it drops as low as 155 metres. Pandas like to dine in the zone from 2300 to 3200 metres, ranging lower in winter.

The earliest known remains of the panda date back 600,000 years. It's stoutly built, rather clumsy, and has a thick pelt of fine hair, a short tail, and a round white face with eyes set in black-rimmed sockets. Though it staggers when it walks, the panda is a good climber, and lives mostly on a vegetarian diet of bamboo and sugar-cane leaves. Mating season has proved a great disappointment to observers at the Wolong Reserve, since pandas are rather particular. Related to the bear and the raccoon, pandas – despite their human-looking shades – can be vicious in self-defence. In captivity they establish remarkable ties with their keepers after a period of time, and can be trained to do a repertoire of tricks.

The giant panda was first discovered in 1896 in Sichuan, and is headed for extinction. Part of the problem is the gradual diminution of their food supply; in the mid-70s more than 130 pandas starved to death when one of the bamboo species on which they feed flowered and withered in the Minshan mountains of Sichuan. Pandas consume enormous amounts of bamboo, although their digestive tracts get little value from the plant (consumption is up to 20 kg of bamboo a day in captivity). They are carnivorous, but they're slow to catch animals. Other problems are genetic defects, internal parasites and a slow reproductive rate (artificial insemination has been used at Beijing Zoo).

The Chinese invited the World Wide Fund for Nature (whose emblem is the lovable panda) to assist in research, itself a rare move. In 1978 a research centre was set up at Wolong. Eminent animal behaviourist Dr George Schaller has paid several visits to the area to work with Chinese biologist Professor Hu Jinchu. There are signs that Wolong will establish observation facilities for tourists – half a dozen pandas are kept at the commune for research. At present, access to this small community is limited to trek-type tours since the road in is a treacherous one. There is little chance of seeing a panda in the wild; Dr Schaller spent two months trekking in the mountains before he got to see one.

One of Schaller's research tasks was to fit wild pandas with radio-monitoring devices. In early 1983, the *People's Daily* reported that Hanhan, one of the very few pandas tagged, was caught in a steel wire trap by a Wolong local. The man strangled the panda, cut off its monitoring ring, skinned it, took it home and ate it. The meal earned the man two years in jail. Since then penalties have increased; in 1990 two Sichuan men who were found with four panda skins were publicly executed. On a brighter note, directives have been issued forbidding locals to hunt, fell trees or make charcoal in the mountainous habitats of the panda. Peasants in the areas are being offered rewards equivalent to double their annual salary if they save a starving panda.

EMEISHAN

(éméi shān) 峨眉山

Emeishan (Mt Emei), locked in a medieval time warp, receives a steady stream of happy pilgrims with their straw hats, makeshift baggage, walking canes and fans. The monasteries hold sombre Buddhist monks, the tinkle of bells, clouds of incense, and firewood and coal lumped in the courtyards for the winter months.

It is more or less a straight mountain climb, with your attention directed to the luxuriant scenery – and, as in *The Canterbury Tales*, to fellow pilgrims. Admirable are the hardened affiliates of Grannies Alpine Club, who slog it up there with the best of them, walking sticks at the ready lest a brazen monkey dare think them easy prey for a food-mugging. They come yearly for the assault, and burn paper money as a Buddhist offering for longevity. The climb no doubt adds to their longevity, so the two factors may be related. For the traveller itching to do something, the Emei climb is a good opportunity to air the respiratory organs, as well as to observe post-76 religious freedoms in action, since you are obliged to stay in the rickety monasteries along the route.

One of the Middle Kingdom's four famous Buddhist mountains (the others are Putuo, Wutai and Jiuhua), Emeishan has little of its original temple-work left. The glittering Jinding (Golden Summit) Temple, with its brass tiling engraved with Tibetan script, was completely gutted by fire. A similar fate befell numerous other temples and monasteries on the mount – war with the Japanese and Red Guard looting have taken their toll.

The original temple structures dated back as far as the advent of Buddhism itself in China; by the 14th century, the estimated 100 or so holy structures housed several thousand monks.

The present temple count is around 20 active after a Cultural Revolution hiatus, bearing only traces of their original splendour. Since 1976 the remnants have been renovated, access to the mountain has been improved, hiking paths widened, lodgings added, and tourists permitted to climb to the sacred summit.

Hiking is spectacular enough. Fir trees, pines and cedars clothe the slopes; lofty crags, cloud-kissing precipices, butterflies and azaleas together form a nature reserve of sorts. The major scenic goal of Chinese hikers is to witness a sunrise or sunset over the sea of clouds at the summit. On the rare afternoon there is a phenomenon known as Buddha's Aureole – rainbow rings, produced by refraction of water particles, attach themselves to a person's shadow in a cloud bank below the summit. Devout Buddhists, thinking this was a call from yonder, used to jump off the Cliff of Self-Sacrifice in ecstasy, so during the Ming and Qing dynasties officials set up iron poles and chain railings to prevent suicides. These days your head can be stuck in a cardboard cutout on the site, and you can be photographed in that same act of attaining Nirvana.

Weather

The best season to visit is from May to October. Winter is not impossible, but will present some trekking problems – iron soles with spikes can be hired to deal with encrusted ice and snow on the trails. At the height of summer, which is scorching elsewhere in Sichuan, Emei presents cool majesty. Temperate zones start at 1000 metres.

Cloud cover and mist are prevalent, and will most likely interfere with the sunrise. If lucky, you'll see Gonggashan to the west; if not, you'll have to settle for the telecom tower 'temple' and the meteorological station. Monthly average temperatures in degrees Celsius are:

	Jan	Apr	Jul	Oct
Emei town	7	21	26	17
Summit	-6	3	12	-1

What to Bring

Emei is a tall one at 3099 metres, so the weather is uncertain and you'd be best advised to prepare for sudden changes without weighing yourself down with a huge

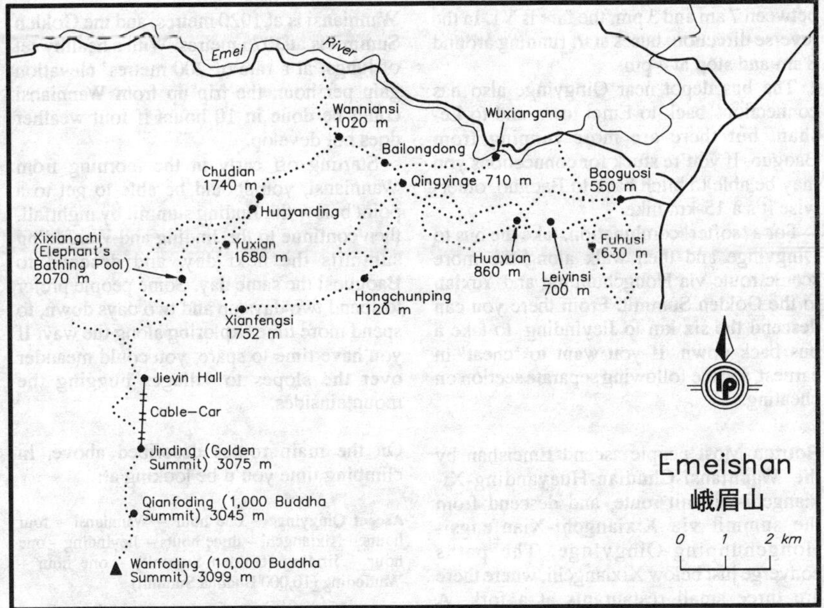

pack (steps can be steep). There is no heating or insulation in the monasteries, but blankets are provided, and you can hire heavy overcoats at the top. Heavy rain can be a problem, calling for a good pair of rough-soled shoes or boots, so you don't go head over heels on the smooth stone steps further up. Flimsy plastic macs are sold by enterprising vendors on the slopes – these will last about 10 minutes before you get wet.

Strange hiking equipment as it may sound, a fixed-length umbrella would be most useful – for the rain, and as a walking stick (scare the hell out of those monkeys by pressing auto-release!). These kinds of umbrellas cost from around Y11 to Y16 in China. If you want to look more authentic you can get yourself a hand-crafted walking stick, very cheap – and while you're at it, get a fan and a straw hat too. A torch would be handy. Food supplies are not necessary, but a pocket of munchies wouldn't hurt. Bring toilet paper with you. Luggage can be left at Emei railway station, at the Hongzhushan Hotel, or at one of the monasteries.

Recent reports indicate that some travellers have been getting sick from contaminated water supplies on the mountain, so you might want to consider carrying bottled water.

Ascending the Heights

Baoguo village is the key transport junction, lying between Baoguosi monastery and the Hongzhushan Hotel at the foot of the mountain. You can dump your bags at the Hongzhushan or Xi Xiang hotels for a modest charge. (It may be possible to dump them at the Baoguosi monastery or the Emei town railway station as well.)

Most people start their ascent of the mountain at Wanniansi (Temple of Myriad Ages) *(wànnián sì)* and come down through Qingyinge (Pure Sound Pavilion). From Baoguo there are buses running close to Wanniansi and to Qingyinge five or six times a day between 7 am and 3 pm; the fare is Y1. In the reverse direction, buses start running around 8 am and stop at 4 pm.

The bus depot near Qingyinge also has connections back to Emei town and to Leshan, but there are more running from Baoguo. If you're stuck for connections you may be able to hitch back to Baoguo, otherwise it's a 15-km hike.

For a 'softer' combination, take the bus to Qingyinge and then walk along the more scenic route via Hongchunping and Yuxian to the Golden Summit. From there you can descend the six km to Jieyinding to take a bus back down. If you want to 'cheat' in earnest, see the following separate section on cheating.

Routes Most people ascend Emeishan by the Wanniansi-Chudian-Huayanding-Xixiangchi-Summit route, and descend from the summit via Xixiangchi-Xianfengsi-Hongchunping-Qingyinge. The paths converge just below Xixiangchi, where there are three small restaurants at a fork. A common route is:

Wanniansi – 15 km – Xixiangchi – 15 km – Jinding – 3.5 km – Wanfoding – 3.5 km – Jinding – 15 km – Xixiangchi – 12.5 km – Xianfengsi – 15 km – Hongchunping – 6 km – Qingyinge – 12.5 km – Leiyinsi – 1.5 km – Fuhusi – 1 km – Baoguosi

Duration Two to three days on site is enough. You usually need one day up and one day down. Enough time should be left for a slow-paced descent, which can be more punishing for the old trotters. A hardy Frenchman made it up and down on the same day, but he must have had unusual legs. Chinese and Western sources have some wildly misleading figures on the length and difficulty of the Emei climb. These figures can be attributed to geriatric or Chinese walking times, or ignorance of the buses running to Wanniansi.

Assuming that most people will want to start climbing from Qingyinge or Wanniansi, buses from Baoguosi run close to these points, so that knocks off the initial 15 km. Wanniansi is at 1020 metres, and the Golden Summit is at 3075 metres. With a healthy set of lungs, at a rate of 200 metres' elevation gain per hour, the trip up from Wanniansi could be done in 10 hours if foul weather does not develop.

Starting off early in the morning from Wanniansi, you should be able to get to a point below the Jinding summit by nightfall, then continue to the Jinding and Wanfoding summits the next day, and descend to Baoguosi the same day. Some people prefer to spend two days up and two days down, to spend more time exploring along the way. If you have time to spare, you could meander over the slopes to villages hugging the mountainsides.

On the main routes described above, in climbing time you'd be looking at:

Ascent Qingyinge – one hour – Wanniansi – four hours – Xixiangchi – three hours – Jieyinding – one hour – Jinding (Golden Summit) – one hour – Wanfoding (10,000 Buddha Summit)

Descent Wanfoding – 45 minutes – Jinding – 45 minutes – Jieyin – 2½ hours – Xixiangchi – two hours – Xianfengsi – 3½ hours – Qingyinge

Cheating Cheating is a popular pastime on Emei (the name Emeishan means 'moth-eyebrow mountain' – raised or lowered these days?). Grannies are portered up on the sturdy backs of young men (likewise healthy-looking young women are carried up).

Several minibuses and buses leave from the square in front of Baoguosi between 7 and 8 am, and run along a recently made dirt road round the back of the mountain up to Jieyinding (2640 metres). From there, it's only 1½ hours to the top. Minibuses (Y10 one way, two hours) and buses (Y6) take about three hours to get up the mountain. Minibuses are usually chartered by prior arrangement.

If even the Jieyin-Jinding climb is too much, you can now accomplish this route in about 20 minutes by cable car for Y9 one way, Y15 return.

Talking of cheating, another traveller has reported that he was recently up on the mountain watching a three-card trickster raking in money when a police patrol suddenly appeared on the scene. As the startled trickster packed his cards, the police opened fire and pursued the man into the undergrowth!

Another spectacular brawl was witnessed at 2640 metres:

The bus was waiting for passengers to go down – well, not exactly waiting...What had happened was that a group of Hong Kong visitors, easily discernible by their clothing and cameras, had set up a deal with the driver to charter the whole bus back down the mountain, leaving no space for locals. The driver, in his wisdom, did not open the main bus door, but his driver's cabin door – to let the Hong Kongers squeeze onto the vehicle. Pandemonium broke out in the crowd of Chinese onlookers – they burst through the main bus door, and old women piled through the windows...Some very nasty scenes ensued as conductor and driver rushed to boot them out again and re-seal the bus.

The remaining Hong Kongers, the ones still on terra firma, regrouped. The Charge of the Light Brigade followed as they smashed through the ranks of the locals and were pulled up by the scruffs of their necks through the driver's cabin. Meanwhile, old and young alike, the locals bashed at the bus with their walking sticks and screamed abuse – finally the bus pulled out, horns blaring, with Chinese running after it, kicking the paintwork for all they were worth, and almost doing in the rear lights with walking sticks.

Places to Stay & Eat

The old monasteries offer food, shelter and sights all rolled into one, and, while spartan, are a delightful change from the regular tourist hotels. They've got maybe as much as 1000 years of character.

You'll probably be asked to pay some ridiculous prices. Bargaining is definitely necessary. Prices range from Y0.80 in a very large dormitory (10 beds or more) to Y10 per person in a single, double or triple room. It's very difficult to get into the dorms – the staff usually let in only the Chinese. In between are other options like a four-bed room at Y4 per person – again, the Chinese get preference for these. Plumbing and electricity are primitive; candles are supplied. Rats can be a nuisance, particularly if you leave food lying around your room.

There are eight monastery guesthouses – at Baoguosi, Qingyinge, Wanniansi, Xixiangchi, Xianfengsi, Hongchunping, Fuhusi and Leiyinsi. There's also a host of smaller lodgings at Chudian, Jieyinding, Yuxian, Bailongdong, the Jinding summit and Huayuan, for instance. The smaller places will accept you if the main monasteries are overloaded. Failing those, you can kip out virtually anywhere – a teahouse, a wayside restaurant – if night is descending.

Be prepared to backtrack or advance under cover of darkness, as key points are often full of pilgrims – old women two to a bed, camped down the corridors, or camping out in the hallowed temple itself, on the floor. Monasteries usually have halfway hygienic restaurants with monk-chefs serving up the vegetarian fare; from Y2 to Y4 should cover a meal. There is often a small retail outlet selling peanuts, biscuits and canned fruit within the monastery precincts. Along the route are small restaurants and food stalls where you can replenish the guts and the tea mug. Food gets more expensive and less varied the higher you mount, due to cartage surcharges and difficulties.

An exception to the monasteries is the *Hongzhushan Hotel (hóngzhūshān bīnguǎn)*, at the foot of Emeishan. It's got dreary brick and plaster dorm accommodation at Y15 per person. Better villa-type rooms are available for Y20 per person and up. This hotel has a very pleasant dining section which is a 10-minute walk back into the forest. There you can dine on a 2nd-floor balcony, where a set menu costs Y10 (copious servings).

About 400 metres uphill from the Baoguo-Leshan bus station is another place *(Xi Xiang Hotel) (xīxiàng fàndiàn)* where comfortable dorm accommodation is available for Y15 per person. At either of these hotels it's a good idea to book a bed or room in advance so you won't be turned away after you've descended the mountain.

Some notes on the monasteries follow. Most of the ones mentioned are sited at key walking junctions and tend to be packed out. If you don't get in, do check out the restaurant and its patrons.

Baoguosi *(bàogúo sì)* The Monastery of Country Rewards was built in the 16th century, enlarged in the 17th by Emperor Kangxi, and recently renovated. Its 3.4-metre porcelain Buddha, made in 1415, is housed near the Sutra Library. To the left of the gate is a rockery for potted miniature trees and rare plants. There's a nice vegetarian restaurant and tearoom with solid wood tables.

Fuhusi *(fúhŭ sì)* The Crouching Tiger Monastery is sunk in the forest. Inside is a seven-metre-high copper pagoda inscribed with Buddhist images and texts. The monastery was completely renovated recently, with the addition of bedding for 400 and restaurant seating for 200. A stay here costs a bit more than at the average Emeishan monastery but is well worth it if you can get in.

Wanniansi *(wànnián sì)* The Temple of 10,000 Years is the oldest surviving Emei monastery (reconstructed in the 9th century). It's dedicated to the man on the white elephant, the bodhisattva Puxian, who is the protector of the mountain. This statue, 8.5 metres high, cast in copper and bronze, weighing an estimated 62,000 kg, is found in Brick Hall, a domed building with small stupas on it. The statue was made in 980 AD. Accommodation in the Wanniansi area is Y10 per person, with good vegetarian food. If it's full, go back towards Qingyinge to Bailongdong, a small guesthouse.

Qingyinge *(qīngyīn gé)* Named the Pure Sound Pavilion because of the sound effects produced by rapid waters coursing around rock formations in the area, the temple itself is built on an outcrop in the middle of a fast-flowing stream. There are small pavilions from which to observe the waterworks and appreciate the natural music. Swimming here is possible.

Xixiangchi *(xĭxiàng chí)* According to legend, the Elephant Bathing Pool is the spot where the monk Puxian flew his elephant in for the big scrub, but now there's not much of a pool to speak of. Being almost at the crossroads of both major trails, this is something of a hang-out and beds are scarce. New extensions are in progress for handling human overload on the trail.

The monkeys have got it all figured out – this is the place to be. If you come across a monkey 'tollgate', the standard procedure is to thrust open palms toward the outlaw to show you have no food. The Chinese find the monkeys an integral part of the Emei trip, and like to tease them. As an aside, monkeys form an important part of Chinese mythology – and there is a saying in Chinese, 'With one monkey in the way, not even 10,000 men can pass' – which may be deeper than you think!

Woyunan *(wòyún ān)* Just below the summit, the Cloud-Reposing Hermitage was built in 1974, a dark, gloomy, primitive wooden structure. Beds here are among the cheapest on the mountain. The hotel will rent padded cotton overcoats for 80 fen a day. Another shop nearby offers the same deal. These are mostly intended for patrons of the sunrise – on a very clear day (rare) the most spectacular sight is not the sunrise but the Gonggashan range rising up like a phantom to the west.

Jinding *(jīndĭng)* At 3077 metres, the magnificent Golden Summit temple is as far as most hikers make it. It has been entirely rebuilt since being gutted by a fire several years ago. Covered with glazed tile and surrounded by white marble balustrades, it now occupies 1695 sq metres. The original temple had a bronze-coated roof, which is how it got the name Jinding (which really means 'Gold Top' rather than 'Golden Summit').

Xianfengsi *(xiānfēng sì)* The surroundings are wonderful, backed into rugged cliffs, and the Magic Peak monastery has loads of character. Try and get a room at the rear, where the floors give pleasant views. It's off the main track so it's not crowded. Nearby is Jiulao Cave, inhabited by big bats.

Getting There & Away

The hubs of the transport links to Emeishan are Baoguo village and Emei town. Emei town itself is best skipped, though it does have markets, a cheap dormitory at the Emei Hotel, a good restaurant, and a long-distance bus station.

Emei town lies 3½ km from the railway station. Baoguo is another 6½ km from Emei town. At Emei station, buses will be waiting for train arrivals – the short trip to Baoguo is Y1 in a minibus, and Y0.60 in a local bus. From Baoguo there are 11 buses a day to Emei town, the first at 7 am and the last at 6 pm – no service during lunch hour. There are also occasional direct buses between Emei and Qingyin for Y5.

There are also direct buses running from Baoguo to Leshan and Chengdu. Eight buses a day run from Baoguo to Leshan, the first at 7 am and the last at 5.30 pm. The trip takes one hour and the fare is Y1.40. There are good bus connections between Leshan and Chengdu. The bus from Baoguo to Chengdu costs Y6.50 and takes four hours.

Emei railway station is on the Chengdu-Kunming railway line, and the three-hour trip to Chengdu costs Y7 hard-seat (Chinese price). The train from Emei town is more comfortable than the bus, but does not offer the convenience of leaving from Baoguo (trains are also less frequent and timing may be off). You can purchase one-day advance train tickets at two little booths by the pavilion in Baoguo square.

LESHAN

(lèshān) 乐山

The opportunity to delve into small-town life in the PRC should always be followed up. While Leshan is no village, it's on a scale that you can be comfortable with. It's an old town which has parts that have that lived-in-forever look, while the trendiest addition from this century is the odd soda-bar with garish fluorescent tubes, disco music, and patrons huddled over fizzy orange drinks. The hotel situation is good, decent food can be unearthed and it's a good resting spot for those Emei-weary legs – plus there's a major archaeological site, the Grand Buddha.

Things to See

The **Grand Buddha** *(dàfó)* is 71 metres high, carved into a cliff face overlooking the confluence of the Dadu and Min rivers. It qualifies as the largest Buddha in the world, with the one at Bamian, Afghanistan, as runner-up (besides, the Leshan model is sitting down!). Dafo's ears are seven metres long, insteps 8.5 metres broad, and a picnic could be conducted on the nail of his big toe, which is 1.6 metres long – the toe itself is 8.3 metres long.

This lunatic project was begun in the year 713 AD, engineered by a Buddhist monk called Haitong who organised fund raising and hired workers; it was completed 90 years later. Below the Buddha was a hollow where boatmen used to vanish – Haitong hoped that the Buddha's presence would subdue the swift currents and protect the boatmen, and Dafo did do a lot of good, as the surplus rocks from the sculpting filled the river hollow. Haitong gouged out his own eyes in an effort to protect funding from disappearing into the hands of officers, but he died before the completion of his life's work. A building used to shelter the giant statue, but it was destroyed during a Ming Dynasty war.

Inside the body, hidden from view, is a water-drainage system to prevent weathering, although the stone statue has seen its fair share. Dafo is so old that foliage is trying to reclaim him – flowers growing on the giant hands, a bushy chest, ferns in his topknots, and weeds winding out of his earholes. He gazes down, perhaps in alarm, at the drifting pollutants in the river that presumably come from the paper mill at the industrial end of town (which started large-scale operation in 1979).

Officials are now worried about the possibility of a collapse due to soil erosion; one

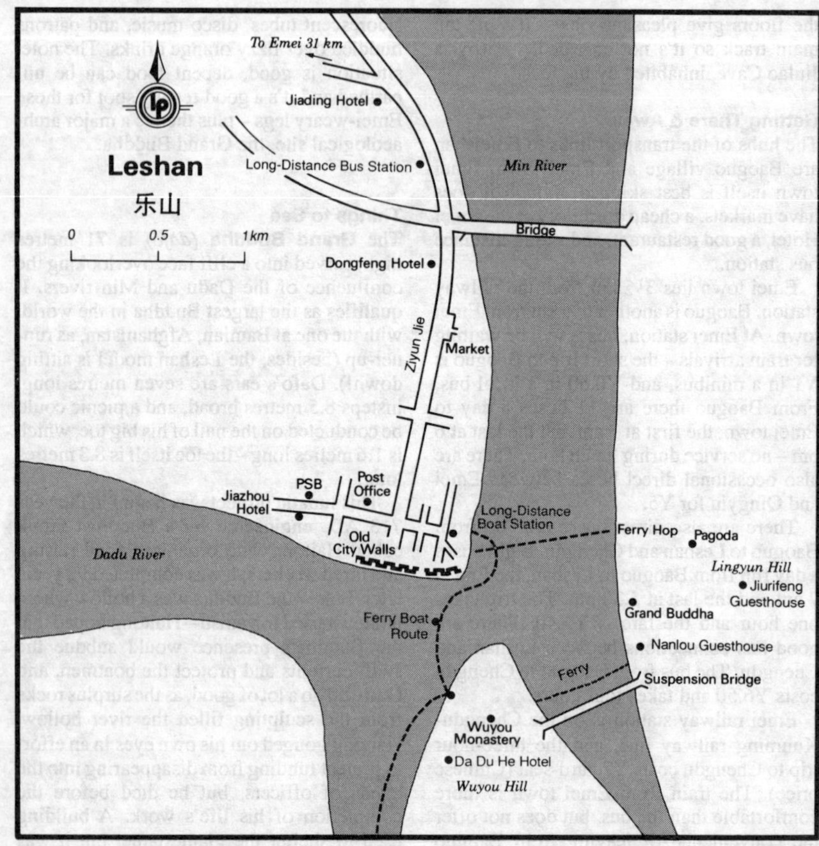

suggestion that has not met with an enthusiastic response is to cover the Buddha with a huge transparent shell.

It's worth making several passes at big Buddha, as there are all kinds of angles on him. You can go to the top, opposite the head, and then descend a short stairway to the feet for a Lilliputian perspective. A local boat passes by for a frontal view, which reveals two guardians in the cliff side, not visible from land.

To make a round tour that encompasses these possibilities, take the passenger vessel from the Leshan pier. It leaves from the pier every 40 minutes or so until 5.30 pm and costs Y1; sit on the upper deck facing the dock, since the boat turns around when leaving. You pass in close by the Grand Buddha and the first stop is at the **Wulong Monastery** *(wūlóng sì)*. The monastery dates, like the Grand Buddha, from the Tang Dynasty with Ming and Qing renovations; it's a museum piece containing calligraphy, painting and artefacts, and commands panoramic views. Wulong also has a hall of 1000 arhats, terracotta monks displaying an incredible variety of postures and facial expressions – no two are alike. The food at the temple's veggie restaurant is cheap and tasty.

You can get off the boat here if you want and go cross-country over the top of Wulong Hill, continue on to the ferry (Y1) linking it to Lingyun Hill (the suspension bridge has been condemned), and reach the semi-active **Grand Buddha Temple** *(dàfó sì)* which sits near Dafo's head. To get back to Leshan walk south to the small ferry going direct across the Min River.

This whole exercise can be done in less than 1½ hours from the Leshan dock; however, it's worth making a day of it. If you want to avoid the crowds, you should consider doing this route in reverse, that is, starting with the Dafo Temple and Grand Buddha in the morning and on to Wulong Monastery in the afternoon.

It would be a mistake to think of Leshan as one big Buddha, for the area is steeped in history. Over 1000 rock tombs were built here in the Eastern Han Dynasty (25-220 AD). By the remains of the town ramparts is an older section of town with cobbled streets and green, blue and red-shuttered buildings; the area around the ferry docks and the old town buzzes with market activity. In season, the markets yield a surprising array of fresh fruit and vegetables, so you can do more than look at them. Further out, by the Jiazhou Hotel, are teahouses with bamboo chairs spilling onto the street.

If you happen to be in town on a Sunday evening, you might like to visit the English Corner which takes place in the riverside park close to the Jiazhou Hotel.

Places to Stay & Eat

Near the Wulong Monastery is the friendly and economical *Da Du He Hotel (dàdù hé fàndiàn)*. Beds can be had for as little as Y5 with bargaining; the dining room has good Sichuan food.

There are two Chinese hostelries in the area above the head of the Grand Buddha, *Nanlou Guesthouse (nánlóu bīnguǎn)* and *Jiurifeng Guesthouse (jiùrìfēng bīnguǎn)*. Perhaps due to the Buddha's drainage system, the cliff around here is wet, and the dampness can extend to the rooms. Aside from this, the guesthouses are nice; each has rooms at Y10 a head, and lower rates are possible. There is an excellent restaurant nearby, in a building to the right of the Buddha as you look towards the river.

If you want to stay in the town centre, try the *Leshan Educational Research Centre* (☎ 22964) *(lèshān jiàoyù yánjiūsuǒ)* at 156 Liren, around the corner from the bus station. Adequate doubles here are Y20, triples Y10-15 per person.

Top-of-the-line is the *Jiazhou Hotel (jiāzhōu bīnguǎn)* which has comfortable, clean rooms with attached bathroom for Y40; Y15 in a triple. The dining room serves amazing set dinners for around Y8 – they're only for hotel guests with advance orders, but friends can creep in. The hotel is in a pleasant area; to get there take the town's sole bus line to the terminal.

You could try the two Chinese hotels, which are sleazy but conveniently located. The *Dongfeng (dōngfēng fàndiàn)* has doubles and triples from Y5 per person. At the dull end of town near the bus station is the *Jiading Hotel (jiādìng lǚguǎn)*, which will accept stray foreign faces. The overflow of patrons is stuffed down the hallways, and the washrooms are hard to find (you might throw up when you see them anyway). Rooms have simple beds and seem to cost Y8 regardless of whether two, three or four people occupy one. A single person pays Y4 or Y5. Make sure you lock your room when you leave it. Down the main street from here are sidewalk stalls dispensing victuals.

Getting There & Away

Bus From the Leshan long-distance bus station there are five daily buses running to Chengdu (the first at 7.20 am and the last at 1 pm). The 165-km trip takes over five hours; fares are Y7.50 in an ordinary bus and Y9.50 in a soft-seat coach. Get the driver to drop you at the Jin Jiang Hotel in Chengdu if you're staying in that area. From Chengdu, faster minibuses also do the route to Leshan for Y10.50 from the major tourist hotels (Traffic, Jin Jiang, Tibet).

From Emeishan to Leshan is 30 km; buses run to Emei town, Baoguosi, or Qingyinge. Most buses go to Baoguosi, and there are only two buses a day to Qingyinge.

There's an express soft-seat coach daily at 7.30 am and 4.40 pm to Chongqing. The trip takes 12 hours and costs Y29.

Boat There is a boat to Chongqing, departing Leshan at 5.30 and 7.30 am every few days, but it's difficult to get aboard. The trip takes 36 hours and costs about Y40 in 3rd class. A shorter run to Yibin departs at 7 am, and costs Y18 in 3rd class. Yibin is part-way to Chongqing and has a railway station.

Getting Around

Bus There is one bus line in Leshan, running from the bus station to the Jiazhou Hotel. The timetable is posted at the Jiazhou bus stop. The bus runs from 6 am to 6 pm, at roughly 20-minute intervals with no service at lunch-time (about 11.20 am to 1.20 pm). On foot, it's a half-hour walk from one end of town to the other.

Bicycle You can hire a bike just near the bridge across the Min River. The price is Y0.50 an hour, which is expensive (for China), and watch out if you hire overnight as charges continue while you snore, unless otherwise negotiated. Bikes are of limited use if visiting the Grand Buddha since uphill work is required, and the track to Wuyou Hill is a dirt one. However, if you wish to explore the surrounding countryside, the bike will be useful – a suggested start is to continue out of town past the Jiazhou Hotel.

MEISHAN

(méishān) 眉山

Meishan, 90 km south-west of Chengdu by road or rail (it's on the Kunming-Chengdu railway line) is largely of interest to those with a knowledge of Chinese language, literature and calligraphy. It was the residence of Su Xun and his two sons, Su Shi and Su Zhe, the three noted literati of the Northern Song Dynasty (960-1127). Their residence was converted into a temple in the early Ming Dynasty, with renovations under the Qing emperor Hongwu (1875-1909). The mansion and pavilions now operate as a museum for the study of the writings of the Northern Song period. Historical documents, relics of the Su family, writings, calligraphy – some 4500 items all told are on display at the Sansu (Three Sus) shrine.

CHONGQING

(chóngqìng) 重庆

Chongqing (known in pre-pinyin China as 'Chungking') was opened as a treaty port in 1890, but not very many foreigners made it up the river to this isolated outpost, and those that did had little impact. A programme of industrialisation got under way in 1928, but it was in the wake of the Japanese invasion that Chongqing really took off as a major centre; the city was the wartime capital of the Kuomintang from 1938 onwards and refugees from all over China flooded in, swelling the population to over two million. The irony of this overpopulated, overstrained city with its bomb-shattered houses is that the name means something like 'double jubilation' or 'repeated good luck'. Emperor Zhao Dun of the Song Dynasty succeeded to the throne in 1190, having previously been made the prince of the city of Gongzhou; as a celebration of these two happy events, he renamed Gongzhou as Chongqing.

Edgar Snow arrived in the city in 1939 and found it:

> a place of moist heat, dirt and wide confusion, into which, between air raids, the imported central government...made an effort to introduce some technique of order and construction. Acres of buildings had been destroyed in the barbaric raids of May and June. The Japanese preferred moonlit nights for their calls, when from their base in Hankow they could follow the silver banner of the Yangtse up to its confluence with the Jialing, which identified the capital in a way no blackout could obscure. The city had no defending air force and only a few anti-aircraft guns....Spacious public shelters were being dug, but it was estimated that a third of the population still had no protection. Government officials, given advance warning, sped outside the city in their motor cars – cabinet ministers first, then vice-ministers, then minor bureaucrats. The populace soon caught on; when they saw a string of

official cars racing to the west, they dropped everything and ran. A mad scramble of rickshaws, carts, animals and humanity blew up the main streets like a great wind, carrying all before it.

The war is over, and today the city is hardly a backwater; six million people live here and it's a heavily industrialised port – as all those belching chimneys along the river front testify. Chongqing sets itself apart from other Chinese cities by the curious absence of bicycles! There's barely a cyclist to be found, as the steep hills on which the city is built make it coronary country for any would-be pedaller.

Chongqing is an enormous industrial city, and the smoke hangs heavily in the air. It's almost what you'd imagine industrial London to look like, circa 1890. This is not a city of 'sights' but there's a certain picturesque quality to the grey place, built as it is on hills that surround the confluence of two great rivers. The 'sights' are usually connected with the Communist Revolution.

Orientation

The heart of Chongqing spreads across a hilly peninsula of land wedged between the Jialing River to the north and the Yangtse River to the south. The rivers meet at the tip of the peninsula at the eastern end of the city.

The city centre is the main shopping and cinema district around the intersection of Zourong, Minquan and Minzu Lu in the eastern part of the town; the large Chaotianmen Dock is at the tip of the peninsula. The hotels, tourist facilities, railway and long-distance bus stations and most of the sights are scattered about the city, and there are a number of sights outside the city limits.

Chongqing's railway station is built on low ground, at the foot of one of the city's innumerable hills in the south-eastern part of town. When you go out of the gates of the station, walk straight ahead along the concrete path – on your left is a long row of noticeboards, followed by a left-luggage room, and on the right and further up are the ticket windows. Go through the concrete archway at the end of the pathway. On your right is Caiyuanbazheng Jie. In front of you is Nanqu Lu and on the left is Shangqingsi Lu.

Over on the left, on the other side of Shangqingsi Lu, is the beginning of a long flight of steps. About 340 of these will take you up to Changjiang Lu, which runs into Zhongshan Lu where you can get buses to the tourist hotels. If you don't feel like walking then beside the steps is a building with the ticket office and cable car up to Zhongshan Lu – a 45-degree, one-minute ride to the top. Taking the cable car to the top, you exit from a subway; turn right to go to the other side of Zhongshan Lu, or turn left and up the short flight of steps to Changjiang Lu. For details of the buses to the tourist hotels, see the section on Places to Stay.

Much of Chongqing makes for good (if hilly) walking, and the Chaotianmen Dock is a good place to start climbing. Walk up Xinhua Lu past the booking hall for the Yangtse boats and turn into Minzu Lu; from here you can carry on up to Cangbai Lu, where you can catch the cable car which flies over the Jialing River. If you carry on up Minzu Lu you'll eventually see on your left a deteriorated but very ornate gateway which is the entrance to a large temple not visible from the street. You walk through the gateway and past Buddha rock carvings on either side – at the end of the pathway on the left is the colourful Luohansi temple.

Further down Minzu Lu towards the Liberation Monument (the clock tower) is the Huixianlou Hotel. You can take the elevator to the rooftop where there's a fine 360-degree view of the city.

The area around the clock tower is the main shopping district. It also has many cinemas, a few street markets, and quite a few bookshops.

Despite the modern apartment and industrial blocks there's enough of old Chongqing left to give the city an oddly ramshackle, picturesque quality. Other Chinese cities such as Beijing have been rebuilt almost in their entirety in the post-1949 urban development programmes, but Chongqing still conveys something of what an old Chinese

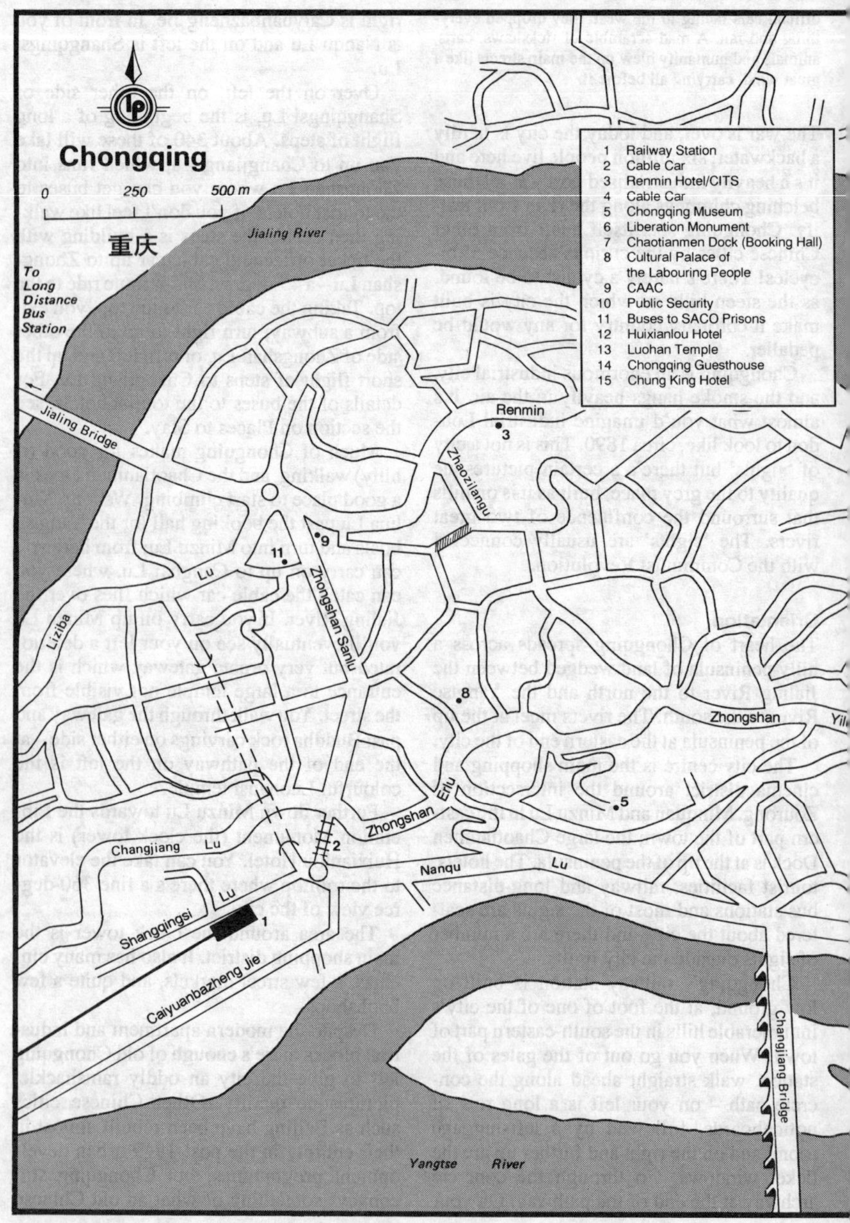
Chongqing
重庆
0
250
500 m
Jialing River
To Long Distance Bus Station
Jialing Bridge
Liziba
Lu
Zhongshan Sanlu
Renmin
Zhaozilangu
Zhongshan
Yil
Zhongshan
Erlu
Changjiang
Lu
Nanqu
Lu
Shangqingsi
Lu
Caiyuanbazheng Jie
Changjiang Bridge
Yangtse
River
1 Railway Station
2 Cable Car
3 Renmin Hotel/CITS
4 Cable Car
5 Chongqing Museum
6 Liberation Monument
7 Chaotianmen Dock (Booking Hall)
8 Cultural Palace of the Labouring People
9 CAAC
10 Public Security
11 Buses to SACO Prisons
12 Huixianlou Hotel
13 Luohan Temple
14 Chongqing Guesthouse
15 Chung King Hotel

Yangtse River
Jialing River
4
7
Chaoqian
Lu
Xinhua Lu
Shaanxi Lu
Beiqu
Lu
Cangbai
Lu
Linjiang
Lu
10
12
Minzu
Lu
15
13
Zourong Lu
6
14
Minsheng
Zhongshan Yilu
Bayi Lu
Wuyi Lu
Lu
Minquan Lu
Zhonghua
Lu
Xinhua Lu
Lu
Jiefang
Jiefang Lu
Yangtse River
1 火车站
2 缆车铁道
3 人民宾馆
4 嘉陵缆车铁道
5 博物馆
6 解放碑
7 朝天门码头（售票处）
8 劳动人民文化宫
9 中国民船
10 公安局外事科
11 至中美合作所汽车站
12 会仙楼宾馆
13 罗汉寺
14 重庆宾馆
15 重庆饭店

city looked like: neighbourhoods with stone steps meandering down narrow streets and alleys, and unkempt, grotty wooden houses.

Information

CITS The travel service (☎ 51449) has its office in a building in the Renmin Hotel compound. They're a friendly mob but hopelessly disorganised. They have been known to charge 100% extra on the price of train tickets (as against the usual 75%), and they never seem to know what tickets are available on the Yangtse boats. The Chung King Hotel has a much better booking service.

Public Security Bureau The office (☎ 43973) is on Linjiang Lu. A bus No 103 from the front of the Renmin Hotel will take you there. They're a friendly lot, but don't expect any permits for strange places.

Money The main Chongqing branch of Bank of China is on Xinhua Lu, diagonally opposite the Chung King Hotel. There are also foreign exchange counters at all the hotels mentioned in Places to Stay.

Post There is a branch post office on Minzu Lu within walking distance of the Chung King and Huixianlou hotels. Both the Renmin and Chung King hotels offer limited postal services.

Maps Good maps in Chinese – one with the bus routes and another without – are available from the shop in the Renmin Hotel.

Luohansi (Arhat Temple)

(luóhàn sì) 罗汉寺

Luohan is the Chinese rendering of the Sanskrit 'arhat', which is a Buddhist term referring to people who have released themselves from the psychological bondage of greed, hate, and delusion. Built around 1000 years ago, Luohansi features a long entranceway flanked by rock carvings, a hall of painted terracotta arhat sculptures (the usual 500) and a hall containing a large gold Buddha figure. Behind the Buddha altar is an Indian-style jataka mural depicting Prince Siddhartha in the process of cutting his hair to renounce the world.

At its peak, Luohansi hosted some 70 monks; there are around 18 in residence these days. The temple appears to be extremely popular with local worshippers, however, who burn tonnes of fragrant incense.

The vegetarian restaurant here is excellent and very cheap, but it's only open for lunch (approximately from 11.30 am to 1.30 pm).

Red Cliff Village

(hóngyán cūn) 红岩村

During the tenuous Kuomintang-Communist alliance against the Japanese during WW II, Red Cliff Village outside Chongqing was used as the offices and living quarters of the Communist representatives to the Kuomintang. Among others, Ye Jianying, Zhou Enlai and Zhou's wife Deng Yingchao lived here. After the Japanese surrender in 1945, it was also to Chongqing that Mao Zedong – at the instigation of American ambassador Patrick Hurley – came in August of that year to join in the peace negotiations with the Kuomintang. The talks lasted 42 days and resulted in a formal agreement which Mao described as 'words on paper'.

One of the better revolutionary history museums now stands at the site, and has a large collection of photos, though none of the captions are in English. A short walk from the museum is the building which housed the South Bureau of the Communist Party's Central Committee and the office of the representatives of the Eighth Route Army – though there's little to see except a few sparse furnishings and photographs.

To get to Red Cliff Village, take bus No 216 four stops from the station on Liziba Lu.

US-Chiang Kaishek Criminal Acts Exhibition Hall & SACO Prisons

In 1941 the United States and Chiang Kaishek signed a secret agreement to set up the Sino-American Cooperation Organisation (SACO), under which the United States helped to train and dispatch secret agents for the Kuomintang government. The chief of

Top: Bikes travelling piggy-bike! (RS)
Bottom Left: Junk under sail (RS)
Bottom Right: Sheep-hide raft, Binglingsi (AS)

Top: View from Moon Hill, Yangshuo (AS)
Bottom Left: Fastest fish-trap on two legs, Shapin market (RS)
Bottom Right: Mt. Maijishan (RS)

SACO was Tai Li, head of the Kuomintang military secret service; its deputy chief was a US Navy officer, Commodore M E Miles.

The SACO prisons were set up outside Chongqing during WW II. The Kuomintang never recognised the Communist Party as a legal political entity, only the Army. Civilian Communists remained subject to the same repressive laws, and though these were not enforced at the time, they were not actually rescinded. Hundreds of political prisoners were still kept captive by the Kuomintang in these prisons and others, and according to the Communists many were executed.

One of the prisoners held in the Chongqing SACO prisons for five years was General Ye Ting, a Whampoa Military Academy cadet, commander of a Nationalist division during the Northern Expedition of 1926-27 and one of the principal leaders of the Nanchang uprising of 1 August 1927. After the failure of the insurrection Ye retreated to Shantou with some of the Red Army and then took part in the disastrous Canton uprising of December 1927. He escaped to Hong Kong and withdrew from politics for a decade.

In 1937, with the anti-Japanese alliance between the Kuomintang and the Communists established, he was authorised by Chiang Kaishek to reorganise the surviving Red partisans on the Jiangxi-Fujian-Hunan borders, and to create the New Fourth Army – these were soldiers who had been left behind as a rearguard when the main part of the army began its Long March to Shaanxi in 1934. In 1941, Chiang Kaishek's troops ambushed the rear detachment of the New Fourth Army while it was moving in an area entirely behind Japanese lines to which it had been assigned by Chiang. This non-combat detachment was annihilated and Ye Ting was imprisoned in Chongqing.

Chiang ruled that the massacre was caused by the New Fourth's 'insubordination' and henceforth all aid was withdrawn from that army and also from the Communists' Eighth Route Army; from this time on the Communists received no pay and no ammunition, and a blockade was thrown up around their areas to prevent access to supplies. Although the Communists did not retaliate against the Kuomintang – which would have made Japan's task much simpler – clashes between Kuomintang and Communist armies were continuous, at times amounting to major civil war.

After Ye's release in 1946 he died en route to Yan'an, in a plane crash which also killed among others Deng Fa (chief of the Red Army's Security Police) and Bo Gu (general secretary of the Communist Party from 1932 to 1935 and a supporter of urban-insurrection policies which had cost the Communists dearly in the 1930s).

While the events that surround them are fairly dramatic, the prisons and the exhibition hall are not and you'll probably find them fairly boring unless you're an enthusiast. The exhibition hall has lots of photos on display but no English captions. There are manacles and chains but nothing to ghoul over. The hall is open 8.30 am to 5 pm and admission is 20 fen. To get there take bus No 217 from the station on Liziba Lu. It's about a 20-minute ride. Make sure that the driver knows where you want to get off, as the place is not obvious. The SACO Prisons are a long hour's walk from the hall (there appears to be no transport, though you could try waving down a truck or jeep), and there's really nothing to see there.

Bridges

Worth checking out are the enormous Jialing and Yangtse bridges. The Jialing Bridge, which crosses the river north of central Chongqing, was built between 1963 and 1966. It is 150 metres long and 60 metres high and for 15 years was one of the few means of access to the rest of China. The Yangtse Bridge to the south was finished in 1981. In 1989 the new Shimen Bridge over the Chang (Yangtse) River was completed.

Chongqing Museum

(chóngqìng bówùguǎn) 重庆博物馆

The museum is a reasonably interesting place, though nothing outstanding. They usually have some dinosaur skeletons on display, unearthed between 1974 and 1977 at Zigong, Yangchuan and elsewhere in Sichuan Province. Hours are from 9 to 11.30 am and from 2 to 5.30 pm.

The museum is at the foot of Pipashan in the southern part of town, walking distance from the Renmin Hotel. Walk up Zaozilanya along the eastern side of the hotel compound; on the right you'll come to a little street market. Walk down this street and turn left where it branches into two smaller streets. Follow the street up to the entrance of a park; head through the park, past the 'Cultural Palace of the Labouring People' and at the other end you'll come out on Zhongshan Lu.

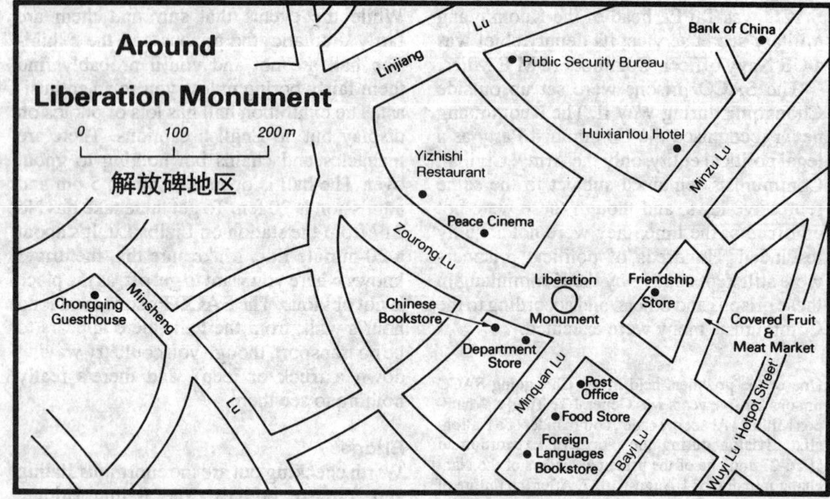

Directly opposite the entrance to the park, on the other side of the road, is a small street which leads uphill to the Chongqing Museum.

Chongqing Zoo

(chóngqìng dòngwùyuán) 重庆动物园

The zoo is little more than the hideous sight of badly kept animals in bare concrete cages. There are a couple of slumbering, dirty pandas here. Whatever you do, don't come on a Sunday, because you'll be the main attraction. From near the entrance to the cable car on Zhongshan Lu, take bus No 3 up Changjiang Lu to its terminal. From the terminal walk along the road directly in front of you for about 10 minutes and this will get you to the zoo.

Northern Hot Springs

(běi wēnquán gōngyuán) 北温泉公园

North-east of the city, overlooking the Jialing River, the Northern Hot Springs are in a large park which is the site of a 5th-century Buddhist temple. The springs have an Olympic-size swimming pool where you can bathe to an audience. There are also private rooms with hot baths – big tubs where the water comes up to your neck if you sit and up to your waist if you stand. Swimsuits can be hired here – they're coloured red, symbolising happiness. There's another group of springs 20 km south of Chongqing but the northern group is said to be better.

Places to Stay

The *Huixianlou Hotel (huìxiān bīnguǎn)*, close to the Liberation Monument, has eight-bed dorms (Y15 per bed) with panoramic views. The air-conditioning doesn't always work and they don't clean the dorms often enough, but you can't beat the location – right in the business district and within walking distance of the pier and Luohansi. There doesn't appear to be anything else in town in this price range. To reach the Huixianlou from the railway station, take a trolley bus No 402 from the top of the steps and get out on Zourong Lu near the Liberation Monument; the hotel is a short walk from the monument.

On the other end of the scale, the *Renmin Hotel* (☎ 351421) *(rénmín bīnguǎn)* is one of the most incredible hotels in China, and if you don't stay here you have got to at least visit the place. It's quite literally a palace,

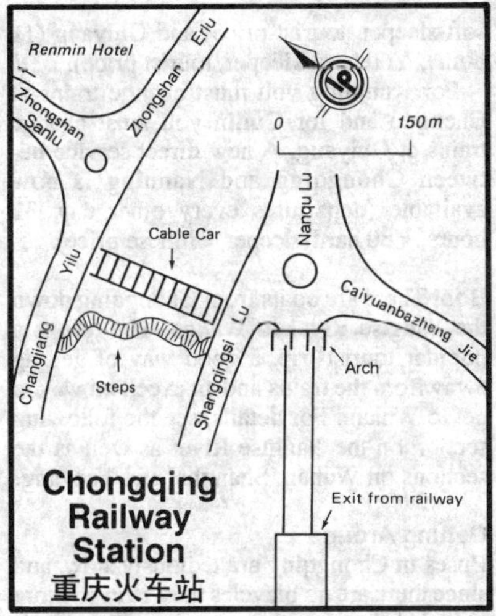

with a design that seems inspired by the Temple of Heaven and the Forbidden City in Beijing. Two wings make up the hotel, and these are separated by an enormous circular concert hall that is 65 metres high and seats 4000 people. The hotel was constructed in 1953.

For all the grandeur of the facade, the rooms themselves are as basic as in any other modern two-star Chinese hotel and the service is generally on the inefficient side. Nevertheless, there's a certain something about being able to come home to half a palace at the end of the day.

Dorms and multi-bed rooms have disappeared in the face of hotel upgrading. The cheapest accommodation is in Y147 singles though bargaining might be possible. Doubles are from Y209 to Y297 – overpriced for the kind of rooms available.

To get there, take trolley bus No 101 from above the railway station (top of the steps) up Zhongshan Sanlu as far as the first traffic circle. Then change to bus Nos 103 or 105, which will take you down past the hotel. It may be just as easy to walk from the traffic circle.

Better in terms of service and value is the newish *Chung King Hotel* (☎ 49301) *(chóngqìng fàndiàn)*, a joint-venture operation on Xinhua Lu near the Chaotianmen pier area. Immaculate singles are Y95 and doubles are from Y160 to Y200. Facilities include a small gift shop (with a few English titles), foreign exchange, post and telecommunications, taxi and clinic. The hotel has its own shuttle bus to and from the railway station.

The *Chongqing Guesthouse* (☎ 45662) *(chóngqìng bīnguǎn)* on Minsheng Lu currently undergoing renovations. Its original condition didn't have much to recommend it, but when renovations are complete who knows? The cheapest room is Y80; most rooms are in the Y125 to Y150 range. Take bus No 101 from Zhongshan Lu, above the railway station.

Places to Eat

The central business district in the eastern section of the city near the docks abounds with small restaurants and street vendors. For tasty noodles and baozi, check out Xinhua Lu and Shaanxi Lu towards Chaotianmen. Behind the Huixianlou Hotel and in the vicinity of Luohansi are a couple of good night markets.

Chongqing's number one speciality is *hǔo gūo* or hotpot. Skewers of pre-sliced meat and vegetables are placed in boiling hot, spiced oil; you're charged by the skewer and it's usually cheap (ask the price of each skewer before cooking if you're concerned about cost). Although hotpot can be found wherever there are street vendors or small restaurants, Wuyi Lu has the greatest variety and is locally known as *huoguo jie* or 'hotpot street'. Wuyi Lu runs off Minzu Lu between Xinhua Lu and Bayi Lu, a couple of blocks away from the Huixianlou and Chung King hotels. Bayi Lu is also a great street for snack-hunting.

Zourong Lu is a good street for larger, sit-down restaurants when you've got a group and feel like feasting on Sichuanese main courses. Among them is the well-known *Yizhishi Restaurant*, which serves Sichuan-style pastries in the morning and local specialities like tea-smoked duck and dry-stewed fish at lunch and dinner.

Of the hotel restaurants, *Chung King Hotel* has the best food – expensive by Chinese standards but moderately priced for most foreigners. The hotel was in fact built next door to the famous *Chung King Restaurant (chóngqìng fàndiàn)*, which is still going strong. The hotel's coffee shop serves Western breakfasts.

Getting There & Away

Air The CAAC office (☎ 52970 or 52643) is at the corner of Zhongshan Sanlu and Renmin Lu. You can also book flights at the Chung King Hotel.

Chongqing is connected by air to Beijing (Y525), Canton (Y380), Changsha (Y222), Chengdu (Y100), Guilin (Y212), Kunming (Y208), Nanjing (Y418), Shanghai (Y492), Wuhan (Y256) and Xi'an (Y193).

Air China (CAAC's international line) flies between Chongqing and Hong Kong on Monday, Thursday, and Saturday for Y855 one way. Tickets can be booked at the CAAC office or at the Chung King Hotel.

Bus The long-distance bus station is on the northern side of the Jialing River, across the Jialing Bridge. Getting to the station isn't so straightforward. Take bus No 105 from the intersection of Zhongshan Lu and Renmin Lu, cross the Jialing Bridge, and get off at the terminal. The bus station is further up ahead and you can walk if you're not carrying too much, or take bus No 210 the last stretch.

Buses from here to Dazu depart at 7.20 and 8 am; the fare is Y10 and the trip takes about eight hours.

A company called Kang Fu Lai (KFL), about a 10-minute walk from the Renmin Hotel, runs modern buses to Dazu. Tickets cost Y14 and buses depart at 7.40 am and 2.10 pm.

Train From Chongqing there are direct trains to Beijing, Chengdu (11 hours, Y30 hard-seat, Y50 soft-seat, Y80 hard-sleeper, Y150 soft-sleeper, tourist price) and Guiyang (11 hours, Y60 hard-sleeper, tourist price).

For Kunming you must change trains at Chengdu and for Guilin you must change trains at Guiyang. A new direct service between Chongqing and Nanning is now available (departures every other day, 32 hours, Y80 hard-sleeper, Chinese price).

Boat There are boats from Chongqing down the Yangtse River to Wuhan. The ride is a popular tourist trip, a good way of getting away from the trains and an excellent way to get to Wuhan. For details, see the following section on the Yangtse River as well as the sections on Wuhan, Shanghai and Yueyang.

Getting Around

Buses in Chongqing are tediously slow, and since there are no bicycles they're even more crowded than in other Chinese cities. Taxis can be hired from CITS or the reception desk of the Renmin Hotel.

A cable car line crosses the Jialing River between the Chaotianmen district of east Chongqing and Jinyangmen on the other side. The entrance is on the south side of Cangbai Lu. In 1988, a new cable car system was established that lifts passengers across the Chang (Yangtse) River from Xinhua Lu.

DOWN RIVER ON THE YANGTSE: CHONGQING TO WUHAN

The dramatic scenery and rushing waters of China's greatest river have been a great artistic inspiration to many painters and poets but for those forced to navigate the tricky waters the reality has been harsh. Tackling the Yangtse could mean danger as well as hard work; a large boat pushing upstream often needed hundreds of coolies ('trackers'), who lined the banks of the river and hauled the boat with long ropes against the surging waters. Today smaller boats can still be seen being pulled up the river by their crews.

The Yangtse is China's longest river and the third longest in the world at 6300 km, emanating from the snow-covered Tanggulashan mountains in south-west Qinghai

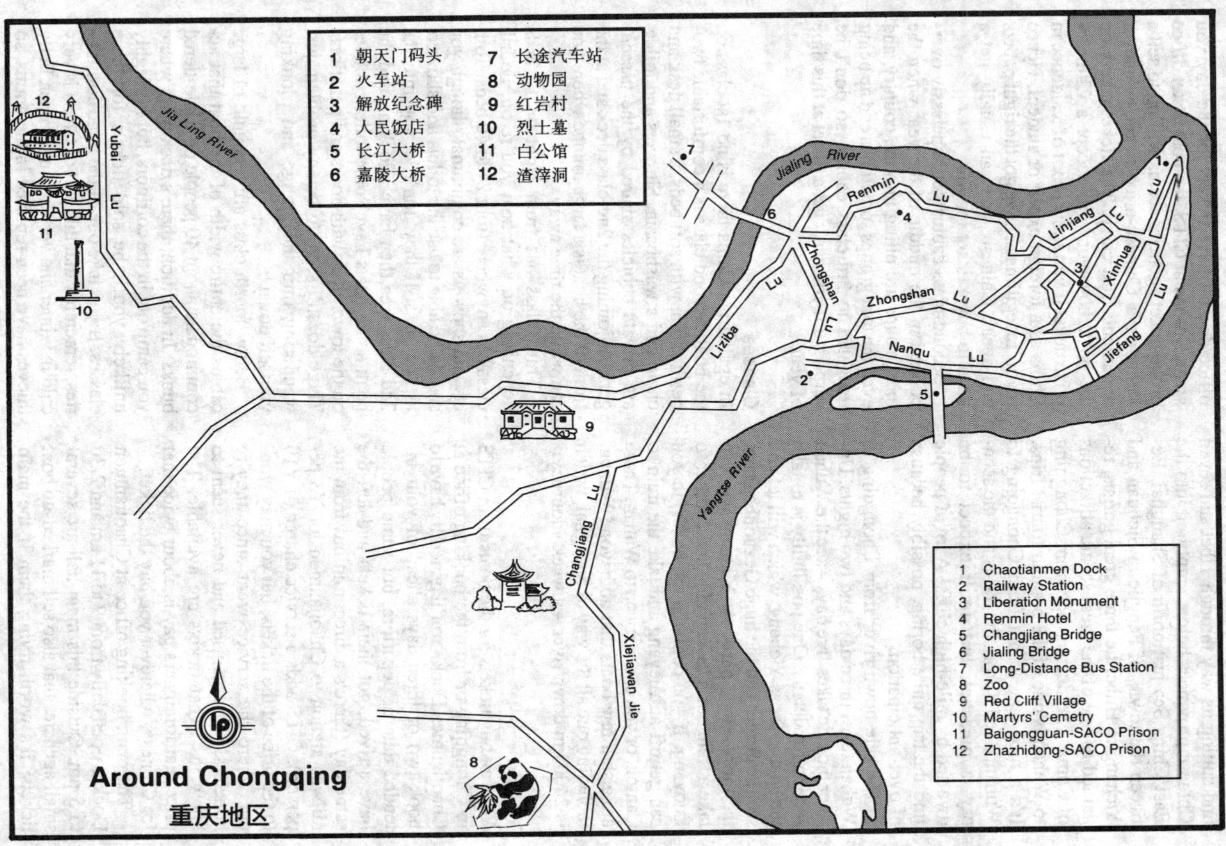

Around Chongqing
重庆地区
1 朝天门码头
2 火车站
3 解放纪念碑
4 人民饭店
5 长江大桥
6 嘉陵大桥
7 长途汽车站
8 动物园
9 红岩村
10 烈士墓
11 白公馆
12 渣滓洞
1 Chaotianmen Dock
2 Railway Station
3 Liberation Monument
4 Renmin Hotel
5 Changjiang Bridge
6 Jialing Bridge
7 Long-Distance Bus Station
8 Zoo
9 Red Cliff Village
10 Martyrs' Cemetery
11 Baigongguan-SACO Prison
12 Zhazhidong-SACO Prison
Jia Ling River
Jialing River
Yangtse River
Yubai Lu
Renmin Lu
Linjiang Lu
Xinhua Lu
Jiefang Lu
Zhongshan Lu
Zhongshan Lu
Nanqu Lu
Liziba Lu
Changjiang Lu
Xiejiawan Jie

and cutting its way through Tibet and seven Chinese provinces before emptying into the East China Sea just north of Shanghai. Between the towns of Fengjie in Sichuan and Yichang in Hubei lie three great gorges, regarded as one of the great scenic attractions of China. The steamer ride from Chongqing to Wuhan is one of the popular tourist trips. It's a nice way to get from Chongqing to Wuhan, a relief from the trains and the scenery is pleasant, but don't expect to be dwarfed by mile-high cliffs! A lot of people find the trip quite boring, possibly because of over-anticipation.

The ride down river from Chongqing to Wuhan takes three days and two nights. Upriver the ride takes five days – see the Wuhan section for details. One possibility is to take the boat as far as Yichang, which will let you see the gorges and the huge Gezhouba Dam, the most scenic parts. At Yichang you can take a train north to Xiangfan and another to Luoyang. If you continue the boat ride you can get off at Yueyang and take the train to Canton, or you can carry on to Wuhan. There are also a few boats that go beyond Wuhan, including one all the way to Shanghai, which is 2400 km down river – a week's journey.

Tickets

You can buy tickets for the boats from CITS in Chongqing or from the booking office at Chaotianmen Dock. You'll generally have to book two or three days ahead of your intended date of departure, but some people have arrived, got their tickets and left the same day (there's a direct minibus from the railway station to Chaotianmen for Y3 per person). CITS adds a service charge of Y10 to the price of the tickets, but you may wonder where the service went since they're hopelessly disorganised and never seem to know just what tickets are available. The price that foreigners pay is about twice that for Chinese, wherever you buy the ticket.

The main booking office at Chaotianmen Dock is open daily from 9 to 11 am and 2.30 to 5 pm. Outside this main hall are several small agencies that also sell marked-up boat tickets; it's worth trying them if the main office doesn't have tickets for the day you want. No-one at CITS, the boat ticket office or the ticket agencies seems willing to sell a foreigner a Chinese-price ticket, whatever documents you carry. The ticket-takers on the boat, however, will accept a Chinese-price ticket if you show proof of residence in China as a foreign expert or student. Hence if you're legitimate, have got the right papers and speak Chinese, you can usually get a local to buy a ticket for you.

Second-class cabins get hopelessly overbooked in the middle of the year when the tour groups are piling into the country, and even the tour groups sometimes end up being relegated to 3rd-class cabins, so don't be surprised if you can't get a ticket at this time of year.

Classes

In egalitarian China there is no 1st class on the boat. Second class is a comfortable two-berth cabin, with soft beds, a small desk and chair, and a washbasin. Showers and toilets are private cubicles shared by the passengers. Adjoining the 2nd-class deck and at the front of the boat is a large lounge where you can while the time away.

Third class has from eight or 12 beds depending on what boat you're on. Fourth class has anywhere from 24 to 40 beds. Toilets and showers are communal, though you should be able to use the toilets and showers in 2nd class. If they don't let you into the 2nd-class area then have a look around the boat; some boats have some toilet cubicles on the lower deck with doors and partitions. There doesn't seem to be any problem just wandering into the lounge and plonking yourself down.

Below fourth class are a couple of large cabins the entire width of the boat that accommodate about 40 people on triple-tiered bunks. In addition, there's deck class where you camp out in the corridors, but it's highly unlikely you'll be sold tickets for these classes. If you take one of the large dormitories, remember that this part of China is very cold in winter and very hot in summer. Petty thieves have been reported in the dorms, so keep valuable items safe – particularly at night.

Fares

The main booking hall in Chongqing charges the following fares for foreigners in yuan per person:

destination	2nd class (Y)	3rd class (Y)	4th class (Y)
Wanxian	189.70	88	67.20
Yichang	345.10	160.20	122.40
Shashi	388.90	180	130
Wuhan (Hankou)	510.40	237	181.20
Shanghai	783.30	363.80	278.20

There are lots of other intermediate destinations including Jiujiang and Wuhu (potential jumping off points for Lushan and Huangshan) and Nanjing on the Shanghai route. Between Nanjing and Wuhan a hydrofoil service cuts travelling time down from 40 hours to just 10 – see the Wuhan section for details.

Departure Times

Boats that terminate in Yichang generally depart Chongqing at 7.30 am. Those that go beyond to Shashi and Wuhan depart at 6.30 and 8 am. Boats to Shanghai leave at 9 am. These times can change from season to season depending on the river level, so check at the signboards at the main ticket hall to be sure. On the signboards, Wuhan is listed as Hankou, since this is the district of Wuhan where the boat docks.

You can sleep on the boat the night before departure for a nominal fee (Y8 foreigners, Y4 Chinese) – which is easier than getting up early and hoofing it down to the pier or trying to find a taxi in the morning. Your ticket should give the number of the pier where your boat will be waiting the night before.

Once you've boarded, a steward will exchange your ticket for a numbered, colour-coded tag that denotes your bed assignment. Hang onto the tag, since it must be exchanged for your ticket at the end of the voyage – without it they won't let you off the boat.

Food

There are a couple of restaurants on the boat. The one on the lower deck caters for the masses and is pretty terrible. The restaurant on the upper deck is quite good, but how much you're charged seems to vary from boat to boat. It's a good idea to bring some of your own food with you. When the boat stops at a town for any length of time, passengers may disembark and eat at little restaurants near the pier.

First Day

For the first few hours the river is lined with factories, though this gives way to some pretty, green terraced countryside with the occasional small town.

Around noon (depending on the boat) you arrive at the town of **Fuling**. The town overlooks the mouth of the Wu River which runs southwards into Guizhou; it controls the river traffic between Guizhou and eastern Sichuan. Near Fuling in the middle of the Yangtse River is a huge rock called Baihe Ridge. On one side of the rock are three carvings known as 'stone fish' which date back to ancient times and are thought to have served as watermarks – the rock can be seen only when the river is at its very lowest. In addition to the carvings, there is a large number of inscriptions describing the culture, art and technology of these ancient times.

The next major town is **Fengdu** *(fēngdū)*. Nearby Pingdushan mountain is said to be the abode of devils. The story goes that during the Han Dynasty two men, Yin Changsheng and Wang Fangping, lived on the mountain, and when their family names were joined together they were mistakenly thought to be the Yinwang, the King of Hell. Numerous temples containing sculptures of demons and devils have been built on the mountain since the Tang Dynasty, with heartening names like 'Between the Living and the Dead', 'Bridge of Helplessness' and 'Palace of the King of Hell'.

The boat then passes through **Zhongxian County**. North-east of the county seat of Zhongzhou is the **Qian Jinggou** site where primitive stone artefacts including axes, hoes and stone weights attached to fishing nets were unearthed.

In the afternoon the boat passes by **Shibaozhai (Stone Treasure Stronghold)** on the northern bank of the river. Shibaozhai is a 30-metre-high rock which is supposed to look something like a stone seal. During the early years of Emperor Qianlong's reign (1736-97) an impressive red wooden temple, the Lanruodian, shaped like a pagoda and 11 storeys high, was built on the rock. It houses a statue of Buddha and inscriptions which commemorate its construction.

Around 7 pm the boat arrives in the large town of **Wanxian** where it ties up for the night. Wanxian is the hub of transportation and communications along the river between eastern Sichuan and western Hubei and has traditionally been known as the gateway to Sichuan. It was opened to foreign trade in 1917. It's a neat, hilly town and a great place to wander around for a few hours while the boat is in port. There's a pleasant park around the tower in the centre of town. A long flight of steps leads from the pier up the river bank to a bustling night market where you can get something to eat or buy very cheap wickerwork baskets, chairs and stools.

Second Day

Boats generally depart Wanxian before dawn. Before entering the gorges the boat passes by (and may stop at) the town of **Fengjie**. This ancient town was the capital of the state of Kui during the Spring and Autumn and Warring States periods from 770 to 221 BC. The town overlooks the Qutang Gorge, the first of the three Yangtse gorges. Just east of Fengjie is a one km-long shoal where the remains of stone piles could be seen when the water level was low. These piles were erected in the Stone and Bronze ages, possibly for commemorative and sacrificial purposes, but their remains were removed in 1964 since they were considered a danger to navigation. Another set of similar structures can be found east of Fengjie outside a place called Baidicheng.

At the entrance to the Qutang Gorge is **Baidicheng** or White King Town on the river's north bank, 7½ km from Fengjie. The story goes that a high official proclaimed himself king during the Western Han Dynasty, and moved his capital to this town. A well was discovered which emitted a fragrant white vapour; this struck him as such an auspicious omen that he renamed himself the White King and his capital 'White King Town'.

The spectacular **Sanxia** (Three Gorges), Qutang, Wu and Xiling, start just after Fengjie and end near Yichang, a stretch of about 200 km. The gorges vary from 300 metres at their widest to less than 100 metres at their narrowest. The seasonal difference in water level can be as much as 50 metres.

Qutang Gorge *(qūtáng xiǎ)* is the smallest and shortest gorge (only eight km long), though the water flows most rapidly here. High on the north bank, at a place called Fengxiang (Bellows) Gorge, are a series of crevices. There is said to have been an ancient tribe in this area whose custom was to place the coffins of their dead in high mountain caves. Nine coffins were discovered in these crevices, some containing bronze swords, armour and other artefacts, but they are believed to date back only as far as the Warring States Period.

Wu Gorge *(wū xiǎ)* is about 40 km in length and the cliffs on either side rise to just over 900 metres. The gorge is noted for the Kong Ming tablet, a large slab of rock at the foot of the Peak of the Immortals. Kong Ming was prime minister of the state of Shu during the period of the Three Kingdoms (220-280 AD). On the tablet is a description of his stance upholding the alliance between the states of Shu and Wu against the state of Wei. **Badong** is a town on the southern bank of the river within the gorge. The town is a communications centre from which roads span out into western Hubei Province. The boat usually stops here.

Xiling Gorge *(xīlíng xiǎ)* is the longest of the three gorges at 80 km. At the end of the gorge everyone crowds out onto the deck to watch the boat pass through the locks of the huge **Gezhouba Dam**.

The next stop is the industrial town of **Yichang**, at about 3 pm if the boat is on time. From here you can take a train north to Xiangfan, where you can catch a train to Luoyang. Yichang is regarded as the gateway to the Upper Yangtse and was once a walled city dating back at least as far as the Sui Dynasty. The town was opened to foreign trade in 1877 by a treaty between Britain and China, and a foreign concession area was set up along the river front to the south-east of the walled city. Near the Yichang railway station you can take a No 10 bus to **White Horse Cave** *(báimǎdòng)*. For Y2, you can boat and walk through caverns with impressive stalactites and stalagmites. Five minutes' walk from the other end is an equally impressive place – **Three Visitors Cave** *(sānyǒudòng)*, along with a cliff trail that overlooks the Yangtse River.

After leaving Yichang, the boat passes under the immense **Changjiang Bridge** at the town of **Zhicheng**. The bridge is 1700 metres long and supports a double-track railway with roads for trucks and cars on either side. It came into operation in 1971.

The next major town is **Shashi**, a light-industrial town. As early as the Tang Dynasty Shashi was a trading centre of some importance, enjoying great prosperity during the Taiping Rebellion when trade lower down the Yangtse was largely at a standstill. It was opened up to foreign trade in 1896 by the Treaty of Shimonoseki between China and Japan, and though an area outside the town was assigned as a Japanese concession it was never developed. About 7½ km from Shashi is the ancient town of **Jingzhou**, to which you can catch a bus.

Third Day

There is absolutely nothing to see on the third day; you're out on the flat plains of eastern China, the river widens immensely and you can see little of the shore. The boat continues down river during the night and passes by the town of **Chenglingji**, which lies at the confluence of Lake Dongting and the Yangtse River. East of Lake Dongting is the town of **Yueyang**, which you'll reach at around about 6 am. If the boat is on time then you'll get into **Wuhan** late that afternoon, around 5 pm. (For details on Yueyang and Wuhan and the Yangtse River between Wuhan and Shanghai, see the separate sections in this book.)

DAZU

(dàzú) 大足

The grotto art of Dazu County, 160 km north-west of Chongqing, is rated alongside China's other great Buddhist cave sculpture at Dunhuang, Luoyang and Datong. Historical records for Dazu are sketchy. The cliff carvings and statues (with Buddhist, Taoist and Confucian influences) amount to thousands of pieces, large and small, scattered over the county in some 40-odd places. The main groupings are at Beishan (North Hill) and the more interesting Baoding. They date from the Tang Dynasty (9th century) to the Song (13th century).

The town of Dazu is a small, unhurried place. It's also been relatively unvisited by Westerners, and the surrounding countryside is superb.

Beishan

(běishān) 北山

Beishan is about a 30-minute hike from Dazu town – aim straight for the pagoda visible from the bus station. There are good overall views from the top of the hill. The dark niches hold small statues, many in poor condition; only one or two are of interest.

Niche No 136 depicts Puxian the patron saint (male) of Emeishan, riding a white elephant. The same niche has the androgynous Sun and Moon Guanyin. Niche 155 holds a bit more talent, the Peacock King. According to inscriptions, the Beishan site was originally a military camp, with the earliest carvings commissioned by a general.

Baoding

(bǎodǐngshān) 宝顶山

Fifteen km north-east of Dazu town, the

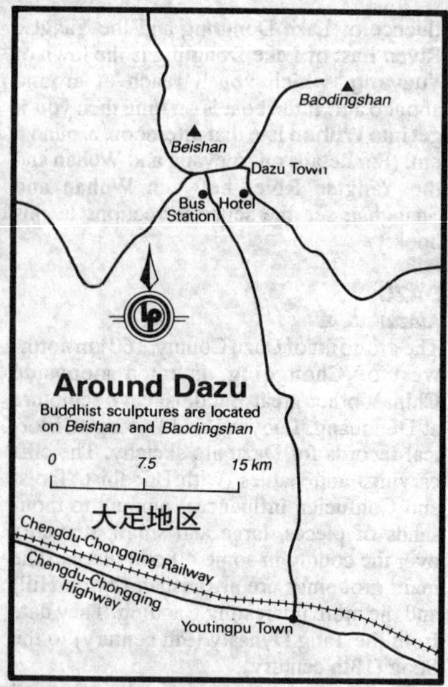

Baoding sculptures are definitely more interesting than those at Beishan. The founding work is attributed to Zhao Zhifeng, a monk from an obscure Yoga sect of Tantric Buddhism. There's a monastery in the throes of renovation with nice woodwork and throngs of pilgrims. On the lower section of the hill on which the monastery sits is a horseshoe-shaped cliff sculpted with coloured figures, some of them up to eight metres high. The centrepiece is a 31-metre-long, five-metre-high reclining Buddha, depicted in the state of entering Nirvana, the torso sunk into the cliff face – most peaceful.

Statues around the rest of the 125-metre horseshoe vary considerably: Buddhist preachers and sages, historical figures, realistic scenes (on the rear of a postcard one is described as 'Pastureland – Cowboy at Rest'), and delicate sculptures a few cm in height. Some of them have been eroded by wind and rain, some have lost layers of paint, but generally there is a remarkable survival rate (fanatical Red Guards did descend on the Dazu area bent on defacing the sculptures, but were stopped – so the story goes – by an urgent order from Zhou Enlai).

Baoding differs from other grottoes in that it was based on a preconceived plan which incorporated some of the area's natural features – a sculpture next to the Reclining Buddha, for example, makes use of an underground spring. Completion of the sculptures in 1249 AD is believed to have taken 70 years. Especially vivid are the demonic pieces: an emblem shows the six ways to transmigrate (look for a large dartboard held by the fangs of a Mr Hyde), and a one-storey section contains sobering sculptures on the evils of alcohol and other misdemeanours. Inside a small temple on the carved cliff is the Goddess of Mercy, with a spectacular gilt forest of fingers (1007 hands if you care to check). Each hand has an eye, the symbol of wisdom.

Buses to Baoding leave Dazu town every half hour from 7 am to 3 pm; the fare is 40 fen. The last bus departs Baoding for Dazu at around 5 pm. The sites are open from 8 am to 6 pm. As you pass by in the bus, keep an eye on the cliff faces for solo sculptures that may occasionally pop up.

CITS (inside the Dazu Binguan) can arrange a four-hour trip by taxi (Y30) or minibus (Y40).

Places to Stay & Eat

The *Dazu Guesthouse (dàzú bīnguǎn)* charges Y15 per person for a room with bath, it's rudimentary but comfortable. The hotel is a major hike from the bus station. Turn left from the station, cross a bridge to a place which bears a sign 'Cold Drinks/Dining-room', turn right after it and walk for about 10 minutes – the hotel is on your left.

The *Cold Drink* place has the best fare in town. Next door is a Chinese hotel which charges Y10.

Getting There & Away

Bus There are several options by bus. The first is the direct bus from Chongqing to Dazu which leaves at 7.20 am from

Chongqing's north-west bus station; there are seven buses a day, the fare is Y10, and the trip takes five to seven hours depending on whether there is a lunch break. The second is the Kang Fu Lai (KFL) bus company, which is a 10-minute walk from the Renmin Hotel (ask reception for directions), and runs modern buses to Dazu. Tickets cost Y14 and buses depart at 7.40 am and 2.10 pm. There is also the daily bus from Chengdu to Dazu; departs 6.50am, takes 10 hours, farc Y20.

Train To get to Dazu by rail, you should drop off the Chengdu-Chongqing railway line at Youtingpu town (five hours from Chongqing, seven hours from Chengdu), which is the nearest stop to Dazu. The 7.20 am train from Chengdu arrives at 2.34 pm in time for a connecting bus to Dazu outside the station. It's a 30-km ride and the fare is Y2. Buses for Youtingpu depart Dazu irregularly on the hour or half-hour from 11.30 am to 3.30 pm. There are six buses a day.

WESTERN SICHUAN & THE ROAD TO TIBET

Literally the next best thing to Tibet are the Sichuan mountains to the north and west of Chengdu – heaps of whipping cream that rise above 4500 metres, with deep valleys and rapid rivers. Tibetans and Tibetan-related peoples (Qiang) live by herding yaks, sheep and goats on the high-altitude Kangba Plateau Grasslands to the far north-west. Another zone, the Zoigê Grassland (north of Chengdu, towards the Gansu border) is over 3000 metres above sea level. Closer to Chengdu, the Tibetans have been assimilated, speak Chinese and have little memory of their origins, although they're regarded as a separate minority and are exempt from birth control quotas. Further out, however, Tibetan customs and clothing are much more in evidence.

Towns on the Kangba Plateau experience cold temperatures, with up to 200 freezing days per year; summers are blistering by day and the high altitude invites particularly bad sunburn. Lightning storms are frequent from May to October; cloud cover can shroud the scenic pcaks. On a pleasanter note, there appear to be sufficient hot springs in these areas to have a solid bath along the route.

A theme often echoed by ancient Chinese poets is that the road to Sichuan is harder to travel than the road to heaven. In the present era, with the province more accessible by road, we can shift the poetry to Tibet and the highway connecting it with western Sichuan.

The Sichuan-Tibet Highway, begun in 1950 and finished in 1954, is one of the world's highest, roughest, most dangerous and most beautiful roads. The highway has been split into northern and southern routes. The northern route runs via Kangding, Ganzi and Dêgê before crossing the boundary into Tibet. The southern route runs via Kangding, Litang and Batang before entering Tibet.

The Public Security Bureau in Chengdu isn't issuing individual permits to Lhasa or anywhere else in Tibet at the time of writing and is directing all foreigners to CITS. Even with a CITS tour, the land route between Chengdu and Lhasa is closed to foreigners for safety reasons. Some palefaces have succeeded and arrived intact in Lhasa. Less fortunate were some Americans and Australians on the back of a truck which overturned close to Dêgê; one member of the group lost half an arm and another member sustained multiple injuries to her back. It took several days for medical help to be sent and even longer before the injured could be brought back to Chengdu.

A couple of years ago there was a legendary crate, the Chengdu-Lhasa bus, which suffered countless breakdowns and took weeks to arrive. In 1985, a monumental mudslip on the southern route took out the road for dozens of km and the service was discontinued. Trucks are the only transport travelling consistently long hauls on this highway. The major truck depots are in Chengdu, Chamdo and Lhasa. Trucks usually run from Lhasa or from Chengdu only as far as Chamdo, where you have to find another lift. The police have now clamped down on truckers giving lifts to foreigners; there is rumoured to be a sign in

Chinese near Dêgê which warns drivers not to take foreigners. Certainly at Dêgê itself, there is a checkpoint on the bridge where guards turn back foreigners. If drivers are caught, they could lose their licences or receive massive fines. Foreigners caught arriving from Chengdu are often fined and always sent back. If you're arriving from Tibet nobody gives a damn.

In sum, the odds are stacked much higher against you when travelling into, rather than out of, Tibet. Whatever you do, bear in mind the risk and equip yourself properly with food and warm clothing. For information on Tibet and Qinghai see the separate chapters in this book. The Sichuan-Tibet Highway is given in-depth coverage in Lonely Planet's *Tibet – a travel survival kit*.

At present, the bus service on the Sichuan-Tibet Highway only seems to function well as far as Kangding. The Exit-Entry Administration Office of Chengdu's PSB hands out permits to Kangding, Ganzi and Dêgê and other towns in the Garzê (Ganzi) Autonomous Prefecture fairly regularly. Some travellers have followed the highway across the Kangba Plateau to the following places.

Kangding (Dardo)

(kāngdìng) 康定

Kangding (2620 metres) is a small town nestled in majestic scenery. Swift currents from the rapids of the Zhepuo River give Kangding hydropower, the source of heating and electricity for the town. There is a daily bus service from Chengdu main bus station to Kangding via Ya'an and Luding.

Towering above Kangding is the mighty peak of Gonggashan (7556 metres) – to behold it is worth 10 years of meditation, says an inscription in a ruined monastery by the base. The mountain is apparently often covered with cloud so patience is required for the beholding. It sits in a mountain range, with a sister peak just below it towering to 5200 metres. Pilgrims used to circle the two for several hundred km to pay homage.

Gonggashan is on the open list for foreign mountaineers – in 1981 it buried eight Japanese climbers in an avalanche. Known conquests of this awesome 'goddess' are those by two Americans in 1939, and by six Chinese in 1957.

There are three or four lamaseries in town in various stages of reconstruction. The most active is **Nanwusi** in the western part of the town on the north bank of the Zhepuo River. *Kangding Da Lamasi* is the most picturesque, sitting on a mountain 500 metres above the north side of town; the five pavilions and surrounding trails afford good views of Kangding and nearby snow peaks.

Foreigners are usually directed to the *Ganzijun Fenqu No 2 Hotel*, a truck stop with rooms for Y10.

Hailuogou Glacier Park

(hǎiluógōu) 海罗沟

This recently opened area near Kangding is a must for glacier freaks. It's part of Gonggashan and is the lowest glacier in Asia. Guides from the town of Moxixian lead inexpensive four to seven-day pony treks along glacier trails (which are virtually impossible to follow without a guide). There are daily buses to Moxixian from Kangding via Luding. To attempt this trip, you'll need down gear, sunglasses and a store of high-calorie food to supplement camp food along the way.

Ganzi

(gānzī) 甘孜

The capital of the Ganzi (Garzê) Tibetan Autonomous Region sits high in a Cholashan mountain valley (3800 metres) north-west of Kangding, and is populated by mostly Tibetans and Khampas. Very few Westerners have sojourned here, though as the Xining-Chengdu route between Qinghai and Sichuan becomes more popular it may yet get its due. For now it's little more than an intermediate stop between Serxü and Kangding for travellers in a hurry to reach 'civilisation' after the rigours of the Xining-Serxü road.

The **Ganzisi** lamasery just north of the town's Tibetan quarter is worth a visit for views of the Ganzi valley, although it's not a particularly spectacular structure.

The *Ganzixian Hotel* has beds for Y10, a decent dining room, friendly staff and plenty of hot water.

For details on the trip north to Xining via Serxü, see the Xining to Chengdu section in the Qinghai chapter.

Dêge

(dégé) 德格

This is the last town on the Chengdu-Lhasa highway before it enters Tibet proper. The 250-year-old **Bakong Scripture Printing Lamasery** houses an extensive collection of Tibetan scriptures of the five Lamaist sects which are revered by followers the world over. Under the direction of the abbot are some 300 workers; housed within the monastery are over 200,000 hardwood printing plates. Texts include ancient works on astronomy, geography, music, medicine and Buddhist classics. A history of Indian Buddhism, comprising 555 woodblock plates, is the only surviving copy in the world (written in Hindi, Sanskrit and Tibetan). Protecting the monastery from fire and earthquake is a guardian goddess, a green Avalokitesvara.

Litang

(lǐtáng) 理塘

West of Kangding on the southern route to Tibet is Litang, which at 4700 metres is 1000 metres higher than Lhasa and a few hundred metres short of the world record for high towns (Wenchuan, on the Tibet-Qinghai Plateau). Litang rests at the edge of a vast grassland. A trading fair and festival lasting 10 days is held here annually beginning on the 13th day of the sixth lunar month; it's sponsored by the Panchen Lama.

NORTHERN SICHUAN

The Aba (Tibet & Qiang) Autonomous Prefecture of northern Sichuan is perhaps the most Tibetan area of the province and doesn't require any special permits from the Chengdu PSB.

Jiuzhaigou

(jiǔzhàigōu) 九寨沟

In northern Sichuan, close to the Gansu border, is Jiuzhaigou (literally: Nine Stockade Gully), which was 'discovered' in the '70s and is now being groomed for an annual influx of 300,000 visitors. In 1984, Zhao Ziyang made the famous comment which all Sichuanese tourism officials love to quote: 'Guilin's scenery ranks top in the world, but Jiuzhaigou's scenery even tops Guilin's'.

Jiuzhaigou, which has several Tibetan settlements, offers a number of dazzling features – it is a nature reserve area (with some panda conservation zones) with North-American-type alpine scenes (peaks, clear lakes, forests). Scattered throughout the region are Tibetan prayer wheels and *chortens*, Tibetan stupas. The remoteness of the region and the chaotic transport connections have kept it clean and relatively untouristed.

Despite the good intentions of the authorities, all this looks certain to change fast. A helicopter landing pad is under construction even though the mountain ranges between Chengdu and Jiuzhaigou are not ideal terrain for helicopters. Tourism officials are already going one step further and planning an airport for small jets.

You should calculate between a week and 10 days for the round trip by road. It takes from two to three days to get there and you can easily spend three or four days, or even weeks, doing superb hikes along trails which cross spectacular scenery of waterfalls, ponds, lakes and forests – just the place to rejuvenate polluted urban senses.

The entrance to Jiuzhaigou National Park is close to the Yangdong Hotel. From there a dirt road runs as far as the Nuorilang Falls where the road splits: branch right for Swan Lake; branch left for Long Lake. Nuorilang is becoming a tourist centre of sorts. From Yangdong to Nuorilang is 13.8 km, Nuorilang to Long Lake is 17.8 km, Nuorilang to Rizi is nine km, Rizi to Swan Lake is eight km.

Jiuzhaigou and Huanglongsi are both around 3000 metres in altitude. Between October and April snow often cuts off access

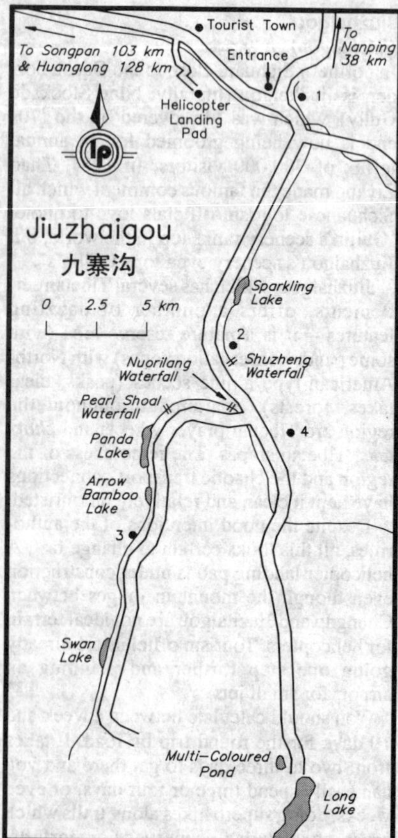

1 Yangdong Hotel
2 Xiniu Haishi Sushe
3 Rize Zhaodaisuo
4 Nuorilang Hotel

1 羊峒招待所
2 犀牛海食宿店
3 日则招待所
4 诺日朗招待所

for weeks on end. Make sure you take warm clothing. Food can be abysmal so take iron rations with you. The rainy season lasts from June to August.

Roads in these regions are dangerous so don't expect more than minimum standards of vehicle, driver or road maintenance. Shock horror stories circulating recently about Jiuzhaigou included a minibus-load of Hong Kongers which reported sighting a UFO; another bus-load plunged over a precipice killing all 20 passengers. An outbreak of plague in the area caught two more Hong Kongers, who were immediately cremated.

Transport is not plentiful and unless you catch a bus at its originating point, be prepared when boarding en route for some tough competition for any seats. To maximise your chances of a seat on a bus out of Jiuzhaigou, it's best to book your ticket three days in advance at the entrance to the reserve. Hitching has worked.

Huanglong

(huánglóng) 黄龙

This valley studded with terraced, coloured ponds (blue, yellow, white and green) and waterfalls is about 56 km from Songpan, on the main road to Jiuzhaigou. The Yellow Dragon Temple *(huánglóng sì)* and the surrounding area were designated a national park in 1983. The most spectacular terraced ponds are behind the temple, about a two-hour walk from the main road. Huanglong is almost always included on the itinerary for a Jiuzhaigou tour, but some people find it disappointing and think an extra day at Jiuzhaigou is preferable. An annual Miao Hui (Temple Fair) held here around the middle of the sixth lunar month (roughly mid-August) attracts large numbers of traders from the Qiang minority.

Places to Stay

In Songpan, three small hostelries offer doubles, triples and five-bed rooms; prices average Y5 to Y7.50 per bed. *Songpan*

Guesthouse is a current favourite for its friendly service.

In Jiuzhaigou, the state-run *Rizi Zhaodaisuo* hotel *(rìzé zhāodàisuǒ)* and the better, privately run *Xiniu Haishi Sushe (xīniú hǎishí sùdiàn)* compete happily for FEC. At the *Yangdong Hotel (yángtóng zhāodàisuǒ)* prices range between Y28 and Y40 for a double, Y10 and Y15 for a triple.

Further up near the Nuorilang Falls is the *Minzulou Tibetan Guesthouse*, a wooden building with basic but friendly accommodation for around Y5 per person. There are other Tibetan guesthouses in the area (check Shuzheng village, between Nuorilang and the park entrance) that charge only Y3 to Y4 for a bed. Tourists usually put up at the *Nuorilang Hotel (nuòrìláng zhāodàisuǒ)* where there's a tourist office. Rooms are around Y20 per person.

In Huanglongsi National Park are several small guesthouses with beds for Y5 or less – no frills, just hard beds and maybe a coal burner in the winter.

Nobody has a decent word for food in this region. Chengdu would be a good place to stock up.

Getting There & Away

Warning Beginning in 1990, the ticket office in Chengdu was requiring that foreigners present a PICC (People Insurance Company of China) card certifying that they're carrying a PICC insurance policy for bus travel in northern Sichuan (the same applies for most of Gansu Province further north). This policy apparently follows from a lawsuit brought upon the Chinese government by the family of a Japanese tourist who was killed in a bus crash in the Jiuzhaigou area. The card costs Y20 and is available from the PICC office on Renmin Donglu in Chengdu. The bus station won't accept any other type of travel insurance. It's a good idea to have this card with you at all times while travelling in northern Sichuan – any bus driver could ask to see it.

Bus Until helicopters and jets send shock waves over Jiuzhaigou, the local bus remains the best means of transport. It can be taken in one dose or as part of a bus/train combination. Several intriguing routes follow.

The bus going directly north from Chengdu (Ximen bus station) to Songpan takes 12 hours and costs Y20 on an ordinary bus, Y34 for a deluxe coach. From Songpan to Jiuzhaigou is another 2½ hours, Y11. Tour buses direct to Jiuzhaigou charge an extortionate Y134 to travel the 438-km route.

Another option is to travel north on the Chengdu-Baoji railway line as far as Zhaohua, where you should immediately book your bus ticket (Y14), stay overnight, and take the bus to Nanping the next day at 6.20 am. The trip takes 12 hours along a notoriously dangerous road which briefly enters Gansu Province. In Nanping, another overnight stay is required before taking the 7.30 am bus to Jiuzhaigou; the trip takes three hours and there is no bus on Wednesdays.

A third option is to take a train or bus to either Mianyang or Jiangyou, both north of Chengdu. Then take a bus to Pingwu, where you can change for a bus to Jiuzhaigou. This road is reportedly superior to the one between Zhaohua and Nanping.

Other possibilities include dropping down from Gannan and cutting across from Qinghai.

Tours During the summer, various companies in Chengdu operate tours to Jiuzhaigou. Some include side trips in the general region. The most welcome customers are Hong Kongers, who tend to travel in miniature armies and can easily book out a whole bus. Most of the trips are advertised for a certain day, but the bus will only go if full. If you are unlucky you may spend days waiting. Find out exactly how many days the trip lasts and which places are to be visited. If you're not sure about the tour company, avoid paying in advance. If there's a booking list, have a look and see how many people have registered. You can register first and pay before departure.

A standard tour includes Huanglongsi and Jiuzhaigou, lasts seven days and costs an average of Y170 to Y250 per person. There are longer tours which include visits to the

Tibetan grassland areas of Barkam and Zoigê. Prices vary according to the colour of your skin, availability of FEC and scruples of the companies involved. An agency next to Chengdu's northern railway station was offering four-day Jiuzhaigou tours for only Y140 per person – according to a couple of travellers who took the tour, it was good value.

In Songpan, you can also arrange pony treks to nearby Munigou, where there is a waterfall, hot springs and temple – and few tourists. The cost is Y20 per person per day, plus a nominal charge for tents and bedding.

The following places in Chengdu have been known to offer tours: Ximen bus station, travel agencies in the Jiaotong (Traffic) Hotel, the Jin Jiang Hotel, the Sichuan Province Tourism Bureau (opposite the Jin Jiang Hotel on Renmin Nanlu) and CITS. The latter two are the most expensive. There is an agency next to the northern railway station

A word of warning. Several tour operators in Chengdu have been blacklisted by Hong Kong travellers for lousy service, rip-offs and rudeness. Ask around among travellers to pinpoint a reliable agency.

Yunnan 云南

Geographically, Yunnan *(yúnnán)* is the most varied of all of China's provinces, with terrains as widely divergent as tropical rainforest and icy Tibetan highlands. It is also the sixth largest province in China and the home of a third of all China's ethnic minorities, and it harbours half of all China's plant and animal species.

When Qin Shihuang and the Han emperors first held tentative sway over the south-west, Yunnan was occupied by a large number of non-Chinese aboriginal peoples without any strong political organisation. But by the 7th century AD the Bai people had established a powerful kingdom, the Nanzhao, south of Dali. Initially allying its power with the Chinese against the Tibetans, this kingdom extended its power until, in the middle of the 8th century, it was able to challenge and defeat the Tang armies. It took control of a large slice of the south-west and established itself as a fully independent entity, dominating the trade routes from China to India and Burma. The Nanzhao kingdom fell in the 10th century and was replaced by the kingdom of Dali, an independent state which lasted until it was overrun by the Mongols in the mid-13th century. After 15 centuries of resistance to northern rule, this part of the south-west was finally integrated into the empire as the province of Yunnan.

Even so it remained an isolated frontier region, with scattered Chinese garrisons and settlements in the valleys and basins, a mixed aboriginal population occupying the uplands, and various Dai (Thai) and other minorities along the Lancang (Mekong) River. Like the rest of the south-west, it was always one of the first regions to break with the northern government. Today, however, Yunnan Province looks to be firmly back in the Chinese fold; it's a province of 34 million people, including a veritable constellation of minorities (24 registered): the Zhuang, Hui, Yi, Miao, Tibetans, Mongols, Yao, Bai, Hani,

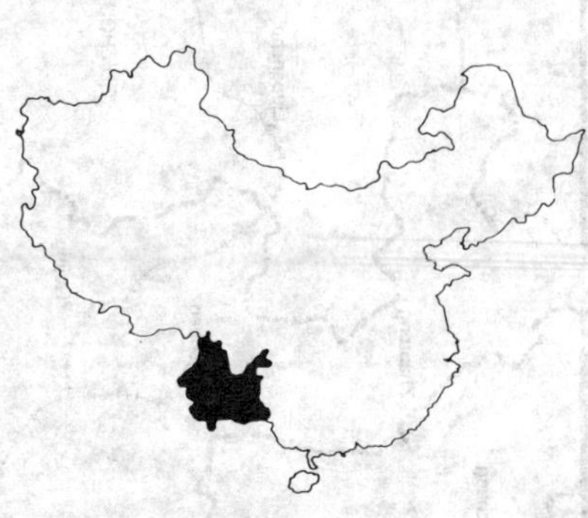

Dai, Lisu, Lahu, Wa, Naxi, Jingpo, Bulang, Pumi, Nu, Achang, Benglong, Jinuo and Dulong. Its chief attraction is, in fact, those pockets of the province that have successfully resisted Chinese influence and exhibit strong local identities. Even Kunming, the provincial capital, has a flavour all its own that seems more than half a world away from Beijing. The province is also well-known for its mild climate; the name 'Yunnan' is a reference to this reputation, meaning 'South of the Clouds'.

KUNMING

(kūnmíng) 昆明

The region of Kunming has been inhabited for 2000 years. Tomb excavations around Lake Dian to the south of the city have unearthed thousands of artefacts from that period – weapons, drums, paintings, and silver, jade and turquoise jewellery – that suggest a well-developed culture and provide clues to a very sketchy early history of the city. Until the 8th century the town was a remote Chinese outpost, but the kingdom of Nanzhao, centred to the north-west of Kunming at Dali, captured it and made it a secondary capital. In 1274 the Mongols came through sweeping all and sundry before them. Marco Polo, who put his big feet

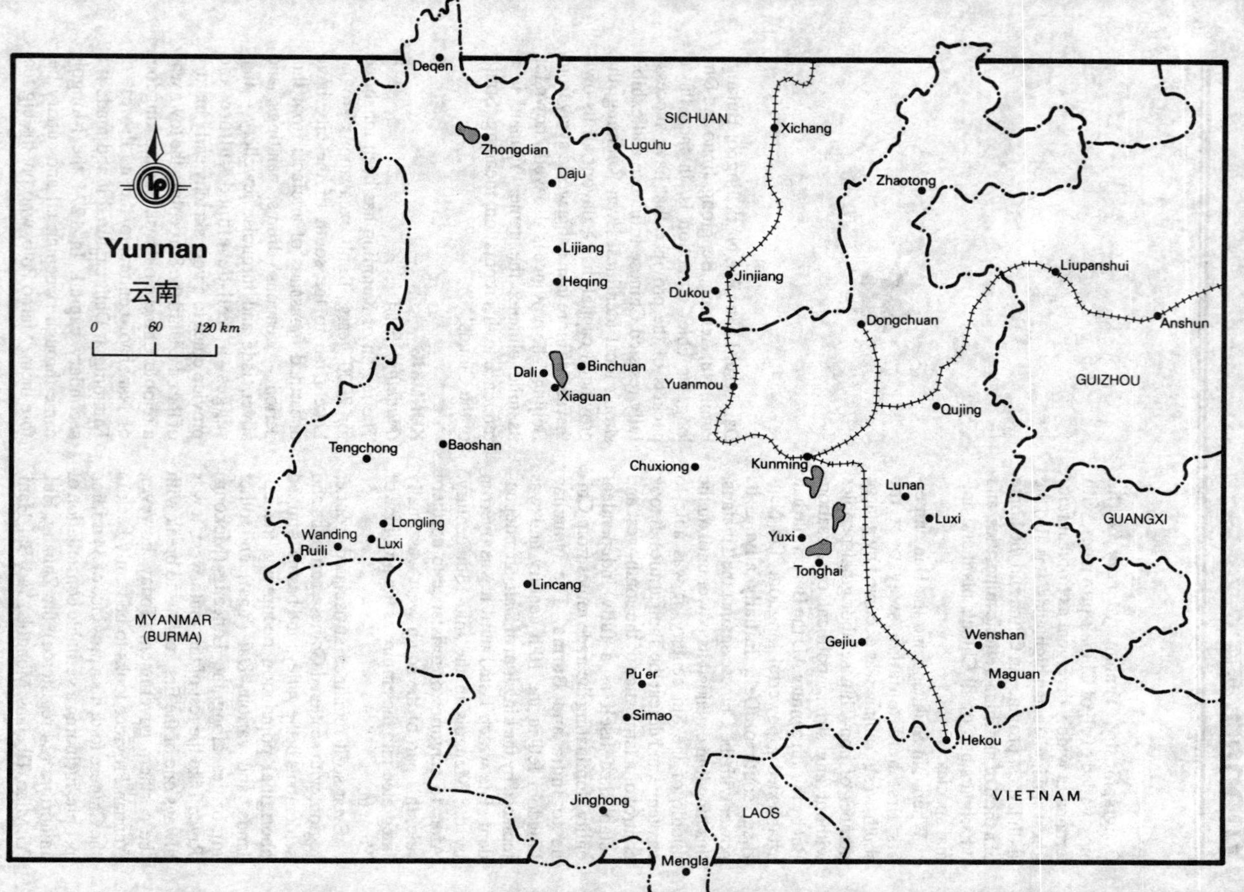
Yunnan
云南
0
60
120 km
SICHUAN
GUIZHOU
GUANGXI
MYANMAR
(BURMA)
LAOS
VIETNAM
Deqen
Zhongdian
Luguhu
Xichang
Daju
Zhaotong
Lijiang
Heqing
Jinjiang
Dukou
Liupanshui
Anshun
Dongchuan
Dali
Binchuan
Xiaguan
Yuanmou
Qujing
Tengchong
Baoshan
Chuxiong
Kunming
Lunan
Luxi
Longling
Wanding
Luxi
Ruili
Yuxi
Tonghai
Lincang
Gejiu
Wenshan
Maguan
Pu'er
Simao
Hekou
Jinghong
Mengla

and top hat in everywhere, gives us a fascinating picture of Kunming's commerce in the late 13th century:

> At the end of these five days journeys you arrive at the capital city, which is named Yachi, and is very great and noble. In it are found merchants and artisans, with a mixed population, consisting of idolaters, Nestorian Christians and Saracens or Mohametans... The land is fertile in rice and wheat...For money they employ the white porcelain shell, found in the sea, and which they also wear as ornaments about their necks. Eighty of the shells are equal in value to...two Venetian groats. In this country also there are salt springs...the duty levied on this salt produces large revenues to the Emperor. The natives do not consider it an injury done to them when others have connection with their wives, provided the act is voluntary on the woman's part. Here there is a lake almost a hundred miles in circuit, in which great quantities of fish are caught. The people are accustomed to eat the raw flesh of fowls, sheep, oxen and buffalo...the poorer sorts only dip it in a sauce of garlic... they eat it as well we do the cooked.

In the 14th century the Ming set up shop in Yunnanfu, as Kunming was then known, building a walled town on the present site. From the 17th century onwards the history of this city becomes rather grisly. The last Ming resistance to the invading Manchu took place in Yunnan in the 1650s and was crushed by General Wu Sangui. Wu in turn rebelled against the king and held out until his death in 1678. His successor was overthrown by the Manchu Emperor Kangxi and killed himself in Kunming in 1681. In the 19th century, the city suffered several bloodbaths as the rebel Muslim leader Du Wenxiu, the Sultan of Dali, attacked and besieged the city several times between 1858 and 1868. A large number of buildings were destroyed and it was not until 1873 that the rebellion was finally and bloodily crushed. The intrusion of the West into Kunming began in the middle of the 19th century when Britain took control of Burma and France took control of Indochina, providing access to the city from the south. By 1900 Kunming, Hekou, Simao and Mengzi were opened to foreign trade. The French were keen on exploiting the region's copper, tin and lumber resources, and in 1910 their Indochina railroad, started in 1898, reached the city.

Kunming's expansion began with WW II, when factories were established here and refugees fleeing the Japanese poured in from eastern China. To keep the Japanese tied up in China, Anglo-American forces sent supplies to Nationalist troops entrenched in Sichuan and Yunnan. Supplies came overland on a dirt road carved out of the mountains in 1937-38 by 160,000 Chinese with virtually no equipment. This was the famous Burma Road, a 1000-km haul from Lashio to Kunming (today, the western extension of Kunming's Renmin Lu, leading in the direction of Heilinpu, is the tail end of the Road). Then in early 1942 the Japanese captured Lashio, cutting the line. Kunming continued to handle most of the incoming aid during 1942-45 when American planes flew the dangerous mission of crossing the 'Hump', the towering 5000-metre mountain ranges between India and Yunnan. A black market sprang up and a fair proportion of the medicines, canned food, petrol and other goods intended for the military were siphoned off into other hands.

The face of Kunming has been radically altered since then: streets widened, office buildings and housing projects flung up. With the coming of the railways, industry has expanded rapidly, and a surprising range of goods and machinery available in China now bears the 'made in Yunnan' stamp. Kunming also has its own steel plant. The city's production includes foodstuffs, trucks, machine tools, electrical equipment, textiles, chemicals, building materials and plastics. The population hovers around the two million mark; minority groups have drifted toward the big lights in search of work, and some have made their home there. At most the minorities account for 6% of Kunming's population, although the farming areas in the outlying counties have some Yi, Hui and Miao groups native to the area. Also calling Kunming home are some 150,000 Vietnamese refugees from the Chinese-Vietnamese wars and border clashes that started in 1977.

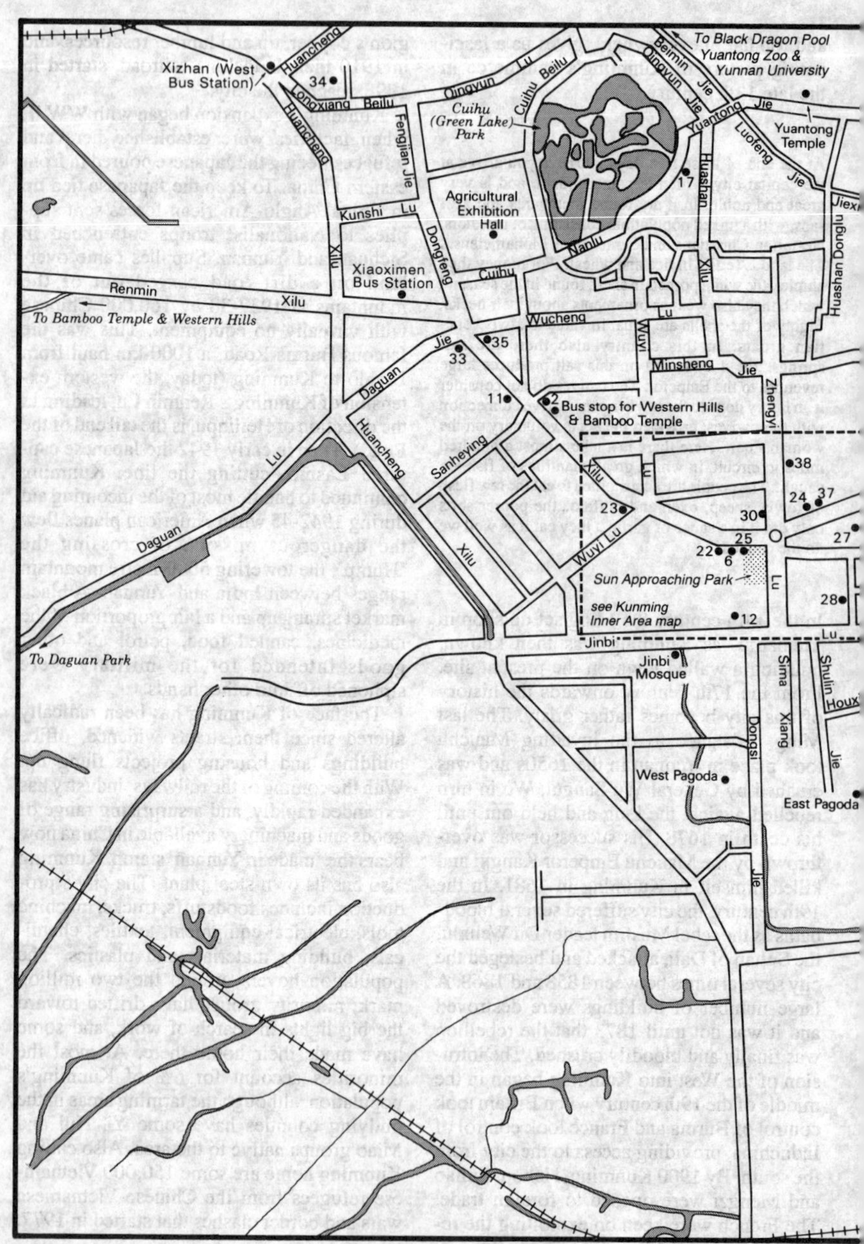

To Black Dragon Pool
Yuantong Zoo &
Yunnan University
Xizhan (West
Bus Station)
Huancheng
34
Longxiang Beilu
Huancheng
Fengjian Jie
Qingyun Lu
Cuihu Beilu
Beimin Jie
Qingyun Jie
Cuihu
(Green Lake)
Park
Yuantong Jie
Yuantong
Temple
Luofeng Jie
Huashan
17
Jiexi
Huashan Donglu
Agricultural
Exhibition
Hall
Kunshi Lu
Xilu
Dongfeng
Nanlu
Cuihu
Xilu
Xiaoximen
Bus Station
Renmin
Xilu
To Bamboo Temple & Western Hills
Wucheng
Lu
Wuyi
35
33
Jie
Daguan
Minsheng
Jie
Zhengyi
11
2
Bus stop for Western Hills
& Bamboo Temple
Huancheng
Sanheying
Xilu
38
24
37
23
30
Lu
27
Daguan
Wuyi Lu
22
6
25
Sun Approaching Park
Lu
Xilu
28
see Kunming
Inner Area map
12
To Daguan Park
Jinbi
Lu
Jinbi
Mosque
Sima
Xiang
Shulin
Houxi
Jie
Dongsi
Jie
West Pagoda
East Pagoda

To North Railway Station
Chuanxingulou Bus Station
Lingguang Jie
Qingnian
Taoyuan
Beijing
Huancheng
Kunming
昆明
Xiang
Jie
Lu
Renmin Donglu
Changchun
Lu
Huguo
Lu
Baita
Donglu
Dongfeng
Donglu
To Stone Forest
The Square
Lu
Lu
Tuodong
Lu
Chongshan Jie
Jie
Beijing
Huangianzhuang
Dongzhan Bus Station
Nanlu
To Airport
Tour Bus Company for Shilin
Bus stop for Western Hills & Bamboo Temple
Huancheng
Lu
See Key on following page

1 Kunming Hotel/CITS
2 Yunnan Hotel
3 Camellia Hotel
4 Kunhu Hotel
5 Three Leaves Hotel
6 Chuncheng Hotel/Restaurant
7 Post Office & Telecom Building
8 CAAC
9 Dianchi Cinema
10 Public Security Bureau
11 Hongxing Theatre
12 Yunnan Across the Bridge Noodles Restaurant
13 Yingjianglou Moslem Restaurant
14 Riverside Cafe
15 Cooking School
16 Coffee Shop
17 Ciuhu Guesthouse
18 Overseas Chinese Restaurant
19 Olympic Restaurant
20 Kunming Railway Station
21 Main Bus Station
22 Advance Rail Booking Office
23 Provincial Museum
24 Poster Shop
25 Tour Operators
26 Guanshengyuan Restaurant
27 Beijing Restaurant
28 Chuanwei Restaurant
29 Gongnongbing Restaurant
30 Kunming Department Store
31 Yunnan Antique Store
32 Kunming Arts & Crafts Store
33 Yunnan Arts & Crafts Store
34 Zhengyi Department Store
35 Dongfeng Department Store
36 Foreign Languages Bookstore
37 Xinhua Bookstore
38 Zhengyi Chinese Pharmacy
39 Three Teahouses
40 Jinlong Fandian
41 International Post Office
42 South Railway Station
43 Liu's Cafe

1 昆明饭店
2 云南饭店
3 茶花宾馆
4 昆湖饭店
5 三叶饭店
6 春城饭店
7 邮电局
8 中国民航
9 滇池电影院
10 公安局外事科
11 红星剧院
12 云南过桥米线
13 映江楼饭店
14 河边的饭店
15 学厨饭店
16 咖啡店
17 翠湖宾馆
18 华侨饭店
19 奥林匹克饭店
20 昆明火车站
21 昆明汽车客运站
22 火车售票处
23 云南省博物馆
24 广告画商店
25 旅游服务处
26 冠生园饭店
27 北京饭店
28 川味饭店
29 工农兵饭店
30 百货商店
31 云南文物商店
32 昆明工艺美术服务部
33 云南工艺美术服务部
34 三招百货商店
35 东风百货商店
36 外文书店
37 新华书店
38 正义中药店
39 桃源街茶馆
40 金龙饭店
41 国际邮局
42 明南火车站
43 咖啡馆

There's very little to see in the way of temples and such in Kunming. The city is however a great place to wander around on foot, once you get off the wide boulevards and away from the Kunming Hotel end of town.

Opposite the Green Lake Hotel is the Green Lake Park. Pleasantly decked out with foliage and waterways, it offers several roller-skating rinks and the possibility of art exhibitions, floral displays or special shows. Sidewalk masseurs in front of the hotel offer Y5 massages. The walking distance so far is about two km. From the park you could head east to Yuantong Temple or cross down to Daguan Jie (south-east), which has an extensive free market (from the southern end of Daguan you can pick up a bus No 4 direct to Yuantong Temple).

In both the north-west sector of Kunming (in the Green Lake vicinity) and along Daguan Jie are green-shuttered, double-storey shop fronts – a rare glimpse of that elusive traditional wooden architecture that glossy travel magazines would have us believe is all over the country. The stretch of Daguan Jie between Dongfeng Xilu and Huancheng Xilu is lined with a large range of produce coming from out-of-town farms, along with cobblers and other merchants.

Another section to perambulate is the shopping bit south of Dongfeng (east of Zhengyi), around Jinbi Lu – plenty of back alleys there too.

Keep an eye out for street performers – we're still puzzling over an artiste who stuck knives in his stomach and pulled skewers through his cheeks – he seemed quite well enough to pass around the hat as he plugged the wounds with a blood-soaked towel.

Climate

At an elevation of 1890 metres, Kunming has a mild climate, and can be visited at any time of year. Light clothes will usually be adequate. There's a fairly even spread of temperatures from April till September. Winters are short, sunny and dry. In summer (from June to August) Kunming offers cool respite, although rain is more prevalent then.

Orientation

The jurisdiction of Kunming covers 6200 sq km, including four city districts and four rural counties (which supply the city with fruit and vegetables). The centre of the city is the roundabout near that prominent landmark the Kunming Department Store. The main shopping-eating-theatre district is the sector immediately south-east of this. The older back-alley maze is north and north-west of Zhengyi Department Store. Most of the recreational features are beyond this old quarter (Cuihu Park, the zoo, Yuantong Temple). The main markets are on Daguan Jie, at the western side of the town – and this is also the direction for the best out-of-town sights.

Information

CITS The travel service (☎ 23922) has a desk on the ground floor of the Kunming Hotel (the wing that is farthest off the street) and is reasonable for information. If you're buying your railway tickets at CITS then you should take advantage of the confusion at the desk. It is shared with CTS, from whom Hong Kongers buy their tickets, so sometimes the wires get crossed and you may be able to get a Chinese-price ticket. CYTS (China Youth Travel Service) has a desk in the lobby of the older building next to the street and offers the same services.

There is also a CITS office in the Golden Dragon Hotel (☎ 33015 and ask for CITS).

Almost any type of ticket is in short supply at short notice. You should book a ticket out as soon as you arrive – allow at least four days lead time. There's easily enough in Kunming and the surrounding area to keep you busy for that long. You may find that flights to Xishuangbanna are booked out for several weeks. In that case, you have to take the bus or fill out the waiting time with a visit to Dali/Lijiang.

If your stay is shorter, arrive at the advance railway ticket office close to the Chuncheng Hotel at the crack of dawn, or try and get a ticket at the station after 6.30 pm on the night before departure.

CITS also books international plane tickets and has tour buses to destinations around Kunming. Some travellers have successfully made reservations by telex to Beijing for tickets on the Trans-Siberian.

Public Security Bureau This is at 525 Beijing Lu and is open from 8 to 11.30 am and 2 to 5.30 pm. It's a tiny office with a small plaque in English on the wall outside. The officers on duty in the Foreign Affairs branch usually speak excellent English and are quite friendly.

Money The Kunming, Green Lake, Camellia and Golden Dragon hotels each have foreign exchange counters. The highest concentration of moneychangers is in front of the Kunming Hotel. Rates are usually among the best in China.

Post There is a post office on the east side of Beijing Lu. It's midway between Tuodong Lu and Huancheng Nanlu and has a very efficient poste restante and parcel service – this is where poste restante mail ends up if not addressed to the Kunming Hotel. Every poste restante letter or parcel that comes in is listed in a ledger that's kept on the counter. To claim a letter, you must show your passport or ID. At least one of the clerks speaks English.

There is another post office to the north of this one, on Beijing Lu near the intersection with Dongfeng Donglu.

The Kunming Hotel has a cardboard box on the desk in the second building for mail addressed c/o Kunming Hotel: this has worked fine for some travellers and not at all for others – don't rely on it.

Maps There are at least five varieties of map, some with a smattering of English names, available from hotels and the Foreign Language Bookstore. The *Kunming Tourist Map* has street and hotel names in English and shows bus lines.

Medical Services The Yanan Hospital (Yanan Yiyuan) is on Jiaosanqiao Lu, about one km north-east of the Kunming Hotel – there's a foreigners' clinic (☎ 2184) on the 1st floor of the outpatients' building.

The Yunnan Comprehensive Quick Recovery Qigong Sanatorium is one of the four main qigong research bases in China. Their recent advertisement in the *China Daily* concluded:

> We give preferential treatment to model workers, heroes, scientific and technical cadres, teachers and patients seeking treatment at their own expense.

If you think you might qualify for treatment, their contact address is: Shenzhen Yunxing Kunming Touring Company (☎ 24318, cable 5150), Chuanjin Lukou, Kunming.

Tang Dynasty Pagodas

To the south of Jinbi Lu are a couple of crumbled Tang pagodas. The East Pagoda was, according to Chinese sources, destroyed by an earthquake; Western sources say it was destroyed by the Muslim revolt. It was rebuilt in the 19th century, though the temples are no longer attached. Walk west on Jinbi Lu from Beijing Lu, cross the canal, and after about five blocks turn left (south) on Shulin Jie till you come to the pagoda. The 13-tiered pagoda stands 41 metres high. The West Pagoda, a bit shorter, is inside a private compound.

Nationalities Institute

(mínzú xuéyuàn) 民族学院

Chance spottings of minority groups in town for shopping sprees add to the spice of Kunming. To the north-west of the city beyond the zoo is the Nationalities Institute where minority leaders and trainees study Marxism and science.

Kunming Provincial Museum

(kūnmíng bówùguǎn) 昆明博物馆

The museum, on Wuyi Lu, houses an exhibition on the minorities, as well as a collection of artefacts from tomb excavations at Jinning on the south side of Lake Dian. The Exhibition of Slave Culture in Ancient Yunnan on the 2nd floor is closed – lack of demand? The minority section has some interesting old photos of minorities in traditional dress – before the era of Mao caps, baggy trousers and army surplus gym shoes. It's closed Sunday.

Yuantong Temple

(yuántōng sì) 圆通寺

The Yuantong Temple, to the north-east of

the Green Lake Hotel, is the largest Buddhist complex in Kunming, and is a target for pilgrims. It is over 1000 years old, and has seen many renovations. Leading up to the main hall from the entrance is an extensive display of flowers and potted landscapes. The central courtyard holds a large square pond intersected by walkways and bridges, and has an octagonal pavilion at the centre. Art exhibitions and potted landscape miniatures are often to be seen at the temple.

Zoo

(dòngwù yuán) 动物园

Behind Yuantong Temple is the zoo, and as Chinese zoos go it's not too shabby. It's pleasantly leafy, high up, and gives a bird's-eye vista of the city. The zoo and the temple are not linked, and you have to leave the temple and go around it to get to the zoo.

Ancient Mosque

(qīngzhēn sì) 清真寺

Today, while Kunming's Buddhist shrines, desecrated during the Cultural Revolution, are humming with renovations for the tourist trade, the local Muslim population seems to have been left out of the action. The 400-year-old Ancient Mosque, a ramshackle building at the city centre next to the Kunming Department Store at 51 Zhengyi Lu, was turned into a factory during the Cultural Revolution. In 1977, the machinery was removed and the mosque reopened, but a dozen households remained living in its courtyard. Three other mosques have also been reopened, and the one on Jinbi Lu has had some restoration work done on it. To repair the Ancient Mosque would cost an estimated 350,000 yuan – which would have to be raised by the Muslims themselves. Ten million yuan has been allocated for renovation projects of a historical nature, but the mosque is certainly not on the priority list.

Yunnan's Muslim population seems to be largely forgotten, despite the Muslim Rebellion of the last century, a period when China was being torn end to end by one rebellion or another.

The one best known to the West was the Taiping Rebellion, mainly because it affected areas which were accessible to Western observers and because the Christian beliefs of the Taipings attracted Western interest. But there were several other major rebellions: the Nien Rebellion which afflicted the Hunan-Hubei-Shaanxi region from 1850 to 1868, the Muslim Rebellion in the north-west from 1862 to 1873, and the rebellion of the Miao minority in the south coinciding with the Taiping Rebellion.

In Yunnan the Muslims rose up in 1855. Their revolt was put down by the imperial armies after years of destruction; untold numbers fled or were massacred, reducing Yunnan's total population from eight million to four or even less.

The Cultural Revolution was the next major assault on the Yunnan minorities, whose rights were severely curtailed. There was a clampdown on religious activity of any nature. Kunming's Muslims came under much pressure during the Cultural Revolution to change their beliefs and fall in line with the new orders from Beijing; one story goes that a delegation of young Muslims went to Beijing to lodge a protest – they were promptly imprisoned, some for up to 10 years, and accused of being anti-revolutionary and anti-socialist. Punishments included being bound and gagged for up to two days at a time.

Once again the mosques are open, but Kunming's Muslim community is a struggling one, with little access to educational resources by which to spread their faith – or, in this case, hang onto it – though apparently they have their own underground press.

Places to Stay – bottom end

The *Three Leaves Hotel (sānyè fàndiàn)* is a short walk from Kunming main railway station and right opposite Kunming main bus station on Beijing Lu. Doubles cost Y40; a bed in a triple costs Y10. There is hot water in the evenings only – as the hot water pressure drops quickly, hotel residents leap down from floor to floor to finish their showers. Try the 2nd floor if you want to know where the hot water stays for the rest of the day. The noisy, grubby hotel is in a very handy location for transport and there is a counter in the lobby that sells bus tickets to Dali, Xishuangbanna and Shilin. The adjacent luggage check will keep your gear for a week or more – useful if you're going on a round trip to any of these places.

The *Kunhu Hotel* (☎ 27732) *(kūnhú fàndiàn)* is a bit farther up Beijing Lu from the railway station, just north of Huancheng Nanlu and the Golden Dragon Hotel (opposite side of the street). This is one of the few places in China where accommodation rates have actually decreased since the last edition of this book. A bed in one of the dorms, which are a bit packed but comfortable enough, is only Y3. Singles and doubles with shared bath are Y12 and Y14; with private bath they're Y30 and Y45. There's no English or pinyin sign on the outside of the hotel – look for a sign reading 'To the Dali bus station office' (tickets for buses to Dali are sold at reception). Conditions at the Kunhu are quite okay (there appears to be hot water throughout the day now), but some people find the halls too noisy. By midnight the noise usually dies down. The hotel is two stops from the station on bus Nos 3, 23 or 25.

The rambling *Yunnan Hotel (yúnnán fàndiàn)* on Dongfeng Xilu, near the Yunnan Provincial Museum and the Zhengyi Department Store, was Kunming's first tourist hotel. Nowadays it's mostly inhabited by mainland Chinese on private or government business. If you want to practise your Mandarin, this is the place to stay; little or no English is spoken here. Singles are Y38, doubles Y65.

Places to Stay – middle

The *Kunming Hotel* (☎ 22063) *(kūnmíng fàndiàn)* at 145 Dongfeng Donglu is split into two wings, a squat older building and a 15-storey newer high-rise, each with its own reception counter. If one wing is full, you must walk to the other to see if they have rooms – reception staff usually won't pick up the telephone and check for you.

In 1990, the refurbished old wing had the better (and more expensive) rooms, though the new wing was undergoing a floor-by-floor renovation. The wonderful 4th-floor dorms in the old wing have given way to modern doubles and the dorm floor of the new wing seems slated for the same fate. Doubles in the old wing are from Y98 to Y108, in the new wing Y75 to Y85.

The Kunming Hotel has some useful facilities: CITS/poste restante, post office, photocopying, bike hire, a good restaurant and a couple of shops. To get there from the main station, take bus No 23 to the intersection of Dongfeng Lu and Beijing Lu, and then take a bus east or walk. From the west bus station (Xizhan) take bus No 5.

A couple of blocks east of the Kunming Hotel on the same side of Dongfeng Donglu is the *Camellia Hotel* (☎ 23000) *(cháhuā bīnguǎn)*. The hotel is on the left of a square entered under a red banner. It's as good as the Kunming Hotel but a bit cheaper, and it still has a dormitory. Doubles (no singles) are Y72. Dorm beds are Y10 and the room is usually tightly packed; lack of cleanliness is sometimes a problem.

The *Green Lake Hotel* (☎ 22192) *(cuìhú bīnguǎn)* is at 16 Cuihu Nanlu. It's at the edge of an older section of Kunming and is quiet and pleasant. In the tradition of China's first 'deluxe' tourist hotels, it's now a bit worn. Double rooms are Y120; triples are Y75. Bus No 1 runs between Xizhan (the west bus station) and the centre of town via the Cuihu. From Beijing Lu, take bus No 2.

The *Xiyuan (West Garden) Hotel* (☎ 29969) *(xīyuán fàndiàn)* is a villa-style hotel. The inner section has rooms with private baths, and the outer section has rooms with a communal bathroom. The hotel is at the western edge of Lake Dian, on the shores below Taihua Temple. It seems to serve a dual purpose – group tours in the inner section, and convalescing Chinese in the outer section. The hotel is worth keeping in mind if you're doing an extended tour of Lake Dian, but also keep in mind the low frequency of transport back to Kunming. The outer section is said to have cheap rates. To get to the hotel, take bus No 33 from the Xiaoximen bus station in Kunming; it departs around 8 am, and 2 and 4 pm.

Places to Stay – top end

Kunming finally has its first joint-venture (HK-China) hotel: the *Golden Dragon Hotel* (☎ 33104) *(jīnlóng fàndiàn)* on the south-east corner of Beijing Nanlu and Huancheng Nanlu. Rates are from Y180 to Y200 for doubles (no singles), Y280 for a deluxe room or Y460 to Y1200 for a suite (plus 10% service charge). CITS, CAAC and Dragon

Air all have offices here and there is a business centre on the premises as well. The Golden Dragon caters largely to European and Asian tour groups and is often full; the reception staff is snobbish toward individual travellers and the restaurants are very poor value.

Places to Eat

Kunming has some great food, especially in the snack line. Regional specialities are herb-infused chicken in an earthenware steampot (qiguoji), Yunnan ham (xuanwei huotei), across-the-bridge noodles (guoqiao mixian), goat cheese (rubing) and various Muslim beef and mutton dishes. One of the best side dishes in the restaurants is toasted goat cheese – very tasty.

Gourmets with money to burn may perhaps be interested in a whole banquet based on Jizhong fungus (mushrooms) or 30 courses of cold mutton, not to mention fried grasshoppers or elephant nose braised in soy sauce.

The chief breakfast in Kunming, as throughout most of Yunnan, is noodles (choice of rice or wheat), usually served in a meat broth and a chilli sauce.

Local Specialities There are several eating places near the Kunming and Camellia hotels on Dongfeng Donglu that feature bilingual menus. The overrated *Cooking School* on Dongfeng Lu specialises in local fish and vegetable dishes. Across-the-bridge noodles must be ordered one day in advance, but come with lots of side dishes. The *Olympic Restaurant (àolínpīkè fàndiàn)* (east of the Cooking School and so named because of its proximity to the stadium) is a large restaurant popular with both foreigners and locals. The staff can be surly. The English menu includes steampot chicken, toasted goat cheese (marked on the menu as 'fried milk curb'), French toast ('creamy toast') and salad.

A smaller, more intimate place near the Kunming and Camellia is the *Che Che Cafe*, which is diagonally opposite the CAAC office. It's privately run and serves great Chinese and Western standards, cold beer, delicious honey-roasted walnuts and probably the best toasted goat cheese in town. Prices are very reasonable. As in many Chinese restaurants, the tablecloths never seem to get changed.

Another small, private restaurant where foreigners tend to hang out is *Liu's Cafe* (formerly Nes Cafe) at 536 Beijing Lu, a block south of Jinbi Lu. Liu's menu features several vegetarian dishes, Yunnanese coffee and very good local yoghurt. There are also a couple of travellers' notebooks lying around and an excellent pinyin/Chinese character map of Yunnan on the wall.

Several small restaurants in the vicinity of Yunnan University's main gate are highly recommended, especially the popular *Tong Da Li Restaurant*. Coming out of the Yunnan University gate, go left on the main road and then take the first left onto a small back street; Tong Da Li is the first restaurant on the right. This area is about a 15-minute walk north from the Green Lake Hotel.

Two of the better-known places for qiguoji (steampot chicken) are the *Chuncheng Hotel* (☎ 23962) and the *Dongfeng Hotel* (☎ 24808), around the corner of Wuyi Lu and Wucheng Lu, in the direction of the Cuihu Hotel. Try the 2nd floor of the Chuncheng Hotel, though service can be bad. Several small, private restaurants on Beijing Lu in the vicinity of the main bus station sell cheaper versions of steampot chicken. Steampot chicken is served in dark brown Jianshui County casserole pots, and is imbued with medicinal properties depending on the spicing – caterpillar fungus (chongcao), pseudo-ginseng (sanqi) or gastrodia.

The best Hui or Chinese Muslim food in Kunming is reportedly served at the *Yingjianglou Muslim Restaurant* (☎ 25198) *(yìngjiānglóu fàndiàn)* at 360 Changchun Jie. As with most Chinese Muslim places, the menu is heavy on mutton and beef.

Yunnan's best-known dish is across-the-bridge noodles *(guòqiáo mǐxiàn)*. You are provided with a bowl of very hot soup (stewed with chicken, duck and spare ribs) on which a thin layer of oil is floating, along

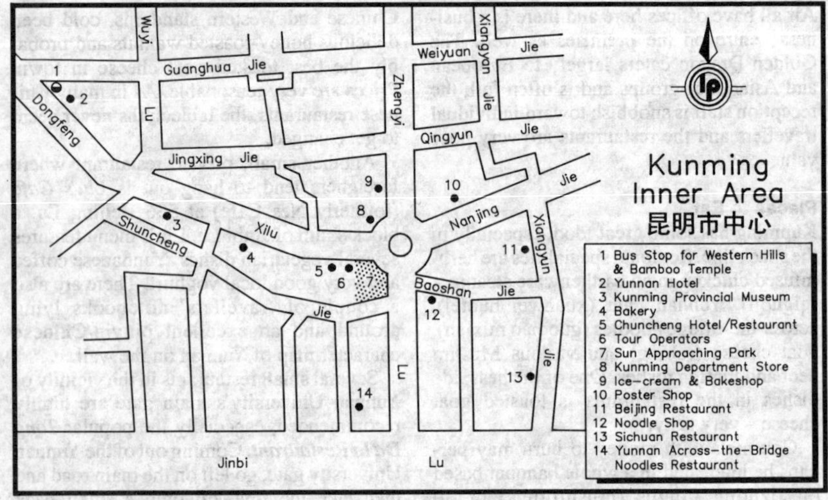

1 至西山汽车站
2 云南饭店
3 云南博物馆
4 面包店
5 春城饭店
6 旅游服务处
7 近日公园
8 昆明百货商店
9 冰淇淋店店
10 广告画商店
11 北京饭店
12 面条店
13 四川饭店
14 云南过桥米线

with a side dish of raw pork slivers (in classier places this might be chicken or fish) and vegetables, and a bowl of rice noodles. Diners place all of the ingredients quickly into the soup bowl, where they are cooked by the steamy broth.

There is a story to the dish:

Once upon a time there was a scholar at the South Lake in Mengzi (Southern Yunnan) who was attracted by the peace and quiet of an island there. He settled into a cottage on the island, in preparation for official examinations. His wife, meanwhile, had to cross a long wooden bridge over the lake to bring the bookworm his meals. The fodder was always cold in winter by the time she got to the study bower. Oversleeping one day, she made a curious discovery – she'd stewed a fat chicken and was puzzled to find the soup still hot, though it gave off no steam – the oil layer on the surface had preserved the food temperature. Subsequent experiments showed that she could cook the rest of the ingredients for her husband's meal in the hot broth after she crossed the bridge.

You can get hold of the same at other central spots for less than Y2 at two restaurants which serve only the noodles. Language is therefore no problem, and all you have to do is get your meal tickets and let the company at the table give you all the necessary instructions for etiquette.

The *Yunnan Across-the-Bridge Noodles Restaurant (guòqiáo mǐxiànguǎn)* on Nantong Jie serves huge bowls at rock-bottom prices. Decor is, shall we say, basic – the predominant noise is a chorus of hissing and slurping; tattered beggars circulate among the stainless-steel-topped tables, pursued by management. Never mind the beggars or the decor – the food is absolutely delicious! Atmosphere, as can be imagined, is very different from the tourist hotels, where this fare will cost you exponentially more.

Asecond across-the-bridge noodles establishment is as cheap as the Yunnan but has less space to play around in (try the 2nd floor) – it's at 99 Baoshan Jie.

Continental Breakfast Filtered through the cultures of France, Vietnam and Yunnan is a wonderful mating of French bread and Yunnanese coffee. Seek out the wooden stools of the *Nanlaisheng Coffee & Bread Shop* at No 299 Jinbi Lu where you pay Y1.50 for a tall porcelain cup of *real*, heart-starting coffee. Three types of bread, including French rolls made of unbleached flour, are sold at the front. Coffee tickets and bread are sold at the front of the shop; take your coffee ticket into the kitchen at the back to pick up the black, freshly brewed coffee (milk costs extra, sugar is free). If the first floor tables are all taken, proceed to the 2nd floor where there are usually free stools and tables, plus a window that overlooks the street.

Other Chinese On Jinbi Lu the *Gangshengyuan Guangwei Restaurant* (☎ 22970) *(guànshēng yuán)* has Cantonese-style food including dim sum, fried chicken, sweet & sour pork, and fried beef curry. The restaurant has a special section for foreigners. For northern Chinese and Sichuan-style cuisine, try the *Worker-Peasant-Soldier Restaurant* (☎ 25679) *(gōngnóngbīng fàndiàn)* at 262 Huguo Lu.

There is a string of eateries on Xiangyun Jie between Jinbi Lu and Dongfeng Donglu. At the Dongfeng end at No 77 is the *Beijing Restaurant* (☎ 3214) *(běijīng fàndiàn)* with northern-style seafood, chicken and duck. The service can be annoying here and the restaurant has foreigner cubicles – stand up for your right to eat alongside your Chinese brothers and sisters. At the Jinbi end of Xiangyun Jie is the *Chuanwei Restaurant* (☎ 23171) *(chuānwèi fàndiàn)*, which serves Sichuan-style chicken, spicy bean curd, hot pork, duck and seafood. In between are lots of street vendors and small private restaurants.

Pick of the pleb restaurants is the *Shanghai* (☎ 22987) *(shànghǎi fàndiàn)* at 73 Dongfeng Xilu, in a yellow-fronted building. To the left side you'll get cheap noodles, to the right are steampot chicken, cold cuts and dumplings.

Snack Tracking There are some good bakeries in Kunming – flatbreads, shortbreads and highly edible cakes make a change from those biscuits sold on store shelves. For on-the-premises baking go to the *Hsing He Yuan*, near the Provincial Museum on Dongfeng Xilu. Just north of the Kunming Department Store on Zhengyi Lu is a bakery and ice-cream parlour. There are also several small bakeries along Beijing Lu in the vicinity of the Kunhu Hotel.

On the narrow street just north of the Kunhu Hotel are a couple of sidewalk noodle restaurants with very reasonable prices. On either side of the hotel are several fairly clean, cheap places selling noodles, baozi (steamed meat buns), youtiao (fried bread sticks) and doujiang (soy milk).

Another place to go snack-hunting is Huguo Lu, north of Nantaiqiao, for simmering noodle bars and a teashop. The intersection of Changchun and Huguo yields lots of small eateries. Along the canal near the Arts & Crafts Shop is a pleasant riverside cafe with beach umbrellas – for a split second it looks like you got lost and ended up in the wrong country. Also try Baoshan Jie, an east-west street running between Zhengyi Lu and Huguo Lu – Baoshan is known as No 1 Food Street because of the retail shops, but it also has noodle bars and eateries.

The whole area around here is a hub of restaurant activity. The stretch of Daguan Jie from Dongfeng to Huancheng is a busy free market, and in season you'll get fruit – mangoes, pineapples, 'ox-belly' fruit from Xishuangbanna, and pears from the Chenggong orchards or from Dali.

Hotel Food The *Kunming Hotel* has a restaurant on the ground floor of the new wing which has good food, reasonable prices and fairly friendly and efficient service (occasionally the harried servers forget to bring a dish). The menu includes Yunnan specialities and Western breakfasts as well as Chinese standards.

The *Camellia Hotel* has a similar restaurant set-up, also quite good. The bar-lounge area makes a pleasant meeting spot.

At the *Green Lake Hotel* there is a bar and cafe on the 3rd floor, a Western restaurant on the 5th floor and a Chinese restaurant on the 2nd floor. The food in these has a good reputation.

Both the *Kunhu* and *Three Leaves* hotels have large, cheap and noisy cafeteria-style restaurants – nothing special unless you like large, cheap and noisy.

Avoid the *Golden Dragon Hotel* coffee shop at all costs – the food is terrible and prices are astronomical.

Nightlife & Entertainment

The Municipal Worker's Cultural Palace *(shì gōngrén wénhuàgōng)* is the gigantic steel-and-concrete building towering to the west of the Kunming Hotel. Very popular with local photographers as a 'modern' backdrop, the rabbit warren of entertainment and hobbies on at least 14 floors is worth ascending. Keep climbing the floors, each of which offers something different: a gallery with sheepish portraits of valiant workers; video and computer games which cost a few jiao; English-language lessons (skip that floor quick); hair-cutting class; body-building class (very trendy for young Chinese, male and female); stuffed Yunnan fauna; table tennis. There's an open-air teahouse on the roof of a side-building.

You might be able to chase up minority dancing displays (more often held for the benefit of group tours), travelling troupes or Yunnan Opera (Hongxing Theatre on Dongfeng Xilu is one of the performing arts venues).

The teahouse to the right-hand side of the canal (off Taoyuan Jie), north of Changchun Lu, has plain-clothes Yunnan Opera in an old temple structure with fluorescent tubes. It is, however, extremely difficult to recognise from the front – there's a side entrance. Teahouses come and go; if this one has disappeared by the time you get there, ask around for the latest spots.

Things to Buy

You have to do a fair bit of digging to come up with inspiring purchases in Kunming. Yunnan specialities are jade (related to Burmese), marble (from the Dali area), batik, minority embroidery (also musical instruments and dress accessories) and spotted brass utensils.

Other crafts to consider are some of the basic utilitarian items that are part of everyday Yunnanese life, eg the large bamboo waterpipes for smoking angel-haired Yunnan tobacco, local herbal medicines (Yunnan-made *baiyao* is a blend of over 100 herbs and is highly prized by Chinese throughout the world) and the *qiguo* or ceramic steampot.

Yunnanese tea is also an excellent buy and comes in several varieties, from bowl-shaped bricks of smoked green tea called *tuocha* (which haven't changed form since Marco Polo's time) to leafy black tea that rivals some of India's best.

One of the main shopping drags is Zhengyi Lu, which has the Zhengyi Department Store *(zhèngyì bǎihuò shāngdiàn)*, Overseas Chinese Department Store and the Kunming Department Store, but these mainly sell consumer goods. The Friendship Store is on the 3rd floor of the Kunming Department Store. Other shopping areas are Jinbi Lu by the Zhengyi Lu intersection (lots of small speciality shops), and Dongfeng Donglu, between Zhengyi Lu and Huguo Lu.

The Kunming Arts & Crafts Shop *(gōngyì měishù fúwùbù)*, on Qingnian Lu, has some batik, pottery, porcelain and handicrafts, but it's pretty dull. Better to look among the privately run shops on Beijing Lu and Dongfeng Donglu. Outside the Kunming Hotel you will probably be ambushed by minority 'bag' ladies flogging their handiwork –

bargain if you want a sane price. Both the Green Lake and Kunming hotels sell batik which you can also find in Dali. Delve into the smaller shops around Jinbi Lu if you're into embroidery. For Yunnan herbal medicines, check the large pharmacy on Zhengyi Lu (on the east side, several blocks up from the Kunming Department Store).

Kunming is a fairly good place to stock up on film. Fuji and other film can be bought at the larger tourist hotels, and the Kunming Hotel's stock includes Ektachrome.

Getting There & Away

Air CAAC (☎ 24270) is at 146 Dongfeng Donglu, next door to the Kunming Hotel. The local CITS and CAAC apparently don't get along too well, so it's usually easier to book your own air tickets directly from CAAC. The 'international' window is for flights to Hong Kong and Bangkok only.

CAAC also has an office in the Golden Dragon Hotel at the corner of Huancheng Nanlu and Beijing Lu. Dragon Air has an office in the hotel as well.

Kunming's most useful air connections are those to Beijing (Y760), Canton (Y391), Changsha (Y375), Chengdu (Y238), Chongqing (Y218), Guilin (Y288), Guiyang (Y150), Nanning (Y685), Shanghai (Y653), Jinghong (Y144) and Xi'an (Y393).

There are also international flights to Hong Kong (Y595, four times a week), to Bangkok (Y762, twice weekly) and to Rangoon (Y810, weekly). CITS was vague about details for the flights to Myanmar (Burma), and gave a sort of 'the plane flies when it's full' comment. Don't put too much faith in punctuality for this destination.

Plane reservations out of Kunming should be made at least a week in advance. During April (Water-Splashing Festival) and summer, the air connection for Xishuangbanna (Jinghong) can be booked rock solid for two to three weeks. The CAAC office is jammed with maniacs pushing, shoving and trying to pull rank. Make your plans for Xishuangbanna as flexible as possible: consider the bus option or book your flight several weeks ahead and spend the intervening time in Dali or elsewhere.

Bus The two most useful bus stations are the main bus station (Kunming Chezhan) close to the main railway station and the west bus station (Xizhan).

For Dali there are minibuses and buses (mostly soft-seat) travelling by day or night. The journey takes a minimum of 10 hours, sometimes 14. Tickets cost Y24 for the Polish 'Autosan' buses or Y37 for the more comfortable Hungarian 'Ikarus' buses. The cheaper bus may stop just short of Dali in Xiaguan, from where it's a 30-minute, Y1 hop to Dali on one of the frequent local buses. The more expensive Ikarus bus has more legroom and includes a meal stop. Dali buses from the main bus station on Beijing Lu leave at 6.30 pm. Buses are also available from the Kunhu Hotel but the night bus from the main station is more reliable.

There are direct buses to Lijiang from the main bus station and the west bus station. They take two days, usually overnight in Xiaguan and cost Y24 on a Chinese bus, Y37 on a Polish bus. The big Ikarus buses don't ply the Kunming-Lijiang route, so if it's maximum comfort you want, take an Ikarus to Dali and get a connecting minibus (Y12) on to Lijiang.

Some people have travelled for four or five days on different buses between Kunming and Guiyang (Guizhou Province), via Qujing and Zhenning (Huangguoshu Falls).

For details on Shilin (Stone Forest), see the Getting There & Away section under Shilin.

Train There are only two rail approaches to Kunming, via Guiyang or Chengdu (a new line is under construction from Nanning to Kunming).

During peak season Kunming can become a real trap for railway travellers. Make a point of booking your tickets at least four days in advance. The advance booking office close to the Chuncheng Hotel is only worth a try if you queue there at 6.30 am. The ticket office in the main station sells tickets from

6.30 pm for trains departing the next day, but these are probably rare returns. CITS and the railway ticket offices often muddle their prices, so it's worth enquiring about soft-sleepers for which you might be given a Chinese price. Black-market train tickets are sometimes available.

If you are heading for Guilin, it's sometimes possible to escape the railway congestion by flying to Nanning and then taking a train to Guilin, although for a little more money you can fly direct to Guilin.

There are direct trains from Kunming to Shanghai, via Guiyang, Guilin, Zhuzhou, Nanchang and Hangzhou. There are also direct trains from Kunming to Beijing. For Chongqing you must change at Guiyang, and for Canton you must change at Hengyang. For hard-sleeper train travel from Kunming to Guiyang it is 15 hours, Y44; to Anshun, 13 hours, Y42; to Emei, 21 hours, Y60; Chengdu, 25 hours, Y77 (tourist prices).

Getting Around

Most of the major sights are within a 15-km radius of Kunming. Local transport to these places is awkward, crowded and time-consuming; it tends to be an out-and-back job, with few crossovers for combined touring. If you wish to take in everything, you'd be looking at something like five return trips, which would consume about three days. You can simplify this by pushing Black Dragon Pool, Anning Hot Springs and the Golden Temple to the background, and concentrating on the trips of high interest – the Bamboo Temple and Western Hills, both of which have decent transport connections with special express buses in the mornings. Lake Dian presents some engrossing circular-tour possibilities on its own. Better yet, buy a map, hire a good bicycle and tour the area by bike.

Bus The relevant bus stations in Kunming for catching buses to various sites around the city and around the lake are:

Chuanxingulou This is on the north end of Beijing Lu. Take bus No 9 to the Black Dragon Pool (Heilongtan); bus No 10 to the Golden Temple (Jindian).

Xiaoximen This is on Renmin Lu, just west of Dongfeng Lu. Take bus No 6 to the Gaoyao station at the foot of the Western Hills, where you can connect with another bus which travels up the mountain. Bus No 19 goes to Fumin via the Bamboo Temple. Bus No 18 goes to Anning Hot Springs. The following buses run to spots around Lake Dian: bus No 33 to Baiyukou (western side of Lake Dian); bus No 13 to Chenggong and Jincheng (eastern side); bus No 14 to Jinning (southern side).

Xizhan The west bus station is near the Yunnan Hotel. A direct bus runs from here to the Bamboo Temple.

Nantaiqiao This bus station, previously west of the Kunming Hotel, appears to have ceased functioning. The Xiaoximen station now handles the relevant bus services.

Zhuantang This station appears to have been phased out for buses, including bus No 24 to Haigeng Beach. Kunming main bus station is now the terminal for bus No 24.

Express buses are the best option; they cost only a fraction more than local transport and will save considerable mucking around.

There are two routes to the Bamboo Temple and to the Western Hills. The starting point is the south end of Beijing Lu, where there are specially posted bus stops near Dianchi Cinema (the tour company that operates the buses has an office across the street from the bus stop). No advance booking is necessary. The buses make a few stops along the route – the first one is to the left of the Yunnan Hotel in the city centre, where there are two more special bus stops; the bus will wait here till it fills up before proceeding, so there is little point in trying to board the bus any further down the line than this hotel. Returning buses may not go back to the Dianchi Cinema; they could stop at the Yunnan Hotel, turn around with a fresh load of passengers and head back out again.

Three buses a day depart from the Dianchi Cinema via the Yunnan Hotel to the Bamboo Temple between 8 and 9 am. More buses leave from the Yunnan Hotel only at 11 am, noon, and 1 and 2 pm. Return buses usually

Top: Shepherds and flock approaching Sunday market, Kashgar (RS)
Bottom Left: Uyghur crowds, Kashgar (RS)
Bottom Right: Mosque at Ürümqi (AS)

Top: Genghis Khan's mausoleum, Dongsheng (RS)
Bottom Left: Kebab arcade, Ürümqi (RS)
Bottom Right: Disturbed camel (RS)

go to the Yunnan Hotel only, leaving the Bamboo Temple from 10.30 am to 3 pm at hourly or half-hourly intervals.

Buses from the Dianchi Cinema, via the Yunnan Hotel, to the Dragon Gate (with stops at the temples on the mountainside along the way if you want to get off before the top) depart between 7.30 and 8.30 am (with possible extra departures at 9 and 9.30 am, probably from the Yunnan Hotel). The bus leaves the Dragon Gate from 2 to 4 pm at hourly or half-hourly intervals.

Bicycle Bikes are a fast way to get around town. The Kunming Hotel offers a rip-off rental rate of Y10 per day. The bike hire at Liu's Cafe on Beijing Lu charges Y0.50 per hour or Y5 per day.

Tours Several outfits cover the ground faster than the express buses, but certainly not cheaper. They include downright boring sights like the Black Dragon Pool, and downtown sights like Yuantong Temple (which is not difficult to get to).

The Kunming Bus Service Company at Sun-Approaching Tower (booths opposite main Department Store) caters mainly for locals and Overseas Chinese, and they speak little if any English. They organise a Golden Temple, Black Dragon Pool, Bamboo Temple, Daguan Park tour, Monday, Wednesday or Friday, departing at 8.30 am and returning at 5 pm. The cost is Y7 per person. They also do a Western Hills-Anning Hot Springs tour (stops at Huating and Taihua temples and Dragon Gate), leaving Tuesday, Thursday or Saturday. The cost is Y15.50 per person.

The Yunnan Tourist Bus Company with departures and bookings from the Kunming Hotel offers a Western Hills, Bamboo Temple, Daguan Park, Yuantong Temple tour. The Kunming Hotel also has taxi-trips to the Stone Forest – enquire at the counter on the ground floor.

The Xiyuan Hotel, at the western shores of Lake Dian, has tour boats which you can most likely crash. Some tours such as buses to the Stone Forest are operated from the Kunhu Hotel, (you should at least be able to get tickets for the buses there).

AROUND KUNMING

Golden Temple

(jīndiàn) 金殿

This Taoist temple is perched amid a pine forest on Phoenix Song Mountain, 11 km north-east of Kunming. The original model was carted off to Dali; the present one dates from the Ming Dynasty and was enlarged by General Wu Sangui, who was dispatched by the Manchus in 1659 to quell the uprisings in the region. Wu Sangui turned against the Manchus and set himself up as a rebel warlord, with the Golden Temple as his summer residence.

The pillars, ornate door frames, walls, fittings and roof tiles of the 6.5-metre temple are all made of copper; the entire structure, laid on a white Dali marble foundation, is estimated to weigh more than 300 tonnes. In the courtyard are ancient camellia trees. At the back is a 14-tonne bronze bell, cast in 1423. The gardens around the temple offer secluded areas for picnicking. In the compound are teahouses and a miantiao (noodle) stand.

To get there take bus Nos 3, 23 or 23 to the northern railway station, and then take bus No 10 to the temple. There are also slightly more expensive minibuses from the station direct to the temple. Many travellers ride hired bikes to the temple – it's fairly level going all the way to the base of the hill. Unless you come by minibus, you'll have to climb an easy hill path to the temple compound.

Black Dragon Pool

(hēilóng tǎn) 黑龙潭

Eleven km north of Kunming is this uninspiring garden, with old cypresses, dull Taoist pavilions and no bubble in the springs. The view of the surrounding mountains from the garden is however inspiring. Within walking distance is the **Kunming Botanical Institute**, where the collection of flora is of interest to specialists.

From the Chuanxingulou bus terminal take bus No 9. The Golden Temple and the Black Dragon Pool require separate trips from Chuanxingulou bus terminal.

Bamboo Temple

(qióngzhú sì) 筇竹寺

Twelve km north-west of Kunming, this temple dates back to the Tang Dynasty. Burned down and rebuilt in the 15th century, it was restored from 1883 to 1890 when the abbot employed the master Sichuan sculptor Li Guangxiu and his apprentices to fashion 500 *luohan* (arhats or 'noble ones'). These life-size clay figures are stunning – either very realistic or very surrealistic – a sculptural tour de force.

Down one huge wall come the incredible surfing buddhas, some 70-odd, riding the waves on a variety of mounts – blue dogs, giant crabs, shrimp, turtles, unicorns. One gentleman has metre-long eyebrows; another has an arm that shoots clear across the hall to the ceiling.

In the main section are housed row upon row of standing figures. The statues have been done with the precision of a split-second photograph – a monk about to chomp into a large peach (the face contorted into almost a scream), a figure caught turning around to emphasise a discussion point, another about to clap two cymbals together or cursing a pet monster. The old, the sick, the emaciated – nothing is spared; the expressions of joy, anger, grief or boredom are extremely vivid.

So accurate are the sculptures that they can be read as an anthropological documentation of the times. The sculptor's work was considered in bad taste by his contemporaries (some of whom no doubt appeared in caricature), and upon the project's completion Li Guangxiu disappeared into thin air. The temple actually had no bamboo on the grounds until the present, when bamboo was transplanted from Chengdu. The main halls were restored in 1958 and again, extensively, in 1981.

By far the easiest way to get there is to take an express bus (Y3, departing every 40 minutes) from the Yunnan Hotel directly to the temple. To get there from the Kunming Hotel, take bus No 5 to Xizhan (the west bus station), where there's a direct public bus to the temple.

Anning Hot Springs

(ānníng wēnquán) 安宁温泉

Forty km south-west of Kunming, this is basically a hotel where the mineral waters are piped into baths. Large, private bathrooms are Y5 per person, or Y3 per person if you're sharing – but no mixed couples allowed! The springs themselves are hidden from view. Anning is a bore; it's a sanatorium for privileged Chinese vacationers and there's also a military hospital here.

One km south of the springs is Caoxi Temple, a wooden structure from the Song Dynasty, and within the region are muddy Miao villages, but they're not overly interesting. If you miss the last bus back to Kunming you might be able to coerce the hotel staff into letting you stay (Y8 double, or Y4 per person in a four-bed dorm).

Several buses run to Anning from Xiaoximen bus terminal. The best one to take is bus No 18, which leaves Kunming at 8 and 11.30 am, 2 and 2.30 pm. It leaves Anning for Kunming at 10.30 am and 2 and 4.30 pm. Other possible buses (involving a bit of hiking in) are bus Nos 35, 16, 17 – also departing from Xiaoximen.

Lake Dian

(diān chí) 滇池

Lake Dian, to the south of Kunming, is dotted with settlements, farms and fishing enterprises around the shores; the western side is hilly, while the eastern side is flat country. The southern end of the lake, particularly the south-east, is industrial, but other than that there are lots of possibilities for extended touring and village-crashing. The lake is an elongated one, about 150 km in circumference, about 40 km from north to

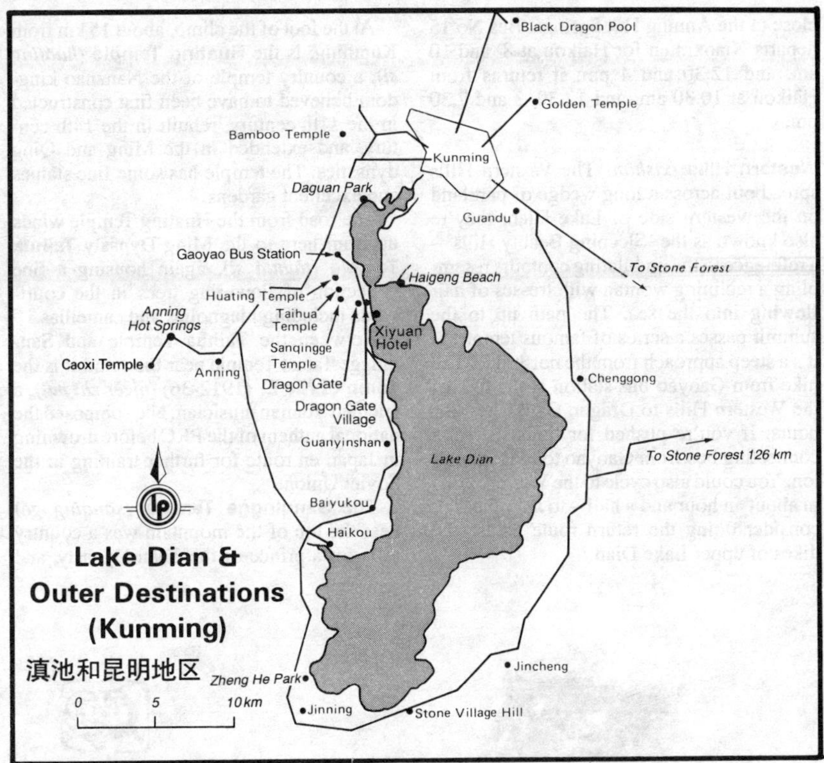

south, and covering 300 sq km. Plying the waters are *fanchuan*, pirate-sized junks with bamboo-battened canvas sails. It's mainly an area for scenic touring and hiking, and there are some fabulous aerial views from the ridges up at Dragon Gate in the Western Hills.

Daguan (Grand View) Park *(dàguān gōngyuán)*. This park, at the northernmost tip of Lake Dian and three km south-west of the city centre, was redesigned by the governor of Yunnan in 1866. It covers 60 hectares and includes a nursery with potted plants, children's playground, rowing boats and pavilions. The Daguan Tower *(dàguān lóu)* is a vantage point for Lake Dian. Its facades are inscribed with a long poem by Qing poet Sun Ranweng. Bus No 4 runs to Daguan Park from Yuantong Temple via the city centre area.

At the north-east end of the park is a boat dock where an 8 am departure takes you from Daguan to Haikou on Lake Dian, passing by Dragon Gate Village. The boat departs Haikou for Daguan at 2 pm and the one-way trip takes four hours. One-hour boat trips on the lake are possible from Daguan Park. Pay the Y1 aboard.

From Haikou you can pick up a bus No 15 which runs back to the Xiaoximen terminal in Kunming. On the way back the bus comes close to the Anning Hot Springs. Bus No 15 departs Xiaoximen for Haikou at 8 and 10 am, and 12.30 and 4 pm; it returns from Haikou at 10.30 am, and 12.30, 3 and 7.30 pm.

Western Hills *(xīshān)* The Western Hills spread out across a long wedge of parkland on the western side of Lake Dian; they're also known as the 'Sleeping Beauty Hills' – a reference to the undulating contours resembling a reclining woman with tresses of hair flowing into the sea. The path up to the summit passes a series of famous temples – it's a steep approach from the north side. The hike from Gaoyao bus station at the foot of the Western Hills to Dragon Gate takes 2½ hours. If you're pushed for time, there's a connecting bus from Gaoyao to the top section. You could also cycle to the Western Hills in about an hour and a half – to vary the trip, consider doing the return route across the dikes of upper Lake Dian.

At the foot of the climb, about 15 km from Kunming, is the **Huating Temple** *(huátíng sì)*, a country temple of the Nanzhao kingdom believed to have been first constructed in the 11th century, rebuilt in the 14th century, and extended in the Ming and Qing dynasties. The temple has some fine statues and excellent gardens.

The road from the Huating Temple winds up from here to the Ming Dynasty **Taihua Temple** *(tàihuá sì)*, again housing a fine collection of flowering trees in the courtyards including magnolias and camellias.

Between the Taihua Temple and Sanqingge Taoist Temple near the summit is the **Tomb of Nie Er** (1912-36) *(nièěr zhī mù)*, a talented Yunnan musician. Nie composed the national anthem of the PRC before drowning in Japan en route for further training in the Soviet Union.

The **Sanqingge Temple** *(sānqīng gé)* near the top of the mountain was a country villa for a prince of the Yuan Dynasty, and

was later turned into a temple dedicated to the three main Taoist deities.

Further up is **Dragon Gate** *(lóngmén)*, a group of grottoes, sculptures, corridors and pavilions hacked from the cliff between 1781 and 1835 by a Taoist monk and co-workers, who must have been hanging up there by their fingertips. That's what the locals do when they visit – seek the most precarious perches for views of Lake Dian. The tunnelling along the outer cliff edge is so narrow that only one or two people can squeeze by at a time, so avoid public holidays! One of the last grottoes is dedicated to the deity who assisted those preparing for imperial exams – there is graffiti on the walls from grateful graduates, but nowadays the Chinese use it as a urinal.

From Kunming to the Western Hills the most convenient connection is the express bus which runs direct to the Sanqingge temple at the top, though you could get off at, say, the Taihua Temple and do the rest on foot.

Alternatively, there's a regular bus combination: take bus No 5 from the Kunming Hotel to Xiaoximen bus station, and then change to bus No 6, which will take you to the Gaoyao bus station at the foot of the hills.

From the Western Hills to Kunming you can either take the bus or scramble down from the Dragon Gate area directly to the lakeside along a zigzag dirt path and steps that lead to Dragon Gate Village. A narrow spit of land leads from here across the lake. At the western side of the 'spit' is a nice fish restaurant with simple food, wooden hut, fish from the lake – just go into the kitchen to organise some tasty food. Continuing across the land spit, you arrive at a narrow stretch of water which is negotiated by a tiny ferry. It's worthwhile hanging around here to see what passes by as this is the bottleneck of the lake, and junks, fishing vessels and other craft must come through.

Having made the short ferry crossing, you proceed by foot through a village area to Haigeng Beach, where you can pick up bus No 24 for the run back to Kunming main bus station (Kunming Zhan).

The tour can easily be done in reverse; start with bus No 24 to Haigeng Beach, walk to Dragon Gate Village, climb straight up to Dragon Gate, then make your way down through the temples to the Gaoyao bus station, where you can get bus No 6 back to the Xiaoximen station. Alternatively, bus No 33 runs along the coast through Dragon Gate Village, or you can take the early-morning boat from Daguan Park.

In 1986, I met an American in Xishuangbanna who told me he'd been doing a little bushwalking around the Western Hills when he was suddenly confronted by a 'large puma'. The American froze and the 'puma' blended swiftly into the undergrowth. At the time, I assumed this was an exaggerated story since no puma in its right mind would leave the virgin forest for a lungful of Kunming's polluted air. However, I believed the story when, a couple of months later, I came across an article on the subject in the *China Daily*. The tiger killed a couple of farmers in Kunming itself before being shot by police.

2 killed, 3 injured by tiger in Kunming

A tiger killed two people and injured three others on Wednesday morning in the city of Kunming, Yunnan Province, then was shot to death by police after it roamed the city for more than six hours, the Shanghai Evening News reported yesterday.

The tiger was first spotted, about 6:30 in the morning by Li Deming, a worker at the Yunnan Tyre Repair Factory, who was doing morning exercises.

He was knocked to the ground by the tiger, which sprang from behind tall grass.

After a fierce scuffle with the tiger, Li got free. Li's face and both shoulders were badly cut by the animal's paws. He was able to get to his factory, where he reported the attack. Police immediately started a search of the city.

But it wasn't until well after noon that the tiger was reported attacking another victim. It bit to death a farmer cutting grass in the fields and another farmer transporting manure to the field, the paper reported. The tiger also injured two people walking on the streets.

According to the paper, the tiger jumped onto a highway and ran toward a crowd of people as police rushed to the scene. They surrounded the tiger, in an attempt to catch it alive, but were forced to open fire as the tiger pounced toward them.

According to the paper, the tiger did not come from any of the city's zoos or animal research institutes. Investigation is under way to find out where the animal came from.

China Daily, 6 December 1986

Baiyukou On the south-western side of Lake Dian, this is a sanatorium and scenic spot. Bus No 33 from the Xiaoximen station runs via Dragon Gate Village to the sanatorium, departing Xiaoximen at around 8 am and 2 and 4 pm, and returning at 10 am, and 4 and 7.30 pm.

Zheng He Park *(zhènghé gōngyuán)* At the south-east corner of the lake, this commemorates the Ming Dynasty navigator Zheng He (known as Admiral Cheng Ho throughout most of the world). A mausoleum here holds tablets describing his life and works. Zheng He, a Muslim, made seven voyages to over 30 Asian and African countries in the 15th century in command of a huge imperial fleet (for details, see the section on the town of Quanzhou in Fujian Province).

Bus No 21 from the Xiaoximen station terminates at the Phosphate Fertiliser Factory near Gucheng at the south-west side of the lake, and north-west of Zheng He Park. From here it may be possible to hike along the hills to the bus No 15 terminal at Haikou; bus No 15 will take you back to Xiaoximen.

Jinning County This is the site of archaeological discoveries from early Kunming, and you'll find it at the southern end of the lake. Bronze vessels, a gold seal and other artefacts were unearthed at Stone Village Hill, and some items are displayed at the Provincial Museum in Kunming. Bus No 14 runs to Jinning from Xiaoximen station, via Chenggong and Jincheng.

Chenggong County This is an orchard region on the eastern side of the lake. Climate has a lot to do with Kunming's reputation as the florist of China. Flowers bloom all year round, with the 'flower tide' in January, February and March – which is the best time to visit. Camellias, azaleas, magnolias and orchids are not usually associated with China by Westerners although many of the Western varieties derive from south-west China varieties. They were introduced to the West by adventuring botanists who carted off samples in the 19th and 20th centuries. Azaleas are native to China – of the 800 varieties in the world, 650 are found in Yunnan. During the Spring Festival (February/March) a profusion of blooming species can be found at temple sites around Kunming – notably Taihua, Huating and Golden temples, as well as Black Dragon Pool and Yuantong Hill.

Bus No 13 from Kunming's Xiaoximen station runs to Chenggong via Jincheng; departures from Xiaoximen are at 7.30 and 8 am, and 2, 2.30, 4.30 and 5 pm. The bus departs Chenggong for Xiaoximen at 9.30 and 10 am, and 4 and 4.30 pm.

Haigeng Beach *(hǎigěng)* This is on the north-eastern side of the lake. It has adequate swimming frontage and a mini-resort area (roller-skating, restaurants, snacks, and you can hire airbeds for swimming). Take bus No 24 from Kunming main bus station on Beijing Lu. Haigeng Beach is a useful approach to the Western Hills from the eastern side of the lake.

STONE FOREST
(shílín) 石林

The Stone Forest is a massive collection of grey limestone pillars, split by rain water and eroded to their present fanciful forms, the tallest standing 30 metres high. Marine fossils found in the area suggest that it was once under the sea. Legend has it that the immortals smashed a mountain into a labyrinth for lovers seeking some privacy – and picnicking Chinese couples take heed of this myth (it can get busy in there!).

The maze of grey pinnacles and peaks, with the odd pool, is treated as an oversized rockery, with a walkway here, a pavilion there, some railings along paths and, if you look more closely, some mind-bending weeds. The larger formations have titles like Baby Elephant, Everlasting Fungus, Baby Buffalo, Moon-Gazing Rhino, Sword Pond. The maze is cooler and quieter by moonlight, and would enthral a surrealist painter.

There are actually several stone forests in the region – the section open to foreign tourists covers 80 hectares. Twelve km to the north-east is a larger (300-hectare) rock series called Fungi Forest (Lingzhi), with karst caves and a large waterfall.

The Stone Forest is basically a Chinese tour attraction and some Westerners find it grossly overrated on the scale of geographical wonders. The important thing, if you venture there, is to get away from the main tourist area – within a couple of km of the centre are some idyllic, secluded walks.

The villages in the Lunan County vicinity are inhabited by the Sani branch of the Yi tribespeople. Considering that so many other 'ethnic' areas of Yunnan are now open, you could be disappointed if you make the trip just to see the Sani branch of the Yi tribespeople who live in this area. Their craftwork (embroidery, purses, footwear) is sold at stalls by the entrance to the forest, and Sani women act as tour guides for groups. Off to the side is Five-Tree Village, which is an easy walk and has the flavour of a Mexican pueblo, but the tribespeople have been somewhat influenced by commercialism. For those keen on genuine village and farming life, well, the Stone Forest is a big place – and you can easily get lost. Just take your butterfly net and a lunch box along and keep walking – you'll get somewhere eventually.

There is a Y3.50 entry fee for foreigners, Y2.50 for Chinese, into the main Stone Forest. Getting into other sections costs Y2.

Activities

The Shilin and Yunlin hotels put on Sani song-and-dance evenings – usually when there are enough tourists around. Surprisingly, these events turn into good-natured exchanges between Homo Ektachromo and Sani Dollari, and neither comes off the worse for wear. The short performances display ethnic costumery and musical instruments. Years ago the hotels charged a small fee for the performances; recently they've been admitting tourists for free (once tourism picks up again the fees will probably be reinstated). The performances start around 8.30 pm. The Torch Festival (wrestling, bullfighting, singing and dancing) takes place on 24 June at a natural outdoor amphitheatre by Hidden Lake.

Places to Stay

The *Shilin Hotel (shílín bīnguǎn)*, near the main entrance to the Stone Forest, is a villa-type place with souvenir shop and dining hall. A double room costs Y100, a single Y60. Similar in size and room rates is the *Yunlin Hotel (yúnlín fàndiàn)*, which is off the road that forks to the right in front of the entrance. In addition to Y60 singles and Y100 doubles, the Yunlin has concrete cells with soft beds for Y10 per person. These cheaper rooms have an attached washing area where you can bathe using a metal basin; toilets are down the hall. Both the Yunlin and Shilin hotels cater mostly to Overseas Chinese tour groups.

Near the bus terminal are several smaller hotels with basic rooms for Y10 per person – similar bathing facilities to the Y10 rooms at the Yunlin but not as clean.

Places to Eat

Several restaurants next to the bus terminal specialise in duck roasted in extremely hot clay ovens with pine needles. A whole duck costs Y15 and takes about 20 minutes to cook – have the restaurant staff put a beer in their freezer and it'll be just right when the duck comes out. The ducks are massaged with a local sesame oil mixture before roasting.

Near the main Stone Forest entrance is a cluster of food vendors that purvey a variety of pastries and noodles from dawn to dusk. The *Shilin Hotel* and *Yunlin Hotel* offer fixed price meals that aren't bad. The Y15 dinner at the Yunlin Hotel includes 12 different dishes, rice, tea and beer – quite a bargain. Western breakfasts are available at either hotel for around Y6.

Getting There & Away

There is a variety of options for getting to the Stone Forest. In all cases the trip takes around 3½ hours one way. If you know exactly how long you intend to stay, book return transport in advance in Kunming. It's best to take an overnight stop in the Forest for further exploration – though if you're just looking at the Forest itself then a day trip will do.

Bus Departures are same-day return, next-day return, or one-way tickets.

The regular long-distance bus costs Y5.50

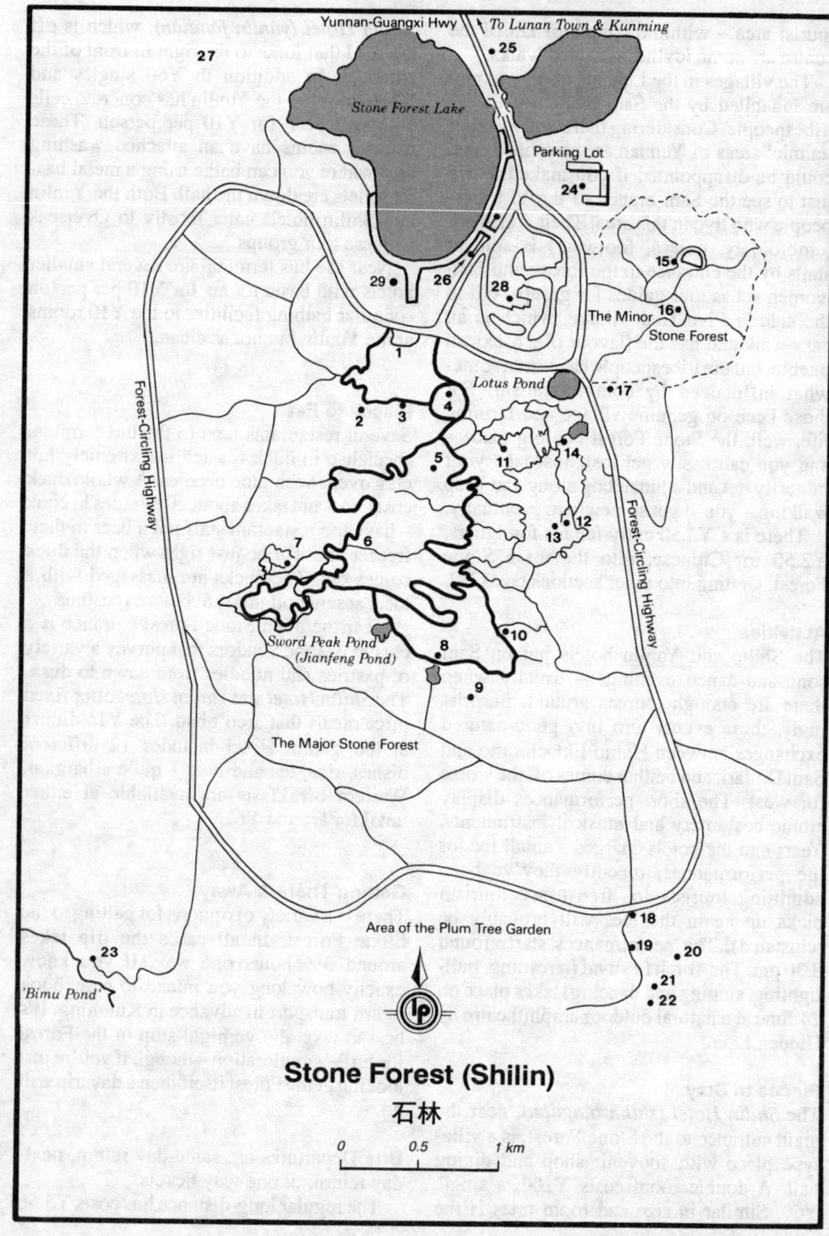
Yunnan-Guangxi Hwy
To Lunan Town & Kunming
Stone Forest Lake
Parking Lot
The Minor
Stone Forest
Lotus Pond
Forest-Circling Highway
Forest-Circling Highway
Sword Peak Pond
(Jianfeng Pond)
The Major Stone Forest
Area of the Plum Tree Garden
'Bimu Pond'
Stone Forest (Shilin)
石林
0
0.5
1 km

1 Lion Pond
2 Sweet Water Well
3 Stone Buffalo
4 Stone Screen
5 Open Stage
6 Steps to the Sky
7 Lotus Peak
8 Two Birds Feeding Each Other
9 Rhinoceros Looking at the Moon
10 Stone Bell
11 Resting Peak for Wild Geese
12 Phoenix Combing its Wings
13 Stone Mushroom
14 Stone Prison
15 Inscription of Mao Zedong's Poem 'Ode to the Plum Blossom'
16 Rock Arrowhead Pointing to the Sky
17 The Figure of Monk Tanseng
18 Wife Waiting for Her Husband
19 Goddess of Mercy
20 A Camel Riding on an Elephant
21 Swan Gazing Afar
22 Old Man Taking a Stroll
23 Stone Mushroom
24 Bus Departures
25 Truck Stop
26 Local Handicraft Stalls
27 Five-Tree Village
28 Shilin Hotel/CITS
29 Yunlin Hotel

1 狮子池
2 甜水井
3 小水牛
4 石屏风
5 舞场
6 耸天阶
7 莲花峰
8 双鸟渡食
9 犀牛望月
10 石钟
11 落雁峰
12 凤凤梳翅
13 灵芝石
14 石监狱
15 泳梅石
16 石簇擎天
17 唐僧石
18 望夫石
19 观音石
20 骆驼骑象
21 天鹅远瞩
22 漫步从容
23 万年灵芝
24 汽车站
25 卡车停场
26 工艺摊
27 五木村
28 石林宾馆
29 云林宾馆

one way or Y11 return. This bus leaves the Kunming main bus station at 8.30 am and 2.30 pm. The Kunming Hotel sells tickets for a tour bus to Shilin for the same rates, but they won't sell one-way tickets for their morning departures; furthermore, if you buy a round-trip ticket you must return the same day (3.30 pm departure from Shilin) or the ticket is invalid. It's much better to buy the tickets at the bus station and leave yourself the option of staying overnight or returning the same day as you please.

Opposite the department store at the centre of Kunming, two booths sell tickets for tour buses to the Stone Forest, but these are mainly for Chinese visitors and are difficult to book. The cost is Y15 return (leaves 7 am, returns 3 pm), which includes stops at two caves along the way (but not the Y2 admission fee at each cave). Other agents operate near the Kunhu and Sanye hotels.

CITS and CTS, operating out of the Kunming Hotel, have a three-day trip to the Western Hills, Bamboo Temple and Stone Forest for around Y100 per person, reducible for larger groups.

To get from the Stone Forest to Kunming, take one of the local buses leaving at 7 am and 3 pm from the bus parking lot. They make another departure at 1 pm from the

Shilin Hotel. These may be pre-booked, but empty seats can be found due to passengers staying overnight. You could also try hitching back to Kunming from the Stone Forest.

Bus & Rail The railway line you see on your trip between Kunming and the Stone Forest is the old French narrow-gauge line that runs all the way from Kunming to Hanoi (Chinese trains now terminate near the Vietnamese border). Historic railway buffs can make half the trip to Shilin on this line and experience one of China's unique train routes (stations along the way sport steep roofs and painted shutters in the French style). The intermediate stop is Yiliang; from here the railway line diverges away from the Shilin area towards Kaiyuan and you must complete your journey by bus.

There are three departures a day from Kunming's northern railway station *(běizhán)*, but the only one that won't require an overnight stay in Yiliang is train No 501, which leaves Kunming at 8.50 am, arriving in Yiliang at 11.30. In Yiliang there are frequent buses to Shilin, 45 minutes away. The total time and money expenditure is roughly the same as a straight bus to Shilin, around 3½ hours, Y12.

LUNAN

(lùnán) 路南

Lunan is a small market town about 10 km from the Stone Forest. It's not worth making a special effort to visit, but if you do go, try and catch a market day (Wednesday or Saturday), when Lunan becomes a colossal jam of donkeys, horse carts and bicycles. The streets are packed with produce, poultry and wares, and Sani women are dressed in their finest.

To get to Lunan from the Stone Forest, head back towards Kunming and take the first major crossroads left, then the second crossroads straight on but veering to the right. You'll have to hitch a truck or hire a three-wheeler (Y1.50 for a 20-minute ride). Plenty of trucks head that way on market day, some from the truck stop near the Forest.

XIAGUAN

(xiàguān) 下关

Xiaguan lies at the southern tip of Erhai Lake about 400 km west of Kunming. It was once an important staging-post on the Burma Road and is still a key centre for transport in north-west Yunnan. Xiaguan is the capital of Dali Prefecture and was previously known as Dali; if your destination is Dali, you can avoid misunderstanding by asking for *dàlǐ gǔ chéng* (Dali Old City).

Things to See

Xiaguan has developed into an industrial city specialising in tea processing, cigarette making and the production of textiles and chemicals. There is little to keep you here other than transport connections.

There are good views of the lake and mountains from **Erhai Lake Park** *(érhǎi gōngyuán)*. You can reach the park by boat. A larger boat runs round the lake; get details at Xinqiao Matou, the pier beside the new bridge.

Places to Stay

The official tourist abode is the *Erhai Guesthouse) (érhǎi bīnguǎn)*, which has doubles for Y50 and dorm beds for Y10. Outside the bus station a sign pointing in the right direction informs foreigners that they should only stay at the hotel. Other hotels with lower prices (Y12 for a double) can be found if you walk in the opposite direction and ask around.

Getting There & Away

There are frequent buses running between Xiaguan and Kunming. You have the choice of hard or soft-seat on a day or night bus. Depending on your bus, tickets cost between Y24 and Y36.

Minibuses provide a shuttle service for the 15 km between Xiaguan and Dali. The fare varies between Y0.50 and Y1, depending on the vehicle.

As recently as early 1990, foreigners were being fined for taking the direct route from Xiaguan to Xishuangbanna via Baoshan. In July 1990, however, this route was supposedly opened although small-town officials along the way may not know it yet. If you decide to try it, get a letter from Kunming or Jinghong PSB in advance. This would mean not having to backtrack through Kunming when moving between Dali and Xishuangbanna; timewise it's not a great saving since you must change buses either way.

Xiaguan also has bus connections for Lijiang, Binchuan (Jizushan), Weishan and Yongping.

AROUND XIAGUAN

There are several places around Xiaguan which are already on the Chinese tour circuit so perhaps even a big-nose can investigate them on a day trip or overnight basis. They involve just a little trial and error, with no satisfaction guaranteed.

Jizushan *(jīzú shān)* is one of China's sacred mountains and attracts Buddhist pilgrims, including Tibetans. Kasyapa, one of Sakyamuni's 10 disciples, is said to have booted out the mountain's resident deity and settled down here in 833 BC. The mountain is called Jizushan (Chicken-Foot Mountain) because the three slopes resemble the claws of a chicken. The Cultural Revolution damaged many of the temples, which have been gradually renovated from 1979 onwards. Over 150,000 tourists and pilgrims clamber up the mountain every year to watch the dawn. Tianzhufeng, the main peak, is a cool 3240 metres high, so you will need some warm clothing.

To reach Jizushan from Xiaguan you should first take a bus to Binchuan, which is 70 km east of Xiaguan. Then take another bus from Binchuan for the 33-km ride to Shazhi, a village at the foot of Jizushan. During peak tourist season there may be a direct bus between Xiaguan and Shazhi.

Weishan is famous for the Taoist temples on nearby Weibaoshan. There are reportedly some fine Taoist murals here. It's 61 km due south of Xiaguan so it could be done as a day trip. You might have to convince the ticket clerk at Xiaguan bus station that you are not taking this route to Xishuangbanna.

Yongping is 55 km south-west of Xiaguan on the old Burma Road. The Jinguang Monastery (Jinguangsi) is the attraction here.

DALI

(dàlǐ) 大理

Dali lies on the western edge of Erhai Lake at an altitude of 1900 metres, with the imposing Cangshan mountain range (average 4,000 metres) behind it. The main inhabitants of the region are the Bai, who number about 1.1 million in Yunnan.

Dali has a long history. In 126 BC a Han ambassador to Afghanistan was amazed to see bamboo wares and bolts of cloth from Sichuan there; the traders were ahead of him and had found a corridor through to India and Burma from Sichuan and Yunnan. Dali lies just off the Burma road and was a centre of the Bai Nanzhao kingdom. After that the kingdom of Dali held sway in south-western China up until the 13th century, when it was overrun by the Mongols and then by the Chinese. Dali has long been famous for its marble, which has been used in temples and palaces around China. A major drive is now being made to gain income from tourism.

Chinese indulge their fantasies by acclaiming this region as China's Switzerland; foreigners blow rings of sweet-smelling smoke and hazily discuss a 'new Kathmandu'. Dali is unlikely to match the sophistication of such places, but it's already a haven for foreigners who want to slow the pace and tune out for a while.

Orientation

Dali is a midget-sized city which has preserved some cobbled streets and traditional stone architecture within its old walls. Unless you are in a mad hurry (in which case use a bike), you can get your bearings just by taking a walk for an hour or so. It takes about half an hour to walk from the South Gate across town to the North Gate. Many of the sights around Dali couldn't be considered stunning on their own, but they do provide a destination towards which you can happily dawdle even if you don't arrive.

Maps of Dali are available at the reception desks of the two hotels.

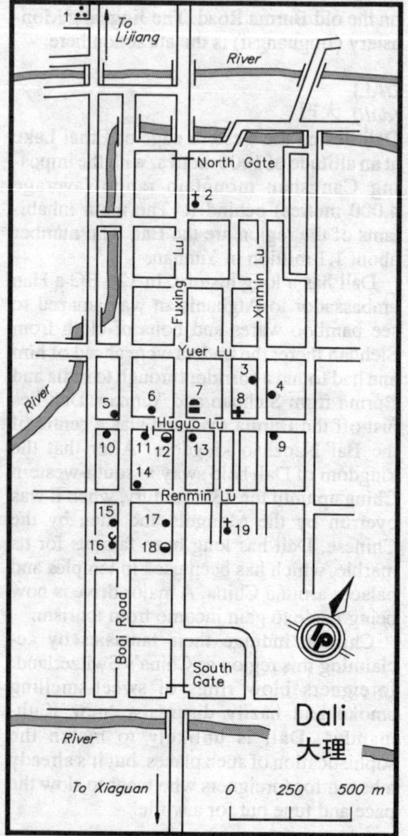

1 Three Pagodas
2 Protestant Church
3 Garden Restaurant
4 Garden Teahouse
5 Teahouse Restaurant
6 Yin Yang Cafe
7 Post Office
8 Hospital
9 Cinema
10 Public Security Bureau
11 No 2 Guesthouse
12 Bus Ticket Office (Kunming)
13 Bank of China
14 Men's Bathhouse
15 Cinema
16 Mosque
17 No 1 Guesthouse
18 Bus Stop (Lijiang)
19 Catholic Church

1 三塔
2 新教堂
3 花园饭馆
4 花园茶馆
5 茶馆饭店
6 阴阳咖啡馆
7 邮局
8 医院
9 电影院
10 公安局外事科
11 第二招待所
12 汽车售票处（昆明）
13 中国银行
14 男浴室
15 电影院
16 清真寺
17 第一招待所
18 汽车站（丽江）
19 主教堂

Information

Public Security Bureau This is at the northern end of the block behind the No 2 Guesthouse. Previous goodwill has been overtaxed by some travellers, so this is no longer the place to get a second or third visa extension.

Money The Bank of China is in the centre of town, at the corner of Huguo Lu and Fuxing Lu.

Post The post office is on Fuxing Lu, with the Bank of China nearby across Huguo Lu.

Three Pagodas

(sān tǎ) 三塔

Standing on the hillside behind Dali, the pagodas look pretty, particularly when seen reflected in the nearby lake. They are, in fact, among the oldest standing structures in south-west China. The tallest of the three, Qianxunta, has 16 tiers that reach a height of 70 metres. It was originally erected in the mid-9th century by Xi'an engineers. It is flanked by two smaller pagodas that are 10-tiered and measure 42 metres high each.

The temple behind the pagodas, Chongshengsi, is laid out in the traditional Yunnanese style, with three layers of buildings lined up with a sacred peak in the background. The temple has been recently restored and converted into a museum that chronicles the history, construction and renovation of the pagodas. Also on exhibit are marble slabs that have been cut and framed so that the patterns of the marble appear to depict landscapes.

Goddess of Mercy Temple

(guānyīn táng) 观音堂

The temple is built over a large boulder said to have been placed there by the Goddess of Mercy to block an invading enemy's advance. It is five km south of Dali.

Erhai Lake

(érhǎi) 洱海

The lake is a 40-minute walk from town or a 10-minute downhill zip on a bike. You can watch the large junks or the smaller boats with their queue of captive cormorants waiting on the edge of the boat for their turn to do the fishing. A ring placed round their necks stops them from guzzling the catch.

From Caicun, the lakeside village east of Dali, there's a ferry at 4 pm to Wase on the other side of the lake. You can stay overnight and catch a ferry back at 5.30 am. Plenty of locals take their bikes over. Since ferries crisscross the lake at various points, there could be some scope for extended touring. Close to Wase is Putuo Island *(pǔtuó dǎo)* with the Lesser Putuo Temple *(xiǎo pǔtuó sì)*. Other ferries run between Longkan and Haidong, and between Xiaguan and Jinsuo Island. Ferries appear to leave early in the morning (for market) and return around 4 pm; timetables are flexible.

Zhonghe Temple

(zhonghesi)

The temple is a long, steep hike up the mountainside behind Dali. When you finally get there, you may be received with a cup of tea and a smile.

Festivals

Probably the best time to be here is during the Third Moon Street Fair *(sān yùe jíe)*, which begins on the 15th day of the third lunar month (usually April) and ends on the 21st day. The fair developed from the original festival of Buddhist rites into a commercial gathering which attracts thousands of people from all over Yunnan to buy, sell, dance, race and sing.

Walkabout Festival *(rào shān lín)* is held between the 23rd and 25th days of the fourth lunar month (usually May). Villagers from the Dali area spend these days on a mass outing, dancing and singing their way from one temple to another.

Torch Festival *(hǔo bǎ jíe)* is held on the 24th day of the sixth lunar month (usually July). Flaming torches are paraded at night through homes and fields. Other events include firework displays and dragon-boat racing.

Places to Wash

On Renmin Lu, the next street south of Huguo Lu (behind the No 2 Guesthouse), is a bathhouse where men can have a hot bath and a massage for a few yuan (rates are posted). The best masseur is O Jing Bao, a deaf man who knows all the right pressure points. His wife has a massage house for women directly opposite the No 2 Guesthouse gate.

Places to Stay

Just about everyone who makes it to Dali heads for the *No 2 Guesthouse (Dali City Hotel No 2) (dìer zhāodàisuǒ)* on Huguo Lu

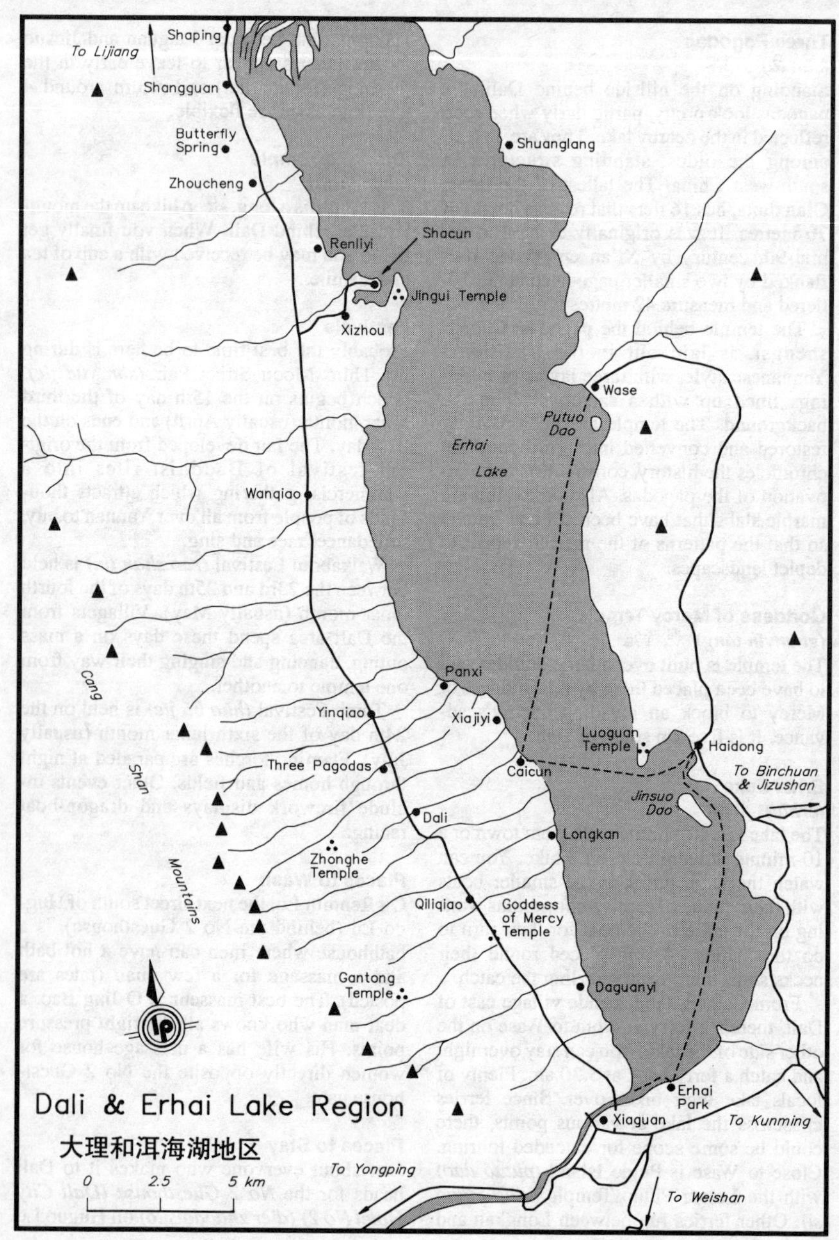

Dali & Erhai Lake Region

大理和洱海湖地区

in the centre of town. The staff is friendly, there's hot water in the evening and rates are low. A bed in the five to eight-bed dorms is Y5; in a three-bed it's Y6 per person. Doubles without bath are Y12 and doubles with bath are Y24.

The only other place in town is the *No 1 Guesthouse (Dali Hotel) (dìyī zhāodàisuǒ)* off Fuxing Lu, which is slightly more upscale at Y6 for dorms, Y40 to Y60 for doubles. This is where the odd tour group puts up and the staff are somewhat churlish.

Next to the gates of each hotel are small agencies where you can purchase bus tickets to Lijiang or Kunming.

Places to Eat

There are plenty of restaurants in Dali serving Western or Chinese dishes. Restaurants seem to open and close rapidly here – do your own exploring or ask other foreigners in town for the latest gourmet opinions. Prices are generally lower at the less-frequented restaurants, which can be just as good as the trendy hang-outs where prices tend to rise with their fame.

Several small, family-run restaurants along Huguo Lu near the No 2 Guesthouse cater to foreigners, with muesli, yoghurt, pancakes, pizza, sandwiches and other world traveller standards. Long-termers include *Jim's Peace Cafe*, the *Yin Yang Cafe* (also called the *Tibetan Cafe* – with the karmic 'Dalai Lama's Breakfast'), the *Coca-Cola Restaurant*, *Happy Restaurant* and the lovely *Teahouse Restaurant.*

If something more local in flavour is required, try the rambling, leafy *Garden Teahouse* or the very Chinese *Garden Restaurant* on Xinmin Lu.

Things to Buy

Dali is famous for its marble. You may not want to load your backpack with marble slabs, but local entrepreneurs produce everything from ashtrays to model pagodas.

Several tailor shops along Fuxing Lu and Huguo Lu are willing and able to produce clothing from local batik cloth at low cost and high speed. They also sell ready-made clothing based on local designs but adapted to Western sizing.

Most of the 'silver' jewellery sold in Dali is actually brass. It looks nice but you shouldn't pay more than, say, Y4 for a bracelet.

Getting There & Away

Public buses to Lijiang leave at 7.20 am from Dali Hotel (No 1 Guesthouse) on Fuxing Lu. Tickets cost Y11 and the trip takes 6½ hours. You can also purchase tickets for private minibuses to Lijiang at the office next to No 2 Guesthouse; these are Y12 and as much as an hour faster than the large public buses. The scenery on the Dali-Lijiang road is stupendous in parts.

Polish-made buses to Kunming leave from diagonally opposite the post office on Fuxing Lu at 6.30 am. The trip takes 11 hours and tickets cost Y27. Deluxe night buses to Kunming leave at 6 pm and cost Y37 (including a midnight meal along the way). Tickets for either bus should be purchased in advance at the ticket office (corner of Fuxing Lu and Huguo Lu), which is open from 7.30 am to 8 pm.

Minibuses to Xiaguan leave frequently (when full) during the day from the minibus station on the main street. The price varies between Y0.50 and Y1, depending on the vehicle.

Getting Around

Bikes are the best way to get around. Prices average Y3 per day, though cheaper rates are available.

The No 2 Guesthouse hires out bikes, but requires your passport as a deposit. The Rising Sun Bike Rental, in front of the guesthouse, has maps of the area and doesn't require a passport as a deposit. A couple of restaurants on Huguo Lu also hire bikes.

AROUND DALI

Gantong Temple

(gāntōng si) 甘通寺

This temple is close to the town of Guanyin, which is about six km from Dali in the direction of Xiaguan. In Guanyin you should follow the path uphill for three km. Ask friendly locals in the tea bushes for directions.

Qinbi Stream

(qinbixi)

This scenic picnic spot near the village of Qiliqiao is three km from Dali in the direction of Xiaguan. After hiking four km up a path running close to the river, you'll reach three ponds.

Butterfly Spring

(húdié quán) 蝴蝶泉

Butterfly Spring is a pleasant spot about 26 km north of Dali. The inevitable legend associated with the spring is that two lovers committed suicide here to escape a cruel king. After jumping into the bottomless pond, they turned into two of the butterflies which gather here en masse during May.

If you're energetic you could bike to the spring. Since it is only four km from Shapin, you could combine it with a visit to the Shapin market.

Shapin Market

The market happens every Monday at Shapin, which is 30 km north of Dali. An extraordinary mixture of livestock, handicrafts and farm produce changes hands here. The colourful costumes of the local Bai minority and the antics of the fair-goers make it a good photographic trip. What looks like a fishing basket with two legs turns out to be a fisherman transporting his huge fish-traps; a woman suddenly appears round the corner being towed by piglets on multiple leashes; some of the men wear a feathery-looking cape, made from palm fibres, which expands when wet to form a waterproof covering. The view across the lake from the top of the hill is superb.

In the market itself, you will be approached by persistent women who want to change money or sell jewellery, coins, snuff boxes and needle-holders. They may demonstrate a combined ear, nose and tooth-pick. The market starts humming at 10 am and ends around 2.30 pm. You can buy everything from tobacco, melon seeds and noodles to meat, pots and wardrobes. In the ethnic clothing line, you can look at shirts, headdresses, embroidered shoes and moneybelts. Prices asked from foreigners are often in FEC and always too high so bargain hard and long – as the market cools down, the women who've been pursuing you also drop their prices.

Getting to Shapin Market from Dali is easy. You can book a minibus ticket in advance at the booth next to the No 2 Guesthouse. The ticket costs Y7 (one way) and the minibus leaves the restaurant at 8.30 am – time for a quick breakfast before you go. The same minibus returns from Shapin around 1 pm; if you want to stay longer, you can flag down a local bus. From 2.30 pm onwards there seems to be a rush hour when everyone leaves, so expect a tussle to haul yourself on board.

An alternative is to take the local bus at 7.30 am from the crossroads north of town. To get to the stop, walk out of the northern gate and follow the road to the left until you reach the main road; the bus stops on the opposite side of the road. It will cost you Y2 and probably fray a few nerves since the bus has to accommodate half the town.

DALI TO LIJIANG

Most travellers take a direct route between Dali and Lijiang. However, a couple of places visited by Chinese tourists might make interesting detours for foreigners. Transport could be a case of potluck with buses or hitching.

Jianchuan

(jìanchūan) 剑川

This town is 92 km north of Dali on the Dali-Lijiang road. Approaching from the direction of Dali, you'll come to the small village of Diannan about eight km before Jianchuan. At Diannan, a small road branches south-west from the main road and passes through the village of Shaxi (23 km from the junction). Close to this village are the Shibaoshan Grottoes (Shibaoshan Shiku). There are three temple groups: Stone

Bell (Shizhong), Lion Pass (Shiziguan) and Shadeng Village (Shadeng Cun).

Heqing

(hèqìng) 鹤庆

About 46 km south of Lijiang, Heqing is on the road which joins the main Dali-Lijiang road just above Lake Erhai at Dengchuan. In the centre of town is the Yun He Lou, a wooden structure built during the Ming Dynasty.

LIJIANG

(lìjiāng) 丽江

North of Dali, bordering Tibet, is the town of Lijiang with its spectacular mountain backdrop. Lijiang is the base of the Naxi (also spelt Nakhi and Nahi) minority, who number about 245,000 in Yunnan and Sichuan. The Naxi are descended from Tibetan nomads and lived until recently in a matriarchal society. Women still seem to run the show, certainly in the old part of Lijiang.

The Naxi matriarchs maintained their hold over the men with flexible arrangements for love affairs. The *azhu* (friend) system allowed a couple to become lovers without setting up joint residence. Both partners would continue to live in their respective homes; the boyfriend would spend the nights at his girlfriend's house but return to live and work at his mother's house during the day. Any children born to the couple belonged to the woman, who was responsible for bringing them up. The father provided support, but once the relationship was over, so was the support. Children lived with their mothers; no special effort was made to recognise paternity. Women inherited all property, and disputes were adjudicated by female elders. The matriarchal system appears to have survived around Yongning, north of Lijiang.

Naxi women wear blue blouses and trousers covered by blue or black aprons. The T-shaped, traditional cape not only stops the basket always worn on the back from chafing, but also symbolises the heavens. Day and night are represented by the light and dark halves of the cape; seven embroidered circles symbolise the stars. The sun and moon used to be depicted with two larger circles, but these have gone out of fashion.

The Naxi created a written language over 1000 years ago using an extraordinary system of pictographs. The most famous Naxi text is the Dongba classic in 500 volumes. Dongba were Naxi shamans who were caretakers of the written language and mediators between the Naxi and the spirit world. The Dongba religion eventually absorbed itself into an amalgam of Lamaist Buddhism, Islam and Taoism. The Tibetan origins of the Naxi are confirmed by references in Naxi literature to Lake Manasarovar and Mt Kailas, both in Western Tibet.

There are strong matriarchal influences in the Naxi language. Nouns enlarge their meaning when the word for 'female' is added; conversely, the addition of the word for 'male' will decrease the meaning. For example, 'stone' plus 'female' conveys the idea of a boulder; 'stone' plus 'male' conveys the idea of a pebble.

Yunnan was a hunting ground for famous foreign plant-hunters such as Kingdon Ward, Forrest and Joseph Rock. Joseph Rock, an Austro-American, lived almost continuously in Lijiang between 1922 and 1949. Rock is still remembered by some locals. A man of quick and violent temper, he required a special chair to accommodate his corpulent frame. He burdened his large caravans with a gold dinner service and a collapsible bathtub from Abercrombie & Fitch. He also wrote the best guide to Hawaiian flora before devoting the rest of his life to researching Naxi culture and collecting the flora of the region.

The Ancient Nakhi Kingdom of Southwest China (Harvard University Press, 1947) is Joseph Rock's definitive work; the two volumes are heavy-duty reading. For a lighter treatment of the man and his work, take a look at *In China's Border Provinces: The Turbulent Career of Joseph Rock, Botanist-Explorer* by J B Sutton (Hastings House, 1974).

Another venerable work on Lijiang worth reading if you can find it is *The Forgotten*

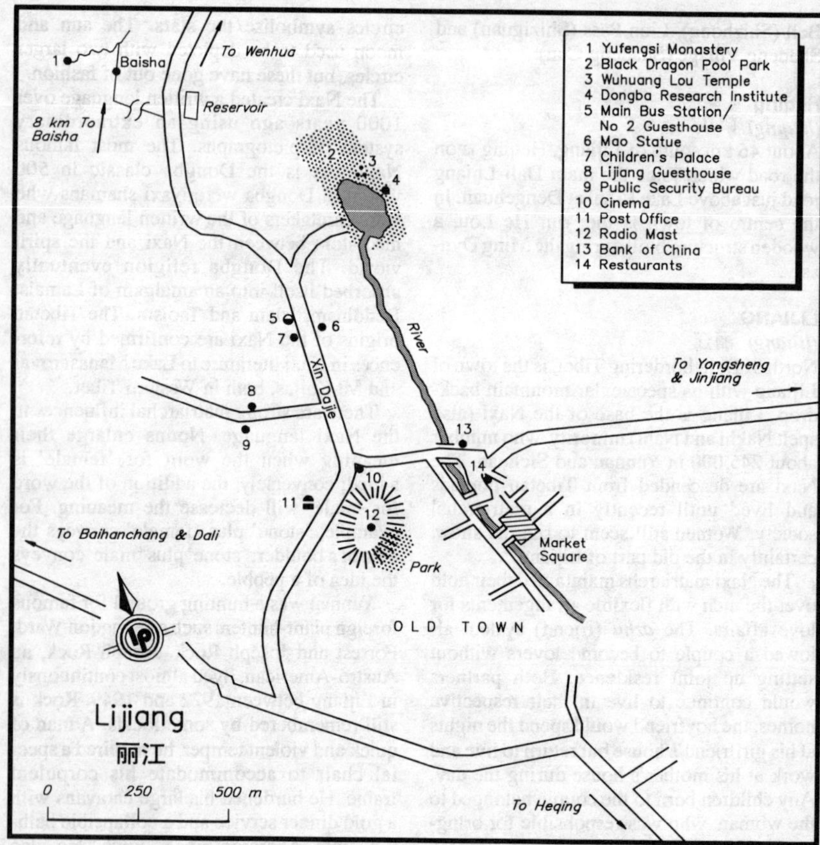

1 雨风寺
2 黑龙潭公园
3 五凰楼
4 东巴研究所
5 汽车总站/第二招待所
6 毛泽东像
7 儿童宫
8 丽江宾馆
9 公安局外事科
10 电影院
11 邮局
12 广播楼
13 中国银行
14 饭馆

Kingdom by Peter Goulart (John Murray Co, 1955). Goulart was a White Russian who studied Naxi culture and lived in Lijiang from 1940 to 1949.

One of the strangest expeditions to pass through Lijiang was that of Theodore and Kermit Roosevelt, who spent several months in 1935 searching for the giant panda. After stumbling through snow, the brothers finally hunted down an old panda which had been snoozing in a hollow tree. They fired in unison and killed it. One of their Kashmiri *shikaris* (gun-bearer) remarked that the bear was a 'sahib', a gentleman, for when hit he did not cry out as a bear would have. It was the first giant panda killed by a white man, and the Roosevelts were exultant.

In retrospect, this seems a dubious distinction: latest reports from China indicate that there are less than 700 giant pandas left in the wild and that they are heading for extinction by the end of the century.

Naxi Glossary

The transliteration used for the Naxi language is pretty mind-boggling, but you might like to try the following tongue gymnastics:

where are you going?
zeh gkv bbeu
Lijiang
ggubbv
going to Lijiang
ggubbv bbeu
you understand Nakhi
nakhi kou chi kv
drink wine!
zhi teh

Information & Orientation

Lijiang is a small town in a beautiful valley. The main attractions are in the surrounding area, so use a bike to get out of town to the mountains, where you can hike around. You may need time to acclimatise to the height (2400 metres).

Lijiang is neatly divided into a standard, boring Chinese section and an old town full of character, cobbled streets, gushing canals and the hurly-burly of market life. The approximate line of division is a hill topped with a radio mast. Everything west of the hill is the new town, and everything east of the hill is the old town.

Information is available from the Lijiang Guesthouse (No 1 Hotel), or you might bump into some of the English-speaking locals.

Public Security Bureau This is opposite the Lijiang Guesthouse.

Money The Bank of China is next to the bridge on the main road beside the old town. Hours are from 10 am to noon, and from 1 to 5 pm. It's closed on Mondays.

Old Town

Crisscrossed by canals and a maze of narrow streets, the old town is not to be missed. Arrive by mid-morning to see the market square full of Naxi women in traditional dress. Parrots and plants adorn the front porches, old women sell griddle cakes in front of tea shops, men walk past with hunting falcons *(lǎo yīng)* proudly keeping balance on their gloved fists, grannies energetically slam down the trumps on a card table in the middle of the street. You can buy embroidery and lengths of striped cloth in shops around the market. Some women offered intricate Tibetan locks for Y8.

Above the old town is a beautiful park which can be reached on the path leading past the radio antenna. Sit on the slope in the early morning and watch the mist clearing as the old town comes to life.

Black Dragon Pool Park
(hēilóng tán gōngyuán)

The park is on the northern edge of town. Apart from strolling around the pool, you can visit the Dongba Research Institute, which is part of a renovated complex on the hillside. At the far side of the pond are renovated buildings used for an art exhibition, a pavilion with its own bridge across the water and the Ming Dynasty Wuhuang Lou temple.

Jade Dragon Snow Mountain

(yùlóngxǔeshān) 玉龙雪山

Soaring 5500 metres above Lijiang is Mt Satseto, also known as Yulongxueshan (Jade Dragon Snow Mountain). In 1963, the peak was climbed for the first time by a research team from Beijing. You can reach the snow line on one of the adjoining peaks if you continue along the base of the hillside but ignore the track to Yufengsi. On the other side of the next obvious valley, a well-worn path leads uphill to a lake.

Museum of Naxi Culture

Mr Xuan Ke, a Naxi scholar who spent 20 years in labour camps following the suppression of the Hundred Flowers movement, has turned his family Lijiang home into a small repository for Naxi and Lijiang cultural items. Besides clothing and musical instruments (including an original Persian lute that has been used in Naxi music for centuries), his home displays Dr Joseph Rock's large, handmade furniture and has a small library of out-of-print books on Lijiang. Dr Rock was a close family friend.

Xuan Ke speaks English and is always willing to discuss his original ideas about world culture (eg, that music and dance originated as rites of exorcism). His home is in the old town, opposite the No 40 Restaurant.

Music

One of the few things to do in the evening in Lijiang is to attend performances of the Naxi orchestra, usually given at the Lijiang Hotel. What's distinctive about the group is not only that all 16 to 18 members are Naxis, but that they play a type of Taoist temple music that has been lost elsewhere in China. The pieces they perform are supposedly faithful renditions of music from the Han, Song and Tang dynasties, played on original instruments (in most of China such instruments didn't survive the Communist revolution). This is a very rare chance to hear Chinese music as it must have sounded in classical China. Xuan Ke usually speaks for the group at performances, explaining each musical piece and describing the instruments.

Festivals

The 13th day of the third moon (late March or early April) is the traditional day to hold a Fertility Festival.

July brings Huopao Jie (Jumping Over Fire Festival), also celebrated as the Torch Festival by the Bai in the Dali region. The origin of this festival is traced back to the Nanzhao Kingdom.

The King of Nanzhao, intent on securing more power, invited all the kings from the surrounding area to a feast. Amongst those invited was the King of Eryuan. The Queen of Eryuan suspected the motives for such a feast and did all she could to dissuade her husband from going. He insisted he was honour bound to accept the invitation and went to the feast.

When the kings had become properly drunk, the King of Nanzhao withdrew from the scene, ordered his servants to lock the doors of the banquet hall and then set it alight. All the kings were burnt to a cinder. The Queen of Eryuan had had premonitions of treachery and had given her husband engraved metal rings to wear around his wrists and ankles. On the basis of these rings she was able to identify the remains of her husband, who was then buried with full honours.

The King of Nanzhao kept sending marriage proposals to the bereaved queen. Finally, she realised she had no option so she accepted on condition that she could dispose of her husband's ceremonial robes first. A huge fire was prepared for the robes; as the flames rose higher and higher to consume them, the queen leapt into the heart of the fire.

Places to Stay

The very basic *No 2 Guesthouse (dìèr zhāodài suǒ)*, next to the main bus station, offers doubles for Y6 per person with shared bath or Y24 per person with private bath. Hard dorm beds are Y3 per person. Evenings can be a bit noisy as there's a Chinese disco on the premises that operates nightly, but by midnight all is usually quiet.

The *Lijiang Guesthouse (No 1 Hotel) (dìyī zhāodàisuǒ)* has more comfortable four-bed dorms for Y5 per bed. A double without bath costs Y24, double with bath Y48. The hotel has two blocks; the one at the back is deluxe. The Hotel Service Bureau is on your left when you come out of the lobby. This is the place to ask about hiring a vehicle, and you might like to look at the excellent map on their wall. Next door to the Service Bureau is the shower room – ask at the reception desk for the precise opening time. To the right of the showers, a few doors down, is the bike depot.

Places to Eat

Like Dali, Lijiang has a legion of small, family-operated restaurants catering to the fantasies of China backpackers. Kitchens are tiny and waits are long (if one of the ubiquitous Dutch tour groups is in town, forget it), but the food is usually interesting. There are always several 'Naxi' items on the menu, including the famous 'Naxi omelette' and 'Naxi sandwich' (goat cheese, tomato and fried egg between two pieces of local baba flatbread). Try locally produced yinjiu, a lychee-based wine with a 500-year history – tastes like a decent semi-sweet sherry.

Diagonally opposite the bus station, next to the Mao statue, is *Peter's*, a small restaurant operated by a former Yunnan opera diva. Down next to the canal in the old town are the similar *Old Town House* (operated by a Bai family), *Mimi's* (Chinese family) and *No 40 Restaurant* (Naxi family). All serve Naxi, Western and Chinese dishes, but according to local wisdom No 40 has the most authentic Naxi food. On the opposite side of the canal, a young Naxi woman has opened the friendly *Kele*.

The *Lijiang Guesthouse* dining room is not a taste-bud experience. On the same street near the intersection with Xin Dajie is the *Xuefengyuan Restaurant*, which offers a respite from all the foreigner places. The speciality of the house is various forms of baba, the Lijiang national dish – thick flatbreads of wheat, served plain or stuffed with meats, vegetable or sweets. Morning is the best time to check out the baba selection. The restaurant also serves other Naxi dishes and a variety of Chinese standards. In the old town, you can buy baba from street vendors. Close to the cinema is a place which serves only baba, noodles and doujiang, the standard soya bean drink – a very inexpensive and filling breakfast. There are several smaller restaurants just before the entrance to the Black Dragon Lake Park. Xin Dajie has several pastry shops.

Getting There & Away

Buses run daily between Lijiang and Dali. The trip takes about six hours and the fare is Y12 by minibus, Y11 by ordinary bus. Buses to Dali and Xiaguan leave at 7 and 11 am from the bus station next to the No 2 Guesthouse opposite the Mao statue. This appears to be the main bus station. A couple of other places serve as bus depots or sell tickets.

There is a bus connection between Lijiang and Jinjiang, a town on the Kunming-Chengdu railway. The trip takes nine hours and the ticket costs Y18. The bus leaves at 6.30 am from the bus station in front of the Mao statue, where train tickets from Jinjiang to Kunming or Chengdu can be booked in advance as well. The bus arrives in Jinjiang in time to connect with the train departing for Chengdu at 7 pm. During the rainy season, from July to September, the Lijiang-Jinjiang road is often washed out and Chengdu-bound travellers have no alternative but to return to Kunming to catch a train or plane onward.

Getting Around

The modern part of town is a tedious place to walk around. The old town, however, is best seen on foot. The Lijiang Guesthouse hires bikes for Y0.60 per hour or Y5 per day. Bikes are good for anything within a radius of 15 km, but after that you'd be better off hiring a vehicle. The Lijiang Guesthouse rents Beijing jeeps at Y0.60 per km and Y2 for each hour of waiting time.

Lijiang (nicknamed 'Land of Horses') is famous for its easily trained horses, which are usually white or chestnut with distinctive white stripes on the back. It might be possible to arrange an excursion on horseback.

AROUND LIJIANG

Monasteries

Lijiang originally had five monasteries, which all belonged to the Karmapa (Red Hat sect) of Tibetan Buddhism introduced to Lijiang in the 16th century by Lama Chuchin

Chone. This lama founded the Chinyunsi monastery close to Lashiba Lake.

About 16 km south of Lijiang is **Shangri Moupo**, a mountain considered sacred by the Tibetans. Half-way up the mountain there was once a large monastery, **Yunfengsi**, which was a popular destination for pilgrims. The present condition of the monastery might be worth investigating. Behind the mountain is a large white cliff where shamanistic rites were once performed by Dongbas.

Stone Drum

(shígǔ) 石鼓

The marble drum is housed in a small pavilion overlooking a bend in the Yangtse, 70 km west of Lijiang. In April 1936 the Red Army crossed the river at Shigu (Stone Drum) on the Long March. During the Cultural Revolution, Red Guards split the drum in defiance of an old prophecy that calamity would befall the country when the drum split. The parts have since been patched together again.

To reach Shigu, you can either hire a jeep from Lijiang or try your luck with local transport. You should try to catch a local bus going in the direction of Judian and make it clear that you want to get off at Shigu. Another useful place to pick up a lift to Shigu is Baihanchang, an important road junction about 24 km before Shigu. If you want to make the sortie, be patient and prepared with warm clothes, food and water.

Tiger Leap Gorge

(hǔyàoxiá) 虎越峡

At this 15-km gorge the Yangtse (here called Jinshajiang) drops nearly 300 metres in a series of 34 rapids. No kayak or raft team has ever successfully navigated the rapids, though a 1986 Chinese expedition using inner-tube barrel made it with a loss of two lives. A narrow path clings to vertical cliffs at a height of over 3700 metres and attracts daredevil trekkers from around the world – take it easy if you're susceptible to vertigo. At some places the gorge is only 30 metres wide. Warm clothes, food, water and sturdy footwear are recommended. Some trekkers also carry a sleeping bag since the guesthouse beds are often short of blankets. A few hardy trekkers camp out on the trail along the way.

To reach Huyaoxia, 94 km from Lijiang, take the 7 am bus from the shopfront just north of the Mao statue (Y12); the bus arrives at Daju, near the northern mouth of the gorge, at about noon. The Tiger Leaping Hotel has dorms for Y2 a bed.

To start the 30-km trek, cross the bridge towards the cliff and follow a track to the left until you come to the river (a 90-minute walk – or an hour for brisk walkers). A gang of local extortionists at the river will ask Y20 per person to operate the ferry the short distance across the river but with some arguing back and forth will usually settle for Y10 per person (the traveller notebooks in Lijiang are full of maledictions hurled at these ferrymen). The first part of the hike takes about 4 ½ hours, at which point most hikers call it a day and spend the night at one of two small guesthouses in the village of He Tao Yuan.

The second day's trek to the other end of the gorge takes about seven hours, after which it's another 90 minutes or so to the next village with accommodation, Qiaotou (Xiaqiaotou).

Those who want to see the gorge without making the somewhat dangerous trek can follow a a trail from Daju to an observation point (and camping area) on the south bank of the Jinsha River.

Baisha

(báishā) 白沙

Baisha is a small village on the plain north of Lijiang in the vicinity of several old temples. Before Kublai Khan made it part of his Yuan Empire (1279-1368), it was the capital of the Naxi kingdom. It's hardly changed since then and though at first sight it seems nothing more than a motley collection of dirt roads and stone houses, it offers a close-up glimpse of Naxi culture for those willing to spend some time nosing around.

The star attraction of Baisha will probably hail you in the street. Dr Ho (or He) looks like the stereotype of a Taoist physician and there's a sign outside his door: 'The Clinic of Chinese Herbs in Jade-Dragon Mountains of Lijiang'. The doctor speaks English and is keen to catch up on foreign contacts. Over a cup of healthy tea, you can discuss herbal medicine and sign his visitors' book. He can mix up a herbal remedy on the spot for whatever ails you. Dr Ho and his family gather all the herbs for his practice from various locations on the Jade Dragon Snow Mountain.

Dr Ho can also give you directions to nearby **Dabaoji Palace**, which has some frescoes executed in the Tibetan style with Tibetan Buddhist, Muslim, Taoist and Dongba elements. Naxi religion developed along such mixed lines due to its position as a crossroads for Islamic Mongols from the north, Tibetans from the west, and Chinese to the south and east. The temple is dedicated to Saddok, the patron god of Lijiang; the indigenous Dongba faith was craftily blended with neighbouring religions, thereby denying potential conquerors an excuse to destroy Naxi places of worship.

Yufengsi This small Karmapa lamasery is on a hillside about five km past Baisha. The last three km of the track require a steep climb. If you decide to leave your bike at the foot of the hill, don't leave it too close to the village below – the local kids have been known to let the air out of the tyres!

The monastery has a magnificent view across the valley to Lijiang. The Cultural Revolution ejected the monks and destroyed the original religious objects. A large statue of Sakyamuni was heaved out of the main temple and smashed in front of the horrified monks. The temples are all silent shells and quiet courtyards filled with orchids, hydrangeas and camellias. Above the temple is a building containing the famous camellia tree which produces hundreds of flowers between February and April. This tree is a favourite with the occasional group of noisy Han tourists. A stone-faced old monk patiently explains its 500-year history; he risked his life during the Cultural Revolution to water the tree secretly at night.

Another Naxi temple worth seeing if you're in the area is between Baisha and Yufengsi in the village of Yulongchun. Called Bai You Sado Go, it contains an image of the Naxi god Sado, flanked by wife and concubine.

Getting There & Away If you're going to Baisha by bike, follow Lijiang's main street past the Mao statue and keep to the left. About two km out of town you'll see a reservoir on your right. Turn left off the main road and follow the trail for another eight km. You can also hire a three-wheeled taxi in Lijiang to drive you to all the sights in and around Baisha for about Y25 per vehicle (figuring on a half-day trip – you'll have to spend more for longer outings).

NORTH-WEST YUNNAN

Zhongdian

(zhōngdìan) 中甸

Located 104 km north of Qiaotou, Zhongdian is not officially open to foreigners yet, but there's a CITS brochure in English about the area. PSB are fining any Tibet-bound foreigners found on this closed route.

The nearby lake region of Baishuitang is said to approach the splendour of Jiuzhaigou in northern Sichuan.

Luguhu

(lúgǔ hú)

This remote lake overlaps the Yunnan-Sichuan border and is a centre for several Tibetan, Yi and Mosu (a Naxi subgroup) villages. The Mosu still practice matriarchy. Several islands on the lake can be visited by dugout canoe, which can be rented for Y3 to Y4 per day. Twelve km west of the lake is **Yongningsi**, a lamasery with at least 20 lamas in residence.

The *Luguhu Guesthouse* at the west end of the lake has basic rooms for Y4 to Y7 per bed. A new, larger hotel was under construction at the time of writing. Food at Luguhu seems to be limited most of the year to potatoes and squash.

From Lijiang it's a nine-hour bus trip to Ninglang, the Luguhu County seat, and then a four-hour hitch or three-day hike to Luguhu. In Ninglang a government guesthouse has rooms for Y20. Luguhu can also be reached from Xichang (via Muli) in Sichuan Province.

JINJIANG

(jìnjiāng) 金江

Jinjiang is the tiny railhead for the large town of Dukou (also known as Panzhihua), just over the line in Sichuan Province. For travellers it's an important junction for the Lijiang-Chengdu route. To reach Jinjiang from Chengdu, one of the better trains is the No 91 which leaves Chengdu at 10.07 pm and reaches Jinjiang at 1.20 pm the next day. A local-price hard-sleeper for this trip costs Y42. At Jinjiang station ticket-sellers usually meet the train and sell bus tickets to Lijiang for the next day. Shortly after leaving Dukou, the bus enters Yunnan Province. The landscape changes to banana groves, terraced fields and small villages of brown mud-brick houses with grey tiled roofs. After several hours of giddy and dramatic climbing above the Jinsha Jiang (upper reaches of the Yangtse River), the bus continues through Yongsheng to Lijiang.

In the opposite direction, train No 92 leaves Jinjiang an hour earlier (9.08 pm) and arrives in Chengdu at the same hour, 1.20 pm. It can be difficult finding anything besides hard-seat tickets in Jinjiang. Sometimes hard-sleeper tickets from Jinjiang to Chengdu can be bought in Lijiang on the black market.

If you must spend a night in Jinjiang (very likely if you're heading north from Lijiang), the Guesthouse *(zhāodàisuǒ)* is a clean, friendly place to stay, charging Y3 per person. They also sell Lijiang bus tickets.

In the square outside Jinjiang station are several open-air restaurants serving excellent food. Try their bean curd (tofu) hotpot (doufu huoguo) and the small pots of beef or pork in batter. They were also cooking a more expensive snake hotpot.

XISHUANGBANNA

(xīshuāngbǎnnà) 西双版纳

The region of Xishuangbanna is in the deep south of Yunnan Province, next to the Burmese and Laotian borders. The name Xishuangbanna is a Chinese approximation of the original Thai name Sip Sawng Panna (12 rice-growing districts). Xishuangbanna Dai Autonomous Prefecture, as it is known officially, is subdivided into the three counties of Jinghong, Menghai and Mengla. Mengla County is closed to foreign tourists at present though permits are easily obtained at the PSB office in Jinghong.

About half the 650,000-strong population of this region is Dai; another 25% or so is Han Chinese and the rest is a hotchpotch of minorities which includes the Miao, Zhuang, Yao and lesser known hill tribes such as the Aini, Jinuo, Bulang, Lahu and Wa.

The Dai people are concentrated in this pocket of Yunnan and exercise a clear upper hand in the economy of Xishuangbanna. During the Cultural Revolution many Dai people simply voted with their feet and slipped across the border to join their fellow Dai who are sprinkled throughout Thailand,

Yao Minority Person

Laos, Burma and Vietnam. Not only the Dai but also most of the other minorities in these areas display a nonchalant disregard for borders and authority in general.

The Dai are Buddhists who were driven southwards by the Mongol invasion of the 13th century. The Dai state of Xishuangbanna was annexed by the Mongols and then by the Chinese, and a Chinese governor was installed in the regional capital of Jinglan (present-day Jinghong). Countless Buddhist temples were built in the early days of the Dai state and now lie in the jungles in ruins. During the Cultural Revolution Xishuangbanna's temples were desecrated and destroyed. Some were saved by being used as granaries, but many are now being rebuilt from scratch. Temples are also recovering their role, with or without official blessing, as village schools where young children are accepted for religious training as monks.

To keep themselves off the damp earth in the tropical rainforest weather, the Dai live in spacious wooden houses raised on stilts in the classic style, with the pigs and chickens below. The common dress for the Dai women is a straw hat or towel-wrap headdress; a tight, short blouse in a bright colour;

and a printed sarong with a belt of silver links. Some Dai men tattoo their bodies with animal designs. Betel-nut chewing is popular and many Dai youngsters get their teeth capped with gold; otherwise they are considered ugly.

Ethnolinguistically, the Dai are part of the very large Thai family that includes the Siamese, Lao, Shan, Thai Dam and Ahom peoples found scattered throughout the river valleys of Thailand, Burma, Laos, north Vietnam and Assam. The Xishuangbanna Dai are broken into four subgroups, the Shui Dai, Han Dai, Huayai Dai and Kemu Dai, each distinguished by variations in costume. All speak the Dai language, which is quite similar to Lao and northern Thai dialects. For the written language, they use their own script, which looks like a cross between Lao and Burmese scripts.

You can make some headway with Chinese, but you'll also find a Thai phrasebook (Lonely Planet produces one) useful in remoter parts.

Both Xishuangbanna and Hainan Island have fascinating collections of plant and animal life which are a unique resource for research into rare species. Unfortunately, recent scientific studies have demonstrated the devastating effect of previous government policies on land use; the tropical rainforest areas of Hainan and Xishuangbanna are now as acutely endangered as similar rainforest areas elsewhere on the planet. The jungle areas that remain still contain dwindling numbers of wild elephants (200), tigers, leopards and also golden-haired monkeys. The Tropical Institute in Jinghong has gardens with a limited selection of plants which give an idea of the spectacular plant life in the deep forests, but foreign visitors are not welcome.

Festivals celebrated by the Dai also attract hordes of foreigners and Han Chinese. The Water-Splashing Festival held around mid-April (usually 13-15 April) washes away the dirt, sorrow and demons of the old year and brings in the happiness of the new. The first day of the festival is devoted to a giant market. The second day features dragon-boat racing (races in Jinghong are held on the Mekong River below the bridge), swimming races and rocket-launching. The third day features the water-splashing freakout – be prepared to get drenched all day by the locals. In the evenings there is dancing, launching of hot-air paper balloons and game-playing.

The festivities attract loads of tourists, so all the planes are booked out, but the bus may be an alternative. Hotels in Jinghong town are booked solid, but you could stay in a nearby Dai village and commute. Festivities take place all over Xishuangbanna, so you might be lucky further away from Jinghong.

During the Tanpa Festival in February young boys are sent to the local temple for initiation as novice monks. At approximately the same time (between February and March), Tan Jing Festival participants honour Buddhist texts housed in local temples.

The Tan Ta Festival is held during the last 10-day period of October or November with temple ceremonies, rocket launches from special towers and hot-air balloons. The rockets, which often contain lucky amulets, blast off with a curious droning sound like mini-space shuttles before exploding high above; those who find the amulets are assured of good luck.

The farming season (from July to October) is the time for the Closed-Door Festival, when marriages or festivals are banned. Traditionally, this is also the time of year that men aged 20 or older ordain as monks for a period of time. The season ends with the Open-Door Festival, when everyone lets their hair down again to celebrate the harvest.

Climate

Xishuangbanna has wet and dry seasons. The wet season is between June and August, when it rains ferociously almost every day. From September to February there is less rainfall but thick fog descends during the late evening and doesn't lift until 10 am. Between May and August there are frequent and spectacular thunderstorms.

Between November and March temperatures average about 19°C. The hottest months of the year are from April to September, when you can expect an average of 25°C.

SIMAO

(sīmáo) 思茅

Before Jinghong got its airport, Simao was a drab but important stepping-stone to Xishuangbanna for those who didn't want to brave the three-day Kunming-Jinghong bus trip. Now the Simao airport is in disrepair following an earthquake and most travellers give it a miss unless the bus from Kunming makes an overnight stop here (unlikely unless there's a breakdown along the way).

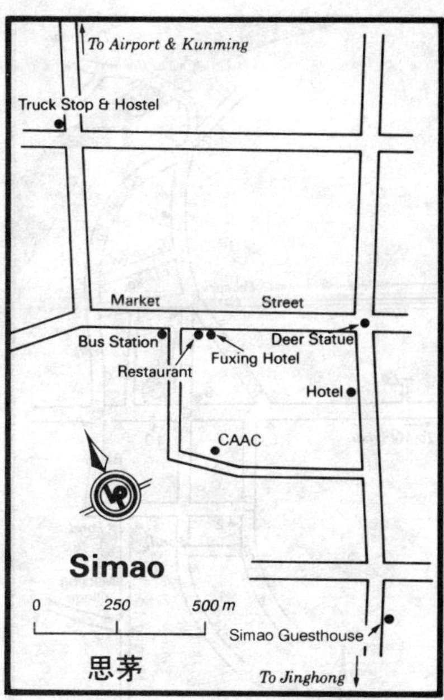

Places to Stay

The tourist joint is *Simao Guesthouse (sīmáo bīnguǎn)*. Doubles with bath cost Y32; triples without bath are Y8 per person.

There are several other hotels in Simao. One is close to the bus station; another is on the main street, close to the CAAC office. The bus from Kunming stops at a depot which is also a hotel. They are all basic and cost around Y3 per person.

Getting There & Away

Air The CAAC office (☎ 2234) is just off the main street at Hongqi Guangchang Beice. It's open from 8 to 11 am and 2.30 to 5.30 pm; closed on Saturday afternoon and Sunday.

When the airport is operative, there are flights between Kunming and Simao. The fare is around Y87 and flights depart five days a week. There are two flights on Monday and Thursday.

The airport bus for the midday flight from Simao takes no more than 10 minutes to reach the airport, where everyone gets thoroughly bored for several hours. The control-tower staff use binoculars to sight the incoming plane, a turboprop Antonov. The flight lasts barely an hour.

Bus There are daily buses between Kunming and Simao. The trip takes 2½ days and costs Y37.50 soft-seat.

The haul is long but not punishing. The bus leaves Kunming at 7.45 am. After skirting Lake Dian, it climbs hills which become less and less populated, but have gushing streams and waterfalls surrounded by lush foliage. Traffic very gingerly crosses the Yuan River over a rickety suspension bridge. After staying overnight, probably at Anding (Y2 per bed in a three-bed room), the bus arrives in Simao at around 5 pm.

Various private and public buses to Jinghong leave early in the morning from the bus station or from the hotel on the main road. Tickets cost Y8.80 and the trip takes five hours.

At Simao bus station, PSB have posted a warning to foreigners not to take the direct bus from Simao to Xiaguan. There must be something exciting out there, but travellers who've done the route have nothing special to report except for the man at Simao CITS, who gets very agitated when you casually tell him you've taken this road. It might have something to do with dope country. Now that

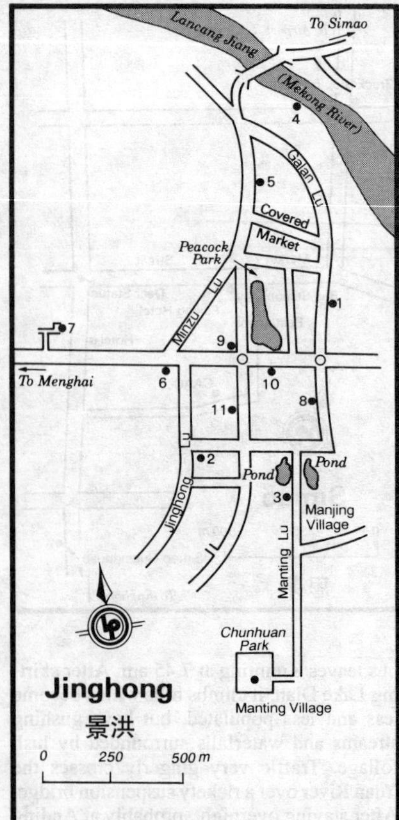

1 Banna Hotel
2 CAAC
3 Dai Minority Guest House
4 Pier for Menghan
5 Main Bus Station
6 Minibus Station
7 Tropical Plant Research Institute
8 Bank of China
9 Post Office
10 Public Security Bureau
11 Workers' Cultural Palace

1 版纳宾馆
2 中国民航
3 傣族饭店
4 码头（勐罕）
5 汽车总站
6 面包车站
7 热带植物研究所
8 中国银行
9 邮局
10 公安局外事科
11 工人文化宫

Baoshan (the intermediate point between Simao and Xiaguan) is officially open, there shouldn't be any problem doing this route. To be on the safe side, however, you should carry a letter from the Jinghong or Kunming PSB that states that this journey is permitted.

JINGHONG

(jǐnghóng) 景洪

Jinghong, the capital of Xishuangbanna prefecture, lies beside the Lancang Jiang (Mekong River). It's a sleepy town with streets lined with palms, which help mask the Chinese-built concrete boxes until they merge with the stilt-houses in the surrounding villages. It doesn't have much to keep you beyond a couple of days. It's more a base for operations or a place for lazing in the midday shade beside the river.

Information

CITS The travel service (☎ 2708) is on the Banna Hotel grounds opposite reception (enter via the stairs on the left). Friendly staff hand round fruit and try to solve your problems.

Ask here about vehicle hire for excursions into the forest: Beijing jeeps cost Y0.60 per km. A private firm provides Toyota Landcruisers for Y1 per km. You can hire a vehicle to take you to Mangsha (five km north of Jinghong), engage a guide in the village and spend the day hacking your way through virgin jungle. Keep gear to a minimum so both your hands are free, and be prepared for bloodthirsty leeches.

CITS can also help you book your return flight to Kunming. If you can form a small group and plan two days in advance, they may be able to arrange a visit to the Tropical Plant Research Institute.

Public Security Bureau This is opposite Peacock Park in the centre of town. They seem to tolerate foreigners making side trips from open towns, providing you don't stay overnight in local villages. They can crack down hard on foreigners caught bushwhacking along the border.

Money The Bank of China is on Galan Lu south of the big traffic circle. The Banna Hotel has a foreign exchange counter.

As far as we could tell, there's still no black market for FEC in Jinghong. As a matter of fact, in most of Xishuangbanna people prefer to accept RMB for all goods and services; hence, it's a good idea to bring lots of RMB with you from Kunming. Even in Jinghong, you'll find little call for FEC except for CAAC tickets and for Banna Hotel accommodation.

Villages

In the southern part of town is **Manjing**, a traditional Dai village. You'll also find several Dai guesthouses here.

If you continue past this village for 500 metres, you'll come to a rustic Dai Buddhist temple. Just beyond it is the village of **Manting** and **Chunhuan Park**, which contains two replica pagodas. The originals are further away in Xishuangbanna, so this is meant to be a chance for tourists to see the pagodas without actually going there. The gardens are full of blooming acacias, hibiscus, wild ginger, pomelo trees and Dai-style pavilions – popular for picnics. West of the park, across a long pond, is the recently constructed **Wat Bajie**, which contains a large Buddha image donated by a Buddhist foundation in Thailand. The gold-leaved image is in the Lanna or northern Thai (Chiang Saen) style and was installed in 1990. As at most Xishuangbanna temples, the monks study modern Thai as part of the curriculum, since most of their Buddhist textbooks come from Thailand.

There's a renovated temple at **Manjao** village. It's on the other side of the bridge over the Mekong. Walk there or hire a bike and explore down by the river. Other nearby villages within cycling or hiking distance are **Mangsha** and **Mengdian.**

Tropical Plant Research Institute
(rèdài zhíwù yánjiūsuǒ) 热带植物研究所

Worth a visit, but the management is too busy guiding cadres on inspection tours to bother with foreigners. Beside a large pond there's an exclusive guesthouse built in imitation Dai style, that is frequented by bigwigs attending conferences.

You can wander through the avenue of oil palms and around the outer grounds, but the inner sanctum requires special permission via CITS. After two days of valiant effort by the CITS woman, we were grudgingly granted entry. Since the minimum group size is five persons and there were two in our group, we paid the maximum price of Y5. Photography was only allowed in one part of the gardens – secret rubber plants elsewhere?

The walls of the institute building are smothered with a fantastic display of flowers. In the research gardens grow all sorts of tropical flowers and medicinal or food plants (cocoa, coffee, liquorice, cinnamon, mango). On the way out we were shown the rubber trees and the leaves of the 'sensitive' plant which curl when touched.

Peacock Lake
(gǎnlán bà)

This artificial lake in the centre of town isn't much but the small park next to it is pleasant. There's also a zoo, but the animals in the zoo are so ferociously baited by onlookers that you can't help feeling depressed. The gibbons just sat in their cage with no escape from the jabbing; one ape finally pulled the stick away from its attacker, then threw up its arms and grimaced in perfect imitation of its tormentor. There's a sad bear in a tiny cage, giant salamanders and a pair of huge pythons.

The 'English Language Corner' takes place here every Sunday evening, so this is your chance to exchange views or practise your English with the locals.

Workers' Cultural Palace

(gōngrén wénhuàgōng) 工人文化宫

Evening dances are staged here. Several travellers have raved about the Dance of the Peacock, a traditional Dai dance sometimes staged for visiting dignitaries here or at the Banna Hotel. You might be able to ferret out details from the Banna Hotel reception desk or CITS.

Bridge Over the Mekong

(mǐgòng qiáo) 湄公桥

The bridge is no technical wonder, but it does have a guard at each end and photography is forbidden. If rumour is correct, there was an attempt several years ago by a member of a disaffected minority to blow up the bridge. Jinghong is such a splendidly torpid town, it's hard to imagine the excitement.

I took my bike for a spin across the bridge and thought it would be great to stop halfway for one of those corny sunset pictures of the river. While taking a couple of photos I heard some strange noises behind me and turned to find a gun-toting soldier shouting what sounded like 'bike, bike' at me. I assumed this was an attempt at issuing a parking ticket so pointed at my bicycle and confirmed that it was a bike. The soldier became very excited and started pushing me back so I concluded that he was trying to say 'back, back'. After dutifully pushing my bike back to his guard house, I made signs to ask if I could leave the bike there while I took photos. His answer was to grab my arm and march me over to a mangy tree on the other side of the road. I indicated that the tree was indeed impressive, and was wondering if the soldier wasn't perhaps a frustrated gardener when I discerned a tiny, rusty, mangled sign: 'No photographs'.

At the other end of the bridge was another sign, in a slightly worse state of decomposition, which was wrapped round a steel support like a piece of washing. Ten minutes later I was taking photos beneath the bridge without any signs of disapproval from above.

The Chinese bridge fetish is alive and well in Jinghong.

Places to Stay

The *Banna Hotel (bǎnnà bīnguǎn)* close to the centre of town, about 15 minutes from the bus station on foot, is a colonial relic in a tropical garden with huge palm trees. Dubbed the 'Banana Hotel', it's a travellers' favourite, one of those rare hotels in China that hasn't murdered its character – yet. The double rooms at the back are great value at Y12 per person; the balcony outside has a view across the heat haze to the Lancang (Mekong). You can draw up a chair, open your Somerset Maugham short stories and drowse through the afternoon surrounded by bougainvillea. The dorm (Y8 per person) has a complete set of wicker furniture for elegant tea parties. The showers behind the dining room produce hot water from 5 to 7 pm. Double rooms with bath are Y40 a night.

The building to the right inside the entrance is the reception office. Impressionist postcards and special stamp issues are also sold. A small shop beside the entrance sells maps, brochures, Dai newspapers, ethnic clothing, wooden pipes, cold beverages and cigarettes.

Along Manting Lu in the Dai neighbourhood are about a dozen traditional Dai homes that double as restaurants and guesthouses. Basic rooms cost from Y3 to Y4 per person; you get a hard bed with a mosquito net in a small cubicle with plyboard walls and that's it. Washing facilities are outdoors, in the traditional Dai style.

Places to Eat

The *Dai Minority Guesthouse (dàizú fànguǎn)* does tremendous Dai food and is very popular with both foreign and Chinese customers. Try their roast fish, eel or roast beef cooked with lemon grass or served with peanut-and-tomato sauce. Vegetarians can order roast bamboo shoot prepared in the same fashion – sublime. Other mouthwatering specialities include fried river moss (sounds gross but it's excellent with beer) and spicy bamboo-shoot soup. For a different kind of rice, try the black glutinous kind. The upstairs balcony is a pleasant place to sit with a beer in the winter and read about the subzero temperatures in Beijing. The several other Dai restaurants along Manting Lu have similar menus.

The Banna Hotel dining room has a bilingual menu that includes several Dai dishes; it overlooks the river and is quite pleasant. It's often booked out with tour groups or visiting cadres, but the staff is usually happy to prepare a table off to the side for individual travellers.

There are several good restaurants along the road in front of the bus station.

Street markets sell coconuts, bananas, papayas, pomelos (a type of grapefruit), and pineapples. The pineapples, served peeled on a stick, are probably the best in China. The covered market near the Banna Hotel is at its busiest in the morning.

Getting There & Away

Air Jinghong's airport opened in the late '80s, thus allowing travellers with limited time away to visit Xishuangbanna without spending six days on buses back and forth from Kunming. The only problem is that it can be very difficult to book a seat in either direction without at least a week's advance notice. During holiday periods (especially the Water-Splashing Festival in April), figure on at least two or three weeks for advance booking. Flights go both ways on Monday, Tuesday, Saturday and Sunday; the fare is Y144 one way.

The CAAC booking office is closed most of the time; when it is open, anyone interested in air tickets is referred to the CITS office at the Banna Hotel. The locals say that this is because the CAAC staff receive a kickback from CITS's ticket surcharges.

Bus There are daily buses between Kunming and Jinghong. Buses booked at the Three Leaves Hotel cost Y40 and take only two days if there are no breakdowns or road blockages along the way. The road is notoriously treacherous, winding and prone to landslides but on the second (or third) day passes through incredible mountain scenery with rice terraces and groves of teak, banana, rubber and papaya. Buses from the main Kunming bus station cost the same but take from 2½ to three days. The only real difference between the two bus services is that the one from the Three Leaves Hotel departs a bit earlier in the morning and runs longer each day of the journey.

The usual towns selected by the bus driver for overnights along the route are Tongguan and Mojiang. Both have basic transit hotels next to their bus terminals that cost only Y2 for a bed, but there's always a mad scramble for bed assignments among passengers at the reception desk. In Tongguan, you can avoid the crowds by slipping out the back of the large transit hotel to a smaller guesthouse on a hillside. In Mojiang there are a couple of hotels just around the corner from the transit hotel/bus terminal with double rooms for Y10.

The bus station in Jinghong has frequent departures to Menghan, Menghai and Damenglong.

Getting Around

The Banna Hotel hires out bikes for Y3 a day. If you want a jeep or a minibus, CITS can help.

AROUND JINGHONG

There are several possibilities for side trips from Jinghong into the countryside by bus, boat, bicycle or foot. Many Dai villages have the word 'Meng' in their names, which is a Chinese rendering of the Thai-Lao-Dai word *muang*, an ancient Thai term for river valley settlements.

Menghai

(měnghǎi) 勐海

This uninspiring place serves as a centre for trips into the surrounding area. Perched on top of a nearby hill is an atrocious loudspeaker system which pounds the hapless inhabitants with distorted noise. The Sunday market attracts members of the hill tribes and the best way to find it is to follow the early-morning crowds. This is the only time when the town shows signs of life other than the dogs, chickens, pigs and cows cruising the street. There are a couple of drab hotels (Y3 per bed); one is at the main bus station.

Minibuses run from the minibus centre in Jinghong to Menghai every hour on the half hour from 7.30 am to 5.30 pm; the fare is Y2.8 and the trip takes about 90 minutes. Minibuses to Jinghong, Menghun and Jingzhen leave from a minibus centre in Menghai, about one km down the street from the main bus station.

Menghun

This tiny village is about 26 km south-west of Menghai. The Sunday market here begins buzzing around 7 am and lingers on through noon. The swirl of hill tribes and women sprouting fancy leggings, headdresses, earrings and bracelets alone makes the trip worthwhile. Although the market seems to be the main attraction, a temple and footpaths that wind through the lush hills behind the White Tower Hotel are also worth an extra day or two.

Places to Stay & Eat The *Phoenix Hotel (fènghuáng fàndiàn)* offers a view of main street activity and costs Y3 per night. The more secluded *White Tower Hotel* (through the archway to the right of the bus stop) is roomier and quieter; rates are also Y3. There are several good Dai restaurants along the main street, including the popular *Bienvenue*.

Getting There & Away There are no direct buses from Jinghong to Menghun. Catch one of the frequent minibuses from the minibus centre in Menghai for Y1.90 (45 minutes).

Jingzhen

In the village of Jingzhen, about 14 km north-west of Menghai, is the **Octagonal Pavilion (Bajiao Ting)** first built in 1701. The original structure was severely damaged during the Cultural Revolution, so the present renovated building isn't exactly thrilling. Take a close look at the new paintings on the wall of the temple. There are some interesting scenes which appear to depict PLA soldiers causing death and destruction during the Cultural Revolution; adjoining scenes depict Buddha vanquishing PLA soldiers, one of whom is waving goodbye as he drowns in a pond!

Jingzhen is a pleasant rural spot for walks along the river or the fishponds behind the village. Frequent minibuses from the minibus centre in Menghai go via Jingzhen.

Nannuoshan

(nánnúoshān) 南罗山

Nannuoshan is on the road between Jinghong and Menghai (17 km from Menghai). It's best done as a day trip from Menghai, providing you start early and return to the main road before dusk. The bus will drop you off close to a bridge; cross the bridge and follow the dirt track about six km uphill until you join a newly constructed main road.

About one km before the junction, you'll round a bend in the road and see a fence with a stile and stone benches beyond. This is the turn-off for the steps down to the overrated **King of Tea Trees (Cha Wang)**. According to the Hani, their ancestors have been growing tea for 55 generations and this tree was the first one planted. The tree is definitely not worth descending hundreds of steps to see; it is half-dead and covered with moss, graffiti and signs forbidding graffiti. A crumbling concrete pavilion daubed with red paint completes the picture.

The new highway has been bulldozed out of the mountain for the comfort of tourists who can now visit the hill tribes further up the mountain. When we were there, the Hani and Lahu villagers were quite friendly. Repeated exposure to tour buses is certain to cause changes. If you leave the main road, there's some pleasant hiking in the area, but don't expect villagers to automatically give you a bed for the night. A Hani villager did invite us into his stilt house for an excellent meal and some firewater that left us wobbling downhill.

The Hani (also known in adjacent countries as the Akha) are of Tibetan origin but according to folklore they are descended from frogs' eyes. They stick to the hills cultivating rice, corn and the occasional poppy. Trading takes place at weekly markets where the Dai obviously dominate the Hani, who seem only too keen to scamper back to their mountain retreats. Hani women wear headdresses of beads, feathers, coins and silver rings. At one remote market the women were very nervous and it was only when their backs were turned that I could inspect their headdresses constructed with French (Vietnamese), Burmese and Indian coins from the turn of the century.

Damenglong

(dà měnglóng) 大勐龙

Damenglong is about 70 km south of Jinghong and a few km from the Burmese border. This is another sleepy village worth visiting if you want to hike around the surrounding hills.

Things to See The much-touted tourist attraction here is the **White Pagoda** *(báită)* built in 1204. According to legend, Sakyamuni once visited Xishuangbanna and left behind footprints. The pagoda was built to honour a footprint which you can see under a niche below one of the nine stupas.

Old photos of the stupas show that they were once white; renovation has been effected with a hastily applied coat of silver paint which looks plain ugly. It's a peaceful spot with a handful of monks and fine views across the river towards Burma. Damenglong is worth a visit during the Tan Ta festival (late October or early November) when the White Pagoda attracts hundreds of locals to spectacular celebrations (dancing, rockets, paper balloons).

To reach the pagoda, walk back along the main road towards Jinghong for two km until you reach a small village with a temple on your left, close to the main road. Take the track to the left, pass the temple and continue uphill for 20 minutes to reach the pagoda. There are other temples in the area. The village of **Xiaojie**, about 15 km before Damenglong, is surrounded by Bulang, Lahu and Hani villages. Lahu women shave their heads; apparently the younger Lahu women aren't happy about this any more and use Mao caps to hide their shaven heads. The Bulang are possibly descended from the Lolo in northern Yunnan. The women wear black turbans with silver decorations; many of the designs are of shells, fish and marine life.

There's plenty of room for exploration in this area, although you're not allowed over the border.

Places to Stay & Eat There's a decrepit hotel next to the bus station or the slightly less decrepit *Damenglong Guesthouse (dàměnglóng bīnguăn)*. To reach the guesthouse, turn left out of the bus station and take the next street to the right – the guesthouse is at the end of the street. The manager has a severe drinking problem; hold onto your receipts and complete all arrangements with him before evening, when he tends to pass out under the table. Don't keep your valuables in your room because he likes to move beds and baggage around when he's sober. Beds cost Y2 in a four-bed dorm or Y3.50 in a double. Behind the guesthouse is a slimy reservoir and an even more turgid toilet.

Turn left out of the bus station and continue for a couple of minutes until you see a restaurant at the foot of the slope on your left. This is probably the only restaurant in town; here food is ladled from large bowls. The market women in the street sell fruit and a type of pancake. The Sunday market is worth visiting early in the morning to see the Hani and the Burmese who are officially allowed to cross the border.

Getting There & Away From the minibus centre in Jinghong there are frequent buses to Damenglong (Y4, 2½ hours). Buses for the return trip leave the Damenglong bus station between 6.40 am and 2 pm.

Menghan

Menghan (Gao En Bang) lies on the Mekong south-east of Jinghong. Half the reason for going here is the boat ride down the Mekong; the other half is the boat ride back. There is some Dai village life to watch – a market, temple and ferry on the other side of the river. Keep your eyes peeled for a glimpse of the

Crim, a monster in the Mekong which is said to devour cattle and people; an explorer called Baber described it less vividly as a blanket fish.

Places to Stay Follow the signs from the ferry landing to reach the clean and quiet *Farm Hotel* about 200 metres to the right. A huge triple with bath is Y6; doubles without bath are Y4.

The family-run *Dai Bamboo House* is a house on stilts with a dorm for Y4 per bed, small rooms for Y5 or larger rooms for Y6; all beds are on the floor in the traditional Dai style. The friendly family serves Dai food on tiny lacquered tables. A previous Japanese guest has drawn a map of the surrounding area to assist with exploration. To find the guesthouse, walk through the market, turn right and proceed past the post office till you see the house on the right.

Getting There & Away Most people visit Menghan by boat from Jinghong. The boat leaves daily at 8 am from the pier below the bridge in Jinghong. The pier is reached via a cobbled road which branches off to the right about 20 metres before the bridge. Mornings are cold on the river so take some warm clothing. Tickets cost Y2.50 on the lower deck or Y4.6 on the upper (better views) and the trip lasts about 1½ hours going downstream and three hours for the return upstream. The captain does some fancy manoeuvring to make a couple of stops en route. The return boat leaves at 1 pm. Some locals take their bikes, which they lash to the railings.

The buses from Jinghong to Menghan (Y2) ply an unbelievably potholed road that takes 1½ hours each way – consider taking the boat down river and the bus on the return trip.

Around Menghan

The stately **Wat Ban Suan Men**, a couple of km south-west of Menghan (ask at the Dai Bamboo House for directions) is said to be 730 years old and is one of the best surviving examples of Dai temple architecture in Yunnan.

South-east of Menghan, the Lancang (Mekong) River meets the Luosuo River from the north-east; up this river a bit is **Menglun**, the easternmost Dai village open to foreigners (by permit only). The Tropical Botanical Gardens here harbour some 3,000 species; a guesthouse on the grounds has basic rooms for Y5 per bed or Y12 for a room with bath. It is possible to boat here from Menghan, or from Jinghong you can catch a bus. A few travellers have done the trip in a day by bicycle from Jinghong. The PSB in Jinghong readily dispenses three-day permits for Menglun.

A Frenchman had his money stolen in Menghan by a kid from Canton who had been travelling with him for several days. When the Frenchman went to the shower, the Canton kid escaped with Y2000 FEC. The police assumed he'd taken one of the roads to the border. I heard vague reports about individuals from other parts of China who occasionally surfaced in this region either to escape across the border region or to buy *da yan* ('big smoke').

Back in 1981, border guards near Menghan were amazed to see a raft with a foreigner perched on top rushing down the river towards them. After pursuing and intercepting the raft, they discovered that the foreigner was a Canadian intent on floating into Thailand. The Canadian was reprimanded, packed off to his embassy in Beijing and turned loose again. Within a month, mystified Chinese security guards picked up the same man on the Sichuan-Tibet borders and had him deported.

The attraction, of course, was the Golden Triangle, the famous opium-growing area on the northern borders of Burma, Thailand and Laos.

Although the Chinese border guards don't always shoot on sight, there is firm evidence that plenty of bandits, militia or similar types on either side of the Mekong beyond the Chinese border do shoot. It is not clever to play around on the borders of the Golden Triangle.

Mengyang

Mengyang is 34 km east of Jinghong on the road to Simao. It's a centre for the Hani, Lahu and Floral-Belt Dai. Chinese tourists stop here to see a banyan tree shaped like an elephant.

From Mengyang it's another 19 km to Jinuo, which is home base for the Jinuo minority. Travellers have reported that the Jinuo are unfriendly, so you'll probably have to stay in Mengyang. Some minorities dislike tourists, and if this is the case with the Jinuo they should be left alone.

The Jinuo, sometimes known as the Youle, were officially 'discovered' as a minority in 1979. The women wear a white cowl, a cotton tunic with bright horizontal stripes, and a tubular black skirt. Ear-lobe decoration is an elaborate custom – the larger the hole and the more flowers it can contain the better. The teeth are sometimes painted black with the sap of the lacquer tree which serves the dual dental purpose of beautifying the mouth and preventing tooth decay or halitosis. Previously, the Jinuo lived in long houses with as many as 27 families occupying rooms on either side of the central corridor. Each family had its own hearth, but the oldest man owned the largest hearth, which was the first at the door. Long houses are rarely used now and it looks like the Jinuo are quickly losing their distinctive way of life.

DEHONG

(déhóng) 德宏

Dehong Dai-Jinpo Autonomous Prefecture is a remote, mountainous, densely forested area that juts into Myanmar (Burma) toward Myitkyina. As the name suggests, the main minorities living here are Dai and Jinpo. In July 1990, five towns in Dehong were opened to foreign tourists for the first time: **Baoshan**, **Tengchong**, **Longling**, **Luxi**, **Wanding** and **Ruili**. Although early reports say that Dehong is not as visually impressive as Xishuangbanna, its very remoteness is bound to be a major attraction for travellers – Wanding and Ruili are right on the Burmese border.

Baoshan is the gateway to Dehong; there are daily buses from both Xiaguan and Kunming (west bus station). Buses from Simao are also a possibility but rumour has it that the PSB in Simao won't allow foreigners to board Baoshan-bound buses there.

There's also a direct bus between from Kunming's No 3 Hostel (see the Kunming map) and Yingjiang, a town in the western part of Dehong; it leaves daily at 6 am. Passengers spend the night in Baoshan.

THE NORTH AND NORTH-WEST

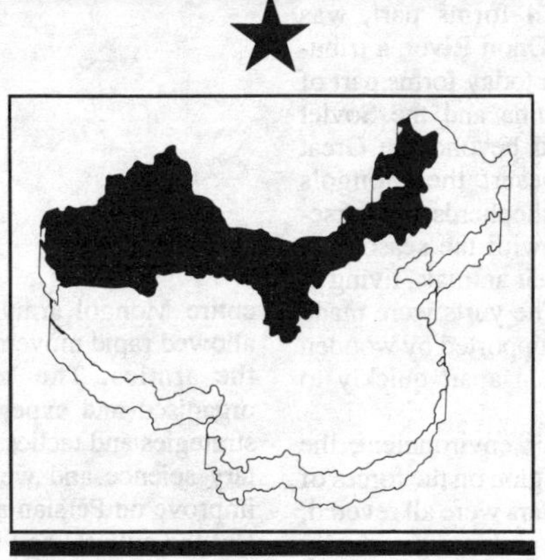

Inner Mongolia 内蒙古

HISTORY

The nomadic tribes to the north of China had always been a problem for China's rulers. The first emperor of the Qin Dynasty, Qin Shihuang, had the Great Wall built simply to keep them out.

The Mongol homeland, of which Inner Mongolia *(nèi měnggǔ)* forms part, was along the banks of the Onon River, a tributary of the Amur, which today forms part of the border between China and the Soviet Union. In the grassland beyond the Great Wall and the Gobi Desert the Mongols endured a rough life as shepherds and horse-breeders. They moved with the seasons in search of pastures for their animals, living in tents known as *yurts*. The yurts were made of animal hide usually supported by wooden rods, and could be taken apart quickly to pack onto wagons.

At the mercy of their environment, the Mongols based their religion on the forces of nature: moon, sun and stars were all revered, as were the rivers. The gods were virtually infinite in number, signifying a universal supernatural presence; the Mongol priests could speak to the gods and communicate their orders to the tribal chief, the Khan. The story goes that Genghis Khan overcame the power of the priests by allowing one to be killed for alleging the disloyalty of the Khan's brother – a calculated act of sacrilege which proclaimed the Khan's absolute power.

Mongol Empire

The Mongols were united by Genghis Khan after 20 years of warfare; by the year 1206 all opposition to his rule among the tribes had surrendered or been wiped out and the Mongol armies stood ready to invade China. Not only did the Mongols conquer China, they went on to conquer most of the known world, founding an empire which stretched from Burma to Russia.

It was an empire won on horseback; the

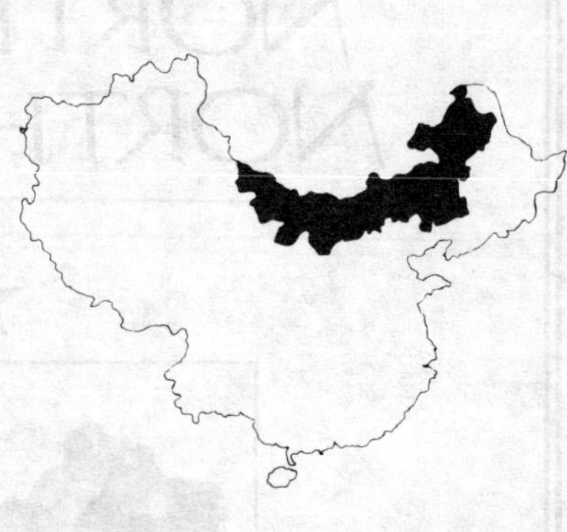

entire Mongol army was cavalry and this allowed rapid movement and deployment of the armies. The Mongols were highly organised and expert at planning complex strategies and tactics. They excelled in military science and were quick to adopt and improve on Persian and Chinese weaponry. But the cultural and scientific legacy of the Mongols was meagre. Once they abandoned their policies of terror and destruction, they became patrons of science and art, although not practitioners. Under the influence of the people they had conquered, they also adopted the local religions – mainly Buddhism and Islam.

The Mongol conquest of China was slow, delayed by campaigns in the west and by internal strife. Secure behind their Great Wall, the Chinese rulers had little inkling of the fury the Mongols would unleash in 1211, when the invasion of China began. For two years the Great Wall deterred them, but it was eventually penetrated through a 27-km gorge which led to the north Chinese plains. In 1215 a Chinese general went over to the Mongols and led them into Beijing. Nevertheless, the Chinese stubbornly held out, and the war in China was placed under the command of one of Genghis' generals so the Khan could turn his attention to the west.

Despite the death of Genghis Khan in 1227, the Mongols lost none of their vigour. The empire had been divided up by Genghis into separate domains, each domain ruled by one of his sons or other descendants. Ogadai was given China and was also elected the Great Khan in 1229 by an assemblage of princes. Northern China was subdued but the conquest of the south was delayed while the Khan turned his attention to the invasion and subjugation of Russia. With the death of Ogadai in 1241, the invasion of Europe was cancelled and Mangu Khan, a grandson of Genghis Khan, continued the conquest of China. He sent his brother Kublai and the general Subotai (who had been responsible for Mongol successes in Russia and Europe) to attack the south of China, which was ruled by the Song emperors. Mangu died of dysentery while fighting in China in 1259. Once again, the death of the Khan brought an end to a Mongol campaign on the brink of success.

Kublai was elected Great Khan in China, but his brother Arik-Boko challenged him for the title. Between the two there was a profound ideological difference. Arik-Boko led a faction of Mongols who wanted to preserve the traditional Mongol way of life, extracting wealth from the empire without intermingling with other races. Kublai, however, realised that an empire won on horseback could not be governed on horseback and intended to establish a government in China with permanent power concentrated in the cities and towns. The deaths of Kublai's enemies in the 'Golden Horde' (the Mongol faction which controlled the far west of the empire) and the defeat of Arik-Boko's forces by Kublai's generals enabled Kublai Khan to complete the conquest of southern China by 1279. It was the first and only time

Inner Mongolian Horseman

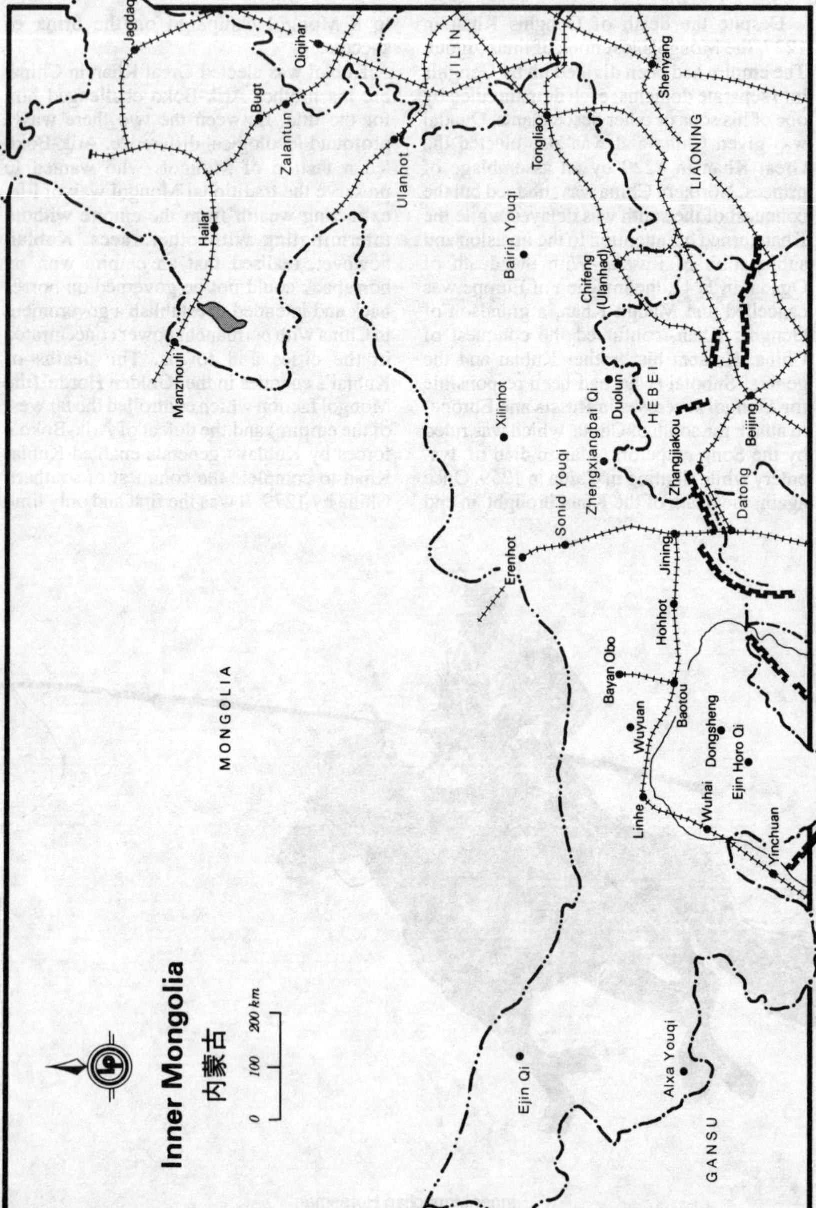
Inner Mongolia
内蒙古
0 100 200 km
MONGOLIA
JILIN
LIAONING
HEBEI
SHANXI
SHAANXI
NINGXIA
GANSU
Jagdaqi
Qiqihar
Bugt
Zalantun
Ulanhot
Hailar
Manzhouli
Shenyang
Tongliao
Bairin Youqi
Chifeng (Ulanhad)
Duolun
Xilinhot
Zhengxiangbai Qi
Sonid Youqi
Zhangjiakou
Beijing
Datong
Erenhot
Jining
Hohhot
Bayan Obo
Baotou
Wuyuan
Dongsheng
Ejin Horo Qi
Linhe
Wuhai
Yinchuan
Ejin Qi
Alxa Youqi

that China has been ruled in its entirety by foreigners.

The Mongols established their capital at Beijing, and Kublai Khan became the first emperor of the Yuan Dynasty. The Mongols improved the road system linking China with Russia, promoted trade throughout the empire and with Europe, instituted a famine-relief scheme and expanded the canal system which brought food from the countryside to the cities. It was into this China that foreigners like Marco Polo wandered, and his book *Description of the World* revealed the secrets of Asia to an amazed Europe.

The Mongols' conquest of China was also to lead to their demise. They alienated the Chinese by staffing the government bureaucracy with Mongols, Muslims and other foreigners. The Chinese were excluded from government and relegated to the level of second-class citizens in their own country. Landowners and wealthy traders were favoured, taxation was high and the prosperity of the empire did little to improve the lot of the peasant. Even if the Mongols did not mix with their Chinese subjects, they did succumb to Chinese civilisation: the warriors grew soft. Kublai died in 1294, the last Khan to rule over a united Mongol empire. He was followed by a series of weak and incompetent rulers who were unable to contain the revolts that spread all over China. In 1368 Chinese rebels converged on Beijing and the Mongols were driven out by an army led by Zhu Yuanzhang, who then founded the Ming Dynasty.

The entire Mongol empire had disintegrated by the end of the 14th century, and the Mongol homeland returned to the way of life it knew before Genghis Khan. Once again the Mongols became a collection of disorganised roaming tribes, warring among themselves and occasionally raiding China until the Qing emperors finally gained control over them in the 18th century.

Divided Mongolia

The eastern expansion of the Russian empire placed the Mongols in the middle of the border struggles between the Russians and the Chinese, and the Russian empire set up a 'protectorate' over the northern part of Mongolia. The rest of Mongolia was governed by the Chinese until 1911, when the Qing fell. For eight years Mongolia remained an independent state until the Chinese returned. Then in 1924 during the Soviet Civil War the Soviet Red Army pursued White Russian leaders to Urga (now Ulan Bator), where they helped create the Mongolian People's Republic by ousting the lama priesthood and the Mongol princes. The new republic has remained very much under Soviet domination.

During the war between China and Japan in the 1930s and '40s, parts of what is now Inner Mongolia were occupied by the Japanese, and Communist guerrillas also operated there. In 1936 Mao Zedong told Edgar Snow in Yan'an:

> As for Inner Mongolia, which is populated by both Chinese and Mongolians, we will struggle to drive Japan from there and help Inner Mongolia to establish an autonomous state...when the people's revolution has been victorious in China, the Outer Mongolian republic will automatically become part of the Chinese federation, at its own will.

But that was not to be. In 1945 Stalin extracted full recognition of the independence of Outer Mongolia from Chiang Kaishek when the two signed an anti-Japanese Sino-Soviet alliance. Two years later, with the resumption of the civil war in China, the Chinese Communists designated what was left to China of the Mongol territories as the 'Autonomous Region of Inner Mongolia'. With the Communist victory in 1949, Outer Mongolia did not join the People's Republic as Mao had said it would. The region remained firmly under Soviet control.

Since the Revolution

About 1½ million people live in the Mongolian People's Republic (Outer Mongolia). Inner Mongolia stretches across half of northern China and is inhabited by almost 19 million people. About two million of these are Mongols, a predominantly Buddhist people with some Muslims among them. The rest of the population is made up of about 16 million Han Chinese (concentrated in Baotou and Hohhot) and minority Huis, Manchus, Daurs and EEwenkis. The Mongolians are very much a minority in their own land.

Since 1949 the Chinese have followed a policy of assimilation of the Mongols. The Chinese language became a compulsory subject in schools, the populace was organised into sheep-farming co-ops and communes, and new railways and roads brought in Chinese settlers. Some of the old nomadic spirit can still be seen at the annual Nadam Fair, held at various grassland locations sometime between mid-July and early August. The fair has its origins in the ancient Obo-Worshipping Festival (an *obo* is a pile of stones with a hollow space for offerings – a kind of shaman shrine). The Mongolian clans make a beeline for the fairs on any form of transport they can muster, and create an impromptu yurt city. The event is a splash of

Inner Mongolian Farmer

colour if you can catch up with it, with competition archery, wrestling and horse-racing – sports the Mongolians excel at, having learned them at an early age. There's also occasional camel racing. Prizes vary from a goat to a fully-equipped horse. There are signs that the fair may be staged more often with the addition of shooting, motorcycling, storytelling, dancing and more trading.

Much of the Inner Mongolia region comprises vast areas of natural grazing land. The economy is based on stock breeding of cattle, sheep, horses and camels, and the region is the main source of tanned hides, wool and dairy products for China. The Greater Hinggan range makes up about one-sixth of the country's forests and is an important source of timber and paper pulp. The region is also rich in mineral reserves, particularly coal and iron ore. As it borders the Soviet Union, it is of paramount military importance to the Chinese.

The Mongolians are scattered throughout China's north-eastern provinces, as well as through Qinghai and Xinjiang. Their 'Inner Mongolia Autonomous Region' enjoys little or no autonomy at all. Outer Mongolia, ostensibly an independent nation, is dominated by the Soviet Union. Then there's a strange little piece of land to the north-west of Outer Mongolia called the Tuva Autonomous Soviet Socialist Republic. Originally called Tannu Tuva, it emerged as a semi-autonomous Mongolian state in 1926, and was renamed in 1945. (A smattering of Chinese have also ended up on the wrong side of the borders-in-triplicate; by a Beijing count there are 10,000 ethnic Chinese residing in Outer Mongolia, 6000 of them in Ulan Bator. Back in mid-1983 more than 600 were suddenly expelled by the Mongolian government and sent to China.)

Excessive fragmentation has led to a few absurdities; the Mongolian areas remain one of the biggest headaches for cartographers. It was not until 1962 that the border with Outer Mongolia was finally settled, though parts of the far north-east were disputed by the Soviet Union. Then in 1969 the Chinese carved up Inner Mongolia and donated bits of it to other provinces – they were reinstated in 1979. The Chinese seem sufficiently confident about the assimilation of the Mongols to talk about historical absurdities like 'Genghis Khan's Chinese armies' or the 'minority assistance in building the Great Wall'.

In 1981 when an Italian film crew rented the courtyard of Beijing's Forbidden City as a Marco Polo film location (at a reported cost of US$4000 a day – the Chinese originally wanted US$10,000 a day), a splendid assembly of horses and soldiers was laid on, the soldiers portrayed by PLA troops. The Chinese claimed the money was secondary and that historical accuracy was the thing at stake. However, they didn't like the Mongols being depicted as hated by the Song Dynasty Chinese they overran – after all, that conflicts with the Communist claim that China's minorities get along famously with the Han majority. It's rather an odd claim, since the Great Wall was built to keep out the ethnic minorities (referred to at the time less politely as 'barbarians'). More predictably, the Chinese vetoed some seduction scenes involving Chinese concubines and Mongol lechers.

CLIMATE

Siberian blizzards and cold currents rake the plains in winter – forget it! In winter you'll even witness the curious phenomenon of snow on the desert sand dunes. Summer (from June to August) brings pleasant temperatures, but the region is prone to occasional thunderstorms. Visiting from May to September is feasible, but pack warm clothing for spring or autumn.

HOHHOT

(hūhéhàotè) 呼和浩特

Hohhot became the capital of Inner Mongolia in 1952, serving as the administrative and educational centre. It was founded in the 16th century and, like the other towns, grew around its temples and lamaseries, now in ruins. Hide and wool industries are the mainstay, backed up by machine-building, a sugar refinery, fertiliser plants, a diesel-engine factory and iron and steel production. The population is around 700,000 – more than a million if the outlying areas are included.

'Hohhot' means 'green city' in Mongolian, and although it can be bleak in the dead of winter, it's reasonably green in summer and is certainly one of China's more pleasant cities.

Information

CITS The office (☎ 24494) is in the Inner Mongolia Hotel. The staff is helpful and friendly – good English spoken.

CITS turns on the culture in Hohhot, from the grasslands tour to the equestrian displays at the horse-racing ground. Horse-racing, polo and stunt riding are put on for large tour groups, if you latch onto one somehow – otherwise they take place only on rare festive occasions. Likewise with song and dance soirées. Check out local entertainment, such as events at the Red Theatre. Other things you might be able to wangle out of CITS if combining in-town sights with a grasslands sortie are a visit to the carpet works, or to the underground tunnelling system built to evacuate Hohhot residents to the Daqing mountains in the event of a Soviet bear hug.

Public Security Bureau This is in the vicinity of Renmin Park, near the corner of Zhongshan Lu and Xilin Guole Lu.

Money Most convenient for changing money are the Bank of China branches inside the Inner Mongolia Hotel and Zhaojun Hotel. The main branch is on Xinhua Dajie.

Inner Mongolia Museum

(nèi měnggǔ bówùgǔan) 内蒙古博物馆

Well presented and definitely worth a visit, this is the biggest attraction in town. The museum includes a large mammoth skeleton dug out of a coal mine; a fantastic array of Mongolian costumery, artefacts, archery equipment and saddles; and a yurt. The top floors are sometimes closed off. The flying horse on top of the museum is meant to symbolise the forward spirit of the Mongo-

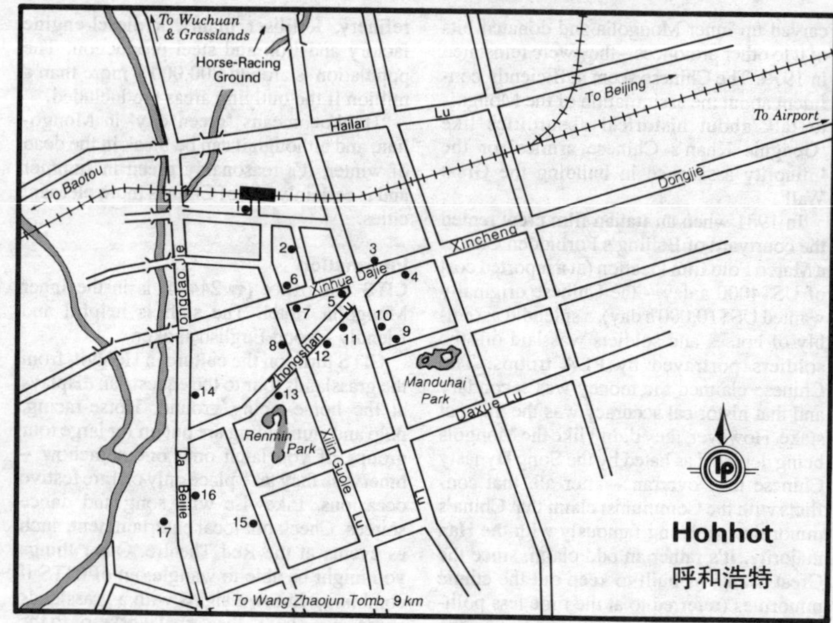

1 Long-Distance Bus Station
2 Hohhot Hotel
3 Department Store
4 Malaqin Restaurant
5 Inner Mongolia Museum
6 Zhaojun Hotel
7 Bank of China
8 CAAC
9 Inner Mongolia Hotel & CITS
10 Xincheng Hotel
11 Yikesai Restaurant
12 Post Office
13 Public Security Bureau
14 Great Mosque
15 Five Pagoda Temple
16 Xiletuzhao Temple
17 Dazhao Temple

1 长途汽车站
2 呼和浩特宾馆
3 百货大楼
4 马拉沁
5 内蒙古博物馆
6 昭君大酒店
7 中国银行
8 中国民航
9 内蒙古饭店
10 新城宾馆
11 伊克赛
12 邮局
13 公安局外事科
14 清真大寺
15 五塔寺
16 席勒图召
17 大召

lian people. The museum is at 1 Xinhua Dajie and only costs Y0.30.

Five Pagoda Temple

(wǔtǎ sì) 五塔寺

This miniaturised structure dating back to 1740 is now bereft of its temple, leaving the Five Pagodas standing on a rectangular block. The pagodas are built with glazed bricks and are inscribed in Mongolian, Sanskrit and Tibetan. Cut into niches are small Buddhist figures; around the back is a screen wall with an astronomical chart inscribed in Mongolian. The Five Pagodas are on the bus No 1 route.

Old Town

(jiùchéng) 旧城

The old part of town directly north of the tomb of Wang Zhaojun has some interesting sights. Down some alleys off a main street is the Dazhao Temple *(dàzhào)*, which has almost fallen apart – a cottage-industry clothing concern now occupies the grounds.

Not far from it is the Xiletuzhao Temple *(xílètúzhào)*. It's the stomping ground of the 11th Grand Living Buddha, who dresses in civvies and is apparently active. There's nothing special to see though. The original temple burned down and the present one was built in the 19th century; the Chinese-style building has a few Tibetan touches. The swastika symbols on the exterior have long been used in Persian, Indian, Greek and Jewish cultures – they symbolise truth and eternity (no relation to the mirror-image Nazi swastika).

Further north of Xiletuzhao is the Great Mosque *(qīngzhēn dà sì)*, which is not so great and is in sad shape. It dates to the Qing Dynasty, with later expansions.

These temples are incidentals; the main action is on the streets. Around the area of the Dazhao Temple are some fascinating adobe houses, low and squat with decorated glass windows. Markets in Hohhot are brisk – in summer at least. Recommended is the north-south strip running from west of the bus station (Tongdao Lu) as far as the two temples. The busy corner of Tongdao Lu and Xinhua Lu is the place for housewares and storytelling. A food market with a courtyard entrance can be found near the Museum of Inner Mongolia. There's another market on the east side of Renmin Park.

Wang Zhaojun Tomb

(zhāojūn mù) 王昭君墓

The tomb of this Han Dynasty concubine to Emperor Yuandi (1st century BC) is a bit of a bore – although it does permit some countryside viewing at the edge of town. The tomb is nine km from the city on the bus No 14 route.

Places to Stay

Hohhot Hotel (hūhéhàotè bīngǔan) is near the train station and has dorms for Y13 to Y18. Doubles are Y36. In terms of convenience, it's a good place to stay, but not a particularly nice hotel.

Most budget travellers prefer the *Xincheng Hotel (xīnchéng bīngǔan)* (☎ 27231). It's the cheapest place in town with nice dorms with three beds each for Y10. Magnificent double rooms with private bath go for Y60. With large rooms and lovely spacious grounds, it's rather like living in a park. The gift shop has maps and there are bicycle rentals. It's two km from the railway station. Unfortunately, no bus runs nearby. Take bus No 5 two stops from the station to get within 10 minutes' walking distance.

Just next door to the Xincheng Hotel is the *Inner Mongolia Hotel (nèi ménggǔ fàndiàn)*, a shiny new high-rise where CITS is located. Doubles cost Y80 and there are some so-so dormitories for Y15 in the old wing.

Hohhot's fancy joint-venture hotel is the *Zhaojun Hotel* (☎ 28230) *(zhāojūn dàjiǔdiàn)*, 11 Xinhua Dajie, where doubles cost from Y80 to Y120.

Places to Eat

The Chinese restaurant in the *Inner Mongolia Hotel* is very cheap and very good. The *Zhaojun Hotel Restaurant* is outrageously expensive. The *Malaqin* (horseman) restaurant is great – they have Chinese and Mongolian food. Try their Mongolian hotpot, roasted lamb and kebab. Their prices are moderate even though they cater to foreign tour groups. *Yikesai* is another good restaurant.

Things to Buy

The Minority Handicraft Factory at the south side of town on the bus No 1 route has a retail shop for tour visits. There is a limited selection, but wares include inlaid knife and chopstick sets, daggers, boots, embroidered shoes, costumes, brassware, blankets and curios. There is a better selection of minority clothing on the 2nd floor of the government department store next to the huge sign 'Minority Markets' on Xinhua Lu.

Getting There & Away

Air CAAC's office (☎ 42722) is on Xilin Guole Lu (see map). Hohhot airport is about 15 km east of the city.

There are flights to Baotou; Beijing (six times weekly, Y148); Canton (four times weekly, Y933); Chifeng; Hailar; Nanjing; Shanghai (twice weekly, Y542); Shenyang; Shijiazhuang; Taiyuan; Tongliao; Ulanhot; Wuhan; Xi'an (twice weekly, Y495); and Xilinhot (three times weekly, Y170).

Inner Mongolian Vendor

Bus There are sporadic bus connections between Hohhot and Datong. Buses to Baotou go once every two hours or so. The most useful bus connection for travellers is to Dongsheng, departing at 7.30 am.

Train Hohhot is on the Beijing-Lanzhou railway line that cuts a long loop through Inner Mongolia; about 2½ hours out of Beijing you'll pass fragments of the Great Wall. On the fastest trains Beijing-Hohhot is a 12-hour trip, Datong-Hohhot is five hours, Baotou-Hohhot is three hours, Yinchuan-Hohhot is 12 hours. It's possible to buy one ticket from Beijing to Lanzhou, get off and have a look at each town and continue on with the same ticket. Train frequency is highest between Hohhot and Beijing, lower between Yinchuan and Hohhot, and gets down to twice a day between Lanzhou and Yinchuan. There are twice-daily connections between Taiyuan and Datong, where a connection to Hohhot can be made.

Getting Around

Hohhot is reasonably small and you can go a long way on a pair of wheels, weather permitting. Bikes can be hired at both the Xincheng and Inner Mongolia hotels, and there are numerous bike stalls along the main road to the left of the station. Prices average Y0.50 per hour, Y2 for half a day, and Y4.50 for the whole day. Passport or similar ID is required.

You can get a detailed city map (in Chinese only), which includes surrounding regions, from the Xincheng Hotel. Check with CITS or the hotel staff for bus numbers for your proposed route. Bus No 1 runs from the railway station to the old part of the city in the south-west corner.

AROUND HOHHOT

About 15 km west of Hohhot, the Sino-Tibetan monastery Wusutuzhao is hardly worth looking at although the surrounding arid landscape is spectacular. About 20 km east of Hohhot, along the airport road, is the topless Wanbuhuayanjing Pagoda, a seven-storey octagonal tower built with bricks and wood. It dates from the Liao Dynasty (10th-12th centuries). The pagoda can be reached by a half-hour suburban train ride.

Grasslands
(cǎoyúan) 草原

These are not really worth the cost or effort in getting there, since you can see much the same thing at Dongsheng and even stay there in a yurt for a fraction of what CITS charges. Or if you want to see real Mongols, read the section of this book about Xilinhot. Nevertheless, the grassland tours continue to attract travellers, so if you can afford the ticket you might want to consider it.

Tours Tours to the grasslands are organised by the Hohhot CITS, which has a stable of vehicles ranging from jeeps to buses to take you out there. The rules of the game – negotiate! Cashing in on the magic draw of 'Mongolia' is the name of the game here, and the less you bargain the bigger the rip-off. Most of Hohhot's population is Han Chinese. The Mongolians are out on the grasslands, supposedly roaming around on their horses or drinking cream tea (a mixture of camel's milk and salt) in their yurts. For pure theatre, nothing beats the CITS Grasslands Tour.

As for visions of the descendants of the mighty Khan riding the endless plains, the herds of wild horses, the remnants of Xanadu – make sure you worm a detailed itinerary out of CITS so you can work out if it's worth the price. The 'real' country for Mongolians is closer to the border further north. Grasslands and yurt dwellings can be seen in other parts of China – in Xinjiang for example. Also, deprived of rain for a week or so, the verdant pasturelands can turn a shrivelled shade of yellow. Take warm, windproof clothing – there's a considerable wind-chill factor even at the height of summer.

There are three grasslands open for CITS tours: Xilamuren, 80 km from Hohhot; Gegentala 170 km away in Siziwang Qi; Huitengxile 120 km from Hohhot – the most beautiful but least visited. There are no group tours to Huitengxile unless you make special arrangements. All tours *must* be arranged through CITS – you can't simply hire a taxi and go yourself. Prices payable in FEC are as follows:

to Xilamuren

Persons	1 Day	2 Days	3 Days
1	369	452	559
2-3	210	267	338
4-6	112	149	188
7-10	83	114	147
11-20	78	108	139
over 20	79	108	140

to Gegentala

Persons	2 Days	3 Days
1	608	715
2-3	345	416
4-6	186	225
7-10	138	171
11-20	130	161
over 20	132	164

to Huitengxile

Persons	2 Days	3 Days
1	512	619
2-3	297	368
4-6	161	200
7-10	122	155
11-20	115	146
over 20	115	147

Being There Here's a two-day itinerary to give you some idea of the picnics and outings in Inner Mongolia.

Day 1 2.30 pm. We discover the first day is half over – the tour is by calendar days. After a three-hour drive over the mountains to the grasslands plateau we arrive at Ulantuge commune. The major industry here seems to be shepherding tourists. It's the first commune from Hohhot, so lots of groups are processed through this meatworks. On arrival a woman pops out of a door in Mongolian costume to greet us (still, however, wearing slacks underneath and a tell-tale pair of tennis shoes). Dinner is very good – baozi and meat dishes. The guide motions toward the yurt compound at the edge of town. These are on fixed brick and concrete foundations with 75-watt light bulbs dangling from each yurt-hole. Only for tourists – the natives live in sensibly thick-walled brick structures. The outhouse is primitive – I'm wondering if the joke is on us, and whether the locals are sitting on porcelain models with flushers. A clammy damp cold permeates the yurts, sufficient to send an arthritic into spasms.

Day 2 Breakfast is at 8.30, a decidedly Western hour. We take advantage of the lull to poke around – post office, school, souvenir shop. There's a large temple structure with Sino-Tibetan features, probably 18th-century, with colonnade, intricate windows and doorways, devilish frescoes – but entry is barred. Part of the complex around it has been turned into a dining hall for receiving the likes of us. At breakfast I ask the guide (who sits at a separate table with the driver) a few questions in relation to the tourist industry which he either ignores, evades, or pretends not to understand. Back at the yurts are two ruddy-cheeked gentlemen waiting with two moth-eaten animals. The ruddy complexion comes from wind chill – the animals have not weathered it so well. One is, I guess you might call it, yes, a horse. The other is the worst-looking excuse for a camel I've seen. I mean, camels are ugly, but this one had just about fallen apart. It's strictly a mounted picture-taking session; the attendants keep these pathetic specimens on leashes, explaining that they're too dangerous to be ridden solo.

At 9.30 am the driver whips over the grasslands – very nice, peaceful, dirt paths. It's reassuring to see some real grass in China. Hong Kongers get most enthralled about this; there isn't too much of the stuff around Kowloon. We stop to observe a flock of sheep – the shepherd poses for photos. Then, the highlight of the tour, a visit to a typical Mongolian family. They live in a three-room brick dwelling, and there, smack on the wall as you enter, is a giant poster of a koala (New South Wales Tourist Authority) which confirms my impression that perhaps I'd be better off on an Australian sheep farm. The typical family is wearing standard Han ration clothing (did we catch them with their pants down?) but they bring out Mongolian garb for dress-up photo-sessions – for us to dress up, that is. They've obviously given up. Parked out the back is their form of transport – bicycles. It puzzles me why we are brought here when there are yurt dwellers in the area. The only explanation I can think of is that they're further out from the Ulantuge commune, and the driver is too lazy or has been given other directions. Or perhaps any real Mongolian wants nothing to do with CITS – a view with which I can sympathise.

Motoring off again, we visit an obo, a pile of stones in the middle of nowhere. When nomads used to gather for mid-May festivals, each would bring a stone and lay it here. We go back to Ulantuge for a banquet-style lunch; a sheep is slaughtered and barbecued for a surcharge. After lunch, the guide announces that it's time for *xiūxi* – the rest period will be 2½ hours. We wave goodbye to the woman near the yurt compound (as she struggles to get into her Mongolian robes in time), and head back for Hohhot. We arrive around 4.30 that afternoon; the tour is supposed to last until 6 pm and there is a filler of sights around town that I've already seen and which don't require a guide.

In sum, the guides are lethargic and unhelpful; your real time on the grasslands amounts to about two hours, plus the drive there and back. You spend a lot of time sleeping, eating, waiting and taking pictures of each other. The three and four-day itineraries are probably much the same, with feeble archery or song and dance routines thrown in. The best part of the trip is, unexpectedly, the food – the meals were banquet-size and tasty, something that the individual traveller is not used to.

Perhaps you could try to lose your guides; horse-drawn carts seem to be a common form of transport on the communes, and of course the grassland is perfect horse country – though this suggestion would probably horrify CITS. (A Hohhot tourist leaflet shows foreigners riding in a decorated camel cart with suspension and truck tyres.) Anyway, even the small Mongolian horse is being phased out – herdsmen can now purchase motorcycles (preferred over bicycles because of substantial wind force), and helicopters and light aircraft are used to round up steers and spot grazing herds.

XILINHOT

(xīlínhàotè) 锡林浩特

From all accounts, if you're interested in pursuing the topic of the disappearing Mongols this is your best bet. Xilinhot is 500 km north-east of Hohhot as the crow flies. It is the headquarters of the large Xilin Gol League, which is subdivided into 10 districts and over 100 communes. The league covers an area of 172,000 sq km, with a population of under a million – a quarter of whom are Mongolian. The Xilin Gol League was a centre of Mongolian nationalism in the 1930s but today the major occupation is the tending of sheep, cattle, goats, camels and horses – some five million of them. Industry is minimal, though petroleum deposits have been discovered. Ensconced in Xilinhot is the Beizimiao, a large, dilapidated lamasery in Chinese style dating from the Qing Dynasty.

The bus station in Hohhot is unwilling to sell tickets, so you must fly from Hohhot. There are three flights weekly and the fare is Y170. Fortunately, you can return overland. To visit Xilinhot, a travel permit *(tōngxíngzhèng)* is needed but can be easily obtained from Public Security.

Once you arrive in Xilinhot, you can only stay in the Baima Fandian, where triple rooms are Y60. CITS is in the same building. Both CITS and the manager of the Baima Fandian are nothing but trouble. One group of foreigners booked an overpriced CITS tour, but the hotel manager cancelled it because he wanted to force them to go on an even more expensive tour with his hotel. The foreigners said forget it and went out on the local bus to visit nearby villages. This also requires another permit, but it's readily available from Public Security in Xilinhot.

Because we speak Chinese and had a lot of luck we could manage in Xilinhot. The CITS is ruled by someone who is interested in your money and nothing more! In Xilinhot itself there is nothing to do – there are no buses in town nor taxis. We would advise other tourists to arrange a tour via CITS Hohhot. Xilinhot isn't worth all the trouble (permits for everything).

Henneke & Erzsebet

If you can put up with the avarice and antics of CITS, they have jeep excursions to communes 50 km and 130 km away, with overnight stops in yurts, tea-tasting and campfires. Should you strike a guaranteed Mongol you might get a cup of their cream tea. It's made of camel's milk and salt, and apparently tastes revolting; it's also most impolite to refuse a cup.

You can leave Xilinhot overland by a combination of bus and train. This also requires another permit – again, Xilinhot Public Security will readily issue these permits (smile at them, we want to keep them friendly). To return to Hohhot or Beijing, you must take the bus to Sonid Youqi *(sūnítè yòuqí)* on the Erenhot-Jining railway line. From Sonid Youqi, there is only one train weekly to Jining (Jining is on the Beijing-Hohhot line). At the time of this writing, the train departs Sonid Youqi on Saturday, but check with the local authorities in Xilinhot because the schedule could change.

CITS and the Baima Fandian management have been telling travellers that they must exit Xilinhot by taxi for Y1600. Your best bet is to ask at the Public Security Bureau or the bus company.

BAOTOU

(bāotóu) 包头

The largest city in Inner Mongolia lies on the northernmost reaches of the Yellow River, to the west of Hohhot. Previously set in an area of underdeveloped grasslands inhabited by the Mongols, the town underwent a radical change when the Communists came to power in 1949. In the next decade, a 1923 railway line linking the town with Beijing was extended south-east to Yinchuan, and roads were constructed to facilitate access to the region's iron, coal and other mineral deposits. Today, Baotou is an industrial city of around 800,000 people.

Baotou is a huge town; 20 km of dismal urban sprawl separate the eastern and western parts of the city. The station for the western section is Baotou station *(bāotóu zhàn)*; for the eastern section it's Baotou east station *(bāotóu dōng zhàn)*. A bus from Baotou east station to Hohhot is Y10 for the three hour trip – an extra Y2 for Baotou station. This extra fare will be collected on the bus, not when you buy your ticket in Hohhot.

Information

CITS This office (☎ 24615) is in the Baotou Guesthouse. They have some excellent English speakers and can provide maps.

Public Security Bureau This is in the same compound as the Baotou Guesthouse.

Money The Bank of China is in western Baotou at the corner of A'erding Dajie and Gangtie Dajie, close to the Baotou Guesthouse.

Things to See

A purple cloud hangs over the western horizon of the city. The source of these colourful sunsets is the Baotou Iron & Steel Company *(bāotóu gāngtiě gōngsī)* which was supervised by the Soviets until their exit in 1960. The original plan foresaw use of ore from Bayan Obo (about 140 km further north). Unfortunately, the local ore couldn't make the grade and the company now imports the

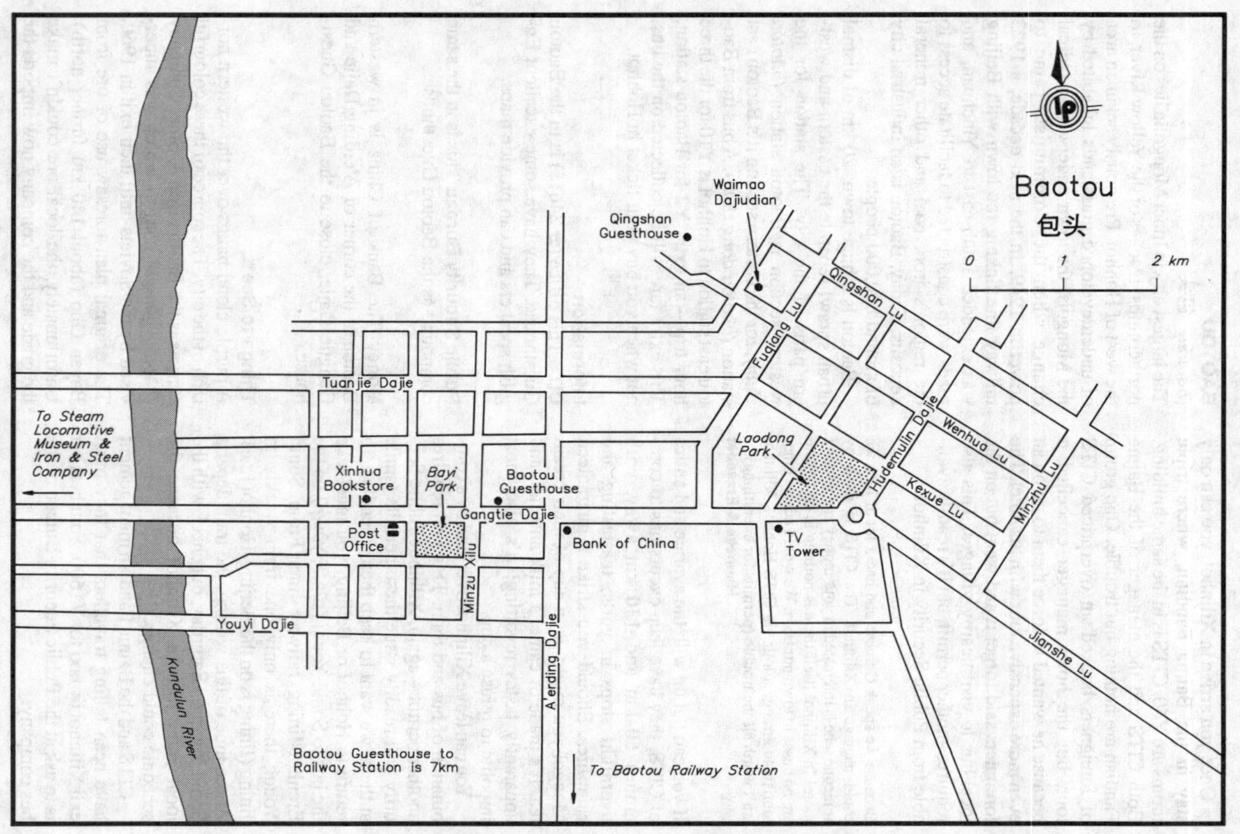
Baotou
包头
0
1
2 km
Waimao Dajiudian
Qingshan Guesthouse
Qingshan Lu
Fuqiang Lu
Hudemulin Dajie
Wenhua Lu
Minzhu Lu
Kexue Lu
Laodong Park
TV Tower
Jianshe Lu
Tuanjie Dajie
To Steam Locomotive Museum & Iron & Steel Company
Xinhua Bookstore
Bayi Park
Baotou Guesthouse
Gangtie Dajie
Post Office
Bank of China
Minzu Xilu
Youyi Dajie
A'erding Dajie
Kundulun River
Baotou Guesthouse to Railway Station is 7km
To Baotou Railway Station

stuff from Australia. If you're interested, CITS does tours of the steelworks.

There is a small Steam Locomotive Museum *(zhēngqì hŭochē bówùgŭan)*. CITS offers tours but they get few takers.

Places to Stay – West Baotou

The *Baotou Guesthouse (bāotóu bīngŭan)* on Gangtie Dajie is where most travellers stay. A pretty hostess dressed in colourful Mongolian robes stands by the front door looking incredibly bored. Doubles cost from Y40 to Y200. In theory, the dormitories only cost Y15, but if you are by yourself you must book the whole room *(bāofáng)*. If arriving by train, get off at Baotou Zhan. The station is seven km from the hotel – take bus No 1. If arriving by bus from Hohhot, you can ask them to drop you off right in front of the hotel.

Your other alternative is a dumpy little hotel, the *A'erding Fandian* next to Baotou station. Doubles are Y20. It's just to your right as you exit the station. There is nothing around the railway station other than a few pushcarts, but if you're only staying in Baotou to catch some sleep before heading elsewhere, this hotel will do.

Cadres like to stay at the *Qingshan Guesthouse* (☎ 34091) *(qīngshān bīngŭan)* where doubles are Y120. There is no public transport to this isolated hotel, only taxis.

Places to Stay – East Baotou

If you are not staying long, but are stopping to see Wudangzhao Monastery or Genghis Khan's Mausoleum near Dongsheng, get off the bus or train at Baotou east station. The *Donghe Guesthouse* (☎ 43352) *(dōnghé bīngŭan)* is about a 15-minute walk (or take bus No 5) up Nanmenwai Dajie in front of the station. Doubles range from Y40 to Y100. There's a convenient, run-down Chinese hotel on the right of the square in front of the station and they take foreigners. Triples cost Y20. It may be noisy at night, but the bus station (for Wudangzhao Monastery, Dongsheng and Hohhot) is opposite the railway station.

Getting There & Away

You can get tickets at the airport, which is two km south of Baotou east station *(bāotóu dōng zhàn)*. You can also buy tickets at the Baotou Guesthouse. There are flights from Baotou to Beijing, Hohhot, Taiyuan and Xi'an.

Getting Around

Bus No 10 stops close to the Baotou Guesthouse and shuttles between the western and eastern sections of Baotou in 45 minutes.

AROUND BAOTOU

Wudangzhao Monastery

(wŭdāngzhào) 五当召

The main tourist attraction is the large Wudangzhao Monastery about 2½ hours from the city by bus. This monastery of the Gelukpa (Yellow Sect) of Tibetan Buddhism was built around 1749 in typical Tibetan style with flat-roofed buildings. It once housed 1200 monks. The ashes of seven reincarnations of the monastery's Living Buddha are kept in a special hall. Today all religious activity is restricted to a handful of pilgrims and dispirited doorkeeper monks who take the Y1 admission fee.

For the crowds of day-tripping, photo-clicking Han Chinese this is no place for religion. The surrounding hillsides are carpeted with hundreds of smashed bottles and piles of garbage. Try and walk into the hills away from the pandemonium; the site has a peculiar strength in its secretive, brooding atmosphere.

Bus No 7 leaves for the monastery at 7 am from the bus station at Baotou east station. To make sure of a seat, it's best to buy tickets the evening before. Only the 7 am bus goes all the way to the monastery; the other departures stop about 15 km before it, so you'd be left with some hitching or a long walk. The bus drops you off about one km below the monastery.

For the return trip, catch the same bus from the same place at 4 pm (check with the driver when you arrive). You may also be able to get a lift back with other vehicles from the car park in front of the monastery.

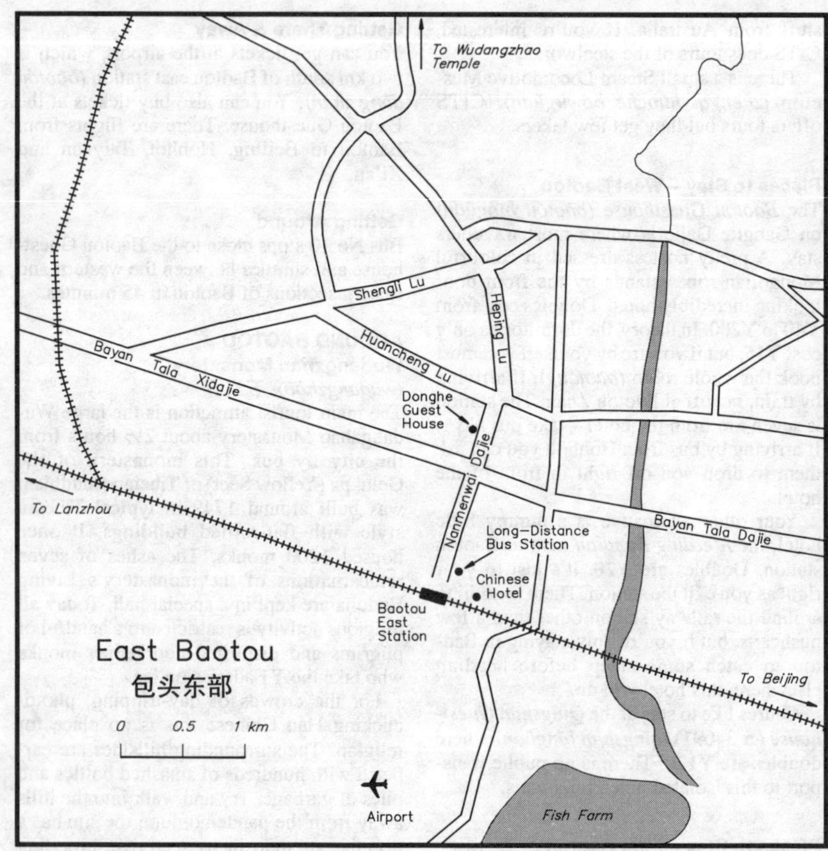

There's a basic dorm with beds for Y5 on the west side of the monastery, and a slightly better deal for Y7 on the east side. CITS organises tours, but you can easily manage on your own. Take a torch if you want to see anything inside the monastery.

DONGSHENG

(dōngshēng) 东胜

Dongsheng lies south of Baotou and serves as a staging post for Ejin Horo Qi *(yījīn hùolùo qí)*, the site of Genghis Khan's Mausoleum. Looks a bit like a Wild West town, with wind, dust, sand and donkeys. A lot of building is going on though, but it will probably be a while before they turn it into another Beijing.

There are at least two hotels for foreigners. The Waimao Dajiudian is a 100-metre walk to the right of this junction on the opposite side of the road. Chinese on conference junkets and groups of foreign tourists often book out the small hotel, but independent travellers are quoted prices between Y10 and Y30 per person, depending on the room. Most travellers stay at the cheaper Yimeng Binguan, 150 metres to the left of the junction on the same side of the road. This is a much larger hotel with triples at Y6.50 per person. The receptionist takes your passport and goes to the hotel's 'Passport Security Office' presumably to check if you're on the list of foreign spies. Assuming you're not from the CIA, your passport will be returned and you can check in.

The best restaurant in town is the Minzu Canting. It's diagonally opposite the Yimeng Binguan, just past the first crossroads to the right. Delicious yoghurt is on sale from stands all around the town.

Getting There & Away

Most travellers take the bus directly from Hohhot – departs at 7.30 am, takes six hours and costs Y21. This bus is amazingly comfortable, with videos included, and there's good scenery along the way.

Another early morning bus runs to Dongsheng from Baotou east station *(bāotóu dōng zhàn)* and takes three hours.

GENGHIS KHAN'S MAUSOLEUM

(chéngjí sīhàn língyúan) 成吉思汗陵国

Buses leave Dongsheng bus station at 7 am and take one hour to get to Ejin Horo Qi *(yījīn hùolùo qí)*, which is 25 km from the Genghis Khan Mausoleum. The fare is Y1.20. Some of these buses continue all the way to the mausoleum, others will only drop you off in Ejin Horo Qi from where you take a minibus (30 minutes, Y3) to the mausoleum. Buy tickets the day before – the bus to Ejin Horo Qi is usually packed solid by departure time, and even more passengers are added en route.

In 1954 what are said to be the ashes of the Khan were brought back from Qinghai (where they had been taken to prevent them from falling into the hands of the Japanese), and a large Mongolian-style mausoleum was built near Ejin Horo Qi. The Cultural Revolution did enough damage to keep the renovators busy for eight years and the result looks new. Interestingly enough, the cult of Genghis Khan has picked up again in Inner Mongolia today. Ceremonies are held four times a year at the mausoleum to honour his memory. Butter lamps are lit, *khadas* (ritual scarves) presented and whole cooked sheep piled high before the Khan's stone statue while chanting is performed by Mongolian monks and specially chosen elders from the Daur nationality.

Photographers outside the mausoleum have robes so you can dress up and have your photo taken posing as the Great Khan. Inside are displays of Genghis Khan's martial gear and statue. Various yurts contain the biers of Genghis and his close relatives. The huge frescoes around the walls are done in cartoon style to depict important stages in the Khan's rise to megastardom – all that's missing are bubble captions with 'pow' or 'zap'.

At the end of the dirt road to the right of the mausoleum's entrance, go one km to reach a tourist yurt campground *(ménggǔbāo)*. It costs Y2 to get in, at least Y10 to stay there, but it's worth looking at even if you don't spend the night. Nice grasslands with horses, sheep, goats and cows, plus some interesting buildings with traditional clothing, warrior outfits and riding equipment inside.

XANADU

About 320 km north of Beijing, tucked away near

Duolun in Inner Mongolia, are the remains of Xanadu, the great Kublai Khan's palace of legendary splendour. Marco Polo visited the Khan in the 13th century and recorded his impressions of the palace:

> There is at this place a very fine marble palace, the rooms of which are all gilt and painted with figures of men and beasts and birds, and with a variety of trees and flowers, all executed with such exquisite art that you regard them with delight and astonishment.
>
> Round this palace a wall is built enclosing a compass of 16 miles, and inside the Park there are fountains and rivers and brooks, and beautiful meadows, with all kinds of wild animals (excluding such as are of ferocious nature), which the Emperor has procured and placed there to supply food for his gerfalcons and hawks. Moreover (at a spot in the Park where there is a charming wood) he has another Palace built of cane. It is gilt all over, and most elaborately finished inside. The Lord abides at this Park of his, dwelling sometimes in the Marble Palace and sometimes in the Cane Palace for three months of

the year, to wit, June, July and August; preferring this residence because it is by no means hot; in fact it is a very cool place. When the 28th day of August arrives, he takes his departure, and the Cane Palace is taken to pieces.

In the 19th century Samuel Taylor Coleridge (who never went near the place) stoked his imagination with some opium and composed 'Kubla Khan', a glowing poem about Xanadu that has been on the set menu for students of English literature ever since.

Over the centuries the deserted palace has crumbled back to dust and the site has been visited by very few foreigners. In 1986 a couple of British students, Louisa Slack and William Hamilton-Dalrymple, followed Marco Polo's original route from Jerusalem to Xanadu. The palace remains are close to Duolun, which is off limits to foreigners, so the local PSB ejected the British duo from the region but compassionately arranged their exit via the legendary site, where all photography was forbidden. The PSB officers must have doubted the sanity of the foreigners, who proceeded to chant Coleridge's poem while pouring a small bottle of oil from the Holy Sepulchre in Jerusalem (the same gift Marco Polo had once brought for the Khan) onto the dilapidated site of the

Kublai Khan

Khan's throne. According to the students, very little now remains of Xanadu (locals call it Shang-du) and it is scheduled for clearance as a wheat prairie. Roll over Kublai!

JAGDAQI

(jiāgédáqí) 加格达奇

This is an unexciting railway junction and the administrative centre of the Oroqen Autonomous Area in the region of the Greater Hinggan mountain range. For more information about the Oroqens, see the Heilongjiang chapter in this book.

You have to approach this area from Harbin in Heilongjiang Province. An express train runs once daily from Harbin via Qiqihar to Jagdaqi, in about 14 hours. A travel permit is needed – apply at PSB in Harbin. From Jagdaqi, you could get to Mohe, China's northernmost town. See the chapter on Heilongjiang Province for more details about Mohe.

TOURING OUTER MONGOLIA

It should not be forgotten that outer Mongolia is in theory an independent country, and this is no doubt the place to go to see genuine Mongolian culture as well as some magnificent natural scenery. A trip to Mongolia can be arranged as part of the Trans-Siberian journey, but you'll pay through the nose for the privilege. By all accounts, it's very expensive and the tourist guides – if you can call them that – are worse than useless. Unfortunately, individual travel is still not permitted in Mongolia. One traveller wrote:

The Mongolian countryside was as beautiful as the tourist guide was horrible. The restaurant car had been disconnected at the border before we had our evening meal the night before, and we were starving! But the guide (who spoke German but hardly any English) took us all around town on the bus to make reservations for accommodation and onward travel before taking us to a touristy fake 'nomad camp' about an hour's drive out of town. By now we had not eaten for almost 24 hours, and when we arrived at the camp there was another long wait for the ghastly food to be prepared...The next day the abominable guide took us back into town and dropped us off at the museum, no English-speaking guide was available, and we were left on our own while the guide and the bus driver got drunk in the bus...Arriving in China late the next night was a great relief, and never again will I go to Mongolia, or at least not have anything to do with the government tourist agency. A genuine rip-off!

Mats Reimer

Footnote

Over the Great Wall and below the Bamboo Curtain is the world's most ambitious reafforestation and afforestation programme – a shelter belt creeping toward its ultimate length of 6000 km. Known as the 'Green Wall', the belt is designed to protect precious farmland from the sands of the Gobi Desert when the winter winds blow. It will eventually stretch from Xinjiang to Heilongjiang (China's last great timber preserve). This huge tree-planting programme is only a small part of the PRC's schedule – there's a similar belt along the south-east coast to break the force of summer typhoons. It's an attempt to reverse the effects of centuries of careless tree-cutting which, combined with slash-and-burn farming, has contributed to disastrous flooding and other ecological catastrophes.

Tree-planting is the duty of every able-bodied person in China. In the early years of the PRC forest cover was decimated to about 9%, but since the formation of the communes and production brigades in 1958, the cover has been raised to almost 13%.

The goal for the year 2000 is 20% cover, which would require tree-planting on 70 million hectares. Planting in the northern frontier zones is done in one-km-wide strips; between 1978 and 1982, almost five million hectares were reafforested with a survival rate of 55%, and a further 1.1 million hectares were added in 1983. Wasteland and barren hills are allocated to rural households for planting and farming (also done on a contract basis), and the government provides seeds, saplings and know-how.

Ningxia 宁夏

Ningxia *(níngxià)* was carved out as a separate administrative region in 1928 and remained a province until 1954, when it was absorbed into Gansu Province. In 1958 Ningxia re-emerged, this time as an Autonomous Region with a large Hui population. The boundaries of the region have ebbed and flowed since then – Inner Mongolia was included at one time, but the borders are now somewhat reduced.

Part of the arid north-west of China, much of Ningxia is populated by a few hardy nomads who make their living grazing sheep and goats. Winters are hard and cold, with plummeting temperatures; blistering summers make irrigation a necessity. In fact, the province would be virtually uninhabitable if it were not for the Yellow River, Ningxia's lifeline. Most of the population lives near the river or the irrigation channels which run off of it. These channels have their beginnings in the Han Dynasty, when the area was first settled by the Han Chinese in the 1st century BC.

Almost four million people live in Ningxia, but only about a third are Hui, living mostly in the south of the province. The rest are Han Chinese. The Hui minority are descended from Arab and Iranian traders who travelled to China during the Tang Dynasty. Their numbers were later increased during the Yuan Dynasty by immigrants from Central Asia. Apart from their continued adherence to Islam, the Hui have been assimilated into Han culture.

In 1958 the building of the Baotou-Lanzhou railway, which cuts through Ningxia, helped to relieve the area's isolation and develop some industry in this otherwise almost exclusively agricultural region.

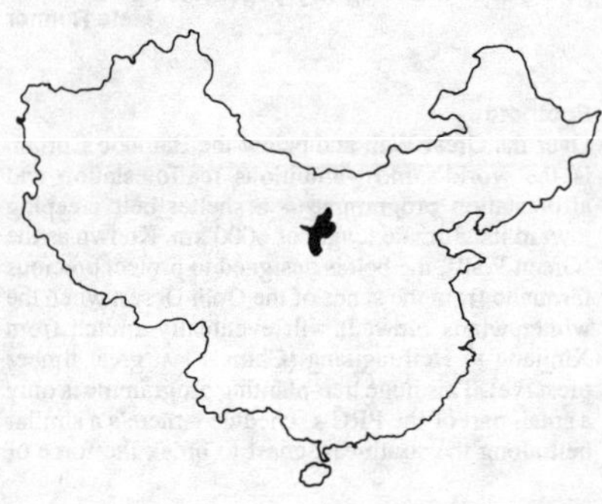

YINCHUAN

(yínchūan) 银川

Yinchuan was once the capital of the Western Xia, a mysterious kingdom founded during the 11th century. Today it's divided into two parts: a new industrial section close to the railway station, and the old town about four km away. At the old town's centre is a large Drum Tower, from which the main streets radiate.

Information

CITS There is an office (☎ 22131) in Room 129 of the Ningxia Hotel. The main CITS office (☎ 33720, 33466) is inside the Bank of China on the 4th floor, 150 Jiefang Xijie.

Public Security Bureau This is on Jiefang Xijie in a white building called Gong'an Ting. Ask for the foreign affairs office *(wàishìkē)*.

Money The Bank of China is at 150 Jiefang Xijie.

Post & Telecommunications The post and telephone office is right in the centre of town at the corner of Minzu Jie and Jiefang Jie.

North Pagoda

(běi tǎ) 北塔

It's easy to spot this pagoda (also known as Haibao Ta), standing like a stone spaceship to the north. Records of the structure date from the 5th century. In 1739 an earthquake

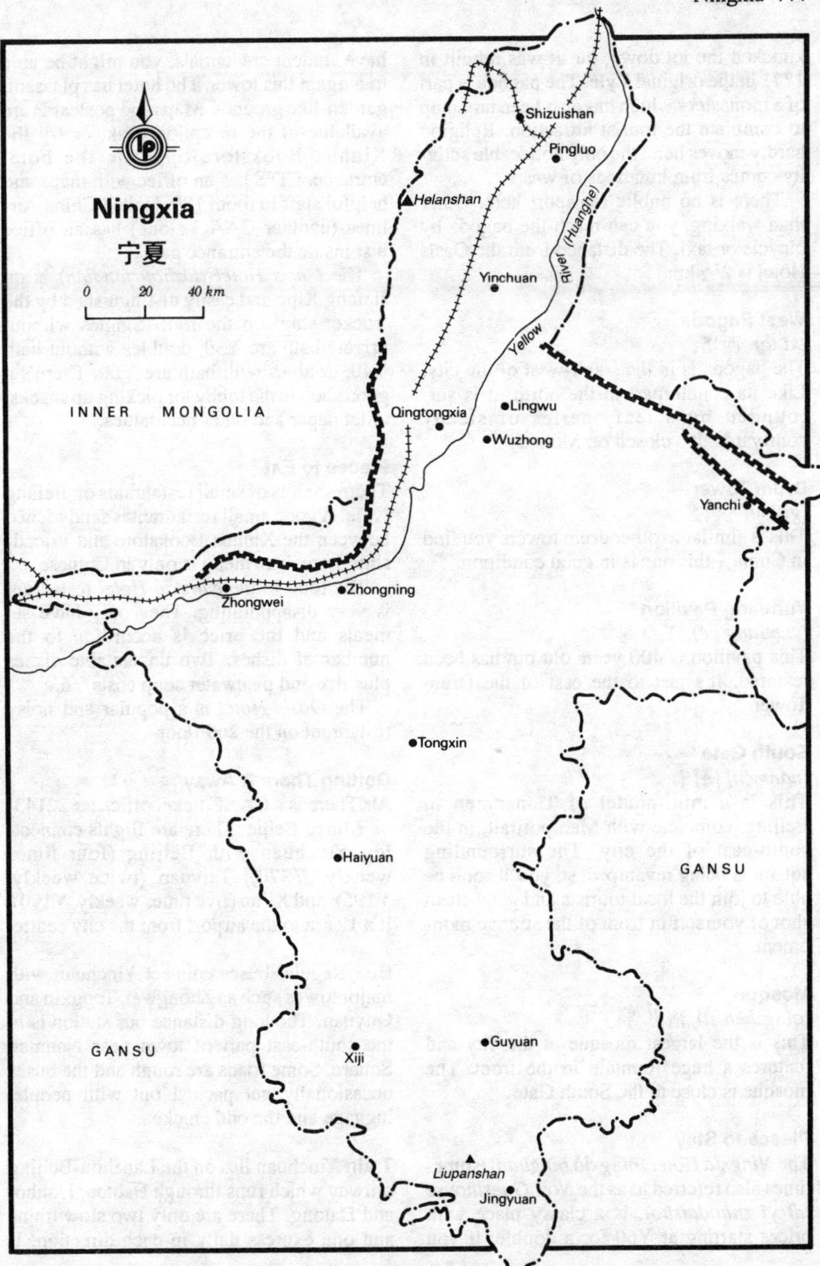
Ningxia
宁夏
0
20
40 km
INNER MONGOLIA
Shizuishan
Pingluo
Helanshan
Yinchuan
Yellow
River (Huanghe)
Qingtongxia
Lingwu
Wuzhong
Yanchi
Zhongwei
Zhongning
Tongxin
Haiyuan
GANSU
GANSU
Xiji
Guyuan
Liupanshan
Jingyuan

knocked the lot down, but it was rebuilt in 1771 in the original style. The pagoda is part of a monastery which has also been tarted up to complete the tourist attraction. Religion hardly moves here; the only noticeable activity comes from hundreds of wasps.

There is no public transport here. Other than walking, you can reach the pagoda by bicycle or taxi. The distance from the Oasis Hotel is 2½ km.

West Pagoda

(xī tǎ) 西塔

The pagoda is in the south-west of the city. Like its counterpart in the north, it is surrounded by a leafy series of sleepy courtyards. It's closed on Monday.

Drum Tower

(gǔlóu) 鼓楼

This is similar to other drum towers you find in China – this one is in good condition.

Yuhuang Pavilion

(yùhúang gé) 玉皇阁

This pavilion is 400 years old but has been restored. It's just to the east of the Drum Tower.

South Gate

(nánmén) 南门

This is a mini-model of Tiananmen in Beijing, complete with Mao portrait, in the south-east of the city. The surrounding square is being revamped, so you'll soon be able to join the local tourists and get a clean shot of yourself in front of the strange monument.

Mosque

(qīngzhēn sì) 清真寺

This is the largest mosque in the city and features a huge fountain in the front. The mosque is close to the South Gate.

Places to Stay

The *Ningxia Hotel (níngxià bīngǔan)*, sometimes also referred to as the *No 1 Guesthouse (dì yī zhāodàisǔo)*, is a classy place with prices starting at Y60 for a double. If you have student credentials, you might be able to bargain this lower. The hotel has pleasant, garden-like grounds. Maps and postcards are available at the reception desk, or try the Xinhua Bookstore opposite the hotel entrance. CITS has an office with maps and helpful staff in room 129. United China Airlines (another CAAC clone) has an office just inside the entrance gate.

The *Oasis Hotel (lüzhōu fàndiàn)* is on Jiefang Xijie and easily distinguished by the 'rocket ship' on the roof. Singles without private bath are Y30; doubles without bath Y40; doubles with bath are Y60. There's a good shop in the lobby for picking up snacks, toilet paper and other necessities.

Places to Eat

There are lots of small restaurants on Jiefang Xijie. A good small restaurant is sandwiched between the Xinhua Bookstore and Friendship Store. The menu is only in Chinese.

The food in the *Ningxia Hotel* restaurant is very disappointing. They only have set meals and the price is according to the number of dishes. Two unpalatable dishes plus rice and dishwater soup costs Y6.

The *Oasis Hotel* is a popular and noisy restaurant on the 2nd floor.

Getting There & Away

Air There is a CAAC ticket office (☎ 22143) on Minzu Beijie. There are flights connecting Yinchuan with Beijing (four times weekly, Y370); Taiyuan (twice weekly, Y195); and Xi'an (five times weekly, Y190). It's 17 km to the airport from the city centre.

Bus Regular buses connect Yinchuan with major towns such as Zhongwei, Tongxin and Guyuan. The long-distance bus station is in the south-east part of town near Nanmen Square. Some roads are rough and the buses occasionally get packed out with people, luggage and the odd chicken.

Train Yinchuan lies on the Lanzhou-Beijing railway which runs through Baotou, Hohhot and Datong. There are only two slow trains and one express daily in each direction. It

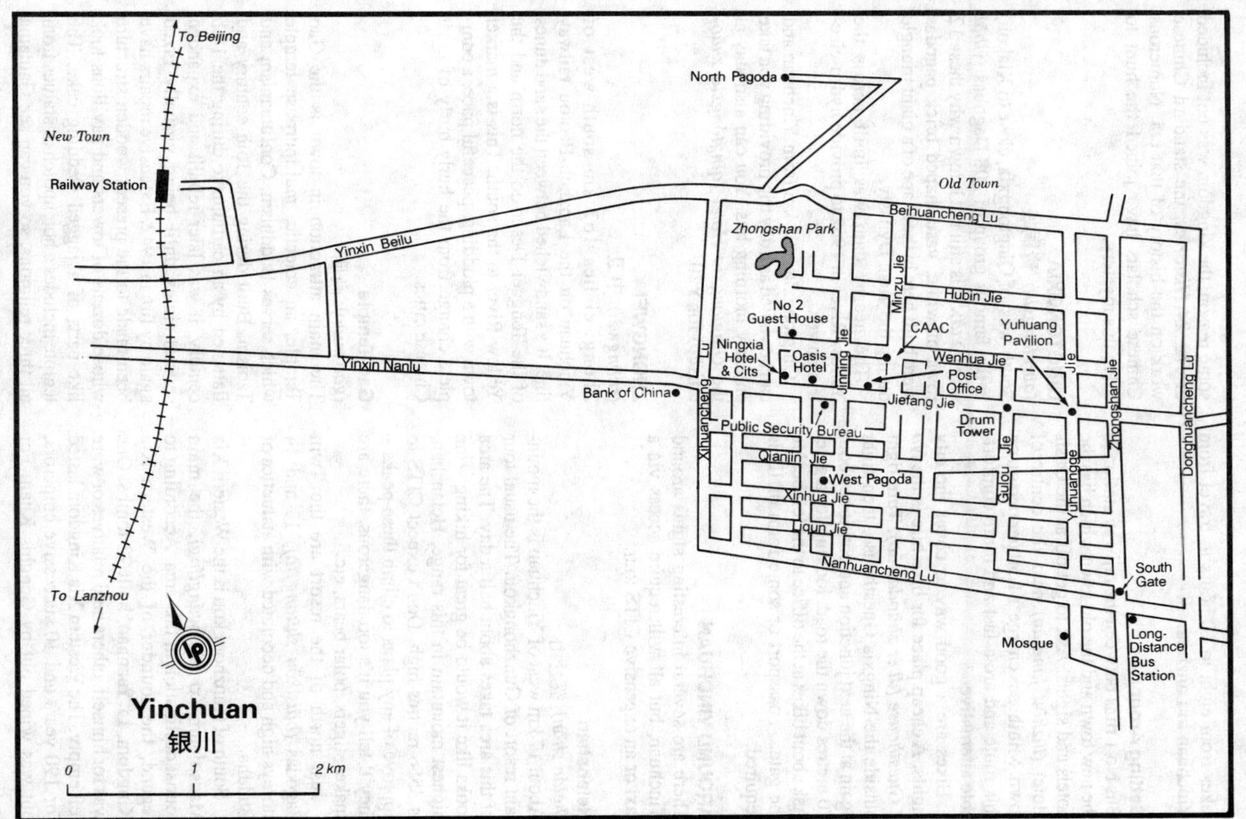

To Beijing
New Town
Railway Station
North Pagoda
Old Town
Zhongshan Park
Beihuancheng Lu
Yinxin Beilu
Yinxin Nanlu
Minzu Jie
Hubin Jie
No 2 Guest House
Ningxia Hotel & Cits
Oasis Hotel
Jinning Jie
CAAC
Wenhua Jie
Post Office
Yuhuang Pavilion
Jie
Zhongshan Jie
Donghuancheng Lu
Bank of China
Xihuancheng Lu
Jiefang Jie
Drum Tower
Public Security Bureau
Qianjin Jie
West Pagoda
Gulou Jie
Yuhuangge
Xinhua Jie
Liqun Jie
Nanhuancheng Lu
South Gate
Mosque
Long-Distance Bus Station
To Lanzhou
Yinchuan
银川
0
1
2 km

takes from eight to 10 hours to travel from Yinchuan to Lanzhou.

Getting Around

Bus No 1 runs between the railway station in the new town and the old town which has the hotels and sights. Ask to get off at the Oasis Hotel *(lüzhōu fàndiàn)* near the centre of town. Minibuses charge Y1.50 per person on this route and are a fast and more comfortable alternative.

Bikes are a good way to cover the city sights. A cheap place for bike hire is the *No 2 Guesthouse (dì èr zhāodàisuo)*. Turn right outside the Ningxia Guesthouse, then right again at the next junction and continue about 70 metres down the road, looking for a gate. Ask about bikes at the office to the left beside the gate. A passport or some form of ID is required.

AROUND YINCHUAN

There are several interesting sights around Yinchuan, but all will require access via a taxi or an expensive CITS tour.

Helanshan

(hèlán shān) 贺兰山

About 17 km west of Yinchuan is the mountain resort of Gunzhongkou. The usual tour of this area takes about half a day. The area looks like it would be great for hiking – the highest mountain in this range, Helanshan, is 3556 metres high. Don't expect CITS to approve of any plans to climb these peaks – they'll tell you it's too dangerous, there are snakes, tigers, polar bears, etc.

Just north of the resort are the Twin Pagodas *(báisìkǒu shūang tǎ)*, 13 and 14 storeys high and decorated with statuettes of Buddha.

South of Gunzhongkou is the Western Xia Mausoleum *(xī xià wánglíng)*, the main tourist destination in this area. According to legend, the founder of the Western Xia Kingdom, Li Yuanhao, built 72 tombs. One was for himself, others held relatives or were left empty. The Western Xia Kingdom lasted for 190 years and 10 successive emperors, but was wiped out by Genghis Khan. For some reason, the kingdom was not included in *The 24 Histories*, the standard Chinese work on the history of that era. Numerous Chinese scholars have joined the hunt to solve this mystery.

QINGTONGXIA

(qīngtóngxiá) 青铜峡

South-west of Qingtongxia, close to Xiakou, is the famous group of 108 Dagobas *(yìbǎi líng bā tǎ)*. It is still not known why these 12 rows of white, vase-shaped brick pagodas were built here in the shape of a giant triangle during the Yuan Dynasty.

The nearby dam was built across the Yellow River in 1962 to provide hydro-electric power.

Qingtongxia is 98 km from Yinchuan and can be visited as a day trip providing you take an early morning bus. You can also stay at the *Qingtongxia Hotel (qīngtóngxiá zhāodàisuo)* for Y20.

ZHONGWEI

(zhōngwèi) 中卫

Zhongwei lies 167 km south-west of Yinchuan on the Lanzhou-Baotou railway line. It's sandwiched between the sand dunes of the Tengger Desert to the north and the Yellow River to the south. This is a market town with a plodding, peaceful pace, a complete change from the hurly-burly of most Chinese cities.

Gao Temple

(gāo miào) 高庙

The main attraction in town is the Gao Temple, an eclectic, multipurpose temple which serves Buddhism, Confucianism and Taoism. Built during the 15th century and flattened by an earthquake during the 18th century, it was later rebuilt and expanded several times until being virtually razed again by fire in 1942. Extensive repairs have been made to the present wooden structure whose dozens of towers and pavilions look like parts of a jagged wedding cake. The temple includes a hotchpotch of statues from all three religions, so you can see Gautama

Buddha, bodhisattvas, the Jade Emperor and the Holy Mother under one roof.

Places to Stay
The *Yellow River Guesthouse (húanghé bīngǔan)* is where most people stay. Rooms can be had for Y30. CITS (☎ 2620) can be contacted here if you want to organise visits to see camels, the Shapotou Desert Research Centre, sheepskin rafts, etc. Ask at reception about hiring bikes.

Getting There & Away
Zhongwei has two train connections daily to Yinchuan or Lanzhou. The express train does not stop here, only the slow trains. There are bus connections with Yinchuan and Guyuan.

AROUND ZHONGWEI

Water Wheels
(shǔi chē) 水车

If you bike or hitch west of Zhongwei down the road towards Shapotou, the road branches halfway. Take the left-hand fork to the Yellow River, where a ferry will take you across to Xiaheye. Follow the dirt road east for about two km to reach the water wheels.

Since the Han Dynasty, water wheels have been a common sight in Ningxia Province and in other regions crossed by the Yellow River. Mechanical pumps have now taken over, though water wheels are occasionally still in use to pump water from the river down a complicated system of ducts and canals to the fields.

Leather Rafts
(yáng pífázi) 羊皮筏子

A few km due south of the town, you can see these rafts in action on the Yellow River – you might even want to have a go!

Leather rafts have been a traditional mode of transport on the Yellow River for centuries. They usually served for short crossings, although thousands of rafts were used during the '50s to freight huge loads of tobacco, herbs or people on a two-week trip covering nearly 2000 km between Lanzhou and Baotou. The largest raft then in use was made from 600 sheepskins, measured 12 metres by seven metres and could carry loads of up to 30 tonnes.

The raft-making process begins with careful skinning of cattle or sheep carcasses. The skins are then soaked for several days in oil and brine before being taken out and inflated. An average of 14 hides are tied together under a wooden framework to make a strong raft capable of carrying four persons and four bikes. Single-skin rafts are also used in parts of Gansu and Qinghai, where you either lie on top of your raft or crawl inside while the rafter lies on top to direct your passage across the river. There is usually enough air inside a large cowhide to last for 15 minutes which, reportedly, is about twice the time needed for an average crossing.

Shapotou Desert Research Centre
(shāpōtóu shāmò yánjiù sǔo)
沙波头沙漠研究所

Shapotou lies about 16 km west of Zhongwei on the fringe of the Tengger Desert. The Desert Research Centre was founded here in 1956 with the task of researching methods to fix or hold back the moving sand dunes from the railway. From 1962 onwards, the researchers have been using the 'checkerboard method' for sand blockage and fixation introduced in the '50s by a Soviet adviser. Plants are protected inside small checkerboards composed of straw bales which are replaced every five years. Even with this protection, plants still require 15 years for full growth. Several thousand hectares of land have now been reclaimed to create an impressive ribbon of greenery beside the railway.

TONGXIN
(tóngxīn) 同心

Tongxin lies on the road between Zhongning and Guyuan. The main attraction is the Great Mosque *(qīngzhēn dà sì)* built during the Ming Dynasty. One of the largest mosques in Ningxia Province, this is a traditional Chinese wooden structure with Islamic woodcuts and decorations of carved brick.

GUYUAN

(gùyúan) 固原

Guyuan is in the south of Ningxia Province and seldom visited by foreigners. There is a fine set of Buddhist grottoes at Xumishan *(xūmíshān shíkū)* about 50 km north-west of Guyuan. Xumi is the Chinese version of the Sanskrit word *sumeru*, which means 'treasure mountain'.

Cut into five adjacent peaks are 132 caves containing over 300 Buddhist statues dating back 1400 years, from the Northern Wei to the Sui and Tang dynasties. The finest Buddhist statues are found in Caves 14, 45, 46, 51, 67 and 70. Cave 5 contains the most famous statue on Xumishan: a colossal Maitreya Buddha, 19 metres high. It remains remarkably well preserved even though the protective tower has long since collapsed and left it exposed to the elements.

Over 60 miniature Buddhist statues and tombs dating from the Han Dynasty have been found in Xiji County, about 60 km west of Guyuan.

It's 460 km from Yinchuan to Guyuan – the trip takes about nine hours. Daily buses leave in the morning at 7 am and arrive about 4 pm. It might be interesting to continue from Guyuan towards Tianshui in Gansu Province.

Gansu 甘肃

Gansu *(gānsù)* is a rugged and barren state, consisting mostly of mountains and deserts. It's hard to imagine that through this narrow corridor China maintained political, cultural and commercial contacts with central Asia and the lands beyond. A frontier with a semi-arid climate, liable to frequent droughts and famines, it has always been on the edge of the empire (except when that empire spilled over into Xinjiang as it did under the Han and the Qing). It was an impoverished region and its inhabitants played little part in the destiny of their country.

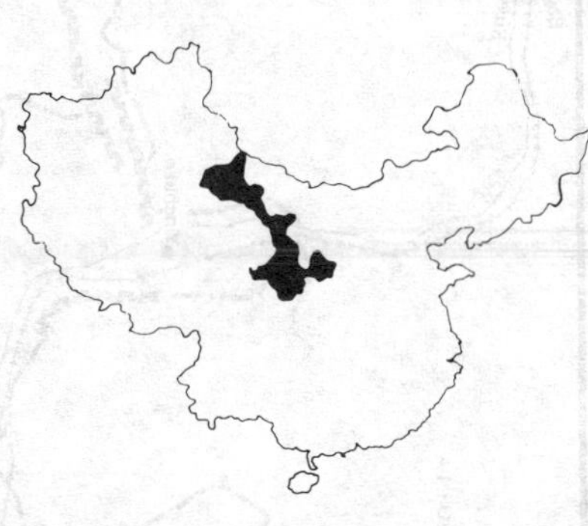

However, the famed 'Silk Road', along which camel caravans carried goods in and out of China, threaded its way through Gansu. The most common export was the highly prized Chinese silk, from which the road took its name. Travellers and merchants from as far away as the Roman Empire entered the Middle Kingdom via this route, using the string of oasis towns as stepping-stones through the barren wastes. Buddhism was also carried into China along the Silk Road, and the Buddhist cave temples found all the way from Xinjiang through Gansu and up through northern China are reminders of the influx of ideas the road made possible.

The Great Wall snaked its way across northern China and into Gansu, finishing up not far past the town of Jiayuguan. All was not peaceful within the wall, however. The Muslim rebellion of 1862 to 1878 was put down with incredible savagery by the Chinese; untold numbers of people, probably millions, were killed and the destruction of cities and property brought the province to ruin – and finally established Chinese control. The century was topped off by a massive famine.

Traditionally the towns of Gansu have been established in the oases along the major caravan route where agriculture is possible. With the coming of modern methods of transport some industrial development and the exploitation of oil, iron ore and coal deposits has taken place. The foothills of the mountainous regions which border Qinghai Province to the south support a pastoral economy based on horses, cattle, sheep and camels. To the north of the 'Gansu corridor' – that narrow part of Gansu that extends north-west from the capital of Lanzhou – lies a barren desert which extends into Inner Mongolia, much of it true desert, some of it sparse grassland.

Just over 19½ million people inhabit Gansu. The province has a considerable variety of minority peoples, among them the Hui, Mongols, Tibetans and Kazakhs. The Han Chinese have built their own settlements, places like Jiayuguan and Jiuquan which have been Chinese outposts for centuries.

Rail – Gansu to Xinjiang

The Lanzhou-Ürümqi railway line was completed in 1963. It is definitely one of the great achievements of the Communist regime, and has done much to relieve the isolation and backwardness of this region.

The railway line stretches north-west along the Gansu corridor from Lanzhou. The Marco Polos of the railway age can break their journey at Jiayuguan (the end of the Great Wall) and at the remarkable Buddhist

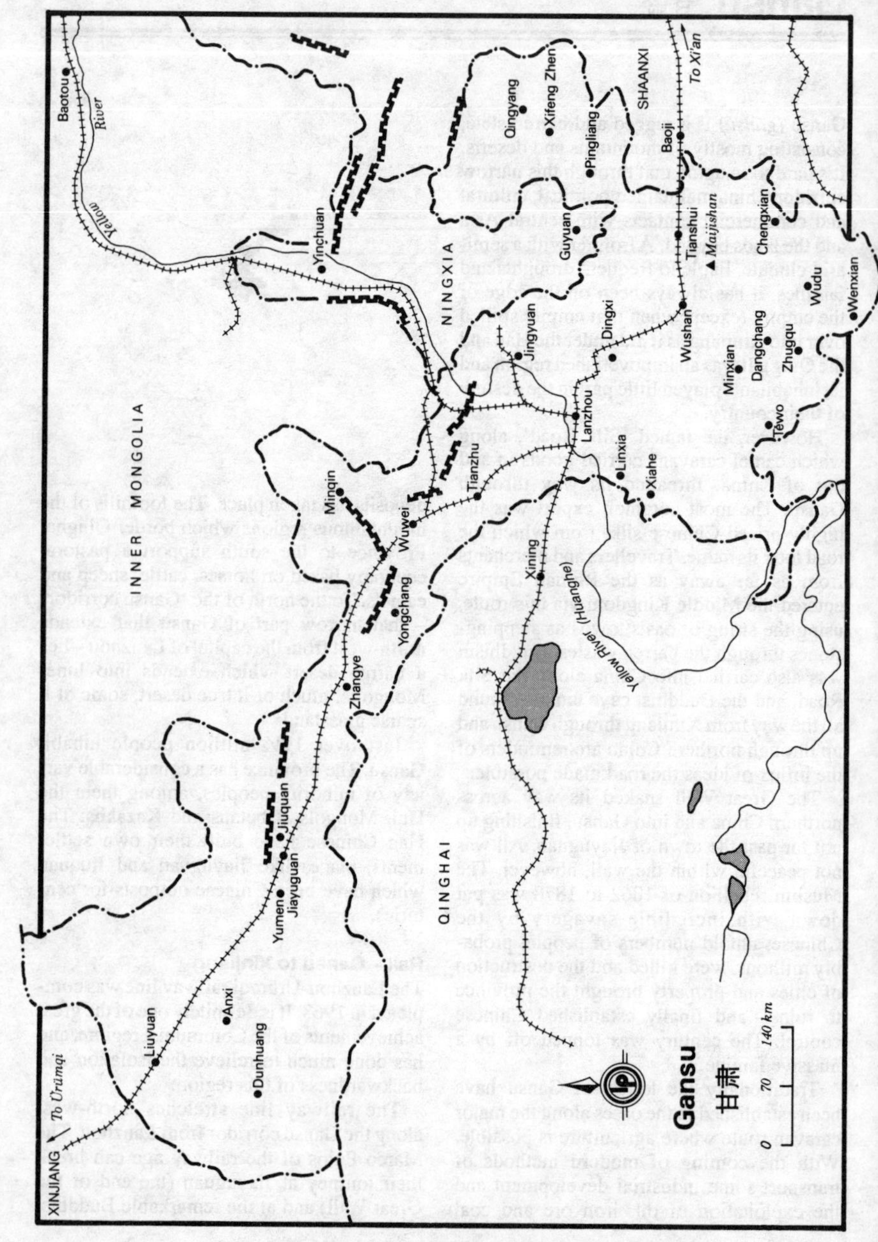
Gansu
甘肃
0
70
140 km
XINJIANG
To Ürümqi
INNER MONGOLIA
NINGXIA
QINGHAI
SHAANXI
To Xi'an
Baotou
Yellow River
Yinchuan
Liuyuan
Dunhuang
Anxi
Yumen
Jiayuguan
Jiuquan
Zhangye
Yongchang
Minqin
Wuwei
Tianzhu
Lanzhou
Jingyuan
Xining
Yellow River (Huanghe)
Linxia
Xiahe
Dingxi
Guyuan
Pingliang
Qingyang
Xifeng Zhen
Tianshui
Maijishan
Baoji
Wushan
Minxian
Tewo
Dangchang
Zhugqu
Chengxian
Wudu
Wenxian

Caves of Dunhuang (the jumping-off point for Dunhuang is Liuyuan, and from here you bus south to Dunhuang). A lot of travellers now head directly from Xi'an to Ürümqi, which is a 2½-day trip, and then work their way back down the line, stopping off at the other open towns.

From Jiayuguan or Liuyuan you can take trains either west to Turpan and Ürümqi (the latter being the terminus of the line) or eastwards. Someday soon it may be possible to carry on to the USSR when the new line from Ürümqi is completed. Many trains from Lanzhou will take you direct to Beijing via Baotou and Hohhot, to Beijing via Xi'an and Zhengzhou, or east to Shanghai via Xi'an and Zhengzhou.

If you do the rail trip straight through from Lanzhou or Xi'an to Ürümqi, then bring a large quantity of water with you – the boiler on the train sometimes runs out. Bring something to eat; there's food on the train in the dining car (rice, meat, vegetables, rice-noodles and eggs), but you might want something extra. Food is also sold on the rail platforms when the train makes its occasional stops (eggs, roast chickens, melons, plums, jars of fruit).

As you head westward, the real desolation begins after Lanzhou, when the scenery changes to endless rugged stony plains. Sometimes you'll spot the Qilianshan mountain range to the south, so high that even in June the peaks are snow-capped, and some have glaciers. Every so often along the line you pass some collection of mud huts, or a tiny railway station in the middle of nowhere, or a large stretch of agricultural land – a stark contrast to the surrounding desert. The approach to Ürümqi is dramatic: the railway line passes over rugged mountains and the train emerges onto an immense plain of grasslands, grazed by horses, sheep and cattle. Far to the north are snow-topped mountains. Gradually the grasslands give way to dry desert and an hour or so later you arrive in Ürümqi, with its concrete jungle of apartment blocks, factories and smokestacks.

There are no direct trains between Ürümqi and Baotou/Hohhot. All trains through Inner Mongolia run from Beijing to Lanzhou only. The connector line from Wuwei to Gantang which would slice about 300 km off the Ürümqi trip is officially closed to foreigners.

MAIJISHAN

(màijīshān) 麦积山

Maijishan, a mountain famed for its grottoes, lies about 35 km south of Tianshui town in south-east Gansu Province. The mountain bears some resemblance to a corn rick, hence the name Maijishan (Corn Rick Mountain).

The Maijishan grottoes are rated one of China's four largest temple groups; the others are at Datong, Luoyang and Dunhuang. The caves date back to the Northern Wei and Song dynasties and contain clay figures and wall paintings. It's not certain just how the artists managed to clamber so high; one theory is that they piled up blocks of wood to the top of the mountain before moving down, gradually removing blocks of wood as they descended. Stone sculptures were evidently brought in from elsewhere, since the local rock is too soft for carving, as at Dunhuang. Earthquakes have demolished many of the caves in the central part while murals have tended to drop off due to damp or rain; fire has destroyed many of the wooden structures.

Catwalks and steep spiral stairs have been built across the cliff face. It's scary to look down, but perfectly safe. Most of the remaining 194 caves can only be seen through wire netting or barred doors – take a torch. Apart from the Qifo Pavilion and the huge Buddha statues which are easily accessible, you may find it hard to get a rewarding peek into many of the caves unless you take a guide. The guides have been known to offer a peek into some of the closed caves in return for ridiculously vast sums of money. One foreigner was quoted a price of Y4000 per cave!

Visitors often pause above the statue of Buddha and attempt to throw coins or even cigarettes on his head. If the objects stay there, so the story goes, the thrower's mind is pure. The visitor may be pure, but Buddha certainly cops a load of rubbish.

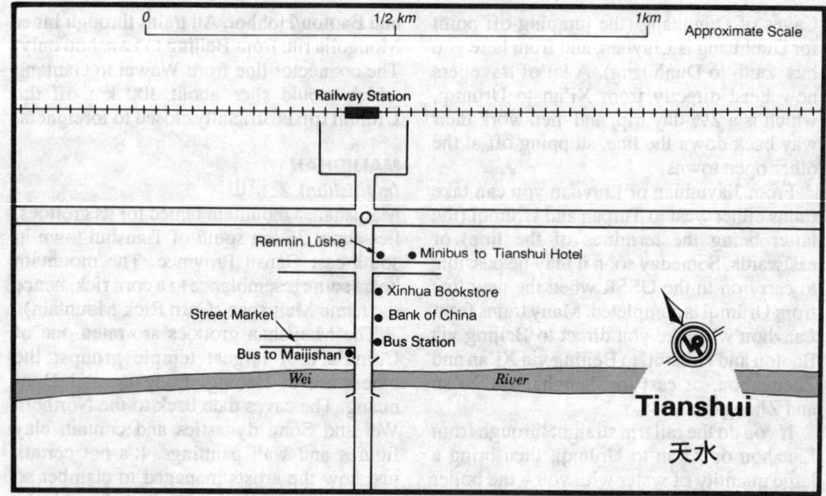

Admission costs Y5. The ticket office is about a 15-minute walk from the bus stop. Follow the road uphill, round a sharp bend to the left, and continue uphill past a statue until you see the ticket office on your right. Local squirrels wait for hand-outs here. Enquire about guides in the management office just past the statue. The ticket office also has a left-luggage office. The caves are open from 9 am to 5 pm.

To reach the high ridge rising behind the ticket office, follow the road up towards the ticket office, but when you get to the sharp bend to the left, take the forest track to the right. Continue uphill along this track for about 15 minutes and then look for a track climbing off to the left. If you follow this, you'll find yourself on a dizzying, knife-edge route with fine views of the grottoes on the cliff face.

Places to Stay

Accommodation is such a serious problem that few foreigners actually visit Maijishan. For budget travellers, the situation is particularly bleak. The only place that accepts foreigners without argument is the *Tianshui Hotel (tiānshǔi bīngǔan)*. All rooms cost Y80 for a double with private bath, but there are no dorms. It's a nice-looking hotel on the outside, but inside it's falling apart. To make matters worse, it's 19 km from the railway station in the *wrong* direction (away from Maijishan). From the railway station, it takes 30 minutes by minibus (Y1) – tell them you want to get off at the *Tianshui Binguan* – they will drop you off within a block of the hotel. Bring food with you – the hotel restaurant is open only from 7.30 to 8.30 am and 6.30 to 7.30 pm. They try to charge Y24 for breakfast – this can be bargained down to Y8. The hotel is in a remote area and there is no other place nearby to buy food. The hotel store doesn't sell food, just cheap junk like plastic toys for children. The hotel post office has no stamps, the hotel bank has no FEC and you'd better have small bills because the front desk has no FEC either to give you change. Overall, it's one of the most grotesquely mismanaged tourist hotels in China. However, the staff is friendly.

There is a number of Chinese hotels right by the railway station, all of which claim to be full when a foreigner shows up. Some travellers have managed to get into some of these Chinese hotels, but you'll have to employ every trick you can think of – getting the local police to introduce you, bribing the desk clerk with cigarettes, collapsing in the hotel lobby, etc. If you can talk your way in, a good place to stay is the 'all full' *Renmin Lüshe* where doubles are Y20.

Getting There & Away

The railway station closest to Maijishan is the one at Tianshui. There is only one good thing about Tianshui – leaving it. Tianshui is a miserably dirty town but there's no way to avoid the place. Dozens of trains going both east and west follow this busy line daily. If you want to make a day trip out of Maijishan, you should try to arrive early. It's most convenient to insert Maijishan as part of your itinerary between Lanzhou and Xi'an. It's eight hours to Lanzhou and seven hours to Xi'an.

There is a military airport in Tianshui and CAAC is 'thinking about' opening up civilian air service. Perhaps they ought to first think about opening up a decent hotel.

Buses and minibuses to Maijishan depart from a terminal at the end of the main street by the Wei River (see map). On weekends it can be really crowded. The trip takes over an hour one way. Bring whatever you need (food, drinks) because there's precious little available at Maijishan.

LANZHOU

(lánzhōu) 兰州

Lanzhou, the capital of Gansu, has been an important garrison town and transport centre since ancient times. The city is in a large valley 1600 metres above sea level. Situated on the major routes along the Gansu corridor into central Asia, westward into Qinghai and Tibet, south into Sichuan and north-west along the Yellow River, Lanzhou was a major centre of caravan traffic into the border regions up until WW II.

Lanzhou's development as an industrial centre began after the Communist victory and the subsequent building of railway lines to link the city with the rest of the country. The line from Baoji in Shaanxi was extended here in 1952; another line came from Baotou in 1958. Construction also began on the Lanzhou-Ürümqi line, probably with the intention that it would one day join up with a Soviet Union line. Another line was built linking Lanzhou with Xining. This transformed Lanzhou into a major industrial city, destined to become the principal industrial base of north-west China. About 200,000 people lived in Lanzhou in 1949; by 1959 the number was 900,000, and today it's over two million.

Though there are few major attractions in the city itself, Lanzhou is a reasonably attractive place. If you get a chance, don't miss the utterly brilliant Dance Ensemble of Gansu Province – try the People's Theatre near the Victory Hotel or get someone at your hotel reception desk to check the *People's Daily (rénmín rìbào)* for the current venue. Also not to be missed are the Bingling Si Buddhist Caves outside the city.

Orientation

Lanzhou stretches for 20 km along the southern bank of the Yellow River. The eastern segment of town, between the railway station and the large Xiguan traffic circle, is the centre of town, and in this area you'll find most of the tourist facilities.

Information

Each Friday at 8.30 pm there's an 'English Corner' at Lanzhou University. The students here speak surprisingly good English and are anxious to meet foreigners.

CITS The office (☎ 26798, 26181) is in a building in the walled-in compound of the Jincheng Hotel. They're open vaguely from 8 am to 6.30 pm, with a couple of hours' break in the middle of the day. The only way to get anything out of this CITS office is to stick your fingers down their throats. Unless you wave FEC in their faces, they don't want to talk to you. Ask them how to get to anywhere, and the answer is 'take a CITS tour'.

The Overseas Travel Company is supposed to be opening an office in the same building, and if so, may prove to be more

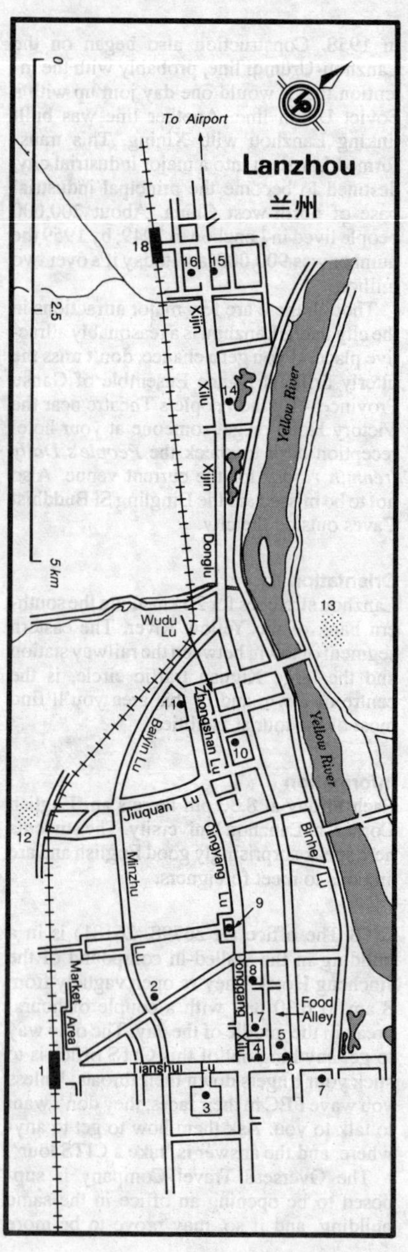

1 Main Railway Station
2 Post Office
3 Lanzhou University
4 Lanzhou Hotel
5 CITS
6 Jincheng Hotel
7 Ningwozhuang Guesthouse
8 Bank of China
9 The East is Red Square
10 Public Security Bureau
11 Victory Hotel
12 Five Springs Park
13 White Pagoda Hill & Park
14 West Bus Station
15 Friendship Hotel
16 Gansu Museum
17 CAAC
18 West Railway Station

1 火车总站
2 邮局
3 兰州大学
4 兰州饭店
5 中国国际旅行社
6 金城饭店
7 宁卧庄宾馆
8 中国银行
9 东方红广场
10 公安局外事科
11 胜利宾馆
12 五泉公园
13 白塔山公园
14 汽车西站
15 友谊饭店
16 甘肃省博物馆
17 中国民航
18 火车西站

helpful. Another source of information can be the front desk clerks in your hotel.

Public Security Bureau This is on Wudu Lu in a large compound with no English sign (see map).

Money The Bank of China (☎ 418044) is at 70 Donggang Lu, just west of the Lanzhou Hotel.

Post The main post office is inconveniently located on Minzhu Lu. There is a post office on the ground floor of the Friendship Hotel. The Jincheng Hotel sells stamps and you can post letters there. There is also a small post office diagonally opposite the Lanzhou Hotel on Donggang Xilu that takes foreign mail and parcels. There is a post office across from the railway station that was still insisting the price for sending international postcards was Y1.30 – a year after it had been raised to Y1.60.

White Pagoda Hill
(báitǎ shān) 白塔山

This is a very pleasant park indeed. There are three mosques, two pagodas, numerous pavilions and terraces where you can sit and drink tea. Most of the buildings are new, but the mountain is topped by a much older white Buddhist shrine. White Pagoda Hill lies opposite the city on the north bank of the Yellow River. Admission for Chinese is Y0.30, but Y3 for foreigners and they want FEC. Bus No 7 from the railway station goes there. You have to cross a bridge, but there is also an occasional ferry.

Gansu Provincial Museum
(gānsù shěng bówùgǔan) 甘肃省博物馆

Unfortunately, this museum was closed at the time of writing – a pity because it's worthwhile. Hopefully, it will be reopened by the time you read this, but nothing is certain. Check with CITS or your hotel before heading out there.

The museum is directly across the street from the Friendship Hotel. It used to be open daily except Sunday and Monday. There are/were exhibits devoted to Gansu's flora, fauna, geology, minerals and natural parks, plus extensive displays of decorated earthenware pottery; the Gansu painted pottery dates from the Yangshuo culture around 4000 to 2000 BC. Also exhibits from the Bingling Si Caves and glazed clay statues. The model bronze chariots and mounted horsemen came from the Letai Han Tomb at Wuwei in Gansu – altogether 220 figures and chariots were unearthed, including the 'Galloping Horse of Gansu'. The 3rd floor had the entire skeleton of a mammoth exhumed in 1973, as well as fragments of skeletons, teeth and tusks from other extinct members of the pachyderm family. The Long March, another mammoth event, was also the subject of a display.

Places to Stay

Lanzhou is good for cheap accommodation. The *Friendship Hotel* (☎ 33051) *(yǒuyí fàndiàn)* is an immense Soviet-built structure consisting of two large buildings – the rear block is used to stow away foreigners. The dormitories have three beds per room and are exceptionally pleasant and clean – a bargain at Y10. Doubles are Y92 to Y114. The post office on the ground floor stays open until 9 pm and is next to a glossy coffee shop that sells maps. The shop in the front building is useful for putting together a cheap meal if you arrive after the restaurant closes. To get to the hotel take bus No 1, 10 stops from the square in front of the railway station – it's a long ride on a crowded bus. Much more pleasant are the minibuses which charge Y5. If you are on your way to Xiahe, you might prefer to stay at this hotel the night before departure, since it's just a 15-minute walk from the west bus station.

The *Lanzhou Hotel* (☎ 22131) *(lánzhōu fàndiàn)* is another cavernous construction, not quite as nice but much better located than the Friendship Hotel. Doubles with shared bath are Y30 – with private bath the price jumps to Y120. Reception sells maps and will store your baggage, which is useful if you plan to spend a week or longer touring the area. There is an all-night grocery by the main gate, a great convenience if you get the urge for midnight munchies. The hotel is a 20-minute walk from the main railway station or you can take bus No 1 two stops. Lots of minibuses ply this route – fare is Y2.

The *Jincheng Hotel* (☎ 27931) *(jīnchéng fàndiàn)* is a plush hotel a few minutes down the street past the Lanzhou Hotel. Doubles cost Y95 in the south building, Y158 in the west building. The dorm accommodation is on the 4th floor of the block at the back (it can also be reached via the CITS entrance). Dorms cost Y12 and are not particularly nice. The hotel has several useful facilities such as a post office, clinic, fruit stall and shop with good maps.

The *Victory Hotel (shènglì bīngŭan)* charges Y10 for a dorm bed in the basement and Y40 for a double. Bus No 31 from the railway station drops you off nearby.

The *Ningwozhuang Guesthouse (níngwòzhūang bīngŭan)* has doubles for Y120. You might be forgiven if you think you've wandered into Communist Party headquarters – the park-like grounds are surrounded by high walls and guards. This is an exclusive cadre hang-out, but is also for visiting foreign dignitaries. A Thai princess was staying here during our last visit. The hotel is mostly empty and the staff look bored. Travellers can stay here, but who would want to?

Places to Eat

The *Friendship Hotel* restaurant offers unexciting set meals at Y15 RMB per head. The *Jincheng Hotel* has a reasonably good Chinese restaurant with English menu. The *Lanzhou Hotel* has an awful restaurant with no English menu – breakfast was memorable for the 'butter' which the waitress spooned out of a huge barrel with a label saying 'Edible Fat – A Gift of Norway'.

Out on the streets, some good noodle stalls serve Lanzhou's spicy speciality, beef noodles *(niúròu miàn)*. The street running behind the Bank of China and parallel to Donggang Xilu has a lot of cheap stalls in the evening serving up beef noodles, or mutton *(yángròu)* with flatbread.

Getting There & Away

Air CAAC's office (☎ 23431, 23432) is at 46 Donggang Xilu, a five-minute walk west of the Lanzhou Hotel. It's open from 7.30 to 11.30 am and from 3 to 6 pm.

Lanzhou is connected by air to Beijing (Y454), Canton (Y697), Chengdu, Dunhuang, Jiayuguan, Nanjing, Qingyang, Shanghai (Y634), Taiyuan, Ürümqi, Xi'an (Y184), Xining and Zhengzhou.

Lanzhou airport is 75 km from the city. The airport bus leaves at 7 pm from the CAAC office and costs Y5 one way – as opposed to Y300 quoted for a taxi! If you are booked on an early-morning flight you have to stay at an airport hotel. There are two: Hotel No 1 *(dì yī bīngŭan)* is cleaner and charges Y40 for a bed in a double with bath; Hotel No 2 *(dì èr bīngŭan)* charges Y20 for a bed in a double without washing facilities. High winds often delay flights, and CAAC can find plenty of other excuses.

Bus The west bus station *(qìchē xīzhàn)* handles departures to Linxia and Xiahe. The buses to Xiahe all go to Linxia first. The first one is at 6.30 am, or 7.30 am in summer. Take an early bus if you want to make it to Xiahe the same day.

Train Trains run to Ürümqi; to Beijing via Hohhot and Datong; to Golmud via Xining; to Shanghai via Xi'an and Zhengzhou; and to Beijing via Xi'an and Zhengzhou, or you can head south to Chengdu. Heading west, it takes 18 hours to reach Jiayuguan; 24 hours to Liuyuan; 37 hours to Turpan and 40 hours to Ürümqi.

The station has a separate window for foreigners (No 15), but it seems to be difficult to get anything but a hard seat. You can try for a sleeper, but you might have to buy a hard seat and then upgrade your ticket to a sleeper after boarding the train. CITS might be able to book the ticket for you, but don't count on it. Black-market tickets are widely available from hawkers at the railway station, but take care that you know what you're buying. Many students in Lanzhou speak English – they can sometimes help you get tickets. If they get you Chinese price you should respond with a tip – they desperately need the money.

Getting Around
Apart from the buses, there are heaps of minibuses plying the main streets. Fares run from Y1 to Y5 depending on distance. Ask at the Victory Hotel about bike hire. A word of warning: Lanzhou has a reputation among many Chinese from other provinces as a centre for proficient pickpockets and petty thieves. Be especially careful on crowded buses, at post offices and at the station. Minibuses are pretty safe as well as much more comfortable, so could be worth the extra price.

AROUND LANZHOU

Bingling Si Caves

(bǐnglíng sì) 炳灵寺

One of the highlights of Gansu Province, the Bingling Si Buddhist Caves are unusual in that they are located in an area that looks rather like America's Grand Canyon. The caves themselves are small, but the setting is stunning. One has to marvel at how anyone ever built these caves on the canyon walls.

Buddha at Bingling Si Caves

The oldest caves have been repaired and added to on numerous occasions since they were built during the Western Qin Dynasty (385-431 AD). The 183 caves are cut into a cliff face 60 metres high and stretch for about 200 metres. They contain 694 statues, 82 clay sculptures and a number of murals. Cave 169 is the oldest and contains one buddha and two bodhisattvas; inscriptions on the wall give the date of the statues as 420 AD. Most of the other caves were completed during the prosperous Tang period. The star of the caves is the 27-metre-high seated statue of Maitreya, the future Buddha.

It's a 12-hour round trip, half of that time on a bus and half on a boat. During spring and early summer it's not always possible to reach the caves because of flooding. Be warned that even though the ride to the caves is beautiful and the caves themselves are magnificent, you're likely to get no more than one hour to look around them – if everything goes on time. Nor will they let you take photographs – and they do enforce that rule! Also, make sure you take food and drink with you – 12 hours can be a long time to abstain.

Getting There & Away The Victory Hotel *(shènglì bīngŭan)* runs minibuses (maximum 10 passengers) to the caves. Tickets are best booked in advance. The price per person is Y45 – student discounts available. There is an additional Y3 charge to enter the site. Show up at 7.30 am to board the bus at 8 am. You can also arrange to have the bus pick you up at your hotel.

CITS does more pricey tours. They pick you up in a minibus from the Friendship Hotel at 7.30 am. The tour from the Victory Hotel is better.

Some travellers have managed to use public transport by taking the early-morning local bus to Yongjing from outside the Victory Hotel. After arriving in Yongjing they boarded the tour boats to the Bingling Si Caves. Yongjing has a hotel which charges Y10 per bed. Overall, it's worth doing the tour because public transport on this route is not reliable.

LINXIA

(línxià) 临夏

Linxia, once an important town on the Silk Road route between Lanzhou and Yangguan, is now a regional centre for the Hui and Dongxiang minorities.

The Dongxiang minority speak their own Altaic language and fascinate scholars, who believe them to be descendants of Central Asians who migrated to Linxia during the 13th century. Some may have been forcibly transferred to China after Kublai Khan's conquest of Afghanistan, Iraq, Syria and Egypt. They have blue eyes, high cheekbones and large noses.

The Yugur minority, numbering only 8000, lives around the town of Jishishan near the Yellow River about 75 km from Linxia. The Yugur speak a language partly derived from Uigur and are followers of Tibetan Buddhism.

Not far from Jishishan, at Dahejia or San'erjia, it is reportedly possible to cross the river into Ningxia by means of a cowhide raft – see the Zhongwei section in the Ningxia chapter.

Linxia is a fascinating slice of Arabia with the full Muslim trimmings. The main attractions of the town are the markets, mosques and people.

Linxia does a thriving trade in spectacles made with ground crystal lenses and metal frames. Carved gourds, daggers and rugs are other local items in the market.

Places to Stay & Eat

The only place accepting foreigners is the *Linxia Hotel (línxià bīnguǎn)*. Doubles are Y40 but bargaining can produce better results.

The best place to eat is at the Minzu Binguan, a Chinese hotel. You can't spend the night here, but the restaurant is good. The hotel looks almost like a temple and has a sign in English that says 'Restaurant'. There are no English menus, so be careful about overcharging.

Getting There & Away

You might have trouble. At the time of this writing, the bus company in Lanzhou was refusing to sell tickets to foreigners. The logic (if you can call it that) seems to be that buses are too dangerous for foreigners (they're OK for Chinese though). Foreigners are expected to go on expensive CITS tours, even though the CITS minibuses are even more vulnerable in a crash than the large public buses.

You have three ways around this restriction. One is to get a Chinese person to buy your ticket. The bus drivers don't seem to care if foreigners get on the bus – only the people at the ticket windows give you a hard time. Another option is to just get on the bus and then buy your ticket. If both these methods fail, you can also round up a group of foreigners at the bus station (usually easy to do) and negotiate a price for a minibus to take you to Linxia. Many minibus drivers hang around the station looking for customers. This will be a little more expensive than the public bus – about Y15 per person depending on the size of the group – but the minibuses will usually be much more comfortable and faster. They might pick up some additional passengers along the way, but they usually won't overload a minibus (the police can fine them if they do).

The place to get buses from Lanzhou to Linxia is the west bus station *(qìchē xīzhàn)*. Buses run from around 6.30 am until about 2 pm. The trip takes three to four hours. It's worth remembering that if you plan to reach Xiahe from Lanzhou in one day, you must take one of the early buses, no later than 8.30 am. Alternatively, you could spend the night in Linxia, but Xiahe draws travellers like a magnet and few devote much time to Linxia. Even though the bus company refuses to sell tickets to foreigners from Lanzhou to Linxia, there seems to be no problem buying tickets from Linxia to Xiahe.

There is a bus between Linxia and Xining (Y9). There are two departures – 6.30 am and 9.30 am.

It is possible to go all the way from Linxia to Chengdu in Sichuan Province. It's a beautiful ride, but a bit dangerous and Public Security is trying to discourage foreigners. To do this trip, you have to take a bus from Linxia to Zoigê *(rùo ěr gài)*, then Zoigê to Chengdu. Depending on the schedule, you may have to first take a bus from Linxia to Hezuo, then on to Zoigê the next day. From Zoigê, it is possible to make a side trip to the national park at Jiuzhaigou. From Zoigê to Chengdu takes two days.

XIAHE

(xiàhé) 夏河

Xiahe is one of the most enchanting places to visit in China, especially if you can't get to Tibet. Outside of Lhasa, it's the leading Tibetan monastery town. Indeed, in some ways it's better than Tibet – the people who come here are mostly on pilgrimage and therefore dress in their finest, most colourful clothing. The pilgrims, the monks, the monastery, the mountain scenery – when you enter Xiahe, you feel like you've entered another world. Indeed, you have.

The religious activity is focused on the Labrang Monastery, one of the six major Tibetan monasteries of the Gelukpa (Yellow Hat sect of Tibetan Buddhism). The others are Ganden, Sera and Drepung monasteries in the Lhasa area; Tashilhunpo monastery in Shigatse; and Ta'er monastery in Huanzhong, Qinghai Province.

At 2920 metres above sea level, Xiahe is a great place for hiking in clean, peaceful surroundings. Take food, water, warm clothing and rain gear. Follow the river or head up into the surrounding valleys, but carry a stick as dogs are a serious problem.

You may be able to organise transport (ask at the Xiahe Binguan) or hitch-and-walk to smaller monasteries in Ganjia (28 km) or Sanke (14 km). Don't expect to get anywhere quickly: traffic in this region is mostly walking tractors, or horses and carts.

Labrang Monastery

(lābǔlèng sì) 拉卜楞寺

The monastery was built in 1709 by E'angzongzhe, the first-generation Jiamuyang

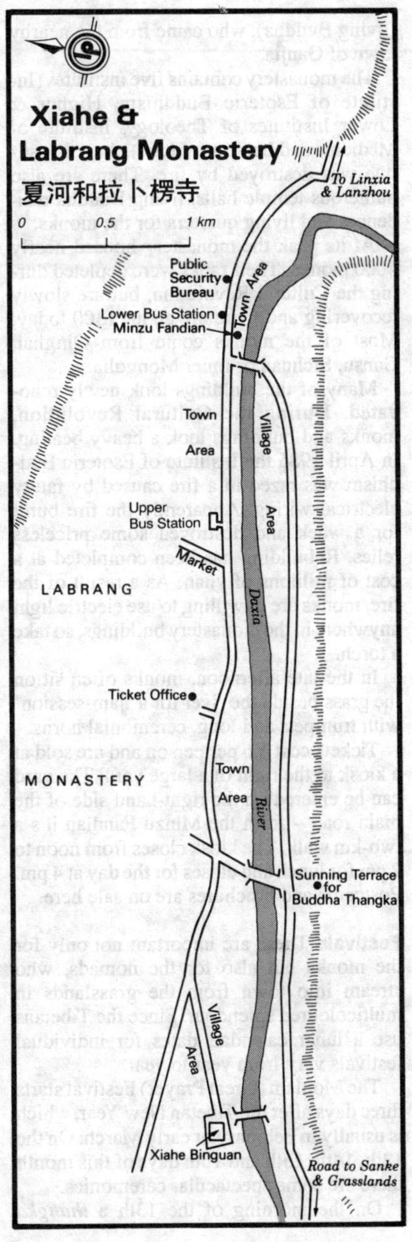

(living Buddha), who came from the nearby town of Ganjia.

The monastery contains five institutes (Institute of Esoteric Buddhism, Higher & Lower Institutes of Theology, Institute of Medicine and Institute of Law). A sixth institute was destroyed by fire. There are also numerous temple halls, living Buddha residences and living quarters for the monks.

At its peak the monastery housed nearly 4000 monks. Their ranks were depleted during the Cultural Revolution, but are slowly recovering and there are about 1300 today. Most of the monks come from Qinghai, Gansu, Sichuan or Inner Mongolia.

Many of the buildings look newly renovated. During the Cultural Revolution, monks and buildings took a heavy beating. In April 1985 the Institute of Esoteric Buddhism was razed in a fire caused by faulty electrical wiring. Apparently the fire burnt for a week and destroyed some priceless relics. Rebuilding has been completed at a cost of millions of yuan. As a result of the fire, monks are unwilling to use electric light anywhere in the monastery buildings, so take a torch.

In the late afternoon, monks often sit on the grass beside the river for a 'jam-session' with trumpets and long, ceremonial horns.

Tickets cost Y6 per person and are sold at a kiosk to the right of a large yard. The yard can be entered on the right-hand side of the main road – from the Minzu Fandian it's a two-km walk. The kiosk closes from noon to 2 pm for lunch and closes for the day at 4 pm. Postcards and brochures are on sale here.

Festivals These are important not only for the monks but also for the nomads, who stream into town from the grasslands in multicoloured splendour. Since the Tibetans use a lunar calendar, dates for individual festivals vary from year to year.

The Monlam (Great Prayer) Festival starts three days after the Tibetan New Year, which is usually in February or early March. On the 13th, 14th, 15th and 16th days of this month there are some spectacular ceremonies.

On the morning of the 13th a *thangka* (sacred painting on cloth) of Buddha measuring over 30 metres by 20 metres is unfurled on the other side of the Daxia River from the hillside facing the monastery. This event is accompanied by processions, bathing rituals and prayer assemblies. On the 14th there is an all-day session of Cham dances performed by 35 masked dancers, with Yama, the King of Religion, playing the leading role. On the 15th there is an evening display of butter lanterns and butter sculptures. On the 16th the Maitreya statue is paraded around the monastery all day.

During the second month (usually starting in March or early April) there are several interesting festivals, especially those held on the seventh and eighth days.

The Fiend-Banishing Ceremony, which takes place on the seventh day, centres around a 'fiend' who is, in fact, a villager hired to play the part of a scapegoat. The fiend, his face painted white and black, is ceremoniously driven out to the other side of the river and is forbidden to enter the monastery during the next week. On the morning of the eighth day, hundreds of monks in full regalia take part in a grand parade to display the monastery's huge collection of treasures and the paraphernalia of the living buddhas.

Scriptural debates, ritual bathing, lighting of butter lamps, collective prayers and blessings take place at other times during the year to commemorate Sakyamuni, Tsong Khapa or individual generations of the living buddhas.

Places to Stay

The up-market place to stay is the *Xiahe Binguan*, the former Summer Residence of living buddhas, a multicoloured haven of peace and architectural taste. It is miles away from the bus station (allow 45 minutes for the walk). To get there from the bus station continue straight down the main street, through the village and down to the river. A bed in an eight-bed dorm costs Y10, and Y13 in a three-bed dorm. Staff are very friendly. The hotel has hot showers.

Much closer to the bus station and less expensive is the *Minzu Fandian*, near the bridge in the centre of town. Beds in a four-bed dorm costs Y6; a two-bed dorm costs Y10; a single room costs Y12. It's not very attractive and there is no place to bathe, but you're best off staying here the night before departure if you want to catch the 6.30 am bus. They lock it up securely at night – the staff sleep in the room nearest the door and you'll have to wake them up so you can get out.

In the winter, when temperatures can drop to -23°C, wood for the stove in your room is extra.

Places to Eat

The *Xiahe Binguan* has a restaurant serving good food. There are several very good noodle shops near the bus station and monastery area. Any place where you see monks eating is bound to be good. Don't expect vegetarian food – practically all the monks here eat meat.

Things to Buy

The main street has an abundance of shops and stalls selling patterned cloth, daggers, half-swords, yak-hair shoe-liners (to keep your feet warm), Dalai Lama pics, turquoise jewellery and trinkets. Don't take claims of authenticity too seriously, and bargain like everyone else. On occasion you may see lynx skins and even a snow-leopard skin for sale – whatever you do, don't buy these skins. If you do, you are contributing directly to the extermination of these rare beasts.

Getting There & Away

Most people reach Xiahe by bus from Lanzhou. Sometimes you can book a direct ticket from Lanzhou to Xiahe, but often you will have to first go to Linxia and then change buses. It's a hassle for foreigners to buy a ticket to either Linxia or Xiahe – see the previous section on Linxia for a full explanation. You might prefer to stay the night before departure at the Friendship Hotel, which is a lot closer to the bus station than the Lanzhou Hotel. The bus departs from Lanzhou's west bus station *(qìchē xīzhàn)* at 6.30 am (7.30 am in summer) and takes about nine hours. The road isn't bad, but the bus sometimes gets overloaded and has to cough, wheeze and sputter its way up the mountain. The bus stops at Linxia for a lunch break.

To leave Xiahe, buy your bus ticket a day in advance at the bus station. Buses depart from the lower bus station, so it's much more convenient to stay at the Minzu Fandian the night before you leave. The bus is meant to leave at 6.30 am, but try to arrive at least 15 minutes earlier, especially if you need to load your luggage onto the roof.

TIANZHU

(tiānzhù) 天祝

This town is simply a place to avoid! It's on the rail line between Lanzhou and Jiayuguan. When the train stops here, don't even get off to buy anything – buy whatever you need on the train or through the windows. Tianzhu is closed to foreigners, and the Public Security Bureau here takes special delight in arresting foreigners, confiscating film and imposing steep fines. One group travelling on an organised CITS tour was arrested despite the fact that Lanzhou CITS told them that they had permission.

> In spite of being officially arranged through CITS, our group met trouble at Tianzhu, between Lanzhou and Wuwei, being arrested for being in a closed area without permission. As the agent had specifically asked for permission, as the party had paid for it, and as I had been told several times during the trip that we had it, it was a bit of a shock to find that we had not in fact got it. Anyway, we were tried and fined by the police in Wuwei.

Back in ancient times, travellers along the Silk Road had to worry about bandits, warlords, lack of water and shortages of food. These days, the main hazards are CITS, Public Security, FEC and the bungling bureaucracy. Visit Tianzhu at your own risk.

JIAYUGUAN

(jiāyùguān) 嘉峪关

Jiayuguan (Jiayu Pass) is an ancient Han Chinese outpost. The Great Wall once extended beyond here, but in 1372, during the

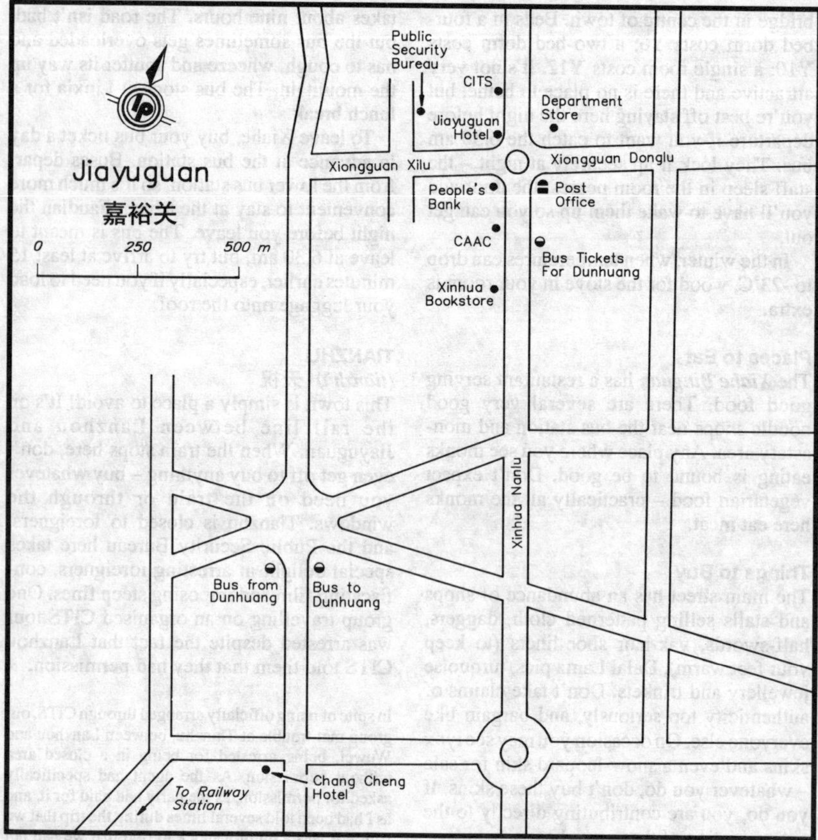

first few years of the Ming Dynasty, a fortress was built. From then on Jiayuguan was considered the terminal of the wall and the end of the empire.

The town lies on the Lanzhou-Ürümqi railway line, and is mainly made up of apartment blocks interspersed with factories and smokestacks. Not an unpleasant place, but drab and dusty. The main attraction is the fort, a worthy structure at which to stop off and have a look around. The mountains form a dramatic backdrop when the weather is clear.

Not far out of Jiayuguan is the Jiuquan Satellite Launching Centre. It was here that China launched its first satellite in 1970 which startled the world by broadcasting 'The East is Red' from space. The satellite centre is still in active use and would probably be an interesting place to visit, but it's not open to tourism.

Orientation

Someone has obviously given some thought to individual travellers because there are signs in English where you need them.

Jiayuguan is an easy place to find your way around since everything is easily accessible from the Jiayuguan Hotel. The railway station is four km to the south of the Jiayuguan Hotel. Minibuses connect the station and the hotel. A bus to the fort near town leaves from outside the hotel. The pick-up point for buses to Dunhuang is a 15 to 20-minute walk from the Jiayuguan Hotel.

Most travellers just do the trip to Jiayuguan Fort because transport is easy. However, if you really want to see everything that this area has to offer, it's best to organise a minibus trip to take in all the sights. Getting together a group of travellers brings down the cost. Most of the sights are for those interested in art and history. You can easily see everything in one day except for the July 1st Glacier, which is a bit of an expedition that most travellers don't bother with.

CITS The office (☎26931) is on the 2nd floor of the building behind the Jiayuguan Hotel.

Public Security Bureau This is close to the hotel. Turn right at the front gate and then right again at the first crossroads. The Public Security compound is around the corner, and the office handling foreigners is just inside the gateway.

Post There is a post office diagonally opposite the Jiayuguan Hotel.

Money There is no Bank of China in Jiayuguan, but you can change money at the People's Bank *(rénmín yínháng)* which is opposite the Jiayuguan Hotel.

Jiayuguan Fort
(jiāyùgūan chénglóu) 嘉峪关城楼
This is the main attraction of Jiayuguan. The fort guards the pass, which lies between the snow-capped Qilianshan peaks and Black Mountain *(hēishān)* of the Mazong range. During the Ming Dynasty this was considered the terminus of the Great Wall, though crumbling fragments can be seen to the west.

The fort was dubbed by the Chinese the 'Impregnable Defile Under the Sun' or the 'Impregnable Pass Under Heaven'. Although the Chinese often controlled territory far beyond Jiayuguan, this was the last major stronghold of the empire to the west.

The fort was first built in 1372, with additional towers and battlements added in subsequent years. The outer wall is about 733 metres in circumference and almost 10 metres high. At the eastern end of the fort is the Gate of Enlightenment *(gūanghùa mén)* and in the west is the Gate of Conciliation *(róuyǔan mén)*. Over each gate stand towers which rise to a height of 17 metres, with upturned flying eaves. On the inside of each gate are horse lanes leading up to the top of the wall. At the fort's four corners are blockhouses, bowmen's turrets and watchtowers. Outside the Gate of Enlightenment but inside the outer wall are three interesting buildings: the Wenchang Pavilion, Guandi Temple and the open-air theatre stage *(zhàntái)*.

A minibus runs from the front of the Jiayuguan Hotel to the fort. There are frequent

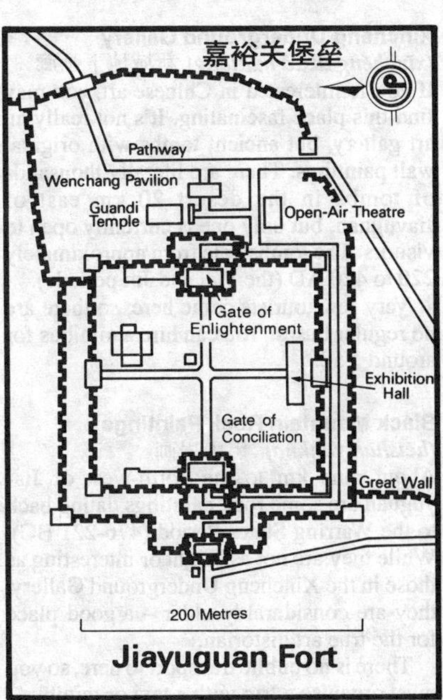

departures. Be sure to determine the fare before boarding. The distance is five km.

Overhanging Great Wall

(xúanbì chángchéng) 悬壁长城

This place is actually a lot more interesting than Jiayuguan Fort. Linking Jiayuguan with Black Mountain, the Overhanging Great Wall was believed to have been constructed in 1540. It pretty much crumbled to dust but was reconstructed in 1987. Students were brought in to do the reconstruction work and were paid one fen for each brick laid. Climb to the top for a great view.

It's seven km from Jiayuguan to the Overhanging Great Wall, but there is no regular transport. Either arrange a trip with a taxi, or see if you can jump on a tour bus with Hong Kongers or Japanese stopping at Jiayuguan Fort. This isn't hard to do – a little gift for the driver (a pack of cigarettes) will help pave the way. A number of travellers have successfully used this means of transport.

Xincheng Underground Gallery

(xīnchéng dìxià hùaláng) 新城地下画廊

If you're interested in Chinese art, you may find this place fascinating. It's not really an art gallery, but ancient tombs with original wall paintings. There are literally thousands of tombs in the desert 20 km east of Jiayuguan, but only one is currently open to visitors. The tombs date from approximately 220 to 420 AD (the Wei and Jin periods).

Very few tourists come here, so there are no regular buses. You can hire a minibus for around Y50.

Black Mountain Rock Paintings

(hēishān yánhùa) 黑山岩画

About nine km to the north-west of Jiayuguan are some rock paintings dating back to the Warring States Period (476-221 BC). While they are not as bright or interesting as those in the Xincheng Underground Gallery, they are considerably older – a good place for the true art historian.

There is no public transport to here, so you must organise a trip with a taxi or minibus.

First Beacon Tower

(dìyī dūn) 第一墩

This is the crumbling remains of a tower built on top of a cliff in 1539 at what was once the westernmost edge of the Great Wall. There isn't much to this place now, but you could include it with a taxi trip to Jiayuguan pass. It's six km south-west of Jiayuguan.

Places to Stay

There are only two hotels in town. Most popular is the *Jiayuguan Hotel* (☎ 26983, 25804) *(jiāyùgūan bīngǔan)*. It's conveniently located right in the centre of town. Dorms cost Y10 and doubles range from Y18 to Y200.

The *Chang Cheng Hotel (chángchéng bīngǔan)* is a shiny new hotel meant for tour groups. The dormitories have three beds with a private bath – the lap of luxury for Y30. Double rooms are Y200. It's on the south end of town and far from everything, but you can walk from here to the train station in 35 minutes. Very few individual travellers stay here.

Places to Eat

The Jiayuguan Hotel does set meals for Y4 – not great food, but reasonably nutritious. There are a few small restaurants outside the hotel.

Getting There & Away

Air The CAAC office is on Xinhua Nanlu a short distance south of the Jiayuguan Hotel (see map). There are flights from Jiayuguan to Lanzhou and Dunhuang. Apparently, reservations to Dunhuang are only confirmed once the aircraft has taken off in Lanzhou. The flights are dependent on tourism, so during the slow season they may not be running. The airport is 14 km from the city.

Bus You can buy tickets for Dunhuang a day in advance at a dinky ticket window diagonally opposite the Jiayuguan Hotel. However, the buses depart from an inconveniently located tiny station near a large intersection (six crossroads converge on this point). It's a 15 to 20-minute walk from the

Jiayuguan Hotel and a little hard to find, so check out the location the day before or give yourself some extra time to find this place. The first departure is at 7 am and there are four buses daily. The trip takes seven hours and costs Y18.

Buses to the nearby city of Jiuquan leave from the stop just next to the post office diagonally across the road from the guesthouse. The first bus is at 6.30 am and the last at 7.45 pm, with buses departing at half to one-hour intervals.

Train A train schedule is posted in the lobby of the Jiayuguan Hotel. Jiayuguan lies on the Lanzhou-Ürümqi railway line. There are five trains a day in each direction. The trip to Liuyuan takes from six to seven hours. Buses to the railway station depart from the stop outside the People's Bank.

The workers in the Jiayuguan railway station are possibly the laziest in China, if not the whole world. Four virtually unemployed women run the tiny station, and spend the whole day sleeping, eating, chatting, drinking tea, picking lint from their bellybuttons and totally ignoring the people who want to buy tickets. Only as the train pulls into the station do they finally open the ticket window, by which time there is a panicked mob of would-be passengers all desperately trying to get a ticket before the train leaves.

Getting Around

Bicycles are available for hire from the Jiayuguan Hotel. There is a workable bus system for the city, but it's a small place so a bicycle should be sufficient. You'll need to use minibuses to reach most of the sights.

AROUND JIAYUGUAN

July 1st Glacier

(qīyī bīngchūan) 七一冰川

This glacier is 120 km south-west of Jiayuguan in the Qilianshan mountains. The elevation is 4300 metres and hikers can walk a five-km-long path by the side of the glacier. At this elevation, it gets cold even in summer, so come prepared. The glacier can only be reached by taxi. Prices are negotiable, but figure on at least Y200 for the vehicle. The area looks like it could present an interesting challenge to genuine mountaineers, but any suggestion of climbing the peaks would undoubtedly horrify CITS.

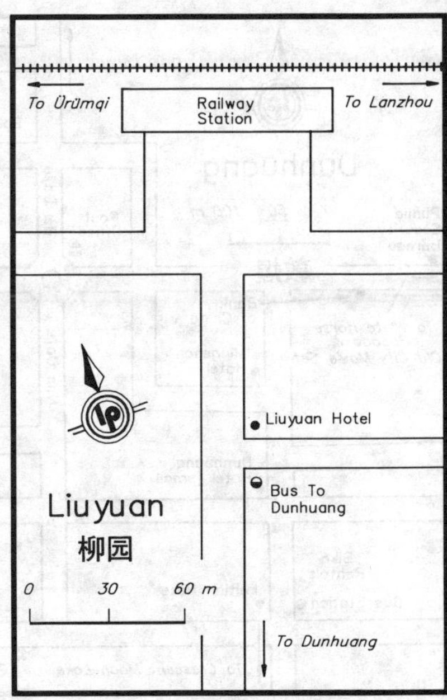

LIUYUAN

(liǔyúan) 柳园

Liuyuan on the Lanzhou-Ürümqi railway line is the jumping-off point for Dunhuang. It's a small, forlorn-looking town in the middle of the desert, and any traveller who comes here should bring a costume and a song-and-dance act to cheer up the Chinese.

There are six trains daily in each direction. Going east, it takes six hours to reach Jiayuguan and 18 hours to reach Lanzhou. Heading west, it's 13 hours to Turpan and 16 hours to Ürümqi.

Buses for Dunhuang depart eight times daily from a small bus terminal one block south of the station. It's 130 km – the fare is Y6 and the trip takes from 2½ to three hours.

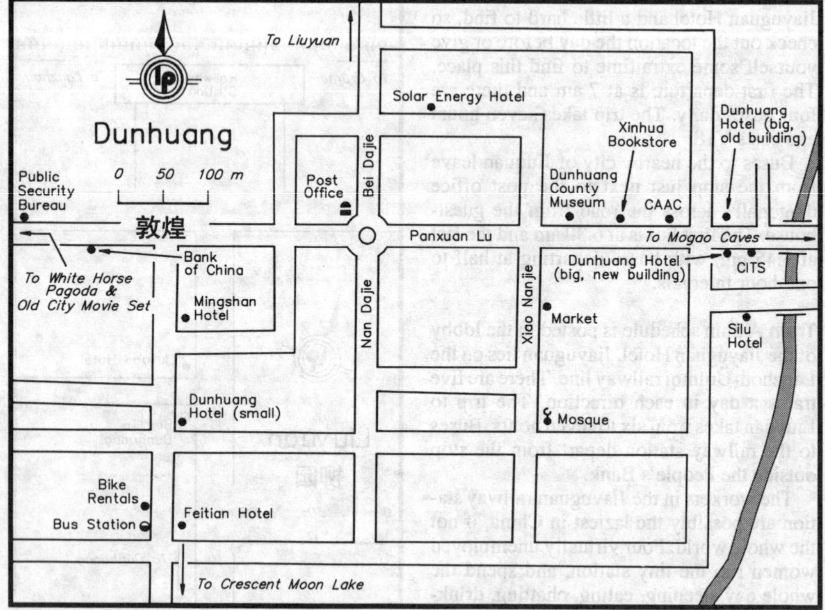

If you arrive late, you'll have to spend the night in the town.

The only place that accepts foreigners is the Liuyuan Hotel *(liǔyúan bīngǔan)* on the main street right by the bus station. There is an English sign on the building. Dorm beds in a three-person room are Y14, or Y25 in a two-person room. The two-person rooms have a private bath, but it hardly matters since the plumbing seldom works. Some travellers have managed to stay in the meeting room for just Y5.

DUNHUANG

(dūnhúang) 墩皇

Dunhuang is a large oasis in one of the most arid regions of China. As you approach by bus, the lush, green oasis suddenly looms out of nowhere like a mirage floating on the giant sand dunes. The area has a certain haunting beauty, especially at night under a star-studded sky.

However, it is not the desert sand dunes and romantic nights that attracts visitors. Tourists come to Dunhuang because of the superb Buddhist art on view in the nearby Mogao Caves. During the Han and Tang dynasties Dunhuang was a pivotal point of interchange between China and the outside world, a major staging-post for both incoming and outgoing trading caravans. Although it no longer plays a role in China's foreign trade, Dunhuang's economic fortunes have been revived by tourism – today it's one of the leading travel destinations in the country.

Information & Orientation

The centre of Dunhuang is little more than two intersecting roads. All life-support systems are within easy walking distance of each other.

CITS There is a CITS office on the second floor of the new section of the bigger Dunhuang Hotel near the CAAC (not to be confused with the smaller Dunhuang Hotel nearer the bus station, see Places to Stay). Since you can't buy train tickets in Dunhuang, there isn't a whole lot they can do for you other than to tell you the current departure times for the various means of transport. Of course, they can arrange tours to some of the more remote sights such as Yumen Pass.

Public Security Bureau This is within walking distance of all the hotels (see map). It's open from 7.30 am to noon and from 3 to 6.30 pm but is closed on Sundays.

Money You can change money at the Bank of China, which is within walking distance from all the hotels (see map). The bank is open from 9.15 am to noon and from 3 to 5.30 pm.

Maps There's a simple map of Dunhuang on sale in the foyer of the bigger Dunhuang Hotel. It's not terribly helpful but has a few nice pictures on the back so you can see what the various tourist sites look like.

Dunhuang County Museum

(dūnhúang xiàn bówùgŭan) 墩皇县博物馆

Walk down the main street towards the Dunhuang Hotel, and the museum is on the left side, about 50 metres after the traffic circle.

The museum is divided into three sections. The first section displays some of the scriptures written in Tibetan and Chinese unearthed from Cave No 17 at Mogao. The second section shows sacrificial objects from the Han to the Tang dynasties. The third section includes relics such as silks, brocades, bamboo slips and reed torches (for the beacons) from the Yangguan and Yumen passes. A pleasant museum for a browse.

Crescent Moon Lake

(yùeyáqúan) 月牙泉

The lake itself is just a small, crescent-shaped pond, but it's well worth visiting. Nestled among the giant sand dunes on the south side of the oasis, the setting is dramatic. It's a steep, hard climb to the top of the dunes, but you get a great view of the oasis in one direction and the infinite stretch of desert in the other. The Chinese call this particular set of dunes the Singing Sand Mountains *(míngshāshān)*.

You can bicycle out to the dunes, but most visitors take the once-daily bus which departs the bus terminal at 6 pm and returns at 8 pm. The fare is just Y1.50 for the round trip. Buy the ticket on the bus. There is a Y2 admission fee to the dunes area (Chinese pay Y0.30) but at least they accept RMB. You'll get plenty of offers to ride a camel. Rates are Y8 (one person) for 20 minutes, Y10 for two persons) or Y40 to the top of the dunes.

If you decide to come out here by yourself in the daytime to do some hiking, bring plenty of water, food and a compass – this would be a bad place to get lost.

White Horse Pagoda

(báimă tă) 白马塔

It's not the most impressive pagoda you'll ever see, but it's only four km west of Dunhuang and you can easily get there by bicycle.

Old City – Movie Set

(diànyĭng gŭchéng) 电影古城

If you're wondering why all those Japanese tour groups flock to Dunhuang, this is the reason. A Chinese-Japanese joint venture filmed a movie here in 1987. The title was *Dunhuang* and it became an award-winning hit in Japan. Lots of local people and a number of camels were hired as stand-ins. The actors and directors lived in Dunhuang for over six months, and it was undoubtedly the biggest invasion of foreigners the town had seen since Kublai Khan. The movie set – an imitation of a Song Dynasty town – was constructed at a cost of over Y3,000,000. While it's really not so exciting to see, the Japanese tourists love it. You can try tagging on to one of their tours. The movie set is 20 km west of Dunhuang – it is possible to get there by bicycle if you're really determined.

Mogao Caves

(mògāo kū) 莫高窑

The Mogao (Desert High) Caves are the highlight of Dunhuang and one of the highlights of north-west China. The story goes that in 366 AD the vision of a thousand buddhas inspired a wandering monk to cut the first of hundreds of caves into the sandstone cliff face. Over the next 10 centuries Dunhuang became a flourishing centre of Buddhist culture on the Silk Road.

The grottoes were then abandoned and eventually forgotten. At the turn of the 20th century a Taoist monk stumbled across a cave filled with a treasure trove of documents and paintings. The cave had been bricked up to stop the contents falling into the hands of invaders and the dry desert air had preserved much of the material.

In 1907, the British explorer Sir Aurel Stein heard a rumour of the hoard, tracked down the monk and was allowed to inspect the contents of the cave. It was an archaeological gold mine of Buddhist texts in Chinese, Tibetan and many other central Asian languages, some known and some long forgotten. There were paintings on silk and linen, and what may be the oldest printed book in existence (dating from 868 AD).

The sacking of the caves began in earnest. Stein convinced Wang to part with a large section of the library in return for a donation towards the restoration of some of the grottoes. He carted away 24 packing cases of manuscripts and five of paintings, embroideries and art relics, all of which were deposited in the British Museum. The following year a French explorer, Pelliot, passed through Dunhuang and bought more of the manuscripts from the monk. He was followed by others from the United States, Japan and Russia, who all carted off their booty. News of the find filtered through to Beijing, and the imperial court ordered the remainder of the collection to be transported to the capital. Many items were pilfered while they sat in the Dunhuang government offices, and Stein reported in 1914 when he returned to the area that fine Buddhist manuscripts were brought to him for sale. He also said that Wang had regretted not taking up his original offer to buy the entire collection.

For the Chinese it's another example of the plundering of the country by foreigners in the 19th and early 20th centuries, though one hates to think what would have happened to the collection if Stein had left it where it was – most likely it would have been looted and either destroyed or sold off piecemeal. Half the world seems to have ended up in the British Museum – the Greeks want their Parthenon frieze back and the Chinese want the Dunhuang manuscripts back.

The Mogao Caves are set into desert cliffs above a river valley about 25 km south-east of Dunhuang. Unfortunately, the area is highly exposed to the elements and the erosion of wind and water have severely damaged quite a few of the caves. Cave 94, for example, is badly damaged and is now used to store junk. Today, 492 grottoes are still standing. The grottoes honeycomb the 1600-metre-long cliff face which sits on a north-south axis. Altogether they contain over 2000 statues and over 45,000 separate murals. Cave 17 is where the Taoist monk, Wang Yuan, discovered the hoard of manuscripts and artworks.

Most of the Dunhuang art dates from the Northern and Western Wei, Northern Zhou, Sui and Tang dynasties, though examples from the Five Dynasties, Northern Song, Western Xia and Yuan can also be found. The Northern Wei, Western Wei, Northern Zhou and Tang caves are in the best state of preservation.

The caves tend to be rectangular or square with recessed, decorated ceilings. The focal point of each is the group of brightly painted statues representing Buddha and the bodhisattvas or Buddha's disciples. The smaller statues are made of terracotta, coated with a kind of plaster surface so that intricate details could be etched into the surface. The walls and ceilings were also plastered with layers of cement and clay and then painted with watercolour. Large sections of the mural are made up of decorative patterns using motifs from nature, architecture, or textiles.

Northern Wei, Western Wei & Northern Zhou Dynasties (386-581 AD) The Turkic-speaking Tobas who inhabited the region north of China invaded and conquered the country in the 4th century and founded the Northern Wei Dynasty around 386 AD. They deliberately adopted a policy of copying Chinese customs and lifestyle. But friction between groups who wanted to maintain the traditional Toba lifestyle and those who wanted to assimilate with the Chinese eventually split the Toba empire in two in the middle of the 6th century; the eastern part adopted the Chinesc way of life and the rulers took the dynasty name of Northern Qi. The western part took the dynastic name of Northern Zhou and tried to revert to Toba customs without success. By 567 AD, however, they had defeated the Qi and taken control of all of northern China.

The fall of the Han Dynasty in 220 AD had sent Confucianism into decline. With the turmoil produced by the Toba invasions, Buddhism's teachings of nirvana and personal salvation became highly appealing. The religion spread rapidly under the patronage of the new rulers, and made a new and decisive impact on Chinese art which can be seen in the Buddhist statues at Mogao.

The art of this period is characterised by its attempt to depict the spirituality of those who had achieved enlightenment and transcended the material world through their asceticism. The Wei statues are slim, ethereal figures with finely chiselled features and comparatively large heads. The bodhisattvas in Northern Wei Caves 248 and 257 are a good example of the later Wei. Like the sculptures of the same period at Luoyang, the expressions on the faces of the buddhas and bodhisattvas are benevolently saccharine – Cave 259 of the Northern Wei period is a good example.

The Wei and Zhou paintings at Mogao are some of the most interesting in the grottoes. The figures are simple, almost cartoon-like, with round heads, elongated ears and puppet-like, segmented bodies which are boldly outlined. The female figures are all naked to the waist, with large breasts, which suggests an Indian influence. Northern Zhou Cave 299 shows musicians and dancers in this style, and Cave 290 shows flying celestial maidens. The paintings in Northern Zhou Cave 428 are a good example of this style.

The wall painting in Northern Wei Cave 254, done in the same style, portrays the story of Buddha vanquishing Mara. It refers to the night that Buddha sat beneath a fig tree south of the Indian city of Patna, and entered into deep meditation. Mara, the Evil One, realising that Sakyamuni was on the verge of enlightenment, rushed to the spot. Mara tempted him with desire, parading three voluptuous goddesses before him, but Sakyamuni resisted. Then Mara assailed him with hurricanes, torrential rains and showers of flaming rocks, but the missiles turned to lotus petals. Finally Mara challenged Buddha's right to do what he was doing, but Buddha touched the earth with his fingertip and the roaring it summoned up drove away Mara and his army of demons. Sakyamuni had achieved enlightenment – but Mara was waiting with one last temptation. This time it was an appeal to reason, that speech-defying revelations could not be translated into words and no one would understand so profound a truth as the Buddha had attained; but Buddha said that there would be some who would understand, and Mara was finally banished forever.

Murals tend to be highly detailed and figures are relatively small. During the Wei Dynasty portraits of noble patrons began to be depicted alongside the more religious themes that they had sponsored. These figures depict the lifestyle and fashions of the Wei nobles. The men are usually shown in the Chinese robe and the women in a tight-fitting gown with loose sleeves.

Sui Dynasty (581-618 AD) The throne of the Northern Zhou Dynasty was usurped by a general of Chinese or mixed Chinese-Toba origin. Prudently putting to death all the sons of the former emperor, he embarked on a series of wars which by 589 had reunited northern and southern China for the first time in 360 years. The Tobas simply disappeared from history, either mixing with other Turkish tribes from Central Asia or assimilating with the Chinese.

The Sui Dynasty was short-lived, and very much a transition between the Wei and Tang periods. It did not leave any great masterpieces. Again, the best Sui art was of Buddhist origin. What separates the Sui style from that of the Wei is the rigidity of its sculpture. The figures of the Buddha and bodhisattvas are stiff and immobile; their heads are curiously oversized and their torsos elongated. They wear Chinese robes and show none of the Indian-inspired softness and grace of the Wei figures.

At Mogao the Sui caves are north of the Wei caves. Buddha's disciples Ananda and Kasyapa are both seen here for the first time – see cave 419 for example. There are also a number of examples of the lotus flower symbol and designs from Middle Asian and Persian brocades. Stories from the life of Buddha provide the main themes of the wall paintings. Other Sui caves include 204, 244, 302 and 427. Some of the paintings show processions of musicians, attendants, wagons and horses.

Tang Dynasty (618-907 AD) The reign of the last Sui emperor, Yang Ti, was characterised by imperial extravagance, cruelty and social injustice. Taking advantage of the inevitable peasant revolts which had arisen in eastern China, a noble family of Chinese-Turkish descent assassinated the emperor, took control of the capital, Chang'an, and assumed the throne, taking the dynasty name of Tang.

During the Tang period China extended its domain by force of arms into central Asia, pushing outward as far as Lake Balkhash in what is today Soviet Kazakhstan. Trade with the outside world expanded and foreign merchants and people of diverse religions poured into the Tang capital of Chang'an. Tang art took on incomparable vigour, moving towards greater realism and nobility of form. Buddhism had become prominent and Buddhist art reached its peak; the proud bearing of the Buddhist figures in the Mogao Caves reflects the feelings of the times, the prevailing image of the brave Tang warrior, and the strength and steadfastness of the empire.

Extravagant robes drape many of the figures, which show an element of sensuality typical of Persian and Indian art. The Tang figures are notable for their overwhelming size and power. The best examples are the colossal Buddhas of caves 96 and 130; the one in 96 stands over 30 metres high. The statues can be viewed from platforms constructed in the cave wall opposite their chests and faces. The roof and walls of Cave 130 are adorned with paintings.

Portraits of Tang nobles are considerably larger than those of the Wei and Sui dynasties and figures tend to occupy important positions within the murals. In some cases patrons are portrayed within the same scene as the Buddha

Unlike the figures of the Wei, Zhou and Sui periods, the Tang figures are realistic with a range of very human expressions. The portrait of a Buddhist nun in cave 17 and the statue of Buddha's older disciple Kasyapa in Cave 45 are good examples of this. There are also notable exceptions such as the statues in Cave 16 with their heavy eyebrows, long slitted eyes and enormous hands.

Other Tang Dynasty caves include 45, 57, 103, 112, 156, 159, 196, 217, 220, 320, 321, 328 and 329. Cave 156 has an interesting wall mural showing a Tang army on the march and Cave 158 has a huge statue of the dead Buddha with a group of grieving 'foreigners'.

Later Dynasties The ultimate development of the cave paintings was reached under the Tang Dynasty. During the later dynasties the economy around Dunhuang went into decline and the luxuriousness and vigour typical of Tang Dynasty painting began to be replaced by simpler drawing techniques and flatter figures. However, during the Northern Song period a number of important breakthroughs were made in landscape painting. Wutaishan in Cave 61 is a good example of this style. People are integrated into the landscape and scenery is depicted for its own sake, rather than just as an abstract backdrop.

No 3 is an example of a Yuan Dynasty cave. Cave 346 is an example of a Five Dynasties cave. Cave 55 is another example of a Northern Song construction.

Admission Chinese pay Y1 for 10 caves, but foreigners must pay Y16 and are permitted to see 30 caves. The fee includes a guide, and a few of them speak surprisingly good English. Unfortunately, no attempt is made to separate the Chinese and foreigners into separate groups – so half of your group could be Chinese-speaking and the other half English-speaking. In this case, the guides will usually just speak in Chinese. With some effort, you can try to round up the foreigners into one group and try to get an English-speaking guide – you are not committed to stick with the guide they assign you. There is a sign by the ticket window saying they can arrange an English-speaking guide, but they charge an excessive fee for this and it isn't necessary. You can work the situation with the guides even after you've entered the cave area – there are many guides around (at least during the tourist season).

Except for the small niches (most of them in very bad condition or bare of statues and paintings) all the caves have locked gates. Many of the locked caves are in such poor condition that they are simply not worth opening to the general public. Some, like Cave 462 – the Mizong Cave – contain Tantric art whose explicit sexual portrayals have been deemed too corrupting for the public to view. A few caves are in the process of being restored. Only 40 have been cleared for public view.

You're not allowed to take photos in the caves; you have to leave your camera and bags in the luggage hut near the entrance. Photos are sometimes permitted after payment of an appropriately vast sum of money. Banning flash photos is understandable, but you're not even allowed to take time-exposures. Instead a shop outside the cave sells slides, postcards and books. Bring your own torch as most of the caves are very dark and it's hard to see much detail, particularly in the niches. Torches can be hired at the caves for Y2.

Getting There & Away It's 25 km and 30 minutes by bus. There are only two buses daily – the first departs at 7.30 am (8 am in summer) and returns at 11 am. The afternoon bus departs at 1.30 pm and returns at 4.30 pm. The cost is Y3 for a round-trip ticket. They sell the tickets on the bus. These buses may not run in the dead of winter.

Alternatively, you could hire a taxi at the Dunhuang Hotel to take you to the caves. You'll have to pay the driver for his waiting time – be sure to agree on the fare in advance.

You could also bicycle out there, but be warned that half the ride is entirely through desert and would be absolute murder.

For Y12 per person you can stay in the hotel *(mògāokū zhāodàisǔo)* at the caves. It's a good hotel and the Y8 lunch is served punctually at noon and is very filling.

Places to Stay

Unfortunately, there are two places that go by the English name *Dunhuang Hotel* (their Chinese names are different). In this chapter, when we refer to the Dunhuang Hotel *(dūnhúang bīngǔan)*, we are talking about the big, touristy one near the CAAC office and CITS. The smaller Dunhuang Hotel *(dūnhúang fàndiàn)* is near the bus station.

The large *Dunhuang Hotel* (☎ 2415) *(dūnhúang bīngǔan)* has dorms for Y15 in the old building and Y20 in the new building. Doubles are Y90 (old building) and Y116 (new building). There are student discounts on the double rooms.

Right behind the large Dunhuang Hotel is the *Silu Hotel* (☎ 2371) *(sīlù bīngǔan)* where good clean doubles with private bath can be had for Y40. One traveller we know bargained them down to Y30 after agreeing to stay for three nights and paying in advance.

The small Dunhuang Hotel *(dūnhúang fàndiàn)* charges Y10 for a dorm and Y25 for a double room. The double rooms have private baths but the plumbing is pretty unre-

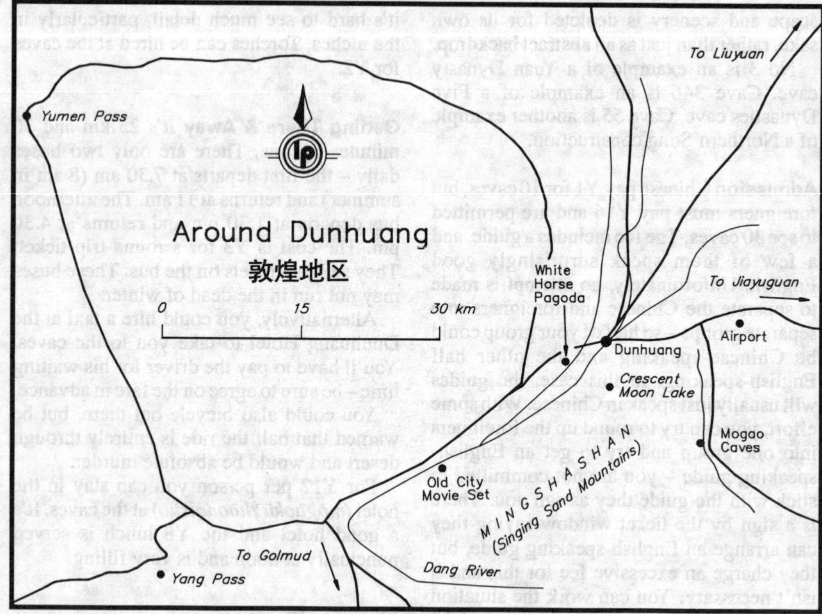

liable. This hotel is a little bleak, but the location is good.

The *Mingshan Hotel* (☎ 2132) *(míngshān bīngŭan)* is near the small Dunhuang Hotel. Doubles cost from Y15 to Y20, but it's somewhat gloomy and the plumbing also leaves much to be desired.

Probably the best deal in town is *Feitian Hotel* (☎ 2337) *(fēitiān bīngŭan)*. The eight-bed dorms cost Y10 and doubles are Y39. It's directly opposite the bus station. Clean, bright and friendly, and you can't beat the location.

Places to Eat

Food at the large *Dunhuang Hotel* is good and reasonably cheap.

During summer evenings, the best place to eat is around the traffic circle by the post office. Literally hundreds of tables are set up here. Shish kebab and other meat dishes are popular – not much for vegetarians though.

Getting There & Away

Air You can book CAAC flights at CITS in the bigger Dunhuang Hotel or walk across the street and book yourself at the CAAC office (☎ 2389). The airport is 13 km from town.

Dunhuang is connected by air to Jiayuguan and to Lanzhou, but the flights aren't very reliable. There are charter flights to Beijing during the peak tourist season (from July to October).

Bus & Rail Buses to Liuyuan (130 km) depart eight times daily from the bus station between 7.30 am and 6 pm. The fare is Y6 and the trip takes about 2½ hours. Liuyuan is on the Lanzhou-Ürümqi railway line. See the Liuyuan section for details about the trains.

If you're going east, you can save yourself some time and hassle by taking a direct bus to Jiayuguan. Departures are at 7.30, 9 and 11.30 am, and at 1.30 pm. It's 380 km, takes seven hours and costs Y18. The bus actually goes to Jiuquan, stopping only briefly in Jiayuguan – make sure you get off or else you'll have to backtrack. There is nothing to see in Jiuquan.

Buses to Golmud leave at 6.30 am (7.30 am in summer). The fare is Y24 and the trip takes 13 hours. You have to store your luggage on the roof, but keep a warm jacket handy even in summer (no matter how hot it is in Dunhuang) because it gets cold suddenly as you ascend the mountains.

Getting Around

Bicycles are for hire outside the large Dunhuang Hotel and by the bus station.

AROUND DUNHUANG

Yang & Yumen Passes

(yánggūan, yùméngūan) 阳关，玉门关

Approximately 76 km south-west of Dunhuang is the Yang (South) Pass. The Han Dynasty beacon towers which marked the route westwards for the camel caravans, and which warned the populace of invaders, have almost disappeared under the drifting sand. Nearby are the ruins of the ancient Han town of Shouchang.

From Dunhuang, it's 98 km to the north-west to reach Yumen (Jade Gate) Pass, also noted for its ancient ruins. If you want to go on safari to either of these passes you'd have to go with a tour group or hire a taxi from the hotel. There are English signs around Dunhuang at various locations advertising trips to these passes.

Caravans heading out of China would travel up the Gansu corridor to Dunhuang; the Yumen Pass was the starting point of the road which ran across the north of what is now Xinjiang Province, and the Yang Pass was the start of the route which cut through the south of the region.

Xinjiang 新疆

Xinjiang *(xīnjiāng)* is one of China's 'autonomous regions', inhabited predominantly by the Turkish-speaking Muslim Uigur *(wéiwǔěr)* people whose autonomy from their Chinese overlords is only nominal.

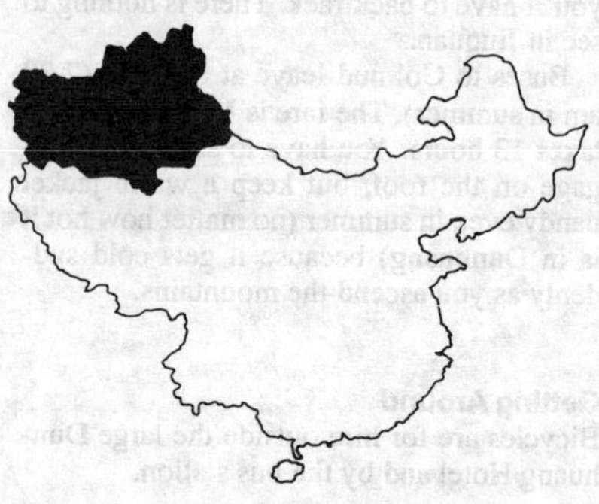

HISTORY

The history of this desolate north-western region has largely been one of continuing wars and conflicts between the native populations, coupled with repeated Chinese invasions and subjugations.

The Chinese were interested in the region for two reasons. Firstly, a lucrative trade plied the 'silk roads' that cut through the oasis towns north and south of the Taklimakan Desert. Along this route camel caravans would carry goods from China to central Asia (from where they eventually found their way to Europe). The trade had been going on at least since Roman days when silk, the principal Chinese export, was prized by fashionable Roman women. Whoever controlled the oasis towns could also tax the flow of goods, so the conquest of Xinjiang was a highly profitable venture.

Secondly, subjugation of the region would help control the troublesome nomadic border tribes, the 'barbarians', who made frequent raids into China to carry off prisoners and booty.

The Chinese never really subdued the region and their hold over it waxed and waned with the power of the central government. The area was constantly subjected to waves of invasions by the Huns and Tibetans, as well as by the Mongols under Genghis Khan, and later on by the Turkic Timur (known as Tamerlane or Tamburlaine in English) at the beginning of the 15th century.

The Han were the first Chinese rulers to conquer Xinjiang. They did so between 73 and 97 AD, even crossing the Tianshan mountains and marching an army of 70,000 people as far as the Caspian Sea, although the Chinese only held onto an area slightly to the east of Lake Balkash. With the demise of the Han in the 3rd century the Chinese lost control of the region until the Tang expeditions reconquered it and extended Chinese power as far as Lake Balkash.

Qing Dynasty

Then, with the fall of the Tang, the region was once again lost to the Chinese; it was not recovered until the Qing Dynasty, when the second Qing emperor, Kangxi, came to the throne at 16 years of age. His long rule from 1661 to 1722 allowed him enough time to conquer Mongolia and Tibet as well, giving the Chinese power over the largest area ever.

The 19th century was a bloody one of general unrest for Xinjiang with internal and external threats. A raging rebellion had been staged between the Yellow and Yangtse rivers in 1796, followed by the massive Taiping Rebellion from 1851 to 1864. There were also two major Muslim rebellions: one in Yunnan from 1855 to 1873, and another in the north-west which spread across Shaanxi, Ningxia, Gansu and Xinjiang from 1862 to 1873. Both were put down with extreme savagery by the Chinese. The north-western rebellion had grown out of decades of Chinese misrule, religious controversy, and contact with the Taipings. The massacre of

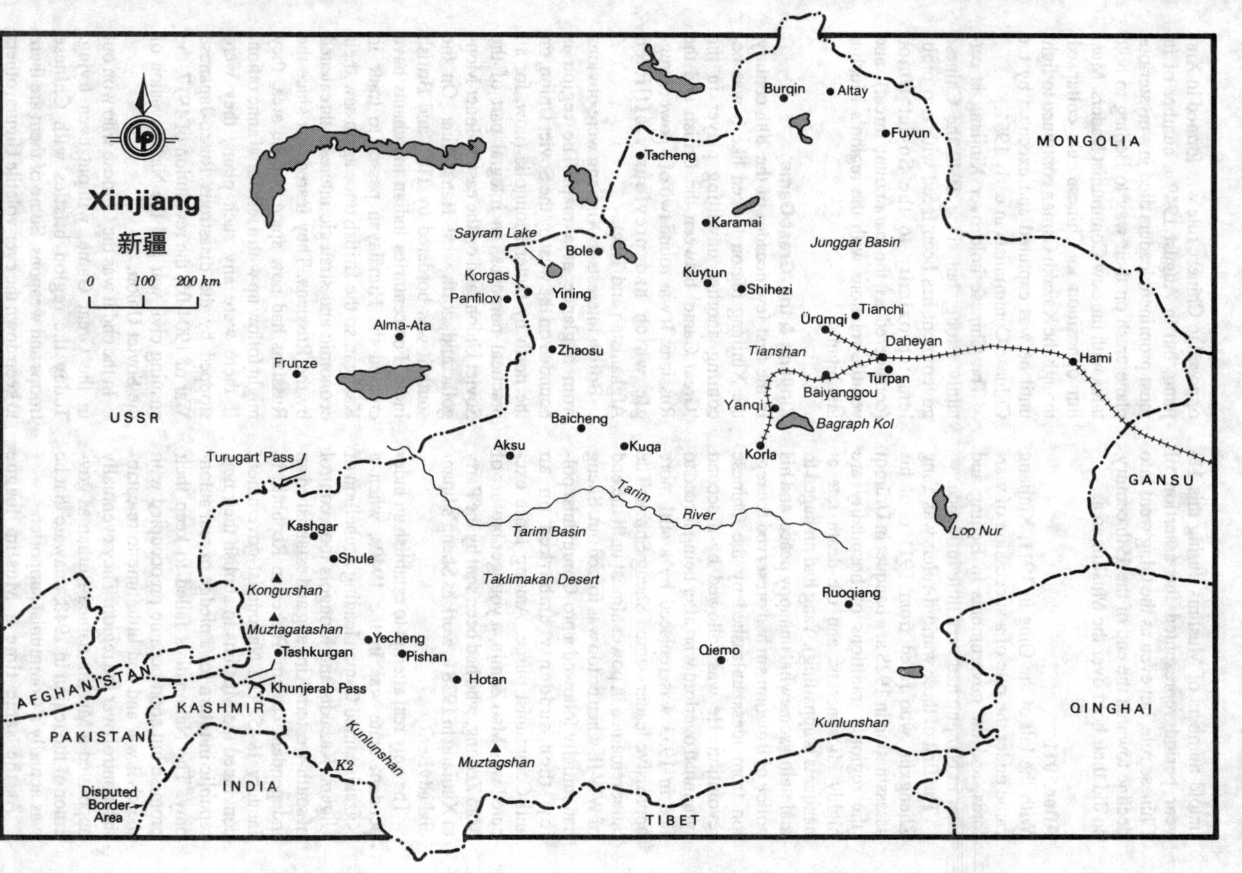
Xinjiang
新疆
0 100 200 km
MONGOLIA
GANSU
QINGHAI
TIBET
INDIA
KASHMIR
PAKISTAN
AFGHANISTAN
USSR
Disputed Border Area
Burqin
Altay
Fuyun
Tacheng
Karamai
Junggar Basin
Sayram Lake
Bole
Korgas
Panfilov
Yining
Kuytun
Shihezi
Ürümqi
Tianchi
Daheyan
Hami
Tianshan
Turpan
Baiyanggou
Yanqi
Bagraph Kol
Korla
Alma-Ata
Zhaosu
Frunze
Baicheng
Aksu
Kuqa
Turugart Pass
Tarim River
Tarim Basin
Lop Nur
Kashgar
Shule
Kongurshan
Taklimakan Desert
Ruoqiang
Muztagatashan
Yecheng
Tashkurgan
Pishan
Qiemo
Hotan
Khunjerab Pass
Kunlunshan
K2
Muztagshan

untold numbers of Muslims during this 11-year period represented the assertion of Chinese rule, but even as the Qing went into decline towards the end of the 19th century, so did their hold over the Muslim areas.

After 1911

With the fall of the Qing in 1911, Xinjiang came under the rule of a succession of warlords, and the governments in Beijing and later in Nanjing had very little influence.

The first of these warlord-rulers was Yang Zhengxin, who ruled from 1911 until his assassination in 1928 at a banquet in Ürümqi (the region's traditions of hospitality are highly idiosyncratic and the death rate at banquets is appalling). Yang had managed to maintain a somewhat unhappy peace, and his policy of isolationism had preserved the region from ideas unleashed by the Chinese revolution. He was followed by a second tyrannical overlord who after being forced to flee in 1933 was replaced by a still more oppressive leader named Sheng Shizai. The latter remained in power almost until the end of WW II, when he too was forced out. Sheng had initially followed a pro-Communist policy, then suddenly embarked on an anti-Communist purge. Among those executed was Mao Zemin, a younger brother of Mao Zedong, who had been sent by the Party to Xinjiang in 1938 to work as Sheng's financial adviser.

The only real attempt to establish an independent state was in the 1940s, when a Kazakh named Osman leading a rebellion of Uigurs, Kazakhs and Mongols took control of south-western Xinjiang and established an independent eastern Turkestan Republic in January 1945. The Nationalist government convinced the Muslims to abolish their new republic in return for a pledge of real autonomy. The Nationalists failed to keep their promise but soon became preoccupied with the civil war and had little time to re-establish control over the region. They eventually appointed a Muslim named Burhan as governor of the region in 1948, unaware that he was actually a Communist supporter.

At the same time a Muslim league opposed to Chinese rule was formed in Xinjiang, but in August 1949 a number of its most prominent leaders died in a mysterious plane crash on their way to Beijing to hold talks with the new Communist leaders. Muslim opposition to Chinese rule collapsed, though the Kazakh Osman continued to fight until he was captured and executed by the Chinese Communists in early 1951.

The Chinese hold over Xinjiang is certainly strong, but since 1949 the Chinese government has been faced with two problems: proximity to the Soviet Union (considered as the paramount threat), and volatile relations with the region's Muslim inhabitants.

Xinjiang & the 'Great Game'

In the first few decades of the 20th century, the Xinjiang region looked like it was becoming another unwilling player in the 'Great Game' between the British and the Russians. It was round two of a power struggle which had previously afflicted Afghanistan and Tibet.

British interests in Xinjiang were obvious from a glance at a map. The region is bounded on the west by the Soviet Union, on the north by Outer Mongolia (now, for all practical purposes, an integral part of the Soviet Union) and on the east by Inner Mongolia and north-west Han China. On the south it was bordered by Tibet and British India. For centuries Indian merchants have crossed the Himalayan passes to trade in Kashgar, so the British once again saw their economic and strategic interests threatened by the Russians. They feared that since the Russians had now spied out the area, they might follow up with a territorial annexation. If there were any such plans, they were stopped by the disastrous Russo-Japanese War of 1904-05, the revolution of 1917, the ensuing civil war and the Nazi invasion of the Soviet Union.

In the end it was the Chinese who won out in the Great Game, without even trying. Today the region bristles with Chinese troops and weapons. Some of them are there to keep down the ever-volatile Uigurs; others hold back the real or imagined threat from the Soviet Union.

GEOGRAPHY

Xinjiang is divided by the east-west Tianshan range into two major regions. To the south of the range is the Tarim Basin, and to the north is the Junggar Basin.

The Tarim Basin, a huge depression whose centre is the sands of the Taklimakan Desert and where streams from the surrounding mountains lose themselves, is bordered to the south by the Kunlunshan range.

Other streams run from the Tianshan range into the Tarim River, which flows eastward and empties into the vast salt marsh and lake of Lop Nur. The boundaries of Lop Nur vary greatly from year to year as a result of climatic variation; it's an area of almost uninhabited poor grassland and semi-desert. Since 1964 the Chinese have been testing nuclear bombs here.

The Taklimakan Desert is a true desert. Cultivation is only possible in the oases of irrigated land centred on the streams flowing into the basin from the surrounding mountains. These oases, largely populated by Uigur people, have had flourishing cultures of their own for 2000 years and were important stopover points on the Silk Road.

They support an irrigated agricultural industry based mainly on food grains and fruit, while the grasslands of the foothills support a pastoral industry based on sheep and horses. The agriculture of places like the Turpan and Hami depressions depends entirely on irrigation, using water drawn from underground streams. Only in the Ili Valley, west of Ürümqi, is rainfall sufficient to support a flourishing agricultural and pastoral industry.

The Junggar Basin has been the centre of extensive colonisation by the Chinese since the 1950s. Large state farms have been established on formerly uncultivated land. The major towns are Ürümqi (the capital of Xinjiang), Shihezi and Manas. Their importance grew with the completion of the Xinjiang railway from Lanzhou to Ürümqi in 1963, the rapid growth in the population, and the exploitation of rich oil resources in the basin.

The Junggar Basin is less arid than the Tarim Basin and is mostly grassland supporting a pastoral population. The people are primarily nomadic Kazakhs or Torgut Mongols, herding sheep, some horses, cattle and camels. The north and north-west of the Junggar Basin are bounded by the Altaishan range of 3000 to 4000-metre-high peaks on the Mongolian border. It's an area of substantial rainfall, and the mountains are either tree-covered or have rich pasturelands. Mainly nomadic Kazakh or Oirat Mongol herders live here.

CLIMATE

Xinjiang's weather tends towards extremes – sizzling summers and frigid winters. As much of the province is desert, humidity is low. Although Ürümqi is tolerable in summer, the Turpan Basin more than deserves the title of 'hottest place in China' with maximums of up to 49°C.

In winter, though, you'll need your woollies in Xinjiang. In Ürümqi the average temperature in January is around -10°C, with minimums of around -30°C. Winter temperatures in Turpan are only about 5°C warmer.

POPULATION

Xinjiang is inhabited by something like 13 of China's official total of 55 national minorities. One problem for the Chinese is that 50% of their country isn't even inhabited by Chinese, but by minority people who mostly don't like them. What's more, these minority people inhabit regions bordering Vietnam, India, Afghanistan and the USSR – all places of past or possible future conflict with China.

In 1955 the province of Xinjiang was renamed the Uigur Autonomous Region. At that time more than 90% of the population was non-Chinese. With the building of the railway from Lanzhou to Ürümqi and the development of industry in the region, there was a large influx of Chinese people who now form a majority in the northern area while the Uigurs continue to predominate in the south.

In 1953 Xinjiang had a population of about 4.9 million, of whom 3.6 million were Uigurs and only a very small number were Han Chinese. By 1970 the number of Hans was estimated to have grown to about four million. There are now over 13 million people in Xinjiang, of whom only about six million are Uigurs. It's a trend that will inevitably continue as the region develops, with the result that the Uigurs will be subjugated and pacified by sheer weight of numbers.

Relations between the Han and the minority people in the region vary. The nomadic Kazakhs were angered by the forced introduction of the communes. About 60,000 of them are supposed to have crossed into the Soviet Union in 1962. This figure represents a sizeable proportion of the population, since at present there are only 900,000 Kazakhs spread across Xinjiang, Gansu and Qinghai. Other groups of Kazakhs escaped to India or Pakistan and were granted political asylum in Turkey, where they were resettled. Chinese relations with the Tajiks (numbering 26,000) are said to be better.

Unfortunately for the Han Chinese, relations with the fairly numerous minority Uigurs can be best described as volatile. The Chinese have done a great deal to reduce the backwardness of the region, building roads, railways and hospitals, and industrialising the towns. The Chinese presence also prevents the Uigurs from fighting among themselves, which has been a problem whenever centralised rule has toppled. So it's difficult for the Chinese to understand the hostility with which they are greeted. Part of this ill will probably originates from centuries of Chinese misrule and from the savage way in which the 19th-century rebellions were put down; part of it simply because the Uigurs don't have much in common with the Chinese. The Uigur religion is monotheistic Islam, their written script is Arabic, their language is closely related to Turkish, and their physical features are basically Caucasian – many could easily be mistaken for Greeks, southern Italians or other southern Europeans.

Part of the problem may also stem from the intentional or unintentional Chinese policy of blurring the distinctions between Han and Uigur cultures. The recent reintroduction of Arabic script in primary schools is offset by the almost exclusive and hence requisite use of Chinese language at tertiary level. Arabic script has been given a romanised form to speed up the learning process and promote literacy. During the Cultural Revolution mosques were closed – a very sensitive issue with the local devout. With the death of Mao and the rise of a more liberal regime to power, the mosques have since been reopened.

In spite of simmering ethnic tensions, there is little likelihood of Xinjiang ever achieving any real autonomy – the recent influx of Chinese soldiers and settlers means that it is almost certainly out of the question. However, even now there is some sort of anti-Chinese riot or demonstration in one Xinjiang town or another every year. For many years the Lop Nur *(lóbù bó)* region in the Tarim Basin has been used for nuclear tests. Reports of livestock and locals suffering from radiation poisoning were confirmed when Uigur protesters took to the streets in Xinjiang and even Beijing. In 1990, serious ethnic riots prompted the Chinese to close the Kashgar area to foreigners and seal off the border with Pakistan. For the Uigurs the Chinese are very much a foreign occupation force.

Minority Nationalities

The minority nationalities of Xinjiang are probably some of the most interesting in China. To the west of Ürümqi, where the Tianshan range divides in two, is the Ili Valley. The population in the valley consists of Kirghiz, Kazakhs and Chinese, and even includes a colony of Sibo (the descendants of the Manchu garrison which was stationed here after the conquests of the 18th century). Another peculiar army to hit Xinjiang was that of the refugee White Russian troops who fled after their defeat in the Russian Civil War. Some settled here and founded scattered colonies.

The most interesting minority has a popu-

Kazakh Person

lation of one; in the 1930s there was a bizarre story that T E Lawrence (of Arabia) was active in the British cause against the Russians in Xinjiang, and had gone wandering off with a band of local tribespeople to raise hell and high sandstorms. It was a rumour which continued even after Lawrence's fatal motorcycle accident in Britain in 1936 and is not the least fantastic part of the Lawrence legend.

LANGUAGE

Uigur Mini-Glossary

If you have Caucasian features and speak Turkish, you will blend perfectly into Xinjiang provided you wear the right clothing. Once you leave the beaten path, Russian can sometimes prove even more useful than Chinese! Even if your command of Turkish, Russian or Uigur is minimal, the Uigurs love to hear an attempt being made at their language – it helps them to forget their isolation. With no apologies for transliteration, here are some linguistic pointers for bargaining, travelling or just passing the time of day:

hello (peace be upon you)
  salaam aleikum
how much?
  khanj pul
good
  yakshi
not good
  yok yakshi
what's your name?
  sen ismi nemä
goodbye
  khosh
bus
  optus
bus stop
  baket
ticket
  bilhet
food/restaurant
  ash/ashkhana
yes
  ah
no
  emess

TIME

Xinjiang is several time zones removed from Beijing, which prefers to ignore the fact. Officially, Beijing time applies; in practice, Xinjiang time is used haphazardly for meal times in hotels, bus departures, etc. Xinjiang time is one hour behind Beijing time – however, daylight-saving time is not used, so during the summer Xinjiang time is two hours behind Beijing time. Try and straighten out any confusion by asking whether the stated time is Beijing time *(běijīng shíjiān)*, Beijing daylight-saving time *(xiàlìng shíjiān)* or Xinjiang time *(xīnjiāng shíjiān)*. Kashgar time is one hour behind Xinjiang time.

HAMI

(hāmì) 哈密

The town of Hami is a small oasis at the remotest end of China. Known in the past as Kumul, it was once an important caravan stop on the northern route of the Silk Road. Hami's most famous product is the delicious Hami melon *(hāmì gūa)*, highly prized by thirsty train passengers who scramble to buy them during the short stop at Hami station. You can also buy these melons in Turpan.

DAHEYAN

(dàhéyán) 大河沿

The jumping-off point for Turpan is a place on the railway line signposted 'Turpan Zhan' *(tǔlǔfān zhàn)*. In fact, you are actually in Daheyan, and the Turpan oasis is an hour's drive south across the desert. Daheyan is not a place you'll want to hang around in, so spare a thought for the locals who have to eke out a sane living here.

The bus station is a five-minute walk from the railway station. Walk up the road leading from the railway station and turn right at the first main intersection; the bus station is a few minutes' walk ahead on the left-hand side of the road. There are four buses a day to Turpan, two in the morning and two in the afternoon, and the fare is Y2 for the 58-km trip, which takes 1½ hours. The bus gets extremely crowded and it's quite a push-and-shove match to get on. There are lots of trucks on these roads and you may be able to hitch if you miss the bus. If you miss the bus and can't get there hitching, you'll have to spend the night in this exotic outpost. The hotel (Y5 per bed) is behind the bus station.

TURPAN

(tǔlǔfān) 吐鲁番

East of Ürümqi the Taishan mountains split into a southern and a northern range; between the two lie the Hami and Turpan basins. Both are below sea level and receive practically no rain; summers are searingly hot. Part of the Turpan Basin is 154 metres below sea level – the lowest spot in China and the second lowest depression in the world.

Turpan County is inhabited by about 170,000 people: about 120,000 are Uigurs and the rest mostly Chinese. The centre of the county is the large Turpan oasis. It's little more than a few main streets set in a vast tract of grain fields, and more importantly it's been spared the architectural horrors that have been inflicted on Ürümqi. Most of the streets are planted with trees and are lined with mud-brick walls enclosing mud houses. Open channels with flowing water run down the sides of the streets; the inhabitants draw water from these and use them to wash their clothes, dishes and themselves in.

Of the places in Xinjiang currently open to foreigners, Turpan and Kashgar remain closest to traditional Uigur culture; Ürümqi and Shihezi are Chinese settlements. Turpan also holds a special place in Uigur history since nearby Gaochang was once the capital of the Uigurs. It was an important staging post on the Silk Road and was a centre of Buddhism before being converted to Islam in the 8th century. During the Chinese occupation it served as a garrison town.

Turpan is a quiet place (one of the few in China) and the Turpan Guesthouse is a good spot to sit underneath the vine trellises and contemplate the moon and stars. The living is cheap, the food is good and the people are friendly, and there are numerous interesting sights scattered around to keep you occupied. Along with Hangzhou and Yangshuo, it's one of the few places in the country where you can relax and withdraw a bit from China. It's also the hottest – the highest recorded temperature here was 49.6°C. Fortunately, the humidity is low – so low that your laundry is practically dry by the time you get it hung up!

Orientation

The centre of the Turpan oasis is little more than a few main roads and a couple of side streets. You'll find the shops, market, long-distance bus station, tourist guesthouse and a couple of plodding donkey carts all within easy walking distance of each other. The centre is called 'Old City' *(lǎochéng)* and the western part is 'New City' *(xīnchéng)*. Most of the sights are scattered on the outskirts of the oasis or in the surrounding desert.

Information

CITS This office (☎ 22768) is at the Oasis Hotel. The friendly manager is an Uigur and speaks excellent English. The office is open from 10 am to 2 pm, and then from 6 to 9 pm.

Public Security Bureau This office is one block west of the Bank of China (see map).

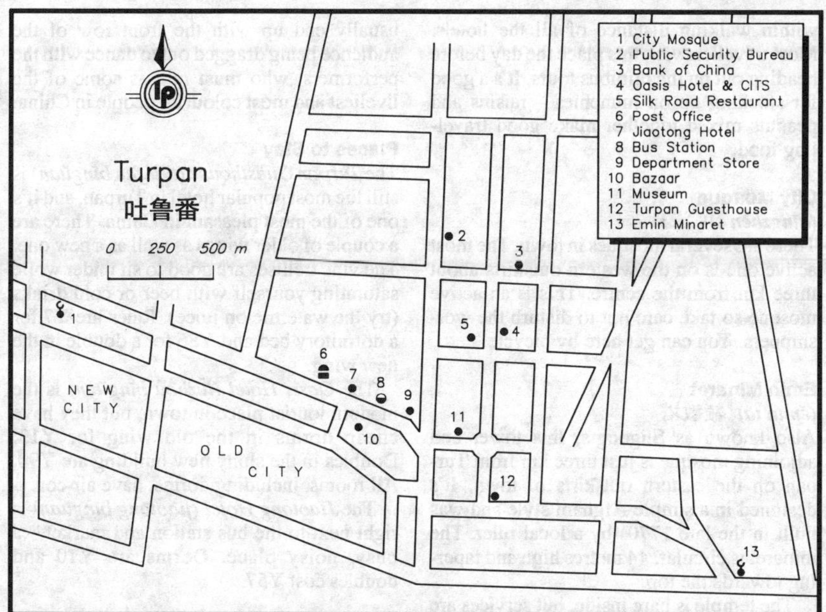

1	清真寺	6	邮局	11	博物馆
2	公安局外事科	7	交通宾馆	12	吐鲁番宾馆
3	中国银行	8	长途汽车站	13	额敏塔
4	绿洲宾馆	9	百货商店		
5	丝路酒家	10	巴扎（集市）		

Money The most convenient place to change money is the Oasis Hotel. There is also a Bank of China about a 10-minute walk from the hotel (see map).

Post The post office is right near the bus station and the bazaar. More convenient is the post office inside the Oasis Hotel – they can handle parcels.

Maps Only CITS has maps of the oasis and the surrounding area.

Bazaar
(nóngmào shìchǎng) 农贸市场
This is one of the most fascinating markets in China – only Kashgar's can match it. You'll find lots of exotica on sale, including brightly decorated knives, Muslim clothing, delicious flatbread, goats (both living and cooked), and unusual fruits. Bargaining is expected, but it's mostly good-natured, not the usual tug of war experienced elsewhere in China.

The market is across from the bus station,

within walking distance of all the hotels. Most travellers visit this place the day before heading out on the minibus tours. It's a good for stocking up on munchies – raisins and peanuts mixed together make good travelling food.

City Mosque

(qīngzhēn sì) 清真寺

There are several mosques in town. The most active one is on the western outskirts about three km from the centre. This is an active mosque so take care not to disturb the worshippers. You can get here by bicycle.

Emin Minaret

(émǐn tǎ) 额敏塔

Also known as Sugongta, this tower and adjoining mosque is just three km from Turpan on the eastern outskirts of town. It's designed in a simple Afghani style and was built in the late 1770s by a local ruler. The minaret is circular, 44 metres high and tapering towards the top.

The temple is bare inside, but services are held every Friday and on holidays.

You could possibly walk or bicycle here from the Turpan Guesthouse, but most people stop here on a minibus tour. Turn left out of the guesthouse and left again at the first crossroad; this road leads straight down to the mosque. There is a hole in the wall at the side of the mosque so you can get into the main building. If you want to climb the minaret you'll have to ask the keeper to unlock the door to the stairway; he lives in the small whitewashed building beside the mosque.

Song & Dance Show

If someone is willing to pay Y400, CITS will organise a performance of traditional Uigur music, song & dance in the courtyard of the Turpan Guesthouse under the trellises. Visiting Japanese tour groups often cough up the money, but they usually have no objection to other travellers watching for free. Most of the singers and dancers are women, but there is usually at least one man. During the summer, the shows are held almost every night from around 10 pm. They're fun nights that usually end up with the front row of the audience being dragged out to dance with the performers, who must rate as some of the liveliest and most colourful people in China.

Places to Stay

The *Turpan Guesthouse (tǔlǔfān bīngǔan)* is still the most popular hotel in Turpan, and it's one of the most pleasant in China. There are a couple of older wings as well as a new one. The vine trellises are good to sit under while saturating yourself with beer or cold drinks (try the watermelon juice). Rates are Y7 for a dormitory bed and Y86 for a double in the new wing.

The *Oasis Hotel (lǜzhōu bīngǔan)* is the modern tourist place in town, but they have cheap dorms in the old wing for Y13. Doubles in the shiny new building are Y90. All rooms, including dorms, have air-con.

The *Jiaotong Hotel (jiāotōng bīngǔan)* is right next to the bus station and market – a busy, noisy place. Dorms are Y10 and doubles cost Y57.

Places to Eat

The *Turpan Guesthouse* is the best place to eat – the food is excellent and cheap, however, the service may not be the friendliest.

Food at the *Oasis Hotel* is outstanding but expensive – figure about Y40 per meal per person. Right across the street from the entrance to the Oasis Hotel is the *Silk Road Restaurant (sīlù jiǔjiā)* – good cheap food, ice-cold drinks and friendly management.

Getting There & Away

Getting out of Turpan is a confused affair but most people make it to the outside world by some means or another.

Air The nearest airport is at Ürümqi.

Bus The bus station is near the market. Make sure you get to the station an hour before departure, because there is invariably a long queue for tickets. The Uigurs are even worse than the Chinese about standing in line, but

Top: Fishing boat on Erhai Lake, Dali (RS)
Bottom Left: Lijiang valley with Mt. Satseto in the background (RS)
Bottom Right: Dai monk on his bike, Menghun (RS)

Top: Survival – Potala Palace, Lhasa (RS)
Bottom: Destruction – Ganden Monastery, Ganden (RS)

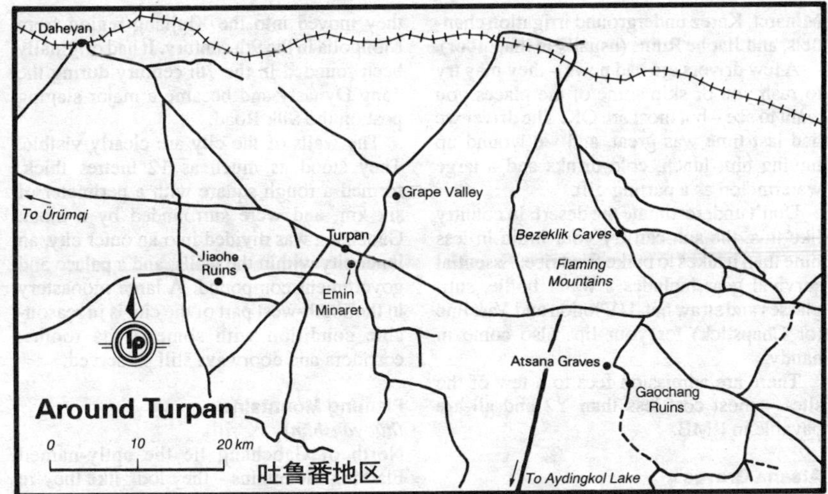

Turpan employs an 'enforcer' to keep order – if only more stations would do this! There are buses from here to Ürümqi and to Daheyan.

There are at least four buses daily to Ürümqi plus private minibuses about once every hour. In Turpan, the public buses want FEC! You can often manage to pay in RMB with a student card or some other ID with your picture (try a driver's licence).

It's great scenery along the route to Ürümqi – immense grey sand dunes, and snow-capped mountains visible in the distance. The fare is Y7.50 and the 180 km trip takes four hours.

Train The nearest railway line is the Ürümqi-Lanzhou line, north of Turpan. The nearest station is at Daheyan. (There are four buses daily between Daheyan and Turpan.) There are six trains daily in both directions. If you're travelling between Ürümqi and Turpan, the direct bus is faster and more convenient than the train. The train from Daheyan to Ürümqi takes three hours, from Daheyan to Liuyuan is 13 hours, to Jiayuguan is 19 hours, and to Lanzhou takes 37 hours.

Getting Around

Public transport around Turpan is by minibus, bicycle or donkey cart. Bicycles are most convenient for the town itself. The only place hiring bicycles is the Turpan Guesthouse. Minibus drivers usually hang around the hotel gates – negotiate the fare in advance. Donkey carts can be found around the market, but this mode of transport is gradually fading away.

AROUND TURPAN

There are many sights in the countryside around Turpan, and it requires at least a day to see everything of importance.

The only way to see the sights is to hire a minibus for a full day (about 10 hours). You won't have to look for them – the drivers will come looking for you. It's easy to find other travellers to share the expense. Figure on spending around Y120 for the whole group. The minibuses normally hold six passengers – any more than eight would be uncomfortable. Make sure it's clearly understood which places you want to see. A typical trip should include the Atsana Graves, Gaochang Ruins, Bezeklik Caves, Grape Valley, Emin

Minaret, Karez underground irrigation channels, and Jiaohe Ruins (usually in that order).

A few drivers are bad news – they may try to rush you or skip some of the places you want to see – but most are OK. The driver we had last time was great, and we wound up buying him lunch, cold drinks and a large watermelon as a parting gift.

Don't underestimate the desert. In country like this, the sun can fry your brain in less time than it takes to make fried rice. Essential survival gear includes a water bottle, sunglasses and straw hat. UV lotion and Vaseline (or Chapstick) for your lips also come in handy.

There are admission fees to a few of the sites – most cost less than Y2 and all are payable in RMB.

Atsana Graves

(āsītǎnà gǔmùqū) 阿斯塔娜古墓区

These graves where the dead of Gaochang are buried lie north-west of the ancient city. Only three of the tombs are open to tourists, and each of these is approached by a short flight of steps which leads down to the burial chamber about six metres below ground level.

One tomb contains portraits of the deceased painted on the walls, while another has paintings of birds. The third tomb holds two well-preserved corpses (one mummy from the original trio seems to have been removed to Turpan's museum) like those in the museums at Ürümqi and Hangzhou. Some of the artefacts date back as far as the Jin Dynasty, from the 3rd to 5th centuries AD. The finds included silks, brocades, embroideries and many funerary objects such as shoes, hats and sashes made of recycled paper. The last turned out to be quite special for the archaeologists, since the paper included deeds, records of slave purchases, orders for silk and other everyday transactions.

Gaochang Ruins

(gāochāng gùchéng) 高昌故城

About 46 km east of Turpan are the ruins of Gaochang, the capital of the Uigurs when they moved into the Xinjiang region from Mongolia in the 9th century. It had originally been founded in the 7th century during the Tang Dynasty and became a major staging post on the Silk Road.

The walls of the city are clearly visible. They stood as much as 12 metres thick, formed a rough square with a perimeter of six km, and were surrounded by a moat. Gaochang was divided into an outer city, an inner city within the walls, and a palace and government compound. A large monastery in the south-west part of the city is in reasonable condition with some of its rooms, corridors and doorways still preserved.

Flaming Mountains

(hǔoyànshān) 火焰山

North of Gaochang lie the aptly-named Flaming Mountains – they look like they're on fire in the midday sun. Purplish-brown in colour, they are 100 km long and 10 km wide. The minibus tours don't usually include a stop here, but they drive through on the way to Bezeklik Caves.

The Flaming Mountains were made famous in Chinese literature by the classic novel *Journey to the West*. The story is about the monk Xuan Zang and his followers who travelled west in search of the Buddhist sutra. The mountains were a formidable barrier which they had to cross.

Should you contemplate actually climbing these mountains, you'd better equip yourself with insulated insoles for your shoes – temperatures on the sunbaked surface have been known to reach 80°C, hot enough to fry an egg.

Bezeklik Thousand Buddha Caves

(bózīkèlǐ qiānfó dòng) 柏孜克里千佛洞

On the western side of the Flaming Mountains, on a cliff face fronting a river valley, are the remains of these Buddhist cave temples. All the caves are in dreadful condition, most having been devastated by Muslims or robbed by all and sundry. The large statues which stood at the back of each cave have been destroyed or stolen and the faces of the buddhas ornamenting the walls have either been scrapped or completely gouged out. Particularly active in the export of murals was a German, Albert von Le Coq, who removed whole frescoes from the stone walls and transported them back to the Berlin Museum – where Allied bombing wiped most of them out during WW II. Today the caves reveal little more than a hint of what these works of art were like in their heyday.

Photography is forbidden inside the caves, but there isn't much reason to bother. Fortunately, the scenery just outside the caves is fine.

Grape Valley

(pútáo gōu) 葡萄沟

In this small paradise – a thick maze of vines and grape trellises – stark desert surrounds you. Most of the minibus tours stop here for lunch – the food isn't bad, and there are plenty of grapes in season (early September is best). The children here are remarkably friendly and like to pose for photos – they don't ask any money for this so please don't turn them into beggars by offering anything.

There is a winery *(gǔojiǔchǎng)* near the valley and lots of well-ventilated brick buildings for drying grapes – wine and raisins are major exports of Turpan. CITS is trying to organise an annual 'grape festival' which they expect to hold during the third week of August.

Tempting as it might be, don't pick the grapes here or anywhere else in Turpan. There is a Y15 fine if you do. Considerable effort goes into raising these grapes and the farmers don't appreciate tourists eating their profits.

Karez Underground Irrigation Channels

(dì xià shǔi) 地下水

The word 'karez' means wells. The wells are sunk at various points to the north of Turpan to collect ground water, which comes from melting snow in the Bogdashan mountains. The ground water then passes through underground channels to irrigate farms in the valley below. The city of Turpan owes its existence to these vital wells and channels, some of which were constructed over 2000 years ago. Some of the channels are on the surface, but putting them underground greatly reduces water loss from evaporation. They are entirely fed by gravity, thus eliminating the need for pumps. There are over a thousand wells, and the total length of the channels exceeds 3000 km. It's remarkable to think that this extensive irrigation system was all constructed by hand and without modern building materials. Locals like to boast that this is one of China's greatest public works projects, on a par with the Great Wall and Grand Canal.

There are a number of places to view the channels, but most of the minibus tours stop at one particular spot on the west side of Turpan. Unfortunately, there are a few children here who ask foreigners for money.

Jiaohe Ruins

(jiāohé gùchéng) 交河古城

During the Han Dynasty Jiaohe was established by the Chinese as a garrison town to defend the borderlands. The city was totally decimated by Genghis Khan's 'travelling roadshow' but you'd be forgiven if you thought it had been struck by an A-bomb. The buildings are rather more obvious than the ruins of Gaochang though, and you can walk through the old streets and along the roads. A main road cuts through the city, and at the end is a large monastery with figures of the Buddha still visible.

The ruins are 20 km west of Turpan and stand on an island bounded by two small rivers – thus the name Jiaohe, which means 'confluence of two rivers'.

Sand Therapy Clinic

(shā liáo zhàn) 沙疗站

Over 5000 people a year – mostly Kazakhs – come to Turpan to get buried up to their necks in the sand. It is believed that the hot sand can greatly relieve the aches of rheumatism. The Sand Therapy Clinic is pretty much an outdoor sandbox, and it only operates from June to August. There's not much to see here and the minibuses usually don't include this as part of your tour except by special request. If you're plagued by rheumatism, you might want to give this therapy a try.

Aydingkol Salt Lake

(àidīng hú) 艾丁湖

At the very bottom of the Turpan depression is Aydingkol Lake, 154 metres below sea level. The 'lake' usually has little water – it's a huge, muddy evaporating pond with a surface of crystallised salt, but technically it's the second lowest lake in the world, only surpassed by the Dead Sea in Israel and Jordan.

Most of the tours do not stop here. If you want to see Aydingkol Lake, tell your driver and expect to pay extra for the additional distance.

ÜRÜMQI

(wūlǔmùqí) 乌鲁木齐

The capital of Xinjiang, this city boomed after the Communists built the railway line from Lanzhou across the Xinjiang desert. About 950,000 people live here now, 80% of them Han Chinese – the place has always been a Chinese island in a sea of Muslims. The inspired concrete-block architecture of socialist eastern China has been imported lock, stock and barrel, and Ürümqi essentially looks little different from its northern Han-China counterparts 2000 km east. There are few 'sights' as such, but it's an intrinsically interesting place to visit.

Two and a half days up the railway line from Xi'an and in the same country, you couldn't come across a people more different from the Chinese than the Uigurs. Ürümqi is the first place where you'll see these swarthy Turkic descendants in any number. They are larger and heavier than the Han Chinese and many of them could easily pass for southern Italians or Greeks. The Uigur women wear skirts or dresses and brightly coloured scarves, in contrast to the slacks and baggy trousers of the Han Chinese, and they pierce their ears – a practice which repels the Han. At arm's distance from the Uigurs are the Han Chinese immigrants as well as the PLA soldiers who are not only there to keep the Russians at bay and maintain Chinese control over Xinjiang, but also to keep the tenuous peace between the Uigurs and the Han. It's hard not to feel you're in the provincial capital of a foreign occupation force.

Orientation

One of the difficulties of finding your way around is that the streets have a notorious habit of changing names every few blocks – a nightmare for mapmakers. Most of the sights, tourist facilities and hotels are scattered across the city, though they're all easily reached on local buses.

The railway and long-distance bus stations are in the south-western corner of the city. There are two candidates for the title of 'city centre': the first is the area around the large Hongshan Department Store where some of the major arteries intersect; the other is in the eastern part of the city, where you'll find the main shopping district, CITS office, Public Security Bureau and Bank of China.

Information

CITS This office (☎ 25794) is in a compound on the east side of Renmin Square in the drab concrete building on your left as you enter the compound. There's a sign in front of the gate – it's open Monday to Saturday, from 9.30 am to 1 pm and 4 to 8 pm.

You might want to come here for the entertainment value – seldom will you encounter a more confused CITS office than this one. Each worker quotes you a different price on tickets and gives conflicting information for transport. Some of the staff claim that a certain place is open – others claim it's closed.

At the time of this writing, Kashgar and the Pakistani border are closed to all *except* those on expensive CITS tours. This means that if you want to visit those places you'll have to deal with this travelling circus. Good luck.

CTS This organisation has an office in the Overseas Chinese Hotel which seems to be more efficient than CITS, but don't expect much English to be spoken. They might give you a better price on tours to Kashgar – try bargaining. Still another possibility is the Xinjiang Overseas Tourist Corporation (☎ 78691, 23782) *(xīnjiāng hǎiwài lǚyóu zǒng gōngsī)*, 32 Xinhua Nanlu.

Pakistan Tourism Office This is in room 8006 in the Overseas Chinese Hotel.

Public Security Bureau This is a 10-minute walk from the CITS office, in a large government building just to the north-west of Renmin Square (see map).

Money The Bank of China is at 343 Jiefang Nanlu close to Renmin Square. It's open from 10 am to 2 pm and 3.30 to 4.30 pm and is closed Wednesday and Friday afternoons and all day Sunday. International credit cards are accepted here too. The 'other' money marketeers conveniently prowl this beat. Take bus No 1 from the Overseas Chinese Hotel or Kunlun Guesthouse.

Post The main post office is a big Corinthian-colonnaded building directly across the traffic circle from the Hongshan Department Store. The foreign section is efficient and has a packing service. Keep an eye on the Customs inspection counter to see what local Uigurs send their Soviet comrades and vice-versa – one export hit from China is stockings. Outside the post office are various seal engravers keen to count you among their customers.

There is a post office on the ground floor of the Kunlun Guesthouse.

Maps Good maps, in Chinese and showing the bus routes, are available from the railway station, bus station, department stores, bookstores and most of the hotels. The Hongshan Department Store has some excellent maps of Xinjiang.

Xinjiang Autonomous Region Museum

(xīnjiāng wéiwúěr zìzhìqū bówùgǔan)
新疆维吾尔自治区博物馆

Xinjiang covers 16% of China's total land surface. It is inhabited not only by the Han Chinese but also by 13 of China's official total of 55 minority peoples. One wing of the museum contains an interesting exhibition relating to some of the Xinjiang minority groups and it's well worth a look.

Notable among the exhibits are the Daur hats (made from animal heads) with large fur rims – there are about 94,000 Daur people spread across Xinjiang, Inner Mongolia and Heilongjiang. The Tajik exhibition features silver and coral beads supporting silver pendants – the people number about 26,500 and are found only in Xinjiang. There are about 900,000 Kazakhs living in Xinjiang and their exhibition in the museum features a heavily furnished yurt. The Mongol exhibit includes particularly ornate silver bridles and saddles studded with semi-precious stones, stringed musical instruments and decorated riding boots.

Another wing of the museum has a fascinating section devoted to history. Prime exhibits are the preserved bodies of two men and two women discovered in tombs in Xinjiang, similar to those you may have seen in the museum at Hangzhou. Also interesting is the collection of multicoloured clay figurines unearthed from Turpan, dating back to the Tang Dynasty. Note the collection of silk fragments with various patterns from different dynasties.

The distinctive Soviet-style building with a green dome is on Xibei Lu, about 20 minutes' walk from the Kunlun Guesthouse.

Ürümqi
乌鲁木齐
0
0.5
1 km
Hongshan
Hongshan Park
Renmin Park
Xibei
Youhao
Hetan Lu
Lu
Lu
Yangzijiang
Lu
Heilongjiang
Lu
Qitai
Lu
Changjiang Lu
Huanghe
Lu
Guangming Lu
Xinhua
Beilu
Jiefang Beilu
Qingnian Lu
Renmin Square
Zhongshan
Lu
Renmin Lu
Nanlu
Jiefang Nanlu
Xinhua
Tuanjie
Lu
1
2
3
4
5
6
7
8
9
10
11
12
13
14
15
16
17
18
19

1	Kunlun Guesthouse	1	昆仑宾馆
2	Xinjiang Autonomous Region Museum	2	新疆维吾尔自治区博物馆
3	CAAC	3	中国民航
4	Hongshan Market	4	红山市场
5	Hongshan Department Store	5	红山商场
6	Main Post Office	6	邮局
7	Buses to Tianchi & Baiyanggou	7	往天池/白扬沟汽车
8	Hongshan Hotel	8	红山宾馆
9	Bogda Hotel	9	博格达宾馆
10	Hongchunyuan Restaurants	10	鸿春园饭店
11	Public Security Bureau	11	公安局外事科
12	CITS	12	中国国际旅行社
13	Bank of China	13	中国银行
14	Erdaoqiao Market	14	二道桥市场
15	Overseas Chinese Hotel	15	华侨宾馆
16	Guangdong Jiujia	16	广东酒家
17	Xinjiang Hotel	17	新疆饭店
18	Long-Distance Bus Station	18	长途汽车站
19	Railway Station	19	火车站

From Hongshan Department Store take bus No 7 for four stops and ask to get off at the museum *(bówùgǔan)*.

Renmin Park

(rénmín gōngyúan) 人民公园

This beautiful, tree-shaded park is about one km in length and can be entered from either the north or south gates. The best time to visit is early in the morning when the Chinese are out here doing their exercises. There are plenty of birds in the park and a few pavilions. Near the north end is a lake where you can hire rowing boats – a pleasant way to relax after dinner. Try to avoid the park on Sunday when the locals descend on the place in force.

Hongshan Park & Pagoda

(hóngshān gōngyúan) 红山公园

It's not exactly one of the world's eight wonders, but the pagoda sits on top of a big hill just to the north of Renmin Park and affords sweeping views of the city.

Places to Stay

The *Hongshan Hotel* (☎ 24761) *(hóngshān bīngǔan)* is a good base in the centre of town and is very popular with budget travellers. The dorms cost Y15 in a three-bed room without private bath. For Y25, they also have two-bed dorms with private bath – these are excellent value if you don't mind paying a little more for the luxury.

At the reception desk, you can get tickets for the shower unit across the yard at the back of the compound. There is often a long queue to use the showers which are frequently out-of-order. The waiting room has a thought-provoking sign in Chinese: 'It is forbidden to do the big one (defecate) in the showers. Y5 fine if you do!'

From the railway station, take bus No 2 for four stops. You'll then be close to the main post office, which is a short walk from the hotel. From the main bus station, turn right out of the station gates and walk about 150 metres along Heilongjiang Lu until you cross an intersection and reach the stop for bus No 8. Take this bus east for four stops and then switch to either bus Nos 7 or 17 going north for one stop. If coming from the airport, the CAAC bus drops you off by their ticket office which is within walking distance of the hotel.

Another alternative for budget travellers is the *Xinjiang Hotel* (☎ 54002) *(xīnjiāng fàndiàn)* at the southern end of Changjiang Lu. It's the only hotel within walking distance of the railway station. Dorms cost Y10 per person.

One other hotel which has a sensible location is the *Bogda Hotel (bǒgědǎ bīngǔan)*. They have nice double rooms for Y50. They have some three-bed dormitories for Y12 per person, but they try to deny the fact.

The *Overseas Chinese Hotel* (☎ 77793, 70529) *(húaqiáo bīngǔan)*, is much further from the town centre than the Hongshan Hotel, but still easy to reach from there on bus No 7. The comfortable rooms are a good place to let your bones knit after a long bus trip. Doubles cost from Y70 to Y90; dorm beds cost Y20 in a five-bed room.

From the railway station, take bus No 10 for four stops, and then walk 50 metres east to Xinhua Nanlu and take bus No 7 south for one stop. From the main bus station, turn right out of the station gates and walk about 150 metres along Heilongjiang Lu until you cross an intersection and reach the stop for bus No 8. Take this bus east for two stops, then hop onto bus No 7 and go south for four stops.

The *Kunlun Guesthouse* (☎ 42411, 43801) *(kūnlún bīngǔan)* is Ürümqi's main tourist joint, but it's only worth keeping in mind as a second choice because it's a long way from everything. Cheapest accommodation is Y20 per bed in a four-bed room – the problem is that apart from the small basin in the room there is nowhere to wash. Double rooms are Y90 with private bath. From the railway station take bus No 2 (the stop is right outside the station), which will drop you off just a few minutes' walk from the hotel.

The *Friendship Hotel* (☎ 77791) *(yǒuyí bīngǔan)* has a very inconvenient location, about seven km south-east of the railway station. Cadres, who usually arrive in chauffeur-driven limousines, like to stay here. Interestingly, this is the hotel recommended by CITS to budget travellers, which just goes to show how detached from reality they are.

Places to Eat

Ürümqi is a good place to try Uigur foods such as shish kebab or noodles with spicy vegetables *(lāmiàn)*. During the summer, the markets are packed with delicious fruit, both fresh and dried. Try the *Hongshan Market* across from the Hongshan Department Store. An even better place is the *Erdaoqiao Market* near the Overseas Chinese Hotel.

The *Hongchunyuan Restaurant (hóngchūnyúan fàndiàn)*, close to the Public Security Bureau, is actually a Chinese-only hotel with two restaurants. One serves Chinese food *(zhōng cān)* and the other – called the *Pumpkin Restaurant* – serves Western food *(xī cān)*. The Western restaurant has an English menu – the Chinese restaurant doesn't. Prices are cheap.

Near the Overseas Chinese Hotel is a good Cantonese restaurant called *Guangdong Jiujia*. In the morning they serve dim sum, and Hong Kongers flock to this place. From the Overseas Chinese Hotel, go one block north and turn left – the restaurant is on the left side.

The restaurant at the *Overseas Chinese Hotel* isn't bad; the one at the *Hongshan Hotel* is best avoided except by the famished. There are small private restaurants just to the south of the Hongshan Hotel on both sides of the street – be sure to negotiate the price in advance.

Getting There & Away

Air Ürümqi is connected by air with Beijing (Y954), Canton (Y1220), Chengdu (Y758), Dalian (Y1240), Fuzhou, Hangzhou, Harbin (Y1293), Lanzhou (Y590), Luoyang, Shanghai (Y1225), Shenyang, Xi'an (Y774), and Zhengzhou.

There are also flights from Ürümqi to the following places in Xinjiang: Aksu (Y289), Altai (Y151), Fuyun (Y136), Hotan (Y464),

Karamai, Kashgar (Y453), Khotan and Korla (Y124), Kuqa (Y216), Qiemo (Y259), and Yining (Y176).

There are international flights to Istanbul for Y5000. Sadly, there are no flights to Pakistan even though this is where most travellers want to go.

CAAC (☎ 41536) is on Youhao Lu, the same road that the Kunlun Guesthouse is on, and it's open from 10 am to 1.30 pm and 4 to 8 pm. Bus Nos 1 and 2 from the Kunlun Guesthouse go past the office.

Bus The long-distance bus station is in the western part of town. The departure time given on your ticket is normally Beijing time; check if you're not sure. There are buses for most cities in Xinjiang. The most popular destinations for travellers are Turpan, Yining and Kashgar (good luck). They ask for FEC here.

Accidents occur frequently on Xinjiang's highways. Check out the small, colourful mosque opposite the bus station – you might want to put in a few prayers for your safe arrival.

Train From Ürümqi there are eastbound trains at least six times daily. Popular destinations include Beijing via Lanzhou, Yinchuan, Baotou, Hohhot and Datong; to Xi'an via Lanzhou; to Beijing via Xi'an, Zhengzhou and Shijiazhuang; to Shanghai via Xi'an, Zhengzhou and Nanjing; to Chengdu via Lanzhou.

There is intense competition for tickets at the railway station, where the market has been cornered by a variety of touts both inside and outside the system. Try and book as far in advance as possible and join the queue before 8 am. If you only manage to get a hard-seat ticket, you can sometimes buy hard-sleepers on the train for at least part of your journey – providing you queue persistently within a few minutes of the train's departure. You might want to get the ticket through CITS or CTS.

There is a rail link between Ürümqi and Korla via Daheyan (Turpan station). At present, only 500-series trains (hard-seat only) run on this route, which may be scenic but is hardly worth 18 hours of hard-seat travel.

Getting Around

Bicycles are available for hire from the Hongshan Hotel for Y1 per hour. They want some sort of ID – an expired passport works fine. The buses go everywhere, but are extremely crowded – the pushing and shoving is incredible! By comparison, the battles you fought on Beijing and Shanghai buses were just practice sessions.

There have been numerous reports of pickpocketing and bag slashing on Ürümqi buses – take care.

AROUND ÜRÜMQI

Tianchi

(tiānchí) 天池

Tianchi (Lake of Heaven) is a sight you'll never forget. Half-way up a mountain in the middle of a desert, it looks like a chunk of Switzerland or Canada that's been exiled to western China. The small, deep-blue lake is surrounded by hills covered with fir trees and grazed by horses. Scattered around are the yurts of the Kazakh people who inhabit the mountains; in the distance are the snow-covered peaks of the Tianshan range, and you can climb the hills right up to the snow line.

The lake is 115 km east of Ürümqi at an elevation of 1900 metres. Nearby is the 5445-metre-high Bogda Feng, the Peak of God. The lake freezes over in Xinjiang's bitter winter and the roads up here are only open in the summer months – a pity since it would make an excellent place for ice-skating.

Buses leave Ürümqi at around 8 am from both the north and south gates of Renmin Park – the north side is more convenient if you're staying at the Hongshan Hotel. Departures are from where the sign says (in English) 'Taxi Service'. Buy your ticket about 30 minutes ahead of time to ensure getting a seat. The trip takes over three hours. The bus will probably drop you off at the end of the lake – from there it's a 20-minute walk to the hotel on the banks. The bus back to Ürümqi leaves at around 4 pm from a bus park just over a low ridge at the back of the hotel. If you stay overnight then you'll have the place pretty much to yourself in the morning and after 4 pm, since most people only come here on day trips. Some people have hitched on trucks to the lake.

A one-way ticket costs Y11. You can buy round-trip tickets – these are valid for any day but you only have a reserved seat if you come back on the same day. If you buy a return ticket and want to come back another day but still want a reserved seat, it will cost you extra.

The Heavenly Lake Hotel on the banks of the lake is a garish building utterly out of place compared with the blues and greens of the surroundings. There are rooms for six people at Y10 per bed. There are boat cruises on the lake.

The other possibility, of course, is to hike into the hills and go camping – it's a great opportunity, and a rare one in China. The surrounding countryside is absolutely stunning. Follow the track skirting the lake for about four km to the far end and walk up the valley. During the summer Kazakhs set up yurts in this area and charge Y8 per person. Horses are also offered (at Y40 to Y60 per day) for a trek to the snow line. The return trek takes 10 hours. Water is best taken from the spring gushing straight out of the mountain at the edge of the lake rather than further up the valley where humans and livestock have contributed to the liquid.

Baiyanggou

(báiyánggōu) 白扬沟

Baiyanggou, also known as the Southern Pastures, is a vast expanse of grazing land south of Ürümqi. The land is inhabited by Kazakh herdsmen who graze sheep, cattle and horses here during the summer months.

Curious stories have been told of the gangs of Hong Kong Chinese who come down here by the minibus-load. Unused to vast open spaces or to the sight of animals almost in the wild, they leap from the bus and charge at the unsuspecting creatures, who scatter in all directions. A distraught Kazakh herdsman usually rides up waving his arms in the air and shouting abuse, and must be placated by the tour guide with apologies and cigarettes.

It's a 1½-hour ride (56 km). The directions for getting there are the same as for Tianchi – at the north and south gates of Renmin Park in Ürümqi there are buses departing at approximately 9 am from where the sign says 'Taxi Service'. There is also a local bus leaving from the bus station close to Lijiaoqiao (see map). There are two buses each day leaving approximately at at 8.40 am and 5.40 pm in the summer; 8.30 am and 3.30 pm in the winter.

It is possible to stay up in the pasturelands at some of the Kazakh yurts.

SHIHEZI

(shíhézi) 石河子

A couple of hours' drive north-west of Ürümqi is the town of Shihezi, or Stony Creek. It's a Chinese outpost and almost all the inhabitants are Hans. The town is officially open to foreigners, but it looks so boring that even a statue would pack up and leave town. The bus between Ürümqi and Yining passes through here.

KUQA

(kùchē) 库车

On the Silk Road between Turpan and Kashgar lies Kuqa. Scattered around the Kuqa region are at least seven 'Thousand Buddha Caves' *(qiānfó dòng)* which rival those of Dunhuang and Datong. There are also at least four ancient ruined cities in the area. Unfortunately, you aren't likely to see them unless things change by the time you read this. Kuqa was closed at the time of this writing, but CITS has indicated it might be opened to those who are willing to pay for an ultra-expensive tour. It wouldn't do much good to try and sneak into Kuqa – the caves themselves are closed unless you get permission to enter, and there's no way you'll get permission unless you pay a huge ransom.

On the odd chance that Kuqa has opened to individual travellers by the time you read this, transport should be as follows: bus from Ürümqi (a two-day trip) or direct flight to Kuqa. CAAC presently runs two flights weekly from Ürümqi, but this number would no doubt increase if the area was opened to foreigners. Since the cave sites are scattered around a large area, it would only be feasible to see them with a taxi or minibus tour. If the area opens to tourists, it's almost certain that local entrepreneurs will start offering such tours out of Kuqa, just like in Turpan – something to look forward to.

KASHGAR

(kāshí) 喀什

Kashgar is a giant oasis 1290 metres above sea level. Like Timbuktu, it's one of those fabled cities that everyone seems to know about but no-one seems to get to. A thousand years ago it was a key centre on the Silk Road and Marco Polo passed through commenting that:

> The inhabitants live by trade and industry. They have fine orchards and vineyards and flourishing estates. Cotton grows here in plenty, besides flax and hemp. The soil is fruitful and productive of all the means of life. The country is the starting-point from which many merchants set out to market their wares all over the world.

In the early part of this century, Kashgar was a relatively major town on the edge of a vast nowhere and separated from the rest of China by an endless sandpit. Traders from India tramped to Kashgar via Gilgit and the Hunza Valley; in 1890 the British sent a trade agent to Kashgar to represent their interests and in 1908 they established a consulate. As with Tibet in the 1890s, the rumours soon spread that the Russians were on the verge of gobbling up Xinjiang.

Bactrian Camel

> To most people Kashgar, which is five or six weeks' journey over 15,000-foot passes from the nearest railhead in India, must seem a place barbarously remote; but for us its outlandish name spelt civilisation. The raptures of arrival were unqualified. Discovery is a delightful process, but rediscovery is better; few people can ever have enjoyed a bath more than we did, who had not had one for 5½ months.

That is how Peter Fleming described his arrival in Kashgar back in 1935, after he and Kini Maillart had spent almost half a year on the backs of camels and donkeys getting there from Beijing. Fleming described the city as being 'in effect run by the secret police, the Russian advisers, and the Soviet Consulate, and most of the high officials were only figureheads'. The rest of the foreign community consisted of the British Consul and his wife, their 15 Hunza guards from the north of Pakistan, and a couple of Swedish missionaries.

Contact with the Soviet Union seemed to make sense given the geographical location of Kashgar. Ethnically, culturally, linguistically and theologically the inhabitants of Kashgar had absolutely nothing in common with the Chinese and everything in common with the Muslim inhabitants on the other side of the border. Whereas it took a five-month camel and donkey ride to get to Beijing and a five or six-week hike to reach the nearest railhead in British India (although mail runners could do it in two), the Soviet railhead at Osh was more accessible, and from Kashgar strings of camels would stalk westward with their bales of wool, returning with cargoes of Russian cigarettes, matches and sugar.

Rumours and also banquets seemed to be at their most eccentric in Kashgar. Fleming describes his last night there at a banquet given by the city officials 'half in their honour and half in ours...You never know what may happen at a banquet in Kashgar and each of our official hosts had prudently brought his own bodyguard. Turkic and Chinese soldiers lounged everywhere; automatic rifles and executioner's swords were much in evidence, and the Mauser pistols of the waiters knocked ominously against the back of your chair as they leant over you with the dishes'. Speeches made by just about everyone, were feverishly translated into English, Russian, Chinese and Turkish, and no one was assassinated.

The Kashgar of today has lost much of the 'romantic' value that made eating there in the '30s a slightly nervous experience. When the Communists came to power the city walls were ripped down and a huge, glistening white statue of Chairman Mao was erected on the main street. The statue stands today, hand (minus a thumb) outstretched to the sky above and the lands beyond, a constant reminder to the local populace of the alien regime that controls the city. About 200,000 people live here, and apart from the Uigur majority this number includes Tajiks, Kirghiz and Uzbekh. The number of Han Chinese living here is relatively small, nothing like the horde that dominates Ürümqi, although PLA troops are always conspicuous and there are plenty of Han plainclothes police. Nor does it take six months to reach Kashgar now; it's a three-day bus ride from Ürümqi or you can fly out in a couple of hours if you have more consideration for your bum. No longer as remote, nor as fabled, the city sounds like a disappointment – yet the peculiar quality of Kashgar is that every so often you chance on some scene that suggests a different age and a world removed from China.

Kashgar is renowned for playing diabolical tricks on the stomach; it's possibly a bug in the water, but whatever it is, your enjoyment of the place can be ruined.

Some foreign women wandering the streets on their own have been sexually harassed. This may be remotely connected with style of dress or even the town's diet of bawdy films. Whatever the reason, it's best for women travellers to dress as you would in any Muslim country.

In Kashgar, the adults don't gather round foreigners like the Han Chinese, but the Uigur children do – they come in plague proportions. If you've got a camera, spare plenty of film for photos of every kid on the block! A foreign face, rare as it is, is usually assumed to be American, but quite often the locals will ask if you're a Pakistani.

Off Limits? Whether or not you will be able to visit Kashgar by the time you read this is uncertain. There were serious anti-Chinese riots in April 1990 and, apparently, several Han Chinese were killed by a Uigur mob; troops were rushed into Kashgar. Foreigners were kicked out so there would be no witnesses to the crackdown that followed. The border with Pakistan was closed due to 'landslides'. No one but the Chinese government knows just how many were arrested or killed. The Chinese have remained tight-lipped about the whole affair, and the outside world will probably never know exactly what happened.

The effect on travellers is that if you're coming from Ürümqi, both Kashgar and the Pakistani border can only be reached by taking an expensive CITS tour. Ironically, travellers coming from Pakistan are still getting into Kashgar without a tour.

Prices announced by CITS were as follows. From Ürümqi, it costs Y1700 for a two-day trip to Kashgar (flying both ways). To cross the Pakistani border with a two-day stop-off in Kashgar will cost Y3000. These prices can probably be bargained down somewhat, especially if you can form a small group with other travellers. Prices include transport, hotels and a guide. Arrangements are to be made with CITS in Ürümqi. Unfortunately, this particular CITS office is a bastion of avarice and incompetence – you might be able to negotiate more favourable terms with CTS or the Xinjiang Overseas Tourist Corporation (addresses are given in Ürümqi section of this book). Many travellers trying to book trips to Kashgar have

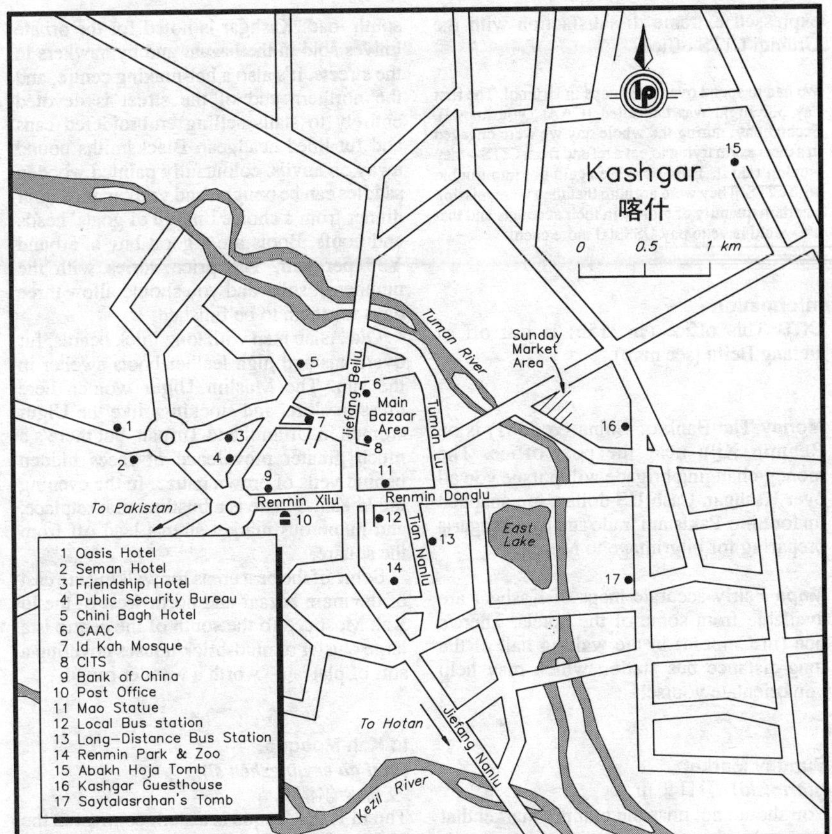

1	绿洲宾馆	10	邮局
2	色满宾馆	11	毛泽东塑像
3	友谊宾馆	12	市公共汽车站
4	公安局外事科	13	长途汽车站
5	其尼巴合宾馆	14	人民公园
6	中国民航	15	香妃墓
7	艾提尕清真寺	16	喀什噶尔宾馆
8	中国国际旅行社	17	赛衣提艾里艾斯拉罕墓
9	中国银行		

expressed extreme dissatisfaction with the Ürümqi CITS office.

We had to spend over three days in Ürümqi. The first day our flight was cancelled (CAAC· you know!). Second day: during the whole day we were engaged in a discussion trying to get a refund from CITS – they wouldn't do it. Third day: We again got into trouble with CITS. They were arguing that they were missing a certain quantity of money in their accounts and that we would have to pay US$300 more each!

Information

CITS This office (☎ 3156) is just off of Jiefang Beilu (see map).

Money The Bank of China (☎ 2461) is on Renmin Xilu near the post office. The money-changing brigade will pursue you all over Kashgar. Cash US dollars are snapped up for Sino-Pakistani trade and by Kashgaris preparing for pilgrimage to Mecca.

Maps Fairly accurate maps of Kashgar are available from some of the hotels. There's one (in Chinese) in the waiting hall of the long-distance bus station which may help you orientate yourself.

Sunday Market

(jiàrì jíshì) 假日集市

You should not miss the bumper market that takes place every Sunday on the eastern fringe of town. Hundreds of donkey carts, horsemen, pedestrians and animals thunder into town for a bargaining extravaganza. It's best to just wander at random through the huge market area and watch camels, goats, horses, melons, grapes, hats, knives, beds and doorframes being bought and sold. Beware of pickpockets.

Bazaar

(jíshì) 集市

Sundays excepted, the bazaar is the focus of activity in Kashgar. The main market-street can be reached from the lanes opposite the Id Kah Square which run off the main north-south road. Kashgar is noted for the ornate knives sold in the bazaar and by hawkers in the streets. It's also a hat-making centre, and the northern end of the street is devoted entirely to stalls selling embroidered caps and fur-lined headgear. Blacksmiths pound away on anvils, colourfully painted wooden saddles can be bought, and you can pick your dinner from a choice line-up of goats' heads and hoofs. Boots are a good buy at around Y35 per pair. The price varies with the number of soles and you should allow three days for them to be finished.

Old Asian men with long thick beards, fur overcoats and high leather boots swelter in the sun. The Muslim Uigur women here dress in skirts and stockings like the Uigur women in Ürümqi and Turpan, but there's a much greater prevalence of faces hidden behind veils of brown gauze. In the evening the Id Kah Square is a bustling marketplace, and numerous market-streets lead off from the square.

Some of the best areas for walking are east of the main bazaar and north-west of the Id Kah Mosque. To the south of the centre is a large cluster of mud-brick houses covering a sort of plateau – worth a wander round.

Id Kah Mosque

(ài tí gǎ ér qīngzhēn sì)
艾提朵尔清真寺

The Id Kah Mosque is a stark contrast to the Chinese-style mosques in eastern cities like Canton and Xi'an. The Id Kah looks like it's been lifted out of Pakistan or Afghanistan, and has the central dome and flanking minarets which Westerners usually associate with a mosque. Prayer time is around 10 pm, though that may vary throughout the year. During the festival of Korban Bairam, usually held in September and October, pilgrims gather in front of the mosque and gradually twirl themselves into a frenzy of dancing which is driven by wailing music from a small band perched on the mosque's portal.

Smaller mosques are scattered among the houses on the streets around the town centre.

Abakh Hoja Tomb

(xiāngfēi mù) 香妃墓

This strange construction is in the eastern part of the oasis. It looks something like a stubby, multicoloured miniature of the Taj Mahal, with green tiles on the walls and dome. To one side of the mosque is a cemetery, with a rectangular base surmounted by fat, conical mud structures. The tomb is the burial place of Hidajetulla Hoja, a Muslim missionary and saint, and his 72 descendants. It's an hour's walk from the Kashgar Guesthouse, but you should be able to hitch a lift on a donkey cart – just show the driver a photo of where you want to go. The tomb lies on a side street off a long east-west road.

The Chinese call this place the Fragrant Concubine's Tomb *(xiāngfēi mù)* in honour of one daughter of the Hoja clan who was married to the emperor Qianlong. However, her body was later moved to Hebei Province and is not actually entombed here.

Renmin Park & Zoo

(rénmín gōngyúan) 人民公园

The park is a pleasant place in which to sit, but the zoo is depressing. The kindest thing you could do for some of the animals would be to put a bullet through their heads. In front of the entrance to the park is Renmin Square and on the opposite side of the road is the massive white statue of Mao Zedong.

Places to Stay

If you are forced to visit Kashgar on a CITS group tour, you won't have much choice about where you stay – CITS will make all the arrangements and you'll be required to pay in advance. If you manage to get in as an individual traveller, you can choose from the few places that accept foreigners.

The *Seman Hotel* (☎ 2129, 2060) *(sèmǎn bīngǔan)* is in the former Soviet consulate on the western edge of town. It's a pleasant place to stay, with relaxing grounds. A double with bath costs Y35 – check to make sure the plumbing works. A bed in the dormitory costs Y10. At the moment, this is probably the best place to stay.

The *Kashgar Guesthouse* (☎ 2367, 2368) *(kāshí gě'ěr bīngǔan)* is the top-rated hotel in town and is up to the same good standard of any other basic Chinese tourist hotel further east. The problem with this place is that it's too far from the town centre – the main intersection is a good hour's walk away, and there's no bus. You can usually wave down a jeep or a truck, or hitch a lift on a donkey cart. Double rooms in building No 1 go for Y100 (with shower and toilet). A bed in a four-bed room in one of the other buildings is Y12, but the building is a real echo chamber. There's a post office, dining rooms, souvenir shops and a small store (just inside the front gate) which sells bottled fruit.

There are three other hotels in Kashgar that are supposed to take foreigners, but at the time of writing they were either closed or 'temporarily off limits' and filled with Han Chinese plain-clothes police. The following information is supplied in case things change for the better which they currently seem to be doing.

The *Chini Bagh Hotel* (☎ 2291, 2103) *(qíníbāhé bīngǔan)* in the former British consulate used to be popular with Pakistani traders commuting along the Karakoram Highway. Doubles without bath cost Y30; a bed in a chaotic six-bed room costs Y10. The shower block is a slime pit. There are rumours that this hotel will be torn down. There's barely a trace of the colonial grandeur left.

The *Oasis Hotel (lǜzhōu bīngǔan)* is opposite the Seman Hotel. Assuming it reopens to foreigners, dorm beds cost Y12 in a four-bed room. There are no showers – use those at the Seman Hotel.

The *Friendship Hotel (yǒuyí bīngǔan)* is no longer friendly to foreigners. It's near the Id Kah Mosque. Dorms cost Y15 and doubles are Y50.

Places to Eat

You won't starve in Kashgar, but restaurant city it ain't. The *Kashgar Guesthouse* serves Chinese meals for Y25 each!

For a wide variety of Uigur foods, pop into the food market close to the Id Kah Mosque.

There you can try shish kebab, rice with mutton, fried fish, samsa (rectangles of crisp pastry enclosing fried mincemeat) and fruit. To the left of the mosque is a teahouse with a balcony above the bustling crowds. Flat bread and shish kebab are sold at the huddle of stalls on the main road, just west of the big square opposite the Mao statue. There are a couple of excellent ice-cream stalls here too – selling very cold and very vanilla ice-cream. There are more ice-cream stalls in the Id Kah Square, and you should find eggs and roast chicken being sold near the main intersection at night. You might also want to consider the following food for thought:

> After dark, Kashgar can still get pretty rough. Prices you bartered down while it was still light (i.e. if you're sitting at a stall eating kebabs) mysteriously go back up to Western levels as night falls. Should you complain, the number of Uigurs around you then multiplies rapidly! Always pay *as soon as* you get the goods.
>
> **Philip Clarke**

Bottled and canned fruit are available from the large food store opposite the Id Kah Square on the main north-south road. There's a smaller store next to the cinema on the main intersection selling the same. You can buy eggs near the long-distance bus station; the ones painted red are hard-boiled.

The *Oasis Cafe* serves good Western food and is underneath the Friendship Hotel. However, this restaurant now charges Western prices. The *Seman Restaurant*, across the street from the Seman Hotel, isn't bad but you can eat more cheaply in the market areas.

Getting There & Away

Air There are daily flights from Kashgar to Ürümqi, and the fare is Y435. The flight takes slightly under two hours.

The CAAC office(☎ 2113) is on Jiefang Beilu north of the Id Kah Mosque (see map).

Bus At the time of writing, CITS was saying foreigners could only go to Kashgar by air. However, if you manage to get into Kashgar, it's possible that you can still depart by bus, at least to Ürümqi. If Kashgar opens up again to individual travellers, bus trips to/from other destinations should be possible. There are buses from the Kashgar long-distance bus station to Ürümqi, Daheyan, Aksu, Maralbixi, Khotan, Yengisar, Payziwat, Yopuria, Makit, Yakam and Kargilik.

There is a daily bus to Ürümqi via Aksu, Korla and Toksun. Tickets can only be bought one day before departure and the bus is scheduled to depart Kashgar at 8 am. The trip takes three days.

The bus to Turpan actually goes to Daheyan, stopping overnight at Aksu and Korla and going straight through Toksun on to Daheyan. The trip takes three days. Daheyan is a small railway town on the line from Lanzhou to Ürümqi, and to get to nearby Turpan there are three buses a day. See the Daheyan section for details.

You won't have access to baggage stored on the roof of the bus during the trip. Take a small bag of essentials with you on board. Be warned that buses don't always run on schedule. You could take four days to do the trip, driving anything between eight and 14 hours a day depending on breakdowns or other factors.

Korla and Aksu were once officially open to foreigners – they are now closed again but this could change anytime. The town of Yanqi, 52 km north of Korla, is a possible stopover (by rail or bus) for a visit to Buddhist caves in the area or to the nearby lake, Bagragh Kol *(bŏsīténg hú)*. From Yanqi to the lakeside centre of Bohu is about 12 km. Access to the lake from Bohu could involve a mud-wading expedition, but the fishing villages might be worth a visit. Prices charged for transport can be as high as Y100 per day for a motorised three-wheeler – bargaining is advised. Korla has bus and rail connections with Daheyan (Turpan station), Ürümqi and Yining. Aksu has bus and air connections. The major problem with stopping off on the way between Kashgar and Ürümqi is that you will need great patience to commandeer a seat in buses already packed to the gills.

The road between Xinjiang and Tibet, one

of the roughest in the world, passes through the disputed territory of Aksai Chin. This route is not officially open to foreigners; some have hitched unofficially from Lhasa to Kashgar in as little as 16 days, others have taken months. Plenty of foreigners have been fined travelling towards Lhasa from Kashgar, and Public Security's worries about safety are understandable in this instance. *Tibet – a travel survival kit* (Lonely Planet Publications) contains more details on this route, which should not be attempted without full preparations for high-altitude travel. At least two foreigners have died on this route: one was thrown from the back of a truck when it hit a pothole; the other died of a combination of hypothermia and altitude sickness, also while riding on the back of a truck.

The road connection between China and Pakistan via the Karakoram Highway is described later in this chapter.

Getting Around

The city buses are of no use; to get around you have to walk or hire a bike, donkey cart or jeep, or take a CITS tour. The most common transport in Kashgar is by bicycle or donkey cart, and there's also the odd horse-drawn cart.

Bikes can be hired from the Oasis Hotel, but there have been numerous stories of cheating, 'misplaced' deposits and lost identity documents. It's probably better to try the bike-hire place close to the Seman Hotel (ask at the hotel for directions). There is another bike hire place in a white building inside the courtyard of the large yellow building to the left of the Mao statue.

Jeeps are available for hire at CITS and at the Kashgar Guesthouse. Be prepared to bargain down to a reasonable price.

AROUND KASHGAR

Hanoi

(hànnùoyī gŭchéng) 罕诺依古城

The ruins of this ancient city lie about 30 km east of Kashgar. The town reached its zenith during the Tang and Song dynasties but appears to have been abandoned after the 11th century. To get out here you'll probably have to try and hire a jeep at the Kashgar Guesthouse – apparently it's a rough ride to see mediocre rubble.

Three Immortals Buddhist Caves

(sānxiān dòng) 三仙洞

These Buddhist caves are on a sheer cliff on the south bank of the Qiakmakh River about 20 km north of Kashgar. There are three caves, one with frescoes which are still discernible. Going to the caves make a pleasant excursion, but it's not worth it just for the art.

KARAKORAM HIGHWAY

(zhōngbā gōnglù) 中巴公路

This highway over Khunjerab Pass (4800 metres) was opened to foreigners in May 1986 and closed again in April 1990. The official excuse was landslides, but the real reason was a political 'earthquake'. However, in August of the same year it opened again but only for individual travel from Pakistan to Kashgar – from Kashgar to Pakistan requires an expensive CITS tour! If the highway is opened again to individuals, you can go from Kashgar as far as Pirali (the Chinese border checkpoint) just for the trip (or some hiking en route) without crossing the border. Ask the bus company or the Public Security Bureau – not CITS – if you want to know the current situation.

For centuries this route was used by caravans plodding down the Silk Road. Back in 400 AD, the Chinese pilgrim Fa Xian recorded feelings of vertigo:

> The way was difficult and rugged, running along a bank exceedingly precipitous. When one approached the edge of it, his eyes became unsteady; and if he wished to go forward in the same direction, there was no place on which he could place his foot, and beneath were the waters of the river called the Indus.

Khunjerab means 'valley of blood', a reference to local bandits who took advantage of the terrain to plunder caravans and slaughter the merchants.

Nearly 20 years were required to plan, push, blast and level the present road between Islamabad and Kashgar; over 400 road-builders died. The rough section between Kashgar and the Pakistan border still needs a few more years before it can be called a road. Facilities en route are being steadily improved, but take warm clothing, food and drink on board with you – once stowed on the roof of the bus your baggage is not easily accessible.

Information

For information or advice, contact the Pakistan Tourism Development Corporation, H-2, St 61, F – 7/4, Islamabad, Pakistan. CITS in Ürümqi has no maps, no knowledge of the highway and no interest other than to sell you an outrageously expensive tour.

A separate guide, *The Karakoram Highway – a travel survival kit* (Lonely Planet Publications), is available.

Visas

Pakistani visas are compulsory for visitors from most Western countries. Visas are *not* given at the border; Hong Kong and Beijing are the closest places to obtain your Pakistan visa, so plan ahead if you want to enter or exit China on this road.

Chinese visas can be obtained in your own country, in Hong Kong and in Islamabad. The Chinese embassy in Islamabad takes between one and five days to issue the visa and charges 70 rupees.

Border

Opening & Closing Times These are officially given as 1 May and 31 October respectively. However, the border can open late or close early depending on conditions at the Khunjerab Pass.

Formalities Travel formalities are performed at Sust, on the Pakistan border; the Chinese borderpost is at Pirali. Pirali now has a post office, restaurants, hotels (charging from Y4 to Y10 per person) and a bank. You can't change Pakistan rupees at Pirali, only Western currencies. Don't worry, Kashgar street marketeers love cash rupees and US dollars.

Routing

The Karakoram Highway stretches between Islamabad and Kashgar. The following chart provides a rough guide to distances and average journey times:

	Distance (km)	Duration
Kashgar-Tashkurgan	280	7 hrs
Tashkurgan-Pirali	84	90 mins
Pirali-Khunjerab (Sino-Pakistan border)	35	1 hr
Khunjerab-Sust	86	2¼ hrs
Sust-Passu	35	45 mins
Passu-Gulmit	14	20 mins
Gulmit-Karimabad	37	1 hr
Karimabad (Hunza)-Gilgit	98	2 hrs
Gilgit-Rawalpindi	631	18 hrs

From China to Pakistan At the time of writing, CITS (in collusion with Public Security) was forcing travellers heading for Pakistan to buy expensive package tours. However, it pays to shop around. In Kashgar, several other tour agencies have sprung up selling trips to the border at less than CITS prices. One such operation is based in the rear of the Chini Bagh Hotel. The best thing to do is talk to other travellers in Kashgar – the rates are cheaper for larger groups. Prices quoted by CITS vary wildly – from Y500 to Y2000 depending on what the CITS staff ate for lunch that day.

In case the rules change and individual travel again becomes possible, you can get to the border cheaply by bus. Buses for Pakistan leave from the bus station in Kashgar, but weekly departure dates are flexible – the normal departure day is Wednesday. Some buses only go as far as Pirali and charge Y15; others go to Sust and charge Y150. It's a good idea to traipse around hotels to see if Pakistani traders have chartered their own bus.

From Kashgar, the bus crosses the Pamir Plateau (3000 metres) before overnighting just short of the foothills of Kongurshan *(gōnggé'ér shān)*, which is 7719 metres high, and nearby Muztag-Atashan *(mùshìtǎgé shān)* at 7546 metres. The journey on the next day passes through stunning scenery: high mountain pastures with grazing camels and yaks tended by Tajiks who live in yurts. Some travellers have stayed in yurts beside Karakol Lake *(kǎlākùlì hú)*, close to both these mountains. Sven Hedin, the Swedish explorer, nearly drowned in this lake!

The bus spends the second night at Tashkurgan *(tǎshíkù'ěrgān)*, a predominantly Tajik town which could be used as a base to explore the nearby ruined fort, local cemeteries and surrounding high country.

From Tashkurgan (3600 metres) the road climbs higher to Pirali, which wouldn't be worth a stop if it wasn't the Chinese checkpost. If you're on a Pakistani bus, you'll have no need to change buses; if you've taken the local bus from Kashgar, you'll need to change to a Pakistani bus from Pirali onwards.

From Pakistan to China The situation is awfully confused out there, but at the time of this writing, individual travellers from Pakistan were managing to get across the border into Kashgar and then on to Ürümqi by bus. However, going in the other direction seems to be impossible except with a ridiculously expensive CITS tour.

From Rawalpindi to Gilgit there are five buses daily. An ordinary coach costs 85 rupees; deluxe will cost 120 rupees. If you can't stand the pace of the bus ride, the flight between Rawalpindi and Gilgit is good value at 180 rupees.

From Gilgit to Sust, there's a NATCO bus which costs 22 rupees; buy your ticket on the morning of departure at 7 am – the bus leaves at 9 am. The tourist hotel at Sust charges 25 rupees for a bed in the dormitory.

From Sust to Pirali, there's a bus for 160 rupees or US$10. At Pirali everyone changes to a Chinese bus to Kashgar. This bus stops overnight at Tashkurgan. Trucks offer lifts (negotiate the price); ditto for jeeps. From Tashkurgan to Kashgar takes aeons over an atrocious boulder-strewn road.

YINING

(yīníng) 伊宁

Also known as Gulja, Yining lies close to the Soviet border, about 700 km west of Ürümqi. It is the centre of Ili Kazakh Autonomous Prefecture.

On the death of Genghis Khan in 1227, his four sons inherited responsibility for the Mongol empire. Chaghatai, the second eldest, took over a huge area which included Turkestan, Xinjiang and, further south, most of Khorasan. Chaghatai is said to have made his capital at Almalik, close to Yining in the valley of the Ili River.

The Ili Valley became an easy access point for invaders and later for the northern route of the Silk Road, which stretched to the Caspian Sea. Russian and Chinese control over this borderland was at best tenuous. Yining was occupied by the Tsar's troops in 1876 during Yakub Beg's independent rule of Kashgaria. Five years later, the Chinese cracked down on Yakub Beg and Yining was handed back by the Russians. The border is still a nervous one; in 1962, there were major Sino-Soviet clashes along the Ili River. In late 1986, the Chinese claimed to have shot six Soviet infiltrators.

Chinese appear uneasy here and warn against staying out after dark, when knives are fast and streets unsafe. They probably do have some problems keeping order in an alien environment. The local Kazakhs and Uzbekhs can be a rough bunch (regularly drunk in the evenings and occasionally involved in street fights) but very friendly towards foreigners, whom they put in a different category from those in authority.

If nothing else, you might want to visit Yining just for fun – or to cry. Nothing seems to work here and no one cares – planes don't arrive, banks run out of money, telephones are perpetually out of order, government workers don't show up for work and much of the population is drunk. Indeed, it seems more like the Soviet Union than China.

Information

CITS This office (☎ 22439) is in room 324 of a large administration building at 27

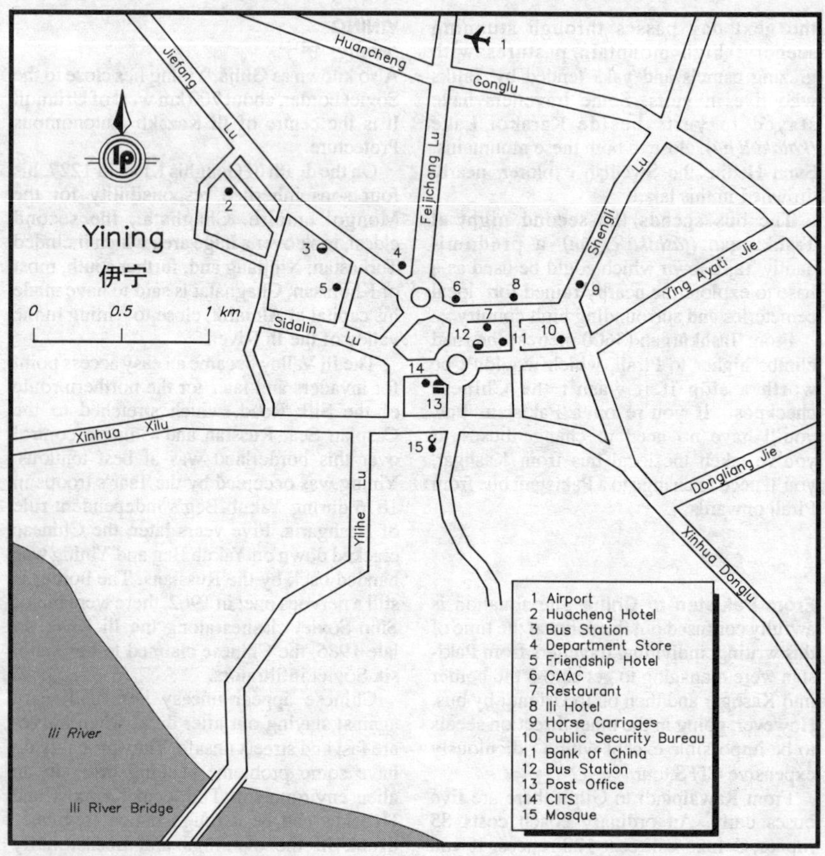

1 飞机场
2 花城宾馆
3 长途汽车站
4 百货大楼
5 友谊宾馆
6 中国民航
7 餐厅
8 伊犁宾馆
9 马车
10 公安局外事科
11 中国银行
12 长途汽车站
13 邮局
14 中国国际旅行社
15 清真寺

Sidalin Beilu, which is just to the west of the post office. You might want to call first to wake up the staff and let them know you're coming.

Public Security Bureau This is two blocks from the Ili Hotel, near a big radio tower (see map).

Money It would be prudent to bring a sufficient supply of FEC with you rather than to depend on the banks in Yining.

There is a sign by the entrance of the Ili Hotel saying 'Bank of China'. Don't believe it. The actual Bank of China is one block south of the Ili Hotel. When you find it, don't be surprised if they don't have any FEC – they often run out, and the man in charge of FEC only shows up for work occasionally.

Post The post office is right on the big traffic circle in the centre of town.

Maps The Friendship Hotel sells a map called *A Tourist Guide to Ili*. This map is also available at the Ili Hotel, but the person in charge of map sales hasn't shown up for work for several years.

Things to See

Yining is a grubby place that has a few faded remnants of Russian architecture, but overall there's not much to the town itself. The main attraction here is the local Uigur, Kazakh and Uzbekh culture. The region is semi-arid, but there are many trees and intensive agriculture thanks to heavy water runoff from the nearby Tianshan mountains. The one true scenic spot in this area is Sayram Lake, high in the mountains about four hours from Yining – the rest is uninspiring. About six km south of the town centre is a bridge over the Ili River. It's worthwhile leaving the main street and following alleys which pass the occasional Russian-style house with carved window-frames, painted shutters and plaster peeling from ornate designs. The street-markets are famous for fruit (especially in August), carpets and leather (boots).

The Ili Valley is pretty – the roads are lined with tall birch trees and there are farms everywhere. The best way to get out and see the countryside is to take a horse carriage *(mǎ chē)*. These cost about Y10 for a 1½-hour tour. Most of the carriage drivers congregate in an area about one block east of the Ili Hotel. Communication can be a real problem – the drivers are Kazakhs and few speak Chinese – the only English they know is 'change money'.

Places to Stay

Most budget travellers stay in the *Ili Hotel* (☎ 22794) *(yīlí bīngǔan)* close to the bus station and CAAC. The hotel features lovely, tree-shaded grounds, but the staff are incredibly lethargic. Dorms cost Y8 and doubles range from Y29 to Y60. Showers are available sometime in the evening and are turned off at 10 pm – buy shower tickets at the front desk for Y0.50.

The only other place worth considering is the *Friendship Hotel* (☎ 24631) *(yǒuyí bīngǔan)*. It doesn't have all the nice trees of the Ili Hotel, but the rooms are very clean and the staff is not only conscious, but actually friendly! The dorms cost Y18 – there are two beds in each room and an attached bath. The main problem with the Friendship Hotel is that it's hard to find – it's down an obscure side-street and the only sign pointing the way is in Chinese.

One other place accepts foreigners – the *Huacheng Hotel* (☎ 2911 ext 296) *(hūachéng bīngǔan)*. Doubles are Y60 and the rooms look decent, but it's too far from everything and there are no cheap dorms.

Places to Eat

The *Ili Hotel* serves filling but unexciting set meals for Y2.70. Buy your meal ticket from the comatose staff at the front desk. Lunch is served around 2 pm.

Go out the main gate of the Ili Hotel, turn right and walk for half a block – there's a small, unnamed restaurant on the left. There's good and cheap food, but lots of hot peppers. If you don't want it hot, say *'bùyào làjiāo'*.

Food markets can be interesting places to

eat. There's one about 10 minutes' walk south-east of the bus station. Apart from the usual kebabs and flat bread (nan), there's another type of kebab which is dipped in batter before roasting. When you try it, make sure that they use meat and not mutton fat or it will taste revolting.

On the main street close to the cinema are two food markets on opposite sides of the street, one catering for Chinese tastes, the other for the wild minority population. The Chinese sector does the usual meat and veg dishes. The wild side is almost medieval, with restaurant proprietors yelling at you over steaming cauldrons, while drunken customers roll around on benches and tables set outside. The staple foods seem to be mutton stew, kebab and flat bread.

Getting There & Away

Foreigners are only allowed to approach Yining from Ürümqi. With the right credentials (lots of money), other possibilities include journeys from Kashgar, Altai or the Soviet Union.

Air It's relatively easy to buy an air ticket from Ürümqi to Yining, but difficult or impossible to get a flight back. The one-way fare is Y176 and the flight takes 1½ hours. Flights run six days a week. If you're determined to fly back to Ürümqi, your best bet is to buy tickets through the hotels. You could also try CITS or go directly to the airport.

The CAAC office is one block west of the Ili Hotel in Yining, but the man in charge seems to be in a coma and the office is normally closed. A lot of foreigners have complained so perhaps things will change – someday.

Figure on spending at least three to four working days to buy an air ticket in Yining. Cancelled and delayed flights are the norm.

Bus Buses leave daily from Ürümqi at 9 am (Beijing summer time) and take two days to get to Yining; the fare is Y28. The station in Ürümqi wants FEC. Departures from Yining are at 8 am during summer, and at 7 am the rest of the year. You can pay in RMB in Yining. It's best to purchase tickets a day in advance. There are two bus stations in Yining – buses from one station do not stop at the other, so you must buy your ticket from the place from which you want to depart.

The bus trip from Ürümqi to Yining takes two days (18 hours). The buses seem to have no shock absorbers – the ride in the back is really rough. Seats in the front are in great demand, so buy your ticket early before all the best seats are given away. Luggage must be stored on the roof, but don't put anything of great value up there.

Buses run daily to Kashgar via Korla, Aksu and Kuqa. The full trip to Kashgar takes three days and the ticket costs Y50. At the time of writing, foreigners were prohibited from making this journey. Ditto for the bus trip to Altai.

AROUND YINING

Sayram Lake

(sàilǐmù hú) 赛里木湖

This large and beautiful alpine lake is to the north of Yining. The bus between Ürümqi and Yining makes a 30-minute rest stop here. The bus from Yining to Sayram Lake takes slightly more than three hours.

If you would like to explore the lake, it's possible to spend the night here, though very few travellers do this. The best place to stay is the Gǔozigōu Zhāodàisǔo where rooms are just Y3. There is one other hotel, the Sàilǐmù Zhāodàisǔo, a terrible place that looks like it might collapse soon. There is food up here, but the selection is limited so bring what you need.

It is possible to hire horses at the lake and go riding with the Kazakh shepherds. It costs about Y40 for a whole day, but be sure to bargain. The area presents some good hiking opportunities. The water from the lake is considered drinkable, but be careful about contamination around the shoreline from sheep.

VISITING THE SOVIET UNION

In theory, it is possible to travel overland by bus from Yining to Panfilov in the Soviet

Union, and then on to Alma-Ata. In practice, the whole exercise is fraught with bureaucratic hurdles and costs a small fortune.

Local Kazakhs, Uigurs, Kirghiz, and others who have relatives on the other side of the border make this trip regularly and inexpensively. Unfortunately, foreigners need tourist visas and must book all hotels in advance through Intourist, the Soviet travel agency. This creates headaches because you must arrive in the Soviet Union on the day you booked for, and transport on the Chinese side is not 100% reliable. For this reason, most travellers are likely to approach the border from the Soviet side and cross into China.

Buses between Yining and Panfilov run daily from 1 May to 1 October via the border town of Korgas *(hùochéng)*, or Khorgos in Russian. This road is actually open all year because of its low elevation, but winter storms could close it for a few days at a time. It's necessary to change buses in Panfilov to reach Alma-Ata.

The bus between Yining and Panfilov costs Y28, assuming you're allowed to get on it, which is unlikely unless you can come up with the necessary papers. There is also a bus between Yining and Korgas, where you cross the border by foot and then catch a bus to Panfilov. Unfortunately, Korgas isn't open to foreigners who aren't crossing the border, so you can't just go up to the border to have a look.

Intourist insists that foreigners cannot spend the night in Panfilov – it is necessary to travel between Korgas and Alma-Ata in one day. This is problematic because the border post is only open from 8.30 am to 4 pm. Intourist will arrange transport from Alma-Ata to Korgas for a heart-stopping US$500. A possibility of doing it more cheaply by taxi exists, but may not be reliable. So far, the only foreigners we know of who have made this journey cheaply by bus are eastern Europeans (Czechs, Hungarians, Poles, etc).

Outside the USSR, Intourist may tell you that you can't exit via Alma-Ata. If so, you can tell them you'll make your own arrangements for exiting the USSR – then you can arrange it with the Alma-Ata Intourist office.

Things may change. A railway line is under construction from Ürümqi to Alma-Ata and is nearing completion. Perhaps it will be open by the time you read this. When completed, it seems logical that foreigners will be able to travel from Xinjiang to eastern Europe without the need to backtrack to Beijing. Whether or not logic prevails is another matter.

Another Soviet-China crossing open since 1989 (if you have the cash) is between Frunze (the capital of Kirghizia) and Kashgar, via Turugart Pass *(tǔ'ěrgǎtè shānkǒu)*. It would be absurdly expensive for individuals – about US$800 for a car and guide, including an overnight stay in a tiny hotel at Naryn (350 km, seven hours from Frunze), then 190 km (five hours) on to the Chinese border, where there are no overnight facilities. This route is only open roughly from June to mid-September. There are no buses on the Chinese side, only a CITS car and driver (by arrangement through Frunze Intourist).

There are also flights (Y635, twice weekly) between Ürümqi and Alma-Ata run jointly by Aeroflot and CAAC. This is probably your cheapest and easiest option to travel between Xinjiang and the USSR. The Alma-Ata CAAC office (☎ 330170 or 336956) is in the Otpar Hotel, Gao Erji St.

ALTAI

(ā'lètài) 阿勒泰

This town is near the northernmost tip of Xinjiang, close to the Soviet border. Just to the north of Altai is a stunning natural area with peaks over 4000 metres. Unfortunately, no tourists (not even Chinese) are permitted in this border area. However, Altai itself is open to foreigners. CAAC has flights from Ürümqi four times weekly for Y151 – the flight takes 1½ hours. Since you cannot visit the mountains and forests at this time, it seems rather pointless to go to Altai. Again, we can only hope that things will change.

TIBET AND QINGHAI

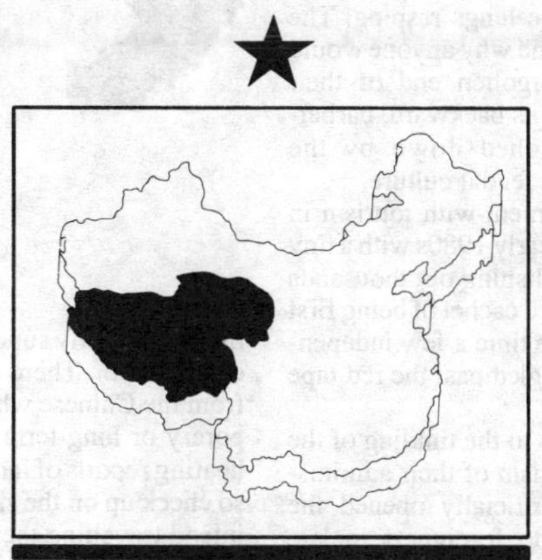

Tibet 西藏

Westerners tend to imagine Tibet *(xīzàng)* as some sort of Shangri-La, a strange projection of one of the world's most barren landscapes: isolated, desolate, bitterly cold in winter, a high plateau where the thin air can set the heart pounding and the lungs rasping. The Chinese can't understand why anyone would want to go to the forgotten end of their Middle Kingdom with its backward, barbarian people still weighed down by the remnants of an archaic feudal culture.

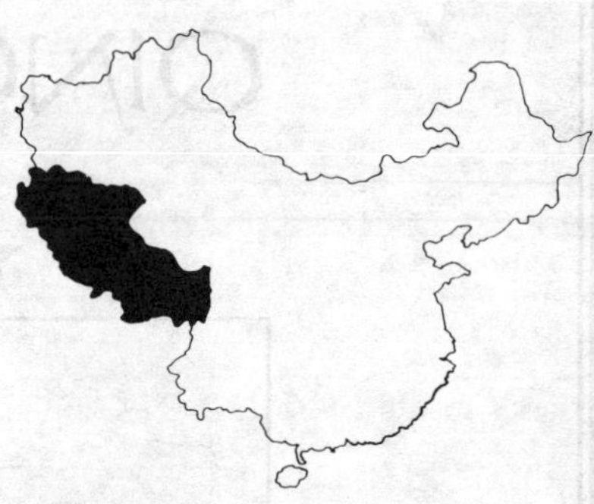

The Chinese experiment with tourism in Tibet kicked off in the early 1980s with a tiny trickle of tour groups dishing out thousands of dollars for the coveted cachet of being first into Tibet. At the same time a few independent backpackers wriggled past the red tape and outrageous prices.

In response, perhaps to the tinkling of the cash register and criticism of their administration, the Chinese officially opened the 'Roof of the World' to foreigners in late 1984. In late 1987 the situation changed quite dramatically when Tibetans in Lhasa gave vent to their feelings about the Chinese and their policies. A series of demonstrations virtually became an uprising. Chinese security forces reportedly opened fire on the demonstrators, many of whom were monks from the monasteries around Lhasa. Both sides suffered casualties and at least one police station was reduced to a smoking pile of rubble. The response of the Chinese authorities was swift; Lhasa was swamped with plain-clothes and uniformed security, who put an abrupt end to the uprising. The embarrassment of foreign press coverage was neatly solved when all members of the foreign media covering events in Lhasa were unceremoniously booted back into China. Within a few weeks, it was the turn of individual travellers to be similarly ejected.

The year 1989 brought more violence in the streets of Lhasa and more restrictions for travellers. At the time of going to press, only official guests and group tours (whose movements are easily supervised) were allowed to enter Tibet. There has been no indication from the Chinese whether this will be a temporary or long-term restriction (we are still hearing reports of individuals entering Tibet) so check up on the situation if and when you intend travelling there.

Despite Chinese administration and the influx of foreign visitors, Tibet retains the fascination of a unique culture quite distinct from that of the Han Chinese. Since full-scale treatment of Tibetan regions would (and should!) take a whole book, Lonely Planet has done just that with its guide ***Tibet – a travel survival kit***.

Travellers to Tibet need to be aware that their movements are likely to be closely watched. It has been reported that Tibetans who have been courageous enough to talk to travelling foreigners about the local situation have got into serious trouble, either at the time or later on when the foreigners went home and published material identifying individual local people. Remember that an interesting conversation for you may mean arrest and imprisonment for your acquaintance.

HISTORY

Recorded Tibetan history begins in the 7th century AD when the Tibetan armies were considered as great a scourge to their neighbours as the Huns were to Europe. Under King Songtsen Gampo the Tibetans occupied Nepal and collected tribute from parts of Yunnan Province. Shortly after the death of Gampo the armies moved north and took control of the Silk Road, including the great city of Kashgar. Opposed by Chinese troops, who occupied all of Xinjiang under the Tang Dynasty, the Tibetans responded by sacking the imperial city of Chang'an (present-day Xi'an). It was not until 842 that Tibetan expansion came to a sudden halt with the assassination of the king, and the region broke up into independent feuding principalities. Never again would the Tibetan armies leave their high plateau.

As secular authority waned, the power of the Buddhist clergy increased. When Buddhism reached Tibet in the 3rd century, it had to compete with Bon, the traditional animistic religion of the region. Buddhism adopted many of the rituals of Bon, like the flying of prayer flags and the turning of prayer wheels. These rituals combined with the esoteric practices of Tantric Buddhism (imported from India) to evolve into Tibetan Buddhism.

The religion had spread through Tibet by the 7th century; after the 9th century the monasteries became increasingly politicised, and in 1641 the Gelukpa (the Yellow Hat sect, a reformist movement advocating stringent monastic discipline) used the support of the Buddhist Mongols to crush the Red Hats, their rivals.

The Yellow Hats' leader adopted the title of Dalai Lama, or Ocean of Wisdom; religion and politics became inextricably entwined, presided over by the Dalai Lama – the god-king. Each Dalai Lama was considered the reincarnation of the last upon whose death the monks searched the land for a newborn child who showed some sign of embodying his predecessor's spirit. The Yellow Hats won the Mongols to their cause by finding the fourth Dalai Lama in the family of the Mongol ruler. The Mongols, however, came to regard Tibet as their own domain and in 1705 ousted the Dalai Lama. Considered a threat to China, the Mongols were targeted by the Qing emperor Kangxi, who sent an expedition to Tibet to expel them. The Chinese left behind representatives to direct Tibetan foreign affairs, and for the next two centuries these Ambans (representatives) maintained a presence, but had scant control in the region.

With the fall of the Qing Dynasty in 1911 Tibet entered a period of independence that was to last until 1950. In that year the PLA entered the region and occupied eastern Tibet. The Dalai Lama sent a delegation to Beijing which reached an agreement with the Chinese that allowed the PLA to occupy the rest of Tibet but left the existing political, social and religious organisation intact. The agreement was to last until 1959. In that year a rebellion broke out. Just why it happened and how widespread it was depends on whether you believe the Chinese or the Tibetans – in any case the rebellion was suppressed by Chinese troops and the Dalai Lama and his retinue fled to India. Another 80,000 Tibetans crossed the high passes, enduring atrocious conditions to escape into India and Nepal.

Tibet became an 'autonomous' region of China. Over the next few years its political organisation was altered drastically.

Tibet Today

Tibetans and Chinese interpret the history of their countries differently. The Tibetans argue that theirs was long an independent country with its own language, religion and literature, and was never really occupied by China. To the Chinese, the region is an 'inalienable' part of China. No effort is spared to reinforce that point, but the 'evidence' that the Chinese conjure up and expect you to believe is an insult to one's intelligence.

The Chinese contend that China and Tibet have for the last 1300 years coexisted peacefully and happily, linked culturally and politically. The marriages of Chinese feudal princesses to Tibetan warlord-kings support this view, as do the audiences the Son of

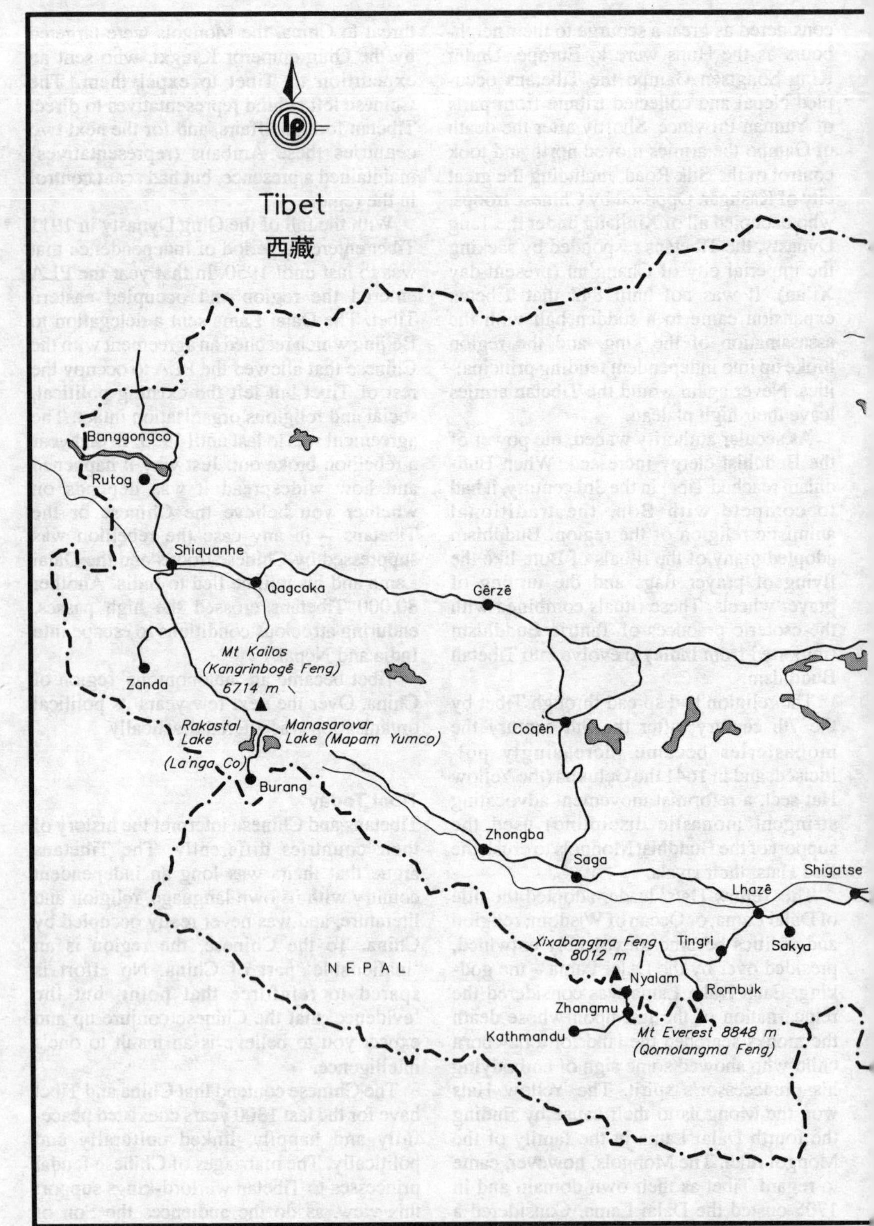
Tibet
西藏
Banggongco
Rutog
Shiquanhe
Qagcaka
Gêrzê
Zanda
Mt Kailas
(Kangrinbogê Feng)
6714 m
Rakastal
Lake
(La'nga Co)
Manasarovar
Lake (Mapam Yumco)
Burang
Coqên
Zhongba
Saga
Shigatse
Lhazê
Sakya
Tingri
Xixabangma Feng
8012 m
Nyalam
Rombuk
Zhangmu
Kathmandu
Mt Everest 8848 m
(Qomolangma Feng)
N E P A L

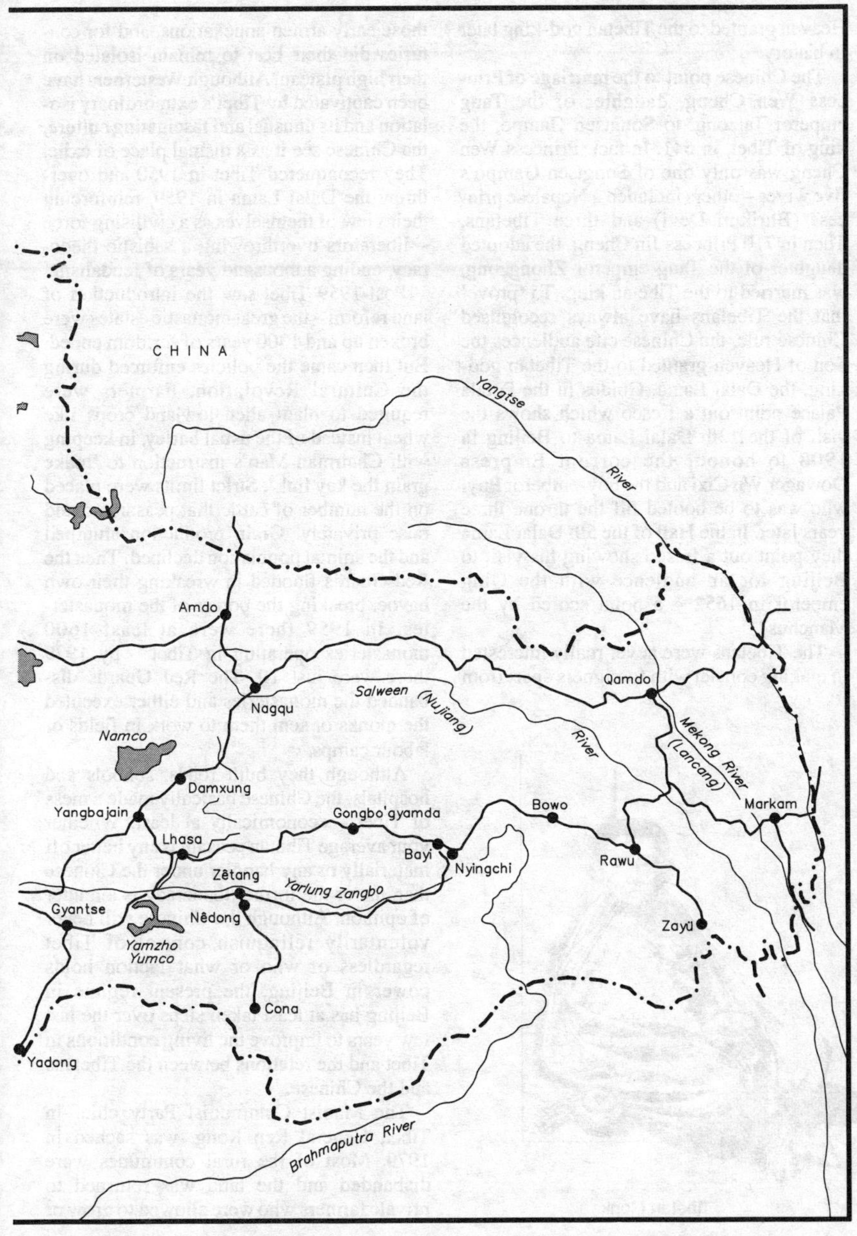
CHINA
Yangtse
River
Amdo
Salween
(Nujiang)
River
Qamdo
Mekong River
(Lancang)
Nagqu
Namco
Damxung
Yangbajain
Gongbo'gyamda
Bowo
Markam
Lhasa
Bayi
Nyingchi
Rawu
Zêtang
Yarlung Zangbo
Nêdong
Gyantse
Yamzho
Yumco
Zayü
Cona
Yadong
Brahmaputra River

Heaven granted to the Tibetan god-king later in history.

The Chinese point to the marriage of Princess Wen Cheng, daughter of the Tang emperor Taizong, to Songtsen Gampo, the king of Tibet, in 641. In fact, Princess Wen Cheng was only one of Songtsen Gampo's five wives – others included a Nepalese princess (Bhrikuti Devi) and three Tibetans. Then in 710 Princess Jin Cheng, the adopted daughter of the Tang emperor Zhongzong, was married to the Tibetan king. To 'prove' that the Tibetans have always recognised Chinese rule, the Chinese cite audiences the Son of Heaven granted to the Tibetan god-king, the Dalai Lama. Guides in the Potala Palace point out a fresco which shows the visit of the 13th Dalai Lama to Beijing in 1908 to honour the corrupt Empress Dowager Wu Cixi and the boy-emperor Puyi who was to be booted off the throne three years later. In the Hall of the 5th Dalai Lama they point out a fresco showing his visit to Beijing for an audience with the Qing emperor in 1652 – a point scored by the Manchus?

The Tibetans were never really interested in making contact with foreigners apart from those early armed annexations, and for centuries did their best to remain isolated on their high plateau. Although Westerners have been captivated by Tibet's extraordinary isolation and its unusual and fascinating culture, the Chinese see it as a dismal place of exile. They reconquered Tibet in 1950 and overthrew the Dalai Lama in 1959, reinforcing their view of themselves as a civilising force – liberators overthrowing a sadistic theocracy, ending a thousand years of feudalism.

Tibetan Monk

Post-1959 Tibet saw the introduction of land reform – the great monastic estates were broken up and 1300 years of serfdom ended. But then came the policies enforced during the Cultural Revolution. Farmers were required to plant alien lowland crops like wheat instead of the usual barley, in keeping with Chairman Mao's instruction to 'make grain the key link'. Strict limits were placed on the number of cattle that peasants could raise privately. Grain production slumped and the animal population declined. Then the Red Guards flooded in wreaking their own havoc, breaking the power of the monasteries. In 1959 there were at least 1600 monasteries operating in Tibet – by 1979 there were just 10. The Red Guards disbanded the monasteries and either executed the monks or sent them to work in fields or labour camps.

Although they built roads, schools and hospitals, the Chinese basically made a mess of Tibet – economically at least. Whether your average Tibetan peasant is any better off materially or any happier under the Chinese than under the former theocracy is a matter of opinion. Although the Chinese will never voluntarily relinquish control of Tibet regardless of who or what faction holds power in Beijing, the present regime in Beijing has at least taken steps over the last few years to improve the living conditions in Tibet and the relations between the Tibetans and the Chinese.

The Maoist Communist Party chief in Tibet, General Ren Rong, was sacked in 1979. Most of the rural communes were disbanded and the land was returned to private farmers who were allowed to grow or graze whatever they wanted and to sell their produce in free markets. Taxes were reduced and state subsidies to the region increased. Some of the monasteries have been reopened on a limited basis, and the Chinese woo the Dalai Lama in the hope that he will return to Tibet. More likely he'll be given an office job in Beijing as a religious figurehead to try and legitimise Chinese control over Tibet. In 1985 the 'celebrations' marking the 20th anniversary of the Tibetan Autonomous Region (TAR) went off like a damp squib. Apart from banning the Western press from the event, the Chinese provided Lhasa with a tight military blanket, including sharpshooters on the roof of the Potala Palace – the general picture looked more like a nervous show of strength than anything else. Certainly a most acute problem for Tibet (as for Qinghai and Xinjiang) is a policy of stealthy resettlement: a massive influx of Han settlers from surrounding provinces threatens to oust Tibetans from employment, occupy arable land and swamp the Tibetan culture with that of the Han Chinese. A large part of what's going on is hidden from world view – most reports come through the eyes and ears of Tibetan refugees, who speak of forced abortion and sterilisation.

Since 1987 Tibetans in Lhasa have given vent to their frustrations in a series of anti-Chinese demonstrations that resulted in untold violence. Claiming that foreign agitators were inspiring the Tibetan riots, the Chinese government stopped all tourist visits to the region for a short period. The current tourism policy allows only groups (minimum of three) into Tibet and restricts them to travel in Lhasa, Xigatse and Gyantse.

It's difficult to say what the future holds for Tibet. The likelihood that the Dalai Lama will return diminishes as his power abroad increases. With his recent acceptance of the Nobel Peace Prize, he's less likely than ever to return without a guarantee of greater home rule for his country. The Chinese government, on the other hand, is not likely to give Tibet back to the Buddhist clerics – they won't allow two dynasties to divide China.

GEOGRAPHY

Most of Tibet is an immense plateau which lies at an altitude from 4000 to 5000 metres. It's a desolate region broken by a series of east-west mountain ranges, and is completely barren except for some poor grasslands to the south-east. The plateau is bounded to the north by the Kunlunshan range which separates Tibet from Xinjiang Province and to the south by the Himalayas and their peaks rising over 7000 metres.

The Qamdo region of Tibet in the east is a somewhat lower section of plateau, drained by the headwaters of the Salween, Mekong and Upper Yangtse rivers. It's an area of considerably greater rainfall than the rest of Tibet and the climate is less extreme. In a number of valleys in the south of the country some agriculture (such as growing the country's main crop, barley) is possible – most of the Tibetan population lives in this area. On the uplands surrounding these valleys the inhabitants are mainly pastoralists raising sheep, yaks and horses.

POPULATION

According to Chinese figures, the population of Tibet is almost 1,900,000. The number comprises Tibetans as well as the pockets of Han Chinese settlers who probably number around 150,000, although it does not include the mobile element of PLA soldiers and migrant Han workers, which could be as high as 400,000 or more. There are, in fact, a total of almost 3,900,000 Tibetans spread out over Tibet, Sichuan, Qinghai, Gansu and Yunnan.

CLIMATE

The climate in Tibet (and neighbouring Qinghai) sometimes gives the impression that all four seasons have been compressed into one day. In general, summer temperatures are pleasantly warm at midday and drop dramatically in the shade and at night. Winter brings intense cold and fierce winds, although Lhasa sees little snow. The best time to travel is between May and September.

In southern and eastern Tibet, the Himalayas act as a barrier against the rain-bearing monsoons, and rainfall decreases as you travel north. The central region of Tibet sees only 25 to 50 cm of rain a year (Sikkim, by contrast, sees some 500 cm). Snowfall is far less common in Tibet than the name 'Land of Snows' implies. The sun is quick to melt off snowfalls. Temperatures can vary from below zero during the early morning and evening to a sizzling 38°C at midday. In the north and west of Tibet rainfall becomes even scarcer, but fewer than 100 days in the year are frost-free and temperatures plummet as low as -40°C. Northern monsoons can sweep across the plains for days on end, often whipping up duststorms, sandstorms, snowstorms, or (rare) rainstorms. In the summer, the snow line in the north and east lies between 5000 and 6000 metres; in the south, even higher at 6000 metres.

LANGUAGE

Although many Tibetans in the cities have a rudimentary command of Chinese, they are pleased (and try hard not to crack up!) when you make an effort to speak in Tibetan. Out on the desolate plateau, you'll have to use Tibetan. In either case, you might be able to save your bacon with a Tibetan phrasebook such as the Lonely Planet one.

Tibetan Mini-Glossary

hello
: *tashi delag*

thank you
: *thuk ji chay*

how are you?
: *kuzak de po yinpe*

how much?
: *di gatse ray*

it's very good
: *shidak yak po dhuk*

cheers!
: *tamdil*

HEALTH

Most visitors to Tibet and Qinghai, high-altitude regions with thin air, will suffer some symptoms of Acute Mountain Sickness (AMS). Until the body has become acclimatised to the lack of oxygen you may experience temporary symptoms such as headaches, sleeping difficulties, nausea and dizziness. If any of these persist or worsen, you should immediately descend to a lower altitude and seek medical help. It's rare for AMS to turn really nasty in Lhasa, but if it does, you should check with the hospital and consider a flight to Chengdu. Certainly, if you intend to do some trekking or mountaineering at higher altitudes, you owe it to yourself to thoroughly understand AMS.

To prepare yourself for higher altitudes, spend the first few days taking your exercise slowly. Drink plenty of liquids (keep your urine a nice pale colour!) to avoid dehydration. Alcohol, tobacco and sedatives are best avoided.

Of the many books available on this subject, *Mountain Sickness: Prevention, Recognition & Treatment* by Peter Hackett (The American Alpine Club) is among the best. If you have any doubts about your health, consult your doctor before you go.

There's no call for instant alarm, but you should not ignore AMS. We met a 65-year-old American with a pacemaker who had taken the bus from Golmud and was happily strolling the streets of Lhasa. On the other hand, Chinese Public Security has reported several foreigners dying from a combination of AMS, cold (hypothermia) and exposure. Oxygen is available at Lhasa tourist hotels – some tourists even carry their own oxygen bags in the streets!

A nasty stomach bug called giardia has travelled from Nepal to Lhasa, where it treks the intestinal paths of unfortunate foreigners – the locals seem immune. Check with your doctor on the pros and cons of anti-giardia drugs such as Tiniba or Flagyl, and take some with you since they are hard to find in Lhasa. Some of the most poignant notices in Lhasa are those by foreigners urgently seeking these magical medicines – two such foreigners in constant search of relief received the nickname of 'flagylantes'.

Coughs and colds are common among foreigners, and everyone in Tibet has a runny nose. Keep yourself well supplied with favourite remedies, vitamins and warm

Top: Defensive Yak, Qinghai Lake (RS)
Bottom Left: Khamba rider, Bamda (RS)
Bottom Right: View from Ganden Monastery (RS)

Top Left: Debating Monk at Sera Monastery, Lhasa (RS)
Top Right: Wandering Monk chanting in the Barkhor, Lhasa (RS)
Bottom Left: Pilgrim wearing "gau" (portable shrine) in Lhasa (RS)
Bottom Right: Tibetan nomad girl with ornate hairband, Qinghai Lake (RS)

clothes. To beat the cold and (most importantly) the dust, join the parade of people wearing surgical or industrial face-masks – the main street in Lhasa sometimes looks like a scene from the movie *MASH*.

Finally, a word of warning about the dogs which roam in packs around monasteries and towns. Several foreigners have been badly bitten, and we have heard reports of rabies. Keep your distance during the day, watch your step in the dark. One French visitor got into the habit of detonating Chinese bangers to send the hounds packing!

GETTING THERE & AWAY

Bus, Truck & Landcruiser

There is a serious shortage of transport in these regions, and drivers enjoy high status. The three main types of vehicle are bus, truck and Landcruiser. On some routes there are modern Japanese buses; other routes are covered by battered wrecks which gasp over each high pass as if it's their last. Trucks are often more comfortable, more fun and faster than the bus. Landcruisers are the chariots of the cadres and those foreigners who can afford CITS rates.

Bus prices in Tibet have been doubled for foreigners. This price hike could be considered acceptable for deluxe buses, but not for the old bangers. Trucks tend to charge the same as buses, but the Chinese government has moved to stop foreigners from hitching on trucks by threatening the drivers with fines or confiscation of their vehicle. Before the elimination of non-group tourism, CITS and several private taxi companies in Lhasa would hire out Landcruisers to foreigners. If this service is ever reinstated, be sure to have the details written into a contract when hiring any vehicle.

Both in Tibet and Qinghai, your safety is entirely at the mercy of the vehicle, the driver and the condition of the road surface. Tibetans take their minds off these variables by praying, and you'd be wise to do likewise unless you want to end up a gibbering bag of nerves. Road accidents are frequent and foreigners have been injured or killed in the past.

During the heyday of individual travel, many foreigners introduced their own means of transport. Small groups of mountain bikers commuted along the road between Lhasa and Kathmandu, stopping at the tops of passes to pose for heroic photos among the prayer flags. Now Chinese border officials have halted the flow of bikes, collapsible kayaks, hang-gliders, rafts, skis and other tourist paraphernalia into Tibet. Although their motives for doing so are questionable they may succeed in slowing the trend towards turning Tibet into a backdrop for the sports-crazed.

Tours

Several different agencies in Kathmandu and Chengdu (Sichuan) arrange group tours to Lhasa and Shigatse only. The Chinese government requires a minimum of three persons for a tour. No matter which company you arrange a tour with, you end up with CITS guides in Tibet. CITS in Chengdu charges Y3350 per person for a four-day Lhasa tour, including round-trip air travel, transfers, meals, tours and hotel (Lhasa Holiday Inn).

For a six-day tour that includes Lhasa and Shigatse, it's Y4800. You can beat these prices by 25% to 50% at other agencies in Chengdu, but the reality is that these cheaper tours usually advertise more days in the itinerary than you actually end up with or in some other way sell you short.

FOOD

The staple diet in Tibet consists of *tsampa* (roasted barley meal) and butter tea. *Momo* (dumplings filled with meat) and *tukpa* (noodles with meat) are usually available at small restaurants. Tibetans consume large quantities of *chang*, a tangy alcoholic drink made from fermented barley.

Most of the larger towns have restaurants serving Chinese or Muslim dishes. Western foods feature on the menus of some hotels and restaurants catering to backpackers in Lhasa.

Outside the towns you should carry your own supply of food since what little is available is often highly priced and poor quality. When entering from Nepal, it's wise to bring food for the journey to Lhasa.

WHAT TO BRING

Clothing, Equipment & Supplies

Department stores in Xining, Golmud and Lhasa have quite a wide selection of warm clothing, but their stock fluctuates so you can't rely on them entirely. Keep the cold at bay with a down jacket, woollen sweater, long underwear, woollen socks, gloves and woolly hat. Protect yourself against the sun with lip salve, sunscreen, sunglasses and something to cover your head.

Trekking is not officially approved in Tibet, but it is feasible for the experienced walker providing you are prepared to be self-sufficient in food, fuel and shelter. Bring equipment suitable for sub-zero temperatures, such as a high quality down sleeping bag, thermal underwear, ground mat, four-season tent, stove and fuel. (Remember that gas canisters and bottles of meths may not be welcome on planes.)

The food situation in Lhasa continues to improve, but it's still advisable to bring in any special foods or supplies – if you intend to trek, you'll appreciate the variety.

DANGERS & ANNOYANCES

Theft

In Tibet, there has been a increase of theft from foreigners. In Xining, a nimble-fingered gang of pickpockets rides the buses. Sneak thieves operate on the train between Golmud and Xining. In Lhasa, the favourite venues for pickpocketing are the bus station, post office, Barkhor market and hotels. Lhasa also has a chronic problem with bike theft.

Cable locks, sold in most cities in China, are useful for bikes and to secure gear on a train. Moneybelts are essential. If something is stolen, you should obtain a loss report from the nearest Public Security Bureau, though the PSB may refuse to include details of cash on the loss report.

In the past, several foreigners trekking in the Everest base camp region have reported thefts. Apparently local villagers or nomads who possess very little find the temptation of foreign goodies too great.

TIBET TOURISM DEVELOPMENT PROGRAMME

The World Tourism Organization (WTO), funded by the United Nations Development Programme, has studied Tibet's tourism potential with an eye toward designing a 'scientific and comprehensive tourism development plan'. The plan's initial two-year stage runs until 1991 (including the policy requiring minimum groups of three), followed by a second stage until 1995 and a final long-term stage until 2010.

The British consultants hired for the job have also designed programmes for the Kingdom of Bhutan, the People's Republic of Mongolia and several South-East Asian nations, so it's difficult to say what the outlook is for non-group travel in the near future. Off-the-record comments by local officials in Chengdu indicate a strong possibility that Tibet will be opened to individuals again within the next two to three years.

LHASA

(lāsà) 拉萨

Lhasa has long been the capital of Tibet and remains the political centre, the most important city and the showpiece of the region. It lies a mere 3683 metres above sea level.

Lhasa is actually two cities: one Chinese and one Tibetan. The Chinese part is the larger and is made up of the same sort of architecture that you see in eastern China. The lively Tibetan side is a ramshackle, scungy place, full of winding streets where the smell of yak butter permeates the air. Towering above the city and encircled by the ugly Chinese blockhouses is the Potala Palace. The other orientation point is the Jokhang Temple, which forms the nucleus of the Tibetan part of town.

Information

General information is sometimes provided by members of the staff at the Lhasa Holiday Inn.

The Traveller's Co-op at the Banak Shol Hotel is no longer functioning since very few non-Chinese tourists stay there anymore. If

Lhasa is ever opened to individuals again, it will probably be worth checking out again.

Alternatively, if the situation improves for individual travel, head for the central Tibetan hotels. Most of the ones that foreigners used displayed noticeboards airing 1001 wishes: Tiniba urgently sought to combat giardia, bus tickets offered to the Nepalese border, etc.

CITS There's an office at the Lhasa Holiday Inn (Room 1219). Although CITS is expected to be the leading light for tours and vehicle hire, they continue to get criticism for bungling inefficiency, price-gouging and unwillingness to correct errors.

Public Security Bureau The office is behind the Potala and is open Monday to Saturday from 10 am to 1 pm and 4 to 6.30 pm. It's closed on Sunday (though there is always someone on duty to deal with emergencies).

Nepalese Consulate General The consulate (☎ 22880) is at 13 Norbulingka Lu. Hours are Monday to Saturday, 10 am to 1.30 pm and 4 to 7.30 pm. An exit stamp from PSB is no longer required. Visa fees vary according to the applicant's nationality: Y170 for British citizens; Y50 for everyone else except the Chinese, who pay just Y10. Bring along the cash with your passport and two photos, and the visa should be ready in a day. The one-month visa is valid for entry within three months.

Bank The Bank of China is close to the PSB, just behind the Potala. Hours are from 10 am to 1.30 pm and 4 to 6.30 pm, Monday to Saturday. It's closed on Sunday. The Lhasa Holiday Inn also has a bank which can be unobliging about serving those who are not staying at the hotel.

There is virtually no black market for FEC anymore in Lhasa. If you need RMB for local purchases (outside Lhasa most people won't accept FEC), your CITS guide will be happy to exchange currencies with you – at a strictly 1 to 1 rate.

Emergency Several hospitals in Lhasa treat foreigners. The Tibetan Autonomous Region People's Hospital and the Regional Military Hospital have been recommended. The Lhasa Holiday Inn may be able to refer you to a doctor at the hotel.

Maps Lhasa maps are available in either the Chinese or Tibetan languages but not in English from Xinhua Shudian (Xinhua Bookstore), which has a branch in the centre of town and another one beside the Lhasa Holiday Inn.

Potala Palace

(bùdǎlā gōng) 布达拉宫

The most imposing attraction of Lhasa is the Potala, once the centre of the Tibetan government and the winter residence of the Dalai Lama. One of the architectural wonders of the world, this immense construction has thousands of rooms, shrines and statues. It dates from the 17th century but is on the site of a former structure built a thousand years earlier. Each day a stream of pilgrims files through this religious maze while chanting, prostrating themselves and offering *khata* (ceremonial scarves) or yak butter.

The general layout of the Potala includes a Red Palace for religious functions and a White Palace for the living quarters of the Dalai Lama. The Red Palace contains many halls and chapels – the most stunning chapels house the jewel-bedecked tombs of previous Dalai Lamas. The apartments of the 13th and 14th Dalai Lamas in the White Palace offer an insight into the high life. The roof has marvellous views, if the monks will let you go there.

The Potala is open Monday and Thursday from 9 am to noon only. Foreigners pay Y5 admission, but this appears to allow them to skip ahead of the pilgrim queue. A torch (flashlight) is very useful. The long climb to the entrance is not recommended on your first day in town – do something relaxing at ground level. Remember photography is not officially allowed.

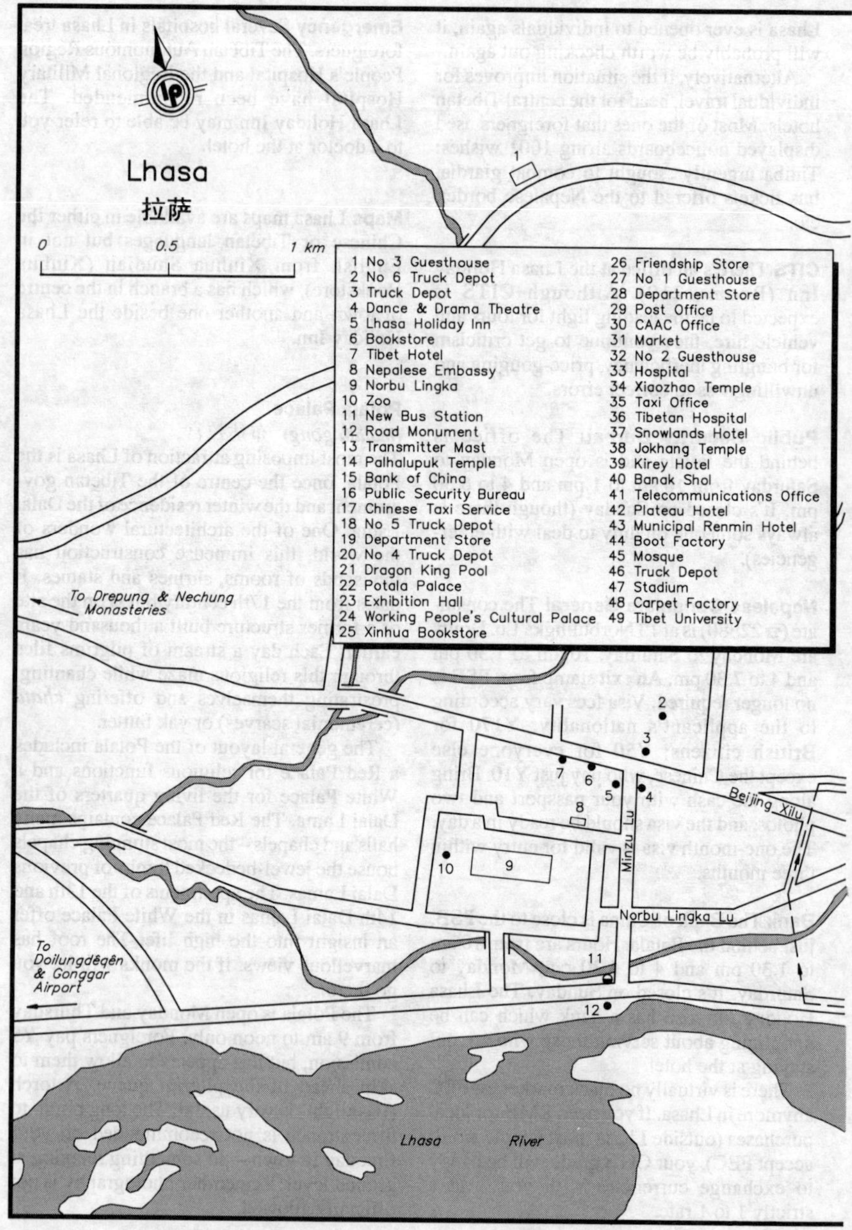
Lhasa
拉萨
0 0.5 1 km
1 No 3 Guesthouse
2 No 6 Truck Depot
3 Truck Depot
4 Dance & Drama Theatre
5 Lhasa Holiday Inn
6 Bookstore
7 Tibet Hotel
8 Nepalese Embassy
9 Norbu Lingka
10 Zoo
11 New Bus Station
12 Road Monument
13 Transmitter Mast
14 Palhalupuk Temple
15 Bank of China
16 Public Security Bureau
17 Chinese Taxi Service
18 No 5 Truck Depot
19 Department Store
20 No 4 Truck Depot
21 Dragon King Pool
22 Potala Palace
23 Exhibition Hall
24 Working People's Cultural Palace
25 Xinhua Bookstore
26 Friendship Store
27 No 1 Guesthouse
28 Department Store
29 Post Office
30 CAAC Office
31 Market
32 No 2 Guesthouse
33 Hospital
34 Xiaozhao Temple
35 Taxi Office
36 Tibetan Hospital
37 Snowlands Hotel
38 Jokhang Temple
39 Kirey Hotel
40 Banak Shol
41 Telecommunications Office
42 Plateau Hotel
43 Municipal Renmin Hotel
44 Boot Factory
45 Mosque
46 Truck Depot
47 Stadium
48 Carpet Factory
49 Tibet University
To Drepung & Nechung Monasteries
Beijing Xilu
Minzu Lu
Norbu Lingka Lu
To Doilungdêqên & Gonggar Airport
Lhasa River

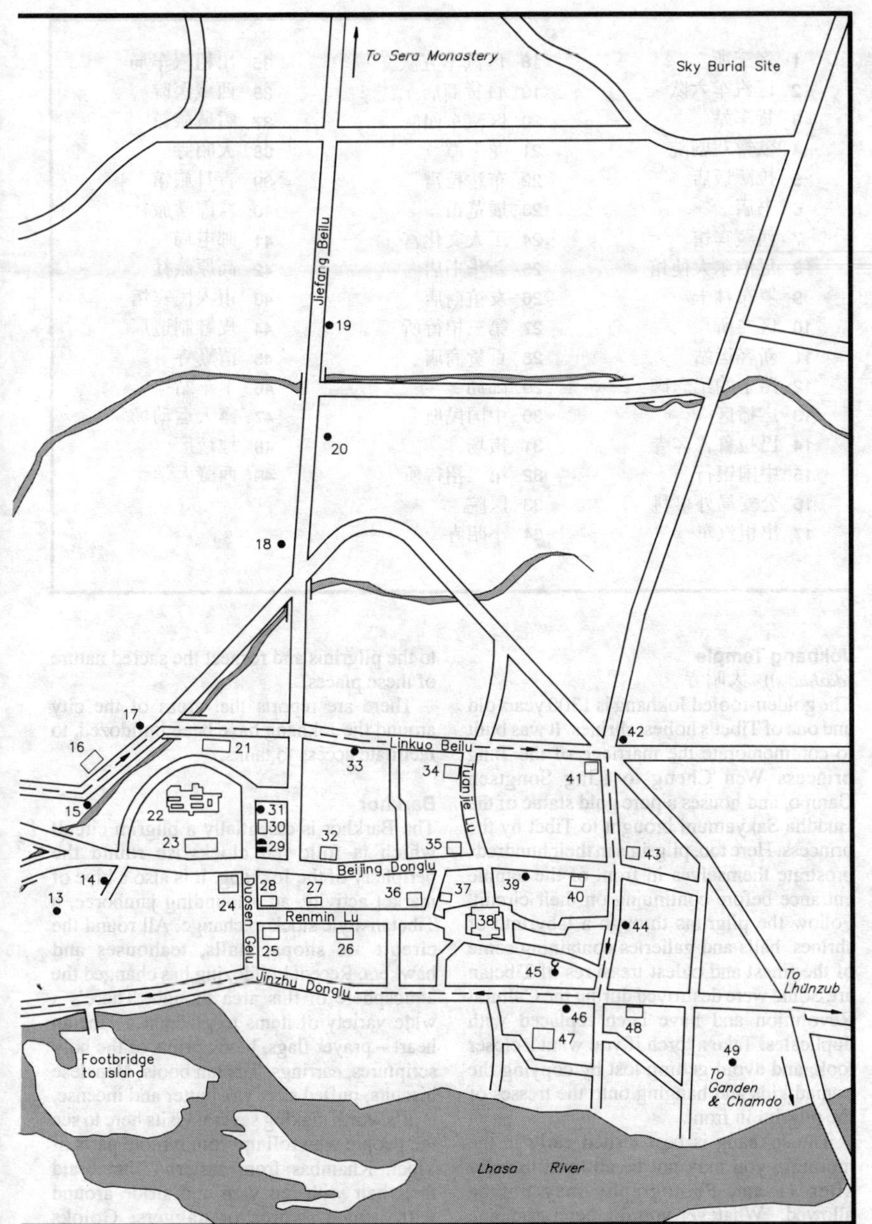

To Sera Monastery
Sky Burial Site
Jiefang Beilu
Linkuo Beilu
Lion jie Lu
Beijing Donglu
Duosen Gelu
Renmin Lu
Jinzhu Donglu
To Lhünzub
To Ganden & Chamdo
Footbridge to island
Lhasa River
13
14
15
16
17
18
19
20
21
22
23
24
25
26
27
28
29
30
31
32
33
34
35
36
37
38
39
40
41
42
43
44
45
46
47
48
49

1 区三所
2 区汽车六队
3 货车站
4 歌舞戏剧院
5 拉萨饭店
6 书店
7 西藏宾馆
8 尼泊尔大使馆
9 罗布林卡
10 区二所
11 新客运站
12 路上的纪念碑
13 广播区
14 巴拉鲁普客寺
15 中国银行
16 公安局外事科
17 出租汽车
18 区汽车五队
19 百货商店
20 区汽车四队
21 龙王潭
22 布达拉宫
23 展览馆
24 工人文化宫
25 新华书店
26 友谊商店
27 第三招待所
28 百货商店
29 邮局
30 中国民航
31 市场
32 第二招待所
33 医院
34 小昭寺
35 出租汽车局
36 西藏医院
37 雪域旅馆
38 大昭寺
39 吉日旅馆
40 八郎学旅社
41 邮电局
42 高原旅社
43 市人民宾馆
44 皮鞋制造厂
45 清真寺
46 卡车站
47 露天运动场
48 地毯厂
49 西藏大学

Jokhang Temple
(dàzhāo sì) 大昭寺
The golden-roofed Jokhang is 1300 years old and one of Tibet's holiest shrines. It was built to commemorate the marriage of the Tang princess Wen Cheng to King Songtsen Gampo, and houses a pure gold statue of the Buddha Sakyamuni brought to Tibet by the princess. Here too, pilgrims in their hundreds prostrate themselves in front of the temple entrance before continuing on their circuit. Follow the pilgrims through a labyrinth of shrines, halls and galleries containing some of the finest and oldest treasures of Tibetan art. Some were destroyed during the Cultural Revolution and have been replaced with duplicates. Take a torch if you want a closer look, and avoid getting lost by copying the nomad kids and hanging onto the tresses of the pilgrim in front.

The Jokhang is best visited early in the morning; you may not be allowed to enter after 11 am. Photography may not be allowed. Whatever you do, be considerate to the pilgrims and respect the sacred nature of these places.

There are reports that areas of the city around the Jokhang have been bulldozed, to facilitate access to tanks.

Barkhor
The Barkhor is essentially a pilgrim circuit which is followed clockwise round the periphery of the Jokhang. It is also a hive of market activity, an astounding jamboree, a Tibetan-style stock exchange. All round the circuit are shops, stalls, teahouses and hawkers. Recent bulldozing has changed the atmosphere of this area though. There's a wide variety of items to gladden a Tibetan heart – prayer flags, block prints of the holy scriptures, earrings, Tibetan boots, Nepalese biscuits, puffed rice, yak butter and incense.

It's worth making several visits here to see the people who roll up from remote parts of Tibet: Khambas from eastern Tibet braid their hair with red yarn and stride around with ornate swords or daggers; Goloks

(Tibetan nomads) from the north wear ragged sheepskins and the women display incredibly ornate hairbands down their backs.

Whether you buy from a shop or a hawker, many of the Tibetan goods on sale have been imported from Nepal and you are most unlikely to find genuine antiques. The prices asked from foreigners have reached absurd heights. Whatever the starting price, be it in RMB or FEC, expect to halvc it. Much of the 'turquoise' in the market is, in fact, a paste of ground turquoise and cement – some keen buyers bite the stones and reject them if the teeth leave white scratch marks. Also, bear in mind that Chinese Customs can confiscate antiques (anything made before 1959) if they think you are carrying out 'too much'.

Norbu Lingka

(luóbù lìnkǎ) 罗布林卡

About three km west of the Potala is the Norbu Lingka, which used to be the summer residence of the Dalai Lama. The pleasant park contains small palaces, chapels and a zoo. For Y2 you can join pilgrims on a tour of the New Palace, built by the 14th Dalai Lama in 1956, which contains vivid murals. The gardens are a favourite spot for picnics.

The animals at the zoo stare balefully at passers-by. As I stood looking at a Himalayan brown bear, an American woman stooped close to the bars to take a picture. The bear obligingly whiffled with his nose and raised a gum to display a fine set of teeth. Then, quick as a flash, his paw zipped between the bars, passing within an inch of the woman's face before his claws ripped the camera case into the cage. The American freaked out entirely, started shaking with fright and squeaking about dangerous bears. As for the bear, he did a few victory canters round the cage before rolling onto the floor to contentedly munch the camera case. The revenge must have tasted sweet: within a few minutes he'd downed the lot and was eyeing my own camera!

Theatre & Exhibition Hall

The ungainly looking building opposite the Lhasa Holiday Inn is the Tibetan Dance & Drama Theatre. Hopefully the shows here will be genuinely Tibetan, not a clumsy Chinese approximation.

At the foot of the Potala is the Exhibition Hall, open from 9 am to 4 pm on Monday, Thursday and Sunday only. The historical exhibition has some interesting photos, but draws predictable conclusions about China and Tibet. The rooms devoted to Tibetan ethnography, monastic life, handicrafts and daily life are well worth a visit. It's fun to observe the reaction of nomads on a pilgrimage to Lhasa when they see the exhibition of nomad life. Most of them get a giggle out of seeing their home in a museum – complete with stuffed dog.

Places to Stay – bottom end

The hotels in this category (mostly clustered in the Barkhor area and managed by Tibetans) rarely see foreigners these days, since tour groups are invariably assigned to the Lhasa Holiday Inn, Sun Light Hotel or Tibet Hotel. Only the occasional wily foreigner who manages by some miracle to arrange a permit to visit Lhasa as an individual tourist has the liberty to select accommodation.

Snowlands (☎ 23687) *(xuěyù lǚguǎn)*, close to the Jokhang Temple, is a friendly place – a legend during the days of 'unorganised' travel – with rooms arranged around a courtyard. Beds cost Y10. Ask at reception about luggage storage and bike hire.

The *Banak Shol* (☎ 23829) *(bālángxuě lǚshè)* is on Beijing Donglu near the Barkhor. This has also achieved star ratings as a travellers' hang-out in Lhasa. It's quite a warren of rooms, ladders and toilets in the ramparts with a friendly atmosphere and staff. Doubles cost Y22; a bed in a dorm costs Y10. There are showers and luggage storage, and bike hire can be arranged.

The *Kirey Hotel (jírì lǚguǎn)*, close to the Banak Shol, charges Y10 for dorm beds. Doubles start at Y15 per person. It lacks atmosphere but has great showers for which you pay a small fee if you're not staying there.

The *Plateau Hotel (gāoyuán lǚshè)* is opposite the telecommunications building on the edge of town. Doubles cost Y12 per person, triples Y9 per person and a four-bed room Y8 per person. The solar-heated showers work sporadically. Ask at the desk about hiring bikes.

The *Yak Hotel (tuōniú lǚshè)* (formerly known by the ponderous name Beijing East Road Tribal Hostelry) is diagonally opposite the Kirey Hotel, on Beijing Donglu. Singles cost Y20, doubles are Y15 per person and dorms cost Y10 per bed.

In the same area are two Chinese-style guesthouses *(zhāodàisǔo)*, known as the No 1 Guesthouse *(qūyī suǒ)* and No 2 Guesthouse *(qūèr suǒ)*. They offer what's common elsewhere in China: uninspired, functional service. Then there are certain places which offer really cheap beds (maybe Y3 per person). Constant harassment by Public Security (who hate to see foreigners paying less than double the local rate) means that these hotels indulge in a creative game of opening and closing – now you see the foreigner, now you don't!

Places to Stay – top end

The *Lhasa Holiday Inn* (☎ 2221) *(lāsà fàndiàn)* is the lap of Lhasa luxury and boasts 500 rooms. Doubles start at Y195 per room. The rates in winter (from 1 November to 1 March) may be dropped 30%. The facilities include Chinese and Western restaurants, a coffee shop, souvenir shops and a wrestling arena (practise the clinches with CITS?). A free shuttle service using minibuses operates between the hotel and the Barkhor. The transport desk arranges day trips to Drepung, Sera or Ganden monasteries (prices range between Y20 and Y100 per person); there's also a daily bus from the hotel to the airport. (It leaves at 6.30 am and costs Y30 per person.) If you want to hire a taxi, Landcruiser, minibus or bus, enquire at the transport desk about the amazingly autonomous prices fixed by the Tibet Autonomous Price Bureau.

The *Tibet Hotel (xīzàng bīnguǎn)* is a few metres up the road from the Lhasa Holiday Inn. Built in mock-Tibetan style, it showed signs of dilapidation within a few months after opening. It's intended for foreign tour groups and Chinese officials. Doubles start at Y176 (US$34) in the high season, Y120 (US$23) in the low. The forecourt is frequented by browsing yaks which nonchalantly obstruct the entrance ramp and are about the only appealing characteristic of the place.

Places to Eat

Food can be mighty scarce out on the high plateau, but Lhasa offers Chinese, Western and Tibetan cuisine.

The *Lhasa Holiday Inn* has a Chinese restaurant which is reasonable value if you eat as a small group; expect to pay Y10 per head for about five dishes. The coffee shop (open from 8 am to 10 pm) serves Western food such as hamburgers, French fries and Lhasa club sandwiches. Prices are relatively high, but breakfast includes endless refills of strong, filtered coffee.

Diagonally across from the Lhasa Holiday Inn, on the opposite side of the crossroads, is a restaurant serving excellent Chinese food.

The *Banak Shol* restaurant has a choose-your-own ingredients system. It deserves reverence as the probable birthplace of the yakburger, and has a popular communal dining room for foreigners.

The Kirey Hotel's *Kailas Restaurant* is a popular place run by a Tibetan who's returned from Kathmandu, where he learned what makes the Western tastebuds dance. The food can be a bit greasy, but the menu includes spring rolls, pancakes, chapatis, French toast and dishes for vegetarians.

Toots Restaurant, diagonally across the street from the Kirey Hotel, does good Chinese food and some Western dishes such as omelettes and fried potatoes. There are plenty of Muslim teahouses around the Barkhor which serve good noodles.

Getting There & Away

Air Lhasa is connected by air with Chengdu (Y656), Beijing (Y1149), Canton (Y1080), Golmud (Y468) and Xi'an (795). Charter flights run between Kathmandu and Lhasa twice a week for about Y950 (US$180) each way.

CAAC The humorous sign 'Lhasa Reception Centre for the Unorganised Tourists', once displayed by this office (☎ 22417) at 88 Jiefang Lu, has disappeared, since all tourists to Tibet are now 'organised'.

Bus The bus station is a deserted monstrosity four km out of town, near the Norbu Lingka. Foreigners are charged double the local price. Buy your tickets several days in advance and roll up early.

Beware of well-dressed pickpockets operating around the buses, particularly in the early morning. They push up close pretending to join the scrum to get on the bus, but instead they pickpocket at lightning speed.

There are daily departures in the early morning for Shigatse (Y54.60 ordinary, Y65.80 deluxe; 12 hours), Zêtang (Y30 ordinary, Y36 deluxe; four hours) and Golmud (Y151.40 ordinary, Y198.10 deluxe; two days). Buses to Zhangmu (Y128 ordinary, Y155 deluxe; three days) leave on Saturday only.

Road Routes

Although there are five major road routes to Lhasa, foreigners are officially allowed to use only the Nepal and Qinghai routes.

Nepal Route The road connecting Lhasa with Nepal is officially called the Friendship Highway and runs from Lhasa to Zhangmu (the Chinese border post) via Gyantse and Shigatse. It's a spectacular trip over high passes and across the plateau. If the weather's good, you'll get a fine view of Mt Everest from the Tibetan village of Tingri. From Zhangmu, it's 11 km to the Nepalese border post at Kodari, which has transport connections to Kathmandu.

Accommodation en route is mostly basic and overpriced, like the food, which can also be scarce. Whichever direction you intend to travel, take warm clothing and food.

For a six-day trip to the Nepalese border in a deluxe minibus (maximum 10 passengers), expect to pay Y1000 per person (a 200% increase since the days of non-group travel). A similar trip in a Landcruiser (maximum seven passengers) costs Y1300 per person; a five-day trip to the border in a modern bus (maximum 25 passengers) costs around Y500 per person. Hiring a Landcruiser will cost around Y6 per km, a minibus Y6.20 per km, and a bus Y7 per km. All these rates must be paid in FEC.

Be careful about paying deposits; it's best to write out a contract which includes exact details of your itinerary (dates, places, time required), the driver's name, the licence-plate number, whether you wish to stop for photography, and a statement that there will be no price increase for technical or climatic reasons. The Public Security Bureau may help with translation. Several readers have complained about transport managers inventing astronomical prices or drivers completely ignoring requests to keep to the agreed itinerary.

Travelling from Nepal to Lhasa the only transport for foreigners is arranged through tour agencies. In the event that individual travel to Tibet is restored local buses, taxis and Tibetan pilgrim buses run regularly to Barabise or as far as the Friendship Bridge. Until the bridge and the road have been restored, the steep and slippery section between the bridge and Zhangmu will have to be negotiated on foot. Sherpas will also act as porters for about Y20 or 50 rupees, but get the price straight (preferably written down!) before hiring them. At Zhangmu (Khasa) you can hunt around for buses, minibuses, Landcruisers or trucks heading towards Lhasa.

Qinghai Route As with the route from Nepal to Lhasa, this is only officially open for members of CITS-sanctioned tour groups. However, of all the land routes into Tibet, this is the one with the greatest potential for unsanctioned travel. An asphalted road connects Xining with Lhasa via Golmud; it crosses the desolate, barren and virtually uninhabited Tibetan Plateau. Modern Japanese buses do the run between Lhasa and

Golmud in 30 hours. Although they are expensive, they are reasonably comfortable and include an overnight stop in Amdo.

Veteran Chinese buses attempt to do the trip in the same time by travelling day and night virtually nonstop. This is not recommended unless you want to save Y56 and like cold, brutally punishing journeys.

Take warm clothing and food on the bus, since baggage is not accessible during the trip.

Other Routes Between Lhasa and Sichuan, Yunnan or Xinjiang provinces are some of the wildest, highest and most dangerous routes in the world; they are not open to foreigners. If you do travel along them, don't underestimate the physical dangers – take food and warm clothing. Public Security tends to fine those heading into Tibet, but travel in the opposite direction is controlled less. Travel on these routes usually takes several weeks of hitching on trucks which have a high accident rate. Lonely Planet's *Tibet – a travel survival kit* describes these routes in detail.

Getting Around

Travelling by bicycle is an excellent way to get around. Most of the hotels used to hire out bikes for an expensive Y1or 2 per hour with a passport or Y200 as a deposit. Near the No 1 Guesthouse, you could be offered cheaper deals.

Buses, minibuses, Landcruisers and jeeps can be hired for day excursions or trips to the Nepalese border (see the Getting There & Away chapter for details).

AROUND LHASA

Monasteries

Prior to 1959, Lhasa had three monasteries which functioned as 'pillars of the Tibetan state'. As part of a concerted effort to smash the influence of these, the Cultural Revolution wiped out the monastic population that once numbered thousands. The buildings of Ganden Monastery were demolished. Today, buildings are being reconstructed for the sake of appearances (rubble is bad for tourism and public relations) and a few hundred caretaker monks go through the motions of religious observance. Visitors who admire the shell may also sense the emptiness.

Drepung *(zhébàng sì)* This dates back to the early 15th century and lies about seven km west of Lhasa. In 1959 there were around 7000 monks living here, whereas the present population numbers between 200 and 300. Admission to the monastery is Y2. You can visit some of the halls and colleges; the kitchen contains huge pots.

Drepung is best reached by bike. You can also take bus No 1 at 9 or 11 am from the stop close to the Banak Shol Hotel.

Sera *(sèlā sì)* About four km north of Lhasa, this monastery was founded in 1419 by a disciple of Tsong Khapa. About a hundred monks are now in residence. It's worth arriving before midday to see them practise debating. Admission costs Y3.

At the base of a mountain, just east of the monastery, is a Tibetan 'sky burial' site where the deceased are chopped up and then served to vultures. Tourism has reduced this admittedly grisly event to an almost daily confrontation between *domden* (undertakers) and scores of photo-hungry visitors. The reactions of the domden have become very violent. Our advice is to leave the place alone.

Bus No 10 runs direct to Sera. From the centre of Lhasa, the trip takes an hour on foot or 20 minutes by bike.

Ganden *(gāndān sì)* About 45 km east of Lhasa, this monastery was founded in 1409 by Tsong Khapa. During the Cultural Revolution it was completely demolished. The efforts of about 200 monks have gone into rebuilding it.

To reach Ganden Monastery, take a bus at 6.30 am from the Barkhor. Pilgrim trucks are now reluctant to take foreigners.

YARLUNG VALLEY

(yálǔ liúyù) 雅鲁流域

About 170 km south-east of Lhasa, this valley is considered to be the birthplace of Tibetan culture. Near the adjacent towns of Zêtang and Nêdong, which form the administrative centre of the region, are several sites of religious importance.

Samye Monastery

This lies about 30 km west of Zêtang, on the opposite bank of the Yarlung Zangbo (Brahmaputra River). It was founded at the end of the 8th century by King Trisong Detsen as the first monastery in Tibet. Getting there is complicated, but the monastery commands a beautiful, secluded position.

To reach Samye, catch a bus from Lhasa or Zêtang. You will be dropped off close to a ferry which functions sporadically and will take you across the river. From there, a tractor, truck or horse and cart will carry you the five km to Samye. Since there's only basic accommodation, you should plan to be self-sufficient.

Yumbu Lhakang

About 12 km south-west of Zêtang, Yumbu Lhakang is the legendary first building in Tibet. Although small in scale, it soars in recently renovated splendour above the valley. Get there by hiring a bike or Landcruiser in Zêtang, or hitch on a walking-tractor.

Tombs of the Kings

At Qonggyai, about 26 km west of Zêtang, these tombs are less of a visual treat; their importance is essentially historical. To get there, hire a Landcruiser or spend half the day pedalling there and back on a bike.

Places to Stay & Eat

The *Zêtang Hotel* is the newest hotel in the area. It is also the shoddiest, with fittings falling to bits and toilets leaking under the lazy gaze of staff. Considering the state of the rooms, the standard charge of Y70 for a double is absurd. Student price for doubles is Y25. The restaurant food was poor. Bikes and Landcruisers may be available for hire – depending on the mood of the staff.

The *Zêtang Zhaodai Suo*, close to the hotel, is a standard Chinese guesthouse which charges Y10 per person in a functional double. It may also be possible to hire Landcruisers here.

Getting There & Away

Buses for Zêtang (Y30) leave Lhasa every morning. Buses for Lhasa leave from the traffic circle in Zêtang every morning – buy your ticket the day before from a tin shack just south of the traffic circle.

SHIGATSE

(Xigazê) (rìkèzé) 日喀则

The second largest urban centre in Tibet is Shigatse. This is the seat of the Panchen Lama, a reincarnation of Amitabha (Buddha of Infinite Light), who ranks close to the Dalai Lama. The 10th Panchen Lama, who died in 1989 reportedly of a heart attack, was taken to Beijing during the '60s and lived a largely puppet existence there, visiting Tibet only occasionally.

Things to See

The main attraction in Shigatse is the seat of the Panchen Lama – Tashilhunpo Monastery. Built in 1447 by a nephew of Tsong Khapa, the monastery once housed over 4000 monks, but now there are only 600. Apart from a giant statue of the Maitreya Buddha (nearly 27 metres high) in the Temple of the Maitreya, the monastery is also famed for its Grand Hall with the opulent tomb (containing 85 kg of gold and masses of jewels) of the 4th Panchen Lama. Admission costs Y8 (!) and closing time is around 4 pm.

Watch out for vicious dogs, especially if you do the pilgrim circuit of the monastery.

Places to Stay & Eat

As in Lhasa, tour group members are usually assigned only to the most expensive hotels.

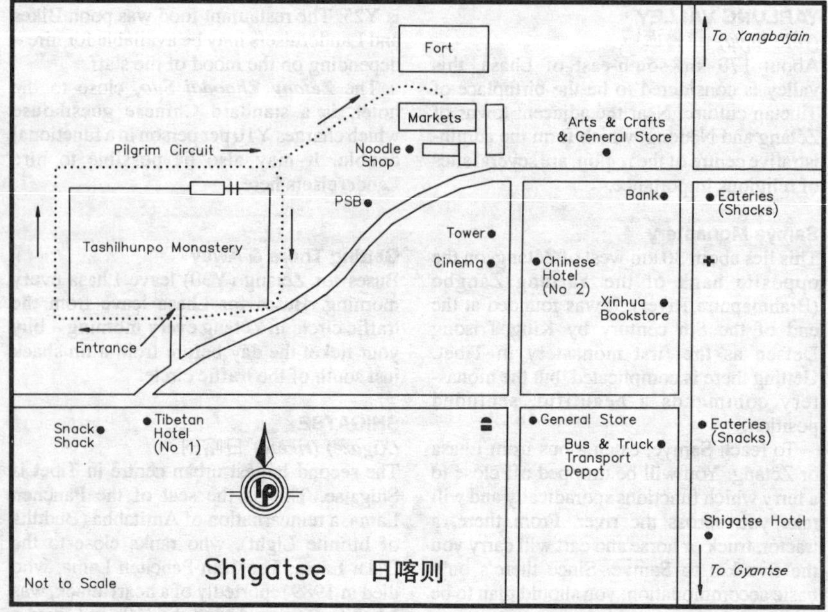

If you're one of the lucky few with an individual permit, you can try the hostel attached to the bus station which charges Y8 per bed. It's nothing special, but is useful if you want to be close to your transport. Across the road from the bus station is another hostel.

The Tibetan-run *Tensin Hotel* is popular for its roof terrace and location opposite the market in the Tibetan part of town. It charges Y10 per person for a double, Y6 in a four-bed room.

The *No 1 Guesthouse (dìyī zhāodài suǒ)*, opposite the entrance to Tashilhunpo Monastery, is a basic place also run by Tibetans. It's popular with pilgrims and bedbugs. A bed costs Y6.

The *Shigatse Hotel (rìkèzé fàndiàn)*, on the outskirts of town, is a Chinese-style hotel built for group tours. Doubles for Y70 are poor value but if you're on a sanctioned tour you'll have no choice.

Shigatse has plenty of free-enterprise restaurants on the streets which serve good Chinese food. Shigatse is also a good place to stock up on supplies – try the department store just round the corner from the bus station.

Getting There & Away

Bus & Truck Shigatse is an important transport centre with connections to the Nepalese border, western Tibet, Lhasa and Golmud. There are two routes linking Lhasa and Shigatse; the most popular one runs via Gyantse.

Buses to Lhasa cost Y55 and leave daily from the bus station. The trip takes an average of 12 hours.

It is almost impossible now to find transport from Shigatse to the Nepalese border. Buses coming from Lhasa are invariably jam-packed and truck drivers are nervous about giving rides to foreigners.

Buses to Sakya leave on Tuesday, Friday and Saturday from the transport depot opposite the bus station. Buy your ticket (Y25) the day before at 10 am.

GYANTSE

(jiāngzī) 江孜

Gyantse is one of southern Tibet's chief centres, although it's more like a small village which retains some Tibetan charm.

Things to See

The **Palkhor Monastery**, built in 1427, is notable for its superb Kumbum (10,000 images) stupa which has nine tiers and, according to Buddhist tradition, 108 chapels. The monks may not allow you to complete the pilgrim circuit to the top, but the lower tiers contain excellent murals. Take a torch.

The **Dzong** (old fort) which towers above Gyantse offers a fine view over the valley. The entrance is usually locked, but you may be able to get the key (for a small fee) from a little house at the foot of the steps leading up the hill; it's close to the tiny bridge on the main road.

Keep a respectful distance from the dogs in Gyantse. They rave all night and sleep until the afternoon.

Places to Stay & Eat

No sanctioned tours include Gyantse on their itineraries, so there aren't any 'tourist hotels'. The bus stop has rough accommodation for Y5 per bed in a six-bed room.

There's a basic hotel closer to town. Coming from Lhasa, turn right at the crossroads and follow the road for 200 metres until you see a yellow building on your right.

If you continue straight across the crossroads, there's a hotel immediately on your right and another one about 100 metres down the road on your left.

Most of these hotels also provide basic meals.

Getting There & Away

The road from Lhasa splits here: one branch goes to Shigatse; the other heads south into Sikkim via the town of Yadong.

Bus connections to Lhasa usually consist of buses from Shigatse or elsewhere which are passing through. They are often packed solid and you'll be lucky to find a seat for the five-hour ride. The fare is around Y60 on a Japanese bus. Wait for the buses at the crossroads; if a bus overnights at the bus station in Gyantse, talk to the driver who might let you on in the morning.

The same problems apply for travel to Shigatse (Y14, two hours) or the border with Nepal.

Transport to Yadong is scarce, and there's a checkpoint en route where foreigners are ordered to turn back.

SAKYA

(sàjiā) 萨迦

Sakya is 152 km west of Shigatse and about 25 km south of the main road. The huge, brooding monastery at Sakya was Tibet's most powerful 700 years ago and was once the centre for the Sakyapa sect founded in the 11th century. The monastery probably contains the finest collection of Tibetan religious relics remaining in Tibet – the monks may restrict you to a couple of halls. Admission costs Y5.

The bus stops at a hotel within a few metres of the monastery. Beds cost Y5 per person. A small restaurant in the hotel can provide basic food, but don't rely on it.

There's a bus from Shigatse to Sakya in the morning on Tuesday and Friday; buy your ticket (Y28) the day before. The bus returns the next day.

Qinghai 青海

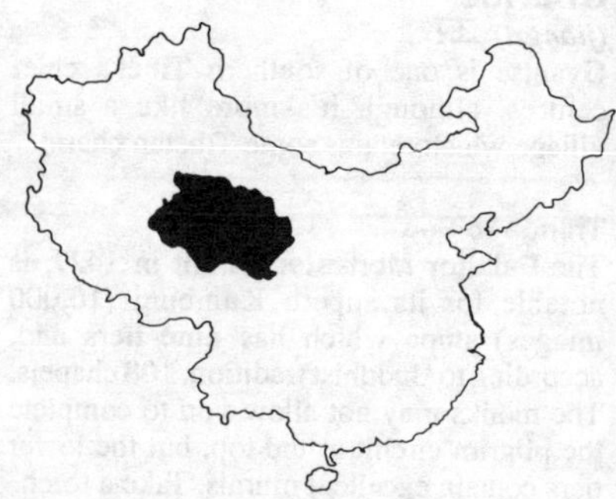

HISTORY

Qinghai *(qīnghǎi)* was part of the Tibetan world and, with the exception of the eastern area around the capital of Xining, the region (formerly known as Amdo) was not incorporated into the Chinese empire until the early 18th century. The province is a sort of Chinese Siberia where common criminals as well as political prisoners are incarcerated. These prisoners have included former Kuomintang army and police officers, 'rightists' arrested in the late 1950s after the Hundred Flowers had their blooms cut off, victims of the Cultural Revolution, former Red Guards arrested for their activities during the Cultural Revolution, supporters of the Gang of Four and opponents of the present regime. Many of the Han Chinese settlers of the region are former prisoners who with their prison records have little or no future in eastern China and so choose to stay in Qinghai. Oddly, the exile of a Soviet dissident to Siberia is headline news in the USA or Europe, but when a Chinese dissident is exiled to Qinghai the story might be cut to a few paragraphs or not printed at all.

GEOGRAPHY

Qinghai Province lies on the north-east border of Tibet and is one of the great cartographical constructions of our time. For centuries this was part of the Tibetan world and today it's separated from the Tibetan homeland by nothing more than the colours on a Chinese-made map.

Eastern Qinghai is a high grassy plateau rising between 2500 and 3000 metres above sea level, and is slashed by a series of mountain ranges whose peaks rise to 5000 metres. It's the source of the Yellow River. Most of the agricultural regions are concentrated in the east around the Xining area, but the surrounding uplands and the regions west of Qinghai Lake have good pasturelands for sheep, horses and cattle.

North-west Qinghai is a great basin surrounded by mountains. It's littered with salt marshes and saline lakes and afflicted with harsh cold winters. Parts of it are barren desert, but it's also rich in mineral deposits, particularly oil.

Southern Qinghai is a high plateau 3500 metres above sea level. It's separated from Tibet by the Tanggulashan range, whose peaks rise to over 6500 metres, and the Yangtse and the Mekong rivers have their source here. Most of the region is grassland and the population is composed almost entirely of semi-nomadic Tibetan herders rearing goats, sheep and yaks.

POPULATION & PEOPLE

Qinghai has a total population of almost 3,800,000 – a figure which may or may not include the unknown number of people imprisoned in the province's labour camps. The people of the region are a mixture of minorities including the Kazakhs, Mongols and Hui. Tibetans are found throughout the province and the Han settlers are concentrated around the area of Xining, the provincial capital.

XINING

(xīníng) 西宁

Xining is the only large city in Qinghai and

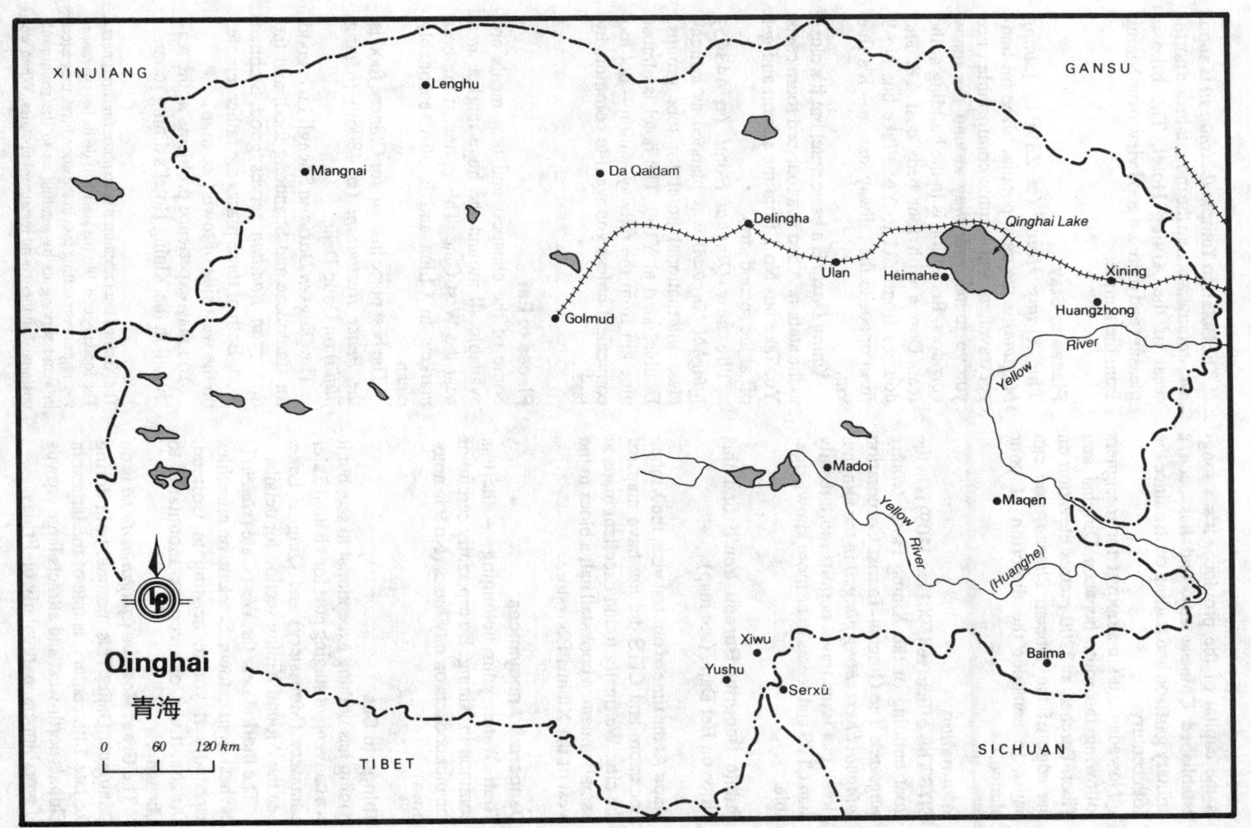
XINJIANG
GANSU
Lenghu
Mangnai
Da Qaidam
Delingha
Qinghai Lake
Ulan
Heimahe
Xining
Huangzhong
Golmud
Yellow
River
Madoi
Maqen
Yellow
River
(Huanghe)
Xiwu
Yushu
Serxü
Baima
Qinghai
青海
0
60
120 km
TIBET
SICHUAN

is the capital of the province. It's a long-established Chinese city, and has been a military garrison and trading centre since the 16th century.

Nowadays, it's a stopover for foreigners following the route between Qinghai and Tibet. Perched at 2200 metres elevation on the edge of the Tibetan Plateau, you can pause to consider the direction of your plunge.

Information

CITS This office (☎ 45901 ext 1109) is in the front building of the Xining Hotel *(xīníng bīnguǎn)*. The Qinghai Tourist Corporation *(qīnghǎi lǚyóu zhōng gōngsī)* in the Qinghai Hotel, can issue travel permits more readily than CITS and seems to be more knowledgeable.

Public Security Bureau You'll find this office on Bei Dajie (see map).

Maps At the time of our last visit, the Xinhua Bookstore and CITS did *not* have maps of the city. We finally found excellent maps at a small unnamed bookstall half a block to the west of the Xinhua Bookstore.

Dangers & Annoyances

Theft Watch your belongings – theft is common in Xining. Be especially careful of the pickpockets on city buses (No 9 is notorious).

Things to See

Xining has nothing exceptional to see, but it is a convenient staging post for visiting Ta'er Lamasery (Monastery) and Qinghai Lake. See the Around Xining section for details.

The **market** near the West Gate *(xīmén)* is the best sight in town. Stock up on munchies especially if you're heading to Golmud, Qinghai Lake or over the mountains to Chengdu.

The **Great Mosque** *(qīngzhēn dà sì)* is on Dongguan Dajie. This mosque, built during the late 14th century, is one of the largest in China's north-west and attracts large crowds of worshippers, particularly on Friday.

The **Beishan Temple** *(běishān sì)* is about a 45-minute walk up the mountainside north-west of the Xining Hotel. The hike is pleasant and there's a good view over Xining from the temple.

Places to Stay

The *Xining Hotel* (☎ 23901) *(xīníng bīnguǎn)* is the most popular place for budget travellers and is quite comfortable once you've found your way around the many corridors. Reception is in the building at the rear. Dorms with four beds cost Y8, and doubles from Y11 to Y65. Take bus No 9 from opposite the railway station – it's five km.

Xining Daxia is a basic hotel but it's close to the station. A bed in a four-bed room costs Y6. Take bus No 1 from the station and get off at the second stop.

The new *Qinghai Hotel* (☎ 44365) *(qīnghǎi bīnguǎn)* was planned as a high-class international hotel for tour groups. Doubles start at Y100. The hotel is almost nine km from the railway station – not too convenient unless you want to commute by taxi.

Places to Eat

Some of the cheapest and best meals are available all around the huge market area near the West Gate. This is one of the best markets in China and is also reasonably clean.

The best place in town for Chinese food is the *Peace Restaurant* (☎ 48069) *(hépíng jiǔjiā)* on Dong Dajie.

The *Qingken Daxia* on Shengli Lu is good for Cantonese and Shandong food, and the *Rongyuan Fandian* serves good Sichuan food. Both of these places are rather remote, on the west side of town (see map).

You may experience problems at the restaurant in the Xining Hotel's dining room.

The Xining Hotel restaurant is no place for foreigners. The food is good, but the staff will do its best to make you regret ever setting foot in the door. First, they tried to avoid serving us by sending us to the restaurant upstairs...but there is no restaurant upstairs. When we

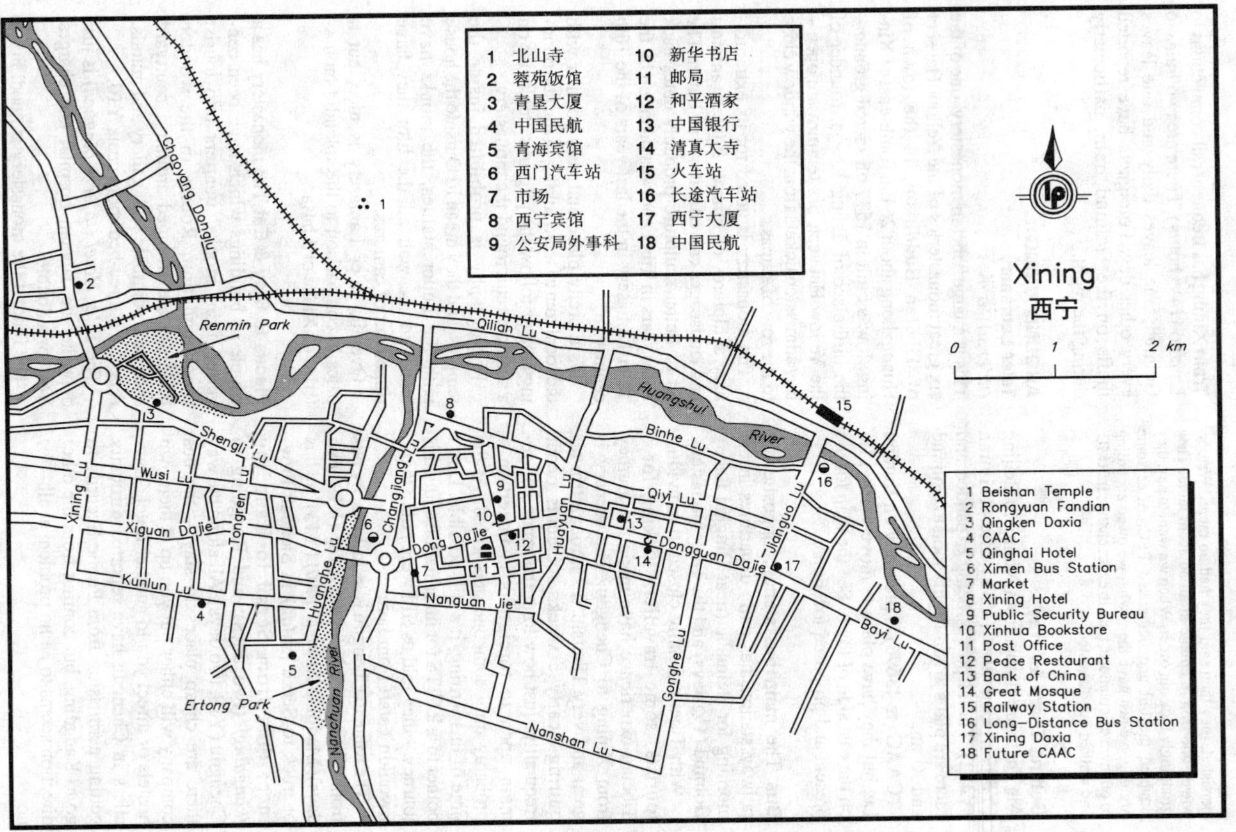
1 北山寺
2 蓉苑饭馆
3 青垦大厦
4 中国民航
5 青海宾馆
6 西门汽车站
7 市场
8 西宁宾馆
9 公安局外事科
10 新华书店
11 邮局
12 和平酒家
13 中国银行
14 清真大寺
15 火车站
16 长途汽车站
17 西宁大厦
18 中国民航
Xining
西宁
0
1
2 km
1 Beishan Temple
2 Rongyuan Fandian
3 Qingken Daxia
4 CAAC
5 Qinghai Hotel
6 Ximen Bus Station
7 Market
8 Xining Hotel
9 Public Security Bureau
10 Xinhua Bookstore
11 Post Office
12 Peace Restaurant
13 Bank of China
14 Great Mosque
15 Railway Station
16 Long–Distance Bus Station
17 Xining Daxia
18 Future CAAC
Chaoyang Donglu
Renmin Park
Qilian Lu
Huangshui River
Binhe Lu
Shengli Lu
Wusi Lu
Xining Lu
Xiguan Dajie
Tongren Lu
Kunlun Lu
Huanghe Lu
Changjiang Lu
Dong Dajie
Nanguan Jie
Huayuan Lu
Qiyi Lu
Dongguan Dajie
Jianguo Lu
Bayi Lu
Gonghe Lu
Nanshan Lu
Ertong Park
Nanchuan River

persisted, they then said they had no menu. We borrowed one from a couple at an adjacent table. They grudgingly took our order. When we went to pay, they doubled the bill and demanded FEC. After some arguing, we just gave them what we owed according to our own calculations, paid in exact change in RMB, and walked out disgusted.

Getting There & Away

Air There are flights from Xining to Beijing (Y597), Lanzhou (Y56) and Taiyuan (Y422). The airport is being expanded and there are plans to add flights soon to Golmud and Xi'an.

CAAC (☎ 43696) is presently on Kunlun Lu, but they have plans to move to Bayi Lu on the east side of town. See the map for the present and proposed locations.

Bus The main bus station, opposite the railway station, has daily departures in the morning for Heimahe (near Qinghai Lake), Golmud (1½ days) and the Ta'er monastery.

With Tibet officially closed to individual tourists, some travellers looking for a Tibetan experience have made the journey from Xining to Chengdu. The scenery is great and very Tibetan. It's a rough trip requiring nearly a week; accidents occur frequently. Just how long this route will remain open to foreigners is uncertain – probably until someone gets killed. At the time of this writing, it's still possible. Don't bother to ask CITS for information about this journey – they told us 'if I were going there, I wouldn't start from here'.

The route to Chengdu is as follows: by bus from Xining to Madoi *(mǎdūo)* (Y19, two days); Madoi to Xiwu *(xiēwǔ)* (Y13); by bus or truck to Serxü *(shíqú)* in Sichuan Province; then from Serxü to Kangding *(kāngdìng)* (two days); and Kangding to Chengdu (Y19, two days). All along the way there are cheap places to stay – the bus company will either put you up at their own hostels or direct you to another hotel. Travellers in Chengdu have reported difficulty getting permission from Public Security to go to Kangding, but coming from the other direction seems to be no problem at all – for now.

Train Xining has frequent rail connections to Lanzhou (4½ hours). There are two trains to Golmud; one leaves daily and one leaves every other day. Foreigners have reported thefts on the Golmud train, particularly during the night.

AROUND XINING

Ta'er Lamasery

(tǎ'ěr sì) 塔尔寺

This is a large Tibetan monastery, one of the six great monasteries of the Yellow Hat sect of Tibetan Buddhism, in the town of Huangzhong about 26 km south-east of Xining. It was built in 1577 on sacred ground – the birthplace of Tsong Khapa, founder of the Yellow Hat sect. Six temples are open – buy admission tickets from the window close to the row of stupas.

The monastery is noted for its extraordinary sculptures of human figures, animals and landscapes carved out of yak butter. The art of butter sculpture probably dates back 1300 years in Tibet and was taken up by the Ta'er Lamasery in the last years of the 16th century.

It's a pretty place and very popular with the local tourists. Go hiking in the surrounding area or follow the pilgrims clockwise on a scenic circuit round the monastery.

Photography is prohibited inside the temples, and they mean it! Outside the house with the butter statues, the monks have nailed to the wall all the film they have ripped out of cameras.

Overall, Ta'er Lamasery is nice, but it pales in comparison to the splendid monasteries of Xiahe or Lhasa.

Places to Stay & Eat The monastery has a couple of buildings which have been converted from monks' quarters into tourist accommodation. Rooms in the wooden buildings are arranged around a courtyard and come complete with gallery and murals. A bed in a three-bed room costs Y10.

The *Ta'er Hotel (tǎ'ěr sì bīngǔan)* is just opposite the Tibetan hospital and charges Y60 for a double.

The food at the monastery is good. For a

change, take a wander down the hill towards town and try some noodles in a Muslim restaurant. Stalls on the approach road to the monastery sell great yoghurt and peaches.

Getting There & Away Buses to Huangzhong leave Ximen bus station *(xīmén qìchē zhàn)* in Xining about every 10 minutes between 7 am and 6.30 pm. The 45-minute ride costs Y2. Minibuses also do the trip faster for a fare of Y5.

Catch your return bus or minibus to Xining from the square in Huangzhong.

QINGHAI LAKE

(qīnghǎi hú) 青海湖

Qinghai Lake (Koko Nor), known as the Western Sea in ancient times, is a somewhat surreal-looking saline lake lying 300 km west of Xining and 3200 metres above sea level. It's the largest lake in China and produces copious quantities of fish.

The main attraction is Bird Island – a breeding ground for thousands of wild geese, gulls, cormorants, sandpipers, extremely rare black-necked cranes and many other bird species. Perhaps most interesting are the bar-headed geese. These hardy birds migrate high over the Himalayas to spend winter on the Indian plains, and have been spotted flying at 10,000 metres.

You will only see birds in any quantity during the breeding season between March and early June – worth remembering if you are considering a CITS tour.

It gets chilly at night so bring warm clothing. The lake water is too salty to drink, so be sure you carry a sufficient supply if you intend to do any hiking. There are nomads around the lake – most are friendly and may invite you for a cup of tea in their tents.

Getting There & Away

North Shore The northern shore of the lake is readily accessible by train. Unfortunately, this is not the part of the lake that has many birds and you might be disappointed if this is all you get to see. Ha'ergai railway station is the jumping-off point and the lake is an hour's walk away. If you are going to Golmud, you get good views of the whole northern shoreline from the train's windows.

Bird Island Most travellers head for Bird Island *(niǎo dǎo)*, 360 km from Xining on the south shore of the lake. It's somewhat difficult to reach. The small settlement of Heimahe *(hēimǎhé)*, 50 km from Bird Island, is the closest town having regular public transport to Xining.

In Heimahe there's a sign which shows the way to the state-run hotel where rooms are just Y5. There's a surprisingly good restaurant and a well-stocked shop, but it's wise to bring some supplies anyway from Xining in case you want to do some hiking.

To reach Bird Island, take the road branching north from Heimahe – an occasional bus goes in this direction as far as Shinaihai *(shínǎihài)* (40 km). From there it's a hike or a hitch for 13 km to the Bird Island Hotel *(niǎo dǎo bīngǔan)* – it's a boring walk. Dorms cost Y10, the hotel staff are very friendly and the food is good. You must

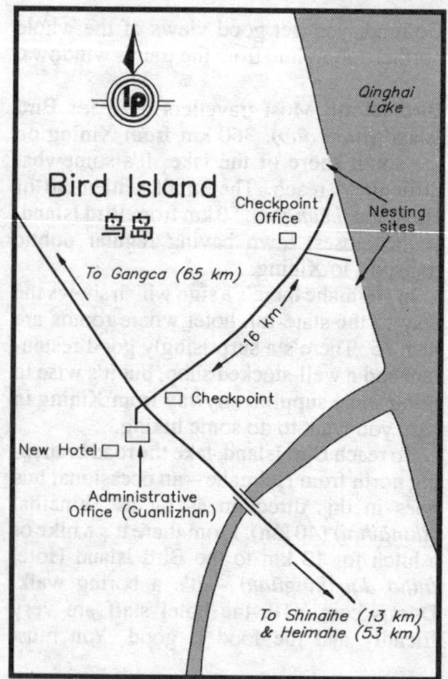

register at the hotel and pay Y5 admission before being shepherded to the island (16 km).

Every Sunday during summer, there is a day trip from Xining to Bird Island for only Y40. Buses depart at 7 am from Ximen bus station and return at 9 pm. Don't expect a tranquil nature experience – your fellow passengers may be very noisy.

If you can get together a group, it is possible to rent minibuses through the Peace Restaurant (☎ 48069) *(hépíng jiǔjiā)*. Go to the 3rd floor to enquire.

CITS organises a three-day trip to Bird Island which costs Y80 (FEC) based on a minimum of 10 passengers. This price is for the bus only – meals and accommodation are an additional Y60 per day.

GOLMUD

(gé ěr mù) 格尔木

Golmud is a pioneering outpost in the desolate centre of Qinghai – the residents will be the first to tell you that from here to hell is a local call. The town owes its existence to potash mining. It's mostly a Chinese city, but there are a few Tibetans around. There really isn't much to see other than the eerie moonscape of the Tibetan Plateau. Golmud used to be the jumping off point on the road to Tibet, but at the present time Tibet is closed except to expensive CITS tours – these can be booked through the Golmud CITS. Some travellers still make Golmud a stop-off point between Xining and Dunhuang, but most now bypass it. Until Tibet reopens to individual travel, the Golmud tourism business can expect very lean times.

Information

CITS This office (☎ 2001 ext 254) is in the Golmud Hotel. They can arrange three day tours to Lhasa for a mere Y3000 (after bargaining).

Public Security Bureau This office is in the Golmud Hotel.

Money The Bank of China is on the corner of Kunlun Lu and Chaidamu Lu.

Post You'll find the post office on the corner of Chaidamu Lu and Jiangyuan Lu.

Climate At 2800 metres elevation, summer days can be very warm but nights are always cool. The daytime sun is incredibly bright – sunglasses are a must. Winters are brutally cold.

Maps A simple map of the city is on sale at the Golmud Hotel.

Things to See

The city itself is devoid of any scenic spots – forget it. It's not unpleasant to walk around, but it doesn't take long to cover the whole town on foot. You might be able to find a taxi to take you to the pasturelands *(cǎoyúan)* on the edge of town. Here the nomads live in

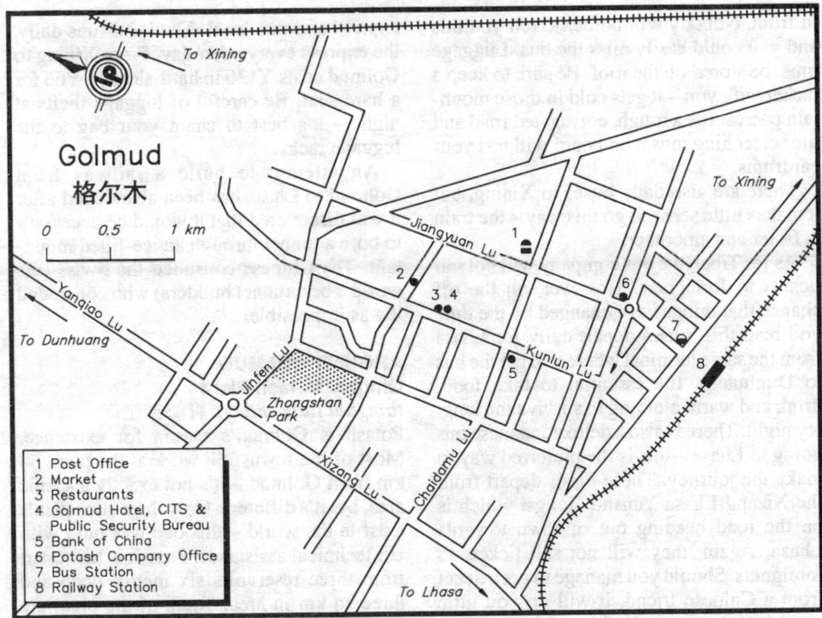

1 邮局
2 市场
3 餐厅
4 格尔木宾馆
5 中国银行
6 青海钾肥厂总工办
7 长途汽车站
8 火车站

yurts and the area has a nice backdrop of snow-capped peaks in the distance.

Places to Stay

There's only one place accepting foreigners, the *Golmud Hotel* (☎ 2001) *(gé ěr mù bīnguǎn)*. Dorms in the old building cost Y10, doubles are Y40. It's not a bad place but the showers seldom work. From the railway station to the hotel costs Y1 on the minibus. Walking takes about 35 minutes.

Places to Eat

Just outside the gate of the Golmud Hotel is the *Golmud Hotel Restaurant*. The food is good and very cheap. Right next door is *The Best Cafe* which is also good and friendly and has a decent English menu.

Getting There & Away

Air There are no flights at present, but there are plans to begin a service between Xining and Golmud. CAAC estimates the airfare will be Y215.

Bus The Golmud bus station is just opposite the railway station. The journey from Golmud to Dunhuang is 524 km and takes 13 hours and costs Y24. It departs at 6.30 am (7.30 am in summer). Foreigners must pay in FEC! Buy your ticket a day in advance. The bus departs from behind the station, not in front. Nobody will bother to tell you this and you could easily miss the bus. Luggage must be stored on the roof. Be sure to keep a jacket with you – it gets cold in those mountain passes. It's a rough, corrugated road and the screeching music on board will test your eardrums.

There are also daily buses to Xining, but it makes little sense to go this way – the train is faster and smoother.

As for Tibet, the bus company will not sell tickets to foreigners. However, on the off chance that things have changed by the time you read this, buses depart daily for Lhasa from the same terminal where you get the bus to Dunhuang. It's essential to take food, drink and warm clothing to survive the long, icy night. There is also a deluxe Japanese bus going to Lhasa – this is the preferred way to make the journey. These buses depart from the Xizang Lhasa Yunshu Gongsi which is on the road heading out of town towards Lhasa. Again, they will not sell tickets to foreigners. Should you manage to get a ticket from a Chinese friend, it will do you little good (unless you look Chinese) because the bus must pass through several police checkpoints.

Trying to sneak into Lhasa is not advised. Many travellers have tried – most have been caught and fined.

Train From Xining, there are two trains, one express and one local. The local runs daily, the express every other day. From Xining to Golmud costs Y130 in hard-sleeper, Y66 for a hard-seat. Be careful of luggage thefts at night – it's best to chain your bag to the luggage racks.

An attempt to build a railway from Golmud to Lhasa has been abandoned after it was discovered that it would be necessary to bore a tunnel through an ice-filled mountain. The Chinese consulted the Swiss (the world's best tunnel builders) who concluded it was impossible.

AROUND GOLMUD

Qinghai Potash Plant

(qīnghǎi jiǎféichǎng) 青海钾肥厂

Potash is Golmud's reason for existence. Most of the townsfolk work at the plant 60 km from Golmud – it's not exactly a scenic area, but it's different. Only three such plants exist in the world – this one was built with US technical assistance. Potash is harvested from three reservoirs six metres deep and three sq km in area. Tours of the plant are free. To arrange a visit, drop in at the potash company office in Golmud – the tall modern steeple building near the railway station. The place you need to find is called the General Engineering Office *(zǒnggōngbàn)*. As you approach the plant, the scenery becomes incredibly desolate – not a blade of grass grows in this salty soil.

Index

ABBREVIATIONS

MAPS

TEXT

Map references in **bold** type

THANKS

Thanks to all the following travellers and others (apologies if we've misspelt your name) who took time to write to us about their experiences of China:

S & L Adelman (Aus), Michael Agelasto (Chi), Marian Anderson (USA), Ingvar Andu, Cary Appenzeller (USA), Gillian Apps (UK), Anabela Arnoldt, Nicole Atherden (UK), Mr & Mrs B Atkinson (C), Bill Avery (USA), Simone Baetens (B), Chris Bain (Aus), H Balev (USA), Georgie & Ian Barber, Julie Barker (UK), Olof Barr (Sw), Lulu Barry (UK), Paul Barton (UK), Jean-Pierre Bazard (Fr), Mary Bean, Claus Becker (A), Jeffrey Benton (USA), Ulrica Bergstrom (Sw), Fredrik Beskow (Sw), Hilde Besser (C), Bernard Biais (USA), Kees Bikker (Nl), Tracey Birney (UK), Greg Bishop (Aus), Lenore Blackwood (Aus), Per Blomqvist (Sw), Elizabeth Bluntzer (UK), Hartmut Bohn, Gordon Bonin, Simon Bourke (UK), Alan Bowen (Aus), Vicky Bower (UK), Mike Bowman (UK), D C Boyall (Aus), Mike Boyall, John Bratton (Taiw), Leo Braudy (USA), Ingrid Bremer (D), Stuart J Britton (UK), Stephen Brown (UK), Jim Buck (UK), Walter Burt (USA), Ian Butler (UK), David Calder (UK), Andrea Carnegie-Smith (Aus), Jay Casey (USA), Evelyne Cevillain (Fr), Daniel Chammiran (Sw), Mr Chen Chi, Chiu Hong-Kuen (HK), Mrs Clarke (NZ), Gary Collinson (Aus), Ian Cotton, Rick & Gilly Craft (UK), Gail Cram (USA), R & S Sutton Crocker (UK), M E Cronin (Aus), Susan Cunningham (HK), Zbigniew Czumaj (P), Matthew Daines (UK), Mikael Darius (Sw), Margaret Darnatt (Aus), Martin Davies (Aus), Michael Dawson (NZ), Maxine Degraaf (Aus), William Dewees, Joe Distler (USA), Sarah Dixon (UK), James Downer, Claire Duiker (B), R A Eagle (UK), Dawn Einwalter (USA), Jane M R Elias, Fred Ellers, Bettina Elten, Pat Eng (UK), Tony English (UK), Niels van Erck (Nl), Hans Evers, R E Farmer (USA), Anna Felcher (It), Robert Felinski (P), Andrew B Ferguson (USA), Marc Foggin (C), Mark J Fromm, Laura Fujii (USA), Robert Furner (Aus), Colin Galbraith (Aus), Nan Gallagher (Aus), Dave Gee (UK), Majida Gibson (USA), Tim Gideon, Manya Giles (A), Ron Gluckman, Dean Goodman (C), Wilfrid & Barb Gratz (A), Jacob de Groot (Nl), Alexandre Grub (D), Carolyn Guy (Aus), Markus Hagen (D), Kim & Cat Haglund (USA), Bonnie Hall (C), Annette Hames (UK), Span Hanna, Rick Hardiman (UK), Kati Harrison (Aus), Julian Haseldine (UK), Philip Hawks (UK), Louise Heinemann (Aus), Richard Herlick (C), Jonathon Hibbs (UK), John Himmen (C), Barry Holzman (USA), Tom Honau (USA), Ki Bong Hong (Kor), Chris & Jenny Hookey (Aus), Jeremy Horner (UK), Carmen Huang (Tai), Erwin Humer (Nl), James & Georgie Hunter (C), T Hutton, Mikael Johansson (Sw), Christine Johns, Trudie Jones (Aus), Kryss Katsiavriades (UK), Humphrey Keenlyside, Anna van Kemenade (Nl), Ruthili Kemmerer (USA), John Kerr (Aus), Riaz Khan, Denise Kirkpatrick (Aus), Keith Kline (HK), M Knossenburg (Nl), Deborah Koons (USA), Bob Korzeniowski (C), J Kungeinden (Aus), Ruth Lacey, Di & Christian Lagoutte (UK), David Lakeman (Aus), Kirsten Laursen (Dk), Sarah & Mike Lawrence (Aus), Florence Lawson (UK), Qin Li (Chi), Miriam Lill (NZ), J W Leech (Aus), Louisa Lera (UK), Nandor Less (Hun), Jacques Lessard (C), Ellis Levin (USA), D Hardy & D Lewinsohn (USA), Wendy Lewis, Richard Lindley (UK), Jim Linker (USA), Rob Lober (UK), Pamela Logan, Jack Longstaff (C), Gaute Losnegard (Nl), Mr Loveridge (Aus), Peter Lund (Dk), Michael Magercord (D), Chantal Maguet (Fr), Eifiona Main (USA), Jenny Major (Fr), Julian Martell (Aus), Janet Martin (Aus), Lisa & Pat McCarthy (UK), John McCormick, David & Helen McIntyre (Aus), Doug McLean (Aus), Mrs M McLean (Ire), Grant McMillan (NZ), Kevin McQuillon, Celia de Mello (USA), Justine Mickle, David Miller (Aus), Boris Minnaert (Nl), Susan Molloy (UK), Stephen Moore (USA), John Morgan, Nicolas Morin (Fr), M Mosetig (A), Johannes Muller (D), Fiona Needham (UK), Iian Neill, Ann Nelson (NZ), Paul Nicholls (UK), Claire Nightingale (UK), Roberto Nocchieri (It), Lucas Noldus (Nl), Asa & Per Olausson (Sw), Rick Olderman (USA), Helene Oldrup (Dk), Keith Pearson (Aus), J Pelienburg (UK), Peter Paget (USA), Peter Palme (D), W Perry (NZ), David Pindar (UK), Dr Rachel Pinniger (UK), Richard Piro (USA), Suzi Pizzi, Alfredo Pizzirani (It), Barbara Pollack (USA), Marcus Pomper (D), Douglas Poole (USA), B Corner & K Pound (NZ), C Poupa (Fr), J D Priestman (UK), Peter Prior (Aus), Vanessa Puniak (USA), Mr & Mrs D L Quant (HK), Peter Quatfass (Nl), Kamilla Ralov (Dk), Jesper Ravn (Dk), David Rees, Mats Reimer (Sw), Joe Rhinewine (USA), Jessica Rigold (NZ), Espen Rinnan (Nl), Gitte & Karin Rix-Hollander (Dk), Annie Roberts (USA), Susie Rockwell (UK), Ruth & Milton Roemer (USA), Ken & Rada Roggle (USA), Tomas Rohlin (Sw), Susanne Hailin Rudolph (USA), Ruth Sanders (Aus), Simon Saubern (Aus), Nancy Scannell (USA), Christiane Schaffer (CH), Peter Schatz (Aus), Danida Schneider (CH), Ron Schroeder (C), Deanne Schultz (C), Peter Sewell (Aus), Richard Sharpley (UK), Gary Siegel (USA), Kimberley Silver (USA), Mark Simon (USA), Jan J Sirks (Nl), Petr Skovajsa (C), John Slaney (HK), Edward Smith (Aus), Heather Smith (Aus), Pauline & Ian Smith (UK), Henrik & Hella Sorud (Dk), M A Spence (Aus), Gunter Spreitzhofer (A), Rachel Starling, John Steedman (UK), Caroline Stevens(UK), Douglas Stevens (C), Peter Stevens (Nl), Angela Stimmedo, Alison Stirland (UK), H P Street 111 (USA), Ted Talbot (UK), Bruce Tamango (Aus), Anna Tanada, James Taylor (UK), Tim Temonink (Nl), Robert Templeton (USA), Warren Tenney-Kor, Riki

Therivel (UK), David Thomas (USA), Suzanne Thomas, Stephen Thompson, Beverley Thomson (UK), D J Thomson (SA), Wouter Tiems (Nl), Edwin Tuchs (CH), Henk Tukker (Thai), Bob Turner, Ewen Turner, Selina Uffhausen (D), Craig Uhler (USA), Monika Uhrig (D), Mike Underhill (NZ), Andrzej Urbanik (P), Sabine Vandenberghe (Fr), Brigitte-Elsa Vanier (Fr), Catherine Vaucherez (UK), C M Velvin, Chantal Vouilloz, Robin Wagner (USA), Caroline Walker (C), Clive Walker, Julia Waterlow (UK), Willy Webb-Purkis (UK), Ian Webster (UK), Scott Welker, Damian White (Aus), Andrew Whyte (Aus), Andrew Wilkinson (C), Alex Wilks (UK), Thomas Wolinski (USA), Mai Yun Wong (Sing), Jan Wood (UK), S Woolf (USA), Melvyn Wright (USA), Gerard Wyfjes (Aus), Martin Wykes (Aus), Xiong Yu Chi, Susie & Joe Yamamoto, Alan Yoshioka (C), Claire Young, Dan & Marty Young (USA), Julie Young, Marisa Zavalloni (C) and Suellen Zima.

A - Austria, Aus - Australia, B - Belgium, C - Canada, CH - Switzerland, Chi - People's Republic of China, D - Germany, Dk - Denmark, Fin - Finland, Fr - France, HK - Hong Kong, Hun - Hungary, It - Italy, Ire - Ireland, Isr - Israel, J - Japan, Kor - Korea, Lux - Luxembourg, Nl - Netherlands, NZ - New Zealand, P - Poland, SA - South Africa, Sing - Singapore, Sp - Spain, Sw - Sweden, Taiw - Taiwan, Thai - Thailand, UK - United Kingdom, USA - United States of America

Guides to North-East Asia

North-East Asia on a shoestring
Concise information for independent low-budget travel in China, Hong Kong, Japan, Macau, South Korea and Taiwan, plus short notes on North Korea.

Hong Kong, Macau & Canton - a travel survival kit
This practical guide had all the travel facts on these three diverse cities, linked by history, culture and geography.

Tibet - a travel survival kit
The fabled mountain-land of Tibet was one of the last areas of China to become accessible to travellers. This guide has full details on this remote and fascinating region, including the border crossing to Nepal.

Japan - a travel survival kit
Japan is a unique contrast of modern cities and remote wilderness areas, of sophisticated technology and ancient tradition. This guide tells you how to find the Japan that many visitors never see.

Korea - a travel survival kit
The second edition of this comprehensive guide includes an exclusive chapter on North Korea, one of the world's most reclusive countries – finally opening its doors to independent travellers.

Also available:
Chinese phrasebook, ***Korean*** phrasebook, ***Tibet*** phrasebook, and ***Japanese*** phrasebook.

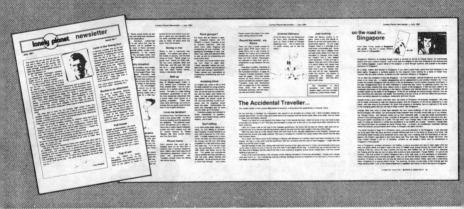

Lonely Planet Guidebooks

Lonely Planet guidebooks cover every accessible part of Asia as well as Australia, the Pacific, South America, Africa, the Middle East and parts of North America and Europe. There are four series: *travel survival kits*, covering a single country for a range of budgets; *shoestring guides* with compact information for low-budget travel in a major region; *walking guides*; and *phrasebooks*.

Australia & the Pacific

Australia
Bushwalking in Australia
Islands of Australia's Great Barrier Reef
Fiji
Micronesia
New Caledonia
New Zealand
Tramping in New Zealand
Papua New Guinea
Papua New Guinea phrasebook
Rarotonga & the Cook Islands
Samoa
Solomon Islands
Sydney
Tahiti & French Polynesia
Tonga
Vanuatu

South-East Asia

Bali & Lombok
Burma
Burmese phrasebook
Indonesia
Indonesia phrasebook
Malaysia, Singapore & Brunei
Philippines
Pilipino phrasebook
Singapore
South-East Asia on a shoestring
Thailand
Thai phrasebook
Vietnam, Laos & Cambodia

North-East Asia

China
Chinese phrasebook
Hong Kong, Macau & Canton
Japan
Japanese phrasebook
Korea
Korean phrasebook
North-East Asia on a shoestring
Taiwan
Tibet
Tibet phrasebook

West Asia

Trekking in Turkey
Turkey
Turkish phrasebook
West Asia on a shoestring

Indian Ocean

Madagascar & Comoros
Maldives & Islands of the East Indian Ocean
Mauritius, Réunion & Seychelles

Mail Order

Lonely Planet guidebooks are distributed worldwide and are sold by good bookshops everywhere. They are also available by mail order from Lonely Planet, so if you have difficulty finding a title please write to us. US and Canadian residents should write to Embarcadero West, 112 Linden St, Oakland CA 94607, USA and residents of other countries to PO Box 617, Hawthorn, Victoria 3122, Australia.

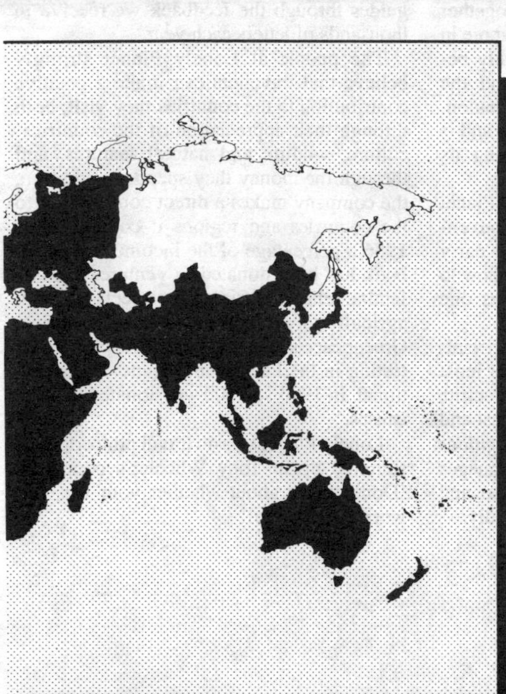

Europe
Eastern Europe on a shoestring
Iceland, Greenland & the Faroe Islands
Trekking in Spain

Indian Subcontinent
Bangladesh
India
Hindi/Urdu phrasebook
Trekking in the Indian Himalaya
Karakoram Highway
Kashmir, Ladakh & Zanskar
Nepal
Trekking in the Nepal Himalaya
Nepal phrasebook
Pakistan
Sri Lanka
Sri Lanka phrasebook

Africa
Africa on a shoestring
Central Africa
East Africa
Kenya
Swahili phrasebook
Morocco, Algeria & Tunisia
Moroccan Arabic phrasebook
West Africa

North America
Alaska
Canada
Hawaii

Mexico
Baja California
Mexico

South America
Argentina
Bolivia
Brazil
Brazilian phrasebook
Chile & Easter Island
Colombia
Ecuador & the Galápagos Islands
Latin American Spanish phrasebook
Peru
Quechua phrasebook
South America on a shoestring

Central America
Costa Rica
La Ruta Maya

Middle East
Egypt & the Sudan
Egyptian Arabic phrasebook
Israel
Jordan & Syria
Yemen

The Lonely Planet Story

Lonely Planet published its first book in 1973 in response to the numerous 'How did you do it?' questions Maureen and Tony Wheeler were asked after driving, bussing, hitching, sailing and railing their way from England to Australia.

Written at a kitchen table and hand collated, trimmed and stapled, *Across Asia on the Cheap* became an instant local bestseller, inspiring thoughts of another book.

Eighteen months in South-East Asia resulted in their second guide, *South-East Asia on a shoestring*, which they put together in a backstreet Chinese hotel in Singapore in 1975. The 'yellow bible' as it quickly became known to backpackers around the world, soon became *the* guide to the region. It has sold well over ½ million copies and is now in its 6th edition, still retaining its familiar yellow cover.

Today there are over 80 Lonely Planet titles – books that have that same adventurous approach to travel as those early guides; books that 'assume you know how to get your luggage off the carousel' as one reviewer put it.

Although Lonely Planet initially specialised in guides to Asia, they now cover most regions of the world, including the Pacific, South America, Africa, the Middle East and Eastern Europe. The list of *walking guides* and *phrasebooks* (for 'unusual' languages such as Quechua, Swahili, Nepalese and Egyptian Arabic) is also growing rapidly.

The emphasis continues to be on travel for independent travellers. Tony and Maureen still travel for several months of each year and play an active part in the writing, updating and quality control of Lonely Planet's guides.

They have been joined by over 50 authors, 40 staff – mainly editors, cartographers, & designers – at our office in Melbourne, Australia, and another 10 at our US office in Oakland, California. Travellers themselves also make a valuable contribution to the guides through the feedback we receive in thousands of letters each year.

The people at Lonely Planet strongly believe that travellers can make a positive contribution to the countries they visit, both through their appreciation of the countries' culture, wildlife and natural features, and through the money they spend. In addition, the company makes a direct contribution to the countries and regions it covers. Since 1986 a percentage of the income from each book has been donated to ventures such as famine relief in Africa; aid projects in India; agricultural projects in Central America; Greenpeace's efforts to halt French nuclear testing in the Pacific and Amnesty International. In 1990 $60,000 was donated to these causes.

Lonely Planet's basic travel philosophy is summed up in Tony Wheeler's comment, 'Don't worry about whether your trip will work out. Just go!'